# MASSACHUSETTS RULES OF COURT: KEYRULES

## VOLUME IIA - FEDERAL

## 2019

**THOMSON REUTERS®**

Mat #42146335

© 2019 Thomson Reuters

**ISBN:** 978-0-314-69811-7

# CONTACT US

For additional information or research assistance call our reference attorneys at 1-800-REF-ATTY (1-800-733-2889). Contact our U.S. legal editorial department directly with your questions and suggestions by email at editors.us-legal@tr.com.

# PREFACE

Massachusetts Rules of Court: KeyRules provides the practitioner with a comprehensive "single source" procedural guide for civil practice in the United States District Court for the District of Massachusetts, combining applicable provisions of the Federal Rules of Civil Procedure, United States Code, local rules of practice, and analytical materials.

This book consists of outlines of the applicable rules of practice, timing requirements, filing and service requirements, hearing requirements, checklists, and other pertinent documents related to pleadings, motions, and discovery requests in United States District Courts.

THE PUBLISHER

February 2019

# UNITED STATES DISTRICT COURT

# DISTRICT OF MASSACHUSETTS

## Pleadings
## Complaint

**Document Last Updated December 2018**

A. **Checklist**

(I) ❑ Matters to be considered by plaintiff

   (a) ❑ Required documents

      (1) ❑ Civil cover sheet

      (2) ❑ Local civil category sheet

      (3) ❑ Complaint

      (4) ❑ Summons

      (5) ❑ Filing fee

      (6) ❑ Affidavit proving service

   (b) ❑ Supplemental documents

      (1) ❑ Notice and request for waiver of service

      (2) ❑ Notice of constitutional question

      (3) ❑ Notice of issue concerning foreign law

      (4) ❑ Nongovernmental corporate disclosure statement

      (5) ❑ Papers for service under state law

      (6) ❑ Request to proceed in forma pauperis

      (7) ❑ Compact disk with copy of document(s) in PDF format

      (8) ❑ Notice of filing with clerk's office

      (9) ❑ Additional copies

     (10) ❑ Courtesy copies

   (c) ❑ Timing

      (1) ❑ A civil action is commenced by filing a complaint with the court

      (2) ❑ If a defendant is not served within ninety (90) days after the complaint is filed, the court—on motion or on its own after notice to the plaintiff—must dismiss the action without prejudice against that defendant or order that service be made within a specified time

(II) ❑ Matters to be considered by defendant

   (a) ❑ Required documents

      (1) ❑ Answer

      (2) ❑ Certificate of service

   (b) ❑ Supplemental documents

      (1) ❑ Waiver of the service of summons

      (2) ❑ Notice of constitutional question

      (3) ❑ Notice of issue concerning foreign law

      (4) ❑ Nongovernmental corporate disclosure statement

(5) ❑ Compact disk with copy of document(s) in PDF format

(6) ❑ Notice of filing with clerk's office

(7) ❑ Additional copies

(8) ❑ Courtesy copies

(c) ❑ Timing

(1) ❑ A defendant must serve an answer:

    (i) ❑ Within twenty-one (21) days after being served with the summons and complaint; or

    (ii) ❑ If it has timely waived service under FRCP 4(d), within sixty (60) days after the request for a waiver was sent, or within ninety (90) days after it was sent to the defendant outside any judicial district of the United States

(2) ❑ The United States, a United States agency, or a United States officer or employee sued only in an official capacity must serve an answer to a complaint, counterclaim, or crossclaim within sixty (60) days after service on the United States attorney

(3) ❑ A United States officer or employee sued in an individual capacity for an act or omission occurring in connection with duties performed on the United States' behalf must serve an answer to a complaint, counterclaim, or crossclaim within sixty (60) days after service on the officer or employee or service on the United States attorney, whichever is later

(4) ❑ Unless the court sets a different time, serving a motion under FRCP 12 alters the periods in FRCP 12(a) as follows:

    (i) ❑ If the court denies the motion or postpones its disposition until trial, the responsive pleading must be served within fourteen (14) days after notice of the court's action; or

    (ii) ❑ If the court grants a motion for a more definite statement, the responsive pleading must be served within fourteen (14) days after the more definite statement is served

(5) ❑ The notice and request for waiver must give the defendant a reasonable time of at least thirty (30) days after the request was sent—or at least sixty (60) days if sent to the defendant outside any judicial district of the United States—to return the waiver

    (i) ❑ A defendant who, before being served with process, timely returns a waiver need not serve an answer to the complaint until sixty (60) days after the request was sent—or until ninety (90) days after it was sent to the defendant outside any judicial district of the United States

(6) ❑ Except as noted in FRCP 33 to FRCP 36, the original of all papers required to be served under FRCP 5(d) shall, unless otherwise submitted to the court, be filed in the office of the clerk within seven (7) days after service has been made

## B. Timing

1. *Commencing an action.* A civil action is commenced by filing a complaint with the court. FRCP 3.

  a. *Statute of limitations.* An action will be barred if it is not commenced within the period set forth in the applicable statute of limitations. Under the Federal Rules of Civil Procedure (FRCP), an action is commenced by filing a complaint with the court. Thus, in a suit on a right created by federal law, filing a complaint suffices to satisfy the statute of limitations. FEDPROF § 61:2.

    i. *Federal question cases.* Absent a specific statutory provision for tolling the statute of limitations, in federal question cases, the filing of the complaint will toll the statute, even if not all filing fees have been paid, although some courts have added the requirement of reasonable diligence in effecting service. FEDPROF § 61:2.

    ii. *Diversity cases.* In diversity actions the matter is less clear. In the landmark Ragan case, the Supreme Court held in construing FRCP 3 that if, under local law, an action is not commenced until the defendant has been served, the statute is not tolled until service has been accomplished. FEDPROF § 61:2; Ragan v. Merchants Transfer & Warehouse Co., 337 U.S. 530, 69 S. Ct. 1233, 93 L. Ed. 1520 (1949). However, in a subsequent case, the Supreme Court distinguished Ragan in holding that the provision of FRCP 4 governing methods of service prevails over a conflicting state rule requiring personal service. FEDPROF § 61:2; Hanna v. Plumer, 380 U.S. 460, 85 S. Ct. 1136, 14 L. Ed. 2d 8 (1965). The court reaffirmed Ragan and held that (1) a state law mandating actual service of a summons to toll the statute of limitations must be followed in a diversity case, and (2) FRCP

# Table of Contents

## DISTRICT OF MASSACHUSETTS

# TABLE OF CONTENTS

3 only governs other timing requirements in the Federal Rules of Civil Procedure. FEDPROF § 61:2; Walker v. Armco Steel Corp., 446 U.S. 740, 100 S. Ct. 1978, 64 L. Ed. 2d 659 (1980).

2. *Service of summons and complaint.* If a defendant is not served within ninety (90) days after the complaint is filed, the court—on motion or on its own after notice to the plaintiff—must dismiss the action without prejudice against that defendant or order that service be made within a specified time. But if the plaintiff shows good cause for the failure, the court must extend the time for service for an appropriate period. FRCP 4(m) does not apply to service in a foreign country under FRCP 4(f), FRCP 4(h)(2), or FRCP 4(j)(1), or to service of a notice under FRCP 71.1(d)(3)(A). FRCP 4(m). Any summons not returned with proof that it was served within ninety (90) days of the filing of the complaint is deemed to be unserved for the purpose of FRCP 4(m). MA R USDCT LR 4.1(a).

   a. *Dismissal for failure to make service.* Counsel and parties appearing pro se who seek to show good cause for the failure to make service within the ninety (90) day period prescribed by FRCP 4(m) shall do so by filing a motion for enlargement of time under FRCP 6(b), together with a supporting affidavit. If on the fourteenth (14th) day following the expiration of the ninety (90) day period good cause has not been shown as provided in MA R USDCT LR 4.1(b), the clerk shall forthwith automatically enter an order of dismissal for failure to effect service of process, without awaiting any further order of the court. The clerk shall furnish a copy of MA R USDCT LR 4.1 to counsel or pro se plaintiffs, together with the summons, and delivery of this copy by the clerk will constitute the notice required by FRCP 4(m). Such notice shall constitute the notice required by FRCP 4(m). No further notice need be given by the court. MA R USDCT LR 4.1(b).

3. *Computation of time*

   a. *Computing time.* FRCP 6 applies in computing any time period specified in the Federal Rules of Civil Procedure, in any local rule or court order, or in any statute that does not specify a method of computing time. FRCP 6(a).

      i. *Period stated in days or a longer unit.* When the period is stated in days or a longer unit of time:
         - Exclude the day of the event that triggers the period;
         - Count every day, including intermediate Saturdays, Sundays, and legal holidays; and
         - Include the last day of the period, but if the last day is a Saturday, Sunday, or legal holiday, the period continues to run until the end of the next day that is not a Saturday, Sunday, or legal holiday. FRCP 6(a)(1).

      ii. *Period stated in hours.* When the period is stated in hours:
         - Begin counting immediately on the occurrence of the event that triggers the period;
         - Count every hour, including hours during intermediate Saturdays, Sundays, and legal holidays; and
         - If the period would end on a Saturday, Sunday, or legal holiday, the period continues to run until the same time on the next day that is not a Saturday, Sunday, or legal holiday. FRCP 6(a)(2).

      iii. *Office of the clerk.* The offices of the Clerk of Court at Boston, Worcester and Springfield shall be open from 8:30 a.m. until 5:00 p.m. on all days except Saturdays, Sundays, legal holidays and other days so ordered by the court and announced in advance, if feasible. MA R USDCT LR 77.2.

      iv. *Inaccessibility of the clerk's office.* Unless the court orders otherwise, if the clerk's office is inaccessible:
         - On the last day for filing under FRCP 6(a)(1), then the time for filing is extended to the first accessible day that is not a Saturday, Sunday, or legal holiday; or
         - During the last hour for filing under FRCP 6(a)(2), then the time for filing is extended to the same time on the first accessible day that is not a Saturday, Sunday, or legal holiday. FRCP 6(a)(3).

      v. *"Last day" defined.* Unless a different time is set by a statute, local rule, or court order, the last day ends:
         - For electronic filing, at midnight in the court's time zone; and
         - For filing by other means, when the clerk's office is scheduled to close. FRCP 6(a)(4).

      vi. *"Next day" defined.* The "next day" is determined by continuing to count forward when the period is measured after an event and backward when measured before an event. FRCP 6(a)(5).

      vii. *"Legal holiday" defined.* "Legal holiday" means:
         - The day set aside by statute for observing New Year's Day, Martin Luther King Jr.'s Birthday, Washington's Birthday, Memorial Day, Independence Day, Labor Day, Columbus Day, Veterans' Day, Thanksgiving Day, or Christmas Day;
         - Any day declared a holiday by the President or Congress; and

- For periods that are measured after an event, any other day declared a holiday by the state where the district court is located. FRCP 6(a)(6).

b. *Computation of electronic filing deadlines.* Filing documents electronically does not alter any filing deadlines. MA R USDCT CM/ECF Admin(K); MA R USDCT LR 5.4(D). Although CM/ECF is generally available twenty-four (24) hours a day for filing, all electronic transmissions of documents must be completed prior to 6:00 PM, Eastern Standard (or Daylight Savings) Time, on the date on which it is due, in order to be considered timely filed that day. MA R USDCT CM/ECF Admin(K); MA R USDCT LR 5.4(D). When a specific time of day deadline is set by court order or stipulation, the electronic filing must be completed by that time. Documents may be filed at any time of the day on days prior to the date on which it is due. MA R USDCT CM/ECF Admin(K). A document filed electronically shall be deemed filed as of the time and date stated on the NEF received from the court. MA R USDCT CM/ECF Admin(G)(2); MA R USDCT CM/ECF Admin(K).

   i. *Technical failures.* A user whose filing is made untimely as the result of a technical failure of the court's CM/ECF system may seek appropriate relief from the court. MA R USDCT CM/ECF Admin(W)(3). Technical difficulties on the filer's end, with telephone, cable lines, the filer's Internet Service Provider (ISP), or hardware or software problems, will not constitute a technical failure under the Administrative Procedures for Electronic Case Filing in the United States District Court for the District of Massachusetts (MA R USDCT CM/ECF Admin) nor excuse an untimely filing. MA R USDCT CM/ECF Admin(W)(3). As help desk support is available during normal business hours, filers are strongly urged to electronically file any documents during that period. MA R USDCT CM/ECF Admin(W)(3).

      - The court has made available a public terminal (computers and scanner) in each clerk's office for registered users to scan and electronically file documents. This equipment is available during normal business hours. Users should bring their prepared document and a valid CM/ECF login and password. MA R USDCT CM/ECF Admin(W)(3).

c. *Extending time.* When an act may or must be done within a specified time, the court may, for good cause, extend the time: (1) with or without motion or notice if the court acts, or if a request is made, before the original time or its extension expires; or (2) on motion made after the time has expired if the party failed to act because of excusable neglect. FRCP 6(b)(1).

   i. *Exceptions.* A court must not extend the time to act under FRCP 50(b), FRCP 50(d), FRCP 52(b), FRCP 59(b), FRCP 59(d), FRCP 59(e), and FRCP 60(b). FRCP 6(b)(2).

   ii. Refer to the United States District Court for the District of Massachusetts KeyRules Motion for Continuance/Extension of Time document for more information on extending time.

## C. General Requirements

1. *Pleading, generally*

   a. *Pleadings allowed.* Only these pleadings are allowed: (1) a complaint; (2) an answer to a complaint; (3) an answer to a counterclaim designated as a counterclaim; (4) an answer to a crossclaim; (5) a third-party complaint; (6) an answer to a third-party complaint; and (7) if the court orders one, a reply to an answer. FRCP 7(a).

   b. *Pleading to be concise and direct.* Each allegation must be simple, concise, and direct. No technical form is required. FRCP 8(d)(1).

   c. *Alternative statements of a claim or defense.* A party may set out 2 or more statements of a claim or defense alternatively or hypothetically, either in a single count or defense or in separate ones. If a party makes alternative statements, the pleading is sufficient if any one of them is sufficient. FRCP 8(d)(2).

   d. *Inconsistent claims or defenses.* A party may state as many separate claims or defenses as it has, regardless of consistency. FRCP 8(d)(3).

   e. *Construing pleadings.* Pleadings must be construed so as to do justice. FRCP 8(e).

2. *Pleading special matters*

   a. *Capacity or authority to sue; Legal existence*

      i. *In general.* Except when required to show that the court has jurisdiction, a pleading need not allege:

         - A party's capacity to sue or be sued;
         - A party's authority to sue or be sued in a representative capacity; or
         - The legal existence of an organized association of persons that is made a party. FRCP 9(a)(1).

ii. *Raising those issues.* To raise any of those issues, a party must do so by a specific denial, which must state any supporting facts that are peculiarly within the party's knowledge. FRCP 9(a)(2).

b. *Fraud or mistake; Conditions of mind.* In alleging fraud or mistake, a party must state with particularity the circumstances constituting fraud or mistake. Malice, intent, knowledge, and other conditions of a person's mind may be alleged generally. FRCP 9(b).

c. *Conditions precedent.* In pleading conditions precedent, it suffices to allege generally that all conditions precedent have occurred or been performed. But when denying that a condition precedent has occurred or been performed, a party must do so with particularity. FRCP 9(c).

d. *Official document or act.* In pleading an official document or official act, it suffices to allege that the document was legally issued or the act legally done. FRCP 9(d).

e. *Judgment.* In pleading a judgment or decision of a domestic or foreign court, a judicial or quasi-judicial tribunal, or a board or officer, it suffices to plead the judgment or decision without showing jurisdiction to render it. FRCP 9(e).

f. *Time and place.* An allegation of time or place is material when testing the sufficiency of a pleading. FRCP 9(f).

g. *Special damages.* If an item of special damage is claimed, it must be specifically stated. FRCP 9(g).

h. *Admiralty or maritime claim*

i. *How designated.* If a claim for relief is within the admiralty or maritime jurisdiction and also within the court's subject-matter jurisdiction on some other ground, the pleading may designate the claim as an admiralty or maritime claim for purposes of FRCP 14(c), FRCP 38(e), and FRCP 82 and the Supplemental Rules for Admiralty or Maritime Claims and Asset Forfeiture Actions. A claim cognizable only in the admiralty or maritime jurisdiction is an admiralty or maritime claim for those purposes, whether or not so designated. FRCP 9(h)(1).

ii. *Designation for appeal.* A case that includes an admiralty or maritime claim within FRCP 9(h) is an admiralty case within 28 U.S.C.A. § 1292(a)(3). FRCP 9(h)(2).

3. *Complaint.* A pleading that states a claim for relief must contain: (1) a short and plain statement of the grounds for the court's jurisdiction, unless the court already has jurisdiction and the claim needs no new jurisdictional support; (2) a short and plain statement of the claim showing that the pleader is entitled to relief; and (3) a demand for the relief sought, which may include relief in the alternative or different types of relief. FRCP 8(a).

a. *Statement of jurisdiction.* Federal courts are courts of limited jurisdiction, and it is presumed that they are without jurisdiction unless the contrary affirmatively appears. FEDPROC § 62:38; Kirkland Masonry, Inc. v. Comm'r, 614 F.2d 532 (5th Cir. 1980). Therefore, in order for a complaint to comply with the requirement that it contain a short and plain statement of the grounds upon which the court's jurisdiction depends, unless the court already has jurisdiction and the claim needs no new jurisdictional support, the jurisdictional basis must be alleged affirmatively and distinctly on the face of the complaint. FEDPROC § 62:38; Spain v. U.S. Through Atomic Nuclear Regulatory Comm'n Through U.S. Atomic Safety & Licensing Bd., 397 F. Supp. 15 (M.D. La. 1975).

i. Although it has been said that the jurisdictional statement requirement contemplates reference to a federal statute, a sufficient jurisdictional statement is not made by simply citing a federal statute without alleging facts which bring the plaintiff within the purview of the statute. FEDPROC § 62:38; Atkins v. Sch. Bd. of Halifax Cty., 379 F. Supp. 1060 (W.D.Va. 1974); Sims v. Mercy Hosp. of Monroe, 451 F.2d 171 (6th Cir. 1971).

ii. Improper venue is an affirmative defense, and a complaint need not include allegations showing venue to be proper. FEDPROC § 62:38; Ripperger v. A.C. Allyn & Co., 113 F.2d 332 (2d Cir. 1940).

b. *Statement of claim*

i. *Notice pleading.* Because the only function left exclusively to the pleadings by the Federal Rules of Civil Procedure is that of giving notice, federal courts frequently have said that the Federal Rules of Civil Procedure have adopted a system of "notice pleading." FPP § 1202; Swierkiewicz v. Sorema N.A., 534 U.S. 506, 122 S.Ct. 992, 152 L.Ed.2d 1 (2002). To comply with the requirement that a complaint contain a short and plain statement of the claim, a pleading must give the opposing party fair notice of the nature of a claim and of the basis or grounds for it, so that the defendant will at least be notified as to which of its actions gave rise to the claim upon which the complaint is based. FEDPROC § 62:45.

• *Plausibility standard.* Bell Atlantic Corporation v. Twombly and Ashcroft v. Iqbal have paved the way for a heightened "plausibility" pleading standard that requires plaintiffs to provide greater factual development in their complaints in order to survive [an] FRCP 12(b)(6) motion to dismiss. FPP § 1202; Bell Atl. Corp.

v. Twombly, 550 U.S. 544, 127 S. Ct. 1955, 167 L. Ed. 2d 929 (2007); Ashcroft v. Iqbal, 556 U.S. 662, 129 S. Ct. 1937, 173 L. Ed. 2d 868 (2009). In discussing what appears to be the new plausibility standard, the Court [in Bell Atlantic Corp. v. Twombly] stated: "While a complaint attacked by a Rule 12(b)(6) motion to dismiss does not need detailed factual allegations. . .a plaintiff's obligation to provide the 'grounds' of his 'entitle[ment] to relief' requires more than labels and conclusions, and a formulaic recitation of the elements of a cause of action will not do. . .Factual allegations must be enough to raise a right to relief above the speculative level." FPP § 1216; Bell Atl. Corp. v. Twombly, 550 U.S. 544, 127 S. Ct. 1955, 167 L. Ed. 2d 929 (2007).

ii.   *Facts and evidence.* The complaint need only state enough facts to raise a reasonable expectation that discovery will reveal evidence of the necessary elements. FEDPROC § 62:52; Phillips v. Cty. of Allegheny, 515 F.3d 224 (3d Cir. 2008). A complaint is not intended to formulate issues or fully summarize the facts involved. FEDPROC § 62:52; Hill v. MCI WorldCom Commc'ns, Inc., 141 F. Supp. 2d 1205 (S.D. Iowa 2001). Under notice pleading, the full development of the facts and the narrowing of contested issues are accomplished through discovery and other pretrial procedures. FEDPROC § 62:52.

iii.   *Particularity.* The claim should be particularized sufficiently for the defendant to prepare an adequate defense, file a responsive pleading, determine whether the defense of res judicata is appropriate, and commence discovery. FEDPROC § 62:45; Kelly v. Schmidberger, 806 F.2d 44 (2d Cir. 1986); Frank v. Mracek, 58 F.R.D. 365 (M.D. Ala. 1973); Barlow v. Pep Boys, Inc., 625 F. Supp. 130 (E.D. Pa. 1985). The statement should be sufficient to [ensure] that the court is sufficiently informed to determine the issue presented and to decide whether the complaint states a claim upon which relief can be had. FEDPROC § 62:45; Philadelphia Dressed Beef Co. v. Wilson & Co., 19 F.R.D. 198 (E.D. Pa. 1956); Luckett v. Cohen, 145 F. Supp. 155 (S.D.N.Y. 1956).

c.   *Demand for relief sought.* FRCP 8(a)(3) does not require a party to frame the demand for judgment according to a prescribed form or set of particular words; any concise statement identifying the remedies and the parties against whom relief is sought will be sufficient. FPP § 1255; Chandler v. McKee Foods Corp., No. CIV.A. 5:08CV00062, 2009 WL 210858 (W.D.Va. Jan. 28, 2009). Moreover, the pleader need only make one demand for relief regardless of the number of claims that are asserted. FPP § 1255; Liberty Mut. Ins. Co. v. Wetzel, 424 U.S. 737, 96 S. Ct. 1202, 47 L. Ed. 2d 435 (1976).

i.   Relief must be requested as to each defendant. FEDPROC § 62:58; RKO-Stanley Warner Theatres, Inc. v. Mellon Nat. Bank & Trust Co., 436 F.2d 1297 (3d Cir. 1970).

4.   *Joinder*

a.   *Joinder of claims.* A party asserting a claim, counterclaim, crossclaim, or third-party claim may join, as independent or alternative claims, as many claims as it has against an opposing party. FRCP 18(a).

i.   *Joinder of contingent claims.* A party may join two claims even though one of them is contingent on the disposition of the other; but the court may grant relief only in accordance with the parties' relative substantive rights. In particular, a plaintiff may state a claim for money and a claim to set aside a conveyance that is fraudulent as to that plaintiff, without first obtaining a judgment for the money. FRCP 18(b).

b.   *Joinder of parties; Required*

i.   *Persons required to be joined if feasible; Required party.* A person who is subject to service of process and whose joinder will not deprive the court of subject-matter jurisdiction must be joined as a party if:

●   In that person's absence, the court cannot accord complete relief among existing parties; or

●   That person claims an interest relating to the subject of the action and is so situated that disposing of the action in the person's absence may: (1) as a practical matter impair or impede the person's ability to protect the interest; or (2) leave an existing party subject to a substantial risk of incurring double, multiple, or otherwise inconsistent obligations because of the interest. FRCP 19(a)(1).

ii.   *Joinder of parties by court order.* If a person has not been joined as required, the court must order that the person be made a party. A person who refuses to join as a plaintiff may be made either a defendant or, in a proper case, an involuntary plaintiff. FRCP 19(a)(2).

iii.   *Venue.* If a joined party objects to venue and the joinder would make venue improper, the court must dismiss that party. FRCP 19(a)(3).

iv.   *When joinder of parties is not feasible.* If a person who is required to be joined if feasible cannot be joined, the court must determine whether, in equity and good conscience, the action should proceed among the existing parties or should be dismissed. FRCP 19(b). For a list of the factors for the court to consider in determining whether joinder of parties is feasible, refer to FRCP 19(b)(1) through FRCP 19(b)(4).

v. *Pleading the reasons for nonjoinder.* When asserting a claim for relief, a party must state:

- The name, if known, of any person who is required to be joined if feasible but is not joined; and

- The reasons for not joining that person. FRCP 19(c).

vi. *Exception for class actions.* FRCP 19 is subject to FRCP 23. FRCP 19(d). For information on class actions, refer to FRCP 23.

c. *Joinder of parties; Permissible*

   i. *Persons who may join or be joined*

   - *Plaintiffs.* Persons may join in one action as plaintiffs if: (1) they assert any right to relief jointly, severally, or in the alternative with respect to or arising out of the same transaction, occurrence, or series of transactions or occurrences; and (2) any question of law or fact common to all plaintiffs will arise in the action. FRCP 20(a)(1).

   - *Defendants.* Persons—as well as a vessel, cargo, or other property subject to admiralty process in rem—may be joined in one action as defendants if: (1) any right to relief is asserted against them jointly, severally, or in the alternative with respect to or arising out of the same transaction, occurrence, or series of transactions or occurrences; and (2) any question of law or fact common to all defendants will arise in the action. FRCP 20(a)(2).

   - *Extent of relief.* Neither a plaintiff nor a defendant need be interested in obtaining or defending against all the relief demanded. The court may grant judgment to one or more plaintiffs according to their rights, and against one or more defendants according to their liabilities. FRCP 20(a)(3).

   ii. *Protective measures.* The court may issue orders—including an order for separate trials—to protect a party against embarrassment, delay, expense, or other prejudice that arises from including a person against whom the party asserts no claim and who asserts no claim against the party. FRCP 20(b).

d. *Misjoinder and nonjoinder of parties.* Misjoinder of parties is not a ground for dismissing an action. On motion or on its own, the court may at any time, on just terms, add or drop a party. The court may also sever any claim against a party. FRCP 21.

5. *Right to a jury trial; Demand*

   a. *Right preserved.* The right of trial by jury as declared by U.S.C.A. Const. Amend. VII, or as provided by a federal statute, is preserved to the parties inviolate. FRCP 38(a).

   b. *Demand.* On any issue triable of right by a jury, a party may demand a jury trial by: (1) serving the other parties with a written demand—which may be included in a pleading—no later than fourteen (14) days after the last pleading directed to the issue is served; and (2) filing the demand in accordance with FRCP 5(d). FRCP 38(b).

   c. *Specifying issues.* In its demand, a party may specify the issues that it wishes to have tried by a jury; otherwise, it is considered to have demanded a jury trial on all the issues so triable. If the party has demanded a jury trial on only some issues, any other party may—within fourteen (14) days after being served with the demand or within a shorter time ordered by the court—serve a demand for a jury trial on any other or all factual issues triable by jury. FRCP 38(c).

   d. *Waiver; Withdrawal.* A party waives a jury trial unless its demand is properly served and filed. A proper demand may be withdrawn only if the parties consent. FRCP 38(d).

   e. *Admiralty and maritime claims.* The rules in FRCP 38 do not create a right to a jury trial on issues in a claim that is an admiralty or maritime claim under FRCP 9(h). FRCP 38(e).

6. *Alternative dispute resolution (ADR).* The judicial officer assigned to preside over the case shall encourage the resolution of disputes by settlement or other alternative dispute resolution programs. MA R USDCT LR 16.4(a).

   a. *Settlement.* At every conference conducted under the Local Rules of the United States District Court for the District of Massachusetts, the judicial officer shall inquire as to the utility of the parties conducting settlement negotiations, explore means of facilitating those negotiations, and offer whatever assistance may be appropriate in the circumstances. Assistance may include a reference of the case to another judicial officer for settlement purposes. MA R USDCT LR 16.4(b).

      i. When a case is settled, the parties shall file with the clerk a signed agreement for judgment or stipulation for dismissal, as appropriate, within twenty-eight (28) days, unless the court otherwise orders. MA R USDCT LR 68.2.

b. *Alternative dispute resolution programs*

    i. *Discretion of judicial officer.* The judicial officer, following an exploration of the matter with all counsel, may refer appropriate cases to alternative dispute resolution programs that have been designated for use in the district court or that the judicial officer may make available. The dispute resolution programs described in MA R USDCT LR 16.4(c)(2) through MA R USDCT LR 16.4(c)(4) are illustrative, not exclusive. Moreover, nothing in MA R USDCT LR 16.4 shall preclude the parties from engaging in private dispute resolution programs as long as they comply with any schedule established by the court. MA R USDCT LR 16.4(c)(1).

    ii. *Mediation.* The judicial officer may refer the case to mediation upon the agreement of all parties. MA R USDCT LR 16.4(c)(2)(A).

    iii. *Other alternative dispute resolution programs.* Use of mediation is not exclusive. At the request of parties, the judicial officer may consider other forms of alternative dispute resolution including, but not limited to, mini-trial, summary jury trial and arbitration. MA R USDCT LR 16.4(c)(3).

c. For more information on alternative dispute resolution (ADR), refer to MA R USDCT LR 16.4.

7. *Sanctions.* Failure to comply with any of the directions or obligations set forth in, or authorized by, these rules may result in dismissal, default, or the imposition of other sanctions as deemed appropriate by the judicial officer. MA R USDCT LR 1.3. Except as provided by law, the court may impose sanctions as provided in MA R USDCT LR 1.3 for failure to comply with the Administrative Procedures for Electronic Case Filing in the United States District Court for the District of Massachusetts (MA R USDCT CM/ECF Admin) or with MA R USDCT LR 5.4. MA R USDCT CM/ECF Admin(C)(3).

## D. Documents

1. *Required documents*

a. *Civil cover sheet.* The party filing the initial pleading shall also file a civil cover sheet in the form prescribed by the Judicial Conference of the United States (JS 44). MA R USDCT LR 3.1; MA R USDCT LR 40.1(A)(2). A civil cover sheet is submitted with each civil complaint filed in the district court. Copies of the cover sheet may be obtained from the Clerk of Court. 2 FEDFORMS § 3:29(Comment).

b. *Local civil category sheet.* The party filing the initial pleading shall also file. . .the local category sheet. MA R USDCT LR 3.1.

    i. *Related civil cases.* If the party filing the initial pleading believes that the case is related to a case already assigned, whether or not the case is then pending, that party shall notify the clerk by notation on the local civil category sheet indicating the title and number of each such earlier case. MA R USDCT LR 40.1(G)(2).

       • For purposes of MA R USDCT LR 40.1, a civil case is related to one previously filed in this court if some or all of the parties are the same and if one or more of the following similarities exist also: the cases involve the same or similar claims or defenses; or the cases involve the same property, transaction or event; or the cases involve insurance coverage for the same property, transaction or event; or the cases involve substantially the same questions of fact and law. In addition, two cases, one criminal and one civil, are related if the civil case involves forfeiture of property from a transaction or event which is the subject of a previously filed criminal case, or the civil case seeks enforcement of a restitution order or fine imposed in a previously filed criminal case. MA R USDCT LR 40.1 shall not apply if more than two (2) years have elapsed since the closing of the previous action. MA R USDCT LR 40.1(G)(1).

       • For more information on related civil cases, refer to MA R USDCT LR 40.1(G).

c. *Complaint.* Refer to the General Requirements section of this document for the form and contents of the complaint.

d. *Summons.* A summons must be served with a copy of the complaint. FRCP 4(c)(1). A summons must:

    i. Name the court and the parties;

    ii. Be directed to the defendant;

    iii. State the name and address of the plaintiff's attorney or—if unrepresented—of the plaintiff;

    iv. State the time within which the defendant must appear and defend;

    v. Notify the defendant that a failure to appear and defend will result in a default judgment against the defendant for the relief demanded in the complaint;

    vi. Be signed by the clerk; and

    vii. Bear the court's seal. FRCP 4(a)(1).

e.  *Filing fee.* The clerk of each district court shall require the parties instituting any civil action, suit or proceeding in such court, whether by original process, removal or otherwise, to pay a filing fee. 28 U.S.C.A. § 1914(a). Except as otherwise provided by law, the clerk and other officers and employees of the court shall not be required to perform any service for a party other than the United States for which a fee is lawfully prescribed, unless the amount of the fee, if it is known, or an amount sufficient to cover the fee reasonably expected by the officer to come due for performance of the service has been deposited with the court. MA R USDCT LR 4.2(a). This provision shall not apply to the United States or a party who is proceeding in forma pauperis, or in any other situation where, in the judgment of the officer entitled to a fee, it is unnecessary to ensure payment of the fee and would work hardship or an injustice. MA R USDCT LR 4.2(b). Each district court by rule or standing order may require advance payment of fees. 28 U.S.C.A. § 1914(c). For information on filing fees and the District Court Miscellaneous Fee Schedule, refer to 28 U.S.C.A. § 1914. For the fee schedule for the United States District Court for the District of Massachusetts, refer to MA R USDCT App. A.

f.  *Affidavit proving service.* Unless service is waived, proof of service must be made to the court. Except for service by a United States marshal or deputy marshal, proof must be by the server's affidavit. FRCP 4(l)(1). Refer to the Filing and Service Requirements section of this document for more information.

2.  *Supplemental documents*

a.  *Notice and request for waiver of service.* An individual, corporation, or association that is subject to service under FRCP 4(e), FRCP 4(f), or FRCP 4(h) has a duty to avoid unnecessary expenses of serving the summons. The plaintiff may notify such a defendant that an action has been commenced and request that the defendant waive service of a summons. The notice and request must:

   i.  Be in writing and be addressed:

      ● To the individual defendant; or

      ● For a defendant subject to service under FRCP 4(h), to an officer, a managing or general agent, or any other agent authorized by appointment or by law to receive service of process;

   ii.  Name the court where the complaint was filed;

   iii.  Be accompanied by a copy of the complaint, two (2) copies of a waiver form appended to FRCP 4, and a prepaid means for returning the form;

   iv.  Inform the defendant, using the form appended to FRCP 4, of the consequences of waiving and not waiving service;

   v.  State the date when the request is sent;

   vi.  Give the defendant a reasonable time of at least thirty (30) days after the request was sent—or at least sixty (60) days if sent to the defendant outside any judicial district of the United States—to return the waiver; and

   vii.  Be sent by first-class mail or other reliable means. FRCP 4(d)(1).

b.  *Notice of constitutional question.* A party that files a pleading, written motion, or other paper drawing into question the constitutionality of a federal or state statute must promptly:

   i.  *File notice.* File a notice of constitutional question stating the question and identifying the paper that raises it, if:

      ● A federal statute is questioned and the parties do not include the United States, one of its agencies, or one of its officers or employees in an official capacity; or

      ● A state statute is questioned and the parties do not include the state, one of its agencies, or one of its officers or employees in an official capacity; and

   ii.  *Serve notice.* Serve the notice and paper on the Attorney General of the United States if a federal statute is questioned—or on the state attorney general if a state statute is questioned—either by certified or registered mail or by sending it to an electronic address designated by the attorney general for this purpose. FRCP 5.1(a).

   iii.  *No forfeiture.* A party's failure to file and serve the notice, or the court's failure to certify, does not forfeit a constitutional claim or defense that is otherwise timely asserted. FRCP 5.1(d).

c.  *Notice of issue concerning foreign law.* A party who intends to raise an issue about a foreign country's law must give notice by a pleading or other writing. In determining foreign law, the court may consider any relevant material or source, including testimony, whether or not submitted by a party or admissible under the Federal Rules of Evidence. The court's determination must be treated as a ruling on a question of law. FRCP 44.1.

    d.  *Nongovernmental corporate disclosure statement*

        i.  *Contents.* A nongovernmental corporate party must file two (2) copies of a disclosure statement that:

- Identifies any parent corporation and any publicly held corporation owning ten percent (10%) or more of its stock; or

- States that there is no such corporation. FRCP 7.1(a).

        ii.  *Time to file; Supplemental filing.* A party must:

- File the disclosure statement with its first appearance, pleading, petition, motion, response, or other request addressed to the court; and

- Promptly file a supplemental statement if any required information changes. FRCP 7.1(b).

    e.  *Papers for service under state law.* In those cases where the Federal Rules of Civil Procedure authorize service of process to be made in accordance with state practice, it shall be the duty of counsel for the party seeking such service to furnish to the Clerk of Court forms of all necessary orders and sufficient copies of all papers to comply with the requirements of the state practice, together with specific instructions for the making of such service, if such service is to be made by the United States marshal. MA R USDCT LR 4.1(c).

    f.  *Request to proceed in forma pauperis.* The clerk shall receive for filing all complaints accompanied by a request to proceed in forma pauperis, and note the date thereon. If the request is denied, the matter will be noted on the miscellaneous business docket. If the request is allowed, or the denial is reversed, the clerk shall file the complaint on the civil docket. MA R USDCT LR 4.2(c).

        i.  *Affidavit.* Requests to proceed in forma pauperis shall be accompanied by an affidavit containing details of the individual's financial status. (The recommended form is available without charge from the clerk's office.) MA R USDCT LR 4.2(c).

    g.  *Compact disk with copy of document(s) in PDF format.* Whenever possible, at the time a civil case is submitted in paper format, the filing party may also file a disk with the clerk's office containing in PDF format the opening documents and any emergency motions and supporting papers not filed electronically. MA R USDCT LR 5.4(E). A filer who cannot file a document electronically because of such technical difficulty on the filer's end [with telephone, cable lines, the filer's Internet Service Provider (ISP), or hardware or software problems] shall file the document conventionally along with a copy of the document in PDF format on a compact disk or contact the clerk's office for permission to submit the PDF document via email. MA R USDCT CM/ECF Admin(W)(3). Refer to the Timing section of this document for more information on technical failures.

    h.  *Notice of filing with clerk's office.* When documents or exhibits (other than those filed ex parte or under seal) are submitted conventionally, a "Notice of Filing with clerk's office" shall be filed electronically and attached to the main document. A paper copy of the "Notice of Filing with clerk's office" must accompany the documents submitted to the court. The "Notice of Filing with clerk's office" (see MA R USDCT CM/ECF Admin(Appendix I)) shall describe each of the documents that will be filed as paper copies in the clerk's office, or shall include an index of the documents if those documents are voluminous. MA R USDCT CM/ECF Admin(P)(5).

    i.  *Additional copies.* Whenever, because of the nature of a proceeding, such as a proceeding before a three-judge district court under 28 U.S.C.A. § 2284, additional copies of a paper required to be filed are necessary either for the use of the court or to enable the clerk to carry out his duties, it is the responsibility of the party filing or having filed the paper to provide the necessary copies. MA R USDCT LR 5.1(d).

    j.  *Courtesy copies.* COURTESY COPIES OF DOCUMENTS FILED ELECTRONICALLY SHALL NOT BE SUBMITTED ROUTINELY. MA R USDCT CM/ECF Admin(J). Judicial officers, on a case-by-case basis, may require courtesy copies for specific cases, or types of motions, etc. A few Judicial Officers have entered Standing Orders, which may be found on their respective pages on the court's website (under Divisions). Any document filed on paper with the court as a courtesy copy must be clearly labeled as such (Example: COURTESY COPY—DO NOT SCAN). Documents delivered to the court as a courtesy copy will not be maintained in the official court record. MA R USDCT CM/ECF Admin(J).

## E. Format

1.  *Form of documents.* The provisions of FRCP 10 and FRCP 11 concerning the form and signing of pleadings, motions, and other papers shall be applicable to all papers filed in any proceeding in this court. The board of bar overseers registration number of each attorney signing such documents, except the United States Attorney and his or her staff, shall be inscribed below the signature. MA R USDCT LR 5.1(a)(1).

    a.  *Paper size and binding.* All papers filed in the court shall be adapted for flat filing, be filed on eight and one-half by eleven (8-1/2 x 11) inch paper without backers and be bound firmly by staple or some such other means (excluding paper or binder clip or rubber band). MA R USDCT LR 5.1(a)(2).

b. *Spacing.* All papers, except discovery requests and responses, shall be double-spaced except for the identification of counsel, title of the case, footnotes, quotations and exhibits. Discovery requests and responses shall be single-spaced. MA R USDCT LR 5.1(a)(2).

c. *Caption.* Every pleading must have a caption with the court's name, a title, a file number, and [an] FRCP 7(a) designation. FRCP 10(a).

    i. *Names of parties.* The title of the complaint must name all the parties; the title of other pleadings, after naming the first party on each side, may refer generally to other parties. FRCP 10(a).

    ii. *Request for special action.* When any pleading or other paper filed in the court includes a request for special process or relief, or any other request such that, if granted, the court will proceed other than in the ordinary course, the request shall, unless it is noted on the category sheet [see MA R USDCT LR 40.1(a)(1)], be noted on the first page to the right of or immediately beneath the caption. MA R USDCT LR 5.1(c).

d. *Claims or defenses*

    i. *Numbered paragraphs.* A party must state its claims or defenses in numbered paragraphs, each limited as far as practicable to a single set of circumstances. A later pleading may refer by number to a paragraph in an earlier pleading. FRCP 10(b).

    ii. *Separate statements.* If doing so would promote clarity, each claim founded on a separate transaction or occurrence—and each defense other than a denial—must be stated in a separate count or defense. FRCP 10(b).

e. *Adoption by reference.* A statement in a pleading may be adopted by reference elsewhere in the same pleading or in any other pleading or motion. FRCP 10(c).

    i. *Exhibits.* A copy of a written instrument that is an exhibit to a pleading is a part of the pleading for all purposes. FRCP 10(c).

f. *Citations*

    i. *Local rules.* These rules shall be known as Local Rules of the United States District Court for the District of Massachusetts and cited as "L.R., D. Mass." or "L.R." MA R USDCT LR 1.1.

    ii. *Electronic case filing procedures.* The procedures governing electronic case filing shall be known as the "Administrative Procedures for Electronic Case Filing in the United States District Court for the District of Massachusetts." They shall be cited as "APECF." MA R USDCT CM/ECF Admin(A)(7).

g. *Acceptance by the clerk.* The clerk must not refuse to file a paper solely because it is not in the form prescribed by the Federal Rules of Civil Procedure or by a local rule or practice. FRCP 5(d)(4).

    i. Except for complaints and notices of appeal, papers that do not conform to the requirements of MA R USDCT LR 5.1(a)(2) shall be returned by the clerk. MA R USDCT LR 5.1(a)(2).

2. *Form of electronic documents.* A paper filed electronically is a written paper for purposes of the Federal Rules of Civil Procedure. FRCP 5(d)(3)(D).

a. *PDF/A format required.* The court will begin requiring submission of documents in PDF/A format in the foreseeable future. PDF/A is an enhanced version of the traditional PDF format. Newer versions of most PDF software will be able to convert to this format. Additional information on PDF/A documents may be found on the court's website. MA R USDCT CM/ECF Admin(Electronic Filing and PDF).

    i. *Electronically converted PDF.* Electronically converted PDF documents are created from word processing documents (MS Word, WordPerfect, etc.) using any appropriate software. These documents are text searchable and the file size is generally smaller than a scanned document. CM/ECF users may use any brand of software to convert documents to PDF. MA R USDCT CM/ECF Admin(Electronic Filing and PDF).

        • Documents converted to PDF, rather than scanned, are preferred for filing in CM/ECF. MA R USDCT CM/ECF Admin(Electronic Filing and PDF).

    ii. *Scanned PDF.* Scanned PDF documents are created from paper documents run through an optical scanner. Scanned PDF documents are generally not searchable and have a larger file size. Please note that software used to create scanned documents may (and should) be set in such a way that the document is "text-searchable." MA R USDCT CM/ECF Admin(Electronic Filing and PDF).

b. *Title.* All pleadings filed electronically shall be titled in accordance with the approved dictionary of civil or criminal

11

events of the CM/ECF system of this court. A list of events is available on the CM/ECF Training Information page of the court's website. The clerk's office may, when necessary and appropriate, modify the docket entry description, or delete and re-enter the docket entry in order to comply with the court's quality assurance standards. MA R USDCT CM/ECF Admin(G)(3).

c. *Attachments to filings and exhibits.* Attachments to filings and exhibits must be filed in accordance with the court's CM/ECF User Manual, unless otherwise ordered by the court. MA R USDCT CM/ECF Admin(O)(1).

    i. Filers must submit as attachments only those excerpts of the referenced documents that are directly germane to the matter under consideration by the court. Excerpted material must be clearly and prominently identified as such. Users who file excerpts of documents do so without prejudice to their right to timely file additional excerpts or the complete document, as may be allowed by the court. Responding parties may timely file additional excerpts or the complete document that they believe are directly germane. MA R USDCT CM/ECF Admin(O)(2).

    ii. Filers shall not attach as an exhibit any pleading or other paper already on file with the court in that case, but shall merely refer to that document. (See MA R USDCT CM/ECF Admin(G) for information on using hyperlinks in PDF documents filed in CM/ECF.) MA R USDCT CM/ECF Admin(O)(3).

d. *Redacted documents.* The parties may request or the court may require the submission of documents that have been redacted/stripped of sensitive or confidential information. The redacted document prepared for electronic filing shall include the original caption of the document, and be clearly labeled as "Redacted Document." A specific event is available for this purpose ("Redacted Document"), found under the Other Filings/Other Documents menu option. MA R USDCT CM/ECF Admin(S).

    i. Attorneys and pro se litigants are advised to take extra care when creating PDF documents intended for submission to CM/ECF. Steps shall be taken to ensure the documents are free of any hidden data (metadata) that may contain redacted information, or traces of information edited or deleted are not hidden in the final document. Even PDF content that has been encrypted may be recovered. An advisory document with additional information on this topic may be found on the court's website. MA R USDCT CM/ECF Admin(S).

e. *Hyperlinks.* Electronically filed documents may contain the following types of hyperlinks: (1) hyperlinks to other portions of the same document; (2) hyperlinks to other documents filed within the CM/ECF system; and (3) hyperlinks to a location on the Internet that contains a source document for a citation. MA R USDCT CM/ECF Admin(G)(7).

    i. Hyperlinks to cited authority may not replace standard citation format. Complete citations must be included in the text of the filed document. Neither a hyperlink, nor any site to which it refers, shall be considered part of the record, but are simply convenient mechanisms for accessing material cited in a document filed in CM/ECF. Instructions on creating hyperlinks may be found in the CM/ECF User Manual. MA R USDCT CM/ECF Admin(G)(7).

    ii. The court accepts no responsibility for, and does not endorse, any product, organization, or content at any hyperlinked site, or at any site to which that site may be linked. The court accepts no responsibility for the availability or functionality of any hyperlink. MA R USDCT CM/ECF Admin(G)(7).

    iii. One feature of PDF/A documents is that hyperlinks are commonly "masked," meaning that the full address of the referenced file is not written out; for example, clicking the word brief may open a brief which was previously filed in CM/ECF. MA R USDCT CM/ECF Admin(G)(7)(NOTE). An "unmasked" hyperlink has the full address visible to the user. MA R USDCT CM/ECF Admin(G)(7)(NOTE).

        • Masked hyperlinks may or may not work in a PDF/A document, depending on how it was created. Currently, masked hyperlinks are preserved in PDF/A documents produced by the "Save As" method in Microsoft Word 2007 and 2010; the "PDFMaker" method in Microsoft Word 2007; and OpenOffice 2.4 ("PDF Export"). With other production methods, such as WordPerfect, the PDF/A document includes underlined words that appear to be links, but clicking them has no effect. MA R USDCT CM/ECF Admin(G)(7)(NOTE).

f. *Documents features not accepted.* CM/ECF will not accept PDF documents containing tracking tags, embedded systems commands, password protections, access restrictions or other security features, special tags or dynamic features. MA R USDCT CM/ECF Admin(G)(8).

g. *File size limitations.* A filing party shall limit the size of each PDF file to no more than twenty (20) megabytes. PDF files larger than seven (7) megabytes will be rejected by the CM/ECF system. The filer will see a message advising of the size limitation. MA R USDCT CM/ECF Admin(P)(2).

   i. Larger documents or exhibits may be submitted electronically if split into separate PDF files each less than seven (7) megabytes, attached to the main document and clearly labeled. MA R USDCT CM/ECF Admin(P)(2).

   ii. Documents submitted electronically or on paper are subject to the page limitations set by MA R USDCT LR 7.1(b)(4) or by order of the court. MA R USDCT CM/ECF Admin(P)(1).

h. *Accuracy and readability.* The filer shall verify the accuracy and readability of any PDF file before electronically filing it in CM/ECF. MA R USDCT CM/ECF Admin(G)(6); MA R USDCT CM/ECF Admin(P)(3).

3. *Signing of pleadings, motions and other papers*

a. *Signature.* Every pleading, written motion, and other paper must be signed by at least one attorney of record in the attorney's name—or by a party personally if the party is unrepresented. The paper must state the signer's address, e-mail address, and telephone number. FRCP 11(a). The provisions of the Federal Rules of Civil Procedure pertaining to the form and signing of pleadings, motions, and other papers shall be applicable to all papers filed in any proceeding in this court. The board of bar overseers registration number of each attorney signing such documents, except the United States Attorney and his staff, shall be inscribed below the signature. MA R USDCT LR 5.1(a)(1).

   i. *Electronic signing.* A filing made through a person's electronic-filing account and authorized by that person, together with that person's name on a signature block, constitutes the person's signature. FRCP 5(d)(3)(C).

   ii. *Appearances.* The filing of an appearance or any other pleading signed on behalf of a party constitutes an entry of appearance for that party. All pleadings shall contain the name, bar admission number, address, telephone number, and e-mail address of the attorney entering an appearance. MA R USDCT LR 83.5.2(a).

     • *Appearances by law firms.* When a party is represented by a law firm, the appearance must include the name and the signature of at least one individual attorney. When a party is represented by more than one attorney from the same or different law firms, the attorney entering the appearance must designate the individual attorney who is authorized to receive all notices in the case. Any notice sent to an attorney so designated shall be deemed to be proper notice unless the court finds that notice was not properly sent. MA R USDCT LR 83.5.2(b).

     • For more information on appearances, refer to MA R USDCT LR 83.5.2.

   iii. *Signatures of attorneys.* The user login and password required to submit documents to the CM/ECF system shall serve as that user's signature for purposes of FRCP 11 and for all other purposes under the Federal Rules of Civil Procedure and the Local Rules of the United States District Court for the District of Massachusetts. All electronically filed documents must include a signature block and must set forth the attorney's name, bar number, address, telephone number and email address. The name of the CM/ECF user under whose log-in and password the document is submitted must be preceded by a "/s/" and typed in the space where the signature would otherwise appear. MA R USDCT CM/ECF Admin(M)(1). For an example, refer to MA R USDCT CM/ECF Admin(M)(1).

   iv. *Signatures of pro se parties.* Any document requiring a signature that is filed by a party appearing pro se shall bear the words "pro se" following that party's signature. Any such document shall also state the party's mailing address, telephone number (if any), and e-mail address (if the party has consented to service by email). MA R USDCT LR 83.5.5(g). For more information on practice by pro se litigants, refer to MA R USDCT LR 83.5.5.

   v. *Multiple signatures.* The filer of any document requiring more than one signature (e.g, stipulations, joint motions, joint status reports, magistrate judge consent forms, etc.) must list thereon all the names of other signatories by means of a "/s/ name of signatory" block for each. By submitting such a document, the filing attorney certifies that each of the other signatories has expressly agreed to the form and substance of the document and that the filing attorney has their actual authority to submit the document electronically. MA R USDCT CM/ECF Admin(M)(2). For more information, refer to MA R USDCT CM/ECF Admin(M)(2).

   vi. *Affidavits.* Except as provided in MA R USDCT CM/ECF Admin(L), affidavits shall be filed electronically; however, the electronically filed version must contain a "/s/ name of signatory" block indicating that the paper document bears an original signature. MA R USDCT CM/ECF Admin(M)(3). The court will also accept a scanned version of the original, signed document. MA R USDCT CM/ECF Admin(M)(3). For more information, refer to MA R USDCT CM/ECF Admin(M)(3).

   vii. *No verification or accompanying affidavit required for pleadings.* Unless a rule or statute specifically states otherwise, a pleading need not be verified or accompanied by an affidavit. FRCP 11(a).

    viii.   *Unsigned papers.* The court must strike an unsigned paper unless the omission is promptly corrected after being called to the attorney's or party's attention. FRCP 11(a).

b.   *Representations to the court.* By presenting to the court a pleading, written motion, or other paper—whether by signing, filing, submitting, or later advocating it—an attorney or unrepresented party certifies that to the best of the person's knowledge, information, and belief, formed after an inquiry reasonable under the circumstances:

    i.   It is not being presented for any improper purpose, such as to harass, cause unnecessary delay, or needlessly increase the cost of litigation;

    ii.   The claims, defenses, and other legal contentions are warranted by existing law or by a nonfrivolous argument for extending, modifying, or reversing existing law or for establishing new law;

    iii.   The factual contentions have evidentiary support or, if specifically so identified, will likely have evidentiary support after a reasonable opportunity for further investigation or discovery; and

    iv.   The denials of factual contentions are warranted on the evidence or, if specifically so identified, are reasonably based on belief or a lack of information. FRCP 11(b).

c.   *Sanctions.* If, after notice and a reasonable opportunity to respond, the court determines that FRCP 11(b) has been violated, the court may impose an appropriate sanction on any attorney, law firm, or party that violated FRCP 11(b) or is responsible for the violation. FRCP 11(c)(1). Refer to the United States District Court for the District of Massachusetts KeyRules Motion for Sanctions document for more information.

4.   *Privacy protection for filings made with the court*

a.   *Redacted filings.* Unless the court orders otherwise, in an electronic or paper filing with the court that contains an individual's Social Security number, taxpayer-identification number, or birth date, the name of an individual known to be a minor, or a financial-account number, a party or nonparty making the filing may include only:

    i.   The last four (4) digits of the Social Security number and taxpayer-identification number;

    ii.   The year of the individual's birth;

    iii.   The minor's initials; and

    iv.   The last four (4) digits of the financial-account number. FRCP 5.2(a); MA R USDCT CM/ECF Admin(N).

b.   *Exemptions from the redaction requirement.* The redaction requirement does not apply to the following:

    i.   A financial-account number that identifies the property allegedly subject to forfeiture in a forfeiture proceeding;

    ii.   The record of an administrative or agency proceeding;

    iii.   The official record of a state-court proceeding;

    iv.   The record of a court or tribunal, if that record was not subject to the redaction requirement when originally filed;

    v.   A filing covered by FRCP 5.2(c) or FRCP 5.2(d); and

    vi.   A pro se filing in an action brought under 28 U.S.C.A. § 2241, 28 U.S.C.A. § 2254, or 28 U.S.C.A. § 2255. FRCP 5.2(b).

c.   *Limitations on remote access to electronic files; Social Security appeals and immigration cases.* Unless the court orders otherwise, in an action for benefits under the Social Security Act, and in an action or proceeding relating to an order of removal, to relief from removal, or to immigration benefits or detention, access to an electronic file is authorized as follows:

    i.   The parties and their attorneys may have remote electronic access to any part of the case file, including the administrative record;

    ii.   Any other person may have electronic access to the full record at the courthouse, but may have remote electronic access only to:

        ●   The docket maintained by the court; and

        ●   An opinion, order, judgment, or other disposition of the court, but not any other part of the case file or the administrative record. FRCP 5.2(c).

d.   *Filings made under seal.* The court may order that a filing be made under seal without redaction. The court may later unseal the filing or order the person who made the filing to file a redacted version for the public record. FRCP 5.2(d).

e.   *Protective orders.* For good cause, the court may by order in a case:

    i.   Require redaction of additional information; or

ii. Limit or prohibit a nonparty's remote electronic access to a document filed with the court. FRCP 5.2(e).

f. *Option for additional unredacted filing under seal.* A person making a redacted filing may also file an unredacted copy under seal. The court must retain the unredacted copy as part of the record. FRCP 5.2(f). For more information, refer to MA R USDCT LR 7.2.

g. *Option for filing a reference list.* A filing that contains redacted information may be filed together with a reference list that identifies each item of redacted information and specifies an appropriate identifier that uniquely corresponds to each item listed. The list must be filed under seal and may be amended as of right. Any reference in the case to a listed identifier will be construed to refer to the corresponding item of information. FRCP 5.2(g).

h. *Responsibility for redaction.* The clerk's office is not responsible for reviewing documents filed with the court to determine whether pleadings have been redacted and are in the proper form. MA R USDCT CM/ECF Admin(N).

i. *Waiver of protection of identifiers.* A person waives the protection of FRCP 5.2(a) as to the person's own information by filing it without redaction and not under seal. FRCP 5.2(h).

## F. Filing and Service Requirements

1. *Filing requirements.* A civil action is commenced by filing a complaint with the court. FRCP 3. The first step in a civil action in a United States district court is the filing of the complaint with the clerk or the judge. FPP § 1052. Filing a complaint requires nothing more than delivery of the document to a court officer authorized to receive it. FPP § 1052; Cent. States, Se. & Sw. Areas Pension Fund v. Paramount Liquor Co., 34 F. Supp. 2d 1092 (N.D. Ill. 1999).

a. *Nonelectronic filing.* A paper not filed electronically is filed by delivering it: (1) to the clerk; or (2) to a judge who agrees to accept it for filing, and who must then note the filing date on the paper and promptly send it to the clerk. FRCP 5(d)(2).

b. *Designation of divisions.* The District of Massachusetts constitutes one judicial district comprising three divisions.

i. *Eastern Division.* The Eastern Division of the District of Massachusetts comprises the counties of Barnstable, Bristol, Dukes, Essex, Middlesex, Nantucket, Norfolk, Plymouth, and Suffolk. Cases assigned to the Eastern Division and all pleadings and documents therein shall be filed in the clerk's office in Boston. MA R USDCT LR 40.1(C)(1).

ii. *Central Division.* The Central Division of the District of Massachusetts is Worcester County. Cases assigned to the Central Division and all pleadings and documents therein shall be filed in the clerk's office in Worcester. MA R USDCT LR 40.1(C)(2).

iii. *Western Division.* The Western Division of the District of Massachusetts comprises the counties of Berkshire, Franklin, Hampden and Hampshire. Cases shall be assigned to the Western Division and all pleadings and documents therein shall be filed at the clerk's office in Springfield. MA R USDCT LR 40.1(C)(3).

c. *Civil case opening documents.* All ECF filers registered in the District of Massachusetts must file civil case opening documents, such as a complaint (or petition or notice of removal), civil action cover sheet, or category sheet, electronically. MA R USDCT LR 5.4(E). Registered CM/ECF users shall file electronically any and all civil ("cv" case type) and miscellaneous (sometimes referred to as MBD or "mc" case type) case opening documents, such as a complaint, petition, or notice of removal in accordance with the guidelines and restrictions described in MA R USDCT CM/ECF Admin(L). For civil cases only, filers shall submit the required civil cover and category sheets, both available on the court's website. MA R USDCT CM/ECF Admin(F)(1).

i. *Cases including sealed or ex parte documents.* Cases which include sealed or ex parte documents and supporting materials presented contemporaneously with civil case opening documents may be filed and served initially in paper format and not electronically. Pro se filers, others exempt from electronic filing, or otherwise ordered by the court, may file case opening documents in paper format and not electronically. MA R USDCT LR 5.4(E).

ii. *Case-related fees.* Pursuant to MA R USDCT LR 67.4, all case-related fees shall be paid by credit card in conjunction with CM/ECF and the United States Treasury's service. MA R USDCT CM/ECF Admin(F)(1).

d. *Pro se incarcerated litigants.* Individuals who are incarcerated and are filing their legal documents pro se may benefit from a special "mailbox rule," which fixes the time of commencement of an action at the point when the complaint enters the prison mail system, rather than when it reaches the court clerk. FPP § 1052; Houston v. Lack, 487 U.S. 266, 276, 108 S.Ct. 2379, 2385, 101 L.Ed.2d 245 (1988).

e. *Electronic filing.* Unless exempt or otherwise ordered by the court, all pleadings and other papers submitted to the court must be filed, signed, and verified by electronic means as provided in MA R USDCT LR 5.4. MA R USDCT LR 5.4(A); MA R USDCT CM/ECF Admin(A)(1). All electronic filings must be made in accordance with the

Administrative Procedures for Electronic Case Filing in the United States District Court for the District of Massachusetts (MA R USDCT CM/ECF Admin). MA R USDCT LR 5.4(B). The court may deviate from the Administrative Procedures for Electronic Case Filing in the United States District Court for the District of Massachusetts (MA R USDCT CM/ECF Admin) in specific cases, without prior notice, if deemed appropriate in the exercise of discretion, considering the need for the just, speedy, and inexpensive determination of matters pending before the court. MA R USDCT CM/ECF Admin(C)(1). The court may excuse a failure to comply with any administrative procedure whenever justice so requires. MA R USDCT CM/ECF Admin(C)(2).

i. *By a represented person; Generally required; Exceptions.* A person represented by an attorney must file electronically, unless nonelectronic filing is allowed by the court for good cause or is allowed or required by local rule. FRCP 5(d)(3)(A).

ii. *By unrepresented person; When allowed or required.* A person not represented by an attorney: (1) may file electronically only if allowed by court order or by local rule; and (2) may be required to file electronically only by court order, or by a local rule that includes reasonable exceptions. FRCP 5(d)(3)(B).

iii. *Exemptions from electronic filing*

- *Documents that should not be filed electronically.* The following types of documents must not be filed electronically, and will not be scanned into the ECF system by the clerk's office: (1) sealed documents; (2) ex parte motions; (3) documents generated as part of an alternative dispute resolution (ADR) process; (4) the administrative record in Social Security and other administrative proceedings; (5) the state court record in proceedings under 28 U.S.C.A. § 2254; and (6) such other types of documents as the clerk may direct in the Administrative Procedures for Electronic Case Filing in the United States District Court for the District of Massachusetts (MA R USDCT CM/ECF Admin). MA R USDCT LR 5.4(G)(1); MA R USDCT CM/ECF Admin(L).

- *Documents that need not be filed electronically.* The following types of documents need not be filed electronically, but may be scanned into the ECF system by a filing party or the clerk's office: (1) handwritten pleadings; (2) documents filed by pro se litigants who are incarcerated or who are not registered ECF users; (3) indictments, informations, criminal complaints, and the criminal JS45 form; (4) affidavits for search or arrest warrants and related documents; (5) documents received from another court under FRCRP 20 or FRCRP 40; (6) appearance bonds; (7) any document in a criminal case containing the original signature of a defendant, such as a waiver of indictment or a plea agreement; (8) petitions for violations of supervised release; (9) executed service of process documents under FRCP 4; and (10) such other types of documents as the clerk may direct in the Administrative Procedures for Electronic Case Filing in the United States District Court for the District of Massachusetts (MA R USDCT CM/ECF Admin). MA R USDCT LR 5.4(G)(2); MA R USDCT CM/ECF Admin(L).

- For more information on exemptions from electronic filing, refer to MA R USDCT CM/ECF Admin(L).

iv. *Consequences of electronic filing.* Electronic transmission of a document to the CM/ECF system, together with the transmission of a Notice of Electronic Filing (NEF) from the court at the completion of the transaction, constitutes the filing of the document for all purposes of the Federal Rules of Procedure and constitutes entry of the document on the docket maintained by the clerk pursuant to FRCP 58 and FRCP 79. MA R USDCT CM/ECF Admin(G)(1).

v. *Payment of filing fees.* When electronically filing any pleading or paper through CM/ECF that requires a fee, all registered ECF users are to pay the fee electronically through the Treasury Department's Internet payment process. MA R USDCT LR 67.4(d); MA R USDCT CM/ECF Admin(A)(1). Pro se filers and those who have been exempted from electronic filing and/or electronic payment of fees may submit payments by check or money order made payable to "Clerk, U.S. District Court". MA R USDCT LR 67.4(d). For more information on filing fees, refer to MA R USDCT LR 67.4 and MA R USDCT CM/ECF Admin(I).

vi. For more information on electronic filing, refer to MA R USDCT CM/ECF Admin.

f. *Email or fax filing.* In general, the court does not accept documents by email or by fax. If the court, in special circumstances, does authorize the submission of a document in that manner, the document shall not be considered filed until an NEF is generated by CM/ECF at the completion of the transaction. MA R USDCT CM/ECF Admin(H)(5).

2. *Issuance of summons.* On or after filing the complaint, the plaintiff may present a summons to the clerk for signature and seal. If the summons is properly completed, the clerk must sign, seal, and issue it to the plaintiff for service on the

defendant. A summons—or a copy of a summons that is addressed to multiple defendants—must be issued for each defendant to be served. FRCP 4(b).

    a. *Electronic issuance.* The clerk's office shall create an electronic summons, when appropriate, and provide it to counsel via CM/ECF. Recipients are directed to download the PDF file from the Notice of Electronic Filing (NEF) and create a summons for each party to be served. MA R USDCT CM/ECF Admin(F)(2).

    b. *Paper issuance.* If the attorney filing the new case is not yet registered to use CM/ECF, the clerk's office will issue the summons on paper, along with a notice regarding MA R USDCT LR 5.4 and the mandatory use of CM/ECF. MA R USDCT CM/ECF Admin(F)(3).

    c. *Amendments.* The court may permit a summons to be amended. FRCP 4(a)(2).

3. *Service requirements.* A summons must be served with a copy of the complaint. The plaintiff is responsible for having the summons and complaint served within the time allowed by FRCP 4(m) and must furnish the necessary copies to the person who makes service. FRCP 4(c)(1). A party may not electronically serve a civil complaint but shall affect service in the manner required by FRCP 4. MA R USDCT CM/ECF Admin(F)(2).

    a. *By whom served.* Any person who is at least 18 years old and not a party may serve a summons and complaint. FRCP 4(c)(2).

      i. *By a marshal or someone specially appointed.* At the plaintiff's request, the court may order that service be made by a United States marshal or deputy marshal or by a person specially appointed by the court. The court must so order if the plaintiff is authorized to proceed in forma pauperis under 28 U.S.C.A. § 1915 or as a seaman under 28 U.S.C.A. § 1916. FRCP 4(c)(3).

    b. *Serving an individual within a judicial district of the United States.* Unless federal law provides otherwise, an individual—other than a minor, an incompetent person, or a person whose waiver has been filed—may be served in a judicial district of the United States by:

      i. Following state law for serving a summons in an action brought in courts of general jurisdiction in the state where the district court is located or where service is made; or

      ii. Doing any of the following:

        • Delivering a copy of the summons and of the complaint to the individual personally;

        • Leaving a copy of each at the individual's dwelling or usual place of abode with someone of suitable age and discretion who resides there; or

        • Delivering a copy of each to an agent authorized by appointment or by law to receive service of process. FRCP 4(e).

    c. *Serving an individual in a foreign country.* Unless federal law provides otherwise, an individual—other than a minor, an incompetent person, or a person whose waiver has been filed—may be served at a place not within any judicial district of the United States:

      i. By any internationally agreed means of service that is reasonably calculated to give notice, such as those authorized by the Hague Convention on the Service Abroad of Judicial and Extrajudicial Documents;

      ii. If there is no internationally agreed means, or if an international agreement allows but does not specify other means, by a method that is reasonably calculated to give notice:

        • As prescribed by the foreign country's law for service in that country in an action in its courts of general jurisdiction;

        • As the foreign authority directs in response to a letter rogatory or letter of request; or

        • Unless prohibited by the foreign country's law, by: (1) delivering a copy of the summons and of the complaint to the individual personally; or (2) using any form of mail that the clerk addresses and sends to the individual and that requires a signed receipt; or

        • By other means not prohibited by international agreement, as the court orders. FRCP 4(f).

    d. *Serving a minor or an incompetent person.* A minor or an incompetent person in a judicial district of the United States must be served by following state law for serving a summons or like process on such a defendant in an action brought in the courts of general jurisdiction of the state where service is made. A minor or an incompetent person who is not within any judicial district of the United States must be served in the manner prescribed by FRCP 4(f)(2)(A), FRCP 4(f)(2)(B), or FRCP 4(f)(3). FRCP 4(g).

e. *Serving a corporation, partnership, or association.* Unless federal law provides otherwise or the defendant's waiver has been filed, a domestic or foreign corporation, or a partnership or other unincorporated association that is subject to suit under a common name, must be served:

    i. In a judicial district of the United States:

- In the manner prescribed by FRCP 4(e)(1) for serving an individual; or

- By delivering a copy of the summons and of the complaint to an officer, a managing or general agent, or any other agent authorized by appointment or by law to receive service of process and—if the agent is one authorized by statute and the statute so requires—by also mailing a copy of each to the defendant; or

    ii. At a place not within any judicial district of the United States, in any manner prescribed by FRCP 4(f) for serving an individual, except personal delivery under FRCP 4(f)(2)(C)(i). FRCP 4(h).

f. *Serving the United States and its agencies, corporations, officers, or employees*

    i. *United States.* To serve the United States, a party must:

- Deliver a copy of the summons and of the complaint to the United States attorney for the district where the action is brought—or to an assistant United States attorney or clerical employee whom the United States attorney designates in a writing filed with the court clerk—or send a copy of each by registered or certified mail to the civil-process clerk at the United States attorney's office;

- Send a copy of each by registered or certified mail to the Attorney General of the United States at Washington, D.C.; and

- If the action challenges an order of a nonparty agency or officer of the United States, send a copy of each by registered or certified mail to the agency or officer. FRCP 4(i)(1).

    ii. *Agency; Corporation; Officer or employee sued in an official capacity.* To serve a United States agency or corporation, or a United States officer or employee sued only in an official capacity, a party must serve the United States and also send a copy of the summons and of the complaint by registered or certified mail to the agency, corporation, officer, or employee. FRCP 4(i)(2).

    iii. *Officer or employee sued individually.* To serve a United States officer or employee sued in an individual capacity for an act or omission occurring in connection with duties performed on the United States' behalf (whether or not the officer or employee is also sued in an official capacity), a party must serve the United States and also serve the officer or employee under FRCP 4(e), FRCP 4(f), or FRCP 4(g). FRCP 4(i)(3).

    iv. *Extending time.* The court must allow a party a reasonable time to cure its failure to:

- Serve a person required to be served under FRCP 4(i)(2), if the party has served either the United States attorney or the Attorney General of the United States; or

- Serve the United States under FRCP 4(i)(3), if the party has served the United States officer or employee. FRCP 4(i)(4).

g. *Serving a foreign, state, or local government*

    i. *Foreign state.* A foreign state or its political subdivision, agency, or instrumentality must be served in accordance with 28 U.S.C.A. § 1608. FRCP 4(j)(1).

    ii. *State or local government.* A state, a municipal corporation, or any other state-created governmental organization that is subject to suit must be served by:

- Delivering a copy of the summons and of the complaint to its chief executive officer; or

- Serving a copy of each in the manner prescribed by that state's law for serving a summons or like process on such a defendant. FRCP 4(j)(2).

h. *Territorial limits of effective service*

    i. *In general.* Serving a summons or filing a waiver of service establishes personal jurisdiction over a defendant:

- Who is subject to the jurisdiction of a court of general jurisdiction in the state where the district court is located;

- Who is a party joined under FRCP 14 or FRCP 19 and is served within a judicial district of the United States and not more than 100 miles from where the summons was issued; or

- When authorized by a federal statute. FRCP 4(k)(1).

    ii. *Federal claim outside state-court jurisdiction.* For a claim that arises under federal law, serving a summons or filing a waiver of service establishes personal jurisdiction over a defendant if:

- The defendant is not subject to jurisdiction in any state's courts of general jurisdiction; and

- Exercising jurisdiction is consistent with the United States Constitution and laws. FRCP 4(k)(2).

  i. *Asserting jurisdiction over property or assets*

    i. *Federal law.* The court may assert jurisdiction over property if authorized by a federal statute. Notice to claimants of the property must be given as provided in the statute or by serving a summons under FRCP 4. FRCP 4(n)(1).

    ii. *State law.* On a showing that personal jurisdiction over a defendant cannot be obtained in the district where the action is brought by reasonable efforts to serve a summons under FRCP 4, the court may assert jurisdiction over the defendant's assets found in the district. Jurisdiction is acquired by seizing the assets under the circumstances and in the manner provided by state law in that district. FRCP 4(n)(2).

  j. *Proving service*

    i. *Affidavit required.* Unless service is waived, proof of service must be made to the court. Except for service by a United States marshal or deputy marshal, proof must be by the server's affidavit. FRCP 4(l)(1).

    ii. *Service outside the United States.* Service not within any judicial district of the United States must be proved as follows:

- If made under FRCP 4(f)(1), as provided in the applicable treaty or convention; or

- If made under FRCP 4(f)(2) or FRCP 4(f)(3), by a receipt signed by the addressee, or by other evidence satisfying the court that the summons and complaint were delivered to the addressee. FRCP 4(l)(2).

    iii. *Validity of service; Amending proof.* Failure to prove service does not affect the validity of service. The court may permit proof of service to be amended. FRCP 4(l)(3).

    iv. *Filing.* The return of service of the summons (or other acknowledgment of service) shall be filed with the court electronically. MA R USDCT CM/ECF Admin(F)(2).

    v. *Results of filing a waiver of service.* When the plaintiff files a waiver, proof of service is not required and FRCP 4 applies as if a summons and complaint had been served at the time of filing the waiver. FRCP 4(d)(4).

  k. *Service of other process.* For information on service of other process, refer to FRCP 4.1.

## G. Hearings

1. There is no hearing contemplated in the federal statutes or rules for the complaint and summons.

## H. Forms

### 1. Official Federal Complaint and Summons Forms

  a. Notice of a lawsuit and request to waive service of summons. FRCP 4.

  b. Duty to avoid unnecessary expenses of serving a summons. FRCP 4.

### 2. Federal Complaint and Summons Forms

  a. Summons. 2 FEDFORMS § 3:23.

  b. Proof of service by U.S. Marshal. 2 FEDFORMS § 3:24.

  c. Summons; Suit against officers of the United States. 2 FEDFORMS § 3:26.

  d. Request for summons. 2 FEDFORMS § 3:27.

  e. Civil cover sheet. 2 FEDFORMS § 3:29.

  f. Motion for appointment of person to serve process. 2 FEDFORMS § 3:30.

  g. Motion for appointment of United States marshal to serve process. 2 FEDFORMS § 3:34.

  h. Notice of lawsuit and request for waiver of service of summons and waiver of summons. 2 FEDFORMS § 3:36.

  i. Motion for payment of costs of personal service. 2 FEDFORMS § 3:37.

  j. Affidavit of personal service; Delivery to individual. 2 FEDFORMS § 3:54.

  k. Declaration of service; Delivery to individual. 2 FEDFORMS § 3:55.

    l.    Declaration of service; Delivery at usual place of abode or residence. 2 FEDFORMS § 3:56.

    m.   Declaration of service; Service on corporation; Delivery to officer. 2 FEDFORMS § 3:57.

    n.    Declaration of service; Service on United States. 2 FEDFORMS § 3:69.

    o.    Declaration of service; Service on officer of United States. 2 FEDFORMS § 3:71.

    p.    Complaint. 2 FEDFORMS § 7:14.

    q.    Pro se complaint for a civil case. 2 FEDFORMS § 7:14.30.

    r.    Pro se complaint and request for injunction. 2 FEDFORMS § 7:14.50.

    s.    Introductory clause; Single claim stated. 2 FEDFORMS § 7:16.

    t.    Introductory clause; Several claims stated in separate counts. 2 FEDFORMS § 7:18.

    u.    Allegations on information and belief. 2 FEDFORMS § 7:19.

    v.    General prayer for relief. 2 FEDFORMS § 7:21.

    w.   Complaint; Single count. FEDPROF § 1A:171.

    x.    Complaint; Multiple counts; With same jurisdictional basis. FEDPROF § 1A:172.

    y.    Complaint; Multiple counts; With different jurisdictional basis for each. FEDPROF § 1A:173.

    z.    Civil cover sheet; General form (form JS-44). FEDPROF § 1A:252.

**3.   Forms for the District of Massachusetts**

    a.    Civil cover sheet. MA R USDCT App. B.

    b.    Local civil category sheet. MA R USDCT App. C.

    c.    Notice of filing with clerk's office. MA R USDCT CM/ECF Admin(Appendix I).

    d.    Notice of filing fee payment. MA R USDCT CM/ECF Admin(Appendix II).

# I.  Applicable Rules

1.   *Federal rules*

    a.    District court; Filing and miscellaneous fees; Rules of court. 28 U.S.C.A. § 1914.

    b.    Commencing an action. FRCP 3.

    c.    Summons. FRCP 4.

    d.    Serving and filing pleadings and other papers. FRCP 5.

    e.    Constitutional challenge to a statute; Notice, certification, and intervention. FRCP 5.1.

    f.    Privacy protection for filings made with the court. FRCP 5.2.

    g.    Computing and extending time; Time for motion papers. FRCP 6.

    h.    Pleadings allowed; Form of motions and other papers. FRCP 7.

    i.    Disclosure statement. FRCP 7.1.

    j.    General rules of pleading. FRCP 8.

    k.    Pleading special matters. FRCP 9.

    l.    Form of pleadings. FRCP 10.

    m.   Signing pleadings, motions, and other papers; Representations to the court; Sanctions. FRCP 11.

    n.    Joinder of claims. FRCP 18.

    o.    Required joinder of parties. FRCP 19.

    p.    Permissive joinder of parties. FRCP 20.

    q.    Misjoinder and nonjoinder of parties. FRCP 21.

    r.    Right to a jury trial; Demand. FRCP 38.

    s.    Determining foreign law. FRCP 44.1.

2. *Local rules*

   a.   Title. MA R USDCT LR 1.1.

   b.   Sanctions. MA R USDCT LR 1.3.

   c.   Civil cover sheet. MA R USDCT LR 3.1.

   d.   Service of process; Dismissal for failure to make service. MA R USDCT LR 4.1.

   e.   Fees. MA R USDCT LR 4.2.

   f.   Form and filing of papers. MA R USDCT LR 5.1.

   g.   Filing and service by electronic means. MA R USDCT LR 5.4.

   h.   Alternative dispute resolution. MA R USDCT LR 16.4.

   i.   Assignment of cases. [MA R USDCT LR 40.1, as amended by MA ORDER 19-3002, effective January 11, 2019].

   j.   Payments and deposits made with the clerk. MA R USDCT LR 67.4.

   k.   Settlement. MA R USDCT LR 68.2.

   l.   Office of the clerk. MA R USDCT LR 77.2.

   m.   Appearances. MA R USDCT LR 83.5.2.

   n.   Practice by pro se litigants. MA R USDCT LR 83.5.5.

   o.   CM/ECF case management/electronic case files administrative procedures. MA R USDCT CM/ECF Admin.

# Pleadings
# Answer

**Document Last Updated December 2018**

## A. Checklist

(I)  ❑ Matters to be considered by plaintiff

  (a)  ❑ Required documents

    (1)  ❑ Civil cover sheet

    (2)  ❑ Local civil category sheet

    (3)  ❑ Complaint

    (4)  ❑ Summons

    (5)  ❑ Filing fee

    (6)  ❑ Affidavit proving service

  (b)  ❑ Supplemental documents

    (1)  ❑ Notice and request for waiver of service

    (2)  ❑ Notice of constitutional question

    (3)  ❑ Notice of issue concerning foreign law

    (4)  ❑ Nongovernmental corporate disclosure statement

    (5)  ❑ Papers for service under state law

    (6)  ❑ Request to proceed in forma pauperis

    (7)  ❑ Compact disk with copy of document(s) in PDF format

    (8)  ❑ Notice of filing with clerk's office

    (9)  ❑ Additional copies

    (10)  ❑ Courtesy copies

  (c)  ❑ Timing

    (1)  ❑ A civil action is commenced by filing a complaint with the court

       (2)  ❑  If a defendant is not served within ninety (90) days after the complaint is filed, the court—on motion or on its own after notice to the plaintiff—must dismiss the action without prejudice against that defendant or order that service be made within a specified time

(II)  ❑  Matters to be considered by defendant

  (a)  ❑  Required documents

      (1)  ❑  Answer

      (2)  ❑  Certificate of service

  (b)  ❑  Supplemental documents

      (1)  ❑  Waiver of the service of summons

      (2)  ❑  Notice of constitutional question

      (3)  ❑  Notice of issue concerning foreign law

      (4)  ❑  Nongovernmental corporate disclosure statement

      (5)  ❑  Compact disk with copy of document(s) in PDF format

      (6)  ❑  Notice of filing with clerk's office

      (7)  ❑  Additional copies

      (8)  ❑  Courtesy copies

  (c)  ❑  Timing

      (1)  ❑  A defendant must serve an answer:

         (i)  ❑  Within twenty-one (21) days after being served with the summons and complaint; or

        (ii)  ❑  If it has timely waived service under FRCP 4(d), within sixty (60) days after the request for a waiver was sent, or within ninety (90) days after it was sent to the defendant outside any judicial district of the United States

      (2)  ❑  The United States, a United States agency, or a United States officer or employee sued only in an official capacity must serve an answer to a complaint, counterclaim, or crossclaim within sixty (60) days after service on the United States attorney

      (3)  ❑  A United States officer or employee sued in an individual capacity for an act or omission occurring in connection with duties performed on the United States' behalf must serve an answer to a complaint, counterclaim, or crossclaim within sixty (60) days after service on the officer or employee or service on the United States attorney, whichever is later

      (4)  ❑  Unless the court sets a different time, serving a motion under FRCP 12 alters the periods in FRCP 12(a) as follows:

         (i)  ❑  If the court denies the motion or postpones its disposition until trial, the responsive pleading must be served within fourteen (14) days after notice of the court's action; or

        (ii)  ❑  If the court grants a motion for a more definite statement, the responsive pleading must be served within fourteen (14) days after the more definite statement is served

      (5)  ❑  The notice and request for waiver must give the defendant a reasonable time of at least thirty (30) days after the request was sent—or at least sixty (60) days if sent to the defendant outside any judicial district of the United States—to return the waiver

         (i)  ❑  A defendant who, before being served with process, timely returns a waiver need not serve an answer to the complaint until sixty (60) days after the request was sent—or until ninety (90) days after it was sent to the defendant outside any judicial district of the United States

      (6)  ❑  Except as noted in FRCP 33 to FRCP 36, the original of all papers required to be served under FRCP 5(d) shall, unless otherwise submitted to the court, be filed in the office of the clerk within seven (7) days after service has been made

## B. Timing

  1.  *Answer.* Unless another time is specified by FRCP 12 or a federal statute. . .a defendant must serve an answer: (1) within twenty-one (21) days after being served with the summons and complaint; or (2) if it has timely waived service under

FRCP 4(d), within sixty (60) days after the request for a waiver was sent, or within ninety (90) days after it was sent to the defendant outside any judicial district of the United States. FRCP 12(a)(1)(A).

    a. *Time to serve other responsive pleadings.* Unless another time is specified by FRCP 12 or a federal statute, the time for serving a responsive pleading is as follows:

        i. *Answer to counterclaim or crossclaim.* A party must serve an answer to a counterclaim or crossclaim within twenty-one (21) days after being served with the pleading that states the counterclaim or crossclaim. FRCP 12(a)(1)(B).

        ii. *Reply to an answer.* A party must serve a reply to an answer within twenty-one (21) days after being served with an order to reply, unless the order specifies a different time. FRCP 12(a)(1)(C).

    b. *United States and its agencies, officers, or employees sued in an official capacity.* The United States, a United States agency, or a United States officer or employee sued only in an official capacity must serve an answer to a complaint, counterclaim, or crossclaim within sixty (60) days after service on the United States attorney. FRCP 12(a)(2).

    c. *United States officers or employees sued in an individual capacity.* A United States officer or employee sued in an individual capacity for an act or omission occurring in connection with duties performed on the United States' behalf must serve an answer to a complaint, counterclaim, or crossclaim within sixty (60) days after service on the officer or employee or service on the United States attorney, whichever is later. FRCP 12(a)(3).

    d. *Effect of FRCP 12 motion on the time to serve a responsive pleading.* Unless the court sets a different time, serving a motion under FRCP 12 alters the periods in FRCP 12(a) as follows:

        i. If the court denies the motion or postpones its disposition until trial, the responsive pleading must be served within fourteen (14) days after notice of the court's action; or

        ii. If the court grants a motion for a more definite statement, the responsive pleading must be served within fourteen (14) days after the more definite statement is served. FRCP 12(a)(4).

2. *Waiver of service.* The notice and request for waiver must give the defendant a reasonable time of at least thirty (30) days after the request was sent—or at least sixty (60) days if sent to the defendant outside any judicial district of the United States—to return the waiver. FRCP 4(d)(1)(F).

    a. *Time to answer after a waiver.* A defendant who, before being served with process, timely returns a waiver need not serve an answer to the complaint until sixty (60) days after the request was sent—or until ninety (90) days after it was sent to the defendant outside any judicial district of the United States. FRCP 4(d)(3).

3. *Filing after service.* Except as noted in FRCP 33 to FRCP 36, the original of all papers required to be served under FRCP 5(d) shall, unless otherwise submitted to the court, be filed in the office of the clerk within seven (7) days after service has been made. MA R USDCT LR 5.1(b).

4. *Computation of time*

    a. *Computing time.* FRCP 6 applies in computing any time period specified in the Federal Rules of Civil Procedure, in any local rule or court order, or in any statute that does not specify a method of computing time. FRCP 6(a).

        i. *Period stated in days or a longer unit.* When the period is stated in days or a longer unit of time:

- Exclude the day of the event that triggers the period;

- Count every day, including intermediate Saturdays, Sundays, and legal holidays; and

- Include the last day of the period, but if the last day is a Saturday, Sunday, or legal holiday, the period continues to run until the end of the next day that is not a Saturday, Sunday, or legal holiday. FRCP 6(a)(1).

        ii. *Period stated in hours.* When the period is stated in hours:

- Begin counting immediately on the occurrence of the event that triggers the period;

- Count every hour, including hours during intermediate Saturdays, Sundays, and legal holidays; and

- If the period would end on a Saturday, Sunday, or legal holiday, the period continues to run until the same time on the next day that is not a Saturday, Sunday, or legal holiday. FRCP 6(a)(2).

        iii. *Office of the clerk.* The offices of the Clerk of Court at Boston, Worcester and Springfield shall be open from 8:30 a.m. until 5:00 p.m. on all days except Saturdays, Sundays, legal holidays and other days so ordered by the court and announced in advance, if feasible. MA R USDCT LR 77.2.

iv. *Inaccessibility of the clerk's office.* Unless the court orders otherwise, if the clerk's office is inaccessible:

- On the last day for filing under FRCP 6(a)(1), then the time for filing is extended to the first accessible day that is not a Saturday, Sunday, or legal holiday; or

- During the last hour for filing under FRCP 6(a)(2), then the time for filing is extended to the same time on the first accessible day that is not a Saturday, Sunday, or legal holiday. FRCP 6(a)(3).

v. *"Last day" defined.* Unless a different time is set by a statute, local rule, or court order, the last day ends:

- For electronic filing, at midnight in the court's time zone; and

- For filing by other means, when the clerk's office is scheduled to close. FRCP 6(a)(4).

vi. *"Next day" defined.* The "next day" is determined by continuing to count forward when the period is measured after an event and backward when measured before an event. FRCP 6(a)(5).

vii. *"Legal holiday" defined.* "Legal holiday" means:

- The day set aside by statute for observing New Year's Day, Martin Luther King Jr.'s Birthday, Washington's Birthday, Memorial Day, Independence Day, Labor Day, Columbus Day, Veterans' Day, Thanksgiving Day, or Christmas Day;

- Any day declared a holiday by the President or Congress; and

- For periods that are measured after an event, any other day declared a holiday by the state where the district court is located. FRCP 6(a)(6).

b. *Computation of electronic filing deadlines.* Filing documents electronically does not alter any filing deadlines. MA R USDCT CM/ECF Admin(K); MA R USDCT LR 5.4(D). Although CM/ECF is generally available twenty-four (24) hours a day for filing, all electronic transmissions of documents must be completed prior to 6:00 PM, Eastern Standard (or Daylight Savings) Time, on the date on which it is due, in order to be considered timely filed that day. MA R USDCT CM/ECF Admin(K); MA R USDCT LR 5.4(D). When a specific time of day deadline is set by court order or stipulation, the electronic filing must be completed by that time. Documents may be filed at any time of the day on days prior to the date on which it is due. MA R USDCT CM/ECF Admin(K). A document filed electronically shall be deemed filed as of the time and date stated on the NEF received from the court. MA R USDCT CM/ECF Admin(G)(2); MA R USDCT CM/ECF Admin(K).

i. *Technical failures.* A user whose filing is made untimely as the result of a technical failure of the court's CM/ECF system may seek appropriate relief from the court. MA R USDCT CM/ECF Admin(W)(3). Technical difficulties on the filer's end, with telephone, cable lines, the filer's Internet Service Provider (ISP), or hardware or software problems, will not constitute a technical failure under the Administrative Procedures for Electronic Case Filing in the United States District Court for the District of Massachusetts (MA R USDCT CM/ECF Admin) nor excuse an untimely filing. MA R USDCT CM/ECF Admin(W)(3). As help desk support is available during normal business hours, filers are strongly urged to electronically file any documents during that period. MA R USDCT CM/ECF Admin(W)(3).

- The court has made available a public terminal (computers and scanner) in each clerk's office for registered users to scan and electronically file documents. This equipment is available during normal business hours. Users should bring their prepared document and a valid CM/ECF login and password. MA R USDCT CM/ECF Admin(W)(3).

c. *Extending time.* When an act may or must be done within a specified time, the court may, for good cause, extend the time: (1) with or without motion or notice if the court acts, or if a request is made, before the original time or its extension expires; or (2) on motion made after the time has expired if the party failed to act because of excusable neglect. FRCP 6(b)(1).

i. *Exceptions.* A court must not extend the time to act under FRCP 50(b), FRCP 50(d), FRCP 52(b), FRCP 59(b), FRCP 59(d), FRCP 59(e), and FRCP 60(b). FRCP 6(b)(2).

ii. Refer to the United States District Court for the District of Massachusetts KeyRules Motion for Continuance/Extension of Time document for more information on extending time.

d. *Additional time after certain kinds of service.* When a party may or must act within a specified time after being served and service is made under FRCP 5(b)(2)(C) (by mail), FRCP 5(b)(2)(D) (by leaving with the clerk), or FRCP 5(b)(2)(F) (by other means consented to), three (3) days are added after the period would otherwise expire under FRCP 6(a). FRCP 6(d).

## C. General Requirements

1. *Pleading, generally*

   a. *Pleadings allowed.* Only these pleadings are allowed: (1) a complaint; (2) an answer to a complaint; (3) an answer to a counterclaim designated as a counterclaim; (4) an answer to a crossclaim; (5) a third-party complaint; (6) an answer to a third-party complaint; and (7) if the court orders one, a reply to an answer. FRCP 7(a).

   b. *Pleading to be concise and direct.* Each allegation must be simple, concise, and direct. No technical form is required. FRCP 8(d)(1).

   c. *Alternative statements of a claim or defense.* A party may set out 2 or more statements of a claim or defense alternatively or hypothetically, either in a single count or defense or in separate ones. If a party makes alternative statements, the pleading is sufficient if any one of them is sufficient. FRCP 8(d)(2).

   d. *Inconsistent claims or defenses.* A party may state as many separate claims or defenses as it has, regardless of consistency. FRCP 8(d)(3).

   e. *Construing pleadings.* Pleadings must be construed so as to do justice. FRCP 8(e).

2. *Pleading special matters*

   a. *Capacity or authority to sue; Legal existence*

      i. *In general.* Except when required to show that the court has jurisdiction, a pleading need not allege:

         • A party's capacity to sue or be sued;

         • A party's authority to sue or be sued in a representative capacity; or

         • The legal existence of an organized association of persons that is made a party. FRCP 9(a)(1).

      ii. *Raising those issues.* To raise any of those issues, a party must do so by a specific denial, which must state any supporting facts that are peculiarly within the party's knowledge. FRCP 9(a)(2).

   b. *Fraud or mistake; Conditions of mind.* In alleging fraud or mistake, a party must state with particularity the circumstances constituting fraud or mistake. Malice, intent, knowledge, and other conditions of a person's mind may be alleged generally. FRCP 9(b).

   c. *Conditions precedent.* In pleading conditions precedent, it suffices to allege generally that all conditions precedent have occurred or been performed. But when denying that a condition precedent has occurred or been performed, a party must do so with particularity. FRCP 9(c).

   d. *Official document or act.* In pleading an official document or official act, it suffices to allege that the document was legally issued or the act legally done. FRCP 9(d).

   e. *Judgment.* In pleading a judgment or decision of a domestic or foreign court, a judicial or quasi-judicial tribunal, or a board or officer, it suffices to plead the judgment or decision without showing jurisdiction to render it. FRCP 9(e).

   f. *Time and place.* An allegation of time or place is material when testing the sufficiency of a pleading. FRCP 9(f).

   g. *Special damages.* If an item of special damage is claimed, it must be specifically stated. FRCP 9(g).

   h. *Admiralty or maritime claim*

      i. *How designated.* If a claim for relief is within the admiralty or maritime jurisdiction and also within the court's subject-matter jurisdiction on some other ground, the pleading may designate the claim as an admiralty or maritime claim for purposes of FRCP 14(c), FRCP 38(e), and FRCP 82 and the Supplemental Rules for Admiralty or Maritime Claims and Asset Forfeiture Actions. A claim cognizable only in the admiralty or maritime jurisdiction is an admiralty or maritime claim for those purposes, whether or not so designated. FRCP 9(h)(1).

      ii. *Designation for appeal.* A case that includes an admiralty or maritime claim within FRCP 9(h) is an admiralty case within 28 U.S.C.A. § 1292(a)(3). FRCP 9(h)(2).

3. *Answer*

   a. *Defenses; Admissions and denials*

      i. *In general.* In responding to a pleading, a party must: (1) state in short and plain terms its defenses to each claim asserted against it; and (2) admit or deny the allegations asserted against it by an opposing party. FRCP 8(b)(1).

         • The purpose of an answer is to formulate issues by means of defenses addressed to the allegations of the complaint, and to give the plaintiff notice of the defenses the plaintiff will be called upon to meet. FEDPROC § 62:70; Lopez v. U.S. Fid. & Guar. Co., 15 Alaska 633 (D. Alaska 1955); Moriarty v. Curran, 18 F.R.D. 461 (S.D.N.Y. 1956).

- An answer is adequate where it accomplishes these purposes, even if it contains general and specific denials and at the same time asserts additional facts by way of justification or explanation, and even if it sets forth conclusions of law. FEDPROC § 62:70; Johnston v. Jones, 178 F.2d 481 (3d Cir. 1949); Burke v. Mesta Mach. Co., 5 F.R.D. 134 (W.D. Pa. 1946).

ii. *Denials; Responding to the substance.* A denial must fairly respond to the substance of the allegation. FRCP 8(b)(2).

iii. *General and specific denials.* A party that intends in good faith to deny all the allegations of a pleading—including the jurisdictional grounds—may do so by a general denial. A party that does not intend to deny all the allegations must either specifically deny designated allegations or generally deny all except those specifically admitted. FRCP 8(b)(3).

iv. *Denying part of an allegation.* A party that intends in good faith to deny only part of an allegation must admit the part that is true and deny the rest. FRCP 8(b)(4).

v. *Lacking knowledge or information.* A party that lacks knowledge or information sufficient to form a belief about the truth of an allegation must so state, and the statement has the effect of a denial. FRCP 8(b)(5).

- An answer merely stating that the defendant lacks knowledge to form a belief as to the plaintiff's allegations, and making no statement as to the defendant's lack of information, has been held to be insufficient, the court suggesting that the phrase might be used in an attempt to mask the defendant's inability to make a good-faith denial of the allegations. FEDPROC § 62:73; Gilbert v. Johnston, 127 F.R.D. 145 (N.D. Ill. 1989).

vi. *Effect of failing to deny.* An allegation—other than one relating to the amount of damages—is admitted if a responsive pleading is required and the allegation is not denied. If a responsive pleading is not required, an allegation is considered denied or avoided. FRCP 8(b)(6).

b. *Affirmative defenses.* In responding to a pleading, a party must affirmatively state any avoidance or affirmative defense, including: (1) accord and satisfaction; (2) arbitration and award; (3) assumption of risk; (4) contributory negligence; (5) duress; (6) estoppel; (7) failure of consideration; (8) fraud; (9) illegality; (10) injury by fellow servant; (11) laches; (12) license; (13) payment; (14) release; (15) res judicata; (16) statute of frauds; (17) statute of limitations; and (18) waiver. FRCP 8(c)(1).

i. *Mistaken designation.* If a party mistakenly designates a defense as a counterclaim, or a counterclaim as a defense, the court must, if justice requires, treat the pleading as though it were correctly designated, and may impose terms for doing so. FRCP 8(c)(2).

c. *How to present defenses.* Every defense to a claim for relief in any pleading must be asserted in the responsive pleading if one is required. But a party may assert the following defenses by motion: (1) lack of subject-matter jurisdiction; (2) lack of personal jurisdiction; (3) improper venue; (4) insufficient process; (5) insufficient service of process; (6) failure to state a claim upon which relief can be granted; and (7) failure to join a party under FRCP 19. FRCP 12(b).

i. A motion asserting any of these defenses must be made before pleading if a responsive pleading is allowed. If a pleading sets out a claim for relief that does not require a responsive pleading, an opposing party may assert at trial any defense to that claim. FRCP 12(b).

ii. Refer to the United States District Court for the District of Massachusetts KeyRules Motion to Dismiss for Lack of Subject Matter Jurisdiction, Motion to Dismiss for Lack of Personal Jurisdiction, Motion to Dismiss for Improper Venue, and Motion to Dismiss for Failure to State a Claim documents for more information on motions under FRCP 12(b)(1), FRCP 12(b)(2), FRCP 12(b)(3), and FRCP 12(b)(6).

d. *Waiving and preserving certain defenses.* No defense or objection is waived by joining it with one or more other defenses or objections in a responsive pleading or in a motion. FRCP 12(b).

i. *When some are waived.* A party waives any defense listed in FRCP 12(b)(2) through FRCP 12(b)(5) by:

- Omitting it from a motion in the circumstances described in FRCP 12(g)(2); or

- Failing to either: (1) make it by motion under FRCP 12; or (2) include it in a responsive pleading or in an amendment allowed by FRCP 15(a)(1) as a matter of course. FRCP 12(h)(1).

    ii. *When to raise others.* Failure to state a claim upon which relief can be granted, to join a person required by FRCP 19(b), or to state a legal defense to a claim may be raised:

- In any pleading allowed or ordered under FRCP 7(a);
- By a motion under FRCP 12(c); or
- At trial. FRCP 12(h)(2).

    iii. *Lack of subject matter jurisdiction.* If the court determines at any time that it lacks subject-matter jurisdiction, the court must dismiss the action. FRCP 12(h)(3).

4. *Counterclaim and crossclaim*

  a. *Compulsory counterclaim*

    i. *In general.* A pleading must state as a counterclaim any claim that—at the time of its service—the pleader has against an opposing party if the claim:

- Arises out of the transaction or occurrence that is the subject matter of the opposing party's claim; and
- Does not require adding another party over whom the court cannot acquire jurisdiction. FRCP 13(a)(1).

    ii. *Exceptions.* The pleader need not state the claim if:

- When the action was commenced, the claim was the subject of another pending action; or
- The opposing party sued on its claim by attachment or other process that did not establish personal jurisdiction over the pleader on that claim, and the pleader does not assert any counterclaim under FRCP 13. FRCP 13(a)(2).

  b. *Permissive counterclaim.* A pleading may state as a counterclaim against an opposing party any claim that is not compulsory. FRCP 13(b).

  c. *Relief sought in a counterclaim.* A counterclaim need not diminish or defeat the recovery sought by the opposing party. It may request relief that exceeds in amount or differs in kind from the relief sought by the opposing party. FRCP 13(c).

  d. *Counterclaim against the United States.* The Federal Rules of Civil Procedure do not expand the right to assert a counterclaim—or to claim a credit—against the United States or a United States officer or agency. FRCP 13(d).

  e. *Counterclaim maturing or acquired after pleading.* The court may permit a party to file a supplemental pleading asserting a counterclaim that matured or was acquired by the party after serving an earlier pleading. FRCP 13(e).

  f. *Crossclaim against a coparty.* A pleading may state as a crossclaim any claim by one party against a coparty if the claim arises out of the transaction or occurrence that is the subject matter of the original action or of a counterclaim, or if the claim relates to any property that is the subject matter of the original action. The crossclaim may include a claim that the coparty is or may be liable to the cross-claimant for all or part of a claim asserted in the action against the cross-claimant. FRCP 13(g).

  g. *Joining additional parties.* FRCP 19 and FRCP 20 govern the addition of a person as a party to a counterclaim or crossclaim. FRCP 13(h).

  h. *Separate trials; Separate judgments.* If the court orders separate trials under FRCP 42(b), it may enter judgment on a counterclaim or crossclaim under FRCP 54(b) when it has jurisdiction to do so, even if the opposing party's claims have been dismissed or otherwise resolved. FRCP 13(i).

5. *Third-party practice*

  a. *Timing of the summons and complaint.* A defending party may, as third-party plaintiff, serve a summons and complaint on a nonparty who is or may be liable to it for all or part of the claim against it. But the third-party plaintiff must, by motion, obtain the court's leave if it files the third-party complaint more than fourteen (14) days after serving its original answer. FRCP 14(a)(1).

  b. *Third-party defendant's claims and defenses.* The person served with the summons and third-party complaint—the "third-party defendant":

    i. Must assert any defense against the third-party plaintiff's claim under FRCP 12;

    ii. Must assert any counterclaim against the third-party plaintiff under FRCP 13(a), and may assert any counterclaim against the third-party plaintiff under FRCP 13(b) or any crossclaim against another third-party defendant under FRCP 13(g);

      iii.  May assert against the plaintiff any defense that the third-party plaintiff has to the plaintiff's claim; and

      iv.  May also assert against the plaintiff any claim arising out of the transaction or occurrence that is the subject matter of the plaintiff's claim against the third-party plaintiff. FRCP 14(a)(2).

  c.  For more information on third-party practice, refer to FRCP 14.

6. *Joinder*

  a.  *Joinder of claims.* A party asserting a claim, counterclaim, crossclaim, or third-party claim may join, as independent or alternative claims, as many claims as it has against an opposing party. FRCP 18(a).

      i.  *Joinder of contingent claims.* A party may join two claims even though one of them is contingent on the disposition of the other; but the court may grant relief only in accordance with the parties' relative substantive rights. In particular, a plaintiff may state a claim for money and a claim to set aside a conveyance that is fraudulent as to that plaintiff, without first obtaining a judgment for the money. FRCP 18(b).

  b.  *Joinder of parties; Required*

      i.  *Persons required to be joined if feasible; Required party.* A person who is subject to service of process and whose joinder will not deprive the court of subject-matter jurisdiction must be joined as a party if:

         • In that person's absence, the court cannot accord complete relief among existing parties; or

         • That person claims an interest relating to the subject of the action and is so situated that disposing of the action in the person's absence may: (1) as a practical matter impair or impede the person's ability to protect the interest; or (2) leave an existing party subject to a substantial risk of incurring double, multiple, or otherwise inconsistent obligations because of the interest. FRCP 19(a)(1).

      ii.  *Joinder of parties by court order.* If a person has not been joined as required, the court must order that the person be made a party. A person who refuses to join as a plaintiff may be made either a defendant or, in a proper case, an involuntary plaintiff. FRCP 19(a)(2).

      iii.  *Venue.* If a joined party objects to venue and the joinder would make venue improper, the court must dismiss that party. FRCP 19(a)(3).

      iv.  *When joinder of parties is not feasible.* If a person who is required to be joined if feasible cannot be joined, the court must determine whether, in equity and good conscience, the action should proceed among the existing parties or should be dismissed. FRCP 19(b). For a list of the factors for the court to consider in determining whether joinder of parties is feasible, refer to FRCP 19(b)(1) through FRCP 19(b)(4).

      v.  *Pleading the reasons for nonjoinder.* When asserting a claim for relief, a party must state:

         • The name, if known, of any person who is required to be joined if feasible but is not joined; and

         • The reasons for not joining that person. FRCP 19(c).

      vi.  *Exception for class actions.* FRCP 19 is subject to FRCP 23. FRCP 19(d). For information on class actions, refer to FRCP 23.

  c.  *Joinder of parties; Permissible*

      i.  *Persons who may join or be joined*

         • *Plaintiffs.* Persons may join in one action as plaintiffs if: (1) they assert any right to relief jointly, severally, or in the alternative with respect to or arising out of the same transaction, occurrence, or series of transactions or occurrences; and (2) any question of law or fact common to all plaintiffs will arise in the action. FRCP 20(a)(1).

         • *Defendants.* Persons—as well as a vessel, cargo, or other property subject to admiralty process in rem—may be joined in one action as defendants if: (1) any right to relief is asserted against them jointly, severally, or in the alternative with respect to or arising out of the same transaction, occurrence, or series of transactions or occurrences; and (2) any question of law or fact common to all defendants will arise in the action. FRCP 20(a)(2).

         • *Extent of relief.* Neither a plaintiff nor a defendant need be interested in obtaining or defending against all the relief demanded. The court may grant judgment to one or more plaintiffs according to their rights, and against one or more defendants according to their liabilities. FRCP 20(a)(3).

      ii.  *Protective measures.* The court may issue orders—including an order for separate trials—to protect a party against embarrassment, delay, expense, or other prejudice that arises from including a person against whom the party asserts no claim and who asserts no claim against the party. FRCP 20(b).

    d.   *Misjoinder and nonjoinder of parties.* Misjoinder of parties is not a ground for dismissing an action. On motion or on its own, the court may at any time, on just terms, add or drop a party. The court may also sever any claim against a party. FRCP 21.

7.  *Right to a jury trial; Demand*

    a.   *Right preserved.* The right of trial by jury as declared by U.S.C.A. Const. Amend. VII, or as provided by a federal statute, is preserved to the parties inviolate. FRCP 38(a).

    b.   *Demand.* On any issue triable of right by a jury, a party may demand a jury trial by: (1) serving the other parties with a written demand—which may be included in a pleading—no later than fourteen (14) days after the last pleading directed to the issue is served; and (2) filing the demand in accordance with FRCP 5(d). FRCP 38(b).

    c.   *Specifying issues.* In its demand, a party may specify the issues that it wishes to have tried by a jury; otherwise, it is considered to have demanded a jury trial on all the issues so triable. If the party has demanded a jury trial on only some issues, any other party may—within fourteen (14) days after being served with the demand or within a shorter time ordered by the court—serve a demand for a jury trial on any other or all factual issues triable by jury. FRCP 38(c).

    d.   *Waiver; Withdrawal.* A party waives a jury trial unless its demand is properly served and filed. A proper demand may be withdrawn only if the parties consent. FRCP 38(d).

    e.   *Admiralty and maritime claims.* The rules in FRCP 38 do not create a right to a jury trial on issues in a claim that is an admiralty or maritime claim under FRCP 9(h). FRCP 38(e).

8.  *Alternative dispute resolution (ADR).* The judicial officer assigned to preside over the case shall encourage the resolution of disputes by settlement or other alternative dispute resolution programs. MA R USDCT LR 16.4(a).

    a.   *Settlement.* At every conference conducted under the Local Rules of the United States District Court for the District of Massachusetts, the judicial officer shall inquire as to the utility of the parties conducting settlement negotiations, explore means of facilitating those negotiations, and offer whatever assistance may be appropriate in the circumstances. Assistance may include a reference of the case to another judicial officer for settlement purposes. MA R USDCT LR 16.4(b).

        i.   When a case is settled, the parties shall file with the clerk a signed agreement for judgment or stipulation for dismissal, as appropriate, within twenty-eight (28) days, unless the court otherwise orders. MA R USDCT LR 68.2.

    b.   *Alternative dispute resolution programs*

        i.   *Discretion of judicial officer.* The judicial officer, following an exploration of the matter with all counsel, may refer appropriate cases to alternative dispute resolution programs that have been designated for use in the district court or that the judicial officer may make available. The dispute resolution programs described in MA R USDCT LR 16.4(c)(2) through MA R USDCT LR 16.4(c)(4) are illustrative, not exclusive. Moreover, nothing in MA R USDCT LR 16.4 shall preclude the parties from engaging in private dispute resolution programs as long as they comply with any schedule established by the court. MA R USDCT LR 16.4(c)(1).

        ii.   *Mediation.* The judicial officer may refer the case to mediation upon the agreement of all parties. MA R USDCT LR 16.4(c)(2)(A).

        iii.   *Other alternative dispute resolution programs.* Use of mediation is not exclusive. At the request of parties, the judicial officer may consider other forms of alternative dispute resolution including, but not limited to, mini-trial, summary jury trial and arbitration. MA R USDCT LR 16.4(c)(3).

    c.   For more information on alternative dispute resolution (ADR), refer to MA R USDCT LR 16.4.

9.  *Sanctions.* Failure to comply with any of the directions or obligations set forth in, or authorized by, these rules may result in dismissal, default, or the imposition of other sanctions as deemed appropriate by the judicial officer. MA R USDCT LR 1.3. Except as provided by law, the court may impose sanctions as provided in MA R USDCT LR 1.3 for failure to comply with the Administrative Procedures for Electronic Case Filing in the United States District Court for the District of Massachusetts (MA R USDCT CM/ECF Admin) or with MA R USDCT LR 5.4. MA R USDCT CM/ECF Admin(C)(3).

## D.  Documents

1.  *Required documents*

    a.   *Answer.* Refer to the General Requirements section of this document for information on the form and contents of the answer.

    b.   *Certificate of service.* No certificate of service is required when a paper is served by filing it with the court's electronic-filing system. When a paper that is required to be served is served by other means: (1) if the paper is filed, a certificate of service must be filed with it or within a reasonable time after service; and (2) if the paper is not filed, a certificate of service need not be filed unless filing is required by court order or by local rule. FRCP 5(d)(1)(B). Except as otherwise provided by the Federal Rules of Civil Procedure, proof of service of all pleadings and other papers required to be served (except discovery papers that in accordance with FRCP 33 to FRCP 36(f) are not to be filed) shall be filed in the office of the clerk promptly after service has been made. The proof shall show the time and manner of service, and may be made by written acknowledgment of service, a certificate of a member of the bar of this court, or an affidavit of the person who served the paper. MA R USDCT LR 5.2(b)(1). A certificate of service of a member of the bar shall appear at the bottom of or on the margin of the last page of the paper to which it relates. MA R USDCT LR 5.2(b)(2).

i.  *Paper service.* The certificate shall be a brief, single-spaced statement and may be in the following form: I hereby certify that a true copy of the above document was served upon (each party appearing pro se and) the attorney of record for each other party by mail (by hand) on (date). (Signature). MA R USDCT LR 5.2(b)(2).

ii.  *Electronic service.* Any pleading or other paper served by electronic means must bear a certificate of service in accordance with MA R USDCT LR 5.2(b). MA R USDCT LR 5.4(C); MA R USDCT CM/ECF Admin(H)(2). The certificate of service shall state that the filer: (1) filed the document electronically, (2) that it will be served electronically to registered CM/ECF participants via the NEF and (3) that the filer will send paper copies to non-registered participants as indicated on the NEF. MA R USDCT CM/ECF Admin(H)(2). For example: I hereby certify that this document filed through the CM/ECF system will be sent electronically to the registered participants as identified on the NEF (NEF) and paper copies will be sent to those indicated as non registered participants on (date). MA R USDCT CM/ECF Admin(H)(2).

iii.  *Return.* Documents not conforming to the requirements of MA R USDCT LR 5.2 (except notices of appeal) shall be returned by the clerk. MA R USDCT LR 5.2(b)(2).

iv.  *Failure to make proof of service.* Failure to make proof of service does not affect the validity of the service. MA R USDCT LR 5.2(b)(3).

2.  *Supplemental documents*

a.  *Waiver of the service of summons.* An individual, corporation, or association that is subject to service under FRCP 4(e), FRCP 4(f), or FRCP 4(h) has a duty to avoid unnecessary expenses of serving the summons. FRCP 4(d)(1). Waiving service of a summons does not waive any objection to personal jurisdiction or to venue. FRCP 4(d)(5). If a defendant located within the United States fails, without good cause, to sign and return a waiver requested by a plaintiff located within the United States, the court must impose on the defendant:

i.  The expenses later incurred in making service; and

ii.  The reasonable expenses, including attorney's fees, of any motion required to collect those service expenses. FRCP 4(d)(2).

b.  *Notice of constitutional question.* A party that files a pleading, written motion, or other paper drawing into question the constitutionality of a federal or state statute must promptly:

i.  *File notice.* File a notice of constitutional question stating the question and identifying the paper that raises it, if:

- A federal statute is questioned and the parties do not include the United States, one of its agencies, or one of its officers or employees in an official capacity; or

- A state statute is questioned and the parties do not include the state, one of its agencies, or one of its officers or employees in an official capacity; and

ii.  *Serve notice.* Serve the notice and paper on the Attorney General of the United States if a federal statute is questioned—or on the state attorney general if a state statute is questioned—either by certified or registered mail or by sending it to an electronic address designated by the attorney general for this purpose. FRCP 5.1(a).

iii.  *No forfeiture.* A party's failure to file and serve the notice, or the court's failure to certify, does not forfeit a constitutional claim or defense that is otherwise timely asserted. FRCP 5.1(d).

c.  *Notice of issue concerning foreign law.* A party who intends to raise an issue about a foreign country's law must give notice by a pleading or other writing. In determining foreign law, the court may consider any relevant material or source, including testimony, whether or not submitted by a party or admissible under the Federal Rules of Evidence. The court's determination must be treated as a ruling on a question of law. FRCP 44.1.

    d. *Nongovernmental corporate disclosure statement.*

        i. *Contents.* A nongovernmental corporate party must file two (2) copies of a disclosure statement that:

- Identifies any parent corporation and any publicly held corporation owning ten percent (10%) or more of its stock; or

- States that there is no such corporation. FRCP 7.1(a).

        ii. *Time to file; Supplemental filing.* A party must:

- File the disclosure statement with its first appearance, pleading, petition, motion, response, or other request addressed to the court; and

- Promptly file a supplemental statement if any required information changes. FRCP 7.1(b).

    e. *Compact disk with copy of document(s) in PDF format.* A filer who cannot file a document electronically because of such technical difficulty on the filer's end [with telephone, cable lines, the filer's Internet Service Provider (ISP), or hardware or software problems] shall file the document conventionally along with a copy of the document in PDF format on a compact disk or contact the clerk's office for permission to submit the PDF document via email. MA R USDCT CM/ECF Admin(W)(3). Refer to the Timing section of this document for more information on technical failures.

    f. *Notice of filing with clerk's office.* When documents or exhibits (other than those filed ex parte or under seal) are submitted conventionally, a "Notice of Filing with clerk's office" shall be filed electronically and attached to the main document. A paper copy of the "Notice of Filing with clerk's office" must accompany the documents submitted to the court. The "Notice of Filing with clerk's office" (see MA R USDCT CM/ECF Admin(Appendix I)) shall describe each of the documents that will be filed as paper copies in the clerk's office, or shall include an index of the documents if those documents are voluminous. MA R USDCT CM/ECF Admin(P)(5).

    g. *Additional copies.* Whenever, because of the nature of a proceeding, such as a proceeding before a three-judge district court under 28 U.S.C.A. § 2284, additional copies of a paper required to be filed are necessary either for the use of the court or to enable the clerk to carry out his duties, it is the responsibility of the party filing or having filed the paper to provide the necessary copies. MA R USDCT LR 5.1(d).

    h. *Courtesy copies.* COURTESY COPIES OF DOCUMENTS FILED ELECTRONICALLY SHALL NOT BE SUBMITTED ROUTINELY. MA R USDCT CM/ECF Admin(J). Judicial officers, on a case-by-case basis, may require courtesy copies for specific cases, or types of motions, etc. A few Judicial Officers have entered Standing Orders, which may be found on their respective pages on the court's website (under Divisions). Any document filed on paper with the court as a courtesy copy must be clearly labeled as such (Example: COURTESY COPY—DO NOT SCAN). Documents delivered to the court as a courtesy copy will not be maintained in the official court record. MA R USDCT CM/ECF Admin(J).

## E. Format

1. *Form of documents.* The provisions of FRCP 10 and FRCP 11 concerning the form and signing of pleadings, motions, and other papers shall be applicable to all papers filed in any proceeding in this court. The board of bar overseers registration number of each attorney signing such documents, except the United States Attorney and his or her staff, shall be inscribed below the signature. MA R USDCT LR 5.1(a)(1).

    a. *Paper size and binding.* All papers filed in the court shall be adapted for flat filing, be filed on eight and one-half by eleven (8-1/2 x 11) inch paper without backers and be bound firmly by staple or some such other means (excluding paper or binder clip or rubber band). MA R USDCT LR 5.1(a)(2).

    b. *Spacing.* All papers, except discovery requests and responses, shall be double-spaced except for the identification of counsel, title of the case, footnotes, quotations and exhibits. Discovery requests and responses shall be single-spaced. MA R USDCT LR 5.1(a)(2).

    c. *Caption.* Every pleading must have a caption with the court's name, a title, a file number, and [an] FRCP 7(a) designation. FRCP 10(a).

        i. *Names of parties.* The title of the complaint must name all the parties; the title of other pleadings, after naming the first party on each side, may refer generally to other parties. FRCP 10(a).

        ii. *Request for special action.* When any pleading or other paper filed in the court includes a request for special process or relief, or any other request such that, if granted, the court will proceed other than in the ordinary course, the request shall, unless it is noted on the category sheet [see MA R USDCT LR 40.1(a)(1)], be noted on the first page to the right of or immediately beneath the caption. MA R USDCT LR 5.1(c).

d. *Claims or defenses*

    i. *Numbered paragraphs.* A party must state its claims or defenses in numbered paragraphs, each limited as far as practicable to a single set of circumstances. A later pleading may refer by number to a paragraph in an earlier pleading. FRCP 10(b).

    ii. *Separate statements.* If doing so would promote clarity, each claim founded on a separate transaction or occurrence—and each defense other than a denial—must be stated in a separate count or defense. FRCP 10(b).

e. *Adoption by reference.* A statement in a pleading may be adopted by reference elsewhere in the same pleading or in any other pleading or motion. FRCP 10(c).

    i. *Exhibits.* A copy of a written instrument that is an exhibit to a pleading is a part of the pleading for all purposes. FRCP 10(c).

f. *Citations*

    i. *Local rules.* These rules shall be known as Local Rules of the United States District Court for the District of Massachusetts and cited as "L.R., D. Mass." or "L.R." MA R USDCT LR 1.1.

    ii. *Electronic case filing procedures.* The procedures governing electronic case filing shall be known as the "Administrative Procedures for Electronic Case Filing in the United States District Court for the District of Massachusetts." They shall be cited as "APECF." MA R USDCT CM/ECF Admin(A)(7).

g. *Acceptance by the clerk.* The clerk must not refuse to file a paper solely because it is not in the form prescribed by the Federal Rules of Civil Procedure or by a local rule or practice. FRCP 5(d)(4).

    i. Except for complaints and notices of appeal, papers that do not conform to the requirements of MA R USDCT LR 5.1(a)(2) shall be returned by the clerk. MA R USDCT LR 5.1(a)(2).

2. *Form of electronic documents.* A paper filed electronically is a written paper for purposes of the Federal Rules of Civil Procedure. FRCP 5(d)(3)(D).

a. *PDF/A format required.* The court will begin requiring submission of documents in PDF/A format in the foreseeable future. PDF/A is an enhanced version of the traditional PDF format. Newer versions of most PDF software will be able to convert to this format. Additional information on PDF/A documents may be found on the court's website. MA R USDCT CM/ECF Admin(Electronic Filing and PDF).

    i. *Electronically converted PDF.* Electronically converted PDF documents are created from word processing documents (MS Word, WordPerfect, etc.) using any appropriate software. These documents are text searchable and the file size is generally smaller than a scanned document. CM/ECF users may use any brand of software to convert documents to PDF. MA R USDCT CM/ECF Admin(Electronic Filing and PDF).

    • Documents converted to PDF, rather than scanned, are preferred for filing in CM/ECF. MA R USDCT CM/ECF Admin(Electronic Filing and PDF).

    ii. *Scanned PDF.* Scanned PDF documents are created from paper documents run through an optical scanner. Scanned PDF documents are generally not searchable and have a larger file size. Please note that software used to create scanned documents may (and should) be set in such a way that the document is "text-searchable." MA R USDCT CM/ECF Admin(Electronic Filing and PDF).

b. *Title.* All pleadings filed electronically shall be titled in accordance with the approved dictionary of civil or criminal events of the CM/ECF system of this court. A list of events is available on the CM/ECF Training Information page of the court's website. The clerk's office may, when necessary and appropriate, modify the docket entry description, or delete and re-enter the docket entry in order to comply with the court's quality assurance standards. MA R USDCT CM/ECF Admin(G)(3).

c. *Attachments to filings and exhibits.* Attachments to filings and exhibits must be filed in accordance with the court's CM/ECF User Manual, unless otherwise ordered by the court. MA R USDCT CM/ECF Admin(O)(1).

    i. Filers must submit as attachments only those excerpts of the referenced documents that are directly germane to the matter under consideration by the court. Excerpted material must be clearly and prominently identified as such. Users who file excerpts of documents do so without prejudice to their right to timely file additional excerpts or the complete document, as may be allowed by the court. Responding parties may timely file additional excerpts or the complete document that they believe are directly germane. MA R USDCT CM/ECF Admin(O)(2).

    ii. Filers shall not attach as an exhibit any pleading or other paper already on file with the court in that case, but shall merely refer to that document. (See MA R USDCT CM/ECF Admin(G) for information on using hyperlinks in PDF documents filed in CM/ECF.) MA R USDCT CM/ECF Admin(O)(3).

d. *Redacted documents.* The parties may request or the court may require the submission of documents that have been redacted/stripped of sensitive or confidential information. The redacted document prepared for electronic filing shall include the original caption of the document, and be clearly labeled as "Redacted Document." A specific event is available for this purpose ("Redacted Document"), found under the Other Filings/Other Documents menu option. MA R USDCT CM/ECF Admin(S).

    i. Attorneys and pro se litigants are advised to take extra care when creating PDF documents intended for submission to CM/ECF. Steps shall be taken to ensure the documents are free of any hidden data (metadata) that may contain redacted information, or traces of information edited or deleted are not hidden in the final document. Even PDF content that has been encrypted may be recovered. An advisory document with additional information on this topic may be found on the court's website. MA R USDCT CM/ECF Admin(S).

e. *Hyperlinks.* Electronically filed documents may contain the following types of hyperlinks: (1) hyperlinks to other portions of the same document; (2) hyperlinks to other documents filed within the CM/ECF system; and (3) hyperlinks to a location on the Internet that contains a source document for a citation. MA R USDCT CM/ECF Admin(G)(7).

    i. Hyperlinks to cited authority may not replace standard citation format. Complete citations must be included in the text of the filed document. Neither a hyperlink, nor any site to which it refers, shall be considered part of the record, but are simply convenient mechanisms for accessing material cited in a document filed in CM/ECF. Instructions on creating hyperlinks may be found in the CM/ECF User Manual. MA R USDCT CM/ECF Admin(G)(7).

    ii. The court accepts no responsibility for, and does not endorse, any product, organization, or content at any hyperlinked site, or at any site to which that site may be linked. The court accepts no responsibility for the availability or functionality of any hyperlink. MA R USDCT CM/ECF Admin(G)(7).

    iii. One feature of PDF/A documents is that hyperlinks are commonly "masked," meaning that the full address of the referenced file is not written out; for example, clicking the word brief may open a brief which was previously filed in CM/ECF. MA R USDCT CM/ECF Admin(G)(7)(NOTE). An "unmasked" hyperlink has the full address visible to the user. MA R USDCT CM/ECF Admin(G)(7)(NOTE).

        • Masked hyperlinks may or may not work in a PDF/A document, depending on how it was created. Currently, masked hyperlinks are preserved in PDF/A documents produced by the "Save As" method in Microsoft Word 2007 and 2010; the "PDFMaker" method in Microsoft Word 2007; and OpenOffice 2.4 ("PDF Export"). With other production methods, such as WordPerfect, the PDF/A document includes underlined words that appear to be links, but clicking them has no effect. MA R USDCT CM/ECF Admin(G)(7)(NOTE).

f. *Documents features not accepted.* CM/ECF will not accept PDF documents containing tracking tags, embedded systems commands, password protections, access restrictions or other security features, special tags or dynamic features. MA R USDCT CM/ECF Admin(G)(8).

g. *File size limitations.* A filing party shall limit the size of each PDF file to no more than twenty (20) megabytes. PDF files larger than seven (7) megabytes will be rejected by the CM/ECF system. The filer will see a message advising of the size limitation. MA R USDCT CM/ECF Admin(P)(2).

    i. Larger documents or exhibits may be submitted electronically if split into separate PDF files each less than seven (7) megabytes, attached to the main document and clearly labeled. MA R USDCT CM/ECF Admin(P)(2).

    ii. Documents submitted electronically or on paper are subject to the page limitations set by MA R USDCT LR 7.1(b)(4) or by order of the court. MA R USDCT CM/ECF Admin(P)(1).

h. *Accuracy and readability.* The filer shall verify the accuracy and readability of any PDF file before electronically filing it in CM/ECF. MA R USDCT CM/ECF Admin(G)(6); MA R USDCT CM/ECF Admin(P)(3).

3. *Signing of pleadings, motions and other papers*

a. *Signature.* Every pleading, written motion, and other paper must be signed by at least one attorney of record in the attorney's name—or by a party personally if the party is unrepresented. The paper must state the signer's address, e-mail address, and telephone number. FRCP 11(a). The provisions of the Federal Rules of Civil Procedure pertaining to the form and signing of pleadings, motions, and other papers shall be applicable to all papers filed in any proceeding in this court. The board of bar overseers registration number of each attorney signing such documents, except the United States Attorney and his staff, shall be inscribed below the signature. MA R USDCT LR 5.1(a)(1).

i. *Electronic signing.* A filing made through a person's electronic-filing account and authorized by that person, together with that person's name on a signature block, constitutes the person's signature. FRCP 5(d)(3)(C).

ii. *Appearances.* The filing of an appearance or any other pleading signed on behalf of a party constitutes an entry of appearance for that party. All pleadings shall contain the name, bar admission number, address, telephone number, and e-mail address of the attorney entering an appearance. MA R USDCT LR 83.5.2(a).

- *Appearances by law firms.* When a party is represented by a law firm, the appearance must include the name and the signature of at least one individual attorney. When a party is represented by more than one attorney from the same or different law firms, the attorney entering the appearance must designate the individual attorney who is authorized to receive all notices in the case. Any notice sent to an attorney so designated shall be deemed to be proper notice unless the court finds that notice was not properly sent. MA R USDCT LR 83.5.2(b).

- For more information on appearances, refer to MA R USDCT LR 83.5.2.

iii. *Signatures of attorneys.* The user login and password required to submit documents to the CM/ECF system shall serve as that user's signature for purposes of FRCP 11 and for all other purposes under the Federal Rules of Civil Procedure and the Local Rules of the United States District Court for the District of Massachusetts. All electronically filed documents must include a signature block and must set forth the attorney's name, bar number, address, telephone number and email address. The name of the CM/ECF user under whose log-in and password the document is submitted must be preceded by a "/s/" and typed in the space where the signature would otherwise appear. MA R USDCT CM/ECF Admin(M)(1). For an example, refer to MA R USDCT CM/ECF Admin(M)(1).

iv. *Signatures of pro se parties.* Any document requiring a signature that is filed by a party appearing pro se shall bear the words "pro se" following that party's signature. Any such document shall also state the party's mailing address, telephone number (if any), and e-mail address (if the party has consented to service by email). MA R USDCT LR 83.5.5(g). For more information on practice by pro se litigants, refer to MA R USDCT LR 83.5.5.

v. *Multiple signatures.* The filer of any document requiring more than one signature (e.g, stipulations, joint motions, joint status reports, magistrate judge consent forms, etc.) must list thereon all the names of other signatories by means of a "/s/ name of signatory" block for each. By submitting such a document, the filing attorney certifies that each of the other signatories has expressly agreed to the form and substance of the document and that the filing attorney has their actual authority to submit the document electronically. MA R USDCT CM/ECF Admin(M)(2). For more information, refer to MA R USDCT CM/ECF Admin(M)(2).

vi. *Affidavits.* Except as provided in MA R USDCT CM/ECF Admin(L), affidavits shall be filed electronically; however, the electronically filed version must contain a "/s/ name of signatory" block indicating that the paper document bears an original signature. MA R USDCT CM/ECF Admin(M)(3). The court will also accept a scanned version of the original, signed document. MA R USDCT CM/ECF Admin(M)(3). For more information, refer to MA R USDCT CM/ECF Admin(M)(3).

vii. *No verification or accompanying affidavit required for pleadings.* Unless a rule or statute specifically states otherwise, a pleading need not be verified or accompanied by an affidavit. FRCP 11(a).

viii. *Unsigned papers.* The court must strike an unsigned paper unless the omission is promptly corrected after being called to the attorney's or party's attention. FRCP 11(a).

b. *Representations to the court.* By presenting to the court a pleading, written motion, or other paper—whether by signing, filing, submitting, or later advocating it—an attorney or unrepresented party certifies that to the best of the person's knowledge, information, and belief, formed after an inquiry reasonable under the circumstances:

i. It is not being presented for any improper purpose, such as to harass, cause unnecessary delay, or needlessly increase the cost of litigation;

ii. The claims, defenses, and other legal contentions are warranted by existing law or by a nonfrivolous argument for extending, modifying, or reversing existing law or for establishing new law;

iii. The factual contentions have evidentiary support or, if specifically so identified, will likely have evidentiary support after a reasonable opportunity for further investigation or discovery; and

iv. The denials of factual contentions are warranted on the evidence or, if specifically so identified, are reasonably based on belief or a lack of information. FRCP 11(b).

   c.   *Sanctions.* If, after notice and a reasonable opportunity to respond, the court determines that FRCP 11(b) has been violated, the court may impose an appropriate sanction on any attorney, law firm, or party that violated FRCP 11(b) or is responsible for the violation. FRCP 11(c)(1). Refer to the United States District Court for the District of Massachusetts KeyRules Motion for Sanctions document for more information.

4.   *Privacy protection for filings made with the court*

   a.   *Redacted filings.* Unless the court orders otherwise, in an electronic or paper filing with the court that contains an individual's Social Security number, taxpayer-identification number, or birth date, the name of an individual known to be a minor, or a financial-account number, a party or nonparty making the filing may include only:

      i.   The last four (4) digits of the Social Security number and taxpayer-identification number;

      ii.   The year of the individual's birth;

      iii.   The minor's initials; and

      iv.   The last four (4) digits of the financial-account number. FRCP 5.2(a); MA R USDCT CM/ECF Admin(N).

   b.   *Exemptions from the redaction requirement.* The redaction requirement does not apply to the following:

      i.   A financial-account number that identifies the property allegedly subject to forfeiture in a forfeiture proceeding;

      ii.   The record of an administrative or agency proceeding;

      iii.   The official record of a state-court proceeding;

      iv.   The record of a court or tribunal, if that record was not subject to the redaction requirement when originally filed;

      v.   A filing covered by FRCP 5.2(c) or FRCP 5.2(d); and

      vi.   A pro se filing in an action brought under 28 U.S.C.A. § 2241, 28 U.S.C.A. § 2254, or 28 U.S.C.A. § 2255. FRCP 5.2(b).

   c.   *Limitations on remote access to electronic files; Social Security appeals and immigration cases.* Unless the court orders otherwise, in an action for benefits under the Social Security Act, and in an action or proceeding relating to an order of removal, to relief from removal, or to immigration benefits or detention, access to an electronic file is authorized as follows:

      i.   The parties and their attorneys may have remote electronic access to any part of the case file, including the administrative record;

      ii.   Any other person may have electronic access to the full record at the courthouse, but may have remote electronic access only to:

         • The docket maintained by the court; and

         • An opinion, order, judgment, or other disposition of the court, but not any other part of the case file or the administrative record. FRCP 5.2(c).

   d.   *Filings made under seal.* The court may order that a filing be made under seal without redaction. The court may later unseal the filing or order the person who made the filing to file a redacted version for the public record. FRCP 5.2(d).

   e.   *Protective orders.* For good cause, the court may by order in a case:

      i.   Require redaction of additional information; or

      ii.   Limit or prohibit a nonparty's remote electronic access to a document filed with the court. FRCP 5.2(e).

   f.   *Option for additional unredacted filing under seal.* A person making a redacted filing may also file an unredacted copy under seal. The court must retain the unredacted copy as part of the record. FRCP 5.2(f). For more information, refer to MA R USDCT LR 7.2.

   g.   *Option for filing a reference list.* A filing that contains redacted information may be filed together with a reference list that identifies each item of redacted information and specifies an appropriate identifier that uniquely corresponds to each item listed. The list must be filed under seal and may be amended as of right. Any reference in the case to a listed identifier will be construed to refer to the corresponding item of information. FRCP 5.2(g).

   h.   *Responsibility for redaction.* The clerk's office is not responsible for reviewing documents filed with the court to determine whether pleadings have been redacted and are in the proper form. MA R USDCT CM/ECF Admin(N).

   i.   *Waiver of protection of identifiers.* A person waives the protection of FRCP 5.2(a) as to the person's own information by filing it without redaction and not under seal. FRCP 5.2(h).

## F. Filing and Service Requirements

1. *Filing requirements*

   a. *Required filings.* Any paper after the complaint that is required to be served must be filed no later than a reasonable time after service. FRCP 5(d)(1).

      i. Except as noted in FRCP 33 to FRCP 36, the original of all papers required to be served under FRCP 5(d) shall, unless otherwise submitted to the court, be filed in the office of the clerk within seven (7) days after service has been made. MA R USDCT LR 5.1(b). Except as otherwise provided by the Federal Rules of Civil Procedure, proof of service of all pleadings and other papers required to be served (except discovery papers that in accordance with FRCP 33 to FRCP 36(f) are not to be filed) shall be filed in the office of the clerk promptly after service has been made. MA R USDCT LR 5.2(b)(1).

   b. *Nonelectronic filing.* A paper not filed electronically is filed by delivering it: (1) to the clerk; or (2) to a judge who agrees to accept it for filing, and who must then note the filing date on the paper and promptly send it to the clerk. FRCP 5(d)(2).

   c. *Electronic filing.* Unless exempt or otherwise ordered by the court, all pleadings and other papers submitted to the court must be filed, signed, and verified by electronic means as provided in MA R USDCT LR 5.4. MA R USDCT LR 5.4(A); MA R USDCT CM/ECF Admin(A)(1). All electronic filings must be made in accordance with the Administrative Procedures for Electronic Case Filing in the United States District Court for the District of Massachusetts (MA R USDCT CM/ECF Admin). MA R USDCT LR 5.4(B). The court may deviate from the Administrative Procedures for Electronic Case Filing in the United States District Court for the District of Massachusetts (MA R USDCT CM/ECF Admin) in specific cases, without prior notice, if deemed appropriate in the exercise of discretion, considering the need for the just, speedy, and inexpensive determination of matters pending before the court. MA R USDCT CM/ECF Admin(C)(1). The court may excuse a failure to comply with any administrative procedure whenever justice so requires. MA R USDCT CM/ECF Admin(C)(2).

      i. *By a represented person; Generally required; Exceptions.* A person represented by an attorney must file electronically, unless nonelectronic filing is allowed by the court for good cause or is allowed or required by local rule. FRCP 5(d)(3)(A).

      ii. *By unrepresented person; When allowed or required.* A person not represented by an attorney: (1) may file electronically only if allowed by court order or by local rule; and (2) may be required to file electronically only by court order, or by a local rule that includes reasonable exceptions. FRCP 5(d)(3)(B).

      iii. *Exemptions from electronic filing*

          • *Documents that should not be filed electronically.* The following types of documents must not be filed electronically, and will not be scanned into the ECF system by the clerk's office: (1) sealed documents; (2) ex parte motions; (3) documents generated as part of an alternative dispute resolution (ADR) process; (4) the administrative record in Social Security and other administrative proceedings; (5) the state court record in proceedings under 28 U.S.C.A. § 2254; and (6) such other types of documents as the clerk may direct in the Administrative Procedures for Electronic Case Filing in the United States District Court for the District of Massachusetts (MA R USDCT CM/ECF Admin). MA R USDCT LR 5.4(G)(1); MA R USDCT CM/ECF Admin(L).

          • *Documents that need not be filed electronically.* The following types of documents need not be filed electronically, but may be scanned into the ECF system by a filing party or the clerk's office: (1) handwritten pleadings; (2) documents filed by pro se litigants who are incarcerated or who are not registered ECF users; (3) indictments, informations, criminal complaints, and the criminal JS45 form; (4) affidavits for search or arrest warrants and related documents; (5) documents received from another court under FRCRP 20 or FRCRP 40; (6) appearance bonds; (7) any document in a criminal case containing the original signature of a defendant, such as a waiver of indictment or a plea agreement; (8) petitions for violations of supervised release; (9) executed service of process documents under FRCP 4; and (10) such other types of documents as the clerk may direct in the Administrative Procedures for Electronic Case Filing in the United States District Court for the District of Massachusetts (MA R USDCT CM/ECF Admin). MA R USDCT LR 5.4(G)(2); MA R USDCT CM/ECF Admin(L).

          • For more information on exemptions from electronic filing, refer to MA R USDCT CM/ECF Admin(L).

      iv. *Consequences of electronic filing.* Electronic transmission of a document to the CM/ECF system, together with the transmission of a Notice of Electronic Filing (NEF) from the court at the completion of the transaction, constitutes the filing of the document for all purposes of the Federal Rules of Procedure and constitutes entry of the document on the docket maintained by the clerk pursuant to FRCP 58 and FRCP 79. MA R USDCT CM/ECF Admin(G)(1).

    v. *Payment of filing fees.* When electronically filing any pleading or paper through CM/ECF that requires a fee, all registered ECF users are to pay the fee electronically through the Treasury Department's Internet payment process. MA R USDCT LR 67.4(d); MA R USDCT CM/ECF Admin(A)(1). Pro se filers and those who have been exempted from electronic filing and/or electronic payment of fees may submit payments by check or money order made payable to "Clerk, U.S. District Court". MA R USDCT LR 67.4(d). For more information on filing fees, refer to MA R USDCT LR 67.4 and MA R USDCT CM/ECF Admin(I).

    vi. For more information on electronic filing, refer to MA R USDCT CM/ECF Admin.

  d. *Email or fax filing.* In general, the court does not accept documents by email or by fax. If the court, in special circumstances, does authorize the submission of a document in that manner, the document shall not be considered filed until an NEF is generated by CM/ECF at the completion of the transaction. MA R USDCT CM/ECF Admin(H)(5).

2. *Service requirements.* Service of all pleadings subsequent to the original complaint and of all other papers required to be served shall be made in the manner specified by FRCP 5. MA R USDCT LR 5.2(a).

  a. *Service; When required*

    i. *In general.* Unless the Federal Rules of Civil Procedure provide otherwise, each of the following papers must be served on every party:

- An order stating that service is required;
- A pleading filed after the original complaint, unless the court orders otherwise under FRCP 5(c) because there are numerous defendants;
- A discovery paper required to be served on a party, unless the court orders otherwise;
- A written motion, except one that may be heard ex parte; and
- A written notice, appearance, demand, or offer of judgment, or any similar paper. FRCP 5(a)(1).

    ii. *If a party fails to appear.* No service is required on a party who is in default for failing to appear. But a pleading that asserts a new claim for relief against such a party must be served on that party under FRCP 4. FRCP 5(a)(2).

    iii. *Seizing property.* If an action is begun by seizing property and no person is or need be named as a defendant, any service required before the filing of an appearance, answer, or claim must be made on the person who had custody or possession of the property when it was seized. FRCP 5(a)(3).

  b. *Service; How made*

    i. *Serving an attorney.* If a party is represented by an attorney, service under FRCP 5 must be made on the attorney unless the court orders service on the party. FRCP 5(b)(1).

- *Nonresident attorney.* On application of a party, the court may order an attorney who represents any other party and who does not maintain an office within this district where service can be made on him by delivery as provided by FRCP 5(b), to designate a member of the bar of this court who does maintain such an office to receive service of all pleadings and other papers in his behalf. MA R USDCT LR 5.2(c)(1).

    ii. *Serving a party acting pro se.* On application of a party, the court may order any other party who is appearing without an attorney and who does not maintain an office or residence within this district where service can be made on him by delivery as provided by FRCP 5(b), to designate an address within the district at which service can be made on him by delivery. MA R USDCT LR 5.2(c)(2).

    iii. *Service in general.* A paper is served under FRCP 5 by:

- Handing it to the person;
- Leaving it: (1) at the person's office with a clerk or other person in charge or, if no one is in charge, in a conspicuous place in the office; or (2) if the person has no office or the office is closed, at the person's dwelling or usual place of abode with someone of suitable age and discretion who resides there;
- Mailing it to the person's last known address—in which event service is complete upon mailing;
- Leaving it with the court clerk if the person has no known address;
- Sending it to a registered user by filing it with the court's electronic-filing system or sending it by other

electronic means that the person consented to in writing—in either of which events service is complete upon filing or sending, but is not effective if the filer or sender learns that it did not reach the person to be served; or

- Delivering it by any other means that the person consented to in writing—in which event service is complete when the person making service delivers it to the agency designated to make delivery. FRCP 5(b)(2).

iv. *Service by electronic means.* Unless exempt or otherwise ordered by the court, all pleadings and other papers must be served on other parties by electronic means. MA R USDCT LR 5.4(C); MA R USDCT CM/ECF Admin(H)(2). Service by electronic means shall be treated the same as service by mail. MA R USDCT CM/ECF Admin(H)(4).

- *Consent to electronic service.* Registering to use CM/ECF constitutes consent to service of all documents by electronic means as provided in the Administrative Procedures for Electronic Case Filing in the United States District Court for the District of Massachusetts (MA R USDCT CM/ECF Admin) and FRCP 5(b) and FRCP 77(d). MA R USDCT CM/ECF Admin(E)(6); MA R USDCT CM/ECF Admin(H)(3).

- *Service on registered ECF users.* Transmission of the Notice of Electronic Filing (NEF) through the court's transmission facilities will constitute service of the filed document upon a registered ECF user. MA R USDCT LR 5.4(C).

- *Service on non-registered users.* The party filing the document electronically is responsible for serving a paper copy of the document by mail in accordance with FRCP 5(b) to those case participants who have not been identified on the NEF as electronic recipients. MA R USDCT CM/ECF Admin(H)(3).

- *Service of conventionally filed papers.* Documents or exhibits submitted conventionally shall be served on other parties by the filer using traditional means. MA R USDCT CM/ECF Admin(P)(4).

c. *Serving numerous defendants*

i. *In general.* If an action involves an unusually large number of defendants, the court may, on motion or on its own, order that:

- Defendants' pleadings and replies to them need not be served on other defendants;

- Any crossclaim, counterclaim, avoidance, or affirmative defense in those pleadings and replies to them will be treated as denied or avoided by all other parties; and

- Filing any such pleading and serving it on the plaintiff constitutes notice of the pleading to all parties. FRCP 5(c)(1).

ii. *Notifying parties.* A copy of every such order must be served on the parties as the court directs. FRCP 5(c)(2).

# G. Hearings

1. *Hearing on certain FRCP 12 defenses before trial.* If a party so moves, any defense listed in FRCP 12(b)(1) through FRCP 12(b)(7)—whether made in a pleading or by motion—and a motion under FRCP 12(c) must be heard and decided before trial unless the court orders a deferral until trial. FRCP 12(i).

# H. Forms

## 1. Official Federal Answer Forms

a. Waiver of the service of summons. FRCP 4.

## 2. Federal Answer Forms

a. Generally. 2B FEDFORMS § 8:10.

b. Introduction to separate defenses. 2B FEDFORMS § 8:11.

c. Presenting defenses. 2B FEDFORMS § 8:12.

d. With counterclaim for interpleader. 2B FEDFORMS § 8:13.

e. Denials and admissions. 2B FEDFORMS § 8:14.

f. Denials, admissions and affirmative defenses. 2B FEDFORMS § 8:15.

g. Separate answer of two defendants; Duty of fair representation. 2B FEDFORMS § 8:16.

h. Separate answer of third defendant. 2B FEDFORMS § 8:17.

i. Reciting paragraphs and subparagraphs of complaint; Account malpractice. 2B FEDFORMS § 8:18.

j. One of multiple defendants. 2B FEDFORMS § 8:21.

k. Pro se answer. 2B FEDFORMS § 8:22.50.

l. Denial of particular averment. 2B FEDFORMS § 8:24.

m. Admission of particular averment. 2B FEDFORMS § 8:25.

n. Denial of all averments of paragraph. 2B FEDFORMS § 8:26.

o. Admission of all averments of paragraph. 2B FEDFORMS § 8:27.

p. Denial in part and admission in part of paragraph. 2B FEDFORMS § 8:28.

q. General denial. 2B FEDFORMS § 8:29.

r. Qualified general denial. 2B FEDFORMS § 8:30.

s. Denial of knowledge or information sufficient to form a belief. 2B FEDFORMS § 8:31.

t. Denial of jurisdictional allegations; Jurisdictional amount. 2B FEDFORMS § 8:32.

u. Denial of jurisdictional allegations; Federal question. 2B FEDFORMS § 8:34.

v. Denial of jurisdictional allegations; Diversity of citizenship. 2B FEDFORMS § 8:37.

w. Contributory negligence. 2B FEDFORMS § 8:58.

x. Fraud. 2B FEDFORMS § 8:74.

y. Mistake. 2B FEDFORMS § 8:85.

z. Statute of limitations. 2B FEDFORMS § 8:103.

**3. Forms for the District of Massachusetts**

    a. Notice of filing with clerk's office. MA R USDCT CM/ECF Admin(Appendix I).

# I. Applicable Rules

1. *Federal rules*

    a. Summons. FRCP 4.

    b. Serving and filing pleadings and other papers. FRCP 5.

    c. Constitutional challenge to a statute; Notice, certification, and intervention. FRCP 5.1.

    d. Privacy protection for filings made with the court. FRCP 5.2.

    e. Computing and extending time; Time for motion papers. FRCP 6.

    f. Pleadings allowed; Form of motions and other papers. FRCP 7.

    g. Disclosure statement. FRCP 7.1.

    h. General rules of pleading. FRCP 8.

    i. Pleading special matters. FRCP 9.

    j. Form of pleadings. FRCP 10.

    k. Signing pleadings, motions, and other papers; Representations to the court; Sanctions. FRCP 11.

    l. Defenses and objections; When and how presented; Motion for judgment on the pleadings; Consolidating motions; Waiving defenses; Pretrial hearing. FRCP 12.

    m. Counterclaim and crossclaim. FRCP 13.

    n. Third-party practice. FRCP 14.

    o. Right to a jury trial; Demand. FRCP 38.

    p. Determining foreign law. FRCP 44.1.

2. *Local rules*

    a. Title. MA R USDCT LR 1.1.

    b. Sanctions. MA R USDCT LR 1.3.

c.  Form and filing of papers. MA R USDCT LR 5.1.

d.  Service and filing of pleadings and other papers. MA R USDCT LR 5.2.

e.  Filing and service by electronic means. MA R USDCT LR 5.4.

f.  Alternative dispute resolution. MA R USDCT LR 16.4.

g.  Payments and deposits made with the clerk. MA R USDCT LR 67.4.

h.  Settlement. MA R USDCT LR 68.2.

i.  Office of the clerk. MA R USDCT LR 77.2.

j.  Appearances. MA R USDCT LR 83.5.2.

k.  Practice by pro se litigants. MA R USDCT LR 83.5.5.

l.  CM/ECF case management/electronic case files administrative procedures. MA R USDCT CM/ECF Admin.

# Pleadings
# Amended Pleading

## Document Last Updated December 2018

### A.  Checklist

(I)  ❏ Matters to be considered by plaintiff or defendant

    (a)  ❏ Required documents

        (1)  ❏ Amended pleading

        (2)  ❏ Certificate of service

    (b)  ❏ Supplemental documents

        (1)  ❏ Notice of constitutional question

        (2)  ❏ Notice of issue concerning foreign law

        (3)  ❏ Compact disk with copy of document(s) in PDF format

        (4)  ❏ Notice of filing with clerk's office

        (5)  ❏ Additional copies

        (6)  ❏ Courtesy copies

    (c)  ❏ Timing

        (1)  ❏ A party may amend its pleading once as a matter of course within:

            (i)  ❏ Twenty-one (21) days after serving it, or

            (ii)  ❏ If the pleading is one to which a responsive pleading is required, twenty-one (21) days after service of a responsive pleading or twenty-one (21) days after service of a motion under FRCP 12(b), FRCP 12(e), or FRCP 12(f), whichever is earlier

        (2)  ❏ Amendments adding parties shall be sought as soon as an attorney reasonably can be expected to have become aware of the identity of the proposed new party

        (3)  ❏ Except as noted in FRCP 33 to FRCP 36, the original of all papers required to be served under FRCP 5(d) shall, unless otherwise submitted to the court, be filed in the office of the clerk within seven (7) days after service has been made

### B.  Timing

1.  *Amended pleading*

    a.  *Amending as a matter of course.* A party may amend its pleading once as a matter of course within:

        i.  Twenty-one (21) days after serving it, or

        ii.  If the pleading is one to which a responsive pleading is required, twenty-one (21) days after service of a responsive pleading or twenty-one (21) days after service of a motion under FRCP 12(b), FRCP 12(e), or FRCP 12(f), whichever is earlier. FRCP 15(a)(1).

    b.   *Amendments adding parties.* Amendments adding parties shall be sought as soon as an attorney reasonably can be expected to have become aware of the identity of the proposed new party. MA R USDCT LR 15.1(a).

    c.   *Extension of time.* If the time for serving the responsive pleading is extended by a motion for enlargement of time under FRCP 6(b), or by a stipulation, the period for amending as of right also may be enlarged. FPP § 1480.

    d.   *Other amendments.* In all other cases, a party may amend its pleading only with the opposing party's written consent or the court's leave. The court should freely give leave when justice so requires. FRCP 15(a)(2). Refer to the United States District Court for the District of Massachusetts KeyRules Motion for Leave to Amend document for more information.

2.   *Filing after service.* Except as noted in FRCP 33 to FRCP 36, the original of all papers required to be served under FRCP 5(d) shall, unless otherwise submitted to the court, be filed in the office of the clerk within seven (7) days after service has been made. MA R USDCT LR 5.1(b).

3.   *Time to respond to an amended pleading.* Unless the court orders otherwise, any required response to an amended pleading must be made within the time remaining to respond to the original pleading or within fourteen (14) days after service of the amended pleading, whichever is later. FRCP 15(a)(3).

4.   *Computation of time*

    a.   *Computing time.* FRCP 6 applies in computing any time period specified in the Federal Rules of Civil Procedure, in any local rule or court order, or in any statute that does not specify a method of computing time. FRCP 6(a).

       i.   *Period stated in days or a longer unit.* When the period is stated in days or a longer unit of time:

- Exclude the day of the event that triggers the period;

- Count every day, including intermediate Saturdays, Sundays, and legal holidays; and

- Include the last day of the period, but if the last day is a Saturday, Sunday, or legal holiday, the period continues to run until the end of the next day that is not a Saturday, Sunday, or legal holiday. FRCP 6(a)(1).

      ii.   *Period stated in hours.* When the period is stated in hours:

- Begin counting immediately on the occurrence of the event that triggers the period;

- Count every hour, including hours during intermediate Saturdays, Sundays, and legal holidays; and

- If the period would end on a Saturday, Sunday, or legal holiday, the period continues to run until the same time on the next day that is not a Saturday, Sunday, or legal holiday. FRCP 6(a)(2).

     iii.   *Office of the clerk.* The offices of the Clerk of Court at Boston, Worcester and Springfield shall be open from 8:30 a.m. until 5:00 p.m. on all days except Saturdays, Sundays, legal holidays and other days so ordered by the court and announced in advance, if feasible. MA R USDCT LR 77.2.

     iv.   *Inaccessibility of the clerk's office.* Unless the court orders otherwise, if the clerk's office is inaccessible:

- On the last day for filing under FRCP 6(a)(1), then the time for filing is extended to the first accessible day that is not a Saturday, Sunday, or legal holiday; or

- During the last hour for filing under FRCP 6(a)(2), then the time for filing is extended to the same time on the first accessible day that is not a Saturday, Sunday, or legal holiday. FRCP 6(a)(3).

      v.   *"Last day" defined.* Unless a different time is set by a statute, local rule, or court order, the last day ends:

- For electronic filing, at midnight in the court's time zone; and

- For filing by other means, when the clerk's office is scheduled to close. FRCP 6(a)(4).

     vi.   *"Next day" defined.* The "next day" is determined by continuing to count forward when the period is measured after an event and backward when measured before an event. FRCP 6(a)(5).

    vii.   *"Legal holiday" defined.* "Legal holiday" means:

- The day set aside by statute for observing New Year's Day, Martin Luther King Jr.'s Birthday, Washington's Birthday, Memorial Day, Independence Day, Labor Day, Columbus Day, Veterans' Day, Thanksgiving Day, or Christmas Day;

- Any day declared a holiday by the President or Congress; and

- For periods that are measured after an event, any other day declared a holiday by the state where the district court is located. FRCP 6(a)(6).

b. *Computation of electronic filing deadlines.* Filing documents electronically does not alter any filing deadlines. MA R USDCT CM/ECF Admin(K); MA R USDCT LR 5.4(D). Although CM/ECF is generally available twenty-four (24) hours a day for filing, all electronic transmissions of documents must be completed prior to 6:00 PM, Eastern Standard (or Daylight Savings) Time, on the date on which it is due, in order to be considered timely filed that day. MA R USDCT CM/ECF Admin(K); MA R USDCT LR 5.4(D). When a specific time of day deadline is set by court order or stipulation, the electronic filing must be completed by that time. Documents may be filed at any time of the day on days prior to the date on which it is due. MA R USDCT CM/ECF Admin(K). A document filed electronically shall be deemed filed as of the time and date stated on the NEF received from the court. MA R USDCT CM/ECF Admin(G)(2); MA R USDCT CM/ECF Admin(K).

   i. *Technical failures.* A user whose filing is made untimely as the result of a technical failure of the court's CM/ECF system may seek appropriate relief from the court. MA R USDCT CM/ECF Admin(W)(3). Technical difficulties on the filer's end, with telephone, cable lines, the filer's Internet Service Provider (ISP), or hardware or software problems, will not constitute a technical failure under the Administrative Procedures for Electronic Case Filing in the United States District Court for the District of Massachusetts (MA R USDCT CM/ECF Admin) nor excuse an untimely filing. MA R USDCT CM/ECF Admin(W)(3). As help desk support is available during normal business hours, filers are strongly urged to electronically file any documents during that period. MA R USDCT CM/ECF Admin(W)(3).

- The court has made available a public terminal (computers and scanner) in each clerk's office for registered users to scan and electronically file documents. This equipment is available during normal business hours. Users should bring their prepared document and a valid CM/ECF login and password. MA R USDCT CM/ECF Admin(W)(3).

c. *Extending time.* When an act may or must be done within a specified time, the court may, for good cause, extend the time: (1) with or without motion or notice if the court acts, or if a request is made, before the original time or its extension expires; or (2) on motion made after the time has expired if the party failed to act because of excusable neglect. FRCP 6(b)(1).

   i. *Exceptions.* A court must not extend the time to act under FRCP 50(b), FRCP 50(d), FRCP 52(b), FRCP 59(b), FRCP 59(d), FRCP 59(e), and FRCP 60(b). FRCP 6(b)(2).

   ii. Refer to the United States District Court for the District of Massachusetts KeyRules Motion for Continuance/Extension of Time document for more information on extending time.

d. *Additional time after certain kinds of service.* When a party may or must act within a specified time after being served and service is made under FRCP 5(b)(2)(C) (by mail), FRCP 5(b)(2)(D) (by leaving with the clerk), or FRCP 5(b)(2)(F) (by other means consented to), three (3) days are added after the period would otherwise expire under FRCP 6(a). FRCP 6(d).

## C. General Requirements

1. *Pleading, generally*

a. *Pleadings allowed.* Only these pleadings are allowed: (1) a complaint; (2) an answer to a complaint; (3) an answer to a counterclaim designated as a counterclaim; (4) an answer to a crossclaim; (5) a third-party complaint; (6) an answer to a third-party complaint; and (7) if the court orders one, a reply to an answer. FRCP 7(a).

b. *Pleading to be concise and direct.* Each allegation must be simple, concise, and direct. No technical form is required. FRCP 8(d)(1).

c. *Alternative statements of a claim or defense.* A party may set out 2 or more statements of a claim or defense alternatively or hypothetically, either in a single count or defense or in separate ones. If a party makes alternative statements, the pleading is sufficient if any one of them is sufficient. FRCP 8(d)(2).

d. *Inconsistent claims or defenses.* A party may state as many separate claims or defenses as it has, regardless of consistency. FRCP 8(d)(3).

e. *Construing pleadings.* Pleadings must be construed so as to do justice. FRCP 8(e).

2. *Pleading special matters*

a. *Capacity or authority to sue; Legal existence*

   i. *In general.* Except when required to show that the court has jurisdiction, a pleading need not allege:

- A party's capacity to sue or be sued;

- A party's authority to sue or be sued in a representative capacity; or

- The legal existence of an organized association of persons that is made a party. FRCP 9(a)(1).

ii. *Raising those issues.* To raise any of those issues, a party must do so by a specific denial, which must state any supporting facts that are peculiarly within the party's knowledge. FRCP 9(a)(2).

b. *Fraud or mistake; Conditions of mind.* In alleging fraud or mistake, a party must state with particularity the circumstances constituting fraud or mistake. Malice, intent, knowledge, and other conditions of a person's mind may be alleged generally. FRCP 9(b).

c. *Conditions precedent.* In pleading conditions precedent, it suffices to allege generally that all conditions precedent have occurred or been performed. But when denying that a condition precedent has occurred or been performed, a party must do so with particularity. FRCP 9(c).

d. *Official document or act.* In pleading an official document or official act, it suffices to allege that the document was legally issued or the act legally done. FRCP 9(d).

e. *Judgment.* In pleading a judgment or decision of a domestic or foreign court, a judicial or quasi-judicial tribunal, or a board or officer, it suffices to plead the judgment or decision without showing jurisdiction to render it. FRCP 9(e).

f. *Time and place.* An allegation of time or place is material when testing the sufficiency of a pleading. FRCP 9(f).

g. *Special damages.* If an item of special damage is claimed, it must be specifically stated. FRCP 9(g).

h. *Admiralty or maritime claim*

   i. *How designated.* If a claim for relief is within the admiralty or maritime jurisdiction and also within the court's subject-matter jurisdiction on some other ground, the pleading may designate the claim as an admiralty or maritime claim for purposes of FRCP 14(c), FRCP 38(e), and FRCP 82 and the Supplemental Rules for Admiralty or Maritime Claims and Asset Forfeiture Actions. A claim cognizable only in the admiralty or maritime jurisdiction is an admiralty or maritime claim for those purposes, whether or not so designated. FRCP 9(h)(1).

   ii. *Designation for appeal.* A case that includes an admiralty or maritime claim within FRCP 9(h) is an admiralty case within 28 U.S.C.A. § 1292(a)(3). FRCP 9(h)(2).

3. *Amended pleading*

   a. *Amendments before trial.* The function of FRCP 15(a), which provides generally for the amendment of pleadings, is to enable a party to assert matters that were overlooked or were unknown at the time the party interposed the original complaint or answer. FPP § 1473; Smiga v. Dean Witter Reynolds, Inc., 766 F.2d 698, 703 (2d Cir. 1985).

      i. *Matters contained in amended pleading under FRCP 15(a).* Although FRCP 15(a) does not expressly state that an amendment must contain only matters that occurred within a particular time period, FRCP 15(d) provides that any "transaction, occurrence, or event that happened after the date of the pleading" should be set forth in a supplemental pleading. FPP § 1473. Thus, impliedly, an amended pleading, whether prepared with or without leave of court, only should relate to matters that have taken place prior to the date of the earlier pleading. FPP § 1473; Ford Motor Co. v. United States, 896 F. Supp. 1224, 1230 (Ct. Int'l Trade 1995).

      ii. *Amending as a matter of course.* The right to amend as of course is not restricted to any particular litigant or pleading. FPP § 1480. It is a right conferred on all of the parties to an action and thus extends to persons who were not original parties to the litigation, but are brought into the action by way of counterclaim, crossclaim, third-party claim, or defensive interpleader. FPP § 1480; Johnson v. Walsh, 65 F.Supp. 157 (W.D.Mo. 1946).

         - *Amending a complaint with multiple defendants.* When a number of defendants are involved in an action, some of whom have answered and some of whom have filed no responsive pleading, the plaintiff can amend as a matter of course as to those defendants who have not answered. FEDPROC § 62:261; Pallant v. Sinatra, 7 F.R.D. 293 (S.D.N.Y. 1945). On the other hand, a plaintiff may not file an amended complaint as of right against those defendants who have not yet answered, if the plaintiff has amended the complaint once already as a matter of course. FEDPROC § 62:261; Glaros v. Perse, 628 F.2d 679 (1st Cir. 1980).

      iii. *Amending with leave of court.* Refer to the United States District Court for the District of Massachusetts KeyRules Motion for Leave to Amend document for information on amending the pleadings with leave of court.

      iv. *Types of amendments permitted under FRCP 15(a)*

         - *Cure a defective pleading.* Perhaps the most common use of FRCP 15(a) is by a party seeking to amend in order to cure a defective pleading. FPP § 1474.

- *Correct insufficiently stated claims or defenses.* A more common use of FRCP 15(a) amendments is to correct insufficiently stated claims or defenses. Typically, amendments of this character involve either adding a necessary allegation in order to state a claim for relief or correcting a misnomer of a party to the action. FPP § 1474.

- *Change nature or theory of claim or capacity of party.* Courts also have allowed a party to amend in order to change the nature or theory of the party's claim or the capacity in which the party is bringing the action. FPP § 1474.

- *State additional claims or defenses or drop claims or defenses.* Plaintiffs and defendants also have been permitted to amend their pleadings to state additional claims, to assert additional defenses, or to drop claims or defenses. FPP § 1474; Weinberger v. Retail Credit Co., 498 F.2d 552, 554, n.4 (4th Cir. 1974).

- *Increase amount of damages or elect a different remedy.* [An] FRCP 15(a) amendment also is appropriate for increasing the amount of damages sought, or for electing a different remedy than the one originally requested. FPP § 1474; McFadden v. Sanchez, 710 F.2d 907 (2d Cir. 1983).

- *Add, substitute, or drop parties.* Finally, a party may make [an] FRCP 15(a) amendment to add, substitute, or drop parties to the action. FPP § 1474.

b. *Amendments during and after trial*

  i. *Based on an objection at trial.* If, at trial, a party objects that evidence is not within the issues raised in the pleadings, the court may permit the pleadings to be amended. The court should freely permit an amendment when doing so will aid in presenting the merits and the objecting party fails to satisfy the court that the evidence would prejudice that party's action or defense on the merits. The court may grant a continuance to enable the objecting party to meet the evidence. FRCP 15(b)(1).

  ii. *For issues tried by consent.* When an issue not raised by the pleadings is tried by the parties' express or implied consent, it must be treated in all respects as if raised in the pleadings. A party may move—at any time, even after judgment—to amend the pleadings to conform them to the evidence and to raise an unpleaded issue. But failure to amend does not affect the result of the trial of that issue. FRCP 15(b)(2).

  iii. Refer to the United States District Court for the District of Massachusetts KeyRules Motion for Leave to Amend document for more information on moving to amend the pleadings.

c. *Relation back of amendments*

  i. *When an amendment relates back.* An amendment to a pleading relates back to the date of the original pleading when:

    - The law that provides the applicable statute of limitations allows relation back;

    - The amendment asserts a claim or defense that arose out of the conduct, transaction, or occurrence set out—or attempted to be set out—in the original pleading; or

    - The amendment changes the party or the naming of the party against whom a claim is asserted, if FRCP 15(c)(1)(B) is satisfied and if, within the period provided by FRCP 4(m) for serving the summons and complaint, the party to be brought in by amendment: (1) received such notice of the action that it will not be prejudiced in defending on the merits; and (2) knew or should have known that the action would have been brought against it, but for a mistake concerning the proper party's identity. FRCP 15(c)(1).

  ii. *Notice to the United States.* When the United States or a United States officer or agency is added as a defendant by amendment, the notice requirements of FRCP 15(c)(1)(C)(i) and FRCP 15(c)(1)(C)(ii) are satisfied if, during the stated period, process was delivered or mailed to the United States attorney or the United States attorney's designee, to the Attorney General of the United States, or to the officer or agency. FRCP 15(c)(2).

d. *Effect of an amended pleading.* A pleading that has been amended under FRCP 15(a) supersedes the pleading it modifies and remains in effect throughout the action unless it subsequently is modified. FPP § 1476. Once an amended pleading is interposed, the original pleading no longer performs any function in the case and any subsequent motion made by an opposing party should be directed at the amended pleading. FPP § 1476; Ferdik v. Bonzelet, 963 F.2d 1258, 1262 (9th Cir. 1992), as amended (May 22, 1992); Davis v. TXO Prod. Corp., 929 F.2d 1515, 1517 (10th Cir. 1991).

4. *Amended complaint.* Refer to the United States District Court for the District of Massachusetts KeyRules Complaint document for the requirements specific to the amended complaint.

5. *Amended answer.* Refer to the United States District Court for the District of Massachusetts KeyRules Answer document for the requirements specific to the amended answer.

6. *Joinder*

   a. *Joinder of claims.* A party asserting a claim, counterclaim, crossclaim, or third-party claim may join, as independent or alternative claims, as many claims as it has against an opposing party. FRCP 18(a).

      i. *Joinder of contingent claims.* A party may join two claims even though one of them is contingent on the disposition of the other; but the court may grant relief only in accordance with the parties' relative substantive rights. In particular, a plaintiff may state a claim for money and a claim to set aside a conveyance that is fraudulent as to that plaintiff, without first obtaining a judgment for the money. FRCP 18(b).

   b. *Joinder of parties; Required*

      i. *Persons required to be joined if feasible; Required party.* A person who is subject to service of process and whose joinder will not deprive the court of subject-matter jurisdiction must be joined as a party if:

- In that person's absence, the court cannot accord complete relief among existing parties; or

- That person claims an interest relating to the subject of the action and is so situated that disposing of the action in the person's absence may: (1) as a practical matter impair or impede the person's ability to protect the interest; or (2) leave an existing party subject to a substantial risk of incurring double, multiple, or otherwise inconsistent obligations because of the interest. FRCP 19(a)(1).

      ii. *Joinder of parties by court order.* If a person has not been joined as required, the court must order that the person be made a party. A person who refuses to join as a plaintiff may be made either a defendant or, in a proper case, an involuntary plaintiff. FRCP 19(a)(2).

      iii. *Venue.* If a joined party objects to venue and the joinder would make venue improper, the court must dismiss that party. FRCP 19(a)(3).

      iv. *When joinder of parties is not feasible.* If a person who is required to be joined if feasible cannot be joined, the court must determine whether, in equity and good conscience, the action should proceed among the existing parties or should be dismissed. FRCP 19(b). For a list of the factors for the court to consider in determining whether joinder of parties is feasible, refer to FRCP 19(b)(1) through FRCP 19(b)(4).

      v. *Pleading the reasons for nonjoinder.* When asserting a claim for relief, a party must state:

- The name, if known, of any person who is required to be joined if feasible but is not joined; and

- The reasons for not joining that person. FRCP 19(c).

      vi. *Exception for class actions.* FRCP 19 is subject to FRCP 23. FRCP 19(d). For information on class actions, refer to FRCP 23.

   c. *Joinder of parties; Permissible*

      i. *Persons who may join or be joined*

- *Plaintiffs.* Persons may join in one action as plaintiffs if: (1) they assert any right to relief jointly, severally, or in the alternative with respect to or arising out of the same transaction, occurrence, or series of transactions or occurrences; and (2) any question of law or fact common to all plaintiffs will arise in the action. FRCP 20(a)(1).

- *Defendants.* Persons—as well as a vessel, cargo, or other property subject to admiralty process in rem—may be joined in one action as defendants if: (1) any right to relief is asserted against them jointly, severally, or in the alternative with respect to or arising out of the same transaction, occurrence, or series of transactions or occurrences; and (2) any question of law or fact common to all defendants will arise in the action. FRCP 20(a)(2).

- *Extent of relief.* Neither a plaintiff nor a defendant need be interested in obtaining or defending against all the relief demanded. The court may grant judgment to one or more plaintiffs according to their rights, and against one or more defendants according to their liabilities. FRCP 20(a)(3).

      ii. *Protective measures.* The court may issue orders—including an order for separate trials—to protect a party against embarrassment, delay, expense, or other prejudice that arises from including a person against whom the party asserts no claim and who asserts no claim against the party. FRCP 20(b).

   d. *Misjoinder and nonjoinder of parties.* Misjoinder of parties is not a ground for dismissing an action. On motion or on its own, the court may at any time, on just terms, add or drop a party. The court may also sever any claim against a party. FRCP 21.

7. *Right to a jury trial; Demand*

   a. *Right preserved.* The right of trial by jury as declared by U.S.C.A. Const. Amend. VII, or as provided by a federal statute, is preserved to the parties inviolate. FRCP 38(a).

   b. *Demand.* On any issue triable of right by a jury, a party may demand a jury trial by: (1) serving the other parties with a written demand—which may be included in a pleading—no later than fourteen (14) days after the last pleading directed to the issue is served; and (2) filing the demand in accordance with FRCP 5(d). FRCP 38(b).

   c. *Specifying issues.* In its demand, a party may specify the issues that it wishes to have tried by a jury; otherwise, it is considered to have demanded a jury trial on all the issues so triable. If the party has demanded a jury trial on only some issues, any other party may—within fourteen (14) days after being served with the demand or within a shorter time ordered by the court—serve a demand for a jury trial on any other or all factual issues triable by jury. FRCP 38(c).

   d. *Waiver; Withdrawal.* A party waives a jury trial unless its demand is properly served and filed. A proper demand may be withdrawn only if the parties consent. FRCP 38(d).

   e. *Admiralty and maritime claims.* The rules in FRCP 38 do not create a right to a jury trial on issues in a claim that is an admiralty or maritime claim under FRCP 9(h). FRCP 38(e).

8. *Alternative dispute resolution (ADR).* The judicial officer assigned to preside over the case shall encourage the resolution of disputes by settlement or other alternative dispute resolution programs. MA R USDCT LR 16.4(a).

   a. *Settlement.* At every conference conducted under the Local Rules of the United States District Court for the District of Massachusetts, the judicial officer shall inquire as to the utility of the parties conducting settlement negotiations, explore means of facilitating those negotiations, and offer whatever assistance may be appropriate in the circumstances. Assistance may include a reference of the case to another judicial officer for settlement purposes. MA R USDCT LR 16.4(b).

      i. When a case is settled, the parties shall file with the clerk a signed agreement for judgment or stipulation for dismissal, as appropriate, within twenty-eight (28) days, unless the court otherwise orders. MA R USDCT LR 68.2.

   b. *Alternative dispute resolution programs*

      i. *Discretion of judicial officer.* The judicial officer, following an exploration of the matter with all counsel, may refer appropriate cases to alternative dispute resolution programs that have been designated for use in the district court or that the judicial officer may make available. The dispute resolution programs described in MA R USDCT LR 16.4(c)(2) through MA R USDCT LR 16.4(c)(4) are illustrative, not exclusive. Moreover, nothing in MA R USDCT LR 16.4 shall preclude the parties from engaging in private dispute resolution programs as long as they comply with any schedule established by the court. MA R USDCT LR 16.4(c)(1).

      ii. *Mediation.* The judicial officer may refer the case to mediation upon the agreement of all parties. MA R USDCT LR 16.4(c)(2)(A).

      iii. *Other alternative dispute resolution programs.* Use of mediation is not exclusive. At the request of parties, the judicial officer may consider other forms of alternative dispute resolution including, but not limited to, mini-trial, summary jury trial and arbitration. MA R USDCT LR 16.4(c)(3).

   c. For more information on alternative dispute resolution (ADR), refer to MA R USDCT LR 16.4.

9. *Sanctions.* Failure to comply with any of the directions or obligations set forth in, or authorized by, these rules may result in dismissal, default, or the imposition of other sanctions as deemed appropriate by the judicial officer. MA R USDCT LR 1.3. Except as provided by law, the court may impose sanctions as provided in MA R USDCT LR 1.3 for failure to comply with the Administrative Procedures for Electronic Case Filing in the United States District Court for the District of Massachusetts (MA R USDCT CM/ECF Admin) or with MA R USDCT LR 5.4. MA R USDCT CM/ECF Admin(C)(3).

## D. Documents

1. *Required documents*

   a. *Amended pleading.* Refer to the General Requirements section of this document for the form and contents of the amended pleading.

   b. *Certificate of service.* No certificate of service is required when a paper is served by filing it with the court's electronic-filing system. When a paper that is required to be served is served by other means: (1) if the paper is filed, a certificate of service must be filed with it or within a reasonable time after service; and (2) if the paper is not filed, a certificate of service need not be filed unless filing is required by court order or by local rule. FRCP 5(d)(1)(B).

Except as otherwise provided by the Federal Rules of Civil Procedure, proof of service of all pleadings and other papers required to be served (except discovery papers that in accordance with FRCP 33 to FRCP 36(f) are not to be filed) shall be filed in the office of the clerk promptly after service has been made. The proof shall show the time and manner of service, and may be made by written acknowledgment of service, a certificate of a member of the bar of this court, or an affidavit of the person who served the paper. MA R USDCT LR 5.2(b)(1). A certificate of service of a member of the bar shall appear at the bottom of or on the margin of the last page of the paper to which it relates. MA R USDCT LR 5.2(b)(2).

 i.  *Paper service.* The certificate shall be a brief, single-spaced statement and may be in the following form: I hereby certify that a true copy of the above document was served upon (each party appearing pro se and) the attorney of record for each other party by mail (by hand) on (date). (Signature). MA R USDCT LR 5.2(b)(2).

 ii.  *Electronic service.* Any pleading or other paper served by electronic means must bear a certificate of service in accordance with MA R USDCT LR 5.2(b). MA R USDCT LR 5.4(C); MA R USDCT CM/ECF Admin(H)(2). The certificate of service shall state that the filer: (1) filed the document electronically, (2) that it will be served electronically to registered CM/ECF participants via the NEF and (3) that the filer will send paper copies to non-registered participants as indicated on the NEF. MA R USDCT CM/ECF Admin(H)(2). For example: I hereby certify that this document filed through the CM/ECF system will be sent electronically to the registered participants as identified on the NEF (NEF) and paper copies will be sent to those indicated as non registered participants on (date). MA R USDCT CM/ECF Admin(H)(2).

 iii.  *Return.* Documents not conforming to the requirements of MA R USDCT LR 5.2 (except notices of appeal) shall be returned by the clerk. MA R USDCT LR 5.2(b)(2).

 iv.  *Failure to make proof of service.* Failure to make proof of service does not affect the validity of the service. MA R USDCT LR 5.2(b)(3).

2.  *Supplemental documents*

 a.  *Notice of constitutional question.* A party that files a pleading, written motion, or other paper drawing into question the constitutionality of a federal or state statute must promptly;

  i.  *File notice.* File a notice of constitutional question stating the question and identifying the paper that raises it, if:

   •  A federal statute is questioned and the parties do not include the United States, one of its agencies, or one of its officers or employees in an official capacity; or

   •  A state statute is questioned and the parties do not include the state, one of its agencies, or one of its officers or employees in an official capacity; and

  ii.  *Serve notice.* Serve the notice and paper on the Attorney General of the United States if a federal statute is questioned—or on the state attorney general if a state statute is questioned—either by certified or registered mail or by sending it to an electronic address designated by the attorney general for this purpose. FRCP 5.1(a).

  iii.  *No forfeiture.* A party's failure to file and serve the notice, or the court's failure to certify, does not forfeit a constitutional claim or defense that is otherwise timely asserted. FRCP 5.1(d).

 b.  *Notice of issue concerning foreign law.* A party who intends to raise an issue about a foreign country's law must give notice by a pleading or other writing. In determining foreign law, the court may consider any relevant material or source, including testimony, whether or not submitted by a party or admissible under the Federal Rules of Evidence. The court's determination must be treated as a ruling on a question of law. FRCP 44.1.

 c.  *Compact disk with copy of document(s) in PDF format.* A filer who cannot file a document electronically because of such technical difficulty on the filer's end [with telephone, cable lines, the filer's Internet Service Provider (ISP), or hardware or software problems] shall file the document conventionally along with a copy of the document in PDF format on a compact disk or contact the clerk's office for permission to submit the PDF document via email. MA R USDCT CM/ECF Admin(W)(3). Refer to the Timing section of this document for more information on technical failures.

 d.  *Notice of filing with clerk's office.* When documents or exhibits (other than those filed ex parte or under seal) are submitted conventionally, a "Notice of Filing with clerk's office" shall be filed electronically and attached to the main document. A paper copy of the "Notice of Filing with clerk's office" must accompany the documents submitted to the court. The "Notice of Filing with clerk's office" (see MA R USDCT CM/ECF Admin(Appendix I)) shall describe each of the documents that will be filed as paper copies in the clerk's office, or shall include an index of the documents if those documents are voluminous. MA R USDCT CM/ECF Admin(P)(5).

 e.  *Additional copies.* Whenever, because of the nature of a proceeding, such as a proceeding before a three-judge district court under 28 U.S.C.A. § 2284, additional copies of a paper required to be filed are necessary either for the use of the court or to enable the clerk to carry out his duties, it is the responsibility of the party filing or having filed the paper to provide the necessary copies. MA R USDCT LR 5.1(d).

f. *Courtesy copies.* COURTESY COPIES OF DOCUMENTS FILED ELECTRONICALLY SHALL NOT BE SUB-MITTED ROUTINELY. MA R USDCT CM/ECF Admin(J). Judicial officers, on a case-by-case basis, may require courtesy copies for specific cases, or types of motions, etc. A few Judicial Officers have entered Standing Orders, which may be found on their respective pages on the court's website (under Divisions). Any document filed on paper with the court as a courtesy copy must be clearly labeled as such (Example: COURTESY COPY—DO NOT SCAN). Documents delivered to the court as a courtesy copy will not be maintained in the official court record. MA R USDCT CM/ECF Admin(J).

3. *Documents required for an amended complaint adding a new claim for relief or new party.* Refer to the United States District Court for the District of Massachusetts KeyRules Complaint document for the documents for an amended complaint adding a new claim for relief or being filed and served against a new party.

## E. Format

1. *Form of documents.* The provisions of FRCP 10 and FRCP 11 concerning the form and signing of pleadings, motions, and other papers shall be applicable to all papers filed in any proceeding in this court. The board of bar overseers registration number of each attorney signing such documents, except the United States Attorney and his or her staff, shall be inscribed below the signature. MA R USDCT LR 5.1(a)(1).

a. *Paper size and binding.* All papers filed in the court shall be adapted for flat filing, be filed on eight and one-half by eleven (8-1/2 x 11) inch paper without backers and be bound firmly by staple or some such other means (excluding paper or binder clip or rubber band). MA R USDCT LR 5.1(a)(2).

b. *Spacing.* All papers, except discovery requests and responses, shall be double-spaced except for the identification of counsel, title of the case, footnotes, quotations and exhibits. Discovery requests and responses shall be single-spaced. MA R USDCT LR 5.1(a)(2).

c. *Caption.* Every pleading must have a caption with the court's name, a title, a file number, and [an] FRCP 7(a) designation. FRCP 10(a).

i. *Names of parties.* The title of the complaint must name all the parties; the title of other pleadings, after naming the first party on each side, may refer generally to other parties. FRCP 10(a).

ii. *Request for special action.* When any pleading or other paper filed in the court includes a request for special process or relief, or any other request such that, if granted, the court will proceed other than in the ordinary course, the request shall, unless it is noted on the category sheet [see MA R USDCT LR 40.1(a)(1)], be noted on the first page to the right of or immediately beneath the caption. MA R USDCT LR 5.1(c).

d. *Claims or defenses*

i. *Numbered paragraphs.* A party must state its claims or defenses in numbered paragraphs, each limited as far as practicable to a single set of circumstances. A later pleading may refer by number to a paragraph in an earlier pleading. FRCP 10(b).

ii. *Separate statements.* If doing so would promote clarity, each claim founded on a separate transaction or occurrence—and each defense other than a denial—must be stated in a separate count or defense. FRCP 10(b).

e. *Adoption by reference.* A statement in a pleading may be adopted by reference elsewhere in the same pleading or in any other pleading or motion. FRCP 10(c).

i. *Exhibits.* A copy of a written instrument that is an exhibit to a pleading is a part of the pleading for all purposes. FRCP 10(c).

f. *Citations*

i. *Local rules.* These rules shall be known as Local Rules of the United States District Court for the District of Massachusetts and cited as "L.R., D. Mass." or "L.R." MA R USDCT LR 1.1.

ii. *Electronic case filing procedures.* The procedures governing electronic case filing shall be known as the "Administrative Procedures for Electronic Case Filing in the United States District Court for the District of Massachusetts." They shall be cited as "APECF." MA R USDCT CM/ECF Admin(A)(7).

g. *Acceptance by the clerk.* The clerk must not refuse to file a paper solely because it is not in the form prescribed by the Federal Rules of Civil Procedure or by a local rule or practice. FRCP 5(d)(4).

    i. Except for complaints and notices of appeal, papers that do not conform to the requirements of MA R USDCT LR 5.1(a)(2) shall be returned by the clerk. MA R USDCT LR 5.1(a)(2).

2. *Form of electronic documents.* A paper filed electronically is a written paper for purposes of the Federal Rules of Civil Procedure. FRCP 5(d)(3)(D).

a. *PDF/A format required.* The court will begin requiring submission of documents in PDF/A format in the foreseeable future. PDF/A is an enhanced version of the traditional PDF format. Newer versions of most PDF software will be able to convert to this format. Additional information on PDF/A documents may be found on the court's website. MA R USDCT CM/ECF Admin(Electronic Filing and PDF).

    i. *Electronically converted PDF.* Electronically converted PDF documents are created from word processing documents (MS Word, WordPerfect, etc.) using any appropriate software. These documents are text searchable and the file size is generally smaller than a scanned document. CM/ECF users may use any brand of software to convert documents to PDF. MA R USDCT CM/ECF Admin(Electronic Filing and PDF).

        • Documents converted to PDF, rather than scanned, are preferred for filing in CM/ECF. MA R USDCT CM/ECF Admin(Electronic Filing and PDF).

    ii. *Scanned PDF.* Scanned PDF documents are created from paper documents run through an optical scanner. Scanned PDF documents are generally not searchable and have a larger file size. Please note that software used to create scanned documents may (and should) be set in such a way that the document is "text-searchable." MA R USDCT CM/ECF Admin(Electronic Filing and PDF).

b. *Title.* All pleadings filed electronically shall be titled in accordance with the approved dictionary of civil or criminal events of the CM/ECF system of this court. A list of events is available on the CM/ECF Training Information page of the court's website. The clerk's office may, when necessary and appropriate, modify the docket entry description, or delete and re-enter the docket entry in order to comply with the court's quality assurance standards. MA R USDCT CM/ECF Admin(G)(3).

c. *Attachments to filings and exhibits.* Attachments to filings and exhibits must be filed in accordance with the court's CM/ECF User Manual, unless otherwise ordered by the court. MA R USDCT CM/ECF Admin(O)(1).

    i. Filers must submit as attachments only those excerpts of the referenced documents that are directly germane to the matter under consideration by the court. Excerpted material must be clearly and prominently identified as such. Users who file excerpts of documents do so without prejudice to their right to timely file additional excerpts or the complete document, as may be allowed by the court. Responding parties may timely file additional excerpts or the complete document that they believe are directly germane. MA R USDCT CM/ECF Admin(O)(2).

    ii. Filers shall not attach as an exhibit any pleading or other paper already on file with the court in that case, but shall merely refer to that document. (See MA R USDCT CM/ECF Admin(G) for information on using hyperlinks in PDF documents filed in CM/ECF.) MA R USDCT CM/ECF Admin(O)(3).

d. *Redacted documents.* The parties may request or the court may require the submission of documents that have been redacted/stripped of sensitive or confidential information. The redacted document prepared for electronic filing shall include the original caption of the document, and be clearly labeled as "Redacted Document." A specific event is available for this purpose ("Redacted Document"), found under the Other Filings/Other Documents menu option. MA R USDCT CM/ECF Admin(S).

    i. Attorneys and pro se litigants are advised to take extra care when creating PDF documents intended for submission to CM/ECF. Steps shall be taken to ensure the documents are free of any hidden data (metadata) that may contain redacted information, or traces of information edited or deleted are not hidden in the final document. Even PDF content that has been encrypted may be recovered. An advisory document with additional information on this topic may be found on the court's website. MA R USDCT CM/ECF Admin(S).

e. *Hyperlinks.* Electronically filed documents may contain the following types of hyperlinks: (1) hyperlinks to other portions of the same document; (2) hyperlinks to other documents filed within the CM/ECF system; and (3) hyperlinks to a location on the Internet that contains a source document for a citation. MA R USDCT CM/ECF Admin(G)(7).

    i. Hyperlinks to cited authority may not replace standard citation format. Complete citations must be included in the text of the filed document. Neither a hyperlink, nor any site to which it refers, shall be considered part of the

record, but are simply convenient mechanisms for accessing material cited in a document filed in CM/ECF. Instructions on creating hyperlinks may be found in the CM/ECF User Manual. MA R USDCT CM/ECF Admin(G)(7).

ii.   The court accepts no responsibility for, and does not endorse, any product, organization, or content at any hyperlinked site, or at any site to which that site may be linked. The court accepts no responsibility for the availability or functionality of any hyperlink. MA R USDCT CM/ECF Admin(G)(7).

iii.  One feature of PDF/A documents is that hyperlinks are commonly "masked," meaning that the full address of the referenced file is not written out; for example, clicking the word brief may open a brief which was previously filed in CM/ECF. MA R USDCT CM/ECF Admin(G)(7)(NOTE). An "unmasked" hyperlink has the full address visible to the user. MA R USDCT CM/ECF Admin(G)(7)(NOTE).

- Masked hyperlinks may or may not work in a PDF/A document, depending on how it was created. Currently, masked hyperlinks are preserved in PDF/A documents produced by the "Save As" method in Microsoft Word 2007 and 2010; the "PDFMaker" method in Microsoft Word 2007; and OpenOffice 2.4 ("PDF Export"). With other production methods, such as WordPerfect, the PDF/A document includes underlined words that appear to be links, but clicking them has no effect. MA R USDCT CM/ECF Admin(G)(7)(NOTE).

f.   *Documents features not accepted.* CM/ECF will not accept PDF documents containing tracking tags, embedded systems commands, password protections, access restrictions or other security features, special tags or dynamic features. MA R USDCT CM/ECF Admin(G)(8).

g.   *File size limitations.* A filing party shall limit the size of each PDF file to no more than twenty (20) megabytes. PDF files larger than seven (7) megabytes will be rejected by the CM/ECF system. The filer will see a message advising of the size limitation. MA R USDCT CM/ECF Admin(P)(2).

i.   Larger documents or exhibits may be submitted electronically if split into separate PDF files each less than seven (7) megabytes, attached to the main document and clearly labeled. MA R USDCT CM/ECF Admin(P)(2).

ii.  Documents submitted electronically or on paper are subject to the page limitations set by MA R USDCT LR 7.1(b)(4) or by order of the court. MA R USDCT CM/ECF Admin(P)(1).

h.   *Accuracy and readability.* The filer shall verify the accuracy and readability of any PDF file before electronically filing it in CM/ECF. MA R USDCT CM/ECF Admin(G)(6); MA R USDCT CM/ECF Admin(P)(3).

3.   *Signing of pleadings, motions and other papers*

a.   *Signature.* Every pleading, written motion, and other paper must be signed by at least one attorney of record in the attorney's name—or by a party personally if the party is unrepresented. The paper must state the signer's address, e-mail address, and telephone number. FRCP 11(a). The provisions of the Federal Rules of Civil Procedure pertaining to the form and signing of pleadings, motions, and other papers shall be applicable to all papers filed in any proceeding in this court. The board of bar overseers registration number of each attorney signing such documents, except the United States Attorney and his staff, shall be inscribed below the signature. MA R USDCT LR 5.1(a)(1).

i.   *Electronic signing.* A filing made through a person's electronic-filing account and authorized by that person, together with that person's name on a signature block, constitutes the person's signature. FRCP 5(d)(3)(C).

ii.  *Appearances.* The filing of an appearance or any other pleading signed on behalf of a party constitutes an entry of appearance for that party. All pleadings shall contain the name, bar admission number, address, telephone number, and e-mail address of the attorney entering an appearance. MA R USDCT LR 83.5.2(a).

- *Appearances by law firms.* When a party is represented by a law firm, the appearance must include the name and the signature of at least one individual attorney. When a party is represented by more than one attorney from the same or different law firms, the attorney entering the appearance must designate the individual attorney who is authorized to receive all notices in the case. Any notice sent to an attorney so designated shall be deemed to be proper notice unless the court finds that notice was not properly sent. MA R USDCT LR 83.5.2(b).

- For more information on appearances, refer to MA R USDCT LR 83.5.2.

iii. *Signatures of attorneys.* The user login and password required to submit documents to the CM/ECF system shall serve as that user's signature for purposes of FRCP 11 and for all other purposes under the Federal Rules of Civil Procedure and the Local Rules of the United States District Court for the District of Massachusetts. All electronically filed documents must include a signature block and must set forth the attorney's name, bar number,

address, telephone number and email address. The name of the CM/ECF user under whose log-in and password the document is submitted must be preceded by a "/s/" and typed in the space where the signature would otherwise appear. MA R USDCT CM/ECF Admin(M)(1). For an example, refer to MA R USDCT CM/ECF Admin(M)(1).

    iv. *Signatures of pro se parties.* Any document requiring a signature that is filed by a party appearing pro se shall bear the words "pro se" following that party's signature. Any such document shall also state the party's mailing address, telephone number (if any), and e-mail address (if the party has consented to service by email). MA R USDCT LR 83.5.5(g). For more information on practice by pro se litigants, refer to MA R USDCT LR 83.5.5.

    v. *Multiple signatures.* The filer of any document requiring more than one signature (e.g, stipulations, joint motions, joint status reports, magistrate judge consent forms, etc.) must list thereon all the names of other signatories by means of a "/s/ name of signatory" block for each. By submitting such a document, the filing attorney certifies that each of the other signatories has expressly agreed to the form and substance of the document and that the filing attorney has their actual authority to submit the document electronically. MA R USDCT CM/ECF Admin(M)(2). For more information, refer to MA R USDCT CM/ECF Admin(M)(2).

    vi. *Affidavits.* Except as provided in MA R USDCT CM/ECF Admin(L), affidavits shall be filed electronically; however, the electronically filed version must contain a "/s/ name of signatory" block indicating that the paper document bears an original signature. MA R USDCT CM/ECF Admin(M)(3). The court will also accept a scanned version of the original, signed document. MA R USDCT CM/ECF Admin(M)(3). For more information, refer to MA R USDCT CM/ECF Admin(M)(3).

    vii. *No verification or accompanying affidavit required for pleadings.* Unless a rule or statute specifically states otherwise, a pleading need not be verified or accompanied by an affidavit. FRCP 11(a).

    viii. *Unsigned papers.* The court must strike an unsigned paper unless the omission is promptly corrected after being called to the attorney's or party's attention. FRCP 11(a).

  b. *Representations to the court.* By presenting to the court a pleading, written motion, or other paper—whether by signing, filing, submitting, or later advocating it—an attorney or unrepresented party certifies that to the best of the person's knowledge, information, and belief, formed after an inquiry reasonable under the circumstances:

    i. It is not being presented for any improper purpose, such as to harass, cause unnecessary delay, or needlessly increase the cost of litigation;

    ii. The claims, defenses, and other legal contentions are warranted by existing law or by a nonfrivolous argument for extending, modifying, or reversing existing law or for establishing new law;

    iii. The factual contentions have evidentiary support or, if specifically so identified, will likely have evidentiary support after a reasonable opportunity for further investigation or discovery; and

    iv. The denials of factual contentions are warranted on the evidence or, if specifically so identified, are reasonably based on belief or a lack of information. FRCP 11(b).

  c. *Sanctions.* If, after notice and a reasonable opportunity to respond, the court determines that FRCP 11(b) has been violated, the court may impose an appropriate sanction on any attorney, law firm, or party that violated FRCP 11(b) or is responsible for the violation. FRCP 11(c)(1). Refer to the United States District Court for the District of Massachusetts KeyRules Motion for Sanctions document for more information.

4. *Privacy protection for filings made with the court*

  a. *Redacted filings.* Unless the court orders otherwise, in an electronic or paper filing with the court that contains an individual's Social Security number, taxpayer-identification number, or birth date, the name of an individual known to be a minor, or a financial-account number, a party or nonparty making the filing may include only:

    i. The last four (4) digits of the Social Security number and taxpayer-identification number;

    ii. The year of the individual's birth;

    iii. The minor's initials; and

    iv. The last four (4) digits of the financial-account number. FRCP 5.2(a); MA R USDCT CM/ECF Admin(N).

  b. *Exemptions from the redaction requirement.* The redaction requirement does not apply to the following:

    i. A financial-account number that identifies the property allegedly subject to forfeiture in a forfeiture proceeding;

    ii. The record of an administrative or agency proceeding;

  iii. The official record of a state-court proceeding;

  iv. The record of a court or tribunal, if that record was not subject to the redaction requirement when originally filed;

  v. A filing covered by FRCP 5.2(c) or FRCP 5.2(d); and

  vi. A pro se filing in an action brought under 28 U.S.C.A. § 2241, 28 U.S.C.A. § 2254, or 28 U.S.C.A. § 2255. FRCP 5.2(b).

 c. *Limitations on remote access to electronic files; Social Security appeals and immigration cases.* Unless the court orders otherwise, in an action for benefits under the Social Security Act, and in an action or proceeding relating to an order of removal, to relief from removal, or to immigration benefits or detention, access to an electronic file is authorized as follows:

  i. The parties and their attorneys may have remote electronic access to any part of the case file, including the administrative record;

  ii. Any other person may have electronic access to the full record at the courthouse, but may have remote electronic access only to:

   • The docket maintained by the court; and

   • An opinion, order, judgment, or other disposition of the court, but not any other part of the case file or the administrative record. FRCP 5.2(c).

 d. *Filings made under seal.* The court may order that a filing be made under seal without redaction. The court may later unseal the filing or order the person who made the filing to file a redacted version for the public record. FRCP 5.2(d).

 e. *Protective orders.* For good cause, the court may by order in a case:

  i. Require redaction of additional information; or

  ii. Limit or prohibit a nonparty's remote electronic access to a document filed with the court. FRCP 5.2(e).

 f. *Option for additional unredacted filing under seal.* A person making a redacted filing may also file an unredacted copy under seal. The court must retain the unredacted copy as part of the record. FRCP 5.2(f). For more information, refer to MA R USDCT LR 7.2.

 g. *Option for filing a reference list.* A filing that contains redacted information may be filed together with a reference list that identifies each item of redacted information and specifies an appropriate identifier that uniquely corresponds to each item listed. The list must be filed under seal and may be amended as of right. Any reference in the case to a listed identifier will be construed to refer to the corresponding item of information. FRCP 5.2(g).

 h. *Responsibility for redaction.* The clerk's office is not responsible for reviewing documents filed with the court to determine whether pleadings have been redacted and are in the proper form. MA R USDCT CM/ECF Admin(N).

 i. *Waiver of protection of identifiers.* A person waives the protection of FRCP 5.2(a) as to the person's own information by filing it without redaction and not under seal. FRCP 5.2(h).

## F. Filing and Service Requirements

 1. *Filing requirements*

  a. *Required filings.* Any paper after the complaint that is required to be served must be filed no later than a reasonable time after service. FRCP 5(d)(1).

   i. Except as noted in FRCP 33 to FRCP 36, the original of all papers required to be served under FRCP 5(d) shall, unless otherwise submitted to the court, be filed in the office of the clerk within seven (7) days after service has been made. MA R USDCT LR 5.1(b). Except as otherwise provided by the Federal Rules of Civil Procedure, proof of service of all pleadings and other papers required to be served (except discovery papers that in accordance with FRCP 33 to FRCP 36(f) are not to be filed) shall be filed in the office of the clerk promptly after service has been made. MA R USDCT LR 5.2(b)(1).

  b. *Nonelectronic filing.* A paper not filed electronically is filed by delivering it: (1) to the clerk; or (2) to a judge who agrees to accept it for filing, and who must then note the filing date on the paper and promptly send it to the clerk. FRCP 5(d)(2).

  c. *Electronic filing.* Unless exempt or otherwise ordered by the court, all pleadings and other papers submitted to the court must be filed, signed, and verified by electronic means as provided in MA R USDCT LR 5.4. MA R USDCT LR 5.4(A); MA R USDCT CM/ECF Admin(A)(1). All electronic filings must be made in accordance with the Administrative Procedures for Electronic Case Filing in the United States District Court for the District of

Massachusetts (MA R USDCT CM/ECF Admin). MA R USDCT LR 5.4(B). The court may deviate from the Administrative Procedures for Electronic Case Filing in the United States District Court for the District of Massachusetts (MA R USDCT CM/ECF Admin) in specific cases, without prior notice, if deemed appropriate in the exercise of discretion, considering the need for the just, speedy, and inexpensive determination of matters pending before the court. MA R USDCT CM/ECF Admin(C)(1). The court may excuse a failure to comply with any administrative procedure whenever justice so requires. MA R USDCT CM/ECF Admin(C)(2).

i. *By a represented person; Generally required; Exceptions.* A person represented by an attorney must file electronically, unless nonelectronic filing is allowed by the court for good cause or is allowed or required by local rule. FRCP 5(d)(3)(A).

ii. *By unrepresented person; When allowed or required.* A person not represented by an attorney: (1) may file electronically only if allowed by court order or by local rule; and (2) may be required to file electronically only by court order, or by a local rule that includes reasonable exceptions. FRCP 5(d)(3)(B).

iii. *Exemptions from electronic filing*

- *Documents that should not be filed electronically.* The following types of documents must not be filed electronically, and will not be scanned into the ECF system by the clerk's office: (1) sealed documents; (2) ex parte motions; (3) documents generated as part of an alternative dispute resolution (ADR) process; (4) the administrative record in Social Security and other administrative proceedings; (5) the state court record in proceedings under 28 U.S.C.A. § 2254; and (6) such other types of documents as the clerk may direct in the Administrative Procedures for Electronic Case Filing in the United States District Court for the District of Massachusetts (MA R USDCT CM/ECF Admin). MA R USDCT LR 5.4(G)(1); MA R USDCT CM/ECF Admin(L).

- *Documents that need not be filed electronically.* The following types of documents need not be filed electronically, but may be scanned into the ECF system by a filing party or the clerk's office: (1) handwritten pleadings; (2) documents filed by pro se litigants who are incarcerated or who are not registered ECF users; (3) indictments, informations, criminal complaints, and the criminal JS45 form; (4) affidavits for search or arrest warrants and related documents; (5) documents received from another court under FRCRP 20 or FRCRP 40; (6) appearance bonds; (7) any document in a criminal case containing the original signature of a defendant, such as a waiver of indictment or a plea agreement; (8) petitions for violations of supervised release; (9) executed service of process documents under FRCP 4; and (10) such other types of documents as the clerk may direct in the Administrative Procedures for Electronic Case Filing in the United States District Court for the District of Massachusetts (MA R USDCT CM/ECF Admin). MA R USDCT LR 5.4(G)(2); MA R USDCT CM/ECF Admin(L).

- For more information on exemptions from electronic filing, refer to MA R USDCT CM/ECF Admin(L).

iv. *Consequences of electronic filing.* Electronic transmission of a document to the CM/ECF system, together with the transmission of a Notice of Electronic Filing (NEF) from the court at the completion of the transaction, constitutes the filing of the document for all purposes of the Federal Rules of Procedure and constitutes entry of the document on the docket maintained by the clerk pursuant to FRCP 58 and FRCP 79. MA R USDCT CM/ECF Admin(G)(1).

v. *Payment of filing fees.* When electronically filing any pleading or paper through CM/ECF that requires a fee, all registered ECF users are to pay the fee electronically through the Treasury Department's Internet payment process. MA R USDCT LR 67.4(d); MA R USDCT CM/ECF Admin(A)(1). Pro se filers and those who have been exempted from electronic filing and/or electronic payment of fees may submit payments by check or money order made payable to "Clerk, U.S. District Court". MA R USDCT LR 67.4(d). For more information on filing fees, refer to MA R USDCT LR 67.4 and MA R USDCT CM/ECF Admin(I).

vi. For more information on electronic filing, refer to MA R USDCT CM/ECF Admin.

d. *Email or fax filing.* In general, the court does not accept documents by email or by fax. If the court, in special circumstances, does authorize the submission of a document in that manner, the document shall not be considered filed until an NEF is generated by CM/ECF at the completion of the transaction. MA R USDCT CM/ECF Admin(H)(5).

2. *Service requirements.* Service of all pleadings subsequent to the original complaint and of all other papers required to be served shall be made in the manner specified by FRCP 5. MA R USDCT LR 5.2(a).

a. *Service; When required*

i. *In general.* Unless the Federal Rules of Civil Procedure provide otherwise, each of the following papers must be served on every party:

- An order stating that service is required;

- A pleading filed after the original complaint, unless the court orders otherwise under FRCP 5(c) because there are numerous defendants;

- A discovery paper required to be served on a party, unless the court orders otherwise;

- A written motion, except one that may be heard ex parte; and

- A written notice, appearance, demand, or offer of judgment, or any similar paper. FRCP 5(a)(1).

ii. *If a party fails to appear.* No service is required on a party who is in default for failing to appear. But a pleading that asserts a new claim for relief against such a party must be served on that party under FRCP 4. FRCP 5(a)(2).

iii. *Seizing property.* If an action is begun by seizing property and no person is or need be named as a defendant, any service required before the filing of an appearance, answer, or claim must be made on the person who had custody or possession of the property when it was seized. FRCP 5(a)(3).

b. *Service; How made*

i. *Serving an attorney.* If a party is represented by an attorney, service under FRCP 5 must be made on the attorney unless the court orders service on the party. FRCP 5(b)(1).

- *Nonresident attorney.* On application of a party, the court may order an attorney who represents any other party and who does not maintain an office within this district where service can be made on him by delivery as provided by FRCP 5(b), to designate a member of the bar of this court who does maintain such an office to receive service of all pleadings and other papers in his behalf. MA R USDCT LR 5.2(c)(1).

ii. *Serving a party acting pro se.* On application of a party, the court may order any other party who is appearing without an attorney and who does not maintain an office or residence within this district where service can be made on him by delivery as provided by FRCP 5(b), to designate an address within the district at which service can be made on him by delivery. MA R USDCT LR 5.2(c)(2).

iii. *Service in general.* A paper is served under FRCP 5 by:

- Handing it to the person;

- Leaving it: (1) at the person's office with a clerk or other person in charge or, if no one is in charge, in a conspicuous place in the office; or (2) if the person has no office or the office is closed, at the person's dwelling or usual place of abode with someone of suitable age and discretion who resides there;

- Mailing it to the person's last known address—in which event service is complete upon mailing;

- Leaving it with the court clerk if the person has no known address;

- Sending it to a registered user by filing it with the court's electronic-filing system or sending it by other electronic means that the person consented to in writing—in either of which events service is complete upon filing or sending, but is not effective if the filer or sender learns that it did not reach the person to be served; or

- Delivering it by any other means that the person consented to in writing—in which event service is complete when the person making service delivers it to the agency designated to make delivery. FRCP 5(b)(2).

iv. *Service by electronic means.* Unless exempt or otherwise ordered by the court, all pleadings and other papers must be served on other parties by electronic means. MA R USDCT LR 5.4(C); MA R USDCT CM/ECF Admin(H)(2). Service by electronic means shall be treated the same as service by mail. MA R USDCT CM/ECF Admin(H)(4).

- *Consent to electronic service.* Registering to use CM/ECF constitutes consent to service of all documents by electronic means as provided in the Administrative Procedures for Electronic Case Filing in the United States District Court for the District of Massachusetts (MA R USDCT CM/ECF Admin) and FRCP 5(b) and FRCP 77(d). MA R USDCT CM/ECF Admin(E)(6); MA R USDCT CM/ECF Admin(H)(3).

- *Service on registered ECF users.* Transmission of the Notice of Electronic Filing (NEF) through the court's transmission facilities will constitute service of the filed document upon a registered ECF user. MA R USDCT LR 5.4(C).

- *Service on non-registered users.* The party filing the document electronically is responsible for serving a paper copy of the document by mail in accordance with FRCP 5(b) to those case participants who have not been identified on the NEF as electronic recipients. MA R USDCT CM/ECF Admin(H)(3).

- *Service of conventionally filed papers.* Documents or exhibits submitted conventionally shall be served on other parties by the filer using traditional means. MA R USDCT CM/ECF Admin(P)(4).

   c. *Serving numerous defendants*

     i. *In general.* If an action involves an unusually large number of defendants, the court may, on motion or on its own, order that:

- Defendants' pleadings and replies to them need not be served on other defendants;

- Any crossclaim, counterclaim, avoidance, or affirmative defense in those pleadings and replies to them will be treated as denied or avoided by all other parties; and

- Filing any such pleading and serving it on the plaintiff constitutes notice of the pleading to all parties. FRCP 5(c)(1).

     ii. *Notifying parties.* A copy of every such order must be served on the parties as the court directs. FRCP 5(c)(2).

3. *Service requirements of an amended complaint asserting new or additional claims for relief.* The service of amended pleadings is generally governed by FRCP 5. Thus, except for an amended pleading against a defaulting party that does not assert new or additional claims for relief, an amended pleading must be served in accordance with FRCP 5. FEDPROC § 62:257; Int'l Controls Corp. v. Vesco, 556 F.2d 665 (2d Cir. 1977). However, while FRCP 5 permits service of an amended complaint on counsel, where the amended complaint contains an entirely different cause of action that could not have been properly served originally by the method used in serving the original complaint, the amended complaint must be served in accordance with the terms of FRCP 4. FEDPROC § 62:257; Lasch v. Antkies, 161 F. Supp. 851 (E.D. Pa. 1958). Refer to the United States District Court for the District of Massachusetts KeyRules Complaint document for more information on serving the amended complaint in accordance with FRCP 4.

## G. Hearings

1. *Hearings, generally.* Generally, there is no hearing contemplated in the federal statutes or rules for the amended pleading.

   a. *Amended answer; Hearing on certain FRCP 12 defenses before trial.* If a party so moves, any defense listed in FRCP 12(b)(1) through FRCP 12(b)(7)—whether made in a pleading or by motion—and a motion under FRCP 12(c) must be heard and decided before trial unless the court orders a deferral until trial. FRCP 12(i).

## H. Forms

## 1. Federal Amended Pleading Forms

   a. Civil cover sheet. 2 FEDFORMS § 3:29.

   b. Notice of lawsuit and request for waiver of service of summons and waiver of summons. 2 FEDFORMS § 3:36.

   c. Complaint. 2 FEDFORMS § 7:14.

   d. Generally. 2B FEDFORMS § 8:10.

   e. Presenting defenses. 2B FEDFORMS § 8:12.

   f. Denials, admissions and affirmative defenses. 2B FEDFORMS § 8:15.

   g. Denial of particular averment. 2B FEDFORMS § 8:24.

   h. Admission of particular averment. 2B FEDFORMS § 8:25.

   i. Denial of all averments of paragraph. 2B FEDFORMS § 8:26.

   j. Admission of all averments of paragraph. 2B FEDFORMS § 8:27.

   k. Denial in part and admission in part of paragraph. 2B FEDFORMS § 8:28.

   l. Notice of amended complaint. 2C FEDFORMS § 14:10.

   m. Amendment to complaint. 2C FEDFORMS § 14:47.

   n. Amendment to complaint; Short version. 2C FEDFORMS § 14:48.

    o.   Amendment to complaint; As of course. 2C FEDFORMS § 14:49.

    p.   Notice; Of filing amended pleading as of course. AMJUR PP FEDPRAC § 162.

    q.   Amendment; Of pleading as of course. AMJUR PP FEDPRAC § 163.

    r.   Complaint; Single count. FEDPROF § 1A:171.

    s.   Complaint; Multiple counts; With same jurisdictional basis. FEDPROF § 1A:172.

    t.   Amendment of pleading; As matter of course. FEDPROF § 1A:332.

    u.   Notice of filing amended pleading; Where amendment is matter of course. FEDPROF § 1A:333.

    v.   Amendment of pleading; Particular clauses. FEDPROF § 1A:336.

    w.   Amendment of pleading; Clause; Change in title of action. FEDPROF § 1A:337.

    x.   Amendment of pleading; Clause; To show amount in controversy. FEDPROF § 1A:339.

    y.   Amendment of pleading; Clause; To show diversity of citizenship. FEDPROF § 1A:340.

    z.   Amendment of pleading; Clause; Demand for relief. FEDPROF § 1A:341.

  **2.**   **Forms for the District of Massachusetts**

    a.   Notice of filing with clerk's office. MA R USDCT CM/ECF Admin(Appendix I).

## I. Applicable Rules

  1.   *Federal rules*

    a.   Serving and filing pleadings and other papers. FRCP 5.

    b.   Constitutional challenge to a statute; Notice, certification, and intervention. FRCP 5.1.

    c.   Privacy protection for filings made with the court. FRCP 5.2.

    d.   Computing and extending time; Time for motion papers. FRCP 6.

    e.   Pleadings allowed; Form of motions and other papers. FRCP 7.

    f.   General rules of pleading. FRCP 8.

    g.   Pleading special matters. FRCP 9.

    h.   Form of pleadings. FRCP 10.

    i.   Signing pleadings, motions, and other papers; Representations to the court; Sanctions. FRCP 11.

    j.   Defenses and objections; When and how presented; Motion for judgment on the pleadings; Consolidating motions; Waiving defenses; Pretrial hearing. FRCP 12.

    k.   Amended and supplemental pleadings. FRCP 15.

    l.   Right to a jury trial; Demand. FRCP 38.

    m.   Determining foreign law. FRCP 44.1.

  2.   *Local rules*

    a.   Title. MA R USDCT LR 1.1.

    b.   Sanctions. MA R USDCT LR 1.3.

    c.   Form and filing of papers. MA R USDCT LR 5.1.

    d.   Service and filing of pleadings and other papers. MA R USDCT LR 5.2.

    e.   Filing and service by electronic means. MA R USDCT LR 5.4.

    f.   Addition of new parties. MA R USDCT LR 15.1.

    g.   Alternative dispute resolution. MA R USDCT LR 16.4.

    h.   Payments and deposits made with the clerk. MA R USDCT LR 67.4.

    i.   Settlement. MA R USDCT LR 68.2.

    j.   Office of the clerk. MA R USDCT LR 77.2.

    k.   Appearances. MA R USDCT LR 83.5.2.

l.   Practice by pro se litigants. MA R USDCT LR 83.5.5.

m.   CM/ECF case management/electronic case files administrative procedures. MA R USDCT CM/ECF Admin.

## Motions, Oppositions and Replies
## Motion to Strike

### Document Last Updated December 2018

**A. Checklist**

(I)  ❑ Matters to be considered by moving party

  (a)  ❑ Required documents

    (1)  ❑ Notice of motion and motion

    (2)  ❑ Memorandum

    (3)  ❑ Certificate of service

  (b)  ❑ Supplemental documents

    (1)  ❑ Deposition

    (2)  ❑ Notice of constitutional question

    (3)  ❑ Nongovernmental corporate disclosure statement

    (4)  ❑ Proposed order

    (5)  ❑ Compact disk with copy of document(s) in PDF format

    (6)  ❑ Notice of filing with clerk's office

    (7)  ❑ Additional copies

    (8)  ❑ Courtesy copies

  (c)  ❑ Timing

    (1)  ❑ The court may act: on motion made by a party either before responding to the pleading or, if a response is not allowed, within twenty-one (21) days after being served with the pleading

    (2)  ❑ A written motion and notice of the hearing must be served at least fourteen (14) days before the time specified for the hearing, with the following exceptions: (i) when the motion may be heard ex parte; (ii) when the Federal Rules of Civil Procedure set a different time; or (iii) when a court order—which a party may, for good cause, apply for ex parte—sets a different time

    (3)  ❑ Any affidavit supporting a motion must be served with the motion

    (4)  ❑ Except as noted in FRCP 33 to FRCP 36, the original of all papers required to be served under FRCP 5(d) shall, unless otherwise submitted to the court, be filed in the office of the clerk within seven (7) days after service has been made

(II)  ❑ Matters to be considered by opposing party

  (a)  ❑ Required documents

    (1)  ❑ Opposition

    (2)  ❑ Certificate of service

  (b)  ❑ Supplemental documents

    (1)  ❑ Deposition

    (2)  ❑ Notice of constitutional question

    (3)  ❑ Compact disk with copy of document(s) in PDF format

    (4)  ❑ Notice of filing with clerk's office

    (5)  ❑ Additional copies

    (6)  ❑ Courtesy copies

(c) ❑ Timing

    (1) ❑ A party opposing a motion, shall file an opposition within fourteen (14) days after the motion is served, unless another period is fixed by rule or statute, or by order of the court

    (2) ❑ Except as FRCP 59(c) provides otherwise, any opposing affidavit must be served at least seven (7) days before the hearing, unless the court permits service at another time

    (3) ❑ Except as noted in FRCP 33 to FRCP 36, the original of all papers required to be served under FRCP 5(d) shall, unless otherwise submitted to the court, be filed in the office of the clerk within seven (7) days after service has been made

## B. Timing

1. *Motion to strike.* The court may act: on motion made by a party either before responding to the pleading or, if a response is not allowed, within twenty-one (21) days after being served with the pleading. FRCP 12(f)(2).

2. *Timing of motions, generally*

    a. *Motion and notice of hearing.* A written motion and notice of the hearing must be served at least fourteen (14) days before the time specified for the hearing, with the following exceptions:

        i. When the motion may be heard ex parte;

        ii. When the Federal Rules of Civil Procedure set a different time; or

        iii. When a court order—which a party may, for good cause, apply for ex parte—sets a different time. FRCP 6(c)(1).

    b. *Supporting affidavit.* Any affidavit supporting a motion must be served with the motion. FRCP 6(c)(2).

3. *Timing of opposing papers.* A party opposing a motion, shall file an opposition within fourteen (14) days after the motion is served, unless (1) the motion is for summary judgment, in which case the opposition shall be filed within twenty-one (21) days after the motion is served, or (2) another period is fixed by rule or statute, or by order of the court. MA R USDCT LR 7.1(b)(2); MA R USDCT CM/ECF Admin(H)(4). The fourteen (14) day period is intended to include the period specified by the civil rules for mailing time and provide for a uniform period regardless of the use of the mails. MA R USDCT LR 7.1(b)(2).

    a. *Opposing affidavit.* Except as FRCP 59(c) provides otherwise, any opposing affidavit must be served at least seven (7) days before the hearing, unless the court permits service at another time. FRCP 6(c)(2).

4. *Timing of reply papers.* [W]here the respondent files an answering affidavit setting up a new matter, the moving party ordinarily is allowed a reasonable time to file a reply affidavit since failure to deny the new matter by affidavit may operate as an admission of its truth. AMJUR MOTIONS § 25.

    a. *Leave of court required.* All other papers not filed as indicated in MA R USDCT LR 7.1(b)(1) and MA R USDCT LR 7.1(b)(2), whether in the form of a reply brief or otherwise, may be submitted only with leave of court. MA R USDCT LR 7.1(b)(3).

5. *Filing after service.* Except as noted in FRCP 33 to FRCP 36, the original of all papers required to be served under FRCP 5(d) shall, unless otherwise submitted to the court, be filed in the office of the clerk within seven (7) days after service has been made. MA R USDCT LR 5.1(b).

6. *Effect of FRCP 12 motion on the time to serve a responsive pleading.* Unless the court sets a different time, serving a motion under FRCP 12 alters the periods in FRCP 12(a) as follows:

    a. If the court denies the motion or postpones its disposition until trial, the responsive pleading must be served within fourteen (14) days after notice of the court's action; or

    b. If the court grants a motion for a more definite statement, the responsive pleading must be served within fourteen (14) days after the more definite statement is served. FRCP 12(a)(4).

7. *Computation of time*

    a. *Computing time.* FRCP 6 applies in computing any time period specified in the Federal Rules of Civil Procedure, in any local rule or court order, or in any statute that does not specify a method of computing time. FRCP 6(a).

        i. *Period stated in days or a longer unit.* When the period is stated in days or a longer unit of time:

            • Exclude the day of the event that triggers the period;

            • Count every day, including intermediate Saturdays, Sundays, and legal holidays; and

            • Include the last day of the period, but if the last day is a Saturday, Sunday, or legal holiday, the period continues to run until the end of the next day that is not a Saturday, Sunday, or legal holiday. FRCP 6(a)(1).

ii. *Period stated in hours.* When the period is stated in hours:

- Begin counting immediately on the occurrence of the event that triggers the period;

- Count every hour, including hours during intermediate Saturdays, Sundays, and legal holidays; and

- If the period would end on a Saturday, Sunday, or legal holiday, the period continues to run until the same time on the next day that is not a Saturday, Sunday, or legal holiday. FRCP 6(a)(2).

iii. *Office of the clerk.* The offices of the Clerk of Court at Boston, Worcester and Springfield shall be open from 8:30 a.m. until 5:00 p.m. on all days except Saturdays, Sundays, legal holidays and other days so ordered by the court and announced in advance, if feasible. MA R USDCT LR 77.2.

iv. *Inaccessibility of the clerk's office.* Unless the court orders otherwise, if the clerk's office is inaccessible:

- On the last day for filing under FRCP 6(a)(1), then the time for filing is extended to the first accessible day that is not a Saturday, Sunday, or legal holiday; or

- During the last hour for filing under FRCP 6(a)(2), then the time for filing is extended to the same time on the first accessible day that is not a Saturday, Sunday, or legal holiday. FRCP 6(a)(3).

v. *"Last day" defined.* Unless a different time is set by a statute, local rule, or court order, the last day ends:

- For electronic filing, at midnight in the court's time zone; and

- For filing by other means, when the clerk's office is scheduled to close. FRCP 6(a)(4).

vi. *"Next day" defined.* The "next day" is determined by continuing to count forward when the period is measured after an event and backward when measured before an event. FRCP 6(a)(5).

vii. *"Legal holiday" defined.* "Legal holiday" means:

- The day set aside by statute for observing New Year's Day, Martin Luther King Jr.'s Birthday, Washington's Birthday, Memorial Day, Independence Day, Labor Day, Columbus Day, Veterans' Day, Thanksgiving Day, or Christmas Day;

- Any day declared a holiday by the President or Congress; and

- For periods that are measured after an event, any other day declared a holiday by the state where the district court is located. FRCP 6(a)(6).

b. *Computation of electronic filing deadlines.* Filing documents electronically does not alter any filing deadlines. MA R USDCT CM/ECF Admin(K); MA R USDCT LR 5.4(D). Although CM/ECF is generally available twenty-four (24) hours a day for filing, all electronic transmissions of documents must be completed prior to 6:00 PM, Eastern Standard (or Daylight Savings) Time, on the date on which it is due, in order to be considered timely filed that day. MA R USDCT CM/ECF Admin(K); MA R USDCT LR 5.4(D). When a specific time of day deadline is set by court order or stipulation, the electronic filing must be completed by that time. Documents may be filed at any time of the day on days prior to the date on which it is due. MA R USDCT CM/ECF Admin(K). A document filed electronically shall be deemed filed as of the time and date stated on the NEF received from the court. MA R USDCT CM/ECF Admin(G)(2); MA R USDCT CM/ECF Admin(K).

i. *Technical failures.* A user whose filing is made untimely as the result of a technical failure of the court's CM/ECF system may seek appropriate relief from the court. MA R USDCT CM/ECF Admin(W)(3). Technical difficulties on the filer's end, with telephone, cable lines, the filer's Internet Service Provider (ISP), or hardware or software problems, will not constitute a technical failure under the Administrative Procedures for Electronic Case Filing in the United States District Court for the District of Massachusetts (MA R USDCT CM/ECF Admin) nor excuse an untimely filing. MA R USDCT CM/ECF Admin(W)(3). As help desk support is available during normal business hours, filers are strongly urged to electronically file any documents during that period. MA R USDCT CM/ECF Admin(W)(3).

- The court has made available a public terminal (computers and scanner) in each clerk's office for registered users to scan and electronically file documents. This equipment is available during normal business hours. Users should bring their prepared document and a valid CM/ECF login and password. MA R USDCT CM/ECF Admin(W)(3).

c. *Extending time.* When an act may or must be done within a specified time, the court may, for good cause, extend the time: (1) with or without motion or notice if the court acts, or if a request is made, before the original time or its extension expires; or (2) on motion made after the time has expired if the party failed to act because of excusable neglect. FRCP 6(b)(1).

 i. *Exceptions.* A court must not extend the time to act under FRCP 50(b), FRCP 50(d), FRCP 52(b), FRCP 59(b), FRCP 59(d), FRCP 59(e), and FRCP 60(b). FRCP 6(b)(2).

 ii. Refer to the United States District Court for the District of Massachusetts KeyRules Motion for Continuance/Extension of Time document for more information on extending time.

d. *Additional time after certain kinds of service.* When a party may or must act within a specified time after being served and service is made under FRCP 5(b)(2)(C) (by mail), FRCP 5(b)(2)(D) (by leaving with the clerk), or FRCP 5(b)(2)(F) (by other means consented to), three (3) days are added after the period would otherwise expire under FRCP 6(a). FRCP 6(d).

## C. General Requirements

1. *Motions, generally*

 a. *Requirements.* A request for a court order must be made by motion. The motion must:

  i. Be in writing unless made during a hearing or trial;

  ii. State with particularity the grounds for seeking the order; and

  iii. State the relief sought. FRCP 7(b)(1).

 b. *Notice of motion.* A party interested in resisting the relief sought by a motion has a right to notice thereof, and an opportunity to be heard. AMJUR MOTIONS § 12.

  i. [I]n addition to statutory or court rule provisions requiring notice of a motion—the purpose of such a notice requirement having been said to be to prevent a party from being prejudicially surprised by a motion—principles of natural justice dictate that an adverse party generally must be given notice that a motion will be presented to the court. AMJUR MOTIONS § 12.

  ii. "Notice," in this regard, means reasonable notice, including a meaningful opportunity to prepare and to defend against allegations of a motion. AMJUR MOTIONS § 12.

 c. *Writing requirement.* The writing requirement is intended to [ensure] that the adverse parties are informed and have a record of both the motion's pendency and the grounds on which the movant seeks an order. FPP § 1191; Feldberg v. Quechee Lakes Corp., 463 F.3d 195 (2d Cir. 2006). [A] single written document can satisfy the writing requirements both for a motion and for [an] FRCP 6(c)(1) notice. FRCP 7(Advisory Committee Notes).

 d. *Particularity requirement.* The particularity requirement [ensures] that the opposing parties will have notice of their opponent's contentions. FEDPROC § 62:358; Goodman v. 1973 26 Foot Trojan Vessel, Arkansas Registration No. AR1439SN, 859 F.2d 71 (8th Cir. 1988). That requirement ensures that notice of the basis for the motion is provided to the court and to the opposing party so as to avoid prejudice, provide the opponent with a meaningful opportunity to respond, and provide the court with enough information to process the motion correctly. FEDPROC § 62:358; Andreas v. Volkswagen of Am., Inc., 336 F.3d 789 (8th Cir. 2003).

  i. Reasonable specification of the grounds for a motion is sufficient. The particularity requirement for motions is satisfied when no party is prejudiced by a lack of particularity or when the court can comprehend the basis for the motion and deal with it fairly. However, where a movant fails to state even one ground for granting the motion in question, the movant has failed to meet the minimal standard of "reasonable specification." FEDPROC § 62:358; Martinez v. Trainor, 556 F.2d 818 (7th Cir. 1977).

  ii. The court may excuse the failure to comply with the particularity requirement if it is inadvertent, and where no prejudice is shown by the opposing party. FEDPROC § 62:358.

 e. *Control of motion practice*

  i. *Plan for the disposition of motions.* At the earliest practicable time, the judicial officer shall establish a framework for the disposition of motions, which, at the discretion of the judicial officer, may include specific deadlines or general time guidelines for filing motions. This framework may be amended from time to time by the judicial officer as required by the progress of the case. MA R USDCT LR 7.1(a)(1).

  ii. *Motion practice.* No motion shall be filed unless counsel certify that they have conferred and have attempted in good faith to resolve or narrow the issue. MA R USDCT LR 7.1(a)(2).

  iii. *Unresolved motions.* The court shall rule on motions as soon as practicable, having in mind the reporting requirements set forth in the Civil Justice Reform Act. MA R USDCT LR 7.1(a)(3).

2. *Motion to strike.* The court may strike from a pleading an insufficient defense or any redundant, immaterial, impertinent, or scandalous matter. The court may act: (1) on its own; or (2) on motion made by a party either before responding to the pleading or, if a response is not allowed, within twenty-one (21) days after being served with the pleading. FRCP 12(f). FRCP 12(f) also is designed to reinforce the requirement in FRCP 8(e) that pleadings be simple, concise, and direct. However, as the cases make clear, it is neither an authorized nor a proper way to procure the dismissal of all or a part of a complaint, or a counterclaim, or to strike an opponent's affidavits. FPP § 1380.

   a. *Practice on a motion to strike.* All well-pleaded facts are taken as admitted on a motion to strike but conclusions of law or conclusions drawn from the facts do not have to be treated in that fashion by the district judge. FPP § 1380. Both because striking a portion of a pleading is a drastic remedy and because it often is sought by the movant simply as a dilatory or harassing tactic, numerous judicial decisions make it clear that motions under FRCP 12(f) are viewed with disfavor by the federal courts and are infrequently granted. FPP § 1380.

   b. *Striking an insufficient defense.* Only if a defense is insufficient as a matter of law will it be stricken. In other words, a defense may be stricken if, on the face of the pleadings, it is patently frivolous, or if it is clearly invalid as a matter of law. FEDPROC § 62:406.

      i. A defense will be stricken if it could not possibly prevent recovery by the plaintiff on its claim. FEDPROC § 62:407. In addition, a defense may be stricken if:

         • The defense requires separate statements;

         • The defense has been previously advanced and rejected; or

         • The defense cannot be waived. FEDPROC § 62:407.

   c. *Striking immaterial or impertinent matter.* Immaterial or impertinent matter will be stricken from a pleading if it is clear that it can have no possible bearing upon the subject matter of the litigation, and that its inclusion will prejudice the movant. If there is any doubt as to whether under any contingency the matter may raise an issue, the motion should be denied. FEDPROC § 62:409.

      i. "Immaterial matter," for purposes of FRCP 12(f), is matter which has no essential or important relationship to the claim for relief or the defenses being pleaded. FEDPROC § 62:408. A statement of unnecessary particulars in connection with and descriptive of that which is material may be stricken as immaterial matter. FEDPROC § 62:410.

      ii. "Impertinent matter," for purposes of FRCP 12(f), consists of statements that do not pertain, and are not necessary, to the issues in question. FEDPROC § 62:408.

   d. *Striking redundant matter.* "Redundant matter," for purposes of FRCP 12(f), consists of allegations that constitute a needless repetition of other averments or which are wholly foreign to the issue to be decided. However, even if allegations are redundant, they need not be stricken if their presence in the pleading cannot prejudice the moving party. FEDPROC § 62:411.

      i. Merely duplicative remedies do not necessarily make claims "redundant," within the meaning of FRCP 12(f), if the claims otherwise require proof of different elements, but a claim that merely recasts the same elements under the guise of a different theory may be stricken as redundant. FEDPROC § 62:411.

   e. *Striking scandalous matter.* A matter is deemed scandalous, for purposes of FRCP 12(f), when it improperly casts a derogatory light on someone, usually a party to the action. Scandalous matter also consists of any unnecessary allegation which reflects cruelly upon the moral character of an individual, or states anything in repulsive language which detracts from the dignity of the court. To be scandalous, degrading charges must be irrelevant, or, if relevant, must go into in unnecessary detail. FEDPROC § 62:412.

      i. Allegations may be stricken as scandalous if the matter bears no possible relation to the controversy or may cause the objecting party prejudice. FEDPROC § 62:412.

      ii. But there are several limitations on the court's willingness to strike scandalous allegations. For example, it is not enough that the matter offends the sensibilities of the objecting party or the person who is the subject of the statements in the pleading, if the challenged allegations describe acts or events that are relevant to the action. FPP § 1382.

   f. *Striking sham or false matter.* FRCP 12(f) does not authorize a motion to strike part or all of a pleading on the ground that it is sham, and the grounds for a motion to strike similarly do not include falsity of the matter alleged. FEDPROC § 62:413; PAE Gov't Servs., Inc. v. MPRI, Inc., 514 F.3d 856 (9th Cir. 2007). However, it has been said that a court will strike a pleading according to FRCP 12(f) when it appears beyond peradventure that it is a sham and false and that its allegations are devoid of factual basis. FEDPROC § 62:413.

g. *Striking conclusions of law.* Unwarranted conclusions of law may be stricken from a pleading pursuant to FRCP 12(f), but ordinarily an allegation is not subject to being stricken merely because it is a conclusion of law. To the contrary, the Federal Rules of Civil Procedure do not condemn conclusions of law, but rather encourage them as at times the clearest and simplest way of stating a claim for relief. Conclusions of law must be unwarranted enough to justify a motion to strike, such as when a plaintiff states causes of action under a federal statute which provides no explicit private right of action. FEDPROC § 62:414.

h. *Striking other particular matter.* Under FRCP 12(f), which permits a court to order stricken from any pleading any redundant, immaterial, impertinent, or scandalous matter, courts have the authority to strike a prayer for relief seeking damages that are not recoverable as a matter of law. A motion to strike may be used to remove an excessive or unauthorized claim for damages. Furthermore, a motion to strike a demand for punitive damages under FRCP 12(f) may be proper if such damages are clearly not collectible, such as in an ordinary breach of contract action. However, there are other ways to raise this issue, and in a particular case, one of these other methods may be more appropriate, such as a motion to dismiss for failure to state a claim pursuant to FRCP 12(b)(6). FEDPROC § 62:415.

i. *Form.* On a motion to strike portions of a pleading, the movant must indicate what paragraphs are being challenged in order to fulfill the particularity requirement; the movant cannot merely state the conclusion that the allegations are too indefinite and insufficient to state a claim or defense. FPP § 1192.

j. *Joining motions*

   i. *Right to join.* A motion under FRCP 12 may be joined with any other motion allowed by FRCP 12. FRCP 12(g)(1).

   ii. *Limitation on further motions.* Except as provided in FRCP 12(h)(2) or FRCP 12(h)(3), a party that makes a motion under FRCP 12 must not make another motion under FRCP 12 raising a defense or objection that was available to the party but omitted from its earlier motion. FRCP 12(g)(2).

3. *Opposing papers.* The Federal Rules of Civil Procedure do not require any formal answer, return, or reply to a motion, except where the Federal Rules of Civil Procedure or local rules may require affidavits, memoranda, or other papers to be filed in opposition to a motion. Such papers are simply to apprise the court of such opposition and the grounds of that opposition. FEDPROC § 62:353.

a. *Effect of failure to respond to motion.* Although in the absence of statutory provision or court rule, a motion ordinarily does not require a written answer, when a party files a motion and the opposing party fails to respond, the court may construe such failure to respond as nonopposition to the motion or an admission that the motion was meritorious, may take the facts alleged in the motion as true—the rule in some jurisdictions being that the failure to respond to a fact set forth in a motion is deemed an admission—and may grant the motion if the relief requested appears to be justified. AMJUR MOTIONS § 28.

b. *Assent or no opposition not determinative.* However, a motion will not be granted automatically simply because an "assent" or a notation of "no opposition" has been filed; federal judges frequently deny motions that have been assented to when it is thought that justice so dictates. FPP § 1190.

c. *Responsive pleading inappropriate as response to motion.* An attempt to answer or oppose a motion with a responsive pleading usually is not appropriate. FPP § 1190.

4. *Reply papers.* A moving party may be required or permitted to prepare papers in addition to his original motion papers. AMJUR MOTIONS § 25. Papers answering or replying to opposing papers may be appropriate, in the interests of justice, where it appears there is a substantial reason for allowing a reply. Thus, a court may accept reply papers where a party demonstrates that the papers to which it seeks to file a reply raise new issues that are material to the disposition of the question before the court, or where the court determines, sua sponte, that it wishes further briefing of an issue raised in those papers and orders the submission of additional papers. FEDPROC § 62:354.

a. *Function of reply papers.* The function of a reply affidavit is to answer the arguments made in opposition to the position taken by the movant and not to permit the movant to introduce new arguments in support of the motion. AMJUR MOTIONS § 25.

b. *Issues raised for the first time in a reply document.* However, the view has been followed in some jurisdictions, that as a matter of judicial economy, where there is no prejudice and where the issues could be raised simply by filing a motion to dismiss, the trial court has discretion to consider arguments raised for the first time in a reply memorandum, and that a trial court may grant a motion to strike issues raised for the first time in a reply memorandum. AMJUR MOTIONS § 26.

5. *Alternative dispute resolution (ADR).* The judicial officer assigned to preside over the case shall encourage the resolution of disputes by settlement or other alternative dispute resolution programs. MA R USDCT LR 16.4(a).

   a. *Settlement.* At every conference conducted under the Local Rules of the United States District Court for the District of Massachusetts, the judicial officer shall inquire as to the utility of the parties conducting settlement negotiations, explore means of facilitating those negotiations, and offer whatever assistance may be appropriate in the circumstances. Assistance may include a reference of the case to another judicial officer for settlement purposes. MA R USDCT LR 16.4(b).

      i. When a case is settled, the parties shall file with the clerk a signed agreement for judgment or stipulation for dismissal, as appropriate, within twenty-eight (28) days, unless the court otherwise orders. MA R USDCT LR 68.2.

   b. *Alternative dispute resolution programs*

      i. *Discretion of judicial officer.* The judicial officer, following an exploration of the matter with all counsel, may refer appropriate cases to alternative dispute resolution programs that have been designated for use in the district court or that the judicial officer may make available. The dispute resolution programs described in MA R USDCT LR 16.4(c)(2) through MA R USDCT LR 16.4(c)(4) are illustrative, not exclusive. Moreover, nothing in MA R USDCT LR 16.4 shall preclude the parties from engaging in private dispute resolution programs as long as they comply with any schedule established by the court. MA R USDCT LR 16.4(c)(1).

      ii. *Mediation.* The judicial officer may refer the case to mediation upon the agreement of all parties. MA R USDCT LR 16.4(c)(2)(A).

      iii. *Other alternative dispute resolution programs.* Use of mediation is not exclusive. At the request of parties, the judicial officer may consider other forms of alternative dispute resolution including, but not limited to, mini-trial, summary jury trial and arbitration. MA R USDCT LR 16.4(c)(3).

   c. For more information on alternative dispute resolution (ADR), refer to MA R USDCT LR 16.4.

6. *Sanctions.* Failure to comply with any of the directions or obligations set forth in, or authorized by, these rules may result in dismissal, default, or the imposition of other sanctions as deemed appropriate by the judicial officer. MA R USDCT LR 1.3. Except as provided by law, the court may impose sanctions as provided in MA R USDCT LR 1.3 for failure to comply with the Administrative Procedures for Electronic Case Filing in the United States District Court for the District of Massachusetts (MA R USDCT CM/ECF Admin) or with MA R USDCT LR 5.4. MA R USDCT CM/ECF Admin(C)(3).

## D. Documents

1. *Documents for moving party*

   a. *Required documents*

      i. *Notice of motion and motion.* Refer to the General Requirements section of this document for information on the notice of motion and motion.

         • *Request for oral argument.* Any party making or opposing a motion who believes that oral argument may assist the court and wishes to be heard shall include a request for oral argument in a separate paragraph of the motion or opposition. The request should be set off with a centered caption, "REQUEST FOR ORAL ARGUMENT." MA R USDCT LR 7.1(d).

      ii. *Memorandum.* A party filing a motion shall at the same time file a memorandum of reasons, including citation of supporting authorities, why the motion should be granted. MA R USDCT LR 7.1(b)(1). Any memorandum of law or other attachment filed in support of a main document shall be filed as a separate document, using the proper event. MA R USDCT CM/ECF Admin(G)(4). Memoranda supporting or opposing allowance of motions shall not, without leave of court, exceed twenty (20) pages, double-spaced. MA R USDCT LR 7.1(b)(4).

      iii. *Certificate of service.* No certificate of service is required when a paper is served by filing it with the court's electronic-filing system. When a paper that is required to be served is served by other means: (1) if the paper is filed, a certificate of service must be filed with it or within a reasonable time after service; and (2) if the paper is not filed, a certificate of service need not be filed unless filing is required by court order or by local rule. FRCP 5(d)(1)(B). Except as otherwise provided by the Federal Rules of Civil Procedure, proof of service of all pleadings and other papers required to be served (except discovery papers that in accordance with FRCP 33 to FRCP 36(f) are not to be filed) shall be filed in the office of the clerk promptly after service has been made. The proof shall show the time and manner of service, and may be made by written acknowledgment of service, a certificate of a member of the bar of this court, or an affidavit of the person who served the paper. MA R USDCT

LR 5.2(b)(1). A certificate of service of a member of the bar shall appear at the bottom of or on the margin of the last page of the paper to which it relates. MA R USDCT LR 5.2(b)(2).

- *Paper service.* The certificate shall be a brief, single-spaced statement and may be in the following form: I hereby certify that a true copy of the above document was served upon (each party appearing pro se and) the attorney of record for each other party by mail (by hand) on (date). (Signature). MA R USDCT LR 5.2(b)(2).

- *Electronic service.* Any pleading or other paper served by electronic means must bear a certificate of service in accordance with MA R USDCT LR 5.2(b). MA R USDCT LR 5.4(C); MA R USDCT CM/ECF Admin(H)(2). The certificate of service shall state that the filer: (1) filed the document electronically, (2) that it will be served electronically to registered CM/ECF participants via the NEF and (3) that the filer will send paper copies to non-registered participants as indicated on the NEF. MA R USDCT CM/ECF Admin(H)(2). For example: I hereby certify that this document filed through the CM/ECF system will be sent electronically to the registered participants as identified on the NEF (NEF) and paper copies will be sent to those indicated as non registered participants on (date). MA R USDCT CM/ECF Admin(H)(2).

- *Return.* Documents not conforming to the requirements of MA R USDCT LR 5.2 (except notices of appeal) shall be returned by the clerk. MA R USDCT LR 5.2(b)(2).

- *Failure to make proof of service.* Failure to make proof of service does not affect the validity of the service. MA R USDCT LR 5.2(b)(3).

b. *Supplemental documents.* Matter outside the pleadings normally is not considered on [an] FRCP 12(f) motion; for example, affidavits in support of or in opposition to the motion typically may not be used. FPP § 1380.

   i. *Deposition.* Notwithstanding the general rule that matters outside the pleadings should ordinarily not be considered in passing upon a motion to strike under FRCP 12(f), a court may consider a deposition in deciding [an] FRCP 12(f) motion if the attorneys for both the plaintiff and the defendant, in their respective briefs, refer to the deposition and to the testimony contained therein. FEDPROC § 62:401.

   ii. *Notice of constitutional question.* A party that files a pleading, written motion, or other paper drawing into question the constitutionality of a federal or state statute must promptly:

   - *File notice.* File a notice of constitutional question stating the question and identifying the paper that raises it, if: (1) a federal statute is questioned and the parties do not include the United States, one of its agencies, or one of its officers or employees in an official capacity; or (2) a state statute is questioned and the parties do not include the state, one of its agencies, or one of its officers or employees in an official capacity; and

   - *Serve notice.* Serve the notice and paper on the Attorney General of the United States if a federal statute is questioned—or on the state attorney general if a state statute is questioned—either by certified or registered mail or by sending it to an electronic address designated by the attorney general for this purpose. FRCP 5.1(a).

   - *No forfeiture.* A party's failure to file and serve the notice, or the court's failure to certify, does not forfeit a constitutional claim or defense that is otherwise timely asserted. FRCP 5.1(d).

   iii. *Nongovernmental corporate disclosure statement*

   - *Contents.* A nongovernmental corporate party must file two (2) copies of a disclosure statement that: (1) identifies any parent corporation and any publicly held corporation owning ten percent (10%) or more of its stock; or (2) states that there is no such corporation. FRCP 7.1(a).

   - *Time to file; Supplemental filing.* A party must: (1) file the disclosure statement with its first appearance, pleading, petition, motion, response, or other request addressed to the court; and (2) promptly file a supplemental statement if any required information changes. FRCP 7.1(b).

   iv. *Proposed order.* Proposed orders usually are not required by this court. However, the court may request the party to submit such a document. In those situations, unless otherwise directed by the clerk's office, electronically file the proposed document/order using the entry for "Proposed Documents submitted to the court," found under the Other Documents menu, or as an attachment to the motion to which it relates. MA R USDCT CM/ECF Admin(T).

   v. *Compact disk with copy of document(s) in PDF format.* A filer who cannot file a document electronically because of such technical difficulty on the filer's end [with telephone, cable lines, the filer's Internet Service Provider (ISP), or hardware or software problems] shall file the document conventionally along with a copy of the document in PDF format on a compact disk or contact the clerk's office for permission to submit the PDF document via email. MA R USDCT CM/ECF Admin(W)(3). Refer to the Timing section of this document for more information on technical failures.

vi. *Notice of filing with clerk's office.* When documents or exhibits (other than those filed ex parte or under seal) are submitted conventionally, a "Notice of Filing with clerk's office" shall be filed electronically and attached to the main document. A paper copy of the "Notice of Filing with clerk's office" must accompany the documents submitted to the court. The "Notice of Filing with clerk's office" (see MA R USDCT CM/ECF Admin(Appendix I)) shall describe each of the documents that will be filed as paper copies in the clerk's office, or shall include an index of the documents if those documents are voluminous. MA R USDCT CM/ECF Admin(P)(5).

vii. *Additional copies.* Whenever, because of the nature of a proceeding, such as a proceeding before a three-judge district court under 28 U.S.C.A. § 2284, additional copies of a paper required to be filed are necessary either for the use of the court or to enable the clerk to carry out his duties, it is the responsibility of the party filing or having filed the paper to provide the necessary copies. MA R USDCT LR 5.1(d).

viii. *Courtesy copies.* COURTESY COPIES OF DOCUMENTS FILED ELECTRONICALLY SHALL NOT BE SUBMITTED ROUTINELY. MA R USDCT CM/ECF Admin(J). Judicial officers, on a case-by-case basis, may require courtesy copies for specific cases, or types of motions, etc. A few Judicial Officers have entered Standing Orders, which may be found on their respective pages on the court's website (under Divisions). Any document filed on paper with the court as a courtesy copy must be clearly labeled as such (Example: COURTESY COPY—DO NOT SCAN). Documents delivered to the court as a courtesy copy will not be maintained in the official court record. MA R USDCT CM/ECF Admin(J).

2. *Documents for opposing party*

   a. *Required documents*

      i. *Opposition.* Refer to the General Requirements section of this document for information on the opposing papers.

         • *Memorandum.* A party opposing a motion shall file, in the same (rather than a separate), document a memorandum of reasons, including citation of supporting authorities, why the motion should not be granted. MA R USDCT LR 7.1(b)(2). Any memorandum of law or other attachment filed in support of a main document shall be filed as a separate document, using the proper event. MA R USDCT CM/ECF Admin(G)(4). Memoranda supporting or opposing allowance of motions shall not, without leave of court, exceed twenty (20) pages, double-spaced. MA R USDCT LR 7.1(b)(4).

         • *Request for oral argument.* Any party making or opposing a motion who believes that oral argument may assist the court and wishes to be heard shall include a request for oral argument in a separate paragraph of the motion or opposition. The request should be set off with a centered caption, "REQUEST FOR ORAL ARGUMENT." MA R USDCT LR 7.1(d).

      ii. *Certificate of service.* No certificate of service is required when a paper is served by filing it with the court's electronic-filing system. When a paper that is required to be served is served by other means: (1) if the paper is filed, a certificate of service must be filed with it or within a reasonable time after service; and (2) if the paper is not filed, a certificate of service need not be filed unless filing is required by court order or by local rule. FRCP 5(d)(1)(B). Except as otherwise provided by the Federal Rules of Civil Procedure, proof of service of all pleadings and other papers required to be served (except discovery papers that in accordance with FRCP 33 to FRCP 36(f) are not to be filed) shall be filed in the office of the clerk promptly after service has been made. The proof shall show the time and manner of service, and may be made by written acknowledgment of service, a certificate of a member of the bar of this court, or an affidavit of the person who served the paper. MA R USDCT LR 5.2(b)(1). A certificate of service of a member of the bar shall appear at the bottom of or on the margin of the last page of the paper to which it relates. MA R USDCT LR 5.2(b)(2).

         • *Paper service.* The certificate shall be a brief, single-spaced statement and may be in the following form: I hereby certify that a true copy of the above document was served upon (each party appearing pro se and) the attorney of record for each other party by mail (by hand) on (date). (Signature). MA R USDCT LR 5.2(b)(2).

         • *Electronic service.* Any pleading or other paper served by electronic means must bear a certificate of service in accordance with MA R USDCT LR 5.2(b). MA R USDCT LR 5.4(C); MA R USDCT CM/ECF Admin(H)(2). The certificate of service shall state that the filer: (1) filed the document electronically, (2) that it will be served electronically to registered CM/ECF participants via the NEF and (3) that the filer will send paper copies to non-registered participants as indicated on the NEF. MA R USDCT CM/ECF

Admin(H)(2). For example: I hereby certify that this document filed through the CM/ECF system will be sent electronically to the registered participants as identified on the NEF (NEF) and paper copies will be sent to those indicated as non registered participants on (date). MA R USDCT CM/ECF Admin(H)(2).

- *Return.* Documents not conforming to the requirements of MA R USDCT LR 5.2 (except notices of appeal) shall be returned by the clerk. MA R USDCT LR 5.2(b)(2).

- *Failure to make proof of service.* Failure to make proof of service does not affect the validity of the service. MA R USDCT LR 5.2(b)(3).

b. *Supplemental documents.* Matter outside the pleadings normally is not considered on [an] FRCP 12(f) motion; for example, affidavits in support of or in opposition to the motion typically may not be used. FPP § 1380.

   i. *Deposition.* Notwithstanding the general rule that matters outside the pleadings should ordinarily not be considered in passing upon a motion to strike under FRCP 12(f), a court may consider a deposition in deciding [an] FRCP 12(f) motion if the attorneys for both the plaintiff and the defendant, in their respective briefs, refer to the deposition and to the testimony contained therein. FEDPROC § 62:401.

   ii. *Notice of constitutional question.* A party that files a pleading, written motion, or other paper drawing into question the constitutionality of a federal or state statute must promptly:

- *File notice.* File a notice of constitutional question stating the question and identifying the paper that raises it, if: (1) a federal statute is questioned and the parties do not include the United States, one of its agencies, or one of its officers or employees in an official capacity; or (2) a state statute is questioned and the parties do not include the state, one of its agencies, or one of its officers or employees in an official capacity; and

- *Serve notice.* Serve the notice and paper on the Attorney General of the United States if a federal statute is questioned—or on the state attorney general if a state statute is questioned—either by certified or registered mail or by sending it to an electronic address designated by the attorney general for this purpose. FRCP 5.1(a).

- *No forfeiture.* A party's failure to file and serve the notice, or the court's failure to certify, does not forfeit a constitutional claim or defense that is otherwise timely asserted. FRCP 5.1(d).

   iii. *Compact disk with copy of document(s) in PDF format.* A filer who cannot file a document electronically because of such technical difficulty on the filer's end [with telephone, cable lines, the filer's Internet Service Provider (ISP), or hardware or software problems] shall file the document conventionally along with a copy of the document in PDF format on a compact disk or contact the clerk's office for permission to submit the PDF document via email. MA R USDCT CM/ECF Admin(W)(3). Refer to the Timing section of this document for more information on technical failures.

   iv. *Notice of filing with clerk's office.* When documents or exhibits (other than those filed ex parte or under seal) are submitted conventionally, a "Notice of Filing with clerk's office" shall be filed electronically and attached to the main document. A paper copy of the "Notice of Filing with clerk's office" must accompany the documents submitted to the court. The "Notice of Filing with clerk's office" (see MA R USDCT CM/ECF Admin(Appendix I)) shall describe each of the documents that will be filed as paper copies in the clerk's office, or shall include an index of the documents if those documents are voluminous. MA R USDCT CM/ECF Admin(P)(5).

   v. *Additional copies.* Whenever, because of the nature of a proceeding, such as a proceeding before a three-judge district court under 28 U.S.C.A. § 2284, additional copies of a paper required to be filed are necessary either for the use of the court or to enable the clerk to carry out his duties, it is the responsibility of the party filing or having filed the paper to provide the necessary copies. MA R USDCT LR 5.1(d).

   vi. *Courtesy copies.* COURTESY COPIES OF DOCUMENTS FILED ELECTRONICALLY SHALL NOT BE SUBMITTED ROUTINELY. MA R USDCT CM/ECF Admin(J). Judicial officers, on a case-by-case basis, may require courtesy copies for specific cases, or types of motions, etc. A few Judicial Officers have entered Standing Orders, which may be found on their respective pages on the court's website (under Divisions). Any document filed on paper with the court as a courtesy copy must be clearly labeled as such (Example: COURTESY COPY—DO NOT SCAN). Documents delivered to the court as a courtesy copy will not be maintained in the official court record. MA R USDCT CM/ECF Admin(J).

# E. Format

1. *Form of documents.* The provisions of FRCP 10 and FRCP 11 concerning the form and signing of pleadings, motions, and other papers shall be applicable to all papers filed in any proceeding in this court. The board of bar overseers registration

number of each attorney signing such documents, except the United States Attorney and his or her staff, shall be inscribed below the signature. MA R USDCT LR 5.1(a)(1).

a. *Paper size and binding.* All papers filed in the court shall be adapted for flat filing, be filed on eight and one-half by eleven (8-1/2 x 11) inch paper without backers and be bound firmly by staple or some such other means (excluding paper or binder clip or rubber band). MA R USDCT LR 5.1(a)(2).

b. *Spacing.* All papers, except discovery requests and responses, shall be double-spaced except for the identification of counsel, title of the case, footnotes, quotations and exhibits. Discovery requests and responses shall be single-spaced. MA R USDCT LR 5.1(a)(2).

c. *Caption.* Every pleading must have a caption with the court's name, a title, a file number, and [an] FRCP 7(a) designation. FRCP 10(a).

    i. *Names of parties.* The title of the complaint must name all the parties; the title of other pleadings, after naming the first party on each side, may refer generally to other parties. FRCP 10(a).

    ii. *Request for special action.* When any pleading or other paper filed in the court includes a request for special process or relief, or any other request such that, if granted, the court will proceed other than in the ordinary course, the request shall, unless it is noted on the category sheet [see MA R USDCT LR 40.1(a)(1)], be noted on the first page to the right of or immediately beneath the caption. MA R USDCT LR 5.1(c).

d. *Claims or defenses*

    i. *Numbered paragraphs.* A party must state its claims or defenses in numbered paragraphs, each limited as far as practicable to a single set of circumstances. A later pleading may refer by number to a paragraph in an earlier pleading. FRCP 10(b).

    ii. *Separate statements.* If doing so would promote clarity, each claim founded on a separate transaction or occurrence—and each defense other than a denial—must be stated in a separate count or defense. FRCP 10(b).

e. *Adoption by reference.* A statement in a pleading may be adopted by reference elsewhere in the same pleading or in any other pleading or motion. FRCP 10(c).

    i. *Exhibits.* A copy of a written instrument that is an exhibit to a pleading is a part of the pleading for all purposes. FRCP 10(c).

f. *Citations*

    i. *Local rules.* These rules shall be known as Local Rules of the United States District Court for the District of Massachusetts and cited as "L.R., D. Mass." or "L.R." MA R USDCT LR 1.1.

    ii. *Electronic case filing procedures.* The procedures governing electronic case filing shall be known as the "Administrative Procedures for Electronic Case Filing in the United States District Court for the District of Massachusetts." They shall be cited as "APECF." MA R USDCT CM/ECF Admin(A)(7).

g. *Acceptance by the clerk.* The clerk must not refuse to file a paper solely because it is not in the form prescribed by the Federal Rules of Civil Procedure or by a local rule or practice. FRCP 5(d)(4).

    i. Except for complaints and notices of appeal, papers that do not conform to the requirements of MA R USDCT LR 5.1(a)(2) shall be returned by the clerk. MA R USDCT LR 5.1(a)(2).

2. *Form of electronic documents.* A paper filed electronically is a written paper for purposes of the Federal Rules of Civil Procedure. FRCP 5(d)(3)(D).

a. *PDF/A format required.* The court will begin requiring submission of documents in PDF/A format in the foreseeable future. PDF/A is an enhanced version of the traditional PDF format. Newer versions of most PDF software will be able to convert to this format. Additional information on PDF/A documents may be found on the court's website. MA R USDCT CM/ECF Admin(Electronic Filing and PDF).

    i. *Electronically converted PDF.* Electronically converted PDF documents are created from word processing documents (MS Word, WordPerfect, etc.) using any appropriate software. These documents are text searchable and the file size is generally smaller than a scanned document. CM/ECF users may use any brand of software to convert documents to PDF. MA R USDCT CM/ECF Admin(Electronic Filing and PDF).

       • Documents converted to PDF, rather than scanned, are preferred for filing in CM/ECF. MA R USDCT CM/ECF Admin(Electronic Filing and PDF).

    ii. *Scanned PDF.* Scanned PDF documents are created from paper documents run through an optical scanner.

Scanned PDF documents are generally not searchable and have a larger file size. Please note that software used to create scanned documents may (and should) be set in such a way that the document is "text-searchable." MA R USDCT CM/ECF Admin(Electronic Filing and PDF).

b. *Title.* All pleadings filed electronically shall be titled in accordance with the approved dictionary of civil or criminal events of the CM/ECF system of this court. A list of events is available on the CM/ECF Training Information page of the court's website. The clerk's office may, when necessary and appropriate, modify the docket entry description, or delete and re-enter the docket entry in order to comply with the court's quality assurance standards. MA R USDCT CM/ECF Admin(G)(3).

c. *Attachments to filings and exhibits.* Attachments to filings and exhibits must be filed in accordance with the court's CM/ECF User Manual, unless otherwise ordered by the court. MA R USDCT CM/ECF Admin(O)(1).

    i. Filers must submit as attachments only those excerpts of the referenced documents that are directly germane to the matter under consideration by the court. Excerpted material must be clearly and prominently identified as such. Users who file excerpts of documents do so without prejudice to their right to timely file additional excerpts or the complete document, as may be allowed by the court. Responding parties may timely file additional excerpts or the complete document that they believe are directly germane. MA R USDCT CM/ECF Admin(O)(2).

    ii. Filers shall not attach as an exhibit any pleading or other paper already on file with the court in that case, but shall merely refer to that document. (See MA R USDCT CM/ECF Admin(G) for information on using hyperlinks in PDF documents filed in CM/ECF.) MA R USDCT CM/ECF Admin(O)(3).

d. *Redacted documents.* The parties may request or the court may require the submission of documents that have been redacted/stripped of sensitive or confidential information. The redacted document prepared for electronic filing shall include the original caption of the document, and be clearly labeled as "Redacted Document." A specific event is available for this purpose ("Redacted Document"), found under the Other Filings/Other Documents menu option. MA R USDCT CM/ECF Admin(S).

    i. Attorneys and pro se litigants are advised to take extra care when creating PDF documents intended for submission to CM/ECF. Steps shall be taken to ensure the documents are free of any hidden data (metadata) that may contain redacted information, or traces of information edited or deleted are not hidden in the final document. Even PDF content that has been encrypted may be recovered. An advisory document with additional information on this topic may be found on the court's website. MA R USDCT CM/ECF Admin(S).

e. *Hyperlinks.* Electronically filed documents may contain the following types of hyperlinks: (1) hyperlinks to other portions of the same document; (2) hyperlinks to other documents filed within the CM/ECF system; and (3) hyperlinks to a location on the Internet that contains a source document for a citation. MA R USDCT CM/ECF Admin(G)(7).

    i. Hyperlinks to cited authority may not replace standard citation format. Complete citations must be included in the text of the filed document. Neither a hyperlink, nor any site to which it refers, shall be considered part of the record, but are simply convenient mechanisms for accessing material cited in a document filed in CM/ECF. Instructions on creating hyperlinks may be found in the CM/ECF User Manual. MA R USDCT CM/ECF Admin(G)(7).

    ii. The court accepts no responsibility for, and does not endorse, any product, organization, or content at any hyperlinked site, or at any site to which that site may be linked. The court accepts no responsibility for the availability or functionality of any hyperlink. MA R USDCT CM/ECF Admin(G)(7).

    iii. One feature of PDF/A documents is that hyperlinks are commonly "masked," meaning that the full address of the referenced file is not written out; for example, clicking the word brief may open a brief which was previously filed in CM/ECF. MA R USDCT CM/ECF Admin(G)(7)(NOTE). An "unmasked" hyperlink has the full address visible to the user. MA R USDCT CM/ECF Admin(G)(7)(NOTE).

        • Masked hyperlinks may or may not work in a PDF/A document, depending on how it was created. Currently, masked hyperlinks are preserved in PDF/A documents produced by the "Save As" method in Microsoft Word 2007 and 2010; the "PDFMaker" method in Microsoft Word 2007; and OpenOffice 2.4 ("PDF Export"). With other production methods, such as WordPerfect, the PDF/A document includes underlined words that appear to be links, but clicking them has no effect. MA R USDCT CM/ECF Admin(G)(7)(NOTE).

f. *Documents features not accepted.* CM/ECF will not accept PDF documents containing tracking tags, embedded systems commands, password protections, access restrictions or other security features, special tags or dynamic features. MA R USDCT CM/ECF Admin(G)(8).

g. *File size limitations.* A filing party shall limit the size of each PDF file to no more than twenty (20) megabytes. PDF files larger than seven (7) megabytes will be rejected by the CM/ECF system. The filer will see a message advising of the size limitation. MA R USDCT CM/ECF Admin(P)(2).

   i. Larger documents or exhibits may be submitted electronically if split into separate PDF files each less than seven (7) megabytes, attached to the main document and clearly labeled. MA R USDCT CM/ECF Admin(P)(2).

   ii. Documents submitted electronically or on paper are subject to the page limitations set by MA R USDCT LR 7.1(b)(4) or by order of the court. MA R USDCT CM/ECF Admin(P)(1).

h. *Accuracy and readability.* The filer shall verify the accuracy and readability of any PDF file before electronically filing it in CM/ECF. MA R USDCT CM/ECF Admin(G)(6); MA R USDCT CM/ECF Admin(P)(3).

3. *Signing of pleadings, motions and other papers*

   a. *Signature.* Every pleading, written motion, and other paper must be signed by at least one attorney of record in the attorney's name—or by a party personally if the party is unrepresented. The paper must state the signer's address, e-mail address, and telephone number. FRCP 11(a). The provisions of the Federal Rules of Civil Procedure pertaining to the form and signing of pleadings, motions, and other papers shall be applicable to all papers filed in any proceeding in this court. The board of bar overseers registration number of each attorney signing such documents, except the United States Attorney and his staff, shall be inscribed below the signature. MA R USDCT LR 5.1(a)(1).

      i. *Electronic signing.* A filing made through a person's electronic-filing account and authorized by that person, together with that person's name on a signature block, constitutes the person's signature. FRCP 5(d)(3)(C).

      ii. *Appearances.* The filing of an appearance or any other pleading signed on behalf of a party constitutes an entry of appearance for that party. All pleadings shall contain the name, bar admission number, address, telephone number, and e-mail address of the attorney entering an appearance. MA R USDCT LR 83.5.2(a).

         • *Appearances by law firms.* When a party is represented by a law firm, the appearance must include the name and the signature of at least one individual attorney. When a party is represented by more than one attorney from the same or different law firms, the attorney entering the appearance must designate the individual attorney who is authorized to receive all notices in the case. Any notice sent to an attorney so designated shall be deemed to be proper notice unless the court finds that notice was not properly sent. MA R USDCT LR 83.5.2(b).

         • For more information on appearances, refer to MA R USDCT LR 83.5.2.

      iii. *Signatures of attorneys.* The user login and password required to submit documents to the CM/ECF system shall serve as that user's signature for purposes of FRCP 11 and for all other purposes under the Federal Rules of Civil Procedure and the Local Rules of the United States District Court for the District of Massachusetts. All electronically filed documents must include a signature block and must set forth the attorney's name, bar number, address, telephone number and email address. The name of the CM/ECF user under whose log-in and password the document is submitted must be preceded by a "/s/" and typed in the space where the signature would otherwise appear. MA R USDCT CM/ECF Admin(M)(1). For an example, refer to MA R USDCT CM/ECF Admin(M)(1).

      iv. *Signatures of pro se parties.* Any document requiring a signature that is filed by a party appearing pro se shall bear the words "pro se" following that party's signature. Any such document shall also state the party's mailing address, telephone number (if any), and e-mail address (if the party has consented to service by email). MA R USDCT LR 83.5.5(g). For more information on practice by pro se litigants, refer to MA R USDCT LR 83.5.5.

      v. *Multiple signatures.* The filer of any document requiring more than one signature (e.g, stipulations, joint motions, joint status reports, magistrate judge consent forms, etc.) must list thereon all the names of other signatories by means of a "/s/ name of signatory" block for each. By submitting such a document, the filing attorney certifies that each of the other signatories has expressly agreed to the form and substance of the document and that the filing attorney has their actual authority to submit the document electronically. MA R USDCT CM/ECF Admin(M)(2). For more information, refer to MA R USDCT CM/ECF Admin(M)(2).

      vi. *Affidavits.* Except as provided in MA R USDCT CM/ECF Admin(L), affidavits shall be filed electronically; however, the electronically filed version must contain a "/s/ name of signatory" block indicating that the paper document bears an original signature. MA R USDCT CM/ECF Admin(M)(3). The court will also accept a scanned version of the original, signed document. MA R USDCT CM/ECF Admin(M)(3). For more information, refer to MA R USDCT CM/ECF Admin(M)(3).

    vii. *No verification or accompanying affidavit required for pleadings.* Unless a rule or statute specifically states otherwise, a pleading need not be verified or accompanied by an affidavit. FRCP 11(a).

    viii. *Unsigned papers.* The court must strike an unsigned paper unless the omission is promptly corrected after being called to the attorney's or party's attention. FRCP 11(a).

b. *Representations to the court.* By presenting to the court a pleading, written motion, or other paper—whether by signing, filing, submitting, or later advocating it—an attorney or unrepresented party certifies that to the best of the person's knowledge, information, and belief, formed after an inquiry reasonable under the circumstances:

    i. It is not being presented for any improper purpose, such as to harass, cause unnecessary delay, or needlessly increase the cost of litigation;

    ii. The claims, defenses, and other legal contentions are warranted by existing law or by a nonfrivolous argument for extending, modifying, or reversing existing law or for establishing new law;

    iii. The factual contentions have evidentiary support or, if specifically so identified, will likely have evidentiary support after a reasonable opportunity for further investigation or discovery; and

    iv. The denials of factual contentions are warranted on the evidence or, if specifically so identified, are reasonably based on belief or a lack of information. FRCP 11(b).

c. *Sanctions.* If, after notice and a reasonable opportunity to respond, the court determines that FRCP 11(b) has been violated, the court may impose an appropriate sanction on any attorney, law firm, or party that violated FRCP 11(b) or is responsible for the violation. FRCP 11(c)(1). Refer to the United States District Court for the District of Massachusetts KeyRules Motion for Sanctions document for more information.

4. *Privacy protection for filings made with the court*

a. *Redacted filings.* Unless the court orders otherwise, in an electronic or paper filing with the court that contains an individual's Social Security number, taxpayer-identification number, or birth date, the name of an individual known to be a minor, or a financial-account number, a party or nonparty making the filing may include only:

    i. The last four (4) digits of the Social Security number and taxpayer-identification number;

    ii. The year of the individual's birth;

    iii. The minor's initials; and

    iv. The last four (4) digits of the financial-account number. FRCP 5.2(a); MA R USDCT CM/ECF Admin(N).

b. *Exemptions from the redaction requirement.* The redaction requirement does not apply to the following:

    i. A financial-account number that identifies the property allegedly subject to forfeiture in a forfeiture proceeding;

    ii. The record of an administrative or agency proceeding;

    iii. The official record of a state-court proceeding;

    iv. The record of a court or tribunal, if that record was not subject to the redaction requirement when originally filed;

    v. A filing covered by FRCP 5.2(c) or FRCP 5.2(d); and

    vi. A pro se filing in an action brought under 28 U.S.C.A. § 2241, 28 U.S.C.A. § 2254, or 28 U.S.C.A. § 2255. FRCP 5.2(b).

c. *Limitations on remote access to electronic files; Social Security appeals and immigration cases.* Unless the court orders otherwise, in an action for benefits under the Social Security Act, and in an action or proceeding relating to an order of removal, to relief from removal, or to immigration benefits or detention, access to an electronic file is authorized as follows:

    i. The parties and their attorneys may have remote electronic access to any part of the case file, including the administrative record;

    ii. Any other person may have electronic access to the full record at the courthouse, but may have remote electronic access only to:

        • The docket maintained by the court; and

        • An opinion, order, judgment, or other disposition of the court, but not any other part of the case file or the administrative record. FRCP 5.2(c).

d. *Filings made under seal.* The court may order that a filing be made under seal without redaction. The court may later unseal the filing or order the person who made the filing to file a redacted version for the public record. FRCP 5.2(d).

e. *Protective orders.* For good cause, the court may by order in a case:

   i. Require redaction of additional information; or

   ii. Limit or prohibit a nonparty's remote electronic access to a document filed with the court. FRCP 5.2(e).

f. *Option for additional unredacted filing under seal.* A person making a redacted filing may also file an unredacted copy under seal. The court must retain the unredacted copy as part of the record. FRCP 5.2(f). For more information, refer to MA R USDCT LR 7.2.

g. *Option for filing a reference list.* A filing that contains redacted information may be filed together with a reference list that identifies each item of redacted information and specifies an appropriate identifier that uniquely corresponds to each item listed. The list must be filed under seal and may be amended as of right. Any reference in the case to a listed identifier will be construed to refer to the corresponding item of information. FRCP 5.2(g).

h. *Responsibility for redaction.* The clerk's office is not responsible for reviewing documents filed with the court to determine whether pleadings have been redacted and are in the proper form. MA R USDCT CM/ECF Admin(N).

i. *Waiver of protection of identifiers.* A person waives the protection of FRCP 5.2(a) as to the person's own information by filing it without redaction and not under seal. FRCP 5.2(h).

## F. Filing and Service Requirements

1. *Filing requirements*

   a. *Required filings.* Any paper after the complaint that is required to be served must be filed no later than a reasonable time after service. FRCP 5(d)(1).

      i. Except as noted in FRCP 33 to FRCP 36, the original of all papers required to be served under FRCP 5(d) shall, unless otherwise submitted to the court, be filed in the office of the clerk within seven (7) days after service has been made. MA R USDCT LR 5.1(b). Except as otherwise provided by the Federal Rules of Civil Procedure, proof of service of all pleadings and other papers required to be served (except discovery papers that in accordance with FRCP 33 to FRCP 36(f) are not to be filed) shall be filed in the office of the clerk promptly after service has been made. MA R USDCT LR 5.2(b)(1).

   b. *Nonelectronic filing.* A paper not filed electronically is filed by delivering it: (1) to the clerk; or (2) to a judge who agrees to accept it for filing, and who must then note the filing date on the paper and promptly send it to the clerk. FRCP 5(d)(2).

   c. *Electronic filing.* Unless exempt or otherwise ordered by the court, all pleadings and other papers submitted to the court must be filed, signed, and verified by electronic means as provided in MA R USDCT LR 5.4. MA R USDCT LR 5.4(A); MA R USDCT CM/ECF Admin(A)(1). All electronic filings must be made in accordance with the Administrative Procedures for Electronic Case Filing in the United States District Court for the District of Massachusetts (MA R USDCT CM/ECF Admin). MA R USDCT LR 5.4(B). The court may deviate from the Administrative Procedures for Electronic Case Filing in the United States District Court for the District of Massachusetts (MA R USDCT CM/ECF Admin) in specific cases, without prior notice, if deemed appropriate in the exercise of discretion, considering the need for the just, speedy, and inexpensive determination of matters pending before the court. MA R USDCT CM/ECF Admin(C)(1). The court may excuse a failure to comply with any administrative procedure whenever justice so requires. MA R USDCT CM/ECF Admin(C)(2).

      i. *By a represented person; Generally required; Exceptions.* A person represented by an attorney must file electronically, unless nonelectronic filing is allowed by the court for good cause or is allowed or required by local rule. FRCP 5(d)(3)(A).

      ii. *By unrepresented person; When allowed or required.* A person not represented by an attorney: (1) may file electronically only if allowed by court order or by local rule; and (2) may be required to file electronically only by court order, or by a local rule that includes reasonable exceptions. FRCP 5(d)(3)(B).

      iii. *Exemptions from electronic filing*

         • *Documents that should not be filed electronically.* The following types of documents must not be filed electronically, and will not be scanned into the ECF system by the clerk's office: (1) sealed documents; (2) ex parte motions; (3) documents generated as part of an alternative dispute resolution (ADR) process; (4) the administrative record in Social Security and other administrative proceedings; (5) the state court record in proceedings under 28 U.S.C.A. § 2254; and (6) such other types of documents as the clerk may direct in the Administrative Procedures for Electronic Case Filing in the United States District Court for the District of Massachusetts (MA R USDCT CM/ECF Admin). MA R USDCT LR 5.4(G)(1); MA R USDCT CM/ECF Admin(L).

- *Documents that need not be filed electronically.* The following types of documents need not be filed electronically, but may be scanned into the ECF system by a filing party or the clerk's office: (1) handwritten pleadings; (2) documents filed by pro se litigants who are incarcerated or who are not registered ECF users; (3) indictments, informations, criminal complaints, and the criminal JS45 form; (4) affidavits for search or arrest warrants and related documents; (5) documents received from another court under FRCRP 20 or FRCRP 40; (6) appearance bonds; (7) any document in a criminal case containing the original signature of a defendant, such as a waiver of indictment or a plea agreement; (8) petitions for violations of supervised release; (9) executed service of process documents under FRCP 4; and (10) such other types of documents as the clerk may direct in the Administrative Procedures for Electronic Case Filing in the United States District Court for the District of Massachusetts (MA R USDCT CM/ECF Admin). MA R USDCT LR 5.4(G)(2); MA R USDCT CM/ECF Admin(L).

- For more information on exemptions from electronic filing, refer to MA R USDCT CM/ECF Admin(L).

iv. *Consequences of electronic filing.* Electronic transmission of a document to the CM/ECF system, together with the transmission of a Notice of Electronic Filing (NEF) from the court at the completion of the transaction, constitutes the filing of the document for all purposes of the Federal Rules of Procedure and constitutes entry of the document on the docket maintained by the clerk pursuant to FRCP 58 and FRCP 79. MA R USDCT CM/ECF Admin(G)(1).

v. *Payment of filing fees.* When electronically filing any pleading or paper through CM/ECF that requires a fee, all registered ECF users are to pay the fee electronically through the Treasury Department's Internet payment process. MA R USDCT LR 67.4(d); MA R USDCT CM/ECF Admin(A)(1). Pro se filers and those who have been exempted from electronic filing and/or electronic payment of fees may submit payments by check or money order made payable to "Clerk, U.S. District Court". MA R USDCT LR 67.4(d). For more information on filing fees, refer to MA R USDCT LR 67.4 and MA R USDCT CM/ECF Admin(I).

vi. For more information on electronic filing, refer to MA R USDCT CM/ECF Admin.

d. *Email or fax filing.* In general, the court does not accept documents by email or by fax. If the court, in special circumstances, does authorize the submission of a document in that manner, the document shall not be considered filed until an NEF is generated by CM/ECF at the completion of the transaction. MA R USDCT CM/ECF Admin(H)(5).

2. *Service requirements.* All papers filed pursuant to MA R USDCT LR 7.1(b) shall be served unless the moving party indicates in writing on the face of the motion that ex parte consideration is requested. Motions filed "ex parte" and related papers need not be served until the motion has been ruled upon or the court orders that service be made. MA R USDCT LR 7.1(c). Service of all pleadings subsequent to the original complaint and of all other papers required to be served shall be made in the manner specified by FRCP 5. MA R USDCT LR 5.2(a).

a. *Service; When required*

i. *In general.* Unless the Federal Rules of Civil Procedure provide otherwise, each of the following papers must be served on every party:

- An order stating that service is required;

- A pleading filed after the original complaint, unless the court orders otherwise under FRCP 5(c) because there are numerous defendants;

- A discovery paper required to be served on a party, unless the court orders otherwise;

- A written motion, except one that may be heard ex parte; and

- A written notice, appearance, demand, or offer of judgment, or any similar paper. FRCP 5(a)(1).

ii. *If a party fails to appear.* No service is required on a party who is in default for failing to appear. But a pleading that asserts a new claim for relief against such a party must be served on that party under FRCP 4. FRCP 5(a)(2).

iii. *Seizing property.* If an action is begun by seizing property and no person is or need be named as a defendant, any service required before the filing of an appearance, answer, or claim must be made on the person who had custody or possession of the property when it was seized. FRCP 5(a)(3).

b. *Service; How made*

i. *Serving an attorney.* If a party is represented by an attorney, service under FRCP 5 must be made on the attorney unless the court orders service on the party. FRCP 5(b)(1).

- *Nonresident attorney.* On application of a party, the court may order an attorney who represents any other

party and who does not maintain an office within this district where service can be made on him by delivery as provided by FRCP 5(b), to designate a member of the bar of this court who does maintain such an office to receive service of all pleadings and other papers in his behalf. MA R USDCT LR 5.2(c)(1).

ii. *Serving a party acting pro se.* On application of a party, the court may order any other party who is appearing without an attorney and who does not maintain an office or residence within this district where service can be made on him by delivery as provided by FRCP 5(b), to designate an address within the district at which service can be made on him by delivery. MA R USDCT LR 5.2(c)(2).

iii. *Service in general.* A paper is served under FRCP 5 by:

- Handing it to the person;

- Leaving it: (1) at the person's office with a clerk or other person in charge or, if no one is in charge, in a conspicuous place in the office; or (2) if the person has no office or the office is closed, at the person's dwelling or usual place of abode with someone of suitable age and discretion who resides there;

- Mailing it to the person's last known address—in which event service is complete upon mailing;

- Leaving it with the court clerk if the person has no known address;

- Sending it to a registered user by filing it with the court's electronic-filing system or sending it by other electronic means that the person consented to in writing—in either of which events service is complete upon filing or sending, but is not effective if the filer or sender learns that it did not reach the person to be served; or

- Delivering it by any other means that the person consented to in writing—in which event service is complete when the person making service delivers it to the agency designated to make delivery. FRCP 5(b)(2).

iv. *Service by electronic means.* Unless exempt or otherwise ordered by the court, all pleadings and other papers must be served on other parties by electronic means. MA R USDCT LR 5.4(C); MA R USDCT CM/ECF Admin(H)(2). Service by electronic means shall be treated the same as service by mail. MA R USDCT CM/ECF Admin(H)(4).

- *Consent to electronic service.* Registering to use CM/ECF constitutes consent to service of all documents by electronic means as provided in the Administrative Procedures for Electronic Case Filing in the United States District Court for the District of Massachusetts (MA R USDCT CM/ECF Admin) and FRCP 5(b) and FRCP 77(d). MA R USDCT CM/ECF Admin(E)(6); MA R USDCT CM/ECF Admin(H)(3).

- *Service on registered ECF users.* Transmission of the Notice of Electronic Filing (NEF) through the court's transmission facilities will constitute service of the filed document upon a registered ECF user. MA R USDCT LR 5.4(C).

- *Service on non-registered users.* The party filing the document electronically is responsible for serving a paper copy of the document by mail in accordance with FRCP 5(b) to those case participants who have not been identified on the NEF as electronic recipients. MA R USDCT CM/ECF Admin(H)(3).

- *Service of conventionally filed papers.* Documents or exhibits submitted conventionally shall be served on other parties by the filer using traditional means. MA R USDCT CM/ECF Admin(P)(4).

c. *Serving numerous defendants*

i. *In general.* If an action involves an unusually large number of defendants, the court may, on motion or on its own, order that:

- Defendants' pleadings and replies to them need not be served on other defendants;

- Any crossclaim, counterclaim, avoidance, or affirmative defense in those pleadings and replies to them will be treated as denied or avoided by all other parties; and

- Filing any such pleading and serving it on the plaintiff constitutes notice of the pleading to all parties. FRCP 5(c)(1).

ii. *Notifying parties.* A copy of every such order must be served on the parties as the court directs. FRCP 5(c)(2).

## G. Hearings

1. *Hearings, generally.* If the court concludes that there should be a hearing on a motion, the motion will be set down for hearing at such time as the court determines. MA R USDCT LR 7.1(e).

a. *Oral argument.* Due process does not require that oral argument be permitted on a motion and, except as otherwise

provided by local rule, the district court has discretion to determine whether it will decide the motion on the papers or hear argument by counsel (and perhaps receive evidence). FPP § 1190; F.D.I.C. v. Deglau, 207 F.3d 153 (3d Cir. 2000).

 i. *Evidence on a motion.* When a motion relies on facts outside the record, the court may hear the matter on affidavits or may hear it wholly or partly on oral testimony or on depositions. FRCP 43(c).

 b. *Providing a regular schedule for oral hearings.* A court may establish regular times and places for oral hearings on motions. FRCP 78(a).

 c. *Providing for submission on briefs.* By rule or order, the court may provide for submitting and determining motions on briefs, without oral hearings. FRCP 78(b). Motions that are not set down for hearing as provided in MA R USDCT LR 7.1(e) will be decided on the papers submitted after an opposition to the motion has been filed, or, if no opposition is filed, after the time for filing an opposition has elapsed. MA R USDCT LR 7.1(f).

2. *Conflict of court appearances.* For information on conflict of court appearances, refer to MA R USDCT LR 40.2.

## H. Forms

### 1. Federal Motion to Strike Forms

 a. Motion to strike insufficient affirmative defenses. 2C FEDFORMS § 11:151.

 b. Motion to strike insufficient defense in answer; Stating particular reason. 2C FEDFORMS § 11:153.

 c. Notice of motion and motion to strike insufficient affirmative defense. 2C FEDFORMS § 11:155.

 d. Motion to strike impertinence and scandal. 2C FEDFORMS § 11:157.

 e. Motion to strike impertinence and immateriality. 2C FEDFORMS § 11:158.

 f. Motion to strike redundancy and scandal. 2C FEDFORMS § 11:159.

 g. Motion to strike immaterial defense. 2C FEDFORMS § 11:160.

 h. Motion to strike for immateriality. 2C FEDFORMS § 11:161.

 i. Motion to strike counterclaim for lack of evidence. 2C FEDFORMS § 11:162.

 j. Motion; By plaintiff; To strike insufficient defense from answer. AMJUR PP FEDPRAC § 453.

 k. Motion; To strike redundant, immaterial, impertinent, or scandalous matter from pleading. AMJUR PP FEDPRAC § 454.

 l. Motion; To strike portions of complaint. AMJUR PP FEDPRAC § 456.

 m. Opposition; To motion. FEDPROF § 1B:175.

 n. Affidavit; Supporting or opposing motion. FEDPROF § 1B:176.

 o. Brief; Supporting or opposing motion. FEDPROF § 1B:177.

 p. Statement of points and authorities; Opposing motion. FEDPROF § 1B:178.

 q. Motion; To strike material outside statute of limitations. FEDPROF § 1B:199.

 r. Opposition to motion; Material not contained in pleading. FEDPROF § 1B:201.

 s. General form. GOLDLTGFMS § 20:8.

 t. General form; Federal form. GOLDLTGFMS § 20:10.

 u. Notice and motion to strike immaterial, redundant or scandalous matter. GOLDLTGFMS § 20:13.

 v. Motion to strike complaint and dismiss action as to one defendant. GOLDLTGFMS § 20:14.

 w. Defendant's motion to strike. GOLDLTGFMS § 20:16.

 x. Defendant's motion to strike; Plaintiff's response. GOLDLTGFMS § 20:17.

 y. Motion to strike answer. GOLDLTGFMS § 20:19.

 z. Objections to motion to strike. GOLDLTGFMS § 20:20.

### 2. Forms for the District of Massachusetts

 a. Notice of filing with clerk's office. MA R USDCT CM/ECF Admin(Appendix I).

# I. Applicable Rules

1. *Federal rules*

   a. Serving and filing pleadings and other papers. FRCP 5.

   b. Constitutional challenge to a statute; Notice, certification, and intervention. FRCP 5.1.

   c. Privacy protection for filings made with the court. FRCP 5.2.

   d. Computing and extending time; Time for motion papers. FRCP 6.

   e. Pleadings allowed; Form of motions and other papers. FRCP 7.

   f. Disclosure statement. FRCP 7.1.

   g. Form of pleadings. FRCP 10.

   h. Signing pleadings, motions, and other papers; Representations to the court; Sanctions. FRCP 11.

   i. Defenses and objections; When and how presented; Motion for judgment on the pleadings; Consolidating motions; Waiving defenses; Pretrial hearing. FRCP 12.

   j. Hearing motions; Submission on briefs. FRCP 78.

2. *Local rules*

   a. Title. MA R USDCT LR 1.1.

   b. Sanctions. MA R USDCT LR 1.3.

   c. Form and filing of papers. MA R USDCT LR 5.1.

   d. Service and filing of pleadings and other papers. MA R USDCT LR 5.2.

   e. Filing and service by electronic means. MA R USDCT LR 5.4.

   f. Motion practice. MA R USDCT LR 7.1.

   g. Alternative dispute resolution. MA R USDCT LR 16.4.

   h. Payments and deposits made with the clerk. MA R USDCT LR 67.4.

   i. Settlement. MA R USDCT LR 68.2.

   j. Office of the clerk. MA R USDCT LR 77.2.

   k. Appearances. MA R USDCT LR 83.5.2.

   l. Practice by pro se litigants. MA R USDCT LR 83.5.5.

   m. CM/ECF case management/electronic case files administrative procedures. MA R USDCT CM/ECF Admin.

# Motions, Oppositions and Replies
# Motion to Dismiss for Improper Venue

### Document Last Updated December 2018

## A. Checklist

(I) ❑ Matters to be considered by moving party

    (a) ❑ Required documents

        (1) ❑ Notice of motion and motion

        (2) ❑ Memorandum

        (3) ❑ Certificate of service

    (b) ❑ Supplemental documents

        (1) ❑ Supporting evidence

        (2) ❑ Notice of constitutional question

        (3) ❑ Nongovernmental corporate disclosure statement

        (4) ❑ Proposed order

    (5) ❑ Compact disk with copy of document(s) in PDF format

    (6) ❑ Notice of filing with clerk's office

    (7) ❑ Additional copies

    (8) ❑ Courtesy copies

(c) ❑ Timing

    (1) ❑ Every defense to a claim for relief in any pleading must be asserted in the responsive pleading if one is required

    (2) ❑ A motion asserting any of the defenses in FRCP 12(b) must be made before pleading if a responsive pleading is allowed

    (3) ❑ If a pleading sets out a claim for relief that does not require a responsive pleading, an opposing party may assert at trial any defense to that claim

    (4) ❑ A written motion and notice of the hearing must be served at least fourteen (14) days before the time specified for the hearing, with the following exceptions: (i) when the motion may be heard ex parte; (ii) when the Federal Rules of Civil Procedure set a different time; or (iii) when a court order—which a party may, for good cause, apply for ex parte—sets a different time

    (5) ❑ Any affidavit supporting a motion must be served with the motion

    (6) ❑ Except as noted in FRCP 33 to FRCP 36, the original of all papers required to be served under FRCP 5(d) shall, unless otherwise submitted to the court, be filed in the office of the clerk within seven (7) days after service has been made

(II) ❑ Matters to be considered by opposing party

  (a) ❑ Required documents

    (1) ❑ Opposition

    (2) ❑ Certificate of service

  (b) ❑ Supplemental documents

    (1) ❑ Supporting evidence

    (2) ❑ Notice of constitutional question

    (3) ❑ Compact disk with copy of document(s) in PDF format

    (4) ❑ Notice of filing with clerk's office

    (5) ❑ Additional copies

    (6) ❑ Courtesy copies

  (c) ❑ Timing

    (1) ❑ A party opposing a motion, shall file an opposition within fourteen (14) days after the motion is served, unless another period is fixed by rule or statute, or by order of the court

    (2) ❑ Except as FRCP 59(c) provides otherwise, any opposing affidavit must be served at least seven (7) days before the hearing, unless the court permits service at another time

    (3) ❑ Except as noted in FRCP 33 to FRCP 36, the original of all papers required to be served under FRCP 5(d) shall, unless otherwise submitted to the court, be filed in the office of the clerk within seven (7) days after service has been made

## B. Timing

1. *Motion to dismiss for improper venue*

  a. *In a responsive pleading.* Every defense to a claim for relief in any pleading must be asserted in the responsive pleading if one is required. FRCP 12(b).

  b. *By motion.* A motion asserting any of the defenses in FRCP 12(b) must be made before pleading if a responsive pleading is allowed. FRCP 12(b). Although FRCP 12(b) encourages the responsive pleader to file a motion to dismiss before filing the answer, nothing in FRCP 12 prohibits the filing of a motion to dismiss with the answer. An untimely motion to dismiss may be considered if the defense asserted in the motion was previously raised in the responsive pleading. FEDPROC § 62:421.

   c. *At trial.* If a pleading sets out a claim for relief that does not require a responsive pleading, an opposing party may assert at trial any defense to that claim. FRCP 12(b).

2. *Timing of motions, generally*

   a. *Motion and notice of hearing.* A written motion and notice of the hearing must be served at least fourteen (14) days before the time specified for the hearing, with the following exceptions:

     i. When the motion may be heard ex parte;

     ii. When the Federal Rules of Civil Procedure set a different time; or

     iii. When a court order—which a party may, for good cause, apply for ex parte—sets a different time. FRCP 6(c)(1).

   b. *Supporting affidavit.* Any affidavit supporting a motion must be served with the motion. FRCP 6(c)(2).

3. *Timing of opposing papers.* A party opposing a motion, shall file an opposition within fourteen (14) days after the motion is served, unless (1) the motion is for summary judgment, in which case the opposition shall be filed within twenty-one (21) days after the motion is served, or (2) another period is fixed by rule or statute, or by order of the court. MA R USDCT LR 7.1(b)(2); MA R USDCT CM/ECF Admin(H)(4). The fourteen (14) day period is intended to include the period specified by the civil rules for mailing time and provide for a uniform period regardless of the use of the mails. MA R USDCT LR 7.1(b)(2).

   a. *Opposing affidavit.* Except as FRCP 59(c) provides otherwise, any opposing affidavit must be served at least seven (7) days before the hearing, unless the court permits service at another time. FRCP 6(c)(2).

4. *Timing of reply papers.* [W]here the respondent files an answering affidavit setting up a new matter, the moving party ordinarily is allowed a reasonable time to file a reply affidavit since failure to deny the new matter by affidavit may operate as an admission of its truth. AMJUR MOTIONS § 25.

   a. *Leave of court required.* All other papers not filed as indicated in MA R USDCT LR 7.1(b)(1) and MA R USDCT LR 7.1(b)(2), whether in the form of a reply brief or otherwise, may be submitted only with leave of court. MA R USDCT LR 7.1(b)(3).

5. *Filing after service.* Except as noted in FRCP 33 to FRCP 36, the original of all papers required to be served under FRCP 5(d) shall, unless otherwise submitted to the court, be filed in the office of the clerk within seven (7) days after service has been made. MA R USDCT LR 5.1(b).

6. *Effect of FRCP 12 motion on the time to serve a responsive pleading.* Unless the court sets a different time, serving a motion under FRCP 12 alters the periods in FRCP 12(a) as follows:

   a. If the court denies the motion or postpones its disposition until trial, the responsive pleading must be served within fourteen (14) days after notice of the court's action; or

   b. If the court grants a motion for a more definite statement, the responsive pleading must be served within fourteen (14) days after the more definite statement is served. FRCP 12(a)(4).

7. *Computation of time*

   a. *Computing time.* FRCP 6 applies in computing any time period specified in the Federal Rules of Civil Procedure, in any local rule or court order, or in any statute that does not specify a method of computing time. FRCP 6(a).

     i. *Period stated in days or a longer unit.* When the period is stated in days or a longer unit of time:

       • Exclude the day of the event that triggers the period;

       • Count every day, including intermediate Saturdays, Sundays, and legal holidays; and

       • Include the last day of the period, but if the last day is a Saturday, Sunday, or legal holiday, the period continues to run until the end of the next day that is not a Saturday, Sunday, or legal holiday. FRCP 6(a)(1).

     ii. *Period stated in hours.* When the period is stated in hours:

       • Begin counting immediately on the occurrence of the event that triggers the period;

       • Count every hour, including hours during intermediate Saturdays, Sundays, and legal holidays; and

       • If the period would end on a Saturday, Sunday, or legal holiday, the period continues to run until the same time on the next day that is not a Saturday, Sunday, or legal holiday. FRCP 6(a)(2).

     iii. *Office of the clerk.* The offices of the Clerk of Court at Boston, Worcester and Springfield shall be open from 8:30 a.m. until 5:00 p.m. on all days except Saturdays, Sundays, legal holidays and other days so ordered by the court and announced in advance, if feasible. MA R USDCT LR 77.2.

    iv.  *Inaccessibility of the clerk's office.* Unless the court orders otherwise, if the clerk's office is inaccessible:

- On the last day for filing under FRCP 6(a)(1), then the time for filing is extended to the first accessible day that is not a Saturday, Sunday, or legal holiday; or

- During the last hour for filing under FRCP 6(a)(2), then the time for filing is extended to the same time on the first accessible day that is not a Saturday, Sunday, or legal holiday. FRCP 6(a)(3).

    v.  *"Last day" defined.* Unless a different time is set by a statute, local rule, or court order, the last day ends:

- For electronic filing, at midnight in the court's time zone; and

- For filing by other means, when the clerk's office is scheduled to close. FRCP 6(a)(4).

    vi.  *"Next day" defined.* The "next day" is determined by continuing to count forward when the period is measured after an event and backward when measured before an event. FRCP 6(a)(5).

    vii.  *"Legal holiday" defined.* "Legal holiday" means:

- The day set aside by statute for observing New Year's Day, Martin Luther King Jr.'s Birthday, Washington's Birthday, Memorial Day, Independence Day, Labor Day, Columbus Day, Veterans' Day, Thanksgiving Day, or Christmas Day;

- Any day declared a holiday by the President or Congress; and

- For periods that are measured after an event, any other day declared a holiday by the state where the district court is located. FRCP 6(a)(6).

  b.  *Computation of electronic filing deadlines.* Filing documents electronically does not alter any filing deadlines. MA R USDCT CM/ECF Admin(K); MA R USDCT LR 5.4(D). Although CM/ECF is generally available twenty-four (24) hours a day for filing, all electronic transmissions of documents must be completed prior to 6:00 PM, Eastern Standard (or Daylight Savings) Time, on the date on which it is due, in order to be considered timely filed that day. MA R USDCT CM/ECF Admin(K); MA R USDCT LR 5.4(D). When a specific time of day deadline is set by court order or stipulation, the electronic filing must be completed by that time. Documents may be filed at any time of the day on days prior to the date on which it is due. MA R USDCT CM/ECF Admin(K). A document filed electronically shall be deemed filed as of the time and date stated on the NEF received from the court. MA R USDCT CM/ECF Admin(G)(2); MA R USDCT CM/ECF Admin(K).

    i.  *Technical failures.* A user whose filing is made untimely as the result of a technical failure of the court's CM/ECF system may seek appropriate relief from the court. MA R USDCT CM/ECF Admin(W)(3). Technical difficulties on the filer's end, with telephone, cable lines, the filer's Internet Service Provider (ISP), or hardware or software problems, will not constitute a technical failure under the Administrative Procedures for Electronic Case Filing in the United States District Court for the District of Massachusetts (MA R USDCT CM/ECF Admin) nor excuse an untimely filing. MA R USDCT CM/ECF Admin(W)(3). As help desk support is available during normal business hours, filers are strongly urged to electronically file any documents during that period. MA R USDCT CM/ECF Admin(W)(3).

- The court has made available a public terminal (computers and scanner) in each clerk's office for registered users to scan and electronically file documents. This equipment is available during normal business hours. Users should bring their prepared document and a valid CM/ECF login and password. MA R USDCT CM/ECF Admin(W)(3).

  c.  *Extending time.* When an act may or must be done within a specified time, the court may, for good cause, extend the time: (1) with or without motion or notice if the court acts, or if a request is made, before the original time or its extension expires; or (2) on motion made after the time has expired if the party failed to act because of excusable neglect. FRCP 6(b)(1).

    i.  *Exceptions.* A court must not extend the time to act under FRCP 50(b), FRCP 50(d), FRCP 52(b), FRCP 59(b), FRCP 59(d), FRCP 59(e), and FRCP 60(b). FRCP 6(b)(2).

    ii.  Refer to the United States District Court for the District of Massachusetts KeyRules Motion for Continuance/Extension of Time document for more information on extending time.

  d.  *Additional time after certain kinds of service.* When a party may or must act within a specified time after being served and service is made under FRCP 5(b)(2)(C) (by mail), FRCP 5(b)(2)(D) (by leaving with the clerk), or FRCP 5(b)(2)(F) (by other means consented to), three (3) days are added after the period would otherwise expire under FRCP 6(a). FRCP 6(d).

## C. General Requirements

1. *Motions, generally*

   a. *Requirements.* A request for a court order must be made by motion. The motion must:

      i. Be in writing unless made during a hearing or trial;

      ii. State with particularity the grounds for seeking the order; and

      iii. State the relief sought. FRCP 7(b)(1).

   b. *Notice of motion.* A party interested in resisting the relief sought by a motion has a right to notice thereof, and an opportunity to be heard. AMJUR MOTIONS § 12.

      i. [I]n addition to statutory or court rule provisions requiring notice of a motion—the purpose of such a notice requirement having been said to be to prevent a party from being prejudicially surprised by a motion—principles of natural justice dictate that an adverse party generally must be given notice that a motion will be presented to the court. AMJUR MOTIONS § 12.

      ii. "Notice," in this regard, means reasonable notice, including a meaningful opportunity to prepare and to defend against allegations of a motion. AMJUR MOTIONS § 12.

   c. *Writing requirement.* The writing requirement is intended to [ensure] that the adverse parties are informed and have a record of both the motion's pendency and the grounds on which the movant seeks an order. FPP § 1191; Feldberg v. Quechee Lakes Corp., 463 F.3d 195 (2d Cir. 2006). [A] single written document can satisfy the writing requirements both for a motion and for [an] FRCP 6(c)(1) notice. FRCP 7(Advisory Committee Notes).

   d. *Particularity requirement.* The particularity requirement [ensures] that the opposing parties will have notice of their opponent's contentions. FEDPROC § 62:358; Goodman v. 1973 26 Foot Trojan Vessel, Arkansas Registration No. AR1439SN, 859 F.2d 71 (8th Cir. 1988). That requirement ensures that notice of the basis for the motion is provided to the court and to the opposing party so as to avoid prejudice, provide the opponent with a meaningful opportunity to respond, and provide the court with enough information to process the motion correctly. FEDPROC § 62:358; Andreas v. Volkswagen of Am., Inc., 336 F.3d 789 (8th Cir. 2003).

      i. Reasonable specification of the grounds for a motion is sufficient. The particularity requirement for motions is satisfied when no party is prejudiced by a lack of particularity or when the court can comprehend the basis for the motion and deal with it fairly. However, where a movant fails to state even one ground for granting the motion in question, the movant has failed to meet the minimal standard of "reasonable specification." FEDPROC § 62:358; Martinez v. Trainor, 556 F.2d 818 (7th Cir. 1977).

      ii. The court may excuse the failure to comply with the particularity requirement if it is inadvertent, and where no prejudice is shown by the opposing party. FEDPROC § 62:358.

   e. *Control of motion practice*

      i. *Plan for the disposition of motions.* At the earliest practicable time, the judicial officer shall establish a framework for the disposition of motions, which, at the discretion of the judicial officer, may include specific deadlines or general time guidelines for filing motions. This framework may be amended from time to time by the judicial officer as required by the progress of the case. MA R USDCT LR 7.1(a)(1).

      ii. *Motion practice.* No motion shall be filed unless counsel certify that they have conferred and have attempted in good faith to resolve or narrow the issue. MA R USDCT LR 7.1(a)(2).

      iii. *Unresolved motions.* The court shall rule on motions as soon as practicable, having in mind the reporting requirements set forth in the Civil Justice Reform Act. MA R USDCT LR 7.1(a)(3).

2. *Motion to dismiss for improper venue.* [A] party may assert the following defense by motion: improper venue. FRCP 12(b)(3). Objections to venue typically stem from a failure to adhere to the requirements specified in the general venue statute, 28 U.S.C.A. § 1391, or some other statutory venue provision. FPP § 1352.

   a. *Forum selection clauses.* In recent years, however, there have been what appears to be an increasing number of venue motions based on the enforcement of forum selection clauses in contracts. FPP § 1352; Tropp v. Corp. of Lloyd's, 385 F. App'x 36, 37 (2d Cir. 2010). The courts of appeal were previously split as to how to treat such motions, treating dismissal of the action as the proper remedy but divided as to whether dismissal was proper pursuant to FRCP 12(b)(3) or FRCP 12(b)(6) when it is based on one of these forum selection clauses rather than on noncompliance with a federal venue statute. FPP § 1352.

      i. The Supreme Court resolved this [split] in its 2013 decision Atlantic Marine Construction Co. Inc. v. United

States District Court for the Western District of Texas by holding that the appropriate method for enforcing a valid forum-selection clause is the use of transfer to the contractually selected forum under 28 U.S.C.A. § 1404(a). FPP § 1352; Atl. Marine Const. Co. Inc. v. U.S. Dist. Court for the W. Dist. of Texas, 571 U.S. 49, 134 S. Ct. 568, 187 L. Ed. 2d 487 (2013); Martinez v. Bloomberg LP, 740 F.3d 211, 216 (2d Cir. 2014).

    ii.   Forum-selection clauses cannot make venue "wrong" or "improper" within the meaning of 28 U.S.C.A. § 1406(a) or FRCP 12(b)(3), which is why FRCP 12(b)(3) is no longer an appropriate method for enforcing forum selection clauses. FPP § 1352; Atl. Marine Const. Co. Inc. v. U.S. Dist. Court for the W. Dist. of Texas, 571 U.S. 49, 134 S. Ct. 568, 187 L. Ed. 2d 487 (2013).

b.  *Burden.* On a motion under FRCP 12(b)(3), facts must be shown that will defeat the plaintiff's assertion of venue. FPP § 1352; Pierce v. Shorty Small's of Branson Inc., 137 F.3d 1190 (10th Cir. 1998). Courts have not agreed as to which party has the burden of proof on a motion for improper venue. FEDPROC § 62:444.

    i.   *On defendant.* A number of federal courts have concluded that the burden of doing so is on the defendant, since venue is a "personal privilege" that can be waived and a lack of venue should be established by the party asserting it. FPP § 1352; Myers v. Am. Dental Ass'n, 695 F.2d 716 (3d Cir. 1982).

    ii.   *On plaintiff.* On the other hand, an equal (perhaps a larger) number of federal courts have imposed the burden on the plaintiff in keeping with the rule applied in the context of subject matter and personal jurisdiction defenses. FPP § 1352. The latter view seems correct inasmuch as it is the plaintiff's obligation to institute his action in a permissible forum, both in terms of jurisdiction and venue. FPP § 1352; Pierce v. Shorty Small's of Branson Inc., 137 F.3d 1190 (10th Cir. 1998).

        •   If the court chooses to rely on pleadings and affidavits, the plaintiff need only make a prima facie showing of venue, but if the court holds an evidentiary hearing, the plaintiff must demonstrate venue by a preponderance of the evidence. FEDPROF § 1C:13; Gulf Ins. Co. v. Glasbrenner, 417 F.3d 353 (2d Cir. 2005).

c.  *Form.* A motion to dismiss for lack of venue must be denied as insufficient where it is not apparent which venue provision the moving party wishes to invoke or, assuming that the general venue statute 28 U.S.C.A. § 1391 is contemplated, which paragraph is considered controlling. FEDPROC § 62:443.

d.  *Practice on an FRCP 12(b)(3) motion.* All well-pleaded allegations in the complaint bearing on the venue question generally are taken as true, unless contradicted by the defendant's affidavits. A district court may examine facts outside the complaint to determine whether its venue is proper. FPP § 1352; Ambraco, Inc. v. Bossclip B.V., 570 F.3d 233 (5th Cir. 2009). And, as is consistent with practice in other contexts, such as construing the complaint, the court must draw all reasonable inferences and resolve all factual conflicts in favor of the plaintiff. FPP § 1352.

e.  *Dismissal versus transfer.* The chances of a motion to dismiss for improper venue being successful have been diminished even further by the liberal attitude of the courts in permitting venue defects to be cured. FPP § 1352.

    i.   A motion to dismiss for improper venue under FRCP 12(b)(3) no longer is necessary in order to object to an inconvenient forum. FPP § 1352. With the enactment of 28 U.S.C.A. § 1404(a) as part of the 1948 revision of the Judicial Code, the district courts now have authority to transfer any case to a more convenient forum if the transfer is in the interest of justice. FPP § 1352; Norwood v. Kirkpatrick, 349 U.S. 29, 75 S.Ct. 544, 99 L.Ed. 789 (1955). Consideration of a dismissal for improper venue must take into account 28 U.S.C.A. § 1406(a) as well as FRCP 12(b)(3). FEDPROC § 62:446.

        •   Any case may be transferred from one division to another division on motion of any party for good cause shown or sua sponte for good cause by the judge to whom the case is assigned. MA R USDCT LR 40.1(F).

        •   The district court of a district in which is filed a case laying venue in the wrong division or district shall dismiss, or if it be in the interest of justice, transfer such case to any district or division in which it could have been brought. 28 U.S.C.A. § 1406(a).

        •   For the convenience of parties and witnesses, in the interest of justice, a district court may transfer any civil action to any other district or division where it might have been brought or to any district or division to which all parties have consented. 28 U.S.C.A. § 1404(a).

    ii.   Technically speaking, motions to transfer are made pursuant to a motion under 28 U.S.C.A. § 1404(a) rather than under FRCP 12(b)(3), although little, other than the possible application of the consolidation requirement in FRCP 12(g), turns on this distinction. FPP § 1352.

f.  *Joining motions*

    i.   *Right to join.* A motion under FRCP 12 may be joined with any other motion allowed by FRCP 12. FRCP 12(g)(1).

    ii.   *Limitation on further motions.* Except as provided in FRCP 12(h)(2) or FRCP 12(h)(3), a party that makes a motion under FRCP 12 must not make another motion under FRCP 12 raising a defense or objection that was available to the party but omitted from its earlier motion. FRCP 12(g)(2).

  g.  *Waiving and preserving certain defenses.* No defense or objection is waived by joining it with one or more other defenses or objections in a responsive pleading or in a motion. FRCP 12(b).

    i.   *Waiver by omission or failure to make or include motion.* A party waives any defense listed in FRCP 12(b)(2) through FRCP 12(b)(5) by:

- Omitting it from a motion in the circumstances described in FRCP 12(g)(2); or

- Failing to either: (1) make it by motion under FRCP 12; or (2) include it in a responsive pleading or in an amendment allowed by FRCP 15(a)(1) as a matter of course. FRCP 12(h)(1).

    ii.   *Waiver by consent.* The defendant. . .may waive the right to obtain a dismissal prior to trial either by express consent to be sued in a certain district or by some conduct that will be construed as implying consent. FPP § 1352.

3.  *Venue, generally*

  a.  *Applicability of 28 U.S.C.A. § 1391.* Except as otherwise provided by law:

    i.   28 U.S.C.A. § 1391 shall govern the venue of all civil actions brought in district courts of the United States; and

    ii.   The proper venue for a civil action shall be determined without regard to whether the action is local or transitory in nature. 28 U.S.C.A. § 1391(a).

  b.  *Venue in general.* A civil action may be brought in:

    i.   A judicial district in which any defendant resides, if all defendants are residents of the State in which the district is located;

    ii.   A judicial district in which a substantial part of the events or omissions giving rise to the claim occurred, or a substantial part of property that is the subject of the action is situated; or

    iii.   If there is no district in which an action may otherwise be brought as provided in 28 U.S.C.A. § 1391, any judicial district in which any defendant is subject to the court's personal jurisdiction with respect to such action. 28 U.S.C.A. § 1391(b).

  c.  *Residency.* For all venue purposes:

    i.   A natural person, including an alien lawfully admitted for permanent residence in the United States, shall be deemed to reside in the judicial district in which that person is domiciled;

    ii.   An entity with the capacity to sue and be sued in its common name under applicable law, whether or not incorporated, shall be deemed to reside, if a defendant, in any judicial district in which such defendant is subject to the court's personal jurisdiction with respect to the civil action in question and, if a plaintiff, only in the judicial district in which it maintains its principal place of business; and

    iii.   A defendant not resident in the United States may be sued in any judicial district, and the joinder of such a defendant shall be disregarded in determining where the action may be brought with respect to other defendants. 28 U.S.C.A. § 1391(c).

  d.  *Residency of corporations in states with multiple districts.* For purposes of venue under this chapter (28 U.S.C.A. § 1390, et seq.), in a State which has more than one judicial district and in which a defendant that is a corporation is subject to personal jurisdiction at the time an action is commenced, such corporation shall be deemed to reside in any district in that State within which its contacts would be sufficient to subject it to personal jurisdiction if that district were a separate State, and, if there is no such district, the corporation shall be deemed to reside in the district within which it has the most significant contacts. 28 U.S.C.A. § 1391(d).

  e.  *Actions where defendant is officer or employee of the United States*

    i.   *In general.* A civil action in which a defendant is an officer or employee of the United States or any agency thereof acting in his official capacity or under color of legal authority, or an agency of the United States, or the United States, may, except as otherwise provided by law, be brought in any judicial district in which: (1) a defendant in the action resides, (2) a substantial part of the events or omissions giving rise to the claim occurred, or a substantial part of property that is the subject of the action is situated, or (3) the plaintiff resides if no real property is involved in the action. Additional persons may be joined as parties to any such action in accordance with the Federal Rules of Civil Procedure and with such other venue requirements as would be applicable if the United States or one of its officers, employees, or agencies were not a party. 28 U.S.C.A. § 1391(e)(1).

    ii. *Service.* The summons and complaint in such an action shall be served as provided by the Federal Rules of Civil Procedure except that the delivery of the summons and complaint to the officer or agency as required by the Federal Rules of Civil Procedure may be made by certified mail beyond the territorial limits of the district in which the action is brought. 28 U.S.C.A. § 1391(e)(2).

f. *Civil actions against a foreign state.* A civil action against a foreign state as defined in 28 U.S.C.A. § 1603(a) may be brought:

    i. In any judicial district in which a substantial part of the events or omissions giving rise to the claim occurred, or a substantial part of property that is the subject of the action is situated;

    ii. In any judicial district in which the vessel or cargo of a foreign state is situated, if the claim is asserted under 28 U.S.C.A. § 1605(b);

    iii. In any judicial district in which the agency or instrumentality is licensed to do business or is doing business, if the action is brought against an agency or instrumentality of a foreign state as defined in 28 U.S.C.A. § 1603(b); or

    iv. In the United States District Court for the District of Columbia if the action is brought against a foreign state or political subdivision thereof. 28 U.S.C.A. § 1391(f).

g. *Multiparty, multiforum litigation.* A civil action in which jurisdiction of the district court is based upon 28 U.S.C.A. § 1369 may be brought in any district in which any defendant resides or in which a substantial part of the accident giving rise to the action took place. 28 U.S.C.A. § 1391(g).

4. *Opposing papers.* The Federal Rules of Civil Procedure do not require any formal answer, return, or reply to a motion, except where the Federal Rules of Civil Procedure or local rules may require affidavits, memoranda, or other papers to be filed in opposition to a motion. Such papers are simply to apprise the court of such opposition and the grounds of that opposition. FEDPROC § 62:353.

a. *Effect of failure to respond to motion.* Although in the absence of statutory provision or court rule, a motion ordinarily does not require a written answer, when a party files a motion and the opposing party fails to respond, the court may construe such failure to respond as nonopposition to the motion or an admission that the motion was meritorious, may take the facts alleged in the motion as true—the rule in some jurisdictions being that the failure to respond to a fact set forth in a motion is deemed an admission—and may grant the motion if the relief requested appears to be justified. AMJUR MOTIONS § 28.

    i. *Unopposed motion to dismiss.* The circuits are split on whether a court may grant a motion to dismiss solely on the basis that the plaintiff did not file a response opposing the motion. FRCP-RC RULE 12.

b. *Assent or no opposition not determinative.* However, a motion will not be granted automatically simply because an "assent" or a notation of "no opposition" has been filed; federal judges frequently deny motions that have been assented to when it is thought that justice so dictates. FPP § 1190.

c. *Responsive pleading inappropriate as response to motion.* An attempt to answer or oppose a motion with a responsive pleading usually is not appropriate. FPP § 1190.

5. *Reply papers.* A moving party may be required or permitted to prepare papers in addition to his original motion papers. AMJUR MOTIONS § 25. Papers answering or replying to opposing papers may be appropriate, in the interests of justice, where it appears there is a substantial reason for allowing a reply. Thus, a court may accept reply papers where a party demonstrates that the papers to which it seeks to file a reply raise new issues that are material to the disposition of the question before the court, or where the court determines, sua sponte, that it wishes further briefing of an issue raised in those papers and orders the submission of additional papers. FEDPROC § 62:354.

a. *Function of reply papers.* The function of a reply affidavit is to answer the arguments made in opposition to the position taken by the movant and not to permit the movant to introduce new arguments in support of the motion. AMJUR MOTIONS § 25.

b. *Issues raised for the first time in a reply document.* However, the view has been followed in some jurisdictions, that as a matter of judicial economy, where there is no prejudice and where the issues could be raised simply by filing a motion to dismiss, the trial court has discretion to consider arguments raised for the first time in a reply memorandum, and that a trial court may grant a motion to strike issues raised for the first time in a reply memorandum. AMJUR MOTIONS § 26.

6. *Alternative dispute resolution (ADR).* The judicial officer assigned to preside over the case shall encourage the resolution of disputes by settlement or other alternative dispute resolution programs. MA R USDCT LR 16.4(a).

   a. *Settlement.* At every conference conducted under the Local Rules of the United States District Court for the District of Massachusetts, the judicial officer shall inquire as to the utility of the parties conducting settlement negotiations, explore means of facilitating those negotiations, and offer whatever assistance may be appropriate in the circumstances. Assistance may include a reference of the case to another judicial officer for settlement purposes. MA R USDCT LR 16.4(b).

      i. When a case is settled, the parties shall file with the clerk a signed agreement for judgment or stipulation for dismissal, as appropriate, within twenty-eight (28) days, unless the court otherwise orders. MA R USDCT LR 68.2.

   b. *Alternative dispute resolution programs*

      i. *Discretion of judicial officer.* The judicial officer, following an exploration of the matter with all counsel, may refer appropriate cases to alternative dispute resolution programs that have been designated for use in the district court or that the judicial officer may make available. The dispute resolution programs described in MA R USDCT LR 16.4(c)(2) through MA R USDCT LR 16.4(c)(4) are illustrative, not exclusive. Moreover, nothing in MA R USDCT LR 16.4 shall preclude the parties from engaging in private dispute resolution programs as long as they comply with any schedule established by the court. MA R USDCT LR 16.4(c)(1).

      ii. *Mediation.* The judicial officer may refer the case to mediation upon the agreement of all parties. MA R USDCT LR 16.4(c)(2)(A).

      iii. *Other alternative dispute resolution programs.* Use of mediation is not exclusive. At the request of parties, the judicial officer may consider other forms of alternative dispute resolution including, but not limited to, mini-trial, summary jury trial and arbitration. MA R USDCT LR 16.4(c)(3).

   c. For more information on alternative dispute resolution (ADR), refer to MA R USDCT LR 16.4.

7. *Sanctions.* Failure to comply with any of the directions or obligations set forth in, or authorized by, these rules may result in dismissal, default, or the imposition of other sanctions as deemed appropriate by the judicial officer. MA R USDCT LR 1.3. Except as provided by law, the court may impose sanctions as provided in MA R USDCT LR 1.3 for failure to comply with the Administrative Procedures for Electronic Case Filing in the United States District Court for the District of Massachusetts (MA R USDCT CM/ECF Admin) or with MA R USDCT LR 5.4. MA R USDCT CM/ECF Admin(C)(3).

## D. Documents

1. *Documents for moving party*

   a. *Required documents*

      i. *Notice of motion and motion.* Refer to the General Requirements section of this document for information on the notice of motion and motion.

         • *Request for oral argument.* Any party making or opposing a motion who believes that oral argument may assist the court and wishes to be heard shall include a request for oral argument in a separate paragraph of the motion or opposition. The request should be set off with a centered caption, "REQUEST FOR ORAL ARGUMENT." MA R USDCT LR 7.1(d).

      ii. *Memorandum.* A party filing a motion shall at the same time file a memorandum of reasons, including citation of supporting authorities, why the motion should be granted. MA R USDCT LR 7.1(b)(1). Any memorandum of law or other attachment filed in support of a main document shall be filed as a separate document, using the proper event. MA R USDCT CM/ECF Admin(G)(4). Memoranda supporting or opposing allowance of motions shall not, without leave of court, exceed twenty (20) pages, double-spaced. MA R USDCT LR 7.1(b)(4).

      iii. *Certificate of service.* No certificate of service is required when a paper is served by filing it with the court's electronic-filing system. When a paper that is required to be served is served by other means: (1) if the paper is filed, a certificate of service must be filed with it or within a reasonable time after service; and (2) if the paper is not filed, a certificate of service need not be filed unless filing is required by court order or by local rule. FRCP 5(d)(1)(B). Except as otherwise provided by the Federal Rules of Civil Procedure, proof of service of all pleadings and other papers required to be served (except discovery papers that in accordance with FRCP 33 to FRCP 36(f) are not to be filed) shall be filed in the office of the clerk promptly after service has been made. The proof shall show the time and manner of service, and may be made by written acknowledgment of service, a certificate of a member of the bar of this court, or an affidavit of the person who served the paper. MA R USDCT

LR 5.2(b)(1). A certificate of service of a member of the bar shall appear at the bottom of or on the margin of the last page of the paper to which it relates. MA R USDCT LR 5.2(b)(2).

- *Paper service.* The certificate shall be a brief, single-spaced statement and may be in the following form: I hereby certify that a true copy of the above document was served upon (each party appearing pro se and) the attorney of record for each other party by mail (by hand) on (date). (Signature). MA R USDCT LR 5.2(b)(2).

- *Electronic service.* Any pleading or other paper served by electronic means must bear a certificate of service in accordance with MA R USDCT LR 5.2(b). MA R USDCT LR 5.4(C); MA R USDCT CM/ECF Admin(H)(2). The certificate of service shall state that the filer: (1) filed the document electronically, (2) that it will be served electronically to registered CM/ECF participants via the NEF and (3) that the filer will send paper copies to non-registered participants as indicated on the NEF. MA R USDCT CM/ECF Admin(H)(2). For example: I hereby certify that this document filed through the CM/ECF system will be sent electronically to the registered participants as identified on the NEF (NEF) and paper copies will be sent to those indicated as non registered participants on (date). MA R USDCT CM/ECF Admin(H)(2).

- *Return.* Documents not conforming to the requirements of MA R USDCT LR 5.2 (except notices of appeal) shall be returned by the clerk. MA R USDCT LR 5.2(b)(2).

- *Failure to make proof of service.* Failure to make proof of service does not affect the validity of the service. MA R USDCT LR 5.2(b)(3).

b. *Supplemental documents*

i. *Supporting evidence.* When a motion relies on facts outside the record, the court may hear the matter on affidavits or may hear it wholly or partly on oral testimony or on depositions. FRCP 43(c). Affidavits and other documents setting forth or evidencing facts on which the motion is based shall be filed with the motion. MA R USDCT LR 7.1(b)(1).

ii. *Notice of constitutional question.* A party that files a pleading, written motion, or other paper drawing into question the constitutionality of a federal or state statute must promptly:

- *File notice.* File a notice of constitutional question stating the question and identifying the paper that raises it, if: (1) a federal statute is questioned and the parties do not include the United States, one of its agencies, or one of its officers or employees in an official capacity; or (2) a state statute is questioned and the parties do not include the state, one of its agencies, or one of its officers or employees in an official capacity; and

- *Serve notice.* Serve the notice and paper on the Attorney General of the United States if a federal statute is questioned—or on the state attorney general if a state statute is questioned—either by certified or registered mail or by sending it to an electronic address designated by the attorney general for this purpose. FRCP 5.1(a).

- *No forfeiture.* A party's failure to file and serve the notice, or the court's failure to certify, does not forfeit a constitutional claim or defense that is otherwise timely asserted. FRCP 5.1(d).

iii. *Nongovernmental corporate disclosure statement*

- *Contents.* A nongovernmental corporate party must file two (2) copies of a disclosure statement that: (1) identifies any parent corporation and any publicly held corporation owning ten percent (10%) or more of its stock; or (2) states that there is no such corporation. FRCP 7.1(a).

- *Time to file; Supplemental filing.* A party must: (1) file the disclosure statement with its first appearance, pleading, petition, motion, response, or other request addressed to the court; and (2) promptly file a supplemental statement if any required information changes. FRCP 7.1(b).

iv. *Proposed order.* Proposed orders usually are not required by this court. However, the court may request the party to submit such a document. In those situations, unless otherwise directed by the clerk's office, electronically file the proposed document/order using the entry for "Proposed Documents submitted to the court," found under the Other Documents menu, or as an attachment to the motion to which it relates. MA R USDCT CM/ECF Admin(T).

v. *Compact disk with copy of document(s) in PDF format.* A filer who cannot file a document electronically because of such technical difficulty on the filer's end [with telephone, cable lines, the filer's Internet Service Provider (ISP), or hardware or software problems] shall file the document conventionally along with a copy of the document in PDF format on a compact disk or contact the clerk's office for permission to submit the PDF document via email. MA R USDCT CM/ECF Admin(W)(3). Refer to the Timing section of this document for more information on technical failures.

vi. *Notice of filing with clerk's office.* When documents or exhibits (other than those filed ex parte or under seal) are submitted conventionally, a "Notice of Filing with clerk's office" shall be filed electronically and attached to the main document. A paper copy of the "Notice of Filing with clerk's office" must accompany the documents submitted to the court. The "Notice of Filing with clerk's office" (see MA R USDCT CM/ECF Admin(Appendix I)) shall describe each of the documents that will be filed as paper copies in the clerk's office, or shall include an index of the documents if those documents are voluminous. MA R USDCT CM/ECF Admin(P)(5).

vii. *Additional copies.* Whenever, because of the nature of a proceeding, such as a proceeding before a three-judge district court under 28 U.S.C.A. § 2284, additional copies of a paper required to be filed are necessary either for the use of the court or to enable the clerk to carry out his duties, it is the responsibility of the party filing or having filed the paper to provide the necessary copies. MA R USDCT LR 5.1(d).

viii. *Courtesy copies.* COURTESY COPIES OF DOCUMENTS FILED ELECTRONICALLY SHALL NOT BE SUBMITTED ROUTINELY. MA R USDCT CM/ECF Admin(J). Judicial officers, on a case-by-case basis, may require courtesy copies for specific cases, or types of motions, etc. A few Judicial Officers have entered Standing Orders, which may be found on their respective pages on the court's website (under Divisions). Any document filed on paper with the court as a courtesy copy must be clearly labeled as such (Example: COURTESY COPY—DO NOT SCAN). Documents delivered to the court as a courtesy copy will not be maintained in the official court record. MA R USDCT CM/ECF Admin(J).

2. *Documents for opposing party*

    a. *Required documents*

        i. *Opposition.* Refer to the General Requirements section of this document for information on the opposing papers.

            • *Memorandum.* A party opposing a motion shall file, in the same (rather than a separate), document a memorandum of reasons, including citation of supporting authorities, why the motion should not be granted. MA R USDCT LR 7.1(b)(2). Any memorandum of law or other attachment filed in support of a main document shall be filed as a separate document, using the proper event. MA R USDCT CM/ECF Admin(G)(4). Memoranda supporting or opposing allowance of motions shall not, without leave of court, exceed twenty (20) pages, double-spaced. MA R USDCT LR 7.1(b)(4).

            • *Request for oral argument.* Any party making or opposing a motion who believes that oral argument may assist the court and wishes to be heard shall include a request for oral argument in a separate paragraph of the motion or opposition. The request should be set off with a centered caption, "REQUEST FOR ORAL ARGUMENT." MA R USDCT LR 7.1(d).

        ii. *Certificate of service.* No certificate of service is required when a paper is served by filing it with the court's electronic-filing system. When a paper that is required to be served is served by other means: (1) if the paper is filed, a certificate of service must be filed with it or within a reasonable time after service; and (2) if the paper is not filed, a certificate of service need not be filed unless filing is required by court order or by local rule. FRCP 5(d)(1)(B). Except as otherwise provided by the Federal Rules of Civil Procedure, proof of service of all pleadings and other papers required to be served (except discovery papers that in accordance with FRCP 33 to FRCP 36(f) are not to be filed) shall be filed in the office of the clerk promptly after service has been made. The proof shall show the time and manner of service, and may be made by written acknowledgment of service, a certificate of a member of the bar of this court, or an affidavit of the person who served the paper. MA R USDCT LR 5.2(b)(1). A certificate of service of a member of the bar shall appear at the bottom of or on the margin of the last page of the paper to which it relates. MA R USDCT LR 5.2(b)(2).

            • *Paper service.* The certificate shall be a brief, single-spaced statement and may be in the following form: I hereby certify that a true copy of the above document was served upon (each party appearing pro se and) the attorney of record for each other party by mail (by hand) on (date). (Signature). MA R USDCT LR 5.2(b)(2).

            • *Electronic service.* Any pleading or other paper served by electronic means must bear a certificate of service in accordance with MA R USDCT LR 5.2(b). MA R USDCT LR 5.4(C); MA R USDCT CM/ECF Admin(H)(2). The certificate of service shall state that the filer: (1) filed the document electronically, (2) that it will be served electronically to registered CM/ECF participants via the NEF and (3) that the filer will send paper copies to non-registered participants as indicated on the NEF. MA R USDCT CM/ECF Admin(H)(2). For example: I hereby certify that this document filed through the CM/ECF system will be sent electronically to the registered participants as identified on the NEF (NEF) and paper copies will be sent to those indicated as non registered participants on (date). MA R USDCT CM/ECF Admin(H)(2).

- *Return.* Documents not conforming to the requirements of MA R USDCT LR 5.2 (except notices of appeal) shall be returned by the clerk. MA R USDCT LR 5.2(b)(2).

- *Failure to make proof of service.* Failure to make proof of service does not affect the validity of the service. MA R USDCT LR 5.2(b)(3).

b. *Supplemental documents*

i. *Supporting evidence.* When a motion relies on facts outside the record, the court may hear the matter on affidavits or may hear it wholly or partly on oral testimony or on depositions. FRCP 43(c). Affidavits and other documents setting forth or evidencing facts on which the opposition is based shall be filed with the opposition. MA R USDCT LR 7.1(b)(2).

ii. *Notice of constitutional question.* A party that files a pleading, written motion, or other paper drawing into question the constitutionality of a federal or state statute must promptly:

- *File notice.* File a notice of constitutional question stating the question and identifying the paper that raises it, if: (1) a federal statute is questioned and the parties do not include the United States, one of its agencies, or one of its officers or employees in an official capacity; or (2) a state statute is questioned and the parties do not include the state, one of its agencies, or one of its officers or employees in an official capacity; and

- *Serve notice.* Serve the notice and paper on the Attorney General of the United States if a federal statute is questioned—or on the state attorney general if a state statute is questioned—either by certified or registered mail or by sending it to an electronic address designated by the attorney general for this purpose. FRCP 5.1(a).

- *No forfeiture.* A party's failure to file and serve the notice, or the court's failure to certify, does not forfeit a constitutional claim or defense that is otherwise timely asserted. FRCP 5.1(d).

iii. *Compact disk with copy of document(s) in PDF format.* A filer who cannot file a document electronically because of such technical difficulty on the filer's end [with telephone, cable lines, the filer's Internet Service Provider (ISP), or hardware or software problems] shall file the document conventionally along with a copy of the document in PDF format on a compact disk or contact the clerk's office for permission to submit the PDF document via email. MA R USDCT CM/ECF Admin(W)(3). Refer to the Timing section of this document for more information on technical failures.

iv. *Notice of filing with clerk's office.* When documents or exhibits (other than those filed ex parte or under seal) are submitted conventionally, a "Notice of Filing with clerk's office" shall be filed electronically and attached to the main document. A paper copy of the "Notice of Filing with clerk's office" must accompany the documents submitted to the court. The "Notice of Filing with clerk's office" (see MA R USDCT CM/ECF Admin(Appendix I)) shall describe each of the documents that will be filed as paper copies in the clerk's office, or shall include an index of the documents if those documents are voluminous. MA R USDCT CM/ECF Admin(P)(5).

v. *Additional copies.* Whenever, because of the nature of a proceeding, such as a proceeding before a three-judge district court under 28 U.S.C.A. § 2284, additional copies of a paper required to be filed are necessary either for the use of the court or to enable the clerk to carry out his duties, it is the responsibility of the party filing or having filed the paper to provide the necessary copies. MA R USDCT LR 5.1(d).

vi. *Courtesy copies.* COURTESY COPIES OF DOCUMENTS FILED ELECTRONICALLY SHALL NOT BE SUBMITTED ROUTINELY. MA R USDCT CM/ECF Admin(J). Judicial officers, on a case-by-case basis, may require courtesy copies for specific cases, or types of motions, etc. A few Judicial Officers have entered Standing Orders, which may be found on their respective pages on the court's website (under Divisions). Any document filed on paper with the court as a courtesy copy must be clearly labeled as such (Example: COURTESY COPY—DO NOT SCAN). Documents delivered to the court as a courtesy copy will not be maintained in the official court record. MA R USDCT CM/ECF Admin(J).

# E. Format

1. *Form of documents.* The rules governing captions and other matters of form in pleadings apply to motions and other papers. FRCP 7(b)(2). The provisions of FRCP 10 and FRCP 11 concerning the form and signing of pleadings, motions, and other papers shall be applicable to all papers filed in any proceeding in this court. The board of bar overseers registration number of each attorney signing such documents, except the United States Attorney and his or her staff, shall be inscribed below the signature. MA R USDCT LR 5.1(a)(1).

a. *Paper size and binding.* All papers filed in the court shall be adapted for flat filing, be filed on eight and one-half by eleven (8-1/2 x 11) inch paper without backers and be bound firmly by staple or some such other means (excluding paper or binder clip or rubber band). MA R USDCT LR 5.1(a)(2).

b.  *Spacing.* All papers, except discovery requests and responses, shall be double-spaced except for the identification of counsel, title of the case, footnotes, quotations and exhibits. Discovery requests and responses shall be single-spaced. MA R USDCT LR 5.1(a)(2).

c.  *Caption.* Every pleading must have a caption with the court's name, a title, a file number, and [an] FRCP 7(a) designation. FRCP 10(a).

  i.  *Names of parties.* The title of the complaint must name all the parties; the title of other pleadings, after naming the first party on each side, may refer generally to other parties. FRCP 10(a).

  ii.  *Request for special action.* When any pleading or other paper filed in the court includes a request for special process or relief, or any other request such that, if granted, the court will proceed other than in the ordinary course, the request shall, unless it is noted on the category sheet [see MA R USDCT LR 40.1(a)(1)], be noted on the first page to the right of or immediately beneath the caption. MA R USDCT LR 5.1(c).

d.  *Claims or defenses*

  i.  *Numbered paragraphs.* A party must state its claims or defenses in numbered paragraphs, each limited as far as practicable to a single set of circumstances. A later pleading may refer by number to a paragraph in an earlier pleading. FRCP 10(b).

  ii.  *Separate statements.* If doing so would promote clarity, each claim founded on a separate transaction or occurrence—and each defense other than a denial—must be stated in a separate count or defense. FRCP 10(b).

e.  *Adoption by reference.* A statement in a pleading may be adopted by reference elsewhere in the same pleading or in any other pleading or motion. FRCP 10(c).

  i.  *Exhibits.* A copy of a written instrument that is an exhibit to a pleading is a part of the pleading for all purposes. FRCP 10(c).

f.  *Citations*

  i.  *Local rules.* These rules shall be known as Local Rules of the United States District Court for the District of Massachusetts and cited as "L.R., D. Mass." or "L.R." MA R USDCT LR 1.1.

  ii.  *Electronic case filing procedures.* The procedures governing electronic case filing shall be known as the "Administrative Procedures for Electronic Case Filing in the United States District Court for the District of Massachusetts." They shall be cited as "APECF." MA R USDCT CM/ECF Admin(A)(7).

g.  *Acceptance by the clerk.* The clerk must not refuse to file a paper solely because it is not in the form prescribed by the Federal Rules of Civil Procedure or by a local rule or practice. FRCP 5(d)(4).

  i.  Except for complaints and notices of appeal, papers that do not conform to the requirements of MA R USDCT LR 5.1(a)(2) shall be returned by the clerk. MA R USDCT LR 5.1(a)(2).

2.  *Form of electronic documents.* A paper filed electronically is a written paper for purposes of the Federal Rules of Civil Procedure. FRCP 5(d)(3)(D).

a.  *PDF/A format required.* The court will begin requiring submission of documents in PDF/A format in the foreseeable future. PDF/A is an enhanced version of the traditional PDF format. Newer versions of most PDF software will be able to convert to this format. Additional information on PDF/A documents may be found on the court's website. MA R USDCT CM/ECF Admin(Electronic Filing and PDF).

  i.  *Electronically converted PDF.* Electronically converted PDF documents are created from word processing documents (MS Word, WordPerfect, etc.) using any appropriate software. These documents are text searchable and the file size is generally smaller than a scanned document. CM/ECF users may use any brand of software to convert documents to PDF. MA R USDCT CM/ECF Admin(Electronic Filing and PDF).

  • Documents converted to PDF, rather than scanned, are preferred for filing in CM/ECF. MA R USDCT CM/ECF Admin(Electronic Filing and PDF).

  ii.  *Scanned PDF.* Scanned PDF documents are created from paper documents run through an optical scanner. Scanned PDF documents are generally not searchable and have a larger file size. Please note that software used to create scanned documents may (and should) be set in such a way that the document is "text-searchable." MA R USDCT CM/ECF Admin(Electronic Filing and PDF).

b.  *Title.* All pleadings filed electronically shall be titled in accordance with the approved dictionary of civil or criminal events of the CM/ECF system of this court. A list of events is available on the CM/ECF Training Information page of the court's website. The clerk's office may, when necessary and appropriate, modify the docket entry description, or delete and re-enter the docket entry in order to comply with the court's quality assurance standards. MA R USDCT CM/ECF Admin(G)(3).

c. *Attachments to filings and exhibits.* Attachments to filings and exhibits must be filed in accordance with the court's CM/ECF User Manual, unless otherwise ordered by the court. MA R USDCT CM/ECF Admin(O)(1).

    i. Filers must submit as attachments only those excerpts of the referenced documents that are directly germane to the matter under consideration by the court. Excerpted material must be clearly and prominently identified as such. Users who file excerpts of documents do so without prejudice to their right to timely file additional excerpts or the complete document, as may be allowed by the court. Responding parties may timely file additional excerpts or the complete document that they believe are directly germane. MA R USDCT CM/ECF Admin(O)(2).

    ii. Filers shall not attach as an exhibit any pleading or other paper already on file with the court in that case, but shall merely refer to that document. (See MA R USDCT CM/ECF Admin(G) for information on using hyperlinks in PDF documents filed in CM/ECF.) MA R USDCT CM/ECF Admin(O)(3).

d. *Redacted documents.* The parties may request or the court may require the submission of documents that have been redacted/stripped of sensitive or confidential information. The redacted document prepared for electronic filing shall include the original caption of the document, and be clearly labeled as "Redacted Document." A specific event is available for this purpose ("Redacted Document"), found under the Other Filings/Other Documents menu option. MA R USDCT CM/ECF Admin(S).

    i. Attorneys and pro se litigants are advised to take extra care when creating PDF documents intended for submission to CM/ECF. Steps shall be taken to ensure the documents are free of any hidden data (metadata) that may contain redacted information, or traces of information edited or deleted are not hidden in the final document. Even PDF content that has been encrypted may be recovered. An advisory document with additional information on this topic may be found on the court's website. MA R USDCT CM/ECF Admin(S).

e. *Hyperlinks.* Electronically filed documents may contain the following types of hyperlinks: (1) hyperlinks to other portions of the same document; (2) hyperlinks to other documents filed within the CM/ECF system; and (3) hyperlinks to a location on the Internet that contains a source document for a citation. MA R USDCT CM/ECF Admin(G)(7).

    i. Hyperlinks to cited authority may not replace standard citation format. Complete citations must be included in the text of the filed document. Neither a hyperlink, nor any site to which it refers, shall be considered part of the record, but are simply convenient mechanisms for accessing material cited in a document filed in CM/ECF. Instructions on creating hyperlinks may be found in the CM/ECF User Manual. MA R USDCT CM/ECF Admin(G)(7).

    ii. The court accepts no responsibility for, and does not endorse, any product, organization, or content at any hyperlinked site, or at any site to which that site may be linked. The court accepts no responsibility for the availability or functionality of any hyperlink. MA R USDCT CM/ECF Admin(G)(7).

    iii. One feature of PDF/A documents is that hyperlinks are commonly "masked," meaning that the full address of the referenced file is not written out; for example, clicking the word brief may open a brief which was previously filed in CM/ECF. MA R USDCT CM/ECF Admin(G)(7)(NOTE). An "unmasked" hyperlink has the full address visible to the user. MA R USDCT CM/ECF Admin(G)(7)(NOTE).

       • Masked hyperlinks may or may not work in a PDF/A document, depending on how it was created. Currently, masked hyperlinks are preserved in PDF/A documents produced by the "Save As" method in Microsoft Word 2007 and 2010; the "PDFMaker" method in Microsoft Word 2007; and OpenOffice 2.4 ("PDF Export"). With other production methods, such as WordPerfect, the PDF/A document includes underlined words that appear to be links, but clicking them has no effect. MA R USDCT CM/ECF Admin(G)(7)(NOTE).

f. *Documents features not accepted.* CM/ECF will not accept PDF documents containing tracking tags, embedded systems commands, password protections, access restrictions or other security features, special tags or dynamic features. MA R USDCT CM/ECF Admin(G)(8).

g. *File size limitations.* A filing party shall limit the size of each PDF file to no more than twenty (20) megabytes. PDF files larger than seven (7) megabytes will be rejected by the CM/ECF system. The filer will see a message advising of the size limitation. MA R USDCT CM/ECF Admin(P)(2).

 i. Larger documents or exhibits may be submitted electronically if split into separate PDF files each less than seven (7) megabytes, attached to the main document and clearly labeled. MA R USDCT CM/ECF Admin(P)(2).

 ii. Documents submitted electronically or on paper are subject to the page limitations set by MA R USDCT LR 7.1(b)(4) or by order of the court. MA R USDCT CM/ECF Admin(P)(1).

h. *Accuracy and readability.* The filer shall verify the accuracy and readability of any PDF file before electronically filing it in CM/ECF. MA R USDCT CM/ECF Admin(G)(6); MA R USDCT CM/ECF Admin(P)(3).

3. *Signing of pleadings, motions and other papers*

a. *Signature.* Every pleading, written motion, and other paper must be signed by at least one attorney of record in the attorney's name—or by a party personally if the party is unrepresented. The paper must state the signer's address, e-mail address, and telephone number. FRCP 11(a). The provisions of the Federal Rules of Civil Procedure pertaining to the form and signing of pleadings, motions, and other papers shall be applicable to all papers filed in any proceeding in this court. The board of bar overseers registration number of each attorney signing such documents, except the United States Attorney and his staff, shall be inscribed below the signature. MA R USDCT LR 5.1(a)(1).

 i. *Electronic signing.* A filing made through a person's electronic-filing account and authorized by that person, together with that person's name on a signature block, constitutes the person's signature. FRCP 5(d)(3)(C).

 ii. *Appearances.* The filing of an appearance or any other pleading signed on behalf of a party constitutes an entry of appearance for that party. All pleadings shall contain the name, bar admission number, address, telephone number, and e-mail address of the attorney entering an appearance. MA R USDCT LR 83.5.2(a).

  &bull; *Appearances by law firms.* When a party is represented by a law firm, the appearance must include the name and the signature of at least one individual attorney. When a party is represented by more than one attorney from the same or different law firms, the attorney entering the appearance must designate the individual attorney who is authorized to receive all notices in the case. Any notice sent to an attorney so designated shall be deemed to be proper notice unless the court finds that notice was not properly sent. MA R USDCT LR 83.5.2(b).

  &bull; For more information on appearances, refer to MA R USDCT LR 83.5.2.

 iii. *Signatures of attorneys.* The user login and password required to submit documents to the CM/ECF system shall serve as that user's signature for purposes of FRCP 11 and for all other purposes under the Federal Rules of Civil Procedure and the Local Rules of the United States District Court for the District of Massachusetts. All electronically filed documents must include a signature block and must set forth the attorney's name, bar number, address, telephone number and email address. The name of the CM/ECF user under whose log-in and password the document is submitted must be preceded by a "/s/" and typed in the space where the signature would otherwise appear. MA R USDCT CM/ECF Admin(M)(1). For an example, refer to MA R USDCT CM/ECF Admin(M)(1).

 iv. *Signatures of pro se parties.* Any document requiring a signature that is filed by a party appearing pro se shall bear the words "pro se" following that party's signature. Any such document shall also state the party's mailing address, telephone number (if any), and e-mail address (if the party has consented to service by email). MA R USDCT LR 83.5.5(g). For more information on practice by pro se litigants, refer to MA R USDCT LR 83.5.5.

 v. *Multiple signatures.* The filer of any document requiring more than one signature (e.g, stipulations, joint motions, joint status reports, magistrate judge consent forms, etc.) must list thereon all the names of other signatories by means of a "/s/ name of signatory" block for each. By submitting such a document, the filing attorney certifies that each of the other signatories has expressly agreed to the form and substance of the document and that the filing attorney has their actual authority to submit the document electronically. MA R USDCT CM/ECF Admin(M)(2). For more information, refer to MA R USDCT CM/ECF Admin(M)(2).

 vi. *Affidavits.* Except as provided in MA R USDCT CM/ECF Admin(L), affidavits shall be filed electronically; however, the electronically filed version must contain a "/s/ name of signatory" block indicating that the paper document bears an original signature. MA R USDCT CM/ECF Admin(M)(3). The court will also accept a scanned version of the original, signed document. MA R USDCT CM/ECF Admin(M)(3). For more information, refer to MA R USDCT CM/ECF Admin(M)(3).

 vii. *No verification or accompanying affidavit required for pleadings.* Unless a rule or statute specifically states otherwise, a pleading need not be verified or accompanied by an affidavit. FRCP 11(a).

      viii.   *Unsigned papers.* The court must strike an unsigned paper unless the omission is promptly corrected after being called to the attorney's or party's attention. FRCP 11(a).

  b.  *Representations to the court.* By presenting to the court a pleading, written motion, or other paper—whether by signing, filing, submitting, or later advocating it—an attorney or unrepresented party certifies that to the best of the person's knowledge, information, and belief, formed after an inquiry reasonable under the circumstances:

      i.   It is not being presented for any improper purpose, such as to harass, cause unnecessary delay, or needlessly increase the cost of litigation;

      ii.   The claims, defenses, and other legal contentions are warranted by existing law or by a nonfrivolous argument for extending, modifying, or reversing existing law or for establishing new law;

      iii.   The factual contentions have evidentiary support or, if specifically so identified, will likely have evidentiary support after a reasonable opportunity for further investigation or discovery; and

      iv.   The denials of factual contentions are warranted on the evidence or, if specifically so identified, are reasonably based on belief or a lack of information. FRCP 11(b).

  c.  *Sanctions.* If, after notice and a reasonable opportunity to respond, the court determines that FRCP 11(b) has been violated, the court may impose an appropriate sanction on any attorney, law firm, or party that violated FRCP 11(b) or is responsible for the violation. FRCP 11(c)(1). Refer to the United States District Court for the District of Massachusetts KeyRules Motion for Sanctions document for more information.

4.  *Privacy protection for filings made with the court*

  a.  *Redacted filings.* Unless the court orders otherwise, in an electronic or paper filing with the court that contains an individual's Social Security number, taxpayer-identification number, or birth date, the name of an individual known to be a minor, or a financial-account number, a party or nonparty making the filing may include only:

      i.   The last four (4) digits of the Social Security number and taxpayer-identification number;

      ii.   The year of the individual's birth;

      iii.   The minor's initials; and

      iv.   The last four (4) digits of the financial-account number. FRCP 5.2(a); MA R USDCT CM/ECF Admin(N).

  b.  *Exemptions from the redaction requirement.* The redaction requirement does not apply to the following:

      i.   A financial-account number that identifies the property allegedly subject to forfeiture in a forfeiture proceeding;

      ii.   The record of an administrative or agency proceeding;

      iii.   The official record of a state-court proceeding;

      iv.   The record of a court or tribunal, if that record was not subject to the redaction requirement when originally filed;

      v.   A filing covered by FRCP 5.2(c) or FRCP 5.2(d); and

      vi.   A pro se filing in an action brought under 28 U.S.C.A. § 2241, 28 U.S.C.A. § 2254, or 28 U.S.C.A. § 2255. FRCP 5.2(b).

  c.  *Limitations on remote access to electronic files; Social Security appeals and immigration cases.* Unless the court orders otherwise, in an action for benefits under the Social Security Act, and in an action or proceeding relating to an order of removal, to relief from removal, or to immigration benefits or detention, access to an electronic file is authorized as follows:

      i.   The parties and their attorneys may have remote electronic access to any part of the case file, including the administrative record;

      ii.   Any other person may have electronic access to the full record at the courthouse, but may have remote electronic access only to:

        •   The docket maintained by the court; and

        •   An opinion, order, judgment, or other disposition of the court, but not any other part of the case file or the administrative record. FRCP 5.2(c).

  d.  *Filings made under seal.* The court may order that a filing be made under seal without redaction. The court may later unseal the filing or order the person who made the filing to file a redacted version for the public record. FRCP 5.2(d).

  e.  *Protective orders.* For good cause, the court may by order in a case:

      i.   Require redaction of additional information; or

ii.   Limit or prohibit a nonparty's remote electronic access to a document filed with the court. FRCP 5.2(e).

f.   *Option for additional unredacted filing under seal.* A person making a redacted filing may also file an unredacted copy under seal. The court must retain the unredacted copy as part of the record. FRCP 5.2(f). For more information, refer to MA R USDCT LR 7.2.

g.   *Option for filing a reference list.* A filing that contains redacted information may be filed together with a reference list that identifies each item of redacted information and specifies an appropriate identifier that uniquely corresponds to each item listed. The list must be filed under seal and may be amended as of right. Any reference in the case to a listed identifier will be construed to refer to the corresponding item of information. FRCP 5.2(g).

h.   *Responsibility for redaction.* The clerk's office is not responsible for reviewing documents filed with the court to determine whether pleadings have been redacted and are in the proper form. MA R USDCT CM/ECF Admin(N).

i.   *Waiver of protection of identifiers.* A person waives the protection of FRCP 5.2(a) as to the person's own information by filing it without redaction and not under seal. FRCP 5.2(h).

## F.   Filing and Service Requirements

1.   *Filing requirements*

a.   *Required filings.* Any paper after the complaint that is required to be served must be filed no later than a reasonable time after service. FRCP 5(d)(1).

i.   Except as noted in FRCP 33 to FRCP 36, the original of all papers required to be served under FRCP 5(d) shall, unless otherwise submitted to the court, be filed in the office of the clerk within seven (7) days after service has been made. MA R USDCT LR 5.1(b). Except as otherwise provided by the Federal Rules of Civil Procedure, proof of service of all pleadings and other papers required to be served (except discovery papers that in accordance with FRCP 33 to FRCP 36(f) are not to be filed) shall be filed in the office of the clerk promptly after service has been made. MA R USDCT LR 5.2(b)(1).

b.   *Nonelectronic filing.* A paper not filed electronically is filed by delivering it: (1) to the clerk; or (2) to a judge who agrees to accept it for filing, and who must then note the filing date on the paper and promptly send it to the clerk. FRCP 5(d)(2).

c.   *Electronic filing.* Unless exempt or otherwise ordered by the court, all pleadings and other papers submitted to the court must be filed, signed, and verified by electronic means as provided in MA R USDCT LR 5.4. MA R USDCT LR 5.4(A); MA R USDCT CM/ECF Admin(A)(1). All electronic filings must be made in accordance with the Administrative Procedures for Electronic Case Filing in the United States District Court for the District of Massachusetts (MA R USDCT CM/ECF Admin). MA R USDCT LR 5.4(B). The court may deviate from the Administrative Procedures for Electronic Case Filing in the United States District Court for the District of Massachusetts (MA R USDCT CM/ECF Admin) in specific cases, without prior notice, if deemed appropriate in the exercise of discretion, considering the need for the just, speedy, and inexpensive determination of matters pending before the court. MA R USDCT CM/ECF Admin(C)(1). The court may excuse a failure to comply with any administrative procedure whenever justice so requires. MA R USDCT CM/ECF Admin(C)(2).

i.   *By a represented person; Generally required; Exceptions.* A person represented by an attorney must file electronically, unless nonelectronic filing is allowed by the court for good cause or is allowed or required by local rule. FRCP 5(d)(3)(A).

ii.   *By unrepresented person; When allowed or required.* A person not represented by an attorney: (1) may file electronically only if allowed by court order or by local rule; and (2) may be required to file electronically only by court order, or by a local rule that includes reasonable exceptions. FRCP 5(d)(3)(B).

iii.   *Exemptions from electronic filing*

●   *Documents that should not be filed electronically.* The following types of documents must not be filed electronically, and will not be scanned into the ECF system by the clerk's office: (1) sealed documents; (2) ex parte motions; (3) documents generated as part of an alternative dispute resolution (ADR) process; (4) the administrative record in Social Security and other administrative proceedings; (5) the state court record in proceedings under 28 U.S.C.A. § 2254; and (6) such other types of documents as the clerk may direct in the Administrative Procedures for Electronic Case Filing in the United States District Court for the District of Massachusetts (MA R USDCT CM/ECF Admin). MA R USDCT LR 5.4(G)(1); MA R USDCT CM/ECF Admin(L).

●   *Documents that need not be filed electronically.* The following types of documents need not be filed electronically, but may be scanned into the ECF system by a filing party or the clerk's office: (1) handwritten pleadings; (2) documents filed by pro se litigants who are incarcerated or who are not registered ECF users; (3) indictments, informations, criminal complaints, and the criminal JS45 form; (4) affidavits for search or arrest warrants and related documents; (5) documents received from another court under FRCRP 20 or FRCRP 40; (6) appearance bonds; (7) any document in a criminal case containing the original signature of a defendant, such as a waiver of indictment or a plea agreement; (8) petitions for violations of supervised release; (9) executed service of process documents under FRCP 4; and (10) such other types of documents as the clerk may direct in the Administrative Procedures for Electronic Case Filing in the United States District Court for the District of Massachusetts (MA R USDCT CM/ECF Admin). MA R USDCT LR 5.4(G)(2); MA R USDCT CM/ECF Admin(L).

- For more information on exemptions from electronic filing, refer to MA R USDCT CM/ECF Admin(L).

    iv. *Consequences of electronic filing.* Electronic transmission of a document to the CM/ECF system, together with the transmission of a Notice of Electronic Filing (NEF) from the court at the completion of the transaction, constitutes the filing of the document for all purposes of the Federal Rules of Procedure and constitutes entry of the document on the docket maintained by the clerk pursuant to FRCP 58 and FRCP 79. MA R USDCT CM/ECF Admin(G)(1).

    v. *Payment of filing fees.* When electronically filing any pleading or paper through CM/ECF that requires a fee, all registered ECF users are to pay the fee electronically through the Treasury Department's Internet payment process. MA R USDCT LR 67.4(d); MA R USDCT CM/ECF Admin(A)(1). Pro se filers and those who have been exempted from electronic filing and/or electronic payment of fees may submit payments by check or money order made payable to "Clerk, U.S. District Court". MA R USDCT LR 67.4(d). For more information on filing fees, refer to MA R USDCT LR 67.4 and MA R USDCT CM/ECF Admin(I).

    vi. For more information on electronic filing, refer to MA R USDCT CM/ECF Admin.

  d. *Email or fax filing.* In general, the court does not accept documents by email or by fax. If the court, in special circumstances, does authorize the submission of a document in that manner, the document shall not be considered filed until an NEF is generated by CM/ECF at the completion of the transaction. MA R USDCT CM/ECF Admin(H)(5).

2. *Service requirements.* All papers filed pursuant to MA R USDCT LR 7.1(b) shall be served unless the moving party indicates in writing on the face of the motion that ex parte consideration is requested. Motions filed "ex parte" and related papers need not be served until the motion has been ruled upon or the court orders that service be made. MA R USDCT LR 7.1(c). Service of all pleadings subsequent to the original complaint and of all other papers required to be served shall be made in the manner specified by FRCP 5. MA R USDCT LR 5.2(a).

  a. *Service; When required*

    i. *In general.* Unless the Federal Rules of Civil Procedure provide otherwise, each of the following papers must be served on every party:

- An order stating that service is required;

- A pleading filed after the original complaint, unless the court orders otherwise under FRCP 5(c) because there are numerous defendants;

- A discovery paper required to be served on a party, unless the court orders otherwise;

- A written motion, except one that may be heard ex parte; and

- A written notice, appearance, demand, or offer of judgment, or any similar paper. FRCP 5(a)(1).

    ii. *If a party fails to appear.* No service is required on a party who is in default for failing to appear. But a pleading that asserts a new claim for relief against such a party must be served on that party under FRCP 4. FRCP 5(a)(2).

    iii. *Seizing property.* If an action is begun by seizing property and no person is or need be named as a defendant, any service required before the filing of an appearance, answer, or claim must be made on the person who had custody or possession of the property when it was seized. FRCP 5(a)(3).

  b. *Service; How made*

    i. *Serving an attorney.* If a party is represented by an attorney, service under FRCP 5 must be made on the attorney unless the court orders service on the party. FRCP 5(b)(1).

- *Nonresident attorney.* On application of a party, the court may order an attorney who represents any other

party and who does not maintain an office within this district where service can be made on him by delivery as provided by FRCP 5(b), to designate a member of the bar of this court who does maintain such an office to receive service of all pleadings and other papers in his behalf. MA R USDCT LR 5.2(c)(1).

ii. *Serving a party acting pro se.* On application of a party, the court may order any other party who is appearing without an attorney and who does not maintain an office or residence within this district where service can be made on him by delivery as provided by FRCP 5(b), to designate an address within the district at which service can be made on him by delivery. MA R USDCT LR 5.2(c)(2).

iii. *Service in general.* A paper is served under FRCP 5 by:

- Handing it to the person;

- Leaving it: (1) at the person's office with a clerk or other person in charge or, if no one is in charge, in a conspicuous place in the office; or (2) if the person has no office or the office is closed, at the person's dwelling or usual place of abode with someone of suitable age and discretion who resides there;

- Mailing it to the person's last known address—in which event service is complete upon mailing;

- Leaving it with the court clerk if the person has no known address;

- Sending it to a registered user by filing it with the court's electronic-filing system or sending it by other electronic means that the person consented to in writing—in either of which events service is complete upon filing or sending, but is not effective if the filer or sender learns that it did not reach the person to be served; or

- Delivering it by any other means that the person consented to in writing—in which event service is complete when the person making service delivers it to the agency designated to make delivery. FRCP 5(b)(2).

iv. *Service by electronic means.* Unless exempt or otherwise ordered by the court, all pleadings and other papers must be served on other parties by electronic means. MA R USDCT LR 5.4(C); MA R USDCT CM/ECF Admin(H)(2). Service by electronic means shall be treated the same as service by mail. MA R USDCT CM/ECF Admin(H)(4).

- *Consent to electronic service.* Registering to use CM/ECF constitutes consent to service of all documents by electronic means as provided in the Administrative Procedures for Electronic Case Filing in the United States District Court for the District of Massachusetts (MA R USDCT CM/ECF Admin) and FRCP 5(b) and FRCP 77(d). MA R USDCT CM/ECF Admin(E)(6); MA R USDCT CM/ECF Admin(H)(3).

- *Service on registered ECF users.* Transmission of the Notice of Electronic Filing (NEF) through the court's transmission facilities will constitute service of the filed document upon a registered ECF user. MA R USDCT LR 5.4(C).

- *Service on non-registered users.* The party filing the document electronically is responsible for serving a paper copy of the document by mail in accordance with FRCP 5(b) to those case participants who have not been identified on the NEF as electronic recipients. MA R USDCT CM/ECF Admin(H)(3).

- *Service of conventionally filed papers.* Documents or exhibits submitted conventionally shall be served on other parties by the filer using traditional means. MA R USDCT CM/ECF Admin(P)(4).

c. *Serving numerous defendants*

i. *In general.* If an action involves an unusually large number of defendants, the court may, on motion or on its own, order that:

- Defendants' pleadings and replies to them need not be served on other defendants;

- Any crossclaim, counterclaim, avoidance, or affirmative defense in those pleadings and replies to them will be treated as denied or avoided by all other parties; and

- Filing any such pleading and serving it on the plaintiff constitutes notice of the pleading to all parties. FRCP 5(c)(1).

ii. *Notifying parties.* A copy of every such order must be served on the parties as the court directs. FRCP 5(c)(2).

## G. Hearings

1. *Hearings, generally.* If the court concludes that there should be a hearing on a motion, the motion will be set down for hearing at such time as the court determines. MA R USDCT LR 7.1(e).

a. *Oral argument.* Due process does not require that oral argument be permitted on a motion and, except as otherwise

provided by local rule, the district court has discretion to determine whether it will decide the motion on the papers or hear argument by counsel (and perhaps receive evidence). FPP § 1190; F.D.I.C. v. Deglau, 207 F.3d 153 (3d Cir. 2000).

    i. *Evidence on a motion.* When a motion relies on facts outside the record, the court may hear the matter on affidavits or may hear it wholly or partly on oral testimony or on depositions. FRCP 43(c).

  b. *Providing a regular schedule for oral hearings.* A court may establish regular times and places for oral hearings on motions. FRCP 78(a).

  c. *Providing for submission on briefs.* By rule or order, the court may provide for submitting and determining motions on briefs, without oral hearings. FRCP 78(b). Motions that are not set down for hearing as provided in MA R USDCT LR 7.1(e) will be decided on the papers submitted after an opposition to the motion has been filed, or, if no opposition is filed, after the time for filing an opposition has elapsed. MA R USDCT LR 7.1(f).

2. *Hearing on certain FRCP 12 defenses before trial.* If a party so moves, any defense listed in FRCP 12(b)(1) through FRCP 12(b)(7)—whether made in a pleading or by motion—and a motion under FRCP 12(c) must be heard and decided before trial unless the court orders a deferral until trial. FRCP 12(i).

3. *Conflict of court appearances.* For information on conflict of court appearances, refer to MA R USDCT LR 40.2.

## H. Forms

### 1. Federal Motion to Dismiss for Improper Venue Forms

  a. Motion; For dismissal or transfer of action on grounds of improper venue; Diversity case. FEDPROF § 1:71.

  b. Motion; For dismissal; Improper venue; Lack of personal jurisdiction. FEDPROF § 1:72.

  c. Defense; Improper venue; Defendant resident of another district. FEDPROF § 1A:292.

  d. Motion; General form. FEDPROF § 1B:171.

  e. Notice; Of motion; General form. FEDPROF § 1B:172.

  f. Notice; Of motion; With costs of motion. FEDPROF § 1B:173.

  g. Notice; Of motion; Containing motion. FEDPROF § 1B:174.

  h. Opposition; To motion. FEDPROF § 1B:175.

  i. Affidavit; Supporting or opposing motion. FEDPROF § 1B:176.

  j. Brief; Supporting or opposing motion. FEDPROF § 1B:177.

  k. Statement of points and authorities; Opposing motion. FEDPROF § 1B:178.

  l. Motion to dismiss; Improper venue; Diversity action. FEDPROF § 1C:101.

  m. Motion to dismiss; Improper venue; Action not founded solely on diversity. FEDPROF § 1C:102.

  n. Motion to dismiss; Improper venue; Corporate defendant not subject to personal jurisdiction in district. FEDPROF § 1C:103.

  o. Motion to dismiss; Improper venue; Action of local nature. FEDPROF § 1C:104.

  p. Motion; To dismiss or, alternatively, to transfer action; Improper venue. FEDPROF § 1C:105.

  q. Affidavit; In support of motion to dismiss for improper venue; Corporate defendant not subject to personal jurisdiction in district. FEDPROF § 1C:106.

  r. Motion; To dismiss action for improper venue. FEDPROF § 22:66.

  s. Motion to dismiss complaint; General form. GOLDLTGFMS § 20:24.

  t. Affidavit in support of motion to dismiss complaint. GOLDLTGFMS § 20:32.

  u. Motion; Federal form. GOLDLTGFMS § 45:4.

  v. Affidavit in support of motion; Improper venue. GOLDLTGFMS § 45:15.

### 2. Forms for the District of Massachusetts

  a. Notice of filing with clerk's office. MA R USDCT CM/ECF Admin(Appendix I).

# I. Applicable Rules

1. *Federal rules*

   a.   Venue generally. 28 U.S.C.A. § 1391.

   b.   Serving and filing pleadings and other papers. FRCP 5.

   c.   Constitutional challenge to a statute; Notice, certification, and intervention. FRCP 5.1.

   d.   Privacy protection for filings made with the court. FRCP 5.2.

   e.   Computing and extending time; Time for motion papers. FRCP 6.

   f.   Pleadings allowed; Form of motions and other papers. FRCP 7.

   g.   Disclosure statement. FRCP 7.1.

   h.   Form of pleadings. FRCP 10.

   i.   Signing pleadings, motions, and other papers; Representations to the court; Sanctions. FRCP 11.

   j.   Defenses and objections; When and how presented; Motion for judgment on the pleadings; Consolidating motions; Waiving defenses; Pretrial hearing. FRCP 12.

   k.   Taking testimony. FRCP 43.

   l.   Hearing motions; Submission on briefs. FRCP 78.

2. *Local rules*

   a.   Title. MA R USDCT LR 1.1.

   b.   Sanctions. MA R USDCT LR 1.3.

   c.   Form and filing of papers. MA R USDCT LR 5.1.

   d.   Service and filing of pleadings and other papers. MA R USDCT LR 5.2.

   e.   Filing and service by electronic means. MA R USDCT LR 5.4.

   f.   Motion practice. MA R USDCT LR 7.1.

   g.   Alternative dispute resolution. MA R USDCT LR 16.4.

   h.   Assignment of cases. [MA R USDCT LR 40.1, as amended by MA ORDER 19-3002, effective January 11, 2019].

   i.   Payments and deposits made with the clerk. MA R USDCT LR 67.4.

   j.   Settlement. MA R USDCT LR 68.2.

   k.   Office of the clerk. MA R USDCT LR 77.2.

   l.   Appearances. MA R USDCT LR 83.5.2.

   m.   Practice by pro se litigants. MA R USDCT LR 83.5.5.

   n.   CM/ECF case management/electronic case files administrative procedures. MA R USDCT CM/ECF Admin.

# Motions, Oppositions and Replies
# Motion for Leave to Amend

**Document Last Updated December 2018**

## A.  Checklist

(I)   ❑  Matters to be considered by moving party

   (a)   ❑  Required documents

      (1)   ❑  Notice of motion and motion

      (2)   ❑  Memorandum

      (3)   ❑  Proposed amended pleading

      (4)   ❑  Certificate of service

(b) ❑ Supplemental documents

    (1) ❑ Supporting evidence

    (2) ❑ Statement of date on which the motion will be filed

    (3) ❑ Certificate of advance service

    (4) ❑ Notice of constitutional question

    (5) ❑ Proposed order

    (6) ❑ Compact disk with copy of document(s) in PDF format

    (7) ❑ Notice of filing with clerk's office

    (8) ❑ Additional copies

    (9) ❑ Courtesy copies

(c) ❑ Timing

    (1) ❑ Unlike amendments as of course, amendments under FRCP 15(a)(2) may be made at any stage of the litigation

    (2) ❑ A party may move—at any time, even after judgment—to amend the pleadings to conform them to the evidence and to raise an unpleaded issue

    (3) ❑ Amendments adding parties shall be sought as soon as an attorney reasonably can be expected to have become aware of the identity of the proposed new party; a party moving to amend a pleading to add a new party shall serve, in the manner contemplated by FRCP 5(b), the motion to amend upon the proposed new party at least fourteen (14) days in advance of filing the motion, together with a separate document stating the date on which the motion will be filed

    (4) ❑ A written motion and notice of the hearing must be served at least fourteen (14) days before the time specified for the hearing, with the following exceptions: (i) when the motion may be heard ex parte; (ii) when the Federal Rules of Civil Procedure set a different time; or (iii) when a court order—which a party may, for good cause, apply for ex parte—sets a different time

    (5) ❑ Any affidavit supporting a motion must be served with the motion

    (6) ❑ Except as noted in FRCP 33 to FRCP 36, the original of all papers required to be served under FRCP 5(d) shall, unless otherwise submitted to the court, be filed in the office of the clerk within seven (7) days after service has been made

(II) ❑ Matters to be considered by opposing party

  (a) ❑ Required documents

    (1) ❑ Opposition

    (2) ❑ Certificate of service

  (b) ❑ Supplemental documents

    (1) ❑ Supporting evidence

    (2) ❑ Notice of constitutional question

    (3) ❑ Compact disk with copy of document(s) in PDF format

    (4) ❑ Notice of filing with clerk's office

    (5) ❑ Additional copies

    (6) ❑ Courtesy copies

  (c) ❑ Timing

    (1) ❑ A party opposing a motion, shall file an opposition within fourteen (14) days after the motion is served, unless another period is fixed by rule or statute, or by order of the court

    (2) ❑ Except as FRCP 59(c) provides otherwise, any opposing affidavit must be served at least seven (7) days before the hearing, unless the court permits service at another time

    (3) ❑ Except as noted in FRCP 33 to FRCP 36, the original of all papers required to be served under FRCP 5(d)

shall, unless otherwise submitted to the court, be filed in the office of the clerk within seven (7) days after service has been made

## B. Timing

1. *Motion for leave to amend.* Unlike amendments as of course, amendments under FRCP 15(a)(2) may be made at any stage of the litigation. FPP § 1484.

   a. *Amendments to conform to the evidence.* A party may move—at any time, even after judgment—to amend the pleadings to conform them to the evidence and to raise an unpleaded issue. FRCP 15(b)(2).

   b. *Amendments to add a new party.* Amendments adding parties shall be sought as soon as an attorney reasonably can be expected to have become aware of the identity of the proposed new party. MA R USDCT LR 15.1(a). A party moving to amend a pleading to add a new party shall serve, in the manner contemplated by FRCP 5(b), the motion to amend upon the proposed new party at least fourteen (14) days in advance of filing the motion, together with a separate document stating the date on which the motion will be filed. MA R USDCT LR 15.1(b).

   c. *Time to respond to an amended pleading.* Unless the court orders otherwise, any required response to an amended pleading must be made within the time remaining to respond to the original pleading or within fourteen (14) days after service of the amended pleading, whichever is later. FRCP 15(a)(3).

2. *Timing of motions, generally*

   a. *Motion and notice of hearing.* A written motion and notice of the hearing must be served at least fourteen (14) days before the time specified for the hearing, with the following exceptions:

      i. When the motion may be heard ex parte;

      ii. When the Federal Rules of Civil Procedure set a different time; or

      iii. When a court order—which a party may, for good cause, apply for ex parte—sets a different time. FRCP 6(c)(1).

   b. *Supporting affidavit.* Any affidavit supporting a motion must be served with the motion. FRCP 6(c)(2).

3. *Timing of opposing papers.* A party opposing a motion, shall file an opposition within fourteen (14) days after the motion is served, unless (1) the motion is for summary judgment, in which case the opposition shall be filed within twenty-one (21) days after the motion is served, or (2) another period is fixed by rule or statute, or by order of the court. MA R USDCT LR 7.1(b)(2); MA R USDCT CM/ECF Admin(H)(4). The fourteen (14) day period is intended to include the period specified by the civil rules for mailing time and provide for a uniform period regardless of the use of the mails. MA R USDCT LR 7.1(b)(2).

   a. *Opposing affidavit.* Except as FRCP 59(c) provides otherwise, any opposing affidavit must be served at least seven (7) days before the hearing, unless the court permits service at another time. FRCP 6(c)(2).

4. *Timing of reply papers.* [W]here the respondent files an answering affidavit setting up a new matter, the moving party ordinarily is allowed a reasonable time to file a reply affidavit since failure to deny the new matter by affidavit may operate as an admission of its truth. AMJUR MOTIONS § 25.

   a. *Leave of court required.* All other papers not filed as indicated in MA R USDCT LR 7.1(b)(1) and MA R USDCT LR 7.1(b)(2), whether in the form of a reply brief or otherwise, may be submitted only with leave of court. MA R USDCT LR 7.1(b)(3).

5. *Filing after service.* Except as noted in FRCP 33 to FRCP 36, the original of all papers required to be served under FRCP 5(d) shall, unless otherwise submitted to the court, be filed in the office of the clerk within seven (7) days after service has been made. MA R USDCT LR 5.1(b).

6. *Computation of time*

   a. *Computing time.* FRCP 6 applies in computing any time period specified in the Federal Rules of Civil Procedure, in any local rule or court order, or in any statute that does not specify a method of computing time. FRCP 6(a).

      i. *Period stated in days or a longer unit.* When the period is stated in days or a longer unit of time:

         • Exclude the day of the event that triggers the period;

         • Count every day, including intermediate Saturdays, Sundays, and legal holidays; and

         • Include the last day of the period, but if the last day is a Saturday, Sunday, or legal holiday, the period continues to run until the end of the next day that is not a Saturday, Sunday, or legal holiday. FRCP 6(a)(1).

      ii. *Period stated in hours.* When the period is stated in hours:

         • Begin counting immediately on the occurrence of the event that triggers the period;

- Count every hour, including hours during intermediate Saturdays, Sundays, and legal holidays; and

- If the period would end on a Saturday, Sunday, or legal holiday, the period continues to run until the same time on the next day that is not a Saturday, Sunday, or legal holiday. FRCP 6(a)(2).

iii. *Office of the clerk.* The offices of the Clerk of Court at Boston, Worcester and Springfield shall be open from 8:30 a.m. until 5:00 p.m. on all days except Saturdays, Sundays, legal holidays and other days so ordered by the court and announced in advance, if feasible. MA R USDCT LR 77.2.

iv. *Inaccessibility of the clerk's office.* Unless the court orders otherwise, if the clerk's office is inaccessible:

- On the last day for filing under FRCP 6(a)(1), then the time for filing is extended to the first accessible day that is not a Saturday, Sunday, or legal holiday; or

- During the last hour for filing under FRCP 6(a)(2), then the time for filing is extended to the same time on the first accessible day that is not a Saturday, Sunday, or legal holiday. FRCP 6(a)(3).

v. *"Last day" defined.* Unless a different time is set by a statute, local rule, or court order, the last day ends:

- For electronic filing, at midnight in the court's time zone; and

- For filing by other means, when the clerk's office is scheduled to close. FRCP 6(a)(4).

vi. *"Next day" defined.* The "next day" is determined by continuing to count forward when the period is measured after an event and backward when measured before an event. FRCP 6(a)(5).

vii. *"Legal holiday" defined.* "Legal holiday" means:

- The day set aside by statute for observing New Year's Day, Martin Luther King Jr.'s Birthday, Washington's Birthday, Memorial Day, Independence Day, Labor Day, Columbus Day, Veterans' Day, Thanksgiving Day, or Christmas Day;

- Any day declared a holiday by the President or Congress; and

- For periods that are measured after an event, any other day declared a holiday by the state where the district court is located. FRCP 6(a)(6).

b. *Computation of electronic filing deadlines.* Filing documents electronically does not alter any filing deadlines. MA R USDCT CM/ECF Admin(K); MA R USDCT LR 5.4(D). Although CM/ECF is generally available twenty-four (24) hours a day for filing, all electronic transmissions of documents must be completed prior to 6:00 PM, Eastern Standard (or Daylight Savings) Time, on the date on which it is due, in order to be considered timely filed that day. MA R USDCT CM/ECF Admin(K); MA R USDCT LR 5.4(D). When a specific time of day deadline is set by court order or stipulation, the electronic filing must be completed by that time. Documents may be filed at any time of the day on days prior to the date on which it is due. MA R USDCT CM/ECF Admin(K). A document filed electronically shall be deemed filed as of the time and date stated on the NEF received from the court. MA R USDCT CM/ECF Admin(G)(2); MA R USDCT CM/ECF Admin(K).

i. *Technical failures.* A user whose filing is made untimely as the result of a technical failure of the court's CM/ECF system may seek appropriate relief from the court. MA R USDCT CM/ECF Admin(W)(3). Technical difficulties on the filer's end, with telephone, cable lines, the filer's Internet Service Provider (ISP), or hardware or software problems, will not constitute a technical failure under the Administrative Procedures for Electronic Case Filing in the United States District Court for the District of Massachusetts (MA R USDCT CM/ECF Admin) nor excuse an untimely filing. MA R USDCT CM/ECF Admin(W)(3). As help desk support is available during normal business hours, filers are strongly urged to electronically file any documents during that period. MA R USDCT CM/ECF Admin(W)(3).

- The court has made available a public terminal (computers and scanner) in each clerk's office for registered users to scan and electronically file documents. This equipment is available during normal business hours. Users should bring their prepared document and a valid CM/ECF login and password. MA R USDCT CM/ECF Admin(W)(3).

c. *Extending time.* When an act may or must be done within a specified time, the court may, for good cause, extend the time: (1) with or without motion or notice if the court acts, or if a request is made, before the original time or its extension expires; or (2) on motion made after the time has expired if the party failed to act because of excusable neglect. FRCP 6(b)(1).

i. *Exceptions.* A court must not extend the time to act under FRCP 50(b), FRCP 50(d), FRCP 52(b), FRCP 59(b), FRCP 59(d), FRCP 59(e), and FRCP 60(b). FRCP 6(b)(2).

    ii.    Refer to the United States District Court for the District of Massachusetts KeyRules Motion for Continuance/Extension of Time document for more information on extending time.

    d.    *Additional time after certain kinds of service.* When a party may or must act within a specified time after being served and service is made under FRCP 5(b)(2)(C) (by mail), FRCP 5(b)(2)(D) (by leaving with the clerk), or FRCP 5(b)(2)(F) (by other means consented to), three (3) days are added after the period would otherwise expire under FRCP 6(a). FRCP 6(d).

## C. General Requirements

1.    *Motions, generally*

    a.    *Requirements.* A request for a court order must be made by motion. The motion must:

        i.    Be in writing unless made during a hearing or trial;

        ii.    State with particularity the grounds for seeking the order; and

        iii.    State the relief sought. FRCP 7(b)(1).

    b.    *Notice of motion.* A party interested in resisting the relief sought by a motion has a right to notice thereof, and an opportunity to be heard. AMJUR MOTIONS § 12.

        i.    [I]n addition to statutory or court rule provisions requiring notice of a motion—the purpose of such a notice requirement having been said to be to prevent a party from being prejudicially surprised by a motion—principles of natural justice dictate that an adverse party generally must be given notice that a motion will be presented to the court. AMJUR MOTIONS § 12.

        ii.    "Notice," in this regard, means reasonable notice, including a meaningful opportunity to prepare and to defend against allegations of a motion. AMJUR MOTIONS § 12.

    c.    *Writing requirement.* The writing requirement is intended to [ensure] that the adverse parties are informed and have a record of both the motion's pendency and the grounds on which the movant seeks an order. FPP § 1191; Feldberg v. Quechee Lakes Corp., 463 F.3d 195 (2d Cir. 2006). [A] single written document can satisfy the writing requirements both for a motion and for [an] FRCP 6(c)(1) notice. FRCP 7(Advisory Committee Notes).

    d.    *Particularity requirement.* The particularity requirement [ensures] that the opposing parties will have notice of their opponent's contentions. FEDPROC § 62:358; Goodman v. 1973 26 Foot Trojan Vessel, Arkansas Registration No. AR1439SN, 859 F.2d 71 (8th Cir. 1988). That requirement ensures that notice of the basis for the motion is provided to the court and to the opposing party so as to avoid prejudice, provide the opponent with a meaningful opportunity to respond, and provide the court with enough information to process the motion correctly. FEDPROC § 62:358; Andreas v. Volkswagen of Am., Inc., 336 F.3d 789 (8th Cir. 2003).

        i.    Reasonable specification of the grounds for a motion is sufficient. The particularity requirement for motions is satisfied when no party is prejudiced by a lack of particularity or when the court can comprehend the basis for the motion and deal with it fairly. However, where a movant fails to state even one ground for granting the motion in question, the movant has failed to meet the minimal standard of "reasonable specification." FEDPROC § 62:358; Martinez v. Trainor, 556 F.2d 818 (7th Cir. 1977).

        ii.    The court may excuse the failure to comply with the particularity requirement if it is inadvertent, and where no prejudice is shown by the opposing party. FEDPROC § 62:358.

    e.    *Control of motion practice*

        i.    *Plan for the disposition of motions.* At the earliest practicable time, the judicial officer shall establish a framework for the disposition of motions, which, at the discretion of the judicial officer, may include specific deadlines or general time guidelines for filing motions. This framework may be amended from time to time by the judicial officer as required by the progress of the case. MA R USDCT LR 7.1(a)(1).

        ii.    *Motion practice.* No motion shall be filed unless counsel certify that they have conferred and have attempted in good faith to resolve or narrow the issue. MA R USDCT LR 7.1(a)(2).

        iii.    *Unresolved motions.* The court shall rule on motions as soon as practicable, having in mind the reporting requirements set forth in the Civil Justice Reform Act. MA R USDCT LR 7.1(a)(3).

2.    *Motion for leave to amend.* FRCP 15(a)(2) provides that after a party has amended a pleading once as of course or the time for amendments of that type has expired, a party may amend only by obtaining leave of the court or if the adverse party consents to it. FPP § 1484; In re Cessna Distributorship Antitrust Litig., 532 F.2d 64 (8th Cir. 1976). FRCP 15(a) does not

set forth any specific procedure for obtaining leave to amend. Typically, it is sought by a motion addressed to the court's discretion. FPP § 1485.

a. *Pleadings to be amended.* As in the case of amendments as of course under FRCP 15(a)(1), any of the pleadings enumerated in FRCP 7(a) may be amended with the court's leave and FRCP 15 does not restrict the purposes for which an amendment may be made or its character. FPP § 1484.

b. *Prerequisites for leave to amend.* The only prerequisites are that the district court have jurisdiction over the case and an appeal must not be pending. FPP § 1484. If these two conditions are met, the court will proceed to examine the effect and the timing of the proposed amendments to determine whether they would prejudice the rights of any of the other parties to the suit. FPP § 1484; Nilsen v. City of Moss Point, Miss., 674 F.2d 379, 388 (5th Cir. 1982), on reh'g, 701 F.2d 556 (5th Cir. 1983).

c. *When leave or consent is not obtained.* In general, if an amendment that cannot be made as of right is served without obtaining the court's leave or the opposing party's consent, it is without legal effect and any new matter it contains will not be considered unless the amendment is resubmitted for the court's approval. Some courts have held, however, that an untimely amended pleading served without judicial permission may be considered as properly introduced when leave to amend would have been granted had it been sought and when it does not appear that any of the parties will be prejudiced by allowing the change. FPP § 1484.

d. *Form.* A motion to amend under FRCP 15(a), as is true of motions generally, is subject to the requirements of FRCP 7(b), and must set forth with particularity the relief or order requested and the grounds supporting the application. In order to satisfy these prerequisites a copy of the amendment should be submitted with the motion so that the court and the adverse party know the precise nature of the pleading changes being proposed. FPP § 1485.

e. *Oral motion for leave to amend.* Courts have held that an oral request to amend a pleading that is made before the court in the presence of opposing party's counsel may be sufficient if the adverse party is put on notice of the nature and purpose of the request and is given the same opportunity to present objections to the proposed amendment as would have occurred if a formal motion had been made. FPP § 1485.

f. *Conditions imposed on leave to amend.* While FRCP 15(a) does not specifically authorize the district court to impose conditions on its granting of leave to amend, it is well settled that the court may impose such conditions to avoid or minimize any prejudice to the opposing party. FEDPROC § 62:270. Conditions frequently are imposed because the amending party knew of the facts sought to be asserted in the amendment but failed to assert such facts until later, to the prejudice of the opposing party. Conversely, the court may decline to impose conditions where the amendment was asserted with relative promptness. FEDPROC § 62:270.

   i. The moving party's refusal to comply with the conditions imposed by the court normally will result in a denial of the right to amend. FPP § 1486.

g. *When leave to amend may be granted.* The Supreme Court, in its opinion in Foman v. Davis, enunciated the following general standard, which is to be employed under FRCP 15(a) by the district courts: If the underlying facts or circumstances relied upon by a plaintiff may be a proper subject of relief, he ought to be afforded an opportunity to test his claim on the merits. In the absence of any apparent or declared reason—such as undue delay, bad faith or dilatory motive on the part of the movant, repeated failure to cure deficiencies by amendments previously allowed, undue prejudice to the opposing party by virtue of allowance of the amendment, futility of amendment, etc.—the leave sought should, as the rules require, be "freely given." FPP § 1487; Foman v. Davis, 371 U.S. 178, 182, 83 S. Ct. 227, 230, 9 L. Ed. 2d 222 (1962).

3. *Amendments, generally*

a. *Amendments before trial.* The function of FRCP 15(a), which provides generally for the amendment of pleadings, is to enable a party to assert matters that were overlooked or were unknown at the time the party interposed the original complaint or answer. FPP § 1473; Smiga v. Dean Witter Reynolds, Inc., 766 F.2d 698, 703 (2d Cir. 1985).

   i. *Matters contained in amended pleading under FRCP 15(a).* Although FRCP 15(a) does not expressly state that an amendment must contain only matters that occurred within a particular time period, FRCP 15(d) provides that any "transaction, occurrence, or event that happened after the date of the pleading" should be set forth in a supplemental pleading. FPP § 1473. Thus, impliedly, an amended pleading, whether prepared with or without leave of court, only should relate to matters that have taken place prior to the date of the earlier pleading. FPP § 1473; Ford Motor Co. v. United States, 896 F. Supp. 1224, 1230 (Ct. Int'l Trade 1995).

   ii. *Amending as a matter of course.* A party may amend its pleading once as a matter of course within: (1) twenty-one (21) days after serving it, or if the pleading is one to which a responsive pleading is required, twenty-one (21) days after service of a responsive pleading or twenty-one (21) days after service of a motion under FRCP 12(b), FRCP 12(e), or FRCP 12(f), whichever is earlier. FRCP 15(a)(1). Refer to the United States District Court for the District of Massachusetts KeyRules Amended Pleading document for more information on amending as a matter of course.

iii. *Other amendments.* In all other cases, a party may amend its pleading only with the opposing party's written consent or the court's leave. The court should freely give leave when justice so requires. FRCP 15(a)(2).

iv. *Types of amendments permitted under FRCP 15(a)*

- *Cure a defective pleading.* Perhaps the most common use of FRCP 15(a) is by a party seeking to amend in order to cure a defective pleading. FPP § 1474.

- *Correct insufficiently stated claims or defenses.* A more common use of FRCP 15(a) amendments is to correct insufficiently stated claims or defenses. Typically, amendments of this character involve either adding a necessary allegation in order to state a claim for relief or correcting a misnomer of a party to the action. FPP § 1474.

- *Change nature or theory of claim or capacity of party.* Courts also have allowed a party to amend in order to change the nature or theory of the party's claim or the capacity in which the party is bringing the action. FPP § 1474.

- *State additional claims or defenses or drop claims or defenses.* Plaintiffs and defendants also have been permitted to amend their pleadings to state additional claims, to assert additional defenses, or to drop claims or defenses. FPP § 1474; Weinberger v. Retail Credit Co., 498 F.2d 552, 554, n.4 (4th Cir. 1974).

- *Increase amount of damages or elect a different remedy.* [An] FRCP 15(a) amendment also is appropriate for increasing the amount of damages sought, or for electing a different remedy than the one originally requested. FPP § 1474; McFadden v. Sanchez, 710 F.2d 907 (2d Cir. 1983).

- *Add, substitute, or drop parties.* Finally, a party may make [an] FRCP 15(a) amendment to add, substitute, or drop parties to the action. FPP § 1474.

b. *Amendments during and after trial*

i. *Based on an objection at trial.* If, at trial, a party objects that evidence is not within the issues raised in the pleadings, the court may permit the pleadings to be amended. The court should freely permit an amendment when doing so will aid in presenting the merits and the objecting party fails to satisfy the court that the evidence would prejudice that party's action or defense on the merits. The court may grant a continuance to enable the objecting party to meet the evidence. FRCP 15(b)(1).

ii. *For issues tried by consent.* When an issue not raised by the pleadings is tried by the parties' express or implied consent, it must be treated in all respects as if raised in the pleadings. A party may move—at any time, even after judgment—to amend the pleadings to conform them to the evidence and to raise an unpleaded issue. But failure to amend does not affect the result of the trial of that issue. FRCP 15(b)(2).

c. *Relation back of amendments*

i. *When an amendment relates back.* An amendment to a pleading relates back to the date of the original pleading when:

- The law that provides the applicable statute of limitations allows relation back;

- The amendment asserts a claim or defense that arose out of the conduct, transaction, or occurrence set out—or attempted to be set out—in the original pleading; or

- The amendment changes the party or the naming of the party against whom a claim is asserted, if FRCP 15(c)(1)(B) is satisfied and if, within the period provided by FRCP 4(m) for serving the summons and complaint, the party to be brought in by amendment: (1) received such notice of the action that it will not be prejudiced in defending on the merits; and (2) knew or should have known that the action would have been brought against it, but for a mistake concerning the proper party's identity. FRCP 15(c)(1).

ii. *Notice to the United States.* When the United States or a United States officer or agency is added as a defendant by amendment, the notice requirements of FRCP 15(c)(1)(C)(i) and FRCP 15(c)(1)(C)(ii) are satisfied if, during the stated period, process was delivered or mailed to the United States attorney or the United States attorney's designee, to the Attorney General of the United States, or to the officer or agency. FRCP 15(c)(2).

d. *Effect of an amended pleading.* A pleading that has been amended under FRCP 15(a) supersedes the pleading it modifies and remains in effect throughout the action unless it subsequently is modified. FPP § 1476. Once an amended pleading is interposed, the original pleading no longer performs any function in the case and any subsequent motion made by an opposing party should be directed at the amended pleading. FPP § 1476; Ferdik v. Bonzelet, 963 F.2d 1258, 1262 (9th Cir. 1992), as amended (May 22, 1992); Davis v. TXO Prod. Corp., 929 F.2d 1515, 1517 (10th Cir. 1991).

4. *Opposing papers.* The Federal Rules of Civil Procedure do not require any formal answer, return, or reply to a motion, except where the Federal Rules of Civil Procedure or local rules may require affidavits, memoranda, or other papers to be filed in opposition to a motion. Such papers are simply to apprise the court of such opposition and the grounds of that opposition. FEDPROC § 62:353.

   a. *Effect of failure to respond to motion.* Although in the absence of statutory provision or court rule, a motion ordinarily does not require a written answer, when a party files a motion and the opposing party fails to respond, the court may construe such failure to respond as nonopposition to the motion or an admission that the motion was meritorious, may take the facts alleged in the motion as true—the rule in some jurisdictions being that the failure to respond to a fact set forth in a motion is deemed an admission—and may grant the motion if the relief requested appears to be justified. AMJUR MOTIONS § 28.

   b. *Assent or no opposition not determinative.* However, a motion will not be granted automatically simply because an "assent" or a notation of "no opposition" has been filed; federal judges frequently deny motions that have been assented to when it is thought that justice so dictates. FPP § 1190.

   c. *Responsive pleading inappropriate as response to motion.* An attempt to answer or oppose a motion with a responsive pleading usually is not appropriate. FPP § 1190.

5. *Reply papers.* A moving party may be required or permitted to prepare papers in addition to his original motion papers. AMJUR MOTIONS § 25. Papers answering or replying to opposing papers may be appropriate, in the interests of justice, where it appears there is a substantial reason for allowing a reply. Thus, a court may accept reply papers where a party demonstrates that the papers to which it seeks to file a reply raise new issues that are material to the disposition of the question before the court, or where the court determines, sua sponte, that it wishes further briefing of an issue raised in those papers and orders the submission of additional papers. FEDPROC § 62:354.

   a. *Function of reply papers.* The function of a reply affidavit is to answer the arguments made in opposition to the position taken by the movant and not to permit the movant to introduce new arguments in support of the motion. AMJUR MOTIONS § 25.

   b. *Issues raised for the first time in a reply document.* However, the view has been followed in some jurisdictions, that as a matter of judicial economy, where there is no prejudice and where the issues could be raised simply by filing a motion to dismiss, the trial court has discretion to consider arguments raised for the first time in a reply memorandum, and that a trial court may grant a motion to strike issues raised for the first time in a reply memorandum. AMJUR MOTIONS § 26.

6. *Alternative dispute resolution (ADR).* The judicial officer assigned to preside over the case shall encourage the resolution of disputes by settlement or other alternative dispute resolution programs. MA R USDCT LR 16.4(a).

   a. *Settlement.* At every conference conducted under the Local Rules of the United States District Court for the District of Massachusetts, the judicial officer shall inquire as to the utility of the parties conducting settlement negotiations, explore means of facilitating those negotiations, and offer whatever assistance may be appropriate in the circumstances. Assistance may include a reference of the case to another judicial officer for settlement purposes. MA R USDCT LR 16.4(b).

      i. When a case is settled, the parties shall file with the clerk a signed agreement for judgment or stipulation for dismissal, as appropriate, within twenty-eight (28) days, unless the court otherwise orders. MA R USDCT LR 68.2.

   b. *Alternative dispute resolution programs*

      i. *Discretion of judicial officer.* The judicial officer, following an exploration of the matter with all counsel, may refer appropriate cases to alternative dispute resolution programs that have been designated for use in the district court or that the judicial officer may make available. The dispute resolution programs described in MA R USDCT LR 16.4(c)(2) through MA R USDCT LR 16.4(c)(4) are illustrative, not exclusive. Moreover, nothing in MA R USDCT LR 16.4 shall preclude the parties from engaging in private dispute resolution programs as long as they comply with any schedule established by the court. MA R USDCT LR 16.4(c)(1).

      ii. *Mediation.* The judicial officer may refer the case to mediation upon the agreement of all parties. MA R USDCT LR 16.4(c)(2)(A).

iii. *Other alternative dispute resolution programs.* Use of mediation is not exclusive. At the request of parties, the judicial officer may consider other forms of alternative dispute resolution including, but not limited to, mini-trial, summary jury trial and arbitration. MA R USDCT LR 16.4(c)(3).

c. For more information on alternative dispute resolution (ADR), refer to MA R USDCT LR 16.4.

7. *Sanctions.* Failure to comply with any of the directions or obligations set forth in, or authorized by, these rules may result in dismissal, default, or the imposition of other sanctions as deemed appropriate by the judicial officer. MA R USDCT LR 1.3. Except as provided by law, the court may impose sanctions as provided in MA R USDCT LR 1.3 for failure to comply with the Administrative Procedures for Electronic Case Filing in the United States District Court for the District of Massachusetts (MA R USDCT CM/ECF Admin) or with MA R USDCT LR 5.4. MA R USDCT CM/ECF Admin(C)(3).

# D. Documents

1. *Documents for moving party*

   a. *Required documents*

      i. *Notice of motion and motion.* Refer to the General Requirements section of this document for information on the notice of motion and motion.

         - *Request for oral argument.* Any party making or opposing a motion who believes that oral argument may assist the court and wishes to be heard shall include a request for oral argument in a separate paragraph of the motion or opposition. The request should be set off with a centered caption, "REQUEST FOR ORAL ARGUMENT." MA R USDCT LR 7.1(d).

      ii. *Memorandum.* A party filing a motion shall at the same time file a memorandum of reasons, including citation of supporting authorities, why the motion should be granted. MA R USDCT LR 7.1(b)(1). Any memorandum of law or other attachment filed in support of a main document shall be filed as a separate document, using the proper event. MA R USDCT CM/ECF Admin(G)(4). Memoranda supporting or opposing allowance of motions shall not, without leave of court, exceed twenty (20) pages, double-spaced. MA R USDCT LR 7.1(b)(4).

      iii. *Proposed amended pleading.* If a party electronically files a motion, pursuant to MA R USDCT LR 7.1, for leave to file a document, or amend a previously filed document, the party shall attach a copy of the proposed document to the motion for leave to file or amend. The attachment must be marked "Proposed [document designation]." MA R USDCT CM/ECF Admin(R). In order to satisfy [the prerequisites of FRCP 7(b)], a copy of the amendment should be submitted with the motion so that the court and the adverse party know the precise nature of the pleading changes being proposed. FPP § 1485. The amending party should submit a copy of the proposed amendment at least by the date of the hearing on the motion for leave to amend. FEDPROC § 62:268; Grombach v. Oerlikon Tool & Arms Corp. of America, 276 F.2d 155 (4th Cir. 1960).

         - *Accompanying documents as a substitute.* The documents accompanying the motion for leave to amend may be an appropriate substitute for a formally proposed amendment, if the documents sufficiently indicate the gist of the amendment. FEDPROC § 62:268.

         - Once leave to file is granted, the party proposing the document shall electronically file the original document, indicating in the caption when leave was granted. MA R USDCT CM/ECF Admin(R). For an example, refer to MA R USDCT CM/ECF Admin(R).

      iv. *Certificate of service.* No certificate of service is required when a paper is served by filing it with the court's electronic-filing system. When a paper that is required to be served is served by other means: (1) if the paper is filed, a certificate of service must be filed with it or within a reasonable time after service; and (2) if the paper is not filed, a certificate of service need not be filed unless filing is required by court order or by local rule. FRCP 5(d)(1)(B). Except as otherwise provided by the Federal Rules of Civil Procedure, proof of service of all pleadings and other papers required to be served (except discovery papers that in accordance with FRCP 33 to FRCP 36(f) are not to be filed) shall be filed in the office of the clerk promptly after service has been made. The proof shall show the time and manner of service, and may be made by written acknowledgment of service, a certificate of a member of the bar of this court, or an affidavit of the person who served the paper. MA R USDCT LR 5.2(b)(1). A certificate of service of a member of the bar shall appear at the bottom of or on the margin of the last page of the paper to which it relates. MA R USDCT LR 5.2(b)(2).

         - *Paper service.* The certificate shall be a brief, single-spaced statement and may be in the following form: I hereby certify that a true copy of the above document was served upon (each party appearing pro se and) the attorney of record for each other party by mail (by hand) on (date). (Signature). MA R USDCT LR 5.2(b)(2).

- *Electronic service.* Any pleading or other paper served by electronic means must bear a certificate of service in accordance with MA R USDCT LR 5.2(b). MA R USDCT LR 5.4(C); MA R USDCT CM/ECF Admin(H)(2). The certificate of service shall state that the filer: (1) filed the document electronically, (2) that it will be served electronically to registered CM/ECF participants via the NEF and (3) that the filer will send paper copies to non-registered participants as indicated on the NEF. MA R USDCT CM/ECF Admin(H)(2). For example: I hereby certify that this document filed through the CM/ECF system will be sent electronically to the registered participants as identified on the NEF (NEF) and paper copies will be sent to those indicated as non registered participants on (date). MA R USDCT CM/ECF Admin(H)(2).

- *Return.* Documents not conforming to the requirements of MA R USDCT LR 5.2 (except notices of appeal) shall be returned by the clerk. MA R USDCT LR 5.2(b)(2).

- *Failure to make proof of service.* Failure to make proof of service does not affect the validity of the service. MA R USDCT LR 5.2(b)(3).

b. *Supplemental documents*

   i. *Supporting evidence.* When a motion relies on facts outside the record, the court may hear the matter on affidavits or may hear it wholly or partly on oral testimony or on depositions. FRCP 43(c). Affidavits and other documents setting forth or evidencing facts on which the motion is based shall be filed with the motion. MA R USDCT LR 7.1(b)(1).

   ii. *Statement of date on which the motion will be filed.* A party moving to amend a pleading to add a new party shall serve, in the manner contemplated by FRCP 5(b), the motion to amend upon the proposed new party at least fourteen (14) days in advance of filing the motion, together with a separate document stating the date on which the motion will be filed. MA R USDCT LR 15.1(b).

   iii. *Certificate of advance service.* A motion to amend a pleading to add a new party shall be accompanied by a certificate stating that it has been served in advance on the new party as required by MA R USDCT LR 15.1. MA R USDCT LR 15.1(b).

   iv. *Notice of constitutional question.* A party that files a pleading, written motion, or other paper drawing into question the constitutionality of a federal or state statute must promptly:

      - *File notice.* File a notice of constitutional question stating the question and identifying the paper that raises it, if: (1) a federal statute is questioned and the parties do not include the United States, one of its agencies, or one of its officers or employees in an official capacity; or (2) a state statute is questioned and the parties do not include the state, one of its agencies, or one of its officers or employees in an official capacity; and

      - *Serve notice.* Serve the notice and paper on the Attorney General of the United States if a federal statute is questioned—or on the state attorney general if a state statute is questioned—either by certified or registered mail or by sending it to an electronic address designated by the attorney general for this purpose. FRCP 5.1(a).

      - *No forfeiture.* A party's failure to file and serve the notice, or the court's failure to certify, does not forfeit a constitutional claim or defense that is otherwise timely asserted. FRCP 5.1(d).

   v. *Proposed order.* Proposed orders usually are not required by this court. However, the court may request the party to submit such a document. In those situations, unless otherwise directed by the clerk's office, electronically file the proposed document/order using the entry for "Proposed Documents submitted to the court," found under the Other Documents menu, or as an attachment to the motion to which it relates. MA R USDCT CM/ECF Admin(T).

   vi. *Compact disk with copy of document(s) in PDF format.* A filer who cannot file a document electronically because of such technical difficulty on the filer's end [with telephone, cable lines, the filer's Internet Service Provider (ISP), or hardware or software problems] shall file the document conventionally along with a copy of the document in PDF format on a compact disk or contact the clerk's office for permission to submit the PDF document via email. MA R USDCT CM/ECF Admin(W)(3). Refer to the Timing section of this document for more information on technical failures.

   vii. *Notice of filing with clerk's office.* When documents or exhibits (other than those filed ex parte or under seal) are submitted conventionally, a "Notice of Filing with clerk's office" shall be filed electronically and attached to the main document. A paper copy of the "Notice of Filing with clerk's office" must accompany the documents submitted to the court. The "Notice of Filing with clerk's office" (see MA R USDCT CM/ECF Admin(Appendix I)) shall describe each of the documents that will be filed as paper copies in the clerk's office, or shall include an index of the documents if those documents are voluminous. MA R USDCT CM/ECF Admin(P)(5).

viii. *Additional copies.* Whenever, because of the nature of a proceeding, such as a proceeding before a three-judge district court under 28 U.S.C.A. § 2284, additional copies of a paper required to be filed are necessary either for the use of the court or to enable the clerk to carry out his duties, it is the responsibility of the party filing or having filed the paper to provide the necessary copies. MA R USDCT LR 5.1(d).

ix. *Courtesy copies.* COURTESY COPIES OF DOCUMENTS FILED ELECTRONICALLY SHALL NOT BE SUBMITTED ROUTINELY. MA R USDCT CM/ECF Admin(J). Judicial officers, on a case-by-case basis, may require courtesy copies for specific cases, or types of motions, etc. A few Judicial Officers have entered Standing Orders, which may be found on their respective pages on the court's website (under Divisions). Any document filed on paper with the court as a courtesy copy must be clearly labeled as such (Example: COURTESY COPY—DO NOT SCAN). Documents delivered to the court as a courtesy copy will not be maintained in the official court record. MA R USDCT CM/ECF Admin(J).

2. *Documents for opposing party*

   a. *Required documents*

      i. *Opposition.* Refer to the General Requirements section of this document for information on the opposing papers.

         • *Memorandum.* A party opposing a motion shall file, in the same (rather than a separate), document a memorandum of reasons, including citation of supporting authorities, why the motion should not be granted. MA R USDCT LR 7.1(b)(2). Any memorandum of law or other attachment filed in support of a main document shall be filed as a separate document, using the proper event. MA R USDCT CM/ECF Admin(G)(4). Memoranda supporting or opposing allowance of motions shall not, without leave of court, exceed twenty (20) pages, double-spaced. MA R USDCT LR 7.1(b)(4).

         • *Request for oral argument.* Any party making or opposing a motion who believes that oral argument may assist the court and wishes to be heard shall include a request for oral argument in a separate paragraph of the motion or opposition. The request should be set off with a centered caption, "REQUEST FOR ORAL ARGUMENT." MA R USDCT LR 7.1(d).

      ii. *Certificate of service.* No certificate of service is required when a paper is served by filing it with the court's electronic-filing system. When a paper that is required to be served is served by other means: (1) if the paper is filed, a certificate of service must be filed with it or within a reasonable time after service; and (2) if the paper is not filed, a certificate of service need not be filed unless filing is required by court order or by local rule. FRCP 5(d)(1)(B). Except as otherwise provided by the Federal Rules of Civil Procedure, proof of service of all pleadings and other papers required to be served (except discovery papers that in accordance with FRCP 33 to FRCP 36(f) are not to be filed) shall be filed in the office of the clerk promptly after service has been made. The proof shall show the time and manner of service, and may be made by written acknowledgment of service, a certificate of a member of the bar of this court, or an affidavit of the person who served the paper. MA R USDCT LR 5.2(b)(1). A certificate of service of a member of the bar shall appear at the bottom of or on the margin of the last page of the paper to which it relates. MA R USDCT LR 5.2(b)(2).

         • *Paper service.* The certificate shall be a brief, single-spaced statement and may be in the following form: I hereby certify that a true copy of the above document was served upon (each party appearing pro se and) the attorney of record for each other party by mail (by hand) on (date). (Signature). MA R USDCT LR 5.2(b)(2).

         • *Electronic service.* Any pleading or other paper served by electronic means must bear a certificate of service in accordance with MA R USDCT LR 5.2(b). MA R USDCT LR 5.4(C); MA R USDCT CM/ECF Admin(H)(2). The certificate of service shall state that the filer: (1) filed the document electronically, (2) that it will be served electronically to registered CM/ECF participants via the NEF and (3) that the filer will send paper copies to non-registered participants as indicated on the NEF. MA R USDCT CM/ECF Admin(H)(2). For example: I hereby certify that this document filed through the CM/ECF system will be sent electronically to the registered participants as identified on the NEF (NEF) and paper copies will be sent to those indicated as non registered participants on (date). MA R USDCT CM/ECF Admin(H)(2).

         • *Return.* Documents not conforming to the requirements of MA R USDCT LR 5.2 (except notices of appeal) shall be returned by the clerk. MA R USDCT LR 5.2(b)(2).

         • *Failure to make proof of service.* Failure to make proof of service does not affect the validity of the service. MA R USDCT LR 5.2(b)(3).

   b. *Supplemental documents*

      i. *Supporting evidence.* When a motion relies on facts outside the record, the court may hear the matter on affidavits or may hear it wholly or partly on oral testimony or on depositions. FRCP 43(c). Affidavits and other documents setting forth or evidencing facts on which the opposition is based shall be filed with the opposition. MA R USDCT LR 7.1(b)(2).

ii. *Notice of constitutional question.* A party that files a pleading, written motion, or other paper drawing into question the constitutionality of a federal or state statute must promptly:

- *File notice.* File a notice of constitutional question stating the question and identifying the paper that raises it, if: (1) a federal statute is questioned and the parties do not include the United States, one of its agencies, or one of its officers or employees in an official capacity; or (2) a state statute is questioned and the parties do not include the state, one of its agencies, or one of its officers or employees in an official capacity; and

- *Serve notice.* Serve the notice and paper on the Attorney General of the United States if a federal statute is questioned—or on the state attorney general if a state statute is questioned—either by certified or registered mail or by sending it to an electronic address designated by the attorney general for this purpose. FRCP 5.1(a).

- *No forfeiture.* A party's failure to file and serve the notice, or the court's failure to certify, does not forfeit a constitutional claim or defense that is otherwise timely asserted. FRCP 5.1(d).

iii. *Compact disk with copy of document(s) in PDF format.* A filer who cannot file a document electronically because of such technical difficulty on the filer's end [with telephone, cable lines, the filer's Internet Service Provider (ISP), or hardware or software problems] shall file the document conventionally along with a copy of the document in PDF format on a compact disk or contact the clerk's office for permission to submit the PDF document via email. MA R USDCT CM/ECF Admin(W)(3). Refer to the Timing section of this document for more information on technical failures.

iv. *Notice of filing with clerk's office.* When documents or exhibits (other than those filed ex parte or under seal) are submitted conventionally, a "Notice of Filing with clerk's office" shall be filed electronically and attached to the main document. A paper copy of the "Notice of Filing with clerk's office" must accompany the documents submitted to the court. The "Notice of Filing with clerk's office" (see MA R USDCT CM/ECF Admin(Appendix I)) shall describe each of the documents that will be filed as paper copies in the clerk's office, or shall include an index of the documents if those documents are voluminous. MA R USDCT CM/ECF Admin(P)(5).

v. *Additional copies.* Whenever, because of the nature of a proceeding, such as a proceeding before a three-judge district court under 28 U.S.C.A. § 2284, additional copies of a paper required to be filed are necessary either for the use of the court or to enable the clerk to carry out his duties, it is the responsibility of the party filing or having filed the paper to provide the necessary copies. MA R USDCT LR 5.1(d).

vi. *Courtesy copies.* COURTESY COPIES OF DOCUMENTS FILED ELECTRONICALLY SHALL NOT BE SUBMITTED ROUTINELY. MA R USDCT CM/ECF Admin(J). Judicial officers, on a case-by-case basis, may require courtesy copies for specific cases, or types of motions, etc. A few Judicial Officers have entered Standing Orders, which may be found on their respective pages on the court's website (under Divisions). Any document filed on paper with the court as a courtesy copy must be clearly labeled as such (Example: COURTESY COPY—DO NOT SCAN). Documents delivered to the court as a courtesy copy will not be maintained in the official court record. MA R USDCT CM/ECF Admin(J).

**E. Format**

1. *Form of documents.* The rules governing captions and other matters of form in pleadings apply to motions and other papers. FRCP 7(b)(2). The provisions of FRCP 10 and FRCP 11 concerning the form and signing of pleadings, motions, and other papers shall be applicable to all papers filed in any proceeding in this court. The board of bar overseers registration number of each attorney signing such documents, except the United States Attorney and his or her staff, shall be inscribed below the signature. MA R USDCT LR 5.1(a)(1).

   a. *Paper size and binding.* All papers filed in the court shall be adapted for flat filing, be filed on eight and one-half by eleven (8-1/2 x 11) inch paper without backers and be bound firmly by staple or some such other means (excluding paper or binder clip or rubber band). MA R USDCT LR 5.1(a)(2).

   b. *Spacing.* All papers, except discovery requests and responses, shall be double-spaced except for the identification of counsel, title of the case, footnotes, quotations and exhibits. Discovery requests and responses shall be single-spaced. MA R USDCT LR 5.1(a)(2).

c. *Caption.* Every pleading must have a caption with the court's name, a title, a file number, and [an] FRCP 7(a) designation. FRCP 10(a).

   i. *Names of parties.* The title of the complaint must name all the parties; the title of other pleadings, after naming the first party on each side, may refer generally to other parties. FRCP 10(a).

   ii. *Request for special action.* When any pleading or other paper filed in the court includes a request for special process or relief, or any other request such that, if granted, the court will proceed other than in the ordinary course, the request shall, unless it is noted on the category sheet [see MA R USDCT LR 40.1(a)(1)], be noted on the first page to the right of or immediately beneath the caption. MA R USDCT LR 5.1(c).

d. *Claims or defenses*

   i. *Numbered paragraphs.* A party must state its claims or defenses in numbered paragraphs, each limited as far as practicable to a single set of circumstances. A later pleading may refer by number to a paragraph in an earlier pleading. FRCP 10(b).

   ii. *Separate statements.* If doing so would promote clarity, each claim founded on a separate transaction or occurrence—and each defense other than a denial—must be stated in a separate count or defense. FRCP 10(b).

e. *Adoption by reference.* A statement in a pleading may be adopted by reference elsewhere in the same pleading or in any other pleading or motion. FRCP 10(c).

   i. *Exhibits.* A copy of a written instrument that is an exhibit to a pleading is a part of the pleading for all purposes. FRCP 10(c).

f. *Citations*

   i. *Local rules.* These rules shall be known as Local Rules of the United States District Court for the District of Massachusetts and cited as "L.R., D. Mass." or "L.R." MA R USDCT LR 1.1.

   ii. *Electronic case filing procedures.* The procedures governing electronic case filing shall be known as the "Administrative Procedures for Electronic Case Filing in the United States District Court for the District of Massachusetts." They shall be cited as "APECF." MA R USDCT CM/ECF Admin(A)(7).

g. *Acceptance by the clerk.* The clerk must not refuse to file a paper solely because it is not in the form prescribed by the Federal Rules of Civil Procedure or by a local rule or practice. FRCP 5(d)(4).

   i. Except for complaints and notices of appeal, papers that do not conform to the requirements of MA R USDCT LR 5.1(a)(2) shall be returned by the clerk. MA R USDCT LR 5.1(a)(2).

2. *Form of electronic documents.* A paper filed electronically is a written paper for purposes of the Federal Rules of Civil Procedure. FRCP 5(d)(3)(D).

   a. *PDF/A format required.* The court will begin requiring submission of documents in PDF/A format in the foreseeable future. PDF/A is an enhanced version of the traditional PDF format. Newer versions of most PDF software will be able to convert to this format. Additional information on PDF/A documents may be found on the court's website. MA R USDCT CM/ECF Admin(Electronic Filing and PDF).

      i. *Electronically converted PDF.* Electronically converted PDF documents are created from word processing documents (MS Word, WordPerfect, etc.) using any appropriate software. These documents are text searchable and the file size is generally smaller than a scanned document. CM/ECF users may use any brand of software to convert documents to PDF. MA R USDCT CM/ECF Admin(Electronic Filing and PDF).

         • Documents converted to PDF, rather than scanned, are preferred for filing in CM/ECF. MA R USDCT CM/ECF Admin(Electronic Filing and PDF).

      ii. *Scanned PDF.* Scanned PDF documents are created from paper documents run through an optical scanner. Scanned PDF documents are generally not searchable and have a larger file size. Please note that software used to create scanned documents may (and should) be set in such a way that the document is "text-searchable." MA R USDCT CM/ECF Admin(Electronic Filing and PDF).

   b. *Title.* All pleadings filed electronically shall be titled in accordance with the approved dictionary of civil or criminal events of the CM/ECF system of this court. A list of events is available on the CM/ECF Training Information page of the court's website. The clerk's office may, when necessary and appropriate, modify the docket entry description, or delete and re-enter the docket entry in order to comply with the court's quality assurance standards. MA R USDCT CM/ECF Admin(G)(3).

c. *Attachments to filings and exhibits.* Attachments to filings and exhibits must be filed in accordance with the court's CM/ECF User Manual, unless otherwise ordered by the court. MA R USDCT CM/ECF Admin(O)(1).

   i. Filers must submit as attachments only those excerpts of the referenced documents that are directly germane to the matter under consideration by the court. Excerpted material must be clearly and prominently identified as such. Users who file excerpts of documents do so without prejudice to their right to timely file additional excerpts or the complete document, as may be allowed by the court. Responding parties may timely file additional excerpts or the complete document that they believe are directly germane. MA R USDCT CM/ECF Admin(O)(2).

   ii. Filers shall not attach as an exhibit any pleading or other paper already on file with the court in that case, but shall merely refer to that document. (See MA R USDCT CM/ECF Admin(G) for information on using hyperlinks in PDF documents filed in CM/ECF.) MA R USDCT CM/ECF Admin(O)(3).

d. *Redacted documents.* The parties may request or the court may require the submission of documents that have been redacted/stripped of sensitive or confidential information. The redacted document prepared for electronic filing shall include the original caption of the document, and be clearly labeled as "Redacted Document." A specific event is available for this purpose ("Redacted Document"), found under the Other Filings/Other Documents menu option. MA R USDCT CM/ECF Admin(S).

   i. Attorneys and pro se litigants are advised to take extra care when creating PDF documents intended for submission to CM/ECF. Steps shall be taken to ensure the documents are free of any hidden data (metadata) that may contain redacted information, or traces of information edited or deleted are not hidden in the final document. Even PDF content that has been encrypted may be recovered. An advisory document with additional information on this topic may be found on the court's website. MA R USDCT CM/ECF Admin(S).

e. *Hyperlinks.* Electronically filed documents may contain the following types of hyperlinks: (1) hyperlinks to other portions of the same document; (2) hyperlinks to other documents filed within the CM/ECF system; and (3) hyperlinks to a location on the Internet that contains a source document for a citation. MA R USDCT CM/ECF Admin(G)(7).

   i. Hyperlinks to cited authority may not replace standard citation format. Complete citations must be included in the text of the filed document. Neither a hyperlink, nor any site to which it refers, shall be considered part of the record, but are simply convenient mechanisms for accessing material cited in a document filed in CM/ECF. Instructions on creating hyperlinks may be found in the CM/ECF User Manual. MA R USDCT CM/ECF Admin(G)(7).

   ii. The court accepts no responsibility for, and does not endorse, any product, organization, or content at any hyperlinked site, or at any site to which that site may be linked. The court accepts no responsibility for the availability or functionality of any hyperlink. MA R USDCT CM/ECF Admin(G)(7).

   iii. One feature of PDF/A documents is that hyperlinks are commonly "masked," meaning that the full address of the referenced file is not written out; for example, clicking the word brief may open a brief which was previously filed in CM/ECF. MA R USDCT CM/ECF Admin(G)(7)(NOTE). An "unmasked" hyperlink has the full address visible to the user. MA R USDCT CM/ECF Admin(G)(7)(NOTE).

   • Masked hyperlinks may or may not work in a PDF/A document, depending on how it was created. Currently, masked hyperlinks are preserved in PDF/A documents produced by the "Save As" method in Microsoft Word 2007 and 2010; the "PDFMaker" method in Microsoft Word 2007; and OpenOffice 2.4 ("PDF Export"). With other production methods, such as WordPerfect, the PDF/A document includes underlined words that appear to be links, but clicking them has no effect. MA R USDCT CM/ECF Admin(G)(7)(NOTE).

f. *Documents features not accepted.* CM/ECF will not accept PDF documents containing tracking tags, embedded systems commands, password protections, access restrictions or other security features, special tags or dynamic features. MA R USDCT CM/ECF Admin(G)(8).

g. *File size limitations.* A filing party shall limit the size of each PDF file to no more than twenty (20) megabytes. PDF files larger than seven (7) megabytes will be rejected by the CM/ECF system. The filer will see a message advising of the size limitation. MA R USDCT CM/ECF Admin(P)(2).

   i. Larger documents or exhibits may be submitted electronically if split into separate PDF files each less than seven (7) megabytes, attached to the main document and clearly labeled. MA R USDCT CM/ECF Admin(P)(2).

   ii. Documents submitted electronically or on paper are subject to the page limitations set by MA R USDCT LR 7.1(b)(4) or by order of the court. MA R USDCT CM/ECF Admin(P)(1).

h. *Accuracy and readability.* The filer shall verify the accuracy and readability of any PDF file before electronically filing it in CM/ECF. MA R USDCT CM/ECF Admin(G)(6); MA R USDCT CM/ECF Admin(P)(3).

3. *Signing of pleadings, motions and other papers*

a. *Signature.* Every pleading, written motion, and other paper must be signed by at least one attorney of record in the attorney's name—or by a party personally if the party is unrepresented. The paper must state the signer's address, e-mail address, and telephone number. FRCP 11(a). The provisions of the Federal Rules of Civil Procedure pertaining to the form and signing of pleadings, motions, and other papers shall be applicable to all papers filed in any proceeding in this court. The board of bar overseers registration number of each attorney signing such documents, except the United States Attorney and his staff, shall be inscribed below the signature. MA R USDCT LR 5.1(a)(1).

i. *Electronic signing.* A filing made through a person's electronic-filing account and authorized by that person, together with that person's name on a signature block, constitutes the person's signature. FRCP 5(d)(3)(C).

ii. *Appearances.* The filing of an appearance or any other pleading signed on behalf of a party constitutes an entry of appearance for that party. All pleadings shall contain the name, bar admission number, address, telephone number, and e-mail address of the attorney entering an appearance. MA R USDCT LR 83.5.2(a).

- *Appearances by law firms.* When a party is represented by a law firm, the appearance must include the name and the signature of at least one individual attorney. When a party is represented by more than one attorney from the same or different law firms, the attorney entering the appearance must designate the individual attorney who is authorized to receive all notices in the case. Any notice sent to an attorney so designated shall be deemed to be proper notice unless the court finds that notice was not properly sent. MA R USDCT LR 83.5.2(b).

- For more information on appearances, refer to MA R USDCT LR 83.5.2.

iii. *Signatures of attorneys.* The user login and password required to submit documents to the CM/ECF system shall serve as that user's signature for purposes of FRCP 11 and for all other purposes under the Federal Rules of Civil Procedure and the Local Rules of the United States District Court for the District of Massachusetts. All electronically filed documents must include a signature block and must set forth the attorney's name, bar number, address, telephone number and email address. The name of the CM/ECF user under whose log-in and password the document is submitted must be preceded by a "/s/" and typed in the space where the signature would otherwise appear. MA R USDCT CM/ECF Admin(M)(1). For an example, refer to MA R USDCT CM/ECF Admin(M)(1).

iv. *Signatures of pro se parties.* Any document requiring a signature that is filed by a party appearing pro se shall bear the words "pro se" following that party's signature. Any such document shall also state the party's mailing address, telephone number (if any), and e-mail address (if the party has consented to service by email). MA R USDCT LR 83.5.5(g). For more information on practice by pro se litigants, refer to MA R USDCT LR 83.5.5.

v. *Multiple signatures.* The filer of any document requiring more than one signature (e.g, stipulations, joint motions, joint status reports, magistrate judge consent forms, etc.) must list thereon all the names of other signatories by means of a "/s/ name of signatory" block for each. By submitting such a document, the filing attorney certifies that each of the other signatories has expressly agreed to the form and substance of the document and that the filing attorney has their actual authority to submit the document electronically. MA R USDCT CM/ECF Admin(M)(2). For more information, refer to MA R USDCT CM/ECF Admin(M)(2).

vi. *Affidavits.* Except as provided in MA R USDCT CM/ECF Admin(L), affidavits shall be filed electronically; however, the electronically filed version must contain a "/s/ name of signatory" block indicating that the paper document bears an original signature. MA R USDCT CM/ECF Admin(M)(3). The court will also accept a scanned version of the original, signed document. MA R USDCT CM/ECF Admin(M)(3). For more information, refer to MA R USDCT CM/ECF Admin(M)(3).

vii. *No verification or accompanying affidavit required for pleadings.* Unless a rule or statute specifically states otherwise, a pleading need not be verified or accompanied by an affidavit. FRCP 11(a).

viii. *Unsigned papers.* The court must strike an unsigned paper unless the omission is promptly corrected after being called to the attorney's or party's attention. FRCP 11(a).

b. *Representations to the court.* By presenting to the court a pleading, written motion, or other paper—whether by signing, filing, submitting, or later advocating it—an attorney or unrepresented party certifies that to the best of the person's knowledge, information, and belief, formed after an inquiry reasonable under the circumstances:

i. It is not being presented for any improper purpose, such as to harass, cause unnecessary delay, or needlessly increase the cost of litigation;

    ii.   The claims, defenses, and other legal contentions are warranted by existing law or by a nonfrivolous argument for extending, modifying, or reversing existing law or for establishing new law;

    iii.  The factual contentions have evidentiary support or, if specifically so identified, will likely have evidentiary support after a reasonable opportunity for further investigation or discovery; and

    iv.  The denials of factual contentions are warranted on the evidence or, if specifically so identified, are reasonably based on belief or a lack of information. FRCP 11(b).

  c.  *Sanctions.* If, after notice and a reasonable opportunity to respond, the court determines that FRCP 11(b) has been violated, the court may impose an appropriate sanction on any attorney, law firm, or party that violated FRCP 11(b) or is responsible for the violation. FRCP 11(c)(1). Refer to the United States District Court for the District of Massachusetts KeyRules Motion for Sanctions document for more information.

4.  *Privacy protection for filings made with the court*

  a.  *Redacted filings.* Unless the court orders otherwise, in an electronic or paper filing with the court that contains an individual's Social Security number, taxpayer-identification number, or birth date, the name of an individual known to be a minor, or a financial-account number, a party or nonparty making the filing may include only:

    i.   The last four (4) digits of the Social Security number and taxpayer-identification number;

    ii.  The year of the individual's birth;

    iii.  The minor's initials; and

    iv.  The last four (4) digits of the financial-account number. FRCP 5.2(a); MA R USDCT CM/ECF Admin(N).

  b.  *Exemptions from the redaction requirement.* The redaction requirement does not apply to the following:

    i.   A financial-account number that identifies the property allegedly subject to forfeiture in a forfeiture proceeding;

    ii.  The record of an administrative or agency proceeding;

    iii.  The official record of a state-court proceeding;

    iv.  The record of a court or tribunal, if that record was not subject to the redaction requirement when originally filed;

    v.  A filing covered by FRCP 5.2(c) or FRCP 5.2(d); and

    vi.  A pro se filing in an action brought under 28 U.S.C.A. § 2241, 28 U.S.C.A. § 2254, or 28 U.S.C.A. § 2255. FRCP 5.2(b).

  c.  *Limitations on remote access to electronic files; Social Security appeals and immigration cases.* Unless the court orders otherwise, in an action for benefits under the Social Security Act, and in an action or proceeding relating to an order of removal, to relief from removal, or to immigration benefits or detention, access to an electronic file is authorized as follows:

    i.   The parties and their attorneys may have remote electronic access to any part of the case file, including the administrative record;

    ii.  Any other person may have electronic access to the full record at the courthouse, but may have remote electronic access only to:

       •  The docket maintained by the court; and

       •  An opinion, order, judgment, or other disposition of the court, but not any other part of the case file or the administrative record. FRCP 5.2(c).

  d.  *Filings made under seal.* The court may order that a filing be made under seal without redaction. The court may later unseal the filing or order the person who made the filing to file a redacted version for the public record. FRCP 5.2(d).

  e.  *Protective orders.* For good cause, the court may by order in a case:

    i.   Require redaction of additional information; or

    ii.  Limit or prohibit a nonparty's remote electronic access to a document filed with the court. FRCP 5.2(e).

  f.  *Option for additional unredacted filing under seal.* A person making a redacted filing may also file an unredacted copy under seal. The court must retain the unredacted copy as part of the record. FRCP 5.2(f). For more information, refer to MA R USDCT LR 7.2.

  g.  *Option for filing a reference list.* A filing that contains redacted information may be filed together with a reference list that identifies each item of redacted information and specifies an appropriate identifier that uniquely corresponds to each item listed. The list must be filed under seal and may be amended as of right. Any reference in the case to a listed identifier will be construed to refer to the corresponding item of information. FRCP 5.2(g).

h. *Responsibility for redaction.* The clerk's office is not responsible for reviewing documents filed with the court to determine whether pleadings have been redacted and are in the proper form. MA R USDCT CM/ECF Admin(N).

i. *Waiver of protection of identifiers.* A person waives the protection of FRCP 5.2(a) as to the person's own information by filing it without redaction and not under seal. FRCP 5.2(h).

## F. Filing and Service Requirements

1. *Filing requirements*

   a. *Required filings.* Any paper after the complaint that is required to be served must be filed no later than a reasonable time after service. FRCP 5(d)(1).

      i. Except as noted in FRCP 33 to FRCP 36, the original of all papers required to be served under FRCP 5(d) shall, unless otherwise submitted to the court, be filed in the office of the clerk within seven (7) days after service has been made. MA R USDCT LR 5.1(b). Except as otherwise provided by the Federal Rules of Civil Procedure, proof of service of all pleadings and other papers required to be served (except discovery papers that in accordance with FRCP 33 to FRCP 36(f) are not to be filed) shall be filed in the office of the clerk promptly after service has been made. MA R USDCT LR 5.2(b)(1).

   b. *Nonelectronic filing.* A paper not filed electronically is filed by delivering it: (1) to the clerk; or (2) to a judge who agrees to accept it for filing, and who must then note the filing date on the paper and promptly send it to the clerk. FRCP 5(d)(2).

   c. *Electronic filing.* Unless exempt or otherwise ordered by the court, all pleadings and other papers submitted to the court must be filed, signed, and verified by electronic means as provided in MA R USDCT LR 5.4. MA R USDCT LR 5.4(A); MA R USDCT CM/ECF Admin(A)(1). All electronic filings must be made in accordance with the Administrative Procedures for Electronic Case Filing in the United States District Court for the District of Massachusetts (MA R USDCT CM/ECF Admin). MA R USDCT LR 5.4(B). The court may deviate from the Administrative Procedures for Electronic Case Filing in the United States District Court for the District of Massachusetts (MA R USDCT CM/ECF Admin) in specific cases, without prior notice, if deemed appropriate in the exercise of discretion, considering the need for the just, speedy, and inexpensive determination of matters pending before the court. MA R USDCT CM/ECF Admin(C)(1). The court may excuse a failure to comply with any administrative procedure whenever justice so requires. MA R USDCT CM/ECF Admin(C)(2).

      i. *By a represented person; Generally required; Exceptions.* A person represented by an attorney must file electronically, unless nonelectronic filing is allowed by the court for good cause or is allowed or required by local rule. FRCP 5(d)(3)(A).

      ii. *By unrepresented person; When allowed or required.* A person not represented by an attorney: (1) may file electronically only if allowed by court order or by local rule; and (2) may be required to file electronically only by court order, or by a local rule that includes reasonable exceptions. FRCP 5(d)(3)(B).

      iii. *Exemptions from electronic filing*

         • *Documents that should not be filed electronically.* The following types of documents must not be filed electronically, and will not be scanned into the ECF system by the clerk's office: (1) sealed documents; (2) ex parte motions; (3) documents generated as part of an alternative dispute resolution (ADR) process; (4) the administrative record in Social Security and other administrative proceedings; (5) the state court record in proceedings under 28 U.S.C.A. § 2254; and (6) such other types of documents as the clerk may direct in the Administrative Procedures for Electronic Case Filing in the United States District Court for the District of Massachusetts (MA R USDCT CM/ECF Admin). MA R USDCT LR 5.4(G)(1); MA R USDCT CM/ECF Admin(L).

         • *Documents that need not be filed electronically.* The following types of documents need not be filed electronically, but may be scanned into the ECF system by a filing party or the clerk's office: (1) handwritten pleadings; (2) documents filed by pro se litigants who are incarcerated or who are not registered ECF users; (3) indictments, informations, criminal complaints, and the criminal JS45 form; (4) affidavits for search or arrest warrants and related documents; (5) documents received from another court under FRCRP 20 or FRCRP 40; (6) appearance bonds; (7) any document in a criminal case containing the original signature of a defendant, such as a waiver of indictment or a plea agreement; (8) petitions for violations of supervised release; (9) executed service of process documents under FRCP 4; and (10) such other types of documents as the clerk may direct in the Administrative Procedures for Electronic Case Filing in the United States District Court for the District of Massachusetts (MA R USDCT CM/ECF Admin). MA R USDCT LR 5.4(G)(2); MA R USDCT CM/ECF Admin(L).

- For more information on exemptions from electronic filing, refer to MA R USDCT CM/ECF Admin(L).

iv. *Consequences of electronic filing.* Electronic transmission of a document to the CM/ECF system, together with the transmission of a Notice of Electronic Filing (NEF) from the court at the completion of the transaction, constitutes the filing of the document for all purposes of the Federal Rules of Procedure and constitutes entry of the document on the docket maintained by the clerk pursuant to FRCP 58 and FRCP 79. MA R USDCT CM/ECF Admin(G)(1).

v. *Payment of filing fees.* When electronically filing any pleading or paper through CM/ECF that requires a fee, all registered ECF users are to pay the fee electronically through the Treasury Department's Internet payment process. MA R USDCT LR 67.4(d); MA R USDCT CM/ECF Admin(A)(1). Pro se filers and those who have been exempted from electronic filing and/or electronic payment of fees may submit payments by check or money order made payable to "Clerk, U.S. District Court". MA R USDCT LR 67.4(d). For more information on filing fees, refer to MA R USDCT LR 67.4 and MA R USDCT CM/ECF Admin(I).

vi. For more information on electronic filing, refer to MA R USDCT CM/ECF Admin.

d. *Email or fax filing.* In general, the court does not accept documents by email or by fax. If the court, in special circumstances, does authorize the submission of a document in that manner, the document shall not be considered filed until an NEF is generated by CM/ECF at the completion of the transaction. MA R USDCT CM/ECF Admin(H)(5).

2. *Service requirements.* All papers filed pursuant to MA R USDCT LR 7.1(b) shall be served unless the moving party indicates in writing on the face of the motion that ex parte consideration is requested. Motions filed "ex parte" and related papers need not be served until the motion has been ruled upon or the court orders that service be made. MA R USDCT LR 7.1(c). Service of all pleadings subsequent to the original complaint and of all other papers required to be served shall be made in the manner specified by FRCP 5. MA R USDCT LR 5.2(a).

a. *Service; When required*

i. *In general.* Unless the Federal Rules of Civil Procedure provide otherwise, each of the following papers must be served on every party:

- An order stating that service is required;
- A pleading filed after the original complaint, unless the court orders otherwise under FRCP 5(c) because there are numerous defendants;
- A discovery paper required to be served on a party, unless the court orders otherwise;
- A written motion, except one that may be heard ex parte; and
- A written notice, appearance, demand, or offer of judgment, or any similar paper. FRCP 5(a)(1).

ii. *If a party fails to appear.* No service is required on a party who is in default for failing to appear. But a pleading that asserts a new claim for relief against such a party must be served on that party under FRCP 4. FRCP 5(a)(2).

iii. *Seizing property.* If an action is begun by seizing property and no person is or need be named as a defendant, any service required before the filing of an appearance, answer, or claim must be made on the person who had custody or possession of the property when it was seized. FRCP 5(a)(3).

b. *Service; How made*

i. *Serving an attorney.* If a party is represented by an attorney, service under FRCP 5 must be made on the attorney unless the court orders service on the party. FRCP 5(b)(1).

- *Nonresident attorney.* On application of a party, the court may order an attorney who represents any other party and who does not maintain an office within this district where service can be made on him by delivery as provided by FRCP 5(b), to designate a member of the bar of this court who does maintain such an office to receive service of all pleadings and other papers in his behalf. MA R USDCT LR 5.2(c)(1).

ii. *Serving a party acting pro se.* On application of a party, the court may order any other party who is appearing without an attorney and who does not maintain an office or residence within this district where service can be made on him by delivery as provided by FRCP 5(b), to designate an address within the district at which service can be made on him by delivery. MA R USDCT LR 5.2(c)(2).

iii. *Service in general.* A paper is served under FRCP 5 by:

- Handing it to the person;

- Leaving it: (1) at the person's office with a clerk or other person in charge or, if no one is in charge, in a conspicuous place in the office; or (2) if the person has no office or the office is closed, at the person's dwelling or usual place of abode with someone of suitable age and discretion who resides there;

- Mailing it to the person's last known address—in which event service is complete upon mailing;

- Leaving it with the court clerk if the person has no known address;

- Sending it to a registered user by filing it with the court's electronic-filing system or sending it by other electronic means that the person consented to in writing—in either of which events service is complete upon filing or sending, but is not effective if the filer or sender learns that it did not reach the person to be served; or

- Delivering it by any other means that the person consented to in writing—in which event service is complete when the person making service delivers it to the agency designated to make delivery. FRCP 5(b)(2).

iv. *Service by electronic means.* Unless exempt or otherwise ordered by the court, all pleadings and other papers must be served on other parties by electronic means. MA R USDCT LR 5.4(C); MA R USDCT CM/ECF Admin(H)(2). Service by electronic means shall be treated the same as service by mail. MA R USDCT CM/ECF Admin(H)(4).

- *Consent to electronic service.* Registering to use CM/ECF constitutes consent to service of all documents by electronic means as provided in the Administrative Procedures for Electronic Case Filing in the United States District Court for the District of Massachusetts (MA R USDCT CM/ECF Admin) and FRCP 5(b) and FRCP 77(d). MA R USDCT CM/ECF Admin(E)(6); MA R USDCT CM/ECF Admin(H)(3).

- *Service on registered ECF users.* Transmission of the Notice of Electronic Filing (NEF) through the court's transmission facilities will constitute service of the filed document upon a registered ECF user. MA R USDCT LR 5.4(C).

- *Service on non-registered users.* The party filing the document electronically is responsible for serving a paper copy of the document by mail in accordance with FRCP 5(b) to those case participants who have not been identified on the NEF as electronic recipients. MA R USDCT CM/ECF Admin(H)(3).

- *Service of conventionally filed papers.* Documents or exhibits submitted conventionally shall be served on other parties by the filer using traditional means. MA R USDCT CM/ECF Admin(P)(4).

c. *Serving numerous defendants*

i. *In general.* If an action involves an unusually large number of defendants, the court may, on motion or on its own, order that:

- Defendants' pleadings and replies to them need not be served on other defendants;

- Any crossclaim, counterclaim, avoidance, or affirmative defense in those pleadings and replies to them will be treated as denied or avoided by all other parties; and

- Filing any such pleading and serving it on the plaintiff constitutes notice of the pleading to all parties. FRCP 5(c)(1).

ii. *Notifying parties.* A copy of every such order must be served on the parties as the court directs. FRCP 5(c)(2).

# G. Hearings

1. *Hearings, generally.* If the court concludes that there should be a hearing on a motion, the motion will be set down for hearing at such time as the court determines. MA R USDCT LR 7.1(e).

a. *Oral argument.* Due process does not require that oral argument be permitted on a motion and, except as otherwise provided by local rule, the district court has discretion to determine whether it will decide the motion on the papers or hear argument by counsel (and perhaps receive evidence). FPP § 1190; F.D.I.C. v. Deglau, 207 F.3d 153 (3d Cir. 2000).

i. *Evidence on a motion.* When a motion relies on facts outside the record, the court may hear the matter on affidavits or may hear it wholly or partly on oral testimony or on depositions. FRCP 43(c).

b. *Providing a regular schedule for oral hearings.* A court may establish regular times and places for oral hearings on motions. FRCP 78(a).

c. *Providing for submission on briefs.* By rule or order, the court may provide for submitting and determining motions on briefs, without oral hearings. FRCP 78(b). Motions that are not set down for hearing as provided in MA R USDCT LR 7.1(e) will be decided on the papers submitted after an opposition to the motion has been filed, or, if no opposition is filed, after the time for filing an opposition has elapsed. MA R USDCT LR 7.1(f).

2. *Conflict of court appearances.* For information on conflict of court appearances, refer to MA R USDCT LR 40.2.

## H. Forms

### 1. Federal Motion for Leave to Amend Forms

a. Leave to amend complaint; Attaching copy of amendment. 2C FEDFORMS § 14:18.

b. Leave to amend complaint; Inserting amendment. 2C FEDFORMS § 14:19.

c. Leave to amend complaint; Interlineation. 2C FEDFORMS § 14:20.

d. Leave to amend complaint; Responding to motion to dismiss complaint. 2C FEDFORMS § 14:21.

e. Leave to amend complaint; Close to trial. 2C FEDFORMS § 14:22.

f. Leave to amend complaint; Adding new count. 2C FEDFORMS § 14:24.

g. Leave to amend complaint; Asserting lack of knowledge of facts at time of original complaint. 2C FEDFORMS § 14:25.

h. Leave to amend complaint; Seeking fourth amendment. 2C FEDFORMS § 14:26.

i. Leave to amend complaint; Substituting plaintiff and dropping defendant. 2C FEDFORMS § 14:27.

j. Leave to amend answer. 2C FEDFORMS § 14:30.

k. Leave to amend answer; With leave endorsed. 2C FEDFORMS § 14:31.

l. Leave to amend answer; Correcting errors, deleting and interlining. 2C FEDFORMS § 14:32.

m. Leave to amend answer; Adding paragraph. 2C FEDFORMS § 14:33.

n. Leave to amend answer; Adding defense. 2C FEDFORMS § 14:34.

o. Leave to amend answer; During trial. 2C FEDFORMS § 14:35.

p. Defendant's response to motion for leave to amend complaint a fourth time. 2C FEDFORMS § 14:36.

q. Motion and notice; For leave to file amended pleading. FEDPROF § 1A:334.

r. Motion; To amend pleading to conform to findings of master. FEDPROF § 1A:335.

s. Affidavit; In support of motion for amendment of pleading. FEDPROF § 1A:342.

t. Opposition; To motion. FEDPROF § 1B:175.

u. Affidavit; Supporting or opposing motion. FEDPROF § 1B:176.

v. Brief; Supporting or opposing motion. FEDPROF § 1B:177.

w. Statement of points and authorities; Opposing motion. FEDPROF § 1B:178.

x. Motion for leave to amend pleading. GOLDLTGFMS § 14:3.

y. Motion to file second amended complaint on ground of newly discovered evidence. GOLDLTGFMS § 14:20.

z. Motion for leave to file amended answer. GOLDLTGFMS § 14:22.

### 2. Forms for the District of Massachusetts

a. Notice of filing with clerk's office. MA R USDCT CM/ECF Admin(Appendix I).

## I. Applicable Rules

### 1. *Federal rules*

a. Serving and filing pleadings and other papers. FRCP 5.

b. Constitutional challenge to a statute; Notice, certification, and intervention. FRCP 5.1.

c. Privacy protection for filings made with the court. FRCP 5.2.

d. Computing and extending time; Time for motion papers. FRCP 6.

e. Pleadings allowed; Form of motions and other papers. FRCP 7.

    f.   Form of pleadings. FRCP 10.

    g.   Signing pleadings, motions, and other papers; Representations to the court; Sanctions. FRCP 11.

    h.   Amended and supplemental pleadings. FRCP 15.

    i.   Taking testimony. FRCP 43.

    j.   Hearing motions; Submission on briefs. FRCP 78.

2.   *Local rules*

    a.   Title. MA R USDCT LR 1.1.

    b.   Sanctions. MA R USDCT LR 1.3.

    c.   Form and filing of papers. MA R USDCT LR 5.1.

    d.   Service and filing of pleadings and other papers. MA R USDCT LR 5.2.

    e.   Filing and service by electronic means. MA R USDCT LR 5.4.

    f.   Motion practice. MA R USDCT LR 7.1.

    g.   Addition of new parties. MA R USDCT LR 15.1.

    h.   Alternative dispute resolution. MA R USDCT LR 16.4.

    i.   Payments and deposits made with the clerk. MA R USDCT LR 67.4.

    j.   Settlement. MA R USDCT LR 68.2.

    k.   Office of the clerk. MA R USDCT LR 77.2.

    l.   Appearances. MA R USDCT LR 83.5.2.

    m.   Practice by pro se litigants. MA R USDCT LR 83.5.5.

    n.   CM/ECF case management/electronic case files administrative procedures. MA R USDCT CM/ECF Admin.

# Motions, Oppositions and Replies
## Motion for Continuance/Extension of Time

### Document Last Updated December 2018

**A. Checklist**

(I)  ❑ Matters to be considered by moving party

  (a)  ❑ Required documents

    (1)  ❑ Notice of motion and motion

    (2)  ❑ Memorandum

    (3)  ❑ Certificate of service

  (b)  ❑ Supplemental documents

    (1)  ❑ Supporting evidence

    (2)  ❑ Medical certificate

    (3)  ❑ Notice of constitutional question

    (4)  ❑ Nongovernmental corporate disclosure statement

    (5)  ❑ Proposed order

    (6)  ❑ Compact disk with copy of document(s) in PDF format

    (7)  ❑ Notice of filing with clerk's office

    (8)  ❑ Additional copies

    (9)  ❑ Courtesy copies

  (c)  ❑ Timing

    (1)  ❑ Motion for continuance: there are no specific timing requirements for moving for a continuance

(2) ☐ Motion for extension of time: when an act may or must be done within a specified time, the court may, for good cause, extend the time: (i) with or without motion or notice if the court acts, or if a request is made, before the original time or its extension expires; or (ii) on motion made after the time has expired if the party failed to act because of excusable neglect

(3) ☐ A written motion and notice of the hearing must be served at least fourteen (14) days before the time specified for the hearing, with the following exceptions: (i) when the motion may be heard ex parte; (ii) when the Federal Rules of Civil Procedure set a different time; or (iii) when a court order—which a party may, for good cause, apply for ex parte—sets a different time

(4) ☐ Any affidavit supporting a motion must be served with the motion

(5) ☐ Except as noted in FRCP 33 to FRCP 36, the original of all papers required to be served under FRCP 5(d) shall, unless otherwise submitted to the court, be filed in the office of the clerk within seven (7) days after service has been made

(II) ☐ Matters to be considered by opposing party

  (a) ☐ Required documents

    (1) ☐ Opposition

    (2) ☐ Certificate of service

  (b) ☐ Supplemental documents

    (1) ☐ Supporting evidence

    (2) ☐ Notice of constitutional question

    (3) ☐ Compact disk with copy of document(s) in PDF format

    (4) ☐ Notice of filing with clerk's office

    (5) ☐ Additional copies

    (6) ☐ Courtesy copies

  (c) ☐ Timing

    (1) ☐ A party opposing a motion, shall file an opposition within fourteen (14) days after the motion is served, unless another period is fixed by rule or statute, or by order of the court

    (2) ☐ Except as FRCP 59(c) provides otherwise, any opposing affidavit must be served at least seven (7) days before the hearing, unless the court permits service at another time

    (3) ☐ Except as noted in FRCP 33 to FRCP 36, the original of all papers required to be served under FRCP 5(d) shall, unless otherwise submitted to the court, be filed in the office of the clerk within seven (7) days after service has been made

## B. Timing

1. *Motion for continuance.* There are no specific timing requirements for moving for a continuance.

2. *Motion for extension of time.* When an act may or must be done within a specified time, the court may, for good cause, extend the time: (1) with or without motion or notice if the court acts, or if a request is made, before the original time or its extension expires; or (2) on motion made after the time has expired if the party failed to act because of excusable neglect. FRCP 6(b)(1).

3. *Timing of motions, generally*

  a. *Motion and notice of hearing.* A written motion and notice of the hearing must be served at least fourteen (14) days before the time specified for the hearing, with the following exceptions:

    i. When the motion may be heard ex parte;

    ii. When the Federal Rules of Civil Procedure set a different time; or

    iii. When a court order—which a party may, for good cause, apply for ex parte—sets a different time. FRCP 6(c)(1).

  b. *Supporting affidavit.* Any affidavit supporting a motion must be served with the motion. FRCP 6(c)(2).

4. *Timing of opposing papers.* A party opposing a motion, shall file an opposition within fourteen (14) days after the motion is served, unless (1) the motion is for summary judgment, in which case the opposition shall be filed within twenty-one (21)

days after the motion is served, or (2) another period is fixed by rule or statute, or by order of the court. MA R USDCT LR 7.1(b)(2); MA R USDCT CM/ECF Admin(H)(4). The fourteen (14) day period is intended to include the period specified by the civil rules for mailing time and provide for a uniform period regardless of the use of the mails. MA R USDCT LR 7.1(b)(2).

  a. *Opposing affidavit.* Except as FRCP 59(c) provides otherwise, any opposing affidavit must be served at least seven (7) days before the hearing, unless the court permits service at another time. FRCP 6(c)(2).

5. *Timing of reply papers.* [W]here the respondent files an answering affidavit setting up a new matter, the moving party ordinarily is allowed a reasonable time to file a reply affidavit since failure to deny the new matter by affidavit may operate as an admission of its truth. AMJUR MOTIONS § 25.

  a. *Leave of court required.* All other papers not filed as indicated in MA R USDCT LR 7.1(b)(1) and MA R USDCT LR 7.1(b)(2), whether in the form of a reply brief or otherwise, may be submitted only with leave of court. MA R USDCT LR 7.1(b)(3).

6. *Filing after service.* Except as noted in FRCP 33 to FRCP 36, the original of all papers required to be served under FRCP 5(d) shall, unless otherwise submitted to the court, be filed in the office of the clerk within seven (7) days after service has been made. MA R USDCT LR 5.1(b).

7. *Computation of time*

  a. *Computing time.* FRCP 6 applies in computing any time period specified in the Federal Rules of Civil Procedure, in any local rule or court order, or in any statute that does not specify a method of computing time. FRCP 6(a).

   i. *Period stated in days or a longer unit.* When the period is stated in days or a longer unit of time:
   - Exclude the day of the event that triggers the period;
   - Count every day, including intermediate Saturdays, Sundays, and legal holidays; and
   - Include the last day of the period, but if the last day is a Saturday, Sunday, or legal holiday, the period continues to run until the end of the next day that is not a Saturday, Sunday, or legal holiday. FRCP 6(a)(1).

   ii. *Period stated in hours.* When the period is stated in hours:
   - Begin counting immediately on the occurrence of the event that triggers the period;
   - Count every hour, including hours during intermediate Saturdays, Sundays, and legal holidays; and
   - If the period would end on a Saturday, Sunday, or legal holiday, the period continues to run until the same time on the next day that is not a Saturday, Sunday, or legal holiday. FRCP 6(a)(2).

   iii. *Office of the clerk.* The offices of the Clerk of Court at Boston, Worcester and Springfield shall be open from 8:30 a.m. until 5:00 p.m. on all days except Saturdays, Sundays, legal holidays and other days so ordered by the court and announced in advance, if feasible. MA R USDCT LR 77.2.

   iv. *Inaccessibility of the clerk's office.* Unless the court orders otherwise, if the clerk's office is inaccessible:
   - On the last day for filing under FRCP 6(a)(1), then the time for filing is extended to the first accessible day that is not a Saturday, Sunday, or legal holiday; or
   - During the last hour for filing under FRCP 6(a)(2), then the time for filing is extended to the same time on the first accessible day that is not a Saturday, Sunday, or legal holiday. FRCP 6(a)(3).

   v. *"Last day" defined.* Unless a different time is set by a statute, local rule, or court order, the last day ends:
   - For electronic filing, at midnight in the court's time zone; and
   - For filing by other means, when the clerk's office is scheduled to close. FRCP 6(a)(4).

   vi. *"Next day" defined.* The "next day" is determined by continuing to count forward when the period is measured after an event and backward when measured before an event. FRCP 6(a)(5).

   vii. *"Legal holiday" defined.* "Legal holiday" means:
   - The day set aside by statute for observing New Year's Day, Martin Luther King Jr.'s Birthday, Washington's Birthday, Memorial Day, Independence Day, Labor Day, Columbus Day, Veterans' Day, Thanksgiving Day, or Christmas Day;
   - Any day declared a holiday by the President or Congress; and
   - For periods that are measured after an event, any other day declared a holiday by the state where the district court is located. FRCP 6(a)(6).

b. *Computation of electronic filing deadlines.* Filing documents electronically does not alter any filing deadlines. MA R USDCT CM/ECF Admin(K); MA R USDCT LR 5.4(D). Although CM/ECF is generally available twenty-four (24) hours a day for filing, all electronic transmissions of documents must be completed prior to 6:00 PM, Eastern Standard (or Daylight Savings) Time, on the date on which it is due, in order to be considered timely filed that day. MA R USDCT CM/ECF Admin(K); MA R USDCT LR 5.4(D). When a specific time of day deadline is set by court order or stipulation, the electronic filing must be completed by that time. Documents may be filed at any time of the day on days prior to the date on which it is due. MA R USDCT CM/ECF Admin(K). A document filed electronically shall be deemed filed as of the time and date stated on the NEF received from the court. MA R USDCT CM/ECF Admin(G)(2); MA R USDCT CM/ECF Admin(K).

   i. *Technical failures.* A user whose filing is made untimely as the result of a technical failure of the court's CM/ECF system may seek appropriate relief from the court. MA R USDCT CM/ECF Admin(W)(3). Technical difficulties on the filer's end, with telephone, cable lines, the filer's Internet Service Provider (ISP), or hardware or software problems, will not constitute a technical failure under the Administrative Procedures for Electronic Case Filing in the United States District Court for the District of Massachusetts (MA R USDCT CM/ECF Admin) nor excuse an untimely filing. MA R USDCT CM/ECF Admin(W)(3). As help desk support is available during normal business hours, filers are strongly urged to electronically file any documents during that period. MA R USDCT CM/ECF Admin(W)(3).

   - The court has made available a public terminal (computers and scanner) in each clerk's office for registered users to scan and electronically file documents. This equipment is available during normal business hours. Users should bring their prepared document and a valid CM/ECF login and password. MA R USDCT CM/ECF Admin(W)(3).

c. *Extending time.* Refer to the General Requirements section of this document for information on extending time.

d. *Additional time after certain kinds of service.* When a party may or must act within a specified time after being served and service is made under FRCP 5(b)(2)(C) (by mail), FRCP 5(b)(2)(D) (by leaving with the clerk), or FRCP 5(b)(2)(F) (by other means consented to), three (3) days are added after the period would otherwise expire under FRCP 6(a). FRCP 6(d).

## C. General Requirements

1. *Motions, generally*

   a. *Requirements.* A request for a court order must be made by motion. The motion must:

      i. Be in writing unless made during a hearing or trial;

      ii. State with particularity the grounds for seeking the order; and

      iii. State the relief sought. FRCP 7(b)(1).

   b. *Notice of motion.* A party interested in resisting the relief sought by a motion has a right to notice thereof, and an opportunity to be heard. AMJUR MOTIONS § 12.

      i. [I]n addition to statutory or court rule provisions requiring notice of a motion—the purpose of such a notice requirement having been said to be to prevent a party from being prejudicially surprised by a motion—principles of natural justice dictate that an adverse party generally must be given notice that a motion will be presented to the court. AMJUR MOTIONS § 12.

      ii. "Notice," in this regard, means reasonable notice, including a meaningful opportunity to prepare and to defend against allegations of a motion. AMJUR MOTIONS § 12.

   c. *Writing requirement.* The writing requirement is intended to [ensure] that the adverse parties are informed and have a record of both the motion's pendency and the grounds on which the movant seeks an order. FPP § 1191; Feldberg v. Quechee Lakes Corp., 463 F.3d 195 (2d Cir. 2006). [A] single written document can satisfy the writing requirements both for a motion and for [an] FRCP 6(c)(1) notice. FRCP 7(Advisory Committee Notes).

   d. *Particularity requirement.* The particularity requirement [ensures] that the opposing parties will have notice of their opponent's contentions. FEDPROC § 62:358; Goodman v. 1973 26 Foot Trojan Vessel, Arkansas Registration No. AR1439SN, 859 F.2d 71 (8th Cir. 1988). That requirement ensures that notice of the basis for the motion is provided to the court and to the opposing party so as to avoid prejudice, provide the opponent with a meaningful opportunity to respond, and provide the court with enough information to process the motion correctly. FEDPROC § 62:358; Andreas v. Volkswagen of Am., Inc., 336 F.3d 789 (8th Cir. 2003).

      i. Reasonable specification of the grounds for a motion is sufficient. The particularity requirement for motions is satisfied when no party is prejudiced by a lack of particularity or when the court can comprehend the basis for the motion and deal with it fairly. However, where a movant fails to state even one ground for granting the motion in question, the movant has failed to meet the minimal standard of "reasonable specification." FEDPROC § 62:358; Martinez v. Trainor, 556 F.2d 818 (7th Cir. 1977).

    ii.    The court may excuse the failure to comply with the particularity requirement if it is inadvertent, and where no prejudice is shown by the opposing party. FEDPROC § 62:358.

e.    *Control of motion practice*

    i.    *Plan for the disposition of motions.* At the earliest practicable time, the judicial officer shall establish a framework for the disposition of motions, which, at the discretion of the judicial officer, may include specific deadlines or general time guidelines for filing motions. This framework may be amended from time to time by the judicial officer as required by the progress of the case. MA R USDCT LR 7.1(a)(1).

    ii.    *Motion practice.* No motion shall be filed unless counsel certify that they have conferred and have attempted in good faith to resolve or narrow the issue. MA R USDCT LR 7.1(a)(2).

    iii.    *Unresolved motions.* The court shall rule on motions as soon as practicable, having in mind the reporting requirements set forth in the Civil Justice Reform Act. MA R USDCT LR 7.1(a)(3).

2.    *Motion for continuance.* A motion for the continuance of a trial, evidentiary hearing, or any other proceeding, will be granted only for good cause. MA R USDCT LR 40.3(a).

a.    *Grounds for continuance.* The grounds upon which a continuance is sought may include the following:

    i.    Unpreparedness of a party. FEDPROC § 77:29; United States v. 110 Bars of Silver, 3 Crucibles of Silver, 11 Bags of Silver Coins, 508 F.2d 799 (5th Cir. 1975).

    ii.    Absence of a party. FEDPROC § 77:29. Since it is generally recognized that a party to a civil action ordinarily has a right to attend the trial, an illness severe enough to prevent a party from appearing in court is always a legitimate ground for asking for a continuance. FEDPROC § 77:30; Davis v. Operation Amigo, Inc., 378 F.2d 101 (10th Cir. 1967). However, the failure of the moving party to produce any competent medical evidence of the reasons and necessities for the party's unavailability will result in the denial of the continuance. FEDPROC § 77:30; Weisman v. Alleco, Inc., 925 F.2d 77 (4th Cir. 1991). Some courts, moreover, require a showing that the party has some particular contribution to make to the trial as a material witness or otherwise before granting a continuance due to the party's illness. FEDPROC § 77:30; Johnston v. Harris Cty. Flood Control Dist., 869 F.2d 1565 (5th Cir. 1989).

    iii.    Absence of counsel. FEDPROC § 77:29. The courts have shown greater leniency when the illness of counsel is the ground for the continuance, especially where the case presents complex issues. FEDPROC § 77:31; Smith-Weik Mach. Corp. v. Murdock Mach. & Eng'g Co., 423 F.2d 842 (5th Cir. 1970). However, many courts do not favor the granting of a continuance where counsel is unavailable due to a claimed engagement elsewhere or where it is not clear that counsel's illness was genuine. FEDPROC § 77:31; Cmty. Nat. Life Ins. Co. v. Parker Square Sav. & Loan Ass'n, 406 F.2d 603 (10th Cir. 1969); Williams v. Johanns, 518 F. Supp. 2d 205 (D.D.C. 2007).

    iv.    Absence of a witness or evidence. FEDPROC § 77:29. The moving party must show. . .that the witness's testimony would be competent and material and that there are no other witnesses who can establish the same facts. FEDPROC § 77:32; Krodel v. Houghtaling, 468 F.2d 887 (4th Cir. 1972); Vitarelle v. Long Island R. Co., 415 F.2d 302 (2d Cir. 1969).

    v.    Surprise and prejudice. FEDPROC § 77:29. The action complained of should not be one which could have been anticipated by due diligence or of which the movant had actual notice. FEDPROC § 77:33; Commc'ns Maint., Inc. v. Motorola, Inc., 761 F.2d 1202 (7th Cir. 1985). Surprise and prejudice are often claimed as a result of the court allowing the other party to amend its pleadings under FRCP 15(b). FEDPROC § 77:29.

b.    *Factors considered in determining whether to grant a continuance.* Absent a controlling statute, the grant or denial of a continuance rests in the discretion of the trial judge, taking into consideration not only the facts of the particular case but also all of the demands on counsel's time and the court's. FEDPROC § 77:28; Star Fin. Servs., Inc. v. AASTAR Mortg. Corp., 89 F.3d 5 (1st Cir. 1996); Streber v. Hunter, 221 F.3d 701 (5th Cir. 2000). In determining whether to grant a continuance, the court will consider a variety of factors, including:

    i.    Good faith on the part of the moving party;

    ii.    Due diligence of the moving party;

iii. The likelihood that the need prompting the request for a continuance will be met if the continuance is granted;

iv. Inconvenience to the court and the nonmoving party, including the witnesses, if the continuance is granted;

v. Possible harm to the moving party if the continuance is denied;

vi. Prior delays in the proceedings;

vii. The court's prior refusal to grant the opposing party a continuance;

viii. Judicial economy. FEDPROC § 77:29; Amarin Plastics, Inc. v. Maryland Cup Corp., 946 F.2d 147 (1st Cir. 1991); Lewis v. Rawson, 564 F.3d 569 (2d Cir. 2009); United States v. 2.61 Acres of Land, More or Less, Situated in Mariposa Cty., State of Cal., 791 F.2d 666 (9th Cir. 1985); In re Homestore.com, Inc. Sec. Litig., 347 F. Supp. 2d 814 (C.D. Cal. 2004).

c. *Conditional granting of continuance.* The judicial officer may condition a continuance upon the payment of expenses caused to the other parties and of jury fees incurred by the court. MA R USDCT LR 40.3(d).

3. *Motion for extension of time*

a. *Generally.* When an act may or must be done within a specified time, the court may, for good cause, extend the time: (1) with or without motion or notice if the court acts, or if a request is made, before the original time or its extension expires; or (2) on motion made after the time has expired if the party failed to act because of excusable neglect. FRCP 6(b)(1).

i. *Exceptions.* A court must not extend the time to act under FRCP 50(b), FRCP 50(d), FRCP 52(b), FRCP 59(b), FRCP 59(d), FRCP 59(e), and FRCP 60(b). FRCP 6(b)(2). FRCP 6(b) does not require the district courts to extend a time period where the [extension] would contravene a local court rule and does not apply to periods of time that are definitely fixed by statute. FEDPROC § 77:4; Truncale v. Universal Pictures Co., 82 F. Supp. 576 (S.D.N.Y. 1949); Lusk v. Lyon Metal Prod., 9 F.R.D. 250 (W.D. Mo. 1949).

b. *Extension of time under FRCP 6(b)(1)(A).* [A]n application for extension of time under FRCP 6(b)(1)(A) normally will be granted in the absence of bad faith on the part of the party seeking relief or prejudice to the adverse party. FPP § 1165. Neither a formal motion for extension nor notice to the adverse party is expressly required by FRCP 6(b). FPP § 1165.

c. *Extension of time under FRCP 6(b)(1)(B).* [N]o relief may be granted under FRCP 6(b)(1)(B) after the expiration of the specified period, even though the failure to act may have been the result of excusable neglect, if no motion is made by the party who failed to act. FEDPROC § 77:3.

i. *Excusable neglect.* Excusable neglect is intended and has proven to be quite elastic in its application. In essence it is an equitable concept that must take account of all relevant circumstances of the party's failure to act within the required time. FPP § 1165.

ii. *Burden.* The burden is on the movant to establish that the failure to act in a timely manner was the result of excusable neglect. FEDPROC § 77:5. Common sense indicates that among the most important factors are the possibility of prejudice to the other parties, the length of the applicant's delay and its impact on the proceeding, the reason for the delay and whether it was within the control of the movant, and whether the movant has acted in good faith. FPP § 1165; Kettle Range Conservation Grp. v. U.S. Forest Serv., 8 F. App'x 729 (9th Cir. 2001). By far the most critical of these factors is the asserted reason for the mistake. FEDPROC § 77:5.

d. *Motion for enlargement of time to serve process.* Counsel and parties appearing pro se who seek to show good cause for the failure to make service within the ninety (90) day period prescribed by FRCP 4(m) shall do so by filing a motion for enlargement of time under FRCP 6(b), together with a supporting affidavit. If on the fourteenth (14th) day following the expiration of the ninety (90) day period good cause has not been shown as provided in MA R USDCT LR 4.1(b), the clerk shall forthwith automatically enter an order of dismissal for failure to effect service of process, without awaiting any further order of the court. MA R USDCT LR 4.1(b). Refer to the United States District Court for the District of Massachusetts KeyRules Complaint document for more information.

4. *Opposing papers.* The Federal Rules of Civil Procedure do not require any formal answer, return, or reply to a motion, except where the Federal Rules of Civil Procedure or local rules may require affidavits, memoranda, or other papers to be filed in opposition to a motion. Such papers are simply to apprise the court of such opposition and the grounds of that opposition. FEDPROC § 62:353.

a. *Effect of failure to respond to motion.* Although in the absence of statutory provision or court rule, a motion ordinarily does not require a written answer, when a party files a motion and the opposing party fails to respond, the court may construe such failure to respond as nonopposition to the motion or an admission that the motion was meritorious, may take the facts alleged in the motion as true—the rule in some jurisdictions being that the failure to respond to a fact set forth in a motion is deemed an admission—and may grant the motion if the relief requested appears to be justified. AMJUR MOTIONS § 28.

b. *Assent or no opposition not determinative.* However, a motion will not be granted automatically simply because an "assent" or a notation of "no opposition" has been filed; federal judges frequently deny motions that have been assented to when it is thought that justice so dictates. FPP § 1190.

c. *Responsive pleading inappropriate as response to motion.* An attempt to answer or oppose a motion with a responsive pleading usually is not appropriate. FPP § 1190.

5. *Reply papers.* A moving party may be required or permitted to prepare papers in addition to his original motion papers. AMJUR MOTIONS § 25. Papers answering or replying to opposing papers may be appropriate, in the interests of justice, where it appears there is a substantial reason for allowing a reply. Thus, a court may accept reply papers where a party demonstrates that the papers to which it seeks to file a reply raise new issues that are material to the disposition of the question before the court, or where the court determines, sua sponte, that it wishes further briefing of an issue raised in those papers and orders the submission of additional papers. FEDPROC § 62:354.

a. *Function of reply papers.* The function of a reply affidavit is to answer the arguments made in opposition to the position taken by the movant and not to permit the movant to introduce new arguments in support of the motion. AMJUR MOTIONS § 25.

b. *Issues raised for the first time in a reply document.* However, the view has been followed in some jurisdictions, that as a matter of judicial economy, where there is no prejudice and where the issues could be raised simply by filing a motion to dismiss, the trial court has discretion to consider arguments raised for the first time in a reply memorandum, and that a trial court may grant a motion to strike issues raised for the first time in a reply memorandum. AMJUR MOTIONS § 26.

6. *Alternative dispute resolution (ADR).* The judicial officer assigned to preside over the case shall encourage the resolution of disputes by settlement or other alternative dispute resolution programs. MA R USDCT LR 16.4(a).

a. *Settlement.* At every conference conducted under the Local Rules of the United States District Court for the District of Massachusetts, the judicial officer shall inquire as to the utility of the parties conducting settlement negotiations, explore means of facilitating those negotiations, and offer whatever assistance may be appropriate in the circumstances. Assistance may include a reference of the case to another judicial officer for settlement purposes. MA R USDCT LR 16.4(b).

i. When a case is settled, the parties shall file with the clerk a signed agreement for judgment or stipulation for dismissal, as appropriate, within twenty-eight (28) days, unless the court otherwise orders. MA R USDCT LR 68.2.

b. *Alternative dispute resolution programs*

i. *Discretion of judicial officer.* The judicial officer, following an exploration of the matter with all counsel, may refer appropriate cases to alternative dispute resolution programs that have been designated for use in the district court or that the judicial officer may make available. The dispute resolution programs described in MA R USDCT LR 16.4(c)(2) through MA R USDCT LR 16.4(c)(4) are illustrative, not exclusive. Moreover, nothing in MA R USDCT LR 16.4 shall preclude the parties from engaging in private dispute resolution programs as long as they comply with any schedule established by the court. MA R USDCT LR 16.4(c)(1).

ii. *Mediation.* The judicial officer may refer the case to mediation upon the agreement of all parties. MA R USDCT LR 16.4(c)(2)(A).

iii. *Other alternative dispute resolution programs.* Use of mediation is not exclusive. At the request of parties, the judicial officer may consider other forms of alternative dispute resolution including, but not limited to, mini-trial, summary jury trial and arbitration. MA R USDCT LR 16.4(c)(3).

c. For more information on alternative dispute resolution (ADR), refer to MA R USDCT LR 16.4.

7. *Sanctions.* Failure to comply with any of the directions or obligations set forth in, or authorized by, these rules may result in dismissal, default, or the imposition of other sanctions as deemed appropriate by the judicial officer. MA R USDCT LR 1.3. Except as provided by law, the court may impose sanctions as provided in MA R USDCT LR 1.3 for failure to comply with the Administrative Procedures for Electronic Case Filing in the United States District Court for the District of Massachusetts (MA R USDCT CM/ECF Admin) or with MA R USDCT LR 5.4. MA R USDCT CM/ECF Admin(C)(3).

**D. Documents**

1. *Documents for moving party*

   a. *Required documents*

      i. *Notice of motion and motion.* Motions to continue discovery and pretrial conferences will not be entertained unless the date and time of the pretrial conference are set out in the motion as well as a statement of how many other requests, if any, for continuances have been sought and granted. MA R USDCT LR 40.3(b). Refer to the General Requirements section of this document for information on the notice of motion and motion.

         - *Request for oral argument.* Any party making or opposing a motion who believes that oral argument may assist the court and wishes to be heard shall include a request for oral argument in a separate paragraph of the motion or opposition. The request should be set off with a centered caption, "REQUEST FOR ORAL ARGUMENT." MA R USDCT LR 7.1(d).

      ii. *Memorandum.* A party filing a motion shall at the same time file a memorandum of reasons, including citation of supporting authorities, why the motion should be granted. MA R USDCT LR 7.1(b)(1). Any memorandum of law or other attachment filed in support of a main document shall be filed as a separate document, using the proper event. MA R USDCT CM/ECF Admin(G)(4). Memoranda supporting or opposing allowance of motions shall not, without leave of court, exceed twenty (20) pages, double-spaced. MA R USDCT LR 7.1(b)(4).

      iii. *Certificate of service.* No certificate of service is required when a paper is served by filing it with the court's electronic-filing system. When a paper that is required to be served is served by other means: (1) if the paper is filed, a certificate of service must be filed with it or within a reasonable time after service; and (2) if the paper is not filed, a certificate of service need not be filed unless filing is required by court order or by local rule. FRCP 5(d)(1)(B). Except as otherwise provided by the Federal Rules of Civil Procedure, proof of service of all pleadings and other papers required to be served (except discovery papers that in accordance with FRCP 33 to FRCP 36(f) are not to be filed) shall be filed in the office of the clerk promptly after service has been made. The proof shall show the time and manner of service, and may be made by written acknowledgment of service, a certificate of a member of the bar of this court, or an affidavit of the person who served the paper. MA R USDCT LR 5.2(b)(1). A certificate of service of a member of the bar shall appear at the bottom of or on the margin of the last page of the paper to which it relates. MA R USDCT LR 5.2(b)(2).

         - *Paper service.* The certificate shall be a brief, single-spaced statement and may be in the following form: I hereby certify that a true copy of the above document was served upon (each party appearing pro se and) the attorney of record for each other party by mail (by hand) on (date). (Signature). MA R USDCT LR 5.2(b)(2).

         - *Electronic service.* Any pleading or other paper served by electronic means must bear a certificate of service in accordance with MA R USDCT LR 5.2(b). MA R USDCT LR 5.4(C); MA R USDCT CM/ECF Admin(H)(2). The certificate of service shall state that the filer: (1) filed the document electronically, (2) that it will be served electronically to registered CM/ECF participants via the NEF and (3) that the filer will send paper copies to non-registered participants as indicated on the NEF. MA R USDCT CM/ECF Admin(H)(2). For example: I hereby certify that this document filed through the CM/ECF system will be sent electronically to the registered participants as identified on the NEF (NEF) and paper copies will be sent to those indicated as non registered participants on (date). MA R USDCT CM/ECF Admin(H)(2).

         - *Return.* Documents not conforming to the requirements of MA R USDCT LR 5.2 (except notices of appeal) shall be returned by the clerk. MA R USDCT LR 5.2(b)(2).

         - *Failure to make proof of service.* Failure to make proof of service does not affect the validity of the service. MA R USDCT LR 5.2(b)(3).

   b. *Supplemental documents*

      i. *Supporting evidence.* When a motion relies on facts outside the record, the court may hear the matter on affidavits or may hear it wholly or partly on oral testimony or on depositions. FRCP 43(c). Affidavits and other documents setting forth or evidencing facts on which the motion is based shall be filed with the motion. MA R USDCT LR 7.1(b)(1).

      ii. *Medical certificate.* Illness of parties and material witnesses must be substantiated by a current medical certificate. MA R USDCT LR 40.3(c).

      iii. *Notice of constitutional question.* A party that files a pleading, written motion, or other paper drawing into question the constitutionality of a federal or state statute must promptly:

         - *File notice.* File a notice of constitutional question stating the question and identifying the paper that raises it, if: (1) a federal statute is questioned and the parties do not include the United States, one of its agencies, or one of its officers or employees in an official capacity; or (2) a state statute is questioned and the parties do not include the state, one of its agencies, or one of its officers or employees in an official capacity; and

- *Serve notice.* Serve the notice and paper on the Attorney General of the United States if a federal statute is questioned—or on the state attorney general if a state statute is questioned—either by certified or registered mail or by sending it to an electronic address designated by the attorney general for this purpose. FRCP 5.1(a).

- *No forfeiture.* A party's failure to file and serve the notice, or the court's failure to certify, does not forfeit a constitutional claim or defense that is otherwise timely asserted. FRCP 5.1(d).

iv. *Nongovernmental corporate disclosure statement*

- *Contents.* A nongovernmental corporate party must file two (2) copies of a disclosure statement that: (1) identifies any parent corporation and any publicly held corporation owning ten percent (10%) or more of its stock; or (2) states that there is no such corporation. FRCP 7.1(a).

- *Time to file; Supplemental filing.* A party must: (1) file the disclosure statement with its first appearance, pleading, petition, motion, response, or other request addressed to the court; and (2) promptly file a supplemental statement if any required information changes. FRCP 7.1(b).

v. *Proposed order.* Proposed orders usually are not required by this court. However, the court may request the party to submit such a document. In those situations, unless otherwise directed by the clerk's office, electronically file the proposed document/order using the entry for "Proposed Documents submitted to the court," found under the Other Documents menu, or as an attachment to the motion to which it relates. MA R USDCT CM/ECF Admin(T).

vi. *Compact disk with copy of document(s) in PDF format.* A filer who cannot file a document electronically because of such technical difficulty on the filer's end [with telephone, cable lines, the filer's Internet Service Provider (ISP), or hardware or software problems] shall file the document conventionally along with a copy of the document in PDF format on a compact disk or contact the clerk's office for permission to submit the PDF document via email. MA R USDCT CM/ECF Admin(W)(3). Refer to the Timing section of this document for more information on technical failures.

vii. *Notice of filing with clerk's office.* When documents or exhibits (other than those filed ex parte or under seal) are submitted conventionally, a "Notice of Filing with clerk's office" shall be filed electronically and attached to the main document. A paper copy of the "Notice of Filing with clerk's office" must accompany the documents submitted to the court. The "Notice of Filing with clerk's office" (see MA R USDCT CM/ECF Admin(Appendix I)) shall describe each of the documents that will be filed as paper copies in the clerk's office, or shall include an index of the documents if those documents are voluminous. MA R USDCT CM/ECF Admin(P)(5).

viii. *Additional copies.* Whenever, because of the nature of a proceeding, such as a proceeding before a three-judge district court under 28 U.S.C.A. § 2284, additional copies of a paper required to be filed are necessary either for the use of the court or to enable the clerk to carry out his duties, it is the responsibility of the party filing or having filed the paper to provide the necessary copies. MA R USDCT LR 5.1(d).

ix. *Courtesy copies.* COURTESY COPIES OF DOCUMENTS FILED ELECTRONICALLY SHALL NOT BE SUBMITTED ROUTINELY. MA R USDCT CM/ECF Admin(J). Judicial officers, on a case-by-case basis, may require courtesy copies for specific cases, or types of motions, etc. A few Judicial Officers have entered Standing Orders, which may be found on their respective pages on the court's website (under Divisions). Any document filed on paper with the court as a courtesy copy must be clearly labeled as such (Example: COURTESY COPY—DO NOT SCAN). Documents delivered to the court as a courtesy copy will not be maintained in the official court record. MA R USDCT CM/ECF Admin(J).

2. *Documents for opposing party*

a. *Required documents*

i. *Opposition.* Refer to the General Requirements section of this document for information on the opposing papers.

- *Memorandum.* A party opposing a motion shall file, in the same (rather than a separate), document a memorandum of reasons, including citation of supporting authorities, why the motion should not be granted. MA R USDCT LR 7.1(b)(2). Any memorandum of law or other attachment filed in support of a main document shall be filed as a separate document, using the proper event. MA R USDCT CM/ECF Admin(G)(4). Memoranda supporting or opposing allowance of motions shall not, without leave of court, exceed twenty (20) pages, double-spaced. MA R USDCT LR 7.1(b)(4).

- *Request for oral argument.* Any party making or opposing a motion who believes that oral argument may assist the court and wishes to be heard shall include a request for oral argument in a separate paragraph of the motion or opposition. The request should be set off with a centered caption, "REQUEST FOR ORAL ARGUMENT." MA R USDCT LR 7.1(d).

ii. *Certificate of service.* No certificate of service is required when a paper is served by filing it with the court's electronic-filing system. When a paper that is required to be served is served by other means: (1) if the paper is filed, a certificate of service must be filed with it or within a reasonable time after service; and (2) if the paper is not filed, a certificate of service need not be filed unless filing is required by court order or by local rule. FRCP 5(d)(1)(B). Except as otherwise provided by the Federal Rules of Civil Procedure, proof of service of all pleadings and other papers required to be served (except discovery papers that in accordance with FRCP 33 to FRCP 36(f) are not to be filed) shall be filed in the office of the clerk promptly after service has been made. The proof shall show the time and manner of service, and may be made by written acknowledgment of service, a certificate of a member of the bar of this court, or an affidavit of the person who served the paper. MA R USDCT LR 5.2(b)(1). A certificate of service of a member of the bar shall appear at the bottom of or on the margin of the last page of the paper to which it relates. MA R USDCT LR 5.2(b)(2).

  - *Paper service.* The certificate shall be a brief, single-spaced statement and may be in the following form: I hereby certify that a true copy of the above document was served upon (each party appearing pro se and) the attorney of record for each other party by mail (by hand) on (date). (Signature). MA R USDCT LR 5.2(b)(2).

  - *Electronic service.* Any pleading or other paper served by electronic means must bear a certificate of service in accordance with MA R USDCT LR 5.2(b). MA R USDCT LR 5.4(C); MA R USDCT CM/ECF Admin(H)(2). The certificate of service shall state that the filer: (1) filed the document electronically, (2) that it will be served electronically to registered CM/ECF participants via the NEF and (3) that the filer will send paper copies to non-registered participants as indicated on the NEF. MA R USDCT CM/ECF Admin(H)(2). For example: I hereby certify that this document filed through the CM/ECF system will be sent electronically to the registered participants as identified on the NEF (NEF) and paper copies will be sent to those indicated as non registered participants on (date). MA R USDCT CM/ECF Admin(H)(2).

  - *Return.* Documents not conforming to the requirements of MA R USDCT LR 5.2 (except notices of appeal) shall be returned by the clerk. MA R USDCT LR 5.2(b)(2).

  - *Failure to make proof of service.* Failure to make proof of service does not affect the validity of the service. MA R USDCT LR 5.2(b)(3).

b. *Supplemental documents*

  i. *Supporting evidence.* When a motion relies on facts outside the record, the court may hear the matter on affidavits or may hear it wholly or partly on oral testimony or on depositions. FRCP 43(c). Affidavits and other documents setting forth or evidencing facts on which the opposition is based shall be filed with the opposition. MA R USDCT LR 7.1(b)(2).

  ii. *Notice of constitutional question.* A party that files a pleading, written motion, or other paper drawing into question the constitutionality of a federal or state statute must promptly:

  - *File notice.* File a notice of constitutional question stating the question and identifying the paper that raises it, if: (1) a federal statute is questioned and the parties do not include the United States, one of its agencies, or one of its officers or employees in an official capacity; or (2) a state statute is questioned and the parties do not include the state, one of its agencies, or one of its officers or employees in an official capacity; and

  - *Serve notice.* Serve the notice and paper on the Attorney General of the United States if a federal statute is questioned—or on the state attorney general if a state statute is questioned—either by certified or registered mail or by sending it to an electronic address designated by the attorney general for this purpose. FRCP 5.1(a).

  - *No forfeiture.* A party's failure to file and serve the notice, or the court's failure to certify, does not forfeit a constitutional claim or defense that is otherwise timely asserted. FRCP 5.1(d).

  iii. *Compact disk with copy of document(s) in PDF format.* A filer who cannot file a document electronically because of such technical difficulty on the filer's end [with telephone, cable lines, the filer's Internet Service Provider (ISP), or hardware or software problems] shall file the document conventionally along with a copy of the document in PDF format on a compact disk or contact the clerk's office for permission to submit the PDF document via email. MA R USDCT CM/ECF Admin(W)(3). Refer to the Timing section of this document for more information on technical failures.

    iv. *Notice of filing with clerk's office.* When documents or exhibits (other than those filed ex parte or under seal) are submitted conventionally, a "Notice of Filing with clerk's office" shall be filed electronically and attached to the main document. A paper copy of the "Notice of Filing with clerk's office" must accompany the documents submitted to the court. The "Notice of Filing with clerk's office" (see MA R USDCT CM/ECF Admin(Appendix I)) shall describe each of the documents that will be filed as paper copies in the clerk's office, or shall include an index of the documents if those documents are voluminous. MA R USDCT CM/ECF Admin(P)(5).

    v. *Additional copies.* Whenever, because of the nature of a proceeding, such as a proceeding before a three-judge district court under 28 U.S.C.A. § 2284, additional copies of a paper required to be filed are necessary either for the use of the court or to enable the clerk to carry out his duties, it is the responsibility of the party filing or having filed the paper to provide the necessary copies. MA R USDCT LR 5.1(d).

    vi. *Courtesy copies.* COURTESY COPIES OF DOCUMENTS FILED ELECTRONICALLY SHALL NOT BE SUBMITTED ROUTINELY. MA R USDCT CM/ECF Admin(J). Judicial officers, on a case-by-case basis, may require courtesy copies for specific cases, or types of motions, etc. A few Judicial Officers have entered Standing Orders, which may be found on their respective pages on the court's website (under Divisions). Any document filed on paper with the court as a courtesy copy must be clearly labeled as such (Example: COURTESY COPY—DO NOT SCAN). Documents delivered to the court as a courtesy copy will not be maintained in the official court record. MA R USDCT CM/ECF Admin(J).

## E. Format

1. *Form of documents.* The rules governing captions and other matters of form in pleadings apply to motions and other papers. FRCP 7(b)(2). The provisions of FRCP 10 and FRCP 11 concerning the form and signing of pleadings, motions, and other papers shall be applicable to all papers filed in any proceeding in this court. The board of bar overseers registration number of each attorney signing such documents, except the United States Attorney and his or her staff, shall be inscribed below the signature. MA R USDCT LR 5.1(a)(1).

    a. *Paper size and binding.* All papers filed in the court shall be adapted for flat filing, be filed on eight and one-half by eleven (8-1/2 x 11) inch paper without backers and be bound firmly by staple or some such other means (excluding paper or binder clip or rubber band). MA R USDCT LR 5.1(a)(2).

    b. *Spacing.* All papers, except discovery requests and responses, shall be double-spaced except for the identification of counsel, title of the case, footnotes, quotations and exhibits. Discovery requests and responses shall be single-spaced. MA R USDCT LR 5.1(a)(2).

    c. *Caption.* Every pleading must have a caption with the court's name, a title, a file number, and [an] FRCP 7(a) designation. FRCP 10(a).

        i. *Names of parties.* The title of the complaint must name all the parties; the title of other pleadings, after naming the first party on each side, may refer generally to other parties. FRCP 10(a).

        ii. *Request for special action.* When any pleading or other paper filed in the court includes a request for special process or relief, or any other request such that, if granted, the court will proceed other than in the ordinary course, the request shall, unless it is noted on the category sheet [see MA R USDCT LR 40.1(a)(1)], be noted on the first page to the right of or immediately beneath the caption. MA R USDCT LR 5.1(c).

    d. *Claims or defenses*

        i. *Numbered paragraphs.* A party must state its claims or defenses in numbered paragraphs, each limited as far as practicable to a single set of circumstances. A later pleading may refer by number to a paragraph in an earlier pleading. FRCP 10(b).

        ii. *Separate statements.* If doing so would promote clarity, each claim founded on a separate transaction or occurrence—and each defense other than a denial—must be stated in a separate count or defense. FRCP 10(b).

    e. *Adoption by reference.* A statement in a pleading may be adopted by reference elsewhere in the same pleading or in any other pleading or motion. FRCP 10(c).

        i. *Exhibits.* A copy of a written instrument that is an exhibit to a pleading is a part of the pleading for all purposes. FRCP 10(c).

    f. *Citations*

        i. *Local rules.* These rules shall be known as Local Rules of the United States District Court for the District of Massachusetts and cited as "L.R., D. Mass." or "L.R." MA R USDCT LR 1.1.

ii.   *Electronic case filing procedures.* The procedures governing electronic case filing shall be known as the "Administrative Procedures for Electronic Case Filing in the United States District Court for the District of Massachusetts." They shall be cited as "APECF." MA R USDCT CM/ECF Admin(A)(7).

g.   *Acceptance by the clerk.* The clerk must not refuse to file a paper solely because it is not in the form prescribed by the Federal Rules of Civil Procedure or by a local rule or practice. FRCP 5(d)(4).

   i.   Except for complaints and notices of appeal, papers that do not conform to the requirements of MA R USDCT LR 5.1(a)(2) shall be returned by the clerk. MA R USDCT LR 5.1(a)(2).

2.   *Form of electronic documents.* A paper filed electronically is a written paper for purposes of the Federal Rules of Civil Procedure. FRCP 5(d)(3)(D).

a.   *PDF/A format required.* The court will begin requiring submission of documents in PDF/A format in the foreseeable future. PDF/A is an enhanced version of the traditional PDF format. Newer versions of most PDF software will be able to convert to this format. Additional information on PDF/A documents may be found on the court's website. MA R USDCT CM/ECF Admin(Electronic Filing and PDF).

   i.   *Electronically converted PDF.* Electronically converted PDF documents are created from word processing documents (MS Word, WordPerfect, etc.) using any appropriate software. These documents are text searchable and the file size is generally smaller than a scanned document. CM/ECF users may use any brand of software to convert documents to PDF. MA R USDCT CM/ECF Admin(Electronic Filing and PDF).

   - Documents converted to PDF, rather than scanned, are preferred for filing in CM/ECF. MA R USDCT CM/ECF Admin(Electronic Filing and PDF).

   ii.   *Scanned PDF.* Scanned PDF documents are created from paper documents run through an optical scanner. Scanned PDF documents are generally not searchable and have a larger file size. Please note that software used to create scanned documents may (and should) be set in such a way that the document is "text-searchable." MA R USDCT CM/ECF Admin(Electronic Filing and PDF).

b.   *Title.* All pleadings filed electronically shall be titled in accordance with the approved dictionary of civil or criminal events of the CM/ECF system of this court. A list of events is available on the CM/ECF Training Information page of the court's website. The clerk's office may, when necessary and appropriate, modify the docket entry description, or delete and re-enter the docket entry in order to comply with the court's quality assurance standards. MA R USDCT CM/ECF Admin(G)(3).

c.   *Attachments to filings and exhibits.* Attachments to filings and exhibits must be filed in accordance with the court's CM/ECF User Manual, unless otherwise ordered by the court. MA R USDCT CM/ECF Admin(O)(1).

   i.   Filers must submit as attachments only those excerpts of the referenced documents that are directly germane to the matter under consideration by the court. Excerpted material must be clearly and prominently identified as such. Users who file excerpts of documents do so without prejudice to their right to timely file additional excerpts or the complete document, as may be allowed by the court. Responding parties may timely file additional excerpts or the complete document that they believe are directly germane. MA R USDCT CM/ECF Admin(O)(2).

   ii.   Filers shall not attach as an exhibit any pleading or other paper already on file with the court in that case, but shall merely refer to that document. (See MA R USDCT CM/ECF Admin(G) for information on using hyperlinks in PDF documents filed in CM/ECF.) MA R USDCT CM/ECF Admin(O)(3).

d.   *Redacted documents.* The parties may request or the court may require the submission of documents that have been redacted/stripped of sensitive or confidential information. The redacted document prepared for electronic filing shall include the original caption of the document, and be clearly labeled as "Redacted Document." A specific event is available for this purpose ("Redacted Document"), found under the Other Filings/Other Documents menu option. MA R USDCT CM/ECF Admin(S).

   i.   Attorneys and pro se litigants are advised to take extra care when creating PDF documents intended for submission to CM/ECF. Steps shall be taken to ensure the documents are free of any hidden data (metadata) that may contain redacted information, or traces of information edited or deleted are not hidden in the final document. Even PDF content that has been encrypted may be recovered. An advisory document with additional information on this topic may be found on the court's website. MA R USDCT CM/ECF Admin(S).

e.   *Hyperlinks.* Electronically filed documents may contain the following types of hyperlinks: (1) hyperlinks to other portions of the same document; (2) hyperlinks to other documents filed within the CM/ECF system; and (3) hyperlinks to a location on the Internet that contains a source document for a citation. MA R USDCT CM/ECF Admin(G)(7).

i. Hyperlinks to cited authority may not replace standard citation format. Complete citations must be included in the text of the filed document. Neither a hyperlink, nor any site to which it refers, shall be considered part of the record, but are simply convenient mechanisms for accessing material cited in a document filed in CM/ECF. Instructions on creating hyperlinks may be found in the CM/ECF User Manual. MA R USDCT CM/ECF Admin(G)(7).

ii. The court accepts no responsibility for, and does not endorse, any product, organization, or content at any hyperlinked site, or at any site to which that site may be linked. The court accepts no responsibility for the availability or functionality of any hyperlink. MA R USDCT CM/ECF Admin(G)(7).

iii. One feature of PDF/A documents is that hyperlinks are commonly "masked," meaning that the full address of the referenced file is not written out; for example, clicking the word brief may open a brief which was previously filed in CM/ECF. MA R USDCT CM/ECF Admin(G)(7)(NOTE). An "unmasked" hyperlink has the full address visible to the user. MA R USDCT CM/ECF Admin(G)(7)(NOTE).

- Masked hyperlinks may or may not work in a PDF/A document, depending on how it was created. Currently, masked hyperlinks are preserved in PDF/A documents produced by the "Save As" method in Microsoft Word 2007 and 2010; the "PDFMaker" method in Microsoft Word 2007; and OpenOffice 2.4 ("PDF Export"). With other production methods, such as WordPerfect, the PDF/A document includes underlined words that appear to be links, but clicking them has no effect. MA R USDCT CM/ECF Admin(G)(7)(NOTE).

f. *Documents features not accepted.* CM/ECF will not accept PDF documents containing tracking tags, embedded systems commands, password protections, access restrictions or other security features, special tags or dynamic features. MA R USDCT CM/ECF Admin(G)(8).

g. *File size limitations.* A filing party shall limit the size of each PDF file to no more than twenty (20) megabytes. PDF files larger than seven (7) megabytes will be rejected by the CM/ECF system. The filer will see a message advising of the size limitation. MA R USDCT CM/ECF Admin(P)(2).

i. Larger documents or exhibits may be submitted electronically if split into separate PDF files each less than seven (7) megabytes, attached to the main document and clearly labeled. MA R USDCT CM/ECF Admin(P)(2).

ii. Documents submitted electronically or on paper are subject to the page limitations set by MA R USDCT LR 7.1(b)(4) or by order of the court. MA R USDCT CM/ECF Admin(P)(1).

h. *Accuracy and readability.* The filer shall verify the accuracy and readability of any PDF file before electronically filing it in CM/ECF. MA R USDCT CM/ECF Admin(G)(6); MA R USDCT CM/ECF Admin(P)(3).

3. *Signing of pleadings, motions and other papers*

a. *Signature.* Every pleading, written motion, and other paper must be signed by at least one attorney of record in the attorney's name—or by a party personally if the party is unrepresented. The paper must state the signer's address, e-mail address, and telephone number. FRCP 11(a). The provisions of the Federal Rules of Civil Procedure pertaining to the form and signing of pleadings, motions, and other papers shall be applicable to all papers filed in any proceeding in this court. The board of bar overseers registration number of each attorney signing such documents, except the United States Attorney and his staff, shall be inscribed below the signature. MA R USDCT LR 5.1(a)(1).

i. *Electronic signing.* A filing made through a person's electronic-filing account and authorized by that person, together with that person's name on a signature block, constitutes the person's signature. FRCP 5(d)(3)(C).

ii. *Appearances.* The filing of an appearance or any other pleading signed on behalf of a party constitutes an entry of appearance for that party. All pleadings shall contain the name, bar admission number, address, telephone number, and e-mail address of the attorney entering an appearance. MA R USDCT LR 83.5.2(a).

- *Appearances by law firms.* When a party is represented by a law firm, the appearance must include the name and the signature of at least one individual attorney. When a party is represented by more than one attorney from the same or different law firms, the attorney entering the appearance must designate the individual attorney who is authorized to receive all notices in the case. Any notice sent to an attorney so designated shall be deemed to be proper notice unless the court finds that notice was not properly sent. MA R USDCT LR 83.5.2(b).

- For more information on appearances, refer to MA R USDCT LR 83.5.2.

    iii. *Signatures of attorneys.* The user login and password required to submit documents to the CM/ECF system shall serve as that user's signature for purposes of FRCP 11 and for all other purposes under the Federal Rules of Civil Procedure and the Local Rules of the United States District Court for the District of Massachusetts. All electronically filed documents must include a signature block and must set forth the attorney's name, bar number, address, telephone number and email address. The name of the CM/ECF user under whose log-in and password the document is submitted must be preceded by a "/s/" and typed in the space where the signature would otherwise appear. MA R USDCT CM/ECF Admin(M)(1). For an example, refer to MA R USDCT CM/ECF Admin(M)(1).

    iv. *Signatures of pro se parties.* Any document requiring a signature that is filed by a party appearing pro se shall bear the words "pro se" following that party's signature. Any such document shall also state the party's mailing address, telephone number (if any), and e-mail address (if the party has consented to service by email). MA R USDCT LR 83.5.5(g). For more information on practice by pro se litigants, refer to MA R USDCT LR 83.5.5.

    v. *Multiple signatures.* The filer of any document requiring more than one signature (e.g, stipulations, joint motions, joint status reports, magistrate judge consent forms, etc.) must list thereon all the names of other signatories by means of a "/s/ name of signatory" block for each. By submitting such a document, the filing attorney certifies that each of the other signatories has expressly agreed to the form and substance of the document and that the filing attorney has their actual authority to submit the document electronically. MA R USDCT CM/ECF Admin(M)(2). For more information, refer to MA R USDCT CM/ECF Admin(M)(2).

    vi. *Affidavits.* Except as provided in MA R USDCT CM/ECF Admin(L), affidavits shall be filed electronically; however, the electronically filed version must contain a "/s/ name of signatory" block indicating that the paper document bears an original signature. MA R USDCT CM/ECF Admin(M)(3). The court will also accept a scanned version of the original, signed document. MA R USDCT CM/ECF Admin(M)(3). For more information, refer to MA R USDCT CM/ECF Admin(M)(3).

    vii. *No verification or accompanying affidavit required for pleadings.* Unless a rule or statute specifically states otherwise, a pleading need not be verified or accompanied by an affidavit. FRCP 11(a).

    viii. *Unsigned papers.* The court must strike an unsigned paper unless the omission is promptly corrected after being called to the attorney's or party's attention. FRCP 11(a).

  b. *Representations to the court.* By presenting to the court a pleading, written motion, or other paper—whether by signing, filing, submitting, or later advocating it—an attorney or unrepresented party certifies that to the best of the person's knowledge, information, and belief, formed after an inquiry reasonable under the circumstances:

    i. It is not being presented for any improper purpose, such as to harass, cause unnecessary delay, or needlessly increase the cost of litigation;

    ii. The claims, defenses, and other legal contentions are warranted by existing law or by a nonfrivolous argument for extending, modifying, or reversing existing law or for establishing new law;

    iii. The factual contentions have evidentiary support or, if specifically so identified, will likely have evidentiary support after a reasonable opportunity for further investigation or discovery; and

    iv. The denials of factual contentions are warranted on the evidence or, if specifically so identified, are reasonably based on belief or a lack of information. FRCP 11(b).

  c. *Sanctions.* If, after notice and a reasonable opportunity to respond, the court determines that FRCP 11(b) has been violated, the court may impose an appropriate sanction on any attorney, law firm, or party that violated FRCP 11(b) or is responsible for the violation. FRCP 11(c)(1). Refer to the United States District Court for the District of Massachusetts KeyRules Motion for Sanctions document for more information.

4. *Privacy protection for filings made with the court*

  a. *Redacted filings.* Unless the court orders otherwise, in an electronic or paper filing with the court that contains an individual's Social Security number, taxpayer-identification number, or birth date, the name of an individual known to be a minor, or a financial-account number, a party or nonparty making the filing may include only:

    i. The last four (4) digits of the Social Security number and taxpayer-identification number;

    ii. The year of the individual's birth;

    iii. The minor's initials; and

    iv. The last four (4) digits of the financial-account number. FRCP 5.2(a); MA R USDCT CM/ECF Admin(N).

b. *Exemptions from the redaction requirement.* The redaction requirement does not apply to the following:

    i. A financial-account number that identifies the property allegedly subject to forfeiture in a forfeiture proceeding;

    ii. The record of an administrative or agency proceeding;

    iii. The official record of a state-court proceeding;

    iv. The record of a court or tribunal, if that record was not subject to the redaction requirement when originally filed;

    v. A filing covered by FRCP 5.2(c) or FRCP 5.2(d); and

    vi. A pro se filing in an action brought under 28 U.S.C.A. § 2241, 28 U.S.C.A. § 2254, or 28 U.S.C.A. § 2255. FRCP 5.2(b).

c. *Limitations on remote access to electronic files; Social Security appeals and immigration cases.* Unless the court orders otherwise, in an action for benefits under the Social Security Act, and in an action or proceeding relating to an order of removal, to relief from removal, or to immigration benefits or detention, access to an electronic file is authorized as follows:

    i. The parties and their attorneys may have remote electronic access to any part of the case file, including the administrative record;

    ii. Any other person may have electronic access to the full record at the courthouse, but may have remote electronic access only to:

       • The docket maintained by the court; and

       • An opinion, order, judgment, or other disposition of the court, but not any other part of the case file or the administrative record. FRCP 5.2(c).

d. *Filings made under seal.* The court may order that a filing be made under seal without redaction. The court may later unseal the filing or order the person who made the filing to file a redacted version for the public record. FRCP 5.2(d).

e. *Protective orders.* For good cause, the court may by order in a case:

    i. Require redaction of additional information; or

    ii. Limit or prohibit a nonparty's remote electronic access to a document filed with the court. FRCP 5.2(e).

f. *Option for additional unredacted filing under seal.* A person making a redacted filing may also file an unredacted copy under seal. The court must retain the unredacted copy as part of the record. FRCP 5.2(f). For more information, refer to MA R USDCT LR 7.2.

g. *Option for filing a reference list.* A filing that contains redacted information may be filed together with a reference list that identifies each item of redacted information and specifies an appropriate identifier that uniquely corresponds to each item listed. The list must be filed under seal and may be amended as of right. Any reference in the case to a listed identifier will be construed to refer to the corresponding item of information. FRCP 5.2(g).

h. *Responsibility for redaction.* The clerk's office is not responsible for reviewing documents filed with the court to determine whether pleadings have been redacted and are in the proper form. MA R USDCT CM/ECF Admin(N).

i. *Waiver of protection of identifiers.* A person waives the protection of FRCP 5.2(a) as to the person's own information by filing it without redaction and not under seal. FRCP 5.2(h).

# F. Filing and Service Requirements

1. *Filing requirements*

a. *Required filings.* Any paper after the complaint that is required to be served must be filed no later than a reasonable time after service. FRCP 5(d)(1).

    i. Except as noted in FRCP 33 to FRCP 36, the original of all papers required to be served under FRCP 5(d) shall, unless otherwise submitted to the court, be filed in the office of the clerk within seven (7) days after service has been made. MA R USDCT LR 5.1(b). Except as otherwise provided by the Federal Rules of Civil Procedure, proof of service of all pleadings and other papers required to be served (except discovery papers that in accordance with FRCP 33 to FRCP 36(f) are not to be filed) shall be filed in the office of the clerk promptly after service has been made. MA R USDCT LR 5.2(b)(1).

b. *Nonelectronic filing.* A paper not filed electronically is filed by delivering it: (1) to the clerk; or (2) to a judge who agrees to accept it for filing, and who must then note the filing date on the paper and promptly send it to the clerk. FRCP 5(d)(2).

c. *Electronic filing.* Unless exempt or otherwise ordered by the court, all pleadings and other papers submitted to the court must be filed, signed, and verified by electronic means as provided in MA R USDCT LR 5.4. MA R USDCT LR 5.4(A); MA R USDCT CM/ECF Admin(A)(1). All electronic filings must be made in accordance with the Administrative Procedures for Electronic Case Filing in the United States District Court for the District of Massachusetts (MA R USDCT CM/ECF Admin). MA R USDCT LR 5.4(B). The court may deviate from the Administrative Procedures for Electronic Case Filing in the United States District Court for the District of Massachusetts (MA R USDCT CM/ECF Admin) in specific cases, without prior notice, if deemed appropriate in the exercise of discretion, considering the need for the just, speedy, and inexpensive determination of matters pending before the court. MA R USDCT CM/ECF Admin(C)(1). The court may excuse a failure to comply with any administrative procedure whenever justice so requires. MA R USDCT CM/ECF Admin(C)(2).

   i. *By a represented person; Generally required; Exceptions.* A person represented by an attorney must file electronically, unless nonelectronic filing is allowed by the court for good cause or is allowed or required by local rule. FRCP 5(d)(3)(A).

   ii. *By unrepresented person; When allowed or required.* A person not represented by an attorney: (1) may file electronically only if allowed by court order or by local rule; and (2) may be required to file electronically only by court order, or by a local rule that includes reasonable exceptions. FRCP 5(d)(3)(B).

   iii. *Exemptions from electronic filing*

   - *Documents that should not be filed electronically.* The following types of documents must not be filed electronically, and will not be scanned into the ECF system by the clerk's office: (1) sealed documents; (2) ex parte motions; (3) documents generated as part of an alternative dispute resolution (ADR) process; (4) the administrative record in Social Security and other administrative proceedings; (5) the state court record in proceedings under 28 U.S.C.A. § 2254; and (6) such other types of documents as the clerk may direct in the Administrative Procedures for Electronic Case Filing in the United States District Court for the District of Massachusetts (MA R USDCT CM/ECF Admin). MA R USDCT LR 5.4(G)(1); MA R USDCT CM/ECF Admin(L).

   - *Documents that need not be filed electronically.* The following types of documents need not be filed electronically, but may be scanned into the ECF system by a filing party or the clerk's office: (1) handwritten pleadings; (2) documents filed by pro se litigants who are incarcerated or who are not registered ECF users; (3) indictments, informations, criminal complaints, and the criminal JS45 form; (4) affidavits for search or arrest warrants and related documents; (5) documents received from another court under FRCRP 20 or FRCRP 40; (6) appearance bonds; (7) any document in a criminal case containing the original signature of a defendant, such as a waiver of indictment or a plea agreement; (8) petitions for violations of supervised release; (9) executed service of process documents under FRCP 4; and (10) such other types of documents as the clerk may direct in the Administrative Procedures for Electronic Case Filing in the United States District Court for the District of Massachusetts (MA R USDCT CM/ECF Admin). MA R USDCT LR 5.4(G)(2); MA R USDCT CM/ECF Admin(L).

   - For more information on exemptions from electronic filing, refer to MA R USDCT CM/ECF Admin(L).

   iv. *Consequences of electronic filing.* Electronic transmission of a document to the CM/ECF system, together with the transmission of a Notice of Electronic Filing (NEF) from the court at the completion of the transaction, constitutes the filing of the document for all purposes of the Federal Rules of Procedure and constitutes entry of the document on the docket maintained by the clerk pursuant to FRCP 58 and FRCP 79. MA R USDCT CM/ECF Admin(G)(1).

   v. *Payment of filing fees.* When electronically filing any pleading or paper through CM/ECF that requires a fee, all registered ECF users are to pay the fee electronically through the Treasury Department's Internet payment process. MA R USDCT LR 67.4(d); MA R USDCT CM/ECF Admin(A)(1). Pro se filers and those who have been exempted from electronic filing and/or electronic payment of fees may submit payments by check or money order made payable to "Clerk, U.S. District Court". MA R USDCT LR 67.4(d). For more information on filing fees, refer to MA R USDCT LR 67.4 and MA R USDCT CM/ECF Admin(I).

   vi. For more information on electronic filing, refer to MA R USDCT CM/ECF Admin.

d. *Email or fax filing.* In general, the court does not accept documents by email or by fax. If the court, in special circumstances, does authorize the submission of a document in that manner, the document shall not be considered filed until an NEF is generated by CM/ECF at the completion of the transaction. MA R USDCT CM/ECF Admin(H)(5).

2. *Service requirements.* All papers filed pursuant to MA R USDCT LR 7.1(b) shall be served unless the moving party indicates in writing on the face of the motion that ex parte consideration is requested. Motions filed "ex parte" and related papers need not be served until the motion has been ruled upon or the court orders that service be made. MA R USDCT LR 7.1(c). Service of all pleadings subsequent to the original complaint and of all other papers required to be served shall be made in the manner specified by FRCP 5. MA R USDCT LR 5.2(a).

a. *Service; When required*

   i. *In general.* Unless the Federal Rules of Civil Procedure provide otherwise, each of the following papers must be served on every party:

   - An order stating that service is required;

   - A pleading filed after the original complaint, unless the court orders otherwise under FRCP 5(c) because there are numerous defendants;

   - A discovery paper required to be served on a party, unless the court orders otherwise;

   - A written motion, except one that may be heard ex parte; and

   - A written notice, appearance, demand, or offer of judgment, or any similar paper. FRCP 5(a)(1).

   ii. *If a party fails to appear.* No service is required on a party who is in default for failing to appear. But a pleading that asserts a new claim for relief against such a party must be served on that party under FRCP 4. FRCP 5(a)(2).

   iii. *Seizing property.* If an action is begun by seizing property and no person is or need be named as a defendant, any service required before the filing of an appearance, answer, or claim must be made on the person who had custody or possession of the property when it was seized. FRCP 5(a)(3).

b. *Service; How made*

   i. *Serving an attorney.* If a party is represented by an attorney, service under FRCP 5 must be made on the attorney unless the court orders service on the party. FRCP 5(b)(1).

   - *Nonresident attorney.* On application of a party, the court may order an attorney who represents any other party and who does not maintain an office within this district where service can be made on him by delivery as provided by FRCP 5(b), to designate a member of the bar of this court who does maintain such an office to receive service of all pleadings and other papers in his behalf. MA R USDCT LR 5.2(c)(1).

   ii. *Serving a party acting pro se.* On application of a party, the court may order any other party who is appearing without an attorney and who does not maintain an office or residence within this district where service can be made on him by delivery as provided by FRCP 5(b), to designate an address within the district at which service can be made on him by delivery. MA R USDCT LR 5.2(c)(2).

   iii. *Service in general.* A paper is served under FRCP 5 by:

   - Handing it to the person;

   - Leaving it: (1) at the person's office with a clerk or other person in charge or, if no one is in charge, in a conspicuous place in the office; or (2) if the person has no office or the office is closed, at the person's dwelling or usual place of abode with someone of suitable age and discretion who resides there;

   - Mailing it to the person's last known address—in which event service is complete upon mailing;

   - Leaving it with the court clerk if the person has no known address;

   - Sending it to a registered user by filing it with the court's electronic-filing system or sending it by other electronic means that the person consented to in writing—in either of which events service is complete upon filing or sending, but is not effective if the filer or sender learns that it did not reach the person to be served; or

   - Delivering it by any other means that the person consented to in writing—in which event service is complete when the person making service delivers it to the agency designated to make delivery. FRCP 5(b)(2).

   iv. *Service by electronic means.* Unless exempt or otherwise ordered by the court, all pleadings and other papers must be served on other parties by electronic means. MA R USDCT LR 5.4(C); MA R USDCT CM/ECF Admin(H)(2). Service by electronic means shall be treated the same as service by mail. MA R USDCT CM/ECF Admin(H)(4).

   - *Consent to electronic service.* Registering to use CM/ECF constitutes consent to service of all documents

by electronic means as provided in the Administrative Procedures for Electronic Case Filing in the United States District Court for the District of Massachusetts (MA R USDCT CM/ECF Admin) and FRCP 5(b) and FRCP 77(d). MA R USDCT CM/ECF Admin(E)(6); MA R USDCT CM/ECF Admin(H)(3).

- *Service on registered ECF users.* Transmission of the Notice of Electronic Filing (NEF) through the court's transmission facilities will constitute service of the filed document upon a registered ECF user. MA R USDCT LR 5.4(C).

- *Service on non-registered users.* The party filing the document electronically is responsible for serving a paper copy of the document by mail in accordance with FRCP 5(b) to those case participants who have not been identified on the NEF as electronic recipients. MA R USDCT CM/ECF Admin(H)(3).

- *Service of conventionally filed papers.* Documents or exhibits submitted conventionally shall be served on other parties by the filer using traditional means. MA R USDCT CM/ECF Admin(P)(4).

c. *Serving numerous defendants*

   i. *In general.* If an action involves an unusually large number of defendants, the court may, on motion or on its own, order that:

      - Defendants' pleadings and replies to them need not be served on other defendants;

      - Any crossclaim, counterclaim, avoidance, or affirmative defense in those pleadings and replies to them will be treated as denied or avoided by all other parties; and

      - Filing any such pleading and serving it on the plaintiff constitutes notice of the pleading to all parties. FRCP 5(c)(1).

   ii. *Notifying parties.* A copy of every such order must be served on the parties as the court directs. FRCP 5(c)(2).

## G. Hearings

1. *Hearings, generally.* If the court concludes that there should be a hearing on a motion, the motion will be set down for hearing at such time as the court determines. MA R USDCT LR 7.1(e).

   a. *Oral argument.* Due process does not require that oral argument be permitted on a motion and, except as otherwise provided by local rule, the district court has discretion to determine whether it will decide the motion on the papers or hear argument by counsel (and perhaps receive evidence). FPP § 1190; F.D.I.C. v. Deglau, 207 F.3d 153 (3d Cir. 2000).

      i. *Evidence on a motion.* When a motion relies on facts outside the record, the court may hear the matter on affidavits or may hear it wholly or partly on oral testimony or on depositions. FRCP 43(c).

   b. *Providing a regular schedule for oral hearings.* A court may establish regular times and places for oral hearings on motions. FRCP 78(a).

   c. *Providing for submission on briefs.* By rule or order, the court may provide for submitting and determining motions on briefs, without oral hearings. FRCP 78(b). Motions that are not set down for hearing as provided in MA R USDCT LR 7.1(e) will be decided on the papers submitted after an opposition to the motion has been filed, or, if no opposition is filed, after the time for filing an opposition has elapsed. MA R USDCT LR 7.1(f).

2. *Conflict of court appearances.* For information on conflict of court appearances, refer to MA R USDCT LR 40.2.

## H. Forms

1. **Federal Motion for Continuance/Extension of Time Forms**

   a. Motion for enlargement of time. 2 FEDFORMS § 5:11.

   b. Motion for enlargement of time; By plaintiff. 2 FEDFORMS § 5:12.

   c. Motion for enlargement of time; To answer motion. 2 FEDFORMS § 5:14.

   d. Motion for continuance. 2 FEDFORMS § 5:36.

   e. Motion for continuance; Reciting supporting facts; New allegations in amended answer. 2 FEDFORMS § 5:37.

   f. Motion for continuance; Reciting supporting facts; Absence of witness. 2 FEDFORMS § 5:38.

   g. Motion for continuance; Reciting supporting facts; Absence of witness; Witness outside the country. 2 FEDFORMS § 5:39.

   h. Motion for continuance or in the alternative for change of venue; Hostility against defendant. 2 FEDFORMS § 5:40.

i. Opposition in federal district court; To motion for continuance; On ground of additional time required to prepare for trial; No excusable neglect shown. AMJUR PP CONTIN § 79.

j. Affidavit in opposition to motion for continuance; By plaintiff's attorney; Lack of due diligence in discovery of documents. AMJUR PP CONTIN § 80.

k. Affidavit in opposition to motion for continuance; By plaintiff's attorney; Defendant's absent witness previously absent; Lack of due diligence in compelling attendance of witness. AMJUR PP CONTIN § 81.

l. Affidavit in opposition to motion for continuance; By plaintiff; Admission that absent witness of defendant would testify according to affidavit. AMJUR PP CONTIN § 83.

m. Affidavit in opposition to defendant's motion for continuance; By plaintiff's counsel; Testimony of absent witness merely cumulative. AMJUR PP CONTIN § 85.

n. Notice; Of motion; Containing motion. FEDPROF § 1B:174.

o. Brief; Supporting or opposing motion. FEDPROF § 1B:177.

p. Opposition to motion; For continuance; No excusable neglect. FEDPROF § 1B:240.

q. Affidavit; Opposing motion for continuance; Offer to stipulate to testimony of unavailable witness. FEDPROF § 1B:246.

r. Reply to motion for extension of time. GOLDLTGFMS § 10:40.

s. Motions; Extension of time to file jury demand. GOLDLTGFMS § 12:6.

t. Motion for extension of time. GOLDLTGFMS § 25:37.

u. Motion for extension of time to answer. GOLDLTGFMS § 26:13.

v. Motion to extend time for serving answers. GOLDLTGFMS § 26:14.

w. Motion for continuance. GOLDLTGFMS § 43:2.

x. Motion for continuance; Lawyer unavailable. GOLDLTGFMS § 43:3.

y. Motion for continuance; Witness unavailable. GOLDLTGFMS § 43:4.

z. Motion for continuance; Party in military service. GOLDLTGFMS § 43:6.

**2. Forms for the District of Massachusetts**

a. Notice of filing with clerk's office. MA R USDCT CM/ECF Admin(Appendix I).

# I. Applicable Rules

1. *Federal rules*

a. Serving and filing pleadings and other papers. FRCP 5.

b. Constitutional challenge to a statute; Notice, certification, and intervention. FRCP 5.1.

c. Privacy protection for filings made with the court. FRCP 5.2.

d. Computing and extending time; Time for motion papers. FRCP 6.

e. Pleadings allowed; Form of motions and other papers. FRCP 7.

f. Disclosure statement. FRCP 7.1.

g. Form of pleadings. FRCP 10.

h. Signing pleadings, motions, and other papers; Representations to the court; Sanctions. FRCP 11.

i. Taking testimony. FRCP 43.

j. Hearing motions; Submission on briefs. FRCP 78.

2. *Local rules*

a. Title. MA R USDCT LR 1.1.

b. Sanctions. MA R USDCT LR 1.3.

c. Service of process; Dismissal for failure to make service. MA R USDCT LR 4.1.

d. Form and filing of papers. MA R USDCT LR 5.1.

e. Service and filing of pleadings and other papers. MA R USDCT LR 5.2.

f.   Filing and service by electronic means. MA R USDCT LR 5.4.

g.   Motion practice. MA R USDCT LR 7.1.

h.   Alternative dispute resolution. MA R USDCT LR 16.4.

i.   Continuances. MA R USDCT LR 40.3.

j.   Payments and deposits made with the clerk. MA R USDCT LR 67.4.

k.   Settlement. MA R USDCT LR 68.2.

l.   Office of the clerk. MA R USDCT LR 77.2.

m.   Appearances. MA R USDCT LR 83.5.2.

n.   Practice by pro se litigants. MA R USDCT LR 83.5.5.

o.   CM/ECF case management/electronic case files administrative procedures. MA R USDCT CM/ECF Admin.

## Motions, Oppositions and Replies
## Motion for Summary Judgment

### Document Last Updated December 2018

**A.  Checklist**

(I)   ❑  Matters to be considered by moving party

   (a)   ❑  Required documents

      (1)   ❑  Notice of motion and motion

      (2)   ❑  Memorandum

      (3)   ❑  Certificate of service

   (b)   ❑  Supplemental documents

      (1)   ❑  Supporting evidence

      (2)   ❑  Notice of constitutional question

      (3)   ❑  Nongovernmental corporate disclosure statement

      (4)   ❑  Proposed order

      (5)   ❑  Compact disk with copy of document(s) in PDF format

      (6)   ❑  Notice of filing with clerk's office

      (7)   ❑  Additional copies

      (8)   ❑  Courtesy copies

   (c)   ❑  Timing

      (1)   ❑  Unless a different time is set by local rule or the court orders otherwise, a party may file a motion for summary judgment at any time until thirty (30) days after the close of all discovery

      (2)   ❑  A written motion and notice of the hearing must be served at least fourteen (14) days before the time specified for the hearing, with the following exceptions: (i) when the motion may be heard ex parte; (ii) when the Federal Rules of Civil Procedure set a different time; or (iii) when a court order—which a party may, for good cause, apply for ex parte—sets a different time

      (3)   ❑  Any affidavit supporting a motion must be served with the motion

      (4)   ❑  Except as noted in FRCP 33 to FRCP 36, the original of all papers required to be served under FRCP 5(d) shall, unless otherwise submitted to the court, be filed in the office of the clerk within seven (7) days after service has been made

(II)   ❑  Matters to be considered by opposing party

   (a)   ❑  Required documents

      (1)   ❑  Opposition

(2) ❑ Certificate of service

(b) ❑ Supplemental documents

(1) ❑ Supporting evidence

(2) ❑ Notice of constitutional question

(3) ❑ Compact disk with copy of document(s) in PDF format

(4) ❑ Notice of filing with clerk's office

(5) ❑ Additional copies

(6) ❑ Courtesy copies

(c) ❑ Timing

(1) ❑ Opposition to motions for summary judgment must be filed, unless the court orders otherwise, within twenty-one (21) days after the motion is served

(2) ❑ Except as FRCP 59(c) provides otherwise, any opposing affidavit must be served at least seven (7) days before the hearing, unless the court permits service at another time

(3) ❑ Except as noted in FRCP 33 to FRCP 36, the original of all papers required to be served under FRCP 5(d) shall, unless otherwise submitted to the court, be filed in the office of the clerk within seven (7) days after service has been made

## B. Timing

1. *Motion for summary judgment.* Unless a different time is set by local rule or the court orders otherwise, a party may file a motion for summary judgment at any time until thirty (30) days after the close of all discovery. FRCP 56(b).

2. *Timing of motions, generally*

   a. *Motion and notice of hearing.* A written motion and notice of the hearing must be served at least fourteen (14) days before the time specified for the hearing, with the following exceptions:

      i. When the motion may be heard ex parte;

      ii. When the Federal Rules of Civil Procedure set a different time; or

      iii. When a court order—which a party may, for good cause, apply for ex parte—sets a different time. FRCP 6(c)(1).

   b. *Supporting affidavit.* Any affidavit supporting a motion must be served with the motion. FRCP 6(c)(2).

3. *Timing of opposing papers.* Opposition to motions for summary judgment must be filed, unless the court orders otherwise, within twenty-one (21) days after the motion is served. MA R USDCT LR 56.1; MA R USDCT LR 7.1(b)(2); MA R USDCT CM/ECF Admin(H)(4). The fourteen (14) day period is intended to include the period specified by the civil rules for mailing time and provide for a uniform period regardless of the use of the mails. MA R USDCT LR 7.1(b)(2).

   a. *Opposing affidavit.* Except as FRCP 59(c) provides otherwise, any opposing affidavit must be served at least seven (7) days before the hearing, unless the court permits service at another time. FRCP 6(c)(2).

4. *Timing of reply papers.* [W]here the respondent files an answering affidavit setting up a new matter, the moving party ordinarily is allowed a reasonable time to file a reply affidavit since failure to deny the new matter by affidavit may operate as an admission of its truth. AMJUR MOTIONS § 25.

   a. *Leave of court required.* All other papers not filed as indicated in MA R USDCT LR 7.1(b)(1) and MA R USDCT LR 7.1(b)(2), whether in the form of a reply brief or otherwise, may be submitted only with leave of court. MA R USDCT LR 7.1(b)(3).

      i. *Reply in support of motion for summary judgment.* Unless the court orders otherwise, the moving party may file a reply within fourteen (14) days after the response is served. MA R USDCT LR 56.1.

5. *Filing after service.* Except as noted in FRCP 33 to FRCP 36, the original of all papers required to be served under FRCP 5(d) shall, unless otherwise submitted to the court, be filed in the office of the clerk within seven (7) days after service has been made. MA R USDCT LR 5.1(b).

6.  *Computation of time*

    a.  *Computing time.* FRCP 6 applies in computing any time period specified in the Federal Rules of Civil Procedure, in any local rule or court order, or in any statute that does not specify a method of computing time. FRCP 6(a).

        i.  *Period stated in days or a longer unit.* When the period is stated in days or a longer unit of time:

            ● Exclude the day of the event that triggers the period;

            ● Count every day, including intermediate Saturdays, Sundays, and legal holidays; and

            ● Include the last day of the period, but if the last day is a Saturday, Sunday, or legal holiday, the period continues to run until the end of the next day that is not a Saturday, Sunday, or legal holiday. FRCP 6(a)(1).

        ii. *Period stated in hours.* When the period is stated in hours:

            ● Begin counting immediately on the occurrence of the event that triggers the period;

            ● Count every hour, including hours during intermediate Saturdays, Sundays, and legal holidays; and

            ● If the period would end on a Saturday, Sunday, or legal holiday, the period continues to run until the same time on the next day that is not a Saturday, Sunday, or legal holiday. FRCP 6(a)(2).

        iii. *Office of the clerk.* The offices of the Clerk of Court at Boston, Worcester and Springfield shall be open from 8:30 a.m. until 5:00 p.m. on all days except Saturdays, Sundays, legal holidays and other days so ordered by the court and announced in advance, if feasible. MA R USDCT LR 77.2.

        iv. *Inaccessibility of the clerk's office.* Unless the court orders otherwise, if the clerk's office is inaccessible:

            ● On the last day for filing under FRCP 6(a)(1), then the time for filing is extended to the first accessible day that is not a Saturday, Sunday, or legal holiday; or

            ● During the last hour for filing under FRCP 6(a)(2), then the time for filing is extended to the same time on the first accessible day that is not a Saturday, Sunday, or legal holiday. FRCP 6(a)(3).

        v.  *"Last day" defined.* Unless a different time is set by a statute, local rule, or court order, the last day ends:

            ● For electronic filing, at midnight in the court's time zone; and

            ● For filing by other means, when the clerk's office is scheduled to close. FRCP 6(a)(4).

        vi. *"Next day" defined.* The "next day" is determined by continuing to count forward when the period is measured after an event and backward when measured before an event. FRCP 6(a)(5).

        vii. *"Legal holiday" defined.* "Legal holiday" means:

            ● The day set aside by statute for observing New Year's Day, Martin Luther King Jr.'s Birthday, Washington's Birthday, Memorial Day, Independence Day, Labor Day, Columbus Day, Veterans' Day, Thanksgiving Day, or Christmas Day;

            ● Any day declared a holiday by the President or Congress; and

            ● For periods that are measured after an event, any other day declared a holiday by the state where the district court is located. FRCP 6(a)(6).

    b.  *Computation of electronic filing deadlines.* Filing documents electronically does not alter any filing deadlines. MA R USDCT CM/ECF Admin(K); MA R USDCT LR 5.4(D). Although CM/ECF is generally available twenty-four (24) hours a day for filing, all electronic transmissions of documents must be completed prior to 6:00 PM, Eastern Standard (or Daylight Savings) Time, on the date on which it is due, in order to be considered timely filed that day. MA R USDCT CM/ECF Admin(K); MA R USDCT LR 5.4(D). When a specific time of day deadline is set by court order or stipulation, the electronic filing must be completed by that time. Documents may be filed at any time of the day on days prior to the date on which it is due. MA R USDCT CM/ECF Admin(K). A document filed electronically shall be deemed filed as of the time and date stated on the NEF received from the court. MA R USDCT CM/ECF Admin(G)(2); MA R USDCT CM/ECF Admin(K).

        i.  *Technical failures.* A user whose filing is made untimely as the result of a technical failure of the court's CM/ECF system may seek appropriate relief from the court. MA R USDCT CM/ECF Admin(W)(3). Technical difficulties on the filer's end, with telephone, cable lines, the filer's Internet Service Provider (ISP), or hardware or software problems, will not constitute a technical failure under the Administrative Procedures for Electronic Case Filing in the United States District Court for the District of Massachusetts (MA R USDCT CM/ECF Admin) nor excuse an untimely filing. MA R USDCT CM/ECF Admin(W)(3). As help desk support is available during normal

business hours, filers are strongly urged to electronically file any documents during that period. MA R USDCT CM/ECF Admin(W)(3).

- The court has made available a public terminal (computers and scanner) in each clerk's office for registered users to scan and electronically file documents. This equipment is available during normal business hours. Users should bring their prepared document and a valid CM/ECF login and password. MA R USDCT CM/ECF Admin(W)(3).

c. *Extending time.* When an act may or must be done within a specified time, the court may, for good cause, extend the time: (1) with or without motion or notice if the court acts, or if a request is made, before the original time or its extension expires; or (2) on motion made after the time has expired if the party failed to act because of excusable neglect. FRCP 6(b)(1).

    i. *Exceptions.* A court must not extend the time to act under FRCP 50(b), FRCP 50(d), FRCP 52(b), FRCP 59(b), FRCP 59(d), FRCP 59(e), and FRCP 60(b). FRCP 6(b)(2).

    ii. Refer to the United States District Court for the District of Massachusetts KeyRules Motion for Continuance/Extension of Time document for more information on extending time.

d. *Additional time after certain kinds of service.* When a party may or must act within a specified time after being served and service is made under FRCP 5(b)(2)(C) (by mail), FRCP 5(b)(2)(D) (by leaving with the clerk), or FRCP 5(b)(2)(F) (by other means consented to), three (3) days are added after the period would otherwise expire under FRCP 6(a). FRCP 6(d).

## C. General Requirements

1. *Motions, generally*

a. *Requirements.* A request for a court order must be made by motion. The motion must:

    i. Be in writing unless made during a hearing or trial;

    ii. State with particularity the grounds for seeking the order; and

    iii. State the relief sought. FRCP 7(b)(1).

b. *Notice of motion.* A party interested in resisting the relief sought by a motion has a right to notice thereof, and an opportunity to be heard. AMJUR MOTIONS § 12.

    i. [I]n addition to statutory or court rule provisions requiring notice of a motion—the purpose of such a notice requirement having been said to be to prevent a party from being prejudicially surprised by a motion—principles of natural justice dictate that an adverse party generally must be given notice that a motion will be presented to the court. AMJUR MOTIONS § 12.

    ii. "Notice," in this regard, means reasonable notice, including a meaningful opportunity to prepare and to defend against allegations of a motion. AMJUR MOTIONS § 12.

c. *Writing requirement.* The writing requirement is intended to [ensure] that the adverse parties are informed and have a record of both the motion's pendency and the grounds on which the movant seeks an order. FPP § 1191; Feldberg v. Quechee Lakes Corp., 463 F.3d 195 (2d Cir. 2006). [A] single written document can satisfy the writing requirements both for a motion and for [an] FRCP 6(c)(1) notice. FRCP 7(Advisory Committee Notes).

d. *Particularity requirement.* The particularity requirement [ensures] that the opposing parties will have notice of their opponent's contentions. FEDPROC § 62:358; Goodman v. 1973 26 Foot Trojan Vessel, Arkansas Registration No. AR1439SN, 859 F.2d 71 (8th Cir. 1988). That requirement ensures that notice of the basis for the motion is provided to the court and to the opposing party so as to avoid prejudice, provide the opponent with a meaningful opportunity to respond, and provide the court with enough information to process the motion correctly. FEDPROC § 62:358; Andreas v. Volkswagen of Am., Inc., 336 F.3d 789 (8th Cir. 2003).

    i. Reasonable specification of the grounds for a motion is sufficient. The particularity requirement for motions is satisfied when no party is prejudiced by a lack of particularity or when the court can comprehend the basis for the motion and deal with it fairly. However, where a movant fails to state even one ground for granting the motion in question, the movant has failed to meet the minimal standard of "reasonable specification." FEDPROC § 62:358; Martinez v. Trainor, 556 F.2d 818 (7th Cir. 1977).

    ii. The court may excuse the failure to comply with the particularity requirement if it is inadvertent, and where no prejudice is shown by the opposing party. FEDPROC § 62:358.

e. *Control of motion practice*

    i. *Plan for the disposition of motions.* At the earliest practicable time, the judicial officer shall establish a framework for the disposition of motions, which, at the discretion of the judicial officer, may include specific deadlines or general time guidelines for filing motions. This framework may be amended from time to time by the judicial officer as required by the progress of the case. MA R USDCT LR 7.1(a)(1).

ii. *Motion practice.* No motion shall be filed unless counsel certify that they have conferred and have attempted in good faith to resolve or narrow the issue. MA R USDCT LR 7.1(a)(2).

iii. *Unresolved motions.* The court shall rule on motions as soon as practicable, having in mind the reporting requirements set forth in the Civil Justice Reform Act. MA R USDCT LR 7.1(a)(3).

2. *Motion for summary judgment.* A party may move for summary judgment, identifying each claim or defense—or the part of each claim or defense—on which summary judgment is sought. The court shall grant summary judgment if the movant shows that there is no genuine dispute as to any material fact and the movant is entitled to judgment as a matter of law. The court should state on the record the reasons for granting or denying the motion. FRCP 56(a).

a. *Burden of proof and presumptions*

i. *Movant's burden.* It is well-settled that the party moving for summary judgment has the burden of demonstrating that the FRCP 56(c) test—"no genuine dispute as to any material fact"—is satisfied and that the movant is entitled to judgment as a matter of law. FPP § 2727; Adickes v. S. H. Kress & Co., 398 U.S. 144, 157, 90 S. Ct. 1598, 1608, 26 L. Ed. 2d 142 (1970).The movant is held to a stringent standard. FPP § 2727. Before summary judgment will be granted it must be clear what the truth is and any doubt as to the existence of a genuine dispute of material fact will be resolved against the movant. FPP § 2727; Poller v. Columbia Broad. Sys., Inc., 368 U.S. 464, 82 S. Ct. 486, 7 L. Ed. 2d 458 (1962); Adickes v. S. H. Kress & Co., 398 U.S. 144, 90 S. Ct. 1598, 26 L. Ed. 2d 142 (1970).

- Because the burden is on the movant, the evidence presented to the court always is construed in favor of the party opposing the motion and the opponent is given the benefit of all favorable inferences that can be drawn from it. FPP § 2727; Scott v. Harris, 550 U.S. 372, 127 S.Ct. 1769, 167 L.Ed.2d 686 (2007).

- Finally, facts asserted by the party opposing the motion, if supported by affidavits or other evidentiary material, are regarded as true. FPP § 2727; McLaughlin v. Liu, 849 F.2d 1205, 1208 (9th Cir. 1988).

ii. *Opponent's burden.* If the summary-judgment movant makes out a prima facie case that would entitle him to a judgment as a matter of law if uncontroverted at trial, summary judgment will be granted unless the opposing party offers some competent evidence that could be presented at trial showing that there is a genuine dispute as to a material fact. FPP § 2727.2; Scott v. Harris, 550 U.S. 372, 127 S.Ct. 1769, 167 L.Ed.2d 686 (2007). In this way the burden of producing evidence is shifted to the party opposing the motion. FPP § 2727.2; Celotex Corp. v. Catrett, 477 U.S. 317, 331, 106 S.Ct. 2548, 2557, 91 L.Ed.2d 265 (1986).

- The burden on the nonmoving party is not a heavy one; the nonmoving party simply is required to show specific facts, as opposed to general allegations, that present a genuine issue worthy of trial. FPP § 2727.2; Lujan v. Defs. of Wildlife, 504 U.S. 555, 112 S. Ct. 2130, 119 L. Ed. 2d 351 (1992).

- A nonmoving party need neither match the moving party witness for witness nor persuade the court that the nonmoving party's case is convincing, but need only come forward with appropriate evidence demonstrating that a dispute of material fact is pending. FEDPROC § 62:589.

b. *Failing to properly support or address a fact.* If a party fails to properly support an assertion of fact or fails to properly address another party's assertion of fact as required by FRCP 56(c), the court may:

i. Give an opportunity to properly support or address the fact;

ii. Consider the fact undisputed for purposes of the motion;

iii. Grant summary judgment if the motion and supporting materials—including the facts considered undisputed—show that the movant is entitled to it; or

iv. Issue any other appropriate order. FRCP 56(e).

c. *Judgment independent of the motion.* After giving notice and a reasonable time to respond, the court may:

i. Grant summary judgment for a nonmovant;

ii. Grant the motion on grounds not raised by a party; or

iii. Consider summary judgment on its own after identifying for the parties material facts that may not be genuinely in dispute. FRCP 56(f).

d. *Failing to grant all the requested relief.* If the court does not grant all the relief requested by the motion, it may enter an order stating any material fact—including an item of damages or other relief—that is not genuinely in dispute and treating the fact as established in the case. FRCP 56(g).

e. *Affidavit or declaration submitted in bad faith.* If satisfied that an affidavit or declaration under FRCP 56 is submitted in bad faith or solely for delay, the court—after notice and a reasonable time to respond—may order the submitting party to pay the other party the reasonable expenses, including attorney's fees, it incurred as a result. An offending party or attorney may also be held in contempt or subjected to other appropriate sanctions. FRCP 56(h).

f. *Conversion of motions under FRCP 12(b)(6) and FRCP 12(c).* If, on a motion under FRCP 12(b)(6) or FRCP 12(c), matters outside the pleadings are presented to and not excluded by the court, the motion must be treated as one for summary judgment under FRCP 56. FRCP 12(d).

3. *Opposing papers*

   a. *Opposing papers, generally.* The Federal Rules of Civil Procedure do not require any formal answer, return, or reply to a motion, except where the Federal Rules of Civil Procedure or local rules may require affidavits, memoranda, or other papers to be filed in opposition to a motion. Such papers are simply to apprise the court of such opposition and the grounds of that opposition. FEDPROC § 62:353.

      i. *Effect of failure to respond to motion.* Although in the absence of statutory provision or court rule, a motion ordinarily does not require a written answer, when a party files a motion and the opposing party fails to respond, the court may construe such failure to respond as nonopposition to the motion or an admission that the motion was meritorious, may take the facts alleged in the motion as true—the rule in some jurisdictions being that the failure to respond to a fact set forth in a motion is deemed an admission—and may grant the motion if the relief requested appears to be justified. AMJUR MOTIONS § 28.

      ii. *Assent or no opposition not determinative.* However, a motion will not be granted automatically simply because an "assent" or a notation of "no opposition" has been filed; federal judges frequently deny motions that have been assented to when it is thought that justice so dictates. FPP § 1190.

      iii. *Responsive pleading inappropriate as response to motion.* An attempt to answer or oppose a motion with a responsive pleading usually is not appropriate. FPP § 1190.

   b. *Opposition to motion for summary judgment.* The party opposing summary judgment does not have a duty to present evidence in opposition to a motion under FRCP 56 in all circumstances. FPP § 2727.2; Jaroma v. Massey, 873 F.2d 17 (1st Cir. 1989).

      i. *When facts are unavailable to the nonmovant.* If a nonmovant shows by affidavit or declaration that, for specified reasons, it cannot present facts essential to justify its opposition, the court may:

         • Defer considering the motion or deny it;

         • Allow time to obtain affidavits or declarations or to take discovery; or

         • Issue any other appropriate order. FRCP 56(d).

4. *Reply papers.* A moving party may be required or permitted to prepare papers in addition to his original motion papers. AMJUR MOTIONS § 25. Papers answering or replying to opposing papers may be appropriate, in the interests of justice, where it appears there is a substantial reason for allowing a reply. Thus, a court may accept reply papers where a party demonstrates that the papers to which it seeks to file a reply raise new issues that are material to the disposition of the question before the court, or where the court determines, sua sponte, that it wishes further briefing of an issue raised in those papers and orders the submission of additional papers. FEDPROC § 62:354.

   a. *Function of reply papers.* The function of a reply affidavit is to answer the arguments made in opposition to the position taken by the movant and not to permit the movant to introduce new arguments in support of the motion. AMJUR MOTIONS § 25.

   b. *Issues raised for the first time in a reply document.* However, the view has been followed in some jurisdictions, that as a matter of judicial economy, where there is no prejudice and where the issues could be raised simply by filing a motion to dismiss, the trial court has discretion to consider arguments raised for the first time in a reply memorandum, and that a trial court may grant a motion to strike issues raised for the first time in a reply memorandum. AMJUR MOTIONS § 26.

5. *Alternative dispute resolution (ADR).* The judicial officer assigned to preside over the case shall encourage the resolution of disputes by settlement or other alternative dispute resolution programs. MA R USDCT LR 16.4(a).

   a. *Settlement.* At every conference conducted under the Local Rules of the United States District Court for the District of Massachusetts, the judicial officer shall inquire as to the utility of the parties conducting settlement negotiations, explore means of facilitating those negotiations, and offer whatever assistance may be appropriate in the circumstances. Assistance may include a reference of the case to another judicial officer for settlement purposes. MA R USDCT LR 16.4(b).

  i. When a case is settled, the parties shall file with the clerk a signed agreement for judgment or stipulation for dismissal, as appropriate, within twenty-eight (28) days, unless the court otherwise orders. MA R USDCT LR 68.2.

b. *Alternative dispute resolution programs*

  i. *Discretion of judicial officer.* The judicial officer, following an exploration of the matter with all counsel, may refer appropriate cases to alternative dispute resolution programs that have been designated for use in the district court or that the judicial officer may make available. The dispute resolution programs described in MA R USDCT LR 16.4(c)(2) through MA R USDCT LR 16.4(c)(4) are illustrative, not exclusive. Moreover, nothing in MA R USDCT LR 16.4 shall preclude the parties from engaging in private dispute resolution programs as long as they comply with any schedule established by the court. MA R USDCT LR 16.4(c)(1).

  ii. *Mediation.* The judicial officer may refer the case to mediation upon the agreement of all parties. MA R USDCT LR 16.4(c)(2)(A).

  iii. *Other alternative dispute resolution programs.* Use of mediation is not exclusive. At the request of parties, the judicial officer may consider other forms of alternative dispute resolution including, but not limited to, mini-trial, summary jury trial and arbitration. MA R USDCT LR 16.4(c)(3).

c. For more information on alternative dispute resolution (ADR), refer to MA R USDCT LR 16.4.

6. *Sanctions.* Failure to comply with any of the directions or obligations set forth in, or authorized by, these rules may result in dismissal, default, or the imposition of other sanctions as deemed appropriate by the judicial officer. MA R USDCT LR 1.3. Except as provided by law, the court may impose sanctions as provided in MA R USDCT LR 1.3 for failure to comply with the Administrative Procedures for Electronic Case Filing in the United States District Court for the District of Massachusetts (MA R USDCT CM/ECF Admin) or with MA R USDCT LR 5.4. MA R USDCT CM/ECF Admin(C)(3).

## D. Documents

1. *Documents for moving party*

  a. *Required documents*

    i. *Notice of motion and motion.* Refer to the General Requirements section of this document for information on the notice of motion and motion.

      • *Statement of material facts.* Motions for summary judgment shall include a concise statement of the material facts of record as to which the moving party contends there is no genuine issue to be tried, with page references to affidavits, depositions and other documentation. Failure to include such a statement constitutes grounds for denial of the motion. MA R USDCT LR 56.1.

      • *Request for oral argument.* Any party making or opposing a motion who believes that oral argument may assist the court and wishes to be heard shall include a request for oral argument in a separate paragraph of the motion or opposition. The request should be set off with a centered caption, "REQUEST FOR ORAL ARGUMENT." MA R USDCT LR 7.1(d).

    ii. *Memorandum.* A party filing a motion shall at the same time file a memorandum of reasons, including citation of supporting authorities, why the motion should be granted. MA R USDCT LR 7.1(b)(1). Any memorandum of law or other attachment filed in support of a main document shall be filed as a separate document, using the proper event. MA R USDCT CM/ECF Admin(G)(4). Memoranda supporting or opposing allowance of motions shall not, without leave of court, exceed twenty (20) pages, double-spaced. MA R USDCT LR 7.1(b)(4).

    iii. *Certificate of service.* No certificate of service is required when a paper is served by filing it with the court's electronic-filing system. When a paper that is required to be served is served by other means: (1) if the paper is filed, a certificate of service must be filed with it or within a reasonable time after service; and (2) if the paper is not filed, a certificate of service need not be filed unless filing is required by court order or by local rule. FRCP 5(d)(1)(B). Except as otherwise provided by the Federal Rules of Civil Procedure, proof of service of all pleadings and other papers required to be served (except discovery papers that in accordance with FRCP 33 to FRCP 36(f) are not to be filed) shall be filed in the office of the clerk promptly after service has been made. The proof shall show the time and manner of service, and may be made by written acknowledgment of service, a certificate of a member of the bar of this court, or an affidavit of the person who served the paper. MA R USDCT LR 5.2(b)(1). A certificate of service of a member of the bar shall appear at the bottom of or on the margin of the last page of the paper to which it relates. MA R USDCT LR 5.2(b)(2).

- *Paper service.* The certificate shall be a brief, single-spaced statement and may be in the following form: I hereby certify that a true copy of the above document was served upon (each party appearing pro se and) the attorney of record for each other party by mail (by hand) on (date). (Signature). MA R USDCT LR 5.2(b)(2).

- *Electronic service.* Any pleading or other paper served by electronic means must bear a certificate of service in accordance with MA R USDCT LR 5.2(b). MA R USDCT LR 5.4(C); MA R USDCT CM/ECF Admin(H)(2). The certificate of service shall state that the filer: (1) filed the document electronically, (2) that it will be served electronically to registered CM/ECF participants via the NEF and (3) that the filer will send paper copies to non-registered participants as indicated on the NEF. MA R USDCT CM/ECF Admin(H)(2). For example: I hereby certify that this document filed through the CM/ECF system will be sent electronically to the registered participants as identified on the NEF (NEF) and paper copies will be sent to those indicated as non registered participants on (date). MA R USDCT CM/ECF Admin(H)(2).

- *Return.* Documents not conforming to the requirements of MA R USDCT LR 5.2 (except notices of appeal) shall be returned by the clerk. MA R USDCT LR 5.2(b)(2).

- *Failure to make proof of service.* Failure to make proof of service does not affect the validity of the service. MA R USDCT LR 5.2(b)(3).

b. *Supplemental documents*

   i. *Supporting evidence.* When a motion relies on facts outside the record, the court may hear the matter on affidavits or may hear it wholly or partly on oral testimony or on depositions. FRCP 43(c). Affidavits and other documents setting forth or evidencing facts on which the motion is based shall be filed with the motion. MA R USDCT LR 7.1(b)(1). Copies of all referenced documentation shall be filed as exhibits to the motion or opposition. MA R USDCT LR 56.1.

- *Supporting factual positions.* A party asserting that a fact cannot be or is genuinely disputed must support the assertion by: (1) citing to particular parts of materials in the record, including depositions, documents, electronically stored information, affidavits or declarations, stipulations (including those made for purposes of the motion only), admissions, interrogatory answers, or other materials; or (2) showing that the materials cited do not establish the absence or presence of a genuine dispute, or that an adverse party cannot produce admissible evidence to support the fact. FRCP 56(c)(1).

- *Objection that a fact is not supported by admissible evidence.* A party may object that the material cited to support or dispute a fact cannot be presented in a form that would be admissible in evidence. FRCP 56(c)(2).

- *Materials not cited.* The court need consider only the cited materials, but it may consider other materials in the record. FRCP 56(c)(3).

- *Affidavits or declarations.* An affidavit or declaration used to support or oppose a motion must be made on personal knowledge, set out facts that would be admissible in evidence, and show that the affiant or declarant is competent to testify on the matters stated. FRCP 56(c)(4).

- *Discovery documents.* If the moving party under FRCP 56 or the opponent relies on discovery documents, copies of the pertinent parts thereof shall be filed with the motion or opposition. MA R USDCT LR 26.6(a).

   ii. *Notice of constitutional question.* A party that files a pleading, written motion, or other paper drawing into question the constitutionality of a federal or state statute must promptly:

- *File notice.* File a notice of constitutional question stating the question and identifying the paper that raises it, if: (1) a federal statute is questioned and the parties do not include the United States, one of its agencies, or one of its officers or employees in an official capacity; or (2) a state statute is questioned and the parties do not include the state, one of its agencies, or one of its officers or employees in an official capacity; and

- *Serve notice.* Serve the notice and paper on the Attorney General of the United States if a federal statute is questioned—or on the state attorney general if a state statute is questioned—either by certified or registered mail or by sending it to an electronic address designated by the attorney general for this purpose. FRCP 5.1(a).

- *No forfeiture.* A party's failure to file and serve the notice, or the court's failure to certify, does not forfeit a constitutional claim or defense that is otherwise timely asserted. FRCP 5.1(d).

iii. *Nongovernmental corporate disclosure statement*

- *Contents.* A nongovernmental corporate party must file two (2) copies of a disclosure statement that: (1) identifies any parent corporation and any publicly held corporation owning ten percent (10%) or more of its stock; or (2) states that there is no such corporation. FRCP 7.1(a).

- *Time to file; Supplemental filing.* A party must: (1) file the disclosure statement with its first appearance, pleading, petition, motion, response, or other request addressed to the court; and (2) promptly file a supplemental statement if any required information changes. FRCP 7.1(b).

iv. *Proposed order.* Proposed orders usually are not required by this court. However, the court may request the party to submit such a document. In those situations, unless otherwise directed by the clerk's office, electronically file the proposed document/order using the entry for "Proposed Documents submitted to the court," found under the Other Documents menu, or as an attachment to the motion to which it relates. MA R USDCT CM/ECF Admin(T).

v. *Compact disk with copy of document(s) in PDF format.* A filer who cannot file a document electronically because of such technical difficulty on the filer's end [with telephone, cable lines, the filer's Internet Service Provider (ISP), or hardware or software problems] shall file the document conventionally along with a copy of the document in PDF format on a compact disk or contact the clerk's office for permission to submit the PDF document via email. MA R USDCT CM/ECF Admin(W)(3). Refer to the Timing section of this document for more information on technical failures.

vi. *Notice of filing with clerk's office.* When documents or exhibits (other than those filed ex parte or under seal) are submitted conventionally, a "Notice of Filing with clerk's office" shall be filed electronically and attached to the main document. A paper copy of the "Notice of Filing with clerk's office" must accompany the documents submitted to the court. The "Notice of Filing with clerk's office" (see MA R USDCT CM/ECF Admin(Appendix I)) shall describe each of the documents that will be filed as paper copies in the clerk's office, or shall include an index of the documents if those documents are voluminous. MA R USDCT CM/ECF Admin(P)(5).

vii. *Additional copies.* Whenever, because of the nature of a proceeding, such as a proceeding before a three-judge district court under 28 U.S.C.A. § 2284, additional copies of a paper required to be filed are necessary either for the use of the court or to enable the clerk to carry out his duties, it is the responsibility of the party filing or having filed the paper to provide the necessary copies. MA R USDCT LR 5.1(d).

viii. *Courtesy copies.* COURTESY COPIES OF DOCUMENTS FILED ELECTRONICALLY SHALL NOT BE SUBMITTED ROUTINELY. MA R USDCT CM/ECF Admin(J). Judicial officers, on a case-by-case basis, may require courtesy copies for specific cases, or types of motions, etc. A few Judicial Officers have entered Standing Orders, which may be found on their respective pages on the court's website (under Divisions). Any document filed on paper with the court as a courtesy copy must be clearly labeled as such (Example: COURTESY COPY—DO NOT SCAN). Documents delivered to the court as a courtesy copy will not be maintained in the official court record. MA R USDCT CM/ECF Admin(J).

2. *Documents for opposing party*

a. *Required documents*

i. *Opposition.* Refer to the General Requirements section of this document for information on the opposing papers.

- *Memorandum.* A party opposing a motion shall file, in the same (rather than a separate), document a memorandum of reasons, including citation of supporting authorities, why the motion should not be granted. MA R USDCT LR 7.1(b)(2). Any memorandum of law or other attachment filed in support of a main document shall be filed as a separate document, using the proper event. MA R USDCT CM/ECF Admin(G)(4). Memoranda supporting or opposing allowance of motions shall not, without leave of court, exceed twenty (20) pages, double-spaced. MA R USDCT LR 7.1(b)(4).

- *Statement of material facts.* A party opposing the motion shall include a concise statement of the material facts of record as to which it is contended that there exists a genuine issue to be tried, with page references to affidavits, depositions and other documentation. MA R USDCT LR 56.1. Material facts of record set forth in the statement required to be served by the moving party will be deemed for purposes of the motion to be admitted by opposing parties unless controverted by the statement required to be served by opposing parties. MA R USDCT LR 56.1.

- *Request for oral argument.* Any party making or opposing a motion who believes that oral argument may assist the court and wishes to be heard shall include a request for oral argument in a separate paragraph of the motion or opposition. The request should be set off with a centered caption, "REQUEST FOR ORAL ARGUMENT." MA R USDCT LR 7.1(d).

ii. *Certificate of service.* No certificate of service is required when a paper is served by filing it with the court's electronic-filing system. When a paper that is required to be served is served by other means: (1) if the paper is filed, a certificate of service must be filed with it or within a reasonable time after service; and (2) if the paper is not filed, a certificate of service need not be filed unless filing is required by court order or by local rule. FRCP 5(d)(1)(B). Except as otherwise provided by the Federal Rules of Civil Procedure, proof of service of all pleadings and other papers required to be served (except discovery papers that in accordance with FRCP 33 to FRCP 36(f) are not to be filed) shall be filed in the office of the clerk promptly after service has been made. The proof shall show the time and manner of service, and may be made by written acknowledgment of service, a certificate of a member of the bar of this court, or an affidavit of the person who served the paper. MA R USDCT LR 5.2(b)(1). A certificate of service of a member of the bar shall appear at the bottom of or on the margin of the last page of the paper to which it relates. MA R USDCT LR 5.2(b)(2).

- *Paper service.* The certificate shall be a brief, single-spaced statement and may be in the following form: I hereby certify that a true copy of the above document was served upon (each party appearing pro se and) the attorney of record for each other party by mail (by hand) on (date). (Signature). MA R USDCT LR 5.2(b)(2).

- *Electronic service.* Any pleading or other paper served by electronic means must bear a certificate of service in accordance with MA R USDCT LR 5.2(b). MA R USDCT LR 5.4(C); MA R USDCT CM/ECF Admin(H)(2). The certificate of service shall state that the filer: (1) filed the document electronically, (2) that it will be served electronically to registered CM/ECF participants via the NEF and (3) that the filer will send paper copies to non-registered participants as indicated on the NEF. MA R USDCT CM/ECF Admin(H)(2). For example: I hereby certify that this document filed through the CM/ECF system will be sent electronically to the registered participants as identified on the NEF (NEF) and paper copies will be sent to those indicated as non registered participants on (date). MA R USDCT CM/ECF Admin(H)(2).

- *Return.* Documents not conforming to the requirements of MA R USDCT LR 5.2 (except notices of appeal) shall be returned by the clerk. MA R USDCT LR 5.2(b)(2).

- *Failure to make proof of service.* Failure to make proof of service does not affect the validity of the service. MA R USDCT LR 5.2(b)(3).

b. *Supplemental documents*

i. *Supporting evidence.* When a motion relies on facts outside the record, the court may hear the matter on affidavits or may hear it wholly or partly on oral testimony or on depositions. FRCP 43(c). Affidavits and other documents setting forth or evidencing facts on which the opposition is based shall be filed with the opposition. MA R USDCT LR 7.1(b)(2). Copies of all referenced documentation shall be filed as exhibits to the motion or opposition. MA R USDCT LR 56.1.

- *Supporting factual positions.* A party asserting that a fact cannot be or is genuinely disputed must support the assertion by: (1) citing to particular parts of materials in the record, including depositions, documents, electronically stored information, affidavits or declarations, stipulations (including those made for purposes of the motion only), admissions, interrogatory answers, or other materials; or (2) showing that the materials cited do not establish the absence or presence of a genuine dispute, or that an adverse party cannot produce admissible evidence to support the fact. FRCP 56(c)(1).

- *Objection that a fact is not supported by admissible evidence.* A party may object that the material cited to support or dispute a fact cannot be presented in a form that would be admissible in evidence. FRCP 56(c)(2).

- *Materials not cited.* The court need consider only the cited materials, but it may consider other materials in the record. FRCP 56(c)(3).

- *Affidavits or declarations.* An affidavit or declaration used to support or oppose a motion must be made on personal knowledge, set out facts that would be admissible in evidence, and show that the affiant or declarant is competent to testify on the matters stated. FRCP 56(c)(4).

- *Discovery documents.* If the moving party under FRCP 56 or the opponent relies on discovery documents, copies of the pertinent parts thereof shall be filed with the motion or opposition. MA R USDCT LR 26.6(a).

ii. *Notice of constitutional question.* A party that files a pleading, written motion, or other paper drawing into question the constitutionality of a federal or state statute must promptly:

- *File notice.* File a notice of constitutional question stating the question and identifying the paper that raises it, if: (1) a federal statute is questioned and the parties do not include the United States, one of its agencies, or one of its officers or employees in an official capacity; or (2) a state statute is questioned and the parties do not include the state, one of its agencies, or one of its officers or employees in an official capacity; and

- *Serve notice.* Serve the notice and paper on the Attorney General of the United States if a federal statute is questioned—or on the state attorney general if a state statute is questioned—either by certified or registered mail or by sending it to an electronic address designated by the attorney general for this purpose. FRCP 5.1(a).

- *No forfeiture.* A party's failure to file and serve the notice, or the court's failure to certify, does not forfeit a constitutional claim or defense that is otherwise timely asserted. FRCP 5.1(d).

iii. *Compact disk with copy of document(s) in PDF format.* A filer who cannot file a document electronically because of such technical difficulty on the filer's end [with telephone, cable lines, the filer's Internet Service Provider (ISP), or hardware or software problems] shall file the document conventionally along with a copy of the document in PDF format on a compact disk or contact the clerk's office for permission to submit the PDF document via email. MA R USDCT CM/ECF Admin(W)(3). Refer to the Timing section of this document for more information on technical failures.

iv. *Notice of filing with clerk's office.* When documents or exhibits (other than those filed ex parte or under seal) are submitted conventionally, a "Notice of Filing with clerk's office" shall be filed electronically and attached to the main document. A paper copy of the "Notice of Filing with clerk's office" must accompany the documents submitted to the court. The "Notice of Filing with clerk's office" (see MA R USDCT CM/ECF Admin(Appendix I)) shall describe each of the documents that will be filed as paper copies in the clerk's office, or shall include an index of the documents if those documents are voluminous. MA R USDCT CM/ECF Admin(P)(5).

v. *Additional copies.* Whenever, because of the nature of a proceeding, such as a proceeding before a three-judge district court under 28 U.S.C.A. § 2284, additional copies of a paper required to be filed are necessary either for the use of the court or to enable the clerk to carry out his duties, it is the responsibility of the party filing or having filed the paper to provide the necessary copies. MA R USDCT LR 5.1(d).

vi. *Courtesy copies.* COURTESY COPIES OF DOCUMENTS FILED ELECTRONICALLY SHALL NOT BE SUBMITTED ROUTINELY. MA R USDCT CM/ECF Admin(J). Judicial officers, on a case-by-case basis, may require courtesy copies for specific cases, or types of motions, etc. A few Judicial Officers have entered Standing Orders, which may be found on their respective pages on the court's website (under Divisions). Any document filed on paper with the court as a courtesy copy must be clearly labeled as such (Example: COURTESY COPY—DO NOT SCAN). Documents delivered to the court as a courtesy copy will not be maintained in the official court record. MA R USDCT CM/ECF Admin(J).

## E. Format

1. *Form of documents.* The rules governing captions and other matters of form in pleadings apply to motions and other papers. FRCP 7(b)(2). The provisions of FRCP 10 and FRCP 11 concerning the form and signing of pleadings, motions, and other papers shall be applicable to all papers filed in any proceeding in this court. The board of bar overseers registration number of each attorney signing such documents, except the United States Attorney and his or her staff, shall be inscribed below the signature. MA R USDCT LR 5.1(a)(1).

   a. *Paper size and binding.* All papers filed in the court shall be adapted for flat filing, be filed on eight and one-half by eleven (8-1/2 x 11) inch paper without backers and be bound firmly by staple or some such other means (excluding paper or binder clip or rubber band). MA R USDCT LR 5.1(a)(2).

   b. *Spacing.* All papers, except discovery requests and responses, shall be double-spaced except for the identification of counsel, title of the case, footnotes, quotations and exhibits. Discovery requests and responses shall be single-spaced. MA R USDCT LR 5.1(a)(2).

   c. *Caption.* Every pleading must have a caption with the court's name, a title, a file number, and [an] FRCP 7(a) designation. FRCP 10(a).

      i. *Names of parties.* The title of the complaint must name all the parties; the title of other pleadings, after naming the first party on each side, may refer generally to other parties. FRCP 10(a).

      ii. *Request for special action.* When any pleading or other paper filed in the court includes a request for special process or relief, or any other request such that, if granted, the court will proceed other than in the ordinary course, the request shall, unless it is noted on the category sheet [see MA R USDCT LR 40.1(a)(1)], be noted on the first page to the right of or immediately beneath the caption. MA R USDCT LR 5.1(c).

d. *Claims or defenses*

   i. *Numbered paragraphs.* A party must state its claims or defenses in numbered paragraphs, each limited as far as practicable to a single set of circumstances. A later pleading may refer by number to a paragraph in an earlier pleading. FRCP 10(b).

   ii. *Separate statements.* If doing so would promote clarity, each claim founded on a separate transaction or occurrence—and each defense other than a denial—must be stated in a separate count or defense. FRCP 10(b).

e. *Adoption by reference.* A statement in a pleading may be adopted by reference elsewhere in the same pleading or in any other pleading or motion. FRCP 10(c).

   i. *Exhibits.* A copy of a written instrument that is an exhibit to a pleading is a part of the pleading for all purposes. FRCP 10(c).

f. *Citations*

   i. *Local rules.* These rules shall be known as Local Rules of the United States District Court for the District of Massachusetts and cited as "L.R., D. Mass." or "L.R." MA R USDCT LR 1.1.

   ii. *Electronic case filing procedures.* The procedures governing electronic case filing shall be known as the "Administrative Procedures for Electronic Case Filing in the United States District Court for the District of Massachusetts." They shall be cited as "APECF." MA R USDCT CM/ECF Admin(A)(7).

g. *Acceptance by the clerk.* The clerk must not refuse to file a paper solely because it is not in the form prescribed by the Federal Rules of Civil Procedure or by a local rule or practice. FRCP 5(d)(4).

   i. Except for complaints and notices of appeal, papers that do not conform to the requirements of MA R USDCT LR 5.1(a)(2) shall be returned by the clerk. MA R USDCT LR 5.1(a)(2).

2. *Form of electronic documents.* A paper filed electronically is a written paper for purposes of the Federal Rules of Civil Procedure. FRCP 5(d)(3)(D).

a. *PDF/A format required.* The court will begin requiring submission of documents in PDF/A format in the foreseeable future. PDF/A is an enhanced version of the traditional PDF format. Newer versions of most PDF software will be able to convert to this format. Additional information on PDF/A documents may be found on the court's website. MA R USDCT CM/ECF Admin(Electronic Filing and PDF).

   i. *Electronically converted PDF.* Electronically converted PDF documents are created from word processing documents (MS Word, WordPerfect, etc.) using any appropriate software. These documents are text searchable and the file size is generally smaller than a scanned document. CM/ECF users may use any brand of software to convert documents to PDF. MA R USDCT CM/ECF Admin(Electronic Filing and PDF).

     • Documents converted to PDF, rather than scanned, are preferred for filing in CM/ECF. MA R USDCT CM/ECF Admin(Electronic Filing and PDF).

   ii. *Scanned PDF.* Scanned PDF documents are created from paper documents run through an optical scanner. Scanned PDF documents are generally not searchable and have a larger file size. Please note that software used to create scanned documents may (and should) be set in such a way that the document is "text-searchable." MA R USDCT CM/ECF Admin(Electronic Filing and PDF).

b. *Title.* All pleadings filed electronically shall be titled in accordance with the approved dictionary of civil or criminal events of the CM/ECF system of this court. A list of events is available on the CM/ECF Training Information page of the court's website. The clerk's office may, when necessary and appropriate, modify the docket entry description, or delete and re-enter the docket entry in order to comply with the court's quality assurance standards. MA R USDCT CM/ECF Admin(G)(3).

c. *Attachments to filings and exhibits.* Attachments to filings and exhibits must be filed in accordance with the court's CM/ECF User Manual, unless otherwise ordered by the court. MA R USDCT CM/ECF Admin(O)(1).

   i. Filers must submit as attachments only those excerpts of the referenced documents that are directly germane to the matter under consideration by the court. Excerpted material must be clearly and prominently identified as such. Users who file excerpts of documents do so without prejudice to their right to timely file additional excerpts or the complete document, as may be allowed by the court. Responding parties may timely file additional excerpts or the complete document that they believe are directly germane. MA R USDCT CM/ECF Admin(O)(2).

ii. Filers shall not attach as an exhibit any pleading or other paper already on file with the court in that case, but shall merely refer to that document. (See MA R USDCT CM/ECF Admin(G) for information on using hyperlinks in PDF documents filed in CM/ECF.) MA R USDCT CM/ECF Admin(O)(3).

d. *Redacted documents.* The parties may request or the court may require the submission of documents that have been redacted/stripped of sensitive or confidential information. The redacted document prepared for electronic filing shall include the original caption of the document, and be clearly labeled as "Redacted Document." A specific event is available for this purpose ("Redacted Document"), found under the Other Filings/Other Documents menu option. MA R USDCT CM/ECF Admin(S).

   i. Attorneys and pro se litigants are advised to take extra care when creating PDF documents intended for submission to CM/ECF. Steps shall be taken to ensure the documents are free of any hidden data (metadata) that may contain redacted information, or traces of information edited or deleted are not hidden in the final document. Even PDF content that has been encrypted may be recovered. An advisory document with additional information on this topic may be found on the court's website. MA R USDCT CM/ECF Admin(S).

e. *Hyperlinks.* Electronically filed documents may contain the following types of hyperlinks: (1) hyperlinks to other portions of the same document; (2) hyperlinks to other documents filed within the CM/ECF system; and (3) hyperlinks to a location on the Internet that contains a source document for a citation. MA R USDCT CM/ECF Admin(G)(7).

   i. Hyperlinks to cited authority may not replace standard citation format. Complete citations must be included in the text of the filed document. Neither a hyperlink, nor any site to which it refers, shall be considered part of the record, but are simply convenient mechanisms for accessing material cited in a document filed in CM/ECF. Instructions on creating hyperlinks may be found in the CM/ECF User Manual. MA R USDCT CM/ECF Admin(G)(7).

   ii. The court accepts no responsibility for, and does not endorse, any product, organization, or content at any hyperlinked site, or at any site to which that site may be linked. The court accepts no responsibility for the availability or functionality of any hyperlink. MA R USDCT CM/ECF Admin(G)(7).

   iii. One feature of PDF/A documents is that hyperlinks are commonly "masked," meaning that the full address of the referenced file is not written out; for example, clicking the word brief may open a brief which was previously filed in CM/ECF. MA R USDCT CM/ECF Admin(G)(7)(NOTE). An "unmasked" hyperlink has the full address visible to the user. MA R USDCT CM/ECF Admin(G)(7)(NOTE).

   • Masked hyperlinks may or may not work in a PDF/A document, depending on how it was created. Currently, masked hyperlinks are preserved in PDF/A documents produced by the "Save As" method in Microsoft Word 2007 and 2010; the "PDFMaker" method in Microsoft Word 2007; and OpenOffice 2.4 ("PDF Export"). With other production methods, such as WordPerfect, the PDF/A document includes underlined words that appear to be links, but clicking them has no effect. MA R USDCT CM/ECF Admin(G)(7)(NOTE).

f. *Documents features not accepted.* CM/ECF will not accept PDF documents containing tracking tags, embedded systems commands, password protections, access restrictions or other security features, special tags or dynamic features. MA R USDCT CM/ECF Admin(G)(8).

g. *File size limitations.* A filing party shall limit the size of each PDF file to no more than twenty (20) megabytes. PDF files larger than seven (7) megabytes will be rejected by the CM/ECF system. The filer will see a message advising of the size limitation. MA R USDCT CM/ECF Admin(P)(2).

   i. Larger documents or exhibits may be submitted electronically if split into separate PDF files each less than seven (7) megabytes, attached to the main document and clearly labeled. MA R USDCT CM/ECF Admin(P)(2).

   ii. Documents submitted electronically or on paper are subject to the page limitations set by MA R USDCT LR 7.1(b)(4) or by order of the court. MA R USDCT CM/ECF Admin(P)(1).

h. *Accuracy and readability.* The filer shall verify the accuracy and readability of any PDF file before electronically filing it in CM/ECF. MA R USDCT CM/ECF Admin(G)(6); MA R USDCT CM/ECF Admin(P)(3).

3. *Signing of pleadings, motions and other papers*

   a. *Signature.* Every pleading, written motion, and other paper must be signed by at least one attorney of record in the attorney's name—or by a party personally if the party is unrepresented. The paper must state the signer's address, e-mail address, and telephone number. FRCP 11(a). The provisions of the Federal Rules of Civil Procedure pertaining to the form and signing of pleadings, motions, and other papers shall be applicable to all papers filed in any proceeding in this court. The board of bar overseers registration number of each attorney signing such documents, except the United States Attorney and his staff, shall be inscribed below the signature. MA R USDCT LR 5.1(a)(1).

i. *Electronic signing.* A filing made through a person's electronic-filing account and authorized by that person, together with that person's name on a signature block, constitutes the person's signature. FRCP 5(d)(3)(C).

ii. *Appearances.* The filing of an appearance or any other pleading signed on behalf of a party constitutes an entry of appearance for that party. All pleadings shall contain the name, bar admission number, address, telephone number, and e-mail address of the attorney entering an appearance. MA R USDCT LR 83.5.2(a).

- *Appearances by law firms.* When a party is represented by a law firm, the appearance must include the name and the signature of at least one individual attorney. When a party is represented by more than one attorney from the same or different law firms, the attorney entering the appearance must designate the individual attorney who is authorized to receive all notices in the case. Any notice sent to an attorney so designated shall be deemed to be proper notice unless the court finds that notice was not properly sent. MA R USDCT LR 83.5.2(b).

- For more information on appearances, refer to MA R USDCT LR 83.5.2.

iii. *Signatures of attorneys.* The user login and password required to submit documents to the CM/ECF system shall serve as that user's signature for purposes of FRCP 11 and for all other purposes under the Federal Rules of Civil Procedure and the Local Rules of the United States District Court for the District of Massachusetts. All electronically filed documents must include a signature block and must set forth the attorney's name, bar number, address, telephone number and email address. The name of the CM/ECF user under whose log-in and password the document is submitted must be preceded by a "/s/" and typed in the space where the signature would otherwise appear. MA R USDCT CM/ECF Admin(M)(1). For an example, refer to MA R USDCT CM/ECF Admin(M)(1).

iv. *Signatures of pro se parties.* Any document requiring a signature that is filed by a party appearing pro se shall bear the words "pro se" following that party's signature. Any such document shall also state the party's mailing address, telephone number (if any), and e-mail address (if the party has consented to service by email). MA R USDCT LR 83.5.5(g). For more information on practice by pro se litigants, refer to MA R USDCT LR 83.5.5.

v. *Multiple signatures.* The filer of any document requiring more than one signature (e.g, stipulations, joint motions, joint status reports, magistrate judge consent forms, etc.) must list thereon all the names of other signatories by means of a "/s/ name of signatory" block for each. By submitting such a document, the filing attorney certifies that each of the other signatories has expressly agreed to the form and substance of the document and that the filing attorney has their actual authority to submit the document electronically. MA R USDCT CM/ECF Admin(M)(2). For more information, refer to MA R USDCT CM/ECF Admin(M)(2).

vi. *Affidavits.* Except as provided in MA R USDCT CM/ECF Admin(L), affidavits shall be filed electronically; however, the electronically filed version must contain a "/s/ name of signatory" block indicating that the paper document bears an original signature. MA R USDCT CM/ECF Admin(M)(3). The court will also accept a scanned version of the original, signed document. MA R USDCT CM/ECF Admin(M)(3). For more information, refer to MA R USDCT CM/ECF Admin(M)(3).

vii. *No verification or accompanying affidavit required for pleadings.* Unless a rule or statute specifically states otherwise, a pleading need not be verified or accompanied by an affidavit. FRCP 11(a).

viii. *Unsigned papers.* The court must strike an unsigned paper unless the omission is promptly corrected after being called to the attorney's or party's attention. FRCP 11(a).

b. *Representations to the court.* By presenting to the court a pleading, written motion, or other paper—whether by signing, filing, submitting, or later advocating it—an attorney or unrepresented party certifies that to the best of the person's knowledge, information, and belief, formed after an inquiry reasonable under the circumstances:

i. It is not being presented for any improper purpose, such as to harass, cause unnecessary delay, or needlessly increase the cost of litigation;

ii. The claims, defenses, and other legal contentions are warranted by existing law or by a nonfrivolous argument for extending, modifying, or reversing existing law or for establishing new law;

iii. The factual contentions have evidentiary support or, if specifically so identified, will likely have evidentiary support after a reasonable opportunity for further investigation or discovery; and

iv.   The denials of factual contentions are warranted on the evidence or, if specifically so identified, are reasonably based on belief or a lack of information. FRCP 11(b).

c.   *Sanctions.* If, after notice and a reasonable opportunity to respond, the court determines that FRCP 11(b) has been violated, the court may impose an appropriate sanction on any attorney, law firm, or party that violated FRCP 11(b) or is responsible for the violation. FRCP 11(c)(1). Refer to the United States District Court for the District of Massachusetts KeyRules Motion for Sanctions document for more information.

4.   *Privacy protection for filings made with the court*

a.   *Redacted filings.* Unless the court orders otherwise, in an electronic or paper filing with the court that contains an individual's Social Security number, taxpayer-identification number, or birth date, the name of an individual known to be a minor, or a financial-account number, a party or nonparty making the filing may include only:

i.   The last four (4) digits of the Social Security number and taxpayer-identification number;

ii.   The year of the individual's birth;

iii.   The minor's initials; and

iv.   The last four (4) digits of the financial-account number. FRCP 5.2(a); MA R USDCT CM/ECF Admin(N).

b.   *Exemptions from the redaction requirement.* The redaction requirement does not apply to the following:

i.   A financial-account number that identifies the property allegedly subject to forfeiture in a forfeiture proceeding;

ii.   The record of an administrative or agency proceeding;

iii.   The official record of a state-court proceeding;

iv.   The record of a court or tribunal, if that record was not subject to the redaction requirement when originally filed;

v.   A filing covered by FRCP 5.2(c) or FRCP 5.2(d); and

vi.   A pro se filing in an action brought under 28 U.S.C.A. § 2241, 28 U.S.C.A. § 2254, or 28 U.S.C.A. § 2255. FRCP 5.2(b).

c.   *Limitations on remote access to electronic files; Social Security appeals and immigration cases.* Unless the court orders otherwise, in an action for benefits under the Social Security Act, and in an action or proceeding relating to an order of removal, to relief from removal, or to immigration benefits or detention, access to an electronic file is authorized as follows:

i.   The parties and their attorneys may have remote electronic access to any part of the case file, including the administrative record;

ii.   Any other person may have electronic access to the full record at the courthouse, but may have remote electronic access only to:

- The docket maintained by the court; and

- An opinion, order, judgment, or other disposition of the court, but not any other part of the case file or the administrative record. FRCP 5.2(c).

d.   *Filings made under seal.* The court may order that a filing be made under seal without redaction. The court may later unseal the filing or order the person who made the filing to file a redacted version for the public record. FRCP 5.2(d).

e.   *Protective orders.* For good cause, the court may by order in a case:

i.   Require redaction of additional information; or

ii.   Limit or prohibit a nonparty's remote electronic access to a document filed with the court. FRCP 5.2(e).

f.   *Option for additional unredacted filing under seal.* A person making a redacted filing may also file an unredacted copy under seal. The court must retain the unredacted copy as part of the record. FRCP 5.2(f). For more information, refer to MA R USDCT LR 7.2.

g.   *Option for filing a reference list.* A filing that contains redacted information may be filed together with a reference list that identifies each item of redacted information and specifies an appropriate identifier that uniquely corresponds to each item listed. The list must be filed under seal and may be amended as of right. Any reference in the case to a listed identifier will be construed to refer to the corresponding item of information. FRCP 5.2(g).

h.   *Responsibility for redaction.* The clerk's office is not responsible for reviewing documents filed with the court to determine whether pleadings have been redacted and are in the proper form. MA R USDCT CM/ECF Admin(N).

    i.   *Waiver of protection of identifiers.* A person waives the protection of FRCP 5.2(a) as to the person's own information by filing it without redaction and not under seal. FRCP 5.2(h).

## F.  Filing and Service Requirements

  1.  *Filing requirements*

    a.  *Required filings.* Any paper after the complaint that is required to be served must be filed no later than a reasonable time after service. FRCP 5(d)(1).

      i.  Except as noted in FRCP 33 to FRCP 36, the original of all papers required to be served under FRCP 5(d) shall, unless otherwise submitted to the court, be filed in the office of the clerk within seven (7) days after service has been made. MA R USDCT LR 5.1(b). Except as otherwise provided by the Federal Rules of Civil Procedure, proof of service of all pleadings and other papers required to be served (except discovery papers that in accordance with FRCP 33 to FRCP 36(f) are not to be filed) shall be filed in the office of the clerk promptly after service has been made. MA R USDCT LR 5.2(b)(1).

    b.  *Nonelectronic filing.* A paper not filed electronically is filed by delivering it: (1) to the clerk; or (2) to a judge who agrees to accept it for filing, and who must then note the filing date on the paper and promptly send it to the clerk. FRCP 5(d)(2).

    c.  *Electronic filing.* Unless exempt or otherwise ordered by the court, all pleadings and other papers submitted to the court must be filed, signed, and verified by electronic means as provided in MA R USDCT LR 5.4. MA R USDCT LR 5.4(A); MA R USDCT CM/ECF Admin(A)(1). All electronic filings must be made in accordance with the Administrative Procedures for Electronic Case Filing in the United States District Court for the District of Massachusetts (MA R USDCT CM/ECF Admin). MA R USDCT LR 5.4(B). The court may deviate from the Administrative Procedures for Electronic Case Filing in the United States District Court for the District of Massachusetts (MA R USDCT CM/ECF Admin) in specific cases, without prior notice, if deemed appropriate in the exercise of discretion, considering the need for the just, speedy, and inexpensive determination of matters pending before the court. MA R USDCT CM/ECF Admin(C)(1). The court may excuse a failure to comply with any administrative procedure whenever justice so requires. MA R USDCT CM/ECF Admin(C)(2).

      i.  *By a represented person; Generally required; Exceptions.* A person represented by an attorney must file electronically, unless nonelectronic filing is allowed by the court for good cause or is allowed or required by local rule. FRCP 5(d)(3)(A).

     ii.  *By unrepresented person; When allowed or required.* A person not represented by an attorney: (1) may file electronically only if allowed by court order or by local rule; and (2) may be required to file electronically only by court order, or by a local rule that includes reasonable exceptions. FRCP 5(d)(3)(B).

     iii.  *Exemptions from electronic filing*

        •  *Documents that should not be filed electronically.* The following types of documents must not be filed electronically, and will not be scanned into the ECF system by the clerk's office: (1) sealed documents; (2) ex parte motions; (3) documents generated as part of an alternative dispute resolution (ADR) process; (4) the administrative record in Social Security and other administrative proceedings; (5) the state court record in proceedings under 28 U.S.C.A. § 2254; and (6) such other types of documents as the clerk may direct in the Administrative Procedures for Electronic Case Filing in the United States District Court for the District of Massachusetts (MA R USDCT CM/ECF Admin). MA R USDCT LR 5.4(G)(1); MA R USDCT CM/ECF Admin(L).

        •  *Documents that need not be filed electronically.* The following types of documents need not be filed electronically, but may be scanned into the ECF system by a filing party or the clerk's office: (1) handwritten pleadings; (2) documents filed by pro se litigants who are incarcerated or who are not registered ECF users; (3) indictments, informations, criminal complaints, and the criminal JS45 form; (4) affidavits for search or arrest warrants and related documents; (5) documents received from another court under FRCRP 20 or FRCRP 40; (6) appearance bonds; (7) any document in a criminal case containing the original signature of a defendant, such as a waiver of indictment or a plea agreement; (8) petitions for violations of supervised release; (9) executed service of process documents under FRCP 4; and (10) such other types of documents as the clerk may direct in the Administrative Procedures for Electronic Case Filing in the United States District Court for the District of Massachusetts (MA R USDCT CM/ECF Admin). MA R USDCT LR 5.4(G)(2); MA R USDCT CM/ECF Admin(L).

        •  For more information on exemptions from electronic filing, refer to MA R USDCT CM/ECF Admin(L).

iv. *Consequences of electronic filing.* Electronic transmission of a document to the CM/ECF system, together with the transmission of a Notice of Electronic Filing (NEF) from the court at the completion of the transaction, constitutes the filing of the document for all purposes of the Federal Rules of Procedure and constitutes entry of the document on the docket maintained by the clerk pursuant to FRCP 58 and FRCP 79. MA R USDCT CM/ECF Admin(G)(1).

v. *Payment of filing fees.* When electronically filing any pleading or paper through CM/ECF that requires a fee, all registered ECF users are to pay the fee electronically through the Treasury Department's Internet payment process. MA R USDCT LR 67.4(d); MA R USDCT CM/ECF Admin(A)(1). Pro se filers and those who have been exempted from electronic filing and/or electronic payment of fees may submit payments by check or money order made payable to "Clerk, U.S. District Court". MA R USDCT LR 67.4(d). For more information on filing fees, refer to MA R USDCT LR 67.4 and MA R USDCT CM/ECF Admin(I).

vi. For more information on electronic filing, refer to MA R USDCT CM/ECF Admin.

d. *Email or fax filing.* In general, the court does not accept documents by email or by fax. If the court, in special circumstances, does authorize the submission of a document in that manner, the document shall not be considered filed until an NEF is generated by CM/ECF at the completion of the transaction. MA R USDCT CM/ECF Admin(H)(5).

2. *Service requirements.* All papers filed pursuant to MA R USDCT LR 7.1(b) shall be served unless the moving party indicates in writing on the face of the motion that ex parte consideration is requested. Motions filed "ex parte" and related papers need not be served until the motion has been ruled upon or the court orders that service be made. MA R USDCT LR 7.1(c). Service of all pleadings subsequent to the original complaint and of all other papers required to be served shall be made in the manner specified by FRCP 5. MA R USDCT LR 5.2(a).

a. *Service; When required*

i. *In general.* Unless the Federal Rules of Civil Procedure provide otherwise, each of the following papers must be served on every party:

- An order stating that service is required;

- A pleading filed after the original complaint, unless the court orders otherwise under FRCP 5(c) because there are numerous defendants;

- A discovery paper required to be served on a party, unless the court orders otherwise;

- A written motion, except one that may be heard ex parte; and

- A written notice, appearance, demand, or offer of judgment, or any similar paper. FRCP 5(a)(1).

ii. *If a party fails to appear.* No service is required on a party who is in default for failing to appear. But a pleading that asserts a new claim for relief against such a party must be served on that party under FRCP 4. FRCP 5(a)(2).

iii. *Seizing property.* If an action is begun by seizing property and no person is or need be named as a defendant, any service required before the filing of an appearance, answer, or claim must be made on the person who had custody or possession of the property when it was seized. FRCP 5(a)(3).

b. *Service; How made*

i. *Serving an attorney.* If a party is represented by an attorney, service under FRCP 5 must be made on the attorney unless the court orders service on the party. FRCP 5(b)(1).

- *Nonresident attorney.* On application of a party, the court may order an attorney who represents any other party and who does not maintain an office within this district where service can be made on him by delivery as provided by FRCP 5(b), to designate a member of the bar of this court who does maintain such an office to receive service of all pleadings and other papers in his behalf. MA R USDCT LR 5.2(c)(1).

ii. *Serving a party acting pro se.* On application of a party, the court may order any other party who is appearing without an attorney and who does not maintain an office or residence within this district where service can be made on him by delivery as provided by FRCP 5(b), to designate an address within the district at which service can be made on him by delivery. MA R USDCT LR 5.2(c)(2).

iii. *Service in general.* A paper is served under FRCP 5 by:

- Handing it to the person;

- Leaving it: (1) at the person's office with a clerk or other person in charge or, if no one is in charge, in a conspicuous place in the office; or (2) if the person has no office or the office is closed, at the person's dwelling or usual place of abode with someone of suitable age and discretion who resides there;

- Mailing it to the person's last known address—in which event service is complete upon mailing;

- Leaving it with the court clerk if the person has no known address;

- Sending it to a registered user by filing it with the court's electronic-filing system or sending it by other electronic means that the person consented to in writing—in either of which events service is complete upon filing or sending, but is not effective if the filer or sender learns that it did not reach the person to be served; or

- Delivering it by any other means that the person consented to in writing—in which event service is complete when the person making service delivers it to the agency designated to make delivery. FRCP 5(b)(2).

iv. *Service by electronic means.* Unless exempt or otherwise ordered by the court, all pleadings and other papers must be served on other parties by electronic means. MA R USDCT LR 5.4(C); MA R USDCT CM/ECF Admin(H)(2). Service by electronic means shall be treated the same as service by mail. MA R USDCT CM/ECF Admin(H)(4).

- *Consent to electronic service.* Registering to use CM/ECF constitutes consent to service of all documents by electronic means as provided in the Administrative Procedures for Electronic Case Filing in the United States District Court for the District of Massachusetts (MA R USDCT CM/ECF Admin) and FRCP 5(b) and FRCP 77(d). MA R USDCT CM/ECF Admin(E)(6); MA R USDCT CM/ECF Admin(H)(3).

- *Service on registered ECF users.* Transmission of the Notice of Electronic Filing (NEF) through the court's transmission facilities will constitute service of the filed document upon a registered ECF user. MA R USDCT LR 5.4(C).

- *Service on non-registered users.* The party filing the document electronically is responsible for serving a paper copy of the document by mail in accordance with FRCP 5(b) to those case participants who have not been identified on the NEF as electronic recipients. MA R USDCT CM/ECF Admin(H)(3).

- *Service of conventionally filed papers.* Documents or exhibits submitted conventionally shall be served on other parties by the filer using traditional means. MA R USDCT CM/ECF Admin(P)(4).

c. *Serving numerous defendants*

i. *In general.* If an action involves an unusually large number of defendants, the court may, on motion or on its own, order that:

- Defendants' pleadings and replies to them need not be served on other defendants;

- Any crossclaim, counterclaim, avoidance, or affirmative defense in those pleadings and replies to them will be treated as denied or avoided by all other parties; and

- Filing any such pleading and serving it on the plaintiff constitutes notice of the pleading to all parties. FRCP 5(c)(1).

ii. *Notifying parties.* A copy of every such order must be served on the parties as the court directs. FRCP 5(c)(2).

## G. Hearings

1. *Hearings, generally.* If the court concludes that there should be a hearing on a motion, the motion will be set down for hearing at such time as the court determines. MA R USDCT LR 7.1(e).

a. *Oral argument.* Due process does not require that oral argument be permitted on a motion and, except as otherwise provided by local rule, the district court has discretion to determine whether it will decide the motion on the papers or hear argument by counsel (and perhaps receive evidence). FPP § 1190; F.D.I.C. v. Deglau, 207 F.3d 153 (3d Cir. 2000).

i. *Evidence on a motion.* When a motion relies on facts outside the record, the court may hear the matter on affidavits or may hear it wholly or partly on oral testimony or on depositions. FRCP 43(c).

b. *Providing a regular schedule for oral hearings.* A court may establish regular times and places for oral hearings on motions. FRCP 78(a).

c. *Providing for submission on briefs.* By rule or order, the court may provide for submitting and determining motions on briefs, without oral hearings. FRCP 78(b). Motions that are not set down for hearing as provided in MA R USDCT

LR 7.1(e) will be decided on the papers submitted after an opposition to the motion has been filed, or, if no opposition is filed, after the time for filing an opposition has elapsed. MA R USDCT LR 7.1(f).

2. *Hearing on motion for summary judgment.* FRCP 56 confers no right to an oral hearing on a summary judgment motion, nor is a hearing required by due process considerations. FEDPROC § 62:671; Forjan v. Leprino Foods, Inc., 209 F. App'x 8 (2d Cir. 2006).

    a. *Oral argument.* Oral argument on a motion for summary judgment may be considered ordinarily appropriate, so that as a general rule, a district court should grant a request for oral argument on all but frivolous summary judgment motions, or a nonmovant's request for oral argument must be granted unless summary judgment is also denied, according to some courts. FEDPROC § 62:672; Season-All Indus., Inc. v. Turkiye Sise Ve Cam Fabrikalari, A. S., 425 F.2d 34 (3d Cir. 1970); Houston v. Bryan, 725 F.2d 516 (9th Cir. 1984); Fernhoff v. Tahoe Reg'l Planning Agency, 803 F.2d 979 (9th Cir. 1986).

        i. *Waiver.* Oral argument on a summary judgment motion may be deemed waived where the opposing party does not request it. FEDPROC § 62:672; McCormack v. Citibank, N.A., 100 F.3d 532 (8th Cir. 1996).

3. *Conflict of court appearances.* For information on conflict of court appearances, refer to MA R USDCT LR 40.2.

## H. Forms

### 1. Federal Motion for Summary Judgment Forms

    a. Motion and notice of motion for summary judgment. 4 FEDFORMS § 39:8.

    b. Motion by plaintiff for summary judgment. 4 FEDFORMS § 39:9.

    c. Motion by defendant for summary judgment. 4 FEDFORMS § 39:13.

    d. Motion by defendant for summary judgment by defendant; Claims of plaintiff and counterclaims of defendant. 4 FEDFORMS § 39:17.

    e. Motion by defendant for summary judgment; Interpleader against another claimant. 4 FEDFORMS § 39:18.

    f. Motion by defendant for summary judgment; Failure of plaintiff to produce evidence. 4 FEDFORMS § 39:19.

    g. Motion by defendant for summary judgment; Statute of limitations. 4 FEDFORMS § 39:20.

    h. Notice of motion for summary judgment. 4 FEDFORMS § 39:44.

    i. Affidavit in support of motion for summary judgment. 4 FEDFORMS § 39:73.

    j. Movant's contention there is no genuine dispute of material facts. 4 FEDFORMS § 39:76.

    k. Opposition to statement of undisputed material facts. 4 FEDFORMS § 39:77.

    l. Response to movant's contention there are no genuine disputes of material facts. 4 FEDFORMS § 39:78.

    m. Answer; To plaintiff's motion for summary judgment. AMJUR PP SUMMARY § 56.

    n. Affidavit opposing defendant's motion for summary judgment; By plaintiff. AMJUR PP SUMMARY § 64.

    o. Affidavit opposing motion for summary judgment; By party; Dispute as to issues of fact. AMJUR PP SUMMARY § 73.

    p. Affidavit opposing motion for summary judgment; By party; Inability to present facts. AMJUR PP SUMMARY § 74.

    q. Affidavit opposing motion for summary judgment; By party; Good defense to part of claim. AMJUR PP SUMMARY § 77.

    r. Statement of disputed and undisputed material facts; In opposition to motion for summary judgment. AMJUR PP SUMMARY § 89.

    s. Motion; For summary judgment; By claimant. FEDPROF § 1C:210.

    t. Motion; For summary judgment; By defending party. FEDPROF § 1C:214.

    u. Motion; By plaintiff; For partial summary judgment. FEDPROF § 1C:217.

    v. Notice of cross motion; For summary judgment; By defending party. FEDPROF § 1C:218.

    w. Statement of material facts; In support of summary judgment motion. FEDPROF § 1C:225.

    x. Statement in support of defendant's summary judgment motion; By codefendant. FEDPROF § 1C:226.

    y. Affidavit; Opposing claimant's motion for summary judgment; Witnesses unavailable. FEDPROF § 1C:230.

z. Affidavit; Opposing part of claim. FEDPROF § 1C:231.

**2. Forms for the District of Massachusetts**

a. Notice of filing with clerk's office. MA R USDCT CM/ECF Admin(Appendix I).

## I. Applicable Rules

1. *Federal rules*

   a. Serving and filing pleadings and other papers. FRCP 5.

   b. Constitutional challenge to a statute; Notice, certification, and intervention. FRCP 5.1.

   c. Privacy protection for filings made with the court. FRCP 5.2.

   d. Computing and extending time; Time for motion papers. FRCP 6.

   e. Pleadings allowed; Form of motions and other papers. FRCP 7.

   f. Disclosure statement. FRCP 7.1.

   g. Form of pleadings. FRCP 10.

   h. Signing pleadings, motions, and other papers; Representations to the court; Sanctions. FRCP 11.

   i. Defenses and objections; When and how presented; Motion for judgment on the pleadings; Consolidating motions; Waiving defenses; Pretrial hearing. FRCP 12.

   j. Taking testimony. FRCP 43.

   k. Summary judgment. FRCP 56.

   l. Hearing motions; Submission on briefs. FRCP 78.

2. *Local rules*

   a. Title. MA R USDCT LR 1.1.

   b. Sanctions. MA R USDCT LR 1.3.

   c. Form and filing of papers. MA R USDCT LR 5.1.

   d. Service and filing of pleadings and other papers. MA R USDCT LR 5.2.

   e. Filing and service by electronic means. MA R USDCT LR 5.4.

   f. Motion practice. MA R USDCT LR 7.1.

   g. Alternative dispute resolution. MA R USDCT LR 16.4.

   h. Court filings and costs. MA R USDCT LR 26.6.

   i. Motions for summary judgment. MA R USDCT LR 56.1.

   j. Payments and deposits made with the clerk. MA R USDCT LR 67.4.

   k. Settlement. MA R USDCT LR 68.2.

   l. Office of the clerk. MA R USDCT LR 77.2.

   m. Appearances. MA R USDCT LR 83.5.2.

   n. Practice by pro se litigants. MA R USDCT LR 83.5.5.

   o. CM/ECF case management/electronic case files administrative procedures. MA R USDCT CM/ECF Admin.

## Motions, Oppositions and Replies
## Motion for Sanctions

**Document Last Updated December 2018**

## A. Checklist

(I)  ❑ Matters to be considered by moving party

   (a)  ❑ Required documents

      (1)  ❑ Notice of motion and motion

    (2)  ❑ Memorandum

    (3)  ❑ Certificate of service

 (b)  ❑ Supplemental documents

    (1)  ❑ Supporting evidence

    (2)  ❑ Notice of constitutional question

    (3)  ❑ Nongovernmental corporate disclosure statement

    (4)  ❑ Proposed order

    (5)  ❑ Compact disk with copy of document(s) in PDF format

    (6)  ❑ Notice of filing with clerk's office

    (7)  ❑ Additional copies

    (8)  ❑ Courtesy copies

 (c)  ❑ Timing

    (1)  ❑ A party who is aware of an FRCP 11 violation should act promptly; however, motions for sanctions can be timely even when filed well after the original pleadings

      (i)  ❑ It must not be filed or be presented to the court if the challenged paper, claim, defense, contention, or denial is withdrawn or appropriately corrected within twenty-one (21) days after service or within another time the court sets

    (2)  ❑ A written motion and notice of the hearing must be served at least fourteen (14) days before the time specified for the hearing, with the following exceptions: (i) when the motion may be heard ex parte; (ii) when the Federal Rules of Civil Procedure set a different time; or (iii) when a court order—which a party may, for good cause, apply for ex parte—sets a different time

    (3)  ❑ Any affidavit supporting a motion must be served with the motion

    (4)  ❑ Except as noted in FRCP 33 to FRCP 36, the original of all papers required to be served under FRCP 5(d) shall, unless otherwise submitted to the court, be filed in the office of the clerk within seven (7) days after service has been made

(II)  ❑ Matters to be considered by opposing party

 (a)  ❑ Required documents

    (1)  ❑ Opposition

    (2)  ❑ Certificate of service

 (b)  ❑ Supplemental documents

    (1)  ❑ Supporting evidence

    (2)  ❑ Notice of constitutional question

    (3)  ❑ Compact disk with copy of document(s) in PDF format

    (4)  ❑ Notice of filing with clerk's office

    (5)  ❑ Additional copies

    (6)  ❑ Courtesy copies

 (c)  ❑ Timing

    (1)  ❑ A party opposing a motion, shall file an opposition within fourteen (14) days after the motion is served, unless another period is fixed by rule or statute, or by order of the court

    (2)  ❑ Except as FRCP 59(c) provides otherwise, any opposing affidavit must be served at least seven (7) days before the hearing, unless the court permits service at another time

    (3)  ❑ Except as noted in FRCP 33 to FRCP 36, the original of all papers required to be served under FRCP 5(d) shall, unless otherwise submitted to the court, be filed in the office of the clerk within seven (7) days after service has been made

## B. Timing

1. *Motion for sanctions.* The deterrent purpose of FRCP 11 can best be served by imposing sanctions at or near the time of

the violation. FEDPROC § 62:775. Accordingly, a party who is aware of [an] FRCP 11 violation should act promptly. FEDPROC § 62:775; Oliveri v. Thompson, 803 F.2d 1265 (2d Cir. 1986). However, whether a case is well-grounded in fact will often not be evident until a plaintiff has been given a chance to conduct discovery. Therefore, motions for sanctions can be timely even when filed well after the original pleadings. FEDPROC § 62:775; Runfola & Assocs., Inc. v. Spectrum Reporting II, Inc., 88 F.3d 368 (6th Cir. 1996).

    a. *Safe harbor provision.* The motion must be served under FRCP 5, but it must not be filed or be presented to the court if the challenged paper, claim, defense, contention, or denial is withdrawn or appropriately corrected within twenty-one (21) days after service or within another time the court sets. FRCP 11(c)(2).

2. *Timing of motions, generally*

    a. *Motion and notice of hearing.* A written motion and notice of the hearing must be served at least fourteen (14) days before the time specified for the hearing, with the following exceptions:

        i. When the motion may be heard ex parte;

        ii. When the Federal Rules of Civil Procedure set a different time; or

        iii. When a court order—which a party may, for good cause, apply for ex parte—sets a different time. FRCP 6(c)(1).

    b. *Supporting affidavit.* Any affidavit supporting a motion must be served with the motion. FRCP 6(c)(2).

3. *Timing of opposing papers.* A party opposing a motion, shall file an opposition within fourteen (14) days after the motion is served, unless (1) the motion is for summary judgment, in which case the opposition shall be filed within twenty-one (21) days after the motion is served, or (2) another period is fixed by rule or statute, or by order of the court. MA R USDCT LR 7.1(b)(2); MA R USDCT CM/ECF Admin(H)(4). The fourteen (14) day period is intended to include the period specified by the civil rules for mailing time and provide for a uniform period regardless of the use of the mails. MA R USDCT LR 7.1(b)(2).

    a. *Opposing affidavit.* Except as FRCP 59(c) provides otherwise, any opposing affidavit must be served at least seven (7) days before the hearing, unless the court permits service at another time. FRCP 6(c)(2).

4. *Timing of reply papers.* [W]here the respondent files an answering affidavit setting up a new matter, the moving party ordinarily is allowed a reasonable time to file a reply affidavit since failure to deny the new matter by affidavit may operate as an admission of its truth. AMJUR MOTIONS § 25.

    a. *Leave of court required.* All other papers not filed as indicated in MA R USDCT LR 7.1(b)(1) and MA R USDCT LR 7.1(b)(2), whether in the form of a reply brief or otherwise, may be submitted only with leave of court. MA R USDCT LR 7.1(b)(3).

5. *Filing after service.* Except as noted in FRCP 33 to FRCP 36, the original of all papers required to be served under FRCP 5(d) shall, unless otherwise submitted to the court, be filed in the office of the clerk within seven (7) days after service has been made. MA R USDCT LR 5.1(b).

6. *Computation of time*

    a. *Computing time.* FRCP 6 applies in computing any time period specified in the Federal Rules of Civil Procedure, in any local rule or court order, or in any statute that does not specify a method of computing time. FRCP 6(a).

        i. *Period stated in days or a longer unit.* When the period is stated in days or a longer unit of time:

           • Exclude the day of the event that triggers the period;

           • Count every day, including intermediate Saturdays, Sundays, and legal holidays; and

           • Include the last day of the period, but if the last day is a Saturday, Sunday, or legal holiday, the period continues to run until the end of the next day that is not a Saturday, Sunday, or legal holiday. FRCP 6(a)(1).

        ii. *Period stated in hours.* When the period is stated in hours:

           • Begin counting immediately on the occurrence of the event that triggers the period;

           • Count every hour, including hours during intermediate Saturdays, Sundays, and legal holidays; and

           • If the period would end on a Saturday, Sunday, or legal holiday, the period continues to run until the same time on the next day that is not a Saturday, Sunday, or legal holiday. FRCP 6(a)(2).

        iii. *Office of the clerk.* The offices of the Clerk of Court at Boston, Worcester and Springfield shall be open from 8:30 a.m. until 5:00 p.m. on all days except Saturdays, Sundays, legal holidays and other days so ordered by the court and announced in advance, if feasible. MA R USDCT LR 77.2.

iv. *Inaccessibility of the clerk's office.* Unless the court orders otherwise, if the clerk's office is inaccessible:

- On the last day for filing under FRCP 6(a)(1), then the time for filing is extended to the first accessible day that is not a Saturday, Sunday, or legal holiday; or

- During the last hour for filing under FRCP 6(a)(2), then the time for filing is extended to the same time on the first accessible day that is not a Saturday, Sunday, or legal holiday. FRCP 6(a)(3).

v. *"Last day" defined.* Unless a different time is set by a statute, local rule, or court order, the last day ends:

- For electronic filing, at midnight in the court's time zone; and

- For filing by other means, when the clerk's office is scheduled to close. FRCP 6(a)(4).

vi. *"Next day" defined.* The "next day" is determined by continuing to count forward when the period is measured after an event and backward when measured before an event. FRCP 6(a)(5).

vii. *"Legal holiday" defined.* "Legal holiday" means:

- The day set aside by statute for observing New Year's Day, Martin Luther King Jr.'s Birthday, Washington's Birthday, Memorial Day, Independence Day, Labor Day, Columbus Day, Veterans' Day, Thanksgiving Day, or Christmas Day;

- Any day declared a holiday by the President or Congress; and

- For periods that are measured after an event, any other day declared a holiday by the state where the district court is located. FRCP 6(a)(6).

b. *Computation of electronic filing deadlines.* Filing documents electronically does not alter any filing deadlines. MA R USDCT CM/ECF Admin(K); MA R USDCT LR 5.4(D). Although CM/ECF is generally available twenty-four (24) hours a day for filing, all electronic transmissions of documents must be completed prior to 6:00 PM, Eastern Standard (or Daylight Savings) Time, on the date on which it is due, in order to be considered timely filed that day. MA R USDCT CM/ECF Admin(K); MA R USDCT LR 5.4(D). When a specific time of day deadline is set by court order or stipulation, the electronic filing must be completed by that time. Documents may be filed at any time of the day on days prior to the date on which it is due. MA R USDCT CM/ECF Admin(K). A document filed electronically shall be deemed filed as of the time and date stated on the NEF received from the court. MA R USDCT CM/ECF Admin(G)(2); MA R USDCT CM/ECF Admin(K).

i. *Technical failures.* A user whose filing is made untimely as the result of a technical failure of the court's CM/ECF system may seek appropriate relief from the court. MA R USDCT CM/ECF Admin(W)(3). Technical difficulties on the filer's end, with telephone, cable lines, the filer's Internet Service Provider (ISP), or hardware or software problems, will not constitute a technical failure under the Administrative Procedures for Electronic Case Filing in the United States District Court for the District of Massachusetts (MA R USDCT CM/ECF Admin) nor excuse an untimely filing. MA R USDCT CM/ECF Admin(W)(3). As help desk support is available during normal business hours, filers are strongly urged to electronically file any documents during that period. MA R USDCT CM/ECF Admin(W)(3).

- The court has made available a public terminal (computers and scanner) in each clerk's office for registered users to scan and electronically file documents. This equipment is available during normal business hours. Users should bring their prepared document and a valid CM/ECF login and password. MA R USDCT CM/ECF Admin(W)(3).

c. *Extending time.* When an act may or must be done within a specified time, the court may, for good cause, extend the time: (1) with or without motion or notice if the court acts, or if a request is made, before the original time or its extension expires; or (2) on motion made after the time has expired if the party failed to act because of excusable neglect. FRCP 6(b)(1).

i. *Exceptions.* A court must not extend the time to act under FRCP 50(b), FRCP 50(d), FRCP 52(b), FRCP 59(b), FRCP 59(d), FRCP 59(e), and FRCP 60(b). FRCP 6(b)(2).

ii. Refer to the United States District Court for the District of Massachusetts KeyRules Motion for Continuance/Extension of Time document for more information on extending time.

d. *Additional time after certain kinds of service.* When a party may or must act within a specified time after being served and service is made under FRCP 5(b)(2)(C) (by mail), FRCP 5(b)(2)(D) (by leaving with the clerk), or FRCP 5(b)(2)(F) (by other means consented to), three (3) days are added after the period would otherwise expire under FRCP 6(a). FRCP 6(d).

## C. General Requirements

1. *Motions, generally*

    a. *Requirements.* A request for a court order must be made by motion. The motion must:

        i. Be in writing unless made during a hearing or trial;

        ii. State with particularity the grounds for seeking the order; and

        iii. State the relief sought. FRCP 7(b)(1).

    b. *Notice of motion.* A party interested in resisting the relief sought by a motion has a right to notice thereof, and an opportunity to be heard. AMJUR MOTIONS § 12.

        i. [I]n addition to statutory or court rule provisions requiring notice of a motion—the purpose of such a notice requirement having been said to be to prevent a party from being prejudicially surprised by a motion—principles of natural justice dictate that an adverse party generally must be given notice that a motion will be presented to the court. AMJUR MOTIONS § 12.

        ii. "Notice," in this regard, means reasonable notice, including a meaningful opportunity to prepare and to defend against allegations of a motion. AMJUR MOTIONS § 12.

    c. *Writing requirement.* The writing requirement is intended to [ensure] that the adverse parties are informed and have a record of both the motion's pendency and the grounds on which the movant seeks an order. FPP § 1191; Feldberg v. Quechee Lakes Corp., 463 F.3d 195 (2d Cir. 2006). [A] single written document can satisfy the writing requirements both for a motion and for [an] FRCP 6(c)(1) notice. FRCP 7(Advisory Committee Notes).

    d. *Particularity requirement.* The particularity requirement [ensures] that the opposing parties will have notice of their opponent's contentions. FEDPROC § 62:358; Goodman v. 1973 26 Foot Trojan Vessel, Arkansas Registration No. AR1439SN, 859 F.2d 71 (8th Cir. 1988). That requirement ensures that notice of the basis for the motion is provided to the court and to the opposing party so as to avoid prejudice, provide the opponent with a meaningful opportunity to respond, and provide the court with enough information to process the motion correctly. FEDPROC § 62:358; Andreas v. Volkswagen of Am., Inc., 336 F.3d 789 (8th Cir. 2003).

        i. Reasonable specification of the grounds for a motion is sufficient. The particularity requirement for motions is satisfied when no party is prejudiced by a lack of particularity or when the court can comprehend the basis for the motion and deal with it fairly. However, where a movant fails to state even one ground for granting the motion in question, the movant has failed to meet the minimal standard of "reasonable specification." FEDPROC § 62:358; Martinez v. Trainor, 556 F.2d 818 (7th Cir. 1977).

        ii. The court may excuse the failure to comply with the particularity requirement if it is inadvertent, and where no prejudice is shown by the opposing party. FEDPROC § 62:358.

    e. *Control of motion practice*

        i. *Plan for the disposition of motions.* At the earliest practicable time, the judicial officer shall establish a framework for the disposition of motions, which, at the discretion of the judicial officer, may include specific deadlines or general time guidelines for filing motions. This framework may be amended from time to time by the judicial officer as required by the progress of the case. MA R USDCT LR 7.1(a)(1).

        ii. *Motion practice.* No motion shall be filed unless counsel certify that they have conferred and have attempted in good faith to resolve or narrow the issue. MA R USDCT LR 7.1(a)(2).

        iii. *Unresolved motions.* The court shall rule on motions as soon as practicable, having in mind the reporting requirements set forth in the Civil Justice Reform Act. MA R USDCT LR 7.1(a)(3).

2. *Motion for sanctions.* A motion for sanctions under FRCP 11 may be filed by either the plaintiff or the defendant. FEDPROC § 62:772. Only parties and other "participants" in an action have standing to seek sanctions, however. FEDPROC § 62:772; New York News, Inc. v. Kheel, 972 F.2d 482 (2d Cir. 1992).

    a. *Basis for motion for sanctions.* FRCP 11(c) authorizes sanctions for misconduct relating to representations to the court. These representations are based on misconduct relating to the presentation (whether by signing, filing, submitting, or later advocating) of a pleading, written motion, or other paper to the court. Improper conduct includes, but is not limited to: (1) the filing of a frivolous suit or document; (2) the filing of a document or lawsuit for an improper purpose; and (3) the filing of actions that needlessly increase the cost or length of litigation. LITGTORT § 20:7. Refer to the Format section of this document for more information on representations to the court.

    b. *Informal notice.* In most cases, . . .counsel should be expected to give informal notice to the other party, whether in person or by a telephone call or letter, of a potential violation before proceeding to prepare and serve [an] FRCP 11 motion. FRCP 11(Advisory Committee Notes).

c. *Safe harbor provision.* A motion for sanctions must be made separately from any other motion and must describe the specific conduct that allegedly violates FRCP 11(b). The motion must be served under FRCP 5, but it must not be filed or be presented to the court if the challenged paper, claim, defense, contention, or denial is withdrawn or appropriately corrected within twenty-one (21) days after service or within another time the court sets. If warranted, the court may award to the prevailing party the reasonable expenses, including attorney's fees, incurred for the motion. FRCP 11(c)(2).

    i. These provisions are intended to provide a type of "safe harbor" against motions under FRCP 11 in that a party will not be subject to sanctions on the basis of another party's motion unless, after receiving the motion, it refuses to withdraw that position or to acknowledge candidly that it does not currently have evidence to support a specified allegation. FRCP 11(Advisory Committee Notes).

d. *Imposition of sanctions.* If, after notice and a reasonable opportunity to respond, the court determines that FRCP 11(b) has been violated, the court may impose an appropriate sanction on any attorney, law firm, or party that violated FRCP 11(b) or is responsible for the violation. Absent exceptional circumstances, a law firm must be held jointly responsible for a violation committed by its partner, associate, or employee. FRCP 11(c)(1).

    i. *Government agencies and their counsel.* FRCP 11 applies to government agencies and their counsel as well as private parties. Thus, the United States is bound by FRCP 11 just as are private parties, and must have reasonable grounds to make allegations within its complaint or answer. FEDPROC § 62:767.

    ii. *Pro se litigants.* The rule governing the imposition of sanctions applies to pro se litigants. FEDPROC § 62:769. Pro se litigants are held to a more lenient standard than professional counsel, with FRCP 11's application determined on a sliding scale according to the litigant's level of sophistication. FEDPROC § 62:769.

e. *Nature of a sanction.* A sanction imposed under FRCP 11 must be limited to what suffices to deter repetition of the conduct or comparable conduct by others similarly situated. The sanction may include nonmonetary directives; an order to pay a penalty into court; or, if imposed on motion and warranted for effective deterrence, an order directing payment to the movant of part or all of the reasonable attorney's fees and other expenses directly resulting from the violation. FRCP 11(c)(4).

f. *Counsel's liability for excessive costs.* Any attorney or other person admitted to conduct cases in any court of the United States or any Territory thereof who so multiplies the proceedings in any case unreasonably and vexatiously may be required by the court to satisfy personally the excess costs, expenses, and attorneys' fees reasonably incurred because of such conduct. 28 U.S.C.A. § 1927.

g. *Limitations on monetary sanctions.* The court must not impose a monetary sanction:

    i. Against a represented party for violating FRCP 11(b)(2); or

    ii. On its own, unless it issued the show-cause order under FRCP 11(c)(3) before voluntary dismissal or settlement of the claims made by or against the party that is, or whose attorneys are, to be sanctioned. FRCP 11(c)(5).

h. *Requirements for an order.* An order imposing a sanction must describe the sanctioned conduct and explain the basis for the sanction. FRCP 11(c)(6).

    i. *On the court's initiative.* On its own, the court may order an attorney, law firm, or party to show cause why conduct specifically described in the order has not violated FRCP 11(b). FRCP 11(c)(3).

3. *Opposing papers.* The Federal Rules of Civil Procedure do not require any formal answer, return, or reply to a motion, except where the Federal Rules of Civil Procedure or local rules may require affidavits, memoranda, or other papers to be filed in opposition to a motion. Such papers are simply to apprise the court of such opposition and the grounds of that opposition. FEDPROC § 62:353.

a. *Effect of failure to respond to motion.* Although in the absence of statutory provision or court rule, a motion ordinarily does not require a written answer, when a party files a motion and the opposing party fails to respond, the court may construe such failure to respond as nonopposition to the motion or an admission that the motion was meritorious, may take the facts alleged in the motion as true—the rule in some jurisdictions being that the failure to respond to a fact set forth in a motion is deemed an admission—and may grant the motion if the relief requested appears to be justified. AMJUR MOTIONS § 28.

b. *Assent or no opposition not determinative.* However, a motion will not be granted automatically simply because an "assent" or a notation of "no opposition" has been filed; federal judges frequently deny motions that have been assented to when it is thought that justice so dictates. FPP § 1190.

c. *Responsive pleading inappropriate as response to motion.* An attempt to answer or oppose a motion with a responsive pleading usually is not appropriate. FPP § 1190.

4. *Reply papers.* A moving party may be required or permitted to prepare papers in addition to his original motion papers. AMJUR MOTIONS § 25. Papers answering or replying to opposing papers may be appropriate, in the interests of justice, where it appears there is a substantial reason for allowing a reply. Thus, a court may accept reply papers where a party demonstrates that the papers to which it seeks to file a reply raise new issues that are material to the disposition of the question before the court, or where the court determines, sua sponte, that it wishes further briefing of an issue raised in those papers and orders the submission of additional papers. FEDPROC § 62:354.

   a. *Function of reply papers.* The function of a reply affidavit is to answer the arguments made in opposition to the position taken by the movant and not to permit the movant to introduce new arguments in support of the motion. AMJUR MOTIONS § 25.

   b. *Issues raised for the first time in a reply document.* However, the view has been followed in some jurisdictions, that as a matter of judicial economy, where there is no prejudice and where the issues could be raised simply by filing a motion to dismiss, the trial court has discretion to consider arguments raised for the first time in a reply memorandum, and that a trial court may grant a motion to strike issues raised for the first time in a reply memorandum. AMJUR MOTIONS § 26.

5. *Alternative dispute resolution (ADR).* The judicial officer assigned to preside over the case shall encourage the resolution of disputes by settlement or other alternative dispute resolution programs. MA R USDCT LR 16.4(a).

   a. *Settlement.* At every conference conducted under the Local Rules of the United States District Court for the District of Massachusetts, the judicial officer shall inquire as to the utility of the parties conducting settlement negotiations, explore means of facilitating those negotiations, and offer whatever assistance may be appropriate in the circumstances. Assistance may include a reference of the case to another judicial officer for settlement purposes. MA R USDCT LR 16.4(b).

      i. When a case is settled, the parties shall file with the clerk a signed agreement for judgment or stipulation for dismissal, as appropriate, within twenty-eight (28) days, unless the court otherwise orders. MA R USDCT LR 68.2.

   b. *Alternative dispute resolution programs*

      i. *Discretion of judicial officer.* The judicial officer, following an exploration of the matter with all counsel, may refer appropriate cases to alternative dispute resolution programs that have been designated for use in the district court or that the judicial officer may make available. The dispute resolution programs described in MA R USDCT LR 16.4(c)(2) through MA R USDCT LR 16.4(c)(4) are illustrative, not exclusive. Moreover, nothing in MA R USDCT LR 16.4 shall preclude the parties from engaging in private dispute resolution programs as long as they comply with any schedule established by the court. MA R USDCT LR 16.4(c)(1).

      ii. *Mediation.* The judicial officer may refer the case to mediation upon the agreement of all parties. MA R USDCT LR 16.4(c)(2)(A).

      iii. *Other alternative dispute resolution programs.* Use of mediation is not exclusive. At the request of parties, the judicial officer may consider other forms of alternative dispute resolution including, but not limited to, mini-trial, summary jury trial and arbitration. MA R USDCT LR 16.4(c)(3).

   c. For more information on alternative dispute resolution (ADR), refer to MA R USDCT LR 16.4.

6. *Sanctions.* Failure to comply with any of the directions or obligations set forth in, or authorized by, these rules may result in dismissal, default, or the imposition of other sanctions as deemed appropriate by the judicial officer. MA R USDCT LR 1.3. Except as provided by law, the court may impose sanctions as provided in MA R USDCT LR 1.3 for failure to comply with the Administrative Procedures for Electronic Case Filing in the United States District Court for the District of Massachusetts (MA R USDCT CM/ECF Admin) or with MA R USDCT LR 5.4. MA R USDCT CM/ECF Admin(C)(3).

**D. Documents**

1. *Documents for moving party*

   a. *Required documents*

      i. *Notice of motion and motion.* Refer to the General Requirements section of this document for information on the notice of motion and motion.

         • *Request for oral argument.* Any party making or opposing a motion who believes that oral argument may

assist the court and wishes to be heard shall include a request for oral argument in a separate paragraph of the motion or opposition. The request should be set off with a centered caption, "REQUEST FOR ORAL ARGUMENT." MA R USDCT LR 7.1(d).

ii. *Memorandum.* A party filing a motion shall at the same time file a memorandum of reasons, including citation of supporting authorities, why the motion should be granted. MA R USDCT LR 7.1(b)(1). Any memorandum of law or other attachment filed in support of a main document shall be filed as a separate document, using the proper event. MA R USDCT CM/ECF Admin(G)(4). Memoranda supporting or opposing allowance of motions shall not, without leave of court, exceed twenty (20) pages, double-spaced. MA R USDCT LR 7.1(b)(4).

iii. *Certificate of service.* No certificate of service is required when a paper is served by filing it with the court's electronic-filing system. When a paper that is required to be served is served by other means: (1) if the paper is filed, a certificate of service must be filed with it or within a reasonable time after service; and (2) if the paper is not filed, a certificate of service need not be filed unless filing is required by court order or by local rule. FRCP 5(d)(1)(B). Except as otherwise provided by the Federal Rules of Civil Procedure, proof of service of all pleadings and other papers required to be served (except discovery papers that in accordance with FRCP 33 to FRCP 36(f) are not to be filed) shall be filed in the office of the clerk promptly after service has been made. The proof shall show the time and manner of service, and may be made by written acknowledgment of service, a certificate of a member of the bar of this court, or an affidavit of the person who served the paper. MA R USDCT LR 5.2(b)(1). A certificate of service of a member of the bar shall appear at the bottom of or on the margin of the last page of the paper to which it relates. MA R USDCT LR 5.2(b)(2).

- *Paper service.* The certificate shall be a brief, single-spaced statement and may be in the following form: I hereby certify that a true copy of the above document was served upon (each party appearing pro se and) the attorney of record for each other party by mail (by hand) on (date). (Signature). MA R USDCT LR 5.2(b)(2).

- *Electronic service.* Any pleading or other paper served by electronic means must bear a certificate of service in accordance with MA R USDCT LR 5.2(b). MA R USDCT LR 5.4(C); MA R USDCT CM/ECF Admin(H)(2). The certificate of service shall state that the filer: (1) filed the document electronically, (2) that it will be served electronically to registered CM/ECF participants via the NEF and (3) that the filer will send paper copies to non-registered participants as indicated on the NEF. MA R USDCT CM/ECF Admin(H)(2). For example: I hereby certify that this document filed through the CM/ECF system will be sent electronically to the registered participants as identified on the NEF (NEF) and paper copies will be sent to those indicated as non registered participants on (date). MA R USDCT CM/ECF Admin(H)(2).

- *Return.* Documents not conforming to the requirements of MA R USDCT LR 5.2 (except notices of appeal) shall be returned by the clerk. MA R USDCT LR 5.2(b)(2).

- *Failure to make proof of service.* Failure to make proof of service does not affect the validity of the service. MA R USDCT LR 5.2(b)(3).

b. *Supplemental documents*

i. *Supporting evidence.* When a motion relies on facts outside the record, the court may hear the matter on affidavits or may hear it wholly or partly on oral testimony or on depositions. FRCP 43(c). Affidavits and other documents setting forth or evidencing facts on which the motion is based shall be filed with the motion. MA R USDCT LR 7.1(b)(1).

ii. *Notice of constitutional question.* A party that files a pleading, written motion, or other paper drawing into question the constitutionality of a federal or state statute must promptly:

- *File notice.* File a notice of constitutional question stating the question and identifying the paper that raises it, if: (1) a federal statute is questioned and the parties do not include the United States, one of its agencies, or one of its officers or employees in an official capacity; or (2) a state statute is questioned and the parties do not include the state, one of its agencies, or one of its officers or employees in an official capacity; and

- *Serve notice.* Serve the notice and paper on the Attorney General of the United States if a federal statute is questioned—or on the state attorney general if a state statute is questioned—either by certified or registered mail or by sending it to an electronic address designated by the attorney general for this purpose. FRCP 5.1(a).

- *No forfeiture.* A party's failure to file and serve the notice, or the court's failure to certify, does not forfeit a constitutional claim or defense that is otherwise timely asserted. FRCP 5.1(d).

iii. *Nongovernmental corporate disclosure statement*

- *Contents.* A nongovernmental corporate party must file two (2) copies of a disclosure statement that: (1) identifies any parent corporation and any publicly held corporation owning ten percent (10%) or more of its stock; or (2) states that there is no such corporation. FRCP 7.1(a).

- *Time to file; Supplemental filing.* A party must: (1) file the disclosure statement with its first appearance, pleading, petition, motion, response, or other request addressed to the court; and (2) promptly file a supplemental statement if any required information changes. FRCP 7.1(b).

iv. *Proposed order.* Proposed orders usually are not required by this court. However, the court may request the party to submit such a document. In those situations, unless otherwise directed by the clerk's office, electronically file the proposed document/order using the entry for "Proposed Documents submitted to the court," found under the Other Documents menu, or as an attachment to the motion to which it relates. MA R USDCT CM/ECF Admin(T).

v. *Compact disk with copy of document(s) in PDF format.* A filer who cannot file a document electronically because of such technical difficulty on the filer's end [with telephone, cable lines, the filer's Internet Service Provider (ISP), or hardware or software problems] shall file the document conventionally along with a copy of the document in PDF format on a compact disk or contact the clerk's office for permission to submit the PDF document via email. MA R USDCT CM/ECF Admin(W)(3). Refer to the Timing section of this document for more information on technical failures.

vi. *Notice of filing with clerk's office.* When documents or exhibits (other than those filed ex parte or under seal) are submitted conventionally, a "Notice of Filing with clerk's office" shall be filed electronically and attached to the main document. A paper copy of the "Notice of Filing with clerk's office" must accompany the documents submitted to the court. The "Notice of Filing with clerk's office" (see MA R USDCT CM/ECF Admin(Appendix I)) shall describe each of the documents that will be filed as paper copies in the clerk's office, or shall include an index of the documents if those documents are voluminous. MA R USDCT CM/ECF Admin(P)(5).

vii. *Additional copies.* Whenever, because of the nature of a proceeding, such as a proceeding before a three-judge district court under 28 U.S.C.A. § 2284, additional copies of a paper required to be filed are necessary either for the use of the court or to enable the clerk to carry out his duties, it is the responsibility of the party filing or having filed the paper to provide the necessary copies. MA R USDCT LR 5.1(d).

viii. *Courtesy copies.* COURTESY COPIES OF DOCUMENTS FILED ELECTRONICALLY SHALL NOT BE SUBMITTED ROUTINELY. MA R USDCT CM/ECF Admin(J). Judicial officers, on a case-by-case basis, may require courtesy copies for specific cases, or types of motions, etc. A few Judicial Officers have entered Standing Orders, which may be found on their respective pages on the court's website (under Divisions). Any document filed on paper with the court as a courtesy copy must be clearly labeled as such (Example: COURTESY COPY—DO NOT SCAN). Documents delivered to the court as a courtesy copy will not be maintained in the official court record. MA R USDCT CM/ECF Admin(J).

2. *Documents for opposing party*

a. *Required documents*

i. *Opposition.* Refer to the General Requirements section of this document for information on the opposing papers.

- *Memorandum.* A party opposing a motion shall file, in the same (rather than a separate), document a memorandum of reasons, including citation of supporting authorities, why the motion should not be granted. MA R USDCT LR 7.1(b)(2). Any memorandum of law or other attachment filed in support of a main document shall be filed as a separate document, using the proper event. MA R USDCT CM/ECF Admin(G)(4). Memoranda supporting or opposing allowance of motions shall not, without leave of court, exceed twenty (20) pages, double-spaced. MA R USDCT LR 7.1(b)(4).

- *Request for oral argument.* Any party making or opposing a motion who believes that oral argument may assist the court and wishes to be heard shall include a request for oral argument in a separate paragraph of the motion or opposition. The request should be set off with a centered caption, "REQUEST FOR ORAL ARGUMENT." MA R USDCT LR 7.1(d).

ii. *Certificate of service.* No certificate of service is required when a paper is served by filing it with the court's electronic-filing system. When a paper that is required to be served is served by other means: (1) if the paper is filed, a certificate of service must be filed with it or within a reasonable time after service; and (2) if the paper is not filed, a certificate of service need not be filed unless filing is required by court order or by local rule. FRCP

5(d)(1)(B). Except as otherwise provided by the Federal Rules of Civil Procedure, proof of service of all pleadings and other papers required to be served (except discovery papers that in accordance with FRCP 33 to FRCP 36(f) are not to be filed) shall be filed in the office of the clerk promptly after service has been made. The proof shall show the time and manner of service, and may be made by written acknowledgment of service, a certificate of a member of the bar of this court, or an affidavit of the person who served the paper. MA R USDCT LR 5.2(b)(1). A certificate of service of a member of the bar shall appear at the bottom of or on the margin of the last page of the paper to which it relates. MA R USDCT LR 5.2(b)(2).

- *Paper service.* The certificate shall be a brief, single-spaced statement and may be in the following form: I hereby certify that a true copy of the above document was served upon (each party appearing pro se and) the attorney of record for each other party by mail (by hand) on (date). (Signature). MA R USDCT LR 5.2(b)(2).

- *Electronic service.* Any pleading or other paper served by electronic means must bear a certificate of service in accordance with MA R USDCT LR 5.2(b). MA R USDCT LR 5.4(C); MA R USDCT CM/ECF Admin(H)(2). The certificate of service shall state that the filer: (1) filed the document electronically, (2) that it will be served electronically to registered CM/ECF participants via the NEF and (3) that the filer will send paper copies to non-registered participants as indicated on the NEF. MA R USDCT CM/ECF Admin(H)(2). For example: I hereby certify that this document filed through the CM/ECF system will be sent electronically to the registered participants as identified on the NEF (NEF) and paper copies will be sent to those indicated as non registered participants on (date). MA R USDCT CM/ECF Admin(H)(2).

- *Return.* Documents not conforming to the requirements of MA R USDCT LR 5.2 (except notices of appeal) shall be returned by the clerk. MA R USDCT LR 5.2(b)(2).

- *Failure to make proof of service.* Failure to make proof of service does not affect the validity of the service. MA R USDCT LR 5.2(b)(3).

b. *Supplemental documents*

i. *Supporting evidence.* When a motion relies on facts outside the record, the court may hear the matter on affidavits or may hear it wholly or partly on oral testimony or on depositions. FRCP 43(c). Affidavits and other documents setting forth or evidencing facts on which the opposition is based shall be filed with the opposition. MA R USDCT LR 7.1(b)(2).

ii. *Notice of constitutional question.* A party that files a pleading, written motion, or other paper drawing into question the constitutionality of a federal or state statute must promptly:

- *File notice.* File a notice of constitutional question stating the question and identifying the paper that raises it, if: (1) a federal statute is questioned and the parties do not include the United States, one of its agencies, or one of its officers or employees in an official capacity; or (2) a state statute is questioned and the parties do not include the state, one of its agencies, or one of its officers or employees in an official capacity; and

- *Serve notice.* Serve the notice and paper on the Attorney General of the United States if a federal statute is questioned—or on the state attorney general if a state statute is questioned—either by certified or registered mail or by sending it to an electronic address designated by the attorney general for this purpose. FRCP 5.1(a).

- *No forfeiture.* A party's failure to file and serve the notice, or the court's failure to certify, does not forfeit a constitutional claim or defense that is otherwise timely asserted. FRCP 5.1(d).

iii. *Compact disk with copy of document(s) in PDF format.* A filer who cannot file a document electronically because of such technical difficulty on the filer's end [with telephone, cable lines, the filer's Internet Service Provider (ISP), or hardware or software problems] shall file the document conventionally along with a copy of the document in PDF format on a compact disk or contact the clerk's office for permission to submit the PDF document via email. MA R USDCT CM/ECF Admin(W)(3). Refer to the Timing section of this document for more information on technical failures.

iv. *Notice of filing with clerk's office.* When documents or exhibits (other than those filed ex parte or under seal) are submitted conventionally, a "Notice of Filing with clerk's office" shall be filed electronically and attached to the main document. A paper copy of the "Notice of Filing with clerk's office" must accompany the documents submitted to the court. The "Notice of Filing with clerk's office" (see MA R USDCT CM/ECF Admin(Appendix I)) shall describe each of the documents that will be filed as paper copies in the clerk's office, or shall include an index of the documents if those documents are voluminous. MA R USDCT CM/ECF Admin(P)(5).

v. *Additional copies.* Whenever, because of the nature of a proceeding, such as a proceeding before a three-judge district court under 28 U.S.C.A. § 2284, additional copies of a paper required to be filed are necessary either for the use of the court or to enable the clerk to carry out his duties, it is the responsibility of the party filing or having filed the paper to provide the necessary copies. MA R USDCT LR 5.1(d).

vi. *Courtesy copies.* COURTESY COPIES OF DOCUMENTS FILED ELECTRONICALLY SHALL NOT BE SUBMITTED ROUTINELY. MA R USDCT CM/ECF Admin(J). Judicial officers, on a case-by-case basis, may require courtesy copies for specific cases, or types of motions, etc. A few Judicial Officers have entered Standing Orders, which may be found on their respective pages on the court's website (under Divisions). Any document filed on paper with the court as a courtesy copy must be clearly labeled as such (Example: COURTESY COPY—DO NOT SCAN). Documents delivered to the court as a courtesy copy will not be maintained in the official court record. MA R USDCT CM/ECF Admin(J).

## E. Format

1. *Form of documents.* The rules governing captions and other matters of form in pleadings apply to motions and other papers. FRCP 7(b)(2). The provisions of FRCP 10 and FRCP 11 concerning the form and signing of pleadings, motions, and other papers shall be applicable to all papers filed in any proceeding in this court. The board of bar overseers registration number of each attorney signing such documents, except the United States Attorney and his or her staff, shall be inscribed below the signature. MA R USDCT LR 5.1(a)(1).

a. *Paper size and binding.* All papers filed in the court shall be adapted for flat filing, be filed on eight and one-half by eleven (8-1/2 x 11) inch paper without backers and be bound firmly by staple or some such other means (excluding paper or binder clip or rubber band). MA R USDCT LR 5.1(a)(2).

b. *Spacing.* All papers, except discovery requests and responses, shall be double-spaced except for the identification of counsel, title of the case, footnotes, quotations and exhibits. Discovery requests and responses shall be single-spaced. MA R USDCT LR 5.1(a)(2).

c. *Caption.* Every pleading must have a caption with the court's name, a title, a file number, and [an] FRCP 7(a) designation. FRCP 10(a).

i. *Names of parties.* The title of the complaint must name all the parties; the title of other pleadings, after naming the first party on each side, may refer generally to other parties. FRCP 10(a).

ii. *Request for special action.* When any pleading or other paper filed in the court includes a request for special process or relief, or any other request such that, if granted, the court will proceed other than in the ordinary course, the request shall, unless it is noted on the category sheet [see MA R USDCT LR 40.1(a)(1)], be noted on the first page to the right of or immediately beneath the caption. MA R USDCT LR 5.1(c).

d. *Claims or defenses*

i. *Numbered paragraphs.* A party must state its claims or defenses in numbered paragraphs, each limited as far as practicable to a single set of circumstances. A later pleading may refer by number to a paragraph in an earlier pleading. FRCP 10(b).

ii. *Separate statements.* If doing so would promote clarity, each claim founded on a separate transaction or occurrence—and each defense other than a denial—must be stated in a separate count or defense. FRCP 10(b).

e. *Adoption by reference.* A statement in a pleading may be adopted by reference elsewhere in the same pleading or in any other pleading or motion. FRCP 10(c).

i. *Exhibits.* A copy of a written instrument that is an exhibit to a pleading is a part of the pleading for all purposes. FRCP 10(c).

f. *Citations*

i. *Local rules.* These rules shall be known as Local Rules of the United States District Court for the District of Massachusetts and cited as "L.R., D. Mass." or "L.R." MA R USDCT LR 1.1.

ii. *Electronic case filing procedures.* The procedures governing electronic case filing shall be known as the "Administrative Procedures for Electronic Case Filing in the United States District Court for the District of Massachusetts." They shall be cited as "APECF." MA R USDCT CM/ECF Admin(A)(7).

g. *Acceptance by the clerk.* The clerk must not refuse to file a paper solely because it is not in the form prescribed by the Federal Rules of Civil Procedure or by a local rule or practice. FRCP 5(d)(4).

i. Except for complaints and notices of appeal, papers that do not conform to the requirements of MA R USDCT LR 5.1(a)(2) shall be returned by the clerk. MA R USDCT LR 5.1(a)(2).

2. *Form of electronic documents.* A paper filed electronically is a written paper for purposes of the Federal Rules of Civil Procedure. FRCP 5(d)(3)(D).

   a. *PDF/A format required.* The court will begin requiring submission of documents in PDF/A format in the foreseeable future. PDF/A is an enhanced version of the traditional PDF format. Newer versions of most PDF software will be able to convert to this format. Additional information on PDF/A documents may be found on the court's website. MA R USDCT CM/ECF Admin(Electronic Filing and PDF).

      i. *Electronically converted PDF.* Electronically converted PDF documents are created from word processing documents (MS Word, WordPerfect, etc.) using any appropriate software. These documents are text searchable and the file size is generally smaller than a scanned document. CM/ECF users may use any brand of software to convert documents to PDF. MA R USDCT CM/ECF Admin(Electronic Filing and PDF).

         • Documents converted to PDF, rather than scanned, are preferred for filing in CM/ECF. MA R USDCT CM/ECF Admin(Electronic Filing and PDF).

      ii. *Scanned PDF.* Scanned PDF documents are created from paper documents run through an optical scanner. Scanned PDF documents are generally not searchable and have a larger file size. Please note that software used to create scanned documents may (and should) be set in such a way that the document is "text-searchable." MA R USDCT CM/ECF Admin(Electronic Filing and PDF).

   b. *Title.* All pleadings filed electronically shall be titled in accordance with the approved dictionary of civil or criminal events of the CM/ECF system of this court. A list of events is available on the CM/ECF Training Information page of the court's website. The clerk's office may, when necessary and appropriate, modify the docket entry description, or delete and re-enter the docket entry in order to comply with the court's quality assurance standards. MA R USDCT CM/ECF Admin(G)(3).

   c. *Attachments to filings and exhibits.* Attachments to filings and exhibits must be filed in accordance with the court's CM/ECF User Manual, unless otherwise ordered by the court. MA R USDCT CM/ECF Admin(O)(1).

      i. Filers must submit as attachments only those excerpts of the referenced documents that are directly germane to the matter under consideration by the court. Excerpted material must be clearly and prominently identified as such. Users who file excerpts of documents do so without prejudice to their right to timely file additional excerpts or the complete document, as may be allowed by the court. Responding parties may timely file additional excerpts or the complete document that they believe are directly germane. MA R USDCT CM/ECF Admin(O)(2).

      ii. Filers shall not attach as an exhibit any pleading or other paper already on file with the court in that case, but shall merely refer to that document. (See MA R USDCT CM/ECF Admin(G) for information on using hyperlinks in PDF documents filed in CM/ECF.) MA R USDCT CM/ECF Admin(O)(3).

   d. *Redacted documents.* The parties may request or the court may require the submission of documents that have been redacted/stripped of sensitive or confidential information. The redacted document prepared for electronic filing shall include the original caption of the document, and be clearly labeled as "Redacted Document." A specific event is available for this purpose ("Redacted Document"), found under the Other Filings/Other Documents menu option. MA R USDCT CM/ECF Admin(S).

      i. Attorneys and pro se litigants are advised to take extra care when creating PDF documents intended for submission to CM/ECF. Steps shall be taken to ensure the documents are free of any hidden data (metadata) that may contain redacted information, or traces of information edited or deleted are not hidden in the final document. Even PDF content that has been encrypted may be recovered. An advisory document with additional information on this topic may be found on the court's website. MA R USDCT CM/ECF Admin(S).

   e. *Hyperlinks.* Electronically filed documents may contain the following types of hyperlinks: (1) hyperlinks to other portions of the same document; (2) hyperlinks to other documents filed within the CM/ECF system; and (3) hyperlinks to a location on the Internet that contains a source document for a citation. MA R USDCT CM/ECF Admin(G)(7).

      i. Hyperlinks to cited authority may not replace standard citation format. Complete citations must be included in the text of the filed document. Neither a hyperlink, nor any site to which it refers, shall be considered part of the record, but are simply convenient mechanisms for accessing material cited in a document filed in CM/ECF. Instructions on creating hyperlinks may be found in the CM/ECF User Manual. MA R USDCT CM/ECF Admin(G)(7).

      ii. The court accepts no responsibility for, and does not endorse, any product, organization, or content at any

hyperlinked site, or at any site to which that site may be linked. The court accepts no responsibility for the availability or functionality of any hyperlink. MA R USDCT CM/ECF Admin(G)(7).

   iii. One feature of PDF/A documents is that hyperlinks are commonly "masked," meaning that the full address of the referenced file is not written out; for example, clicking the word brief may open a brief which was previously filed in CM/ECF. MA R USDCT CM/ECF Admin(G)(7)(NOTE). An "unmasked" hyperlink has the full address visible to the user. MA R USDCT CM/ECF Admin(G)(7)(NOTE).

   - Masked hyperlinks may or may not work in a PDF/A document, depending on how it was created. Currently, masked hyperlinks are preserved in PDF/A documents produced by the "Save As" method in Microsoft Word 2007 and 2010; the "PDFMaker" method in Microsoft Word 2007; and OpenOffice 2.4 ("PDF Export"). With other production methods, such as WordPerfect, the PDF/A document includes underlined words that appear to be links, but clicking them has no effect. MA R USDCT CM/ECF Admin(G)(7)(NOTE).

f. *Documents features not accepted.* CM/ECF will not accept PDF documents containing tracking tags, embedded systems commands, password protections, access restrictions or other security features, special tags or dynamic features. MA R USDCT CM/ECF Admin(G)(8).

g. *File size limitations.* A filing party shall limit the size of each PDF file to no more than twenty (20) megabytes. PDF files larger than seven (7) megabytes will be rejected by the CM/ECF system. The filer will see a message advising of the size limitation. MA R USDCT CM/ECF Admin(P)(2).

   i. Larger documents or exhibits may be submitted electronically if split into separate PDF files each less than seven (7) megabytes, attached to the main document and clearly labeled. MA R USDCT CM/ECF Admin(P)(2).

   ii. Documents submitted electronically or on paper are subject to the page limitations set by MA R USDCT LR 7.1(b)(4) or by order of the court. MA R USDCT CM/ECF Admin(P)(1).

h. *Accuracy and readability.* The filer shall verify the accuracy and readability of any PDF file before electronically filing it in CM/ECF. MA R USDCT CM/ECF Admin(G)(6); MA R USDCT CM/ECF Admin(P)(3).

3. *Signing of pleadings, motions and other papers*

   a. *Signature.* Every pleading, written motion, and other paper must be signed by at least one attorney of record in the attorney's name—or by a party personally if the party is unrepresented. The paper must state the signer's address, e-mail address, and telephone number. FRCP 11(a). The provisions of the Federal Rules of Civil Procedure pertaining to the form and signing of pleadings, motions, and other papers shall be applicable to all papers filed in any proceeding in this court. The board of bar overseers registration number of each attorney signing such documents, except the United States Attorney and his staff, shall be inscribed below the signature. MA R USDCT LR 5.1(a)(1).

      i. *Electronic signing.* A filing made through a person's electronic-filing account and authorized by that person, together with that person's name on a signature block, constitutes the person's signature. FRCP 5(d)(3)(C).

      ii. *Appearances.* The filing of an appearance or any other pleading signed on behalf of a party constitutes an entry of appearance for that party. All pleadings shall contain the name, bar admission number, address, telephone number, and e-mail address of the attorney entering an appearance. MA R USDCT LR 83.5.2(a).

         - *Appearances by law firms.* When a party is represented by a law firm, the appearance must include the name and the signature of at least one individual attorney. When a party is represented by more than one attorney from the same or different law firms, the attorney entering the appearance must designate the individual attorney who is authorized to receive all notices in the case. Any notice sent to an attorney so designated shall be deemed to be proper notice unless the court finds that notice was not properly sent. MA R USDCT LR 83.5.2(b).

         - For more information on appearances, refer to MA R USDCT LR 83.5.2.

      iii. *Signatures of attorneys.* The user login and password required to submit documents to the CM/ECF system shall serve as that user's signature for purposes of FRCP 11 and for all other purposes under the Federal Rules of Civil Procedure and the Local Rules of the United States District Court for the District of Massachusetts. All electronically filed documents must include a signature block and must set forth the attorney's name, bar number, address, telephone number and email address. The name of the CM/ECF user under whose log-in and password the document is submitted must be preceded by a "/s/" and typed in the space where the signature would otherwise appear. MA R USDCT CM/ECF Admin(M)(1). For an example, refer to MA R USDCT CM/ECF Admin(M)(1).

      iv. *Signatures of pro se parties.* Any document requiring a signature that is filed by a party appearing pro se shall

bear the words "pro se" following that party's signature. Any such document shall also state the party's mailing address, telephone number (if any), and e-mail address (if the party has consented to service by email). MA R USDCT LR 83.5.5(g). For more information on practice by pro se litigants, refer to MA R USDCT LR 83.5.5.

v. *Multiple signatures.* The filer of any document requiring more than one signature (e.g, stipulations, joint motions, joint status reports, magistrate judge consent forms, etc.) must list thereon all the names of other signatories by means of a "/s/ name of signatory" block for each. By submitting such a document, the filing attorney certifies that each of the other signatories has expressly agreed to the form and substance of the document and that the filing attorney has their actual authority to submit the document electronically. MA R USDCT CM/ECF Admin(M)(2). For more information, refer to MA R USDCT CM/ECF Admin(M)(2).

vi. *Affidavits.* Except as provided in MA R USDCT CM/ECF Admin(L), affidavits shall be filed electronically; however, the electronically filed version must contain a "/s/ name of signatory" block indicating that the paper document bears an original signature. MA R USDCT CM/ECF Admin(M)(3). The court will also accept a scanned version of the original, signed document. MA R USDCT CM/ECF Admin(M)(3). For more information, refer to MA R USDCT CM/ECF Admin(M)(3).

vii. *No verification or accompanying affidavit required for pleadings.* Unless a rule or statute specifically states otherwise, a pleading need not be verified or accompanied by an affidavit. FRCP 11(a).

viii. *Unsigned papers.* The court must strike an unsigned paper unless the omission is promptly corrected after being called to the attorney's or party's attention. FRCP 11(a).

b. *Representations to the court.* By presenting to the court a pleading, written motion, or other paper—whether by signing, filing, submitting, or later advocating it—an attorney or unrepresented party certifies that to the best of the person's knowledge, information, and belief, formed after an inquiry reasonable under the circumstances:

i. It is not being presented for any improper purpose, such as to harass, cause unnecessary delay, or needlessly increase the cost of litigation;

ii. The claims, defenses, and other legal contentions are warranted by existing law or by a nonfrivolous argument for extending, modifying, or reversing existing law or for establishing new law;

iii. The factual contentions have evidentiary support or, if specifically so identified, will likely have evidentiary support after a reasonable opportunity for further investigation or discovery; and

iv. The denials of factual contentions are warranted on the evidence or, if specifically so identified, are reasonably based on belief or a lack of information. FRCP 11(b).

c. *Sanctions.* Refer to the General Requirements section of this document for information on sanctions.

4. *Privacy protection for filings made with the court*

a. *Redacted filings.* Unless the court orders otherwise, in an electronic or paper filing with the court that contains an individual's Social Security number, taxpayer-identification number, or birth date, the name of an individual known to be a minor, or a financial-account number, a party or nonparty making the filing may include only:

i. The last four (4) digits of the Social Security number and taxpayer-identification number;

ii. The year of the individual's birth;

iii. The minor's initials; and

iv. The last four (4) digits of the financial-account number. FRCP 5.2(a); MA R USDCT CM/ECF Admin(N).

b. *Exemptions from the redaction requirement.* The redaction requirement does not apply to the following:

i. A financial-account number that identifies the property allegedly subject to forfeiture in a forfeiture proceeding;

ii. The record of an administrative or agency proceeding;

iii. The official record of a state-court proceeding;

iv. The record of a court or tribunal, if that record was not subject to the redaction requirement when originally filed;

v. A filing covered by FRCP 5.2(c) or FRCP 5.2(d); and

vi. A pro se filing in an action brought under 28 U.S.C.A. § 2241, 28 U.S.C.A. § 2254, or 28 U.S.C.A. § 2255. FRCP 5.2(b).

c. *Limitations on remote access to electronic files; Social Security appeals and immigration cases.* Unless the court orders otherwise, in an action for benefits under the Social Security Act, and in an action or proceeding relating to an order of removal, to relief from removal, or to immigration benefits or detention, access to an electronic file is authorized as follows:

    i.   The parties and their attorneys may have remote electronic access to any part of the case file, including the administrative record;

    ii.   Any other person may have electronic access to the full record at the courthouse, but may have remote electronic access only to:

- The docket maintained by the court; and
- An opinion, order, judgment, or other disposition of the court, but not any other part of the case file or the administrative record. FRCP 5.2(c).

d.   *Filings made under seal.* The court may order that a filing be made under seal without redaction. The court may later unseal the filing or order the person who made the filing to file a redacted version for the public record. FRCP 5.2(d).

e.   *Protective orders.* For good cause, the court may by order in a case:

    i.   Require redaction of additional information; or

    ii.   Limit or prohibit a nonparty's remote electronic access to a document filed with the court. FRCP 5.2(e).

f.   *Option for additional unredacted filing under seal.* A person making a redacted filing may also file an unredacted copy under seal. The court must retain the unredacted copy as part of the record. FRCP 5.2(f). For more information, refer to MA R USDCT LR 7.2.

g.   *Option for filing a reference list.* A filing that contains redacted information may be filed together with a reference list that identifies each item of redacted information and specifies an appropriate identifier that uniquely corresponds to each item listed. The list must be filed under seal and may be amended as of right. Any reference in the case to a listed identifier will be construed to refer to the corresponding item of information. FRCP 5.2(g).

h.   *Responsibility for redaction.* The clerk's office is not responsible for reviewing documents filed with the court to determine whether pleadings have been redacted and are in the proper form. MA R USDCT CM/ECF Admin(N).

i.   *Waiver of protection of identifiers.* A person waives the protection of FRCP 5.2(a) as to the person's own information by filing it without redaction and not under seal. FRCP 5.2(h).

## F.  Filing and Service Requirements

1.   *Filing requirements*

a.   *Required filings.* Any paper after the complaint that is required to be served must be filed no later than a reasonable time after service. FRCP 5(d)(1).

    i.   Except as noted in FRCP 33 to FRCP 36, the original of all papers required to be served under FRCP 5(d) shall, unless otherwise submitted to the court, be filed in the office of the clerk within seven (7) days after service has been made. MA R USDCT LR 5.1(b). Except as otherwise provided by the Federal Rules of Civil Procedure, proof of service of all pleadings and other papers required to be served (except discovery papers that in accordance with FRCP 33 to FRCP 36(f) are not to be filed) shall be filed in the office of the clerk promptly after service has been made. MA R USDCT LR 5.2(b)(1).

b.   *Nonelectronic filing.* A paper not filed electronically is filed by delivering it: (1) to the clerk; or (2) to a judge who agrees to accept it for filing, and who must then note the filing date on the paper and promptly send it to the clerk. FRCP 5(d)(2).

c.   *Electronic filing.* Unless exempt or otherwise ordered by the court, all pleadings and other papers submitted to the court must be filed, signed, and verified by electronic means as provided in MA R USDCT LR 5.4. MA R USDCT LR 5.4(A); MA R USDCT CM/ECF Admin(A)(1). All electronic filings must be made in accordance with the Administrative Procedures for Electronic Case Filing in the United States District Court for the District of Massachusetts (MA R USDCT CM/ECF Admin). MA R USDCT LR 5.4(B). The court may deviate from the Administrative Procedures for Electronic Case Filing in the United States District Court for the District of Massachusetts (MA R USDCT CM/ECF Admin) in specific cases, without prior notice, if deemed appropriate in the exercise of discretion, considering the need for the just, speedy, and inexpensive determination of matters pending before the court. MA R USDCT CM/ECF Admin(C)(1). The court may excuse a failure to comply with any administrative procedure whenever justice so requires. MA R USDCT CM/ECF Admin(C)(2).

    i.   *By a represented person; Generally required; Exceptions.* A person represented by an attorney must file electronically, unless nonelectronic filing is allowed by the court for good cause or is allowed or required by local rule. FRCP 5(d)(3)(A).

ii. *By unrepresented person; When allowed or required.* A person not represented by an attorney: (1) may file electronically only if allowed by court order or by local rule; and (2) may be required to file electronically only by court order, or by a local rule that includes reasonable exceptions. FRCP 5(d)(3)(B).

iii. *Exemptions from electronic filing*

- *Documents that should not be filed electronically.* The following types of documents must not be filed electronically, and will not be scanned into the ECF system by the clerk's office: (1) sealed documents; (2) ex parte motions; (3) documents generated as part of an alternative dispute resolution (ADR) process; (4) the administrative record in Social Security and other administrative proceedings; (5) the state court record in proceedings under 28 U.S.C.A. § 2254; and (6) such other types of documents as the clerk may direct in the Administrative Procedures for Electronic Case Filing in the United States District Court for the District of Massachusetts (MA R USDCT CM/ECF Admin). MA R USDCT LR 5.4(G)(1); MA R USDCT CM/ECF Admin(L).

- *Documents that need not be filed electronically.* The following types of documents need not be filed electronically, but may be scanned into the ECF system by a filing party or the clerk's office: (1) handwritten pleadings; (2) documents filed by pro se litigants who are incarcerated or who are not registered ECF users; (3) indictments, informations, criminal complaints, and the criminal JS45 form; (4) affidavits for search or arrest warrants and related documents; (5) documents received from another court under FRCRP 20 or FRCRP 40; (6) appearance bonds; (7) any document in a criminal case containing the original signature of a defendant, such as a waiver of indictment or a plea agreement; (8) petitions for violations of supervised release; (9) executed service of process documents under FRCP 4; and (10) such other types of documents as the clerk may direct in the Administrative Procedures for Electronic Case Filing in the United States District Court for the District of Massachusetts (MA R USDCT CM/ECF Admin). MA R USDCT LR 5.4(G)(2); MA R USDCT CM/ECF Admin(L).

- For more information on exemptions from electronic filing, refer to MA R USDCT CM/ECF Admin(L).

iv. *Consequences of electronic filing.* Electronic transmission of a document to the CM/ECF system, together with the transmission of a Notice of Electronic Filing (NEF) from the court at the completion of the transaction, constitutes the filing of the document for all purposes of the Federal Rules of Procedure and constitutes entry of the document on the docket maintained by the clerk pursuant to FRCP 58 and FRCP 79. MA R USDCT CM/ECF Admin(G)(1).

v. *Payment of filing fees.* When electronically filing any pleading or paper through CM/ECF that requires a fee, all registered ECF users are to pay the fee electronically through the Treasury Department's Internet payment process. MA R USDCT LR 67.4(d); MA R USDCT CM/ECF Admin(A)(1). Pro se filers and those who have been exempted from electronic filing and/or electronic payment of fees may submit payments by check or money order made payable to "Clerk, U.S. District Court". MA R USDCT LR 67.4(d). For more information on filing fees, refer to MA R USDCT LR 67.4 and MA R USDCT CM/ECF Admin(I).

vi. For more information on electronic filing, refer to MA R USDCT CM/ECF Admin.

d. *Email or fax filing.* In general, the court does not accept documents by email or by fax. If the court, in special circumstances, does authorize the submission of a document in that manner, the document shall not be considered filed until an NEF is generated by CM/ECF at the completion of the transaction. MA R USDCT CM/ECF Admin(H)(5).

2. *Service requirements.* All papers filed pursuant to MA R USDCT LR 7.1(b) shall be served unless the moving party indicates in writing on the face of the motion that ex parte consideration is requested. Motions filed "ex parte" and related papers need not be served until the motion has been ruled upon or the court orders that service be made. MA R USDCT LR 7.1(c). Service of all pleadings subsequent to the original complaint and of all other papers required to be served shall be made in the manner specified by FRCP 5. MA R USDCT LR 5.2(a).

a. *Service; When required*

i. *In general.* Unless the Federal Rules of Civil Procedure provide otherwise, each of the following papers must be served on every party:

- An order stating that service is required;

- A pleading filed after the original complaint, unless the court orders otherwise under FRCP 5(c) because there are numerous defendants;

- A discovery paper required to be served on a party, unless the court orders otherwise;

- A written motion, except one that may be heard ex parte; and

- A written notice, appearance, demand, or offer of judgment, or any similar paper. FRCP 5(a)(1).

ii. *If a party fails to appear.* No service is required on a party who is in default for failing to appear. But a pleading that asserts a new claim for relief against such a party must be served on that party under FRCP 4. FRCP 5(a)(2).

iii. *Seizing property.* If an action is begun by seizing property and no person is or need be named as a defendant, any service required before the filing of an appearance, answer, or claim must be made on the person who had custody or possession of the property when it was seized. FRCP 5(a)(3).

b. *Service; How made*

  i. *Serving an attorney.* If a party is represented by an attorney, service under FRCP 5 must be made on the attorney unless the court orders service on the party. FRCP 5(b)(1).

  - *Nonresident attorney.* On application of a party, the court may order an attorney who represents any other party and who does not maintain an office within this district where service can be made on him by delivery as provided by FRCP 5(b), to designate a member of the bar of this court who does maintain such an office to receive service of all pleadings and other papers in his behalf. MA R USDCT LR 5.2(c)(1).

  ii. *Serving a party acting pro se.* On application of a party, the court may order any other party who is appearing without an attorney and who does not maintain an office or residence within this district where service can be made on him by delivery as provided by FRCP 5(b), to designate an address within the district at which service can be made on him by delivery. MA R USDCT LR 5.2(c)(2).

  iii. *Service in general.* A paper is served under FRCP 5 by:

  - Handing it to the person;

  - Leaving it: (1) at the person's office with a clerk or other person in charge or, if no one is in charge, in a conspicuous place in the office; or (2) if the person has no office or the office is closed, at the person's dwelling or usual place of abode with someone of suitable age and discretion who resides there;

  - Mailing it to the person's last known address—in which event service is complete upon mailing;

  - Leaving it with the court clerk if the person has no known address;

  - Sending it to a registered user by filing it with the court's electronic-filing system or sending it by other electronic means that the person consented to in writing—in either of which events service is complete upon filing or sending, but is not effective if the filer or sender learns that it did not reach the person to be served; or

  - Delivering it by any other means that the person consented to in writing—in which event service is complete when the person making service delivers it to the agency designated to make delivery. FRCP 5(b)(2).

  iv. *Service by electronic means.* Unless exempt or otherwise ordered by the court, all pleadings and other papers must be served on other parties by electronic means. MA R USDCT LR 5.4(C); MA R USDCT CM/ECF Admin(H)(2). Service by electronic means shall be treated the same as service by mail. MA R USDCT CM/ECF Admin(H)(4).

  - *Consent to electronic service.* Registering to use CM/ECF constitutes consent to service of all documents by electronic means as provided in the Administrative Procedures for Electronic Case Filing in the United States District Court for the District of Massachusetts (MA R USDCT CM/ECF Admin) and FRCP 5(b) and FRCP 77(d). MA R USDCT CM/ECF Admin(E)(6); MA R USDCT CM/ECF Admin(H)(3).

  - *Service on registered ECF users.* Transmission of the Notice of Electronic Filing (NEF) through the court's transmission facilities will constitute service of the filed document upon a registered ECF user. MA R USDCT LR 5.4(C).

  - *Service on non-registered users.* The party filing the document electronically is responsible for serving a paper copy of the document by mail in accordance with FRCP 5(b) to those case participants who have not been identified on the NEF as electronic recipients. MA R USDCT CM/ECF Admin(H)(3).

  - *Service of conventionally filed papers.* Documents or exhibits submitted conventionally shall be served on other parties by the filer using traditional means. MA R USDCT CM/ECF Admin(P)(4).

    c. *Serving numerous defendants*

       i. *In general.* If an action involves an unusually large number of defendants, the court may, on motion or on its own, order that:

- Defendants' pleadings and replies to them need not be served on other defendants;

- Any crossclaim, counterclaim, avoidance, or affirmative defense in those pleadings and replies to them will be treated as denied or avoided by all other parties; and

- Filing any such pleading and serving it on the plaintiff constitutes notice of the pleading to all parties. FRCP 5(c)(1).

       ii. *Notifying parties.* A copy of every such order must be served on the parties as the court directs. FRCP 5(c)(2).

## G. Hearings

1. *Hearings, generally.* If the court concludes that there should be a hearing on a motion, the motion will be set down for hearing at such time as the court determines. MA R USDCT LR 7.1(e).

    a. *Oral argument.* Due process does not require that oral argument be permitted on a motion and, except as otherwise provided by local rule, the district court has discretion to determine whether it will decide the motion on the papers or hear argument by counsel (and perhaps receive evidence). FPP § 1190; F.D.I.C. v. Deglau, 207 F.3d 153 (3d Cir. 2000).

       i. *Evidence on a motion.* When a motion relies on facts outside the record, the court may hear the matter on affidavits or may hear it wholly or partly on oral testimony or on depositions. FRCP 43(c).

    b. *Providing a regular schedule for oral hearings.* A court may establish regular times and places for oral hearings on motions. FRCP 78(a).

    c. *Providing for submission on briefs.* By rule or order, the court may provide for submitting and determining motions on briefs, without oral hearings. FRCP 78(b). Motions that are not set down for hearing as provided in MA R USDCT LR 7.1(e) will be decided on the papers submitted after an opposition to the motion has been filed, or, if no opposition is filed, after the time for filing an opposition has elapsed. MA R USDCT LR 7.1(f).

2. *Conflict of court appearances.* For information on conflict of court appearances, refer to MA R USDCT LR 40.2.

## H. Forms

### 1. Federal Motion for Sanctions Forms

    a. Notice of motion for sanctions. 2C FEDFORMS § 10:74.

    b. Notice of motion and motion for sanctions. 2C FEDFORMS § 10:75.

    c. Notice of motion and motion for sanctions; Including motion for sanctions under FRCP 37(c). 2C FEDFORMS § 10:76.

    d. Motion for sanctions; Including sanctions under FRCP 37(d). 2C FEDFORMS § 10:77.

    e. Defendant's summary of attorney fees. 2C FEDFORMS § 10:78.

    f. Motion; For order imposing sanctions pursuant to FRCP 11; Allegation; Notice of removal frivolous. AMJUR PP FEDPRAC § 375.

    g. Motion; General form. FEDPROF § 1B:171.

    h. Notice; Of motion; General form. FEDPROF § 1B:172.

    i. Notice; Of motion; With costs of motion. FEDPROF § 1B:173.

    j. Notice; Of motion; Containing motion. FEDPROF § 1B:174.

    k. Opposition; To motion. FEDPROF § 1B:175.

    l. Affidavit; Supporting or opposing motion. FEDPROF § 1B:176.

    m. Brief; Supporting or opposing motion. FEDPROF § 1B:177.

    n. Statement of points and authorities; Opposing motion. FEDPROF § 1B:178.

    o. Illustrative forms; FRCP 11; Notice and motion for sanctions. LITGTORT § 20:36.

    p. Illustrative forms; FRCP 11; Memorandum in support of motion. LITGTORT § 20:37.

    q. Illustrative forms; FRCP 11; Declaration in support of motion. LITGTORT § 20:38.

    r.   Illustrative forms; FRCP 11 and 28 U.S.C.A. § 1927; Notice of motion and motion for sanctions. LITGTORT § 20:39.

    s.   Illustrative forms; FRCP 11 and 28 U.S.C.A. § 1927; Brief in support of motion. LITGTORT § 20:40.

**2.   Forms for the District of Massachusetts**

    a.   Notice of filing with clerk's office. MA R USDCT CM/ECF Admin(Appendix I).

## I.  Applicable Rules

1.  *Federal rules*

    a.   Counsel's liability for excessive costs. 28 U.S.C.A. § 1927.

    b.   Serving and filing pleadings and other papers. FRCP 5.

    c.   Constitutional challenge to a statute; Notice, certification, and intervention. FRCP 5.1.

    d.   Privacy protection for filings made with the court. FRCP 5.2.

    e.   Computing and extending time; Time for motion papers. FRCP 6.

    f.   Pleadings allowed; Form of motions and other papers. FRCP 7.

    g.   Disclosure statement. FRCP 7.1.

    h.   Form of pleadings. FRCP 10.

    i.   Signing pleadings, motions, and other papers; Representations to the court; Sanctions. FRCP 11.

    j.   Taking testimony. FRCP 43.

    k.   Hearing motions; Submission on briefs. FRCP 78.

2.  *Local rules*

    a.   Title. MA R USDCT LR 1.1.

    b.   Sanctions. MA R USDCT LR 1.3.

    c.   Form and filing of papers. MA R USDCT LR 5.1.

    d.   Service and filing of pleadings and other papers. MA R USDCT LR 5.2.

    e.   Filing and service by electronic means. MA R USDCT LR 5.4.

    f.   Motion practice. MA R USDCT LR 7.1.

    g.   Alternative dispute resolution. MA R USDCT LR 16.4.

    h.   Payments and deposits made with the clerk. MA R USDCT LR 67.4.

    i.   Settlement. MA R USDCT LR 68.2.

    j.   Office of the clerk. MA R USDCT LR 77.2.

    k.   Appearances. MA R USDCT LR 83.5.2.

    l.   Practice by pro se litigants. MA R USDCT LR 83.5.5.

    m.   CM/ECF case management/electronic case files administrative procedures. MA R USDCT CM/ECF Admin.

## Motions, Oppositions and Replies
## Motion to Compel Discovery

**Document Last Updated December 2018**

## A.  Checklist

(I)  ❑  Matters to be considered by moving party

    (a)  ❑  Required documents

        (1)  ❑  Notice of motion and motion

        (2)  ❑  Certificate of compliance

        (3)  ❑  Memorandum

    (4) ❑ Discovery documents

    (5) ❑ Certificate of service

(b) ❑ Supplemental documents

    (1) ❑ Supporting evidence

    (2) ❑ Notice of constitutional question

    (3) ❑ Proposed order

    (4) ❑ Compact disk with copy of document(s) in PDF format

    (5) ❑ Notice of filing with clerk's office

    (6) ❑ Additional copies

    (7) ❑ Courtesy copies

(c) ❑ Timing

    (1) ❑ The Federal Rules of Civil Procedure do not contain any time limit for filing motions to compel discovery; rather, a motion must simply be submitted within a reasonable time; however, a motion to compel discovery is premature if it is filed before any request for discovery is made

    (2) ❑ A written motion and notice of the hearing must be served at least fourteen (14) days before the time specified for the hearing, with the following exceptions: (i) when the motion may be heard ex parte; (ii) when the Federal Rules of Civil Procedure set a different time; or (iii) when a court order—which a party may, for good cause, apply for ex parte—sets a different time

    (3) ❑ Any affidavit supporting a motion must be served with the motion

    (4) ❑ Except as noted in FRCP 33 to FRCP 36, the original of all papers required to be served under FRCP 5(d) shall, unless otherwise submitted to the court, be filed in the office of the clerk within seven (7) days after service has been made

(II) ❑ Matters to be considered by opposing party

(a) ❑ Required documents

    (1) ❑ Opposition

    (2) ❑ Certificate of service

(b) ❑ Supplemental documents

    (1) ❑ Supporting evidence

    (2) ❑ Notice of constitutional question

    (3) ❑ Compact disk with copy of document(s) in PDF format

    (4) ❑ Notice of filing with clerk's office

    (5) ❑ Additional copies

    (6) ❑ Courtesy copies

(c) ❑ Timing

    (1) ❑ A party opposing a motion, shall file an opposition within fourteen (14) days after the motion is served, unless another period is fixed by rule or statute, or by order of the court

    (2) ❑ Except as FRCP 59(c) provides otherwise, any opposing affidavit must be served at least seven (7) days before the hearing, unless the court permits service at another time

    (3) ❑ Except as noted in FRCP 33 to FRCP 36, the original of all papers required to be served under FRCP 5(d) shall, unless otherwise submitted to the court, be filed in the office of the clerk within seven (7) days after service has been made

## B. Timing

1. *Motion to compel discovery.* The Federal Rules of Civil Procedure do not contain any time limit for filing motions to compel discovery. Rather, a motion must simply be submitted within a reasonable time. FEDPROC § 26:729. However, a motion to compel discovery is premature if it is filed before any request for discovery is made. FEDPROC § 26:729; Bermudez v. Duenas, 936 F.2d 1064 (9th Cir. 1991).

2.  *Timing of motions, generally*

    a.  *Motion and notice of hearing.* A written motion and notice of the hearing must be served at least fourteen (14) days before the time specified for the hearing, with the following exceptions:

        i.   When the motion may be heard ex parte;

        ii.  When the Federal Rules of Civil Procedure set a different time; or

        iii. When a court order—which a party may, for good cause, apply for ex parte—sets a different time. FRCP 6(c)(1).

    b.  *Supporting affidavit.* Any affidavit supporting a motion must be served with the motion. FRCP 6(c)(2).

3.  *Timing of opposing papers.* A party opposing a motion, shall file an opposition within fourteen (14) days after the motion is served, unless (1) the motion is for summary judgment, in which case the opposition shall be filed within twenty-one (21) days after the motion is served, or (2) another period is fixed by rule or statute, or by order of the court. MA R USDCT LR 7.1(b)(2); MA R USDCT CM/ECF Admin(H)(4); MA R USDCT LR 37.1(c). The fourteen (14) day period is intended to include the period specified by the civil rules for mailing time and provide for a uniform period regardless of the use of the mails. MA R USDCT LR 7.1(b)(2).

    a.  *Opposing affidavit.* Except as FRCP 59(c) provides otherwise, any opposing affidavit must be served at least seven (7) days before the hearing, unless the court permits service at another time. FRCP 6(c)(2).

4.  *Timing of reply papers.* [W]here the respondent files an answering affidavit setting up a new matter, the moving party ordinarily is allowed a reasonable time to file a reply affidavit since failure to deny the new matter by affidavit may operate as an admission of its truth. AMJUR MOTIONS § 25.

    a.  *Leave of court required.* All other papers not filed as indicated in MA R USDCT LR 7.1(b)(1) and MA R USDCT LR 7.1(b)(2), whether in the form of a reply brief or otherwise, may be submitted only with leave of court. MA R USDCT LR 7.1(b)(3).

5.  *Filing after service.* Except as noted in FRCP 33 to FRCP 36, the original of all papers required to be served under FRCP 5(d) shall, unless otherwise submitted to the court, be filed in the office of the clerk within seven (7) days after service has been made. MA R USDCT LR 5.1(b).

6.  *Computation of time*

    a.  *Computing time.* FRCP 6 applies in computing any time period specified in the Federal Rules of Civil Procedure, in any local rule or court order, or in any statute that does not specify a method of computing time. FRCP 6(a).

        i.   *Period stated in days or a longer unit.* When the period is stated in days or a longer unit of time:

             - Exclude the day of the event that triggers the period;

             - Count every day, including intermediate Saturdays, Sundays, and legal holidays; and

             - Include the last day of the period, but if the last day is a Saturday, Sunday, or legal holiday, the period continues to run until the end of the next day that is not a Saturday, Sunday, or legal holiday. FRCP 6(a)(1).

        ii.  *Period stated in hours.* When the period is stated in hours:

             - Begin counting immediately on the occurrence of the event that triggers the period;

             - Count every hour, including hours during intermediate Saturdays, Sundays, and legal holidays; and

             - If the period would end on a Saturday, Sunday, or legal holiday, the period continues to run until the same time on the next day that is not a Saturday, Sunday, or legal holiday. FRCP 6(a)(2).

        iii. *Office of the clerk.* The offices of the Clerk of Court at Boston, Worcester and Springfield shall be open from 8:30 a.m. until 5:00 p.m. on all days except Saturdays, Sundays, legal holidays and other days so ordered by the court and announced in advance, if feasible. MA R USDCT LR 77.2.

        iv.  *Inaccessibility of the clerk's office.* Unless the court orders otherwise, if the clerk's office is inaccessible:

             - On the last day for filing under FRCP 6(a)(1), then the time for filing is extended to the first accessible day that is not a Saturday, Sunday, or legal holiday; or

             - During the last hour for filing under FRCP 6(a)(2), then the time for filing is extended to the same time on the first accessible day that is not a Saturday, Sunday, or legal holiday. FRCP 6(a)(3).

        v.   *"Last day" defined.* Unless a different time is set by a statute, local rule, or court order, the last day ends:

             - For electronic filing, at midnight in the court's time zone; and

- For filing by other means, when the clerk's office is scheduled to close. FRCP 6(a)(4).

vi. *"Next day" defined.* The "next day" is determined by continuing to count forward when the period is measured after an event and backward when measured before an event. FRCP 6(a)(5).

vii. *"Legal holiday" defined.* "Legal holiday" means:

- The day set aside by statute for observing New Year's Day, Martin Luther King Jr.'s Birthday, Washington's Birthday, Memorial Day, Independence Day, Labor Day, Columbus Day, Veterans' Day, Thanksgiving Day, or Christmas Day;

- Any day declared a holiday by the President or Congress; and

- For periods that are measured after an event, any other day declared a holiday by the state where the district court is located. FRCP 6(a)(6).

b. *Computation of electronic filing deadlines.* Filing documents electronically does not alter any filing deadlines. MA R USDCT CM/ECF Admin(K); MA R USDCT LR 5.4(D). Although CM/ECF is generally available twenty-four (24) hours a day for filing, all electronic transmissions of documents must be completed prior to 6:00 PM, Eastern Standard (or Daylight Savings) Time, on the date on which it is due, in order to be considered timely filed that day. MA R USDCT CM/ECF Admin(K); MA R USDCT LR 5.4(D). When a specific time of day deadline is set by court order or stipulation, the electronic filing must be completed by that time. Documents may be filed at any time of the day on days prior to the date on which it is due. MA R USDCT CM/ECF Admin(K). A document filed electronically shall be deemed filed as of the time and date stated on the NEF received from the court. MA R USDCT CM/ECF Admin(G)(2); MA R USDCT CM/ECF Admin(K).

i. *Technical failures.* A user whose filing is made untimely as the result of a technical failure of the court's CM/ECF system may seek appropriate relief from the court. MA R USDCT CM/ECF Admin(W)(3). Technical difficulties on the filer's end, with telephone, cable lines, the filer's Internet Service Provider (ISP), or hardware or software problems, will not constitute a technical failure under the Administrative Procedures for Electronic Case Filing in the United States District Court for the District of Massachusetts (MA R USDCT CM/ECF Admin) nor excuse an untimely filing. MA R USDCT CM/ECF Admin(W)(3). As help desk support is available during normal business hours, filers are strongly urged to electronically file any documents during that period. MA R USDCT CM/ECF Admin(W)(3).

- The court has made available a public terminal (computers and scanner) in each clerk's office for registered users to scan and electronically file documents. This equipment is available during normal business hours. Users should bring their prepared document and a valid CM/ECF login and password. MA R USDCT CM/ECF Admin(W)(3).

c. *Extending time.* When an act may or must be done within a specified time, the court may, for good cause, extend the time: (1) with or without motion or notice if the court acts, or if a request is made, before the original time or its extension expires; or (2) on motion made after the time has expired if the party failed to act because of excusable neglect. FRCP 6(b)(1).

i. *Exceptions.* A court must not extend the time to act under FRCP 50(b), FRCP 50(d), FRCP 52(b), FRCP 59(b), FRCP 59(d), FRCP 59(e), and FRCP 60(b). FRCP 6(b)(2).

ii. Refer to the United States District Court for the District of Massachusetts KeyRules Motion for Continuance/Extension of Time document for more information on extending time.

d. *Additional time after certain kinds of service.* When a party may or must act within a specified time after being served and service is made under FRCP 5(b)(2)(C) (by mail), FRCP 5(b)(2)(D) (by leaving with the clerk), or FRCP 5(b)(2)(F) (by other means consented to), three (3) days are added after the period would otherwise expire under FRCP 6(a). FRCP 6(d).

# C. General Requirements

1. *Motions, generally*

a. *Requirements.* A request for a court order must be made by motion. The motion must:

i. Be in writing unless made during a hearing or trial;

ii. State with particularity the grounds for seeking the order; and

iii. State the relief sought. FRCP 7(b)(1).

b. *Notice of motion.* A party interested in resisting the relief sought by a motion has a right to notice thereof, and an opportunity to be heard. AMJUR MOTIONS § 12.

    i. [I]n addition to statutory or court rule provisions requiring notice of a motion—the purpose of such a notice requirement having been said to be to prevent a party from being prejudicially surprised by a motion—principles of natural justice dictate that an adverse party generally must be given notice that a motion will be presented to the court. AMJUR MOTIONS § 12.

    ii. "Notice," in this regard, means reasonable notice, including a meaningful opportunity to prepare and to defend against allegations of a motion. AMJUR MOTIONS § 12.

c. *Writing requirement.* The writing requirement is intended to [ensure] that the adverse parties are informed and have a record of both the motion's pendency and the grounds on which the movant seeks an order. FPP § 1191; Feldberg v. Quechee Lakes Corp., 463 F.3d 195 (2d Cir. 2006). [A] single written document can satisfy the writing requirements both for a motion and for [an] FRCP 6(c)(1) notice. FRCP 7(Advisory Committee Notes).

d. *Particularity requirement.* The particularity requirement [ensures] that the opposing parties will have notice of their opponent's contentions. FEDPROC § 62:358; Goodman v. 1973 26 Foot Trojan Vessel, Arkansas Registration No. AR1439SN, 859 F.2d 71 (8th Cir. 1988). That requirement ensures that notice of the basis for the motion is provided to the court and to the opposing party so as to avoid prejudice, provide the opponent with a meaningful opportunity to respond, and provide the court with enough information to process the motion correctly. FEDPROC § 62:358; Andreas v. Volkswagen of Am., Inc., 336 F.3d 789 (8th Cir. 2003).

    i. Reasonable specification of the grounds for a motion is sufficient. The particularity requirement for motions is satisfied when no party is prejudiced by a lack of particularity or when the court can comprehend the basis for the motion and deal with it fairly. However, where a movant fails to state even one ground for granting the motion in question, the movant has failed to meet the minimal standard of "reasonable specification." FEDPROC § 62:358; Martinez v. Trainor, 556 F.2d 818 (7th Cir. 1977).

    ii. The court may excuse the failure to comply with the particularity requirement if it is inadvertent, and where no prejudice is shown by the opposing party. FEDPROC § 62:358.

e. *Control of motion practice*

    i. *Plan for the disposition of motions.* At the earliest practicable time, the judicial officer shall establish a framework for the disposition of motions, which, at the discretion of the judicial officer, may include specific deadlines or general time guidelines for filing motions. This framework may be amended from time to time by the judicial officer as required by the progress of the case. MA R USDCT LR 7.1(a)(1).

    ii. *Motion practice.* No motion shall be filed unless counsel certify that they have conferred and have attempted in good faith to resolve or narrow the issue. MA R USDCT LR 7.1(a)(2).

    iii. *Unresolved motions.* The court shall rule on motions as soon as practicable, having in mind the reporting requirements set forth in the Civil Justice Reform Act. MA R USDCT LR 7.1(a)(3).

2. *Good faith conference.* Before filing any discovery motion, including any motion for sanctions or for a protective order, counsel for each of the parties shall confer in good faith to narrow the areas of disagreement to the greatest possible extent. It shall be the responsibility of counsel for the moving party to arrange for the conference. Conferences may be conducted over the telephone. Failure of opposing counsel to respond to a request for a discovery conference within seven (7) days of the request shall be grounds for sanctions, which may include automatic allowance of the motion. MA R USDCT LR 37.1(a).

a. *When to file a motion and memorandum.* If (1) opposing counsel has failed to respond to a request for a discovery conference within the seven day period set forth in MA R USDCT LR 37.1(a), (2) opposing counsel has failed to attend a discovery conference within fourteen (14) calendar days of the request, or (3) if disputed issues are not resolved at the discovery conference, a dissatisfied party may file a motion and supporting memorandum. MA R USDCT LR 37.1(b).

3. *Motion to compel discovery.* On notice to other parties and all affected persons, a party may move for an order compelling disclosure or discovery. FRCP 37(a)(1). The moving party must affirmatively demonstrate that the opponent did not produce discoverable information. A party's suspicion that its opponent must have documents that it claims not to have is insufficient to warrant granting a motion to compel. FEDPROC § 26:726.

a. *Appropriate court.* A motion for an order to a party must be made in the court where the action is pending. A motion for an order to a nonparty must be made in the court where the discovery is or will be taken. FRCP 37(a)(2).

b. *Specific motions*

    i. *To compel disclosure.* If a party fails to make a disclosure required by FRCP 26(a), any other party may move to compel disclosure and for appropriate sanctions. FRCP 37(a)(3)(A). Refer to the United States District Court for the District of Massachusetts KeyRules Motion for Discovery Sanctions document for more information on sanctions.

    ii. *To compel a discovery response.* A party seeking discovery may move for an order compelling an answer, designation, production, or inspection. This motion may be made if:

- A deponent fails to answer a question asked under FRCP 30 or FRCP 31;

- A corporation or other entity fails to make a designation under FRCP 30(b)(6) or FRCP 31(a)(4);

- A party fails to answer an interrogatory submitted under FRCP 33; or

- A party fails to produce documents or fails to respond that inspection will be permitted—or fails to permit inspection—as requested under FRCP 34. FRCP 37(a)(3)(B).

    iii. *Related to a deposition.* When taking an oral deposition, the party asking a question may complete or adjourn the examination before moving for an order. FRCP 37(a)(3)(C).

    iv. *Evasive or incomplete disclosure, answer, or response.* For purposes of FRCP 37(a), an evasive or incomplete disclosure, answer, or response must be treated as a failure to disclose, answer, or respond. FRCP 37(a)(4).

c. *Payment of expenses; Protective orders*

    i. *If the motion is granted (or disclosure or discovery is provided after filing).* If the motion is granted—or if the disclosure or requested discovery is provided after the motion was filed—the court must, after giving an opportunity to be heard, require the party or deponent whose conduct necessitated the motion, the party or attorney advising that conduct, or both to pay the movant's reasonable expenses incurred in making the motion, including attorney's fees. But the court must not order this payment if:

- The movant filed the motion before attempting in good faith to obtain the disclosure or discovery without court action;

- The opposing party's nondisclosure, response, or objection was substantially justified; or

- Other circumstances make an award of expenses unjust. FRCP 37(a)(5)(A).

    ii. *If the motion is denied.* If the motion is denied, the court may issue any protective order authorized under FRCP 26(c) and must, after giving an opportunity to be heard, require the movant, the attorney filing the motion, or both to pay the party or deponent who opposed the motion its reasonable expenses incurred in opposing the motion, including attorney's fees. But the court must not order this payment if the motion was substantially justified or other circumstances make an award of expenses unjust. FRCP 37(a)(5)(B).

    iii. *If the motion is granted in part and denied in part.* If the motion is granted in part and denied in part, the court may issue any protective order authorized under FRCP 26(c) and may, after giving an opportunity to be heard, apportion the reasonable expenses for the motion. FRCP 37(a)(5)(C).

4. *Opposing papers.* The Federal Rules of Civil Procedure do not require any formal answer, return, or reply to a motion, except where the Federal Rules of Civil Procedure or local rules may require affidavits, memoranda, or other papers to be filed in opposition to a motion. Such papers are simply to apprise the court of such opposition and the grounds of that opposition. FEDPROC § 62:353.

a. *Effect of failure to respond to motion.* Although in the absence of statutory provision or court rule, a motion ordinarily does not require a written answer, when a party files a motion and the opposing party fails to respond, the court may construe such failure to respond as nonopposition to the motion or an admission that the motion was meritorious, may take the facts alleged in the motion as true—the rule in some jurisdictions being that the failure to respond to a fact set forth in a motion is deemed an admission—and may grant the motion if the relief requested appears to be justified. AMJUR MOTIONS § 28.

b. *Assent or no opposition not determinative.* However, a motion will not be granted automatically simply because an "assent" or a notation of "no opposition" has been filed; federal judges frequently deny motions that have been assented to when it is thought that justice so dictates. FPP § 1190.

c. *Responsive pleading inappropriate as response to motion.* An attempt to answer or oppose a motion with a responsive pleading usually is not appropriate. FPP § 1190.

5. *Reply papers.* A moving party may be required or permitted to prepare papers in addition to his original motion papers.

AMJUR MOTIONS § 25. Papers answering or replying to opposing papers may be appropriate, in the interests of justice, where it appears there is a substantial reason for allowing a reply. Thus, a court may accept reply papers where a party demonstrates that the papers to which it seeks to file a reply raise new issues that are material to the disposition of the question before the court, or where the court determines, sua sponte, that it wishes further briefing of an issue raised in those papers and orders the submission of additional papers. FEDPROC § 62:354.

   a. *Function of reply papers.* The function of a reply affidavit is to answer the arguments made in opposition to the position taken by the movant and not to permit the movant to introduce new arguments in support of the motion. AMJUR MOTIONS § 25.

   b. *Issues raised for the first time in a reply document.* However, the view has been followed in some jurisdictions, that as a matter of judicial economy, where there is no prejudice and where the issues could be raised simply by filing a motion to dismiss, the trial court has discretion to consider arguments raised for the first time in a reply memorandum, and that a trial court may grant a motion to strike issues raised for the first time in a reply memorandum. AMJUR MOTIONS § 26.

6. *Alternative dispute resolution (ADR).* The judicial officer assigned to preside over the case shall encourage the resolution of disputes by settlement or other alternative dispute resolution programs. MA R USDCT LR 16.4(a).

   a. *Settlement.* At every conference conducted under the Local Rules of the United States District Court for the District of Massachusetts, the judicial officer shall inquire as to the utility of the parties conducting settlement negotiations, explore means of facilitating those negotiations, and offer whatever assistance may be appropriate in the circumstances. Assistance may include a reference of the case to another judicial officer for settlement purposes. MA R USDCT LR 16.4(b).

      i. When a case is settled, the parties shall file with the clerk a signed agreement for judgment or stipulation for dismissal, as appropriate, within twenty-eight (28) days, unless the court otherwise orders. MA R USDCT LR 68.2.

   b. *Alternative dispute resolution programs*

      i. *Discretion of judicial officer.* The judicial officer, following an exploration of the matter with all counsel, may refer appropriate cases to alternative dispute resolution programs that have been designated for use in the district court or that the judicial officer may make available. The dispute resolution programs described in MA R USDCT LR 16.4(c)(2) through MA R USDCT LR 16.4(c)(4) are illustrative, not exclusive. Moreover, nothing in MA R USDCT LR 16.4 shall preclude the parties from engaging in private dispute resolution programs as long as they comply with any schedule established by the court. MA R USDCT LR 16.4(c)(1).

      ii. *Mediation.* The judicial officer may refer the case to mediation upon the agreement of all parties. MA R USDCT LR 16.4(c)(2)(A).

      iii. *Other alternative dispute resolution programs.* Use of mediation is not exclusive. At the request of parties, the judicial officer may consider other forms of alternative dispute resolution including, but not limited to, mini-trial, summary jury trial and arbitration. MA R USDCT LR 16.4(c)(3).

   c. For more information on alternative dispute resolution (ADR), refer to MA R USDCT LR 16.4.

7. *Sanctions.* Failure to comply with any of the directions or obligations set forth in, or authorized by, these rules may result in dismissal, default, or the imposition of other sanctions as deemed appropriate by the judicial officer. MA R USDCT LR 1.3. Except as provided by law, the court may impose sanctions as provided in MA R USDCT LR 1.3 for failure to comply with the Administrative Procedures for Electronic Case Filing in the United States District Court for the District of Massachusetts (MA R USDCT CM/ECF Admin) or with MA R USDCT LR 5.4. MA R USDCT CM/ECF Admin(C)(3).

## D. Documents

1. *Documents for moving party*

   a. *Required documents*

      i. *Notice of motion and motion.* Refer to the General Requirements section of this document for information on the notice of motion and motion.

         • *Request for oral argument.* Any party making or opposing a motion who believes that oral argument may assist the court and wishes to be heard shall include a request for oral argument in a separate paragraph of the motion or opposition. The request should be set off with a centered caption, "REQUEST FOR ORAL ARGUMENT." MA R USDCT LR 7.1(d).

      ii. *Certificate of compliance.* The motion shall include a certificate in the margin of the last page that the provisions of MA R USDCT LR 37.1 have been complied with. MA R USDCT LR 37.1(b). The judicial officer shall not consider any discovery motion that is not accompanied by a certification, as required by MA R USDCT LR 7.1(a)(2) and MA R USDCT LR 37.1(b), that the moving party has made a reasonable and good faith effort to reach agreement with opposing counsel on the matters set forth in the motion. In evaluating any discovery motion, the judicial officer may consider the desirability of conducting phased discovery, as contemplated by MA R USDCT LR 26.3. MA R USDCT LR 26.2(c). The motion must include a certification that the movant has in good faith conferred or attempted to confer with the person or party failing to make disclosure or discovery in an effort to obtain it without court action. FRCP 37(a)(1).

iii. *Memorandum.* A party filing a motion shall at the same time file a memorandum of reasons, including citation of supporting authorities, why the motion should be granted. MA R USDCT LR 7.1(b)(1). Any memorandum of law or other attachment filed in support of a main document shall be filed as a separate document, using the proper event. MA R USDCT CM/ECF Admin(G)(4). Memoranda supporting or opposing allowance of motions shall not, without leave of court, exceed twenty (20) pages, double-spaced. MA R USDCT LR 7.1(b)(4). The memorandum shall state with particularity the following:

- If a discovery conference was not held, the reasons why it was not;

- If a discovery conference was held, the time, date, location and duration of the conference; who was present for each party; the matters on which the parties reached agreement; and the issues remaining to be decided by the court;

- The nature of the case and the facts relevant to the discovery matters to be decided;

- Each interrogatory, deposition question, request for production, request for admission or other discovery matter raising an issue to be decided by the court, and the response thereto; and

- A statement of the moving party's position as to each contested issue, with supporting legal authority, which statement shall be set forth separately immediately following each contested item. MA R USDCT LR 37.1(b).

iv. *Discovery documents.* If relief is sought under FRCP 26(c) or FRCP 37, copies of the relevant portions of disputed documents shall be filed with the court contemporaneously with any motion. MA R USDCT LR 26.6(a).

v. *Certificate of service.* No certificate of service is required when a paper is served by filing it with the court's electronic-filing system. When a paper that is required to be served is served by other means: (1) if the paper is filed, a certificate of service must be filed with it or within a reasonable time after service; and (2) if the paper is not filed, a certificate of service need not be filed unless filing is required by court order or by local rule. FRCP 5(d)(1)(B). Except as otherwise provided by the Federal Rules of Civil Procedure, proof of service of all pleadings and other papers required to be served (except discovery papers that in accordance with FRCP 33 to FRCP 36(f) are not to be filed) shall be filed in the office of the clerk promptly after service has been made. The proof shall show the time and manner of service, and may be made by written acknowledgment of service, a certificate of a member of the bar of this court, or an affidavit of the person who served the paper. MA R USDCT LR 5.2(b)(1). A certificate of service of a member of the bar shall appear at the bottom of or on the margin of the last page of the paper to which it relates. MA R USDCT LR 5.2(b)(2).

- *Paper service.* The certificate shall be a brief, single-spaced statement and may be in the following form: I hereby certify that a true copy of the above document was served upon (each party appearing pro se and) the attorney of record for each other party by mail (by hand) on (date). (Signature). MA R USDCT LR 5.2(b)(2).

- *Electronic service.* Any pleading or other paper served by electronic means must bear a certificate of service in accordance with MA R USDCT LR 5.2(b). MA R USDCT LR 5.4(C); MA R USDCT CM/ECF Admin(H)(2). The certificate of service shall state that the filer: (1) filed the document electronically, (2) that it will be served electronically to registered CM/ECF participants via the NEF and (3) that the filer will send paper copies to non-registered participants as indicated on the NEF. MA R USDCT CM/ECF Admin(H)(2). For example: I hereby certify that this document filed through the CM/ECF system will be sent electronically to the registered participants as identified on the NEF (NEF) and paper copies will be sent to those indicated as non registered participants on (date). MA R USDCT CM/ECF Admin(H)(2).

- *Return.* Documents not conforming to the requirements of MA R USDCT LR 5.2 (except notices of appeal) shall be returned by the clerk. MA R USDCT LR 5.2(b)(2).

- *Failure to make proof of service.* Failure to make proof of service does not affect the validity of the service. MA R USDCT LR 5.2(b)(3).

b. *Supplemental documents*

i. *Supporting evidence.* When a motion relies on facts outside the record, the court may hear the matter on affidavits or may hear it wholly or partly on oral testimony or on depositions. FRCP 43(c). Affidavits and other documents setting forth or evidencing facts on which the motion is based shall be filed with the motion. MA R USDCT LR 7.1(b)(1).

ii. *Notice of constitutional question.* A party that files a pleading, written motion, or other paper drawing into question the constitutionality of a federal or state statute must promptly:

- *File notice.* File a notice of constitutional question stating the question and identifying the paper that raises it, if: (1) a federal statute is questioned and the parties do not include the United States, one of its agencies, or one of its officers or employees in an official capacity; or (2) a state statute is questioned and the parties do not include the state, one of its agencies, or one of its officers or employees in an official capacity; and

- *Serve notice.* Serve the notice and paper on the Attorney General of the United States if a federal statute is questioned—or on the state attorney general if a state statute is questioned—either by certified or registered mail or by sending it to an electronic address designated by the attorney general for this purpose. FRCP 5.1(a).

- *No forfeiture.* A party's failure to file and serve the notice, or the court's failure to certify, does not forfeit a constitutional claim or defense that is otherwise timely asserted. FRCP 5.1(d).

iii. *Proposed order.* Proposed orders usually are not required by this court. However, the court may request the party to submit such a document. In those situations, unless otherwise directed by the clerk's office, electronically file the proposed document/order using the entry for "Proposed Documents submitted to the court," found under the Other Documents menu, or as an attachment to the motion to which it relates. MA R USDCT CM/ECF Admin(T).

iv. *Compact disk with copy of document(s) in PDF format.* A filer who cannot file a document electronically because of such technical difficulty on the filer's end [with telephone, cable lines, the filer's Internet Service Provider (ISP), or hardware or software problems] shall file the document conventionally along with a copy of the document in PDF format on a compact disk or contact the clerk's office for permission to submit the PDF document via email. MA R USDCT CM/ECF Admin(W)(3). Refer to the Timing section of this document for more information on technical failures.

v. *Notice of filing with clerk's office.* When documents or exhibits (other than those filed ex parte or under seal) are submitted conventionally, a "Notice of Filing with clerk's office" shall be filed electronically and attached to the main document. A paper copy of the "Notice of Filing with clerk's office" must accompany the documents submitted to the court. The "Notice of Filing with clerk's office" (see MA R USDCT CM/ECF Admin(Appendix I)) shall describe each of the documents that will be filed as paper copies in the clerk's office, or shall include an index of the documents if those documents are voluminous. MA R USDCT CM/ECF Admin(P)(5).

vi. *Additional copies.* Whenever, because of the nature of a proceeding, such as a proceeding before a three-judge district court under 28 U.S.C.A. § 2284, additional copies of a paper required to be filed are necessary either for the use of the court or to enable the clerk to carry out his duties, it is the responsibility of the party filing or having filed the paper to provide the necessary copies. MA R USDCT LR 5.1(d).

vii. *Courtesy copies.* COURTESY COPIES OF DOCUMENTS FILED ELECTRONICALLY SHALL NOT BE SUBMITTED ROUTINELY. MA R USDCT CM/ECF Admin(J). Judicial officers, on a case-by-case basis, may require courtesy copies for specific cases, or types of motions, etc. A few Judicial Officers have entered Standing Orders, which may be found on their respective pages on the court's website (under Divisions). Any document filed on paper with the court as a courtesy copy must be clearly labeled as such (Example: COURTESY COPY—DO NOT SCAN). Documents delivered to the court as a courtesy copy will not be maintained in the official court record. MA R USDCT CM/ECF Admin(J).

2. *Documents for opposing party*

a. *Required documents*

i. *Opposition.* The response, if any, shall conform to the requirements of MA R USDCT LR 37.1(b)(5). MA R USDCT LR 37.1(c). A statement of the moving party's position as to each contested issue, with supporting legal authority, which statement shall be set forth separately immediately following each contested item. MA R USDCT LR 37.1(b)(5). Refer to the General Requirements section of this document for information on the opposing papers.

- *Memorandum.* A party opposing a motion shall file, in the same (rather than a separate), document a memorandum of reasons, including citation of supporting authorities, why the motion should not be granted. MA R USDCT LR 7.1(b)(2). Any memorandum of law or other attachment filed in support of a main document shall be filed as a separate document, using the proper event. MA R USDCT CM/ECF Admin(G)(4). Memoranda supporting or opposing allowance of motions shall not, without leave of court, exceed twenty (20) pages, double-spaced. MA R USDCT LR 7.1(b)(4).

- *Request for oral argument.* Any party making or opposing a motion who believes that oral argument may assist the court and wishes to be heard shall include a request for oral argument in a separate paragraph of the motion or opposition. The request should be set off with a centered caption, "REQUEST FOR ORAL ARGUMENT." MA R USDCT LR 7.1(d).

ii. *Certificate of service.* No certificate of service is required when a paper is served by filing it with the court's electronic-filing system. When a paper that is required to be served is served by other means: (1) if the paper is filed, a certificate of service must be filed with it or within a reasonable time after service; and (2) if the paper is not filed, a certificate of service need not be filed unless filing is required by court order or by local rule. FRCP 5(d)(1)(B). Except as otherwise provided by the Federal Rules of Civil Procedure, proof of service of all pleadings and other papers required to be served (except discovery papers that in accordance with FRCP 33 to FRCP 36(f) are not to be filed) shall be filed in the office of the clerk promptly after service has been made. The proof shall show the time and manner of service, and may be made by written acknowledgment of service, a certificate of a member of the bar of this court, or an affidavit of the person who served the paper. MA R USDCT LR 5.2(b)(1). A certificate of service of a member of the bar shall appear at the bottom of or on the margin of the last page of the paper to which it relates. MA R USDCT LR 5.2(b)(2).

- *Paper service.* The certificate shall be a brief, single-spaced statement and may be in the following form: I hereby certify that a true copy of the above document was served upon (each party appearing pro se and) the attorney of record for each other party by mail (by hand) on (date). (Signature). MA R USDCT LR 5.2(b)(2).

- *Electronic service.* Any pleading or other paper served by electronic means must bear a certificate of service in accordance with MA R USDCT LR 5.2(b). MA R USDCT LR 5.4(C); MA R USDCT CM/ECF Admin(H)(2). The certificate of service shall state that the filer: (1) filed the document electronically, (2) that it will be served electronically to registered CM/ECF participants via the NEF and (3) that the filer will send paper copies to non-registered participants as indicated on the NEF. MA R USDCT CM/ECF Admin(H)(2). For example: I hereby certify that this document filed through the CM/ECF system will be sent electronically to the registered participants as identified on the NEF (NEF) and paper copies will be sent to those indicated as non registered participants on (date). MA R USDCT CM/ECF Admin(H)(2).

- *Return.* Documents not conforming to the requirements of MA R USDCT LR 5.2 (except notices of appeal) shall be returned by the clerk. MA R USDCT LR 5.2(b)(2).

- *Failure to make proof of service.* Failure to make proof of service does not affect the validity of the service. MA R USDCT LR 5.2(b)(3).

b. *Supplemental documents*

i. *Supporting evidence.* When a motion relies on facts outside the record, the court may hear the matter on affidavits or may hear it wholly or partly on oral testimony or on depositions. FRCP 43(c). Affidavits and other documents setting forth or evidencing facts on which the opposition is based shall be filed with the opposition. MA R USDCT LR 7.1(b)(2).

ii. *Notice of constitutional question.* A party that files a pleading, written motion, or other paper drawing into question the constitutionality of a federal or state statute must promptly:

- *File notice.* File a notice of constitutional question stating the question and identifying the paper that raises it, if: (1) a federal statute is questioned and the parties do not include the United States, one of its agencies, or one of its officers or employees in an official capacity; or (2) a state statute is questioned and the parties do not include the state, one of its agencies, or one of its officers or employees in an official capacity; and

- *Serve notice.* Serve the notice and paper on the Attorney General of the United States if a federal statute is questioned—or on the state attorney general if a state statute is questioned—either by certified or registered mail or by sending it to an electronic address designated by the attorney general for this purpose. FRCP 5.1(a).

- *No forfeiture.* A party's failure to file and serve the notice, or the court's failure to certify, does not forfeit a constitutional claim or defense that is otherwise timely asserted. FRCP 5.1(d).

iii. *Compact disk with copy of document(s) in PDF format.* A filer who cannot file a document electronically because of such technical difficulty on the filer's end [with telephone, cable lines, the filer's Internet Service Provider (ISP), or hardware or software problems] shall file the document conventionally along with a copy of the document in PDF format on a compact disk or contact the clerk's office for permission to submit the PDF document via email. MA R USDCT CM/ECF Admin(W)(3). Refer to the Timing section of this document for more information on technical failures.

iv. *Notice of filing with clerk's office.* When documents or exhibits (other than those filed ex parte or under seal) are submitted conventionally, a "Notice of Filing with clerk's office" shall be filed electronically and attached to the main document. A paper copy of the "Notice of Filing with clerk's office" must accompany the documents submitted to the court. The "Notice of Filing with clerk's office" (see MA R USDCT CM/ECF Admin(Appendix I)) shall describe each of the documents that will be filed as paper copies in the clerk's office, or shall include an index of the documents if those documents are voluminous. MA R USDCT CM/ECF Admin(P)(5).

v. *Additional copies.* Whenever, because of the nature of a proceeding, such as a proceeding before a three-judge district court under 28 U.S.C.A. § 2284, additional copies of a paper required to be filed are necessary either for the use of the court or to enable the clerk to carry out his duties, it is the responsibility of the party filing or having filed the paper to provide the necessary copies. MA R USDCT LR 5.1(d).

vi. *Courtesy copies.* COURTESY COPIES OF DOCUMENTS FILED ELECTRONICALLY SHALL NOT BE SUBMITTED ROUTINELY. MA R USDCT CM/ECF Admin(J). Judicial officers, on a case-by-case basis, may require courtesy copies for specific cases, or types of motions, etc. A few Judicial Officers have entered Standing Orders, which may be found on their respective pages on the court's website (under Divisions). Any document filed on paper with the court as a courtesy copy must be clearly labeled as such (Example: COURTESY COPY—DO NOT SCAN). Documents delivered to the court as a courtesy copy will not be maintained in the official court record. MA R USDCT CM/ECF Admin(J).

## E. Format

1. *Form of documents.* The rules governing captions and other matters of form in pleadings apply to motions and other papers. FRCP 7(b)(2). The provisions of FRCP 10 and FRCP 11 concerning the form and signing of pleadings, motions, and other papers shall be applicable to all papers filed in any proceeding in this court. The board of bar overseers registration number of each attorney signing such documents, except the United States Attorney and his or her staff, shall be inscribed below the signature. MA R USDCT LR 5.1(a)(1).

   a. *Paper size and binding.* All papers filed in the court shall be adapted for flat filing, be filed on eight and one-half by eleven (8-1/2 x 11) inch paper without backers and be bound firmly by staple or some such other means (excluding paper or binder clip or rubber band). MA R USDCT LR 5.1(a)(2).

   b. *Spacing.* All papers, except discovery requests and responses, shall be double-spaced except for the identification of counsel, title of the case, footnotes, quotations and exhibits. Discovery requests and responses shall be single-spaced. MA R USDCT LR 5.1(a)(2).

   c. *Caption.* Every pleading must have a caption with the court's name, a title, a file number, and [an] FRCP 7(a) designation. FRCP 10(a).

      i. *Names of parties.* The title of the complaint must name all the parties; the title of other pleadings, after naming the first party on each side, may refer generally to other parties. FRCP 10(a).

      ii. *Request for special action.* When any pleading or other paper filed in the court includes a request for special process or relief, or any other request such that, if granted, the court will proceed other than in the ordinary course, the request shall, unless it is noted on the category sheet [see MA R USDCT LR 40.1(a)(1)], be noted on the first page to the right of or immediately beneath the caption. MA R USDCT LR 5.1(c).

   d. *Claims or defenses*

      i. *Numbered paragraphs.* A party must state its claims or defenses in numbered paragraphs, each limited as far as practicable to a single set of circumstances. A later pleading may refer by number to a paragraph in an earlier pleading. FRCP 10(b).

      ii. *Separate statements.* If doing so would promote clarity, each claim founded on a separate transaction or occurrence—and each defense other than a denial—must be stated in a separate count or defense. FRCP 10(b).

   e. *Adoption by reference.* A statement in a pleading may be adopted by reference elsewhere in the same pleading or in any other pleading or motion. FRCP 10(c).

      i. *Exhibits.* A copy of a written instrument that is an exhibit to a pleading is a part of the pleading for all purposes. FRCP 10(c).

f. *Citations*

    i. *Local rules.* These rules shall be known as Local Rules of the United States District Court for the District of Massachusetts and cited as "L.R., D. Mass." or "L.R." MA R USDCT LR 1.1.

    ii. *Electronic case filing procedures.* The procedures governing electronic case filing shall be known as the "Administrative Procedures for Electronic Case Filing in the United States District Court for the District of Massachusetts." They shall be cited as "APECF." MA R USDCT CM/ECF Admin(A)(7).

g. *Acceptance by the clerk.* The clerk must not refuse to file a paper solely because it is not in the form prescribed by the Federal Rules of Civil Procedure or by a local rule or practice. FRCP 5(d)(4).

    i. Except for complaints and notices of appeal, papers that do not conform to the requirements of MA R USDCT LR 5.1(a)(2) shall be returned by the clerk. MA R USDCT LR 5.1(a)(2).

2. *Form of electronic documents.* A paper filed electronically is a written paper for purposes of the Federal Rules of Civil Procedure. FRCP 5(d)(3)(D).

a. *PDF/A format required.* The court will begin requiring submission of documents in PDF/A format in the foreseeable future. PDF/A is an enhanced version of the traditional PDF format. Newer versions of most PDF software will be able to convert to this format. Additional information on PDF/A documents may be found on the court's website. MA R USDCT CM/ECF Admin(Electronic Filing and PDF).

    i. *Electronically converted PDF.* Electronically converted PDF documents are created from word processing documents (MS Word, WordPerfect, etc.) using any appropriate software. These documents are text searchable and the file size is generally smaller than a scanned document. CM/ECF users may use any brand of software to convert documents to PDF. MA R USDCT CM/ECF Admin(Electronic Filing and PDF).

        • Documents converted to PDF, rather than scanned, are preferred for filing in CM/ECF. MA R USDCT CM/ECF Admin(Electronic Filing and PDF).

    ii. *Scanned PDF.* Scanned PDF documents are created from paper documents run through an optical scanner. Scanned PDF documents are generally not searchable and have a larger file size. Please note that software used to create scanned documents may (and should) be set in such a way that the document is "text-searchable." MA R USDCT CM/ECF Admin(Electronic Filing and PDF).

b. *Title.* All pleadings filed electronically shall be titled in accordance with the approved dictionary of civil or criminal events of the CM/ECF system of this court. A list of events is available on the CM/ECF Training Information page of the court's website. The clerk's office may, when necessary and appropriate, modify the docket entry description, or delete and re-enter the docket entry in order to comply with the court's quality assurance standards. MA R USDCT CM/ECF Admin(G)(3).

c. *Attachments to filings and exhibits.* Attachments to filings and exhibits must be filed in accordance with the court's CM/ECF User Manual, unless otherwise ordered by the court. MA R USDCT CM/ECF Admin(O)(1).

    i. Filers must submit as attachments only those excerpts of the referenced documents that are directly germane to the matter under consideration by the court. Excerpted material must be clearly and prominently identified as such. Users who file excerpts of documents do so without prejudice to their right to timely file additional excerpts or the complete document, as may be allowed by the court. Responding parties may timely file additional excerpts or the complete document that they believe are directly germane. MA R USDCT CM/ECF Admin(O)(2).

    ii. Filers shall not attach as an exhibit any pleading or other paper already on file with the court in that case, but shall merely refer to that document. (See MA R USDCT CM/ECF Admin(G) for information on using hyperlinks in PDF documents filed in CM/ECF.) MA R USDCT CM/ECF Admin(O)(3).

d. *Redacted documents.* The parties may request or the court may require the submission of documents that have been redacted/stripped of sensitive or confidential information. The redacted document prepared for electronic filing shall include the original caption of the document, and be clearly labeled as "Redacted Document." A specific event is available for this purpose ("Redacted Document"), found under the Other Filings/Other Documents menu option. MA R USDCT CM/ECF Admin(S).

    i. Attorneys and pro se litigants are advised to take extra care when creating PDF documents intended for submission to CM/ECF. Steps shall be taken to ensure the documents are free of any hidden data (metadata) that may contain redacted information, or traces of information edited or deleted are not hidden in the final document. Even PDF content that has been encrypted may be recovered. An advisory document with additional information on this topic may be found on the court's website. MA R USDCT CM/ECF Admin(S).

e. *Hyperlinks.* Electronically filed documents may contain the following types of hyperlinks: (1) hyperlinks to other portions of the same document; (2) hyperlinks to other documents filed within the CM/ECF system; and (3) hyperlinks to a location on the Internet that contains a source document for a citation. MA R USDCT CM/ECF Admin(G)(7).

   i. Hyperlinks to cited authority may not replace standard citation format. Complete citations must be included in the text of the filed document. Neither a hyperlink, nor any site to which it refers, shall be considered part of the record, but are simply convenient mechanisms for accessing material cited in a document filed in CM/ECF. Instructions on creating hyperlinks may be found in the CM/ECF User Manual. MA R USDCT CM/ECF Admin(G)(7).

   ii. The court accepts no responsibility for, and does not endorse, any product, organization, or content at any hyperlinked site, or at any site to which that site may be linked. The court accepts no responsibility for the availability or functionality of any hyperlink. MA R USDCT CM/ECF Admin(G)(7).

   iii. One feature of PDF/A documents is that hyperlinks are commonly "masked," meaning that the full address of the referenced file is not written out; for example, clicking the word brief may open a brief which was previously filed in CM/ECF. MA R USDCT CM/ECF Admin(G)(7)(NOTE). An "unmasked" hyperlink has the full address visible to the user. MA R USDCT CM/ECF Admin(G)(7)(NOTE).

   • Masked hyperlinks may or may not work in a PDF/A document, depending on how it was created. Currently, masked hyperlinks are preserved in PDF/A documents produced by the "Save As" method in Microsoft Word 2007 and 2010; the "PDFMaker" method in Microsoft Word 2007; and OpenOffice 2.4 ("PDF Export"). With other production methods, such as WordPerfect, the PDF/A document includes underlined words that appear to be links, but clicking them has no effect. MA R USDCT CM/ECF Admin(G)(7)(NOTE).

f. *Documents features not accepted.* CM/ECF will not accept PDF documents containing tracking tags, embedded systems commands, password protections, access restrictions or other security features, special tags or dynamic features. MA R USDCT CM/ECF Admin(G)(8).

g. *File size limitations.* A filing party shall limit the size of each PDF file to no more than twenty (20) megabytes. PDF files larger than seven (7) megabytes will be rejected by the CM/ECF system. The filer will see a message advising of the size limitation. MA R USDCT CM/ECF Admin(P)(2).

   i. Larger documents or exhibits may be submitted electronically if split into separate PDF files each less than seven (7) megabytes, attached to the main document and clearly labeled. MA R USDCT CM/ECF Admin(P)(2).

   ii. Documents submitted electronically or on paper are subject to the page limitations set by MA R USDCT LR 7.1(b)(4) or by order of the court. MA R USDCT CM/ECF Admin(P)(1).

h. *Accuracy and readability.* The filer shall verify the accuracy and readability of any PDF file before electronically filing it in CM/ECF. MA R USDCT CM/ECF Admin(G)(6); MA R USDCT CM/ECF Admin(P)(3).

3. *Signing disclosures and discovery requests, responses, and objections.* FRCP 11 does not apply to disclosures and discovery requests, responses, objections, and motions under FRCP 26 through FRCP 37. FRCP 11(d).

a. *Signature required.* Every disclosure under FRCP 26(a)(1) or FRCP 26(a)(3) and every discovery request, response, or objection must be signed by at least one attorney of record in the attorney's own name—or by the party personally, if unrepresented—and must state the signer's address, e-mail address, and telephone number. FRCP 26(g)(1). The provisions of the Federal Rules of Civil Procedure pertaining to the form and signing of pleadings, motions, and other papers shall be applicable to all papers filed in any proceeding in this court. The board of bar overseers registration number of each attorney signing such documents, except the United States Attorney and his staff, shall be inscribed below the signature. MA R USDCT LR 5.1(a)(1).

   i. *Electronic signing.* A filing made through a person's electronic-filing account and authorized by that person, together with that person's name on a signature block, constitutes the person's signature. FRCP 5(d)(3)(C).

   ii. *Appearances.* The filing of an appearance or any other pleading signed on behalf of a party constitutes an entry of appearance for that party. All pleadings shall contain the name, bar admission number, address, telephone number, and e-mail address of the attorney entering an appearance. MA R USDCT LR 83.5.2(a).

   • *Appearances by law firms.* When a party is represented by a law firm, the appearance must include the name and the signature of at least one individual attorney. When a party is represented by more than one attorney from the same or different law firms, the attorney entering the appearance must designate the individual attorney who is authorized to receive all notices in the case. Any notice sent to an attorney so designated

shall be deemed to be proper notice unless the court finds that notice was not properly sent. MA R USDCT LR 83.5.2(b).

- For more information on appearances, refer to MA R USDCT LR 83.5.2.

iii. *Signatures of attorneys.* The user login and password required to submit documents to the CM/ECF system shall serve as that user's signature for purposes of FRCP 11 and for all other purposes under the Federal Rules of Civil Procedure and the Local Rules of the United States District Court for the District of Massachusetts. All electronically filed documents must include a signature block and must set forth the attorney's name, bar number, address, telephone number and email address. The name of the CM/ECF user under whose log-in and password the document is submitted must be preceded by a "/s/" and typed in the space where the signature would otherwise appear. MA R USDCT CM/ECF Admin(M)(1). For an example, refer to MA R USDCT CM/ECF Admin(M)(1).

iv. *Signatures of pro se parties.* Any document requiring a signature that is filed by a party appearing pro se shall bear the words "pro se" following that party's signature. Any such document shall also state the party's mailing address, telephone number (if any), and e-mail address (if the party has consented to service by email). MA R USDCT LR 83.5.5(g). For more information on practice by pro se litigants, refer to MA R USDCT LR 83.5.5.

v. *Multiple signatures.* The filer of any document requiring more than one signature (e.g, stipulations, joint motions, joint status reports, magistrate judge consent forms, etc.) must list thereon all the names of other signatories by means of a "/s/ name of signatory" block for each. By submitting such a document, the filing attorney certifies that each of the other signatories has expressly agreed to the form and substance of the document and that the filing attorney has their actual authority to submit the document electronically. MA R USDCT CM/ECF Admin(M)(2). For more information, refer to MA R USDCT CM/ECF Admin(M)(2).

vi. *Affidavits.* Except as provided in MA R USDCT CM/ECF Admin(L), affidavits shall be filed electronically; however, the electronically filed version must contain a "/s/ name of signatory" block indicating that the paper document bears an original signature. MA R USDCT CM/ECF Admin(M)(3). The court will also accept a scanned version of the original, signed document. MA R USDCT CM/ECF Admin(M)(3). For more information, refer to MA R USDCT CM/ECF Admin(M)(3).

b. *Effect of signature.* By signing, an attorney or party certifies that to the best of the person's knowledge, information, and belief formed after a reasonable inquiry:

i. With respect to a disclosure, it is complete and correct as of the time it is made; and

ii. With respect to a discovery request, response, or objection, it is:

- Consistent with the Federal Rules of Civil Procedure and warranted by existing law or by a nonfrivolous argument for extending, modifying, or reversing existing law, or for establishing new law;

- Not interposed for any improper purpose, such as to harass, cause unnecessary delay, or needlessly increase the cost of litigation; and

- Neither unreasonable nor unduly burdensome or expensive, considering the needs of the case, prior discovery in the case, the amount in controversy, and the importance of the issues at stake in the action. FRCP 26(g)(1).

c. *Failure to sign.* Other parties have no duty to act on an unsigned disclosure, request, response, or objection until it is signed, and the court must strike it unless a signature is promptly supplied after the omission is called to the attorney's or party's attention. FRCP 26(g)(2).

d. *Sanction for improper certification.* If a certification violates FRCP 26(g) without substantial justification, the court, on motion or on its own, must impose an appropriate sanction on the signer, the party on whose behalf the signer was acting, or both. The sanction may include an order to pay the reasonable expenses, including attorney's fees, caused by the violation. FRCP 26(g)(3). Refer to the United States District Court for the District of Massachusetts KeyRules Motion for Discovery Sanctions document for more information.

4. *Privacy protection for filings made with the court*

a. *Redacted filings.* Unless the court orders otherwise, in an electronic or paper filing with the court that contains an individual's Social Security number, taxpayer-identification number, or birth date, the name of an individual known to be a minor, or a financial-account number, a party or nonparty making the filing may include only:

i. The last four (4) digits of the Social Security number and taxpayer-identification number;

ii. The year of the individual's birth;

    iii.   The minor's initials; and

    iv.   The last four (4) digits of the financial-account number. FRCP 5.2(a); MA R USDCT CM/ECF Admin(N).

b.   *Exemptions from the redaction requirement.* The redaction requirement does not apply to the following:

    i.   A financial-account number that identifies the property allegedly subject to forfeiture in a forfeiture proceeding;

    ii.   The record of an administrative or agency proceeding;

    iii.   The official record of a state-court proceeding;

    iv.   The record of a court or tribunal, if that record was not subject to the redaction requirement when originally filed;

    v.   A filing covered by FRCP 5.2(c) or FRCP 5.2(d); and

    vi.   A pro se filing in an action brought under 28 U.S.C.A. § 2241, 28 U.S.C.A. § 2254, or 28 U.S.C.A. § 2255. FRCP 5.2(b).

c.   *Limitations on remote access to electronic files; Social Security appeals and immigration cases.* Unless the court orders otherwise, in an action for benefits under the Social Security Act, and in an action or proceeding relating to an order of removal, to relief from removal, or to immigration benefits or detention, access to an electronic file is authorized as follows:

    i.   The parties and their attorneys may have remote electronic access to any part of the case file, including the administrative record;

    ii.   Any other person may have electronic access to the full record at the courthouse, but may have remote electronic access only to:

       ●   The docket maintained by the court; and

       ●   An opinion, order, judgment, or other disposition of the court, but not any other part of the case file or the administrative record. FRCP 5.2(c).

d.   *Filings made under seal.* The court may order that a filing be made under seal without redaction. The court may later unseal the filing or order the person who made the filing to file a redacted version for the public record. FRCP 5.2(d).

e.   *Protective orders.* For good cause, the court may by order in a case:

    i.   Require redaction of additional information; or

    ii.   Limit or prohibit a nonparty's remote electronic access to a document filed with the court. FRCP 5.2(e).

f.   *Option for additional unredacted filing under seal.* A person making a redacted filing may also file an unredacted copy under seal. The court must retain the unredacted copy as part of the record. FRCP 5.2(f). For more information, refer to MA R USDCT LR 7.2.

g.   *Option for filing a reference list.* A filing that contains redacted information may be filed together with a reference list that identifies each item of redacted information and specifies an appropriate identifier that uniquely corresponds to each item listed. The list must be filed under seal and may be amended as of right. Any reference in the case to a listed identifier will be construed to refer to the corresponding item of information. FRCP 5.2(g).

h.   *Responsibility for redaction.* The clerk's office is not responsible for reviewing documents filed with the court to determine whether pleadings have been redacted and are in the proper form. MA R USDCT CM/ECF Admin(N).

i.   *Waiver of protection of identifiers.* A person waives the protection of FRCP 5.2(a) as to the person's own information by filing it without redaction and not under seal. FRCP 5.2(h).

## F.  Filing and Service Requirements

1.   *Filing requirements*

a.   *Required filings.* Any paper after the complaint that is required to be served must be filed no later than a reasonable time after service. FRCP 5(d)(1).

    i.   Except as noted in FRCP 33 to FRCP 36, the original of all papers required to be served under FRCP 5(d) shall, unless otherwise submitted to the court, be filed in the office of the clerk within seven (7) days after service has been made. MA R USDCT LR 5.1(b). Except as otherwise provided by the Federal Rules of Civil Procedure, proof of service of all pleadings and other papers required to be served (except discovery papers that in accordance with FRCP 33 to FRCP 36(f) are not to be filed) shall be filed in the office of the clerk promptly after service has been made. MA R USDCT LR 5.2(b)(1).

b.   *Nonelectronic filing.* A paper not filed electronically is filed by delivering it: (1) to the clerk; or (2) to a judge who agrees to accept it for filing, and who must then note the filing date on the paper and promptly send it to the clerk. FRCP 5(d)(2).

c. *Electronic filing.* Unless exempt or otherwise ordered by the court, all pleadings and other papers submitted to the court must be filed, signed, and verified by electronic means as provided in MA R USDCT LR 5.4. MA R USDCT LR 5.4(A); MA R USDCT CM/ECF Admin(A)(1). All electronic filings must be made in accordance with the Administrative Procedures for Electronic Case Filing in the United States District Court for the District of Massachusetts (MA R USDCT CM/ECF Admin). MA R USDCT LR 5.4(B). The court may deviate from the Administrative Procedures for Electronic Case Filing in the United States District Court for the District of Massachusetts (MA R USDCT CM/ECF Admin) in specific cases, without prior notice, if deemed appropriate in the exercise of discretion, considering the need for the just, speedy, and inexpensive determination of matters pending before the court. MA R USDCT CM/ECF Admin(C)(1). The court may excuse a failure to comply with any administrative procedure whenever justice so requires. MA R USDCT CM/ECF Admin(C)(2).

   i. *By a represented person; Generally required; Exceptions.* A person represented by an attorney must file electronically, unless nonelectronic filing is allowed by the court for good cause or is allowed or required by local rule. FRCP 5(d)(3)(A).

   ii. *By unrepresented person; When allowed or required.* A person not represented by an attorney: (1) may file electronically only if allowed by court order or by local rule; and (2) may be required to file electronically only by court order, or by a local rule that includes reasonable exceptions. FRCP 5(d)(3)(B).

   iii. *Exemptions from electronic filing*

   - *Documents that should not be filed electronically.* The following types of documents must not be filed electronically, and will not be scanned into the ECF system by the clerk's office: (1) sealed documents; (2) ex parte motions; (3) documents generated as part of an alternative dispute resolution (ADR) process; (4) the administrative record in Social Security and other administrative proceedings; (5) the state court record in proceedings under 28 U.S.C.A. § 2254; and (6) such other types of documents as the clerk may direct in the Administrative Procedures for Electronic Case Filing in the United States District Court for the District of Massachusetts (MA R USDCT CM/ECF Admin). MA R USDCT LR 5.4(G)(1); MA R USDCT CM/ECF Admin(L).

   - *Documents that need not be filed electronically.* The following types of documents need not be filed electronically, but may be scanned into the ECF system by a filing party or the clerk's office: (1) handwritten pleadings; (2) documents filed by pro se litigants who are incarcerated or who are not registered ECF users; (3) indictments, informations, criminal complaints, and the criminal JS45 form; (4) affidavits for search or arrest warrants and related documents; (5) documents received from another court under FRCRP 20 or FRCRP 40; (6) appearance bonds; (7) any document in a criminal case containing the original signature of a defendant, such as a waiver of indictment or a plea agreement; (8) petitions for violations of supervised release; (9) executed service of process documents under FRCP 4; and (10) such other types of documents as the clerk may direct in the Administrative Procedures for Electronic Case Filing in the United States District Court for the District of Massachusetts (MA R USDCT CM/ECF Admin). MA R USDCT LR 5.4(G)(2); MA R USDCT CM/ECF Admin(L).

   - For more information on exemptions from electronic filing, refer to MA R USDCT CM/ECF Admin(L).

   iv. *Consequences of electronic filing.* Electronic transmission of a document to the CM/ECF system, together with the transmission of a Notice of Electronic Filing (NEF) from the court at the completion of the transaction, constitutes the filing of the document for all purposes of the Federal Rules of Procedure and constitutes entry of the document on the docket maintained by the clerk pursuant to FRCP 58 and FRCP 79. MA R USDCT CM/ECF Admin(G)(1).

   v. *Payment of filing fees.* When electronically filing any pleading or paper through CM/ECF that requires a fee, all registered ECF users are to pay the fee electronically through the Treasury Department's Internet payment process. MA R USDCT LR 67.4(d); MA R USDCT CM/ECF Admin(A)(1). Pro se filers and those who have been exempted from electronic filing and/or electronic payment of fees may submit payments by check or money order made payable to "Clerk, U.S. District Court". MA R USDCT LR 67.4(d). For more information on filing fees, refer to MA R USDCT LR 67.4 and MA R USDCT CM/ECF Admin(I).

   vi. For more information on electronic filing, refer to MA R USDCT CM/ECF Admin.

d. *Email or fax filing.* In general, the court does not accept documents by email or by fax. If the court, in special circumstances, does authorize the submission of a document in that manner, the document shall not be considered filed until an NEF is generated by CM/ECF at the completion of the transaction. MA R USDCT CM/ECF Admin(H)(5).

2. *Service requirements.* All papers filed pursuant to MA R USDCT LR 7.1(b) shall be served unless the moving party indicates in writing on the face of the motion that ex parte consideration is requested. Motions filed "ex parte" and related papers need not be served until the motion has been ruled upon or the court orders that service be made. MA R USDCT LR 7.1(c). Service of all pleadings subsequent to the original complaint and of all other papers required to be served shall be made in the manner specified by FRCP 5. MA R USDCT LR 5.2(a).

   a. *Service; When required*

      i. *In general.* Unless the Federal Rules of Civil Procedure provide otherwise, each of the following papers must be served on every party:

- An order stating that service is required;
- A pleading filed after the original complaint, unless the court orders otherwise under FRCP 5(c) because there are numerous defendants;
- A discovery paper required to be served on a party, unless the court orders otherwise;
- A written motion, except one that may be heard ex parte; and
- A written notice, appearance, demand, or offer of judgment, or any similar paper. FRCP 5(a)(1).

      ii. *If a party fails to appear.* No service is required on a party who is in default for failing to appear. But a pleading that asserts a new claim for relief against such a party must be served on that party under FRCP 4. FRCP 5(a)(2).

      iii. *Seizing property.* If an action is begun by seizing property and no person is or need be named as a defendant, any service required before the filing of an appearance, answer, or claim must be made on the person who had custody or possession of the property when it was seized. FRCP 5(a)(3).

   b. *Service; How made*

      i. *Serving an attorney.* If a party is represented by an attorney, service under FRCP 5 must be made on the attorney unless the court orders service on the party. FRCP 5(b)(1).

- *Nonresident attorney.* On application of a party, the court may order an attorney who represents any other party and who does not maintain an office within this district where service can be made on him by delivery as provided by FRCP 5(b), to designate a member of the bar of this court who does maintain such an office to receive service of all pleadings and other papers in his behalf. MA R USDCT LR 5.2(c)(1).

      ii. *Serving a party acting pro se.* On application of a party, the court may order any other party who is appearing without an attorney and who does not maintain an office or residence within this district where service can be made on him by delivery as provided by FRCP 5(b), to designate an address within the district at which service can be made on him by delivery. MA R USDCT LR 5.2(c)(2).

      iii. *Service in general.* A paper is served under FRCP 5 by:

- Handing it to the person;
- Leaving it: (1) at the person's office with a clerk or other person in charge or, if no one is in charge, in a conspicuous place in the office; or (2) if the person has no office or the office is closed, at the person's dwelling or usual place of abode with someone of suitable age and discretion who resides there;
- Mailing it to the person's last known address—in which event service is complete upon mailing;
- Leaving it with the court clerk if the person has no known address;
- Sending it to a registered user by filing it with the court's electronic-filing system or sending it by other electronic means that the person consented to in writing—in either of which events service is complete upon filing or sending, but is not effective if the filer or sender learns that it did not reach the person to be served; or
- Delivering it by any other means that the person consented to in writing—in which event service is complete when the person making service delivers it to the agency designated to make delivery. FRCP 5(b)(2).

      iv. *Service by electronic means.* Unless exempt or otherwise ordered by the court, all pleadings and other papers must be served on other parties by electronic means. MA R USDCT LR 5.4(C); MA R USDCT CM/ECF

Admin(H)(2). Service by electronic means shall be treated the same as service by mail. MA R USDCT CM/ECF Admin(H)(4).

- *Consent to electronic service.* Registering to use CM/ECF constitutes consent to service of all documents by electronic means as provided in the Administrative Procedures for Electronic Case Filing in the United States District Court for the District of Massachusetts (MA R USDCT CM/ECF Admin) and FRCP 5(b) and FRCP 77(d). MA R USDCT CM/ECF Admin(E)(6); MA R USDCT CM/ECF Admin(H)(3).

- *Service on registered ECF users.* Transmission of the Notice of Electronic Filing (NEF) through the court's transmission facilities will constitute service of the filed document upon a registered ECF user. MA R USDCT LR 5.4(C).

- *Service on non-registered users.* The party filing the document electronically is responsible for serving a paper copy of the document by mail in accordance with FRCP 5(b) to those case participants who have not been identified on the NEF as electronic recipients. MA R USDCT CM/ECF Admin(H)(3).

- *Service of conventionally filed papers.* Documents or exhibits submitted conventionally shall be served on other parties by the filer using traditional means. MA R USDCT CM/ECF Admin(P)(4).

c. *Serving numerous defendants*

  i. *In general.* If an action involves an unusually large number of defendants, the court may, on motion or on its own, order that:

  - Defendants' pleadings and replies to them need not be served on other defendants;

  - Any crossclaim, counterclaim, avoidance, or affirmative defense in those pleadings and replies to them will be treated as denied or avoided by all other parties; and

  - Filing any such pleading and serving it on the plaintiff constitutes notice of the pleading to all parties. FRCP 5(c)(1).

  ii. *Notifying parties.* A copy of every such order must be served on the parties as the court directs. FRCP 5(c)(2).

# G. Hearings

1. *Hearings, generally.* If the court concludes that there should be a hearing on a motion, the motion will be set down for hearing at such time as the court determines. MA R USDCT LR 7.1(e).

   a. *Oral argument.* Due process does not require that oral argument be permitted on a motion and, except as otherwise provided by local rule, the district court has discretion to determine whether it will decide the motion on the papers or hear argument by counsel (and perhaps receive evidence). FPP § 1190; F.D.I.C. v. Deglau, 207 F.3d 153 (3d Cir. 2000).

      i. *Evidence on a motion.* When a motion relies on facts outside the record, the court may hear the matter on affidavits or may hear it wholly or partly on oral testimony or on depositions. FRCP 43(c).

   b. *Providing a regular schedule for oral hearings.* A court may establish regular times and places for oral hearings on motions. FRCP 78(a).

   c. *Providing for submission on briefs.* By rule or order, the court may provide for submitting and determining motions on briefs, without oral hearings. FRCP 78(b). Motions that are not set down for hearing as provided in MA R USDCT LR 7.1(e) will be decided on the papers submitted after an opposition to the motion has been filed, or, if no opposition is filed, after the time for filing an opposition has elapsed. MA R USDCT LR 7.1(f).

2. *Conflict of court appearances.* For information on conflict of court appearances, refer to MA R USDCT LR 40.2.

# H. Forms

## 1. Federal Motion to Compel Discovery Forms

   a. Notice of motion to compel party to answer deposition questions. 3B FEDFORMS § 27:17.

   b. Motion to compel deposition, request for sanctions and request for expedited hearing. 3B FEDFORMS § 27:20.

   c. Motion to compel answer to interrogatories. 3B FEDFORMS § 27:21.

   d. Affidavit in support of motion. 3B FEDFORMS § 27:24.

   e. Objection to motion for order requiring witness to answer oral questions on deposition. 3B FEDFORMS § 27:27.

   f. Notice of motion; To compel required disclosure of names and addresses of witnesses and persons having knowledge of the claims involved; Civil proceeding. AMJUR PP DEPOSITION § 6.

g. Motion; To compel required disclosure of names and addresses of witnesses and persons having knowledge of the claims involved. AMJUR PP DEPOSITION § 7.

h. Motion; To compel answer to interrogatories; Complete failure to answer. AMJUR PP DEPOSITION § 403.

i. Affidavit; In opposition of motion to compel psychiatric or physical examinations; By attorney. AMJUR PP DEPOSITION § 645.

j. Motion; To compel further responses to interrogatories; Various grounds. AMJUR PP DEPOSITION § 713.

k. Affidavit; In support of motion to compel answers to interrogatories and to impose sanctions. AMJUR PP DEPOSITION § 715.

l. Opposition; To motion to compel electronic discovery; Federal class action. AMJUR PP DEPOSITION § 721.

m. Notice of motion; For order to compel compliance with request to permit entry on real property for inspection. AMJUR PP DEPOSITION § 733.

n. Motion; To compel production of documents; After rejected request; Request for sanctions. AMJUR PP DEPOSITION § 734.

o. Affidavit; In support of motion to compel production of documents; By attorney. AMJUR PP DEPOSITION § 736.

p. Motion; To compel doctor's production of medical records for trial. AMJUR PP DEPOSITION § 744.

q. Motion; To compel answers to outstanding discovery requests. FEDPROF § 23:44.

r. Motion; To compel required disclosure of names and addresses of witnesses and persons having knowledge of the claims involved. FEDPROF § 23:45.

s. Motion; To compel answer to questions asked on oral or written examination. FEDPROF § 23:214.

t. Motion; To compel further answers to questions asked on oral or written examination and to award expenses of motion. FEDPROF § 23:215.

u. Motion; To compel party to produce witness at deposition. FEDPROF § 23:216.

v. Affidavit; By opposing attorney; In opposition to motion to compel answers asked at deposition; Answers tend to incriminate. FEDPROF § 23:219.

w. Motion; To compel answer to interrogatories; Complete failure to answer. FEDPROF § 23:383.

x. Motion; To compel further responses to interrogatories; Various grounds. FEDPROF § 23:384.

y. Motion to compel discovery. GOLDLTGFMS § 21:2.

2. **Forms for the District of Massachusetts**

a. Notice of filing with clerk's office. MA R USDCT CM/ECF Admin(Appendix I).

## I. Applicable Rules

1. *Federal rules*

a. Serving and filing pleadings and other papers. FRCP 5.

b. Constitutional challenge to a statute; Notice, certification, and intervention. FRCP 5.1.

c. Privacy protection for filings made with the court. FRCP 5.2.

d. Computing and extending time; Time for motion papers. FRCP 6.

e. Pleadings allowed; Form of motions and other papers. FRCP 7.

f. Form of pleadings. FRCP 10.

g. Signing pleadings, motions, and other papers; Representations to the court; Sanctions. FRCP 11.

h. Duty to disclose; General provisions governing discovery. FRCP 26.

i. Failure to make disclosures or to cooperate in discovery; Sanctions. FRCP 37.

j. Taking testimony. FRCP 43.

k. Hearing motions; Submission on briefs. FRCP 78.

2. *Local rules*

a. Title. MA R USDCT LR 1.1.

b. Sanctions. MA R USDCT LR 1.3.

c. Form and filing of papers. MA R USDCT LR 5.1.

d. Service and filing of pleadings and other papers. MA R USDCT LR 5.2.

e. Filing and service by electronic means. MA R USDCT LR 5.4.

f. Motion practice. MA R USDCT LR 7.1.

g. Alternative dispute resolution. MA R USDCT LR 16.4.

h. Sequences of discovery. MA R USDCT LR 26.2.

i. Court filings and costs. MA R USDCT LR 26.6.

j. Discovery disputes. MA R USDCT LR 37.1.

k. Payments and deposits made with the clerk. MA R USDCT LR 67.4.

l. Settlement. MA R USDCT LR 68.2.

m. Office of the clerk. MA R USDCT LR 77.2.

n. Appearances. MA R USDCT LR 83.5.2.

o. Practice by pro se litigants. MA R USDCT LR 83.5.5.

p. CM/ECF case management/electronic case files administrative procedures. MA R USDCT CM/ECF Admin.

## Motions, Oppositions and Replies
## Motion for Protective Order

**Document Last Updated December 2018**

A. **Checklist**

(I) ❑ Matters to be considered by moving party

   (a) ❑ Required documents

      (1) ❑ Notice of motion and motion

      (2) ❑ Certificate of compliance

      (3) ❑ Memorandum

      (4) ❑ Discovery documents

      (5) ❑ Certificate of service

   (b) ❑ Supplemental documents

      (1) ❑ Supporting evidence

      (2) ❑ Notice of constitutional question

      (3) ❑ Nongovernmental corporate disclosure statement

      (4) ❑ Proposed order

      (5) ❑ Compact disk with copy of document(s) in PDF format

      (6) ❑ Notice of filing with clerk's office

      (7) ❑ Additional copies

      (8) ❑ Courtesy copies

   (c) ❑ Timing

      (1) ❑ The express language of FRCP 26(c) does not set out time limits within which a motion for a protective order must be made; yet the requirement that a motion be made within a reasonable time remains an implicit condition for obtaining a protective order

         (i) ❑ Although a party or deponent is allowed a reasonable amount of time in which to apply for a protective order, a protective order, as a general rule, must be obtained before the date set for the discovery; a motion for a protective order must be made before or on the date the discovery is due

(2) ❑ A written motion and notice of the hearing must be served at least fourteen (14) days before the time specified for the hearing, with the following exceptions: (i) when the motion may be heard ex parte; (ii) when the Federal Rules of Civil Procedure set a different time; or (iii) when a court order—which a party may, for good cause, apply for ex parte—sets a different time

(3) ❑ Any affidavit supporting a motion must be served with the motion

(4) ❑ Except as noted in FRCP 33 to FRCP 36, the original of all papers required to be served under FRCP 5(d) shall, unless otherwise submitted to the court, be filed in the office of the clerk within seven (7) days after service has been made

(II) ❑ Matters to be considered by opposing party

  (a) ❑ Required documents

    (1) ❑ Opposition

    (2) ❑ Certificate of service

  (b) ❑ Supplemental documents

    (1) ❑ Supporting evidence

    (2) ❑ Notice of constitutional question

    (3) ❑ Compact disk with copy of document(s) in PDF format

    (4) ❑ Notice of filing with clerk's office

    (5) ❑ Additional copies

    (6) ❑ Courtesy copies

  (c) ❑ Timing

    (1) ❑ A party opposing a motion, shall file an opposition within fourteen (14) days after the motion is served, unless another period is fixed by rule or statute, or by order of the court

    (2) ❑ Except as FRCP 59(c) provides otherwise, any opposing affidavit must be served at least seven (7) days before the hearing, unless the court permits service at another time

    (3) ❑ Except as noted in FRCP 33 to FRCP 36, the original of all papers required to be served under FRCP 5(d) shall, unless otherwise submitted to the court, be filed in the office of the clerk within seven (7) days after service has been made

## B. Timing

1. *Motion for protective order.* The express language of FRCP 26(c) does not set out time limits within which a motion for a protective order must be made; yet the requirement that a motion be made within a reasonable time remains an implicit condition for obtaining a protective order. FEDPROC § 26:289.

  a. *Reasonable time.* Although a party or deponent is allowed a reasonable amount of time in which to apply for a protective order, a protective order, as a general rule, must be obtained before the date set for the discovery. A motion for a protective order must be made before or on the date the discovery is due. FEDPROC § 26:289.

2. *Timing of motions, generally*

  a. *Motion and notice of hearing.* A written motion and notice of the hearing must be served at least fourteen (14) days before the time specified for the hearing, with the following exceptions:

    i. When the motion may be heard ex parte;

    ii. When the Federal Rules of Civil Procedure set a different time; or

    iii. When a court order—which a party may, for good cause, apply for ex parte—sets a different time. FRCP 6(c)(1).

  b. *Supporting affidavit.* Any affidavit supporting a motion must be served with the motion. FRCP 6(c)(2).

3. *Timing of opposing papers.* A party opposing a motion, shall file an opposition within fourteen (14) days after the motion is served, unless (1) the motion is for summary judgment, in which case the opposition shall be filed within twenty-one (21) days after the motion is served, or (2) another period is fixed by rule or statute, or by order of the court. MA R USDCT LR 7.1(b)(2); MA R USDCT CM/ECF Admin(H)(4); MA R USDCT LR 37.1(c). The fourteen (14) day period is intended to

include the period specified by the civil rules for mailing time and provide for a uniform period regardless of the use of the mails. MA R USDCT LR 7.1(b)(2).

    a.   *Opposing affidavit.* Except as FRCP 59(c) provides otherwise, any opposing affidavit must be served at least seven (7) days before the hearing, unless the court permits service at another time. FRCP 6(c)(2).

4.   *Timing of reply papers.* [W]here the respondent files an answering affidavit setting up a new matter, the moving party ordinarily is allowed a reasonable time to file a reply affidavit since failure to deny the new matter by affidavit may operate as an admission of its truth. AMJUR MOTIONS § 25.

    a.   *Leave of court required.* All other papers not filed as indicated in MA R USDCT LR 7.1(b)(1) and MA R USDCT LR 7.1(b)(2), whether in the form of a reply brief or otherwise, may be submitted only with leave of court. MA R USDCT LR 7.1(b)(3).

5.   *Filing after service.* Except as noted in FRCP 33 to FRCP 36, the original of all papers required to be served under FRCP 5(d) shall, unless otherwise submitted to the court, be filed in the office of the clerk within seven (7) days after service has been made. MA R USDCT LR 5.1(b).

6.   *Computation of time*

    a.   *Computing time.* FRCP 6 applies in computing any time period specified in the Federal Rules of Civil Procedure, in any local rule or court order, or in any statute that does not specify a method of computing time. FRCP 6(a).

        i.   *Period stated in days or a longer unit.* When the period is stated in days or a longer unit of time:

          •   Exclude the day of the event that triggers the period;

          •   Count every day, including intermediate Saturdays, Sundays, and legal holidays; and

          •   Include the last day of the period, but if the last day is a Saturday, Sunday, or legal holiday, the period continues to run until the end of the next day that is not a Saturday, Sunday, or legal holiday. FRCP 6(a)(1).

        ii.   *Period stated in hours.* When the period is stated in hours:

          •   Begin counting immediately on the occurrence of the event that triggers the period;

          •   Count every hour, including hours during intermediate Saturdays, Sundays, and legal holidays; and

          •   If the period would end on a Saturday, Sunday, or legal holiday, the period continues to run until the same time on the next day that is not a Saturday, Sunday, or legal holiday. FRCP 6(a)(2).

        iii.   *Office of the clerk.* The offices of the Clerk of Court at Boston, Worcester and Springfield shall be open from 8:30 a.m. until 5:00 p.m. on all days except Saturdays, Sundays, legal holidays and other days so ordered by the court and announced in advance, if feasible. MA R USDCT LR 77.2.

        iv.   *Inaccessibility of the clerk's office.* Unless the court orders otherwise, if the clerk's office is inaccessible:

          •   On the last day for filing under FRCP 6(a)(1), then the time for filing is extended to the first accessible day that is not a Saturday, Sunday, or legal holiday; or

          •   During the last hour for filing under FRCP 6(a)(2), then the time for filing is extended to the same time on the first accessible day that is not a Saturday, Sunday, or legal holiday. FRCP 6(a)(3).

        v.   *"Last day" defined.* Unless a different time is set by a statute, local rule, or court order, the last day ends:

          •   For electronic filing, at midnight in the court's time zone; and

          •   For filing by other means, when the clerk's office is scheduled to close. FRCP 6(a)(4).

        vi.   *"Next day" defined.* The "next day" is determined by continuing to count forward when the period is measured after an event and backward when measured before an event. FRCP 6(a)(5).

        vii.   *"Legal holiday" defined.* "Legal holiday" means:

          •   The day set aside by statute for observing New Year's Day, Martin Luther King Jr.'s Birthday, Washington's Birthday, Memorial Day, Independence Day, Labor Day, Columbus Day, Veterans' Day, Thanksgiving Day, or Christmas Day;

          •   Any day declared a holiday by the President or Congress; and

          •   For periods that are measured after an event, any other day declared a holiday by the state where the district court is located. FRCP 6(a)(6).

    b.   *Computation of electronic filing deadlines.* Filing documents electronically does not alter any filing deadlines. MA R

USDCT CM/ECF Admin(K); MA R USDCT LR 5.4(D). Although CM/ECF is generally available twenty-four (24) hours a day for filing, all electronic transmissions of documents must be completed prior to 6:00 PM, Eastern Standard (or Daylight Savings) Time, on the date on which it is due, in order to be considered timely filed that day. MA R USDCT CM/ECF Admin(K); MA R USDCT LR 5.4(D). When a specific time of day deadline is set by court order or stipulation, the electronic filing must be completed by that time. Documents may be filed at any time of the day on days prior to the date on which it is due. MA R USDCT CM/ECF Admin(K). A document filed electronically shall be deemed filed as of the time and date stated on the NEF received from the court. MA R USDCT CM/ECF Admin(G)(2); MA R USDCT CM/ECF Admin(K).

   i.   *Technical failures.* A user whose filing is made untimely as the result of a technical failure of the court's CM/ECF system may seek appropriate relief from the court. MA R USDCT CM/ECF Admin(W)(3). Technical difficulties on the filer's end, with telephone, cable lines, the filer's Internet Service Provider (ISP), or hardware or software problems, will not constitute a technical failure under the Administrative Procedures for Electronic Case Filing in the United States District Court for the District of Massachusetts (MA R USDCT CM/ECF Admin) nor excuse an untimely filing. MA R USDCT CM/ECF Admin(W)(3). As help desk support is available during normal business hours, filers are strongly urged to electronically file any documents during that period. MA R USDCT CM/ECF Admin(W)(3).

   - The court has made available a public terminal (computers and scanner) in each clerk's office for registered users to scan and electronically file documents. This equipment is available during normal business hours. Users should bring their prepared document and a valid CM/ECF login and password. MA R USDCT CM/ECF Admin(W)(3).

   c.   *Extending time.* When an act may or must be done within a specified time, the court may, for good cause, extend the time: (1) with or without motion or notice if the court acts, or if a request is made, before the original time or its extension expires; or (2) on motion made after the time has expired if the party failed to act because of excusable neglect. FRCP 6(b)(1).

   i.   *Exceptions.* A court must not extend the time to act under FRCP 50(b), FRCP 50(d), FRCP 52(b), FRCP 59(b), FRCP 59(d), FRCP 59(e), and FRCP 60(b). FRCP 6(b)(2).

   ii.  Refer to the United States District Court for the District of Massachusetts KeyRules Motion for Continuance/Extension of Time document for more information on extending time.

   d.   *Additional time after certain kinds of service.* When a party may or must act within a specified time after being served and service is made under FRCP 5(b)(2)(C) (by mail), FRCP 5(b)(2)(D) (by leaving with the clerk), or FRCP 5(b)(2)(F) (by other means consented to), three (3) days are added after the period would otherwise expire under FRCP 6(a). FRCP 6(d).

## C. General Requirements

1.  *Motions, generally*

   a.   *Requirements.* A request for a court order must be made by motion. The motion must:

   i.   Be in writing unless made during a hearing or trial;

   ii.  State with particularity the grounds for seeking the order; and

   iii. State the relief sought. FRCP 7(b)(1).

   b.   *Notice of motion.* A party interested in resisting the relief sought by a motion has a right to notice thereof, and an opportunity to be heard. AMJUR MOTIONS § 12.

   i.   [I]n addition to statutory or court rule provisions requiring notice of a motion—the purpose of such a notice requirement having been said to be to prevent a party from being prejudicially surprised by a motion—principles of natural justice dictate that an adverse party generally must be given notice that a motion will be presented to the court. AMJUR MOTIONS § 12.

   ii.  "Notice," in this regard, means reasonable notice, including a meaningful opportunity to prepare and to defend against allegations of a motion. AMJUR MOTIONS § 12.

   c.   *Writing requirement.* The writing requirement is intended to [ensure] that the adverse parties are informed and have a record of both the motion's pendency and the grounds on which the movant seeks an order. FPP § 1191; Feldberg v. Quechee Lakes Corp., 463 F.3d 195 (2d Cir. 2006). [A] single written document can satisfy the writing requirements both for a motion and for [an] FRCP 6(c)(1) notice. FRCP 7(Advisory Committee Notes).

   d.   *Particularity requirement.* The particularity requirement [ensures] that the opposing parties will have notice of their opponent's contentions. FEDPROC § 62:358; Goodman v. 1973 26 Foot Trojan Vessel, Arkansas Registration No. AR1439SN, 859 F.2d 71 (8th Cir. 1988). That requirement ensures that notice of the basis for the motion is provided to the court and to the opposing party so as to avoid prejudice, provide the opponent with a meaningful opportunity to respond, and provide the court with enough information to process the motion correctly. FEDPROC § 62:358; Andreas v. Volkswagen of Am., Inc., 336 F.3d 789 (8th Cir. 2003).

    i.   Reasonable specification of the grounds for a motion is sufficient. The particularity requirement for motions is satisfied when no party is prejudiced by a lack of particularity or when the court can comprehend the basis for the motion and deal with it fairly. However, where a movant fails to state even one ground for granting the motion in question, the movant has failed to meet the minimal standard of "reasonable specification." FEDPROC § 62:358; Martinez v. Trainor, 556 F.2d 818 (7th Cir. 1977).

    ii.   The court may excuse the failure to comply with the particularity requirement if it is inadvertent, and where no prejudice is shown by the opposing party. FEDPROC § 62:358.

  e.  *Control of motion practice*

    i.   *Plan for the disposition of motions.* At the earliest practicable time, the judicial officer shall establish a framework for the disposition of motions, which, at the discretion of the judicial officer, may include specific deadlines or general time guidelines for filing motions. This framework may be amended from time to time by the judicial officer as required by the progress of the case. MA R USDCT LR 7.1(a)(1).

    ii.   *Motion practice.* No motion shall be filed unless counsel certify that they have conferred and have attempted in good faith to resolve or narrow the issue. MA R USDCT LR 7.1(a)(2).

    iii.   *Unresolved motions.* The court shall rule on motions as soon as practicable, having in mind the reporting requirements set forth in the Civil Justice Reform Act. MA R USDCT LR 7.1(a)(3).

2.  *Good faith conference.* Before filing any discovery motion, including any motion for sanctions or for a protective order, counsel for each of the parties shall confer in good faith to narrow the areas of disagreement to the greatest possible extent. It shall be the responsibility of counsel for the moving party to arrange for the conference. Conferences may be conducted over the telephone. Failure of opposing counsel to respond to a request for a discovery conference within seven (7) days of the request shall be grounds for sanctions, which may include automatic allowance of the motion. MA R USDCT LR 37.1(a).

  a.  *When to file a motion and memorandum.* If (1) opposing counsel has failed to respond to a request for a discovery conference within the seven day period set forth in MA R USDCT LR 37.1(a), (2) opposing counsel has failed to attend a discovery conference within fourteen (14) calendar days of the request, or (3) if disputed issues are not resolved at the discovery conference, a dissatisfied party may file a motion and supporting memorandum. MA R USDCT LR 37.1(b).

3.  *Motion for protective order.* A party or any person from whom discovery is sought may move for a protective order in the court where the action is pending—or as an alternative on matters relating to a deposition, in the court for the district where the deposition will be taken. FRCP 26(c)(1). FRCP 26(c) was enacted as a safeguard for the protection of parties and witnesses in view of the broad discovery rights authorized by FRCP 26(b). FEDPROC § 26:260; United States v. Columbia Broad. Sys., Inc., 666 F.2d 364 (9th Cir. 1982).

  a.  *Grounds for protective orders.* The court may, for good cause, issue an order to protect a party or person from annoyance, embarrassment, oppression, or undue burden or expense, including one or more of the following:

    i.   Forbidding the disclosure or discovery;

    ii.   Specifying terms, including time and place or the allocation of expenses, for the disclosure or discovery;

    iii.   Prescribing a discovery method other than the one selected by the party seeking discovery;

    iv.   Forbidding inquiry into certain matters, or limiting the scope of disclosure or discovery to certain matters;

    v.   Designating the persons who may be present while the discovery is conducted;

    vi.   Requiring that a deposition be sealed and opened only on court order;

    vii.   Requiring that a trade secret or other confidential research, development, or commercial information not be revealed or be revealed only in a specified way; and

    viii.   Requiring that the parties simultaneously file specified documents or information in sealed envelopes, to be opened as the court directs. FRCP 26(c)(1).

  b.  *Third-party protection.* A party may not ask for an order to protect the rights of another party or a witness if that party or witness does not claim protection for himself, but a party may seek an order if it believes its own interest is jeopardized by discovery sought from a third person. FPP § 2035.

   c. *Burden.* The party seeking a protective order has the burden of demonstrating that good cause exists for issuance of the order. FEDPROC § 26:273. The good-cause requirement under FRCP 26(c), encompasses a standard of reasonableness. FEDPROC § 26:278.

      i. *Factual demonstration of injury.* The party requesting a protective order must demonstrate that failure to issue the order requested will work a clearly defined harm, and must make a specific demonstration of facts in support of the request as opposed to conclusory or speculative statements about the need for a protective order and the harm which will be suffered without one. FEDPROC § 26:276.

      ii. *Serious injury.* A party seeking a protective order under FRCP 26(c) must demonstrate that failure to issue the order requested will work a serious injury. FEDPROC § 26:277.

   d. *Application of protective orders.* FRCP 26(c) provides no authority for the issuance of protective orders purporting to regulate the use of information or documents obtained through means other than discovery in the pending proceeding, and does not permit the district court to issue protective orders with respect to data obtained through means other than the court's discovery processes. FEDPROC § 26:265.

      i. *Information not discovered.* FRCP 26(c) does not give the court authority to prohibit disclosure of trade data which was compiled by counsel prior the commencing of a lawsuit. Similarly, material received by one party prior to commencement of an action (and therefore before initiation of any discovery and before a request for protective orders) cannot be made a legitimate part of the corpus of any protective order a court enters. FEDPROC § 26:265.

      ii. *Information discovered in other action.* [T]he trial court lacks the discretion and power to issue a valid protective order to compel the return of documents obtained through discovery in a separate action. FEDPROC § 26:266.

   e. *Ordering discovery.* If a motion for a protective order is wholly or partly denied, the court may, on just terms, order that any party or person provide or permit discovery. FRCP 26(c)(2).

   f. *Awarding expenses.* FRCP 37(a)(5) applies to the award of expenses. FRCP 26(c)(3). Refer to the United States District Court for the District of Massachusetts KeyRules Motion for Discovery Sanctions document for more information.

4. *Opposing papers.* The Federal Rules of Civil Procedure do not require any formal answer, return, or reply to a motion, except where the Federal Rules of Civil Procedure or local rules may require affidavits, memoranda, or other papers to be filed in opposition to a motion. Such papers are simply to apprise the court of such opposition and the grounds of that opposition. FEDPROC § 62:353.

   a. *Effect of failure to respond to motion.* Although in the absence of statutory provision or court rule, a motion ordinarily does not require a written answer, when a party files a motion and the opposing party fails to respond, the court may construe such failure to respond as nonopposition to the motion or an admission that the motion was meritorious, may take the facts alleged in the motion as true—the rule in some jurisdictions being that the failure to respond to a fact set forth in a motion is deemed an admission—and may grant the motion if the relief requested appears to be justified. AMJUR MOTIONS § 28.

   b. *Assent or no opposition not determinative.* However, a motion will not be granted automatically simply because an "assent" or a notation of "no opposition" has been filed; federal judges frequently deny motions that have been assented to when it is thought that justice so dictates. FPP § 1190.

   c. *Responsive pleading inappropriate as response to motion.* An attempt to answer or oppose a motion with a responsive pleading usually is not appropriate. FPP § 1190.

5. *Reply papers.* A moving party may be required or permitted to prepare papers in addition to his original motion papers. AMJUR MOTIONS § 25. Papers answering or replying to opposing papers may be appropriate, in the interests of justice, where it appears there is a substantial reason for allowing a reply. Thus, a court may accept reply papers where a party demonstrates that the papers to which it seeks to file a reply raise new issues that are material to the disposition of the question before the court, or where the court determines, sua sponte, that it wishes further briefing of an issue raised in those papers and orders the submission of additional papers. FEDPROC § 62:354.

   a. *Function of reply papers.* The function of a reply affidavit is to answer the arguments made in opposition to the position taken by the movant and not to permit the movant to introduce new arguments in support of the motion. AMJUR MOTIONS § 25.

   b. *Issues raised for the first time in a reply document.* However, the view has been followed in some jurisdictions, that as a matter of judicial economy, where there is no prejudice and where the issues could be raised simply by filing a motion to dismiss, the trial court has discretion to consider arguments raised for the first time in a reply memorandum, and that a trial court may grant a motion to strike issues raised for the first time in a reply memorandum. AMJUR MOTIONS § 26.

6. *Alternative dispute resolution (ADR).* The judicial officer assigned to preside over the case shall encourage the resolution of disputes by settlement or other alternative dispute resolution programs. MA R USDCT LR 16.4(a).

   a. *Settlement.* At every conference conducted under the Local Rules of the United States District Court for the District of Massachusetts, the judicial officer shall inquire as to the utility of the parties conducting settlement negotiations, explore means of facilitating those negotiations, and offer whatever assistance may be appropriate in the circumstances. Assistance may include a reference of the case to another judicial officer for settlement purposes. MA R USDCT LR 16.4(b).

      i. When a case is settled, the parties shall file with the clerk a signed agreement for judgment or stipulation for dismissal, as appropriate, within twenty-eight (28) days, unless the court otherwise orders. MA R USDCT LR 68.2.

   b. *Alternative dispute resolution programs*

      i. *Discretion of judicial officer.* The judicial officer, following an exploration of the matter with all counsel, may refer appropriate cases to alternative dispute resolution programs that have been designated for use in the district court or that the judicial officer may make available. The dispute resolution programs described in MA R USDCT LR 16.4(c)(2) through MA R USDCT LR 16.4(c)(4) are illustrative, not exclusive. Moreover, nothing in MA R USDCT LR 16.4 shall preclude the parties from engaging in private dispute resolution programs as long as they comply with any schedule established by the court. MA R USDCT LR 16.4(c)(1).

      ii. *Mediation.* The judicial officer may refer the case to mediation upon the agreement of all parties. MA R USDCT LR 16.4(c)(2)(A).

      iii. *Other alternative dispute resolution programs.* Use of mediation is not exclusive. At the request of parties, the judicial officer may consider other forms of alternative dispute resolution including, but not limited to, mini-trial, summary jury trial and arbitration. MA R USDCT LR 16.4(c)(3).

   c. For more information on alternative dispute resolution (ADR), refer to MA R USDCT LR 16.4.

7. *Sanctions.* Failure to comply with any of the directions or obligations set forth in, or authorized by, these rules may result in dismissal, default, or the imposition of other sanctions as deemed appropriate by the judicial officer. MA R USDCT LR 1.3. Except as provided by law, the court may impose sanctions as provided in MA R USDCT LR 1.3 for failure to comply with the Administrative Procedures for Electronic Case Filing in the United States District Court for the District of Massachusetts (MA R USDCT CM/ECF Admin) or with MA R USDCT LR 5.4. MA R USDCT CM/ECF Admin(C)(3).

## D. Documents

1. *Documents for moving party*

   a. *Required documents*

      i. *Notice of motion and motion.* Refer to the General Requirements section of this document for information on the notice of motion and motion.

         • *Request for oral argument.* Any party making or opposing a motion who believes that oral argument may assist the court and wishes to be heard shall include a request for oral argument in a separate paragraph of the motion or opposition. The request should be set off with a centered caption, "REQUEST FOR ORAL ARGUMENT." MA R USDCT LR 7.1(d).

      ii. *Certificate of compliance.* The motion shall include a certificate in the margin of the last page that the provisions of MA R USDCT LR 37.1 have been complied with. MA R USDCT LR 37.1(b). The judicial officer shall not consider any discovery motion that is not accompanied by a certification, as required by MA R USDCT LR 7.1(a)(2) and MA R USDCT LR 37.1(b), that the moving party has made a reasonable and good faith effort to reach agreement with opposing counsel on the matters set forth in the motion. In evaluating any discovery motion, the judicial officer may consider the desirability of conducting phased discovery, as contemplated by MA R USDCT LR 26.3. MA R USDCT LR 26.2(c).

      iii. *Memorandum.* A party filing a motion shall at the same time file a memorandum of reasons, including citation of supporting authorities, why the motion should be granted. MA R USDCT LR 7.1(b)(1). Any memorandum of law or other attachment filed in support of a main document shall be filed as a separate document, using the proper event. MA R USDCT CM/ECF Admin(G)(4). Memoranda supporting or opposing allowance of motions shall not, without leave of court, exceed twenty (20) pages, double-spaced. MA R USDCT LR 7.1(b)(4). The memorandum shall state with particularity the following:

- If a discovery conference was not held, the reasons why it was not;

- If a discovery conference was held, the time, date, location and duration of the conference; who was present for each party; the matters on which the parties reached agreement; and the issues remaining to be decided by the court;

- The nature of the case and the facts relevant to the discovery matters to be decided;

- Each interrogatory, deposition question, request for production, request for admission or other discovery matter raising an issue to be decided by the court, and the response thereto; and

- A statement of the moving party's position as to each contested issue, with supporting legal authority, which statement shall be set forth separately immediately following each contested item. MA R USDCT LR 37.1(b).

iv.   *Discovery documents.* If relief is sought under FRCP 26(c) or FRCP 37, copies of the relevant portions of disputed documents shall be filed with the court contemporaneously with any motion. MA R USDCT LR 26.6(a).

v.   *Certificate of service.* No certificate of service is required when a paper is served by filing it with the court's electronic-filing system. When a paper that is required to be served is served by other means: (1) if the paper is filed, a certificate of service must be filed with it or within a reasonable time after service; and (2) if the paper is not filed, a certificate of service need not be filed unless filing is required by court order or by local rule. FRCP 5(d)(1)(B). Except as otherwise provided by the Federal Rules of Civil Procedure, proof of service of all pleadings and other papers required to be served (except discovery papers that in accordance with FRCP 33 to FRCP 36(f) are not to be filed) shall be filed in the office of the clerk promptly after service has been made. The proof shall show the time and manner of service, and may be made by written acknowledgment of service, a certificate of a member of the bar of this court, or an affidavit of the person who served the paper. MA R USDCT LR 5.2(b)(1). A certificate of service of a member of the bar shall appear at the bottom of or on the margin of the last page of the paper to which it relates. MA R USDCT LR 5.2(b)(2).

- *Paper service.* The certificate shall be a brief, single-spaced statement and may be in the following form: I hereby certify that a true copy of the above document was served upon (each party appearing pro se and) the attorney of record for each other party by mail (by hand) on (date). (Signature). MA R USDCT LR 5.2(b)(2).

- *Electronic service.* Any pleading or other paper served by electronic means must bear a certificate of service in accordance with MA R USDCT LR 5.2(b). MA R USDCT LR 5.4(C); MA R USDCT CM/ECF Admin(H)(2). The certificate of service shall state that the filer: (1) filed the document electronically, (2) that it will be served electronically to registered CM/ECF participants via the NEF and (3) that the filer will send paper copies to non-registered participants as indicated on the NEF. MA R USDCT CM/ECF Admin(H)(2). For example: I hereby certify that this document filed through the CM/ECF system will be sent electronically to the registered participants as identified on the NEF (NEF) and paper copies will be sent to those indicated as non registered participants on (date). MA R USDCT CM/ECF Admin(H)(2).

- *Return.* Documents not conforming to the requirements of MA R USDCT LR 5.2 (except notices of appeal) shall be returned by the clerk. MA R USDCT LR 5.2(b)(2).

- *Failure to make proof of service.* Failure to make proof of service does not affect the validity of the service. MA R USDCT LR 5.2(b)(3).

b.   *Supplemental documents*

i.   *Supporting evidence.* When a motion relies on facts outside the record, the court may hear the matter on affidavits or may hear it wholly or partly on oral testimony or on depositions. FRCP 43(c). Affidavits and other documents setting forth or evidencing facts on which the motion is based shall be filed with the motion. MA R USDCT LR 7.1(b)(1).

ii.   *Notice of constitutional question.* A party that files a pleading, written motion, or other paper drawing into question the constitutionality of a federal or state statute must promptly:

- *File notice.* File a notice of constitutional question stating the question and identifying the paper that raises it, if: (1) a federal statute is questioned and the parties do not include the United States, one of its agencies, or one of its officers or employees in an official capacity; or (2) a state statute is questioned and the parties do not include the state, one of its agencies, or one of its officers or employees in an official capacity; and

- *Serve notice.* Serve the notice and paper on the Attorney General of the United States if a federal statute is questioned—or on the state attorney general if a state statute is questioned—either by certified or registered mail or by sending it to an electronic address designated by the attorney general for this purpose. FRCP 5.1(a).

- *No forfeiture.* A party's failure to file and serve the notice, or the court's failure to certify, does not forfeit a constitutional claim or defense that is otherwise timely asserted. FRCP 5.1(d).

iii. *Nongovernmental corporate disclosure statement*

- *Contents.* A nongovernmental corporate party must file two (2) copies of a disclosure statement that: (1) identifies any parent corporation and any publicly held corporation owning ten percent (10%) or more of its stock; or (2) states that there is no such corporation. FRCP 7.1(a).

- *Time to file; Supplemental filing.* A party must: (1) file the disclosure statement with its first appearance, pleading, petition, motion, response, or other request addressed to the court; and (2) promptly file a supplemental statement if any required information changes. FRCP 7.1(b).

iv. *Proposed order.* Proposed orders usually are not required by this court. However, the court may request the party to submit such a document. In those situations, unless otherwise directed by the clerk's office, electronically file the proposed document/order using the entry for "Proposed Documents submitted to the court," found under the Other Documents menu, or as an attachment to the motion to which it relates. MA R USDCT CM/ECF Admin(T).

v. *Compact disk with copy of document(s) in PDF format.* A filer who cannot file a document electronically because of such technical difficulty on the filer's end [with telephone, cable lines, the filer's Internet Service Provider (ISP), or hardware or software problems] shall file the document conventionally along with a copy of the document in PDF format on a compact disk or contact the clerk's office for permission to submit the PDF document via email. MA R USDCT CM/ECF Admin(W)(3). Refer to the Timing section of this document for more information on technical failures.

vi. *Notice of filing with clerk's office.* When documents or exhibits (other than those filed ex parte or under seal) are submitted conventionally, a "Notice of Filing with clerk's office" shall be filed electronically and attached to the main document. A paper copy of the "Notice of Filing with clerk's office" must accompany the documents submitted to the court. The "Notice of Filing with clerk's office" (see MA R USDCT CM/ECF Admin(Appendix I)) shall describe each of the documents that will be filed as paper copies in the clerk's office, or shall include an index of the documents if those documents are voluminous. MA R USDCT CM/ECF Admin(P)(5).

vii. *Additional copies.* Whenever, because of the nature of a proceeding, such as a proceeding before a three-judge district court under 28 U.S.C.A. § 2284, additional copies of a paper required to be filed are necessary either for the use of the court or to enable the clerk to carry out his duties, it is the responsibility of the party filing or having filed the paper to provide the necessary copies. MA R USDCT LR 5.1(d).

viii. *Courtesy copies.* COURTESY COPIES OF DOCUMENTS FILED ELECTRONICALLY SHALL NOT BE SUBMITTED ROUTINELY. MA R USDCT CM/ECF Admin(J). Judicial officers, on a case-by-case basis, may require courtesy copies for specific cases, or types of motions, etc. A few Judicial Officers have entered Standing Orders, which may be found on their respective pages on the court's website (under Divisions). Any document filed on paper with the court as a courtesy copy must be clearly labeled as such (Example: COURTESY COPY—DO NOT SCAN). Documents delivered to the court as a courtesy copy will not be maintained in the official court record. MA R USDCT CM/ECF Admin(J).

2. *Documents for opposing party*

   a. *Required documents*

      i. *Opposition.* The response, if any, shall conform to the requirements of MA R USDCT LR 37.1(b)(5). MA R USDCT LR 37.1(c). A statement of the moving party's position as to each contested issue, with supporting legal authority, which statement shall be set forth separately immediately following each contested item. MA R USDCT LR 37.1(b)(5). Refer to the General Requirements section of this document for information on the opposing papers.

         - *Memorandum.* A party opposing a motion shall file, in the same (rather than a separate), document a memorandum of reasons, including citation of supporting authorities, why the motion should not be granted. MA R USDCT LR 7.1(b)(2). Any memorandum of law or other attachment filed in support of a main document shall be filed as a separate document, using the proper event. MA R USDCT CM/ECF Admin(G)(4). Memoranda supporting or opposing allowance of motions shall not, without leave of court, exceed twenty (20) pages, double-spaced. MA R USDCT LR 7.1(b)(4).

- *Request for oral argument.* Any party making or opposing a motion who believes that oral argument may assist the court and wishes to be heard shall include a request for oral argument in a separate paragraph of the motion or opposition. The request should be set off with a centered caption, "REQUEST FOR ORAL ARGUMENT." MA R USDCT LR 7.1(d).

ii. *Certificate of service.* No certificate of service is required when a paper is served by filing it with the court's electronic-filing system. When a paper that is required to be served is served by other means: (1) if the paper is filed, a certificate of service must be filed with it or within a reasonable time after service; and (2) if the paper is not filed, a certificate of service need not be filed unless filing is required by court order or by local rule. FRCP 5(d)(1)(B). Except as otherwise provided by the Federal Rules of Civil Procedure, proof of service of all pleadings and other papers required to be served (except discovery papers that in accordance with FRCP 33 to FRCP 36(f) are not to be filed) shall be filed in the office of the clerk promptly after service has been made. The proof shall show the time and manner of service, and may be made by written acknowledgment of service, a certificate of a member of the bar of this court, or an affidavit of the person who served the paper. MA R USDCT LR 5.2(b)(1). A certificate of service of a member of the bar shall appear at the bottom of or on the margin of the last page of the paper to which it relates. MA R USDCT LR 5.2(b)(2).

- *Paper service.* The certificate shall be a brief, single-spaced statement and may be in the following form: I hereby certify that a true copy of the above document was served upon (each party appearing pro se and) the attorney of record for each other party by mail (by hand) on (date). (Signature). MA R USDCT LR 5.2(b)(2).

- *Electronic service.* Any pleading or other paper served by electronic means must bear a certificate of service in accordance with MA R USDCT LR 5.2(b). MA R USDCT LR 5.4(C); MA R USDCT CM/ECF Admin(H)(2). The certificate of service shall state that the filer: (1) filed the document electronically, (2) that it will be served electronically to registered CM/ECF participants via the NEF and (3) that the filer will send paper copies to non-registered participants as indicated on the NEF. MA R USDCT CM/ECF Admin(H)(2). For example: I hereby certify that this document filed through the CM/ECF system will be sent electronically to the registered participants as identified on the NEF (NEF) and paper copies will be sent to those indicated as non registered participants on (date). MA R USDCT CM/ECF Admin(H)(2).

- *Return.* Documents not conforming to the requirements of MA R USDCT LR 5.2 (except notices of appeal) shall be returned by the clerk. MA R USDCT LR 5.2(b)(2).

- *Failure to make proof of service.* Failure to make proof of service does not affect the validity of the service. MA R USDCT LR 5.2(b)(3).

b. *Supplemental documents*

i. *Supporting evidence.* When a motion relies on facts outside the record, the court may hear the matter on affidavits or may hear it wholly or partly on oral testimony or on depositions. FRCP 43(c). Affidavits and other documents setting forth or evidencing facts on which the opposition is based shall be filed with the opposition. MA R USDCT LR 7.1(b)(2).

ii. *Notice of constitutional question.* A party that files a pleading, written motion, or other paper drawing into question the constitutionality of a federal or state statute must promptly:

- *File notice.* File a notice of constitutional question stating the question and identifying the paper that raises it, if: (1) a federal statute is questioned and the parties do not include the United States, one of its agencies, or one of its officers or employees in an official capacity; or (2) a state statute is questioned and the parties do not include the state, one of its agencies, or one of its officers or employees in an official capacity; and

- *Serve notice.* Serve the notice and paper on the Attorney General of the United States if a federal statute is questioned—or on the state attorney general if a state statute is questioned—either by certified or registered mail or by sending it to an electronic address designated by the attorney general for this purpose. FRCP 5.1(a).

- *No forfeiture.* A party's failure to file and serve the notice, or the court's failure to certify, does not forfeit a constitutional claim or defense that is otherwise timely asserted. FRCP 5.1(d).

iii. *Compact disk with copy of document(s) in PDF format.* A filer who cannot file a document electronically because of such technical difficulty on the filer's end [with telephone, cable lines, the filer's Internet Service Provider (ISP), or hardware or software problems] shall file the document conventionally along with a copy of the document in PDF format on a compact disk or contact the clerk's office for permission to submit the PDF document via email. MA R USDCT CM/ECF Admin(W)(3). Refer to the Timing section of this document for more information on technical failures.

iv. *Notice of filing with clerk's office.* When documents or exhibits (other than those filed ex parte or under seal) are submitted conventionally, a "Notice of Filing with clerk's office" shall be filed electronically and attached to the main document. A paper copy of the "Notice of Filing with clerk's office" must accompany the documents submitted to the court. The "Notice of Filing with clerk's office" (see MA R USDCT CM/ECF Admin(Appendix I)) shall describe each of the documents that will be filed as paper copies in the clerk's office, or shall include an index of the documents if those documents are voluminous. MA R USDCT CM/ECF Admin(P)(5).

v. *Additional copies.* Whenever, because of the nature of a proceeding, such as a proceeding before a three-judge district court under 28 U.S.C.A. § 2284, additional copies of a paper required to be filed are necessary either for the use of the court or to enable the clerk to carry out his duties, it is the responsibility of the party filing or having filed the paper to provide the necessary copies. MA R USDCT LR 5.1(d).

vi. *Courtesy copies.* COURTESY COPIES OF DOCUMENTS FILED ELECTRONICALLY SHALL NOT BE SUBMITTED ROUTINELY. MA R USDCT CM/ECF Admin(J). Judicial officers, on a case-by-case basis, may require courtesy copies for specific cases, or types of motions, etc. A few Judicial Officers have entered Standing Orders, which may be found on their respective pages on the court's website (under Divisions). Any document filed on paper with the court as a courtesy copy must be clearly labeled as such (Example: COURTESY COPY—DO NOT SCAN). Documents delivered to the court as a courtesy copy will not be maintained in the official court record. MA R USDCT CM/ECF Admin(J).

## E. Format

1. *Form of documents.* The rules governing captions and other matters of form in pleadings apply to motions and other papers. FRCP 7(b)(2). The provisions of FRCP 10 and FRCP 11 concerning the form and signing of pleadings, motions, and other papers shall be applicable to all papers filed in any proceeding in this court. The board of bar overseers registration number of each attorney signing such documents, except the United States Attorney and his or her staff, shall be inscribed below the signature. MA R USDCT LR 5.1(a)(1).

   a. *Paper size and binding.* All papers filed in the court shall be adapted for flat filing, be filed on eight and one-half by eleven (8-1/2 x 11) inch paper without backers and be bound firmly by staple or some such other means (excluding paper or binder clip or rubber band). MA R USDCT LR 5.1(a)(2).

   b. *Spacing.* All papers, except discovery requests and responses, shall be double-spaced except for the identification of counsel, title of the case, footnotes, quotations and exhibits. Discovery requests and responses shall be single-spaced. MA R USDCT LR 5.1(a)(2).

   c. *Caption.* Every pleading must have a caption with the court's name, a title, a file number, and [an] FRCP 7(a) designation. FRCP 10(a).

      i. *Names of parties.* The title of the complaint must name all the parties; the title of other pleadings, after naming the first party on each side, may refer generally to other parties. FRCP 10(a).

      ii. *Request for special action.* When any pleading or other paper filed in the court includes a request for special process or relief, or any other request such that, if granted, the court will proceed other than in the ordinary course, the request shall, unless it is noted on the category sheet [see MA R USDCT LR 40.1(a)(1)], be noted on the first page to the right of or immediately beneath the caption. MA R USDCT LR 5.1(c).

   d. *Claims or defenses*

      i. *Numbered paragraphs.* A party must state its claims or defenses in numbered paragraphs, each limited as far as practicable to a single set of circumstances. A later pleading may refer by number to a paragraph in an earlier pleading. FRCP 10(b).

      ii. *Separate statements.* If doing so would promote clarity, each claim founded on a separate transaction or occurrence—and each defense other than a denial—must be stated in a separate count or defense. FRCP 10(b).

   e. *Adoption by reference.* A statement in a pleading may be adopted by reference elsewhere in the same pleading or in any other pleading or motion. FRCP 10(c).

      i. *Exhibits.* A copy of a written instrument that is an exhibit to a pleading is a part of the pleading for all purposes. FRCP 10(c).

f. *Citations*

    i. *Local rules.* These rules shall be known as Local Rules of the United States District Court for the District of Massachusetts and cited as "L.R., D. Mass." or "L.R." MA R USDCT LR 1.1.

    ii. *Electronic case filing procedures.* The procedures governing electronic case filing shall be known as the "Administrative Procedures for Electronic Case Filing in the United States District Court for the District of Massachusetts." They shall be cited as "APECF." MA R USDCT CM/ECF Admin(A)(7).

g. *Acceptance by the clerk.* The clerk must not refuse to file a paper solely because it is not in the form prescribed by the Federal Rules of Civil Procedure or by a local rule or practice. FRCP 5(d)(4).

    i. Except for complaints and notices of appeal, papers that do not conform to the requirements of MA R USDCT LR 5.1(a)(2) shall be returned by the clerk. MA R USDCT LR 5.1(a)(2).

2. *Form of electronic documents.* A paper filed electronically is a written paper for purposes of the Federal Rules of Civil Procedure. FRCP 5(d)(3)(D).

a. *PDF/A format required.* The court will begin requiring submission of documents in PDF/A format in the foreseeable future. PDF/A is an enhanced version of the traditional PDF format. Newer versions of most PDF software will be able to convert to this format. Additional information on PDF/A documents may be found on the court's website. MA R USDCT CM/ECF Admin(Electronic Filing and PDF).

    i. *Electronically converted PDF.* Electronically converted PDF documents are created from word processing documents (MS Word, WordPerfect, etc.) using any appropriate software. These documents are text searchable and the file size is generally smaller than a scanned document. CM/ECF users may use any brand of software to convert documents to PDF. MA R USDCT CM/ECF Admin(Electronic Filing and PDF).

        • Documents converted to PDF, rather than scanned, are preferred for filing in CM/ECF. MA R USDCT CM/ECF Admin(Electronic Filing and PDF).

    ii. *Scanned PDF.* Scanned PDF documents are created from paper documents run through an optical scanner. Scanned PDF documents are generally not searchable and have a larger file size. Please note that software used to create scanned documents may (and should) be set in such a way that the document is "text-searchable." MA R USDCT CM/ECF Admin(Electronic Filing and PDF).

b. *Title.* All pleadings filed electronically shall be titled in accordance with the approved dictionary of civil or criminal events of the CM/ECF system of this court. A list of events is available on the CM/ECF Training Information page of the court's website. The clerk's office may, when necessary and appropriate, modify the docket entry description, or delete and re-enter the docket entry in order to comply with the court's quality assurance standards. MA R USDCT CM/ECF Admin(G)(3).

c. *Attachments to filings and exhibits.* Attachments to filings and exhibits must be filed in accordance with the court's CM/ECF User Manual, unless otherwise ordered by the court. MA R USDCT CM/ECF Admin(O)(1).

    i. Filers must submit as attachments only those excerpts of the referenced documents that are directly germane to the matter under consideration by the court. Excerpted material must be clearly and prominently identified as such. Users who file excerpts of documents do so without prejudice to their right to timely file additional excerpts or the complete document, as may be allowed by the court. Responding parties may timely file additional excerpts or the complete document that they believe are directly germane. MA R USDCT CM/ECF Admin(O)(2).

    ii. Filers shall not attach as an exhibit any pleading or other paper already on file with the court in that case, but shall merely refer to that document. (See MA R USDCT CM/ECF Admin(G) for information on using hyperlinks in PDF documents filed in CM/ECF.) MA R USDCT CM/ECF Admin(O)(3).

d. *Redacted documents.* The parties may request or the court may require the submission of documents that have been redacted/stripped of sensitive or confidential information. The redacted document prepared for electronic filing shall include the original caption of the document, and be clearly labeled as "Redacted Document." A specific event is available for this purpose ("Redacted Document"), found under the Other Filings/Other Documents menu option. MA R USDCT CM/ECF Admin(S).

    i. Attorneys and pro se litigants are advised to take extra care when creating PDF documents intended for submission to CM/ECF. Steps shall be taken to ensure the documents are free of any hidden data (metadata) that may contain redacted information, or traces of information edited or deleted are not hidden in the final document. Even PDF content that has been encrypted may be recovered. An advisory document with additional information on this topic may be found on the court's website. MA R USDCT CM/ECF Admin(S).

e. *Hyperlinks.* Electronically filed documents may contain the following types of hyperlinks: (1) hyperlinks to other portions of the same document; (2) hyperlinks to other documents filed within the CM/ECF system; and (3) hyperlinks to a location on the Internet that contains a source document for a citation. MA R USDCT CM/ECF Admin(G)(7).

    i. Hyperlinks to cited authority may not replace standard citation format. Complete citations must be included in the text of the filed document. Neither a hyperlink, nor any site to which it refers, shall be considered part of the record, but are simply convenient mechanisms for accessing material cited in a document filed in CM/ECF. Instructions on creating hyperlinks may be found in the CM/ECF User Manual. MA R USDCT CM/ECF Admin(G)(7).

    ii. The court accepts no responsibility for, and does not endorse, any product, organization, or content at any hyperlinked site, or at any site to which that site may be linked. The court accepts no responsibility for the availability or functionality of any hyperlink. MA R USDCT CM/ECF Admin(G)(7).

    iii. One feature of PDF/A documents is that hyperlinks are commonly "masked," meaning that the full address of the referenced file is not written out; for example, clicking the word brief may open a brief which was previously filed in CM/ECF. MA R USDCT CM/ECF Admin(G)(7)(NOTE). An "unmasked" hyperlink has the full address visible to the user. MA R USDCT CM/ECF Admin(G)(7)(NOTE).

        • Masked hyperlinks may or may not work in a PDF/A document, depending on how it was created. Currently, masked hyperlinks are preserved in PDF/A documents produced by the "Save As" method in Microsoft Word 2007 and 2010; the "PDFMaker" method in Microsoft Word 2007; and OpenOffice 2.4 ("PDF Export"). With other production methods, such as WordPerfect, the PDF/A document includes underlined words that appear to be links, but clicking them has no effect. MA R USDCT CM/ECF Admin(G)(7)(NOTE).

f. *Documents features not accepted.* CM/ECF will not accept PDF documents containing tracking tags, embedded systems commands, password protections, access restrictions or other security features, special tags or dynamic features. MA R USDCT CM/ECF Admin(G)(8).

g. *File size limitations.* A filing party shall limit the size of each PDF file to no more than twenty (20) megabytes. PDF files larger than seven (7) megabytes will be rejected by the CM/ECF system. The filer will see a message advising of the size limitation. MA R USDCT CM/ECF Admin(P)(2).

    i. Larger documents or exhibits may be submitted electronically if split into separate PDF files each less than seven (7) megabytes, attached to the main document and clearly labeled. MA R USDCT CM/ECF Admin(P)(2).

    ii. Documents submitted electronically or on paper are subject to the page limitations set by MA R USDCT LR 7.1(b)(4) or by order of the court. MA R USDCT CM/ECF Admin(P)(1).

h. *Accuracy and readability.* The filer shall verify the accuracy and readability of any PDF file before electronically filing it in CM/ECF. MA R USDCT CM/ECF Admin(G)(6); MA R USDCT CM/ECF Admin(P)(3).

3. *Signing disclosures and discovery requests, responses, and objections.* FRCP 11 does not apply to disclosures and discovery requests, responses, objections, and motions under FRCP 26 through FRCP 37. FRCP 11(d).

a. *Signature required.* Every disclosure under FRCP 26(a)(1) or FRCP 26(a)(3) and every discovery request, response, or objection must be signed by at least one attorney of record in the attorney's own name—or by the party personally, if unrepresented—and must state the signer's address, e-mail address, and telephone number. FRCP 26(g)(1). The provisions of the Federal Rules of Civil Procedure pertaining to the form and signing of pleadings, motions, and other papers shall be applicable to all papers filed in any proceeding in this court. The board of bar overseers registration number of each attorney signing such documents, except the United States Attorney and his staff, shall be inscribed below the signature. MA R USDCT LR 5.1(a)(1).

    i. *Electronic signing.* A filing made through a person's electronic-filing account and authorized by that person, together with that person's name on a signature block, constitutes the person's signature. FRCP 5(d)(3)(C).

    ii. *Appearances.* The filing of an appearance or any other pleading signed on behalf of a party constitutes an entry of appearance for that party. All pleadings shall contain the name, bar admission number, address, telephone number, and e-mail address of the attorney entering an appearance. MA R USDCT LR 83.5.2(a).

        • *Appearances by law firms.* When a party is represented by a law firm, the appearance must include the name and the signature of at least one individual attorney. When a party is represented by more than one attorney from the same or different law firms, the attorney entering the appearance must designate the individual attorney who is authorized to receive all notices in the case. Any notice sent to an attorney so designated

shall be deemed to be proper notice unless the court finds that notice was not properly sent. MA R USDCT LR 83.5.2(b).

- For more information on appearances, refer to MA R USDCT LR 83.5.2.

iii. *Signatures of attorneys.* The user login and password required to submit documents to the CM/ECF system shall serve as that user's signature for purposes of FRCP 11 and for all other purposes under the Federal Rules of Civil Procedure and the Local Rules of the United States District Court for the District of Massachusetts. All electronically filed documents must include a signature block and must set forth the attorney's name, bar number, address, telephone number and email address. The name of the CM/ECF user under whose log-in and password the document is submitted must be preceded by a "/s/" and typed in the space where the signature would otherwise appear. MA R USDCT CM/ECF Admin(M)(1). For an example, refer to MA R USDCT CM/ECF Admin(M)(1).

iv. *Signatures of pro se parties.* Any document requiring a signature that is filed by a party appearing pro se shall bear the words "pro se" following that party's signature. Any such document shall also state the party's mailing address, telephone number (if any), and e-mail address (if the party has consented to service by email). MA R USDCT LR 83.5.5(g). For more information on practice by pro se litigants, refer to MA R USDCT LR 83.5.5.

v. *Multiple signatures.* The filer of any document requiring more than one signature (e.g, stipulations, joint motions, joint status reports, magistrate judge consent forms, etc.) must list thereon all the names of other signatories by means of a "/s/ name of signatory" block for each. By submitting such a document, the filing attorney certifies that each of the other signatories has expressly agreed to the form and substance of the document and that the filing attorney has their actual authority to submit the document electronically. MA R USDCT CM/ECF Admin(M)(2). For more information, refer to MA R USDCT CM/ECF Admin(M)(2).

vi. *Affidavits.* Except as provided in MA R USDCT CM/ECF Admin(L), affidavits shall be filed electronically; however, the electronically filed version must contain a "/s/ name of signatory" block indicating that the paper document bears an original signature. MA R USDCT CM/ECF Admin(M)(3). The court will also accept a scanned version of the original, signed document. MA R USDCT CM/ECF Admin(M)(3). For more information, refer to MA R USDCT CM/ECF Admin(M)(3).

b. *Effect of signature.* By signing, an attorney or party certifies that to the best of the person's knowledge, information, and belief formed after a reasonable inquiry:

i. With respect to a disclosure, it is complete and correct as of the time it is made; and

ii. With respect to a discovery request, response, or objection, it is:

- Consistent with the Federal Rules of Civil Procedure and warranted by existing law or by a nonfrivolous argument for extending, modifying, or reversing existing law, or for establishing new law;

- Not interposed for any improper purpose, such as to harass, cause unnecessary delay, or needlessly increase the cost of litigation; and

- Neither unreasonable nor unduly burdensome or expensive, considering the needs of the case, prior discovery in the case, the amount in controversy, and the importance of the issues at stake in the action. FRCP 26(g)(1).

c. *Failure to sign.* Other parties have no duty to act on an unsigned disclosure, request, response, or objection until it is signed, and the court must strike it unless a signature is promptly supplied after the omission is called to the attorney's or party's attention. FRCP 26(g)(2).

d. *Sanction for improper certification.* If a certification violates FRCP 26(g) without substantial justification, the court, on motion or on its own, must impose an appropriate sanction on the signer, the party on whose behalf the signer was acting, or both. The sanction may include an order to pay the reasonable expenses, including attorney's fees, caused by the violation. FRCP 26(g)(3). Refer to the United States District Court for the District of Massachusetts KeyRules Motion for Discovery Sanctions document for more information.

4. *Privacy protection for filings made with the court*

a. *Redacted filings.* Unless the court orders otherwise, in an electronic or paper filing with the court that contains an individual's Social Security number, taxpayer-identification number, or birth date, the name of an individual known to be a minor, or a financial-account number, a party or nonparty making the filing may include only:

i. The last four (4) digits of the Social Security number and taxpayer-identification number;

ii. The year of the individual's birth;

iii. The minor's initials; and

iv. The last four (4) digits of the financial-account number. FRCP 5.2(a); MA R USDCT CM/ECF Admin(N).

b. *Exemptions from the redaction requirement.* The redaction requirement does not apply to the following:

i. A financial-account number that identifies the property allegedly subject to forfeiture in a forfeiture proceeding;

ii. The record of an administrative or agency proceeding;

iii. The official record of a state-court proceeding;

iv. The record of a court or tribunal, if that record was not subject to the redaction requirement when originally filed;

v. A filing covered by FRCP 5.2(c) or FRCP 5.2(d); and

vi. A pro se filing in an action brought under 28 U.S.C.A. § 2241, 28 U.S.C.A. § 2254, or 28 U.S.C.A. § 2255. FRCP 5.2(b).

c. *Limitations on remote access to electronic files; Social Security appeals and immigration cases.* Unless the court orders otherwise, in an action for benefits under the Social Security Act, and in an action or proceeding relating to an order of removal, to relief from removal, or to immigration benefits or detention, access to an electronic file is authorized as follows:

i. The parties and their attorneys may have remote electronic access to any part of the case file, including the administrative record;

ii. Any other person may have electronic access to the full record at the courthouse, but may have remote electronic access only to:

- The docket maintained by the court; and

- An opinion, order, judgment, or other disposition of the court, but not any other part of the case file or the administrative record. FRCP 5.2(c).

d. *Filings made under seal.* The court may order that a filing be made under seal without redaction. The court may later unseal the filing or order the person who made the filing to file a redacted version for the public record. FRCP 5.2(d).

e. *Protective orders.* For good cause, the court may by order in a case:

i. Require redaction of additional information; or

ii. Limit or prohibit a nonparty's remote electronic access to a document filed with the court. FRCP 5.2(e).

f. *Option for additional unredacted filing under seal.* A person making a redacted filing may also file an unredacted copy under seal. The court must retain the unredacted copy as part of the record. FRCP 5.2(f). For more information, refer to MA R USDCT LR 7.2.

g. *Option for filing a reference list.* A filing that contains redacted information may be filed together with a reference list that identifies each item of redacted information and specifies an appropriate identifier that uniquely corresponds to each item listed. The list must be filed under seal and may be amended as of right. Any reference in the case to a listed identifier will be construed to refer to the corresponding item of information. FRCP 5.2(g).

h. *Responsibility for redaction.* The clerk's office is not responsible for reviewing documents filed with the court to determine whether pleadings have been redacted and are in the proper form. MA R USDCT CM/ECF Admin(N).

i. *Waiver of protection of identifiers.* A person waives the protection of FRCP 5.2(a) as to the person's own information by filing it without redaction and not under seal. FRCP 5.2(h).

## F. Filing and Service Requirements

1. *Filing requirements*

a. *Required filings.* Any paper after the complaint that is required to be served must be filed no later than a reasonable time after service. FRCP 5(d)(1).

i. Except as noted in FRCP 33 to FRCP 36, the original of all papers required to be served under FRCP 5(d) shall, unless otherwise submitted to the court, be filed in the office of the clerk within seven (7) days after service has been made. MA R USDCT LR 5.1(b). Except as otherwise provided by the Federal Rules of Civil Procedure, proof of service of all pleadings and other papers required to be served (except discovery papers that in accordance with FRCP 33 to FRCP 36(f) are not to be filed) shall be filed in the office of the clerk promptly after service has been made. MA R USDCT LR 5.2(b)(1).

b. *Nonelectronic filing.* A paper not filed electronically is filed by delivering it: (1) to the clerk; or (2) to a judge who agrees to accept it for filing, and who must then note the filing date on the paper and promptly send it to the clerk. FRCP 5(d)(2).

c. *Electronic filing.* Unless exempt or otherwise ordered by the court, all pleadings and other papers submitted to the court must be filed, signed, and verified by electronic means as provided in MA R USDCT LR 5.4. MA R USDCT LR 5.4(A); MA R USDCT CM/ECF Admin(A)(1). All electronic filings must be made in accordance with the Administrative Procedures for Electronic Case Filing in the United States District Court for the District of Massachusetts (MA R USDCT CM/ECF Admin). MA R USDCT LR 5.4(B). The court may deviate from the Administrative Procedures for Electronic Case Filing in the United States District Court for the District of Massachusetts (MA R USDCT CM/ECF Admin) in specific cases, without prior notice, if deemed appropriate in the exercise of discretion, considering the need for the just, speedy, and inexpensive determination of matters pending before the court. MA R USDCT CM/ECF Admin(C)(1). The court may excuse a failure to comply with any administrative procedure whenever justice so requires. MA R USDCT CM/ECF Admin(C)(2).

i. *By a represented person; Generally required; Exceptions.* A person represented by an attorney must file electronically, unless nonelectronic filing is allowed by the court for good cause or is allowed or required by local rule. FRCP 5(d)(3)(A).

ii. *By unrepresented person; When allowed or required.* A person not represented by an attorney: (1) may file electronically only if allowed by court order or by local rule; and (2) may be required to file electronically only by court order, or by a local rule that includes reasonable exceptions. FRCP 5(d)(3)(B).

iii. *Exemptions from electronic filing*

- *Documents that should not be filed electronically.* The following types of documents must not be filed electronically, and will not be scanned into the ECF system by the clerk's office: (1) sealed documents; (2) ex parte motions; (3) documents generated as part of an alternative dispute resolution (ADR) process; (4) the administrative record in Social Security and other administrative proceedings; (5) the state court record in proceedings under 28 U.S.C.A. § 2254; and (6) such other types of documents as the clerk may direct in the Administrative Procedures for Electronic Case Filing in the United States District Court for the District of Massachusetts (MA R USDCT CM/ECF Admin). MA R USDCT LR 5.4(G)(1); MA R USDCT CM/ECF Admin(L).

- *Documents that need not be filed electronically.* The following types of documents need not be filed electronically, but may be scanned into the ECF system by a filing party or the clerk's office: (1) handwritten pleadings; (2) documents filed by pro se litigants who are incarcerated or who are not registered ECF users; (3) indictments, informations, criminal complaints, and the criminal JS45 form; (4) affidavits for search or arrest warrants and related documents; (5) documents received from another court under FRCRP 20 or FRCRP 40; (6) appearance bonds; (7) any document in a criminal case containing the original signature of a defendant, such as a waiver of indictment or a plea agreement; (8) petitions for violations of supervised release; (9) executed service of process documents under FRCP 4; and (10) such other types of documents as the clerk may direct in the Administrative Procedures for Electronic Case Filing in the United States District Court for the District of Massachusetts (MA R USDCT CM/ECF Admin). MA R USDCT LR 5.4(G)(2); MA R USDCT CM/ECF Admin(L).

- For more information on exemptions from electronic filing, refer to MA R USDCT CM/ECF Admin(L).

iv. *Consequences of electronic filing.* Electronic transmission of a document to the CM/ECF system, together with the transmission of a Notice of Electronic Filing (NEF) from the court at the completion of the transaction, constitutes the filing of the document for all purposes of the Federal Rules of Procedure and constitutes entry of the document on the docket maintained by the clerk pursuant to FRCP 58 and FRCP 79. MA R USDCT CM/ECF Admin(G)(1).

v. *Payment of filing fees.* When electronically filing any pleading or paper through CM/ECF that requires a fee, all registered ECF users are to pay the fee electronically through the Treasury Department's Internet payment process. MA R USDCT LR 67.4(d); MA R USDCT CM/ECF Admin(A)(1). Pro se filers and those who have been exempted from electronic filing and/or electronic payment of fees may submit payments by check or money order made payable to "Clerk, U.S. District Court". MA R USDCT LR 67.4(d). For more information on filing fees, refer to MA R USDCT LR 67.4 and MA R USDCT CM/ECF Admin(I).

vi. For more information on electronic filing, refer to MA R USDCT CM/ECF Admin.

d. *Email or fax filing.* In general, the court does not accept documents by email or by fax. If the court, in special circumstances, does authorize the submission of a document in that manner, the document shall not be considered filed until an NEF is generated by CM/ECF at the completion of the transaction. MA R USDCT CM/ECF Admin(H)(5).

2. *Service requirements.* All papers filed pursuant to MA R USDCT LR 7.1(b) shall be served unless the moving party indicates in writing on the face of the motion that ex parte consideration is requested. Motions filed "ex parte" and related papers need not be served until the motion has been ruled upon or the court orders that service be made. MA R USDCT LR 7.1(c). Service of all pleadings subsequent to the original complaint and of all other papers required to be served shall be made in the manner specified by FRCP 5. MA R USDCT LR 5.2(a).

a. *Service; When required*

i. *In general.* Unless the Federal Rules of Civil Procedure provide otherwise, each of the following papers must be served on every party:

- An order stating that service is required;
- A pleading filed after the original complaint, unless the court orders otherwise under FRCP 5(c) because there are numerous defendants;
- A discovery paper required to be served on a party, unless the court orders otherwise;
- A written motion, except one that may be heard ex parte; and
- A written notice, appearance, demand, or offer of judgment, or any similar paper. FRCP 5(a)(1).

ii. *If a party fails to appear.* No service is required on a party who is in default for failing to appear. But a pleading that asserts a new claim for relief against such a party must be served on that party under FRCP 4. FRCP 5(a)(2).

iii. *Seizing property.* If an action is begun by seizing property and no person is or need be named as a defendant, any service required before the filing of an appearance, answer, or claim must be made on the person who had custody or possession of the property when it was seized. FRCP 5(a)(3).

b. *Service; How made*

i. *Serving an attorney.* If a party is represented by an attorney, service under FRCP 5 must be made on the attorney unless the court orders service on the party. FRCP 5(b)(1).

- *Nonresident attorney.* On application of a party, the court may order an attorney who represents any other party and who does not maintain an office within this district where service can be made on him by delivery as provided by FRCP 5(b), to designate a member of the bar of this court who does maintain such an office to receive service of all pleadings and other papers in his behalf. MA R USDCT LR 5.2(c)(1).

ii. *Serving a party acting pro se.* On application of a party, the court may order any other party who is appearing without an attorney and who does not maintain an office or residence within this district where service can be made on him by delivery as provided by FRCP 5(b), to designate an address within the district at which service can be made on him by delivery. MA R USDCT LR 5.2(c)(2).

iii. *Service in general.* A paper is served under FRCP 5 by:

- Handing it to the person;
- Leaving it: (1) at the person's office with a clerk or other person in charge or, if no one is in charge, in a conspicuous place in the office; or (2) if the person has no office or the office is closed, at the person's dwelling or usual place of abode with someone of suitable age and discretion who resides there;
- Mailing it to the person's last known address—in which event service is complete upon mailing;
- Leaving it with the court clerk if the person has no known address;
- Sending it to a registered user by filing it with the court's electronic-filing system or sending it by other electronic means that the person consented to in writing—in either of which events service is complete upon filing or sending, but is not effective if the filer or sender learns that it did not reach the person to be served; or
- Delivering it by any other means that the person consented to in writing—in which event service is complete when the person making service delivers it to the agency designated to make delivery. FRCP 5(b)(2).

iv. *Service by electronic means.* Unless exempt or otherwise ordered by the court, all pleadings and other papers must be served on other parties by electronic means. MA R USDCT LR 5.4(C); MA R USDCT CM/ECF

Admin(H)(2). Service by electronic means shall be treated the same as service by mail. MA R USDCT CM/ECF Admin(H)(4).

- *Consent to electronic service.* Registering to use CM/ECF constitutes consent to service of all documents by electronic means as provided in the Administrative Procedures for Electronic Case Filing in the United States District Court for the District of Massachusetts (MA R USDCT CM/ECF Admin) and FRCP 5(b) and FRCP 77(d). MA R USDCT CM/ECF Admin(E)(6); MA R USDCT CM/ECF Admin(H)(3).

- *Service on registered ECF users.* Transmission of the Notice of Electronic Filing (NEF) through the court's transmission facilities will constitute service of the filed document upon a registered ECF user. MA R USDCT LR 5.4(C).

- *Service on non-registered users.* The party filing the document electronically is responsible for serving a paper copy of the document by mail in accordance with FRCP 5(b) to those case participants who have not been identified on the NEF as electronic recipients. MA R USDCT CM/ECF Admin(H)(3).

- *Service of conventionally filed papers.* Documents or exhibits submitted conventionally shall be served on other parties by the filer using traditional means. MA R USDCT CM/ECF Admin(P)(4).

c. *Serving numerous defendants*

i. *In general.* If an action involves an unusually large number of defendants, the court may, on motion or on its own, order that:

- Defendants' pleadings and replies to them need not be served on other defendants;

- Any crossclaim, counterclaim, avoidance, or affirmative defense in those pleadings and replies to them will be treated as denied or avoided by all other parties; and

- Filing any such pleading and serving it on the plaintiff constitutes notice of the pleading to all parties. FRCP 5(c)(1).

ii. *Notifying parties.* A copy of every such order must be served on the parties as the court directs. FRCP 5(c)(2).

## G. Hearings

1. *Hearings, generally.* If the court concludes that there should be a hearing on a motion, the motion will be set down for hearing at such time as the court determines. MA R USDCT LR 7.1(e).

a. *Oral argument.* Due process does not require that oral argument be permitted on a motion and, except as otherwise provided by local rule, the district court has discretion to determine whether it will decide the motion on the papers or hear argument by counsel (and perhaps receive evidence). FPP § 1190; F.D.I.C. v. Deglau, 207 F.3d 153 (3d Cir. 2000).

i. *Evidence on a motion.* When a motion relies on facts outside the record, the court may hear the matter on affidavits or may hear it wholly or partly on oral testimony or on depositions. FRCP 43(c).

b. *Providing a regular schedule for oral hearings.* A court may establish regular times and places for oral hearings on motions. FRCP 78(a).

c. *Providing for submission on briefs.* By rule or order, the court may provide for submitting and determining motions on briefs, without oral hearings. FRCP 78(b). Motions that are not set down for hearing as provided in MA R USDCT LR 7.1(e) will be decided on the papers submitted after an opposition to the motion has been filed, or, if no opposition is filed, after the time for filing an opposition has elapsed. MA R USDCT LR 7.1(f).

2. *Conflict of court appearances.* For information on conflict of court appearances, refer to MA R USDCT LR 40.2.

## H. Forms

### 1. Federal Motion for Protective Order Forms

a. Motion for protective order limiting scope of oral examination; Privileged material. 3A FEDFORMS § 21:39.

b. Notice of motion and motion for protective order. 3A FEDFORMS § 21:41.

c. Notice of motion and motion for protective order; Prohibiting taking of deposition. 3A FEDFORMS § 21:42.

d. Notice of motion and motion for protective order; To quash notice of taking deposition or for continuance; Late taking of deposition. 3A FEDFORMS § 21:43.

e. Motion for protective order limiting scope of oral examination. 3A FEDFORMS § 21:55.

f. Motion for protective order limiting examination upon written questions. 3A FEDFORMS § 21:59.

g. Notice of motion; For protective order; Preventing deposition of consultant and production of documents; Federal class action. AMJUR PP DEPOSITION § 334.

h. Motion; For protective order pending court's order on motion to quash deposition notice of plaintiff. AMJUR PP DEPOSITION § 341.

i. Motion; For protective order; To prevent deposition of consultant and production of documents; Federal class action. AMJUR PP DEPOSITION § 343.

j. Opposition; By plaintiffs; To motion by defendants for protective order; Prevention of deposition of consultant and production of documents; Federal class action. AMJUR PP DEPOSITION § 370.

k. Declaration; By plaintiffs' attorney; In support of opposition to defendants' motion for protective order; Federal class action. AMJUR PP DEPOSITION § 371.

l. Notice of motion; For protective order; To vacate notice to produce documents. AMJUR PP DEPOSITION § 592.

m. Notice of motion; For protective order; To limit scope of inspection of premises; Premises liability action; Objection to scope of request. AMJUR PP DEPOSITION § 593.

n. Motion; For protective order; Staying proceedings on production requests; Pending ruling on movant's dispositive motion. AMJUR PP DEPOSITION § 594.

o. Motion; For protective order; Limiting requests for production; Additional protection of trade secrets. AMJUR PP DEPOSITION § 595.

p. Answer; To motion for protective order. FEDPROF § 23:203.

q. Motion; For protective order; Limiting interrogatories. FEDPROF § 23:381.

r. Motion; For protective order; Staying proceedings on production requests. FEDPROF § 23:432.

s. Motion; For protective order; Limiting requests for production. FEDPROF § 23:433.

t. Motion; For protective order staying proceedings on request for admissions. FEDPROF § 23:585.

u. Notice of motion for protective order. GOLDLTGFMS § 31:2.

v. Motion for protective order; Federal form. GOLDLTGFMS § 31:5.

w. Motion for protective order; Deposition not to be taken. GOLDLTGFMS § 31:6.

x. Motion for protective order; Retaking depositions. GOLDLTGFMS § 31:7.

y. Motion for protective order; Certain matters shall not be inquired into. GOLDLTGFMS § 31:8.

z. Motion for protective order; To limit scope of examination. GOLDLTGFMS § 31:10.

2. **Forms for the District of Massachusetts**

a. Notice of filing with clerk's office. MA R USDCT CM/ECF Admin(Appendix I).

## I. Applicable Rules

1. *Federal rules*

a. Serving and filing pleadings and other papers. FRCP 5.

b. Constitutional challenge to a statute; Notice, certification, and intervention. FRCP 5.1.

c. Privacy protection for filings made with the court. FRCP 5.2.

d. Computing and extending time; Time for motion papers. FRCP 6.

e. Pleadings allowed; Form of motions and other papers. FRCP 7.

f. Disclosure statement. FRCP 7.1.

g. Form of pleadings. FRCP 10.

h. Signing pleadings, motions, and other papers; Representations to the court; Sanctions. FRCP 11.

i. Duty to disclose; General provisions governing discovery. FRCP 26.

j. Taking testimony. FRCP 43.

k. Hearing motions; Submission on briefs. FRCP 78.

2. *Local rules*

a. Title. MA R USDCT LR 1.1.

b. Sanctions. MA R USDCT LR 1.3.

c. Form and filing of papers. MA R USDCT LR 5.1.

d. Service and filing of pleadings and other papers. MA R USDCT LR 5.2.

e. Filing and service by electronic means. MA R USDCT LR 5.4.

f. Motion practice. MA R USDCT LR 7.1.

g. Alternative dispute resolution. MA R USDCT LR 16.4.

h. Sequences of discovery. MA R USDCT LR 26.2.

i. Court filings and costs. MA R USDCT LR 26.6.

j. Discovery disputes. MA R USDCT LR 37.1.

k. Payments and deposits made with the clerk. MA R USDCT LR 67.4.

l. Settlement. MA R USDCT LR 68.2.

m. Office of the clerk. MA R USDCT LR 77.2.

n. Appearances. MA R USDCT LR 83.5.2.

o. Practice by pro se litigants. MA R USDCT LR 83.5.5.

p. CM/ECF case management/electronic case files administrative procedures. MA R USDCT CM/ECF Admin.

## Motions, Oppositions and Replies
## Motion for Discovery Sanctions

### Document Last Updated December 2018

**A. Checklist**

(I) ❑ Matters to be considered by moving party

  (a) ❑ Required documents

    (1) ❑ Notice of motion and motion

    (2) ❑ Certificate of compliance

    (3) ❑ Memorandum

    (4) ❑ Discovery documents

    (5) ❑ Certificate of service

  (b) ❑ Supplemental documents

    (1) ❑ Supporting evidence

    (2) ❑ Notice of constitutional question

    (3) ❑ Proposed order

    (4) ❑ Compact disk with copy of document(s) in PDF format

    (5) ❑ Notice of filing with clerk's office

    (6) ❑ Additional copies

    (7) ❑ Courtesy copies

  (c) ❑ Timing

    (1) ❑ There are no specific timing requirements for moving for discovery sanctions

    (2) ❑ A written motion and notice of the hearing must be served at least fourteen (14) days before the time specified for the hearing, with the following exceptions: (i) when the motion may be heard ex parte; (ii) when the Federal Rules of Civil Procedure set a different time; or (iii) when a court order—which a party may, for good cause, apply for ex parte—sets a different time

    (3) ❑ Any affidavit supporting a motion must be served with the motion

(4) ❑ Except as noted in FRCP 33 to FRCP 36, the original of all papers required to be served under FRCP 5(d) shall, unless otherwise submitted to the court, be filed in the office of the clerk within seven (7) days after service has been made

(II) ❑ Matters to be considered by opposing party

(a) ❑ Required documents

(1) ❑ Opposition

(2) ❑ Certificate of service

(b) ❑ Supplemental documents

(1) ❑ Supporting evidence

(2) ❑ Notice of constitutional question

(3) ❑ Compact disk with copy of document(s) in PDF format

(4) ❑ Notice of filing with clerk's office

(5) ❑ Additional copies

(6) ❑ Courtesy copies

(c) ❑ Timing

(1) ❑ A party opposing a motion, shall file an opposition within fourteen (14) days after the motion is served, unless another period is fixed by rule or statute, or by order of the court

(2) ❑ Except as FRCP 59(c) provides otherwise, any opposing affidavit must be served at least seven (7) days before the hearing, unless the court permits service at another time

(3) ❑ Except as noted in FRCP 33 to FRCP 36, the original of all papers required to be served under FRCP 5(d) shall, unless otherwise submitted to the court, be filed in the office of the clerk within seven (7) days after service has been made

## B. Timing

1. *Motion for discovery sanctions.* There are no specific timing requirements for moving for discovery sanctions.

2. *Timing of motions, generally*

   a. *Motion and notice of hearing.* A written motion and notice of the hearing must be served at least fourteen (14) days before the time specified for the hearing, with the following exceptions:

      i. When the motion may be heard ex parte;

      ii. When the Federal Rules of Civil Procedure set a different time; or

      iii. When a court order—which a party may, for good cause, apply for ex parte—sets a different time. FRCP 6(c)(1).

   b. *Supporting affidavit.* Any affidavit supporting a motion must be served with the motion. FRCP 6(c)(2).

3. *Timing of opposing papers.* A party opposing a motion, shall file an opposition within fourteen (14) days after the motion is served, unless (1) the motion is for summary judgment, in which case the opposition shall be filed within twenty-one (21) days after the motion is served, or (2) another period is fixed by rule or statute, or by order of the court. MA R USDCT LR 7.1(b)(2); MA R USDCT CM/ECF Admin(H)(4); MA R USDCT LR 37.1(c). The fourteen (14) day period is intended to include the period specified by the civil rules for mailing time and provide for a uniform period regardless of the use of the mails. MA R USDCT LR 7.1(b)(2).

   a. *Opposing affidavit.* Except as FRCP 59(c) provides otherwise, any opposing affidavit must be served at least seven (7) days before the hearing, unless the court permits service at another time. FRCP 6(c)(2).

4. *Timing of reply papers.* [W]here the respondent files an answering affidavit setting up a new matter, the moving party ordinarily is allowed a reasonable time to file a reply affidavit since failure to deny the new matter by affidavit may operate as an admission of its truth. AMJUR MOTIONS § 25.

   a. *Leave of court required.* All other papers not filed as indicated in MA R USDCT LR 7.1(b)(1) and MA R USDCT LR 7.1(b)(2), whether in the form of a reply brief or otherwise, may be submitted only with leave of court. MA R USDCT LR 7.1(b)(3).

5. *Filing after service.* Except as noted in FRCP 33 to FRCP 36, the original of all papers required to be served under FRCP

5(d) shall, unless otherwise submitted to the court, be filed in the office of the clerk within seven (7) days after service has been made. MA R USDCT LR 5.1(b).

6. *Computation of time*

    a. *Computing time.* FRCP 6 applies in computing any time period specified in the Federal Rules of Civil Procedure, in any local rule or court order, or in any statute that does not specify a method of computing time. FRCP 6(a).

        i. *Period stated in days or a longer unit.* When the period is stated in days or a longer unit of time:

- Exclude the day of the event that triggers the period;

- Count every day, including intermediate Saturdays, Sundays, and legal holidays; and

- Include the last day of the period, but if the last day is a Saturday, Sunday, or legal holiday, the period continues to run until the end of the next day that is not a Saturday, Sunday, or legal holiday. FRCP 6(a)(1).

        ii. *Period stated in hours.* When the period is stated in hours:

- Begin counting immediately on the occurrence of the event that triggers the period;

- Count every hour, including hours during intermediate Saturdays, Sundays, and legal holidays; and

- If the period would end on a Saturday, Sunday, or legal holiday, the period continues to run until the same time on the next day that is not a Saturday, Sunday, or legal holiday. FRCP 6(a)(2).

        iii. *Office of the clerk.* The offices of the Clerk of Court at Boston, Worcester and Springfield shall be open from 8:30 a.m. until 5:00 p.m. on all days except Saturdays, Sundays, legal holidays and other days so ordered by the court and announced in advance, if feasible. MA R USDCT LR 77.2.

        iv. *Inaccessibility of the clerk's office.* Unless the court orders otherwise, if the clerk's office is inaccessible:

- On the last day for filing under FRCP 6(a)(1), then the time for filing is extended to the first accessible day that is not a Saturday, Sunday, or legal holiday; or

- During the last hour for filing under FRCP 6(a)(2), then the time for filing is extended to the same time on the first accessible day that is not a Saturday, Sunday, or legal holiday. FRCP 6(a)(3).

        v. *"Last day" defined.* Unless a different time is set by a statute, local rule, or court order, the last day ends:

- For electronic filing, at midnight in the court's time zone; and

- For filing by other means, when the clerk's office is scheduled to close. FRCP 6(a)(4).

        vi. *"Next day" defined.* The "next day" is determined by continuing to count forward when the period is measured after an event and backward when measured before an event. FRCP 6(a)(5).

        vii. *"Legal holiday" defined.* "Legal holiday" means:

- The day set aside by statute for observing New Year's Day, Martin Luther King Jr.'s Birthday, Washington's Birthday, Memorial Day, Independence Day, Labor Day, Columbus Day, Veterans' Day, Thanksgiving Day, or Christmas Day;

- Any day declared a holiday by the President or Congress; and

- For periods that are measured after an event, any other day declared a holiday by the state where the district court is located. FRCP 6(a)(6).

    b. *Computation of electronic filing deadlines.* Filing documents electronically does not alter any filing deadlines. MA R USDCT CM/ECF Admin(K); MA R USDCT LR 5.4(D). Although CM/ECF is generally available twenty-four (24) hours a day for filing, all electronic transmissions of documents must be completed prior to 6:00 PM, Eastern Standard (or Daylight Savings) Time, on the date on which it is due, in order to be considered timely filed that day. MA R USDCT CM/ECF Admin(K); MA R USDCT LR 5.4(D). When a specific time of day deadline is set by court order or stipulation, the electronic filing must be completed by that time. Documents may be filed at any time of the day on days prior to the date on which it is due. MA R USDCT CM/ECF Admin(K). A document filed electronically shall be deemed filed as of the time and date stated on the NEF received from the court. MA R USDCT CM/ECF Admin(G)(2); MA R USDCT CM/ECF Admin(K).

        i. *Technical failures.* A user whose filing is made untimely as the result of a technical failure of the court's CM/ECF system may seek appropriate relief from the court. MA R USDCT CM/ECF Admin(W)(3). Technical difficulties on the filer's end, with telephone, cable lines, the filer's Internet Service Provider (ISP), or hardware or software problems, will not constitute a technical failure under the Administrative Procedures for Electronic Case Filing in the United States District Court for the District of Massachusetts (MA R USDCT CM/ECF Admin) nor excuse an untimely filing. MA R USDCT CM/ECF Admin(W)(3). As help desk support is available during normal business hours, filers are strongly urged to electronically file any documents during that period. MA R USDCT CM/ECF Admin(W)(3).

- The court has made available a public terminal (computers and scanner) in each clerk's office for registered users to scan and electronically file documents. This equipment is available during normal business hours. Users should bring their prepared document and a valid CM/ECF login and password. MA R USDCT CM/ECF Admin(W)(3).

c. *Extending time.* When an act may or must be done within a specified time, the court may, for good cause, extend the time: (1) with or without motion or notice if the court acts, or if a request is made, before the original time or its extension expires; or (2) on motion made after the time has expired if the party failed to act because of excusable neglect. FRCP 6(b)(1).

   i. *Exceptions.* A court must not extend the time to act under FRCP 50(b), FRCP 50(d), FRCP 52(b), FRCP 59(b), FRCP 59(d), FRCP 59(e), and FRCP 60(b). FRCP 6(b)(2).

   ii. Refer to the United States District Court for the District of Massachusetts KeyRules Motion for Continuance/Extension of Time document for more information on extending time.

d. *Additional time after certain kinds of service.* When a party may or must act within a specified time after being served and service is made under FRCP 5(b)(2)(C) (by mail), FRCP 5(b)(2)(D) (by leaving with the clerk), or FRCP 5(b)(2)(F) (by other means consented to), three (3) days are added after the period would otherwise expire under FRCP 6(a). FRCP 6(d).

## C. General Requirements

1. *Motions, generally*

   a. *Requirements.* A request for a court order must be made by motion. The motion must:

      i. Be in writing unless made during a hearing or trial;

      ii. State with particularity the grounds for seeking the order; and

      iii. State the relief sought. FRCP 7(b)(1).

   b. *Notice of motion.* A party interested in resisting the relief sought by a motion has a right to notice thereof, and an opportunity to be heard. AMJUR MOTIONS § 12.

      i. [I]n addition to statutory or court rule provisions requiring notice of a motion—the purpose of such a notice requirement having been said to be to prevent a party from being prejudicially surprised by a motion—principles of natural justice dictate that an adverse party generally must be given notice that a motion will be presented to the court. AMJUR MOTIONS § 12.

      ii. "Notice," in this regard, means reasonable notice, including a meaningful opportunity to prepare and to defend against allegations of a motion. AMJUR MOTIONS § 12.

   c. *Writing requirement.* The writing requirement is intended to [ensure] that the adverse parties are informed and have a record of both the motion's pendency and the grounds on which the movant seeks an order. FPP § 1191; Feldberg v. Quechee Lakes Corp., 463 F.3d 195 (2d Cir. 2006). [A] single written document can satisfy the writing requirements both for a motion and for [an] FRCP 6(c)(1) notice. FRCP 7(Advisory Committee Notes).

   d. *Particularity requirement.* The particularity requirement [ensures] that the opposing parties will have notice of their opponent's contentions. FEDPROC § 62:358; Goodman v. 1973 26 Foot Trojan Vessel, Arkansas Registration No. AR1439SN, 859 F.2d 71 (8th Cir. 1988). That requirement ensures that notice of the basis for the motion is provided to the court and to the opposing party so as to avoid prejudice, provide the opponent with a meaningful opportunity to respond, and provide the court with enough information to process the motion correctly. FEDPROC § 62:358; Andreas v. Volkswagen of Am., Inc., 336 F.3d 789 (8th Cir. 2003).

      i. Reasonable specification of the grounds for a motion is sufficient. The particularity requirement for motions is satisfied when no party is prejudiced by a lack of particularity or when the court can comprehend the basis for the motion and deal with it fairly. However, where a movant fails to state even one ground for granting the motion in question, the movant has failed to meet the minimal standard of "reasonable specification." FEDPROC § 62:358; Martinez v. Trainor, 556 F.2d 818 (7th Cir. 1977).

      ii. The court may excuse the failure to comply with the particularity requirement if it is inadvertent, and where no prejudice is shown by the opposing party. FEDPROC § 62:358.

e. *Control of motion practice*

    i. *Plan for the disposition of motions.* At the earliest practicable time, the judicial officer shall establish a framework for the disposition of motions, which, at the discretion of the judicial officer, may include specific deadlines or general time guidelines for filing motions. This framework may be amended from time to time by the judicial officer as required by the progress of the case. MA R USDCT LR 7.1(a)(1).

    ii. *Motion practice.* No motion shall be filed unless counsel certify that they have conferred and have attempted in good faith to resolve or narrow the issue. MA R USDCT LR 7.1(a)(2).

    iii. *Unresolved motions.* The court shall rule on motions as soon as practicable, having in mind the reporting requirements set forth in the Civil Justice Reform Act. MA R USDCT LR 7.1(a)(3).

2. *Good faith conference.* Before filing any discovery motion, including any motion for sanctions or for a protective order, counsel for each of the parties shall confer in good faith to narrow the areas of disagreement to the greatest possible extent. It shall be the responsibility of counsel for the moving party to arrange for the conference. Conferences may be conducted over the telephone. Failure of opposing counsel to respond to a request for a discovery conference within seven (7) days of the request shall be grounds for sanctions, which may include automatic allowance of the motion. MA R USDCT LR 37.1(a).

a. *When to file a motion and memorandum.* If (1) opposing counsel has failed to respond to a request for a discovery conference within the seven (7) day period set forth in MA R USDCT LR 37.1(a), (2) opposing counsel has failed to attend a discovery conference within fourteen (14) calendar days of the request, or (3) if disputed issues are not resolved at the discovery conference, a dissatisfied party may file a motion and supporting memorandum. MA R USDCT LR 37.1(b).

3. *Motion for discovery sanctions*

a. *Sanctions, generally.* FRCP 37 is flexible. The court is directed to make such orders as are "just" and is not limited in any case of disregard of the discovery rules or court orders under them to a stereotyped response. The sanctions enumerated in FRCP 37 are not exclusive and arbitrary but flexible, selective, and plural. The district court may, within reason, use as many and as varied sanctions as are necessary to hold the scales of justice even. FPP § 2284.

    i. There is one fixed limitation that should be noted. A party may not be imprisoned or otherwise punished for contempt of court for failure to submit to a physical or mental examination, or for failure to produce a person in his or her custody or under his or her control for such an examination. FPP § 2284; Sibbach v. Wilson & Co., 312 U.S. 1, 312 U.S. 655, 61 S.Ct. 422, 85 L.Ed. 479 (1941).

    ii. Although FRCP 37 is very broad, and the courts have considerable discretion in imposing sanctions as authorized by FRCP 37, there are constitutional limits, stemming from the Due Process Clause of U.S.C.A. Const. Amend. V and U.S.C.A. Const. Amend. XIV, on the imposition of sanctions. There are two principal facets of the due process issues:

        • First, the court must ask whether there is a sufficient relationship between the discovery and the merits sought to be foreclosed by the sanction to legitimate depriving a party of the opportunity to litigate the merits. FPP § 2283.

        • Second, before imposing a serious merits sanction the court should determine whether the party guilty of a failure to provide discovery was unable to comply with the discovery. FPP § 2283.

b. *Sanction for improper certification.* If a certification violates FRCP 26(g) without substantial justification, the court, on motion or on its own, must impose an appropriate sanction on the signer, the party on whose behalf the signer was acting, or both. The sanction may include an order to pay the reasonable expenses, including attorney's fees, caused by the violation. FRCP 26(g)(3).

c. *Motion to compel discovery; Payment of expenses; Protective orders*

    i. *If the motion is granted (or disclosure or discovery is provided after filing).* If the motion is granted—or if the disclosure or requested discovery is provided after the motion was filed—the court must, after giving an opportunity to be heard, require the party or deponent whose conduct necessitated the motion, the party or attorney advising that conduct, or both to pay the movant's reasonable expenses incurred in making the motion, including attorney's fees. But the court must not order this payment if:

        • The movant filed the motion before attempting in good faith to obtain the disclosure or discovery without court action;

        • The opposing party's nondisclosure, response, or objection was substantially justified; or

- Other circumstances make an award of expenses unjust. FRCP 37(a)(5)(A).

ii. *If the motion is denied.* If the motion is denied, the court may issue any protective order authorized under FRCP 26(c) and must, after giving an opportunity to be heard, require the movant, the attorney filing the motion, or both to pay the party or deponent who opposed the motion its reasonable expenses incurred in opposing the motion, including attorney's fees. But the court must not order this payment if the motion was substantially justified or other circumstances make an award of expenses unjust. FRCP 37(a)(5)(B).

iii. *If the motion is granted in part and denied in part.* If the motion is granted in part and denied in part, the court may issue any protective order authorized under FRCP 26(c) and may, after giving an opportunity to be heard, apportion the reasonable expenses for the motion. FRCP 37(a)(5)(C).

d. *Failure to comply with a court order*

   i. *Sanctions in the district where the deposition is taken.* If the court where the discovery is taken orders a deponent to be sworn or to answer a question and the deponent fails to obey, the failure may be treated as contempt of court. If a deposition-related motion is transferred to the court where the action is pending, and that court orders a deponent to be sworn or to answer a question and the deponent fails to obey, the failure may be treated as contempt of either the court where the discovery is taken or the court where the action is pending. FRCP 37(b)(1).

   ii. *Sanctions in the district where the action is pending; For not obeying a discovery order.* If a party or a party's officer, director, or managing agent—or a witness designated under FRCP 30(b)(6) or FRCP 31(a)(4)—fails to obey an order to provide or permit discovery, including an order under FRCP 26(f), FRCP 35, or FRCP 37(a), the court where the action is pending may issue further just orders. They may include the following:

- Directing that the matters embraced in the order or other designated facts be taken as established for purposes of the action, as the prevailing party claims;

- Prohibiting the disobedient party from supporting or opposing designated claims or defenses, or from introducing designated matters in evidence;

- Striking pleadings in whole or in part;

- Staying further proceedings until the order is obeyed;

- Dismissing the action or proceeding in whole or in part;

- Rendering a default judgment against the disobedient party; or

- Treating as contempt of court the failure to obey any order except an order to submit to a physical or mental examination. FRCP 37(b)(2)(A).

   iii. *Sanctions in the district where the action is pending; For not producing a person for examination.* If a party fails to comply with an order under FRCP 35(a) requiring it to produce another person for examination, the court may issue any of the orders listed in FRCP 37(b)(2)(A)(i) through FRCP 37(b)(2)(A)(vi), unless the disobedient party shows that it cannot produce the other person. FRCP 37(b)(2)(B).

   iv. *Sanctions in the district where the action is pending; Payment of expenses.* Instead of or in addition to the orders in FRCP 37(b)(2)(A) and FRCP 37(b)(2)(B), the court must order the disobedient party, the attorney advising that party, or both to pay the reasonable expenses, including attorney's fees, caused by the failure, unless the failure was substantially justified or other circumstances make an award of expenses unjust. FRCP 37(b)(2)(C).

e. *Failure to disclose, to supplement an earlier response, or to admit*

   i. *Failure to disclose or supplement.* If a party fails to provide information or identify a witness as required by FRCP 26(a) or FRCP 26(e), the party is not allowed to use that information or witness to supply evidence on a motion, at a hearing, or at a trial, unless the failure was substantially justified or is harmless. In addition to or instead of this sanction, the court, on motion and after giving an opportunity to be heard:

- May order payment of the reasonable expenses, including attorney's fees, caused by the failure;

- May inform the jury of the party's failure; and

- May impose other appropriate sanctions, including any of the orders listed in FRCP 37(b)(2)(A)(i) through FRCP 37(b)(2)(A)(vi). FRCP 37(c)(1).

   ii. *Failure to admit.* If a party fails to admit what is requested under FRCP 36 and if the requesting party later proves a document to be genuine or the matter true, the requesting party may move that the party who failed to admit pay the reasonable expenses, including attorney's fees, incurred in making that proof. The court must so order unless:

- The request was held objectionable under FRCP 36(a);
- The admission sought was of no substantial importance;
- The party failing to admit had a reasonable ground to believe that it might prevail on the matter; or
- There was other good reason for the failure to admit. FRCP 37(c)(2).

f. *Party's failure to attend its own deposition, serve answers to interrogatories, or respond to a request for inspection*

  i. *Motion; Grounds for sanctions.* The court where the action is pending may, on motion, order sanctions if:

     - A party or a party's officer, director, or managing agent—or a person designated under FRCP 30(b)(6) or FRCP 31(a)(4)—fails, after being served with proper notice, to appear for that person's deposition; or
     - A party, after being properly served with interrogatories under FRCP 33 or a request for inspection under FRCP 34, fails to serve its answers, objections, or written response. FRCP 37(d)(1)(A).

  ii. *Unacceptable excuse for failing to act.* A failure described in FRCP 37(d)(1)(A) is not excused on the ground that the discovery sought was objectionable, unless the party failing to act has a pending motion for a protective order under FRCP 26(c). FRCP 37(d)(2).

  iii. *Types of sanctions.* Sanctions may include any of the orders listed in FRCP 37(b)(2)(A)(i) through FRCP 37(b)(2)(A)(vi). Instead of or in addition to these sanctions, the court must require the party failing to act, the attorney advising that party, or both to pay the reasonable expenses, including attorney's fees, caused by the failure, unless the failure was substantially justified or other circumstances make an award of expenses unjust. FRCP 37(d)(3).

g. *Failure to provide electronically stored information.* If electronically stored information that should have been preserved in the anticipation or conduct of litigation is lost because a party failed to take reasonable steps to preserve it, and it cannot be restored or replaced through additional discovery, the court:

  i. Upon finding prejudice to another party from loss of the information, may order measures no greater than necessary to cure the prejudice; or

  ii. Only upon finding that the party acted with the intent to deprive another party of the information's use in the litigation may: (1) presume that the lost information was unfavorable to the party; (2) instruct the jury that it may or must presume the information was unfavorable to the party; or (3) dismiss the action or enter a default judgment. FRCP 37(e).

h. *Failure to participate in framing a discovery plan.* If a party or its attorney fails to participate in good faith in developing and submitting a proposed discovery plan as required by FRCP 26(f), the court may, after giving an opportunity to be heard, require that party or attorney to pay to any other party the reasonable expenses, including attorney's fees, caused by the failure. FRCP 37(f).

i. *Counsel's liability for excessive costs.* 28 U.S.C.A. § 1927 is a basis for sanctioning attorney misconduct in discovery proceedings. DISCPROFED § 22:3. Any attorney or other person admitted to conduct cases in any court of the United States or any Territory thereof who so multiplies the proceedings in any case unreasonably and vexatiously may be required by the court to satisfy personally the excess costs, expenses, and attorneys' fees reasonably incurred because of such conduct. 28 U.S.C.A. § 1927.

4. *Opposing papers.* The Federal Rules of Civil Procedure do not require any formal answer, return, or reply to a motion, except where the Federal Rules of Civil Procedure or local rules may require affidavits, memoranda, or other papers to be filed in opposition to a motion. Such papers are simply to apprise the court of such opposition and the grounds of that opposition. FEDPROC § 62:353.

a. *Effect of failure to respond to motion.* Although in the absence of statutory provision or court rule, a motion ordinarily does not require a written answer, when a party files a motion and the opposing party fails to respond, the court may construe such failure to respond as nonopposition to the motion or an admission that the motion was meritorious, may take the facts alleged in the motion as true—the rule in some jurisdictions being that the failure to respond to a fact set forth in a motion is deemed an admission—and may grant the motion if the relief requested appears to be justified. AMJUR MOTIONS § 28.

b. *Assent or no opposition not determinative.* However, a motion will not be granted automatically simply because an "assent" or a notation of "no opposition" has been filed; federal judges frequently deny motions that have been assented to when it is thought that justice so dictates. FPP § 1190.

c. *Responsive pleading inappropriate as response to motion.* An attempt to answer or oppose a motion with a responsive pleading usually is not appropriate. FPP § 1190.

5. *Reply papers.* A moving party may be required or permitted to prepare papers in addition to his original motion papers. AMJUR MOTIONS § 25. Papers answering or replying to opposing papers may be appropriate, in the interests of justice, where it appears there is a substantial reason for allowing a reply. Thus, a court may accept reply papers where a party demonstrates that the papers to which it seeks to file a reply raise new issues that are material to the disposition of the question before the court, or where the court determines, sua sponte, that it wishes further briefing of an issue raised in those papers and orders the submission of additional papers. FEDPROC § 62:354.

   a. *Function of reply papers.* The function of a reply affidavit is to answer the arguments made in opposition to the position taken by the movant and not to permit the movant to introduce new arguments in support of the motion. AMJUR MOTIONS § 25.

   b. *Issues raised for the first time in a reply document.* However, the view has been followed in some jurisdictions, that as a matter of judicial economy, where there is no prejudice and where the issues could be raised simply by filing a motion to dismiss, the trial court has discretion to consider arguments raised for the first time in a reply memorandum, and that a trial court may grant a motion to strike issues raised for the first time in a reply memorandum. AMJUR MOTIONS § 26.

6. *Alternative dispute resolution (ADR).* The judicial officer assigned to preside over the case shall encourage the resolution of disputes by settlement or other alternative dispute resolution programs. MA R USDCT LR 16.4(a).

   a. *Settlement.* At every conference conducted under the Local Rules of the United States District Court for the District of Massachusetts, the judicial officer shall inquire as to the utility of the parties conducting settlement negotiations, explore means of facilitating those negotiations, and offer whatever assistance may be appropriate in the circumstances. Assistance may include a reference of the case to another judicial officer for settlement purposes. MA R USDCT LR 16.4(b).

      i. When a case is settled, the parties shall file with the clerk a signed agreement for judgment or stipulation for dismissal, as appropriate, within twenty-eight (28) days, unless the court otherwise orders. MA R USDCT LR 68.2.

   b. *Alternative dispute resolution programs*

      i. *Discretion of judicial officer.* The judicial officer, following an exploration of the matter with all counsel, may refer appropriate cases to alternative dispute resolution programs that have been designated for use in the district court or that the judicial officer may make available. The dispute resolution programs described in MA R USDCT LR 16.4(c)(2) through MA R USDCT LR 16.4(c)(4) are illustrative, not exclusive. Moreover, nothing in MA R USDCT LR 16.4 shall preclude the parties from engaging in private dispute resolution programs as long as they comply with any schedule established by the court. MA R USDCT LR 16.4(c)(1).

      ii. *Mediation.* The judicial officer may refer the case to mediation upon the agreement of all parties. MA R USDCT LR 16.4(c)(2)(A).

      iii. *Other alternative dispute resolution programs.* Use of mediation is not exclusive. At the request of parties, the judicial officer may consider other forms of alternative dispute resolution including, but not limited to, mini-trial, summary jury trial and arbitration. MA R USDCT LR 16.4(c)(3).

   c. For more information on alternative dispute resolution (ADR), refer to MA R USDCT LR 16.4.

7. *Sanctions.* Failure to comply with any of the directions or obligations set forth in, or authorized by, these rules may result in dismissal, default, or the imposition of other sanctions as deemed appropriate by the judicial officer. MA R USDCT LR 1.3. Except as provided by law, the court may impose sanctions as provided in MA R USDCT LR 1.3 for failure to comply with the Administrative Procedures for Electronic Case Filing in the United States District Court for the District of Massachusetts (MA R USDCT CM/ECF Admin) or with MA R USDCT LR 5.4. MA R USDCT CM/ECF Admin(C)(3).

## D. Documents

1. *Documents for moving party*

   a. *Required documents*

      i. *Notice of motion and motion.* Refer to the General Requirements section of this document for information on the notice of motion and motion.

         • *Request for oral argument.* Any party making or opposing a motion who believes that oral argument may

assist the court and wishes to be heard shall include a request for oral argument in a separate paragraph of the motion or opposition. The request should be set off with a centered caption, "REQUEST FOR ORAL ARGUMENT." MA R USDCT LR 7.1(d).

ii. *Certificate of compliance.* The motion shall include a certificate in the margin of the last page that the provisions of MA R USDCT LR 37.1 have been complied with. MA R USDCT LR 37.1(b). The judicial officer shall not consider any discovery motion that is not accompanied by a certification, as required by MA R USDCT LR 7.1(a)(2) and MA R USDCT LR 37.1(b), that the moving party has made a reasonable and good faith effort to reach agreement with opposing counsel on the matters set forth in the motion. In evaluating any discovery motion, the judicial officer may consider the desirability of conducting phased discovery, as contemplated by MA R USDCT LR 26.3. MA R USDCT LR 26.2(c). A motion for sanctions for failing to answer or respond must include a certification that the movant has in good faith conferred or attempted to confer with the party failing to act in an effort to obtain the answer or response without court action. FRCP 37(d)(1)(B).

iii. *Memorandum.* A party filing a motion shall at the same time file a *memorandum* of reasons, including citation of supporting authorities, why the motion should be granted. MA R USDCT LR 7.1(b)(1). Any memorandum of law or other attachment filed in support of a main document shall be filed as a separate document, using the proper event. MA R USDCT CM/ECF Admin(G)(4). Memoranda supporting or opposing allowance of motions shall not, without leave of court, exceed twenty (20) pages, double-spaced. MA R USDCT LR 7.1(b)(4). The memorandum shall state with particularity the following:

- If a discovery conference was not held, the reasons why it was not;

- If a discovery conference was held, the time, date, location and duration of the conference; who was present for each party; the matters on which the parties reached agreement; and the issues remaining to be decided by the court;

- The nature of the case and the facts relevant to the discovery matters to be decided;

- Each interrogatory, deposition question, request for production, request for admission or other discovery matter raising an issue to be decided by the court, and the response thereto; and

- A statement of the moving party's position as to each contested issue, with supporting legal authority, which statement shall be set forth separately immediately following each contested item. MA R USDCT LR 37.1(b).

iv. *Discovery documents.* If relief is sought under FRCP 26(c) or FRCP 37, copies of the relevant portions of disputed documents shall be filed with the court contemporaneously with any motion. MA R USDCT LR 26.6(a).

v. *Certificate of service.* No certificate of service is required when a paper is served by filing it with the court's electronic-filing system. When a paper that is required to be served is served by other means: (1) if the paper is filed, a certificate of service must be filed with it or within a reasonable time after service; and (2) if the paper is not filed, a certificate of service need not be filed unless filing is required by court order or by local rule. FRCP 5(d)(1)(B). Except as otherwise provided by the Federal Rules of Civil Procedure, proof of service of all pleadings and other papers required to be served (except discovery papers that in accordance with FRCP 33 to FRCP 36(f) are not to be filed) shall be filed in the office of the clerk promptly after service has been made. The proof shall show the time and manner of service, and may be made by written acknowledgment of service, a certificate of a member of the bar of this court, or an affidavit of the person who served the paper. MA R USDCT LR 5.2(b)(1). A certificate of service of a member of the bar shall appear at the bottom of or on the margin of the last page of the paper to which it relates. MA R USDCT LR 5.2(b)(2).

- *Paper service.* The certificate shall be a brief, single-spaced statement and may be in the following form: I hereby certify that a true copy of the above document was served upon (each party appearing pro se and) the attorney of record for each other party by mail (by hand) on (date). (Signature). MA R USDCT LR 5.2(b)(2).

- *Electronic service.* Any pleading or other paper served by electronic means must bear a certificate of service in accordance with MA R USDCT LR 5.2(b). MA R USDCT LR 5.4(C); MA R USDCT CM/ECF Admin(H)(2). The certificate of service shall state that the filer: (1) filed the document electronically, (2) that it will be served electronically to registered CM/ECF participants via the NEF and (3) that the filer will send paper copies to non-registered participants as indicated on the NEF. MA R USDCT CM/ECF Admin(H)(2). For example: I hereby certify that this document filed through the CM/ECF system will be sent electronically to the registered participants as identified on the NEF (NEF) and paper copies will be sent to those indicated as non registered participants on (date). MA R USDCT CM/ECF Admin(H)(2).

- *Return.* Documents not conforming to the requirements of MA R USDCT LR 5.2 (except notices of appeal) shall be returned by the clerk. MA R USDCT LR 5.2(b)(2).

- *Failure to make proof of service.* Failure to make proof of service does not affect the validity of the service. MA R USDCT LR 5.2(b)(3).

b. *Supplemental documents*

   i. *Supporting evidence.* When a motion relies on facts outside the record, the court may hear the matter on affidavits or may hear it wholly or partly on oral testimony or on depositions. FRCP 43(c). Affidavits and other documents setting forth or evidencing facts on which the motion is based shall be filed with the motion. MA R USDCT LR 7.1(b)(1).

   ii. *Notice of constitutional question.* A party that files a pleading, written motion, or other paper drawing into question the constitutionality of a federal or state statute must promptly:

- *File notice.* File a notice of constitutional question stating the question and identifying the paper that raises it, if: (1) a federal statute is questioned and the parties do not include the United States, one of its agencies, or one of its officers or employees in an official capacity; or (2) a state statute is questioned and the parties do not include the state, one of its agencies, or one of its officers or employees in an official capacity; and

- *Serve notice.* Serve the notice and paper on the Attorney General of the United States if a federal statute is questioned—or on the state attorney general if a state statute is questioned—either by certified or registered mail or by sending it to an electronic address designated by the attorney general for this purpose. FRCP 5.1(a).

- *No forfeiture.* A party's failure to file and serve the notice, or the court's failure to certify, does not forfeit a constitutional claim or defense that is otherwise timely asserted. FRCP 5.1(d).

   iii. *Proposed order.* Proposed orders usually are not required by this court. However, the court may request the party to submit such a document. In those situations, unless otherwise directed by the clerk's office, electronically file the proposed document/order using the entry for "Proposed Documents submitted to the court," found under the Other Documents menu, or as an attachment to the motion to which it relates. MA R USDCT CM/ECF Admin(T).

   iv. *Compact disk with copy of document(s) in PDF format.* A filer who cannot file a document electronically because of such technical difficulty on the filer's end [with telephone, cable lines, the filer's Internet Service Provider (ISP), or hardware or software problems] shall file the document conventionally along with a copy of the document in PDF format on a compact disk or contact the clerk's office for permission to submit the PDF document via email. MA R USDCT CM/ECF Admin(W)(3). Refer to the Timing section of this document for more information on technical failures.

   v. *Notice of filing with clerk's office.* When documents or exhibits (other than those filed ex parte or under seal) are submitted conventionally, a "Notice of Filing with clerk's office" shall be filed electronically and attached to the main document. A paper copy of the "Notice of Filing with clerk's office" must accompany the documents submitted to the court. The "Notice of Filing with clerk's office" (see MA R USDCT CM/ECF Admin(Appendix I)) shall describe each of the documents that will be filed as paper copies in the clerk's office, or shall include an index of the documents if those documents are voluminous. MA R USDCT CM/ECF Admin(P)(5).

   vi. *Additional copies.* Whenever, because of the nature of a proceeding, such as a proceeding before a three-judge district court under 28 U.S.C.A. § 2284, additional copies of a paper required to be filed are necessary either for the use of the court or to enable the clerk to carry out his duties, it is the responsibility of the party filing or having filed the paper to provide the necessary copies. MA R USDCT LR 5.1(d).

   vii. *Courtesy copies.* COURTESY COPIES OF DOCUMENTS FILED ELECTRONICALLY SHALL NOT BE SUBMITTED ROUTINELY. MA R USDCT CM/ECF Admin(J). Judicial officers, on a case-by-case basis, may require courtesy copies for specific cases, or types of motions, etc. A few Judicial Officers have entered Standing Orders, which may be found on their respective pages on the court's website (under Divisions). Any document filed on paper with the court as a courtesy copy must be clearly labeled as such (Example: COURTESY COPY—DO NOT SCAN). Documents delivered to the court as a courtesy copy will not be maintained in the official court record. MA R USDCT CM/ECF Admin(J).

2. *Documents for opposing party*

a. *Required documents*

   i. *Opposition.* The response, if any, shall conform to the requirements of MA R USDCT LR 37.1(b)(5). MA R

USDCT LR 37.1(c). A statement of the moving party's position as to each contested issue, with supporting legal authority, which statement shall be set forth separately immediately following each contested item. MA R USDCT LR 37.1(b)(5). Refer to the General Requirements section of this document for information on the opposing papers.

- *Memorandum.* A party opposing a motion shall file, in the same (rather than a separate), document a memorandum of reasons, including citation of supporting authorities, why the motion should not be granted. MA R USDCT LR 7.1(b)(2). Any memorandum of law or other attachment filed in support of a main document shall be filed as a separate document, using the proper event. MA R USDCT CM/ECF Admin(G)(4). Memoranda supporting or opposing allowance of motions shall not, without leave of court, exceed twenty (20) pages, double-spaced. MA R USDCT LR 7.1(b)(4).

- *Request for oral argument.* Any party making or opposing a motion who believes that oral argument may assist the court and wishes to be heard shall include a request for oral argument in a separate paragraph of the motion or opposition. The request should be set off with a centered caption, "REQUEST FOR ORAL ARGUMENT." MA R USDCT LR 7.1(d).

ii. *Certificate of service.* No certificate of service is required when a paper is served by filing it with the court's electronic-filing system. When a paper that is required to be served is served by other means: (1) if the paper is filed, a certificate of service must be filed with it or within a reasonable time after service; and (2) if the paper is not filed, a certificate of service need not be filed unless filing is required by court order or by local rule. FRCP 5(d)(1)(B). Except as otherwise provided by the Federal Rules of Civil Procedure, proof of service of all pleadings and other papers required to be served (except discovery papers that in accordance with FRCP 33 to FRCP 36(f) are not to be filed) shall be filed in the office of the clerk promptly after service has been made. The proof shall show the time and manner of service, and may be made by written acknowledgment of service, a certificate of a member of the bar of this court, or an affidavit of the person who served the paper. MA R USDCT LR 5.2(b)(1). A certificate of service of a member of the bar shall appear at the bottom of or on the margin of the last page of the paper to which it relates. MA R USDCT LR 5.2(b)(2).

- *Paper service.* The certificate shall be a brief, single-spaced statement and may be in the following form: I hereby certify that a true copy of the above document was served upon (each party appearing pro se and) the attorney of record for each other party by mail (by hand) on (date). (Signature). MA R USDCT LR 5.2(b)(2).

- *Electronic service.* Any pleading or other paper served by electronic means must bear a certificate of service in accordance with MA R USDCT LR 5.2(b). MA R USDCT LR 5.4(C); MA R USDCT CM/ECF Admin(H)(2). The certificate of service shall state that the filer: (1) filed the document electronically, (2) that it will be served electronically to registered CM/ECF participants via the NEF and (3) that the filer will send paper copies to non-registered participants as indicated on the NEF. MA R USDCT CM/ECF Admin(H)(2). For example: I hereby certify that this document filed through the CM/ECF system will be sent electronically to the registered participants as identified on the NEF (NEF) and paper copies will be sent to those indicated as non registered participants on (date). MA R USDCT CM/ECF Admin(H)(2).

- *Return.* Documents not conforming to the requirements of MA R USDCT LR 5.2 (except notices of appeal) shall be returned by the clerk. MA R USDCT LR 5.2(b)(2).

- *Failure to make proof of service.* Failure to make proof of service does not affect the validity of the service. MA R USDCT LR 5.2(b)(3).

b. *Supplemental documents*

i. *Supporting evidence.* When a motion relies on facts outside the record, the court may hear the matter on affidavits or may hear it wholly or partly on oral testimony or on depositions. FRCP 43(c). Affidavits and other documents setting forth or evidencing facts on which the opposition is based shall be filed with the opposition. MA R USDCT LR 7.1(b)(2).

ii. *Notice of constitutional question.* A party that files a pleading, written motion, or other paper drawing into question the constitutionality of a federal or state statute must promptly:

- *File notice.* File a notice of constitutional question stating the question and identifying the paper that raises it, if: (1) a federal statute is questioned and the parties do not include the United States, one of its agencies, or one of its officers or employees in an official capacity; or (2) a state statute is questioned and the parties do not include the state, one of its agencies, or one of its officers or employees in an official capacity; and

- *Serve notice.* Serve the notice and paper on the Attorney General of the United States if a federal statute is questioned—or on the state attorney general if a state statute is questioned—either by certified or registered mail or by sending it to an electronic address designated by the attorney general for this purpose. FRCP 5.1(a).

- *No forfeiture.* A party's failure to file and serve the notice, or the court's failure to certify, does not forfeit a constitutional claim or defense that is otherwise timely asserted. FRCP 5.1(d).

   iii.  *Compact disk with copy of document(s) in PDF format.* A filer who cannot file a document electronically because of such technical difficulty on the filer's end [with telephone, cable lines, the filer's Internet Service Provider (ISP), or hardware or software problems] shall file the document conventionally along with a copy of the document in PDF format on a compact disk or contact the clerk's office for permission to submit the PDF document via email. MA R USDCT CM/ECF Admin(W)(3). Refer to the Timing section of this document for more information on technical failures.

   iv.  *Notice of filing with clerk's office.* When documents or exhibits (other than those filed ex parte or under seal) are submitted conventionally, a "Notice of Filing with clerk's office" shall be filed electronically and attached to the main document. A paper copy of the "Notice of Filing with clerk's office" must accompany the documents submitted to the court. The "Notice of Filing with clerk's office" (see MA R USDCT CM/ECF Admin(Appendix I)) shall describe each of the documents that will be filed as paper copies in the clerk's office, or shall include an index of the documents if those documents are voluminous. MA R USDCT CM/ECF Admin(P)(5).

   v.  *Additional copies.* Whenever, because of the nature of a proceeding, such as a proceeding before a three-judge district court under 28 U.S.C.A. § 2284, additional copies of a paper required to be filed are necessary either for the use of the court or to enable the clerk to carry out his duties, it is the responsibility of the party filing or having filed the paper to provide the necessary copies. MA R USDCT LR 5.1(d).

   vi.  *Courtesy copies.* COURTESY COPIES OF DOCUMENTS FILED ELECTRONICALLY SHALL NOT BE SUBMITTED ROUTINELY. MA R USDCT CM/ECF Admin(J). Judicial officers, on a case-by-case basis, may require courtesy copies for specific cases, or types of motions, etc. A few Judicial Officers have entered Standing Orders, which may be found on their respective pages on the court's website (under Divisions). Any document filed on paper with the court as a courtesy copy must be clearly labeled as such (Example: COURTESY COPY—DO NOT SCAN). Documents delivered to the court as a courtesy copy will not be maintained in the official court record. MA R USDCT CM/ECF Admin(J).

## E.  Format

1.  *Form of documents.* The rules governing captions and other matters of form in pleadings apply to motions and other papers. FRCP 7(b)(2). The provisions of FRCP 10 and FRCP 11 concerning the form and signing of pleadings, motions, and other papers shall be applicable to all papers filed in any proceeding in this court. The board of bar overseers registration number of each attorney signing such documents, except the United States Attorney and his or her staff, shall be inscribed below the signature. MA R USDCT LR 5.1(a)(1).

   a.  *Paper size and binding.* All papers filed in the court shall be adapted for flat filing, be filed on eight and one-half by eleven (8-1/2 x 11) inch paper without backers and be bound firmly by staple or some such other means (excluding paper or binder clip or rubber band). MA R USDCT LR 5.1(a)(2).

   b.  *Spacing.* All papers, except discovery requests and responses, shall be double-spaced except for the identification of counsel, title of the case, footnotes, quotations and exhibits. Discovery requests and responses shall be single-spaced. MA R USDCT LR 5.1(a)(2).

   c.  *Caption.* Every pleading must have a caption with the court's name, a title, a file number, and [an] FRCP 7(a) designation. FRCP 10(a).

     i.  *Names of parties.* The title of the complaint must name all the parties; the title of other pleadings, after naming the first party on each side, may refer generally to other parties. FRCP 10(a).

     ii.  *Request for special action.* When any pleading or other paper filed in the court includes a request for special process or relief, or any other request such that, if granted, the court will proceed other than in the ordinary course, the request shall, unless it is noted on the category sheet [see MA R USDCT LR 40.1(a)(1)], be noted on the first page to the right of or immediately beneath the caption. MA R USDCT LR 5.1(c).

   d.  *Claims or defenses*

     i.  *Numbered paragraphs.* A party must state its claims or defenses in numbered paragraphs, each limited as far as practicable to a single set of circumstances. A later pleading may refer by number to a paragraph in an earlier pleading. FRCP 10(b).

    ii. *Separate statements.* If doing so would promote clarity, each claim founded on a separate transaction or occurrence—and each defense other than a denial—must be stated in a separate count or defense. FRCP 10(b).

  e. *Adoption by reference.* A statement in a pleading may be adopted by reference elsewhere in the same pleading or in any other pleading or motion. FRCP 10(c).

    i. *Exhibits.* A copy of a written instrument that is an exhibit to a pleading is a part of the pleading for all purposes. FRCP 10(c).

  f. *Citations*

    i. *Local rules.* These rules shall be known as Local Rules of the United States District Court for the District of Massachusetts and cited as "L.R., D. Mass." or "L.R." MA R USDCT LR 1.1.

    ii. *Electronic case filing procedures.* The procedures governing electronic case filing shall be known as the "Administrative Procedures for Electronic Case Filing in the United States District Court for the District of Massachusetts." They shall be cited as "APECF." MA R USDCT CM/ECF Admin(A)(7).

  g. *Acceptance by the clerk.* The clerk must not refuse to file a paper solely because it is not in the form prescribed by the Federal Rules of Civil Procedure or by a local rule or practice. FRCP 5(d)(4).

    i. Except for complaints and notices of appeal, papers that do not conform to the requirements of MA R USDCT LR 5.1(a)(2) shall be returned by the clerk. MA R USDCT LR 5.1(a)(2).

2. *Form of electronic documents.* A paper filed electronically is a written paper for purposes of the Federal Rules of Civil Procedure. FRCP 5(d)(3)(D).

  a. *PDF/A format required.* The court will begin requiring submission of documents in PDF/A format in the foreseeable future. PDF/A is an enhanced version of the traditional PDF format. Newer versions of most PDF software will be able to convert to this format. Additional information on PDF/A documents may be found on the court's website. MA R USDCT CM/ECF Admin(Electronic Filing and PDF).

    i. *Electronically converted PDF.* Electronically converted PDF documents are created from word processing documents (MS Word, WordPerfect, etc.) using any appropriate software. These documents are text searchable and the file size is generally smaller than a scanned document. CM/ECF users may use any brand of software to convert documents to PDF. MA R USDCT CM/ECF Admin(Electronic Filing and PDF).

      • Documents converted to PDF, rather than scanned, are preferred for filing in CM/ECF. MA R USDCT CM/ECF Admin(Electronic Filing and PDF).

    ii. *Scanned PDF.* Scanned PDF documents are created from paper documents run through an optical scanner. Scanned PDF documents are generally not searchable and have a larger file size. Please note that software used to create scanned documents may (and should) be set in such a way that the document is "text-searchable." MA R USDCT CM/ECF Admin(Electronic Filing and PDF).

  b. *Title.* All pleadings filed electronically shall be titled in accordance with the approved dictionary of civil or criminal events of the CM/ECF system of this court. A list of events is available on the CM/ECF Training Information page of the court's website. The clerk's office may, when necessary and appropriate, modify the docket entry description, or delete and re-enter the docket entry in order to comply with the court's quality assurance standards. MA R USDCT CM/ECF Admin(G)(3).

  c. *Attachments to filings and exhibits.* Attachments to filings and exhibits must be filed in accordance with the court's CM/ECF User Manual, unless otherwise ordered by the court. MA R USDCT CM/ECF Admin(O)(1).

    i. Filers must submit as attachments only those excerpts of the referenced documents that are directly germane to the matter under consideration by the court. Excerpted material must be clearly and prominently identified as such. Users who file excerpts of documents do so without prejudice to their right to timely file additional excerpts or the complete document, as may be allowed by the court. Responding parties may timely file additional excerpts or the complete document that they believe are directly germane. MA R USDCT CM/ECF Admin(O)(2).

    ii. Filers shall not attach as an exhibit any pleading or other paper already on file with the court in that case, but shall merely refer to that document. (See MA R USDCT CM/ECF Admin(G) for information on using hyperlinks in PDF documents filed in CM/ECF.) MA R USDCT CM/ECF Admin(O)(3).

  d. *Redacted documents.* The parties may request or the court may require the submission of documents that have been redacted/stripped of sensitive or confidential information. The redacted document prepared for electronic filing shall include the original caption of the document, and be clearly labeled as "Redacted Document." A specific event is available for this purpose ("Redacted Document"), found under the Other Filings/Other Documents menu option. MA R USDCT CM/ECF Admin(S).

   i.  Attorneys and pro se litigants are advised to take extra care when creating PDF documents intended for submission to CM/ECF. Steps shall be taken to ensure the documents are free of any hidden data (metadata) that may contain redacted information, or traces of information edited or deleted are not hidden in the final document. Even PDF content that has been encrypted may be recovered. An advisory document with additional information on this topic may be found on the court's website. MA R USDCT CM/ECF Admin(S).

e.  *Hyperlinks.* Electronically filed documents may contain the following types of hyperlinks: (1) hyperlinks to other portions of the same document; (2) hyperlinks to other documents filed within the CM/ECF system; and (3) hyperlinks to a location on the Internet that contains a source document for a citation. MA R USDCT CM/ECF Admin(G)(7).

   i.  Hyperlinks to cited authority may not replace standard citation format. Complete citations must be included in the text of the filed document. Neither a hyperlink, nor any site to which it refers, shall be considered part of the record, but are simply convenient mechanisms for accessing material cited in a document filed in CM/ECF. Instructions on creating hyperlinks may be found in the CM/ECF User Manual. MA R USDCT CM/ECF Admin(G)(7).

   ii.  The court accepts no responsibility for, and does not endorse, any product, organization, or content at any hyperlinked site, or at any site to which that site may be linked. The court accepts no responsibility for the availability or functionality of any hyperlink. MA R USDCT CM/ECF Admin(G)(7).

   iii.  One feature of PDF/A documents is that hyperlinks are commonly "masked," meaning that the full address of the referenced file is not written out; for example, clicking the word brief may open a brief which was previously filed in CM/ECF. MA R USDCT CM/ECF Admin(G)(7)(NOTE). An "unmasked" hyperlink has the full address visible to the user. MA R USDCT CM/ECF Admin(G)(7)(NOTE).

     • Masked hyperlinks may or may not work in a PDF/A document, depending on how it was created. Currently, masked hyperlinks are preserved in PDF/A documents produced by the "Save As" method in Microsoft Word 2007 and 2010; the "PDFMaker" method in Microsoft Word 2007; and OpenOffice 2.4 ("PDF Export"). With other production methods, such as WordPerfect, the PDF/A document includes underlined words that appear to be links, but clicking them has no effect. MA R USDCT CM/ECF Admin(G)(7)(NOTE).

f.  *Documents features not accepted.* CM/ECF will not accept PDF documents containing tracking tags, embedded systems commands, password protections, access restrictions or other security features, special tags or dynamic features. MA R USDCT CM/ECF Admin(G)(8).

g.  *File size limitations.* A filing party shall limit the size of each PDF file to no more than twenty (20) megabytes. PDF files larger than seven (7) megabytes will be rejected by the CM/ECF system. The filer will see a message advising of the size limitation. MA R USDCT CM/ECF Admin(P)(2).

   i.  Larger documents or exhibits may be submitted electronically if split into separate PDF files each less than seven (7) megabytes, attached to the main document and clearly labeled. MA R USDCT CM/ECF Admin(P)(2).

   ii.  Documents submitted electronically or on paper are subject to the page limitations set by MA R USDCT LR 7.1(b)(4) or by order of the court. MA R USDCT CM/ECF Admin(P)(1).

h.  *Accuracy and readability.* The filer shall verify the accuracy and readability of any PDF file before electronically filing it in CM/ECF. MA R USDCT CM/ECF Admin(G)(6); MA R USDCT CM/ECF Admin(P)(3).

3.  *Signing disclosures and discovery requests, responses, and objections.* FRCP 11 does not apply to disclosures and discovery requests, responses, objections, and motions under FRCP 26 through FRCP 37. FRCP 11(d).

a.  *Signature required.* Every disclosure under FRCP 26(a)(1) or FRCP 26(a)(3) and every discovery request, response, or objection must be signed by at least one attorney of record in the attorney's own name—or by the party personally, if unrepresented—and must state the signer's address, e-mail address, and telephone number. FRCP 26(g)(1). The provisions of the Federal Rules of Civil Procedure pertaining to the form and signing of pleadings, motions, and other papers shall be applicable to all papers filed in any proceeding in this court. The board of bar overseers registration number of each attorney signing such documents, except the United States Attorney and his staff, shall be inscribed below the signature. MA R USDCT LR 5.1(a)(1).

   i.  *Electronic signing.* A filing made through a person's electronic-filing account and authorized by that person, together with that person's name on a signature block, constitutes the person's signature. FRCP 5(d)(3)(C).

    ii. *Appearances.* The filing of an appearance or any other pleading signed on behalf of a party constitutes an entry of appearance for that party. All pleadings shall contain the name, bar admission number, address, telephone number, and e-mail address of the attorney entering an appearance. MA R USDCT LR 83.5.2(a).

- *Appearances by law firms.* When a party is represented by a law firm, the appearance must include the name and the signature of at least one individual attorney. When a party is represented by more than one attorney from the same or different law firms, the attorney entering the appearance must designate the individual attorney who is authorized to receive all notices in the case. Any notice sent to an attorney so designated shall be deemed to be proper notice unless the court finds that notice was not properly sent. MA R USDCT LR 83.5.2(b).

- For more information on appearances, refer to MA R USDCT LR 83.5.2.

    iii. *Signatures of attorneys.* The user login and password required to submit documents to the CM/ECF system shall serve as that user's signature for purposes of FRCP 11 and for all other purposes under the Federal Rules of Civil Procedure and the Local Rules of the United States District Court for the District of Massachusetts. All electronically filed documents must include a signature block and must set forth the attorney's name, bar number, address, telephone number and email address. The name of the CM/ECF user under whose log-in and password the document is submitted must be preceded by a "/s/" and typed in the space where the signature would otherwise appear. MA R USDCT CM/ECF Admin(M)(1). For an example, refer to MA R USDCT CM/ECF Admin(M)(1).

    iv. *Signatures of pro se parties.* Any document requiring a signature that is filed by a party appearing pro se shall bear the words "pro se" following that party's signature. Any such document shall also state the party's mailing address, telephone number (if any), and e-mail address (if the party has consented to service by email). MA R USDCT LR 83.5.5(g). For more information on practice by pro se litigants, refer to MA R USDCT LR 83.5.5.

    v. *Multiple signatures.* The filer of any document requiring more than one signature (e.g, stipulations, joint motions, joint status reports, magistrate judge consent forms, etc.) must list thereon all the names of other signatories by means of a "/s/ name of signatory" block for each. By submitting such a document, the filing attorney certifies that each of the other signatories has expressly agreed to the form and substance of the document and that the filing attorney has their actual authority to submit the document electronically. MA R USDCT CM/ECF Admin(M)(2). For more information, refer to MA R USDCT CM/ECF Admin(M)(2).

    vi. *Affidavits.* Except as provided in MA R USDCT CM/ECF Admin(L), affidavits shall be filed electronically; however, the electronically filed version must contain a "/s/ name of signatory" block indicating that the paper document bears an original signature. MA R USDCT CM/ECF Admin(M)(3). The court will also accept a scanned version of the original, signed document. MA R USDCT CM/ECF Admin(M)(3). For more information, refer to MA R USDCT CM/ECF Admin(M)(3).

b. *Effect of signature.* By signing, an attorney or party certifies that to the best of the person's knowledge, information, and belief formed after a reasonable inquiry:

    i. With respect to a disclosure, it is complete and correct as of the time it is made; and

    ii. With respect to a discovery request, response, or objection, it is:

- Consistent with the Federal Rules of Civil Procedure and warranted by existing law or by a nonfrivolous argument for extending, modifying, or reversing existing law, or for establishing new law;

- Not interposed for any improper purpose, such as to harass, cause unnecessary delay, or needlessly increase the cost of litigation; and

- Neither unreasonable nor unduly burdensome or expensive, considering the needs of the case, prior discovery in the case, the amount in controversy, and the importance of the issues at stake in the action. FRCP 26(g)(1).

c. *Failure to sign.* Other parties have no duty to act on an unsigned disclosure, request, response, or objection until it is signed, and the court must strike it unless a signature is promptly supplied after the omission is called to the attorney's or party's attention. FRCP 26(g)(2).

d. *Sanction for improper certification.* Refer to the General Requirements section of this document for information on the sanction for improper certification.

4. *Privacy protection for filings made with the court*

    a. *Redacted filings.* Unless the court orders otherwise, in an electronic or paper filing with the court that contains an individual's Social Security number, taxpayer-identification number, or birth date, the name of an individual known to be a minor, or a financial-account number, a party or nonparty making the filing may include only:

i. The last four (4) digits of the Social Security number and taxpayer-identification number;

ii. The year of the individual's birth;

iii. The minor's initials; and

iv. The last four (4) digits of the financial-account number. FRCP 5.2(a); MA R USDCT CM/ECF Admin(N).

b. *Exemptions from the redaction requirement.* The redaction requirement does not apply to the following:

i. A financial-account number that identifies the property allegedly subject to forfeiture in a forfeiture proceeding;

ii. The record of an administrative or agency proceeding;

iii. The official record of a state-court proceeding;

iv. The record of a court or tribunal, if that record was not subject to the redaction requirement when originally filed;

v. A filing covered by FRCP 5.2(c) or FRCP 5.2(d); and

vi. A pro se filing in an action brought under 28 U.S.C.A. § 2241, 28 U.S.C.A. § 2254, or 28 U.S.C.A. § 2255. FRCP 5.2(b).

c. *Limitations on remote access to electronic files; Social Security appeals and immigration cases.* Unless the court orders otherwise, in an action for benefits under the Social Security Act, and in an action or proceeding relating to an order of removal, to relief from removal, or to immigration benefits or detention, access to an electronic file is authorized as follows:

i. The parties and their attorneys may have remote electronic access to any part of the case file, including the administrative record;

ii. Any other person may have electronic access to the full record at the courthouse, but may have remote electronic access only to:

- The docket maintained by the court; and

- An opinion, order, judgment, or other disposition of the court, but not any other part of the case file or the administrative record. FRCP 5.2(c).

d. *Filings made under seal.* The court may order that a filing be made under seal without redaction. The court may later unseal the filing or order the person who made the filing to file a redacted version for the public record. FRCP 5.2(d).

e. *Protective orders.* For good cause, the court may by order in a case:

i. Require redaction of additional information; or

ii. Limit or prohibit a nonparty's remote electronic access to a document filed with the court. FRCP 5.2(e).

f. *Option for additional unredacted filing under seal.* A person making a redacted filing may also file an unredacted copy under seal. The court must retain the unredacted copy as part of the record. FRCP 5.2(f). For more information, refer to MA R USDCT LR 7.2.

g. *Option for filing a reference list.* A filing that contains redacted information may be filed together with a reference list that identifies each item of redacted information and specifies an appropriate identifier that uniquely corresponds to each item listed. The list must be filed under seal and may be amended as of right. Any reference in the case to a listed identifier will be construed to refer to the corresponding item of information. FRCP 5.2(g).

h. *Responsibility for redaction.* The clerk's office is not responsible for reviewing documents filed with the court to determine whether pleadings have been redacted and are in the proper form. MA R USDCT CM/ECF Admin(N).

i. *Waiver of protection of identifiers.* A person waives the protection of FRCP 5.2(a) as to the person's own information by filing it without redaction and not under seal. FRCP 5.2(h).

## F. Filing and Service Requirements

1. *Filing requirements*

a. *Required filings.* Any paper after the complaint that is required to be served must be filed no later than a reasonable time after service. FRCP 5(d)(1).

i. Except as noted in FRCP 33 to FRCP 36, the original of all papers required to be served under FRCP 5(d) shall, unless otherwise submitted to the court, be filed in the office of the clerk within seven (7) days after service has been made. MA R USDCT LR 5.1(b). Except as otherwise provided by the Federal Rules of Civil Procedure, proof of service of all pleadings and other papers required to be served (except discovery papers that in accordance with FRCP 33 to FRCP 36(f) are not to be filed) shall be filed in the office of the clerk promptly after service has been made. MA R USDCT LR 5.2(b)(1).

b.  *Nonelectronic filing.* A paper not filed electronically is filed by delivering it: (1) to the clerk; or (2) to a judge who agrees to accept it for filing, and who must then note the filing date on the paper and promptly send it to the clerk. FRCP 5(d)(2).

c.  *Electronic filing.* Unless exempt or otherwise ordered by the court, all pleadings and other papers submitted to the court must be filed, signed, and verified by electronic means as provided in MA R USDCT LR 5.4. MA R USDCT LR 5.4(A); MA R USDCT CM/ECF Admin(A)(1). All electronic filings must be made in accordance with the Administrative Procedures for Electronic Case Filing in the United States District Court for the District of Massachusetts (MA R USDCT CM/ECF Admin). MA R USDCT LR 5.4(B). The court may deviate from the Administrative Procedures for Electronic Case Filing in the United States District Court for the District of Massachusetts (MA R USDCT CM/ECF Admin) in specific cases, without prior notice, if deemed appropriate in the exercise of discretion, considering the need for the just, speedy, and inexpensive determination of matters pending before the court. MA R USDCT CM/ECF Admin(C)(1). The court may excuse a failure to comply with any administrative procedure whenever justice so requires. MA R USDCT CM/ECF Admin(C)(2).

  i.  *By a represented person; Generally required; Exceptions.* A person represented by an attorney must file electronically, unless nonelectronic filing is allowed by the court for good cause or is allowed or required by local rule. FRCP 5(d)(3)(A).

  ii.  *By unrepresented person; When allowed or required.* A person not represented by an attorney: (1) may file electronically only if allowed by court order or by local rule; and (2) may be required to file electronically only by court order, or by a local rule that includes reasonable exceptions. FRCP 5(d)(3)(B).

  iii.  *Exemptions from electronic filing*

  • *Documents that should not be filed electronically.* The following types of documents must not be filed electronically, and will not be scanned into the ECF system by the clerk's office: (1) sealed documents; (2) ex parte motions; (3) documents generated as part of an alternative dispute resolution (ADR) process; (4) the administrative record in Social Security and other administrative proceedings; (5) the state court record in proceedings under 28 U.S.C.A. § 2254; and (6) such other types of documents as the clerk may direct in the Administrative Procedures for Electronic Case Filing in the United States District Court for the District of Massachusetts (MA R USDCT CM/ECF Admin). MA R USDCT LR 5.4(G)(1); MA R USDCT CM/ECF Admin(L).

  • *Documents that need not be filed electronically.* The following types of documents need not be filed electronically, but may be scanned into the ECF system by a filing party or the clerk's office: (1) handwritten pleadings; (2) documents filed by pro se litigants who are incarcerated or who are not registered ECF users; (3) indictments, informations, criminal complaints, and the criminal JS45 form; (4) affidavits for search or arrest warrants and related documents; (5) documents received from another court under FRCRP 20 or FRCRP 40; (6) appearance bonds; (7) any document in a criminal case containing the original signature of a defendant, such as a waiver of indictment or a plea agreement; (8) petitions for violations of supervised release; (9) executed service of process documents under FRCP 4; and (10) such other types of documents as the clerk may direct in the Administrative Procedures for Electronic Case Filing in the United States District Court for the District of Massachusetts (MA R USDCT CM/ECF Admin). MA R USDCT LR 5.4(G)(2); MA R USDCT CM/ECF Admin(L).

  • For more information on exemptions from electronic filing, refer to MA R USDCT CM/ECF Admin(L).

  iv.  *Consequences of electronic filing.* Electronic transmission of a document to the CM/ECF system, together with the transmission of a Notice of Electronic Filing (NEF) from the court at the completion of the transaction, constitutes the filing of the document for all purposes of the Federal Rules of Procedure and constitutes entry of the document on the docket maintained by the clerk pursuant to FRCP 58 and FRCP 79. MA R USDCT CM/ECF Admin(G)(1).

  v.  *Payment of filing fees.* When electronically filing any pleading or paper through CM/ECF that requires a fee, all registered ECF users are to pay the fee electronically through the Treasury Department's Internet payment process. MA R USDCT LR 67.4(d); MA R USDCT CM/ECF Admin(A)(1). Pro se filers and those who have been exempted from electronic filing and/or electronic payment of fees may submit payments by check or money order made payable to "Clerk, U.S. District Court". MA R USDCT LR 67.4(d). For more information on filing fees, refer to MA R USDCT LR 67.4 and MA R USDCT CM/ECF Admin(I).

    vi.    For more information on electronic filing, refer to MA R USDCT CM/ECF Admin.

   d.   *Email or fax filing.* In general, the court does not accept documents by email or by fax. If the court, in special circumstances, does authorize the submission of a document in that manner, the document shall not be considered filed until an NEF is generated by CM/ECF at the completion of the transaction. MA R USDCT CM/ECF Admin(H)(5).

2.   *Service requirements.* All papers filed pursuant to MA R USDCT LR 7.1(b) shall be served unless the moving party indicates in writing on the face of the motion that ex parte consideration is requested. Motions filed "ex parte" and related papers need not be served until the motion has been ruled upon or the court orders that service be made. MA R USDCT LR 7.1(c). Service of all pleadings subsequent to the original complaint and of all other papers required to be served shall be made in the manner specified by FRCP 5. MA R USDCT LR 5.2(a).

   a.   *Service; When required*

      i.    *In general.* Unless the Federal Rules of Civil Procedure provide otherwise, each of the following papers must be served on every party:

- An order stating that service is required;
- A pleading filed after the original complaint, unless the court orders otherwise under FRCP 5(c) because there are numerous defendants;
- A discovery paper required to be served on a party, unless the court orders otherwise;
- A written motion, except one that may be heard ex parte; and
- A written notice, appearance, demand, or offer of judgment, or any similar paper. FRCP 5(a)(1).

     ii.    *If a party fails to appear.* No service is required on a party who is in default for failing to appear. But a pleading that asserts a new claim for relief against such a party must be served on that party under FRCP 4. FRCP 5(a)(2).

    iii.    *Seizing property.* If an action is begun by seizing property and no person is or need be named as a defendant, any service required before the filing of an appearance, answer, or claim must be made on the person who had custody or possession of the property when it was seized. FRCP 5(a)(3).

   b.   *Service; How made*

      i.    *Serving an attorney.* If a party is represented by an attorney, service under FRCP 5 must be made on the attorney unless the court orders service on the party. FRCP 5(b)(1).

- *Nonresident attorney.* On application of a party, the court may order an attorney who represents any other party and who does not maintain an office within this district where service can be made on him by delivery as provided by FRCP 5(b), to designate a member of the bar of this court who does maintain such an office to receive service of all pleadings and other papers in his behalf. MA R USDCT LR 5.2(c)(1).

     ii.    *Serving a party acting pro se.* On application of a party, the court may order any other party who is appearing without an attorney and who does not maintain an office or residence within this district where service can be made on him by delivery as provided by FRCP 5(b), to designate an address within the district at which service can be made on him by delivery. MA R USDCT LR 5.2(c)(2).

    iii.    *Service in general.* A paper is served under FRCP 5 by:

- Handing it to the person;
- Leaving it: (1) at the person's office with a clerk or other person in charge or, if no one is in charge, in a conspicuous place in the office; or (2) if the person has no office or the office is closed, at the person's dwelling or usual place of abode with someone of suitable age and discretion who resides there;
- Mailing it to the person's last known address—in which event service is complete upon mailing;
- Leaving it with the court clerk if the person has no known address;
- Sending it to a registered user by filing it with the court's electronic-filing system or sending it by other electronic means that the person consented to in writing—in either of which events service is complete upon filing or sending, but is not effective if the filer or sender learns that it did not reach the person to be served; or

- Delivering it by any other means that the person consented to in writing—in which event service is complete when the person making service delivers it to the agency designated to make delivery. FRCP 5(b)(2).

 iv. *Service by electronic means.* Unless exempt or otherwise ordered by the court, all pleadings and other papers must be served on other parties by electronic means. MA R USDCT LR 5.4(C); MA R USDCT CM/ECF Admin(H)(2). Service by electronic means shall be treated the same as service by mail. MA R USDCT CM/ECF Admin(H)(4).

- *Consent to electronic service.* Registering to use CM/ECF constitutes consent to service of all documents by electronic means as provided in the Administrative Procedures for Electronic Case Filing in the United States District Court for the District of Massachusetts (MA R USDCT CM/ECF Admin) and FRCP 5(b) and FRCP 77(d). MA R USDCT CM/ECF Admin(E)(6); MA R USDCT CM/ECF Admin(H)(3).

- *Service on registered ECF users.* Transmission of the Notice of Electronic Filing (NEF) through the court's transmission facilities will constitute service of the filed document upon a registered ECF user. MA R USDCT LR 5.4(C).

- *Service on non-registered users.* The party filing the document electronically is responsible for serving a paper copy of the document by mail in accordance with FRCP 5(b) to those case participants who have not been identified on the NEF as electronic recipients. MA R USDCT CM/ECF Admin(H)(3).

- *Service of conventionally filed papers.* Documents or exhibits submitted conventionally shall be served on other parties by the filer using traditional means. MA R USDCT CM/ECF Admin(P)(4).

 c. *Serving numerous defendants*

  i. *In general.* If an action involves an unusually large number of defendants, the court may, on motion or on its own, order that:

- Defendants' pleadings and replies to them need not be served on other defendants;

- Any crossclaim, counterclaim, avoidance, or affirmative defense in those pleadings and replies to them will be treated as denied or avoided by all other parties; and

- Filing any such pleading and serving it on the plaintiff constitutes notice of the pleading to all parties. FRCP 5(c)(1).

  ii. *Notifying parties.* A copy of every such order must be served on the parties as the court directs. FRCP 5(c)(2).

## G. Hearings

 1. *Hearings, generally.* If the court concludes that there should be a hearing on a motion, the motion will be set down for hearing at such time as the court determines. MA R USDCT LR 7.1(e).

 a. *Oral argument.* Due process does not require that oral argument be permitted on a motion and, except as otherwise provided by local rule, the district court has discretion to determine whether it will decide the motion on the papers or hear argument by counsel (and perhaps receive evidence). FPP § 1190; F.D.I.C. v. Deglau, 207 F.3d 153 (3d Cir. 2000).

  i. *Evidence on a motion.* When a motion relies on facts outside the record, the court may hear the matter on affidavits or may hear it wholly or partly on oral testimony or on depositions. FRCP 43(c).

 b. *Providing a regular schedule for oral hearings.* A court may establish regular times and places for oral hearings on motions. FRCP 78(a).

 c. *Providing for submission on briefs.* By rule or order, the court may provide for submitting and determining motions on briefs, without oral hearings. FRCP 78(b). Motions that are not set down for hearing as provided in MA R USDCT LR 7.1(e) will be decided on the papers submitted after an opposition to the motion has been filed, or, if no opposition is filed, after the time for filing an opposition has elapsed. MA R USDCT LR 7.1(f).

 2. *Conflict of court appearances.* For information on conflict of court appearances, refer to MA R USDCT LR 40.2.

## H. Forms

### 1. Federal Motion for Discovery Sanctions Forms

 a. Motion for contempt. 3B FEDFORMS § 27:43.

 b. Motion for sanctions for failure to appear at deposition. 3B FEDFORMS § 27:44.

 c. Motion that facts be taken as established for failure to answer questions upon deposition. 3B FEDFORMS § 27:45.

d. Motion for order refusing to allow disobedient party to support or oppose designated claims or defenses. 3B FEDFORMS § 27:46.

e. Motion for default judgment against defendant for failure to comply with order for production of documents. 3B FEDFORMS § 27:47.

f. Motion for award of expenses incurred to prove matter opponent failed to admit under FRCP 36. 3B FEDFORMS § 27:48.

g. Motion to strike answer or dismiss action for failure to comply with order requiring answer to interrogatories. 3B FEDFORMS § 27:51.

h. Motion to dismiss for failure to comply with previous order requiring answer to interrogatories to party. 3B FEDFORMS § 27:54.

i. Motion; For order that facts be taken to be established, and/or prohibiting certain claims, defenses, or evidence in opposition thereto. FEDPROF § 23:618.

j. Affidavit; By attorney; In support of motion for order that facts be taken to be established, etc; Failure to produce documents for inspection. FEDPROF § 23:619.

k. Affidavit; By attorney; In support of motion for order that facts be taken to be established, etc; Failure to obey order to answer questions. FEDPROF § 23:620.

l. Motion; For order striking pleadings, and for default judgment or dismissal of action. FEDPROF § 23:623.

m. Affidavit; By attorney; In support of motion for default judgment for defendant's failure to obey discovery order. FEDPROF § 23:624.

n. Motion; By defendant; For dismissal of action and other sanctions; For failure to comply with orders to complete deposition. FEDPROF § 23:625.

o. Motion; By defendant; For dismissal of action or other sanctions; For failure and refusal to comply with order to produce documents. FEDPROF § 23:626.

p. Motion; By defendant; For dismissal with prejudice; Failure to answer interrogatories as ordered. FEDPROF § 23:627.

q. Motion; For order staying further proceedings until adverse party obeys order compelling discovery. FEDPROF § 23:628.

r. Affidavit; By attorney; Opposing motion for order striking pleading and directing entry of default judgment; Good-faith attempt to obey discovery order; Production of documents illegal under foreign law. FEDPROF § 23:629.

s. Motion; For sanctions for failure to comply with examination order. FEDPROF § 23:634.

t. Motion; For order finding person in contempt of court; Refusal, after order, to answer question. FEDPROF § 23:636.

u. Affidavit; By attorney; In support of motion for order finding party in contempt. FEDPROF § 23:637.

v. Affidavit; By plaintiff; In support of motion for order holding defendant in contempt of court; Defendant disobeyed order for production of documents. FEDPROF § 23:638.

w. Motion; For order compelling opposing party to pay expenses incurred in proving facts such party refused to admit. FEDPROF § 23:640.

x. Motion; For sanctions; Failure to attend own deposition, serve answers to interrogatories, or respond to request for inspection. FEDPROF § 23:642.

y. Motion; For order staying proceedings until required response to discovery request is made. FEDPROF § 23:643.

z. Affidavit; By attorney; In support of motion for sanctions; Failure to attend own deposition, serve answers to interrogatories, or respond to request for inspection. FEDPROF § 23:645.

2. **Forms for the District of Massachusetts**

   a. Notice of filing with clerk's office. MA R USDCT CM/ECF Admin(Appendix I).

# I. Applicable Rules

1. *Federal rules*

   a. Counsel's liability for excessive costs. 28 U.S.C.A. § 1927.

   b. Serving and filing pleadings and other papers. FRCP 5.

   c.   Constitutional challenge to a statute; Notice, certification, and intervention. FRCP 5.1.

   d.   Privacy protection for filings made with the court. FRCP 5.2.

   e.   Computing and extending time; Time for motion papers. FRCP 6.

   f.   Pleadings allowed; Form of motions and other papers. FRCP 7.

   g.   Form of pleadings. FRCP 10.

   h.   Signing pleadings, motions, and other papers; Representations to the court; Sanctions. FRCP 11.

   i.   Duty to disclose; General provisions governing discovery. FRCP 26.

   j.   Failure to make disclosures or to cooperate in discovery; Sanctions. FRCP 37.

   k.   Taking testimony. FRCP 43.

   l.   Hearing motions; Submission on briefs. FRCP 78.

2.  *Local rules*

   a.   Title. MA R USDCT LR 1.1.

   b.   Sanctions. MA R USDCT LR 1.3.

   c.   Form and filing of papers. MA R USDCT LR 5.1.

   d.   Service and filing of pleadings and other papers. MA R USDCT LR 5.2.

   e.   Filing and service by electronic means. MA R USDCT LR 5.4.

   f.   Motion practice. MA R USDCT LR 7.1.

   g.   Alternative dispute resolution. MA R USDCT LR 16.4.

   h.   Sequences of discovery. MA R USDCT LR 26.2.

   i.   Court filings and costs. MA R USDCT LR 26.6.

   j.   Discovery disputes. MA R USDCT LR 37.1.

   k.   Payments and deposits made with the clerk. MA R USDCT LR 67.4.

   l.   Settlement. MA R USDCT LR 68.2.

   m.   Office of the clerk. MA R USDCT LR 77.2.

   n.   Appearances. MA R USDCT LR 83.5.2.

   o.   Practice by pro se litigants. MA R USDCT LR 83.5.5.

   p.   CM/ECF case management/electronic case files administrative procedures. MA R USDCT CM/ECF Admin.

## Motions, Oppositions and Replies
## Motion for Preliminary Injunction

**Document Last Updated December 2018**

**A.  Checklist**

(I)  ❑ Matters to be considered by moving party

   (a)  ❑ Required documents

      (1)  ❑ Notice of motion and motion

      (2)  ❑ Memorandum

      (3)  ❑ Security

      (4)  ❑ Certificate of service

   (b)  ❑ Supplemental documents

      (1)  ❑ Supporting evidence

      (2)  ❑ Verified pleadings

    (3)  ❑  Notice of constitutional question

    (4)  ❑  Nongovernmental corporate disclosure statement

    (5)  ❑  Proposed order

    (6)  ❑  Compact disk with copy of document(s) in PDF format

    (7)  ❑  Notice of filing with clerk's office

    (8)  ❑  Additional copies

    (9)  ❑  Courtesy copies

(c)  ❑  Timing

    (1)  ❑  There are no specific timing requirements for moving for a preliminary injunction

    (2)  ❑  FRCP 65 is silent about when notice must be given

    (3)  ❑  A written motion and notice of the hearing must be served at least fourteen (14) days before the time specified for the hearing, with the following exceptions: (i) when the motion may be heard ex parte; (ii) when the Federal Rules of Civil Procedure set a different time; or (iii) when a court order—which a party may, for good cause, apply for ex parte—sets a different time

    (4)  ❑  Any affidavit supporting a motion must be served with the motion

    (5)  ❑  Except as noted in FRCP 33 to FRCP 36, the original of all papers required to be served under FRCP 5(d) shall, unless otherwise submitted to the court, be filed in the office of the clerk within seven (7) days after service has been made

(II)  ❑  Matters to be considered by opposing party

  (a)  ❑  Required documents

    (1)  ❑  Opposition

    (2)  ❑  Certificate of service

  (b)  ❑  Supplemental documents

    (1)  ❑  Supporting evidence

    (2)  ❑  Verified pleadings

    (3)  ❑  Notice of constitutional question

    (4)  ❑  Nongovernmental corporate disclosure statement

    (5)  ❑  Compact disk with copy of document(s) in PDF format

    (6)  ❑  Notice of filing with clerk's office

    (7)  ❑  Additional copies

    (8)  ❑  Courtesy copies

  (c)  ❑  Timing

    (1)  ❑  A party opposing a motion, shall file an opposition within fourteen (14) days after the motion is served, unless another period is fixed by rule or statute, or by order of the court

    (2)  ❑  Except as FRCP 59(c) provides otherwise, any opposing affidavit must be served at least seven (7) days before the hearing, unless the court permits service at another time

    (3)  ❑  Except as noted in FRCP 33 to FRCP 36, the original of all papers required to be served under FRCP 5(d) shall, unless otherwise submitted to the court, be filed in the office of the clerk within seven (7) days after service has been made

## B. Timing

1. *Motion for preliminary injunction.* There are no specific timing requirements for moving for a preliminary injunction.

  a.  *Notice.* FRCP 65 is silent about when notice must be given. FPP § 2949.

2. *Timing of motions, generally*

   a. *Motion and notice of hearing.* A written motion and notice of the hearing must be served at least fourteen (14) days before the time specified for the hearing, with the following exceptions:

      i. When the motion may be heard ex parte;

      ii. When the Federal Rules of Civil Procedure set a different time; or

      iii. When a court order—which a party may, for good cause, apply for ex parte—sets a different time. FRCP 6(c)(1).

   b. *Supporting affidavit.* Any affidavit supporting a motion must be served with the motion. FRCP 6(c)(2).

3. *Timing of opposing papers.* A party opposing a motion, shall file an opposition within fourteen (14) days after the motion is served, unless (1) the motion is for summary judgment, in which case the opposition shall be filed within twenty-one (21) days after the motion is served, or (2) another period is fixed by rule or statute, or by order of the court. MA R USDCT LR 7.1(b)(2); MA R USDCT CM/ECF Admin(H)(4). The fourteen (14) day period is intended to include the period specified by the civil rules for mailing time and provide for a uniform period regardless of the use of the mails. MA R USDCT LR 7.1(b)(2).

   a. *Opposing affidavit.* Except as FRCP 59(c) provides otherwise, any opposing affidavit must be served at least seven (7) days before the hearing, unless the court permits service at another time. FRCP 6(c)(2).

4. *Timing of reply papers.* [W]here the respondent files an answering affidavit setting up a new matter, the moving party ordinarily is allowed a reasonable time to file a reply affidavit since failure to deny the new matter by affidavit may operate as an admission of its truth. AMJUR MOTIONS § 25.

   a. *Leave of court required.* All other papers not filed as indicated in MA R USDCT LR 7.1(b)(1) and MA R USDCT LR 7.1(b)(2), whether in the form of a reply brief or otherwise, may be submitted only with leave of court. MA R USDCT LR 7.1(b)(3).

5. *Filing after service.* Except as noted in FRCP 33 to FRCP 36, the original of all papers required to be served under FRCP 5(d) shall, unless otherwise submitted to the court, be filed in the office of the clerk within seven (7) days after service has been made. MA R USDCT LR 5.1(b).

6. *Computation of time*

   a. *Computing time.* FRCP 6 applies in computing any time period specified in the Federal Rules of Civil Procedure, in any local rule or court order, or in any statute that does not specify a method of computing time. FRCP 6(a).

      i. *Period stated in days or a longer unit.* When the period is stated in days or a longer unit of time:

         • Exclude the day of the event that triggers the period;

         • Count every day, including intermediate Saturdays, Sundays, and legal holidays; and

         • Include the last day of the period, but if the last day is a Saturday, Sunday, or legal holiday, the period continues to run until the end of the next day that is not a Saturday, Sunday, or legal holiday. FRCP 6(a)(1).

      ii. *Period stated in hours.* When the period is stated in hours:

         • Begin counting immediately on the occurrence of the event that triggers the period;

         • Count every hour, including hours during intermediate Saturdays, Sundays, and legal holidays; and

         • If the period would end on a Saturday, Sunday, or legal holiday, the period continues to run until the same time on the next day that is not a Saturday, Sunday, or legal holiday. FRCP 6(a)(2).

      iii. *Office of the clerk.* The offices of the Clerk of Court at Boston, Worcester and Springfield shall be open from 8:30 a.m. until 5:00 p.m. on all days except Saturdays, Sundays, legal holidays and other days so ordered by the court and announced in advance, if feasible. MA R USDCT LR 77.2.

      iv. *Inaccessibility of the clerk's office.* Unless the court orders otherwise, if the clerk's office is inaccessible:

         • On the last day for filing under FRCP 6(a)(1), then the time for filing is extended to the first accessible day that is not a Saturday, Sunday, or legal holiday; or

         • During the last hour for filing under FRCP 6(a)(2), then the time for filing is extended to the same time on the first accessible day that is not a Saturday, Sunday, or legal holiday. FRCP 6(a)(3).

      v. *"Last day" defined.* Unless a different time is set by a statute, local rule, or court order, the last day ends:

         • For electronic filing, at midnight in the court's time zone; and

- For filing by other means, when the clerk's office is scheduled to close. FRCP 6(a)(4).

vi. *"Next day" defined.* The "next day" is determined by continuing to count forward when the period is measured after an event and backward when measured before an event. FRCP 6(a)(5).

vii. *"Legal holiday" defined.* "Legal holiday" means:

- The day set aside by statute for observing New Year's Day, Martin Luther King Jr.'s Birthday, Washington's Birthday, Memorial Day, Independence Day, Labor Day, Columbus Day, Veterans' Day, Thanksgiving Day, or Christmas Day;

- Any day declared a holiday by the President or Congress; and

- For periods that are measured after an event, any other day declared a holiday by the state where the district court is located. FRCP 6(a)(6).

b. *Computation of electronic filing deadlines.* Filing documents electronically does not alter any filing deadlines. MA R USDCT CM/ECF Admin(K); MA R USDCT LR 5.4(D). Although CM/ECF is generally available twenty-four (24) hours a day for filing, all electronic transmissions of documents must be completed prior to 6:00 PM, Eastern Standard (or Daylight Savings) Time, on the date on which it is due, in order to be considered timely filed that day. MA R USDCT CM/ECF Admin(K); MA R USDCT LR 5.4(D). When a specific time of day deadline is set by court order or stipulation, the electronic filing must be completed by that time. Documents may be filed at any time of the day on days prior to the date on which it is due. MA R USDCT CM/ECF Admin(K). A document filed electronically shall be deemed filed as of the time and date stated on the NEF received from the court. MA R USDCT CM/ECF Admin(G)(2); MA R USDCT CM/ECF Admin(K).

i. *Technical failures.* A user whose filing is made untimely as the result of a technical failure of the court's CM/ECF system may seek appropriate relief from the court. MA R USDCT CM/ECF Admin(W)(3). Technical difficulties on the filer's end, with telephone, cable lines, the filer's Internet Service Provider (ISP), or hardware or software problems, will not constitute a technical failure under the Administrative Procedures for Electronic Case Filing in the United States District Court for the District of Massachusetts (MA R USDCT CM/ECF Admin) nor excuse an untimely filing. MA R USDCT CM/ECF Admin(W)(3). As help desk support is available during normal business hours, filers are strongly urged to electronically file any documents during that period. MA R USDCT CM/ECF Admin(W)(3).

- The court has made available a public terminal (computers and scanner) in each clerk's office for registered users to scan and electronically file documents. This equipment is available during normal business hours. Users should bring their prepared document and a valid CM/ECF login and password. MA R USDCT CM/ECF Admin(W)(3).

c. *Extending time.* When an act may or must be done within a specified time, the court may, for good cause, extend the time: (1) with or without motion or notice if the court acts, or if a request is made, before the original time or its extension expires; or (2) on motion made after the time has expired if the party failed to act because of excusable neglect. FRCP 6(b)(1).

i. *Exceptions.* A court must not extend the time to act under FRCP 50(b), FRCP 50(d), FRCP 52(b), FRCP 59(b), FRCP 59(d), FRCP 59(e), and FRCP 60(b). FRCP 6(b)(2).

ii. Refer to the United States District Court for the District of Massachusetts KeyRules Motion for Continuance/Extension of Time document for more information on extending time.

d. *Additional time after certain kinds of service.* When a party may or must act within a specified time after being served and service is made under FRCP 5(b)(2)(C) (by mail), FRCP 5(b)(2)(D) (by leaving with the clerk), or FRCP 5(b)(2)(F) (by other means consented to), three (3) days are added after the period would otherwise expire under FRCP 6(a). FRCP 6(d).

## C. General Requirements

1. *Motions, generally*

a. *Requirements.* A request for a court order must be made by motion. The motion must:

i. Be in writing unless made during a hearing or trial;

ii. State with particularity the grounds for seeking the order; and

iii. State the relief sought. FRCP 7(b)(1).

b. *Notice of motion.* A party interested in resisting the relief sought by a motion has a right to notice thereof, and an opportunity to be heard. AMJUR MOTIONS § 12.

    i. [I]n addition to statutory or court rule provisions requiring notice of a motion—the purpose of such a notice requirement having been said to be to prevent a party from being prejudicially surprised by a motion—principles of natural justice dictate that an adverse party generally must be given notice that a motion will be presented to the court. AMJUR MOTIONS § 12.

    ii. "Notice," in this regard, means reasonable notice, including a meaningful opportunity to prepare and to defend against allegations of a motion. AMJUR MOTIONS § 12.

c. *Writing requirement.* The writing requirement is intended to [ensure] that the adverse parties are informed and have a record of both the motion's pendency and the grounds on which the movant seeks an order. FPP § 1191; Feldberg v. Quechee Lakes Corp., 463 F.3d 195 (2d Cir. 2006). [A] single written document can satisfy the writing requirements both for a motion and for [an] FRCP 6(c)(1) notice. FRCP 7(Advisory Committee Notes).

d. *Particularity requirement.* The particularity requirement [ensures] that the opposing parties will have notice of their opponent's contentions. FEDPROC § 62:358; Goodman v. 1973 26 Foot Trojan Vessel, Arkansas Registration No. AR1439SN, 859 F.2d 71 (8th Cir. 1988). That requirement ensures that notice of the basis for the motion is provided to the court and to the opposing party so as to avoid prejudice, provide the opponent with a meaningful opportunity to respond, and provide the court with enough information to process the motion correctly. FEDPROC § 62:358; Andreas v. Volkswagen of Am., Inc., 336 F.3d 789 (8th Cir. 2003).

    i. Reasonable specification of the grounds for a motion is sufficient. The particularity requirement for motions is satisfied when no party is prejudiced by a lack of particularity or when the court can comprehend the basis for the motion and deal with it fairly. However, where a movant fails to state even one ground for granting the motion in question, the movant has failed to meet the minimal standard of "reasonable specification." FEDPROC § 62:358; Martinez v. Trainor, 556 F.2d 818 (7th Cir. 1977).

    ii. The court may excuse the failure to comply with the particularity requirement if it is inadvertent, and where no prejudice is shown by the opposing party. FEDPROC § 62:358.

e. *Control of motion practice*

    i. *Plan for the disposition of motions.* At the earliest practicable time, the judicial officer shall establish a framework for the disposition of motions, which, at the discretion of the judicial officer, may include specific deadlines or general time guidelines for filing motions. This framework may be amended from time to time by the judicial officer as required by the progress of the case. MA R USDCT LR 7.1(a)(1).

    ii. *Motion practice.* No motion shall be filed unless counsel certify that they have conferred and have attempted in good faith to resolve or narrow the issue. MA R USDCT LR 7.1(a)(2).

    iii. *Unresolved motions.* The court shall rule on motions as soon as practicable, having in mind the reporting requirements set forth in the Civil Justice Reform Act. MA R USDCT LR 7.1(a)(3).

2. *Motion for preliminary injunction.* The appropriate procedure for requesting a preliminary injunction is by motion, although it also commonly is requested by an order to show cause. FPP § 2949; James Luterbach Const. Co. v. Adamkus, 781 F.2d 599, 603 (7th Cir. 1986); Studebaker Corp. v. Gittlin, 360 F.2d 692 (2d. Cir. 1966).

a. *Preliminary injunction.* An interim grant of specific relief is a preliminary injunction that may be issued only on notice to the adverse party. FEDPROC § 47:53; Westar Energy, Inc. v. Lake, 552 F.3d 1215 (10th Cir. 2009). Defined broadly, a preliminary injunction is an injunction that is issued to protect plaintiff from irreparable injury and to preserve the court's power to render a meaningful decision after a trial on the merits. FPP § 2947; Evans v. Buchanan, 555 F.2d 373, 387 (3d Cir. 1977).

    i. *Disfavored injunctions.* There are three types of preliminary injunctions that are disfavored:

        • Those that afford the moving party substantially all the relief it might recover after a full trial on the merits;

        • Those that disturb the status quo; and

        • Those that are mandatory as opposed to prohibitory. FEDPROC § 47:55; Prairie Band of Potawatomi Indians v. Pierce, 253 F.3d 1234 (10th Cir. 2001).

b. *Notice.* The court may issue a preliminary injunction only on notice to the adverse party. FRCP 65(a)(1). Although FRCP 65(a)(1) does not define what constitutes proper notice, it has been held that providing a copy of the motion and a specification of the time and place of the hearing are adequate. FPP § 2949.

c. *Security.* The court may issue a preliminary injunction or a temporary restraining order only if the movant gives security in an amount that the court considers proper to pay the costs and damages sustained by any party found to have been wrongfully enjoined or restrained. The United States, its officers, and its agencies are not required to give security. FRCP 65(c).

    i. *Proceedings against a security provider.* Whenever the Federal Rules of Civil Procedure (including the Supplemental Rules for Admiralty or Maritime Claims and Asset Forfeiture Actions) require or allow a party to give security, and security is given with one or more security providers, each provider submits to the court's jurisdiction and irrevocably appoints the court clerk as its agent for receiving service of any papers that affect its liability on the security. The security provider's liability may be enforced on motion without an independent action. The motion and any notice that the court orders may be served on the court clerk, who must promptly send a copy of each to every security provider whose address is known. FRCP 65.1. For more information on sureties, refer to MA R USDCT LR 67.1.

d. *Preliminary injunction versus temporary restraining order.* Care should be taken to distinguish preliminary injunctions under FRCP 65(a) from temporary-restraining orders under FRCP 65(b). FPP § 2947.

    i. *Notice and duration.* [Temporary restraining orders] may be issued ex parte without an adversary hearing in order to prevent an immediate, irreparable injury and are of limited duration—they typically remain in effect for a maximum of twenty-eight (28) days. On the other hand, FRCP 65(a)(1) requires that notice be given to the opposing party before a preliminary injunction may be issued. FPP § 2947. Furthermore, a preliminary injunction normally lasts until the completion of the trial on the merits, unless it is dissolved earlier by court order or the consent of the parties. FPP § 2947. Therefore, its duration varies and is controlled by the nature of the situation in which it is utilized. FPP § 2947; Fundicao Tupy S.A. v. United States, 841 F.2d 1101, 1103 (Fed. Cir. 1988).

    ii. *Hearing.* Some type of a hearing also implicitly is required by FRCP 65(a)(2), which was added in 1966 and provides either for the consolidation of the trial on the merits with the preliminary-injunction hearing or the inclusion in the trial record of any evidence received at the FRCP 65(a) hearing. FPP § 2947.

e. *Grounds for granting or denying a preliminary injunction.* The policies that bear on the propriety of granting a preliminary injunction rarely are discussed directly in the cases. Instead they are taken into account by the court considering a number of factors that have been found useful in deciding whether to grant or deny preliminary injunctions in particular cases. A formulation that has become popular in all kinds of cases, although it originally was devised in connection with stays of administrative orders, is that the four most important factors are: (1) the significance of the threat of irreparable harm to plaintiff if the injunction is not granted; (2) the state of the balance between this harm and the injury that granting the injunction would inflict on defendant; (3) the probability that plaintiff will succeed on the merits; and (4) the public interest. FPP § 2948; Pottgen v. Missouri State High Sch. Activities Ass'n, 40 F.3d 926 (8th Cir. 1994).

    i. *Irreparable harm.* Perhaps the single most important prerequisite for the issuance of a preliminary injunction is a demonstration that if it is not granted the applicant is likely to suffer irreparable harm before a decision on the merits can be rendered. Only when the threatened harm would impair the court's ability to grant an effective remedy is there really a need for preliminary relief. FPP § 2948.1.

- There must be a likelihood that irreparable harm will occur. Speculative injury is not sufficient; there must be more than an unfounded fear on the part of the applicant. FPP § 2948.1.

- Thus, a preliminary injunction will not be issued simply to prevent the possibility of some remote future injury. A presently existing actual threat must be shown. However, the injury need not have been inflicted when application is made or be certain to occur; a strong threat of irreparable injury before trial is an adequate basis. FPP § 2948.1.

    ii. *Balancing hardship to parties.* The second factor bearing on the court's exercise of its discretion as to whether to grant preliminary relief involves an evaluation of the severity of the impact on defendant should the temporary injunction be granted and the hardship that would occur to plaintiff if the injunction should be denied. FPP § 2948.2. Two factors that frequently are considered when balancing the hardship on the respective parties of the grant or denial of relief are whether a preliminary injunction would give plaintiff all or most of the relief to which plaintiff would be entitled if successful at trial and whether mandatory relief is being sought. FPP § 2948.2.

    iii. *Likelihood of prevailing on the merits.* The third factor that enters into the preliminary injunction calculus is the likelihood that plaintiff will prevail on the merits. This is relevant because the need for the court to act is, at least in part, a function of the validity of the applicant's claim. The courts use a bewildering variety of formulations of the need for showing some likelihood of success—the most common being that plaintiff must demonstrate a reasonable probability of success. But the verbal differences do not seem to reflect substantive disagreement. All courts agree that plaintiff must present a prima facie case but need not show a certainty of winning. FPP § 2948.3.

iv. *Public interest.* The final major factor bearing on the court's discretion to issue or deny a preliminary injunction is the public interest. [Focusing] on this factor is another way of inquiring whether there are policy considerations that bear on whether the order should issue. Thus, when granting preliminary relief, courts frequently emphasize that the public interest will be furthered by the injunction. Conversely, preliminary relief will be denied if the court finds that the public interest would be injured were an injunction to be issued. If the court finds there is no public interest supporting preliminary relief, that conclusion also supports denial of any injunction, even if the public interest would not be harmed by one. FPP § 2948.4. Consequently, an evaluation of the public interest should be given considerable weight in determining whether a motion for a preliminary injunction should be granted. FPP § 2948.4; Yakus v. United States, 321 U.S. 414, 64 S. Ct. 660, 88 L. Ed. 834 (1944).

f. *Contents and scope of every injunction and restraining order*

i. *Contents.* Every order granting an injunction and every restraining order must:

- State the reasons why it issued;
- State its terms specifically; and
- Describe in reasonable detail—and not by referring to the complaint or other document—the act or acts restrained or required. FRCP 65(d)(1).

ii. *Persons bound.* The order binds only the following who receive actual notice of it by personal service or otherwise:

- The parties;
- The parties' officers, agents, servants, employees, and attorneys; and
- Other persons who are in active concert or participation with anyone described in FRCP 65(d)(2)(A) or FRCP 65(d)(2)(B). FRCP 65(d)(2).

g. *Other laws not modified.* FRCP 65 does not modify the following:

i. Any federal statute relating to temporary restraining orders or preliminary injunctions in actions affecting employer and employee;

ii. 28 U.S.C.A. § 2361, which relates to preliminary injunctions in actions of interpleader or in the nature of interpleader; or

iii. 28 U.S.C.A. § 2284, which relates to actions that must be heard and decided by a three-judge district court. FRCP 65(e).

h. *Copyright impoundment.* FRCP 65 applies to copyright-impoundment proceedings. FRCP 65(f).

3. *Opposing papers.* The Federal Rules of Civil Procedure do not require any formal answer, return, or reply to a motion, except where the Federal Rules of Civil Procedure or local rules may require affidavits, memoranda, or other papers to be filed in opposition to a motion. Such papers are simply to apprise the court of such opposition and the grounds of that opposition. FEDPROC § 62:353.

a. *Effect of failure to respond to motion.* Although in the absence of statutory provision or court rule, a motion ordinarily does not require a written answer, when a party files a motion and the opposing party fails to respond, the court may construe such failure to respond as nonopposition to the motion or an admission that the motion was meritorious, may take the facts alleged in the motion as true—the rule in some jurisdictions being that the failure to respond to a fact set forth in a motion is deemed an admission—and may grant the motion if the relief requested appears to be justified. AMJUR MOTIONS § 28.

b. *Assent or no opposition not determinative.* However, a motion will not be granted automatically simply because an "assent" or a notation of "no opposition" has been filed; federal judges frequently deny motions that have been assented to when it is thought that justice so dictates. FPP § 1190.

c. *Responsive pleading inappropriate as response to motion.* An attempt to answer or oppose a motion with a responsive pleading usually is not appropriate. FPP § 1190.

4. *Reply papers.* A moving party may be required or permitted to prepare papers in addition to his original motion papers. AMJUR MOTIONS § 25. Papers answering or replying to opposing papers may be appropriate, in the interests of justice,

where it appears there is a substantial reason for allowing a reply. Thus, a court may accept reply papers where a party demonstrates that the papers to which it seeks to file a reply raise new issues that are material to the disposition of the question before the court, or where the court determines, sua sponte, that it wishes further briefing of an issue raised in those papers and orders the submission of additional papers. FEDPROC § 62:354.

    a. *Function of reply papers.* The function of a reply affidavit is to answer the arguments made in opposition to the position taken by the movant and not to permit the movant to introduce new arguments in support of the motion. AMJUR MOTIONS § 25.

    b. *Issues raised for the first time in a reply document.* However, the view has been followed in some jurisdictions, that as a matter of judicial economy, where there is no prejudice and where the issues could be raised simply by filing a motion to dismiss, the trial court has discretion to consider arguments raised for the first time in a reply memorandum, and that a trial court may grant a motion to strike issues raised for the first time in a reply memorandum. AMJUR MOTIONS § 26.

5. *Alternative dispute resolution (ADR).* The judicial officer assigned to preside over the case shall encourage the resolution of disputes by settlement or other alternative dispute resolution programs. MA R USDCT LR 16.4(a).

    a. *Settlement.* At every conference conducted under the Local Rules of the United States District Court for the District of Massachusetts, the judicial officer shall inquire as to the utility of the parties conducting settlement negotiations, explore means of facilitating those negotiations, and offer whatever assistance may be appropriate in the circumstances. Assistance may include a reference of the case to another judicial officer for settlement purposes. MA R USDCT LR 16.4(b).

        i. When a case is settled, the parties shall file with the clerk a signed agreement for judgment or stipulation for dismissal, as appropriate, within twenty-eight (28) days, unless the court otherwise orders. MA R USDCT LR 68.2.

    b. *Alternative dispute resolution programs*

        i. *Discretion of judicial officer.* The judicial officer, following an exploration of the matter with all counsel, may refer appropriate cases to alternative dispute resolution programs that have been designated for use in the district court or that the judicial officer may make available. The dispute resolution programs described in MA R USDCT LR 16.4(c)(2) through MA R USDCT LR 16.4(c)(4) are illustrative, not exclusive. Moreover, nothing in MA R USDCT LR 16.4 shall preclude the parties from engaging in private dispute resolution programs as long as they comply with any schedule established by the court. MA R USDCT LR 16.4(c)(1).

        ii. *Mediation.* The judicial officer may refer the case to mediation upon the agreement of all parties. MA R USDCT LR 16.4(c)(2)(A).

        iii. *Other alternative dispute resolution programs.* Use of mediation is not exclusive. At the request of parties, the judicial officer may consider other forms of alternative dispute resolution including, but not limited to, mini-trial, summary jury trial and arbitration. MA R USDCT LR 16.4(c)(3).

    c. For more information on alternative dispute resolution (ADR), refer to MA R USDCT LR 16.4.

6. *Sanctions.* Failure to comply with any of the directions or obligations set forth in, or authorized by, these rules may result in dismissal, default, or the imposition of other sanctions as deemed appropriate by the judicial officer. MA R USDCT LR 1.3. Except as provided by law, the court may impose sanctions as provided in MA R USDCT LR 1.3 for failure to comply with the Administrative Procedures for Electronic Case Filing in the United States District Court for the District of Massachusetts (MA R USDCT CM/ECF Admin) or with MA R USDCT LR 5.4. MA R USDCT CM/ECF Admin(C)(3).

## D. Documents

1. *Documents for moving party*

    a. *Required documents*

        i. *Notice of motion and motion.* Refer to the General Requirements section of this document for information on the notice of motion and motion.

          • *Request for oral argument.* Any party making or opposing a motion who believes that oral argument may assist the court and wishes to be heard shall include a request for oral argument in a separate paragraph of the motion or opposition. The request should be set off with a centered caption, "REQUEST FOR ORAL ARGUMENT." MA R USDCT LR 7.1(d).

        ii. *Memorandum.* A party filing a motion shall at the same time file a memorandum of reasons, including citation of supporting authorities, why the motion should be granted. MA R USDCT LR 7.1(b)(1). Any memorandum of law or other attachment filed in support of a main document shall be filed as a separate document, using the proper event. MA R USDCT CM/ECF Admin(G)(4). Memoranda supporting or opposing allowance of motions shall not, without leave of court, exceed twenty (20) pages, double-spaced. MA R USDCT LR 7.1(b)(4).

iii. *Security.* Refer to the General Requirements section of this document for information on the security required.

iv. *Certificate of service.* No certificate of service is required when a paper is served by filing it with the court's electronic-filing system. When a paper that is required to be served is served by other means: (1) if the paper is filed, a certificate of service must be filed with it or within a reasonable time after service; and (2) if the paper is not filed, a certificate of service need not be filed unless filing is required by court order or by local rule. FRCP 5(d)(1)(B). Except as otherwise provided by the Federal Rules of Civil Procedure, proof of service of all pleadings and other papers required to be served (except discovery papers that in accordance with FRCP 33 to FRCP 36(f) are not to be filed) shall be filed in the office of the clerk promptly after service has been made. The proof shall show the time and manner of service, and may be made by written acknowledgment of service, a certificate of a member of the bar of this court, or an affidavit of the person who served the paper. MA R USDCT LR 5.2(b)(1). A certificate of service of a member of the bar shall appear at the bottom of or on the margin of the last page of the paper to which it relates. MA R USDCT LR 5.2(b)(2).

- *Paper service.* The certificate shall be a brief, single-spaced statement and may be in the following form: I hereby certify that a true copy of the above document was served upon (each party appearing pro se and) the attorney of record for each other party by mail (by hand) on (date). (Signature). MA R USDCT LR 5.2(b)(2).

- *Electronic service.* Any pleading or other paper served by electronic means must bear a certificate of service in accordance with MA R USDCT LR 5.2(b). MA R USDCT LR 5.4(C); MA R USDCT CM/ECF Admin(H)(2). The certificate of service shall state that the filer: (1) filed the document electronically, (2) that it will be served electronically to registered CM/ECF participants via the NEF and (3) that the filer will send paper copies to non-registered participants as indicated on the NEF. MA R USDCT CM/ECF Admin(H)(2). For example: I hereby certify that this document filed through the CM/ECF system will be sent electronically to the registered participants as identified on the NEF (NEF) and paper copies will be sent to those indicated as non registered participants on (date). MA R USDCT CM/ECF Admin(H)(2).

- *Return.* Documents not conforming to the requirements of MA R USDCT LR 5.2 (except notices of appeal) shall be returned by the clerk. MA R USDCT LR 5.2(b)(2).

- *Failure to make proof of service.* Failure to make proof of service does not affect the validity of the service. MA R USDCT LR 5.2(b)(3).

b. *Supplemental documents*

i. *Supporting evidence.* When a motion relies on facts outside the record, the court may hear the matter on affidavits or may hear it wholly or partly on oral testimony or on depositions. FRCP 43(c). Evidence that goes beyond the unverified allegations of the pleadings and motion papers must be presented to support or oppose a motion for a preliminary injunction. FPP § 2949. Affidavits and other documents setting forth or evidencing facts on which the motion is based shall be filed with the motion. MA R USDCT LR 7.1(b)(1).

- *Affidavits.* Affidavits are appropriate on a preliminary-injunction motion and typically will be offered by both parties. FPP § 2949. All affidavits should state the facts supporting the litigant's position clearly and specifically. Preliminary injunctions frequently are denied if the affidavits are too vague or conclusory to demonstrate a clear right to relief under FRCP 65. FPP § 2949.

ii. *Verified pleadings.* Pleadings may be considered if they have been verified. FPP § 2949; K-2 Ski Co. v. Head Ski Co., 467 F.2d 1087 (9th Cir. 1972).

iii. *Notice of constitutional question.* A party that files a pleading, written motion, or other paper drawing into question the constitutionality of a federal or state statute must promptly:

- *File notice.* File a notice of constitutional question stating the question and identifying the paper that raises it, if: (1) a federal statute is questioned and the parties do not include the United States, one of its agencies, or one of its officers or employees in an official capacity; or (2) a state statute is questioned and the parties do not include the state, one of its agencies, or one of its officers or employees in an official capacity; and

- *Serve notice.* Serve the notice and paper on the Attorney General of the United States if a federal statute is questioned—or on the state attorney general if a state statute is questioned—either by certified or registered mail or by sending it to an electronic address designated by the attorney general for this purpose. FRCP 5.1(a).

- *No forfeiture.* A party's failure to file and serve the notice, or the court's failure to certify, does not forfeit a constitutional claim or defense that is otherwise timely asserted. FRCP 5.1(d).

iv. *Nongovernmental corporate disclosure statement*

- *Contents.* A nongovernmental corporate party must file two (2) copies of a disclosure statement that: (1) identifies any parent corporation and any publicly held corporation owning ten percent (10%) or more of its stock; or (2) states that there is no such corporation. FRCP 7.1(a).

- *Time to file; Supplemental filing.* A party must: (1) file the disclosure statement with its first appearance, pleading, petition, motion, response, or other request addressed to the court; and (2) promptly file a supplemental statement if any required information changes. FRCP 7.1(b).

v. *Proposed order.* Proposed orders usually are not required by this court. However, the court may request the party to submit such a document. In those situations, unless otherwise directed by the clerk's office, electronically file the proposed document/order using the entry for "Proposed Documents submitted to the court," found under the Other Documents menu, or as an attachment to the motion to which it relates. MA R USDCT CM/ECF Admin(T).

vi. *Compact disk with copy of document(s) in PDF format.* A filer who cannot file a document electronically because of such technical difficulty on the filer's end [with telephone, cable lines, the filer's Internet Service Provider (ISP), or hardware or software problems] shall file the document conventionally along with a copy of the document in PDF format on a compact disk or contact the clerk's office for permission to submit the PDF document via email. MA R USDCT CM/ECF Admin(W)(3). Refer to the Timing section of this document for more information on technical failures.

vii. *Notice of filing with clerk's office.* When documents or exhibits (other than those filed ex parte or under seal) are submitted conventionally, a "Notice of Filing with clerk's office" shall be filed electronically and attached to the main document. A paper copy of the "Notice of Filing with clerk's office" must accompany the documents submitted to the court. The "Notice of Filing with clerk's office" (see MA R USDCT CM/ECF Admin(Appendix I)) shall describe each of the documents that will be filed as paper copies in the clerk's office, or shall include an index of the documents if those documents are voluminous. MA R USDCT CM/ECF Admin(P)(5).

viii. *Additional copies.* Whenever, because of the nature of a proceeding, such as a proceeding before a three-judge district court under 28 U.S.C.A. § 2284, additional copies of a paper required to be filed are necessary either for the use of the court or to enable the clerk to carry out his duties, it is the responsibility of the party filing or having filed the paper to provide the necessary copies. MA R USDCT LR 5.1(d).

ix. *Courtesy copies.* COURTESY COPIES OF DOCUMENTS FILED ELECTRONICALLY SHALL NOT BE SUBMITTED ROUTINELY. MA R USDCT CM/ECF Admin(J). Judicial officers, on a case-by-case basis, may require courtesy copies for specific cases, or types of motions, etc. A few Judicial Officers have entered Standing Orders, which may be found on their respective pages on the court's website (under Divisions). Any document filed on paper with the court as a courtesy copy must be clearly labeled as such (Example: COURTESY COPY—DO NOT SCAN). Documents delivered to the court as a courtesy copy will not be maintained in the official court record. MA R USDCT CM/ECF Admin(J).

2. *Documents for opposing party*

   a. *Required documents*

      i. *Opposition.* Refer to the General Requirements section of this document for information on the opposing papers.

      - *Memorandum.* A party opposing a motion shall file, in the same (rather than a separate), document a memorandum of reasons, including citation of supporting authorities, why the motion should not be granted. MA R USDCT LR 7.1(b)(2). Any memorandum of law or other attachment filed in support of a main document shall be filed as a separate document, using the proper event. MA R USDCT CM/ECF Admin(G)(4). Memoranda supporting or opposing allowance of motions shall not, without leave of court, exceed twenty (20) pages, double-spaced. MA R USDCT LR 7.1(b)(4).

      - *Request for oral argument.* Any party making or opposing a motion who believes that oral argument may assist the court and wishes to be heard shall include a request for oral argument in a separate paragraph of the motion or opposition. The request should be set off with a centered caption, "REQUEST FOR ORAL ARGUMENT." MA R USDCT LR 7.1(d).

ii. *Certificate of service.* No certificate of service is required when a paper is served by filing it with the court's electronic-filing system. When a paper that is required to be served is served by other means: (1) if the paper is filed, a certificate of service must be filed with it or within a reasonable time after service; and (2) if the paper is not filed, a certificate of service need not be filed unless filing is required by court order or by local rule. FRCP 5(d)(1)(B). Except as otherwise provided by the Federal Rules of Civil Procedure, proof of service of all pleadings and other papers required to be served (except discovery papers that in accordance with FRCP 33 to FRCP 36(f) are not to be filed) shall be filed in the office of the clerk promptly after service has been made. The proof shall show the time and manner of service, and may be made by written acknowledgment of service, a certificate of a member of the bar of this court, or an affidavit of the person who served the paper. MA R USDCT LR 5.2(b)(1). A certificate of service of a member of the bar shall appear at the bottom of or on the margin of the last page of the paper to which it relates. MA R USDCT LR 5.2(b)(2).

- *Paper service.* The certificate shall be a brief, single-spaced statement and may be in the following form: I hereby certify that a true copy of the above document was served upon (each party appearing pro se and) the attorney of record for each other party by mail (by hand) on (date). (Signature). MA R USDCT LR 5.2(b)(2).

- *Electronic service.* Any pleading or other paper served by electronic means must bear a certificate of service in accordance with MA R USDCT LR 5.2(b). MA R USDCT LR 5.4(C); MA R USDCT CM/ECF Admin(H)(2). The certificate of service shall state that the filer: (1) filed the document electronically, (2) that it will be served electronically to registered CM/ECF participants via the NEF and (3) that the filer will send paper copies to non-registered participants as indicated on the NEF. MA R USDCT CM/ECF Admin(H)(2). For example: I hereby certify that this document filed through the CM/ECF system will be sent electronically to the registered participants as identified on the NEF (NEF) and paper copies will be sent to those indicated as non registered participants on (date). MA R USDCT CM/ECF Admin(H)(2).

- *Return.* Documents not conforming to the requirements of MA R USDCT LR 5.2 (except notices of appeal) shall be returned by the clerk. MA R USDCT LR 5.2(b)(2).

- *Failure to make proof of service.* Failure to make proof of service does not affect the validity of the service. MA R USDCT LR 5.2(b)(3).

b. *Supplemental documents*

i. *Supporting evidence.* When a motion relies on facts outside the record, the court may hear the matter on affidavits or may hear it wholly or partly on oral testimony or on depositions. FRCP 43(c). Evidence that goes beyond the unverified allegations of the pleadings and motion papers must be presented to support or oppose a motion for a preliminary injunction. FPP § 2949. Affidavits and other documents setting forth or evidencing facts on which the opposition is based shall be filed with the opposition. MA R USDCT LR 7.1(b)(2).

- *Affidavits.* Affidavits are appropriate on a preliminary-injunction motion and typically will be offered by both parties. FPP § 2949. All affidavits should state the facts supporting the litigant's position clearly and specifically. Preliminary injunctions frequently are denied if the affidavits are too vague or conclusory to demonstrate a clear right to relief under FRCP 65. FPP § 2949.

ii. *Verified pleadings.* Pleadings may be considered if they have been verified. FPP § 2949; K-2 Ski Co. v. Head Ski Co., 467 F.2d 1087 (9th Cir. 1972).

iii. *Notice of constitutional question.* A party that files a pleading, written motion, or other paper drawing into question the constitutionality of a federal or state statute must promptly:

- *File notice.* File a notice of constitutional question stating the question and identifying the paper that raises it, if: (1) a federal statute is questioned and the parties do not include the United States, one of its agencies, or one of its officers or employees in an official capacity; or (2) a state statute is questioned and the parties do not include the state, one of its agencies, or one of its officers or employees in an official capacity; and

- *Serve notice.* Serve the notice and paper on the Attorney General of the United States if a federal statute is questioned—or on the state attorney general if a state statute is questioned—either by certified or registered mail or by sending it to an electronic address designated by the attorney general for this purpose. FRCP 5.1(a).

- *No forfeiture.* A party's failure to file and serve the notice, or the court's failure to certify, does not forfeit a constitutional claim or defense that is otherwise timely asserted. FRCP 5.1(d).

iv. *Nongovernmental corporate disclosure statement*

- *Contents.* A nongovernmental corporate party must file two (2) copies of a disclosure statement that: (1)

identifies any parent corporation and any publicly held corporation owning ten percent (10%) or more of its stock; or (2) states that there is no such corporation. FRCP 7.1(a).

- *Time to file; Supplemental filing.* A party must: (1) file the disclosure statement with its first appearance, pleading, petition, motion, response, or other request addressed to the court; and (2) promptly file a supplemental statement if any required information changes. FRCP 7.1(b).

v. *Compact disk with copy of document(s) in PDF format.* A filer who cannot file a document electronically because of such technical difficulty on the filer's end [with telephone, cable lines, the filer's Internet Service Provider (ISP), or hardware or software problems] shall file the document conventionally along with a copy of the document in PDF format on a compact disk or contact the clerk's office for permission to submit the PDF document via email. MA R USDCT CM/ECF Admin(W)(3). Refer to the Timing section of this document for more information on technical failures.

vi. *Notice of filing with clerk's office.* When documents or exhibits (other than those filed ex parte or under seal) are submitted conventionally, a "Notice of Filing with clerk's office" shall be filed electronically and attached to the main document. A paper copy of the "Notice of Filing with clerk's office" must accompany the documents submitted to the court. The "Notice of Filing with clerk's office" (see MA R USDCT CM/ECF Admin(Appendix I)) shall describe each of the documents that will be filed as paper copies in the clerk's office, or shall include an index of the documents if those documents are voluminous. MA R USDCT CM/ECF Admin(P)(5).

vii. *Additional copies.* Whenever, because of the nature of a proceeding, such as a proceeding before a three-judge district court under 28 U.S.C.A. § 2284, additional copies of a paper required to be filed are necessary either for the use of the court or to enable the clerk to carry out his duties, it is the responsibility of the party filing or having filed the paper to provide the necessary copies. MA R USDCT LR 5.1(d).

viii. *Courtesy copies.* COURTESY COPIES OF DOCUMENTS FILED ELECTRONICALLY SHALL NOT BE SUBMITTED ROUTINELY. MA R USDCT CM/ECF Admin(J). Judicial officers, on a case-by-case basis, may require courtesy copies for specific cases, or types of motions, etc. A few Judicial Officers have entered Standing Orders, which may be found on their respective pages on the court's website (under Divisions). Any document filed on paper with the court as a courtesy copy must be clearly labeled as such (Example: COURTESY COPY—DO NOT SCAN). Documents delivered to the court as a courtesy copy will not be maintained in the official court record. MA R USDCT CM/ECF Admin(J).

## E. Format

1. *Form of documents.* The rules governing captions and other matters of form in pleadings apply to motions and other papers. FRCP 7(b)(2). The provisions of FRCP 10 and FRCP 11 concerning the form and signing of pleadings, motions, and other papers shall be applicable to all papers filed in any proceeding in this court. The board of bar overseers registration number of each attorney signing such documents, except the United States Attorney and his or her staff, shall be inscribed below the signature. MA R USDCT LR 5.1(a)(1).

    a. *Paper size and binding.* All papers filed in the court shall be adapted for flat filing, be filed on eight and one-half by eleven (8-1/2 x 11) inch paper without backers and be bound firmly by staple or some such other means (excluding paper or binder clip or rubber band). MA R USDCT LR 5.1(a)(2).

    b. *Spacing.* All papers, except discovery requests and responses, shall be double-spaced except for the identification of counsel, title of the case, footnotes, quotations and exhibits. Discovery requests and responses shall be single-spaced. MA R USDCT LR 5.1(a)(2).

    c. *Caption.* Every pleading must have a caption with the court's name, a title, a file number, and [an] FRCP 7(a) designation. FRCP 10(a).

        i. *Names of parties.* The title of the complaint must name all the parties; the title of other pleadings, after naming the first party on each side, may refer generally to other parties. FRCP 10(a).

        ii. *Request for special action.* When any pleading or other paper filed in the court includes a request for special process or relief, or any other request such that, if granted, the court will proceed other than in the ordinary course, the request shall, unless it is noted on the category sheet [see MA R USDCT LR 40.1(a)(1)], be noted on the first page to the right of or immediately beneath the caption. MA R USDCT LR 5.1(c).

    d. *Claims or defenses*

        i. *Numbered paragraphs.* A party must state its claims or defenses in numbered paragraphs, each limited as far as practicable to a single set of circumstances. A later pleading may refer by number to a paragraph in an earlier pleading. FRCP 10(b).

    ii.   *Separate statements.* If doing so would promote clarity, each claim founded on a separate transaction or occurrence—and each defense other than a denial—must be stated in a separate count or defense. FRCP 10(b).

e.  *Adoption by reference.* A statement in a pleading may be adopted by reference elsewhere in the same pleading or in any other pleading or motion. FRCP 10(c).

    i.   *Exhibits.* A copy of a written instrument that is an exhibit to a pleading is a part of the pleading for all purposes. FRCP 10(c).

f.  *Citations*

    i.   *Local rules.* These rules shall be known as Local Rules of the United States District Court for the District of Massachusetts and cited as "L.R., D. Mass." or "L.R." MA R USDCT LR 1.1.

    ii.   *Electronic case filing procedures.* The procedures governing electronic case filing shall be known as the "Administrative Procedures for Electronic Case Filing in the United States District Court for the District of Massachusetts." They shall be cited as "APECF." MA R USDCT CM/ECF Admin(A)(7).

g.  *Acceptance by the clerk.* The clerk must not refuse to file a paper solely because it is not in the form prescribed by the Federal Rules of Civil Procedure or by a local rule or practice. FRCP 5(d)(4).

    i.   Except for complaints and notices of appeal, papers that do not conform to the requirements of MA R USDCT LR 5.1(a)(2) shall be returned by the clerk. MA R USDCT LR 5.1(a)(2).

2.  *Form of electronic documents.* A paper filed electronically is a written paper for purposes of the Federal Rules of Civil Procedure. FRCP 5(d)(3)(D).

a.  *PDF/A format required.* The court will begin requiring submission of documents in PDF/A format in the foreseeable future. PDF/A is an enhanced version of the traditional PDF format. Newer versions of most PDF software will be able to convert to this format. Additional information on PDF/A documents may be found on the court's website. MA R USDCT CM/ECF Admin(Electronic Filing and PDF).

    i.   *Electronically converted PDF.* Electronically converted PDF documents are created from word processing documents (MS Word, WordPerfect, etc.) using any appropriate software. These documents are text searchable and the file size is generally smaller than a scanned document. CM/ECF users may use any brand of software to convert documents to PDF. MA R USDCT CM/ECF Admin(Electronic Filing and PDF).

        •  Documents converted to PDF, rather than scanned, are preferred for filing in CM/ECF. MA R USDCT CM/ECF Admin(Electronic Filing and PDF).

    ii.   *Scanned PDF.* Scanned PDF documents are created from paper documents run through an optical scanner. Scanned PDF documents are generally not searchable and have a larger file size. Please note that software used to create scanned documents may (and should) be set in such a way that the document is "text-searchable." MA R USDCT CM/ECF Admin(Electronic Filing and PDF).

b.  *Title.* All pleadings filed electronically shall be titled in accordance with the approved dictionary of civil or criminal events of the CM/ECF system of this court. A list of events is available on the CM/ECF Training Information page of the court's website. The clerk's office may, when necessary and appropriate, modify the docket entry description, or delete and re-enter the docket entry in order to comply with the court's quality assurance standards. MA R USDCT CM/ECF Admin(G)(3).

c.  *Attachments to filings and exhibits.* Attachments to filings and exhibits must be filed in accordance with the court's CM/ECF User Manual, unless otherwise ordered by the court. MA R USDCT CM/ECF Admin(O)(1).

    i.   Filers must submit as attachments only those excerpts of the referenced documents that are directly germane to the matter under consideration by the court. Excerpted material must be clearly and prominently identified as such. Users who file excerpts of documents do so without prejudice to their right to timely file additional excerpts or the complete document, as may be allowed by the court. Responding parties may timely file additional excerpts or the complete document that they believe are directly germane. MA R USDCT CM/ECF Admin(O)(2).

    ii.   Filers shall not attach as an exhibit any pleading or other paper already on file with the court in that case, but shall merely refer to that document. (See MA R USDCT CM/ECF Admin(G) for information on using hyperlinks in PDF documents filed in CM/ECF.) MA R USDCT CM/ECF Admin(O)(3).

d.  *Redacted documents.* The parties may request or the court may require the submission of documents that have been redacted/stripped of sensitive or confidential information. The redacted document prepared for electronic filing shall include the original caption of the document, and be clearly labeled as "Redacted Document." A specific event is available for this purpose ("Redacted Document"), found under the Other Filings/Other Documents menu option. MA R USDCT CM/ECF Admin(S).

    i.    Attorneys and pro se litigants are advised to take extra care when creating PDF documents intended for submission to CM/ECF. Steps shall be taken to ensure the documents are free of any hidden data (metadata) that may contain redacted information, or traces of information edited or deleted are not hidden in the final document. Even PDF content that has been encrypted may be recovered. An advisory document with additional information on this topic may be found on the court's website. MA R USDCT CM/ECF Admin(S).

e.    *Hyperlinks.* Electronically filed documents may contain the following types of hyperlinks: (1) hyperlinks to other portions of the same document; (2) hyperlinks to other documents filed within the CM/ECF system; and (3) hyperlinks to a location on the Internet that contains a source document for a citation. MA R USDCT CM/ECF Admin(G)(7).

    i.    Hyperlinks to cited authority may not replace standard citation format. Complete citations must be included in the text of the filed document. Neither a hyperlink, nor any site to which it refers, shall be considered part of the record, but are simply convenient mechanisms for accessing material cited in a document filed in CM/ECF. Instructions on creating hyperlinks may be found in the CM/ECF User Manual. MA R USDCT CM/ECF Admin(G)(7).

    ii.    The court accepts no responsibility for, and does not endorse, any product, organization, or content at any hyperlinked site, or at any site to which that site may be linked. The court accepts no responsibility for the availability or functionality of any hyperlink. MA R USDCT CM/ECF Admin(G)(7).

    iii.    One feature of PDF/A documents is that hyperlinks are commonly "masked," meaning that the full address of the referenced file is not written out; for example, clicking the word brief may open a brief which was previously filed in CM/ECF. MA R USDCT CM/ECF Admin(G)(7)(NOTE). An "unmasked" hyperlink has the full address visible to the user. MA R USDCT CM/ECF Admin(G)(7)(NOTE).

    •    Masked hyperlinks may or may not work in a PDF/A document, depending on how it was created. Currently, masked hyperlinks are preserved in PDF/A documents produced by the "Save As" method in Microsoft Word 2007 and 2010; the "PDFMaker" method in Microsoft Word 2007; and OpenOffice 2.4 ("PDF Export"). With other production methods, such as WordPerfect, the PDF/A document includes underlined words that appear to be links, but clicking them has no effect. MA R USDCT CM/ECF Admin(G)(7)(NOTE).

f.    *Documents features not accepted.* CM/ECF will not accept PDF documents containing tracking tags, embedded systems commands, password protections, access restrictions or other security features, special tags or dynamic features. MA R USDCT CM/ECF Admin(G)(8).

g.    *File size limitations.* A filing party shall limit the size of each PDF file to no more than twenty (20) megabytes. PDF files larger than seven (7) megabytes will be rejected by the CM/ECF system. The filer will see a message advising of the size limitation. MA R USDCT CM/ECF Admin(P)(2).

    i.    Larger documents or exhibits may be submitted electronically if split into separate PDF files each less than seven (7) megabytes, attached to the main document and clearly labeled. MA R USDCT CM/ECF Admin(P)(2).

    ii.    Documents submitted electronically or on paper are subject to the page limitations set by MA R USDCT LR 7.1(b)(4) or by order of the court. MA R USDCT CM/ECF Admin(P)(1).

h.    *Accuracy and readability.* The filer shall verify the accuracy and readability of any PDF file before electronically filing it in CM/ECF. MA R USDCT CM/ECF Admin(G)(6); MA R USDCT CM/ECF Admin(P)(3).

3.    *Signing of pleadings, motions and other papers*

a.    *Signature.* Every pleading, written motion, and other paper must be signed by at least one attorney of record in the attorney's name—or by a party personally if the party is unrepresented. The paper must state the signer's address, e-mail address, and telephone number. FRCP 11(a). The provisions of the Federal Rules of Civil Procedure pertaining to the form and signing of pleadings, motions, and other papers shall be applicable to all papers filed in any proceeding in this court. The board of bar overseers registration number of each attorney signing such documents, except the United States Attorney and his staff, shall be inscribed below the signature. MA R USDCT LR 5.1(a)(1).

    i.    *Electronic signing.* A filing made through a person's electronic-filing account and authorized by that person, together with that person's name on a signature block, constitutes the person's signature. FRCP 5(d)(3)(C).

    ii.    *Appearances.* The filing of an appearance or any other pleading signed on behalf of a party constitutes an entry of appearance for that party. All pleadings shall contain the name, bar admission number, address, telephone number, and e-mail address of the attorney entering an appearance. MA R USDCT LR 83.5.2(a).

- *Appearances by law firms.* When a party is represented by a law firm, the appearance must include the name and the signature of at least one individual attorney. When a party is represented by more than one attorney from the same or different law firms, the attorney entering the appearance must designate the individual attorney who is authorized to receive all notices in the case. Any notice sent to an attorney so designated shall be deemed to be proper notice unless the court finds that notice was not properly sent. MA R USDCT LR 83.5.2(b).

- For more information on appearances, refer to MA R USDCT LR 83.5.2.

iii.  *Signatures of attorneys.* The user login and password required to submit documents to the CM/ECF system shall serve as that user's signature for purposes of FRCP 11 and for all other purposes under the Federal Rules of Civil Procedure and the Local Rules of the United States District Court for the District of Massachusetts. All electronically filed documents must include a signature block and must set forth the attorney's name, bar number, address, telephone number and email address. The name of the CM/ECF user under whose log-in and password the document is submitted must be preceded by a "/s/" and typed in the space where the signature would otherwise appear. MA R USDCT CM/ECF Admin(M)(1). For an example, refer to MA R USDCT CM/ECF Admin(M)(1).

iv.  *Signatures of pro se parties.* Any document requiring a signature that is filed by a party appearing pro se shall bear the words "pro se" following that party's signature. Any such document shall also state the party's mailing address, telephone number (if any), and e-mail address (if the party has consented to service by email). MA R USDCT LR 83.5.5(g). For more information on practice by pro se litigants, refer to MA R USDCT LR 83.5.5.

v.  *Multiple signatures.* The filer of any document requiring more than one signature (e.g, stipulations, joint motions, joint status reports, magistrate judge consent forms, etc.) must list thereon all the names of other signatories by means of a "/s/ name of signatory" block for each. By submitting such a document, the filing attorney certifies that each of the other signatories has expressly agreed to the form and substance of the document and that the filing attorney has their actual authority to submit the document electronically. MA R USDCT CM/ECF Admin(M)(2). For more information, refer to MA R USDCT CM/ECF Admin(M)(2).

vi.  *Affidavits.* Except as provided in MA R USDCT CM/ECF Admin(L), affidavits shall be filed electronically; however, the electronically filed version must contain a "/s/ name of signatory" block indicating that the paper document bears an original signature. MA R USDCT CM/ECF Admin(M)(3). The court will also accept a scanned version of the original, signed document. MA R USDCT CM/ECF Admin(M)(3). For more information, refer to MA R USDCT CM/ECF Admin(M)(3).

vii.  *No verification or accompanying affidavit required for pleadings.* Unless a rule or statute specifically states otherwise, a pleading need not be verified or accompanied by an affidavit. FRCP 11(a).

viii.  *Unsigned papers.* The court must strike an unsigned paper unless the omission is promptly corrected after being called to the attorney's or party's attention. FRCP 11(a).

b.  *Representations to the court.* By presenting to the court a pleading, written motion, or other paper—whether by signing, filing, submitting, or later advocating it—an attorney or unrepresented party certifies that to the best of the person's knowledge, information, and belief, formed after an inquiry reasonable under the circumstances:

i.  It is not being presented for any improper purpose, such as to harass, cause unnecessary delay, or needlessly increase the cost of litigation;

ii.  The claims, defenses, and other legal contentions are warranted by existing law or by a nonfrivolous argument for extending, modifying, or reversing existing law or for establishing new law;

iii.  The factual contentions have evidentiary support or, if specifically so identified, will likely have evidentiary support after a reasonable opportunity for further investigation or discovery; and

iv.  The denials of factual contentions are warranted on the evidence or, if specifically so identified, are reasonably based on belief or a lack of information. FRCP 11(b).

c.  *Sanctions.* If, after notice and a reasonable opportunity to respond, the court determines that FRCP 11(b) has been violated, the court may impose an appropriate sanction on any attorney, law firm, or party that violated FRCP 11(b) or is responsible for the violation. FRCP 11(c)(1). Refer to the United States District Court for the District of Massachusetts KeyRules Motion for Sanctions document for more information.

4. *Privacy protection for filings made with the court*

   a. *Redacted filings.* Unless the court orders otherwise, in an electronic or paper filing with the court that contains an individual's Social Security number, taxpayer-identification number, or birth date, the name of an individual known to be a minor, or a financial-account number, a party or nonparty making the filing may include only:

      i. The last four (4) digits of the Social Security number and taxpayer-identification number;

      ii. The year of the individual's birth;

      iii. The minor's initials; and

      iv. The last four (4) digits of the financial-account number. FRCP 5.2(a); MA R USDCT CM/ECF Admin(N).

   b. *Exemptions from the redaction requirement.* The redaction requirement does not apply to the following:

      i. A financial-account number that identifies the property allegedly subject to forfeiture in a forfeiture proceeding;

      ii. The record of an administrative or agency proceeding;

      iii. The official record of a state-court proceeding;

      iv. The record of a court or tribunal, if that record was not subject to the redaction requirement when originally filed;

      v. A filing covered by FRCP 5.2(c) or FRCP 5.2(d); and

      vi. A pro se filing in an action brought under 28 U.S.C.A. § 2241, 28 U.S.C.A. § 2254, or 28 U.S.C.A. § 2255. FRCP 5.2(b).

   c. *Limitations on remote access to electronic files; Social Security appeals and immigration cases.* Unless the court orders otherwise, in an action for benefits under the Social Security Act, and in an action or proceeding relating to an order of removal, to relief from removal, or to immigration benefits or detention, access to an electronic file is authorized as follows:

      i. The parties and their attorneys may have remote electronic access to any part of the case file, including the administrative record;

      ii. Any other person may have electronic access to the full record at the courthouse, but may have remote electronic access only to:

         • The docket maintained by the court; and

         • An opinion, order, judgment, or other disposition of the court, but not any other part of the case file or the administrative record. FRCP 5.2(c).

   d. *Filings made under seal.* The court may order that a filing be made under seal without redaction. The court may later unseal the filing or order the person who made the filing to file a redacted version for the public record. FRCP 5.2(d).

   e. *Protective orders.* For good cause, the court may by order in a case:

      i. Require redaction of additional information; or

      ii. Limit or prohibit a nonparty's remote electronic access to a document filed with the court. FRCP 5.2(e).

   f. *Option for additional unredacted filing under seal.* A person making a redacted filing may also file an unredacted copy under seal. The court must retain the unredacted copy as part of the record. FRCP 5.2(f). For more information, refer to MA R USDCT LR 7.2.

   g. *Option for filing a reference list.* A filing that contains redacted information may be filed together with a reference list that identifies each item of redacted information and specifies an appropriate identifier that uniquely corresponds to each item listed. The list must be filed under seal and may be amended as of right. Any reference in the case to a listed identifier will be construed to refer to the corresponding item of information. FRCP 5.2(g).

   h. *Responsibility for redaction.* The clerk's office is not responsible for reviewing documents filed with the court to determine whether pleadings have been redacted and are in the proper form. MA R USDCT CM/ECF Admin(N).

   i. *Waiver of protection of identifiers.* A person waives the protection of FRCP 5.2(a) as to the person's own information by filing it without redaction and not under seal. FRCP 5.2(h).

## F. Filing and Service Requirements

1. *Filing requirements*

   a. *Required filings.* Any paper after the complaint that is required to be served must be filed no later than a reasonable time after service. FRCP 5(d)(1).

      i. Except as noted in FRCP 33 to FRCP 36, the original of all papers required to be served under FRCP 5(d) shall, unless otherwise submitted to the court, be filed in the office of the clerk within seven (7) days after service has been made. MA R USDCT LR 5.1(b). Except as otherwise provided by the Federal Rules of Civil Procedure, proof of service of all pleadings and other papers required to be served (except discovery papers that in accordance with FRCP 33 to FRCP 36(f) are not to be filed) shall be filed in the office of the clerk promptly after service has been made. MA R USDCT LR 5.2(b)(1).

   b. *Nonelectronic filing.* A paper not filed electronically is filed by delivering it: (1) to the clerk; or (2) to a judge who agrees to accept it for filing, and who must then note the filing date on the paper and promptly send it to the clerk. FRCP 5(d)(2).

   c. *Electronic filing.* Unless exempt or otherwise ordered by the court, all pleadings and other papers submitted to the court must be filed, signed, and verified by electronic means as provided in MA R USDCT LR 5.4. MA R USDCT LR 5.4(A); MA R USDCT CM/ECF Admin(A)(1). All electronic filings must be made in accordance with the Administrative Procedures for Electronic Case Filing in the United States District Court for the District of Massachusetts (MA R USDCT CM/ECF Admin). MA R USDCT LR 5.4(B). The court may deviate from the Administrative Procedures for Electronic Case Filing in the United States District Court for the District of Massachusetts (MA R USDCT CM/ECF Admin) in specific cases, without prior notice, if deemed appropriate in the exercise of discretion, considering the need for the just, speedy, and inexpensive determination of matters pending before the court. MA R USDCT CM/ECF Admin(C)(1). The court may excuse a failure to comply with any administrative procedure whenever justice so requires. MA R USDCT CM/ECF Admin(C)(2).

      i. *By a represented person; Generally required; Exceptions.* A person represented by an attorney must file electronically, unless nonelectronic filing is allowed by the court for good cause or is allowed or required by local rule. FRCP 5(d)(3)(A).

      ii. *By unrepresented person; When allowed or required.* A person not represented by an attorney: (1) may file electronically only if allowed by court order or by local rule; and (2) may be required to file electronically only by court order, or by a local rule that includes reasonable exceptions. FRCP 5(d)(3)(B).

      iii. *Exemptions from electronic filing*

         - *Documents that should not be filed electronically.* The following types of documents must not be filed electronically, and will not be scanned into the ECF system by the clerk's office: (1) sealed documents; (2) ex parte motions; (3) documents generated as part of an alternative dispute resolution (ADR) process; (4) the administrative record in Social Security and other administrative proceedings; (5) the state court record in proceedings under 28 U.S.C.A. § 2254; and (6) such other types of documents as the clerk may direct in the Administrative Procedures for Electronic Case Filing in the United States District Court for the District of Massachusetts (MA R USDCT CM/ECF Admin). MA R USDCT LR 5.4(G)(1); MA R USDCT CM/ECF Admin(L).

         - *Documents that need not be filed electronically.* The following types of documents need not be filed electronically, but may be scanned into the ECF system by a filing party or the clerk's office: (1) handwritten pleadings; (2) documents filed by pro se litigants who are incarcerated or who are not registered ECF users; (3) indictments, informations, criminal complaints, and the criminal JS45 form; (4) affidavits for search or arrest warrants and related documents; (5) documents received from another court under FRCRP 20 or FRCRP 40; (6) appearance bonds; (7) any document in a criminal case containing the original signature of a defendant, such as a waiver of indictment or a plea agreement; (8) petitions for violations of supervised release; (9) executed service of process documents under FRCP 4; and (10) such other types of documents as the clerk may direct in the Administrative Procedures for Electronic Case Filing in the United States District Court for the District of Massachusetts (MA R USDCT CM/ECF Admin). MA R USDCT LR 5.4(G)(2); MA R USDCT CM/ECF Admin(L).

         - For more information on exemptions from electronic filing, refer to MA R USDCT CM/ECF Admin(L).

      iv. *Consequences of electronic filing.* Electronic transmission of a document to the CM/ECF system, together with the transmission of a Notice of Electronic Filing (NEF) from the court at the completion of the transaction, constitutes the filing of the document for all purposes of the Federal Rules of Procedure and constitutes entry of the document on the docket maintained by the clerk pursuant to FRCP 58 and FRCP 79. MA R USDCT CM/ECF Admin(G)(1).

    v. *Payment of filing fees.* When electronically filing any pleading or paper through CM/ECF that requires a fee, all registered ECF users are to pay the fee electronically through the Treasury Department's Internet payment process. MA R USDCT LR 67.4(d); MA R USDCT CM/ECF Admin(A)(1). Pro se filers and those who have been exempted from electronic filing and/or electronic payment of fees may submit payments by check or money order made payable to "Clerk, U.S. District Court". MA R USDCT LR 67.4(d). For more information on filing fees, refer to MA R USDCT LR 67.4 and MA R USDCT CM/ECF Admin(I).

    vi. For more information on electronic filing, refer to MA R USDCT CM/ECF Admin.

  d. *Email or fax filing.* In general, the court does not accept documents by email or by fax. If the court, in special circumstances, does authorize the submission of a document in that manner, the document shall not be considered filed until an NEF is generated by CM/ECF at the completion of the transaction. MA R USDCT CM/ECF Admin(H)(5).

2. *Service requirements.* All papers filed pursuant to MA R USDCT LR 7.1(b) shall be served unless the moving party indicates in writing on the face of the motion that ex parte consideration is requested. Motions filed "ex parte" and related papers need not be served until the motion has been ruled upon or the court orders that service be made. MA R USDCT LR 7.1(c). Service of all pleadings subsequent to the original complaint and of all other papers required to be served shall be made in the manner specified by FRCP 5. MA R USDCT LR 5.2(a).

  a. *Service; When required*

    i. *In general.* Unless the Federal Rules of Civil Procedure provide otherwise, each of the following papers must be served on every party:

- An order stating that service is required;
- A pleading filed after the original complaint, unless the court orders otherwise under FRCP 5(c) because there are numerous defendants;
- A discovery paper required to be served on a party, unless the court orders otherwise;
- A written motion, except one that may be heard ex parte; and
- A written notice, appearance, demand, or offer of judgment, or any similar paper. FRCP 5(a)(1).

    ii. *If a party fails to appear.* No service is required on a party who is in default for failing to appear. But a pleading that asserts a new claim for relief against such a party must be served on that party under FRCP 4. FRCP 5(a)(2).

    iii. *Seizing property.* If an action is begun by seizing property and no person is or need be named as a defendant, any service required before the filing of an appearance, answer, or claim must be made on the person who had custody or possession of the property when it was seized. FRCP 5(a)(3).

  b. *Service; How made*

    i. *Serving an attorney.* If a party is represented by an attorney, service under FRCP 5 must be made on the attorney unless the court orders service on the party. FRCP 5(b)(1).

- *Nonresident attorney.* On application of a party, the court may order an attorney who represents any other party and who does not maintain an office within this district where service can be made on him by delivery as provided by FRCP 5(b), to designate a member of the bar of this court who does maintain such an office to receive service of all pleadings and other papers in his behalf. MA R USDCT LR 5.2(c)(1).

    ii. *Serving a party acting pro se.* On application of a party, the court may order any other party who is appearing without an attorney and who does not maintain an office or residence within this district where service can be made on him by delivery as provided by FRCP 5(b), to designate an address within the district at which service can be made on him by delivery. MA R USDCT LR 5.2(c)(2).

    iii. *Service in general.* A paper is served under FRCP 5 by:

- Handing it to the person;
- Leaving it: (1) at the person's office with a clerk or other person in charge or, if no one is in charge, in a conspicuous place in the office; or (2) if the person has no office or the office is closed, at the person's dwelling or usual place of abode with someone of suitable age and discretion who resides there;

- Mailing it to the person's last known address—in which event service is complete upon mailing;

- Leaving it with the court clerk if the person has no known address;

- Sending it to a registered user by filing it with the court's electronic-filing system or sending it by other electronic means that the person consented to in writing—in either of which events service is complete upon filing or sending, but is not effective if the filer or sender learns that it did not reach the person to be served; or

- Delivering it by any other means that the person consented to in writing—in which event service is complete when the person making service delivers it to the agency designated to make delivery. FRCP 5(b)(2).

    iv. *Service by electronic means.* Unless exempt or otherwise ordered by the court, all pleadings and other papers must be served on other parties by electronic means. MA R USDCT LR 5.4(C); MA R USDCT CM/ECF Admin(H)(2). Service by electronic means shall be treated the same as service by mail. MA R USDCT CM/ECF Admin(H)(4).

- *Consent to electronic service.* Registering to use CM/ECF constitutes consent to service of all documents by electronic means as provided in the Administrative Procedures for Electronic Case Filing in the United States District Court for the District of Massachusetts (MA R USDCT CM/ECF Admin) and FRCP 5(b) and FRCP 77(d). MA R USDCT CM/ECF Admin(E)(6); MA R USDCT CM/ECF Admin(H)(3).

- *Service on registered ECF users.* Transmission of the Notice of Electronic Filing (NEF) through the court's transmission facilities will constitute service of the filed document upon a registered ECF user. MA R USDCT LR 5.4(C).

- *Service on non-registered users.* The party filing the document electronically is responsible for serving a paper copy of the document by mail in accordance with FRCP 5(b) to those case participants who have not been identified on the NEF as electronic recipients. MA R USDCT CM/ECF Admin(H)(3).

- *Service of conventionally filed papers.* Documents or exhibits submitted conventionally shall be served on other parties by the filer using traditional means. MA R USDCT CM/ECF Admin(P)(4).

  c. *Serving numerous defendants*

    i. *In general.* If an action involves an unusually large number of defendants, the court may, on motion or on its own, order that:

- Defendants' pleadings and replies to them need not be served on other defendants;

- Any crossclaim, counterclaim, avoidance, or affirmative defense in those pleadings and replies to them will be treated as denied or avoided by all other parties; and

- Filing any such pleading and serving it on the plaintiff constitutes notice of the pleading to all parties. FRCP 5(c)(1).

    ii. *Notifying parties.* A copy of every such order must be served on the parties as the court directs. FRCP 5(c)(2).

# G. Hearings

1. *Hearings, generally.* If the court concludes that there should be a hearing on a motion, the motion will be set down for hearing at such time as the court determines. MA R USDCT LR 7.1(e).

  a. *Oral argument.* Due process does not require that oral argument be permitted on a motion and, except as otherwise provided by local rule, the district court has discretion to determine whether it will decide the motion on the papers or hear argument by counsel (and perhaps receive evidence). FPP § 1190; F.D.I.C. v. Deglau, 207 F.3d 153 (3d Cir. 2000).

    i. *Evidence on a motion.* When a motion relies on facts outside the record, the court may hear the matter on affidavits or may hear it wholly or partly on oral testimony or on depositions. FRCP 43(c).

  b. *Providing a regular schedule for oral hearings.* A court may establish regular times and places for oral hearings on motions. FRCP 78(a).

  c. *Providing for submission on briefs.* By rule or order, the court may provide for submitting and determining motions on briefs, without oral hearings. FRCP 78(b). Motions that are not set down for hearing as provided in MA R USDCT LR 7.1(e) will be decided on the papers submitted after an opposition to the motion has been filed, or, if no opposition is filed, after the time for filing an opposition has elapsed. MA R USDCT LR 7.1(f).

2. *Hearing on motion for preliminary injunction*

   a. *Consolidating the hearing with the trial on the merits.* Before or after beginning the hearing on a motion for a preliminary injunction, the court may advance the trial on the merits and consolidate it with the hearing. Even when consolidation is not ordered, evidence that is received on the motion and that would be admissible at trial becomes part of the trial record and need not be repeated at trial. But the court must preserve any party's right to a jury trial. FRCP 65(a)(2).

   b. *Expediting the hearing after temporary restraining order is issued without notice.* If the order is issued without notice, the motion for a preliminary injunction must be set for hearing at the earliest possible time, taking precedence over all other matters except hearings on older matters of the same character. At the hearing, the party who obtained the order must proceed with the motion; if the party does not, the court must dissolve the order. FRCP 65(b)(3).

3. *Conflict of court appearances.* For information on conflict of court appearances, refer to MA R USDCT LR 40.2.

## H. Forms

### 1. Federal Motion for Preliminary Injunction Forms

   a. Motion for preliminary injunction. 4A FEDFORMS § 47:14.

   b. Motion enjoining use of information acquired from employment with plaintiff. 4A FEDFORMS § 47:17.

   c. Motion enjoining interference with public access. 4A FEDFORMS § 47:18.

   d. Motion enjoining collection of tax assessment. 4A FEDFORMS § 47:19.

   e. Motion enjoining conducting election or certifying representative. 4A FEDFORMS § 47:20.

   f. Motion enjoining preventing plaintiff's acting as teacher. 4A FEDFORMS § 47:21.

   g. Motion enjoining interference with plaintiff's enforcement of judgment in related case. 4A FEDFORMS § 47:22.

   h. Motion for preliminary injunction in patent infringement action. 4A FEDFORMS § 47:23.

   i. Motion for preliminary injunction on basis of prayer of complaint and for setting hearing on motion. 4A FEDFORMS § 47:24.

   j. Notice of motion. 4A FEDFORMS § 47:39.

   k. Notice of motion and motion. 4A FEDFORMS § 47:41.

   l. Declaration; In support of motion for preliminary injunction. AMJUR PP INJUNCTION § 38.

   m. Memorandum of points and authorities; In support of motion for preliminary injunction. AMJUR PP INJUNCTION § 39.

   n. Notice; Motion for preliminary injunction. AMJUR PP INJUNCTION § 40.

   o. Motion; For preliminary injunction. AMJUR PP INJUNCTION § 41.

   p. Motion; For preliminary injunction; On pleadings and other papers without evidentiary hearing or oral argument. AMJUR PP INJUNCTION § 43.

   q. Affidavit; In support of motion for preliminary injunction. AMJUR PP INJUNCTION § 52.

   r. Bond; To obtain preliminary injunction. FEDPROF § 1:226.

   s. Opposition; To motion. FEDPROF § 1B:175.

   t. Brief; Supporting or opposing motion. FEDPROF § 1B:177.

   u. Motion for temporary restraining order and preliminary injunction. GOLDLTGFMS § 13A:6.

   v. Motion for preliminary injunction. GOLDLTGFMS § 13A:18.

   w. Motion for preliminary injunction; Based upon pleadings and other papers without evidentiary hearing or oral argument. GOLDLTGFMS § 13A:19.

   x. Motion for preliminary injunction; Supporting affidavit. GOLDLTGFMS § 13A:20.

   y. Bond. GOLDLTGFMS § 19:2.

   z. Bond; In support of injunction. GOLDLTGFMS § 19:3.

### 2. Forms for the District of Massachusetts

   a. Notice of filing with clerk's office. MA R USDCT CM/ECF Admin(Appendix I).

## I. Applicable Rules

1. *Federal rules*

   a. Serving and filing pleadings and other papers. FRCP 5.

   b. Constitutional challenge to a statute; Notice, certification, and intervention. FRCP 5.1.

   c. Privacy protection for filings made with the court. FRCP 5.2.

   d. Computing and extending time; Time for motion papers. FRCP 6.

   e. Pleadings allowed; Form of motions and other papers. FRCP 7.

   f. Disclosure statement. FRCP 7.1.

   g. Form of pleadings. FRCP 10.

   h. Signing pleadings, motions, and other papers; Representations to the court; Sanctions. FRCP 11.

   i. Taking testimony. FRCP 43.

   j. Injunctions and restraining orders. FRCP 65.

   k. Proceedings against a security provider. FRCP 65.1.

   l. Hearing motions; Submission on briefs. FRCP 78.

2. *Local rules*

   a. Title. MA R USDCT LR 1.1.

   b. Sanctions. MA R USDCT LR 1.3.

   c. Form and filing of papers. MA R USDCT LR 5.1.

   d. Service and filing of pleadings and other papers. MA R USDCT LR 5.2.

   e. Filing and service by electronic means. MA R USDCT LR 5.4.

   f. Motion practice. MA R USDCT LR 7.1.

   g. Alternative dispute resolution. MA R USDCT LR 16.4.

   h. Payments and deposits made with the clerk. MA R USDCT LR 67.4.

   i. Settlement. MA R USDCT LR 68.2.

   j. Office of the clerk. MA R USDCT LR 77.2.

   k. Appearances. MA R USDCT LR 83.5.2.

   l. Practice by pro se litigants. MA R USDCT LR 83.5.5.

   m. CM/ECF case management/electronic case files administrative procedures. MA R USDCT CM/ECF Admin.

# Motions, Oppositions and Replies
# Motion to Dismiss for Failure to State a Claim

### Document Last Updated December 2018

## A. Checklist

(I) ❑ Matters to be considered by moving party

   (a) ❑ Required documents

      (1) ❑ Notice of motion and motion

      (2) ❑ Memorandum

      (3) ❑ Certificate of service

   (b) ❑ Supplemental documents

      (1) ❑ Pleading

      (2) ❑ Notice of constitutional question

    (3)  ❑ Nongovernmental corporate disclosure statement

    (4)  ❑ Proposed order

    (5)  ❑ Compact disk with copy of document(s) in PDF format

    (6)  ❑ Notice of filing with clerk's office

    (7)  ❑ Additional copies

    (8)  ❑ Courtesy copies

(c)  ❑ Timing

    (1)  ❑ Failure to state a claim upon which relief can be granted may be raised in any pleading allowed or ordered under FRCP 7(a); every defense to a claim for relief in any pleading must be asserted in the responsive pleading if one is required

    (2)  ❑ A motion asserting any of the defenses in FRCP 12(b) must be made before pleading if a responsive pleading is allowed

    (3)  ❑ Failure to state a claim upon which relief can be granted may be raised by a motion under FRCP 12(c); after the pleadings are closed—but early enough not to delay trial—a party may move for judgment on the pleadings

    (4)  ❑ Failure to state a claim upon which relief can be granted may be raised: at trial; if a pleading sets out a claim for relief that does not require a responsive pleading, an opposing party may assert at trial any defense to that claim

    (5)  ❑ A written motion and notice of the hearing must be served at least fourteen (14) days before the time specified for the hearing, with the following exceptions: (i) when the motion may be heard ex parte; (ii) when the Federal Rules of Civil Procedure set a different time; or (iii) when a court order—which a party may, for good cause, apply for ex parte—sets a different time

    (6)  ❑ Any affidavit supporting a motion must be served with the motion

    (7)  ❑ Except as noted in FRCP 33 to FRCP 36, the original of all papers required to be served under FRCP 5(d) shall, unless otherwise submitted to the court, be filed in the office of the clerk within seven (7) days after service has been made

(II)  ❑ Matters to be considered by opposing party

  (a)  ❑ Required documents

    (1)  ❑ Opposition

    (2)  ❑ Certificate of service

  (b)  ❑ Supplemental documents

    (1)  ❑ Pleading

    (2)  ❑ Notice of constitutional question

    (3)  ❑ Compact disk with copy of document(s) in PDF format

    (4)  ❑ Notice of filing with clerk's office

    (5)  ❑ Additional copies

    (6)  ❑ Courtesy copies

  (c)  ❑ Timing

    (1)  ❑ A party opposing a motion, shall file an opposition within fourteen (14) days after the motion is served, unless another period is fixed by rule or statute, or by order of the court

    (2)  ❑ Except as FRCP 59(c) provides otherwise, any opposing affidavit must be served at least seven (7) days before the hearing, unless the court permits service at another time

    (3)  ❑ Except as noted in FRCP 33 to FRCP 36, the original of all papers required to be served under FRCP 5(d) shall, unless otherwise submitted to the court, be filed in the office of the clerk within seven (7) days after service has been made

## B. Timing

1. *Motion to dismiss for failure to state a claim*

   a. *In a pleading under FRCP 7(a).* Failure to state a claim upon which relief can be granted may be raised in any pleading allowed or ordered under FRCP 7(a). FRCP 12(h)(2)(A).

      i. *In a responsive pleading.* Every defense to a claim for relief in any pleading must be asserted in the responsive pleading if one is required. FRCP 12(b).

   b. *By motion.* A motion asserting any of the defenses in FRCP 12(b) must be made before pleading if a responsive pleading is allowed. FRCP 12(b). Although FRCP 12(b) encourages the responsive pleader to file a motion to dismiss before filing the answer, nothing in FRCP 12 prohibits the filing of a motion to dismiss with the answer. An untimely motion to dismiss may be considered if the defense asserted in the motion was previously raised in the responsive pleading. FEDPROC § 62:421.

   c. *By motion under FRCP 12(c).* Failure to state a claim upon which relief can be granted may be raised by a motion under FRCP 12(c). FRCP 12(h)(2)(B). After the pleadings are closed—but early enough not to delay trial—a party may move for judgment on the pleadings. FRCP 12(c).

   d. *At trial.* Failure to state a claim upon which relief can be granted may be raised: at trial. FRCP 12(h)(2)(C). If a pleading sets out a claim for relief that does not require a responsive pleading, an opposing party may assert at trial any defense to that claim. FRCP 12(b).

2. *Timing of motions, generally*

   a. *Motion and notice of hearing.* A written motion and notice of the hearing must be served at least fourteen (14) days before the time specified for the hearing, with the following exceptions:

      i. When the motion may be heard ex parte;

      ii. When the Federal Rules of Civil Procedure set a different time; or

      iii. When a court order—which a party may, for good cause, apply for ex parte—sets a different time. FRCP 6(c)(1).

   b. *Supporting affidavit.* Any affidavit supporting a motion must be served with the motion. FRCP 6(c)(2).

3. *Timing of opposing papers.* A party opposing a motion, shall file an opposition within fourteen (14) days after the motion is served, unless (1) the motion is for summary judgment, in which case the opposition shall be filed within twenty-one (21) days after the motion is served, or (2) another period is fixed by rule or statute, or by order of the court. MA R USDCT LR 7.1(b)(2); MA R USDCT CM/ECF Admin(H)(4). The fourteen (14) day period is intended to include the period specified by the civil rules for mailing time and provide for a uniform period regardless of the use of the mails. MA R USDCT LR 7.1(b)(2).

   a. *Opposing affidavit.* Except as FRCP 59(c) provides otherwise, any opposing affidavit must be served at least seven (7) days before the hearing, unless the court permits service at another time. FRCP 6(c)(2).

4. *Timing of reply papers.* [W]here the respondent files an answering affidavit setting up a new matter, the moving party ordinarily is allowed a reasonable time to file a reply affidavit since failure to deny the new matter by affidavit may operate as an admission of its truth. AMJUR MOTIONS § 25.

   a. *Leave of court required.* All other papers not filed as indicated in MA R USDCT LR 7.1(b)(1) and MA R USDCT LR 7.1(b)(2), whether in the form of a reply brief or otherwise, may be submitted only with leave of court. MA R USDCT LR 7.1(b)(3).

5. *Filing after service.* Except as noted in FRCP 33 to FRCP 36, the original of all papers required to be served under FRCP 5(d) shall, unless otherwise submitted to the court, be filed in the office of the clerk within seven (7) days after service has been made. MA R USDCT LR 5.1(b).

6. *Effect of FRCP 12 motion on the time to serve a responsive pleading.* Unless the court sets a different time, serving a motion under FRCP 12 alters the periods in FRCP 12(a) as follows:

   a. If the court denies the motion or postpones its disposition until trial, the responsive pleading must be served within fourteen (14) days after notice of the court's action; or

   b. If the court grants a motion for a more definite statement, the responsive pleading must be served within fourteen (14) days after the more definite statement is served. FRCP 12(a)(4).

7. *Computation of time*

a. *Computing time.* FRCP 6 applies in computing any time period specified in the Federal Rules of Civil Procedure, in any local rule or court order, or in any statute that does not specify a method of computing time. FRCP 6(a).

  i. *Period stated in days or a longer unit.* When the period is stated in days or a longer unit of time:

    • Exclude the day of the event that triggers the period;

    • Count every day, including intermediate Saturdays, Sundays, and legal holidays; and

    • Include the last day of the period, but if the last day is a Saturday, Sunday, or legal holiday, the period continues to run until the end of the next day that is not a Saturday, Sunday, or legal holiday. FRCP 6(a)(1).

  ii. *Period stated in hours.* When the period is stated in hours:

    • Begin counting immediately on the occurrence of the event that triggers the period;

    • Count every hour, including hours during intermediate Saturdays, Sundays, and legal holidays; and

    • If the period would end on a Saturday, Sunday, or legal holiday, the period continues to run until the same time on the next day that is not a Saturday, Sunday, or legal holiday. FRCP 6(a)(2).

  iii. *Office of the clerk.* The offices of the Clerk of Court at Boston, Worcester and Springfield shall be open from 8:30 a.m. until 5:00 p.m. on all days except Saturdays, Sundays, legal holidays and other days so ordered by the court and announced in advance, if feasible. MA R USDCT LR 77.2.

  iv. *Inaccessibility of the clerk's office.* Unless the court orders otherwise, if the clerk's office is inaccessible:

    • On the last day for filing under FRCP 6(a)(1), then the time for filing is extended to the first accessible day that is not a Saturday, Sunday, or legal holiday; or

    • During the last hour for filing under FRCP 6(a)(2), then the time for filing is extended to the same time on the first accessible day that is not a Saturday, Sunday, or legal holiday. FRCP 6(a)(3).

  v. *"Last day" defined.* Unless a different time is set by a statute, local rule, or court order, the last day ends:

    • For electronic filing, at midnight in the court's time zone; and

    • For filing by other means, when the clerk's office is scheduled to close. FRCP 6(a)(4).

  vi. *"Next day" defined.* The "next day" is determined by continuing to count forward when the period is measured after an event and backward when measured before an event. FRCP 6(a)(5).

  vii. *"Legal holiday" defined.* "Legal holiday" means:

    • The day set aside by statute for observing New Year's Day, Martin Luther King Jr.'s Birthday, Washington's Birthday, Memorial Day, Independence Day, Labor Day, Columbus Day, Veterans' Day, Thanksgiving Day, or Christmas Day;

    • Any day declared a holiday by the President or Congress; and

    • For periods that are measured after an event, any other day declared a holiday by the state where the district court is located. FRCP 6(a)(6).

b. *Computation of electronic filing deadlines.* Filing documents electronically does not alter any filing deadlines. MA R USDCT CM/ECF Admin(K); MA R USDCT LR 5.4(D). Although CM/ECF is generally available twenty-four (24) hours a day for filing, all electronic transmissions of documents must be completed prior to 6:00 PM, Eastern Standard (or Daylight Savings) Time, on the date on which it is due, in order to be considered timely filed that day. MA R USDCT CM/ECF Admin(K); MA R USDCT LR 5.4(D). When a specific time of day deadline is set by court order or stipulation, the electronic filing must be completed by that time. Documents may be filed at any time of the day on days prior to the date on which it is due. MA R USDCT CM/ECF Admin(K). A document filed electronically shall be deemed filed as of the time and date stated on the NEF received from the court. MA R USDCT CM/ECF Admin(G)(2); MA R USDCT CM/ECF Admin(K).

  i. *Technical failures.* A user whose filing is made untimely as the result of a technical failure of the court's CM/ECF system may seek appropriate relief from the court. MA R USDCT CM/ECF Admin(W)(3). Technical difficulties on the filer's end, with telephone, cable lines, the filer's Internet Service Provider (ISP), or hardware or software problems, will not constitute a technical failure under the Administrative Procedures for Electronic Case Filing in the United States District Court for the District of Massachusetts (MA R USDCT CM/ECF Admin) nor excuse an untimely filing. MA R USDCT CM/ECF Admin(W)(3). As help desk support is available during normal

business hours, filers are strongly urged to electronically file any documents during that period. MA R USDCT CM/ECF Admin(W)(3).

- The court has made available a public terminal (computers and scanner) in each clerk's office for registered users to scan and electronically file documents. This equipment is available during normal business hours. Users should bring their prepared document and a valid CM/ECF login and password. MA R USDCT CM/ECF Admin(W)(3).

c. *Extending time.* When an act may or must be done within a specified time, the court may, for good cause, extend the time: (1) with or without motion or notice if the court acts, or if a request is made, before the original time or its extension expires; or (2) on motion made after the time has expired if the party failed to act because of excusable neglect. FRCP 6(b)(1).

   i. *Exceptions.* A court must not extend the time to act under FRCP 50(b), FRCP 50(d), FRCP 52(b), FRCP 59(b), FRCP 59(d), FRCP 59(e), and FRCP 60(b). FRCP 6(b)(2).

   ii. Refer to the United States District Court for the District of Massachusetts KeyRules Motion for Continuance/Extension of Time document for more information on extending time.

d. *Additional time after certain kinds of service.* When a party may or must act within a specified time after being served and service is made under FRCP 5(b)(2)(C) (by mail), FRCP 5(b)(2)(D) (by leaving with the clerk), or FRCP 5(b)(2)(F) (by other means consented to), three (3) days are added after the period would otherwise expire under FRCP 6(a). FRCP 6(d).

## C. General Requirements

1. *Motions, generally*

   a. *Requirements.* A request for a court order must be made by motion. The motion must:

      i. Be in writing unless made during a hearing or trial;

      ii. State with particularity the grounds for seeking the order; and

      iii. State the relief sought. FRCP 7(b)(1).

   b. *Notice of motion.* A party interested in resisting the relief sought by a motion has a right to notice thereof, and an opportunity to be heard. AMJUR MOTIONS § 12.

      i. [I]n addition to statutory or court rule provisions requiring notice of a motion—the purpose of such a notice requirement having been said to be to prevent a party from being prejudicially surprised by a motion—principles of natural justice dictate that an adverse party generally must be given notice that a motion will be presented to the court. AMJUR MOTIONS § 12.

      ii. "Notice," in this regard, means reasonable notice, including a meaningful opportunity to prepare and to defend against allegations of a motion. AMJUR MOTIONS § 12.

   c. *Writing requirement.* The writing requirement is intended to [ensure] that the adverse parties are informed and have a record of both the motion's pendency and the grounds on which the movant seeks an order. FPP § 1191; Feldberg v. Quechee Lakes Corp., 463 F.3d 195 (2d Cir. 2006). [A] single written document can satisfy the writing requirements both for a motion and for [an] FRCP 6(c)(1) notice. FRCP 7(Advisory Committee Notes).

   d. *Particularity requirement.* The particularity requirement [ensures] that the opposing parties will have notice of their opponent's contentions. FEDPROC § 62:358; Goodman v. 1973 26 Foot Trojan Vessel, Arkansas Registration No. AR1439SN, 859 F.2d 71 (8th Cir. 1988). That requirement ensures that notice of the basis for the motion is provided to the court and to the opposing party so as to avoid prejudice, provide the opponent with a meaningful opportunity to respond, and provide the court with enough information to process the motion correctly. FEDPROC § 62:358; Andreas v. Volkswagen of Am., Inc., 336 F.3d 789 (8th Cir. 2003).

      i. Reasonable specification of the grounds for a motion is sufficient. The particularity requirement for motions is satisfied when no party is prejudiced by a lack of particularity or when the court can comprehend the basis for the motion and deal with it fairly. However, where a movant fails to state even one ground for granting the motion in question, the movant has failed to meet the minimal standard of "reasonable specification." FEDPROC § 62:358; Martinez v. Trainor, 556 F.2d 818 (7th Cir. 1977).

      ii. The court may excuse the failure to comply with the particularity requirement if it is inadvertent, and where no prejudice is shown by the opposing party. FEDPROC § 62:358.

   e. *Control of motion practice*

      i. *Plan for the disposition of motions.* At the earliest practicable time, the judicial officer shall establish a framework for the disposition of motions, which, at the discretion of the judicial officer, may include specific deadlines or general time guidelines for filing motions. This framework may be amended from time to time by the judicial officer as required by the progress of the case. MA R USDCT LR 7.1(a)(1).

ii. *Motion practice.* No motion shall be filed unless counsel certify that they have conferred and have attempted in good faith to resolve or narrow the issue. MA R USDCT LR 7.1(a)(2).

iii. *Unresolved motions.* The court shall rule on motions as soon as practicable, having in mind the reporting requirements set forth in the Civil Justice Reform Act. MA R USDCT LR 7.1(a)(3).

2. *Motion to dismiss for failure to state a claim.* [A] party may assert the following defense by motion: failure to state a claim upon which relief can be granted. FRCP 12(b)(6). The motion under FRCP 12(b)(6) is available to test a claim for relief in any pleading, whether it be in the plaintiff's original complaint, a defendant's counterclaim, a defendant's cross-claim or counterclaim thereto, or a third-party claim or any other FRCP 14 claim. Most commonly, of course, [an] FRCP 12(b)(6) motion is directed against the plaintiff's complaint. FPP § 1356.

a. *Applicable standard.* The FRCP 12(b)(6) motion is used to test the sufficiency of the complaint. FEDPROC § 62:455; Petruska v. Gannon Univ., 462 F.3d 294 (3d Cir. 2006). In this regard, the applicable standard is stated in FRCP 8(a)(2), which requires that a pleading setting forth a claim for relief contain a short and plain statement of the claim showing that the pleader is entitled to relief. Thus, a complaint must set forth sufficient information to suggest that there is some recognized legal theory upon which relief can be granted. FEDPROC § 62:455. Only when the plaintiff's complaint fails to meet this liberal pleading standard is it subject to dismissal under FRCP 12(b)(6). FPP § 1356.

   i. In order to withstand a motion to dismiss filed under FRCP 12(b)(6) in response to claims understood to raise a high risk of abusive litigation, addressed by FRCP 9(b), a plaintiff must state factual allegations with greater particularity than that required by FRCP 8. FEDPROC § 62:464; Bell Atl. Corp. v. Twombly, 550 U.S. 544, 127 S. Ct. 1955, 167 L. Ed. 2d 929 (2007).

   ii. FRCP 12(b)(6) motions are looked on with disfavor by the courts, and are granted sparingly and with care. Dismissals for failure to state a claim are especially disfavored in cases where the complaint sets forth a novel legal theory that can best be assessed after factual development. FEDPROC § 62:458.

b. *Construction of allegations of complaint (or other pleading).* In considering [an] FRCP 12(b)(6) motion to dismiss, the complaint is liberally construed and is viewed in the light most favorable to the plaintiff. FEDPROC § 62:461; Bell Atl. Corp. v. Twombly, 550 U.S. 544, 127 S. Ct. 1955, 167 L. Ed. 2d 929 (2007).

   i. On a motion to dismiss, a federal court presumes that general allegations embrace those specific facts that are necessary to support the claim. FEDPROC § 62:461; Steel Co. v. Citizens for a Better Env't, 523 U.S. 83, 118 S. Ct. 1003, 140 L. Ed. 2d 210 (1998).

   ii. In addition, the well-pleaded allegations of fact contained in the complaint and every inference fairly deducible therefrom are accepted as true for purposes of the motion, including facts alleged on information and belief. FEDPROC § 62:461; Bell Atl. Corp. v. Twombly, 550 U.S. 544, 127 S. Ct. 1955, 167 L. Ed. 2d 929 (2007); Tellabs, Inc. v. Makor Issues & Rights, Ltd., 551 U.S. 308, 127 S. Ct. 2499, 168 L. Ed. 2d 179 (2007).

   iii. However, the court will not accept as true the plaintiff's bare statements of opinions, conclusory allegations, including legal conclusion couched as a factual allegation, and unwarranted inferences of fact. FEDPROC § 62:461; Leopoldo Fontanillas, Inc. v. Luis Ayala Colon Sucesores, Inc., 283 F. Supp. 2d 579 (D.P.R. 2003); Hopkins v. Women's Div., Gen. Bd. of Glob. Ministries, 238 F. Supp. 2d 174 (D.D.C. 2002). Nor will the court accept as true facts which are legally impossible, facts which the court can take judicial notice of as being other than as alleged by the plaintiff, or facts which by the record or by a document attached to the complaint appear to be unfounded. FEDPROC § 62:461; Cohen v. United States, 129 F.2d 733 (8th Cir. 1942); Henthorn v. Dep't of Navy, 29 F.3d 682 (D.C. Cir. 1994).

c. *Affirmative defenses.* It is generally agreed that affirmative defenses can be raised by [an] FRCP 12(b)(6) motion to dismiss. FEDPROC § 62:465; McCready v. eBay, Inc., 453 F.3d 882 (7th Cir. 2006). However, in order for these defenses to be raised on [an] FRCP 12(b)(6) motion to dismiss, the complaint must clearly show on its face that the affirmative defense is applicable and bars the action. FEDPROC § 62:465; In re Colonial Mortg. Bankers Corp., 324 F.3d 12 (1st Cir. 2003). Thus, FRCP 12(b)(6) motions may be used to raise the affirmative defenses of: (1) statute of limitations; (2) statute of frauds; (3) res judicata; (4) collateral estoppel; (5) release; (6) waiver; (7) estoppel; (8) sovereign immunity; (9) qualified immunity; (10) illegality; (11) contributory negligence; and (12) preemption. FEDPROC § 62:465.

    d. *Joining motions*

        i. *Right to join.* A motion under FRCP 12 may be joined with any other motion allowed by FRCP 12. FRCP 12(g)(1).

        ii. *Limitation on further motions.* Except as provided in FRCP 12(h)(2) or FRCP 12(h)(3), a party that makes a motion under FRCP 12 must not make another motion under FRCP 12 raising a defense or objection that was available to the party but omitted from its earlier motion. FRCP 12(g)(2).

    e. *Waiving and preserving certain defenses.* No defense or objection is waived by joining it with one or more other defenses or objections in a responsive pleading or in a motion. FRCP 12(b). Failure to state a claim upon which relief can be granted, to join a person required by FRCP 19(b), or to state a legal defense to a claim may be raised:

        i. In any pleading allowed or ordered under FRCP 7(a);

        ii. By a motion under FRCP 12(c); or

        iii. At trial. FRCP 12(h)(2).

3. *Opposing papers.* The Federal Rules of Civil Procedure do not require any formal answer, return, or reply to a motion, except where the Federal Rules of Civil Procedure or local rules may require affidavits, memoranda, or other papers to be filed in opposition to a motion. Such papers are simply to apprise the court of such opposition and the grounds of that opposition. FEDPROC § 62:353.

    a. *Effect of failure to respond to motion.* Although in the absence of statutory provision or court rule, a motion ordinarily does not require a written answer, when a party files a motion and the opposing party fails to respond, the court may construe such failure to respond as nonopposition to the motion or an admission that the motion was meritorious, may take the facts alleged in the motion as true—the rule in some jurisdictions being that the failure to respond to a fact set forth in a motion is deemed an admission—and may grant the motion if the relief requested appears to be justified. AMJUR MOTIONS § 28.

        i. *Unopposed motion to dismiss.* The circuits are split on whether a court may grant a motion to dismiss solely on the basis that the plaintiff did not file a response opposing the motion. FRCP-RC RULE 12.

            • Some circuits hold that FRCP 12(b)(6) motions can be granted solely because they are unopposed. FRCP-RC RULE 12; Fox v. Am. Airlines, Inc., 389 F.3d 1291, 1295 (D.C. Cir. 2004); Cohen v. Bd. of Trustees of the Univ. of the D.C., 819 F.3d 476, 483-484 (D.C. Cir. 2016). Other circuits hold that, while the plaintiff has forfeited its ability to present arguments for why the complaint is sufficient, the court still must assess the sufficiency of the complaint. FRCP-RC RULE 12.

    b. *Assent or no opposition not determinative.* However, a motion will not be granted automatically simply because an "assent" or a notation of "no opposition" has been filed; federal judges frequently deny motions that have been assented to when it is thought that justice so dictates. FPP § 1190.

    c. *Responsive pleading inappropriate as response to motion.* An attempt to answer or oppose a motion with a responsive pleading usually is not appropriate. FPP § 1190.

4. *Reply papers.* A moving party may be required or permitted to prepare papers in addition to his original motion papers. AMJUR MOTIONS § 25. Papers answering or replying to opposing papers may be appropriate, in the interests of justice, where it appears there is a substantial reason for allowing a reply. Thus, a court may accept reply papers where a party demonstrates that the papers to which it seeks to file a reply raise new issues that are material to the disposition of the question before the court, or where the court determines, sua sponte, that it wishes further briefing of an issue raised in those papers and orders the submission of additional papers. FEDPROC § 62:354.

    a. *Function of reply papers.* The function of a reply affidavit is to answer the arguments made in opposition to the position taken by the movant and not to permit the movant to introduce new arguments in support of the motion. AMJUR MOTIONS § 25.

    b. *Issues raised for the first time in a reply document.* However, the view has been followed in some jurisdictions, that as a matter of judicial economy, where there is no prejudice and where the issues could be raised simply by filing a motion to dismiss, the trial court has discretion to consider arguments raised for the first time in a reply memorandum, and that a trial court may grant a motion to strike issues raised for the first time in a reply memorandum. AMJUR MOTIONS § 26.

5. *Alternative dispute resolution (ADR).* The judicial officer assigned to preside over the case shall encourage the resolution of disputes by settlement or other alternative dispute resolution programs. MA R USDCT LR 16.4(a).

    a. *Settlement.* At every conference conducted under the Local Rules of the United States District Court for the District of Massachusetts, the judicial officer shall inquire as to the utility of the parties conducting settlement negotiations, explore means of facilitating those negotiations, and offer whatever assistance may be appropriate in the circumstances. Assistance may include a reference of the case to another judicial officer for settlement purposes. MA R USDCT LR 16.4(b).

    i. When a case is settled, the parties shall file with the clerk a signed agreement for judgment or stipulation for dismissal, as appropriate, within twenty-eight (28) days, unless the court otherwise orders. MA R USDCT LR 68.2.

  b. *Alternative dispute resolution programs*

    i. *Discretion of judicial officer.* The judicial officer, following an exploration of the matter with all counsel, may refer appropriate cases to alternative dispute resolution programs that have been designated for use in the district court or that the judicial officer may make available. The dispute resolution programs described in MA R USDCT LR 16.4(c)(2) through MA R USDCT LR 16.4(c)(4) are illustrative, not exclusive. Moreover, nothing in MA R USDCT LR 16.4 shall preclude the parties from engaging in private dispute resolution programs as long as they comply with any schedule established by the court. MA R USDCT LR 16.4(c)(1).

    ii. *Mediation.* The judicial officer may refer the case to mediation upon the agreement of all parties. MA R USDCT LR 16.4(c)(2)(A).

    iii. *Other alternative dispute resolution programs.* Use of mediation is not exclusive. At the request of parties, the judicial officer may consider other forms of alternative dispute resolution including, but not limited to, mini-trial, summary jury trial and arbitration. MA R USDCT LR 16.4(c)(3).

  c. For more information on alternative dispute resolution (ADR), refer to MA R USDCT LR 16.4.

6. *Sanctions.* Failure to comply with any of the directions or obligations set forth in, or authorized by, these rules may result in dismissal, default, or the imposition of other sanctions as deemed appropriate by the judicial officer. MA R USDCT LR 1.3. Except as provided by law, the court may impose sanctions as provided in MA R USDCT LR 1.3 for failure to comply with the Administrative Procedures for Electronic Case Filing in the United States District Court for the District of Massachusetts (MA R USDCT CM/ECF Admin) or with MA R USDCT LR 5.4. MA R USDCT CM/ECF Admin(C)(3).

# D. Documents

1. *Documents for moving party*

  a. *Required documents*

    i. *Notice of motion and motion.* Refer to the General Requirements section of this document for information on the notice of motion and motion.

      • *Request for oral argument.* Any party making or opposing a motion who believes that oral argument may assist the court and wishes to be heard shall include a request for oral argument in a separate paragraph of the motion or opposition. The request should be set off with a centered caption, "REQUEST FOR ORAL ARGUMENT." MA R USDCT LR 7.1(d).

    ii. *Memorandum.* A party filing a motion shall at the same time file a memorandum of reasons, including citation of supporting authorities, why the motion should be granted. MA R USDCT LR 7.1(b)(1). Any memorandum of law or other attachment filed in support of a main document shall be filed as a separate document, using the proper event. MA R USDCT CM/ECF Admin(G)(4). Memoranda supporting or opposing allowance of motions shall not, without leave of court, exceed twenty (20) pages, double-spaced. MA R USDCT LR 7.1(b)(4).

    iii. *Certificate of service.* No certificate of service is required when a paper is served by filing it with the court's electronic-filing system. When a paper that is required to be served is served by other means: (1) if the paper is filed, a certificate of service must be filed with it or within a reasonable time after service; and (2) if the paper is not filed, a certificate of service need not be filed unless filing is required by court order or by local rule. FRCP 5(d)(1)(B). Except as otherwise provided by the Federal Rules of Civil Procedure, proof of service of all pleadings and other papers required to be served (except discovery papers that in accordance with FRCP 33 to FRCP 36(f) are not to be filed) shall be filed in the office of the clerk promptly after service has been made. The proof shall show the time and manner of service, and may be made by written acknowledgment of service, a certificate of a member of the bar of this court, or an affidavit of the person who served the paper. MA R USDCT LR 5.2(b)(1). A certificate of service of a member of the bar shall appear at the bottom of or on the margin of the last page of the paper to which it relates. MA R USDCT LR 5.2(b)(2).

      • *Paper service.* The certificate shall be a brief, single-spaced statement and may be in the following form:

I hereby certify that a true copy of the above document was served upon (each party appearing pro se and) the attorney of record for each other party by mail (by hand) on (date). (Signature). MA R USDCT LR 5.2(b)(2).

- *Electronic service.* Any pleading or other paper served by electronic means must bear a certificate of service in accordance with MA R USDCT LR 5.2(b). MA R USDCT LR 5.4(C); MA R USDCT CM/ECF Admin(H)(2). The certificate of service shall state that the filer: (1) filed the document electronically, (2) that it will be served electronically to registered CM/ECF participants via the NEF and (3) that the filer will send paper copies to non-registered participants as indicated on the NEF. MA R USDCT CM/ECF Admin(H)(2). For example: I hereby certify that this document filed through the CM/ECF system will be sent electronically to the registered participants as identified on the NEF (NEF) and paper copies will be sent to those indicated as non registered participants on (date). MA R USDCT CM/ECF Admin(H)(2).

- *Return.* Documents not conforming to the requirements of MA R USDCT LR 5.2 (except notices of appeal) shall be returned by the clerk. MA R USDCT LR 5.2(b)(2).

- *Failure to make proof of service.* Failure to make proof of service does not affect the validity of the service. MA R USDCT LR 5.2(b)(3).

b. *Supplemental documents*

   i. *Pleading.* As a general rule, the court may only consider the pleading which is attacked by [an] FRCP 12(b)(6) motion in determining its sufficiency. FEDPROC § 62:460; Armengau v. Cline, 7 F. App'x 336 (6th Cir. 2001). The plaintiff is not entitled to discovery to obtain information relevant to the motion, and the court is not permitted to look at matters outside the record. FEDPROC § 62:460; Cooperativa de Ahorro y Credito Aguada v. Kidder, Peabody & Co., 993 F.2d 269 (1st Cir. 1993).

- *Motion treated as one for summary judgment.* If, on a motion under FRCP 12(b)(6) or FRCP 12(c), matters outside the pleadings are presented to and not excluded by the court, the motion must be treated as one for summary judgment under FRCP 56. All parties must be given a reasonable opportunity to present all the material that is pertinent to the motion. FRCP 12(d).

- *Documents attached to pleadings.* However, the court may consider documents which are attached to or submitted with the complaint, as well as legal arguments presented in memorandums or briefs and arguments of counsel. FEDPROC § 62:460; Tellabs, Inc. v. Makor Issues & Rights, Ltd., 551 U.S. 308, 127 S. Ct. 2499, 168 L. Ed. 2d 179 (2007); E.E.O.C. v. Ohio Edison Co., 7 F.3d 541 (6th Cir. 1993). Documents not attached to the complaint may also be considered if they are incorporated by reference, or their contents are alleged in the complaint, they are central to the claim, integral to or explicitly relied upon, their authenticity is undisputed, and their relevance is uncontested. FEDPROC § 62:460.

   ii. *Notice of constitutional question.* A party that files a pleading, written motion, or other paper drawing into question the constitutionality of a federal or state statute must promptly:

- *File notice.* File a notice of constitutional question stating the question and identifying the paper that raises it, if: (1) a federal statute is questioned and the parties do not include the United States, one of its agencies, or one of its officers or employees in an official capacity; or (2) a state statute is questioned and the parties do not include the state, one of its agencies, or one of its officers or employees in an official capacity; and

- *Serve notice.* Serve the notice and paper on the Attorney General of the United States if a federal statute is questioned—or on the state attorney general if a state statute is questioned—either by certified or registered mail or by sending it to an electronic address designated by the attorney general for this purpose. FRCP 5.1(a).

- *No forfeiture.* A party's failure to file and serve the notice, or the court's failure to certify, does not forfeit a constitutional claim or defense that is otherwise timely asserted. FRCP 5.1(d).

   iii. *Nongovernmental corporate disclosure statement*

- *Contents.* A nongovernmental corporate party must file two (2) copies of a disclosure statement that: (1) identifies any parent corporation and any publicly held corporation owning ten percent (10%) or more of its stock; or (2) states that there is no such corporation. FRCP 7.1(a).

- *Time to file; Supplemental filing.* A party must: (1) file the disclosure statement with its first appearance, pleading, petition, motion, response, or other request addressed to the court; and (2) promptly file a supplemental statement if any required information changes. FRCP 7.1(b).

   iv. *Proposed order.* Proposed orders usually are not required by this court. However, the court may request the party to submit such a document. In those situations, unless otherwise directed by the clerk's office, electronically file the proposed document/order using the entry for "Proposed Documents submitted to the court," found under the Other Documents menu, or as an attachment to the motion to which it relates. MA R USDCT CM/ECF Admin(T).

v. *Compact disk with copy of document(s) in PDF format.* A filer who cannot file a document electronically because of such technical difficulty on the filer's end [with telephone, cable lines, the filer's Internet Service Provider (ISP), or hardware or software problems] shall file the document conventionally along with a copy of the document in PDF format on a compact disk or contact the clerk's office for permission to submit the PDF document via email. MA R USDCT CM/ECF Admin(W)(3). Refer to the Timing section of this document for more information on technical failures.

vi. *Notice of filing with clerk's office.* When documents or exhibits (other than those filed ex parte or under seal) are submitted conventionally, a "Notice of Filing with clerk's office" shall be filed electronically and attached to the main document. A paper copy of the "Notice of Filing with clerk's office" must accompany the documents submitted to the court. The "Notice of Filing with clerk's office" (see MA R USDCT CM/ECF Admin(Appendix I)) shall describe each of the documents that will be filed as paper copies in the clerk's office, or shall include an index of the documents if those documents are voluminous. MA R USDCT CM/ECF Admin(P)(5).

vii. *Additional copies.* Whenever, because of the nature of a proceeding, such as a proceeding before a three-judge district court under 28 U.S.C.A. § 2284, additional copies of a paper required to be filed are necessary either for the use of the court or to enable the clerk to carry out his duties, it is the responsibility of the party filing or having filed the paper to provide the necessary copies. MA R USDCT LR 5.1(d).

viii. *Courtesy copies.* COURTESY COPIES OF DOCUMENTS FILED ELECTRONICALLY SHALL NOT BE SUBMITTED ROUTINELY. MA R USDCT CM/ECF Admin(J). Judicial officers, on a case-by-case basis, may require courtesy copies for specific cases, or types of motions, etc. A few Judicial Officers have entered Standing Orders, which may be found on their respective pages on the court's website (under Divisions). Any document filed on paper with the court as a courtesy copy must be clearly labeled as such (Example: COURTESY COPY—DO NOT SCAN). Documents delivered to the court as a courtesy copy will not be maintained in the official court record. MA R USDCT CM/ECF Admin(J).

2. *Documents for opposing party*

   a. *Required documents*

      i. *Opposition.* Refer to the General Requirements section of this document for information on the opposing papers.

         - *Memorandum.* A party opposing a motion shall file, in the same (rather than a separate), document a memorandum of reasons, including citation of supporting authorities, why the motion should not be granted. MA R USDCT LR 7.1(b)(2). Any memorandum of law or other attachment filed in support of a main document shall be filed as a separate document, using the proper event. MA R USDCT CM/ECF Admin(G)(4). Memoranda supporting or opposing allowance of motions shall not, without leave of court, exceed twenty (20) pages, double-spaced. MA R USDCT LR 7.1(b)(4).

         - *Request for oral argument.* Any party making or opposing a motion who believes that oral argument may assist the court and wishes to be heard shall include a request for oral argument in a separate paragraph of the motion or opposition. The request should be set off with a centered caption, "REQUEST FOR ORAL ARGUMENT." MA R USDCT LR 7.1(d).

      ii. *Certificate of service.* No certificate of service is required when a paper is served by filing it with the court's electronic-filing system. When a paper that is required to be served is served by other means: (1) if the paper is filed, a certificate of service must be filed with it or within a reasonable time after service; and (2) if the paper is not filed, a certificate of service need not be filed unless filing is required by court order or by local rule. FRCP 5(d)(1)(B). Except as otherwise provided by the Federal Rules of Civil Procedure, proof of service of all pleadings and other papers required to be served (except discovery papers that in accordance with FRCP 33 to FRCP 36(f) are not to be filed) shall be filed in the office of the clerk promptly after service has been made. The proof shall show the time and manner of service, and may be made by written acknowledgment of service, a certificate of a member of the bar of this court, or an affidavit of the person who served the paper. MA R USDCT LR 5.2(b)(1). A certificate of service of a member of the bar shall appear at the bottom of or on the margin of the last page of the paper to which it relates. MA R USDCT LR 5.2(b)(2).

         - *Paper service.* The certificate shall be a brief, single-spaced statement and may be in the following form: I hereby certify that a true copy of the above document was served upon (each party appearing pro se and) the attorney of record for each other party by mail (by hand) on (date). (Signature). MA R USDCT LR 5.2(b)(2).

- *Electronic service.* Any pleading or other paper served by electronic means must bear a certificate of service in accordance with MA R USDCT LR 5.2(b). MA R USDCT LR 5.4(C); MA R USDCT CM/ECF Admin(H)(2). The certificate of service shall state that the filer: (1) filed the document electronically, (2) that it will be served electronically to registered CM/ECF participants via the NEF and (3) that the filer will send paper copies to non-registered participants as indicated on the NEF. MA R USDCT CM/ECF Admin(H)(2). For example: I hereby certify that this document filed through the CM/ECF system will be sent electronically to the registered participants as identified on the NEF (NEF) and paper copies will be sent to those indicated as non registered participants on (date). MA R USDCT CM/ECF Admin(H)(2).

- *Return.* Documents not conforming to the requirements of MA R USDCT LR 5.2 (except notices of appeal) shall be returned by the clerk. MA R USDCT LR 5.2(b)(2).

- *Failure to make proof of service.* Failure to make proof of service does not affect the validity of the service. MA R USDCT LR 5.2(b)(3).

b.  *Supplemental documents*

   i.  *Pleading.* As a general rule, the court may only consider the pleading which is attacked by [an] FRCP 12(b)(6) motion in determining its sufficiency. FEDPROC § 62:460; Armengau v. Cline, 7 F. App'x 336 (6th Cir. 2001). The plaintiff is not entitled to discovery to obtain information relevant to the motion, and the court is not permitted to look at matters outside the record. FEDPROC § 62:460; Cooperativa de Ahorro y Credito Aguada v. Kidder, Peabody & Co., 993 F.2d 269 (1st Cir. 1993).

   - *Motion treated as one for summary judgment.* If, on a motion under FRCP 12(b)(6) or FRCP 12(c), matters outside the pleadings are presented to and not excluded by the court, the motion must be treated as one for summary judgment under FRCP 56. All parties must be given a reasonable opportunity to present all the material that is pertinent to the motion. FRCP 12(d).

   - *Documents attached to pleadings.* However, the court may consider documents which are attached to or submitted with the complaint, as well as legal arguments presented in memorandums or briefs and arguments of counsel. FEDPROC § 62:460; Tellabs, Inc. v. Makor Issues & Rights, Ltd., 551 U.S. 308, 127 S. Ct. 2499, 168 L. Ed. 2d 179 (2007); E.E.O.C. v. Ohio Edison Co., 7 F.3d 541 (6th Cir. 1993). Documents not attached to the complaint may also be considered if they are incorporated by reference, or their contents are alleged in the complaint, they are central to the claim, integral to or explicitly relied upon, their authenticity is undisputed, and their relevance is uncontested. FEDPROC § 62:460.

  ii.  *Notice of constitutional question.* A party that files a pleading, written motion, or other paper drawing into question the constitutionality of a federal or state statute must promptly:

   - *File notice.* File a notice of constitutional question stating the question and identifying the paper that raises it, if: (1) a federal statute is questioned and the parties do not include the United States, one of its agencies, or one of its officers or employees in an official capacity; or (2) a state statute is questioned and the parties do not include the state, one of its agencies, or one of its officers or employees in an official capacity; and

   - *Serve notice.* Serve the notice and paper on the Attorney General of the United States if a federal statute is questioned—or on the state attorney general if a state statute is questioned—either by certified or registered mail or by sending it to an electronic address designated by the attorney general for this purpose. FRCP 5.1(a).

   - *No forfeiture.* A party's failure to file and serve the notice, or the court's failure to certify, does not forfeit a constitutional claim or defense that is otherwise timely asserted. FRCP 5.1(d).

 iii.  *Compact disk with copy of document(s) in PDF format.* A filer who cannot file a document electronically because of such technical difficulty on the filer's end [with telephone, cable lines, the filer's Internet Service Provider (ISP), or hardware or software problems] shall file the document conventionally along with a copy of the document in PDF format on a compact disk or contact the clerk's office for permission to submit the PDF document via email. MA R USDCT CM/ECF Admin(W)(3). Refer to the Timing section of this document for more information on technical failures.

 iv.  *Notice of filing with clerk's office.* When documents or exhibits (other than those filed ex parte or under seal) are submitted conventionally, a "Notice of Filing with clerk's office" shall be filed electronically and attached to the main document. A paper copy of the "Notice of Filing with clerk's office" must accompany the documents submitted to the court. The "Notice of Filing with clerk's office" (see MA R USDCT CM/ECF Admin(Appendix I)) shall describe each of the documents that will be filed as paper copies in the clerk's office, or shall include an index of the documents if those documents are voluminous. MA R USDCT CM/ECF Admin(P)(5).

   v. *Additional copies.* Whenever, because of the nature of a proceeding, such as a proceeding before a three-judge district court under 28 U.S.C.A. § 2284, additional copies of a paper required to be filed are necessary either for the use of the court or to enable the clerk to carry out his duties, it is the responsibility of the party filing or having filed the paper to provide the necessary copies. MA R USDCT LR 5.1(d).

   vi. *Courtesy copies.* COURTESY COPIES OF DOCUMENTS FILED ELECTRONICALLY SHALL NOT BE SUBMITTED ROUTINELY. MA R USDCT CM/ECF Admin(J). Judicial officers, on a case-by-case basis, may require courtesy copies for specific cases, or types of motions, etc. A few Judicial Officers have entered Standing Orders, which may be found on their respective pages on the court's website (under Divisions). Any document filed on paper with the court as a courtesy copy must be clearly labeled as such (Example: COURTESY COPY—DO NOT SCAN). Documents delivered to the court as a courtesy copy will not be maintained in the official court record. MA R USDCT CM/ECF Admin(J).

## E. Format

1. *Form of documents.* The rules governing captions and other matters of form in pleadings apply to motions and other papers. FRCP 7(b)(2). The provisions of FRCP 10 and FRCP 11 concerning the form and signing of pleadings, motions, and other papers shall be applicable to all papers filed in any proceeding in this court. The board of bar overseers registration number of each attorney signing such documents, except the United States Attorney and his or her staff, shall be inscribed below the signature. MA R USDCT LR 5.1(a)(1).

   a. *Paper size and binding.* All papers filed in the court shall be adapted for flat filing, be filed on eight and one-half by eleven (8-1/2 x 11) inch paper without backers and be bound firmly by staple or some such other means (excluding paper or binder clip or rubber band). MA R USDCT LR 5.1(a)(2).

   b. *Spacing.* All papers, except discovery requests and responses, shall be double-spaced except for the identification of counsel, title of the case, footnotes, quotations and exhibits. Discovery requests and responses shall be single-spaced. MA R USDCT LR 5.1(a)(2).

   c. *Caption.* Every pleading must have a caption with the court's name, a title, a file number, and [an] FRCP 7(a) designation. FRCP 10(a).

      i. *Names of parties.* The title of the complaint must name all the parties; the title of other pleadings, after naming the first party on each side, may refer generally to other parties. FRCP 10(a).

      ii. *Request for special action.* When any pleading or other paper filed in the court includes a request for special process or relief, or any other request such that, if granted, the court will proceed other than in the ordinary course, the request shall, unless it is noted on the category sheet [see MA R USDCT LR 40.1(a)(1)], be noted on the first page to the right of or immediately beneath the caption. MA R USDCT LR 5.1(c).

   d. *Claims or defenses*

      i. *Numbered paragraphs.* A party must state its claims or defenses in numbered paragraphs, each limited as far as practicable to a single set of circumstances. A later pleading may refer by number to a paragraph in an earlier pleading. FRCP 10(b).

      ii. *Separate statements.* If doing so would promote clarity, each claim founded on a separate transaction or occurrence—and each defense other than a denial—must be stated in a separate count or defense. FRCP 10(b).

   e. *Adoption by reference.* A statement in a pleading may be adopted by reference elsewhere in the same pleading or in any other pleading or motion. FRCP 10(c).

      i. *Exhibits.* A copy of a written instrument that is an exhibit to a pleading is a part of the pleading for all purposes. FRCP 10(c).

   f. *Citations*

      i. *Local rules.* These rules shall be known as Local Rules of the United States District Court for the District of Massachusetts and cited as "L.R., D. Mass." or "L.R." MA R USDCT LR 1.1.

      ii. *Electronic case filing procedures.* The procedures governing electronic case filing shall be known as the "Administrative Procedures for Electronic Case Filing in the United States District Court for the District of Massachusetts." They shall be cited as "APECF." MA R USDCT CM/ECF Admin(A)(7).

g. *Acceptance by the clerk.* The clerk must not refuse to file a paper solely because it is not in the form prescribed by the Federal Rules of Civil Procedure or by a local rule or practice. FRCP 5(d)(4).

　　i. Except for complaints and notices of appeal, papers that do not conform to the requirements of MA R USDCT LR 5.1(a)(2) shall be returned by the clerk. MA R USDCT LR 5.1(a)(2).

2. *Form of electronic documents.* A paper filed electronically is a written paper for purposes of the Federal Rules of Civil Procedure. FRCP 5(d)(3)(D).

　a. *PDF/A format required.* The court will begin requiring submission of documents in PDF/A format in the foreseeable future. PDF/A is an enhanced version of the traditional PDF format. Newer versions of most PDF software will be able to convert to this format. Additional information on PDF/A documents may be found on the court's website. MA R USDCT CM/ECF Admin(Electronic Filing and PDF).

　　i. *Electronically converted PDF.* Electronically converted PDF documents are created from word processing documents (MS Word, WordPerfect, etc.) using any appropriate software. These documents are text searchable and the file size is generally smaller than a scanned document. CM/ECF users may use any brand of software to convert documents to PDF. MA R USDCT CM/ECF Admin(Electronic Filing and PDF).

　　　• Documents converted to PDF, rather than scanned, are preferred for filing in CM/ECF. MA R USDCT CM/ECF Admin(Electronic Filing and PDF).

　　ii. *Scanned PDF.* Scanned PDF documents are created from paper documents run through an optical scanner. Scanned PDF documents are generally not searchable and have a larger file size. Please note that software used to create scanned documents may (and should) be set in such a way that the document is "text-searchable." MA R USDCT CM/ECF Admin(Electronic Filing and PDF).

　b. *Title.* All pleadings filed electronically shall be titled in accordance with the approved dictionary of civil or criminal events of the CM/ECF system of this court. A list of events is available on the CM/ECF Training Information page of the court's website. The clerk's office may, when necessary and appropriate, modify the docket entry description, or delete and re-enter the docket entry in order to comply with the court's quality assurance standards. MA R USDCT CM/ECF Admin(G)(3).

　c. *Attachments to filings and exhibits.* Attachments to filings and exhibits must be filed in accordance with the court's CM/ECF User Manual, unless otherwise ordered by the court. MA R USDCT CM/ECF Admin(O)(1).

　　i. Filers must submit as attachments only those excerpts of the referenced documents that are directly germane to the matter under consideration by the court. Excerpted material must be clearly and prominently identified as such. Users who file excerpts of documents do so without prejudice to their right to timely file additional excerpts or the complete document, as may be allowed by the court. Responding parties may timely file additional excerpts or the complete document that they believe are directly germane. MA R USDCT CM/ECF Admin(O)(2).

　　ii. Filers shall not attach as an exhibit any pleading or other paper already on file with the court in that case, but shall merely refer to that document. (See MA R USDCT CM/ECF Admin(G) for information on using hyperlinks in PDF documents filed in CM/ECF.) MA R USDCT CM/ECF Admin(O)(3).

　d. *Redacted documents.* The parties may request or the court may require the submission of documents that have been redacted/stripped of sensitive or confidential information. The redacted document prepared for electronic filing shall include the original caption of the document, and be clearly labeled as "Redacted Document." A specific event is available for this purpose ("Redacted Document"), found under the Other Filings/Other Documents menu option. MA R USDCT CM/ECF Admin(S).

　　i. Attorneys and pro se litigants are advised to take extra care when creating PDF documents intended for submission to CM/ECF. Steps shall be taken to ensure the documents are free of any hidden data (metadata) that may contain redacted information, or traces of information edited or deleted are not hidden in the final document. Even PDF content that has been encrypted may be recovered. An advisory document with additional information on this topic may be found on the court's website. MA R USDCT CM/ECF Admin(S).

　e. *Hyperlinks.* Electronically filed documents may contain the following types of hyperlinks: (1) hyperlinks to other portions of the same document; (2) hyperlinks to other documents filed within the CM/ECF system; and (3) hyperlinks to a location on the Internet that contains a source document for a citation. MA R USDCT CM/ECF Admin(G)(7).

　　i. Hyperlinks to cited authority may not replace standard citation format. Complete citations must be included in the text of the filed document. Neither a hyperlink, nor any site to which it refers, shall be considered part of the

record, but are simply convenient mechanisms for accessing material cited in a document filed in CM/ECF. Instructions on creating hyperlinks may be found in the CM/ECF User Manual. MA R USDCT CM/ECF Admin(G)(7).

ii. The court accepts no responsibility for, and does not endorse, any product, organization, or content at any hyperlinked site, or at any site to which that site may be linked. The court accepts no responsibility for the availability or functionality of any hyperlink. MA R USDCT CM/ECF Admin(G)(7).

iii. One feature of PDF/A documents is that hyperlinks are commonly "masked," meaning that the full address of the referenced file is not written out; for example, clicking the word brief may open a brief which was previously filed in CM/ECF. MA R USDCT CM/ECF Admin(G)(7)(NOTE). An "unmasked" hyperlink has the full address visible to the user. MA R USDCT CM/ECF Admin(G)(7)(NOTE).

- Masked hyperlinks may or may not work in a PDF/A document, depending on how it was created. Currently, masked hyperlinks are preserved in PDF/A documents produced by the "Save As" method in Microsoft Word 2007 and 2010; the "PDFMaker" method in Microsoft Word 2007; and OpenOffice 2.4 ("PDF Export"). With other production methods, such as WordPerfect, the PDF/A document includes underlined words that appear to be links, but clicking them has no effect. MA R USDCT CM/ECF Admin(G)(7)(NOTE).

f. *Documents features not accepted.* CM/ECF will not accept PDF documents containing tracking tags, embedded systems commands, password protections, access restrictions or other security features, special tags or dynamic features. MA R USDCT CM/ECF Admin(G)(8).

g. *File size limitations.* A filing party shall limit the size of each PDF file to no more than twenty (20) megabytes. PDF files larger than seven (7) megabytes will be rejected by the CM/ECF system. The filer will see a message advising of the size limitation. MA R USDCT CM/ECF Admin(P)(2).

i. Larger documents or exhibits may be submitted electronically if split into separate PDF files each less than seven (7) megabytes, attached to the main document and clearly labeled. MA R USDCT CM/ECF Admin(P)(2).

ii. Documents submitted electronically or on paper are subject to the page limitations set by MA R USDCT LR 7.1(b)(4) or by order of the court. MA R USDCT CM/ECF Admin(P)(1).

h. *Accuracy and readability.* The filer shall verify the accuracy and readability of any PDF file before electronically filing it in CM/ECF. MA R USDCT CM/ECF Admin(G)(6); MA R USDCT CM/ECF Admin(P)(3).

3. *Signing of pleadings, motions and other papers*

a. *Signature.* Every pleading, written motion, and other paper must be signed by at least one attorney of record in the attorney's name—or by a party personally if the party is unrepresented. The paper must state the signer's address, e-mail address, and telephone number. FRCP 11(a). The provisions of the Federal Rules of Civil Procedure pertaining to the form and signing of pleadings, motions, and other papers shall be applicable to all papers filed in any proceeding in this court. The board of bar overseers registration number of each attorney signing such documents, except the United States Attorney and his staff, shall be inscribed below the signature. MA R USDCT LR 5.1(a)(1).

i. *Electronic signing.* A filing made through a person's electronic-filing account and authorized by that person, together with that person's name on a signature block, constitutes the person's signature. FRCP 5(d)(3)(C).

ii. *Appearances.* The filing of an appearance or any other pleading signed on behalf of a party constitutes an entry of appearance for that party. All pleadings shall contain the name, bar admission number, address, telephone number, and e-mail address of the attorney entering an appearance. MA R USDCT LR 83.5.2(a).

- *Appearances by law firms.* When a party is represented by a law firm, the appearance must include the name and the signature of at least one individual attorney. When a party is represented by more than one attorney from the same or different law firms, the attorney entering the appearance must designate the individual attorney who is authorized to receive all notices in the case. Any notice sent to an attorney so designated shall be deemed to be proper notice unless the court finds that notice was not properly sent. MA R USDCT LR 83.5.2(b).

- For more information on appearances, refer to MA R USDCT LR 83.5.2.

iii. *Signatures of attorneys.* The user login and password required to submit documents to the CM/ECF system shall serve as that user's signature for purposes of FRCP 11 and for all other purposes under the Federal Rules of Civil Procedure and the Local Rules of the United States District Court for the District of Massachusetts. All electronically filed documents must include a signature block and must set forth the attorney's name, bar number,

address, telephone number and email address. The name of the CM/ECF user under whose log-in and password the document is submitted must be preceded by a "/s/" and typed in the space where the signature would otherwise appear. MA R USDCT CM/ECF Admin(M)(1). For an example, refer to MA R USDCT CM/ECF Admin(M)(1).

iv. *Signatures of pro se parties.* Any document requiring a signature that is filed by a party appearing pro se shall bear the words "pro se" following that party's signature. Any such document shall also state the party's mailing address, telephone number (if any), and e-mail address (if the party has consented to service by email). MA R USDCT LR 83.5.5(g). For more information on practice by pro se litigants, refer to MA R USDCT LR 83.5.5.

v. *Multiple signatures.* The filer of any document requiring more than one signature (e.g, stipulations, joint motions, joint status reports, magistrate judge consent forms, etc.) must list thereon all the names of other signatories by means of a "/s/ name of signatory" block for each. By submitting such a document, the filing attorney certifies that each of the other signatories has expressly agreed to the form and substance of the document and that the filing attorney has their actual authority to submit the document electronically. MA R USDCT CM/ECF Admin(M)(2). For more information, refer to MA R USDCT CM/ECF Admin(M)(2).

vi. *Affidavits.* Except as provided in MA R USDCT CM/ECF Admin(L), affidavits shall be filed electronically; however, the electronically filed version must contain a "/s/ name of signatory" block indicating that the paper document bears an original signature. MA R USDCT CM/ECF Admin(M)(3). The court will also accept a scanned version of the original, signed document. MA R USDCT CM/ECF Admin(M)(3). For more information, refer to MA R USDCT CM/ECF Admin(M)(3).

vii. *No verification or accompanying affidavit required for pleadings.* Unless a rule or statute specifically states otherwise, a pleading need not be verified or accompanied by an affidavit. FRCP 11(a).

viii. *Unsigned papers.* The court must strike an unsigned paper unless the omission is promptly corrected after being called to the attorney's or party's attention. FRCP 11(a).

b. *Representations to the court.* By presenting to the court a pleading, written motion, or other paper—whether by signing, filing, submitting, or later advocating it—an attorney or unrepresented party certifies that to the best of the person's knowledge, information, and belief, formed after an inquiry reasonable under the circumstances:

i. It is not being presented for any improper purpose, such as to harass, cause unnecessary delay, or needlessly increase the cost of litigation;

ii. The claims, defenses, and other legal contentions are warranted by existing law or by a nonfrivolous argument for extending, modifying, or reversing existing law or for establishing new law;

iii. The factual contentions have evidentiary support or, if specifically so identified, will likely have evidentiary support after a reasonable opportunity for further investigation or discovery; and

iv. The denials of factual contentions are warranted on the evidence or, if specifically so identified, are reasonably based on belief or a lack of information. FRCP 11(b).

c. *Sanctions.* If, after notice and a reasonable opportunity to respond, the court determines that FRCP 11(b) has been violated, the court may impose an appropriate sanction on any attorney, law firm, or party that violated FRCP 11(b) or is responsible for the violation. FRCP 11(c)(1). Refer to the United States District Court for the District of Massachusetts KeyRules Motion for Sanctions document for more information.

4. *Privacy protection for filings made with the court*

a. *Redacted filings.* Unless the court orders otherwise, in an electronic or paper filing with the court that contains an individual's Social Security number, taxpayer-identification number, or birth date, the name of an individual known to be a minor, or a financial-account number, a party or nonparty making the filing may include only:

i. The last four (4) digits of the Social Security number and taxpayer-identification number;

ii. The year of the individual's birth;

iii. The minor's initials; and

iv. The last four (4) digits of the financial-account number. FRCP 5.2(a); MA R USDCT CM/ECF Admin(N).

b. *Exemptions from the redaction requirement.* The redaction requirement does not apply to the following:

i. A financial-account number that identifies the property allegedly subject to forfeiture in a forfeiture proceeding;

ii. The record of an administrative or agency proceeding;

iii. The official record of a state-court proceeding;

iv. The record of a court or tribunal, if that record was not subject to the redaction requirement when originally filed;

v. A filing covered by FRCP 5.2(c) or FRCP 5.2(d); and

vi. A pro se filing in an action brought under 28 U.S.C.A. § 2241, 28 U.S.C.A. § 2254, or 28 U.S.C.A. § 2255. FRCP 5.2(b).

c. *Limitations on remote access to electronic files; Social Security appeals and immigration cases.* Unless the court orders otherwise, in an action for benefits under the Social Security Act, and in an action or proceeding relating to an order of removal, to relief from removal, or to immigration benefits or detention, access to an electronic file is authorized as follows:

i. The parties and their attorneys may have remote electronic access to any part of the case file, including the administrative record;

ii. Any other person may have electronic access to the full record at the courthouse, but may have remote electronic access only to:

- The docket maintained by the court; and

- An opinion, order, judgment, or other disposition of the court, but not any other part of the case file or the administrative record. FRCP 5.2(c).

d. *Filings made under seal.* The court may order that a filing be made under seal without redaction. The court may later unseal the filing or order the person who made the filing to file a redacted version for the public record. FRCP 5.2(d).

e. *Protective orders.* For good cause, the court may by order in a case:

i. Require redaction of additional information; or

ii. Limit or prohibit a nonparty's remote electronic access to a document filed with the court. FRCP 5.2(e).

f. *Option for additional unredacted filing under seal.* A person making a redacted filing may also file an unredacted copy under seal. The court must retain the unredacted copy as part of the record. FRCP 5.2(f). For more information, refer to MA R USDCT LR 7.2.

g. *Option for filing a reference list.* A filing that contains redacted information may be filed together with a reference list that identifies each item of redacted information and specifies an appropriate identifier that uniquely corresponds to each item listed. The list must be filed under seal and may be amended as of right. Any reference in the case to a listed identifier will be construed to refer to the corresponding item of information. FRCP 5.2(g).

h. *Responsibility for redaction.* The clerk's office is not responsible for reviewing documents filed with the court to determine whether pleadings have been redacted and are in the proper form. MA R USDCT CM/ECF Admin(N).

i. *Waiver of protection of identifiers.* A person waives the protection of FRCP 5.2(a) as to the person's own information by filing it without redaction and not under seal. FRCP 5.2(h).

# F. Filing and Service Requirements

1. *Filing requirements*

a. *Required filings.* Any paper after the complaint that is required to be served must be filed no later than a reasonable time after service. FRCP 5(d)(1).

i. Except as noted in FRCP 33 to FRCP 36, the original of all papers required to be served under FRCP 5(d) shall, unless otherwise submitted to the court, be filed in the office of the clerk within seven (7) days after service has been made. MA R USDCT LR 5.1(b). Except as otherwise provided by the Federal Rules of Civil Procedure, proof of service of all pleadings and other papers required to be served (except discovery papers that in accordance with FRCP 33 to FRCP 36(f) are not to be filed) shall be filed in the office of the clerk promptly after service has been made. MA R USDCT LR 5.2(b)(1).

b. *Nonelectronic filing.* A paper not filed electronically is filed by delivering it: (1) to the clerk; or (2) to a judge who agrees to accept it for filing, and who must then note the filing date on the paper and promptly send it to the clerk. FRCP 5(d)(2).

c. *Electronic filing.* Unless exempt or otherwise ordered by the court, all pleadings and other papers submitted to the court must be filed, signed, and verified by electronic means as provided in MA R USDCT LR 5.4. MA R USDCT LR 5.4(A); MA R USDCT CM/ECF Admin(A)(1). All electronic filings must be made in accordance with the Administrative Procedures for Electronic Case Filing in the United States District Court for the District of

Massachusetts (MA R USDCT CM/ECF Admin). MA R USDCT LR 5.4(B). The court may deviate from the Administrative Procedures for Electronic Case Filing in the United States District Court for the District of Massachusetts (MA R USDCT CM/ECF Admin) in specific cases, without prior notice, if deemed appropriate in the exercise of discretion, considering the need for the just, speedy, and inexpensive determination of matters pending before the court. MA R USDCT CM/ECF Admin(C)(1). The court may excuse a failure to comply with any administrative procedure whenever justice so requires. MA R USDCT CM/ECF Admin(C)(2).

   i. *By a represented person; Generally required; Exceptions.* A person represented by an attorney must file electronically, unless nonelectronic filing is allowed by the court for good cause or is allowed or required by local rule. FRCP 5(d)(3)(A).

   ii. *By unrepresented person; When allowed or required.* A person not represented by an attorney: (1) may file electronically only if allowed by court order or by local rule; and (2) may be required to file electronically only by court order, or by a local rule that includes reasonable exceptions. FRCP 5(d)(3)(B).

   iii. *Exemptions from electronic filing*

- *Documents that should not be filed electronically.* The following types of documents must not be filed electronically, and will not be scanned into the ECF system by the clerk's office: (1) sealed documents; (2) ex parte motions; (3) documents generated as part of an alternative dispute resolution (ADR) process; (4) the administrative record in Social Security and other administrative proceedings; (5) the state court record in proceedings under 28 U.S.C.A. § 2254; and (6) such other types of documents as the clerk may direct in the Administrative Procedures for Electronic Case Filing in the United States District Court for the District of Massachusetts (MA R USDCT CM/ECF Admin). MA R USDCT LR 5.4(G)(1); MA R USDCT CM/ECF Admin(L).

- *Documents that need not be filed electronically.* The following types of documents need not be filed electronically, but may be scanned into the ECF system by a filing party or the clerk's office: (1) handwritten pleadings; (2) documents filed by pro se litigants who are incarcerated or who are not registered ECF users; (3) indictments, informations, criminal complaints, and the criminal JS45 form; (4) affidavits for search or arrest warrants and related documents; (5) documents received from another court under FRCRP 20 or FRCRP 40; (6) appearance bonds; (7) any document in a criminal case containing the original signature of a defendant, such as a waiver of indictment or a plea agreement; (8) petitions for violations of supervised release; (9) executed service of process documents under FRCP 4; and (10) such other types of documents as the clerk may direct in the Administrative Procedures for Electronic Case Filing in the United States District Court for the District of Massachusetts (MA R USDCT CM/ECF Admin). MA R USDCT LR 5.4(G)(2); MA R USDCT CM/ECF Admin(L).

- For more information on exemptions from electronic filing, refer to MA R USDCT CM/ECF Admin(L).

   iv. *Consequences of electronic filing.* Electronic transmission of a document to the CM/ECF system, together with the transmission of a Notice of Electronic Filing (NEF) from the court at the completion of the transaction, constitutes the filing of the document for all purposes of the Federal Rules of Procedure and constitutes entry of the document on the docket maintained by the clerk pursuant to FRCP 58 and FRCP 79. MA R USDCT CM/ECF Admin(G)(1).

   v. *Payment of filing fees.* When electronically filing any pleading or paper through CM/ECF that requires a fee, all registered ECF users are to pay the fee electronically through the Treasury Department's Internet payment process. MA R USDCT LR 67.4(d); MA R USDCT CM/ECF Admin(A)(1). Pro se filers and those who have been exempted from electronic filing and/or electronic payment of fees may submit payments by check or money order made payable to "Clerk, U.S. District Court". MA R USDCT LR 67.4(d). For more information on filing fees, refer to MA R USDCT LR 67.4 and MA R USDCT CM/ECF Admin(I).

   vi. For more information on electronic filing, refer to MA R USDCT CM/ECF Admin.

  d. *Email or fax filing.* In general, the court does not accept documents by email or by fax. If the court, in special circumstances, does authorize the submission of a document in that manner, the document shall not be considered filed until an NEF is generated by CM/ECF at the completion of the transaction. MA R USDCT CM/ECF Admin(H)(5).

2. *Service requirements.* All papers filed pursuant to MA R USDCT LR 7.1(b) shall be served unless the moving party indicates in writing on the face of the motion that ex parte consideration is requested. Motions filed "ex parte" and related papers need not be served until the motion has been ruled upon or the court orders that service be made. MA R USDCT LR

7.1(c). Service of all pleadings subsequent to the original complaint and of all other papers required to be served shall be made in the manner specified by FRCP 5. MA R USDCT LR 5.2(a).

a. *Service; When required*

    i. *In general.* Unless the Federal Rules of Civil Procedure provide otherwise, each of the following papers must be served on every party:

- An order stating that service is required;
- A pleading filed after the original complaint, unless the court orders otherwise under FRCP 5(c) because there are numerous defendants;
- A discovery paper required to be served on a party, unless the court orders otherwise;
- A written motion, except one that may be heard ex parte; and
- A written notice, appearance, demand, or offer of judgment, or any similar paper. FRCP 5(a)(1).

    ii. *If a party fails to appear.* No service is required on a party who is in default for failing to appear. But a pleading that asserts a new claim for relief against such a party must be served on that party under FRCP 4. FRCP 5(a)(2).

    iii. *Seizing property.* If an action is begun by seizing property and no person is or need be named as a defendant, any service required before the filing of an appearance, answer, or claim must be made on the person who had custody or possession of the property when it was seized. FRCP 5(a)(3).

b. *Service; How made*

    i. *Serving an attorney.* If a party is represented by an attorney, service under FRCP 5 must be made on the attorney unless the court orders service on the party. FRCP 5(b)(1).

- *Nonresident attorney.* On application of a party, the court may order an attorney who represents any other party and who does not maintain an office within this district where service can be made on him by delivery as provided by FRCP 5(b), to designate a member of the bar of this court who does maintain such an office to receive service of all pleadings and other papers in his behalf. MA R USDCT LR 5.2(c)(1).

    ii. *Serving a party acting pro se.* On application of a party, the court may order any other party who is appearing without an attorney and who does not maintain an office or residence within this district where service can be made on him by delivery as provided by FRCP 5(b), to designate an address within the district at which service can be made on him by delivery. MA R USDCT LR 5.2(c)(2).

    iii. *Service in general.* A paper is served under FRCP 5 by:

- Handing it to the person;
- Leaving it: (1) at the person's office with a clerk or other person in charge or, if no one is in charge, in a conspicuous place in the office; or (2) if the person has no office or the office is closed, at the person's dwelling or usual place of abode with someone of suitable age and discretion who resides there;
- Mailing it to the person's last known address—in which event service is complete upon mailing;
- Leaving it with the court clerk if the person has no known address;
- Sending it to a registered user by filing it with the court's electronic-filing system or sending it by other electronic means that the person consented to in writing—in either of which events service is complete upon filing or sending, but is not effective if the filer or sender learns that it did not reach the person to be served; or
- Delivering it by any other means that the person consented to in writing—in which event service is complete when the person making service delivers it to the agency designated to make delivery. FRCP 5(b)(2).

    iv. *Service by electronic means.* Unless exempt or otherwise ordered by the court, all pleadings and other papers must be served on other parties by electronic means. MA R USDCT LR 5.4(C); MA R USDCT CM/ECF Admin(H)(2). Service by electronic means shall be treated the same as service by mail. MA R USDCT CM/ECF Admin(H)(4).

- *Consent to electronic service.* Registering to use CM/ECF constitutes consent to service of all documents by electronic means as provided in the Administrative Procedures for Electronic Case Filing in the United States District Court for the District of Massachusetts (MA R USDCT CM/ECF Admin) and FRCP 5(b) and FRCP 77(d). MA R USDCT CM/ECF Admin(E)(6); MA R USDCT CM/ECF Admin(H)(3).

- *Service on registered ECF users.* Transmission of the Notice of Electronic Filing (NEF) through the court's transmission facilities will constitute service of the filed document upon a registered ECF user. MA R USDCT LR 5.4(C).

- *Service on non-registered users.* The party filing the document electronically is responsible for serving a paper copy of the document by mail in accordance with FRCP 5(b) to those case participants who have not been identified on the NEF as electronic recipients. MA R USDCT CM/ECF Admin(H)(3).

- *Service of conventionally filed papers.* Documents or exhibits submitted conventionally shall be served on other parties by the filer using traditional means. MA R USDCT CM/ECF Admin(P)(4).

  c. *Serving numerous defendants*

    i. *In general.* If an action involves an unusually large number of defendants, the court may, on motion or on its own, order that:

- Defendants' pleadings and replies to them need not be served on other defendants;

- Any crossclaim, counterclaim, avoidance, or affirmative defense in those pleadings and replies to them will be treated as denied or avoided by all other parties; and

- Filing any such pleading and serving it on the plaintiff constitutes notice of the pleading to all parties. FRCP 5(c)(1).

    ii. *Notifying parties.* A copy of every such order must be served on the parties as the court directs. FRCP 5(c)(2).

## G. Hearings

1. *Hearings, generally.* If the court concludes that there should be a hearing on a motion, the motion will be set down for hearing at such time as the court determines. MA R USDCT LR 7.1(e).

  a. *Oral argument.* Due process does not require that oral argument be permitted on a motion and, except as otherwise provided by local rule, the district court has discretion to determine whether it will decide the motion on the papers or hear argument by counsel (and perhaps receive evidence). FPP § 1190; F.D.I.C. v. Deglau, 207 F.3d 153 (3d Cir. 2000).

    i. *Evidence on a motion.* When a motion relies on facts outside the record, the court may hear the matter on affidavits or may hear it wholly or partly on oral testimony or on depositions. FRCP 43(c).

  b. *Providing a regular schedule for oral hearings.* A court may establish regular times and places for oral hearings on motions. FRCP 78(a).

  c. *Providing for submission on briefs.* By rule or order, the court may provide for submitting and determining motions on briefs, without oral hearings. FRCP 78(b). Motions that are not set down for hearing as provided in MA R USDCT LR 7.1(e) will be decided on the papers submitted after an opposition to the motion has been filed, or, if no opposition is filed, after the time for filing an opposition has elapsed. MA R USDCT LR 7.1(f).

2. *Hearing on certain FRCP 12 defenses before trial.* If a party so moves, any defense listed in FRCP 12(b)(1) through FRCP 12(b)(7)—whether made in a pleading or by motion—and a motion under FRCP 12(c) must be heard and decided before trial unless the court orders a deferral until trial. FRCP 12(i).

3. *Conflict of court appearances.* For information on conflict of court appearances, refer to MA R USDCT LR 40.2.

## H. Forms

### 1. Federal Motion to Dismiss for Failure to State a Claim Forms

  a. Failure to state a claim upon which relief can be granted. 2C FEDFORMS § 11:80.

  b. Failure to state a claim upon which relief can be granted; Long version. 2C FEDFORMS § 11:81.

  c. Failure to state a claim upon which relief can be granted; Dismissal of certain allegations. 2C FEDFORMS § 11:82.

  d. Failure to state a claim upon which relief can be granted; With supporting reasons. 2C FEDFORMS § 11:83.

  e. Failure to state a claim upon which relief can be granted; With supporting reasons; Plaintiff not the real party in interest. 2C FEDFORMS § 11:85.

  f. Failure to state a claim upon which relief can be granted; With supporting reasons; Failure to show implied contract. 2C FEDFORMS § 11:86.

  g. Failure to state a claim upon which relief can be granted; With supporting reasons; Issue not arbitrable. 2C FEDFORMS § 11:87.

h. Failure to state a claim upon which relief can be granted; With supporting affidavits. 2C FEDFORMS § 11:88.

i. Failure to state a claim upon which relief can be granted; In alternative for summary judgment. 2C FEDFORMS § 11:89.

j. Notice in federal court; Motion for involuntary dismissal of action without prejudice; Complaint fails to state a claim on which relief can be granted. AMJUR PP DISMISSAL § 108.

k. Motion; To dismiss; Failure to state a claim on which relief can be granted or facts sufficient to constitute cause of action. AMJUR PP LIMITATION § 100.

l. Motion to dismiss; For failure to state a claim, improper service of process, improper venue, and want of jurisdiction. AMJUR PP MOTIONS § 42.

m. Motion to dismiss; Failure to state sufficient claim; By one of several defendants. FEDPROF § 1C:108.

n. Motion to dismiss; Failure to state sufficient claim; By third-party defendant. FEDPROF § 1C:109.

o. Motion to dismiss; Failure to state sufficient claim after successive attempts. FEDPROF § 1C:110.

p. Motion to dismiss; By individual defendants. FEDPROF § 1C:111.

q. Motion to dismiss; By state agency. FEDPROF § 1C:112.

r. Motion to dismiss counterclaim. FEDPROF § 1C:117.

s. Allegation; In motion to dismiss; Res judicata. FEDPROF § 1C:119.

t. Allegation; In motion to dismiss; Statute of limitations. FEDPROF § 1C:121.

u. Allegation; In motion to dismiss; Strict liability claim barred by statute. FEDPROF § 1C:122.

v. Allegation; In motion to dismiss; By United States; Absence of consent to suit. FEDPROF § 1C:124.

w. Reply; To motion to dismiss for failure to state sufficient claim. FEDPROF § 1C:125.

x. Motion to dismiss counterclaim. GOLDLTGFMS § 13:10.

y. Motion to dismiss complaint; General form. GOLDLTGFMS § 20:24.

z. Affidavit in support of motion to dismiss complaint. GOLDLTGFMS § 20:32.

2. **Forms for the District of Massachusetts**

   a. Notice of filing with clerk's office. MA R USDCT CM/ECF Admin(Appendix I).

# I. Applicable Rules

1. *Federal rules*

   a. Serving and filing pleadings and other papers. FRCP 5.

   b. Constitutional challenge to a statute; Notice, certification, and intervention. FRCP 5.1.

   c. Privacy protection for filings made with the court. FRCP 5.2.

   d. Computing and extending time; Time for motion papers. FRCP 6.

   e. Pleadings allowed; Form of motions and other papers. FRCP 7.

   f. Disclosure statement. FRCP 7.1.

   g. Form of pleadings. FRCP 10.

   h. Signing pleadings, motions, and other papers; Representations to the court; Sanctions. FRCP 11.

   i. Defenses and objections; When and how presented; Motion for judgment on the pleadings; Consolidating motions; Waiving defenses; Pretrial hearing. FRCP 12.

   j. Hearing motions; Submission on briefs. FRCP 78.

2. *Local rules*

   a. Title. MA R USDCT LR 1.1.

   b. Sanctions. MA R USDCT LR 1.3.

   c. Form and filing of papers. MA R USDCT LR 5.1.

   d. Service and filing of pleadings and other papers. MA R USDCT LR 5.2.

e. Filing and service by electronic means. MA R USDCT LR 5.4.

f. Motion practice. MA R USDCT LR 7.1.

g. Alternative dispute resolution. MA R USDCT LR 16.4.

h. Payments and deposits made with the clerk. MA R USDCT LR 67.4.

i. Settlement. MA R USDCT LR 68.2.

j. Office of the clerk. MA R USDCT LR 77.2.

k. Appearances. MA R USDCT LR 83.5.2.

l. Practice by pro se litigants. MA R USDCT LR 83.5.5.

m. CM/ECF case management/electronic case files administrative procedures. MA R USDCT CM/ECF Admin.

## Motions, Oppositions and Replies
## Motion to Dismiss for Lack of Subject Matter Jurisdiction

### Document Last Updated December 2018

A. **Checklist**

(I) ❑ Matters to be considered by moving party

(a) ❑ Required documents

(1) ❑ Notice of motion and motion

(2) ❑ Memorandum

(3) ❑ Certificate of service

(b) ❑ Supplemental documents

(1) ❑ Supporting evidence

(2) ❑ Notice of constitutional question

(3) ❑ Nongovernmental corporate disclosure statement

(4) ❑ Proposed order

(5) ❑ Compact disk with copy of document(s) in PDF format

(6) ❑ Notice of filing with clerk's office

(7) ❑ Additional copies

(8) ❑ Courtesy copies

(c) ❑ Timing

(1) ❑ The defense of lack of subject matter jurisdiction can be raised at any time

(2) ❑ Every defense to a claim for relief in any pleading must be asserted in the responsive pleading if one is required

(3) ❑ A motion asserting any of the defenses in FRCP 12(b) must be made before pleading if a responsive pleading is allowed

(4) ❑ If a pleading sets out a claim for relief that does not require a responsive pleading, an opposing party may assert at trial any defense to that claim

(5) ❑ A written motion and notice of the hearing must be served at least fourteen (14) days before the time specified for the hearing, with the following exceptions: (i) when the motion may be heard ex parte; (ii) when the Federal Rules of Civil Procedure set a different time; or (iii) when a court order—which a party may, for good cause, apply for ex parte—sets a different time

(6) ❑ Any affidavit supporting a motion must be served with the motion

(7) ❑ Except as noted in FRCP 33 to FRCP 36, the original of all papers required to be served under FRCP 5(d) shall, unless otherwise submitted to the court, be filed in the office of the clerk within seven (7) days after service has been made

(II) ❑ Matters to be considered by opposing party

    (a) ❑ Required documents

        (1) ❑ Opposition

        (2) ❑ Certificate of service

    (b) ❑ Supplemental documents

        (1) ❑ Supporting evidence

        (2) ❑ Notice of constitutional question

        (3) ❑ Compact disk with copy of document(s) in PDF format

        (4) ❑ Notice of filing with clerk's office

        (5) ❑ Additional copies

        (6) ❑ Courtesy copies

    (c) ❑ Timing

        (1) ❑ A party opposing a motion, shall file an opposition within fourteen (14) days after the motion is served, unless another period is fixed by rule or statute, or by order of the court

        (2) ❑ Except as FRCP 59(c) provides otherwise, any opposing affidavit must be served at least seven (7) days before the hearing, unless the court permits service at another time

        (3) ❑ Except as noted in FRCP 33 to FRCP 36, the original of all papers required to be served under FRCP 5(d) shall, unless otherwise submitted to the court, be filed in the office of the clerk within seven (7) days after service has been made

## B. Timing

1. *Motion to dismiss for lack of subject matter jurisdiction.* [The defense of lack of subject matter jurisdiction] can be raised at any time. FEDPROC § 62:428.

    a. *In a responsive pleading.* Every defense to a claim for relief in any pleading must be asserted in the responsive pleading if one is required. FRCP 12(b).

    b. *By motion.* A motion asserting any of the defenses in FRCP 12(b) must be made before pleading if a responsive pleading is allowed. FRCP 12(b). Although FRCP 12(b) encourages the responsive pleader to file a motion to dismiss before filing the answer, nothing in FRCP 12 prohibits the filing of a motion to dismiss with the answer. An untimely motion to dismiss may be considered if the defense asserted in the motion was previously raised in the responsive pleading. FEDPROC § 62:421.

    c. *At trial.* If a pleading sets out a claim for relief that does not require a responsive pleading, an opposing party may assert at trial any defense to that claim. FRCP 12(b).

2. *Timing of motions, generally*

    a. *Motion and notice of hearing.* A written motion and notice of the hearing must be served at least fourteen (14) days before the time specified for the hearing, with the following exceptions:

        i. When the motion may be heard ex parte;

        ii. When the Federal Rules of Civil Procedure set a different time; or

        iii. When a court order—which a party may, for good cause, apply for ex parte—sets a different time. FRCP 6(c)(1).

    b. *Supporting affidavit.* Any affidavit supporting a motion must be served with the motion. FRCP 6(c)(2).

3. *Timing of opposing papers.* A party opposing a motion, shall file an opposition within fourteen (14) days after the motion is served, unless (1) the motion is for summary judgment, in which case the opposition shall be filed within twenty-one (21) days after the motion is served, or (2) another period is fixed by rule or statute, or by order of the court. MA R USDCT LR 7.1(b)(2); MA R USDCT CM/ECF Admin(H)(4). The fourteen (14) day period is intended to include the period specified by the civil rules for mailing time and provide for a uniform period regardless of the use of the mails. MA R USDCT LR 7.1(b)(2).

    a. *Opposing affidavit.* Except as FRCP 59(c) provides otherwise, any opposing affidavit must be served at least seven (7) days before the hearing, unless the court permits service at another time. FRCP 6(c)(2).

4. *Timing of reply papers.* [W]here the respondent files an answering affidavit setting up a new matter, the moving party

ordinarily is allowed a reasonable time to file a reply affidavit since failure to deny the new matter by affidavit may operate as an admission of its truth. AMJUR MOTIONS § 25.

    a.   *Leave of court required.* All other papers not filed as indicated in MA R USDCT LR 7.1(b)(1) and MA R USDCT LR 7.1(b)(2), whether in the form of a reply brief or otherwise, may be submitted only with leave of court. MA R USDCT LR 7.1(b)(3).

5.   *Filing after service.* Except as noted in FRCP 33 to FRCP 36, the original of all papers required to be served under FRCP 5(d) shall, unless otherwise submitted to the court, be filed in the office of the clerk within seven (7) days after service has been made. MA R USDCT LR 5.1(b).

6.   *Effect of FRCP 12 motion on the time to serve a responsive pleading.* Unless the court sets a different time, serving a motion under FRCP 12 alters the periods in FRCP 12(a) as follows:

    a.   If the court denies the motion or postpones its disposition until trial, the responsive pleading must be served within fourteen (14) days after notice of the court's action; or

    b.   If the court grants a motion for a more definite statement, the responsive pleading must be served within fourteen (14) days after the more definite statement is served. FRCP 12(a)(4).

7.   *Computation of time*

    a.   *Computing time.* FRCP 6 applies in computing any time period specified in the Federal Rules of Civil Procedure, in any local rule or court order, or in any statute that does not specify a method of computing time. FRCP 6(a).

        i.   *Period stated in days or a longer unit.* When the period is stated in days or a longer unit of time:

           •  Exclude the day of the event that triggers the period;

           •  Count every day, including intermediate Saturdays, Sundays, and legal holidays; and

           •  Include the last day of the period, but if the last day is a Saturday, Sunday, or legal holiday, the period continues to run until the end of the next day that is not a Saturday, Sunday, or legal holiday. FRCP 6(a)(1).

        ii.   *Period stated in hours.* When the period is stated in hours:

           •  Begin counting immediately on the occurrence of the event that triggers the period;

           •  Count every hour, including hours during intermediate Saturdays, Sundays, and legal holidays; and

           •  If the period would end on a Saturday, Sunday, or legal holiday, the period continues to run until the same time on the next day that is not a Saturday, Sunday, or legal holiday. FRCP 6(a)(2).

        iii.   *Office of the clerk.* The offices of the Clerk of Court at Boston, Worcester and Springfield shall be open from 8:30 a.m. until 5:00 p.m. on all days except Saturdays, Sundays, legal holidays and other days so ordered by the court and announced in advance, if feasible. MA R USDCT LR 77.2.

        iv.   *Inaccessibility of the clerk's office.* Unless the court orders otherwise, if the clerk's office is inaccessible:

           •  On the last day for filing under FRCP 6(a)(1), then the time for filing is extended to the first accessible day that is not a Saturday, Sunday, or legal holiday; or

           •  During the last hour for filing under FRCP 6(a)(2), then the time for filing is extended to the same time on the first accessible day that is not a Saturday, Sunday, or legal holiday. FRCP 6(a)(3).

        v.   *"Last day" defined.* Unless a different time is set by a statute, local rule, or court order, the last day ends:

           •  For electronic filing, at midnight in the court's time zone; and

           •  For filing by other means, when the clerk's office is scheduled to close. FRCP 6(a)(4).

        vi.   *"Next day" defined.* The "next day" is determined by continuing to count forward when the period is measured after an event and backward when measured before an event. FRCP 6(a)(5).

        vii.   *"Legal holiday" defined.* "Legal holiday" means:

           •  The day set aside by statute for observing New Year's Day, Martin Luther King Jr.'s Birthday, Washington's Birthday, Memorial Day, Independence Day, Labor Day, Columbus Day, Veterans' Day, Thanksgiving Day, or Christmas Day;

           •  Any day declared a holiday by the President or Congress; and

           •  For periods that are measured after an event, any other day declared a holiday by the state where the district court is located. FRCP 6(a)(6).

b. *Computation of electronic filing deadlines.* Filing documents electronically does not alter any filing deadlines. MA R USDCT CM/ECF Admin(K); MA R USDCT LR 5.4(D). Although CM/ECF is generally available twenty-four (24) hours a day for filing, all electronic transmissions of documents must be completed prior to 6:00 PM, Eastern Standard (or Daylight Savings) Time, on the date on which it is due, in order to be considered timely filed that day. MA R USDCT CM/ECF Admin(K); MA R USDCT LR 5.4(D). When a specific time of day deadline is set by court order or stipulation, the electronic filing must be completed by that time. Documents may be filed at any time of the day on days prior to the date on which it is due. MA R USDCT CM/ECF Admin(K). A document filed electronically shall be deemed filed as of the time and date stated on the NEF received from the court. MA R USDCT CM/ECF Admin(G)(2); MA R USDCT CM/ECF Admin(K).

   i. *Technical failures.* A user whose filing is made untimely as the result of a technical failure of the court's CM/ECF system may seek appropriate relief from the court. MA R USDCT CM/ECF Admin(W)(3). Technical difficulties on the filer's end, with telephone, cable lines, the filer's Internet Service Provider (ISP), or hardware or software problems, will not constitute a technical failure under the Administrative Procedures for Electronic Case Filing in the United States District Court for the District of Massachusetts (MA R USDCT CM/ECF Admin) nor excuse an untimely filing. MA R USDCT CM/ECF Admin(W)(3). As help desk support is available during normal business hours, filers are strongly urged to electronically file any documents during that period. MA R USDCT CM/ECF Admin(W)(3).

   ● The court has made available a public terminal (computers and scanner) in each clerk's office for registered users to scan and electronically file documents. This equipment is available during normal business hours. Users should bring their prepared document and a valid CM/ECF login and password. MA R USDCT CM/ECF Admin(W)(3).

c. *Extending time.* When an act may or must be done within a specified time, the court may, for good cause, extend the time: (1) with or without motion or notice if the court acts, or if a request is made, before the original time or its extension expires; or (2) on motion made after the time has expired if the party failed to act because of excusable neglect. FRCP 6(b)(1).

   i. *Exceptions.* A court must not extend the time to act under FRCP 50(b), FRCP 50(d), FRCP 52(b), FRCP 59(b), FRCP 59(d), FRCP 59(e), and FRCP 60(b). FRCP 6(b)(2).

   ii. Refer to the United States District Court for the District of Massachusetts KeyRules Motion for Continuance/Extension of Time document for more information on extending time.

d. *Additional time after certain kinds of service.* When a party may or must act within a specified time after being served and service is made under FRCP 5(b)(2)(C) (by mail), FRCP 5(b)(2)(D) (by leaving with the clerk), or FRCP 5(b)(2)(F) (by other means consented to), three (3) days are added after the period would otherwise expire under FRCP 6(a). FRCP 6(d).

## C. General Requirements

1. *Motions, generally*

   a. *Requirements.* A request for a court order must be made by motion. The motion must:

      i. Be in writing unless made during a hearing or trial;

      ii. State with particularity the grounds for seeking the order; and

      iii. State the relief sought. FRCP 7(b)(1).

   b. *Notice of motion.* A party interested in resisting the relief sought by a motion has a right to notice thereof, and an opportunity to be heard. AMJUR MOTIONS § 12.

      i. [I]n addition to statutory or court rule provisions requiring notice of a motion—the purpose of such a notice requirement having been said to be to prevent a party from being prejudicially surprised by a motion—principles of natural justice dictate that an adverse party generally must be given notice that a motion will be presented to the court. AMJUR MOTIONS § 12.

      ii. "Notice," in this regard, means reasonable notice, including a meaningful opportunity to prepare and to defend against allegations of a motion. AMJUR MOTIONS § 12.

   c. *Writing requirement.* The writing requirement is intended to [ensure] that the adverse parties are informed and have a record of both the motion's pendency and the grounds on which the movant seeks an order. FPP § 1191; Feldberg v. Quechee Lakes Corp., 463 F.3d 195 (2d Cir. 2006). [A] single written document can satisfy the writing requirements both for a motion and for [an] FRCP 6(c)(1) notice. FRCP 7(Advisory Committee Notes).

d. *Particularity requirement.* The particularity requirement [ensures] that the opposing parties will have notice of their opponent's contentions. FEDPROC § 62:358; Goodman v. 1973 26 Foot Trojan Vessel, Arkansas Registration No. AR1439SN, 859 F.2d 71 (8th Cir. 1988). That requirement ensures that notice of the basis for the motion is provided to the court and to the opposing party so as to avoid prejudice, provide the opponent with a meaningful opportunity to respond, and provide the court with enough information to process the motion correctly. FEDPROC § 62:358; Andreas v. Volkswagen of Am., Inc., 336 F.3d 789 (8th Cir. 2003).

    i. Reasonable specification of the grounds for a motion is sufficient. The particularity requirement for motions is satisfied when no party is prejudiced by a lack of particularity or when the court can comprehend the basis for the motion and deal with it fairly. However, where a movant fails to state even one ground for granting the motion in question, the movant has failed to meet the minimal standard of "reasonable specification." FEDPROC § 62:358; Martinez v. Trainor, 556 F.2d 818 (7th Cir. 1977).

    ii. The court may excuse the failure to comply with the particularity requirement if it is inadvertent, and where no prejudice is shown by the opposing party. FEDPROC § 62:358.

e. *Control of motion practice*

    i. *Plan for the disposition of motions.* At the earliest practicable time, the judicial officer shall establish a framework for the disposition of motions, which, at the discretion of the judicial officer, may include specific deadlines or general time guidelines for filing motions. This framework may be amended from time to time by the judicial officer as required by the progress of the case. MA R USDCT LR 7.1(a)(1).

    ii. *Motion practice.* No motion shall be filed unless counsel certify that they have conferred and have attempted in good faith to resolve or narrow the issue. MA R USDCT LR 7.1(a)(2).

    iii. *Unresolved motions.* The court shall rule on motions as soon as practicable, having in mind the reporting requirements set forth in the Civil Justice Reform Act. MA R USDCT LR 7.1(a)(3).

2. *Motion to dismiss for lack of subject matter jurisdiction.* [A] party may assert the following defense by motion: lack of subject-matter jurisdiction. FRCP 12(b)(1). The objection presented by a motion under FRCP 12(b)(1) challenging the court's subject matter jurisdiction is that the district judge has no authority or competence to hear and decide the case before it. [An] FRCP 12(b)(1) motion most typically is employed when the movant believes that the claim asserted by the plaintiff does not involve a federal question, and there is no diversity of citizenship between the parties or, in a diversity of citizenship case, the amount in controversy does not exceed the required jurisdictional amount. FPP § 1350.

a. *Subject matter jurisdiction.* It always must be remembered that the federal courts are courts of limited jurisdiction and only can adjudicate those cases that fall within Article III of the Constitution (see U.S.C.A. Const. Art. III § 1, et seq.) and a congressional authorization enacted thereunder. FPP § 1350.

    i. *Federal question.* The district courts shall have original jurisdiction of all civil actions arising under the Constitution, laws, or treaties of the United States. 28 U.S.C.A. § 1331.

    ii. *Diversity of citizenship; Amount in controversy.* The district courts shall have original jurisdiction of all civil actions where the matter in controversy exceeds the sum or value of seventy-five thousand dollars ($75,000), exclusive of interest and costs, and is between:

- Citizens of different States;
- Citizens of a State and citizens or subjects of a foreign state, except that the district courts shall not have original jurisdiction under 28 U.S.C.A. § 1332 of an action between citizens of a State and citizens or subjects of a foreign state who are lawfully admitted for permanent residence in the United States and are domiciled in the same State;
- Citizens of different States and in which citizens or subjects of a foreign state are additional parties; and
- A foreign state, defined in 28 U.S.C.A. § 1603(a), as plaintiff and citizens of a State or of different States. 28 U.S.C.A. § 1332(a).

b. *Types of FRCP 12(b)(1) motions.* There are two separate types of FRCP 12(b)(1) motions to dismiss for lack of subject-matter jurisdiction: the "facial attack" and the "factual attack." FEDPROC § 62:434.

    i. *Facial attack.* The facial attack is addressed to the sufficiency of the allegations of the complaint itself. FEDPROC § 62:434; Stalley ex rel. U.S. v. Orlando Reg'l Healthcare Sys., Inc., 524 F.3d 1229 (11th Cir. 2008). On such a motion, the court is merely required to determine whether the plaintiff has sufficiently alleged a basis of subject-matter jurisdiction. FEDPROC § 62:434; U.S. ex rel. Atkinson v. PA. Shipbuilding Co., 473 F.3d 506 (3d Cir. 2007).

ii. *Factual attack.* A factual attack challenges the factual existence of subject-matter jurisdiction, irrespective of the pleadings, and matters outside the pleadings, such as testimony and affidavits, may be considered by the court. FEDPROC § 62:434; Kligman v. I.R.S., 272 F. App'x 166 (3d Cir. 2008); Paper, Allied-Indus., Chem. And Energy Workers Int'l Union v. Cont'l Carbon Co., 428 F.3d 1285 (10th Cir. 2005). The trial court in such a situation is free to weigh the evidence and satisfy itself as to the existence of its power to hear the case; therefore, no presumptive truthfulness attaches to the plaintiff's factual allegations. FEDPROC § 62:434; Land v. Dollar, 330 U.S. 731, 67 S. Ct. 1009, 91 L. Ed. 1209 (1947).

c. *Burden.* With the limited exception of the question whether the amount in controversy requirement in diversity of citizenship cases has been satisfied, the extensive case law on the subject makes clear that the burden of proof on [an] FRCP 12(b)(1) motion is on the party asserting that subject matter jurisdiction exists, which, of course, typically is the plaintiff. FPP § 1350; Thomson v. Gaskill, 315 U.S. 442, 62 S. Ct. 673, 86 L. Ed. 951 (1942). A plaintiff meets the burden of establishing subject-matter jurisdiction at the pleading stage by pleading sufficient allegations to show the proper basis for the court to assert subject-matter jurisdiction over the action. 2 FEDFORMS § 7:6.

  i. *Federal question.* If subject matter jurisdiction is based on the existence of a federal question, the pleader must show that he or she has alleged a claim for relief arising under federal law and that the claim is not frivolous. FPP § 1350; Baker v. Carr, 369 U.S. 186, 82 S.Ct. 691, 7 L.Ed.2d 663 (1962).

  ii. *Diversity of citizenship.* If jurisdiction is based on diversity of citizenship, on the other hand, the pleader must show that real and complete diversity exists between all of the plaintiffs and all of the defendants, and also that the assertion that the claim exceeds the requisite jurisdictional amount in controversy is made in good faith. FPP § 1350; City of Indianapolis v. Chase Nat. Bank of City of New York, 314 U.S. 63, 62 S. Ct. 15, 86 L. Ed. 47 (1941). Satisfying this last requirement is a relatively simple task, however, because the claim is deemed to be made in good faith so long as it is not clear to a legal certainty that the claimant could not recover a judgment exceeding the statutorily mandated jurisdictional amount, a matter on which the party challenging the district court's jurisdiction has the burden. FPP § 1350.

d. *Joining motions.* [W]hen the motion is based on more than one ground, the cases are legion stating that the district court should consider the FRCP 12(b)(1) challenge first because if it must dismiss the complaint for lack of subject matter jurisdiction, the accompanying defenses and objections become moot and do not need to be determined by the judge. FPP § 1350; Steel Co. v. Citizens for a Better Env't, 523 U.S. 83, 118 S. Ct. 1003, 140 L. Ed. 2d 210 (1998). However, there are a number of decisions in which the court has decided one or more defenses in addition to the subject matter jurisdiction question or simply assumed the existence of jurisdiction and gone on to decide another matter. FPP § 1350.

  i. *Right to join.* A motion under FRCP 12 may be joined with any other motion allowed by FRCP 12. FRCP 12(g)(1).

  ii. *Limitation on further motions.* Except as provided in FRCP 12(h)(2) or FRCP 12(h)(3), a party that makes a motion under FRCP 12 must not make another motion under FRCP 12 raising a defense or objection that was available to the party but omitted from its earlier motion. FRCP 12(g)(2).

e. *Waiving and preserving certain defenses.* No defense or objection is waived by joining it with one or more other defenses or objections in a responsive pleading or in a motion. FRCP 12(b). If the court determines at any time that it lacks subject-matter jurisdiction, the court must dismiss the action. FRCP 12(h)(3).

3. *Opposing papers.* The Federal Rules of Civil Procedure do not require any formal answer, return, or reply to a motion, except where the Federal Rules of Civil Procedure or local rules may require affidavits, memoranda, or other papers to be filed in opposition to a motion. Such papers are simply to apprise the court of such opposition and the grounds of that opposition. FEDPROC § 62:353.

a. *Effect of failure to respond to motion.* Although in the absence of statutory provision or court rule, a motion ordinarily does not require a written answer, when a party files a motion and the opposing party fails to respond, the court may construe such failure to respond as nonopposition to the motion or an admission that the motion was meritorious, may take the facts alleged in the motion as true—the rule in some jurisdictions being that the failure to respond to a fact set forth in a motion is deemed an admission—and may grant the motion if the relief requested appears to be justified. AMJUR MOTIONS § 28.

  i. *Unopposed motion to dismiss.* The circuits are split on whether a court may grant a motion to dismiss solely on the basis that the plaintiff did not file a response opposing the motion. FRCP-RC RULE 12.

b. *Assent or no opposition not determinative.* However, a motion will not be granted automatically simply because an "assent" or a notation of "no opposition" has been filed; federal judges frequently deny motions that have been assented to when it is thought that justice so dictates. FPP § 1190.

c. *Responsive pleading inappropriate as response to motion.* An attempt to answer or oppose a motion with a responsive pleading usually is not appropriate. FPP § 1190.

4. *Reply papers.* A moving party may be required or permitted to prepare papers in addition to his original motion papers. AMJUR MOTIONS § 25. Papers answering or replying to opposing papers may be appropriate, in the interests of justice, where it appears there is a substantial reason for allowing a reply. Thus, a court may accept reply papers where a party demonstrates that the papers to which it seeks to file a reply raise new issues that are material to the disposition of the question before the court, or where the court determines, sua sponte, that it wishes further briefing of an issue raised in those papers and orders the submission of additional papers. FEDPROC § 62:354.

a. *Function of reply papers.* The function of a reply affidavit is to answer the arguments made in opposition to the position taken by the movant and not to permit the movant to introduce new arguments in support of the motion. AMJUR MOTIONS § 25.

b. *Issues raised for the first time in a reply document.* However, the view has been followed in some jurisdictions, that as a matter of judicial economy, where there is no prejudice and where the issues could be raised simply by filing a motion to dismiss, the trial court has discretion to consider arguments raised for the first time in a reply memorandum, and that a trial court may grant a motion to strike issues raised for the first time in a reply memorandum. AMJUR MOTIONS § 26.

5. *Alternative dispute resolution (ADR).* The judicial officer assigned to preside over the case shall encourage the resolution of disputes by settlement or other alternative dispute resolution programs. MA R USDCT LR 16.4(a).

a. *Settlement.* At every conference conducted under the Local Rules of the United States District Court for the District of Massachusetts, the judicial officer shall inquire as to the utility of the parties conducting settlement negotiations, explore means of facilitating those negotiations, and offer whatever assistance may be appropriate in the circumstances. Assistance may include a reference of the case to another judicial officer for settlement purposes. MA R USDCT LR 16.4(b).

i. When a case is settled, the parties shall file with the clerk a signed agreement for judgment or stipulation for dismissal, as appropriate, within twenty-eight (28) days, unless the court otherwise orders. MA R USDCT LR 68.2.

b. *Alternative dispute resolution programs*

i. *Discretion of judicial officer.* The judicial officer, following an exploration of the matter with all counsel, may refer appropriate cases to alternative dispute resolution programs that have been designated for use in the district court or that the judicial officer may make available. The dispute resolution programs described in MA R USDCT LR 16.4(c)(2) through MA R USDCT LR 16.4(c)(4) are illustrative, not exclusive. Moreover, nothing in MA R USDCT LR 16.4 shall preclude the parties from engaging in private dispute resolution programs as long as they comply with any schedule established by the court. MA R USDCT LR 16.4(c)(1).

ii. *Mediation.* The judicial officer may refer the case to mediation upon the agreement of all parties. MA R USDCT LR 16.4(c)(2)(A).

iii. *Other alternative dispute resolution programs.* Use of mediation is not exclusive. At the request of parties, the judicial officer may consider other forms of alternative dispute resolution including, but not limited to, mini-trial, summary jury trial and arbitration. MA R USDCT LR 16.4(c)(3).

c. For more information on alternative dispute resolution (ADR), refer to MA R USDCT LR 16.4.

6. *Sanctions.* Failure to comply with any of the directions or obligations set forth in, or authorized by, these rules may result in dismissal, default, or the imposition of other sanctions as deemed appropriate by the judicial officer. MA R USDCT LR 1.3. Except as provided by law, the court may impose sanctions as provided in MA R USDCT LR 1.3 for failure to comply with the Administrative Procedures for Electronic Case Filing in the United States District Court for the District of Massachusetts (MA R USDCT CM/ECF Admin) or with MA R USDCT LR 5.4. MA R USDCT CM/ECF Admin(C)(3).

**D. Documents**

1. *Documents for moving party*

a. *Required documents*

i. *Notice of motion and motion.* Refer to the General Requirements section of this document for information on the notice of motion and motion.

- *Request for oral argument.* Any party making or opposing a motion who believes that oral argument may

275

assist the court and wishes to be heard shall include a request for oral argument in a separate paragraph of the motion or opposition. The request should be set off with a centered caption, "REQUEST FOR ORAL ARGUMENT." MA R USDCT LR 7.1(d).

   ii. *Memorandum.* A party filing a motion shall at the same time file a memorandum of reasons, including citation of supporting authorities, why the motion should be granted. MA R USDCT LR 7.1(b)(1). Any memorandum of law or other attachment filed in support of a main document shall be filed as a separate document, using the proper event. MA R USDCT CM/ECF Admin(G)(4). Memoranda supporting or opposing allowance of motions shall not, without leave of court, exceed twenty (20) pages, double-spaced. MA R USDCT LR 7.1(b)(4).

   iii. *Certificate of service.* No certificate of service is required when a paper is served by filing it with the court's electronic-filing system. When a paper that is required to be served is served by other means: (1) if the paper is filed, a certificate of service must be filed with it or within a reasonable time after service; and (2) if the paper is not filed, a certificate of service need not be filed unless filing is required by court order or by local rule. FRCP 5(d)(1)(B). Except as otherwise provided by the Federal Rules of Civil Procedure, proof of service of all pleadings and other papers required to be served (except discovery papers that in accordance with FRCP 33 to FRCP 36(f) are not to be filed) shall be filed in the office of the clerk promptly after service has been made. The proof shall show the time and manner of service, and may be made by written acknowledgment of service, a certificate of a member of the bar of this court, or an affidavit of the person who served the paper. MA R USDCT LR 5.2(b)(1). A certificate of service of a member of the bar shall appear at the bottom of or on the margin of the last page of the paper to which it relates. MA R USDCT LR 5.2(b)(2).

- *Paper service.* The certificate shall be a brief, single-spaced statement and may be in the following form: I hereby certify that a true copy of the above document was served upon (each party appearing pro se and) the attorney of record for each other party by mail (by hand) on (date). (Signature). MA R USDCT LR 5.2(b)(2).

- *Electronic service.* Any pleading or other paper served by electronic means must bear a certificate of service in accordance with MA R USDCT LR 5.2(b). MA R USDCT LR 5.4(C); MA R USDCT CM/ECF Admin(H)(2). The certificate of service shall state that the filer: (1) filed the document electronically, (2) that it will be served electronically to registered CM/ECF participants via the NEF and (3) that the filer will send paper copies to non-registered participants as indicated on the NEF. MA R USDCT CM/ECF Admin(H)(2). For example: I hereby certify that this document filed through the CM/ECF system will be sent electronically to the registered participants as identified on the NEF (NEF) and paper copies will be sent to those indicated as non registered participants on (date). MA R USDCT CM/ECF Admin(H)(2).

- *Return.* Documents not conforming to the requirements of MA R USDCT LR 5.2 (except notices of appeal) shall be returned by the clerk. MA R USDCT LR 5.2(b)(2).

- *Failure to make proof of service.* Failure to make proof of service does not affect the validity of the service. MA R USDCT LR 5.2(b)(3).

  b. *Supplemental documents*

   i. *Supporting evidence.* When a motion relies on facts outside the record, the court may hear the matter on affidavits or may hear it wholly or partly on oral testimony or on depositions. FRCP 43(c). Affidavits and other documents setting forth or evidencing facts on which the motion is based shall be filed with the motion. MA R USDCT LR 7.1(b)(1).

   ii. *Notice of constitutional question.* A party that files a pleading, written motion, or other paper drawing into question the constitutionality of a federal or state statute must promptly:

- *File notice.* File a notice of constitutional question stating the question and identifying the paper that raises it, if: (1) a federal statute is questioned and the parties do not include the United States, one of its agencies, or one of its officers or employees in an official capacity; or (2) a state statute is questioned and the parties do not include the state, one of its agencies, or one of its officers or employees in an official capacity; and

- *Serve notice.* Serve the notice and paper on the Attorney General of the United States if a federal statute is questioned—or on the state attorney general if a state statute is questioned—either by certified or registered mail or by sending it to an electronic address designated by the attorney general for this purpose. FRCP 5.1(a).

- *No forfeiture.* A party's failure to file and serve the notice, or the court's failure to certify, does not forfeit a constitutional claim or defense that is otherwise timely asserted. FRCP 5.1(d).

iii. *Nongovernmental corporate disclosure statement*

- *Contents.* A nongovernmental corporate party must file two (2) copies of a disclosure statement that: (1) identifies any parent corporation and any publicly held corporation owning ten percent (10%) or more of its stock; or (2) states that there is no such corporation. FRCP 7.1(a).

- *Time to file; Supplemental filing.* A party must: (1) file the disclosure statement with its first appearance, pleading, petition, motion, response, or other request addressed to the court; and (2) promptly file a supplemental statement if any required information changes. FRCP 7.1(b).

iv. *Proposed order.* Proposed orders usually are not required by this court. However, the court may request the party to submit such a document. In those situations, unless otherwise directed by the clerk's office, electronically file the proposed document/order using the entry for "Proposed Documents submitted to the court," found under the Other Documents menu, or as an attachment to the motion to which it relates. MA R USDCT CM/ECF Admin(T).

v. *Compact disk with copy of document(s) in PDF format.* A filer who cannot file a document electronically because of such technical difficulty on the filer's end [with telephone, cable lines, the filer's Internet Service Provider (ISP), or hardware or software problems] shall file the document conventionally along with a copy of the document in PDF format on a compact disk or contact the clerk's office for permission to submit the PDF document via email. MA R USDCT CM/ECF Admin(W)(3). Refer to the Timing section of this document for more information on technical failures.

vi. *Notice of filing with clerk's office.* When documents or exhibits (other than those filed ex parte or under seal) are submitted conventionally, a "Notice of Filing with clerk's office" shall be filed electronically and attached to the main document. A paper copy of the "Notice of Filing with clerk's office" must accompany the documents submitted to the court. The "Notice of Filing with clerk's office" (see MA R USDCT CM/ECF Admin(Appendix I)) shall describe each of the documents that will be filed as paper copies in the clerk's office, or shall include an index of the documents if those documents are voluminous. MA R USDCT CM/ECF Admin(P)(5).

vii. *Additional copies.* Whenever, because of the nature of a proceeding, such as a proceeding before a three-judge district court under 28 U.S.C.A. § 2284, additional copies of a paper required to be filed are necessary either for the use of the court or to enable the clerk to carry out his duties, it is the responsibility of the party filing or having filed the paper to provide the necessary copies. MA R USDCT LR 5.1(d).

viii. *Courtesy copies.* COURTESY COPIES OF DOCUMENTS FILED ELECTRONICALLY SHALL NOT BE SUBMITTED ROUTINELY. MA R USDCT CM/ECF Admin(J). Judicial officers, on a case-by-case basis, may require courtesy copies for specific cases, or types of motions, etc. A few Judicial Officers have entered Standing Orders, which may be found on their respective pages on the court's website (under Divisions). Any document filed on paper with the court as a courtesy copy must be clearly labeled as such (Example: COURTESY COPY—DO NOT SCAN). Documents delivered to the court as a courtesy copy will not be maintained in the official court record. MA R USDCT CM/ECF Admin(J).

2. *Documents for opposing party*

a. *Required documents*

i. *Opposition.* Refer to the General Requirements section of this document for information on the opposing papers.

- *Memorandum.* A party opposing a motion shall file, in the same (rather than a separate), document a memorandum of reasons, including citation of supporting authorities, why the motion should not be granted. MA R USDCT LR 7.1(b)(2). Any memorandum of law or other attachment filed in support of a main document shall be filed as a separate document, using the proper event. MA R USDCT CM/ECF Admin(G)(4). Memoranda supporting or opposing allowance of motions shall not, without leave of court, exceed twenty (20) pages, double-spaced. MA R USDCT LR 7.1(b)(4).

- *Request for oral argument.* Any party making or opposing a motion who believes that oral argument may assist the court and wishes to be heard shall include a request for oral argument in a separate paragraph of the motion or opposition. The request should be set off with a centered caption, "REQUEST FOR ORAL ARGUMENT." MA R USDCT LR 7.1(d).

ii. *Certificate of service.* No certificate of service is required when a paper is served by filing it with the court's electronic-filing system. When a paper that is required to be served is served by other means: (1) if the paper is filed, a certificate of service must be filed with it or within a reasonable time after service; and (2) if the paper is not filed, a certificate of service need not be filed unless filing is required by court order or by local rule. FRCP

5(d)(1)(B). Except as otherwise provided by the Federal Rules of Civil Procedure, proof of service of all pleadings and other papers required to be served (except discovery papers that in accordance with FRCP 33 to FRCP 36(f) are not to be filed) shall be filed in the office of the clerk promptly after service has been made. The proof shall show the time and manner of service, and may be made by written acknowledgment of service, a certificate of a member of the bar of this court, or an affidavit of the person who served the paper. MA R USDCT LR 5.2(b)(1). A certificate of service of a member of the bar shall appear at the bottom of or on the margin of the last page of the paper to which it relates. MA R USDCT LR 5.2(b)(2).

- *Paper service.* The certificate shall be a brief, single-spaced statement and may be in the following form: I hereby certify that a true copy of the above document was served upon (each party appearing pro se and) the attorney of record for each other party by mail (by hand) on (date). (Signature). MA R USDCT LR 5.2(b)(2).

- *Electronic service.* Any pleading or other paper served by electronic means must bear a certificate of service in accordance with MA R USDCT LR 5.2(b). MA R USDCT LR 5.4(C); MA R USDCT CM/ECF Admin(H)(2). The certificate of service shall state that the filer: (1) filed the document electronically, (2) that it will be served electronically to registered CM/ECF participants via the NEF and (3) that the filer will send paper copies to non-registered participants as indicated on the NEF. MA R USDCT CM/ECF Admin(H)(2). For example: I hereby certify that this document filed through the CM/ECF system will be sent electronically to the registered participants as identified on the NEF (NEF) and paper copies will be sent to those indicated as non registered participants on (date). MA R USDCT CM/ECF Admin(H)(2).

- *Return.* Documents not conforming to the requirements of MA R USDCT LR 5.2 (except notices of appeal) shall be returned by the clerk. MA R USDCT LR 5.2(b)(2).

- *Failure to make proof of service.* Failure to make proof of service does not affect the validity of the service. MA R USDCT LR 5.2(b)(3).

b. *Supplemental documents*

  i. *Supporting evidence.* When a motion relies on facts outside the record, the court may hear the matter on affidavits or may hear it wholly or partly on oral testimony or on depositions. FRCP 43(c). Affidavits and other documents setting forth or evidencing facts on which the opposition is based shall be filed with the opposition. MA R USDCT LR 7.1(b)(2).

  ii. *Notice of constitutional question.* A party that files a pleading, written motion, or other paper drawing into question the constitutionality of a federal or state statute must promptly:

  - *File notice.* File a notice of constitutional question stating the question and identifying the paper that raises it, if: (1) a federal statute is questioned and the parties do not include the United States, one of its agencies, or one of its officers or employees in an official capacity; or (2) a state statute is questioned and the parties do not include the state, one of its agencies, or one of its officers or employees in an official capacity; and

  - *Serve notice.* Serve the notice and paper on the Attorney General of the United States if a federal statute is questioned—or on the state attorney general if a state statute is questioned—either by certified or registered mail or by sending it to an electronic address designated by the attorney general for this purpose. FRCP 5.1(a).

  - *No forfeiture.* A party's failure to file and serve the notice, or the court's failure to certify, does not forfeit a constitutional claim or defense that is otherwise timely asserted. FRCP 5.1(d).

  iii. *Compact disk with copy of document(s) in PDF format.* A filer who cannot file a document electronically because of such technical difficulty on the filer's end [with telephone, cable lines, the filer's Internet Service Provider (ISP), or hardware or software problems] shall file the document conventionally along with a copy of the document in PDF format on a compact disk or contact the clerk's office for permission to submit the PDF document via email. MA R USDCT CM/ECF Admin(W)(3). Refer to the Timing section of this document for more information on technical failures.

  iv. *Notice of filing with clerk's office.* When documents or exhibits (other than those filed ex parte or under seal) are submitted conventionally, a "Notice of Filing with clerk's office" shall be filed electronically and attached to the main document. A paper copy of the "Notice of Filing with clerk's office" must accompany the documents submitted to the court. The "Notice of Filing with clerk's office" (see MA R USDCT CM/ECF Admin(Appendix I)) shall describe each of the documents that will be filed as paper copies in the clerk's office, or shall include an index of the documents if those documents are voluminous. MA R USDCT CM/ECF Admin(P)(5).

    v. *Additional copies.* Whenever, because of the nature of a proceeding, such as a proceeding before a three-judge district court under 28 U.S.C.A. § 2284, additional copies of a paper required to be filed are necessary either for the use of the court or to enable the clerk to carry out his duties, it is the responsibility of the party filing or having filed the paper to provide the necessary copies. MA R USDCT LR 5.1(d).

    vi. *Courtesy copies.* COURTESY COPIES OF DOCUMENTS FILED ELECTRONICALLY SHALL NOT BE SUBMITTED ROUTINELY. MA R USDCT CM/ECF Admin(J). Judicial officers, on a case-by-case basis, may require courtesy copies for specific cases, or types of motions, etc. A few Judicial Officers have entered Standing Orders, which may be found on their respective pages on the court's website (under Divisions). Any document filed on paper with the court as a courtesy copy must be clearly labeled as such (Example: COURTESY COPY—DO NOT SCAN). Documents delivered to the court as a courtesy copy will not be maintained in the official court record. MA R USDCT CM/ECF Admin(J).

## E. Format

1. *Form of documents.* The rules governing captions and other matters of form in pleadings apply to motions and other papers. FRCP 7(b)(2). The provisions of FRCP 10 and FRCP 11 concerning the form and signing of pleadings, motions, and other papers shall be applicable to all papers filed in any proceeding in this court. The board of bar overseers registration number of each attorney signing such documents, except the United States Attorney and his or her staff, shall be inscribed below the signature. MA R USDCT LR 5.1(a)(1).

    a. *Paper size and binding.* All papers filed in the court shall be adapted for flat filing, be filed on eight and one-half by eleven (8-1/2 x 11) inch paper without backers and be bound firmly by staple or some such other means (excluding paper or binder clip or rubber band). MA R USDCT LR 5.1(a)(2).

    b. *Spacing.* All papers, except discovery requests and responses, shall be double-spaced except for the identification of counsel, title of the case, footnotes, quotations and exhibits. Discovery requests and responses shall be single-spaced. MA R USDCT LR 5.1(a)(2).

    c. *Caption.* Every pleading must have a caption with the court's name, a title, a file number, and [an] FRCP 7(a) designation. FRCP 10(a).

        i. *Names of parties.* The title of the complaint must name all the parties; the title of other pleadings, after naming the first party on each side, may refer generally to other parties. FRCP 10(a).

        ii. *Request for special action.* When any pleading or other paper filed in the court includes a request for special process or relief, or any other request such that, if granted, the court will proceed other than in the ordinary course, the request shall, unless it is noted on the category sheet [see MA R USDCT LR 40.1(a)(1)], be noted on the first page to the right of or immediately beneath the caption. MA R USDCT LR 5.1(c).

    d. *Claims or defenses*

        i. *Numbered paragraphs.* A party must state its claims or defenses in numbered paragraphs, each limited as far as practicable to a single set of circumstances. A later pleading may refer by number to a paragraph in an earlier pleading. FRCP 10(b).

        ii. *Separate statements.* If doing so would promote clarity, each claim founded on a separate transaction or occurrence—and each defense other than a denial—must be stated in a separate count or defense. FRCP 10(b).

    e. *Adoption by reference.* A statement in a pleading may be adopted by reference elsewhere in the same pleading or in any other pleading or motion. FRCP 10(c).

        i. *Exhibits.* A copy of a written instrument that is an exhibit to a pleading is a part of the pleading for all purposes. FRCP 10(c).

    f. *Citations*

        i. *Local rules.* These rules shall be known as Local Rules of the United States District Court for the District of Massachusetts and cited as "L.R., D. Mass." or "L.R." MA R USDCT LR 1.1.

        ii. *Electronic case filing procedures.* The procedures governing electronic case filing shall be known as the "Administrative Procedures for Electronic Case Filing in the United States District Court for the District of Massachusetts." They shall be cited as "APECF." MA R USDCT CM/ECF Admin(A)(7).

    g. *Acceptance by the clerk.* The clerk must not refuse to file a paper solely because it is not in the form prescribed by the Federal Rules of Civil Procedure or by a local rule or practice. FRCP 5(d)(4).

        i. Except for complaints and notices of appeal, papers that do not conform to the requirements of MA R USDCT LR 5.1(a)(2) shall be returned by the clerk. MA R USDCT LR 5.1(a)(2).

2. *Form of electronic documents.* A paper filed electronically is a written paper for purposes of the Federal Rules of Civil Procedure. FRCP 5(d)(3)(D).

 a. *PDF/A format required.* The court will begin requiring submission of documents in PDF/A format in the foreseeable future. PDF/A is an enhanced version of the traditional PDF format. Newer versions of most PDF software will be able to convert to this format. Additional information on PDF/A documents may be found on the court's website. MA R USDCT CM/ECF Admin(Electronic Filing and PDF).

  i. *Electronically converted PDF.* Electronically converted PDF documents are created from word processing documents (MS Word, WordPerfect, etc.) using any appropriate software. These documents are text searchable and the file size is generally smaller than a scanned document. CM/ECF users may use any brand of software to convert documents to PDF. MA R USDCT CM/ECF Admin(Electronic Filing and PDF).

   • Documents converted to PDF, rather than scanned, are preferred for filing in CM/ECF. MA R USDCT CM/ECF Admin(Electronic Filing and PDF).

  ii. *Scanned PDF.* Scanned PDF documents are created from paper documents run through an optical scanner. Scanned PDF documents are generally not searchable and have a larger file size. Please note that software used to create scanned documents may (and should) be set in such a way that the document is "text-searchable." MA R USDCT CM/ECF Admin(Electronic Filing and PDF).

 b. *Title.* All pleadings filed electronically shall be titled in accordance with the approved dictionary of civil or criminal events of the CM/ECF system of this court. A list of events is available on the CM/ECF Training Information page of the court's website. The clerk's office may, when necessary and appropriate, modify the docket entry description, or delete and re-enter the docket entry in order to comply with the court's quality assurance standards. MA R USDCT CM/ECF Admin(G)(3).

 c. *Attachments to filings and exhibits.* Attachments to filings and exhibits must be filed in accordance with the court's CM/ECF User Manual, unless otherwise ordered by the court. MA R USDCT CM/ECF Admin(O)(1).

  i. Filers must submit as attachments only those excerpts of the referenced documents that are directly germane to the matter under consideration by the court. Excerpted material must be clearly and prominently identified as such. Users who file excerpts of documents do so without prejudice to their right to timely file additional excerpts or the complete document, as may be allowed by the court. Responding parties may timely file additional excerpts or the complete document that they believe are directly germane. MA R USDCT CM/ECF Admin(O)(2).

  ii. Filers shall not attach as an exhibit any pleading or other paper already on file with the court in that case, but shall merely refer to that document. (See MA R USDCT CM/ECF Admin(G) for information on using hyperlinks in PDF documents filed in CM/ECF.) MA R USDCT CM/ECF Admin(O)(3).

 d. *Redacted documents.* The parties may request or the court may require the submission of documents that have been redacted/stripped of sensitive or confidential information. The redacted document prepared for electronic filing shall include the original caption of the document, and be clearly labeled as "Redacted Document." A specific event is available for this purpose ("Redacted Document"), found under the Other Filings/Other Documents menu option. MA R USDCT CM/ECF Admin(S).

  i. Attorneys and pro se litigants are advised to take extra care when creating PDF documents intended for submission to CM/ECF. Steps shall be taken to ensure the documents are free of any hidden data (metadata) that may contain redacted information, or traces of information edited or deleted are not hidden in the final document. Even PDF content that has been encrypted may be recovered. An advisory document with additional information on this topic may be found on the court's website. MA R USDCT CM/ECF Admin(S).

 e. *Hyperlinks.* Electronically filed documents may contain the following types of hyperlinks: (1) hyperlinks to other portions of the same document; (2) hyperlinks to other documents filed within the CM/ECF system; and (3) hyperlinks to a location on the Internet that contains a source document for a citation. MA R USDCT CM/ECF Admin(G)(7).

  i. Hyperlinks to cited authority may not replace standard citation format. Complete citations must be included in the text of the filed document. Neither a hyperlink, nor any site to which it refers, shall be considered part of the record, but are simply convenient mechanisms for accessing material cited in a document filed in CM/ECF. Instructions on creating hyperlinks may be found in the CM/ECF User Manual. MA R USDCT CM/ECF Admin(G)(7).

  ii. The court accepts no responsibility for, and does not endorse, any product, organization, or content at any

hyperlinked site, or at any site to which that site may be linked. The court accepts no responsibility for the availability or functionality of any hyperlink. MA R USDCT CM/ECF Admin(G)(7).

   iii.   One feature of PDF/A documents is that hyperlinks are commonly "masked," meaning that the full address of the referenced file is not written out; for example, clicking the word brief may open a brief which was previously filed in CM/ECF. MA R USDCT CM/ECF Admin(G)(7)(NOTE). An "unmasked" hyperlink has the full address visible to the user. MA R USDCT CM/ECF Admin(G)(7)(NOTE).

- Masked hyperlinks may or may not work in a PDF/A document, depending on how it was created. Currently, masked hyperlinks are preserved in PDF/A documents produced by the "Save As" method in Microsoft Word 2007 and 2010; the "PDFMaker" method in Microsoft Word 2007; and OpenOffice 2.4 ("PDF Export"). With other production methods, such as WordPerfect, the PDF/A document includes underlined words that appear to be links, but clicking them has no effect. MA R USDCT CM/ECF Admin(G)(7)(NOTE).

  f.  *Documents features not accepted.* CM/ECF will not accept PDF documents containing tracking tags, embedded systems commands, password protections, access restrictions or other security features, special tags or dynamic features. MA R USDCT CM/ECF Admin(G)(8).

  g.  *File size limitations.* A filing party shall limit the size of each PDF file to no more than twenty (20) megabytes. PDF files larger than seven (7) megabytes will be rejected by the CM/ECF system. The filer will see a message advising of the size limitation. MA R USDCT CM/ECF Admin(P)(2).

   i.   Larger documents or exhibits may be submitted electronically if split into separate PDF files each less than seven (7) megabytes, attached to the main document and clearly labeled. MA R USDCT CM/ECF Admin(P)(2).

   ii.   Documents submitted electronically or on paper are subject to the page limitations set by MA R USDCT LR 7.1(b)(4) or by order of the court. MA R USDCT CM/ECF Admin(P)(1).

  h.  *Accuracy and readability.* The filer shall verify the accuracy and readability of any PDF file before electronically filing it in CM/ECF. MA R USDCT CM/ECF Admin(G)(6); MA R USDCT CM/ECF Admin(P)(3).

3.  *Signing of pleadings, motions and other papers*

  a.  *Signature.* Every pleading, written motion, and other paper must be signed by at least one attorney of record in the attorney's name—or by a party personally if the party is unrepresented. The paper must state the signer's address, e-mail address, and telephone number. FRCP 11(a). The provisions of the Federal Rules of Civil Procedure pertaining to the form and signing of pleadings, motions, and other papers shall be applicable to all papers filed in any proceeding in this court. The board of bar overseers registration number of each attorney signing such documents, except the United States Attorney and his staff, shall be inscribed below the signature. MA R USDCT LR 5.1(a)(1).

   i.   *Electronic signing.* A filing made through a person's electronic-filing account and authorized by that person, together with that person's name on a signature block, constitutes the person's signature. FRCP 5(d)(3)(C).

   ii.   *Appearances.* The filing of an appearance or any other pleading signed on behalf of a party constitutes an entry of appearance for that party. All pleadings shall contain the name, bar admission number, address, telephone number, and e-mail address of the attorney entering an appearance. MA R USDCT LR 83.5.2(a).

- *Appearances by law firms.* When a party is represented by a law firm, the appearance must include the name and the signature of at least one individual attorney. When a party is represented by more than one attorney from the same or different law firms, the attorney entering the appearance must designate the individual attorney who is authorized to receive all notices in the case. Any notice sent to an attorney so designated shall be deemed to be proper notice unless the court finds that notice was not properly sent. MA R USDCT LR 83.5.2(b).

- For more information on appearances, refer to MA R USDCT LR 83.5.2.

   iii.   *Signatures of attorneys.* The user login and password required to submit documents to the CM/ECF system shall serve as that user's signature for purposes of FRCP 11 and for all other purposes under the Federal Rules of Civil Procedure and the Local Rules of the United States District Court for the District of Massachusetts. All electronically filed documents must include a signature block and must set forth the attorney's name, bar number, address, telephone number and email address. The name of the CM/ECF user under whose log-in and password the document is submitted must be preceded by a "/s/" and typed in the space where the signature would otherwise appear. MA R USDCT CM/ECF Admin(M)(1). For an example, refer to MA R USDCT CM/ECF Admin(M)(1).

   iv.   *Signatures of pro se parties.* Any document requiring a signature that is filed by a party appearing pro se shall

bear the words "pro se" following that party's signature. Any such document shall also state the party's mailing address, telephone number (if any), and e-mail address (if the party has consented to service by email). MA R USDCT LR 83.5.5(g). For more information on practice by pro se litigants, refer to MA R USDCT LR 83.5.5.

v.  *Multiple signatures.* The filer of any document requiring more than one signature (e.g, stipulations, joint motions, joint status reports, magistrate judge consent forms, etc.) must list thereon all the names of other signatories by means of a "/s/ name of signatory" block for each. By submitting such a document, the filing attorney certifies that each of the other signatories has expressly agreed to the form and substance of the document and that the filing attorney has their actual authority to submit the document electronically. MA R USDCT CM/ECF Admin(M)(2). For more information, refer to MA R USDCT CM/ECF Admin(M)(2).

vi.  *Affidavits.* Except as provided in MA R USDCT CM/ECF Admin(L), affidavits shall be filed electronically; however, the electronically filed version must contain a "/s/ name of signatory" block indicating that the paper document bears an original signature. MA R USDCT CM/ECF Admin(M)(3). The court will also accept a scanned version of the original, signed document. MA R USDCT CM/ECF Admin(M)(3). For more information, refer to MA R USDCT CM/ECF Admin(M)(3).

vii.  *No verification or accompanying affidavit required for pleadings.* Unless a rule or statute specifically states otherwise, a pleading need not be verified or accompanied by an affidavit. FRCP 11(a).

viii.  *Unsigned papers.* The court must strike an unsigned paper unless the omission is promptly corrected after being called to the attorney's or party's attention. FRCP 11(a).

b.  *Representations to the court.* By presenting to the court a pleading, written motion, or other paper—whether by signing, filing, submitting, or later advocating it—an attorney or unrepresented party certifies that to the best of the person's knowledge, information, and belief, formed after an inquiry reasonable under the circumstances:

i.  It is not being presented for any improper purpose, such as to harass, cause unnecessary delay, or needlessly increase the cost of litigation;

ii.  The claims, defenses, and other legal contentions are warranted by existing law or by a nonfrivolous argument for extending, modifying, or reversing existing law or for establishing new law;

iii.  The factual contentions have evidentiary support or, if specifically so identified, will likely have evidentiary support after a reasonable opportunity for further investigation or discovery; and

iv.  The denials of factual contentions are warranted on the evidence or, if specifically so identified, are reasonably based on belief or a lack of information. FRCP 11(b).

c.  *Sanctions.* If, after notice and a reasonable opportunity to respond, the court determines that FRCP 11(b) has been violated, the court may impose an appropriate sanction on any attorney, law firm, or party that violated FRCP 11(b) or is responsible for the violation. FRCP 11(c)(1). Refer to the United States District Court for the District of Massachusetts KeyRules Motion for Sanctions document for more information.

4.  *Privacy protection for filings made with the court*

a.  *Redacted filings.* Unless the court orders otherwise, in an electronic or paper filing with the court that contains an individual's Social Security number, taxpayer-identification number, or birth date, the name of an individual known to be a minor, or a financial-account number, a party or nonparty making the filing may include only:

i.  The last four (4) digits of the Social Security number and taxpayer-identification number;

ii.  The year of the individual's birth;

iii.  The minor's initials; and

iv.  The last four (4) digits of the financial-account number. FRCP 5.2(a); MA R USDCT CM/ECF Admin(N).

b.  *Exemptions from the redaction requirement.* The redaction requirement does not apply to the following:

i.  A financial-account number that identifies the property allegedly subject to forfeiture in a forfeiture proceeding;

ii.  The record of an administrative or agency proceeding;

iii.  The official record of a state-court proceeding;

iv.  The record of a court or tribunal, if that record was not subject to the redaction requirement when originally filed;

v.  A filing covered by FRCP 5.2(c) or FRCP 5.2(d); and

vi.  A pro se filing in an action brought under 28 U.S.C.A. § 2241, 28 U.S.C.A. § 2254, or 28 U.S.C.A. § 2255. FRCP 5.2(b).

c. *Limitations on remote access to electronic files; Social Security appeals and immigration cases.* Unless the court orders otherwise, in an action for benefits under the Social Security Act, and in an action or proceeding relating to an order of removal, to relief from removal, or to immigration benefits or detention, access to an electronic file is authorized as follows:

   i. The parties and their attorneys may have remote electronic access to any part of the case file, including the administrative record;

   ii. Any other person may have electronic access to the full record at the courthouse, but may have remote electronic access only to:

   - The docket maintained by the court; and

   - An opinion, order, judgment, or other disposition of the court, but not any other part of the case file or the administrative record. FRCP 5.2(c).

d. *Filings made under seal.* The court may order that a filing be made under seal without redaction. The court may later unseal the filing or order the person who made the filing to file a redacted version for the public record. FRCP 5.2(d).

e. *Protective orders.* For good cause, the court may by order in a case:

   i. Require redaction of additional information; or

   ii. Limit or prohibit a nonparty's remote electronic access to a document filed with the court. FRCP 5.2(e).

f. *Option for additional unredacted filing under seal.* A person making a redacted filing may also file an unredacted copy under seal. The court must retain the unredacted copy as part of the record. FRCP 5.2(f). For more information, refer to MA R USDCT LR 7.2.

g. *Option for filing a reference list.* A filing that contains redacted information may be filed together with a reference list that identifies each item of redacted information and specifies an appropriate identifier that uniquely corresponds to each item listed. The list must be filed under seal and may be amended as of right. Any reference in the case to a listed identifier will be construed to refer to the corresponding item of information. FRCP 5.2(g).

h. *Responsibility for redaction.* The clerk's office is not responsible for reviewing documents filed with the court to determine whether pleadings have been redacted and are in the proper form. MA R USDCT CM/ECF Admin(N).

i. *Waiver of protection of identifiers.* A person waives the protection of FRCP 5.2(a) as to the person's own information by filing it without redaction and not under seal. FRCP 5.2(h).

## F. Filing and Service Requirements

1. *Filing requirements*

   a. *Required filings.* Any paper after the complaint that is required to be served must be filed no later than a reasonable time after service. FRCP 5(d)(1).

      i. Except as noted in FRCP 33 to FRCP 36, the original of all papers required to be served under FRCP 5(d) shall, unless otherwise submitted to the court, be filed in the office of the clerk within seven (7) days after service has been made. MA R USDCT LR 5.1(b). Except as otherwise provided by the Federal Rules of Civil Procedure, proof of service of all pleadings and other papers required to be served (except discovery papers that in accordance with FRCP 33 to FRCP 36(f) are not to be filed) shall be filed in the office of the clerk promptly after service has been made. MA R USDCT LR 5.2(b)(1).

   b. *Nonelectronic filing.* A paper not filed electronically is filed by delivering it: (1) to the clerk; or (2) to a judge who agrees to accept it for filing, and who must then note the filing date on the paper and promptly send it to the clerk. FRCP 5(d)(2).

   c. *Electronic filing.* Unless exempt or otherwise ordered by the court, all pleadings and other papers submitted to the court must be filed, signed, and verified by electronic means as provided in MA R USDCT LR 5.4. MA R USDCT LR 5.4(A); MA R USDCT CM/ECF Admin(A)(1). All electronic filings must be made in accordance with the Administrative Procedures for Electronic Case Filing in the United States District Court for the District of Massachusetts (MA R USDCT CM/ECF Admin). MA R USDCT LR 5.4(B). The court may deviate from the Administrative Procedures for Electronic Case Filing in the United States District Court for the District of Massachusetts (MA R USDCT CM/ECF Admin) in specific cases, without prior notice, if deemed appropriate in the exercise of discretion, considering the need for the just, speedy, and inexpensive determination of matters pending before the court. MA R USDCT CM/ECF Admin(C)(1). The court may excuse a failure to comply with any administrative procedure whenever justice so requires. MA R USDCT CM/ECF Admin(C)(2).

      i. *By a represented person; Generally required; Exceptions.* A person represented by an attorney must file

electronically, unless nonelectronic filing is allowed by the court for good cause or is allowed or required by local rule. FRCP 5(d)(3)(A).

ii. *By unrepresented person; When allowed or required.* A person not represented by an attorney: (1) may file electronically only if allowed by court order or by local rule; and (2) may be required to file electronically only by court order, or by a local rule that includes reasonable exceptions. FRCP 5(d)(3)(B).

iii. *Exemptions from electronic filing*

- *Documents that should not be filed electronically.* The following types of documents must not be filed electronically, and will not be scanned into the ECF system by the clerk's office: (1) sealed documents; (2) ex parte motions; (3) documents generated as part of an alternative dispute resolution (ADR) process; (4) the administrative record in Social Security and other administrative proceedings; (5) the state court record in proceedings under 28 U.S.C.A. § 2254; and (6) such other types of documents as the clerk may direct in the Administrative Procedures for Electronic Case Filing in the United States District Court for the District of Massachusetts (MA R USDCT CM/ECF Admin). MA R USDCT LR 5.4(G)(1); MA R USDCT CM/ECF Admin(L).

- *Documents that need not be filed electronically.* The following types of documents need not be filed electronically, but may be scanned into the ECF system by a filing party or the clerk's office: (1) handwritten pleadings; (2) documents filed by pro se litigants who are incarcerated or who are not registered ECF users; (3) indictments, informations, criminal complaints, and the criminal JS45 form; (4) affidavits for search or arrest warrants and related documents; (5) documents received from another court under FRCRP 20 or FRCRP 40; (6) appearance bonds; (7) any document in a criminal case containing the original signature of a defendant, such as a waiver of indictment or a plea agreement; (8) petitions for violations of supervised release; (9) executed service of process documents under FRCP 4; and (10) such other types of documents as the clerk may direct in the Administrative Procedures for Electronic Case Filing in the United States District Court for the District of Massachusetts (MA R USDCT CM/ECF Admin). MA R USDCT LR 5.4(G)(2); MA R USDCT CM/ECF Admin(L).

- For more information on exemptions from electronic filing, refer to MA R USDCT CM/ECF Admin(L).

iv. *Consequences of electronic filing.* Electronic transmission of a document to the CM/ECF system, together with the transmission of a Notice of Electronic Filing (NEF) from the court at the completion of the transaction, constitutes the filing of the document for all purposes of the Federal Rules of Procedure and constitutes entry of the document on the docket maintained by the clerk pursuant to FRCP 58 and FRCP 79. MA R USDCT CM/ECF Admin(G)(1).

v. *Payment of filing fees.* When electronically filing any pleading or paper through CM/ECF that requires a fee, all registered ECF users are to pay the fee electronically through the Treasury Department's Internet payment process. MA R USDCT LR 67.4(d); MA R USDCT CM/ECF Admin(A)(1). Pro se filers and those who have been exempted from electronic filing and/or electronic payment of fees may submit payments by check or money order made payable to "Clerk, U.S. District Court". MA R USDCT LR 67.4(d). For more information on filing fees, refer to MA R USDCT LR 67.4 and MA R USDCT CM/ECF Admin(I).

vi. For more information on electronic filing, refer to MA R USDCT CM/ECF Admin.

d. *Email or fax filing.* In general, the court does not accept documents by email or by fax. If the court, in special circumstances, does authorize the submission of a document in that manner, the document shall not be considered filed until an NEF is generated by CM/ECF at the completion of the transaction. MA R USDCT CM/ECF Admin(H)(5).

2. *Service requirements.* All papers filed pursuant to MA R USDCT LR 7.1(b) shall be served unless the moving party indicates in writing on the face of the motion that ex parte consideration is requested. Motions filed "ex parte" and related papers need not be served until the motion has been ruled upon or the court orders that service be made. MA R USDCT LR 7.1(c). Service of all pleadings subsequent to the original complaint and of all other papers required to be served shall be made in the manner specified by FRCP 5. MA R USDCT LR 5.2(a).

a. *Service; When required*

i. *In general.* Unless the Federal Rules of Civil Procedure provide otherwise, each of the following papers must be served on every party:

- An order stating that service is required;

- A pleading filed after the original complaint, unless the court orders otherwise under FRCP 5(c) because there are numerous defendants;

- A discovery paper required to be served on a party, unless the court orders otherwise;
- A written motion, except one that may be heard ex parte; and
- A written notice, appearance, demand, or offer of judgment, or any similar paper. FRCP 5(a)(1).

ii. *If a party fails to appear.* No service is required on a party who is in default for failing to appear. But a pleading that asserts a new claim for relief against such a party must be served on that party under FRCP 4. FRCP 5(a)(2).

iii. *Seizing property.* If an action is begun by seizing property and no person is or need be named as a defendant, any service required before the filing of an appearance, answer, or claim must be made on the person who had custody or possession of the property when it was seized. FRCP 5(a)(3).

b. *Service; How made*

i. *Serving an attorney.* If a party is represented by an attorney, service under FRCP 5 must be made on the attorney unless the court orders service on the party. FRCP 5(b)(1).

- *Nonresident attorney.* On application of a party, the court may order an attorney who represents any other party and who does not maintain an office within this district where service can be made on him by delivery as provided by FRCP 5(b), to designate a member of the bar of this court who does maintain such an office to receive service of all pleadings and other papers in his behalf. MA R USDCT LR 5.2(c)(1).

ii. *Serving a party acting pro se.* On application of a party, the court may order any other party who is appearing without an attorney and who does not maintain an office or residence within this district where service can be made on him by delivery as provided by FRCP 5(b), to designate an address within the district at which service can be made on him by delivery. MA R USDCT LR 5.2(c)(2).

iii. *Service in general.* A paper is served under FRCP 5 by:

- Handing it to the person;
- Leaving it: (1) at the person's office with a clerk or other person in charge or, if no one is in charge, in a conspicuous place in the office; or (2) if the person has no office or the office is closed, at the person's dwelling or usual place of abode with someone of suitable age and discretion who resides there;
- Mailing it to the person's last known address—in which event service is complete upon mailing;
- Leaving it with the court clerk if the person has no known address;
- Sending it to a registered user by filing it with the court's electronic-filing system or sending it by other electronic means that the person consented to in writing—in either of which events service is complete upon filing or sending, but is not effective if the filer or sender learns that it did not reach the person to be served; or
- Delivering it by any other means that the person consented to in writing—in which event service is complete when the person making service delivers it to the agency designated to make delivery. FRCP 5(b)(2).

iv. *Service by electronic means.* Unless exempt or otherwise ordered by the court, all pleadings and other papers must be served on other parties by electronic means. MA R USDCT LR 5.4(C); MA R USDCT CM/ECF Admin(H)(2). Service by electronic means shall be treated the same as service by mail. MA R USDCT CM/ECF Admin(H)(4).

- *Consent to electronic service.* Registering to use CM/ECF constitutes consent to service of all documents by electronic means as provided in the Administrative Procedures for Electronic Case Filing in the United States District Court for the District of Massachusetts (MA R USDCT CM/ECF Admin) and FRCP 5(b) and FRCP 77(d). MA R USDCT CM/ECF Admin(E)(6); MA R USDCT CM/ECF Admin(H)(3).

- *Service on registered ECF users.* Transmission of the Notice of Electronic Filing (NEF) through the court's transmission facilities will constitute service of the filed document upon a registered ECF user. MA R USDCT LR 5.4(C).

- *Service on non-registered users.* The party filing the document electronically is responsible for serving a paper copy of the document by mail in accordance with FRCP 5(b) to those case participants who have not been identified on the NEF as electronic recipients. MA R USDCT CM/ECF Admin(H)(3).

- *Service of conventionally filed papers.* Documents or exhibits submitted conventionally shall be served on other parties by the filer using traditional means. MA R USDCT CM/ECF Admin(P)(4).

    c. *Serving numerous defendants*

        i. *In general.* If an action involves an unusually large number of defendants, the court may, on motion or on its own, order that:

- Defendants' pleadings and replies to them need not be served on other defendants;

- Any crossclaim, counterclaim, avoidance, or affirmative defense in those pleadings and replies to them will be treated as denied or avoided by all other parties; and

- Filing any such pleading and serving it on the plaintiff constitutes notice of the pleading to all parties. FRCP 5(c)(1).

        ii. *Notifying parties.* A copy of every such order must be served on the parties as the court directs. FRCP 5(c)(2).

## G. Hearings

1. *Hearings, generally.* If the court concludes that there should be a hearing on a motion, the motion will be set down for hearing at such time as the court determines. MA R USDCT LR 7.1(e).

    a. *Oral argument.* Due process does not require that oral argument be permitted on a motion and, except as otherwise provided by local rule, the district court has discretion to determine whether it will decide the motion on the papers or hear argument by counsel (and perhaps receive evidence). FPP § 1190; F.D.I.C. v. Deglau, 207 F.3d 153 (3d Cir. 2000).

        i. *Evidence on a motion.* When a motion relies on facts outside the record, the court may hear the matter on affidavits or may hear it wholly or partly on oral testimony or on depositions. FRCP 43(c).

    b. *Providing a regular schedule for oral hearings.* A court may establish regular times and places for oral hearings on motions. FRCP 78(a).

    c. *Providing for submission on briefs.* By rule or order, the court may provide for submitting and determining motions on briefs, without oral hearings. FRCP 78(b). Motions that are not set down for hearing as provided in MA R USDCT LR 7.1(e) will be decided on the papers submitted after an opposition to the motion has been filed, or, if no opposition is filed, after the time for filing an opposition has elapsed. MA R USDCT LR 7.1(f).

2. *Hearing on certain FRCP 12 defenses before trial.* If a party so moves, any defense listed in FRCP 12(b)(1) through FRCP 12(b)(7)—whether made in a pleading or by motion—and a motion under FRCP 12(c) must be heard and decided before trial unless the court orders a deferral until trial. FRCP 12(i).

3. *Hearing on motion to dismiss for lack of subject matter jurisdiction.* It may be error for a court to dismiss a case on the defendant's motion to dismiss for lack of subject-matter jurisdiction without first holding a hearing, as FRCP 12(b)(1) requires a preliminary hearing or hearing at trial to determine any disputed facts upon which the motion or opposition to it is predicated. FEDPROC § 62:429.

4. *Conflict of court appearances.* For information on conflict of court appearances, refer to MA R USDCT LR 40.2.

## H. Forms

### 1. Federal Motion to Dismiss for Lack of Subject Matter Jurisdiction Forms

    a. Motion to dismiss for lack of subject-matter jurisdiction. 2C FEDFORMS § 11:35.

    b. Motion to dismiss for lack of subject-matter jurisdiction; Want of diversity of citizenship because requisite diversity not alleged. 2C FEDFORMS § 11:37.

    c. Motion to dismiss for lack of subject-matter jurisdiction; Want of diversity on a factual basis and because requisite diversity not alleged. 2C FEDFORMS § 11:38.

    d. Motion to dismiss for lack of subject-matter jurisdiction; Want of diversity of citizenship because state of incorporation and principal place of business of defendant not as alleged. 2C FEDFORMS § 11:39.

    e. Motion to dismiss for lack of subject-matter jurisdiction; Want of diversity of citizenship because principal place of business of defendant not as alleged. 2C FEDFORMS § 11:40.

    f. Motion to dismiss for lack of subject-matter jurisdiction; Failure to comply with procedural requirements. 2C FEDFORMS § 11:41.

    g. Motion to dismiss for lack of subject-matter jurisdiction; Want of diversity upon realignment of parties according to interest. 2C FEDFORMS § 11:42.

    h. Motion to dismiss for lack of subject-matter jurisdiction; Want of federal question. 2C FEDFORMS § 11:43.

i. Motion to dismiss for lack of subject-matter jurisdiction; Unsubstantial federal question. 2C FEDFORMS § 11:44.

j. Motion to dismiss for lack of subject-matter jurisdiction; Want of amount in controversy. 2C FEDFORMS § 11:45.

k. Motion to dismiss for lack of subject-matter jurisdiction; Want of amount in controversy; Insurance policy limits do not exceed required jurisdictional amount. 2C FEDFORMS § 11:46.

l. Motion to dismiss for lack of subject-matter jurisdiction; Want of amount in controversy; Claim for damages in excess of jurisdictional amount not made in good faith. 2C FEDFORMS § 11:47.

m. Motion to dismiss for lack of subject-matter jurisdiction; Want of amount in controversy; Made after judgment. 2C FEDFORMS § 11:48.

n. Motion to dismiss for lack of subject-matter jurisdiction; Want of consent by the United States to be sued. 2C FEDFORMS § 11:49.

o. Motion to dismiss for lack of subject-matter jurisdiction; Want of consent by United States to be sued; United States indispensable party. 2C FEDFORMS § 11:50.

p. Motion; To dismiss; Plaintiff and defendant citizens of same state when action filed. FEDPROF § 1C:72.

q. Motion to dismiss; Assignment to nonresident for purpose of invoking federal jurisdiction sham and ineffective to confer jurisdiction. FEDPROF § 1C:73.

r. Motion to dismiss; For lack of diversity in third-party complaint. FEDPROF § 1C:74.

s. Affidavit; In support of motion to dismiss for want of diversity of citizenship; Plaintiff and defendant citizens of same state on date action filed. FEDPROF § 1C:76.

t. Affidavit; In opposition to motion to dismiss for lack of diversity; Assignment of claim to plaintiff bona fide. FEDPROF § 1C:78.

u. Motion to dismiss; Insufficiency of amount in controversy. FEDPROF § 1C:81.

v. Motion to dismiss; Bad faith in claiming jurisdictional amount. FEDPROF § 1C:82.

w. Motion to dismiss; Lack of jurisdiction over subject matter, generally. FEDPROF § 1C:87.

x. Motion to dismiss; Absence of federal question. FEDPROF § 1C:88.

y. Motion to dismiss; Absence of federal question; Failure to exhaust state remedies. FEDPROF § 1C:89.

z. Affidavit; In opposition to motion to dismiss for absence of jurisdiction over subject matter. FEDPROF § 1C:90.

**2. Forms for the District of Massachusetts**

a. Notice of filing with clerk's office. MA R USDCT CM/ECF Admin(Appendix I).

# I. Applicable Rules

1. *Federal rules*

a. Federal question. 28 U.S.C.A. § 1331.

b. Diversity of citizenship; Amount in controversy; Costs. 28 U.S.C.A. § 1332.

c. Serving and filing pleadings and other papers. FRCP 5.

d. Constitutional challenge to a statute; Notice, certification, and intervention. FRCP 5.1.

e. Privacy protection for filings made with the court. FRCP 5.2.

f. Computing and extending time; Time for motion papers. FRCP 6.

g. Pleadings allowed; Form of motions and other papers. FRCP 7.

h. Disclosure statement. FRCP 7.1.

i. Form of pleadings. FRCP 10.

j. Signing pleadings, motions, and other papers; Representations to the court; Sanctions. FRCP 11.

k. Defenses and objections; When and how presented; Motion for judgment on the pleadings; Consolidating motions; Waiving defenses; Pretrial hearing. FRCP 12.

l. Taking testimony. FRCP 43.

m. Hearing motions; Submission on briefs. FRCP 78.

2. *Local rules*

   a.  Title. MA R USDCT LR 1.1.

   b.  Sanctions. MA R USDCT LR 1.3.

   c.  Form and filing of papers. MA R USDCT LR 5.1.

   d.  Service and filing of pleadings and other papers. MA R USDCT LR 5.2.

   e.  Filing and service by electronic means. MA R USDCT LR 5.4.

   f.  Motion practice. MA R USDCT LR 7.1.

   g.  Alternative dispute resolution. MA R USDCT LR 16.4.

   h.  Payments and deposits made with the clerk. MA R USDCT LR 67.4.

   i.  Settlement. MA R USDCT LR 68.2.

   j.  Office of the clerk. MA R USDCT LR 77.2.

   k.  Appearances. MA R USDCT LR 83.5.2.

   l.  Practice by pro se litigants. MA R USDCT LR 83.5.5.

   m.  CM/ECF case management/electronic case files administrative procedures. MA R USDCT CM/ECF Admin.

## Motions, Oppositions and Replies
## Motion to Dismiss for Lack of Personal Jurisdiction

### Document Last Updated December 2018

**A. Checklist**

(I)  ❏  Matters to be considered by moving party

  (a)  ❏  Required documents

    (1)  ❏  Notice of motion and motion

    (2)  ❏  Memorandum

    (3)  ❏  Certificate of service

  (b)  ❏  Supplemental documents

    (1)  ❏  Supporting evidence

    (2)  ❏  Notice of constitutional question

    (3)  ❏  Nongovernmental corporate disclosure statement

    (4)  ❏  Proposed order

    (5)  ❏  Compact disk with copy of document(s) in PDF format

    (6)  ❏  Notice of filing with clerk's office

    (7)  ❏  Additional copies

    (8)  ❏  Courtesy copies

  (c)  ❏  Timing

    (1)  ❏  Every defense to a claim for relief in any pleading must be asserted in the responsive pleading if one is required

    (2)  ❏  A motion asserting any of the defenses in FRCP 12(b) must be made before pleading if a responsive pleading is allowed

    (3)  ❏  If a pleading sets out a claim for relief that does not require a responsive pleading, an opposing party may assert at trial any defense to that claim

    (4)  ❏  A written motion and notice of the hearing must be served at least fourteen (14) days before the time specified for the hearing, with the following exceptions: (i) when the motion may be heard ex parte; (ii) when the Federal Rules of Civil Procedure set a different time; or (iii) when a court order—which a party may, for good cause, apply for ex parte—sets a different time

(5) ❑ Any affidavit supporting a motion must be served with the motion

(6) ❑ Except as noted in FRCP 33 to FRCP 36, the original of all papers required to be served under FRCP 5(d) shall, unless otherwise submitted to the court, be filed in the office of the clerk within seven (7) days after service has been made

(II) ❑ Matters to be considered by opposing party

    (a) ❑ Required documents

        (1) ❑ Opposition

        (2) ❑ Certificate of service

    (b) ❑ Supplemental documents

        (1) ❑ Supporting evidence

        (2) ❑ Notice of constitutional question

        (3) ❑ Compact disk with copy of document(s) in PDF format

        (4) ❑ Notice of filing with clerk's office

        (5) ❑ Additional copies

        (6) ❑ Courtesy copies

    (c) ❑ Timing

        (1) ❑ A party opposing a motion, shall file an opposition within fourteen (14) days after the motion is served, unless another period is fixed by rule or statute, or by order of the court

        (2) ❑ Except as FRCP 59(c) provides otherwise, any opposing affidavit must be served at least seven (7) days before the hearing, unless the court permits service at another time

        (3) ❑ Except as noted in FRCP 33 to FRCP 36, the original of all papers required to be served under FRCP 5(d) shall, unless otherwise submitted to the court, be filed in the office of the clerk within seven (7) days after service has been made

**B. Timing**

  1. *Motion to dismiss for lack of personal jurisdiction*

    a. *In a responsive pleading.* Every defense to a claim for relief in any pleading must be asserted in the responsive pleading if one is required. FRCP 12(b).

    b. *By motion.* A motion asserting any of the defenses in FRCP 12(b) must be made before pleading if a responsive pleading is allowed. FRCP 12(b). Although FRCP 12(b) encourages the responsive pleader to file a motion to dismiss before filing the answer, nothing in FRCP 12 prohibits the filing of a motion to dismiss with the answer. An untimely motion to dismiss may be considered if the defense asserted in the motion was previously raised in the responsive pleading. FEDPROC § 62:421.

    c. *At trial.* If a pleading sets out a claim for relief that does not require a responsive pleading, an opposing party may assert at trial any defense to that claim. FRCP 12(b).

  2. *Timing of motions, generally*

    a. *Motion and notice of hearing.* A written motion and notice of the hearing must be served at least fourteen (14) days before the time specified for the hearing, with the following exceptions:

      i. When the motion may be heard ex parte;

      ii. When the Federal Rules of Civil Procedure set a different time; or

      iii. When a court order—which a party may, for good cause, apply for ex parte—sets a different time. FRCP 6(c)(1).

    b. *Supporting affidavit.* Any affidavit supporting a motion must be served with the motion. FRCP 6(c)(2).

  3. *Timing of opposing papers.* A party opposing a motion, shall file an opposition within fourteen (14) days after the motion is served, unless (1) the motion is for summary judgment, in which case the opposition shall be filed within twenty-one (21) days after the motion is served, or (2) another period is fixed by rule or statute, or by order of the court. MA R USDCT LR 7.1(b)(2); MA R USDCT CM/ECF Admin(H)(4). The fourteen (14) day period is intended to include the period specified

by the civil rules for mailing time and provide for a uniform period regardless of the use of the mails. MA R USDCT LR 7.1(b)(2).

    a.   *Opposing affidavit.* Except as FRCP 59(c) provides otherwise, any opposing affidavit must be served at least seven (7) days before the hearing, unless the court permits service at another time. FRCP 6(c)(2).

4.   *Timing of reply papers.* [W]here the respondent files an answering affidavit setting up a new matter, the moving party ordinarily is allowed a reasonable time to file a reply affidavit since failure to deny the new matter by affidavit may operate as an admission of its truth. AMJUR MOTIONS § 25.

    a.   *Leave of court required.* All other papers not filed as indicated in MA R USDCT LR 7.1(b)(1) and MA R USDCT LR 7.1(b)(2), whether in the form of a reply brief or otherwise, may be submitted only with leave of court. MA R USDCT LR 7.1(b)(3).

5.   *Filing after service.* Except as noted in FRCP 33 to FRCP 36, the original of all papers required to be served under FRCP 5(d) shall, unless otherwise submitted to the court, be filed in the office of the clerk within seven (7) days after service has been made. MA R USDCT LR 5.1(b).

6.   *Effect of FRCP 12 motion on the time to serve a responsive pleading.* Unless the court sets a different time, serving a motion under FRCP 12 alters the periods in FRCP 12(a) as follows:

    a.   If the court denies the motion or postpones its disposition until trial, the responsive pleading must be served within fourteen (14) days after notice of the court's action; or

    b.   If the court grants a motion for a more definite statement, the responsive pleading must be served within fourteen (14) days after the more definite statement is served. FRCP 12(a)(4).

7.   *Computation of time*

    a.   *Computing time.* FRCP 6 applies in computing any time period specified in the Federal Rules of Civil Procedure, in any local rule or court order, or in any statute that does not specify a method of computing time. FRCP 6(a).

       i.   *Period stated in days or a longer unit.* When the period is stated in days or a longer unit of time:

           • Exclude the day of the event that triggers the period;

           • Count every day, including intermediate Saturdays, Sundays, and legal holidays; and

           • Include the last day of the period, but if the last day is a Saturday, Sunday, or legal holiday, the period continues to run until the end of the next day that is not a Saturday, Sunday, or legal holiday. FRCP 6(a)(1).

       ii.   *Period stated in hours.* When the period is stated in hours:

           • Begin counting immediately on the occurrence of the event that triggers the period;

           • Count every hour, including hours during intermediate Saturdays, Sundays, and legal holidays; and

           • If the period would end on a Saturday, Sunday, or legal holiday, the period continues to run until the same time on the next day that is not a Saturday, Sunday, or legal holiday. FRCP 6(a)(2).

       iii.   *Office of the clerk.* The offices of the Clerk of Court at Boston, Worcester and Springfield shall be open from 8:30 a.m. until 5:00 p.m. on all days except Saturdays, Sundays, legal holidays and other days so ordered by the court and announced in advance, if feasible. MA R USDCT LR 77.2.

       iv.   *Inaccessibility of the clerk's office.* Unless the court orders otherwise, if the clerk's office is inaccessible:

           • On the last day for filing under FRCP 6(a)(1), then the time for filing is extended to the first accessible day that is not a Saturday, Sunday, or legal holiday; or

           • During the last hour for filing under FRCP 6(a)(2), then the time for filing is extended to the same time on the first accessible day that is not a Saturday, Sunday, or legal holiday. FRCP 6(a)(3).

       v.   *"Last day" defined.* Unless a different time is set by a statute, local rule, or court order, the last day ends:

           • For electronic filing, at midnight in the court's time zone; and

           • For filing by other means, when the clerk's office is scheduled to close. FRCP 6(a)(4).

       vi.   *"Next day" defined.* The "next day" is determined by continuing to count forward when the period is measured after an event and backward when measured before an event. FRCP 6(a)(5).

       vii.   *"Legal holiday" defined.* "Legal holiday" means:

           • The day set aside by statute for observing New Year's Day, Martin Luther King Jr.'s Birthday, Washington's

Birthday, Memorial Day, Independence Day, Labor Day, Columbus Day, Veterans' Day, Thanksgiving Day, or Christmas Day;

- Any day declared a holiday by the President or Congress; and

- For periods that are measured after an event, any other day declared a holiday by the state where the district court is located. FRCP 6(a)(6).

b. *Computation of electronic filing deadlines.* Filing documents electronically does not alter any filing deadlines. MA R USDCT CM/ECF Admin(K); MA R USDCT LR 5.4(D). Although CM/ECF is generally available twenty-four (24) hours a day for filing, all electronic transmissions of documents must be completed prior to 6:00 PM, Eastern Standard (or Daylight Savings) Time, on the date on which it is due, in order to be considered timely filed that day. MA R USDCT CM/ECF Admin(K); MA R USDCT LR 5.4(D). When a specific time of day deadline is set by court order or stipulation, the electronic filing must be completed by that time. Documents may be filed at any time of the day on days prior to the date on which it is due. MA R USDCT CM/ECF Admin(K). A document filed electronically shall be deemed filed as of the time and date stated on the NEF received from the court. MA R USDCT CM/ECF Admin(G)(2); MA R USDCT CM/ECF Admin(K).

  i. *Technical failures.* A user whose filing is made untimely as the result of a technical failure of the court's CM/ECF system may seek appropriate relief from the court. MA R USDCT CM/ECF Admin(W)(3). Technical difficulties on the filer's end, with telephone, cable lines, the filer's Internet Service Provider (ISP), or hardware or software problems, will not constitute a technical failure under the Administrative Procedures for Electronic Case Filing in the United States District Court for the District of Massachusetts (MA R USDCT CM/ECF Admin) nor excuse an untimely filing. MA R USDCT CM/ECF Admin(W)(3). As help desk support is available during normal business hours, filers are strongly urged to electronically file any documents during that period. MA R USDCT CM/ECF Admin(W)(3).

    - The court has made available a public terminal (computers and scanner) in each clerk's office for registered users to scan and electronically file documents. This equipment is available during normal business hours. Users should bring their prepared document and a valid CM/ECF login and password. MA R USDCT CM/ECF Admin(W)(3).

c. *Extending time.* When an act may or must be done within a specified time, the court may, for good cause, extend the time: (1) with or without motion or notice if the court acts, or if a request is made, before the original time or its extension expires; or (2) on motion made after the time has expired if the party failed to act because of excusable neglect. FRCP 6(b)(1).

  i. *Exceptions.* A court must not extend the time to act under FRCP 50(b), FRCP 50(d), FRCP 52(b), FRCP 59(b), FRCP 59(d), FRCP 59(e), and FRCP 60(b). FRCP 6(b)(2).

  ii. Refer to the United States District Court for the District of Massachusetts KeyRules Motion for Continuance/Extension of Time document for more information on extending time.

d. *Additional time after certain kinds of service.* When a party may or must act within a specified time after being served and service is made under FRCP 5(b)(2)(C) (by mail), FRCP 5(b)(2)(D) (by leaving with the clerk), or FRCP 5(b)(2)(F) (by other means consented to), three (3) days are added after the period would otherwise expire under FRCP 6(a). FRCP 6(d).

## C. General Requirements

1. *Motions, generally*

a. *Requirements.* A request for a court order must be made by motion. The motion must:

  i. Be in writing unless made during a hearing or trial;

  ii. State with particularity the grounds for seeking the order; and

  iii. State the relief sought. FRCP 7(b)(1).

b. *Notice of motion.* A party interested in resisting the relief sought by a motion has a right to notice thereof, and an opportunity to be heard. AMJUR MOTIONS § 12.

  i. [I]n addition to statutory or court rule provisions requiring notice of a motion—the purpose of such a notice requirement having been said to be to prevent a party from being prejudicially surprised by a motion—principles of natural justice dictate that an adverse party generally must be given notice that a motion will be presented to the court. AMJUR MOTIONS § 12.

ii. "Notice," in this regard, means reasonable notice, including a meaningful opportunity to prepare and to defend against allegations of a motion. AMJUR MOTIONS § 12.

c. *Writing requirement.* The writing requirement is intended to [ensure] that the adverse parties are informed and have a record of both the motion's pendency and the grounds on which the movant seeks an order. FPP § 1191; Feldberg v. Quechee Lakes Corp., 463 F.3d 195 (2d Cir. 2006). [A] single written document can satisfy the writing requirements both for a motion and for [an] FRCP 6(c)(1) notice. FRCP 7(Advisory Committee Notes).

d. *Particularity requirement.* The particularity requirement [ensures] that the opposing parties will have notice of their opponent's contentions. FEDPROC § 62:358; Goodman v. 1973 26 Foot Trojan Vessel, Arkansas Registration No. AR1439SN, 859 F.2d 71 (8th Cir. 1988). That requirement ensures that notice of the basis for the motion is provided to the court and to the opposing party so as to avoid prejudice, provide the opponent with a meaningful opportunity to respond, and provide the court with enough information to process the motion correctly. FEDPROC § 62:358; Andreas v. Volkswagen of Am., Inc., 336 F.3d 789 (8th Cir. 2003).

   i. Reasonable specification of the grounds for a motion is sufficient. The particularity requirement for motions is satisfied when no party is prejudiced by a lack of particularity or when the court can comprehend the basis for the motion and deal with it fairly. However, where a movant fails to state even one ground for granting the motion in question, the movant has failed to meet the minimal standard of "reasonable specification." FEDPROC § 62:358; Martinez v. Trainor, 556 F.2d 818 (7th Cir. 1977).

   ii. The court may excuse the failure to comply with the particularity requirement if it is inadvertent, and where no prejudice is shown by the opposing party. FEDPROC § 62:358.

e. *Control of motion practice*

   i. *Plan for the disposition of motions.* At the earliest practicable time, the judicial officer shall establish a framework for the disposition of motions, which, at the discretion of the judicial officer, may include specific deadlines or general time guidelines for filing motions. This framework may be amended from time to time by the judicial officer as required by the progress of the case. MA R USDCT LR 7.1(a)(1).

   ii. *Motion practice.* No motion shall be filed unless counsel certify that they have conferred and have attempted in good faith to resolve or narrow the issue. MA R USDCT LR 7.1(a)(2).

   iii. *Unresolved motions.* The court shall rule on motions as soon as practicable, having in mind the reporting requirements set forth in the Civil Justice Reform Act. MA R USDCT LR 7.1(a)(3).

2. *Motion to dismiss for lack of personal jurisdiction.* [A] party may assert the following defense by motion: lack of personal jurisdiction. FRCP 12(b)(2). The most common use of the FRCP 12(b)(2) motion is to challenge the use of a state long-arm statute in a diversity action. FEDPROC § 62:439; Best Van Lines, Inc. v. Walker, 490 F.3d 239 (2d Cir. 2007). A dismissal pursuant to FRCP 12(b)(2) is proper where it appears that the assertion of jurisdiction over the defendant offends traditional notions of fair play and substantial justice—that is, where neither the defendant nor the controversy has a substantial enough connection with the forum state to make the exercise of jurisdiction reasonable. FEDPROC § 62:439; Neogen Corp. v. Neo Gen Screening, Inc., 282 F.3d 883 (6th Cir. 2002).

   a. *Personal jurisdiction, generally*

      i. *Due process limitations.* Due process requires that a court obtain jurisdiction over a defendant before it may adjudicate that defendant's personal rights. FEDPROC § 65:1; Omni Capital Int'l, Ltd. v. Rudolf Wolff & Co., Ltd., 484 U.S. 97, 108 S. Ct. 404, 98 L. Ed. 2d 415 (1987).

         • Originally, it was believed that a judgment in personam could only be entered against a defendant found and served within a state, but the increased flow of commerce between the states and the disuse of the writ of capias ad respondendum, which directed the sheriff to secure the defendant's appearance by taking the defendant into custody, in civil cases led to the liberalization of the concept of personal jurisdiction over nonresidents, and the flexible "minimum contacts" test is now followed. FEDPROC § 65:1.

         • Today the rule is that no binding judgment may be rendered against an individual or corporate defendant unless the defendant has sufficient contacts, ties, or relations with the jurisdiction. FEDPROC § 65:1; Burger King Corp. v. Rudzewicz, 471 U.S. 462, 105 S. Ct. 2174, 85 L. Ed. 2d 528 (1985); Int'l Shoe Co. v. State of Wash., Office of Unemployment Comp. & Placement, 326 U.S. 310, 66 S. Ct. 154, 90 L. Ed. 95 (1945).

         • Moreover, even if the defendant has sufficient contacts with the forum state to satisfy due process, a court nevertheless does not obtain personal jurisdiction over the defendant unless the defendant has notice sufficient to satisfy due process and, if such notice requires service of a summons, that there is authorization for the type and manner of service used. FEDPROC § 65:1; Omni Capital Int'l, Ltd. v. Rudolf Wolff & Co., Ltd., 484 U.S. 97, 108 S. Ct. 404, 98 L. Ed. 2d 415 (1987).

- Personal jurisdiction is a prerequisite to the maintenance of an action and must exist even though subject matter jurisdiction and venue are proper. FEDPROC § 65:1; Bookout v. Beck, 354 F.2d 823 (9th Cir. 1965).

- Personal jurisdiction over a nonresident defendant is appropriate under the Due Process Clause only where the defendant has sufficient minimum contacts with the forum state that are more than random, fortuitous, or attenuated contacts made by interacting with other persons affiliated with the state, such that summoning the defendant would not offend traditional notions of fair play and substantial justice. FEDPROC § 65:1; Pecoraro v. Sky Ranch for Boys, Inc., 340 F.3d 558 (8th Cir. 2003).

ii. *Methods of obtaining jurisdiction over an individual.* There are four basic methods of obtaining jurisdiction over an individual:

- Personal service within the jurisdiction. FEDPROC § 65:22.

- Service on a domiciliary of the forum state who is temporarily outside the jurisdiction, on the theory that the authority of a state over one of its citizens is not terminated by the mere fact of his absence. FEDPROC § 65:22; Milliken v. Meyer, 311 U.S. 457, 61 S. Ct. 339, 85 L. Ed. 278 (1940).

- Service on a nonresident who has sufficient contacts with the forum state, since the test of International Shoe is applicable to individuals. FEDPROC § 65:22; Kulko v. Superior Court of California In & For City & Cty. of San Francisco, 436 U.S. 84, 98 S. Ct. 1690, 56 L. Ed. 2d 132 (1978).

- Service on an agent who has been expressly appointed or appointed by operation of law, such as under a nonresident motorist statute. FEDPROC § 65:22; Nat'l Equip. Rental, Ltd. v. Szukhent, 375 U.S. 311, 84 S. Ct. 411, 11 L. Ed. 2d 354 (1964).

iii. *Territorial limits of effective service*

- *In general.* Serving a summons or filing a waiver of service establishes personal jurisdiction over a defendant: (1) who is subject to the jurisdiction of a court of general jurisdiction in the state where the district court is located; (2) who is a party joined under FRCP 14 or FRCP 19 and is served within a judicial district of the United States and not more than 100 miles from where the summons was issued; or (3) when authorized by a federal statute. FRCP 4(k)(1).

- *Federal claim outside state-court jurisdiction.* For a claim that arises under federal law, serving a summons or filing a waiver of service establishes personal jurisdiction over a defendant if: (1) the defendant is not subject to jurisdiction in any state's courts of general jurisdiction; and (2) exercising jurisdiction is consistent with the United States Constitution and laws. FRCP 4(k)(2).

b. *Motion based on lack of in rem or quasi-in-rem jurisdiction.* Although FRCP 12(b)(2) only refers to "lack of personal jurisdiction," the provision presumably is sufficiently elastic to embrace a defense or objection that the district court lacks in rem or quasi-in-rem jurisdiction, admittedly a subject that rarely arises in contemporary practice. FPP § 1351.

c. *Motion based on insufficient process or insufficient service of process.* FRCP 12(b)(2) motions to dismiss are frequently based on the failure to serve the defendant with process or a defective service of process, on the theory that if the defendant was not properly served with process, the court lacks personal jurisdiction over the defendant. FEDPROC § 62:440; Prokopiou v. Long Island R. Co., No. 06 CIV. 2558 KNF, 2007 WL 1098696 (S.D.N.Y. Apr. 9, 2007).

d. *Independent ground for dismissal.* Lack of overall reasonableness in the assertion of personal jurisdiction constitutes an independent ground for dismissal under FRCP 12(b)(2). FEDPROC § 62:442; Fed. Ins. Co. v. Lake Shore Inc., 886 F.2d 654 (4th Cir. 1989).

e. *Burden.* On the motion, the plaintiff bears the burden to establish the court's jurisdiction, which normally is not a heavy one, although the standard of proof may vary depending on the procedure used by the court in making its determination and whether the defendant is successful in rebutting the plaintiff's initial showing. Moreover, the Supreme Court has intimated that in the case of a challenge to the constitutional fairness and reasonableness of the chosen forum, the burden is on the defendant. FPP § 1351; Burger King Corp. v. Rudzewicz, 471 U.S. 462, 105 S. Ct. 2174, 85 L. Ed. 2d 528 (1985).

i. The most common formulation found in the judicial opinions is that the plaintiff bears the ultimate burden of demonstrating that the court's personal jurisdiction over the defendant exists by a preponderance of the evidence, but needs only make a prima facie showing when the district judge restricts her review of the FRCP 12(b)(2) motion solely to affidavits and other written evidence. FPP § 1351; Mullins v. TestAmerica, Inc., 564 F.3d 386 (5th Cir. 2009).

    ii. In addition, for purposes of such a review, federal courts will, as they do on other motions under FRCP 12(b), take as true the allegations of the nonmoving party with regard to the jurisdictional issues and resolve all factual disputes in his or her favor. FPP § 1351.

f. *Motion denied.* A party who has unsuccessfully raised an objection under FRCP 12(b)(2) may proceed to trial on the merits without waiving the ability to renew the objection to the court's jurisdiction. FPP § 1351.

g. *Joining motions.* As a general rule, when the court is confronted by a motion raising a combination of FRCP 12(b) defenses, it will pass on the jurisdictional issues before considering whether a claim was stated by the complaint. FPP § 1351.

    i. *Right to join.* A motion under FRCP 12 may be joined with any other motion allowed by FRCP 12. FRCP 12(g)(1).

    ii. *Limitation on further motions.* Except as provided in FRCP 12(h)(2) or FRCP 12(h)(3), a party that makes a motion under FRCP 12 must not make another motion under FRCP 12 raising a defense or objection that was available to the party but omitted from its earlier motion. FRCP 12(g)(2).

h. *Waiving and preserving certain defenses.* No defense or objection is waived by joining it with one or more other defenses or objections in a responsive pleading or in a motion. FRCP 12(b).

    i. *Waiver by omission or failure to make or include motion.* A party waives any defense listed in FRCP 12(b)(2) through FRCP 12(b)(5) by:

- Omitting it from a motion in the circumstances described in FRCP 12(g)(2); or

- Failing to either: (1) make it by motion under FRCP 12; or (2) include it in a responsive pleading or in an amendment allowed by FRCP 15(a)(1) as a matter of course. FRCP 12(h)(1).

    ii. *Waiver by consent or stipulation.* [A] valid consent or a stipulation that the court has jurisdiction prevents the successful assertion of [an] FRCP 12(b)(2) defense. FPP § 1351.

    iii. *Waiver by filing permissive counterclaim.* [A] defendant may be deemed to have waived an objection to personal jurisdiction if he or she files a permissive counterclaim under FRCP 13(b). FPP § 1351.

3. *Opposing papers.* The Federal Rules of Civil Procedure do not require any formal answer, return, or reply to a motion, except where the Federal Rules of Civil Procedure or local rules may require affidavits, memoranda, or other papers to be filed in opposition to a motion. Such papers are simply to apprise the court of such opposition and the grounds of that opposition. FEDPROC § 62:353.

a. *Effect of failure to respond to motion.* Although in the absence of statutory provision or court rule, a motion ordinarily does not require a written answer, when a party files a motion and the opposing party fails to respond, the court may construe such failure to respond as nonopposition to the motion or an admission that the motion was meritorious, may take the facts alleged in the motion as true—the rule in some jurisdictions being that the failure to respond to a fact set forth in a motion is deemed an admission—and may grant the motion if the relief requested appears to be justified. AMJUR MOTIONS § 28.

    i. *Unopposed motion to dismiss.* The circuits are split on whether a court may grant a motion to dismiss solely on the basis that the plaintiff did not file a response opposing the motion. FRCP-RC RULE 12.

b. *Assent or no opposition not determinative.* However, a motion will not be granted automatically simply because an "assent" or a notation of "no opposition" has been filed; federal judges frequently deny motions that have been assented to when it is thought that justice so dictates. FPP § 1190.

c. *Responsive pleading inappropriate as response to motion.* An attempt to answer or oppose a motion with a responsive pleading usually is not appropriate. FPP § 1190.

4. *Reply papers.* A moving party may be required or permitted to prepare papers in addition to his original motion papers. AMJUR MOTIONS § 25. Papers answering or replying to opposing papers may be appropriate, in the interests of justice, where it appears there is a substantial reason for allowing a reply. Thus, a court may accept reply papers where a party demonstrates that the papers to which it seeks to file a reply raise new issues that are material to the disposition of the question before the court, or where the court determines, sua sponte, that it wishes further briefing of an issue raised in those papers and orders the submission of additional papers. FEDPROC § 62:354.

a. *Function of reply papers.* The function of a reply affidavit is to answer the arguments made in opposition to the position taken by the movant and not to permit the movant to introduce new arguments in support of the motion. AMJUR MOTIONS § 25.

b. *Issues raised for the first time in a reply document.* However, the view has been followed in some jurisdictions, that as a matter of judicial economy, where there is no prejudice and where the issues could be raised simply by filing a motion to dismiss, the trial court has discretion to consider arguments raised for the first time in a reply memorandum, and that a trial court may grant a motion to strike issues raised for the first time in a reply memorandum. AMJUR MOTIONS § 26.

5. *Alternative dispute resolution (ADR).* The judicial officer assigned to preside over the case shall encourage the resolution of disputes by settlement or other alternative dispute resolution programs. MA R USDCT LR 16.4(a).

a. *Settlement.* At every conference conducted under the Local Rules of the United States District Court for the District of Massachusetts, the judicial officer shall inquire as to the utility of the parties conducting settlement negotiations, explore means of facilitating those negotiations, and offer whatever assistance may be appropriate in the circumstances. Assistance may include a reference of the case to another judicial officer for settlement purposes. MA R USDCT LR 16.4(b).

   i. When a case is settled, the parties shall file with the clerk a signed agreement for judgment or stipulation for dismissal, as appropriate, within twenty-eight (28) days, unless the court otherwise orders. MA R USDCT LR 68.2.

b. *Alternative dispute resolution programs*

   i. *Discretion of judicial officer.* The judicial officer, following an exploration of the matter with all counsel, may refer appropriate cases to alternative dispute resolution programs that have been designated for use in the district court or that the judicial officer may make available. The dispute resolution programs described in MA R USDCT LR 16.4(c)(2) through MA R USDCT LR 16.4(c)(4) are illustrative, not exclusive. Moreover, nothing in MA R USDCT LR 16.4 shall preclude the parties from engaging in private dispute resolution programs as long as they comply with any schedule established by the court. MA R USDCT LR 16.4(c)(1).

   ii. *Mediation.* The judicial officer may refer the case to mediation upon the agreement of all parties. MA R USDCT LR 16.4(c)(2)(A).

   iii. *Other alternative dispute resolution programs.* Use of mediation is not exclusive. At the request of parties, the judicial officer may consider other forms of alternative dispute resolution including, but not limited to, mini-trial, summary jury trial and arbitration. MA R USDCT LR 16.4(c)(3).

c. For more information on alternative dispute resolution (ADR), refer to MA R USDCT LR 16.4.

6. *Sanctions.* Failure to comply with any of the directions or obligations set forth in, or authorized by, these rules may result in dismissal, default, or the imposition of other sanctions as deemed appropriate by the judicial officer. MA R USDCT LR 1.3. Except as provided by law, the court may impose sanctions as provided in MA R USDCT LR 1.3 for failure to comply with the Administrative Procedures for Electronic Case Filing in the United States District Court for the District of Massachusetts (MA R USDCT CM/ECF Admin) or with MA R USDCT LR 5.4. MA R USDCT CM/ECF Admin(C)(3).

## D. Documents

1. *Documents for moving party*

   a. *Required documents*

      i. *Notice of motion and motion.* Refer to the General Requirements section of this document for information on the notice of motion and motion.

         • *Request for oral argument.* Any party making or opposing a motion who believes that oral argument may assist the court and wishes to be heard shall include a request for oral argument in a separate paragraph of the motion or opposition. The request should be set off with a centered caption, "REQUEST FOR ORAL ARGUMENT." MA R USDCT LR 7.1(d).

      ii. *Memorandum.* A party filing a motion shall at the same time file a memorandum of reasons, including citation of supporting authorities, why the motion should be granted. MA R USDCT LR 7.1(b)(1). Any memorandum of law or other attachment filed in support of a main document shall be filed as a separate document, using the proper event. MA R USDCT CM/ECF Admin(G)(4). Memoranda supporting or opposing allowance of motions shall not, without leave of court, exceed twenty (20) pages, double-spaced. MA R USDCT LR 7.1(b)(4).

      iii. *Certificate of service.* No certificate of service is required when a paper is served by filing it with the court's electronic-filing system. When a paper that is required to be served is served by other means: (1) if the paper is filed, a certificate of service must be filed with it or within a reasonable time after service; and (2) if the paper is not filed, a certificate of service need not be filed unless filing is required by court order or by local rule. FRCP 5(d)(1)(B). Except as otherwise provided by the Federal Rules of Civil Procedure, proof of service of all pleadings and other papers required to be served (except discovery papers that in accordance with FRCP 33 to FRCP 36(f) are not to be filed) shall be filed in the office of the clerk promptly after service has been made. The proof shall show the time and manner of service, and may be made by written acknowledgment of service, a certificate of a member of the bar of this court, or an affidavit of the person who served the paper. MA R USDCT LR 5.2(b)(1). A certificate of service of a member of the bar shall appear at the bottom of or on the margin of the last page of the paper to which it relates. MA R USDCT LR 5.2(b)(2).

- *Paper service.* The certificate shall be a brief, single-spaced statement and may be in the following form: I hereby certify that a true copy of the above document was served upon (each party appearing pro se and) the attorney of record for each other party by mail (by hand) on (date). (Signature). MA R USDCT LR 5.2(b)(2).

- *Electronic service.* Any pleading or other paper served by electronic means must bear a certificate of service in accordance with MA R USDCT LR 5.2(b). MA R USDCT LR 5.4(C); MA R USDCT CM/ECF Admin(H)(2). The certificate of service shall state that the filer: (1) filed the document electronically, (2) that it will be served electronically to registered CM/ECF participants via the NEF and (3) that the filer will send paper copies to non-registered participants as indicated on the NEF. MA R USDCT CM/ECF Admin(H)(2). For example: I hereby certify that this document filed through the CM/ECF system will be sent electronically to the registered participants as identified on the NEF (NEF) and paper copies will be sent to those indicated as non registered participants on (date). MA R USDCT CM/ECF Admin(H)(2).

- *Return.* Documents not conforming to the requirements of MA R USDCT LR 5.2 (except notices of appeal) shall be returned by the clerk. MA R USDCT LR 5.2(b)(2).

- *Failure to make proof of service.* Failure to make proof of service does not affect the validity of the service. MA R USDCT LR 5.2(b)(3).

b.  *Supplemental documents*

   i.  *Supporting evidence.* When a motion relies on facts outside the record, the court may hear the matter on affidavits or may hear it wholly or partly on oral testimony or on depositions. FRCP 43(c). Affidavits and other documents setting forth or evidencing facts on which the motion is based shall be filed with the motion. MA R USDCT LR 7.1(b)(1).

   ii.  *Notice of constitutional question.* A party that files a pleading, written motion, or other paper drawing into question the constitutionality of a federal or state statute must promptly:

   - *File notice.* File a notice of constitutional question stating the question and identifying the paper that raises it, if: (1) a federal statute is questioned and the parties do not include the United States, one of its agencies, or one of its officers or employees in an official capacity; or (2) a state statute is questioned and the parties do not include the state, one of its agencies, or one of its officers or employees in an official capacity; and

   - *Serve notice.* Serve the notice and paper on the Attorney General of the United States if a federal statute is questioned—or on the state attorney general if a state statute is questioned—either by certified or registered mail or by sending it to an electronic address designated by the attorney general for this purpose. FRCP 5.1(a).

   - *No forfeiture.* A party's failure to file and serve the notice, or the court's failure to certify, does not forfeit a constitutional claim or defense that is otherwise timely asserted. FRCP 5.1(d).

   iii.  *Nongovernmental corporate disclosure statement*

   - *Contents.* A nongovernmental corporate party must file two (2) copies of a disclosure statement that: (1) identifies any parent corporation and any publicly held corporation owning ten percent (10%) or more of its stock; or (2) states that there is no such corporation. FRCP 7.1(a).

   - *Time to file; Supplemental filing.* A party must: (1) file the disclosure statement with its first appearance, pleading, petition, motion, response, or other request addressed to the court; and (2) promptly file a supplemental statement if any required information changes. FRCP 7.1(b).

   iv.  *Proposed order.* Proposed orders usually are not required by this court. However, the court may request the party to submit such a document. In those situations, unless otherwise directed by the clerk's office, electronically file the proposed document/order using the entry for "Proposed Documents submitted to the court," found under the Other Documents menu, or as an attachment to the motion to which it relates. MA R USDCT CM/ECF Admin(T).

v. *Compact disk with copy of document(s) in PDF format.* A filer who cannot file a document electronically because of such technical difficulty on the filer's end [with telephone, cable lines, the filer's Internet Service Provider (ISP), or hardware or software problems] shall file the document conventionally along with a copy of the document in PDF format on a compact disk or contact the clerk's office for permission to submit the PDF document via email. MA R USDCT CM/ECF Admin(W)(3). Refer to the Timing section of this document for more information on technical failures.

vi. *Notice of filing with clerk's office.* When documents or exhibits (other than those filed ex parte or under seal) are submitted conventionally, a "Notice of Filing with clerk's office" shall be filed electronically and attached to the main document. A paper copy of the "Notice of Filing with clerk's office" must accompany the documents submitted to the court. The "Notice of Filing with clerk's office" (see MA R USDCT CM/ECF Admin(Appendix I)) shall describe each of the documents that will be filed as paper copies in the clerk's office, or shall include an index of the documents if those documents are voluminous. MA R USDCT CM/ECF Admin(P)(5).

vii. *Additional copies.* Whenever, because of the nature of a proceeding, such as a proceeding before a three-judge district court under 28 U.S.C.A. § 2284, additional copies of a paper required to be filed are necessary either for the use of the court or to enable the clerk to carry out his duties, it is the responsibility of the party filing or having filed the paper to provide the necessary copies. MA R USDCT LR 5.1(d).

viii. *Courtesy copies.* COURTESY COPIES OF DOCUMENTS FILED ELECTRONICALLY SHALL NOT BE SUBMITTED ROUTINELY. MA R USDCT CM/ECF Admin(J). Judicial officers, on a case-by-case basis, may require courtesy copies for specific cases, or types of motions, etc. A few Judicial Officers have entered Standing Orders, which may be found on their respective pages on the court's website (under Divisions). Any document filed on paper with the court as a courtesy copy must be clearly labeled as such (Example: COURTESY COPY—DO NOT SCAN). Documents delivered to the court as a courtesy copy will not be maintained in the official court record. MA R USDCT CM/ECF Admin(J).

2. *Documents for opposing party*

   a. *Required documents*

      i. *Opposition.* Refer to the General Requirements section of this document for information on the opposing papers.

         - *Memorandum.* A party opposing a motion shall file, in the same (rather than a separate), document a memorandum of reasons, including citation of supporting authorities, why the motion should not be granted. MA R USDCT LR 7.1(b)(2). Any memorandum of law or other attachment filed in support of a main document shall be filed as a separate document, using the proper event. MA R USDCT CM/ECF Admin(G)(4). Memoranda supporting or opposing allowance of motions shall not, without leave of court, exceed twenty (20) pages, double-spaced. MA R USDCT LR 7.1(b)(4).

         - *Request for oral argument.* Any party making or opposing a motion who believes that oral argument may assist the court and wishes to be heard shall include a request for oral argument in a separate paragraph of the motion or opposition. The request should be set off with a centered caption, "REQUEST FOR ORAL ARGUMENT." MA R USDCT LR 7.1(d).

      ii. *Certificate of service.* No certificate of service is required when a paper is served by filing it with the court's electronic-filing system. When a paper that is required to be served is served by other means: (1) if the paper is filed, a certificate of service must be filed with it or within a reasonable time after service; and (2) if the paper is not filed, a certificate of service need not be filed unless filing is required by court order or by local rule. FRCP 5(d)(1)(B). Except as otherwise provided by the Federal Rules of Civil Procedure, proof of service of all pleadings and other papers required to be served (except discovery papers that in accordance with FRCP 33 to FRCP 36(f) are not to be filed) shall be filed in the office of the clerk promptly after service has been made. The proof shall show the time and manner of service, and may be made by written acknowledgment of service, a certificate of a member of the bar of this court, or an affidavit of the person who served the paper. MA R USDCT LR 5.2(b)(1). A certificate of service of a member of the bar shall appear at the bottom of or on the margin of the last page of the paper to which it relates. MA R USDCT LR 5.2(b)(2).

         - *Paper service.* The certificate shall be a brief, single-spaced statement and may be in the following form: I hereby certify that a true copy of the above document was served upon (each party appearing pro se and) the attorney of record for each other party by mail (by hand) on (date). (Signature). MA R USDCT LR 5.2(b)(2).

- *Electronic service.* Any pleading or other paper served by electronic means must bear a certificate of service in accordance with MA R USDCT LR 5.2(b). MA R USDCT LR 5.4(C); MA R USDCT CM/ECF Admin(H)(2). The certificate of service shall state that the filer: (1) filed the document electronically, (2) that it will be served electronically to registered CM/ECF participants via the NEF and (3) that the filer will send paper copies to non-registered participants as indicated on the NEF. MA R USDCT CM/ECF Admin(H)(2). For example: I hereby certify that this document filed through the CM/ECF system will be sent electronically to the registered participants as identified on the NEF (NEF) and paper copies will be sent to those indicated as non registered participants on (date). MA R USDCT CM/ECF Admin(H)(2).

- *Return.* Documents not conforming to the requirements of MA R USDCT LR 5.2 (except notices of appeal) shall be returned by the clerk. MA R USDCT LR 5.2(b)(2).

- *Failure to make proof of service.* Failure to make proof of service does not affect the validity of the service. MA R USDCT LR 5.2(b)(3).

b. *Supplemental documents*

i. *Supporting evidence.* When a motion relies on facts outside the record, the court may hear the matter on affidavits or may hear it wholly or partly on oral testimony or on depositions. FRCP 43(c). Affidavits and other documents setting forth or evidencing facts on which the opposition is based shall be filed with the opposition. MA R USDCT LR 7.1(b)(2).

ii. *Notice of constitutional question.* A party that files a pleading, written motion, or other paper drawing into question the constitutionality of a federal or state statute must promptly:

- *File notice.* File a notice of constitutional question stating the question and identifying the paper that raises it, if: (1) a federal statute is questioned and the parties do not include the United States, one of its agencies, or one of its officers or employees in an official capacity; or (2) a state statute is questioned and the parties do not include the state, one of its agencies, or one of its officers or employees in an official capacity; and

- *Serve notice.* Serve the notice and paper on the Attorney General of the United States if a federal statute is questioned—or on the state attorney general if a state statute is questioned—either by certified or registered mail or by sending it to an electronic address designated by the attorney general for this purpose. FRCP 5.1(a).

- *No forfeiture.* A party's failure to file and serve the notice, or the court's failure to certify, does not forfeit a constitutional claim or defense that is otherwise timely asserted. FRCP 5.1(d).

iii. *Compact disk with copy of document(s) in PDF format.* A filer who cannot file a document electronically because of such technical difficulty on the filer's end [with telephone, cable lines, the filer's Internet Service Provider (ISP), or hardware or software problems] shall file the document conventionally along with a copy of the document in PDF format on a compact disk or contact the clerk's office for permission to submit the PDF document via email. MA R USDCT CM/ECF Admin(W)(3). Refer to the Timing section of this document for more information on technical failures.

iv. *Notice of filing with clerk's office.* When documents or exhibits (other than those filed ex parte or under seal) are submitted conventionally, a "Notice of Filing with clerk's office" shall be filed electronically and attached to the main document. A paper copy of the "Notice of Filing with clerk's office" must accompany the documents submitted to the court. The "Notice of Filing with clerk's office" (see MA R USDCT CM/ECF Admin(Appendix I)) shall describe each of the documents that will be filed as paper copies in the clerk's office, or shall include an index of the documents if those documents are voluminous. MA R USDCT CM/ECF Admin(P)(5).

v. *Additional copies.* Whenever, because of the nature of a proceeding, such as a proceeding before a three-judge district court under 28 U.S.C.A. § 2284, additional copies of a paper required to be filed are necessary either for the use of the court or to enable the clerk to carry out his duties, it is the responsibility of the party filing or having filed the paper to provide the necessary copies. MA R USDCT LR 5.1(d).

vi. *Courtesy copies.* COURTESY COPIES OF DOCUMENTS FILED ELECTRONICALLY SHALL NOT BE SUBMITTED ROUTINELY. MA R USDCT CM/ECF Admin(J). Judicial officers, on a case-by-case basis, may require courtesy copies for specific cases, or types of motions, etc. A few Judicial Officers have entered Standing Orders, which may be found on their respective pages on the court's website (under Divisions). Any document filed on paper with the court as a courtesy copy must be clearly labeled as such (Example: COURTESY COPY—DO NOT SCAN). Documents delivered to the court as a courtesy copy will not be maintained in the official court record. MA R USDCT CM/ECF Admin(J).

## E. Format

1. *Form of documents.* The rules governing captions and other matters of form in pleadings apply to motions and other papers. FRCP 7(b)(2). The provisions of FRCP 10 and FRCP 11 concerning the form and signing of pleadings, motions, and other papers shall be applicable to all papers filed in any proceeding in this court. The board of bar overseers registration number of each attorney signing such documents, except the United States Attorney and his or her staff, shall be inscribed below the signature. MA R USDCT LR 5.1(a)(1).

   a. *Paper size and binding.* All papers filed in the court shall be adapted for flat filing, be filed on eight and one-half by eleven (8-1/2 x 11) inch paper without backers and be bound firmly by staple or some such other means (excluding paper or binder clip or rubber band). MA R USDCT LR 5.1(a)(2).

   b. *Spacing.* All papers, except discovery requests and responses, shall be double-spaced except for the identification of counsel, title of the case, footnotes, quotations and exhibits. Discovery requests and responses shall be single-spaced. MA R USDCT LR 5.1(a)(2).

   c. *Caption.* Every pleading must have a caption with the court's name, a title, a file number, and [an] FRCP 7(a) designation. FRCP 10(a).

      i. *Names of parties.* The title of the complaint must name all the parties; the title of other pleadings, after naming the first party on each side, may refer generally to other parties. FRCP 10(a).

      ii. *Request for special action.* When any pleading or other paper filed in the court includes a request for special process or relief, or any other request such that, if granted, the court will proceed other than in the ordinary course, the request shall, unless it is noted on the category sheet [see MA R USDCT LR 40.1(a)(1)], be noted on the first page to the right of or immediately beneath the caption. MA R USDCT LR 5.1(c).

   d. *Claims or defenses*

      i. *Numbered paragraphs.* A party must state its claims or defenses in numbered paragraphs, each limited as far as practicable to a single set of circumstances. A later pleading may refer by number to a paragraph in an earlier pleading. FRCP 10(b).

      ii. *Separate statements.* If doing so would promote clarity, each claim founded on a separate transaction or occurrence—and each defense other than a denial—must be stated in a separate count or defense. FRCP 10(b).

   e. *Adoption by reference.* A statement in a pleading may be adopted by reference elsewhere in the same pleading or in any other pleading or motion. FRCP 10(c).

      i. *Exhibits.* A copy of a written instrument that is an exhibit to a pleading is a part of the pleading for all purposes. FRCP 10(c).

   f. *Citations*

      i. *Local rules.* These rules shall be known as Local Rules of the United States District Court for the District of Massachusetts and cited as "L.R., D. Mass." or "L.R." MA R USDCT LR 1.1.

      ii. *Electronic case filing procedures.* The procedures governing electronic case filing shall be known as the "Administrative Procedures for Electronic Case Filing in the United States District Court for the District of Massachusetts." They shall be cited as "APECF." MA R USDCT CM/ECF Admin(A)(7).

   g. *Acceptance by the clerk.* The clerk must not refuse to file a paper solely because it is not in the form prescribed by the Federal Rules of Civil Procedure or by a local rule or practice. FRCP 5(d)(4).

      i. Except for complaints and notices of appeal, papers that do not conform to the requirements of MA R USDCT LR 5.1(a)(2) shall be returned by the clerk. MA R USDCT LR 5.1(a)(2).

2. *Form of electronic documents.* A paper filed electronically is a written paper for purposes of the Federal Rules of Civil Procedure. FRCP 5(d)(3)(D).

   a. *PDF/A format required.* The court will begin requiring submission of documents in PDF/A format in the foreseeable future. PDF/A is an enhanced version of the traditional PDF format. Newer versions of most PDF software will be able to convert to this format. Additional information on PDF/A documents may be found on the court's website. MA R USDCT CM/ECF Admin(Electronic Filing and PDF).

      i. *Electronically converted PDF.* Electronically converted PDF documents are created from word processing documents (MS Word, WordPerfect, etc.) using any appropriate software. These documents are text searchable

and the file size is generally smaller than a scanned document. CM/ECF users may use any brand of software to convert documents to PDF. MA R USDCT CM/ECF Admin(Electronic Filing and PDF).

- Documents converted to PDF, rather than scanned, are preferred for filing in CM/ECF. MA R USDCT CM/ECF Admin(Electronic Filing and PDF).

ii. *Scanned PDF.* Scanned PDF documents are created from paper documents run through an optical scanner. Scanned PDF documents are generally not searchable and have a larger file size. Please note that software used to create scanned documents may (and should) be set in such a way that the document is "text-searchable." MA R USDCT CM/ECF Admin(Electronic Filing and PDF).

b. *Title.* All pleadings filed electronically shall be titled in accordance with the approved dictionary of civil or criminal events of the CM/ECF system of this court. A list of events is available on the CM/ECF Training Information page of the court's website. The clerk's office may, when necessary and appropriate, modify the docket entry description, or delete and re-enter the docket entry in order to comply with the court's quality assurance standards. MA R USDCT CM/ECF Admin(G)(3).

c. *Attachments to filings and exhibits.* Attachments to filings and exhibits must be filed in accordance with the court's CM/ECF User Manual, unless otherwise ordered by the court. MA R USDCT CM/ECF Admin(O)(1).

i. Filers must submit as attachments only those excerpts of the referenced documents that are directly germane to the matter under consideration by the court. Excerpted material must be clearly and prominently identified as such. Users who file excerpts of documents do so without prejudice to their right to timely file additional excerpts or the complete document, as may be allowed by the court. Responding parties may timely file additional excerpts or the complete document that they believe are directly germane. MA R USDCT CM/ECF Admin(O)(2).

ii. Filers shall not attach as an exhibit any pleading or other paper already on file with the court in that case, but shall merely refer to that document. (See MA R USDCT CM/ECF Admin(G) for information on using hyperlinks in PDF documents filed in CM/ECF.) MA R USDCT CM/ECF Admin(O)(3).

d. *Redacted documents.* The parties may request or the court may require the submission of documents that have been redacted/stripped of sensitive or confidential information. The redacted document prepared for electronic filing shall include the original caption of the document, and be clearly labeled as "Redacted Document." A specific event is available for this purpose ("Redacted Document"), found under the Other Filings/Other Documents menu option. MA R USDCT CM/ECF Admin(S).

i. Attorneys and pro se litigants are advised to take extra care when creating PDF documents intended for submission to CM/ECF. Steps shall be taken to ensure the documents are free of any hidden data (metadata) that may contain redacted information, or traces of information edited or deleted are not hidden in the final document. Even PDF content that has been encrypted may be recovered. An advisory document with additional information on this topic may be found on the court's website. MA R USDCT CM/ECF Admin(S).

e. *Hyperlinks.* Electronically filed documents may contain the following types of hyperlinks: (1) hyperlinks to other portions of the same document; (2) hyperlinks to other documents filed within the CM/ECF system; and (3) hyperlinks to a location on the Internet that contains a source document for a citation. MA R USDCT CM/ECF Admin(G)(7).

i. Hyperlinks to cited authority may not replace standard citation format. Complete citations must be included in the text of the filed document. Neither a hyperlink, nor any site to which it refers, shall be considered part of the record, but are simply convenient mechanisms for accessing material cited in a document filed in CM/ECF. Instructions on creating hyperlinks may be found in the CM/ECF User Manual. MA R USDCT CM/ECF Admin(G)(7).

ii. The court accepts no responsibility for, and does not endorse, any product, organization, or content at any hyperlinked site, or at any site to which that site may be linked. The court accepts no responsibility for the availability or functionality of any hyperlink. MA R USDCT CM/ECF Admin(G)(7).

iii. One feature of PDF/A documents is that hyperlinks are commonly "masked," meaning that the full address of the referenced file is not written out; for example, clicking the word brief may open a brief which was previously filed in CM/ECF. MA R USDCT CM/ECF Admin(G)(7)(NOTE). An "unmasked" hyperlink has the full address visible to the user. MA R USDCT CM/ECF Admin(G)(7)(NOTE).

- Masked hyperlinks may or may not work in a PDF/A document, depending on how it was created. Currently, masked hyperlinks are preserved in PDF/A documents produced by the "Save As" method in

Microsoft Word 2007 and 2010; the "PDFMaker" method in Microsoft Word 2007; and OpenOffice 2.4 ("PDF Export"). With other production methods, such as WordPerfect, the PDF/A document includes underlined words that appear to be links, but clicking them has no effect. MA R USDCT CM/ECF Admin(G)(7)(NOTE).

f. *Documents features not accepted.* CM/ECF will not accept PDF documents containing tracking tags, embedded systems commands, password protections, access restrictions or other security features, special tags or dynamic features. MA R USDCT CM/ECF Admin(G)(8).

g. *File size limitations.* A filing party shall limit the size of each PDF file to no more than twenty (20) megabytes. PDF files larger than seven (7) megabytes will be rejected by the CM/ECF system. The filer will see a message advising of the size limitation. MA R USDCT CM/ECF Admin(P)(2).

   i. Larger documents or exhibits may be submitted electronically if split into separate PDF files each less than seven (7) megabytes, attached to the main document and clearly labeled. MA R USDCT CM/ECF Admin(P)(2).

   ii. Documents submitted electronically or on paper are subject to the page limitations set by MA R USDCT LR 7.1(b)(4) or by order of the court. MA R USDCT CM/ECF Admin(P)(1).

h. *Accuracy and readability.* The filer shall verify the accuracy and readability of any PDF file before electronically filing it in CM/ECF. MA R USDCT CM/ECF Admin(G)(6); MA R USDCT CM/ECF Admin(P)(3).

3. *Signing of pleadings, motions and other papers*

a. *Signature.* Every pleading, written motion, and other paper must be signed by at least one attorney of record in the attorney's name—or by a party personally if the party is unrepresented. The paper must state the signer's address, e-mail address, and telephone number. FRCP 11(a). The provisions of the Federal Rules of Civil Procedure pertaining to the form and signing of pleadings, motions, and other papers shall be applicable to all papers filed in any proceeding in this court. The board of bar overseers registration number of each attorney signing such documents, except the United States Attorney and his staff, shall be inscribed below the signature. MA R USDCT LR 5.1(a)(1).

   i. *Electronic signing.* A filing made through a person's electronic-filing account and authorized by that person, together with that person's name on a signature block, constitutes the person's signature. FRCP 5(d)(3)(C).

   ii. *Appearances.* The filing of an appearance or any other pleading signed on behalf of a party constitutes an entry of appearance for that party. All pleadings shall contain the name, bar admission number, address, telephone number, and e-mail address of the attorney entering an appearance. MA R USDCT LR 83.5.2(a).

   - *Appearances by law firms.* When a party is represented by a law firm, the appearance must include the name and the signature of at least one individual attorney. When a party is represented by more than one attorney from the same or different law firms, the attorney entering the appearance must designate the individual attorney who is authorized to receive all notices in the case. Any notice sent to an attorney so designated shall be deemed to be proper notice unless the court finds that notice was not properly sent. MA R USDCT LR 83.5.2(b).

   - For more information on appearances, refer to MA R USDCT LR 83.5.2.

   iii. *Signatures of attorneys.* The user login and password required to submit documents to the CM/ECF system shall serve as that user's signature for purposes of FRCP 11 and for all other purposes under the Federal Rules of Civil Procedure and the Local Rules of the United States District Court for the District of Massachusetts. All electronically filed documents must include a signature block and must set forth the attorney's name, bar number, address, telephone number and email address. The name of the CM/ECF user under whose log-in and password the document is submitted must be preceded by a "/s/" and typed in the space where the signature would otherwise appear. MA R USDCT CM/ECF Admin(M)(1). For an example, refer to MA R USDCT CM/ECF Admin(M)(1).

   iv. *Signatures of pro se parties.* Any document requiring a signature that is filed by a party appearing pro se shall bear the words "pro se" following that party's signature. Any such document shall also state the party's mailing address, telephone number (if any), and e-mail address (if the party has consented to service by email). MA R USDCT LR 83.5.5(g). For more information on practice by pro se litigants, refer to MA R USDCT LR 83.5.5.

   v. *Multiple signatures.* The filer of any document requiring more than one signature (e.g, stipulations, joint motions, joint status reports, magistrate judge consent forms, etc.) must list thereon all the names of other signatories by means of a "/s/ name of signatory" block for each. By submitting such a document, the filing attorney certifies that each of the other signatories has expressly agreed to the form and substance of the document and that the filing attorney has their actual authority to submit the document electronically. MA R USDCT CM/ECF Admin(M)(2). For more information, refer to MA R USDCT CM/ECF Admin(M)(2).

vi. *Affidavits.* Except as provided in MA R USDCT CM/ECF Admin(L), affidavits shall be filed electronically; however, the electronically filed version must contain a "/s/ name of signatory" block indicating that the paper document bears an original signature. MA R USDCT CM/ECF Admin(M)(3). The court will also accept a scanned version of the original, signed document. MA R USDCT CM/ECF Admin(M)(3). For more information, refer to MA R USDCT CM/ECF Admin(M)(3).

vii. *No verification or accompanying affidavit required for pleadings.* Unless a rule or statute specifically states otherwise, a pleading need not be verified or accompanied by an affidavit. FRCP 11(a).

viii. *Unsigned papers.* The court must strike an unsigned paper unless the omission is promptly corrected after being called to the attorney's or party's attention. FRCP 11(a).

b. *Representations to the court.* By presenting to the court a pleading, written motion, or other paper—whether by signing, filing, submitting, or later advocating it—an attorney or unrepresented party certifies that to the best of the person's knowledge, information, and belief, formed after an inquiry reasonable under the circumstances:

i. It is not being presented for any improper purpose, such as to harass, cause unnecessary delay, or needlessly increase the cost of litigation;

ii. The claims, defenses, and other legal contentions are warranted by existing law or by a nonfrivolous argument for extending, modifying, or reversing existing law or for establishing new law;

iii. The factual contentions have evidentiary support or, if specifically so identified, will likely have evidentiary support after a reasonable opportunity for further investigation or discovery; and

iv. The denials of factual contentions are warranted on the evidence or, if specifically so identified, are reasonably based on belief or a lack of information. FRCP 11(b).

c. *Sanctions.* If, after notice and a reasonable opportunity to respond, the court determines that FRCP 11(b) has been violated, the court may impose an appropriate sanction on any attorney, law firm, or party that violated FRCP 11(b) or is responsible for the violation. FRCP 11(c)(1). Refer to the United States District Court for the District of Massachusetts KeyRules Motion for Sanctions document for more information.

4. *Privacy protection for filings made with the court*

a. *Redacted filings.* Unless the court orders otherwise, in an electronic or paper filing with the court that contains an individual's Social Security number, taxpayer-identification number, or birth date, the name of an individual known to be a minor, or a financial-account number, a party or nonparty making the filing may include only:

i. The last four (4) digits of the Social Security number and taxpayer-identification number;

ii. The year of the individual's birth;

iii. The minor's initials; and

iv. The last four (4) digits of the financial-account number. FRCP 5.2(a); MA R USDCT CM/ECF Admin(N).

b. *Exemptions from the redaction requirement.* The redaction requirement does not apply to the following:

i. A financial-account number that identifies the property allegedly subject to forfeiture in a forfeiture proceeding;

ii. The record of an administrative or agency proceeding;

iii. The official record of a state-court proceeding;

iv. The record of a court or tribunal, if that record was not subject to the redaction requirement when originally filed;

v. A filing covered by FRCP 5.2(c) or FRCP 5.2(d); and

vi. A pro se filing in an action brought under 28 U.S.C.A. § 2241, 28 U.S.C.A. § 2254, or 28 U.S.C.A. § 2255. FRCP 5.2(b).

c. *Limitations on remote access to electronic files; Social Security appeals and immigration cases.* Unless the court orders otherwise, in an action for benefits under the Social Security Act, and in an action or proceeding relating to an order of removal, to relief from removal, or to immigration benefits or detention, access to an electronic file is authorized as follows:

i. The parties and their attorneys may have remote electronic access to any part of the case file, including the administrative record;

ii. Any other person may have electronic access to the full record at the courthouse, but may have remote electronic access only to:

- The docket maintained by the court; and

- An opinion, order, judgment, or other disposition of the court, but not any other part of the case file or the administrative record. FRCP 5.2(c).

d. *Filings made under seal.* The court may order that a filing be made under seal without redaction. The court may later unseal the filing or order the person who made the filing to file a redacted version for the public record. FRCP 5.2(d).

e. *Protective orders.* For good cause, the court may by order in a case:

   i. Require redaction of additional information; or

   ii. Limit or prohibit a nonparty's remote electronic access to a document filed with the court. FRCP 5.2(e).

f. *Option for additional unredacted filing under seal.* A person making a redacted filing may also file an unredacted copy under seal. The court must retain the unredacted copy as part of the record. FRCP 5.2(f). For more information, refer to MA R USDCT LR 7.2.

g. *Option for filing a reference list.* A filing that contains redacted information may be filed together with a reference list that identifies each item of redacted information and specifies an appropriate identifier that uniquely corresponds to each item listed. The list must be filed under seal and may be amended as of right. Any reference in the case to a listed identifier will be construed to refer to the corresponding item of information. FRCP 5.2(g).

h. *Responsibility for redaction.* The clerk's office is not responsible for reviewing documents filed with the court to determine whether pleadings have been redacted and are in the proper form. MA R USDCT CM/ECF Admin(N).

i. *Waiver of protection of identifiers.* A person waives the protection of FRCP 5.2(a) as to the person's own information by filing it without redaction and not under seal. FRCP 5.2(h).

## F. Filing and Service Requirements

1. *Filing requirements*

   a. *Required filings.* Any paper after the complaint that is required to be served must be filed no later than a reasonable time after service. FRCP 5(d)(1).

      i. Except as noted in FRCP 33 to FRCP 36, the original of all papers required to be served under FRCP 5(d) shall, unless otherwise submitted to the court, be filed in the office of the clerk within seven (7) days after service has been made. MA R USDCT LR 5.1(b). Except as otherwise provided by the Federal Rules of Civil Procedure, proof of service of all pleadings and other papers required to be served (except discovery papers that in accordance with FRCP 33 to FRCP 36(f) are not to be filed) shall be filed in the office of the clerk promptly after service has been made. MA R USDCT LR 5.2(b)(1).

   b. *Nonelectronic filing.* A paper not filed electronically is filed by delivering it: (1) to the clerk; or (2) to a judge who agrees to accept it for filing, and who must then note the filing date on the paper and promptly send it to the clerk. FRCP 5(d)(2).

   c. *Electronic filing.* Unless exempt or otherwise ordered by the court, all pleadings and other papers submitted to the court must be filed, signed, and verified by electronic means as provided in MA R USDCT LR 5.4. MA R USDCT LR 5.4(A); MA R USDCT CM/ECF Admin(A)(1). All electronic filings must be made in accordance with the Administrative Procedures for Electronic Case Filing in the United States District Court for the District of Massachusetts (MA R USDCT CM/ECF Admin). MA R USDCT LR 5.4(B). The court may deviate from the Administrative Procedures for Electronic Case Filing in the United States District Court for the District of Massachusetts (MA R USDCT CM/ECF Admin) in specific cases, without prior notice, if deemed appropriate in the exercise of discretion, considering the need for the just, speedy, and inexpensive determination of matters pending before the court. MA R USDCT CM/ECF Admin(C)(1). The court may excuse a failure to comply with any administrative procedure whenever justice so requires. MA R USDCT CM/ECF Admin(C)(2).

      i. *By a represented person; Generally required; Exceptions.* A person represented by an attorney must file electronically, unless nonelectronic filing is allowed by the court for good cause or is allowed or required by local rule. FRCP 5(d)(3)(A).

      ii. *By unrepresented person; When allowed or required.* A person not represented by an attorney: (1) may file electronically only if allowed by court order or by local rule; and (2) may be required to file electronically only by court order, or by a local rule that includes reasonable exceptions. FRCP 5(d)(3)(B).

      iii. *Exemptions from electronic filing*

         - *Documents that should not be filed electronically.* The following types of documents must not be filed electronically, and will not be scanned into the ECF system by the clerk's office: (1) sealed documents; (2)

ex parte motions; (3) documents generated as part of an alternative dispute resolution (ADR) process; (4) the administrative record in Social Security and other administrative proceedings; (5) the state court record in proceedings under 28 U.S.C.A. § 2254; and (6) such other types of documents as the clerk may direct in the Administrative Procedures for Electronic Case Filing in the United States District Court for the District of Massachusetts (MA R USDCT CM/ECF Admin). MA R USDCT LR 5.4(G)(1); MA R USDCT CM/ECF Admin(L).

- *Documents that need not be filed electronically.* The following types of documents need not be filed electronically, but may be scanned into the ECF system by a filing party or the clerk's office: (1) handwritten pleadings; (2) documents filed by pro se litigants who are incarcerated or who are not registered ECF users; (3) indictments, informations, criminal complaints, and the criminal JS45 form; (4) affidavits for search or arrest warrants and related documents; (5) documents received from another court under FRCRP 20 or FRCRP 40; (6) appearance bonds; (7) any document in a criminal case containing the original signature of a defendant, such as a waiver of indictment or a plea agreement; (8) petitions for violations of supervised release; (9) executed service of process documents under FRCP 4; and (10) such other types of documents as the clerk may direct in the Administrative Procedures for Electronic Case Filing in the United States District Court for the District of Massachusetts (MA R USDCT CM/ECF Admin). MA R USDCT LR 5.4(G)(2); MA R USDCT CM/ECF Admin(L).

- For more information on exemptions from electronic filing, refer to MA R USDCT CM/ECF Admin(L).

iv. *Consequences of electronic filing.* Electronic transmission of a document to the CM/ECF system, together with the transmission of a Notice of Electronic Filing (NEF) from the court at the completion of the transaction, constitutes the filing of the document for all purposes of the Federal Rules of Procedure and constitutes entry of the document on the docket maintained by the clerk pursuant to FRCP 58 and FRCP 79. MA R USDCT CM/ECF Admin(G)(1).

v. *Payment of filing fees.* When electronically filing any pleading or paper through CM/ECF that requires a fee, all registered ECF users are to pay the fee electronically through the Treasury Department's Internet payment process. MA R USDCT LR 67.4(d); MA R USDCT CM/ECF Admin(A)(1). Pro se filers and those who have been exempted from electronic filing and/or electronic payment of fees may submit payments by check or money order made payable to "Clerk, U.S. District Court". MA R USDCT LR 67.4(d). For more information on filing fees, refer to MA R USDCT LR 67.4 and MA R USDCT CM/ECF Admin(I).

vi. For more information on electronic filing, refer to MA R USDCT CM/ECF Admin.

d. *Email or fax filing.* In general, the court does not accept documents by email or by fax. If the court, in special circumstances, does authorize the submission of a document in that manner, the document shall not be considered filed until an NEF is generated by CM/ECF at the completion of the transaction. MA R USDCT CM/ECF Admin(H)(5).

2. *Service requirements.* All papers filed pursuant to MA R USDCT LR 7.1(b) shall be served unless the moving party indicates in writing on the face of the motion that ex parte consideration is requested. Motions filed "ex parte" and related papers need not be served until the motion has been ruled upon or the court orders that service be made. MA R USDCT LR 7.1(c). Service of all pleadings subsequent to the original complaint and of all other papers required to be served shall be made in the manner specified by FRCP 5. MA R USDCT LR 5.2(a).

a. *Service; When required*

i. *In general.* Unless the Federal Rules of Civil Procedure provide otherwise, each of the following papers must be served on every party:

- An order stating that service is required;

- A pleading filed after the original complaint, unless the court orders otherwise under FRCP 5(c) because there are numerous defendants;

- A discovery paper required to be served on a party, unless the court orders otherwise;

- A written motion, except one that may be heard ex parte; and

- A written notice, appearance, demand, or offer of judgment, or any similar paper. FRCP 5(a)(1).

ii. *If a party fails to appear.* No service is required on a party who is in default for failing to appear. But a pleading that asserts a new claim for relief against such a party must be served on that party under FRCP 4. FRCP 5(a)(2).

iii. *Seizing property.* If an action is begun by seizing property and no person is or need be named as a defendant, any service required before the filing of an appearance, answer, or claim must be made on the person who had custody or possession of the property when it was seized. FRCP 5(a)(3).

b. *Service; How made*

   i. *Serving an attorney.* If a party is represented by an attorney, service under FRCP 5 must be made on the attorney unless the court orders service on the party. FRCP 5(b)(1).

   - *Nonresident attorney.* On application of a party, the court may order an attorney who represents any other party and who does not maintain an office within this district where service can be made on him by delivery as provided by FRCP 5(b), to designate a member of the bar of this court who does maintain such an office to receive service of all pleadings and other papers in his behalf. MA R USDCT LR 5.2(c)(1).

   ii. *Serving a party acting pro se.* On application of a party, the court may order any other party who is appearing without an attorney and who does not maintain an office or residence within this district where service can be made on him by delivery as provided by FRCP 5(b), to designate an address within the district at which service can be made on him by delivery. MA R USDCT LR 5.2(c)(2).

   iii. *Service in general.* A paper is served under FRCP 5 by:

   - Handing it to the person;
   - Leaving it: (1) at the person's office with a clerk or other person in charge or, if no one is in charge, in a conspicuous place in the office; or (2) if the person has no office or the office is closed, at the person's dwelling or usual place of abode with someone of suitable age and discretion who resides there;
   - Mailing it to the person's last known address—in which event service is complete upon mailing;
   - Leaving it with the court clerk if the person has no known address;
   - Sending it to a registered user by filing it with the court's electronic-filing system or sending it by other electronic means that the person consented to in writing—in either of which events service is complete upon filing or sending, but is not effective if the filer or sender learns that it did not reach the person to be served; or
   - Delivering it by any other means that the person consented to in writing—in which event service is complete when the person making service delivers it to the agency designated to make delivery. FRCP 5(b)(2).

   iv. *Service by electronic means.* Unless exempt or otherwise ordered by the court, all pleadings and other papers must be served on other parties by electronic means. MA R USDCT LR 5.4(C); MA R USDCT CM/ECF Admin(H)(2). Service by electronic means shall be treated the same as service by mail. MA R USDCT CM/ECF Admin(H)(4).

   - *Consent to electronic service.* Registering to use CM/ECF constitutes consent to service of all documents by electronic means as provided in the Administrative Procedures for Electronic Case Filing in the United States District Court for the District of Massachusetts (MA R USDCT CM/ECF Admin) and FRCP 5(b) and FRCP 77(d). MA R USDCT CM/ECF Admin(E)(6); MA R USDCT CM/ECF Admin(H)(3).

   - *Service on registered ECF users.* Transmission of the Notice of Electronic Filing (NEF) through the court's transmission facilities will constitute service of the filed document upon a registered ECF user. MA R USDCT LR 5.4(C).

   - *Service on non-registered users.* The party filing the document electronically is responsible for serving a paper copy of the document by mail in accordance with FRCP 5(b) to those case participants who have not been identified on the NEF as electronic recipients. MA R USDCT CM/ECF Admin(H)(3).

   - *Service of conventionally filed papers.* Documents or exhibits submitted conventionally shall be served on other parties by the filer using traditional means. MA R USDCT CM/ECF Admin(P)(4).

c. *Serving numerous defendants*

   i. *In general.* If an action involves an unusually large number of defendants, the court may, on motion or on its own, order that:

   - Defendants' pleadings and replies to them need not be served on other defendants;
   - Any crossclaim, counterclaim, avoidance, or affirmative defense in those pleadings and replies to them will be treated as denied or avoided by all other parties; and

- Filing any such pleading and serving it on the plaintiff constitutes notice of the pleading to all parties. FRCP 5(c)(1).

    ii. *Notifying parties.* A copy of every such order must be served on the parties as the court directs. FRCP 5(c)(2).

## G. Hearings

1. *Hearings, generally.* If the court concludes that there should be a hearing on a motion, the motion will be set down for hearing at such time as the court determines. MA R USDCT LR 7.1(e).

    a. *Oral argument.* Due process does not require that oral argument be permitted on a motion and, except as otherwise provided by local rule, the district court has discretion to determine whether it will decide the motion on the papers or hear argument by counsel (and perhaps receive evidence). FPP § 1190; F.D.I.C. v. Deglau, 207 F.3d 153 (3d Cir. 2000).

        i. *Evidence on a motion.* When a motion relies on facts outside the record, the court may hear the matter on affidavits or may hear it wholly or partly on oral testimony or on depositions. FRCP 43(c).

    b. *Providing a regular schedule for oral hearings.* A court may establish regular times and places for oral hearings on motions. FRCP 78(a).

    c. *Providing for submission on briefs.* By rule or order, the court may provide for submitting and determining motions on briefs, without oral hearings. FRCP 78(b). Motions that are not set down for hearing as provided in MA R USDCT LR 7.1(e) will be decided on the papers submitted after an opposition to the motion has been filed, or, if no opposition is filed, after the time for filing an opposition has elapsed. MA R USDCT LR 7.1(f).

2. *Hearing on certain FRCP 12 defenses before trial.* If a party so moves, any defense listed in FRCP 12(b)(1) through FRCP 12(b)(7)—whether made in a pleading or by motion—and a motion under FRCP 12(c) must be heard and decided before trial unless the court orders a deferral until trial. FRCP 12(i).

3. *Conflict of court appearances.* For information on conflict of court appearances, refer to MA R USDCT LR 40.2.

## H. Forms

### 1. Federal Motion to Dismiss for Lack of Personal Jurisdiction Forms

a. Motion to dismiss for lack of personal jurisdiction; Corporate defendant. 2C FEDFORMS § 11:52.

b. Motion to dismiss for lack of personal jurisdiction; By corporate defendant; With citation. 2C FEDFORMS § 11:53.

c. Motion to dismiss for lack of personal jurisdiction; By a foreign corporation. 2C FEDFORMS § 11:54.

d. Motion to dismiss for lack of personal jurisdiction; For insufficiency of service. 2C FEDFORMS § 11:55.

e. Motion to dismiss for lack of personal jurisdiction; Insufficiency of process and insufficiency of service of process. 2C FEDFORMS § 11:56.

f. Motion and notice; To dismiss; Defendant not present within state where district court is located. AMJUR PP FEDPRAC § 501.

g. Motion and notice; To dismiss; Lack of jurisdiction over person. AMJUR PP FEDPRAC § 502.

h. Motion and notice; To dismiss; Lack of jurisdiction over person; Ineffective service of process on foreign state. AMJUR PP FEDPRAC § 503.

i. Motion and notice; To dismiss; Lack of jurisdiction over person; Consul not agent of country represented for purpose of receiving service of process. AMJUR PP FEDPRAC § 504.

j. Motion and notice; To dismiss; Lack of jurisdiction over corporate defendant. AMJUR PP FEDPRAC § 505.

k. Motion and notice; To dismiss; International organization immune from suit. AMJUR PP FEDPRAC § 506.

l. Motion and notice; To dismiss; Officer or employee of international organization acting within official capacity; Immune from suit. AMJUR PP FEDPRAC § 507.

m. Motion and notice; To dismiss; Family member of member of foreign mission immune from suit. AMJUR PP FEDPRAC § 508.

n. Motion and notice; To dismiss complaint or, in alternative, to quash service of summons; Lack of jurisdiction over corporate defendant. AMJUR PP FEDPRAC § 509.

o. Motion to dismiss; Lack of personal jurisdiction; No minimum contacts. AMJUR PP FEDPRAC § 510.

p. Declaration; For motion to dismiss for lack of personal jurisdiction; No minimum contacts. AMJUR PP FEDPRAC § 512.

q. Opposition; To motion. FEDPROF § 1B:175.

r. Affidavit; Supporting or opposing motion. FEDPROF § 1B:176.

s. Brief; Supporting or opposing motion. FEDPROF § 1B:177.

t. Statement of points and authorities; Opposing motion. FEDPROF § 1B:178.

u. Motion to dismiss; Lack of jurisdiction over person of defendant. FEDPROF § 1C:94.

v. Motion to dismiss; Lack of jurisdiction over person of defendant; Short form. FEDPROF § 1C:95.

w. Motion to dismiss; Lack of jurisdiction over person of defendant; Accident in foreign country and defendants have no contacts with forum state. FEDPROF § 1C:96.

x. Motion to dismiss; Lack of jurisdiction over corporate defendant. FEDPROF § 1C:97.

y. Motion; To dismiss complaint or, in the alternative, to quash service of summons; Lack of jurisdiction over corporate defendant. FEDPROF § 1C:98.

z. Motion to dismiss complaint; General form. GOLDLTGFMS § 20:24.

**2. Forms for the District of Massachusetts**

a. Notice of filing with clerk's office. MA R USDCT CM/ECF Admin(Appendix I).

# I. Applicable Rules

1. *Federal rules*

a. Summons. FRCP 4.

b. Serving and filing pleadings and other papers. FRCP 5.

c. Constitutional challenge to a statute; Notice, certification, and intervention. FRCP 5.1.

d. Privacy protection for filings made with the court. FRCP 5.2.

e. Computing and extending time; Time for motion papers. FRCP 6.

f. Pleadings allowed; Form of motions and other papers. FRCP 7.

g. Disclosure statement. FRCP 7.1.

h. Form of pleadings. FRCP 10.

i. Signing pleadings, motions, and other papers; Representations to the court; Sanctions. FRCP 11.

j. Defenses and objections; When and how presented; Motion for judgment on the pleadings; Consolidating motions; Waiving defenses; Pretrial hearing. FRCP 12.

k. Taking testimony. FRCP 43.

l. Hearing motions; Submission on briefs. FRCP 78.

2. *Local rules*

a. Title. MA R USDCT LR 1.1.

b. Sanctions. MA R USDCT LR 1.3.

c. Form and filing of papers. MA R USDCT LR 5.1.

d. Service and filing of pleadings and other papers. MA R USDCT LR 5.2.

e. Filing and service by electronic means. MA R USDCT LR 5.4.

f. Motion practice. MA R USDCT LR 7.1.

g. Alternative dispute resolution. MA R USDCT LR 16.4.

h. Payments and deposits made with the clerk. MA R USDCT LR 67.4.

i. Settlement. MA R USDCT LR 68.2.

j. Office of the clerk. MA R USDCT LR 77.2.

k. Appearances. MA R USDCT LR 83.5.2.

l. Practice by pro se litigants. MA R USDCT LR 83.5.5.

m. CM/ECF case management/electronic case files administrative procedures. MA R USDCT CM/ECF Admin.

# Motions, Oppositions and Replies
# Motion for Judgment on the Pleadings

## Document Last Updated December 2018

### A. Checklist

(I) ❑ Matters to be considered by moving party

  (a) ❑ Required documents

    (1) ❑ Notice of motion and motion

    (2) ❑ Memorandum

    (3) ❑ Certificate of service

  (b) ❑ Supplemental documents

    (1) ❑ Pleadings

    (2) ❑ Notice of constitutional question

    (3) ❑ Nongovernmental corporate disclosure statement

    (4) ❑ Proposed order

    (5) ❑ Compact disk with copy of document(s) in PDF format

    (6) ❑ Notice of filing with clerk's office

    (7) ❑ Additional copies

    (8) ❑ Courtesy copies

  (c) ❑ Timing

    (1) ❑ After the pleadings are closed—but early enough not to delay trial—a party may move for judgment on the pleadings

    (2) ❑ A written motion and notice of the hearing must be served at least fourteen (14) days before the time specified for the hearing, with the following exceptions: (i) when the motion may be heard ex parte; (ii) when the Federal Rules of Civil Procedure set a different time; or (iii) when a court order—which a party may, for good cause, apply for ex parte—sets a different time

    (3) ❑ Any affidavit supporting a motion must be served with the motion

    (4) ❑ Except as noted in FRCP 33 to FRCP 36, the original of all papers required to be served under FRCP 5(d) shall, unless otherwise submitted to the court, be filed in the office of the clerk within seven (7) days after service has been made

(II) ❑ Matters to be considered by opposing party

  (a) ❑ Required documents

    (1) ❑ Opposition

    (2) ❑ Certificate of service

  (b) ❑ Supplemental documents

    (1) ❑ Pleadings

    (2) ❑ Notice of constitutional question

    (3) ❑ Compact disk with copy of document(s) in PDF format

    (4) ❑ Notice of filing with clerk's office

    (5) ❑ Additional copies

    (6) ❑ Courtesy copies

  (c) ❑ Timing

    (1) ❑ A party opposing a motion, shall file an opposition within fourteen (14) days after the motion is served, unless another period is fixed by rule or statute, or by order of the court

(2) ❑ Except as FRCP 59(c) provides otherwise, any opposing affidavit must be served at least seven (7) days before the hearing, unless the court permits service at another time

(3) ❑ Except as noted in FRCP 33 to FRCP 36, the original of all papers required to be served under FRCP 5(d) shall, unless otherwise submitted to the court, be filed in the office of the clerk within seven (7) days after service has been made

## B. Timing

1. *Motion for judgment on the pleadings.* After the pleadings are closed—but early enough not to delay trial—a party may move for judgment on the pleadings. FRCP 12(c).

    a. *When pleadings are closed.* FRCP 7(a) provides that the pleadings are closed upon the filing of a complaint and an answer (absent a court-ordered reply), unless a counterclaim, cross-claim, or third-party claim is interposed, in which event the filing of a reply to a counterclaim, cross-claim answer, or third-party answer normally will mark the close of the pleadings. FPP § 1367.

    b. *Timeliness and delay.* Ordinarily, a motion for judgment on the pleadings should be made promptly after the close of the pleadings. Generally, however, [an] FRCP 12(c) motion is considered timely if it is made early enough not to delay trial or cause prejudice to the non-movant. FPP § 1367.

2. *Timing of motions, generally*

    a. *Motion and notice of hearing.* A written motion and notice of the hearing must be served at least fourteen (14) days before the time specified for the hearing, with the following exceptions:

        i. When the motion may be heard ex parte;

        ii. When the Federal Rules of Civil Procedure set a different time; or

        iii. When a court order—which a party may, for good cause, apply for ex parte—sets a different time. FRCP 6(c)(1).

    b. *Supporting affidavit.* Any affidavit supporting a motion must be served with the motion. FRCP 6(c)(2).

3. *Timing of opposing papers.* A party opposing a motion, shall file an opposition within fourteen (14) days after the motion is served, unless (1) the motion is for summary judgment, in which case the opposition shall be filed within twenty-one (21) days after the motion is served, or (2) another period is fixed by rule or statute, or by order of the court. MA R USDCT LR 7.1(b)(2); MA R USDCT CM/ECF Admin(H)(4). The fourteen (14) day period is intended to include the period specified by the civil rules for mailing time and provide for a uniform period regardless of the use of the mails. MA R USDCT LR 7.1(b)(2).

    a. *Opposing affidavit.* Except as FRCP 59(c) provides otherwise, any opposing affidavit must be served at least seven (7) days before the hearing, unless the court permits service at another time. FRCP 6(c)(2).

4. *Timing of reply papers.* [W]here the respondent files an answering affidavit setting up a new matter, the moving party ordinarily is allowed a reasonable time to file a reply affidavit since failure to deny the new matter by affidavit may operate as an admission of its truth. AMJUR MOTIONS § 25.

    a. *Leave of court required.* All other papers not filed as indicated in MA R USDCT LR 7.1(b)(1) and MA R USDCT LR 7.1(b)(2), whether in the form of a reply brief or otherwise, may be submitted only with leave of court. MA R USDCT LR 7.1(b)(3).

5. *Filing after service.* Except as noted in FRCP 33 to FRCP 36, the original of all papers required to be served under FRCP 5(d) shall, unless otherwise submitted to the court, be filed in the office of the clerk within seven (7) days after service has been made. MA R USDCT LR 5.1(b).

6. *Effect of FRCP 12 motion on the time to serve a responsive pleading.* Unless the court sets a different time, serving a motion under FRCP 12 alters the periods in FRCP 12(a) as follows:

    a. If the court denies the motion or postpones its disposition until trial, the responsive pleading must be served within fourteen (14) days after notice of the court's action; or

    b. If the court grants a motion for a more definite statement, the responsive pleading must be served within fourteen (14) days after the more definite statement is served. FRCP 12(a)(4).

7. *Computation of time*

    a. *Computing time.* FRCP 6 applies in computing any time period specified in the Federal Rules of Civil Procedure, in any local rule or court order, or in any statute that does not specify a method of computing time. FRCP 6(a).

        i. *Period stated in days or a longer unit.* When the period is stated in days or a longer unit of time:

            • Exclude the day of the event that triggers the period;

- Count every day, including intermediate Saturdays, Sundays, and legal holidays; and

- Include the last day of the period, but if the last day is a Saturday, Sunday, or legal holiday, the period continues to run until the end of the next day that is not a Saturday, Sunday, or legal holiday. FRCP 6(a)(1).

ii. *Period stated in hours.* When the period is stated in hours:

- Begin counting immediately on the occurrence of the event that triggers the period;

- Count every hour, including hours during intermediate Saturdays, Sundays, and legal holidays; and

- If the period would end on a Saturday, Sunday, or legal holiday, the period continues to run until the same time on the next day that is not a Saturday, Sunday, or legal holiday. FRCP 6(a)(2).

iii. *Office of the clerk.* The offices of the Clerk of Court at Boston, Worcester and Springfield shall be open from 8:30 a.m. until 5:00 p.m. on all days except Saturdays, Sundays, legal holidays and other days so ordered by the court and announced in advance, if feasible. MA R USDCT LR 77.2.

iv. *Inaccessibility of the clerk's office.* Unless the court orders otherwise, if the clerk's office is inaccessible:

- On the last day for filing under FRCP 6(a)(1), then the time for filing is extended to the first accessible day that is not a Saturday, Sunday, or legal holiday; or

- During the last hour for filing under FRCP 6(a)(2), then the time for filing is extended to the same time on the first accessible day that is not a Saturday, Sunday, or legal holiday. FRCP 6(a)(3).

v. *"Last day" defined.* Unless a different time is set by a statute, local rule, or court order, the last day ends:

- For electronic filing, at midnight in the court's time zone; and

- For filing by other means, when the clerk's office is scheduled to close. FRCP 6(a)(4).

vi. *"Next day" defined.* The "next day" is determined by continuing to count forward when the period is measured after an event and backward when measured before an event. FRCP 6(a)(5).

vii. *"Legal holiday" defined.* "Legal holiday" means:

- The day set aside by statute for observing New Year's Day, Martin Luther King Jr.'s Birthday, Washington's Birthday, Memorial Day, Independence Day, Labor Day, Columbus Day, Veterans' Day, Thanksgiving Day, or Christmas Day;

- Any day declared a holiday by the President or Congress; and

- For periods that are measured after an event, any other day declared a holiday by the state where the district court is located. FRCP 6(a)(6).

b. *Computation of electronic filing deadlines.* Filing documents electronically does not alter any filing deadlines. MA R USDCT CM/ECF Admin(K); MA R USDCT LR 5.4(D). Although CM/ECF is generally available twenty-four (24) hours a day for filing, all electronic transmissions of documents must be completed prior to 6:00 PM, Eastern Standard (or Daylight Savings) Time, on the date on which it is due, in order to be considered timely filed that day. MA R USDCT CM/ECF Admin(K); MA R USDCT LR 5.4(D). When a specific time of day deadline is set by court order or stipulation, the electronic filing must be completed by that time. Documents may be filed at any time of the day on days prior to the date on which it is due. MA R USDCT CM/ECF Admin(K). A document filed electronically shall be deemed filed as of the time and date stated on the NEF received from the court. MA R USDCT CM/ECF Admin(G)(2); MA R USDCT CM/ECF Admin(K).

i. *Technical failures.* A user whose filing is made untimely as the result of a technical failure of the court's CM/ECF system may seek appropriate relief from the court. MA R USDCT CM/ECF Admin(W)(3). Technical difficulties on the filer's end, with telephone, cable lines, the filer's Internet Service Provider (ISP), or hardware or software problems, will not constitute a technical failure under the Administrative Procedures for Electronic Case Filing in the United States District Court for the District of Massachusetts (MA R USDCT CM/ECF Admin) nor excuse an untimely filing. MA R USDCT CM/ECF Admin(W)(3). As help desk support is available during normal business hours, filers are strongly urged to electronically file any documents during that period. MA R USDCT CM/ECF Admin(W)(3).

- The court has made available a public terminal (computers and scanner) in each clerk's office for registered users to scan and electronically file documents. This equipment is available during normal business hours. Users should bring their prepared document and a valid CM/ECF login and password. MA R USDCT CM/ECF Admin(W)(3).

    c.  *Extending time.* When an act may or must be done within a specified time, the court may, for good cause, extend the time: (1) with or without motion or notice if the court acts, or if a request is made, before the original time or its extension expires; or (2) on motion made after the time has expired if the party failed to act because of excusable neglect. FRCP 6(b)(1).

        i.  *Exceptions.* A court must not extend the time to act under FRCP 50(b), FRCP 50(d), FRCP 52(b), FRCP 59(b), FRCP 59(d), FRCP 59(e), and FRCP 60(b). FRCP 6(b)(2).

        ii.  Refer to the United States District Court for the District of Massachusetts KeyRules Motion for Continuance/Extension of Time document for more information on extending time.

    d.  *Additional time after certain kinds of service.* When a party may or must act within a specified time after being served and service is made under FRCP 5(b)(2)(C) (by mail), FRCP 5(b)(2)(D) (by leaving with the clerk), or FRCP 5(b)(2)(F) (by other means consented to), three (3) days are added after the period would otherwise expire under FRCP 6(a). FRCP 6(d).

## C. General Requirements

1.  *Motions, generally*

    a.  *Requirements.* A request for a court order must be made by motion. The motion must:

        i.  Be in writing unless made during a hearing or trial;

        ii.  State with particularity the grounds for seeking the order; and

        iii.  State the relief sought. FRCP 7(b)(1).

    b.  *Notice of motion.* A party interested in resisting the relief sought by a motion has a right to notice thereof, and an opportunity to be heard. AMJUR MOTIONS § 12.

        i.  [I]n addition to statutory or court rule provisions requiring notice of a motion—the purpose of such a notice requirement having been said to be to prevent a party from being prejudicially surprised by a motion—principles of natural justice dictate that an adverse party generally must be given notice that a motion will be presented to the court. AMJUR MOTIONS § 12.

        ii.  "Notice," in this regard, means reasonable notice, including a meaningful opportunity to prepare and to defend against allegations of a motion. AMJUR MOTIONS § 12.

    c.  *Writing requirement.* The writing requirement is intended to [ensure] that the adverse parties are informed and have a record of both the motion's pendency and the grounds on which the movant seeks an order. FPP § 1191; Feldberg v. Quechee Lakes Corp., 463 F.3d 195 (2d Cir. 2006). [A] single written document can satisfy the writing requirements both for a motion and for [an] FRCP 6(c)(1) notice. FRCP 7(Advisory Committee Notes).

    d.  *Particularity requirement.* The particularity requirement [ensures] that the opposing parties will have notice of their opponent's contentions. FEDPROC § 62:358; Goodman v. 1973 26 Foot Trojan Vessel, Arkansas Registration No. AR1439SN, 859 F.2d 71 (8th Cir. 1988). That requirement ensures that notice of the basis for the motion is provided to the court and to the opposing party so as to avoid prejudice, provide the opponent with a meaningful opportunity to respond, and provide the court with enough information to process the motion correctly. FEDPROC § 62:358; Andreas v. Volkswagen of Am., Inc., 336 F.3d 789 (8th Cir. 2003).

        i.  Reasonable specification of the grounds for a motion is sufficient. The particularity requirement for motions is satisfied when no party is prejudiced by a lack of particularity or when the court can comprehend the basis for the motion and deal with it fairly. However, where a movant fails to state even one ground for granting the motion in question, the movant has failed to meet the minimal standard of "reasonable specification." FEDPROC § 62:358; Martinez v. Trainor, 556 F.2d 818 (7th Cir. 1977).

        ii.  The court may excuse the failure to comply with the particularity requirement if it is inadvertent, and where no prejudice is shown by the opposing party. FEDPROC § 62:358.

    e.  *Control of motion practice*

        i.  *Plan for the disposition of motions.* At the earliest practicable time, the judicial officer shall establish a framework for the disposition of motions, which, at the discretion of the judicial officer, may include specific deadlines or general time guidelines for filing motions. This framework may be amended from time to time by the judicial officer as required by the progress of the case. MA R USDCT LR 7.1(a)(1).

        ii.  *Motion practice.* No motion shall be filed unless counsel certify that they have conferred and have attempted in good faith to resolve or narrow the issue. MA R USDCT LR 7.1(a)(2).

iii. *Unresolved motions.* The court shall rule on motions as soon as practicable, having in mind the reporting requirements set forth in the Civil Justice Reform Act. MA R USDCT LR 7.1(a)(3).

2. *Motion for judgment on the pleadings.* After the pleadings are closed—but early enough not to delay trial—a party may move for judgment on the pleadings. FRCP 12(c).

   a. *Relationship to other motions*

      i. *Common law demurrer.* The motion for judgment on the pleadings under FRCP 12(c) has its historical roots in common law practice, which permitted either party, at any point in the proceeding, to demur to his opponent's pleading and secure a dismissal or final judgment on the basis of the pleadings. FPP § 1367.

         • The common law demurrer could be used to search the record and raise procedural defects, or it could be employed to resolve the substantive merits of the controversy as disclosed on the face of the pleadings. FPP § 1367.

         • In contrast to the common law practice, the FRCP 12(c) judgment on the pleadings procedure primarily is addressed to the latter function of disposing of cases on the basis of the underlying substantive merits of the parties' claims and defenses as they are revealed in the formal pleadings. FPP § 1367. The purpose of FRCP 12(c) is to save time and expense in cases where the ultimate issues of fact are not in dispute, and to prevent the piecemeal process of judicial determination which prevailed under the old common-law practice. FEDPROC § 62:560.

      ii. *Motions to dismiss.* While FRCP 12(b) motions to dismiss and FRCP 12(c) motions for judgment on the pleadings are to some extent merely interchangeable weapons in a party's arsenal of pretrial challenges, there are differences in the scope and effect of the two motions. [An] FRCP 12(b) motion to dismiss is directed solely toward the defects of the plaintiff's claim for relief, without concern for the merits of the controversy, while [an] FRCP 12(c) motion for judgment on the pleadings at least theoretically requires some scrutiny of the merits of the controversy. FEDPROC § 62:562.

      iii. *Motion to strike.* The FRCP 12(c) motion also should be contrasted with the motion to strike under FRCP 12(f). The latter motion permits either party to strike redundant, immaterial, impertinent, or scandalous matter from an adversary's pleading and may be used to challenge the sufficiency of defenses asserted by that adversary. The motion serves as a pruning device to eliminate objectionable matter from an opponent's pleadings and, unlike the FRCP 12(c) procedure, it is not directed at gaining a final judgment on the merits, although [an] FRCP 12(f) motion that succeeds in eliminating the defenses to the action may have that purpose and, in some cases, may have that effect. FPP § 1369.

         • If a plaintiff seeks to dispute the legal sufficiency of fewer than all of the defenses raised in the defendant's pleading, he should proceed under FRCP 12(f) rather than under FRCP 12(c) because the latter leads to the entry of a judgment. FPP § 1369.

      iv. *Motion for summary judgment.* In most circumstances a party will find it preferable to proceed under FRCP 56 rather than FRCP 12(c) for a variety of reasons. For example, the summary judgment procedure is available when the defendant fails to file an answer, whereas technically no relief would be available under FRCP 12(c) because the pleadings have not been closed. If a party believes that it will be necessary to introduce evidence outside the formal pleadings in order to demonstrate that no material issue of fact exists and he is clearly entitled to judgment, it is advisable to proceed directly under FRCP 56 rather than taking the circuitous route through FRCP 12(c). Moreover, the FRCP 12(c) path may present certain risks because the court, in its discretion, may refuse to permit the introduction of matters beyond the pleadings and insist on treating the motion as one under FRCP 12(c) or apply the general motion time period set out in FRCP 6(d), rather than the special time provision in FRCP 56. FPP § 1369.

   b. *Bringing an FRCP 12(c) motion.* As numerous judicial opinions make clear, [an] FRCP 12(c) motion is designed to provide a means of disposing of cases when the material facts are not in dispute between the parties and a judgment on the merits can be achieved by focusing on the content of the competing pleadings, exhibits thereto, matters incorporated by reference in the pleadings, whatever is central or integral to the claim for relief or defense, and any facts of which the district court will take judicial notice. FPP § 1367; DiCarlo v. St. Mary Hosp., 530 F.3d 255 (3d Cir. 2008); Buddy Bean Lumber Co. v. Axis Surplus Ins. Co., 715 F.3d 695, 697 (8th Cir. 2013).

      i. The motion for a judgment on the pleadings only has utility when all material allegations of fact are admitted or not controverted in the pleadings and only questions of law remain to be decided by the district court. FPP § 1367; Stafford v. Jewelers Mut. Ins. Co., 554 F. App'x 360, 370 (6th Cir. 2014).

   c. *Partial judgment on the pleadings.* Although not provided for by FRCP 12(c), a party may properly move for partial judgment on the pleadings to further the policy goal of the efficient resolution of actions when there are no material facts in dispute. This conclusion has been said to be buttressed by FRCP 56(a), which provides that a party may move for summary judgment, identifying each claim or defense—or the part of each claim or defense—on which summary judgment is sought. FEDPROC § 62:565.

d. *Granting of a motion for judgment on the pleadings.* The federal courts have followed a fairly restrictive standard in ruling on motions for judgment on the pleadings. FPP § 1368. A motion for judgment on the pleadings is a motion for judgment on the merits, and should be granted only if no material issue of fact remains to be resolved and the movant establishes their entitlement to judgment as a matter of law. FEDPROC § 62:563; Great Plains Tr. Co. v. Morgan Stanley Dean Witter & Co., 313 F.3d 305 (5th Cir. 2002); Sikirica v. Nationwide Ins. Co., 416 F.3d 214 (3d Cir. 2005). A motion for a judgment on the pleadings must be sustained where the undisputed facts appearing in the pleadings, supplemented by any facts of which the court will take judicial notice, show that no relief can be granted. On a motion for judgment on the pleadings, dismissal can be based on either the lack of a cognizable legal theory or the absence of sufficient facts alleged under a cognizable legal theory. FEDPROC § 62:563.

   i. A motion for judgment on the pleadings admits, for purposes of the motion, the truth of all well-pleaded facts in the pleadings of the opposing party, together with all fair inferences to be drawn therefrom, even where the defendant asserts, in the FRCP 12(c) motion, [an] FRCP 12(b)(6) defense of failure to state a claim upon which relief can be granted. FEDPROC § 62:564; In re World Trade Ctr. Disaster Site Litig., 521 F.3d 169 (2d Cir. 2008); Massachusetts Nurses Ass'n v. N. Adams Reg'l Hosp., 467 F.3d 27 (1st Cir. 2006). However, all allegations of the moving party which have been denied are taken as false. FEDPROC § 62:564; Volvo Const. Equip. N. Am., Inc. v. CLM Equip. Co., Inc., 386 F.3d 581 (4th Cir. 2004). In considering a motion for judgment on the pleadings, the trial court is thus required to view the facts presented in the pleadings and inferences to be drawn therefrom in the light most favorable to the nonmoving party. In this fashion the courts hope to [ensure] that the rights of the nonmoving party are decided as fully and fairly on [an] FRCP 12(c) motion as if there had been a trial. FEDPROC § 62:564.

   ii. On a motion for judgment on the pleadings, the court may consider facts upon the basis of judicial notice. FEDPROC § 62:564; R.G. Fin. Corp. v. Vergara-Nunez, 446 F.3d 178 (1st Cir. 2006). However, a motion for judgment on the pleadings does not admit conclusions of law or unwarranted factual inferences. FEDPROC § 62:564; JPMorgan Chase Bank, N.A. v. Winget, 510 F.3d 577 (6th Cir. 2007).

e. *Joining motions*

   i. *Right to join.* A motion under FRCP 12 may be joined with any other motion allowed by FRCP 12. FRCP 12(g)(1).

   ii. *Limitation on further motions.* Except as provided in FRCP 12(h)(2) or FRCP 12(h)(3), a party that makes a motion under FRCP 12 must not make another motion under FRCP 12 raising a defense or objection that was available to the party but omitted from its earlier motion. FRCP 12(g)(2).

3. *Opposing papers.* The Federal Rules of Civil Procedure do not require any formal answer, return, or reply to a motion, except where the Federal Rules of Civil Procedure or local rules may require affidavits, memoranda, or other papers to be filed in opposition to a motion. Such papers are simply to apprise the court of such opposition and the grounds of that opposition. FEDPROC § 62:353.

a. *Effect of failure to respond to motion.* Although in the absence of statutory provision or court rule, a motion ordinarily does not require a written answer, when a party files a motion and the opposing party fails to respond, the court may construe such failure to respond as nonopposition to the motion or an admission that the motion was meritorious, may take the facts alleged in the motion as true—the rule in some jurisdictions being that the failure to respond to a fact set forth in a motion is deemed an admission—and may grant the motion if the relief requested appears to be justified. AMJUR MOTIONS § 28.

b. *Assent or no opposition not determinative.* However, a motion will not be granted automatically simply because an "assent" or a notation of "no opposition" has been filed; federal judges frequently deny motions that have been assented to when it is thought that justice so dictates. FPP § 1190.

c. *Responsive pleading inappropriate as response to motion.* An attempt to answer or oppose a motion with a responsive pleading usually is not appropriate. FPP § 1190.

4. *Reply papers.* A moving party may be required or permitted to prepare papers in addition to his original motion papers. AMJUR MOTIONS § 25. Papers answering or replying to opposing papers may be appropriate, in the interests of justice, where it appears there is a substantial reason for allowing a reply. Thus, a court may accept reply papers where a party demonstrates that the papers to which it seeks to file a reply raise new issues that are material to the disposition of the

question before the court, or where the court determines, sua sponte, that it wishes further briefing of an issue raised in those papers and orders the submission of additional papers. FEDPROC § 62:354.

    a. *Function of reply papers.* The function of a reply affidavit is to answer the arguments made in opposition to the position taken by the movant and not to permit the movant to introduce new arguments in support of the motion. AMJUR MOTIONS § 25.

    b. *Issues raised for the first time in a reply document.* However, the view has been followed in some jurisdictions, that as a matter of judicial economy, where there is no prejudice and where the issues could be raised simply by filing a motion to dismiss, the trial court has discretion to consider arguments raised for the first time in a reply memorandum, and that a trial court may grant a motion to strike issues raised for the first time in a reply memorandum. AMJUR MOTIONS § 26.

5. *Alternative dispute resolution (ADR).* The judicial officer assigned to preside over the case shall encourage the resolution of disputes by settlement or other alternative dispute resolution programs. MA R USDCT LR 16.4(a).

    a. *Settlement.* At every conference conducted under the Local Rules of the United States District Court for the District of Massachusetts, the judicial officer shall inquire as to the utility of the parties conducting settlement negotiations, explore means of facilitating those negotiations, and offer whatever assistance may be appropriate in the circumstances. Assistance may include a reference of the case to another judicial officer for settlement purposes. MA R USDCT LR 16.4(b).

        i. When a case is settled, the parties shall file with the clerk a signed agreement for judgment or stipulation for dismissal, as appropriate, within twenty-eight (28) days, unless the court otherwise orders. MA R USDCT LR 68.2.

    b. *Alternative dispute resolution programs*

        i. *Discretion of judicial officer.* The judicial officer, following an exploration of the matter with all counsel, may refer appropriate cases to alternative dispute resolution programs that have been designated for use in the district court or that the judicial officer may make available. The dispute resolution programs described in MA R USDCT LR 16.4(c)(2) through MA R USDCT LR 16.4(c)(4) are illustrative, not exclusive. Moreover, nothing in MA R USDCT LR 16.4 shall preclude the parties from engaging in private dispute resolution programs as long as they comply with any schedule established by the court. MA R USDCT LR 16.4(c)(1).

        ii. *Mediation.* The judicial officer may refer the case to mediation upon the agreement of all parties. MA R USDCT LR 16.4(c)(2)(A).

        iii. *Other alternative dispute resolution programs.* Use of mediation is not exclusive. At the request of parties, the judicial officer may consider other forms of alternative dispute resolution including, but not limited to, mini-trial, summary jury trial and arbitration. MA R USDCT LR 16.4(c)(3).

    c. For more information on alternative dispute resolution (ADR), refer to MA R USDCT LR 16.4.

6. *Sanctions.* Failure to comply with any of the directions or obligations set forth in, or authorized by, these rules may result in dismissal, default, or the imposition of other sanctions as deemed appropriate by the judicial officer. MA R USDCT LR 1.3. Except as provided by law, the court may impose sanctions as provided in MA R USDCT LR 1.3 for failure to comply with the Administrative Procedures for Electronic Case Filing in the United States District Court for the District of Massachusetts (MA R USDCT CM/ECF Admin) or with MA R USDCT LR 5.4. MA R USDCT CM/ECF Admin(C)(3).

## D. Documents

1. *Documents for moving party*

    a. *Required documents*

        i. *Notice of motion and motion.* Refer to the General Requirements section of this document for information on the notice of motion and motion.

          • *Request for oral argument.* Any party making or opposing a motion who believes that oral argument may assist the court and wishes to be heard shall include a request for oral argument in a separate paragraph of the motion or opposition. The request should be set off with a centered caption, "REQUEST FOR ORAL ARGUMENT." MA R USDCT LR 7.1(d).

        ii. *Memorandum.* A party filing a motion shall at the same time file a memorandum of reasons, including citation of supporting authorities, why the motion should be granted. MA R USDCT LR 7.1(b)(1). Any memorandum of law or other attachment filed in support of a main document shall be filed as a separate document, using the proper event. MA R USDCT CM/ECF Admin(G)(4). Memoranda supporting or opposing allowance of motions shall not, without leave of court, exceed twenty (20) pages, double-spaced. MA R USDCT LR 7.1(b)(4).

iii. *Certificate of service.* No certificate of service is required when a paper is served by filing it with the court's electronic-filing system. When a paper that is required to be served is served by other means: (1) if the paper is filed, a certificate of service must be filed with it or within a reasonable time after service; and (2) if the paper is not filed, a certificate of service need not be filed unless filing is required by court order or by local rule. FRCP 5(d)(1)(B). Except as otherwise provided by the Federal Rules of Civil Procedure, proof of service of all pleadings and other papers required to be served (except discovery papers that in accordance with FRCP 33 to FRCP 36(f) are not to be filed) shall be filed in the office of the clerk promptly after service has been made. The proof shall show the time and manner of service, and may be made by written acknowledgment of service, a certificate of a member of the bar of this court, or an affidavit of the person who served the paper. MA R USDCT LR 5.2(b)(1). A certificate of service of a member of the bar shall appear at the bottom of or on the margin of the last page of the paper to which it relates. MA R USDCT LR 5.2(b)(2).

- *Paper service.* The certificate shall be a brief, single-spaced statement and may be in the following form: I hereby certify that a true copy of the above document was served upon (each party appearing pro se and) the attorney of record for each other party by mail (by hand) on (date). (Signature). MA R USDCT LR 5.2(b)(2).

- *Electronic service.* Any pleading or other paper served by electronic means must bear a certificate of service in accordance with MA R USDCT LR 5.2(b). MA R USDCT LR 5.4(C); MA R USDCT CM/ECF Admin(H)(2). The certificate of service shall state that the filer: (1) filed the document electronically, (2) that it will be served electronically to registered CM/ECF participants via the NEF and (3) that the filer will send paper copies to non-registered participants as indicated on the NEF. MA R USDCT CM/ECF Admin(H)(2). For example: I hereby certify that this document filed through the CM/ECF system will be sent electronically to the registered participants as identified on the NEF (NEF) and paper copies will be sent to those indicated as non registered participants on (date). MA R USDCT CM/ECF Admin(H)(2).

- *Return.* Documents not conforming to the requirements of MA R USDCT LR 5.2 (except notices of appeal) shall be returned by the clerk. MA R USDCT LR 5.2(b)(2).

- *Failure to make proof of service.* Failure to make proof of service does not affect the validity of the service. MA R USDCT LR 5.2(b)(3).

b. *Supplemental documents*

i. *Pleadings.* In considering a motion for judgment on the pleadings, the trial court is. . .required to view the facts presented in the pleadings and inferences to be drawn therefrom in the light most favorable to the nonmoving party. FEDPROC § 62:564.

- *Motion treated as one for summary judgment.* If, on a motion under FRCP 12(b)(6) or FRCP 12(c), matters outside the pleadings are presented to and not excluded by the court, the motion must be treated as one for summary judgment under FRCP 56. All parties must be given a reasonable opportunity to present all the material that is pertinent to the motion. FRCP 12(d).

ii. *Notice of constitutional question.* A party that files a pleading, written motion, or other paper drawing into question the constitutionality of a federal or state statute must promptly:

- *File notice.* File a notice of constitutional question stating the question and identifying the paper that raises it, if: (1) a federal statute is questioned and the parties do not include the United States, one of its agencies, or one of its officers or employees in an official capacity; or (2) a state statute is questioned and the parties do not include the state, one of its agencies, or one of its officers or employees in an official capacity; and

- *Serve notice.* Serve the notice and paper on the Attorney General of the United States if a federal statute is questioned—or on the state attorney general if a state statute is questioned—either by certified or registered mail or by sending it to an electronic address designated by the attorney general for this purpose. FRCP 5.1(a).

- *No forfeiture.* A party's failure to file and serve the notice, or the court's failure to certify, does not forfeit a constitutional claim or defense that is otherwise timely asserted. FRCP 5.1(d).

iii. *Nongovernmental corporate disclosure statement*

- *Contents.* A nongovernmental corporate party must file two (2) copies of a disclosure statement that: (1) identifies any parent corporation and any publicly held corporation owning ten percent (10%) or more of its stock; or (2) states that there is no such corporation. FRCP 7.1(a).

- *Time to file; Supplemental filing.* A party must: (1) file the disclosure statement with its first appearance, pleading, petition, motion, response, or other request addressed to the court; and (2) promptly file a supplemental statement if any required information changes. FRCP 7.1(b).

iv. *Proposed order.* Proposed orders usually are not required by this court. However, the court may request the party to submit such a document. In those situations, unless otherwise directed by the clerk's office, electronically file the proposed document/order using the entry for "Proposed Documents submitted to the court," found under the Other Documents menu, or as an attachment to the motion to which it relates. MA R USDCT CM/ECF Admin(T).

v. *Compact disk with copy of document(s) in PDF format.* A filer who cannot file a document electronically because of such technical difficulty on the filer's end [with telephone, cable lines, the filer's Internet Service Provider (ISP), or hardware or software problems] shall file the document conventionally along with a copy of the document in PDF format on a compact disk or contact the clerk's office for permission to submit the PDF document via email. MA R USDCT CM/ECF Admin(W)(3). Refer to the Timing section of this document for more information on technical failures.

vi. *Notice of filing with clerk's office.* When documents or exhibits (other than those filed ex parte or under seal) are submitted conventionally, a "Notice of Filing with clerk's office" shall be filed electronically and attached to the main document. A paper copy of the "Notice of Filing with clerk's office" must accompany the documents submitted to the court. The "Notice of Filing with clerk's office" (see MA R USDCT CM/ECF Admin(Appendix I)) shall describe each of the documents that will be filed as paper copies in the clerk's office, or shall include an index of the documents if those documents are voluminous. MA R USDCT CM/ECF Admin(P)(5).

vii. *Additional copies.* Whenever, because of the nature of a proceeding, such as a proceeding before a three-judge district court under 28 U.S.C.A. § 2284, additional copies of a paper required to be filed are necessary either for the use of the court or to enable the clerk to carry out his duties, it is the responsibility of the party filing or having filed the paper to provide the necessary copies. MA R USDCT LR 5.1(d).

viii. *Courtesy copies.* COURTESY COPIES OF DOCUMENTS FILED ELECTRONICALLY SHALL NOT BE SUBMITTED ROUTINELY. MA R USDCT CM/ECF Admin(J). Judicial officers, on a case-by-case basis, may require courtesy copies for specific cases, or types of motions, etc. A few Judicial Officers have entered Standing Orders, which may be found on their respective pages on the court's website (under Divisions). Any document filed on paper with the court as a courtesy copy must be clearly labeled as such (Example: COURTESY COPY—DO NOT SCAN). Documents delivered to the court as a courtesy copy will not be maintained in the official court record. MA R USDCT CM/ECF Admin(J).

2. *Documents for opposing party*

  a. *Required documents*

    i. *Opposition.* Refer to the General Requirements section of this document for information on the opposing papers.

      - *Memorandum.* A party opposing a motion shall file, in the same (rather than a separate), document a memorandum of reasons, including citation of supporting authorities, why the motion should not be granted. MA R USDCT LR 7.1(b)(2). Any memorandum of law or other attachment filed in support of a main document shall be filed as a separate document, using the proper event. MA R USDCT CM/ECF Admin(G)(4). Memoranda supporting or opposing allowance of motions shall not, without leave of court, exceed twenty (20) pages, double-spaced. MA R USDCT LR 7.1(b)(4).

      - *Request for oral argument.* Any party making or opposing a motion who believes that oral argument may assist the court and wishes to be heard shall include a request for oral argument in a separate paragraph of the motion or opposition. The request should be set off with a centered caption, "REQUEST FOR ORAL ARGUMENT." MA R USDCT LR 7.1(d).

    ii. *Certificate of service.* No certificate of service is required when a paper is served by filing it with the court's electronic-filing system. When a paper that is required to be served is served by other means: (1) if the paper is filed, a certificate of service must be filed with it or within a reasonable time after service; and (2) if the paper is not filed, a certificate of service need not be filed unless filing is required by court order or by local rule. FRCP 5(d)(1)(B). Except as otherwise provided by the Federal Rules of Civil Procedure, proof of service of all pleadings and other papers required to be served (except discovery papers that in accordance with FRCP 33 to FRCP 36(f) are not to be filed) shall be filed in the office of the clerk promptly after service has been made. The proof shall show the time and manner of service, and may be made by written acknowledgment of service, a certificate of a member of the bar of this court, or an affidavit of the person who served the paper. MA R USDCT

LR 5.2(b)(1). A certificate of service of a member of the bar shall appear at the bottom of or on the margin of the last page of the paper to which it relates. MA R USDCT LR 5.2(b)(2).

- *Paper service.* The certificate shall be a brief, single-spaced statement and may be in the following form: I hereby certify that a true copy of the above document was served upon (each party appearing pro se and) the attorney of record for each other party by mail (by hand) on (date). (Signature). MA R USDCT LR 5.2(b)(2).

- *Electronic service.* Any pleading or other paper served by electronic means must bear a certificate of service in accordance with MA R USDCT LR 5.2(b). MA R USDCT LR 5.4(C); MA R USDCT CM/ECF Admin(H)(2). The certificate of service shall state that the filer: (1) filed the document electronically, (2) that it will be served electronically to registered CM/ECF participants via the NEF and (3) that the filer will send paper copies to non-registered participants as indicated on the NEF. MA R USDCT CM/ECF Admin(H)(2). For example: I hereby certify that this document filed through the CM/ECF system will be sent electronically to the registered participants as identified on the NEF (NEF) and paper copies will be sent to those indicated as non registered participants on (date). MA R USDCT CM/ECF Admin(H)(2).

- *Return.* Documents not conforming to the requirements of MA R USDCT LR 5.2 (except notices of appeal) shall be returned by the clerk. MA R USDCT LR 5.2(b)(2).

- *Failure to make proof of service.* Failure to make proof of service does not affect the validity of the service. MA R USDCT LR 5.2(b)(3).

b. *Supplemental documents*

i. *Pleadings.* In considering a motion for judgment on the pleadings, the trial court is. . .required to view the facts presented in the pleadings and inferences to be drawn therefrom in the light most favorable to the nonmoving party. FEDPROC § 62:564.

- *Motion treated as one for summary judgment.* If, on a motion under FRCP 12(b)(6) or FRCP 12(c), matters outside the pleadings are presented to and not excluded by the court, the motion must be treated as one for summary judgment under FRCP 56. All parties must be given a reasonable opportunity to present all the material that is pertinent to the motion. FRCP 12(d).

ii. *Notice of constitutional question.* A party that files a pleading, written motion, or other paper drawing into question the constitutionality of a federal or state statute must promptly:

- *File notice.* File a notice of constitutional question stating the question and identifying the paper that raises it, if: (1) a federal statute is questioned and the parties do not include the United States, one of its agencies, or one of its officers or employees in an official capacity; or (2) a state statute is questioned and the parties do not include the state, one of its agencies, or one of its officers or employees in an official capacity; and

- *Serve notice.* Serve the notice and paper on the Attorney General of the United States if a federal statute is questioned—or on the state attorney general if a state statute is questioned—either by certified or registered mail or by sending it to an electronic address designated by the attorney general for this purpose. FRCP 5.1(a).

- *No forfeiture.* A party's failure to file and serve the notice, or the court's failure to certify, does not forfeit a constitutional claim or defense that is otherwise timely asserted. FRCP 5.1(d).

iii. *Compact disk with copy of document(s) in PDF format.* A filer who cannot file a document electronically because of such technical difficulty on the filer's end [with telephone, cable lines, the filer's Internet Service Provider (ISP), or hardware or software problems] shall file the document conventionally along with a copy of the document in PDF format on a compact disk or contact the clerk's office for permission to submit the PDF document via email. MA R USDCT CM/ECF Admin(W)(3). Refer to the Timing section of this document for more information on technical failures.

iv. *Notice of filing with clerk's office.* When documents or exhibits (other than those filed ex parte or under seal) are submitted conventionally, a "Notice of Filing with clerk's office" shall be filed electronically and attached to the main document. A paper copy of the "Notice of Filing with clerk's office" must accompany the documents submitted to the court. The "Notice of Filing with clerk's office" (see MA R USDCT CM/ECF Admin(Appendix I)) shall describe each of the documents that will be filed as paper copies in the clerk's office, or shall include an index of the documents if those documents are voluminous. MA R USDCT CM/ECF Admin(P)(5).

v. *Additional copies.* Whenever, because of the nature of a proceeding, such as a proceeding before a three-judge district court under 28 U.S.C.A. § 2284, additional copies of a paper required to be filed are necessary either for the use of the court or to enable the clerk to carry out his duties, it is the responsibility of the party filing or having filed the paper to provide the necessary copies. MA R USDCT LR 5.1(d).

vi. *Courtesy copies.* COURTESY COPIES OF DOCUMENTS FILED ELECTRONICALLY SHALL NOT BE SUBMITTED ROUTINELY. MA R USDCT CM/ECF Admin(J). Judicial officers, on a case-by-case basis, may require courtesy copies for specific cases, or types of motions, etc. A few Judicial Officers have entered Standing Orders, which may be found on their respective pages on the court's website (under Divisions). Any document filed on paper with the court as a courtesy copy must be clearly labeled as such (Example: COURTESY COPY—DO NOT SCAN). Documents delivered to the court as a courtesy copy will not be maintained in the official court record. MA R USDCT CM/ECF Admin(J).

## E. Format

1. *Form of documents.* The rules governing captions and other matters of form in pleadings apply to motions and other papers. FRCP 7(b)(2). The provisions of FRCP 10 and FRCP 11 concerning the form and signing of pleadings, motions, and other papers shall be applicable to all papers filed in any proceeding in this court. The board of bar overseers registration number of each attorney signing such documents, except the United States Attorney and his or her staff, shall be inscribed below the signature. MA R USDCT LR 5.1(a)(1).

   a. *Paper size and binding.* All papers filed in the court shall be adapted for flat filing, be filed on eight and one-half by eleven (8-1/2 x 11) inch paper without backers and be bound firmly by staple or some such other means (excluding paper or binder clip or rubber band). MA R USDCT LR 5.1(a)(2).

   b. *Spacing.* All papers, except discovery requests and responses, shall be double-spaced except for the identification of counsel, title of the case, footnotes, quotations and exhibits. Discovery requests and responses shall be single-spaced. MA R USDCT LR 5.1(a)(2).

   c. *Caption.* Every pleading must have a caption with the court's name, a title, a file number, and [an] FRCP 7(a) designation. FRCP 10(a).

      i. *Names of parties.* The title of the complaint must name all the parties; the title of other pleadings, after naming the first party on each side, may refer generally to other parties. FRCP 10(a).

      ii. *Request for special action.* When any pleading or other paper filed in the court includes a request for special process or relief, or any other request such that, if granted, the court will proceed other than in the ordinary course, the request shall, unless it is noted on the category sheet [see MA R USDCT LR 40.1(a)(1)], be noted on the first page to the right of or immediately beneath the caption. MA R USDCT LR 5.1(c).

   d. *Claims or defenses*

      i. *Numbered paragraphs.* A party must state its claims or defenses in numbered paragraphs, each limited as far as practicable to a single set of circumstances. A later pleading may refer by number to a paragraph in an earlier pleading. FRCP 10(b).

      ii. *Separate statements.* If doing so would promote clarity, each claim founded on a separate transaction or occurrence—and each defense other than a denial—must be stated in a separate count or defense. FRCP 10(b).

   e. *Adoption by reference.* A statement in a pleading may be adopted by reference elsewhere in the same pleading or in any other pleading or motion. FRCP 10(c).

      i. *Exhibits.* A copy of a written instrument that is an exhibit to a pleading is a part of the pleading for all purposes. FRCP 10(c).

   f. *Citations*

      i. *Local rules.* These rules shall be known as Local Rules of the United States District Court for the District of Massachusetts and cited as "L.R., D. Mass." or "L.R." MA R USDCT LR 1.1.

      ii. *Electronic case filing procedures.* The procedures governing electronic case filing shall be known as the "Administrative Procedures for Electronic Case Filing in the United States District Court for the District of Massachusetts." They shall be cited as "APECF." MA R USDCT CM/ECF Admin(A)(7).

   g. *Acceptance by the clerk.* The clerk must not refuse to file a paper solely because it is not in the form prescribed by the Federal Rules of Civil Procedure or by a local rule or practice. FRCP 5(d)(4).

      i. Except for complaints and notices of appeal, papers that do not conform to the requirements of MA R USDCT LR 5.1(a)(2) shall be returned by the clerk. MA R USDCT LR 5.1(a)(2).

2. *Form of electronic documents.* A paper filed electronically is a written paper for purposes of the Federal Rules of Civil Procedure. FRCP 5(d)(3)(D).

    a. *PDF/A format required.* The court will begin requiring submission of documents in PDF/A format in the foreseeable future. PDF/A is an enhanced version of the traditional PDF format. Newer versions of most PDF software will be able to convert to this format. Additional information on PDF/A documents may be found on the court's website. MA R USDCT CM/ECF Admin(Electronic Filing and PDF).

        i. *Electronically converted PDF.* Electronically converted PDF documents are created from word processing documents (MS Word, WordPerfect, etc.) using any appropriate software. These documents are text searchable and the file size is generally smaller than a scanned document. CM/ECF users may use any brand of software to convert documents to PDF. MA R USDCT CM/ECF Admin(Electronic Filing and PDF).

            • Documents converted to PDF, rather than scanned, are preferred for filing in CM/ECF. MA R USDCT CM/ECF Admin(Electronic Filing and PDF).

        ii. *Scanned PDF.* Scanned PDF documents are created from paper documents run through an optical scanner. Scanned PDF documents are generally not searchable and have a larger file size. Please note that software used to create scanned documents may (and should) be set in such a way that the document is "text-searchable." MA R USDCT CM/ECF Admin(Electronic Filing and PDF).

    b. *Title.* All pleadings filed electronically shall be titled in accordance with the approved dictionary of civil or criminal events of the CM/ECF system of this court. A list of events is available on the CM/ECF Training Information page of the court's website. The clerk's office may, when necessary and appropriate, modify the docket entry description, or delete and re-enter the docket entry in order to comply with the court's quality assurance standards. MA R USDCT CM/ECF Admin(G)(3).

    c. *Attachments to filings and exhibits.* Attachments to filings and exhibits must be filed in accordance with the court's CM/ECF User Manual, unless otherwise ordered by the court. MA R USDCT CM/ECF Admin(O)(1).

        i. Filers must submit as attachments only those excerpts of the referenced documents that are directly germane to the matter under consideration by the court. Excerpted material must be clearly and prominently identified as such. Users who file excerpts of documents do so without prejudice to their right to timely file additional excerpts or the complete document, as may be allowed by the court. Responding parties may timely file additional excerpts or the complete document that they believe are directly germane. MA R USDCT CM/ECF Admin(O)(2).

        ii. Filers shall not attach as an exhibit any pleading or other paper already on file with the court in that case, but shall merely refer to that document. (See MA R USDCT CM/ECF Admin(G) for information on using hyperlinks in PDF documents filed in CM/ECF.) MA R USDCT CM/ECF Admin(O)(3).

    d. *Redacted documents.* The parties may request or the court may require the submission of documents that have been redacted/stripped of sensitive or confidential information. The redacted document prepared for electronic filing shall include the original caption of the document, and be clearly labeled as "Redacted Document." A specific event is available for this purpose ("Redacted Document"), found under the Other Filings/Other Documents menu option. MA R USDCT CM/ECF Admin(S).

        i. Attorneys and pro se litigants are advised to take extra care when creating PDF documents intended for submission to CM/ECF. Steps shall be taken to ensure the documents are free of any hidden data (metadata) that may contain redacted information, or traces of information edited or deleted are not hidden in the final document. Even PDF content that has been encrypted may be recovered. An advisory document with additional information on this topic may be found on the court's website. MA R USDCT CM/ECF Admin(S).

    e. *Hyperlinks.* Electronically filed documents may contain the following types of hyperlinks: (1) hyperlinks to other portions of the same document; (2) hyperlinks to other documents filed within the CM/ECF system; and (3) hyperlinks to a location on the Internet that contains a source document for a citation. MA R USDCT CM/ECF Admin(G)(7).

        i. Hyperlinks to cited authority may not replace standard citation format. Complete citations must be included in the text of the filed document. Neither a hyperlink, nor any site to which it refers, shall be considered part of the record, but are simply convenient mechanisms for accessing material cited in a document filed in CM/ECF. Instructions on creating hyperlinks may be found in the CM/ECF User Manual. MA R USDCT CM/ECF Admin(G)(7).

        ii. The court accepts no responsibility for, and does not endorse, any product, organization, or content at any

hyperlinked site, or at any site to which that site may be linked. The court accepts no responsibility for the availability or functionality of any hyperlink. MA R USDCT CM/ECF Admin(G)(7).

iii. One feature of PDF/A documents is that hyperlinks are commonly "masked," meaning that the full address of the referenced file is not written out; for example, clicking the word brief may open a brief which was previously filed in CM/ECF. MA R USDCT CM/ECF Admin(G)(7)(NOTE). An "unmasked" hyperlink has the full address visible to the user. MA R USDCT CM/ECF Admin(G)(7)(NOTE).

- Masked hyperlinks may or may not work in a PDF/A document, depending on how it was created. Currently, masked hyperlinks are preserved in PDF/A documents produced by the "Save As" method in Microsoft Word 2007 and 2010; the "PDFMaker" method in Microsoft Word 2007; and OpenOffice 2.4 ("PDF Export"). With other production methods, such as WordPerfect, the PDF/A document includes underlined words that appear to be links, but clicking them has no effect. MA R USDCT CM/ECF Admin(G)(7)(NOTE).

f. *Documents features not accepted.* CM/ECF will not accept PDF documents containing tracking tags, embedded systems commands, password protections, access restrictions or other security features, special tags or dynamic features. MA R USDCT CM/ECF Admin(G)(8).

g. *File size limitations.* A filing party shall limit the size of each PDF file to no more than twenty (20) megabytes. PDF files larger than seven (7) megabytes will be rejected by the CM/ECF system. The filer will see a message advising of the size limitation. MA R USDCT CM/ECF Admin(P)(2).

i. Larger documents or exhibits may be submitted electronically if split into separate PDF files each less than seven (7) megabytes, attached to the main document and clearly labeled. MA R USDCT CM/ECF Admin(P)(2).

ii. Documents submitted electronically or on paper are subject to the page limitations set by MA R USDCT LR 7.1(b)(4) or by order of the court. MA R USDCT CM/ECF Admin(P)(1).

h. *Accuracy and readability.* The filer shall verify the accuracy and readability of any PDF file before electronically filing it in CM/ECF. MA R USDCT CM/ECF Admin(G)(6); MA R USDCT CM/ECF Admin(P)(3).

3. *Signing of pleadings, motions and other papers*

a. *Signature.* Every pleading, written motion, and other paper must be signed by at least one attorney of record in the attorney's name—or by a party personally if the party is unrepresented. The paper must state the signer's address, e-mail address, and telephone number. FRCP 11(a). The provisions of the Federal Rules of Civil Procedure pertaining to the form and signing of pleadings, motions, and other papers shall be applicable to all papers filed in any proceeding in this court. The board of bar overseers registration number of each attorney signing such documents, except the United States Attorney and his staff, shall be inscribed below the signature. MA R USDCT LR 5.1(a)(1).

i. *Electronic signing.* A filing made through a person's electronic-filing account and authorized by that person, together with that person's name on a signature block, constitutes the person's signature. FRCP 5(d)(3)(C).

ii. *Appearances.* The filing of an appearance or any other pleading signed on behalf of a party constitutes an entry of appearance for that party. All pleadings shall contain the name, bar admission number, address, telephone number, and e-mail address of the attorney entering an appearance. MA R USDCT LR 83.5.2(a).

- *Appearances by law firms.* When a party is represented by a law firm, the appearance must include the name and the signature of at least one individual attorney. When a party is represented by more than one attorney from the same or different law firms, the attorney entering the appearance must designate the individual attorney who is authorized to receive all notices in the case. Any notice sent to an attorney so designated shall be deemed to be proper notice unless the court finds that notice was not properly sent. MA R USDCT LR 83.5.2(b).

- For more information on appearances, refer to MA R USDCT LR 83.5.2.

iii. *Signatures of attorneys.* The user login and password required to submit documents to the CM/ECF system shall serve as that user's signature for purposes of FRCP 11 and for all other purposes under the Federal Rules of Civil Procedure and the Local Rules of the United States District Court for the District of Massachusetts. All electronically filed documents must include a signature block and must set forth the attorney's name, bar number, address, telephone number and email address. The name of the CM/ECF user under whose log-in and password the document is submitted must be preceded by a "/s/" and typed in the space where the signature would otherwise appear. MA R USDCT CM/ECF Admin(M)(1). For an example, refer to MA R USDCT CM/ECF Admin(M)(1).

iv. *Signatures of pro se parties.* Any document requiring a signature that is filed by a party appearing pro se shall

bear the words "pro se" following that party's signature. Any such document shall also state the party's mailing address, telephone number (if any), and e-mail address (if the party has consented to service by email). MA R USDCT LR 83.5.5(g). For more information on practice by pro se litigants, refer to MA R USDCT LR 83.5.5.

v. *Multiple signatures.* The filer of any document requiring more than one signature (e.g, stipulations, joint motions, joint status reports, magistrate judge consent forms, etc.) must list thereon all the names of other signatories by means of a "/s/ name of signatory" block for each. By submitting such a document, the filing attorney certifies that each of the other signatories has expressly agreed to the form and substance of the document and that the filing attorney has their actual authority to submit the document electronically. MA R USDCT CM/ECF Admin(M)(2). For more information, refer to MA R USDCT CM/ECF Admin(M)(2).

vi. *Affidavits.* Except as provided in MA R USDCT CM/ECF Admin(L), affidavits shall be filed electronically; however, the electronically filed version must contain a "/s/ name of signatory" block indicating that the paper document bears an original signature. MA R USDCT CM/ECF Admin(M)(3). The court will also accept a scanned version of the original, signed document. MA R USDCT CM/ECF Admin(M)(3). For more information, refer to MA R USDCT CM/ECF Admin(M)(3).

vii. *No verification or accompanying affidavit required for pleadings.* Unless a rule or statute specifically states otherwise, a pleading need not be verified or accompanied by an affidavit. FRCP 11(a).

viii. *Unsigned papers.* The court must strike an unsigned paper unless the omission is promptly corrected after being called to the attorney's or party's attention. FRCP 11(a).

b. *Representations to the court.* By presenting to the court a pleading, written motion, or other paper—whether by signing, filing, submitting, or later advocating it—an attorney or unrepresented party certifies that to the best of the person's knowledge, information, and belief, formed after an inquiry reasonable under the circumstances:

i. It is not being presented for any improper purpose, such as to harass, cause unnecessary delay, or needlessly increase the cost of litigation;

ii. The claims, defenses, and other legal contentions are warranted by existing law or by a nonfrivolous argument for extending, modifying, or reversing existing law or for establishing new law;

iii. The factual contentions have evidentiary support or, if specifically so identified, will likely have evidentiary support after a reasonable opportunity for further investigation or discovery; and

iv. The denials of factual contentions are warranted on the evidence or, if specifically so identified, are reasonably based on belief or a lack of information. FRCP 11(b).

c. *Sanctions.* If, after notice and a reasonable opportunity to respond, the court determines that FRCP 11(b) has been violated, the court may impose an appropriate sanction on any attorney, law firm, or party that violated FRCP 11(b) or is responsible for the violation. FRCP 11(c)(1). Refer to the United States District Court for the District of Massachusetts KeyRules Motion for Sanctions document for more information.

4. *Privacy protection for filings made with the court*

a. *Redacted filings.* Unless the court orders otherwise, in an electronic or paper filing with the court that contains an individual's Social Security number, taxpayer-identification number, or birth date, the name of an individual known to be a minor, or a financial-account number, a party or nonparty making the filing may include only:

i. The last four (4) digits of the Social Security number and taxpayer-identification number;

ii. The year of the individual's birth;

iii. The minor's initials; and

iv. The last four (4) digits of the financial-account number. FRCP 5.2(a); MA R USDCT CM/ECF Admin(N).

b. *Exemptions from the redaction requirement.* The redaction requirement does not apply to the following:

i. A financial-account number that identifies the property allegedly subject to forfeiture in a forfeiture proceeding;

ii. The record of an administrative or agency proceeding;

iii. The official record of a state-court proceeding;

iv. The record of a court or tribunal, if that record was not subject to the redaction requirement when originally filed;

v. A filing covered by FRCP 5.2(c) or FRCP 5.2(d); and

vi. A pro se filing in an action brought under 28 U.S.C.A. § 2241, 28 U.S.C.A. § 2254, or 28 U.S.C.A. § 2255. FRCP 5.2(b).

c. *Limitations on remote access to electronic files; Social Security appeals and immigration cases.* Unless the court orders otherwise, in an action for benefits under the Social Security Act, and in an action or proceeding relating to an order of removal, to relief from removal, or to immigration benefits or detention, access to an electronic file is authorized as follows:

    i. The parties and their attorneys may have remote electronic access to any part of the case file, including the administrative record;

    ii. Any other person may have electronic access to the full record at the courthouse, but may have remote electronic access only to:

- The docket maintained by the court; and
- An opinion, order, judgment, or other disposition of the court, but not any other part of the case file or the administrative record. FRCP 5.2(c).

d. *Filings made under seal.* The court may order that a filing be made under seal without redaction. The court may later unseal the filing or order the person who made the filing to file a redacted version for the public record. FRCP 5.2(d).

e. *Protective orders.* For good cause, the court may by order in a case:

    i. Require redaction of additional information; or

    ii. Limit or prohibit a nonparty's remote electronic access to a document filed with the court. FRCP 5.2(e).

f. *Option for additional unredacted filing under seal.* A person making a redacted filing may also file an unredacted copy under seal. The court must retain the unredacted copy as part of the record. FRCP 5.2(f). For more information, refer to MA R USDCT LR 7.2.

g. *Option for filing a reference list.* A filing that contains redacted information may be filed together with a reference list that identifies each item of redacted information and specifies an appropriate identifier that uniquely corresponds to each item listed. The list must be filed under seal and may be amended as of right. Any reference in the case to a listed identifier will be construed to refer to the corresponding item of information. FRCP 5.2(g).

h. *Responsibility for redaction.* The clerk's office is not responsible for reviewing documents filed with the court to determine whether pleadings have been redacted and are in the proper form. MA R USDCT CM/ECF Admin(N).

i. *Waiver of protection of identifiers.* A person waives the protection of FRCP 5.2(a) as to the person's own information by filing it without redaction and not under seal. FRCP 5.2(h).

## F. Filing and Service Requirements

1. *Filing requirements*

a. *Required filings.* Any paper after the complaint that is required to be served must be filed no later than a reasonable time after service. FRCP 5(d)(1).

    i. Except as noted in FRCP 33 to FRCP 36, the original of all papers required to be served under FRCP 5(d) shall, unless otherwise submitted to the court, be filed in the office of the clerk within seven (7) days after service has been made. MA R USDCT LR 5.1(b). Except as otherwise provided by the Federal Rules of Civil Procedure, proof of service of all pleadings and other papers required to be served (except discovery papers that in accordance with FRCP 33 to FRCP 36(f) are not to be filed) shall be filed in the office of the clerk promptly after service has been made. MA R USDCT LR 5.2(b)(1).

b. *Nonelectronic filing.* A paper not filed electronically is filed by delivering it: (1) to the clerk; or (2) to a judge who agrees to accept it for filing, and who must then note the filing date on the paper and promptly send it to the clerk. FRCP 5(d)(2).

c. *Electronic filing.* Unless exempt or otherwise ordered by the court, all pleadings and other papers submitted to the court must be filed, signed, and verified by electronic means as provided in MA R USDCT LR 5.4. MA R USDCT LR 5.4(A); MA R USDCT CM/ECF Admin(A)(1). All electronic filings must be made in accordance with the Administrative Procedures for Electronic Case Filing in the United States District Court for the District of Massachusetts (MA R USDCT CM/ECF Admin). MA R USDCT LR 5.4(B). The court may deviate from the Administrative Procedures for Electronic Case Filing in the United States District Court for the District of Massachusetts (MA R USDCT CM/ECF Admin) in specific cases, without prior notice, if deemed appropriate in the exercise of discretion, considering the need for the just, speedy, and inexpensive determination of matters pending before the court. MA R USDCT CM/ECF Admin(C)(1). The court may excuse a failure to comply with any administrative procedure whenever justice so requires. MA R USDCT CM/ECF Admin(C)(2).

    i. *By a represented person; Generally required; Exceptions.* A person represented by an attorney must file

electronically, unless nonelectronic filing is allowed by the court for good cause or is allowed or required by local rule. FRCP 5(d)(3)(A).

    ii. *By unrepresented person; When allowed or required.* A person not represented by an attorney: (1) may file electronically only if allowed by court order or by local rule; and (2) may be required to file electronically only by court order, or by a local rule that includes reasonable exceptions. FRCP 5(d)(3)(B).

    iii. *Exemptions from electronic filing*

- *Documents that should not be filed electronically.* The following types of documents must not be filed electronically, and will not be scanned into the ECF system by the clerk's office: (1) sealed documents; (2) ex parte motions; (3) documents generated as part of an alternative dispute resolution (ADR) process; (4) the administrative record in Social Security and other administrative proceedings; (5) the state court record in proceedings under 28 U.S.C.A. § 2254; and (6) such other types of documents as the clerk may direct in the Administrative Procedures for Electronic Case Filing in the United States District Court for the District of Massachusetts (MA R USDCT CM/ECF Admin). MA R USDCT LR 5.4(G)(1); MA R USDCT CM/ECF Admin(L).

- *Documents that need not be filed electronically.* The following types of documents need not be filed electronically, but may be scanned into the ECF system by a filing party or the clerk's office: (1) handwritten pleadings; (2) documents filed by pro se litigants who are incarcerated or who are not registered ECF users; (3) indictments, informations, criminal complaints, and the criminal JS45 form; (4) affidavits for search or arrest warrants and related documents; (5) documents received from another court under FRCRP 20 or FRCRP 40; (6) appearance bonds; (7) any document in a criminal case containing the original signature of a defendant, such as a waiver of indictment or a plea agreement; (8) petitions for violations of supervised release; (9) executed service of process documents under FRCP 4; and (10) such other types of documents as the clerk may direct in the Administrative Procedures for Electronic Case Filing in the United States District Court for the District of Massachusetts (MA R USDCT CM/ECF Admin). MA R USDCT LR 5.4(G)(2); MA R USDCT CM/ECF Admin(L).

- For more information on exemptions from electronic filing, refer to MA R USDCT CM/ECF Admin(L).

    iv. *Consequences of electronic filing.* Electronic transmission of a document to the CM/ECF system, together with the transmission of a Notice of Electronic Filing (NEF) from the court at the completion of the transaction, constitutes the filing of the document for all purposes of the Federal Rules of Procedure and constitutes entry of the document on the docket maintained by the clerk pursuant to FRCP 58 and FRCP 79. MA R USDCT CM/ECF Admin(G)(1).

    v. *Payment of filing fees.* When electronically filing any pleading or paper through CM/ECF that requires a fee, all registered ECF users are to pay the fee electronically through the Treasury Department's Internet payment process. MA R USDCT LR 67.4(d); MA R USDCT CM/ECF Admin(A)(1). Pro se filers and those who have been exempted from electronic filing and/or electronic payment of fees may submit payments by check or money order made payable to "Clerk, U.S. District Court". MA R USDCT LR 67.4(d). For more information on filing fees, refer to MA R USDCT LR 67.4 and MA R USDCT CM/ECF Admin(I).

    vi. For more information on electronic filing, refer to MA R USDCT CM/ECF Admin.

  d. *Email or fax filing.* In general, the court does not accept documents by email or by fax. If the court, in special circumstances, does authorize the submission of a document in that manner, the document shall not be considered filed until an NEF is generated by CM/ECF at the completion of the transaction. MA R USDCT CM/ECF Admin(H)(5).

2. *Service requirements.* All papers filed pursuant to MA R USDCT LR 7.1(b) shall be served unless the moving party indicates in writing on the face of the motion that ex parte consideration is requested. Motions filed "ex parte" and related papers need not be served until the motion has been ruled upon or the court orders that service be made. MA R USDCT LR 7.1(c). Service of all pleadings subsequent to the original complaint and of all other papers required to be served shall be made in the manner specified by FRCP 5. MA R USDCT LR 5.2(a).

  a. *Service; When required*

    i. *In general.* Unless the Federal Rules of Civil Procedure provide otherwise, each of the following papers must be served on every party:

- An order stating that service is required;

- A pleading filed after the original complaint, unless the court orders otherwise under FRCP 5(c) because there are numerous defendants;

- A discovery paper required to be served on a party, unless the court orders otherwise;

- A written motion, except one that may be heard ex parte; and

- A written notice, appearance, demand, or offer of judgment, or any similar paper. FRCP 5(a)(1).

ii. *If a party fails to appear.* No service is required on a party who is in default for failing to appear. But a pleading that asserts a new claim for relief against such a party must be served on that party under FRCP 4. FRCP 5(a)(2).

iii. *Seizing property.* If an action is begun by seizing property and no person is or need be named as a defendant, any service required before the filing of an appearance, answer, or claim must be made on the person who had custody or possession of the property when it was seized. FRCP 5(a)(3).

b. *Service; How made*

i. *Serving an attorney.* If a party is represented by an attorney, service under FRCP 5 must be made on the attorney unless the court orders service on the party. FRCP 5(b)(1).

- *Nonresident attorney.* On application of a party, the court may order an attorney who represents any other party and who does not maintain an office within this district where service can be made on him by delivery as provided by FRCP 5(b), to designate a member of the bar of this court who does maintain such an office to receive service of all pleadings and other papers in his behalf. MA R USDCT LR 5.2(c)(1).

ii. *Serving a party acting pro se.* On application of a party, the court may order any other party who is appearing without an attorney and who does not maintain an office or residence within this district where service can be made on him by delivery as provided by FRCP 5(b), to designate an address within the district at which service can be made on him by delivery. MA R USDCT LR 5.2(c)(2).

iii. *Service in general.* A paper is served under FRCP 5 by:

- Handing it to the person;

- Leaving it: (1) at the person's office with a clerk or other person in charge or, if no one is in charge, in a conspicuous place in the office; or (2) if the person has no office or the office is closed, at the person's dwelling or usual place of abode with someone of suitable age and discretion who resides there;

- Mailing it to the person's last known address—in which event service is complete upon mailing;

- Leaving it with the court clerk if the person has no known address;

- Sending it to a registered user by filing it with the court's electronic-filing system or sending it by other electronic means that the person consented to in writing—in either of which events service is complete upon filing or sending, but is not effective if the filer or sender learns that it did not reach the person to be served; or

- Delivering it by any other means that the person consented to in writing—in which event service is complete when the person making service delivers it to the agency designated to make delivery. FRCP 5(b)(2).

iv. *Service by electronic means.* Unless exempt or otherwise ordered by the court, all pleadings and other papers must be served on other parties by electronic means. MA R USDCT LR 5.4(C); MA R USDCT CM/ECF Admin(H)(2). Service by electronic means shall be treated the same as service by mail. MA R USDCT CM/ECF Admin(H)(4).

- *Consent to electronic service.* Registering to use CM/ECF constitutes consent to service of all documents by electronic means as provided in the Administrative Procedures for Electronic Case Filing in the United States District Court for the District of Massachusetts (MA R USDCT CM/ECF Admin) and FRCP 5(b) and FRCP 77(d). MA R USDCT CM/ECF Admin(E)(6); MA R USDCT CM/ECF Admin(H)(3).

- *Service on registered ECF users.* Transmission of the Notice of Electronic Filing (NEF) through the court's transmission facilities will constitute service of the filed document upon a registered ECF user. MA R USDCT LR 5.4(C).

- *Service on non-registered users.* The party filing the document electronically is responsible for serving a paper copy of the document by mail in accordance with FRCP 5(b) to those case participants who have not been identified on the NEF as electronic recipients. MA R USDCT CM/ECF Admin(H)(3).

- *Service of conventionally filed papers.* Documents or exhibits submitted conventionally shall be served on other parties by the filer using traditional means. MA R USDCT CM/ECF Admin(P)(4).

    c.  *Serving numerous defendants*

        i.  *In general.* If an action involves an unusually large number of defendants, the court may, on motion or on its own, order that:

- Defendants' pleadings and replies to them need not be served on other defendants;

- Any crossclaim, counterclaim, avoidance, or affirmative defense in those pleadings and replies to them will be treated as denied or avoided by all other parties; and

- Filing any such pleading and serving it on the plaintiff constitutes notice of the pleading to all parties. FRCP 5(c)(1).

        ii.  *Notifying parties.* A copy of every such order must be served on the parties as the court directs. FRCP 5(c)(2).

## G. Hearings

1.  *Hearings, generally.* If the court concludes that there should be a hearing on a motion, the motion will be set down for hearing at such time as the court determines. MA R USDCT LR 7.1(e).

    a.  *Oral argument.* Due process does not require that oral argument be permitted on a motion and, except as otherwise provided by local rule, the district court has discretion to determine whether it will decide the motion on the papers or hear argument by counsel (and perhaps receive evidence). FPP § 1190; F.D.I.C. v. Deglau, 207 F.3d 153 (3d Cir. 2000).

        i.  *Evidence on a motion.* When a motion relies on facts outside the record, the court may hear the matter on affidavits or may hear it wholly or partly on oral testimony or on depositions. FRCP 43(c).

    b.  *Providing a regular schedule for oral hearings.* A court may establish regular times and places for oral hearings on motions. FRCP 78(a).

    c.  *Providing for submission on briefs.* By rule or order, the court may provide for submitting and determining motions on briefs, without oral hearings. FRCP 78(b). Motions that are not set down for hearing as provided in MA R USDCT LR 7.1(e) will be decided on the papers submitted after an opposition to the motion has been filed, or, if no opposition is filed, after the time for filing an opposition has elapsed. MA R USDCT LR 7.1(f).

2.  *Hearing on certain FRCP 12 defenses before trial.* If a party so moves, any defense listed in FRCP 12(b)(1) through FRCP 12(b)(7)—whether made in a pleading or by motion—and a motion under FRCP 12(c) must be heard and decided before trial unless the court orders a deferral until trial. FRCP 12(i).

3.  *Conflict of court appearances.* For information on conflict of court appearances, refer to MA R USDCT LR 40.2.

## H. Forms

### 1. Federal Motion for Judgment on the Pleadings Forms

    a.  Motion for judgment on the pleadings. 2C FEDFORMS § 11:131.

    b.  Motion for judgment on the pleadings; Alternate wording. 2C FEDFORMS § 11:132.

    c.  Motion for judgment on the pleadings; Long version. 2C FEDFORMS § 11:133.

    d.  Motion for judgment on the pleadings; Several grounds. 2C FEDFORMS § 11:134.

    e.  Notice of motion and motion for judgment on the pleadings. 2C FEDFORMS § 11:135.

    f.  Notice of motion for judgment on the pleadings (partial) or for partial summary judgment. 2C FEDFORMS § 11:136.

    g.  Order granting judgment on the pleadings. 2C FEDFORMS § 11:137.

    h.  Order granting judgment on the pleadings; Motion by plaintiff. 2C FEDFORMS § 11:138.

    i.  Judgment on the pleadings. 2C FEDFORMS § 11:139.

    j.  Motion and notice; For judgment on pleadings. AMJUR PP FEDPRAC § 551.

    k.  Countermotion and notice; For judgment on pleadings; By defendants. AMJUR PP FEDPRAC § 552.

    l.  Order; For judgment on pleadings; In favor of plaintiff. AMJUR PP FEDPRAC § 553.

    m.  Order; For judgment on pleadings; In favor of defendant. AMJUR PP FEDPRAC § 554.

    n.  Motion; General form. FEDPROF § 1B:171.

    o.  Notice; Of motion; General form. FEDPROF § 1B:172.

    p.  Notice; Of motion; With costs of motion. FEDPROF § 1B:173.

q. Notice; Of motion; Containing motion. FEDPROF § 1B:174.

r. Opposition; To motion. FEDPROF § 1B:175.

s. Affidavit; Supporting or opposing motion. FEDPROF § 1B:176.

t. Brief; Supporting or opposing motion. FEDPROF § 1B:177.

u. Statement of points and authorities; Opposing motion. FEDPROF § 1B:178.

v. Motion; For judgment on the pleadings. FEDPROF § 1C:206.

w. Order; For judgment on the pleadings; In favor of plaintiff. FEDPROF § 1C:208.

x. Order; For judgment on the pleadings; In favor of defendant. FEDPROF § 1C:209.

y. Motion for judgment on pleadings; Plaintiff. GOLDLTGFMS § 20:38.

z. Motion for judgment on pleadings; Defendant. GOLDLTGFMS § 20:39.

2. **Forms for the District of Massachusetts**

a. Notice of filing with clerk's office. MA R USDCT CM/ECF Admin(Appendix I).

## I. Applicable Rules

1. *Federal rules*

a. Serving and filing pleadings and other papers. FRCP 5.

b. Constitutional challenge to a statute; Notice, certification, and intervention. FRCP 5.1.

c. Privacy protection for filings made with the court. FRCP 5.2.

d. Computing and extending time; Time for motion papers. FRCP 6.

e. Pleadings allowed; Form of motions and other papers. FRCP 7.

f. Disclosure statement. FRCP 7.1.

g. Form of pleadings. FRCP 10.

h. Signing pleadings, motions, and other papers; Representations to the court; Sanctions. FRCP 11.

i. Defenses and objections; When and how presented; Motion for judgment on the pleadings; Consolidating motions; Waiving defenses; Pretrial hearing. FRCP 12.

j. Hearing motions; Submission on briefs. FRCP 78.

2. *Local rules*

a. Title. MA R USDCT LR 1.1.

b. Sanctions. MA R USDCT LR 1.3.

c. Form and filing of papers. MA R USDCT LR 5.1.

d. Service and filing of pleadings and other papers. MA R USDCT LR 5.2.

e. Filing and service by electronic means. MA R USDCT LR 5.4.

f. Motion practice. MA R USDCT LR 7.1.

g. Alternative dispute resolution. MA R USDCT LR 16.4.

h. Payments and deposits made with the clerk. MA R USDCT LR 67.4.

i. Settlement. MA R USDCT LR 68.2.

j. Office of the clerk. MA R USDCT LR 77.2.

k. Appearances. MA R USDCT LR 83.5.2.

l. Practice by pro se litigants. MA R USDCT LR 83.5.5.

m. CM/ECF case management/electronic case files administrative procedures. MA R USDCT CM/ECF Admin.

# Motions, Oppositions and Replies
# Motion for More Definite Statement

## Document Last Updated December 2018

**A. Checklist**

(I) ❑ Matters to be considered by moving party

    (a) ❑ Required documents

        (1) ❑ Notice of motion and motion

        (2) ❑ Memorandum

        (3) ❑ Certificate of service

    (b) ❑ Supplemental documents

        (1) ❑ Supporting evidence

        (2) ❑ Notice of constitutional question

        (3) ❑ Nongovernmental corporate disclosure statement

        (4) ❑ Proposed order

        (5) ❑ Compact disk with copy of document(s) in PDF format

        (6) ❑ Notice of filing with clerk's office

        (7) ❑ Additional copies

        (8) ❑ Courtesy copies

    (c) ❑ Timing

        (1) ❑ The motion must be made before filing a responsive pleading

        (2) ❑ A written motion and notice of the hearing must be served at least fourteen (14) days before the time specified for the hearing, with the following exceptions: (i) when the motion may be heard ex parte; (ii) when the Federal Rules of Civil Procedure set a different time; or (iii) when a court order—which a party may, for good cause, apply for ex parte—sets a different time

        (3) ❑ Any affidavit supporting a motion must be served with the motion

        (4) ❑ Except as noted in FRCP 33 to FRCP 36, the original of all papers required to be served under FRCP 5(d) shall, unless otherwise submitted to the court, be filed in the office of the clerk within seven (7) days after service has been made

(II) ❑ Matters to be considered by opposing party

    (a) ❑ Required documents

        (1) ❑ Opposition

        (2) ❑ Certificate of service

    (b) ❑ Supplemental documents

        (1) ❑ Supporting evidence

        (2) ❑ Notice of constitutional question

        (3) ❑ Compact disk with copy of document(s) in PDF format

        (4) ❑ Notice of filing with clerk's office

        (5) ❑ Additional copies

        (6) ❑ Courtesy copies

    (c) ❑ Timing

        (1) ❑ A party opposing a motion, shall file an opposition within fourteen (14) days after the motion is served, unless another period is fixed by rule or statute, or by order of the court

        (2) ❑ Except as FRCP 59(c) provides otherwise, any opposing affidavit must be served at least seven (7) days before the hearing, unless the court permits service at another time

(3) ☐ Except as noted in FRCP 33 to FRCP 36, the original of all papers required to be served under FRCP 5(d) shall, unless otherwise submitted to the court, be filed in the office of the clerk within seven (7) days after service has been made

## B. Timing

1. *Motion for more definite statement.* The motion must be made before filing a responsive pleading. FRCP 12(e). Thus, a motion for a more definite statement must be made before an answer. FEDPROC § 62:380.

2. *Timing of motions, generally*

   a. *Motion and notice of hearing.* A written motion and notice of the hearing must be served at least fourteen (14) days before the time specified for the hearing, with the following exceptions:

      i. When the motion may be heard ex parte;

      ii. When the Federal Rules of Civil Procedure set a different time; or

      iii. When a court order—which a party may, for good cause, apply for ex parte—sets a different time. FRCP 6(c)(1).

   b. *Supporting affidavit.* Any affidavit supporting a motion must be served with the motion. FRCP 6(c)(2).

3. *Timing of opposing papers.* A party opposing a motion, shall file an opposition within fourteen (14) days after the motion is served, unless (1) the motion is for summary judgment, in which case the opposition shall be filed within twenty-one (21) days after the motion is served, or (2) another period is fixed by rule or statute, or by order of the court. MA R USDCT LR 7.1(b)(2); MA R USDCT CM/ECF Admin(H)(4). The fourteen (14) day period is intended to include the period specified by the civil rules for mailing time and provide for a uniform period regardless of the use of the mails. MA R USDCT LR 7.1(b)(2).

   a. *Opposing affidavit.* Except as FRCP 59(c) provides otherwise, any opposing affidavit must be served at least seven (7) days before the hearing, unless the court permits service at another time. FRCP 6(c)(2).

4. *Timing of reply papers.* [W]here the respondent files an answering affidavit setting up a new matter, the moving party ordinarily is allowed a reasonable time to file a reply affidavit since failure to deny the new matter by affidavit may operate as an admission of its truth. AMJUR MOTIONS § 25.

   a. *Leave of court required.* All other papers not filed as indicated in MA R USDCT LR 7.1(b)(1) and MA R USDCT LR 7.1(b)(2), whether in the form of a reply brief or otherwise, may be submitted only with leave of court. MA R USDCT LR 7.1(b)(3).

5. *Filing after service.* Except as noted in FRCP 33 to FRCP 36, the original of all papers required to be served under FRCP 5(d) shall, unless otherwise submitted to the court, be filed in the office of the clerk within seven (7) days after service has been made. MA R USDCT LR 5.1(b).

6. *Effect of FRCP 12 motion on the time to serve a responsive pleading.* Unless the court sets a different time, serving a motion under FRCP 12 alters the periods in FRCP 12(a) as follows:

   a. If the court denies the motion or postpones its disposition until trial, the responsive pleading must be served within fourteen (14) days after notice of the court's action; or

   b. If the court grants a motion for a more definite statement, the responsive pleading must be served within fourteen (14) days after the more definite statement is served. FRCP 12(a)(4).

7. *Computation of time*

   a. *Computing time.* FRCP 6 applies in computing any time period specified in the Federal Rules of Civil Procedure, in any local rule or court order, or in any statute that does not specify a method of computing time. FRCP 6(a).

      i. *Period stated in days or a longer unit.* When the period is stated in days or a longer unit of time:

         - Exclude the day of the event that triggers the period;

         - Count every day, including intermediate Saturdays, Sundays, and legal holidays; and

         - Include the last day of the period, but if the last day is a Saturday, Sunday, or legal holiday, the period continues to run until the end of the next day that is not a Saturday, Sunday, or legal holiday. FRCP 6(a)(1).

      ii. *Period stated in hours.* When the period is stated in hours:

         - Begin counting immediately on the occurrence of the event that triggers the period;

         - Count every hour, including hours during intermediate Saturdays, Sundays, and legal holidays; and

- If the period would end on a Saturday, Sunday, or legal holiday, the period continues to run until the same time on the next day that is not a Saturday, Sunday, or legal holiday. FRCP 6(a)(2).

iii. *Office of the clerk.* The offices of the Clerk of Court at Boston, Worcester and Springfield shall be open from 8:30 a.m. until 5:00 p.m. on all days except Saturdays, Sundays, legal holidays and other days so ordered by the court and announced in advance, if feasible. MA R USDCT LR 77.2.

iv. *Inaccessibility of the clerk's office.* Unless the court orders otherwise, if the clerk's office is inaccessible:

- On the last day for filing under FRCP 6(a)(1), then the time for filing is extended to the first accessible day that is not a Saturday, Sunday, or legal holiday; or

- During the last hour for filing under FRCP 6(a)(2), then the time for filing is extended to the same time on the first accessible day that is not a Saturday, Sunday, or legal holiday. FRCP 6(a)(3).

v. *"Last day" defined.* Unless a different time is set by a statute, local rule, or court order, the last day ends:

- For electronic filing, at midnight in the court's time zone; and

- For filing by other means, when the clerk's office is scheduled to close. FRCP 6(a)(4).

vi. *"Next day" defined.* The "next day" is determined by continuing to count forward when the period is measured after an event and backward when measured before an event. FRCP 6(a)(5).

vii. *"Legal holiday" defined.* "Legal holiday" means:

- The day set aside by statute for observing New Year's Day, Martin Luther King Jr.'s Birthday, Washington's Birthday, Memorial Day, Independence Day, Labor Day, Columbus Day, Veterans' Day, Thanksgiving Day, or Christmas Day;

- Any day declared a holiday by the President or Congress; and

- For periods that are measured after an event, any other day declared a holiday by the state where the district court is located. FRCP 6(a)(6).

b. *Computation of electronic filing deadlines.* Filing documents electronically does not alter any filing deadlines. MA R USDCT CM/ECF Admin(K); MA R USDCT LR 5.4(D). Although CM/ECF is generally available twenty-four (24) hours a day for filing, all electronic transmissions of documents must be completed prior to 6:00 PM, Eastern Standard (or Daylight Savings) Time, on the date on which it is due, in order to be considered timely filed that day. MA R USDCT CM/ECF Admin(K); MA R USDCT LR 5.4(D). When a specific time of day deadline is set by court order or stipulation, the electronic filing must be completed by that time. Documents may be filed at any time of the day on days prior to the date on which it is due. MA R USDCT CM/ECF Admin(K). A document filed electronically shall be deemed filed as of the time and date stated on the NEF received from the court. MA R USDCT CM/ECF Admin(G)(2); MA R USDCT CM/ECF Admin(K).

i. *Technical failures.* A user whose filing is made untimely as the result of a technical failure of the court's CM/ECF system may seek appropriate relief from the court. MA R USDCT CM/ECF Admin(W)(3). Technical difficulties on the filer's end, with telephone, cable lines, the filer's Internet Service Provider (ISP), or hardware or software problems, will not constitute a technical failure under the Administrative Procedures for Electronic Case Filing in the United States District Court for the District of Massachusetts (MA R USDCT CM/ECF Admin) nor excuse an untimely filing. MA R USDCT CM/ECF Admin(W)(3). As help desk support is available during normal business hours, filers are strongly urged to electronically file any documents during that period. MA R USDCT CM/ECF Admin(W)(3).

- The court has made available a public terminal (computers and scanner) in each clerk's office for registered users to scan and electronically file documents. This equipment is available during normal business hours. Users should bring their prepared document and a valid CM/ECF login and password. MA R USDCT CM/ECF Admin(W)(3).

c. *Extending time.* When an act may or must be done within a specified time, the court may, for good cause, extend the time: (1) with or without motion or notice if the court acts, or if a request is made, before the original time or its extension expires; or (2) on motion made after the time has expired if the party failed to act because of excusable neglect. FRCP 6(b)(1).

i. *Exceptions.* A court must not extend the time to act under FRCP 50(b), FRCP 50(d), FRCP 52(b), FRCP 59(b), FRCP 59(d), FRCP 59(e), and FRCP 60(b). FRCP 6(b)(2).

ii. Refer to the United States District Court for the District of Massachusetts KeyRules Motion for Continuance/Extension of Time document for more information on extending time.

d. *Additional time after certain kinds of service.* When a party may or must act within a specified time after being served and service is made under FRCP 5(b)(2)(C) (by mail), FRCP 5(b)(2)(D) (by leaving with the clerk), or FRCP 5(b)(2)(F) (by other means consented to), three (3) days are added after the period would otherwise expire under FRCP 6(a). FRCP 6(d).

## C. General Requirements

1. *Motions, generally*

   a. *Requirements.* A request for a court order must be made by motion. The motion must:

      i. Be in writing unless made during a hearing or trial;

      ii. State with particularity the grounds for seeking the order; and

      iii. State the relief sought. FRCP 7(b)(1).

   b. *Notice of motion.* A party interested in resisting the relief sought by a motion has a right to notice thereof, and an opportunity to be heard. AMJUR MOTIONS § 12.

      i. [I]n addition to statutory or court rule provisions requiring notice of a motion—the purpose of such a notice requirement having been said to be to prevent a party from being prejudicially surprised by a motion—principles of natural justice dictate that an adverse party generally must be given notice that a motion will be presented to the court. AMJUR MOTIONS § 12.

      ii. "Notice," in this regard, means reasonable notice, including a meaningful opportunity to prepare and to defend against allegations of a motion. AMJUR MOTIONS § 12.

   c. *Writing requirement.* The writing requirement is intended to [ensure] that the adverse parties are informed and have a record of both the motion's pendency and the grounds on which the movant seeks an order. FPP § 1191; Feldberg v. Quechee Lakes Corp., 463 F.3d 195 (2d Cir. 2006). [A] single written document can satisfy the writing requirements both for a motion and for [an] FRCP 6(c)(1) notice. FRCP 7(Advisory Committee Notes).

   d. *Particularity requirement.* The particularity requirement [ensures] that the opposing parties will have notice of their opponent's contentions. FEDPROC § 62:358; Goodman v. 1973 26 Foot Trojan Vessel, Arkansas Registration No. AR1439SN, 859 F.2d 71 (8th Cir. 1988). That requirement ensures that notice of the basis for the motion is provided to the court and to the opposing party so as to avoid prejudice, provide the opponent with a meaningful opportunity to respond, and provide the court with enough information to process the motion correctly. FEDPROC § 62:358; Andreas v. Volkswagen of Am., Inc., 336 F.3d 789 (8th Cir. 2003).

      i. Reasonable specification of the grounds for a motion is sufficient. The particularity requirement for motions is satisfied when no party is prejudiced by a lack of particularity or when the court can comprehend the basis for the motion and deal with it fairly. However, where a movant fails to state even one ground for granting the motion in question, the movant has failed to meet the minimal standard of "reasonable specification." FEDPROC § 62:358; Martinez v. Trainor, 556 F.2d 818 (7th Cir. 1977).

      ii. The court may excuse the failure to comply with the particularity requirement if it is inadvertent, and where no prejudice is shown by the opposing party. FEDPROC § 62:358.

   e. *Control of motion practice*

      i. *Plan for the disposition of motions.* At the earliest practicable time, the judicial officer shall establish a framework for the disposition of motions, which, at the discretion of the judicial officer, may include specific deadlines or general time guidelines for filing motions. This framework may be amended from time to time by the judicial officer as required by the progress of the case. MA R USDCT LR 7.1(a)(1).

      ii. *Motion practice.* No motion shall be filed unless counsel certify that they have conferred and have attempted in good faith to resolve or narrow the issue. MA R USDCT LR 7.1(a)(2).

      iii. *Unresolved motions.* The court shall rule on motions as soon as practicable, having in mind the reporting requirements set forth in the Civil Justice Reform Act. MA R USDCT LR 7.1(a)(3).

2. *Motion for more definite statement.* A party may move for a more definite statement of a pleading to which a responsive pleading is allowed but which is so vague or ambiguous that the party cannot reasonably prepare a response. FRCP 12(e). A motion for a more definite statement under FRCP 12(e) is inappropriate where a responsive pleading is not required or permitted. FEDPROC § 62:379.

   a. *Contents.* The motion must be made before filing a responsive pleading and must point out the defects complained of and the details desired. FRCP 12(e). A motion for a more definite statement must point out the defects complained of and the details desired, should offer discussion or legal analysis in support of the FRCP 12(e) claim, and will be denied where the motion fails to satisfy this requirement. FEDPROC § 62:381.

    i. Regardless of whether the plaintiff or the defendant moves under FRCP 12(e), she must identify the deficiencies in the pleading believed to be objectionable, point out the details she desires to have pleaded in a more intelligible form, and assert her inability to prepare a responsive pleading. These requirements are designed to enable the district judge to test the propriety of the motion and formulate an appropriate order in the light of its limited purpose of enabling the framing of a responsive pleading. FPP § 1378.

    ii. Since FRCP 12(e) must be construed in light of the federal rules relating to liberal pleading, a motion for a more definite statement need not particularize the requested information in great detail and should not request an excessive amount of information. Indeed, if the movant does ask for too much, his motion may be denied on the ground that evidentiary matter is being sought. FPP § 1378.

  b. *Burden.* Most federal courts cast the burden of establishing the need for a more definite statement on the movant. Whether he will succeed in discharging that burden depends on such factors as the availability of information from other sources that may clear up the pleading for the movant and a coparty's ability to answer. FPP § 1378.

  c. *Motion disfavored.* Motions for a more definite statement are not favored by the courts, and thus, are rarely granted, since pleadings in the federal courts are only required to fairly notify the opposing party of the nature of the claim, and since there are ample provisions for discovery under FRCP 26 to FRCP 37 as well as for pretrial procedure under FRCP 16. Generally, motions for more definite statement are disfavored because of their dilatory effect on the progress of litigation, and the preferred course is to encourage the use of discovery procedures to apprise the parties of the factual basis of the claims made in the pleadings. FEDPROC § 62:382.

    i. *Discretion of court.* A motion for a more definite statement pursuant to FRCP 12(e) is addressed to the discretion of the court. Whether the motion should be granted or denied depends primarily on the facts of each individual case. FEDPROC § 62:382.

  d. *Joining motions*

    i. *Right to join.* A motion under FRCP 12 may be joined with any other motion allowed by FRCP 12. FRCP 12(g)(1).

    ii. *Limitation on further motions.* Except as provided in FRCP 12(h)(2) or FRCP 12(h)(3), a party that makes a motion under FRCP 12 must not make another motion under FRCP 12 raising a defense or objection that was available to the party but omitted from its earlier motion. FRCP 12(g)(2).

    • If the movant legitimately is unable to assert his other defenses at the time a motion is made under FRCP 12(e), the movant will not be penalized when he actually does interpose a second motion. FPP § 1378.

  e. *General standard for granting motion.* The general standard for granting a motion for a more definite statement is set forth in FRCP 12(e) itself, which provides that a party may move for a more definite statement if a pleading to which a responsive pleading is allowed is so vague or ambiguous that the party cannot reasonably prepare a response. The clear trend of judicial decisions is to deny motions for a more definite statement unless the complaint is so excessively vague and ambiguous as to prejudice the defendant seriously in attempting to answer it. The burden is on the movant to demonstrate that the complaint is so vague or ambiguous that they cannot respond, even with a simple denial, in good faith or without prejudice to itself. FEDPROC § 62:383.

  f. *Compliance and enforcement of order.* If the court orders a more definite statement and the order is not obeyed within fourteen (14) days after notice of the order or within the time the court sets, the court may strike the pleading or issue any other appropriate order. FRCP 12(e).

3. *Opposing papers.* The Federal Rules of Civil Procedure do not require any formal answer, return, or reply to a motion, except where the Federal Rules of Civil Procedure or local rules may require affidavits, memoranda, or other papers to be filed in opposition to a motion. Such papers are simply to apprise the court of such opposition and the grounds of that opposition. FEDPROC § 62:353.

  a. *Effect of failure to respond to motion.* Although in the absence of statutory provision or court rule, a motion ordinarily does not require a written answer, when a party files a motion and the opposing party fails to respond, the court may construe such failure to respond as nonopposition to the motion or an admission that the motion was meritorious, may take the facts alleged in the motion as true—the rule in some jurisdictions being that the failure to respond to a fact set forth in a motion is deemed an admission—and may grant the motion if the relief requested appears to be justified. AMJUR MOTIONS § 28.

  b. *Assent or no opposition not determinative.* However, a motion will not be granted automatically simply because an "assent" or a notation of "no opposition" has been filed; federal judges frequently deny motions that have been assented to when it is thought that justice so dictates. FPP § 1190.

    c.   *Responsive pleading inappropriate as response to motion.* An attempt to answer or oppose a motion with a responsive pleading usually is not appropriate. FPP § 1190.

4.  *Reply papers.* A moving party may be required or permitted to prepare papers in addition to his original motion papers. AMJUR MOTIONS § 25. Papers answering or replying to opposing papers may be appropriate, in the interests of justice, where it appears there is a substantial reason for allowing a reply. Thus, a court may accept reply papers where a party demonstrates that the papers to which it seeks to file a reply raise new issues that are material to the disposition of the question before the court, or where the court determines, sua sponte, that it wishes further briefing of an issue raised in those papers and orders the submission of additional papers. FEDPROC § 62:354.

    a.   *Function of reply papers.* The function of a reply affidavit is to answer the arguments made in opposition to the position taken by the movant and not to permit the movant to introduce new arguments in support of the motion. AMJUR MOTIONS § 25.

    b.   *Issues raised for the first time in a reply document.* However, the view has been followed in some jurisdictions, that as a matter of judicial economy, where there is no prejudice and where the issues could be raised simply by filing a motion to dismiss, the trial court has discretion to consider arguments raised for the first time in a reply memorandum, and that a trial court may grant a motion to strike issues raised for the first time in a reply memorandum. AMJUR MOTIONS § 26.

5.  *Alternative dispute resolution (ADR).* The judicial officer assigned to preside over the case shall encourage the resolution of disputes by settlement or other alternative dispute resolution programs. MA R USDCT LR 16.4(a).

    a.   *Settlement.* At every conference conducted under the Local Rules of the United States District Court for the District of Massachusetts, the judicial officer shall inquire as to the utility of the parties conducting settlement negotiations, explore means of facilitating those negotiations, and offer whatever assistance may be appropriate in the circumstances. Assistance may include a reference of the case to another judicial officer for settlement purposes. MA R USDCT LR 16.4(b).

        i.   When a case is settled, the parties shall file with the clerk a signed agreement for judgment or stipulation for dismissal, as appropriate, within twenty-eight (28) days, unless the court otherwise orders. MA R USDCT LR 68.2.

    b.   *Alternative dispute resolution programs*

        i.   *Discretion of judicial officer.* The judicial officer, following an exploration of the matter with all counsel, may refer appropriate cases to alternative dispute resolution programs that have been designated for use in the district court or that the judicial officer may make available. The dispute resolution programs described in MA R USDCT LR 16.4(c)(2) through MA R USDCT LR 16.4(c)(4) are illustrative, not exclusive. Moreover, nothing in MA R USDCT LR 16.4 shall preclude the parties from engaging in private dispute resolution programs as long as they comply with any schedule established by the court. MA R USDCT LR 16.4(c)(1).

        ii.   *Mediation.* The judicial officer may refer the case to mediation upon the agreement of all parties. MA R USDCT LR 16.4(c)(2)(A).

        iii.   *Other alternative dispute resolution programs.* Use of mediation is not exclusive. At the request of parties, the judicial officer may consider other forms of alternative dispute resolution including, but not limited to, mini-trial, summary jury trial and arbitration. MA R USDCT LR 16.4(c)(3).

    c.   For more information on alternative dispute resolution (ADR), refer to MA R USDCT LR 16.4.

6.  *Sanctions.* Failure to comply with any of the directions or obligations set forth in, or authorized by, these rules may result in dismissal, default, or the imposition of other sanctions as deemed appropriate by the judicial officer. MA R USDCT LR 1.3. Except as provided by law, the court may impose sanctions as provided in MA R USDCT LR 1.3 for failure to comply with the Administrative Procedures for Electronic Case Filing in the United States District Court for the District of Massachusetts (MA R USDCT CM/ECF Admin) or with MA R USDCT LR 5.4. MA R USDCT CM/ECF Admin(C)(3).

## D.  Documents

1.  *Documents for moving party*

    a.   *Required documents*

        i.   *Notice of motion and motion.* Refer to the General Requirements section of this document for information on the notice of motion and motion.

            •  *Request for oral argument.* Any party making or opposing a motion who believes that oral argument may

assist the court and wishes to be heard shall include a request for oral argument in a separate paragraph of the motion or opposition. The request should be set off with a centered caption, "REQUEST FOR ORAL ARGUMENT." MA R USDCT LR 7.1(d).

ii. *Memorandum.* A party filing a motion shall at the same time file a memorandum of reasons, including citation of supporting authorities, why the motion should be granted. MA R USDCT LR 7.1(b)(1). Any memorandum of law or other attachment filed in support of a main document shall be filed as a separate document, using the proper event. MA R USDCT CM/ECF Admin(G)(4). Memoranda supporting or opposing allowance of motions shall not, without leave of court, exceed twenty (20) pages, double-spaced. MA R USDCT LR 7.1(b)(4).

iii. *Certificate of service.* No certificate of service is required when a paper is served by filing it with the court's electronic-filing system. When a paper that is required to be served is served by other means: (1) if the paper is filed, a certificate of service must be filed with it or within a reasonable time after service; and (2) if the paper is not filed, a certificate of service need not be filed unless filing is required by court order or by local rule. FRCP 5(d)(1)(B). Except as otherwise provided by the Federal Rules of Civil Procedure, proof of service of all pleadings and other papers required to be served (except discovery papers that in accordance with FRCP 33 to FRCP 36(f) are not to be filed) shall be filed in the office of the clerk promptly after service has been made. The proof shall show the time and manner of service, and may be made by written acknowledgment of service, a certificate of a member of the bar of this court, or an affidavit of the person who served the paper. MA R USDCT LR 5.2(b)(1). A certificate of service of a member of the bar shall appear at the bottom of or on the margin of the last page of the paper to which it relates. MA R USDCT LR 5.2(b)(2).

- *Paper service.* The certificate shall be a brief, single-spaced statement and may be in the following form: I hereby certify that a true copy of the above document was served upon (each party appearing pro se and) the attorney of record for each other party by mail (by hand) on (date). (Signature). MA R USDCT LR 5.2(b)(2).

- *Electronic service.* Any pleading or other paper served by electronic means must bear a certificate of service in accordance with MA R USDCT LR 5.2(b). MA R USDCT LR 5.4(C); MA R USDCT CM/ECF Admin(H)(2). The certificate of service shall state that the filer: (1) filed the document electronically, (2) that it will be served electronically to registered CM/ECF participants via the NEF and (3) that the filer will send paper copies to non-registered participants as indicated on the NEF. MA R USDCT CM/ECF Admin(H)(2). For example: I hereby certify that this document filed through the CM/ECF system will be sent electronically to the registered participants as identified on the NEF (NEF) and paper copies will be sent to those indicated as non registered participants on (date). MA R USDCT CM/ECF Admin(H)(2).

- *Return.* Documents not conforming to the requirements of MA R USDCT LR 5.2 (except notices of appeal) shall be returned by the clerk. MA R USDCT LR 5.2(b)(2).

- *Failure to make proof of service.* Failure to make proof of service does not affect the validity of the service. MA R USDCT LR 5.2(b)(3).

b. *Supplemental documents*

i. *Supporting evidence.* When a motion relies on facts outside the record, the court may hear the matter on affidavits or may hear it wholly or partly on oral testimony or on depositions. FRCP 43(c). Affidavits and other documents setting forth or evidencing facts on which the motion is based shall be filed with the motion. MA R USDCT LR 7.1(b)(1).

- *Supporting affidavit(s).* Good practice for a party seeking relief under FRCP 12(e) is to support the motion by an affidavit showing the necessity for a more definite statement. FEDPROC § 62:381. Courts differ in their attitude toward the use of affidavits on [an] FRCP 12(e) motion. Some insist on affidavits delineating the ways in which the pleading should be made more definite; others feel that affidavits would be helpful but do not insist upon them; and a few courts, usually when a more definite statement obviously is appropriate, do not seem to require supporting affidavits. FPP § 1378.

ii. *Notice of constitutional question.* A party that files a pleading, written motion, or other paper drawing into question the constitutionality of a federal or state statute must promptly:

- *File notice.* File a notice of constitutional question stating the question and identifying the paper that raises it, if: (1) a federal statute is questioned and the parties do not include the United States, one of its agencies, or one of its officers or employees in an official capacity; or (2) a state statute is questioned and the parties do not include the state, one of its agencies, or one of its officers or employees in an official capacity; and

- *Serve notice.* Serve the notice and paper on the Attorney General of the United States if a federal statute is questioned—or on the state attorney general if a state statute is questioned—either by certified or registered mail or by sending it to an electronic address designated by the attorney general for this purpose. FRCP 5.1(a).

- *No forfeiture.* A party's failure to file and serve the notice, or the court's failure to certify, does not forfeit a constitutional claim or defense that is otherwise timely asserted. FRCP 5.1(d).

iii. *Nongovernmental corporate disclosure statement*

- *Contents.* A nongovernmental corporate party must file two (2) copies of a disclosure statement that: (1) identifies any parent corporation and any publicly held corporation owning ten percent (10%) or more of its stock; or (2) states that there is no such corporation. FRCP 7.1(a).

- *Time to file; Supplemental filing.* A party must: (1) file the disclosure statement with its first appearance, pleading, petition, motion, response, or other request addressed to the court; and (2) promptly file a supplemental statement if any required information changes. FRCP 7.1(b).

iv. *Proposed order.* Proposed orders usually are not required by this court. However, the court may request the party to submit such a document. In those situations, unless otherwise directed by the clerk's office, electronically file the proposed document/order using the entry for "Proposed Documents submitted to the court," found under the Other Documents menu, or as an attachment to the motion to which it relates. MA R USDCT CM/ECF Admin(T).

v. *Compact disk with copy of document(s) in PDF format.* A filer who cannot file a document electronically because of such technical difficulty on the filer's end [with telephone, cable lines, the filer's Internet Service Provider (ISP), or hardware or software problems] shall file the document conventionally along with a copy of the document in PDF format on a compact disk or contact the clerk's office for permission to submit the PDF document via email. MA R USDCT CM/ECF Admin(W)(3). Refer to the Timing section of this document for more information on technical failures.

vi. *Notice of filing with clerk's office.* When documents or exhibits (other than those filed ex parte or under seal) are submitted conventionally, a "Notice of Filing with clerk's office" shall be filed electronically and attached to the main document. A paper copy of the "Notice of Filing with clerk's office" must accompany the documents submitted to the court. The "Notice of Filing with clerk's office" (see MA R USDCT CM/ECF Admin(Appendix I)) shall describe each of the documents that will be filed as paper copies in the clerk's office, or shall include an index of the documents if those documents are voluminous. MA R USDCT CM/ECF Admin(P)(5).

vii. *Additional copies.* Whenever, because of the nature of a proceeding, such as a proceeding before a three-judge district court under 28 U.S.C.A. § 2284, additional copies of a paper required to be filed are necessary either for the use of the court or to enable the clerk to carry out his duties, it is the responsibility of the party filing or having filed the paper to provide the necessary copies. MA R USDCT LR 5.1(d).

viii. *Courtesy copies.* COURTESY COPIES OF DOCUMENTS FILED ELECTRONICALLY SHALL NOT BE SUBMITTED ROUTINELY. MA R USDCT CM/ECF Admin(J). Judicial officers, on a case-by-case basis, may require courtesy copies for specific cases, or types of motions, etc. A few Judicial Officers have entered Standing Orders, which may be found on their respective pages on the court's website (under Divisions). Any document filed on paper with the court as a courtesy copy must be clearly labeled as such (Example: COURTESY COPY—DO NOT SCAN). Documents delivered to the court as a courtesy copy will not be maintained in the official court record. MA R USDCT CM/ECF Admin(J).

2. *Documents for opposing party*

a. *Required documents*

i. *Opposition.* Refer to the General Requirements section of this document for information on the opposing papers.

- *Memorandum.* A party opposing a motion shall file, in the same (rather than a separate), document a memorandum of reasons, including citation of supporting authorities, why the motion should not be granted. MA R USDCT LR 7.1(b)(2). Any memorandum of law or other attachment filed in support of a main document shall be filed as a separate document, using the proper event. MA R USDCT CM/ECF Admin(G)(4). Memoranda supporting or opposing allowance of motions shall not, without leave of court, exceed twenty (20) pages, double-spaced. MA R USDCT LR 7.1(b)(4).

- *Request for oral argument.* Any party making or opposing a motion who believes that oral argument may assist the court and wishes to be heard shall include a request for oral argument in a separate paragraph of the motion or opposition. The request should be set off with a centered caption, "REQUEST FOR ORAL ARGUMENT." MA R USDCT LR 7.1(d).

ii. *Certificate of service.* No certificate of service is required when a paper is served by filing it with the court's electronic-filing system. When a paper that is required to be served is served by other means: (1) if the paper is filed, a certificate of service must be filed with it or within a reasonable time after service; and (2) if the paper is not filed, a certificate of service need not be filed unless filing is required by court order or by local rule. FRCP 5(d)(1)(B). Except as otherwise provided by the Federal Rules of Civil Procedure, proof of service of all pleadings and other papers required to be served (except discovery papers that in accordance with FRCP 33 to FRCP 36(f) are not to be filed) shall be filed in the office of the clerk promptly after service has been made. The proof shall show the time and manner of service, and may be made by written acknowledgment of service, a certificate of a member of the bar of this court, or an affidavit of the person who served the paper. MA R USDCT LR 5.2(b)(1). A certificate of service of a member of the bar shall appear at the bottom of or on the margin of the last page of the paper to which it relates. MA R USDCT LR 5.2(b)(2).

- *Paper service.* The certificate shall be a brief, single-spaced statement and may be in the following form: I hereby certify that a true copy of the above document was served upon (each party appearing pro se and) the attorney of record for each other party by mail (by hand) on (date). (Signature). MA R USDCT LR 5.2(b)(2).

- *Electronic service.* Any pleading or other paper served by electronic means must bear a certificate of service in accordance with MA R USDCT LR 5.2(b). MA R USDCT LR 5.4(C); MA R USDCT CM/ECF Admin(H)(2). The certificate of service shall state that the filer: (1) filed the document electronically, (2) that it will be served electronically to registered CM/ECF participants via the NEF and (3) that the filer will send paper copies to non-registered participants as indicated on the NEF. MA R USDCT CM/ECF Admin(H)(2). For example: I hereby certify that this document filed through the CM/ECF system will be sent electronically to the registered participants as identified on the NEF (NEF) and paper copies will be sent to those indicated as non registered participants on (date). MA R USDCT CM/ECF Admin(H)(2).

- *Return.* Documents not conforming to the requirements of MA R USDCT LR 5.2 (except notices of appeal) shall be returned by the clerk. MA R USDCT LR 5.2(b)(2).

- *Failure to make proof of service.* Failure to make proof of service does not affect the validity of the service. MA R USDCT LR 5.2(b)(3).

b. *Supplemental documents*

i. *Supporting evidence.* When a motion relies on facts outside the record, the court may hear the matter on affidavits or may hear it wholly or partly on oral testimony or on depositions. FRCP 43(c). Affidavits and other documents setting forth or evidencing facts on which the opposition is based shall be filed with the opposition. MA R USDCT LR 7.1(b)(2).

ii. *Notice of constitutional question.* A party that files a pleading, written motion, or other paper drawing into question the constitutionality of a federal or state statute must promptly:

- *File notice.* File a notice of constitutional question stating the question and identifying the paper that raises it, if: (1) a federal statute is questioned and the parties do not include the United States, one of its agencies, or one of its officers or employees in an official capacity; or (2) a state statute is questioned and the parties do not include the state, one of its agencies, or one of its officers or employees in an official capacity; and

- *Serve notice.* Serve the notice and paper on the Attorney General of the United States if a federal statute is questioned—or on the state attorney general if a state statute is questioned—either by certified or registered mail or by sending it to an electronic address designated by the attorney general for this purpose. FRCP 5.1(a).

- *No forfeiture.* A party's failure to file and serve the notice, or the court's failure to certify, does not forfeit a constitutional claim or defense that is otherwise timely asserted. FRCP 5.1(d).

iii. *Compact disk with copy of document(s) in PDF format.* A filer who cannot file a document electronically because of such technical difficulty on the filer's end [with telephone, cable lines, the filer's Internet Service Provider (ISP), or hardware or software problems] shall file the document conventionally along with a copy of the document in PDF format on a compact disk or contact the clerk's office for permission to submit the PDF document via email. MA R USDCT CM/ECF Admin(W)(3). Refer to the Timing section of this document for more information on technical failures.

iv. *Notice of filing with clerk's office.* When documents or exhibits (other than those filed ex parte or under seal) are submitted conventionally, a "Notice of Filing with clerk's office" shall be filed electronically and attached to the main document. A paper copy of the "Notice of Filing with clerk's office" must accompany the documents submitted to the court. The "Notice of Filing with clerk's office" (see MA R USDCT CM/ECF Admin(Appendix I)) shall describe each of the documents that will be filed as paper copies in the clerk's office, or shall include an index of the documents if those documents are voluminous. MA R USDCT CM/ECF Admin(P)(5).

v.  *Additional copies.* Whenever, because of the nature of a proceeding, such as a proceeding before a three-judge district court under 28 U.S.C.A. § 2284, additional copies of a paper required to be filed are necessary either for the use of the court or to enable the clerk to carry out his duties, it is the responsibility of the party filing or having filed the paper to provide the necessary copies. MA R USDCT LR 5.1(d).

vi. *Courtesy copies.* COURTESY COPIES OF DOCUMENTS FILED ELECTRONICALLY SHALL NOT BE SUBMITTED ROUTINELY. MA R USDCT CM/ECF Admin(J). Judicial officers, on a case-by-case basis, may require courtesy copies for specific cases, or types of motions, etc. A few Judicial Officers have entered Standing Orders, which may be found on their respective pages on the court's website (under Divisions). Any document filed on paper with the court as a courtesy copy must be clearly labeled as such (Example: COURTESY COPY—DO NOT SCAN). Documents delivered to the court as a courtesy copy will not be maintained in the official court record. MA R USDCT CM/ECF Admin(J).

## E. Format

1.  *Form of documents.* The rules governing captions and other matters of form in pleadings apply to motions and other papers. FRCP 7(b)(2). The provisions of FRCP 10 and FRCP 11 concerning the form and signing of pleadings, motions, and other papers shall be applicable to all papers filed in any proceeding in this court. The board of bar overseers registration number of each attorney signing such documents, except the United States Attorney and his or her staff, shall be inscribed below the signature. MA R USDCT LR 5.1(a)(1).

    a.  *Paper size and binding.* All papers filed in the court shall be adapted for flat filing, be filed on eight and one-half by eleven (8-1/2 x 11) inch paper without backers and be bound firmly by staple or some such other means (excluding paper or binder clip or rubber band). MA R USDCT LR 5.1(a)(2).

    b.  *Spacing.* All papers, except discovery requests and responses, shall be double-spaced except for the identification of counsel, title of the case, footnotes, quotations and exhibits. Discovery requests and responses shall be single-spaced. MA R USDCT LR 5.1(a)(2).

    c.  *Caption.* Every pleading must have a caption with the court's name, a title, a file number, and [an] FRCP 7(a) designation. FRCP 10(a).

        i.  *Names of parties.* The title of the complaint must name all the parties; the title of other pleadings, after naming the first party on each side, may refer generally to other parties. FRCP 10(a).

        ii. *Request for special action.* When any pleading or other paper filed in the court includes a request for special process or relief, or any other request such that, if granted, the court will proceed other than in the ordinary course, the request shall, unless it is noted on the category sheet [see MA R USDCT LR 40.1(a)(1)], be noted on the first page to the right of or immediately beneath the caption. MA R USDCT LR 5.1(c).

    d.  *Claims or defenses*

        i.  *Numbered paragraphs.* A party must state its claims or defenses in numbered paragraphs, each limited as far as practicable to a single set of circumstances. A later pleading may refer by number to a paragraph in an earlier pleading. FRCP 10(b).

        ii. *Separate statements.* If doing so would promote clarity, each claim founded on a separate transaction or occurrence—and each defense other than a denial—must be stated in a separate count or defense. FRCP 10(b).

    e.  *Adoption by reference.* A statement in a pleading may be adopted by reference elsewhere in the same pleading or in any other pleading or motion. FRCP 10(c).

        i.  *Exhibits.* A copy of a written instrument that is an exhibit to a pleading is a part of the pleading for all purposes. FRCP 10(c).

    f.  *Citations*

        i.  *Local rules.* These rules shall be known as Local Rules of the United States District Court for the District of Massachusetts and cited as "L.R., D. Mass." or "L.R." MA R USDCT LR 1.1.

        ii. *Electronic case filing procedures.* The procedures governing electronic case filing shall be known as the "Administrative Procedures for Electronic Case Filing in the United States District Court for the District of Massachusetts." They shall be cited as "APECF." MA R USDCT CM/ECF Admin(A)(7).

g. *Acceptance by the clerk.* The clerk must not refuse to file a paper solely because it is not in the form prescribed by the Federal Rules of Civil Procedure or by a local rule or practice. FRCP 5(d)(4).

   i. Except for complaints and notices of appeal, papers that do not conform to the requirements of MA R USDCT LR 5.1(a)(2) shall be returned by the clerk. MA R USDCT LR 5.1(a)(2).

2. *Form of electronic documents.* A paper filed electronically is a written paper for purposes of the Federal Rules of Civil Procedure. FRCP 5(d)(3)(D).

   a. *PDF/A format required.* The court will begin requiring submission of documents in PDF/A format in the foreseeable future. PDF/A is an enhanced version of the traditional PDF format. Newer versions of most PDF software will be able to convert to this format. Additional information on PDF/A documents may be found on the court's website. MA R USDCT CM/ECF Admin(Electronic Filing and PDF).

      i. *Electronically converted PDF.* Electronically converted PDF documents are created from word processing documents (MS Word, WordPerfect, etc.) using any appropriate software. These documents are text searchable and the file size is generally smaller than a scanned document. CM/ECF users may use any brand of software to convert documents to PDF. MA R USDCT CM/ECF Admin(Electronic Filing and PDF).

         • Documents converted to PDF, rather than scanned, are preferred for filing in CM/ECF. MA R USDCT CM/ECF Admin(Electronic Filing and PDF).

      ii. *Scanned PDF.* Scanned PDF documents are created from paper documents run through an optical scanner. Scanned PDF documents are generally not searchable and have a larger file size. Please note that software used to create scanned documents may (and should) be set in such a way that the document is "text-searchable." MA R USDCT CM/ECF Admin(Electronic Filing and PDF).

   b. *Title.* All pleadings filed electronically shall be titled in accordance with the approved dictionary of civil or criminal events of the CM/ECF system of this court. A list of events is available on the CM/ECF Training Information page of the court's website. The clerk's office may, when necessary and appropriate, modify the docket entry description, or delete and re-enter the docket entry in order to comply with the court's quality assurance standards. MA R USDCT CM/ECF Admin(G)(3).

   c. *Attachments to filings and exhibits.* Attachments to filings and exhibits must be filed in accordance with the court's CM/ECF User Manual, unless otherwise ordered by the court. MA R USDCT CM/ECF Admin(O)(1).

      i. Filers must submit as attachments only those excerpts of the referenced documents that are directly germane to the matter under consideration by the court. Excerpted material must be clearly and prominently identified as such. Users who file excerpts of documents do so without prejudice to their right to timely file additional excerpts or the complete document, as may be allowed by the court. Responding parties may timely file additional excerpts or the complete document that they believe are directly germane. MA R USDCT CM/ECF Admin(O)(2).

      ii. Filers shall not attach as an exhibit any pleading or other paper already on file with the court in that case, but shall merely refer to that document. (See MA R USDCT CM/ECF Admin(G) for information on using hyperlinks in PDF documents filed in CM/ECF.) MA R USDCT CM/ECF Admin(O)(3).

   d. *Redacted documents.* The parties may request or the court may require the submission of documents that have been redacted/stripped of sensitive or confidential information. The redacted document prepared for electronic filing shall include the original caption of the document, and be clearly labeled as "Redacted Document." A specific event is available for this purpose ("Redacted Document"), found under the Other Filings/Other Documents menu option. MA R USDCT CM/ECF Admin(S).

      i. Attorneys and pro se litigants are advised to take extra care when creating PDF documents intended for submission to CM/ECF. Steps shall be taken to ensure the documents are free of any hidden data (metadata) that may contain redacted information, or traces of information edited or deleted are not hidden in the final document. Even PDF content that has been encrypted may be recovered. An advisory document with additional information on this topic may be found on the court's website. MA R USDCT CM/ECF Admin(S).

   e. *Hyperlinks.* Electronically filed documents may contain the following types of hyperlinks: (1) hyperlinks to other portions of the same document; (2) hyperlinks to other documents filed within the CM/ECF system; and (3) hyperlinks to a location on the Internet that contains a source document for a citation. MA R USDCT CM/ECF Admin(G)(7).

      i. Hyperlinks to cited authority may not replace standard citation format. Complete citations must be included in the text of the filed document. Neither a hyperlink, nor any site to which it refers, shall be considered part of the

record, but are simply convenient mechanisms for accessing material cited in a document filed in CM/ECF. Instructions on creating hyperlinks may be found in the CM/ECF User Manual. MA R USDCT CM/ECF Admin(G)(7).

ii.   The court accepts no responsibility for, and does not endorse, any product, organization, or content at any hyperlinked site, or at any site to which that site may be linked. The court accepts no responsibility for the availability or functionality of any hyperlink. MA R USDCT CM/ECF Admin(G)(7).

iii.   One feature of PDF/A documents is that hyperlinks are commonly "masked," meaning that the full address of the referenced file is not written out; for example, clicking the word brief may open a brief which was previously filed in CM/ECF. MA R USDCT CM/ECF Admin(G)(7)(NOTE). An "unmasked" hyperlink has the full address visible to the user. MA R USDCT CM/ECF Admin(G)(7)(NOTE).

- Masked hyperlinks may or may not work in a PDF/A document, depending on how it was created. Currently, masked hyperlinks are preserved in PDF/A documents produced by the "Save As" method in Microsoft Word 2007 and 2010; the "PDFMaker" method in Microsoft Word 2007; and OpenOffice 2.4 ("PDF Export"). With other production methods, such as WordPerfect, the PDF/A document includes underlined words that appear to be links, but clicking them has no effect. MA R USDCT CM/ECF Admin(G)(7)(NOTE).

f.   *Documents features not accepted.* CM/ECF will not accept PDF documents containing tracking tags, embedded systems commands, password protections, access restrictions or other security features, special tags or dynamic features. MA R USDCT CM/ECF Admin(G)(8).

g.   *File size limitations.* A filing party shall limit the size of each PDF file to no more than twenty (20) megabytes. PDF files larger than seven (7) megabytes will be rejected by the CM/ECF system. The filer will see a message advising of the size limitation. MA R USDCT CM/ECF Admin(P)(2).

i.   Larger documents or exhibits may be submitted electronically if split into separate PDF files each less than seven (7) megabytes, attached to the main document and clearly labeled. MA R USDCT CM/ECF Admin(P)(2).

ii.   Documents submitted electronically or on paper are subject to the page limitations set by MA R USDCT LR 7.1(b)(4) or by order of the court. MA R USDCT CM/ECF Admin(P)(1).

h.   *Accuracy and readability.* The filer shall verify the accuracy and readability of any PDF file before electronically filing it in CM/ECF. MA R USDCT CM/ECF Admin(G)(6); MA R USDCT CM/ECF Admin(P)(3).

3.   *Signing of pleadings, motions and other papers*

a.   *Signature.* Every pleading, written motion, and other paper must be signed by at least one attorney of record in the attorney's name—or by a party personally if the party is unrepresented. The paper must state the signer's address, e-mail address, and telephone number. FRCP 11(a). The provisions of the Federal Rules of Civil Procedure pertaining to the form and signing of pleadings, motions, and other papers shall be applicable to all papers filed in any proceeding in this court. The board of bar overseers registration number of each attorney signing such documents, except the United States Attorney and his staff, shall be inscribed below the signature. MA R USDCT LR 5.1(a)(1).

i.   *Electronic signing.* A filing made through a person's electronic-filing account and authorized by that person, together with that person's name on a signature block, constitutes the person's signature. FRCP 5(d)(3)(C).

ii.   *Appearances.* The filing of an appearance or any other pleading signed on behalf of a party constitutes an entry of appearance for that party. All pleadings shall contain the name, bar admission number, address, telephone number, and e-mail address of the attorney entering an appearance. MA R USDCT LR 83.5.2(a).

- *Appearances by law firms.* When a party is represented by a law firm, the appearance must include the name and the signature of at least one individual attorney. When a party is represented by more than one attorney from the same or different law firms, the attorney entering the appearance must designate the individual attorney who is authorized to receive all notices in the case. Any notice sent to an attorney so designated shall be deemed to be proper notice unless the court finds that notice was not properly sent. MA R USDCT LR 83.5.2(b).

- For more information on appearances, refer to MA R USDCT LR 83.5.2.

iii.   *Signatures of attorneys.* The user login and password required to submit documents to the CM/ECF system shall serve as that user's signature for purposes of FRCP 11 and for all other purposes under the Federal Rules of Civil Procedure and the Local Rules of the United States District Court for the District of Massachusetts. All electronically filed documents must include a signature block and must set forth the attorney's name, bar number,

address, telephone number and email address. The name of the CM/ECF user under whose log-in and password the document is submitted must be preceded by a "/s/" and typed in the space where the signature would otherwise appear. MA R USDCT CM/ECF Admin(M)(1). For an example, refer to MA R USDCT CM/ECF Admin(M)(1).

iv. *Signatures of pro se parties.* Any document requiring a signature that is filed by a party appearing pro se shall bear the words "pro se" following that party's signature. Any such document shall also state the party's mailing address, telephone number (if any), and e-mail address (if the party has consented to service by email). MA R USDCT LR 83.5.5(g). For more information on practice by pro se litigants, refer to MA R USDCT LR 83.5.5.

v. *Multiple signatures.* The filer of any document requiring more than one signature (e.g, stipulations, joint motions, joint status reports, magistrate judge consent forms, etc.) must list thereon all the names of other signatories by means of a "/s/ name of signatory" block for each. By submitting such a document, the filing attorney certifies that each of the other signatories has expressly agreed to the form and substance of the document and that the filing attorney has their actual authority to submit the document electronically. MA R USDCT CM/ECF Admin(M)(2). For more information, refer to MA R USDCT CM/ECF Admin(M)(2).

vi. *Affidavits.* Except as provided in MA R USDCT CM/ECF Admin(L), affidavits shall be filed electronically; however, the electronically filed version must contain a "/s/ name of signatory" block indicating that the paper document bears an original signature. MA R USDCT CM/ECF Admin(M)(3). The court will also accept a scanned version of the original, signed document. MA R USDCT CM/ECF Admin(M)(3). For more information, refer to MA R USDCT CM/ECF Admin(M)(3).

vii. *No verification or accompanying affidavit required for pleadings.* Unless a rule or statute specifically states otherwise, a pleading need not be verified or accompanied by an affidavit. FRCP 11(a).

viii. *Unsigned papers.* The court must strike an unsigned paper unless the omission is promptly corrected after being called to the attorney's or party's attention. FRCP 11(a).

b. *Representations to the court.* By presenting to the court a pleading, written motion, or other paper—whether by signing, filing, submitting, or later advocating it—an attorney or unrepresented party certifies that to the best of the person's knowledge, information, and belief, formed after an inquiry reasonable under the circumstances:

i. It is not being presented for any improper purpose, such as to harass, cause unnecessary delay, or needlessly increase the cost of litigation;

ii. The claims, defenses, and other legal contentions are warranted by existing law or by a nonfrivolous argument for extending, modifying, or reversing existing law or for establishing new law;

iii. The factual contentions have evidentiary support or, if specifically so identified, will likely have evidentiary support after a reasonable opportunity for further investigation or discovery; and

iv. The denials of factual contentions are warranted on the evidence or, if specifically so identified, are reasonably based on belief or a lack of information. FRCP 11(b).

c. *Sanctions.* If, after notice and a reasonable opportunity to respond, the court determines that FRCP 11(b) has been violated, the court may impose an appropriate sanction on any attorney, law firm, or party that violated FRCP 11(b) or is responsible for the violation. FRCP 11(c)(1). Refer to the United States District Court for the District of Massachusetts KeyRules Motion for Sanctions document for more information.

4. *Privacy protection for filings made with the court*

a. *Redacted filings.* Unless the court orders otherwise, in an electronic or paper filing with the court that contains an individual's Social Security number, taxpayer-identification number, or birth date, the name of an individual known to be a minor, or a financial-account number, a party or nonparty making the filing may include only:

i. The last four (4) digits of the Social Security number and taxpayer-identification number;

ii. The year of the individual's birth;

iii. The minor's initials; and

iv. The last four (4) digits of the financial-account number. FRCP 5.2(a); MA R USDCT CM/ECF Admin(N).

b. *Exemptions from the redaction requirement.* The redaction requirement does not apply to the following:

i. A financial-account number that identifies the property allegedly subject to forfeiture in a forfeiture proceeding;

ii. The record of an administrative or agency proceeding;

iii. The official record of a state-court proceeding;

iv. The record of a court or tribunal, if that record was not subject to the redaction requirement when originally filed;

v. A filing covered by FRCP 5.2(c) or FRCP 5.2(d); and

vi. A pro se filing in an action brought under 28 U.S.C.A. § 2241, 28 U.S.C.A. § 2254, or 28 U.S.C.A. § 2255. FRCP 5.2(b).

c. *Limitations on remote access to electronic files; Social Security appeals and immigration cases.* Unless the court orders otherwise, in an action for benefits under the Social Security Act, and in an action or proceeding relating to an order of removal, to relief from removal, or to immigration benefits or detention, access to an electronic file is authorized as follows:

i. The parties and their attorneys may have remote electronic access to any part of the case file, including the administrative record;

ii. Any other person may have electronic access to the full record at the courthouse, but may have remote electronic access only to:

- The docket maintained by the court; and

- An opinion, order, judgment, or other disposition of the court, but not any other part of the case file or the administrative record. FRCP 5.2(c).

d. *Filings made under seal.* The court may order that a filing be made under seal without redaction. The court may later unseal the filing or order the person who made the filing to file a redacted version for the public record. FRCP 5.2(d).

e. *Protective orders.* For good cause, the court may by order in a case:

i. Require redaction of additional information; or

ii. Limit or prohibit a nonparty's remote electronic access to a document filed with the court. FRCP 5.2(e).

f. *Option for additional unredacted filing under seal.* A person making a redacted filing may also file an unredacted copy under seal. The court must retain the unredacted copy as part of the record. FRCP 5.2(f). For more information, refer to MA R USDCT LR 7.2.

g. *Option for filing a reference list.* A filing that contains redacted information may be filed together with a reference list that identifies each item of redacted information and specifies an appropriate identifier that uniquely corresponds to each item listed. The list must be filed under seal and may be amended as of right. Any reference in the case to a listed identifier will be construed to refer to the corresponding item of information. FRCP 5.2(g).

h. *Responsibility for redaction.* The clerk's office is not responsible for reviewing documents filed with the court to determine whether pleadings have been redacted and are in the proper form. MA R USDCT CM/ECF Admin(N).

i. *Waiver of protection of identifiers.* A person waives the protection of FRCP 5.2(a) as to the person's own information by filing it without redaction and not under seal. FRCP 5.2(h).

## F. Filing and Service Requirements

1. *Filing requirements*

a. *Required filings.* Any paper after the complaint that is required to be served must be filed no later than a reasonable time after service. FRCP 5(d)(1).

i. Except as noted in FRCP 33 to FRCP 36, the original of all papers required to be served under FRCP 5(d) shall, unless otherwise submitted to the court, be filed in the office of the clerk within seven (7) days after service has been made. MA R USDCT LR 5.1(b). Except as otherwise provided by the Federal Rules of Civil Procedure, proof of service of all pleadings and other papers required to be served (except discovery papers that in accordance with FRCP 33 to FRCP 36(f) are not to be filed) shall be filed in the office of the clerk promptly after service has been made. MA R USDCT LR 5.2(b)(1).

b. *Nonelectronic filing.* A paper not filed electronically is filed by delivering it: (1) to the clerk; or (2) to a judge who agrees to accept it for filing, and who must then note the filing date on the paper and promptly send it to the clerk. FRCP 5(d)(2).

c. *Electronic filing.* Unless exempt or otherwise ordered by the court, all pleadings and other papers submitted to the court must be filed, signed, and verified by electronic means as provided in MA R USDCT LR 5.4. MA R USDCT LR 5.4(A); MA R USDCT CM/ECF Admin(A)(1). All electronic filings must be made in accordance with the Administrative Procedures for Electronic Case Filing in the United States District Court for the District of

Massachusetts (MA R USDCT CM/ECF Admin). MA R USDCT LR 5.4(B). The court may deviate from the Administrative Procedures for Electronic Case Filing in the United States District Court for the District of Massachusetts (MA R USDCT CM/ECF Admin) in specific cases, without prior notice, if deemed appropriate in the exercise of discretion, considering the need for the just, speedy, and inexpensive determination of matters pending before the court. MA R USDCT CM/ECF Admin(C)(1). The court may excuse a failure to comply with any administrative procedure whenever justice so requires. MA R USDCT CM/ECF Admin(C)(2).

i. *By a represented person; Generally required; Exceptions.* A person represented by an attorney must file electronically, unless nonelectronic filing is allowed by the court for good cause or is allowed or required by local rule. FRCP 5(d)(3)(A).

ii. *By unrepresented person; When allowed or required.* A person not represented by an attorney: (1) may file electronically only if allowed by court order or by local rule; and (2) may be required to file electronically only by court order, or by a local rule that includes reasonable exceptions. FRCP 5(d)(3)(B).

iii. *Exemptions from electronic filing*

- *Documents that should not be filed electronically.* The following types of documents must not be filed electronically, and will not be scanned into the ECF system by the clerk's office: (1) sealed documents; (2) ex parte motions; (3) documents generated as part of an alternative dispute resolution (ADR) process; (4) the administrative record in Social Security and other administrative proceedings; (5) the state court record in proceedings under 28 U.S.C.A. § 2254; and (6) such other types of documents as the clerk may direct in the Administrative Procedures for Electronic Case Filing in the United States District Court for the District of Massachusetts (MA R USDCT CM/ECF Admin). MA R USDCT LR 5.4(G)(1); MA R USDCT CM/ECF Admin(L).

- *Documents that need not be filed electronically.* The following types of documents need not be filed electronically, but may be scanned into the ECF system by a filing party or the clerk's office: (1) handwritten pleadings; (2) documents filed by pro se litigants who are incarcerated or who are not registered ECF users; (3) indictments, informations, criminal complaints, and the criminal JS45 form; (4) affidavits for search or arrest warrants and related documents; (5) documents received from another court under FRCRP 20 or FRCRP 40; (6) appearance bonds; (7) any document in a criminal case containing the original signature of a defendant, such as a waiver of indictment or a plea agreement; (8) petitions for violations of supervised release; (9) executed service of process documents under FRCP 4; and (10) such other types of documents as the clerk may direct in the Administrative Procedures for Electronic Case Filing in the United States District Court for the District of Massachusetts (MA R USDCT CM/ECF Admin). MA R USDCT LR 5.4(G)(2); MA R USDCT CM/ECF Admin(L).

- For more information on exemptions from electronic filing, refer to MA R USDCT CM/ECF Admin(L).

iv. *Consequences of electronic filing.* Electronic transmission of a document to the CM/ECF system, together with the transmission of a Notice of Electronic Filing (NEF) from the court at the completion of the transaction, constitutes the filing of the document for all purposes of the Federal Rules of Procedure and constitutes entry of the document on the docket maintained by the clerk pursuant to FRCP 58 and FRCP 79. MA R USDCT CM/ECF Admin(G)(1).

v. *Payment of filing fees.* When electronically filing any pleading or paper through CM/ECF that requires a fee, all registered ECF users are to pay the fee electronically through the Treasury Department's Internet payment process. MA R USDCT LR 67.4(d); MA R USDCT CM/ECF Admin(A)(1). Pro se filers and those who have been exempted from electronic filing and/or electronic payment of fees may submit payments by check or money order made payable to "Clerk, U.S. District Court". MA R USDCT LR 67.4(d). For more information on filing fees, refer to MA R USDCT LR 67.4 and MA R USDCT CM/ECF Admin(I).

vi. For more information on electronic filing, refer to MA R USDCT CM/ECF Admin.

d. *Email or fax filing.* In general, the court does not accept documents by email or by fax. If the court, in special circumstances, does authorize the submission of a document in that manner, the document shall not be considered filed until an NEF is generated by CM/ECF at the completion of the transaction. MA R USDCT CM/ECF Admin(H)(5).

2. *Service requirements.* All papers filed pursuant to MA R USDCT LR 7.1(b) shall be served unless the moving party indicates in writing on the face of the motion that ex parte consideration is requested. Motions filed "ex parte" and related papers need not be served until the motion has been ruled upon or the court orders that service be made. MA R USDCT LR

7.1(c). Service of all pleadings subsequent to the original complaint and of all other papers required to be served shall be made in the manner specified by FRCP 5. MA R USDCT LR 5.2(a).

a. *Service; When required*

i. *In general.* Unless the Federal Rules of Civil Procedure provide otherwise, each of the following papers must be served on every party:

- An order stating that service is required;

- A pleading filed after the original complaint, unless the court orders otherwise under FRCP 5(c) because there are numerous defendants;

- A discovery paper required to be served on a party, unless the court orders otherwise;

- A written motion, except one that may be heard ex parte; and

- A written notice, appearance, demand, or offer of judgment, or any similar paper. FRCP 5(a)(1).

ii. *If a party fails to appear.* No service is required on a party who is in default for failing to appear. But a pleading that asserts a new claim for relief against such a party must be served on that party under FRCP 4. FRCP 5(a)(2).

iii. *Seizing property.* If an action is begun by seizing property and no person is or need be named as a defendant, any service required before the filing of an appearance, answer, or claim must be made on the person who had custody or possession of the property when it was seized. FRCP 5(a)(3).

b. *Service; How made*

i. *Serving an attorney.* If a party is represented by an attorney, service under FRCP 5 must be made on the attorney unless the court orders service on the party. FRCP 5(b)(1).

- *Nonresident attorney.* On application of a party, the court may order an attorney who represents any other party and who does not maintain an office within this district where service can be made on him by delivery as provided by FRCP 5(b), to designate a member of the bar of this court who does maintain such an office to receive service of all pleadings and other papers in his behalf. MA R USDCT LR 5.2(c)(1).

ii. *Serving a party acting pro se.* On application of a party, the court may order any other party who is appearing without an attorney and who does not maintain an office or residence within this district where service can be made on him by delivery as provided by FRCP 5(b), to designate an address within the district at which service can be made on him by delivery. MA R USDCT LR 5.2(c)(2).

iii. *Service in general.* A paper is served under FRCP 5 by:

- Handing it to the person;

- Leaving it: (1) at the person's office with a clerk or other person in charge or, if no one is in charge, in a conspicuous place in the office; or (2) if the person has no office or the office is closed, at the person's dwelling or usual place of abode with someone of suitable age and discretion who resides there;

- Mailing it to the person's last known address—in which event service is complete upon mailing;

- Leaving it with the court clerk if the person has no known address;

- Sending it to a registered user by filing it with the court's electronic-filing system or sending it by other electronic means that the person consented to in writing—in either of which events service is complete upon filing or sending, but is not effective if the filer or sender learns that it did not reach the person to be served; or

- Delivering it by any other means that the person consented to in writing—in which event service is complete when the person making service delivers it to the agency designated to make delivery. FRCP 5(b)(2).

iv. *Service by electronic means.* Unless exempt or otherwise ordered by the court, all pleadings and other papers must be served on other parties by electronic means. MA R USDCT LR 5.4(C); MA R USDCT CM/ECF Admin(H)(2). Service by electronic means shall be treated the same as service by mail. MA R USDCT CM/ECF Admin(H)(4).

- *Consent to electronic service.* Registering to use CM/ECF constitutes consent to service of all documents by electronic means as provided in the Administrative Procedures for Electronic Case Filing in the United States District Court for the District of Massachusetts (MA R USDCT CM/ECF Admin) and FRCP 5(b) and FRCP 77(d). MA R USDCT CM/ECF Admin(E)(6); MA R USDCT CM/ECF Admin(H)(3).

- *Service on registered ECF users.* Transmission of the Notice of Electronic Filing (NEF) through the court's transmission facilities will constitute service of the filed document upon a registered ECF user. MA R USDCT LR 5.4(C).

- *Service on non-registered users.* The party filing the document electronically is responsible for serving a paper copy of the document by mail in accordance with FRCP 5(b) to those case participants who have not been identified on the NEF as electronic recipients. MA R USDCT CM/ECF Admin(H)(3).

- *Service of conventionally filed papers.* Documents or exhibits submitted conventionally shall be served on other parties by the filer using traditional means. MA R USDCT CM/ECF Admin(P)(4).

c. *Serving numerous defendants*

   i. *In general.* If an action involves an unusually large number of defendants, the court may, on motion or on its own, order that:

- Defendants' pleadings and replies to them need not be served on other defendants;

- Any crossclaim, counterclaim, avoidance, or affirmative defense in those pleadings and replies to them will be treated as denied or avoided by all other parties; and

- Filing any such pleading and serving it on the plaintiff constitutes notice of the pleading to all parties. FRCP 5(c)(1).

   ii. *Notifying parties.* A copy of every such order must be served on the parties as the court directs. FRCP 5(c)(2).

## G. Hearings

1. *Hearings, generally.* If the court concludes that there should be a hearing on a motion, the motion will be set down for hearing at such time as the court determines. MA R USDCT LR 7.1(e).

a. *Oral argument.* Due process does not require that oral argument be permitted on a motion and, except as otherwise provided by local rule, the district court has discretion to determine whether it will decide the motion on the papers or hear argument by counsel (and perhaps receive evidence). FPP § 1190; F.D.I.C. v. Deglau, 207 F.3d 153 (3d Cir. 2000).

   i. *Evidence on a motion.* When a motion relies on facts outside the record, the court may hear the matter on affidavits or may hear it wholly or partly on oral testimony or on depositions. FRCP 43(c).

b. *Providing a regular schedule for oral hearings.* A court may establish regular times and places for oral hearings on motions. FRCP 78(a).

c. *Providing for submission on briefs.* By rule or order, the court may provide for submitting and determining motions on briefs, without oral hearings. FRCP 78(b). Motions that are not set down for hearing as provided in MA R USDCT LR 7.1(e) will be decided on the papers submitted after an opposition to the motion has been filed, or, if no opposition is filed, after the time for filing an opposition has elapsed. MA R USDCT LR 7.1(f).

2. *Conflict of court appearances.* For information on conflict of court appearances, refer to MA R USDCT LR 40.2.

## H. Forms

### 1. Federal Motion for More Definite Statement Forms

a. Motion for more definite statement. 2C FEDFORMS § 11:144.

b. Motion for more definite statement; Describing allegations requiring more definite statement. 2C FEDFORMS § 11:145.

c. Motion for more definite statement; Damages. 2C FEDFORMS § 11:146.

d. Motion for more definite statement; Patent case. 2C FEDFORMS § 11:147.

e. Compliance with order for more definite statement of complaint. 2C FEDFORMS § 11:149.

f. Motion to strike complaint upon failure of plaintiff to furnish more definite statement ordered by the court. 2C FEDFORMS § 11:150.

g. Motion; To strike pleading for failure to comply with order for more definite statement. AMJUR PP FEDPRAC § 455.

h. Notice of motion; To strike complaint and dismiss action for failure to furnish more definite statement. AMJUR PP FEDPRAC § 457.

i. Motion and notice; For more definite statement; General form. AMJUR PP FEDPRAC § 560.

j.  Motion and notice; To strike complaint and to dismiss action for failure of plaintiff to furnish more definite statement in compliance with order. AMJUR PP FEDPRAC § 561.

k.  Motion; By multiple defendants; For more definite statement. AMJUR PP FEDPRAC § 562.

l.  More definite statement. AMJUR PP FEDPRAC § 565.

m.  Motion; For more definite statement as to date of transaction alleged in complaint. AMJUR PP FEDPRAC § 1426.

n.  Motion; For more definite statement concerning jurisdictional amount. AMJUR PP FEDPRAC § 1448.

o.  Notice; Of motion; Containing motion. FEDPROF § 1B:174.

p.  Opposition; To motion. FEDPROF § 1B:175.

q.  Affidavit; Supporting or opposing motion. FEDPROF § 1B:176.

r.  Brief; Supporting or opposing motion. FEDPROF § 1B:177.

s.  Statement of points and authorities; Opposing motion. FEDPROF § 1B:178.

t.  Motion; For more definite statement. FEDPROF § 1B:207.

u.  Motion; By plaintiff; For more definite statement. FEDPROF § 1B:208.

v.  Motion; By defendant; For more definite statement. FEDPROF § 1B:209.

w.  Motion; By defendant; For more definite statement; By trustee. FEDPROF § 1B:211.

x.  Motion; By multiple defendants; For more definite statement. FEDPROF § 1B:212.

y.  Response; By plaintiff; To motion for more definite statement. FEDPROF § 1B:213.

z.  Notice and motion for more definite statement. GOLDLTGFMS § 20:6.

**2. Forms for the District of Massachusetts**

a.  Notice of filing with clerk's office. MA R USDCT CM/ECF Admin(Appendix I).

## I. Applicable Rules

1.  *Federal rules*

a.  Serving and filing pleadings and other papers. FRCP 5.

b.  Constitutional challenge to a statute; Notice, certification, and intervention. FRCP 5.1.

c.  Privacy protection for filings made with the court. FRCP 5.2.

d.  Computing and extending time; Time for motion papers. FRCP 6.

e.  Pleadings allowed; Form of motions and other papers. FRCP 7.

f.  Disclosure statement. FRCP 7.1.

g.  Form of pleadings. FRCP 10.

h.  Signing pleadings, motions, and other papers; Representations to the court; Sanctions. FRCP 11.

i.  Defenses and objections; When and how presented; Motion for judgment on the pleadings; Consolidating motions; Waiving defenses; Pretrial hearing. FRCP 12.

j.  Taking testimony. FRCP 43.

k.  Hearing motions; Submission on briefs. FRCP 78.

2.  *Local rules*

a.  Title. MA R USDCT LR 1.1.

b.  Sanctions. MA R USDCT LR 1.3.

c.  Form and filing of papers. MA R USDCT LR 5.1.

d.  Service and filing of pleadings and other papers. MA R USDCT LR 5.2.

e.  Filing and service by electronic means. MA R USDCT LR 5.4.

f.  Motion practice. MA R USDCT LR 7.1.

g.  Alternative dispute resolution. MA R USDCT LR 16.4.

h.  Payments and deposits made with the clerk. MA R USDCT LR 67.4.

i.  Settlement. MA R USDCT LR 68.2.

j.  Office of the clerk. MA R USDCT LR 77.2.

k.  Appearances. MA R USDCT LR 83.5.2.

l.  Practice by pro se litigants. MA R USDCT LR 83.5.5.

m.  CM/ECF case management/electronic case files administrative procedures. MA R USDCT CM/ECF Admin.

## Motions, Oppositions and Replies
## Motion for Post-Trial Relief

### Document Last Updated December 2018

**A. Checklist**

(I)  ❏ Matters to be considered by moving party

　(a)  ❏ Required documents

　　(1)  ❏ Notice of motion and motion

　　(2)  ❏ Memorandum

　　(3)  ❏ Certificate of service

　(b)  ❏ Supplemental documents

　　(1)  ❏ Supporting evidence

　　(2)  ❏ Notice of constitutional question

　　(3)  ❏ Proposed order

　　(4)  ❏ Compact disk with copy of document(s) in PDF format

　　(5)  ❏ Notice of filing with clerk's office

　　(6)  ❏ Additional copies

　　(7)  ❏ Courtesy copies

　(c)  ❏ Timing

　　(1)  ❏ Motion for new trial: a motion for a new trial must be filed no later than twenty-eight (28) days after the entry of judgment

　　　(i)  ❏ When a motion for a new trial is based on affidavits, they must be filed with the motion

　　(2)  ❏ Motion to alter or amend judgment: a motion to alter or amend a judgment must be filed no later than twenty-eight (28) days after the entry of the judgment

　　(3)  ❏ Motion for relief from judgment:

　　　(i)  ❏ Clerical mistakes and errors of oversight or omission may be corrected at any time

　　　(ii)  ❏ A motion under FRCP 60(b) must be made within a reasonable time—and for reasons under FRCP 60(b)(1), FRCP 60(b)(2), and FRCP 60(b)(3) no more than a year after the entry of the judgment or order or the date of the proceeding

　　(4)  ❏ A written motion and notice of the hearing must be served at least fourteen (14) days before the time specified for the hearing, with the following exceptions: (i) when the motion may be heard ex parte; (ii) when the Federal Rules of Civil Procedure set a different time; or (iii) when a court order—which a party may, for good cause, apply for ex parte—sets a different time

　　(5)  ❏ Any affidavit supporting a motion must be served with the motion

　　(6)  ❏ Except as noted in FRCP 33 to FRCP 36, the original of all papers required to be served under FRCP 5(d) shall, unless otherwise submitted to the court, be filed in the office of the clerk within seven (7) days after service has been made

(II) ❑ Matters to be considered by opposing party

   (a) ❑ Required documents

      (1) ❑ Opposition

      (2) ❑ Certificate of service

   (b) ❑ Supplemental documents

      (1) ❑ Supporting evidence

      (2) ❑ Notice of constitutional question

      (3) ❑ Compact disk with copy of document(s) in PDF format

      (4) ❑ Notice of filing with clerk's office

      (5) ❑ Additional copies

      (6) ❑ Courtesy copies

   (c) ❑ Timing

      (1) ❑ A party opposing a motion, shall file an opposition within fourteen (14) days after the motion is served, unless another period is fixed by rule or statute, or by order of the court

      (2) ❑ Except as FRCP 59(c) provides otherwise, any opposing affidavit must be served at least seven (7) days before the hearing, unless the court permits service at another time

         (i) ❑ Opposing affidavits in support of motion for new trial: the opposing party has fourteen (14) days after being served to file opposing affidavits

      (3) ❑ Except as noted in FRCP 33 to FRCP 36, the original of all papers required to be served under FRCP 5(d) shall, unless otherwise submitted to the court, be filed in the office of the clerk within seven (7) days after service has been made

## B. Timing

1. *Motion for post-trial relief*

   a. *Motion for new trial.* A motion for a new trial must be filed no later than twenty-eight (28) days after the entry of judgment. FRCP 59(b). A motion for a new trial on the ground of newly discovered evidence is subject to the same time limit as any other motion under FRCP 59 and must be made within twenty-eight (28) days after entry of judgment. However, under FRCP 60(b)(2) a party may move for relief from the judgment on this ground within a year of the entry of the judgment. FPP § 2808. The same standard applies for establishing this ground for relief, whether the motion is under FRCP 59 or FRCP 60(b)(2). FPP § 2808; WMS Gaming, Inc. v. Int'l Game Tech., 184 F.3d 1339, 1361 n.10 (Fed. Cir. 1999).

      i. *Supporting affidavit.* When a motion for a new trial is based on affidavits, they must be filed with the motion. FRCP 59(c).

   b. *Motion to alter or amend judgment.* A motion to alter or amend a judgment must be filed no later than twenty-eight (28) days after the entry of the judgment. FRCP 59(e).

   c. *Motion for relief from judgment*

      i. *Correction of clerical mistakes, oversights and omissions in judgment, order, or proceeding.* Clerical mistakes and errors of oversight or omission may be corrected at any time. FPP § 2855.

      ii. *Relief from judgment, order, or proceeding.* A motion under FRCP 60(b) must be made within a reasonable time—and for reasons under FRCP 60(b)(1), FRCP 60(b)(2), and FRCP 60(b)(3) no more than a year after the entry of the judgment or order or the date of the proceeding. FRCP 60(c)(1).

         • *Exception for motions under FRCP 60(b)(4).* [T]he time limitations applicable generally to FRCP 60(b) motions ordinarily [do not] apply to motions seeking relief for voidness, and the moving party need not show diligence in seeking to overturn the judgment or a meritorious defense. FEDPROC § 51:149.

2. *Timing of motions, generally*

   a. *Motion and notice of hearing.* A written motion and notice of the hearing must be served at least fourteen (14) days before the time specified for the hearing, with the following exceptions:

      i. When the motion may be heard ex parte;

      ii.   When the Federal Rules of Civil Procedure set a different time; or

      iii.   When a court order—which a party may, for good cause, apply for ex parte—sets a different time. FRCP 6(c)(1).

  b.  *Supporting affidavit.* Any affidavit supporting a motion must be served with the motion. FRCP 6(c)(2).

3.  *Timing of opposing papers.* A party opposing a motion, shall file an opposition within fourteen (14) days after the motion is served, unless (1) the motion is for summary judgment, in which case the opposition shall be filed within twenty-one (21) days after the motion is served, or (2) another period is fixed by rule or statute, or by order of the court. MA R USDCT LR 7.1(b)(2); MA R USDCT CM/ECF Admin(H)(4). The fourteen (14) day period is intended to include the period specified by the civil rules for mailing time and provide for a uniform period regardless of the use of the mails. MA R USDCT LR 7.1(b)(2).

  a.  *Opposing affidavit.* Except as FRCP 59(c) provides otherwise, any opposing affidavit must be served at least seven (7) days before the hearing, unless the court permits service at another time. FRCP 6(c)(2).

      i.   *Opposing affidavits in support of motion for new trial.* The opposing party has fourteen (14) days after being served to file opposing affidavits. FRCP 59(c).

4.  *Timing of reply papers.* Where the respondent files an answering affidavit setting up a new matter, the moving party ordinarily is allowed a reasonable time to file a reply affidavit since failure to deny the new matter by affidavit may operate as an admission of its truth. AMJUR MOTIONS § 25.

  a.  *Generally.* All other papers not filed as indicated in MA R USDCT LR 7.1(b)(1) and MA R USDCT LR 7.1(b)(2), whether in the form of a reply brief or otherwise, may be submitted only with leave of court. MA R USDCT LR 7.1(b)(3).

      i.   *Reply affidavits in support of motion for new trial.* The court may permit reply affidavits. FRCP 59(c).

5.  *Filing after service.* Except as noted in FRCP 33 to FRCP 36, the original of all papers required to be served under FRCP 5(d) shall, unless otherwise submitted to the court, be filed in the office of the clerk within seven (7) days after service has been made. MA R USDCT LR 5.1(b).

6.  *Computation of time*

  a.  *Computing time.* FRCP 6 applies in computing any time period specified in the Federal Rules of Civil Procedure, in any local rule or court order, or in any statute that does not specify a method of computing time. FRCP 6(a).

      i.   *Period stated in days or a longer unit.* When the period is stated in days or a longer unit of time:

        •  Exclude the day of the event that triggers the period;

        •  Count every day, including intermediate Saturdays, Sundays, and legal holidays; and

        •  Include the last day of the period, but if the last day is a Saturday, Sunday, or legal holiday, the period continues to run until the end of the next day that is not a Saturday, Sunday, or legal holiday. FRCP 6(a)(1).

      ii.   *Period stated in hours.* When the period is stated in hours:

        •  Begin counting immediately on the occurrence of the event that triggers the period;

        •  Count every hour, including hours during intermediate Saturdays, Sundays, and legal holidays; and

        •  If the period would end on a Saturday, Sunday, or legal holiday, the period continues to run until the same time on the next day that is not a Saturday, Sunday, or legal holiday. FRCP 6(a)(2).

      iii.   *Office of the clerk.* The offices of the Clerk of Court at Boston, Worcester and Springfield shall be open from 8:30 a.m. until 5:00 p.m. on all days except Saturdays, Sundays, legal holidays and other days so ordered by the court and announced in advance, if feasible. MA R USDCT LR 77.2.

      iv.   *Inaccessibility of the clerk's office.* Unless the court orders otherwise, if the clerk's office is inaccessible:

        •  On the last day for filing under FRCP 6(a)(1), then the time for filing is extended to the first accessible day that is not a Saturday, Sunday, or legal holiday; or

        •  During the last hour for filing under FRCP 6(a)(2), then the time for filing is extended to the same time on the first accessible day that is not a Saturday, Sunday, or legal holiday. FRCP 6(a)(3).

      v.   *"Last day" defined.* Unless a different time is set by a statute, local rule, or court order, the last day ends:

        •  For electronic filing, at midnight in the court's time zone; and

        •  For filing by other means, when the clerk's office is scheduled to close. FRCP 6(a)(4).

vi. *"Next day" defined.* The "next day" is determined by continuing to count forward when the period is measured after an event and backward when measured before an event. FRCP 6(a)(5).

vii. *"Legal holiday" defined.* "Legal holiday" means:

- The day set aside by statute for observing New Year's Day, Martin Luther King Jr.'s Birthday, Washington's Birthday, Memorial Day, Independence Day, Labor Day, Columbus Day, Veterans' Day, Thanksgiving Day, or Christmas Day;

- Any day declared a holiday by the President or Congress; and

- For periods that are measured after an event, any other day declared a holiday by the state where the district court is located. FRCP 6(a)(6).

b. *Computation of electronic filing deadlines.* Filing documents electronically does not alter any filing deadlines. MA R USDCT CM/ECF Admin(K); MA R USDCT LR 5.4(D). Although CM/ECF is generally available twenty-four (24) hours a day for filing, all electronic transmissions of documents must be completed prior to 6:00 PM, Eastern Standard (or Daylight Savings) Time, on the date on which it is due, in order to be considered timely filed that day. MA R USDCT CM/ECF Admin(K); MA R USDCT LR 5.4(D). When a specific time of day deadline is set by court order or stipulation, the electronic filing must be completed by that time. Documents may be filed at any time of the day on days prior to the date on which it is due. MA R USDCT CM/ECF Admin(K). A document filed electronically shall be deemed filed as of the time and date stated on the NEF received from the court. MA R USDCT CM/ECF Admin(G)(2); MA R USDCT CM/ECF Admin(K).

i. *Technical failures.* A user whose filing is made untimely as the result of a technical failure of the court's CM/ECF system may seek appropriate relief from the court. MA R USDCT CM/ECF Admin(W)(3). Technical difficulties on the filer's end, with telephone, cable lines, the filer's Internet Service Provider (ISP), or hardware or software problems, will not constitute a technical failure under the Administrative Procedures for Electronic Case Filing in the United States District Court for the District of Massachusetts (MA R USDCT CM/ECF Admin) nor excuse an untimely filing. MA R USDCT CM/ECF Admin(W)(3). As help desk support is available during normal business hours, filers are strongly urged to electronically file any documents during that period. MA R USDCT CM/ECF Admin(W)(3).

- The court has made available a public terminal (computers and scanner) in each clerk's office for registered users to scan and electronically file documents. This equipment is available during normal business hours. Users should bring their prepared document and a valid CM/ECF login and password. MA R USDCT CM/ECF Admin(W)(3).

c. *Extending time.* When an act may or must be done within a specified time, the court may, for good cause, extend the time: (1) with or without motion or notice if the court acts, or if a request is made, before the original time or its extension expires; or (2) on motion made after the time has expired if the party failed to act because of excusable neglect. FRCP 6(b)(1).

i. *Exceptions.* A court must not extend the time to act under FRCP 50(b), FRCP 50(d), FRCP 52(b), FRCP 59(b), FRCP 59(d), FRCP 59(e), and FRCP 60(b). FRCP 6(b)(2).

ii. Refer to the United States District Court for the District of Massachusetts KeyRules Motion for Continuance/Extension of Time document for more information on extending time.

d. *Additional time after certain kinds of service.* When a party may or must act within a specified time after being served and service is made under FRCP 5(b)(2)(C) (by mail), FRCP 5(b)(2)(D) (by leaving with the clerk), or FRCP 5(b)(2)(F) (by other means consented to), three (3) days are added after the period would otherwise expire under FRCP 6(a). FRCP 6(d).

# C. General Requirements

1. *Motions, generally*

a. *Requirements.* A request for a court order must be made by motion. The motion must:

i. Be in writing unless made during a hearing or trial;

ii. State with particularity the grounds for seeking the order; and

iii. State the relief sought. FRCP 7(b)(1).

b. *Notice of motion.* A party interested in resisting the relief sought by a motion has a right to notice thereof, and an opportunity to be heard. AMJUR MOTIONS § 12.

i. [I]n addition to statutory or court rule provisions requiring notice of a motion—the purpose of such a notice requirement having been said to be to prevent a party from being prejudicially surprised by a motion—principles of natural justice dictate that an adverse party generally must be given notice that a motion will be presented to the court. AMJUR MOTIONS § 12.

    ii. "Notice," in this regard, means reasonable notice, including a meaningful opportunity to prepare and to defend against allegations of a motion. AMJUR MOTIONS § 12.

c. *Writing requirement.* The writing requirement is intended to [ensure] that the adverse parties are informed and have a record of both the motion's pendency and the grounds on which the movant seeks an order. FPP § 1191; Feldberg v. Quechee Lakes Corp., 463 F.3d 195 (2d Cir. 2006). [A] single written document can satisfy the writing requirements both for a motion and for [an] FRCP 6(c)(1) notice. FRCP 7(Advisory Committee Notes).

d. *Particularity requirement.* The particularity requirement [ensures] that the opposing parties will have notice of their opponent's contentions. FEDPROC § 62:358; Goodman v. 1973 26 Foot Trojan Vessel, Arkansas Registration No. AR1439SN, 859 F.2d 71 (8th Cir. 1988). That requirement ensures that notice of the basis for the motion is provided to the court and to the opposing party so as to avoid prejudice, provide the opponent with a meaningful opportunity to respond, and provide the court with enough information to process the motion correctly. FEDPROC § 62:358; Andreas v. Volkswagen of Am., Inc., 336 F.3d 789 (8th Cir. 2003).

    i. Reasonable specification of the grounds for a motion is sufficient. The particularity requirement for motions is satisfied when no party is prejudiced by a lack of particularity or when the court can comprehend the basis for the motion and deal with it fairly. However, where a movant fails to state even one ground for granting the motion in question, the movant has failed to meet the minimal standard of "reasonable specification." FEDPROC § 62:358; Martinez v. Trainor, 556 F.2d 818 (7th Cir. 1977).

    ii. The court may excuse the failure to comply with the particularity requirement if it is inadvertent, and where no prejudice is shown by the opposing party. FEDPROC § 62:358.

e. *Control of motion practice*

    i. *Plan for the disposition of motions.* At the earliest practicable time, the judicial officer shall establish a framework for the disposition of motions, which, at the discretion of the judicial officer, may include specific deadlines or general time guidelines for filing motions. This framework may be amended from time to time by the judicial officer as required by the progress of the case. MA R USDCT LR 7.1(a)(1).

    ii. *Motion practice.* No motion shall be filed unless counsel certify that they have conferred and have attempted in good faith to resolve or narrow the issue. MA R USDCT LR 7.1(a)(2).

    iii. *Unresolved motions.* The court shall rule on motions as soon as practicable, having in mind the reporting requirements set forth in the Civil Justice Reform Act. MA R USDCT LR 7.1(a)(3).

2. *Motion for post-trial relief*

a. *Motion for new trial.* FRCP 59 gives the trial judge ample power to prevent what the judge considers to be a miscarriage of justice. It is the judge's right, and indeed duty, to order a new trial if it is deemed in the interest of justice to do so. FPP § 2803; Juneau Square Corp. v. First Wisconsin Nat. Bank of Milwaukee, 624 F.2d 798, 807 (7th Cir. 1980).

    i. *Grounds for new trial.* The court may, on motion, grant a new trial on all or some of the issues—and to any party—as follows: (1) after a jury trial, for any reason for which a new trial has heretofore been granted in an action at law in federal court; or (2) after a nonjury trial, for any reason for which a rehearing has heretofore been granted in a suit in equity in federal court. FRCP 59(a)(1). Any error of law, if prejudicial, is a good ground for a new trial. The other grounds most commonly raised. . .are that the verdict is against the weight of the evidence, that the verdict is too large or too small, that there is newly discovered evidence, that conduct of counsel or of the court has tainted the verdict, or that there has been misconduct affecting the jury. FPP § 2805.

        • *Weight of the evidence.* The power of a federal judge to grant a new trial on the ground that the verdict was against the weight of the evidence is clear. FPP § 2806; Byrd v. Blue Ridge Rural Elec. Co-op., Inc., 356 U.S. 525, 540, 78 S.Ct. 893, 902, 2 L.Ed.2d 953 (1958); Montgomery Ward & Co. v. Duncan, 311 U.S. 243, 251, 61 S.Ct. 189, 194, 85 L.Ed. 147 (1940). On a motion for a new trial—unlike a motion for a judgment as a matter of law—the judge may set aside the verdict even though there is substantial evidence to support it. FPP § 2806; ATD Corp. v. Lydall, Inc., 159 F.3d 534, 549 (Fed. Cir. 1998). The judge is not required to take that view of the evidence most favorable to the verdict-winner. FPP § 2806; Bates v. Hensley, 414 F.2d 1006, 1011 (8th Cir. 1969). The mere fact that the evidence is in conflict is not enough to set aside the verdict, however. Indeed the more sharply the evidence conflicts, the more reluctant the judge should be to substitute his judgment for that of the jury. FPP § 2806; Dawson v. Wal-Mart Stores, Inc., 978 F.2d 205 (5th Cir. 1992); Williams v. City of Valdosta, 689 F.2d 964, 974 (11th Cir. 1982). But on a motion for a new trial on the ground that the verdict is against the weight of the evidence, the judge is free to weigh the evidence. FPP § 2806; Uniloc USA, Inc. v. Microsoft Corp., 632 F.3d 1292 (Fed. Cir. 2011). Indeed, it has been said that the granting of a new trial on the ground that the verdict is against the weight of the evidence "involves an element of discretion which goes further than the mere sufficiency of the evidence. It embraces all the reasons which inhere in the integrity of the jury system itself." FPP § 2806; Tidewater Oil Co. v. Waller, 302 F.2d 638, 643 (10th Cir. 1962).

- *Size of the verdict.* A motion under FRCP 59 is an appropriate means to challenge the size of the verdict. The court always may grant relief if the verdict is excessive or inadequate as a matter of law, but this is not the limit of the court's power. FPP § 2807. It also may grant a new trial if the size of the verdict is against the weight of the evidence. FPP § 2807; Sprague v. Boston & Maine Corp., 769 F.2d 26, 28 (1st Cir. 1985). If the court finds that a verdict is unreasonably high, it may condition denial of the motion for a new trial on plaintiff's consent to a remittitur. FPP § 2807. If the verdict is too low, it may not provide for an additur as an alternative to a new trial. FPP § 2807; Dimick v. Schiedt, 293 U.S. 474, 55 S. Ct. 296, 79 L. Ed. 603 (1935).

- *Newly discovered evidence.* Newly discovered evidence must be of facts existing at the time of trial. FPP § 2808; Alicea v. Machete Music, 744 F.3d 773, 781 (1st Cir. 2014). The moving party must have been excusably ignorant of the facts despite using due diligence to learn about them. FPP § 2808; United States v. 41 Cases, More or Less, 420 F.2d 1126 (5th Cir. 1970); Huff v. Metro. Life Ins. Co., 675 F.2d 119 (6th Cir. 1982). If the facts were known to the party and no excusable ignorance can be shown, a new-trial motion will not be granted. Failure to show due diligence also generally will result in the denial of the motion. FPP § 2808. However, it has been held that a new trial may be granted even though proper diligence was not used if this is necessary to prevent a manifest miscarriage of justice. FPP § 2808; Ferrell v. Trailmobile, Inc., 223 F.2d 697 (5th Cir. 1955).

- *Conduct of counsel and judge.* If a verdict has been unfairly influenced by the misconduct of counsel, a new trial should be granted. Misconduct of counsel that may necessitate a new trial may involve things such as improper comments or arguments to the jury, including presenting arguments about evidence not properly before the court. FPP § 2809. Improper conduct by the trial judge also is a ground for a new trial. Motions raising this ground happily are rare and a new trial is not required if the judge's behavior has not made the trial unfair. The moving party must meet a heavy burden to prevail on the ground of judicial misconduct. FPP § 2809.

- *Misconduct affecting jury.* A common ground for a motion for a new trial is that the jury, or members of it, has not performed in the fashion expected of juries. FPP § 2810. Because of the limitations on the use of testimony by the jurors and because a new trial is required in any event only if conduct affecting the jury has been harmful to the losing party, most motions for a new trial on this ground are denied. It is ground for a new trial if a juror was prejudiced from the start but claims that a juror did not disclose all that he should at voir dire usually fail, unless it can be found that the information omitted would have supported a challenge for cause. Motions for a new trial asserting that the jury did not deliberate for a sufficient length of time also usually fail. FPP § 2810.

ii. *Partial new trial.* FRCP 59(a) provides that a new trial may be granted "on all or some of the issues—and to any party—. . ." Thus it recognizes the court's power to grant a partial new trial. FPP § 2814. If a partial new trial is granted, those portions of the first judgment not set aside become part of the judgment entered following the jury verdict at the new trial. Thus, the end result is a single judgment. FPP § 2814.

iii. *Further action after a nonjury trial.* After a nonjury trial, the court may, on motion for a new trial, open the judgment if one has been entered, take additional testimony, amend findings of fact and conclusions of law or make new ones, and direct the entry of a new judgment. FRCP 59(a)(2).

iv. *New trial on the court's initiate or for reasons not in the motion.* No later than twenty-eight (28) days after the entry of judgment, the court, on its own, may order a new trial for any reason that would justify granting one on a party's motion. After giving the parties notice and an opportunity to be heard, the court may grant a timely motion for a new trial for a reason not stated in the motion. In either event, the court must specify the reasons in its order. FRCP 59(d).

b. *Motion to alter or amend judgment.* FRCP 59(e) authorizes a motion to alter or amend a judgment after its entry.

FRCP 59(e) also has been interpreted as permitting a motion to vacate a judgment rather than merely amend it. FPP § 2810.1.

i. *Types of motions covered under FRCP 59(e).* FRCP 59(e) covers a broad range of motions, and the only real limitation on the type of the motion permitted is that it must request a substantive alteration of the judgment, not merely the correction of a clerical error, or relief of a type wholly collateral to the judgment. FPP § 2810.1; Osterneck v. Ernst & Whinney, 489 U.S. 169, 109 S. Ct. 987, 103 L. Ed. 2d 146 (1989). The type of relief requested in postjudgment motions for attorney's fees and costs, for instance, is considered collateral unless it is specifically addressed in the judgment, and thus these motions generally do not fall under FRCP 59(e). FPP § 2810.1; Hastert v. Illinois State Bd. of Election Comm'rs, 28 F.3d 1430, 1438 n.8 (7th Cir. 1993), as amended on reh'g (June 1, 1994). FRCP 59(e) does, however, include motions for reconsideration. FPP § 2810.1; United States v. $23,000 in U.S. Currency, 356 F.3d 157, 165 n.9 (1st Cir. 2004). A motion under FRCP 59(e) also is appropriate if the court in the original judgment has failed to give relief on a certain claim on which it has found that the party is entitled to relief. Finally, the motion may be used to request an amendment of the judgment to provide for prejudgment interest. The court may not, however, give relief under FRCP 59(e) if this would defeat a party's right to jury trial on an issue. FPP § 2810.1.

ii. *Grounds for granting an FRCP 59(e) motion.* There are four basic grounds upon which [an] FRCP 59(e) motion may be granted. FPP § 2810.1; F.D.I.C. v. World Univ. Inc., 978 F.2d 10 (1st Cir. 1992). First, the movant may demonstrate that the motion is necessary to correct manifest errors of law or fact upon which the judgment is based. Of course, the corollary principle applies and the movant's failure to show any manifest error may result in the motion's denial. FPP § 2810.1. Second, the motion may be granted so that the moving party may present newly discovered or previously unavailable evidence. FPP § 2810.1; GenCorp, Inc. v. Am. Int'l Underwriters, 178 F.3d 804, 834 (6th Cir. 1999). Third, the motion will be granted if necessary to prevent manifest injustice. Serious misconduct of counsel may justify relief under this theory. Fourth, [an] FRCP 59(e) motion may be justified by an intervening change in controlling law. FPP § 2810.1.

iii. *Limitations on an FRCP 59(e) motion.* The FRCP 59(e) motion may not be used to relitigate old matters, or to raise arguments or present evidence that could have been raised prior to the entry of judgment. Also, amendment of the judgment will be denied if it would serve no useful purpose. In practice, because of the narrow purposes for which they are intended, FRCP 59(e) motions typically are denied. FPP § 2810.1.

c. *Motion for relief from judgment*

i. *Corrections based on clerical mistakes; Oversights and omissions.* The court may correct a clerical mistake or a mistake arising from oversight or omission whenever one is found in a judgment, order, or other part of the record. The court may do so on motion or on its own, with or without notice. But after an appeal has been docketed in the appellate court and while it is pending, such a mistake may be corrected only with the appellate court's leave. FRCP 60(a).

- *Correctable mistakes.* A motion under FRCP 60(a) only can be used to make the judgment or record speak the truth and cannot be used to make it say something other than what originally was pronounced. FPP § 2854. FRCP 60(a) is not a vehicle for relitigating matters that already have been litigated and decided, nor to change what has been deliberately done. FPP § 2854. The mistake correctable under FRCP 60(a) need not be committed by the clerk or the court; FRCP 60(a) may be utilized to correct mistakes by the parties as well. FPP § 2854.

- *Substantive changes.* When the change sought is substantive in nature, such as a change in the calculation of interest not originally intended, the addition of an amount to a judgment to compensate for depreciation in stock awarded, or the broadening of a summary-judgment motion to dismiss all claims, relief is not appropriate under FRCP 60(a). FPP § 2854. Errors of a more substantial nature are to be corrected by a motion under FRCP 59(e) or FRCP 60(b). FPP § 2854.

ii. *Relief from judgment, order, or proceeding.* Relief under FRCP 60(b) ordinarily is obtained by motion in the court that rendered the judgment. FPP § 2865.

- *Grounds for relief from a final judgment, order, or proceeding.* On motion and just terms, the court may relieve a party or its legal representative from a final judgment, order, or proceeding for the following reasons: (1) mistake, inadvertence, surprise, or excusable neglect; (2) newly discovered evidence that, with reasonable diligence, could not have been discovered in time to move for a new trial under FRCP 59(b); (3) fraud (whether previously called intrinsic or extrinsic), misrepresentation, or misconduct by an opposing party; (4) the judgment is void; (5) the judgment has been satisfied, released or discharged; it is based on an earlier judgment that has been reversed or vacated; or applying it prospectively is no longer equitable; or (6) any other reason that justifies relief. FRCP 60(b).

- *Mistake, inadvertence, surprise, or excusable neglect.* Although FRCP 60(b)(1) speaks only of mistake, inadvertence, surprise, or excusable neglect, a defendant must prove the existence of a meritorious defense as a prerequisite to obtaining relief on these grounds. FEDPROC § 51:131; Augusta Fiberglass Coatings, Inc. v. Fodor Contracting Corp., 843 F.2d 808 (4th Cir. 1988). In all averments of fraud or mistake, the circumstances constituting fraud or mistake must be stated with particularity. This requirement applies with respect to averments of mistake in motion papers under FRCP 60(b)(1). FEDPROC § 51:138. In assessing whether conduct is excusable, several factors must be taken into account, including: (1) the danger of prejudice to the nonmoving party; (2) the length of the delay and its potential impact on judicial proceedings; (3) whether the movant acted in good faith; and (4) the reason for the delay, including whether it was within the reasonable control of the movant. FEDPROC § 51:132; Nara v. Frank, 488 F.3d 187 (3d Cir. 2007), as amended (June 12, 2007).

- *Newly discovered evidence.* The standards for relief from a judgment on the basis of newly discovered evidence are, in summary: (1) the motion must involve legally admissible "evidence" in some technical sense, rather than just factual information of some variety; (2) the evidence must have been in existence at the time of the trial or consists of facts existing at the time of trial; (3) the evidence must be newly discovered since the trial; (4) the evidence must not have been discoverable by the exercise of due diligence in time for use at the trial or to move for a new trial; (5) the evidence must be material and not merely cumulative or impeaching; and (6) the evidence must be such that, if received, it will probably produce a different result. FEDPROC § 51:140.

- *Fraud, misrepresentation, or other misconduct of opposing party.* Many other cases support the propositions that the burden of proof of fraud is on the moving party and that fraud must be established by clear and convincing evidence. Further, the fraud must have prevented the moving party from fully and fairly presenting his case. It also must be chargeable to an adverse party; the moving party cannot get relief because of the party's own fraud. FPP § 2860. There is some disagreement about the meaning of "fraud" or "misconduct" in this context. One view is that the moving party must show that the adverse party committed a deliberate act that adversely impacted the fairness of the relevant legal proceeding in question. FEDPROC § 51:144; Jordan v. Paccar, Inc., 97 F.3d 1452 (6th Cir. 1996). The prevailing view is broader, however, and allows a motion for relief to be granted regardless of whether the adverse party acted with an evil, nefarious, malicious, innocent, or careless purpose. FEDPROC § 51:144.

- *Void judgment.* A judgment is not void merely because it is erroneous. It is void only if the court that rendered it lacked jurisdiction of the subject matter, or of the parties, or if it acted in a manner inconsistent with due process of law. Of course, although a challenge on one of those three grounds can be made under FRCP 60(b)(4), if the court finds that there was subject-matter or personal jurisdiction, or that no due-process violation has occurred, the motion will be denied. FPP § 2862.

- *Judgment satisfied or no longer equitable.* The significant portion of FRCP 60(b)(5) is the final ground, allowing relief if it is no longer equitable for the judgment to be applied prospectively. FPP § 2863. In order to obtain relief on these grounds, the judgment itself must have prospective application and such application must be inequitable due to a change in circumstances since the judgment was rendered. FEDPROC § 51:156. The mere possibility that a judgment has some future effect does not mean that it is "prospective," for purposes of applying FRCP 60(b)(5), because virtually every court order causes at least some reverberations into the future and has some prospective effect; the essential inquiry into the prospective nature of a judgment revolves around whether it is executory, or involves the supervision of changing conduct or conditions. FEDPROC § 51:157; Kalamazoo River Study Grp. v. Rockwell Int'l Corp., 355 F.3d 574 (6th Cir. 2004). The court's duty when confronted with such a motion is not to examine the correctness of the existing decree at the time it was entered, or even whether it is needed today, but to determine whether, assuming it was needed when entered, intervening changes have eliminated that need. FEDPROC § 51:158; Swift & Co. v. United States, 367 U.S. 909, 81 S. Ct. 1918, 6 L. Ed. 2d 1249 (1961).

- *Any other reason justifying relief.* The broad power granted by FRCP 60(b)(6) is not for the purpose of relieving a party from free, calculated, and deliberate choices the party has made. A party remains under a duty to take legal steps to protect his own interests. FPP § 2864. [Case law] certainly seemed to establish that FRCP 60(b)(6) and the first five clauses are mutually exclusive and that relief cannot be had under FRCP 60(b)(6) if it would have been available under the earlier clauses. FPP § 2864.

- *Effect of motion.* The motion does not affect the judgment's finality or suspend its operation. FRCP 60(c)(2).
- *Other powers to grant relief.* FRCP 60 does not limit a court's power to: (1) entertain an independent action to relieve a party from a judgment, order, or proceeding; (2) grant relief under 28 U.S.C.A. § 1655 to a defendant who was not personally notified of the action; or (3) set aside a judgment for fraud on the court. FRCP 60(d).

   iii. *Bills and writs abolished.* The following are abolished: bills of review, bills in the nature of bills of review, and writs of coram nobis, coram vobis, and audita querela. FRCP 60(e).

3. *Opposing papers.* The Federal Rules of Civil Procedure do not require any formal answer, return, or reply to a motion, except where the Federal Rules of Civil Procedure or local rules may require affidavits, memoranda, or other papers to be filed in opposition to a motion. Such papers are simply to apprise the court of such opposition and the grounds of that opposition. FEDPROC § 62:353.

   a. *Effect of failure to respond to motion.* Although in the absence of statutory provision or court rule, a motion ordinarily does not require a written answer, when a party files a motion and the opposing party fails to respond, the court may construe such failure to respond as nonopposition to the motion or an admission that the motion was meritorious, may take the facts alleged in the motion as true—the rule in some jurisdictions being that the failure to respond to a fact set forth in a motion is deemed an admission—and may grant the motion if the relief requested appears to be justified. AMJUR MOTIONS § 28.

   b. *Assent or no opposition not determinative.* However, a motion will not be granted automatically simply because an "assent" or a notation of "no opposition" has been filed; federal judges frequently deny motions that have been assented to when it is thought that justice so dictates. FPP § 1190.

   c. *Responsive pleading inappropriate as response to motion.* An attempt to answer or oppose a motion with a responsive pleading usually is not appropriate. FPP § 1190.

4. *Reply papers.* A moving party may be required or permitted to prepare papers in addition to his original motion papers. AMJUR MOTIONS § 25. Papers answering or replying to opposing papers may be appropriate, in the interests of justice, where it appears there is a substantial reason for allowing a reply. Thus, a court may accept reply papers where a party demonstrates that the papers to which it seeks to file a reply raise new issues that are material to the disposition of the question before the court, or where the court determines, sua sponte, that it wishes further briefing of an issue raised in those papers and orders the submission of additional papers. FEDPROC § 62:354.

   a. *Function of reply papers.* The function of a reply affidavit is to answer the arguments made in opposition to the position taken by the movant and not to permit the movant to introduce new arguments in support of the motion. AMJUR MOTIONS § 25.

   b. *Issues raised for the first time in a reply document.* However, the view has been followed in some jurisdictions, that as a matter of judicial economy, where there is no prejudice and where the issues could be raised simply by filing a motion to dismiss, the trial court has discretion to consider arguments raised for the first time in a reply memorandum, and that a trial court may grant a motion to strike issues raised for the first time in a reply memorandum. AMJUR MOTIONS § 26.

5. *Alternative dispute resolution (ADR).* The judicial officer assigned to preside over the case shall encourage the resolution of disputes by settlement or other alternative dispute resolution programs. MA R USDCT LR 16.4(a).

   a. *Settlement.* At every conference conducted under the Local Rules of the United States District Court for the District of Massachusetts, the judicial officer shall inquire as to the utility of the parties conducting settlement negotiations, explore means of facilitating those negotiations, and offer whatever assistance may be appropriate in the circumstances. Assistance may include a reference of the case to another judicial officer for settlement purposes. MA R USDCT LR 16.4(b).

     i. When a case is settled, the parties shall file with the clerk a signed agreement for judgment or stipulation for dismissal, as appropriate, within twenty-eight (28) days, unless the court otherwise orders. MA R USDCT LR 68.2.

   b. *Alternative dispute resolution programs*

     i. *Discretion of judicial officer.* The judicial officer, following an exploration of the matter with all counsel, may refer appropriate cases to alternative dispute resolution programs that have been designated for use in the district court or that the judicial officer may make available. The dispute resolution programs described in MA R USDCT LR 16.4(c)(2) through MA R USDCT LR 16.4(c)(4) are illustrative, not exclusive. Moreover, nothing in MA R USDCT LR 16.4 shall preclude the parties from engaging in private dispute resolution programs as long as they comply with any schedule established by the court. MA R USDCT LR 16.4(c)(1).

ii. *Mediation.* The judicial officer may refer the case to mediation upon the agreement of all parties. MA R USDCT LR 16.4(c)(2)(A).

iii. *Other alternative dispute resolution programs.* Use of mediation is not exclusive. At the request of parties, the judicial officer may consider other forms of alternative dispute resolution including, but not limited to, mini-trial, summary jury trial and arbitration. MA R USDCT LR 16.4(c)(3).

c. For more information on alternative dispute resolution (ADR), refer to MA R USDCT LR 16.4.

6. *Sanctions.* Failure to comply with any of the directions or obligations set forth in, or authorized by, these rules may result in dismissal, default, or the imposition of other sanctions as deemed appropriate by the judicial officer. MA R USDCT LR 1.3. Except as provided by law, the court may impose sanctions as provided in MA R USDCT LR 1.3 for failure to comply with the Administrative Procedures for Electronic Case Filing in the United States District Court for the District of Massachusetts (MA R USDCT CM/ECF Admin) or with MA R USDCT LR 5.4. MA R USDCT CM/ECF Admin(C)(3).

## D. Documents

1. *Documents for moving party*

   a. *Required documents*

      i. *Notice of motion and motion.* Refer to the General Requirements section of this document for information on the notice of motion and motion.

      - *Request for oral argument.* Any party making or opposing a motion who believes that oral argument may assist the court and wishes to be heard shall include a request for oral argument in a separate paragraph of the motion or opposition. The request should be set off with a centered caption, "REQUEST FOR ORAL ARGUMENT." MA R USDCT LR 7.1(d).

      ii. *Memorandum.* A party filing a motion shall at the same time file a memorandum of reasons, including citation of supporting authorities, why the motion should be granted. MA R USDCT LR 7.1(b)(1). Any memorandum of law or other attachment filed in support of a main document shall be filed as a separate document, using the proper event. MA R USDCT CM/ECF Admin(G)(4). Memoranda supporting or opposing allowance of motions shall not, without leave of court, exceed twenty (20) pages, double-spaced. MA R USDCT LR 7.1(b)(4).

      iii. *Certificate of service.* No certificate of service is required when a paper is served by filing it with the court's electronic-filing system. When a paper that is required to be served is served by other means: (1) if the paper is filed, a certificate of service must be filed with it or within a reasonable time after service; and (2) if the paper is not filed, a certificate of service need not be filed unless filing is required by court order or by local rule. FRCP 5(d)(1)(B). Except as otherwise provided by the Federal Rules of Civil Procedure, proof of service of all pleadings and other papers required to be served (except discovery papers that in accordance with FRCP 33 to FRCP 36(f) are not to be filed) shall be filed in the office of the clerk promptly after service has been made. The proof shall show the time and manner of service, and may be made by written acknowledgment of service, a certificate of a member of the bar of this court, or an affidavit of the person who served the paper. MA R USDCT LR 5.2(b)(1). A certificate of service of a member of the bar shall appear at the bottom of or on the margin of the last page of the paper to which it relates. MA R USDCT LR 5.2(b)(2).

      - *Paper service.* The certificate shall be a brief, single-spaced statement and may be in the following form: I hereby certify that a true copy of the above document was served upon (each party appearing pro se and) the attorney of record for each other party by mail (by hand) on (date). (Signature). MA R USDCT LR 5.2(b)(2).

      - *Electronic service.* Any pleading or other paper served by electronic means must bear a certificate of service in accordance with MA R USDCT LR 5.2(b). MA R USDCT LR 5.4(C); MA R USDCT CM/ECF Admin(H)(2). The certificate of service shall state that the filer: (1) filed the document electronically, (2) that it will be served electronically to registered CM/ECF participants via the NEF and (3) that the filer will send paper copies to non-registered participants as indicated on the NEF. MA R USDCT CM/ECF Admin(H)(2). For example: I hereby certify that this document filed through the CM/ECF system will be sent electronically to the registered participants as identified on the NEF (NEF) and paper copies will be sent to those indicated as non registered participants on (date). MA R USDCT CM/ECF Admin(H)(2).

      - *Return.* Documents not conforming to the requirements of MA R USDCT LR 5.2 (except notices of appeal) shall be returned by the clerk. MA R USDCT LR 5.2(b)(2).

      - *Failure to make proof of service.* Failure to make proof of service does not affect the validity of the service. MA R USDCT LR 5.2(b)(3).

b. *Supplemental documents*

    i. *Supporting evidence.* When a motion relies on facts outside the record, the court may hear the matter on affidavits or may hear it wholly or partly on oral testimony or on depositions. FRCP 43(c). Affidavits and other documents setting forth or evidencing facts on which the motion is based shall be filed with the motion. MA R USDCT LR 7.1(b)(1).

    ii. *Notice of constitutional question.* A party that files a pleading, written motion, or other paper drawing into question the constitutionality of a federal or state statute must promptly:

- *File notice.* File a notice of constitutional question stating the question and identifying the paper that raises it, if: (1) a federal statute is questioned and the parties do not include the United States, one of its agencies, or one of its officers or employees in an official capacity; or (2) a state statute is questioned and the parties do not include the state, one of its agencies, or one of its officers or employees in an official capacity; and

- *Serve notice.* Serve the notice and paper on the Attorney General of the United States if a federal statute is questioned—or on the state attorney general if a state statute is questioned—either by certified or registered mail or by sending it to an electronic address designated by the attorney general for this purpose. FRCP 5.1(a).

- *No forfeiture.* A party's failure to file and serve the notice, or the court's failure to certify, does not forfeit a constitutional claim or defense that is otherwise timely asserted. FRCP 5.1(d).

    iii. *Proposed order.* Proposed orders usually are not required by this court. However, the court may request the party to submit such a document. In those situations, unless otherwise directed by the clerk's office, electronically file the proposed document/order using the entry for "Proposed Documents submitted to the court," found under the Other Documents menu, or as an attachment to the motion to which it relates. MA R USDCT CM/ECF Admin(T).

    iv. *Compact disk with copy of document(s) in PDF format.* A filer who cannot file a document electronically because of such technical difficulty on the filer's end [with telephone, cable lines, the filer's Internet Service Provider (ISP), or hardware or software problems] shall file the document conventionally along with a copy of the document in PDF format on a compact disk or contact the clerk's office for permission to submit the PDF document via email. MA R USDCT CM/ECF Admin(W)(3). Refer to the Timing section of this document for more information on technical failures.

    v. *Notice of filing with clerk's office.* When documents or exhibits (other than those filed ex parte or under seal) are submitted conventionally, a "Notice of Filing with clerk's office" shall be filed electronically and attached to the main document. A paper copy of the "Notice of Filing with clerk's office" must accompany the documents submitted to the court. The "Notice of Filing with clerk's office" (see MA R USDCT CM/ECF Admin(Appendix I)) shall describe each of the documents that will be filed as paper copies in the clerk's office, or shall include an index of the documents if those documents are voluminous. MA R USDCT CM/ECF Admin(P)(5).

    vi. *Additional copies.* Whenever, because of the nature of a proceeding, such as a proceeding before a three-judge district court under 28 U.S.C.A. § 2284, additional copies of a paper required to be filed are necessary either for the use of the court or to enable the clerk to carry out his duties, it is the responsibility of the party filing or having filed the paper to provide the necessary copies. MA R USDCT LR 5.1(d).

    vii. *Courtesy copies.* COURTESY COPIES OF DOCUMENTS FILED ELECTRONICALLY SHALL NOT BE SUBMITTED ROUTINELY. MA R USDCT CM/ECF Admin(J). Judicial officers, on a case-by-case basis, may require courtesy copies for specific cases, or types of motions, etc. A few Judicial Officers have entered Standing Orders, which may be found on their respective pages on the court's website (under Divisions). Any document filed on paper with the court as a courtesy copy must be clearly labeled as such (Example: COURTESY COPY—DO NOT SCAN). Documents delivered to the court as a courtesy copy will not be maintained in the official court record. MA R USDCT CM/ECF Admin(J).

2. *Documents for opposing party*

a. *Required documents*

    i. *Opposition.* Refer to the General Requirements section of this document for information on the opposing papers.

- *Memorandum.* A party opposing a motion shall file, in the same (rather than a separate), document a memorandum of reasons, including citation of supporting authorities, why the motion should not be granted. MA R USDCT LR 7.1(b)(2). Any memorandum of law or other attachment filed in support of a main document shall be filed as a separate document, using the proper event. MA R USDCT CM/ECF

Admin(G)(4). Memoranda supporting or opposing allowance of motions shall not, without leave of court, exceed twenty (20) pages, double-spaced. MA R USDCT LR 7.1(b)(4).

- *Request for oral argument.* Any party making or opposing a motion who believes that oral argument may assist the court and wishes to be heard shall include a request for oral argument in a separate paragraph of the motion or opposition. The request should be set off with a centered caption, "REQUEST FOR ORAL ARGUMENT." MA R USDCT LR 7.1(d).

ii. *Certificate of service.* No certificate of service is required when a paper is served by filing it with the court's electronic-filing system. When a paper that is required to be served is served by other means: (1) if the paper is filed, a certificate of service must be filed with it or within a reasonable time after service; and (2) if the paper is not filed, a certificate of service need not be filed unless filing is required by court order or by local rule. FRCP 5(d)(1)(B). Except as otherwise provided by the Federal Rules of Civil Procedure, proof of service of all pleadings and other papers required to be served (except discovery papers that in accordance with FRCP 33 to FRCP 36(f) are not to be filed) shall be filed in the office of the clerk promptly after service has been made. The proof shall show the time and manner of service, and may be made by written acknowledgment of service, a certificate of a member of the bar of this court, or an affidavit of the person who served the paper. MA R USDCT LR 5.2(b)(1). A certificate of service of a member of the bar shall appear at the bottom of or on the margin of the last page of the paper to which it relates. MA R USDCT LR 5.2(b)(2).

- *Paper service.* The certificate shall be a brief, single-spaced statement and may be in the following form: I hereby certify that a true copy of the above document was served upon (each party appearing pro se and) the attorney of record for each other party by mail (by hand) on (date). (Signature). MA R USDCT LR 5.2(b)(2).

- *Electronic service.* Any pleading or other paper served by electronic means must bear a certificate of service in accordance with MA R USDCT LR 5.2(b). MA R USDCT LR 5.4(C); MA R USDCT CM/ECF Admin(H)(2). The certificate of service shall state that the filer: (1) filed the document electronically, (2) that it will be served electronically to registered CM/ECF participants via the NEF and (3) that the filer will send paper copies to non-registered participants as indicated on the NEF. MA R USDCT CM/ECF Admin(H)(2). For example: I hereby certify that this document filed through the CM/ECF system will be sent electronically to the registered participants as identified on the NEF (NEF) and paper copies will be sent to those indicated as non registered participants on (date). MA R USDCT CM/ECF Admin(H)(2).

- *Return.* Documents not conforming to the requirements of MA R USDCT LR 5.2 (except notices of appeal) shall be returned by the clerk. MA R USDCT LR 5.2(b)(2).

- *Failure to make proof of service.* Failure to make proof of service does not affect the validity of the service. MA R USDCT LR 5.2(b)(3).

b. *Supplemental documents*

i. *Supporting evidence.* When a motion relies on facts outside the record, the court may hear the matter on affidavits or may hear it wholly or partly on oral testimony or on depositions. FRCP 43(c). Affidavits and other documents setting forth or evidencing facts on which the opposition is based shall be filed with the opposition. MA R USDCT LR 7.1(b)(2).

ii. *Notice of constitutional question.* A party that files a pleading, written motion, or other paper drawing into question the constitutionality of a federal or state statute must promptly:

- *File notice.* File a notice of constitutional question stating the question and identifying the paper that raises it, if: (1) a federal statute is questioned and the parties do not include the United States, one of its agencies, or one of its officers or employees in an official capacity; or (2) a state statute is questioned and the parties do not include the state, one of its agencies, or one of its officers or employees in an official capacity; and

- *Serve notice.* Serve the notice and paper on the Attorney General of the United States if a federal statute is questioned—or on the state attorney general if a state statute is questioned—either by certified or registered mail or by sending it to an electronic address designated by the attorney general for this purpose. FRCP 5.1(a).

- *No forfeiture.* A party's failure to file and serve the notice, or the court's failure to certify, does not forfeit a constitutional claim or defense that is otherwise timely asserted. FRCP 5.1(d).

iii. *Compact disk with copy of document(s) in PDF format.* A filer who cannot file a document electronically because of such technical difficulty on the filer's end [with telephone, cable lines, the filer's Internet Service

Provider (ISP), or hardware or software problems] shall file the document conventionally along with a copy of the document in PDF format on a compact disk or contact the clerk's office for permission to submit the PDF document via email. MA R USDCT CM/ECF Admin(W)(3). Refer to the Timing section of this document for more information on technical failures.

iv. *Notice of filing with clerk's office.* When documents or exhibits (other than those filed ex parte or under seal) are submitted conventionally, a "Notice of Filing with clerk's office" shall be filed electronically and attached to the main document. A paper copy of the "Notice of Filing with clerk's office" must accompany the documents submitted to the court. The "Notice of Filing with clerk's office" (see MA R USDCT CM/ECF Admin(Appendix I)) shall describe each of the documents that will be filed as paper copies in the clerk's office, or shall include an index of the documents if those documents are voluminous. MA R USDCT CM/ECF Admin(P)(5).

v. *Additional copies.* Whenever, because of the nature of a proceeding, such as a proceeding before a three-judge district court under 28 U.S.C.A. § 2284, additional copies of a paper required to be filed are necessary either for the use of the court or to enable the clerk to carry out his duties, it is the responsibility of the party filing or having filed the paper to provide the necessary copies. MA R USDCT LR 5.1(d).

vi. *Courtesy copies.* COURTESY COPIES OF DOCUMENTS FILED ELECTRONICALLY SHALL NOT BE SUBMITTED ROUTINELY. MA R USDCT CM/ECF Admin(J). Judicial officers, on a case-by-case basis, may require courtesy copies for specific cases, or types of motions, etc. A few Judicial Officers have entered Standing Orders, which may be found on their respective pages on the court's website (under Divisions). Any document filed on paper with the court as a courtesy copy must be clearly labeled as such (Example: COURTESY COPY—DO NOT SCAN). Documents delivered to the court as a courtesy copy will not be maintained in the official court record. MA R USDCT CM/ECF Admin(J).

## E. Format

1. *Form of documents.* The rules governing captions and other matters of form in pleadings apply to motions and other papers. FRCP 7(b)(2). The provisions of FRCP 10 and FRCP 11 concerning the form and signing of pleadings, motions, and other papers shall be applicable to all papers filed in any proceeding in this court. The board of bar overseers registration number of each attorney signing such documents, except the United States Attorney and his or her staff, shall be inscribed below the signature. MA R USDCT LR 5.1(a)(1).

   a. *Paper size and binding.* All papers filed in the court shall be adapted for flat filing, be filed on eight and one-half by eleven (8-1/2 x 11) inch paper without backers and be bound firmly by staple or some such other means (excluding paper or binder clip or rubber band). MA R USDCT LR 5.1(a)(2).

   b. *Spacing.* All papers, except discovery requests and responses, shall be double-spaced except for the identification of counsel, title of the case, footnotes, quotations and exhibits. Discovery requests and responses shall be single-spaced. MA R USDCT LR 5.1(a)(2).

   c. *Caption.* Every pleading must have a caption with the court's name, a title, a file number, and [an] FRCP 7(a) designation. FRCP 10(a).

      i. *Names of parties.* The title of the complaint must name all the parties; the title of other pleadings, after naming the first party on each side, may refer generally to other parties. FRCP 10(a).

      ii. *Request for special action.* When any pleading or other paper filed in the court includes a request for special process or relief, or any other request such that, if granted, the court will proceed other than in the ordinary course, the request shall, unless it is noted on the category sheet [see MA R USDCT LR 40.1(a)(1)], be noted on the first page to the right of or immediately beneath the caption. MA R USDCT LR 5.1(c).

   d. *Claims or defenses*

      i. *Numbered paragraphs.* A party must state its claims or defenses in numbered paragraphs, each limited as far as practicable to a single set of circumstances. A later pleading may refer by number to a paragraph in an earlier pleading. FRCP 10(b).

      ii. *Separate statements.* If doing so would promote clarity, each claim founded on a separate transaction or occurrence—and each defense other than a denial—must be stated in a separate count or defense. FRCP 10(b).

   e. *Adoption by reference.* A statement in a pleading may be adopted by reference elsewhere in the same pleading or in any other pleading or motion. FRCP 10(c).

      i. *Exhibits.* A copy of a written instrument that is an exhibit to a pleading is a part of the pleading for all purposes. FRCP 10(c).

f.   *Citations*

    i.   *Local rules.* These rules shall be known as Local Rules of the United States District Court for the District of Massachusetts and cited as "L.R., D. Mass." or "L.R." MA R USDCT LR 1.1.

    ii.  *Electronic case filing procedures.* The procedures governing electronic case filing shall be known as the "Administrative Procedures for Electronic Case Filing in the United States District Court for the District of Massachusetts." They shall be cited as "APECF." MA R USDCT CM/ECF Admin(A)(7).

g.   *Acceptance by the clerk.* The clerk must not refuse to file a paper solely because it is not in the form prescribed by the Federal Rules of Civil Procedure or by a local rule or practice. FRCP 5(d)(4).

    i.   Except for complaints and notices of appeal, papers that do not conform to the requirements of MA R USDCT LR 5.1(a)(2) shall be returned by the clerk. MA R USDCT LR 5.1(a)(2).

2.   *Form of electronic documents.* A paper filed electronically is a written paper for purposes of the Federal Rules of Civil Procedure. FRCP 5(d)(3)(D).

a.   *PDF/A format required.* The court will begin requiring submission of documents in PDF/A format in the foreseeable future. PDF/A is an enhanced version of the traditional PDF format. Newer versions of most PDF software will be able to convert to this format. Additional information on PDF/A documents may be found on the court's website. MA R USDCT CM/ECF Admin(Electronic Filing and PDF).

    i.   *Electronically converted PDF.* Electronically converted PDF documents are created from word processing documents (MS Word, WordPerfect, etc.) using any appropriate software. These documents are text searchable and the file size is generally smaller than a scanned document. CM/ECF users may use any brand of software to convert documents to PDF. MA R USDCT CM/ECF Admin(Electronic Filing and PDF).

        •   Documents converted to PDF, rather than scanned, are preferred for filing in CM/ECF. MA R USDCT CM/ECF Admin(Electronic Filing and PDF).

    ii.  *Scanned PDF.* Scanned PDF documents are created from paper documents run through an optical scanner. Scanned PDF documents are generally not searchable and have a larger file size. Please note that software used to create scanned documents may (and should) be set in such a way that the document is "text-searchable." MA R USDCT CM/ECF Admin(Electronic Filing and PDF).

b.   *Title.* All pleadings filed electronically shall be titled in accordance with the approved dictionary of civil or criminal events of the CM/ECF system of this court. A list of events is available on the CM/ECF Training Information page of the court's website. The clerk's office may, when necessary and appropriate, modify the docket entry description, or delete and re-enter the docket entry in order to comply with the court's quality assurance standards. MA R USDCT CM/ECF Admin(G)(3).

c.   *Attachments to filings and exhibits.* Attachments to filings and exhibits must be filed in accordance with the court's CM/ECF User Manual, unless otherwise ordered by the court. MA R USDCT CM/ECF Admin(O)(1).

    i.   Filers must submit as attachments only those excerpts of the referenced documents that are directly germane to the matter under consideration by the court. Excerpted material must be clearly and prominently identified as such. Users who file excerpts of documents do so without prejudice to their right to timely file additional excerpts or the complete document, as may be allowed by the court. Responding parties may timely file additional excerpts or the complete document that they believe are directly germane. MA R USDCT CM/ECF Admin(O)(2).

    ii.  Filers shall not attach as an exhibit any pleading or other paper already on file with the court in that case, but shall merely refer to that document. (See MA R USDCT CM/ECF Admin(G) for information on using hyperlinks in PDF documents filed in CM/ECF.) MA R USDCT CM/ECF Admin(O)(3).

d.   *Redacted documents.* The parties may request or the court may require the submission of documents that have been redacted/stripped of sensitive or confidential information. The redacted document prepared for electronic filing shall include the original caption of the document, and be clearly labeled as "Redacted Document." A specific event is available for this purpose ("Redacted Document"), found under the Other Filings/Other Documents menu option. MA R USDCT CM/ECF Admin(S).

    i.   Attorneys and pro se litigants are advised to take extra care when creating PDF documents intended for submission to CM/ECF. Steps shall be taken to ensure the documents are free of any hidden data (metadata) that may contain redacted information, or traces of information edited or deleted are not hidden in the final document. Even PDF content that has been encrypted may be recovered. An advisory document with additional information on this topic may be found on the court's website. MA R USDCT CM/ECF Admin(S).

e. *Hyperlinks.* Electronically filed documents may contain the following types of hyperlinks: (1) hyperlinks to other portions of the same document; (2) hyperlinks to other documents filed within the CM/ECF system; and (3) hyperlinks to a location on the Internet that contains a source document for a citation. MA R USDCT CM/ECF Admin(G)(7).

   i. Hyperlinks to cited authority may not replace standard citation format. Complete citations must be included in the text of the filed document. Neither a hyperlink, nor any site to which it refers, shall be considered part of the record, but are simply convenient mechanisms for accessing material cited in a document filed in CM/ECF. Instructions on creating hyperlinks may be found in the CM/ECF User Manual. MA R USDCT CM/ECF Admin(G)(7).

   ii. The court accepts no responsibility for, and does not endorse, any product, organization, or content at any hyperlinked site, or at any site to which that site may be linked. The court accepts no responsibility for the availability or functionality of any hyperlink. MA R USDCT CM/ECF Admin(G)(7).

   iii. One feature of PDF/A documents is that hyperlinks are commonly "masked," meaning that the full address of the referenced file is not written out; for example, clicking the word brief may open a brief which was previously filed in CM/ECF. MA R USDCT CM/ECF Admin(G)(7)(NOTE). An "unmasked" hyperlink has the full address visible to the user. MA R USDCT CM/ECF Admin(G)(7)(NOTE).

      • Masked hyperlinks may or may not work in a PDF/A document, depending on how it was created. Currently, masked hyperlinks are preserved in PDF/A documents produced by the "Save As" method in Microsoft Word 2007 and 2010; the "PDFMaker" method in Microsoft Word 2007; and OpenOffice 2.4 ("PDF Export"). With other production methods, such as WordPerfect, the PDF/A document includes underlined words that appear to be links, but clicking them has no effect. MA R USDCT CM/ECF Admin(G)(7)(NOTE).

f. *Documents features not accepted.* CM/ECF will not accept PDF documents containing tracking tags, embedded systems commands, password protections, access restrictions or other security features, special tags or dynamic features. MA R USDCT CM/ECF Admin(G)(8).

g. *File size limitations.* A filing party shall limit the size of each PDF file to no more than twenty (20) megabytes. PDF files larger than seven (7) megabytes will be rejected by the CM/ECF system. The filer will see a message advising of the size limitation. MA R USDCT CM/ECF Admin(P)(2).

   i. Larger documents or exhibits may be submitted electronically if split into separate PDF files each less than seven (7) megabytes, attached to the main document and clearly labeled. MA R USDCT CM/ECF Admin(P)(2).

   ii. Documents submitted electronically or on paper are subject to the page limitations set by MA R USDCT LR 7.1(b)(4) or by order of the court. MA R USDCT CM/ECF Admin(P)(1).

h. *Accuracy and readability.* The filer shall verify the accuracy and readability of any PDF file before electronically filing it in CM/ECF. MA R USDCT CM/ECF Admin(G)(6); MA R USDCT CM/ECF Admin(P)(3).

3. *Signing of pleadings, motions and other papers*

a. *Signature.* Every pleading, written motion, and other paper must be signed by at least one attorney of record in the attorney's name—or by a party personally if the party is unrepresented. The paper must state the signer's address, e-mail address, and telephone number. FRCP 11(a). The provisions of the Federal Rules of Civil Procedure pertaining to the form and signing of pleadings, motions, and other papers shall be applicable to all papers filed in any proceeding in this court. The board of bar overseers registration number of each attorney signing such documents, except the United States Attorney and his staff, shall be inscribed below the signature. MA R USDCT LR 5.1(a)(1).

   i. *Electronic signing.* A filing made through a person's electronic-filing account and authorized by that person, together with that person's name on a signature block, constitutes the person's signature. FRCP 5(d)(3)(C).

   ii. *Appearances.* The filing of an appearance or any other pleading signed on behalf of a party constitutes an entry of appearance for that party. All pleadings shall contain the name, bar admission number, address, telephone number, and e-mail address of the attorney entering an appearance. MA R USDCT LR 83.5.2(a).

      • *Appearances by law firms.* When a party is represented by a law firm, the appearance must include the name and the signature of at least one individual attorney. When a party is represented by more than one attorney from the same or different law firms, the attorney entering the appearance must designate the individual attorney who is authorized to receive all notices in the case. Any notice sent to an attorney so designated shall be deemed to be proper notice unless the court finds that notice was not properly sent. MA R USDCT LR 83.5.2(b).

- For more information on appearances, refer to MA R USDCT LR 83.5.2.

iii. *Signatures of attorneys.* The user login and password required to submit documents to the CM/ECF system shall serve as that user's signature for purposes of FRCP 11 and for all other purposes under the Federal Rules of Civil Procedure and the Local Rules of the United States District Court for the District of Massachusetts. All electronically filed documents must include a signature block and must set forth the attorney's name, bar number, address, telephone number and email address. The name of the CM/ECF user under whose log-in and password the document is submitted must be preceded by a "/s/" and typed in the space where the signature would otherwise appear. MA R USDCT CM/ECF Admin(M)(1). For an example, refer to MA R USDCT CM/ECF Admin(M)(1).

iv. *Signatures of pro se parties.* Any document requiring a signature that is filed by a party appearing pro se shall bear the words "pro se" following that party's signature. Any such document shall also state the party's mailing address, telephone number (if any), and e-mail address (if the party has consented to service by email). MA R USDCT LR 83.5.5(g). For more information on practice by pro se litigants, refer to MA R USDCT LR 83.5.5.

v. *Multiple signatures.* The filer of any document requiring more than one signature (e.g, stipulations, joint motions, joint status reports, magistrate judge consent forms, etc.) must list thereon all the names of other signatories by means of a "/s/ name of signatory" block for each. By submitting such a document, the filing attorney certifies that each of the other signatories has expressly agreed to the form and substance of the document and that the filing attorney has their actual authority to submit the document electronically. MA R USDCT CM/ECF Admin(M)(2). For more information, refer to MA R USDCT CM/ECF Admin(M)(2).

vi. *Affidavits.* Except as provided in MA R USDCT CM/ECF Admin(L), affidavits shall be filed electronically; however, the electronically filed version must contain a "/s/ name of signatory" block indicating that the paper document bears an original signature. MA R USDCT CM/ECF Admin(M)(3). The court will also accept a scanned version of the original, signed document. MA R USDCT CM/ECF Admin(M)(3). For more information, refer to MA R USDCT CM/ECF Admin(M)(3).

vii. *No verification or accompanying affidavit required for pleadings.* Unless a rule or statute specifically states otherwise, a pleading need not be verified or accompanied by an affidavit. FRCP 11(a).

viii. *Unsigned papers.* The court must strike an unsigned paper unless the omission is promptly corrected after being called to the attorney's or party's attention. FRCP 11(a).

b. *Representations to the court.* By presenting to the court a pleading, written motion, or other paper—whether by signing, filing, submitting, or later advocating it—an attorney or unrepresented party certifies that to the best of the person's knowledge, information, and belief, formed after an inquiry reasonable under the circumstances:

i. It is not being presented for any improper purpose, such as to harass, cause unnecessary delay, or needlessly increase the cost of litigation;

ii. The claims, defenses, and other legal contentions are warranted by existing law or by a nonfrivolous argument for extending, modifying, or reversing existing law or for establishing new law;

iii. The factual contentions have evidentiary support or, if specifically so identified, will likely have evidentiary support after a reasonable opportunity for further investigation or discovery; and

iv. The denials of factual contentions are warranted on the evidence or, if specifically so identified, are reasonably based on belief or a lack of information. FRCP 11(b).

c. *Sanctions.* If, after notice and a reasonable opportunity to respond, the court determines that FRCP 11(b) has been violated, the court may impose an appropriate sanction on any attorney, law firm, or party that violated FRCP 11(b) or is responsible for the violation. FRCP 11(c)(1). Refer to the United States District Court for the District of Massachusetts KeyRules Motion for Sanctions document for more information.

4. *Privacy protection for filings made with the court*

a. *Redacted filings.* Unless the court orders otherwise, in an electronic or paper filing with the court that contains an individual's Social Security number, taxpayer-identification number, or birth date, the name of an individual known to be a minor, or a financial-account number, a party or nonparty making the filing may include only:

i. The last four (4) digits of the Social Security number and taxpayer-identification number;

ii. The year of the individual's birth;

iii. The minor's initials; and

iv. The last four (4) digits of the financial-account number. FRCP 5.2(a); MA R USDCT CM/ECF Admin(N).

b. *Exemptions from the redaction requirement.* The redaction requirement does not apply to the following:

   i. A financial-account number that identifies the property allegedly subject to forfeiture in a forfeiture proceeding;

   ii. The record of an administrative or agency proceeding;

   iii. The official record of a state-court proceeding;

   iv. The record of a court or tribunal, if that record was not subject to the redaction requirement when originally filed;

   v. A filing covered by FRCP 5.2(c) or FRCP 5.2(d); and

   vi. A pro se filing in an action brought under 28 U.S.C.A. § 2241, 28 U.S.C.A. § 2254, or 28 U.S.C.A. § 2255. FRCP 5.2(b).

c. *Limitations on remote access to electronic files; Social Security appeals and immigration cases.* Unless the court orders otherwise, in an action for benefits under the Social Security Act, and in an action or proceeding relating to an order of removal, to relief from removal, or to immigration benefits or detention, access to an electronic file is authorized as follows:

   i. The parties and their attorneys may have remote electronic access to any part of the case file, including the administrative record;

   ii. Any other person may have electronic access to the full record at the courthouse, but may have remote electronic access only to:

   - The docket maintained by the court; and

   - An opinion, order, judgment, or other disposition of the court, but not any other part of the case file or the administrative record. FRCP 5.2(c).

d. *Filings made under seal.* The court may order that a filing be made under seal without redaction. The court may later unseal the filing or order the person who made the filing to file a redacted version for the public record. FRCP 5.2(d).

e. *Protective orders.* For good cause, the court may by order in a case:

   i. Require redaction of additional information; or

   ii. Limit or prohibit a nonparty's remote electronic access to a document filed with the court. FRCP 5.2(e).

f. *Option for additional unredacted filing under seal.* A person making a redacted filing may also file an unredacted copy under seal. The court must retain the unredacted copy as part of the record. FRCP 5.2(f). For more information, refer to MA R USDCT LR 7.2.

g. *Option for filing a reference list.* A filing that contains redacted information may be filed together with a reference list that identifies each item of redacted information and specifies an appropriate identifier that uniquely corresponds to each item listed. The list must be filed under seal and may be amended as of right. Any reference in the case to a listed identifier will be construed to refer to the corresponding item of information. FRCP 5.2(g).

h. *Responsibility for redaction.* The clerk's office is not responsible for reviewing documents filed with the court to determine whether pleadings have been redacted and are in the proper form. MA R USDCT CM/ECF Admin(N).

i. *Waiver of protection of identifiers.* A person waives the protection of FRCP 5.2(a) as to the person's own information by filing it without redaction and not under seal. FRCP 5.2(h).

# F. Filing and Service Requirements

1. *Filing requirements*

   a. *Required filings.* Any paper after the complaint that is required to be served must be filed no later than a reasonable time after service. FRCP 5(d)(1).

   i. Except as noted in FRCP 33 to FRCP 36, the original of all papers required to be served under FRCP 5(d) shall, unless otherwise submitted to the court, be filed in the office of the clerk within seven (7) days after service has been made. MA R USDCT LR 5.1(b). Except as otherwise provided by the Federal Rules of Civil Procedure, proof of service of all pleadings and other papers required to be served (except discovery papers that in accordance with FRCP 33 to FRCP 36(f) are not to be filed) shall be filed in the office of the clerk promptly after service has been made. MA R USDCT LR 5.2(b)(1).

   b. *Nonelectronic filing.* A paper not filed electronically is filed by delivering it: (1) to the clerk; or (2) to a judge who agrees to accept it for filing, and who must then note the filing date on the paper and promptly send it to the clerk. FRCP 5(d)(2).

c. *Electronic filing.* Unless exempt or otherwise ordered by the court, all pleadings and other papers submitted to the court must be filed, signed, and verified by electronic means as provided in MA R USDCT LR 5.4. MA R USDCT LR 5.4(A); MA R USDCT CM/ECF Admin(A)(1). All electronic filings must be made in accordance with the Administrative Procedures for Electronic Case Filing in the United States District Court for the District of Massachusetts (MA R USDCT CM/ECF Admin). MA R USDCT LR 5.4(B). The court may deviate from the Administrative Procedures for Electronic Case Filing in the United States District Court for the District of Massachusetts (MA R USDCT CM/ECF Admin) in specific cases, without prior notice, if deemed appropriate in the exercise of discretion, considering the need for the just, speedy, and inexpensive determination of matters pending before the court. MA R USDCT CM/ECF Admin(C)(1). The court may excuse a failure to comply with any administrative procedure whenever justice so requires. MA R USDCT CM/ECF Admin(C)(2).

   i. *By a represented person; Generally required; Exceptions.* A person represented by an attorney must file electronically, unless nonelectronic filing is allowed by the court for good cause or is allowed or required by local rule. FRCP 5(d)(3)(A).

   ii. *By unrepresented person; When allowed or required.* A person not represented by an attorney: (1) may file electronically only if allowed by court order or by local rule; and (2) may be required to file electronically only by court order, or by a local rule that includes reasonable exceptions. FRCP 5(d)(3)(B).

   iii. *Exemptions from electronic filing*

   • *Documents that should not be filed electronically.* The following types of documents must not be filed electronically, and will not be scanned into the ECF system by the clerk's office: (1) sealed documents; (2) ex parte motions; (3) documents generated as part of an alternative dispute resolution (ADR) process; (4) the administrative record in Social Security and other administrative proceedings; (5) the state court record in proceedings under 28 U.S.C.A. § 2254; and (6) such other types of documents as the clerk may direct in the Administrative Procedures for Electronic Case Filing in the United States District Court for the District of Massachusetts (MA R USDCT CM/ECF Admin). MA R USDCT LR 5.4(G)(1); MA R USDCT CM/ECF Admin(L).

   • *Documents that need not be filed electronically.* The following types of documents need not be filed electronically, but may be scanned into the ECF system by a filing party or the clerk's office: (1) handwritten pleadings; (2) documents filed by pro se litigants who are incarcerated or who are not registered ECF users; (3) indictments, informations, criminal complaints, and the criminal JS45 form; (4) affidavits for search or arrest warrants and related documents; (5) documents received from another court under FRCRP 20 or FRCRP 40; (6) appearance bonds; (7) any document in a criminal case containing the original signature of a defendant, such as a waiver of indictment or a plea agreement; (8) petitions for violations of supervised release; (9) executed service of process documents under FRCP 4; and (10) such other types of documents as the clerk may direct in the Administrative Procedures for Electronic Case Filing in the United States District Court for the District of Massachusetts (MA R USDCT CM/ECF Admin). MA R USDCT LR 5.4(G)(2); MA R USDCT CM/ECF Admin(L).

   • For more information on exemptions from electronic filing, refer to MA R USDCT CM/ECF Admin(L).

   iv. *Consequences of electronic filing.* Electronic transmission of a document to the CM/ECF system, together with the transmission of a Notice of Electronic Filing (NEF) from the court at the completion of the transaction, constitutes the filing of the document for all purposes of the Federal Rules of Procedure and constitutes entry of the document on the docket maintained by the clerk pursuant to FRCP 58 and FRCP 79. MA R USDCT CM/ECF Admin(G)(1).

   v. *Payment of filing fees.* When electronically filing any pleading or paper through CM/ECF that requires a fee, all registered ECF users are to pay the fee electronically through the Treasury Department's Internet payment process. MA R USDCT LR 67.4(d); MA R USDCT CM/ECF Admin(A)(1). Pro se filers and those who have been exempted from electronic filing and/or electronic payment of fees may submit payments by check or money order made payable to "Clerk, U.S. District Court". MA R USDCT LR 67.4(d). For more information on filing fees, refer to MA R USDCT LR 67.4 and MA R USDCT CM/ECF Admin(I).

   vi. For more information on electronic filing, refer to MA R USDCT CM/ECF Admin.

d. *Email or fax filing.* In general, the court does not accept documents by email or by fax. If the court, in special circumstances, does authorize the submission of a document in that manner, the document shall not be considered filed until an NEF is generated by CM/ECF at the completion of the transaction. MA R USDCT CM/ECF Admin(H)(5).

2. *Service requirements.* All papers filed pursuant to MA R USDCT LR 7.1(b) shall be served unless the moving party indicates in writing on the face of the motion that ex parte consideration is requested. Motions filed "ex parte" and related papers need not be served until the motion has been ruled upon or the court orders that service be made. MA R USDCT LR 7.1(c). Service of all pleadings subsequent to the original complaint and of all other papers required to be served shall be made in the manner specified by FRCP 5. MA R USDCT LR 5.2(a).

a. *Service; When required*

   i. *In general.* Unless the Federal Rules of Civil Procedure provide otherwise, each of the following papers must be served on every party:

   - An order stating that service is required;

   - A pleading filed after the original complaint, unless the court orders otherwise under FRCP 5(c) because there are numerous defendants;

   - A discovery paper required to be served on a party, unless the court orders otherwise;

   - A written motion, except one that may be heard ex parte; and

   - A written notice, appearance, demand, or offer of judgment, or any similar paper. FRCP 5(a)(1).

   ii. *If a party fails to appear.* No service is required on a party who is in default for failing to appear. But a pleading that asserts a new claim for relief against such a party must be served on that party under FRCP 4. FRCP 5(a)(2).

   iii. *Seizing property.* If an action is begun by seizing property and no person is or need be named as a defendant, any service required before the filing of an appearance, answer, or claim must be made on the person who had custody or possession of the property when it was seized. FRCP 5(a)(3).

b. *Service; How made*

   i. *Serving an attorney.* If a party is represented by an attorney, service under FRCP 5 must be made on the attorney unless the court orders service on the party. FRCP 5(b)(1).

   - *Nonresident attorney.* On application of a party, the court may order an attorney who represents any other party and who does not maintain an office within this district where service can be made on him by delivery as provided by FRCP 5(b), to designate a member of the bar of this court who does maintain such an office to receive service of all pleadings and other papers in his behalf. MA R USDCT LR 5.2(c)(1).

   ii. *Serving a party acting pro se.* On application of a party, the court may order any other party who is appearing without an attorney and who does not maintain an office or residence within this district where service can be made on him by delivery as provided by FRCP 5(b), to designate an address within the district at which service can be made on him by delivery. MA R USDCT LR 5.2(c)(2).

   iii. *Service in general.* A paper is served under FRCP 5 by:

   - Handing it to the person;

   - Leaving it: (1) at the person's office with a clerk or other person in charge or, if no one is in charge, in a conspicuous place in the office; or (2) if the person has no office or the office is closed, at the person's dwelling or usual place of abode with someone of suitable age and discretion who resides there;

   - Mailing it to the person's last known address—in which event service is complete upon mailing;

   - Leaving it with the court clerk if the person has no known address;

   - Sending it to a registered user by filing it with the court's electronic-filing system or sending it by other electronic means that the person consented to in writing—in either of which events service is complete upon filing or sending, but is not effective if the filer or sender learns that it did not reach the person to be served; or

   - Delivering it by any other means that the person consented to in writing—in which event service is complete when the person making service delivers it to the agency designated to make delivery. FRCP 5(b)(2).

   iv. *Service by electronic means.* Unless exempt or otherwise ordered by the court, all pleadings and other papers must be served on other parties by electronic means. MA R USDCT LR 5.4(C); MA R USDCT CM/ECF Admin(H)(2). Service by electronic means shall be treated the same as service by mail. MA R USDCT CM/ECF Admin(H)(4).

   - *Consent to electronic service.* Registering to use CM/ECF constitutes consent to service of all documents

by electronic means as provided in the Administrative Procedures for Electronic Case Filing in the United States District Court for the District of Massachusetts (MA R USDCT CM/ECF Admin) and FRCP 5(b) and FRCP 77(d). MA R USDCT CM/ECF Admin(E)(6); MA R USDCT CM/ECF Admin(H)(3).

- *Service on registered ECF users.* Transmission of the Notice of Electronic Filing (NEF) through the court's transmission facilities will constitute service of the filed document upon a registered ECF user. MA R USDCT LR 5.4(C).

- *Service on non-registered users.* The party filing the document electronically is responsible for serving a paper copy of the document by mail in accordance with FRCP 5(b) to those case participants who have not been identified on the NEF as electronic recipients. MA R USDCT CM/ECF Admin(H)(3).

- *Service of conventionally filed papers.* Documents or exhibits submitted conventionally shall be served on other parties by the filer using traditional means. MA R USDCT CM/ECF Admin(P)(4).

  c. *Serving numerous defendants*

    i. *In general.* If an action involves an unusually large number of defendants, the court may, on motion or on its own, order that:

- Defendants' pleadings and replies to them need not be served on other defendants;

- Any crossclaim, counterclaim, avoidance, or affirmative defense in those pleadings and replies to them will be treated as denied or avoided by all other parties; and

- Filing any such pleading and serving it on the plaintiff constitutes notice of the pleading to all parties. FRCP 5(c)(1).

    ii. *Notifying parties.* A copy of every such order must be served on the parties as the court directs. FRCP 5(c)(2).

## G. Hearings

1. *Hearings, generally.* If the court concludes that there should be a hearing on a motion, the motion will be set down for hearing at such time as the court determines. MA R USDCT LR 7.1(e).

  a. *Oral argument.* Due process does not require that oral argument be permitted on a motion and, except as otherwise provided by local rule, the district court has discretion to determine whether it will decide the motion on the papers or hear argument by counsel (and perhaps receive evidence). FPP § 1190; F.D.I.C. v. Deglau, 207 F.3d 153 (3d Cir. 2000).

    i. *Evidence on a motion.* When a motion relies on facts outside the record, the court may hear the matter on affidavits or may hear it wholly or partly on oral testimony or on depositions. FRCP 43(c).

  b. *Providing a regular schedule for oral hearings.* A court may establish regular times and places for oral hearings on motions. FRCP 78(a).

  c. *Providing for submission on briefs.* By rule or order, the court may provide for submitting and determining motions on briefs, without oral hearings. FRCP 78(b). Motions that are not set down for hearing as provided in MA R USDCT LR 7.1(e) will be decided on the papers submitted after an opposition to the motion has been filed, or, if no opposition is filed, after the time for filing an opposition has elapsed. MA R USDCT LR 7.1(f).

2. *Conflict of court appearances.* For information on conflict of court appearances, refer to MA R USDCT LR 40.2.

## H. Forms

### 1. Federal Motion for Post-Trial Relief Forms

  a. Motion for new trial. 4 FEDFORMS § 42:10.

  b. Motion for new trial with statement of grounds. 4 FEDFORMS § 42:11.

  c. Motion for partial new trial. 4 FEDFORMS § 42:14.

  d. Affidavit in support of motion. 4 FEDFORMS § 42:30.

  e. Motion for new trial in nonjury action. 4 FEDFORMS § 42:43.

  f. Motion for new trial or to amend findings and judgment. 4 FEDFORMS § 42:47.

  g. Motion for new trial or to amend judgment. 4 FEDFORMS § 42:50.

  h. Motion for new trial and amendment of findings. 4 FEDFORMS § 42:51.

  i. Motion to amend judgment. 4 FEDFORMS § 42:56.

j.   Notice of motion to amend judgment by correcting amount. 4 FEDFORMS § 42:57.

k.   Motion to correct clerical error. 4 FEDFORMS § 43:13.

l.   Motion to vacate judgment. 4 FEDFORMS § 43:21.

m.   Motion to vacate consent decree on ground of excusable neglect, mistake or surprise. 4 FEDFORMS § 43:23.

n.   Affidavit to vacate judgment; Excusable neglect, mistake, inadvertence or surprise. 4 FEDFORMS § 43:25.

o.   Notice of motion; To amend or correct judgment. AMJUR PP JUDGMENTS § 38.

p.   Motion for additur or new trial; Plaintiff awarded only medical bills without consideration of pain and suffering; No-fault automobile insurances. AMJUR PP JUDGMENTS § 47.

q.   Motion for judgment; In federal court; By plaintiff; In accordance with motion for directed verdict or for new trial. AMJUR PP JUDGMENTS § 257.

r.   Motion for judgment; By defendant; In accordance with motion for directed verdict or for new trial; In federal court. AMJUR PP JUDGMENTS § 258.

s.   Notice of motion; To vacate judgment. AMJUR PP JUDGMENTS § 344.

t.   Motion; Correction of clerical mistake in judgment. FEDPROF § 1E:117.

u.   Motion; For relief from judgment; General form. FEDPROF § 1E:118.

v.   Motion; For relief from judgment; Newly discovered evidence. FEDPROF § 1E:119.

w.   Affidavit; Supporting motion for relief from judgment; Newly discovered evidence. FEDPROF § 1E:123.

x.   Motion for new trial; General form. GOLDLTGFMS § 61:3.

y.   Motion to vacate judgment; General form. GOLDLTGFMS § 63:2.

z.   Motion to vacate judgment; Date of discovery of facts. GOLDLTGFMS § 63:3.

**2.   Forms for the District of Massachusetts**

    a.   Notice of filing with clerk's office. MA R USDCT CM/ECF Admin(Appendix I).

# I.  Applicable Rules

1.   *Federal rules*

    a.   Serving and filing pleadings and other papers. FRCP 5.

    b.   Constitutional challenge to a statute; Notice, certification, and intervention. FRCP 5.1.

    c.   Privacy protection for filings made with the court. FRCP 5.2.

    d.   Computing and extending time; Time for motion papers. FRCP 6.

    e.   Pleadings allowed; Form of motions and other papers. FRCP 7.

    f.   Form of pleadings. FRCP 10.

    g.   Signing pleadings, motions, and other papers; Representations to the court; Sanctions. FRCP 11.

    h.   Taking testimony. FRCP 43.

    i.   New trial; Altering or amending a judgment. FRCP 59.

    j.   Relief from a judgment or order. FRCP 60.

    k.   Hearing motions; Submission on briefs. FRCP 78.

2.   *Local rules*

    a.   Title. MA R USDCT LR 1.1.

    b.   Sanctions. MA R USDCT LR 1.3.

    c.   Form and filing of papers. MA R USDCT LR 5.1.

    d.   Service and filing of pleadings and other papers. MA R USDCT LR 5.2.

    e.   Filing and service by electronic means. MA R USDCT LR 5.4.

    f.   Motion practice. MA R USDCT LR 7.1.

    g.   Alternative dispute resolution. MA R USDCT LR 16.4.

h.  Payments and deposits made with the clerk. MA R USDCT LR 67.4.

i.  Settlement. MA R USDCT LR 68.2.

j.  Office of the clerk. MA R USDCT LR 77.2.

k.  Appearances. MA R USDCT LR 83.5.2.

l.  Practice by pro se litigants. MA R USDCT LR 83.5.5.

m.  CM/ECF case management/electronic case files administrative procedures. MA R USDCT CM/ECF Admin.

# Requests, Notices and Applications
# Interrogatories

### Document Last Updated December 2018

## A.  Checklist

(I)  ❑ Matters to be considered by requesting party

    (a)  ❑ Required documents

        (1)  ❑ Interrogatories

    (b)  ❑ Supplemental documents

        (1)  ❑ Certificate of service

    (c)  ❑ Timing

        (1)  ❑ A party may not seek discovery from any source before the parties have conferred as required by FRCP 26(f), except in a proceeding exempted from initial disclosure under FRCP 26(a)(1)(B), or when authorized by the Federal Rules of Civil Procedure, by stipulation, or by court order

(II)  ❑ Matters to be considered by responding party

    (a)  ❑ Required documents

        (1)  ❑ Response to interrogatories

    (b)  ❑ Supplemental documents

        (1)  ❑ Certificate of service

    (c)  ❑ Timing

        (1)  ❑ The responding party must serve its answers and any objections within thirty (30) days after being served with the interrogatories

        (2)  ❑ Answers to interrogatories with respect to which objections were served and which are subsequently required to be answered shall be served within fourteen (14) days after it is determined that they should be answered, unless the court directs otherwise

## B.  Timing

1.  *Interrogatories.* FRCP 33(a) contains no limit on when interrogatories may first be served. FPP § 2170. FRCP 33 is also silent on how late in a case interrogatories may be served. But FRCP 16(b)(3)(A) provides that the scheduling order in the case "must limit the time to . . . complete discovery." Although the scheduling order requirement does not apply to cases exempted by local rule, ordinarily there should be a scheduling order that sets a discovery cutoff. FPP § 2170.

2.  *Commencement of discovery.* A party may not seek discovery from any source before the parties have conferred as required by FRCP 26(f), except in a proceeding exempted from initial disclosure under FRCP 26(a)(1)(B), or when authorized by the Federal Rules of Civil Procedure, by stipulation, or by court order. FRCP 26(d)(1).

3.  *Computation of time*

    a.  *Computing time.* FRCP 6 applies in computing any time period specified in the Federal Rules of Civil Procedure, in any local rule or court order, or in any statute that does not specify a method of computing time. FRCP 6(a).

        i.  *Period stated in days or a longer unit.* When the period is stated in days or a longer unit of time:

            •  Exclude the day of the event that triggers the period;

- Count every day, including intermediate Saturdays, Sundays, and legal holidays; and

- Include the last day of the period, but if the last day is a Saturday, Sunday, or legal holiday, the period continues to run until the end of the next day that is not a Saturday, Sunday, or legal holiday. FRCP 6(a)(1).

ii. *Period stated in hours.* When the period is stated in hours:

- Begin counting immediately on the occurrence of the event that triggers the period;

- Count every hour, including hours during intermediate Saturdays, Sundays, and legal holidays; and

- If the period would end on a Saturday, Sunday, or legal holiday, the period continues to run until the same time on the next day that is not a Saturday, Sunday, or legal holiday. FRCP 6(a)(2).

iii. *Office of the clerk.* The offices of the Clerk of Court at Boston, Worcester and Springfield shall be open from 8:30 a.m. until 5:00 p.m. on all days except Saturdays, Sundays, legal holidays and other days so ordered by the court and announced in advance, if feasible. MA R USDCT LR 77.2.

iv. *Inaccessibility of the clerk's office.* Unless the court orders otherwise, if the clerk's office is inaccessible:

- On the last day for filing under FRCP 6(a)(1), then the time for filing is extended to the first accessible day that is not a Saturday, Sunday, or legal holiday; or

- During the last hour for filing under FRCP 6(a)(2), then the time for filing is extended to the same time on the first accessible day that is not a Saturday, Sunday, or legal holiday. FRCP 6(a)(3).

v. *"Last day" defined.* Unless a different time is set by a statute, local rule, or court order, the last day ends:

- For electronic filing, at midnight in the court's time zone; and

- For filing by other means, when the clerk's office is scheduled to close. FRCP 6(a)(4).

vi. *"Next day" defined.* The "next day" is determined by continuing to count forward when the period is measured after an event and backward when measured before an event. FRCP 6(a)(5).

vii. *"Legal holiday" defined.* "Legal holiday" means:

- The day set aside by statute for observing New Year's Day, Martin Luther King Jr.'s Birthday, Washington's Birthday, Memorial Day, Independence Day, Labor Day, Columbus Day, Veterans' Day, Thanksgiving Day, or Christmas Day;

- Any day declared a holiday by the President or Congress; and

- For periods that are measured after an event, any other day declared a holiday by the state where the district court is located. FRCP 6(a)(6).

b. *Computation of electronic filing deadlines.* Filing documents electronically does not alter any filing deadlines. MA R USDCT CM/ECF Admin(K); MA R USDCT LR 5.4(D). Although CM/ECF is generally available twenty-four (24) hours a day for filing, all electronic transmissions of documents must be completed prior to 6:00 PM, Eastern Standard (or Daylight Savings) Time, on the date on which it is due, in order to be considered timely filed that day. MA R USDCT CM/ECF Admin(K); MA R USDCT LR 5.4(D). When a specific time of day deadline is set by court order or stipulation, the electronic filing must be completed by that time. Documents may be filed at any time of the day on days prior to the date on which it is due. MA R USDCT CM/ECF Admin(K). A document filed electronically shall be deemed filed as of the time and date stated on the NEF received from the court. MA R USDCT CM/ECF Admin(G)(2); MA R USDCT CM/ECF Admin(K).

i. *Technical failures.* A user whose filing is made untimely as the result of a technical failure of the court's CM/ECF system may seek appropriate relief from the court. MA R USDCT CM/ECF Admin(W)(3). Technical difficulties on the filer's end, with telephone, cable lines, the filer's Internet Service Provider (ISP), or hardware or software problems, will not constitute a technical failure under the Administrative Procedures for Electronic Case Filing in the United States District Court for the District of Massachusetts (MA R USDCT CM/ECF Admin) nor excuse an untimely filing. MA R USDCT CM/ECF Admin(W)(3). As help desk support is available during normal business hours, filers are strongly urged to electronically file any documents during that period. MA R USDCT CM/ECF Admin(W)(3).

- The court has made available a public terminal (computers and scanner) in each clerk's office for registered users to scan and electronically file documents. This equipment is available during normal business hours. Users should bring their prepared document and a valid CM/ECF login and password. MA R USDCT CM/ECF Admin(W)(3).

    c. *Extending time.* When an act may or must be done within a specified time, the court may, for good cause, extend the time: (1) with or without motion or notice if the court acts, or if a request is made, before the original time or its extension expires; or (2) on motion made after the time has expired if the party failed to act because of excusable neglect. FRCP 6(b)(1).

        i. *Exceptions.* A court must not extend the time to act under FRCP 50(b), FRCP 50(d), FRCP 52(b), FRCP 59(b), FRCP 59(d), FRCP 59(e), and FRCP 60(b). FRCP 6(b)(2).

        ii. Refer to the United States District Court for the District of Massachusetts KeyRules Motion for Continuance/Extension of Time document for more information on extending time.

    d. *Additional time after certain kinds of service.* When a party may or must act within a specified time after being served and service is made under FRCP 5(b)(2)(C) (by mail), FRCP 5(b)(2)(D) (by leaving with the clerk), or FRCP 5(b)(2)(F) (by other means consented to), three (3) days are added after the period would otherwise expire under FRCP 6(a). FRCP 6(d).

## C. General Requirements

1. *General provisions governing discovery*

    a. *Discovery scope and limits*

        i. *Scope in general.* Unless otherwise limited by court order, the scope of discovery is as follows: Parties may obtain discovery regarding any nonprivileged matter that is relevant to any party's claim or defense and proportional to the needs of the case, considering the importance of the issues at stake in the action, the amount in controversy, the parties' relative access to relevant information, the parties' resources, the importance of the discovery in resolving the issues, and whether the burden or expense of the proposed discovery outweighs its likely benefit. Information within this scope of discovery need not be admissible in evidence to be discoverable. FRCP 26(b)(1).

        ii. *Limitations on frequency and extent*

           • *When permitted.* By order, the court may alter the limits in the Federal Rules of Civil Procedure on the number of depositions and interrogatories or on the length of depositions under FRCP 30. By order or local rule, the court may also limit the number of requests under FRCP 36. FRCP 26(b)(2)(A).

           • *Specific limitations on electronically stored information.* A party need not provide discovery of electronically stored information from sources that the party identifies as not reasonably accessible because of undue burden or cost. On motion to compel discovery or for a protective order, the party from whom discovery is sought must show that the information is not reasonably accessible because of undue burden or cost. If that showing is made, the court may nonetheless order discovery from such sources if the requesting party shows good cause, considering the limitations of FRCP 26(b)(2)(C). The court may specify conditions for the discovery. FRCP 26(b)(2)(B).

           • *When required.* On motion or on its own, the court must limit the frequency or extent of discovery otherwise allowed by the Federal Rules of Civil Procedure or by local rule if it determines that: (1) the discovery sought is unreasonably cumulative or duplicative, or can be obtained from some other source that is more convenient, less burdensome, or less expensive; (2) the party seeking discovery has had ample opportunity to obtain the information by discovery in the action; or (3) the proposed discovery is outside the scope permitted by FRCP 26(b)(1). FRCP 26(b)(2)(C).

        iii. *Trial preparation; Materials*

           • *Documents and tangible things.* Ordinarily, a party may not discover documents and tangible things that are prepared in anticipation of litigation or for trial by or for another party or its representative (including the other party's attorney, consultant, surety, indemnitor, insurer, or agent). But, subject to FRCP 26(b)(4), those materials may be discovered if: (1) they are otherwise discoverable under FRCP 26(b)(1); and (2) the party shows that it has substantial need for the materials to prepare its case and cannot, without undue hardship, obtain their substantial equivalent by other means. FRCP 26(b)(3)(A).

           • *Protection against disclosure.* If the court orders discovery of those materials, it must protect against disclosure of the mental impressions, conclusions, opinions, or legal theories of a party's attorney or other representative concerning the litigation. FRCP 26(b)(3)(B).

           • *Previous statement.* Any party or other person may, on request and without the required showing, obtain the person's own previous statement about the action or its subject matter. If the request is refused, the person may move for a court order, and FRCP 37(a)(5) applies to the award of expenses. A previous statement is either: (1) a written statement that the person has signed or otherwise adopted or approved; or (2) a contemporaneous stenographic, mechanical, electrical, or other recording—or a transcription of it—that recites substantially verbatim the person's oral statement. FRCP 26(b)(3)(C).

iv. *Trial preparation; Experts*

- *Deposition of an expert who may testify.* A party may depose any person who has been identified as an expert whose opinions may be presented at trial. If FRCP 26(a)(2)(B) requires a report from the expert, the deposition may be conducted only after the report is provided. FRCP 26(b)(4)(A).

- *Trial-preparation protection for draft reports or disclosures.* FRCP 26(b)(3)(A) and FRCP 26(b)(3)(B) protect drafts of any report or disclosure required under FRCP 26(a)(2), regardless of the form in which the draft is recorded. FRCP 26(b)(4)(B).

- *Trial-preparation protection for communications between a party's attorney and expert witnesses.* FRCP 26(b)(3)(A) and FRCP 26(b)(3)(B) protect communications between the party's attorney and any witness required to provide a report under FRCP 26(a)(2)(B), regardless of the form of the communications, except to the extent that the communications: (1) relate to compensation for the expert's study or testimony; (2) identify facts or data that the party's attorney provided and that the expert considered in forming the opinions to be expressed; or (3) identify assumptions that the party's attorney provided and that the expert relied on in forming the opinions to be expressed. FRCP 26(b)(4)(C).

- *Expert employed only for trial preparation.* Ordinarily, a party may not, by interrogatories or deposition, discover facts known or opinions held by an expert who has been retained or specially employed by another party in anticipation of litigation or to prepare for trial and who is not expected to be called as a witness at trial. But a party may do so only: (1) as provided in FRCP 35(b); or (2) on showing exceptional circumstances under which it is impracticable for the party to obtain facts or opinions on the same subject by other means. FRCP 26(b)(4)(D).

- *Payment.* Unless manifest injustice would result, the court must require that the party seeking discovery: (1) pay the expert a reasonable fee for time spent in responding to discovery under FRCP 26(b)(4)(A) or FRCP 26(b)(4)(D); and (2) for discovery under FRCP 26(b)(4)(D), also pay the other party a fair portion of the fees and expenses it reasonably incurred in obtaining the expert's facts and opinions. FRCP 26(b)(4)(E).

v. *Claiming privilege or protecting trial-preparation materials*

- *Information withheld.* When a party withholds information otherwise discoverable by claiming that the information is privileged or subject to protection as trial-preparation material, the party must: (1) expressly make the claim; and (2) describe the nature of the documents, communications, or tangible things not produced or disclosed—and do so in a manner that, without revealing information itself privileged or protected, will enable other parties to assess the claim. FRCP 26(b)(5)(A).

- *Information produced.* If information produced in discovery is subject to a claim of privilege or of protection as trial-preparation material, the party making the claim may notify any party that received the information of the claim and the basis for it. After being notified, a party must promptly return, sequester, or destroy the specified information and any copies it has; must not use or disclose the information until the claim is resolved; must take reasonable steps to retrieve the information if the party disclosed it before being notified; and may promptly present the information to the court under seal for a determination of the claim. The producing party must preserve the information until the claim is resolved. FRCP 26(b)(5)(B).

b. *Protective orders.* A party or any person from whom discovery is sought may move for a protective order in the court where the action is pending—or as an alternative on matters relating to a deposition, in the court for the district where the deposition will be taken. FRCP 26(c)(1). Refer to the United States District Court for the District of Massachusetts KeyRules Motion for Protective Order document for more information.

c. *Disclosure orders.* The judicial officer may order the parties to submit at the scheduling conference, or at any subsequent time the officer deems appropriate, sworn statements disclosing certain information to every other party. At the discretion of the judicial officer, this order may direct the submission of:

i. A sworn statement from a claimant, whether plaintiff, third-party plaintiff, cross-claimant, or counter-claimant, that:

- Itemizes all economic loss and provides a computation of damages for which recovery is sought, if any, sustained before the date of service of process;

- Identifies all persons then known to the claimant or the claimant's attorney who witnessed or participated in the transaction or occurrence giving rise to the claim or otherwise known or believed to have substantial discoverable information about the claim or defenses, together with a statement of the subject and a brief summary of that information;

- Identifies all opposing parties, and all officers, directors, and employees of opposing parties, from whom statements have been obtained by or on behalf of the claimant regarding the subject matter of the claim; and

- Identifies all governmental agencies or officials then known to the claimant or the claimant's attorney to have investigated the transaction or occurrence giving rise to the claim; and

 ii. A sworn statement from a defendant, whether the direct defendant, third-party defendant, cross-claim defendant, or counterclaim defendant, that identifies:

- All persons then known to the defendant or the defendant's attorneys who witnessed the transaction or occurrence giving rise to the claim or otherwise is known or believed to have substantial discoverable information about the claims or defenses, together with a statement of the subject and a brief summary of that information;

- All opposing parties, and all officers, directors, and employees of opposing parties, from whom statements have been obtained by or on behalf of the defendant regarding the subject matter of the claims or defenses; and

- All government agencies or officials then known to the defendant or the defendant's attorneys to have investigated the transaction or occurrence giving rise to the claims or defenses. MA R USDCT LR 26.1(b).

 iii. Noncompliance may be excused only by order of the judicial officer. MA R USDCT LR 26.1(b).

d. *Uniform definitions in discovery requests*

 i. *Incorporation by reference and limitations.* The full text of the definitions set forth in MA R USDCT LR 26.5(c) is deemed incorporated by reference into all discovery requests, but shall not preclude:

- The definition of other terms specific to the particular litigation;

- The use of abbreviations; or

- A narrower definition of a term defined in MA R USDCT LR 26.5(c). MA R USDCT LR 26.5(a).

 ii. *Effect on scope of discovery.* MA R USDCT LR 26.5 is not intended to broaden or narrow the scope of discovery permitted by the Federal Rules of Civil Procedure. MA R USDCT LR 26.5(b).

 iii. *Definitions.* The following definitions apply to all discovery requests:

- *Communication.* The term "communication" means the transmittal of information (in the form of facts, ideas, inquiries, or otherwise). MA R USDCT LR 26.5(c)(1).

- *Document.* The term "document" is defined to be synonymous in meaning and equal in scope to the usage of this term in FRCP 34(a). A draft or non-identical copy is a separate document within the meaning of this term. MA R USDCT LR 26.5(c)(2).

- *Identify (with respect to persons).* When referring to a person, "to identify" means to give, to the extent known, the person's full name, present or last known address, and, when referring to a natural person, the present or last known place of employment. Once a person has been identified in accordance with this subparagraph, only the name of that person need be listed in response to subsequent discovery requesting the identification of that person. MA R USDCT LR 26.5(c)(3).

- *Identify (with respect to documents).* When referring to documents, "to identify" means to give, to the extent known, the: (1) type of document; (2) general subject matter; (3) date of the document; and (4) author(s), addressee(s), and recipient(s). MA R USDCT LR 26.5(c)(4).

- *Parties.* The terms "plaintiff" and "defendant" as well as a party's full or abbreviated name or a pronoun referring to a party mean the party and, where applicable, its officers, directors, employees, partners, corporate parent, subsidiaries, or affiliates. This definition is not intended to impose a discovery obligation on any person who is not a party to the litigation. MA R USDCT LR 26.5(c)(5).

- *Person.* The term "person" is defined as any natural person or any business, legal, or governmental entity or association. MA R USDCT LR 26.5(c)(6).

- *Concerning.* The term "concerning" means referring to, describing, evidencing, or constituting. MA R USDCT LR 26.5(c)(7).

- *State the basis.* When an interrogatory calls upon a party to "state the basis" of or for a particular claim, assertion, allegation, or contention, the party shall: (1) identify each and every document (and, where pertinent, the section, article, or subparagraph thereof), which forms any part of the source of the party's information regarding the alleged facts or legal conclusions referred to by the interrogatory; (2) identify each and every communication which forms any part of the source of the party's information regarding the alleged facts or legal conclusions referred to by the interrogatory; (3) state separately the acts or omissions to act on the part of any person (identifying the acts or omissions to act by stating their nature, time, and place and identifying the persons involved) which form any part of the party's information regarding the alleged facts or legal conclusions referred to in the interrogatory; and (4) state separately any other fact which forms the basis of the party's information regarding the alleged facts or conclusions referred to in the interrogatory. MA R USDCT LR 26.5(c)(8).

e.  *Cooperative discovery.* The judicial officer should encourage cost effective discovery by means of voluntary exchange of information among litigants and their attorneys. This may be accomplished through the use of: (1) informal, cooperative discovery practices in which counsel provide information to opposing counsel without resort to formal discovery procedures; or (2) stipulations entered into by the parties with respect to deposition notices, waiver of signing, and other matters, except that the parties may not enter into stipulations extending the time for responding to discovery requests or otherwise modify discovery procedures ordered by the judicial officer. MA R USDCT LR 26.1(a).

f.  *Phasing of discovery.* In order to facilitate settlement and the efficient completion of discovery, the judicial officer has discretion to structure discovery activities by phasing and sequencing the topics which are the subject of discovery. For example, an order may be framed limiting the first phase to developing information needed for a realistic assessment of the case. If the case does not terminate, the second phase would be directed at information needed to prepare for trial. MA R USDCT LR 26.3.

g.  *Sequence of discovery.* Unless the parties stipulate or the court orders otherwise for the parties' and witnesses' convenience and in the interests of justice: (1) methods of discovery may be used in any sequence; and (2) discovery by one party does not require any other party to delay its discovery. FRCP 26(d)(3).

2.  *Interrogatories*

a.  *Number.* Unless otherwise stipulated or ordered by the court, a party may serve on any other party no more than twenty-five (25) written interrogatories, including all discrete subparts. Leave to serve additional interrogatories may be granted to the extent consistent with FRCP 26(b)(1) and FRCP 26(b)(2). FRCP 33(a)(1). Unless the judicial officer orders otherwise, the number of discovery events shall be limited for each side (or group of parties with a common interest) to twenty-five (25) interrogatories. MA R USDCT LR 26.1(c). For purposes of determining the number of interrogatories propounded, subparts of a basic interrogatory which are logical extensions of the basic interrogatory and seek only to obtain specified additional particularized information with respect to the basic interrogatory shall not be counted separately from the basic interrogatory. MA R USDCT LR 26.1(c).

i.  *Further discovery.* Should a party exhaust the opportunities for any type of discovery events under MA R USDCT LR 26.1(c), any requests that such party may make for additional interrogatories, depositions, admissions or the production of documents beyond that allowed pursuant to MA R USDCT LR 26.1(c) shall be by discovery motion. All requests for additional discovery events, extensions of deadlines, for the completion of discovery or for postponement of the trial must be signed by the attorney and the party making the request. MA R USDCT LR 26.2(b).

b.  *Scope.* An interrogatory may relate to any matter that may be inquired into under FRCP 26(b). An interrogatory is not objectionable merely because it asks for an opinion or contention that relates to fact or the application of law to fact, but the court may order that the interrogatory need not be answered until designated discovery is complete, or until a pretrial conference or some other time. FRCP 33(a)(2).

c.  *Parties subject to interrogatories.* Depositions may be taken of any person but interrogatories are limited to parties to the litigation. FPP § 2171. Interrogatories may not be directed to the attorney for a party. They must be addressed to the party, who is then required to give all information known to it or its attorney. FPP § 2171; Hickman v. Taylor, 329 U.S. 495, 504, 67 S.Ct. 385, 390, 91 L.Ed. 451 (1947). For more information, refer to FPP § 2171.

d.  *Form.* Ideally an interrogatory should be a single direct question phrased in a fashion that will inform the other party what is requested. In fact the courts have given parties considerable latitude in framing interrogatories. Rather general language has been permitted so long as the interrogatory gives the other party a reasonably clear indication of the information to be included in its answer. FPP § 2168.

i.  *Use of definitions.* There is no prohibition against the use of definitions in interrogatories, and definitions may be

371

helpful in clarifying the meaning of obscure terms or avoiding repetitions in a long set of interrogatories. FPP §
2168.

ii. *Use of standardized form interrogatories.* There have been mixed reactions to the use of standardized form
interrogatories. They have been referred to opprobriously as "canned sets of interrogatories of the shotgun
variety" and it has been said that their indiscriminate use is an "undesirable practice." FPP § 2168.

e. *Copying expense for discovery materials*

   i. *Inspection of documents.* Except as otherwise provided in an order entered pursuant to FRCP 26(c), all parties
   to an action shall be entitled to inspect documents produced by another party pursuant to FRCP 33(c) or FRCP
   34 at the location where they are produced. MA R USDCT LR 26.6(b)(1).

   ii. *Copies of documents.* Except as otherwise provided in an order entered pursuant to FRCP 26(c), upon request of
   any party, and upon that party's agreement to pay the copying costs at the time of delivery, a party who produces
   documents pursuant to FRCP 33(c) or FRCP 34 shall provide copies of all or any specified part of the documents.
   No party shall be entitled to obtain copies of documents produced by another party pursuant to FRCP 33(c) or
   FRCP 34 without paying the costs thereof. MA R USDCT LR 26.6(b)(2).

f. *Motion to compel.* [T]he party submitting the interrogatories must attempt to confer with the responding party in an
effort to secure the information without court action and, if that fails, move for an order under FRCP 37(a) compelling
answers. FPP § 2182. Refer to the United States District Court for the District of Massachusetts KeyRules Motion to
Compel Discovery document for more information.

3. *Sanctions for failure to cooperate in discovery.* The court where the action is pending may, on motion, order sanctions if
a party, after being properly served with interrogatories under FRCP 33 or a request for inspection under FRCP 34, fails to
serve its answers, objections, or written response. FRCP 37(d)(1)(A)(ii). If a motion to compel is granted, the court must,
after giving an opportunity to be heard, require the party or deponent whose conduct necessitated the motion, the party or
attorney advising that conduct, or both to pay the movant's reasonable expenses incurred in making the motion, including
attorney's fees. But the court must not order this payment if the opposing party's nondisclosure, response, or objection was
substantially justified. FRCP 37(a)(5)(A)(ii). Refer to the United States District Court for the District of Massachusetts
KeyRules Motion for Discovery Sanctions document for more information.

4. *Stipulations about discovery procedure.* Unless the court orders otherwise, the parties may stipulate that: (1) a deposition
may be taken before any person, at any time or place, on any notice, and in the manner specified—in which event it may
be used in the same way as any other deposition; and (2) other procedures governing or limiting discovery be
modified—but a stipulation extending the time for any form of discovery must have court approval if it would interfere
with the time set for completing discovery, for hearing a motion, or for trial. FRCP 29.

5. *Alternative dispute resolution (ADR).* The judicial officer assigned to preside over the case shall encourage the resolution
of disputes by settlement or other alternative dispute resolution programs. MA R USDCT LR 16.4(a).

a. *Settlement.* At every conference conducted under the Local Rules of the United States District Court for the District
of Massachusetts, the judicial officer shall inquire as to the utility of the parties conducting settlement negotiations,
explore means of facilitating those negotiations, and offer whatever assistance may be appropriate in the
circumstances. Assistance may include a reference of the case to another judicial officer for settlement purposes. MA
R USDCT LR 16.4(b).

   i. When a case is settled, the parties shall file with the clerk a signed agreement for judgment or stipulation for
   dismissal, as appropriate, within twenty-eight (28) days, unless the court otherwise orders. MA R USDCT LR
   68.2.

b. *Alternative dispute resolution programs*

   i. *Discretion of judicial officer.* The judicial officer, following an exploration of the matter with all counsel, may
   refer appropriate cases to alternative dispute resolution programs that have been designated for use in the district
   court or that the judicial officer may make available. The dispute resolution programs described in MA R
   USDCT LR 16.4(c)(2) through MA R USDCT LR 16.4(c)(4) are illustrative, not exclusive. Moreover, nothing
   in MA R USDCT LR 16.4 shall preclude the parties from engaging in private dispute resolution programs as
   long as they comply with any schedule established by the court. MA R USDCT LR 16.4(c)(1).

   ii. *Mediation.* The judicial officer may refer the case to mediation upon the agreement of all parties. MA R USDCT
   LR 16.4(c)(2)(A).

   iii. *Other alternative dispute resolution programs.* Use of mediation is not exclusive. At the request of parties, the
   judicial officer may consider other forms of alternative dispute resolution including, but not limited to,
   mini-trial, summary jury trial and arbitration. MA R USDCT LR 16.4(c)(3).

   c.   For more information on alternative dispute resolution (ADR), refer to MA R USDCT LR 16.4.

6.   *Sanctions.* Failure to comply with any of the directions or obligations set forth in, or authorized by, these rules may result in dismissal, default, or the imposition of other sanctions as deemed appropriate by the judicial officer. MA R USDCT LR 1.3. Except as provided by law, the court may impose sanctions as provided in MA R USDCT LR 1.3 for failure to comply with the Administrative Procedures for Electronic Case Filing in the United States District Court for the District of Massachusetts (MA R USDCT CM/ECF Admin) or with MA R USDCT LR 5.4. MA R USDCT CM/ECF Admin(C)(3).

## D.  Documents

1.  *Required documents*

   a.   *Interrogatories.* Refer to the General Requirements section of this document for information on interrogatories.

2.  *Supplemental documents*

   a.   *Certificate of service.* No certificate of service is required when a paper is served by filing it with the court's electronic-filing system. When a paper that is required to be served is served by other means: (1) if the paper is filed, a certificate of service must be filed with it or within a reasonable time after service; and (2) if the paper is not filed, a certificate of service need not be filed unless filing is required by court order or by local rule. FRCP 5(d)(1)(B).

## E.  Format

1.  *Form of documents.* The rules governing captions and other matters of form in pleadings apply to motions and other papers. FRCP 7(b)(2). The provisions of FRCP 10 and FRCP 11 concerning the form and signing of pleadings, motions, and other papers shall be applicable to all papers filed in any proceeding in this court. The board of bar overseers registration number of each attorney signing such documents, except the United States Attorney and his or her staff, shall be inscribed below the signature. MA R USDCT LR 5.1(a)(1).

   a.   *Paper size and binding.* All papers filed in the court shall be adapted for flat filing, be filed on eight and one-half by eleven (8-1/2 x 11) inch paper without backers and be bound firmly by staple or some such other means (excluding paper or binder clip or rubber band). MA R USDCT LR 5.1(a)(2).

   b.   *Spacing.* All papers, except discovery requests and responses, shall be double-spaced except for the identification of counsel, title of the case, footnotes, quotations and exhibits. Discovery requests and responses shall be single-spaced. MA R USDCT LR 5.1(a)(2).

   c.   *Caption.* Every pleading must have a caption with the court's name, a title, a file number, and [an] FRCP 7(a) designation. FRCP 10(a).

      i.   *Names of parties.* The title of the complaint must name all the parties; the title of other pleadings, after naming the first party on each side, may refer generally to other parties. FRCP 10(a).

     ii.   *Request for special action.* When any pleading or other paper filed in the court includes a request for special process or relief, or any other request such that, if granted, the court will proceed other than in the ordinary course, the request shall, unless it is noted on the category sheet [see MA R USDCT LR 40.1(a)(1)], be noted on the first page to the right of or immediately beneath the caption. MA R USDCT LR 5.1(c).

   d.   *Claims or defenses*

      i.   *Numbered paragraphs.* A party must state its claims or defenses in numbered paragraphs, each limited as far as practicable to a single set of circumstances. A later pleading may refer by number to a paragraph in an earlier pleading. FRCP 10(b).

     ii.   *Separate statements.* If doing so would promote clarity, each claim founded on a separate transaction or occurrence—and each defense other than a denial—must be stated in a separate count or defense. FRCP 10(b).

   e.   *Adoption by reference.* A statement in a pleading may be adopted by reference elsewhere in the same pleading or in any other pleading or motion. FRCP 10(c).

      i.   *Exhibits.* A copy of a written instrument that is an exhibit to a pleading is a part of the pleading for all purposes. FRCP 10(c).

   f.   *Citations*

      i.   *Local rules.* These rules shall be known as Local Rules of the United States District Court for the District of Massachusetts and cited as "L.R., D. Mass." or "L.R." MA R USDCT LR 1.1.

     ii.   *Electronic case filing procedures.* The procedures governing electronic case filing shall be known as the "Administrative Procedures for Electronic Case Filing in the United States District Court for the District of Massachusetts." They shall be cited as "APECF." MA R USDCT CM/ECF Admin(A)(7).

g. *Acceptance by the clerk.* The clerk must not refuse to file a paper solely because it is not in the form prescribed by the Federal Rules of Civil Procedure or by a local rule or practice. FRCP 5(d)(4).

    i. Except for complaints and notices of appeal, papers that do not conform to the requirements of MA R USDCT LR 5.1(a)(2) shall be returned by the clerk. MA R USDCT LR 5.1(a)(2).

2. *Form of electronic documents.* A paper filed electronically is a written paper for purposes of the Federal Rules of Civil Procedure. FRCP 5(d)(3)(D).

    a. *PDF/A format required.* The court will begin requiring submission of documents in PDF/A format in the foreseeable future. PDF/A is an enhanced version of the traditional PDF format. Newer versions of most PDF software will be able to convert to this format. Additional information on PDF/A documents may be found on the court's website. MA R USDCT CM/ECF Admin(Electronic Filing and PDF).

        i. *Electronically converted PDF.* Electronically converted PDF documents are created from word processing documents (MS Word, WordPerfect, etc.) using any appropriate software. These documents are text searchable and the file size is generally smaller than a scanned document. CM/ECF users may use any brand of software to convert documents to PDF. MA R USDCT CM/ECF Admin(Electronic Filing and PDF).

            • Documents converted to PDF, rather than scanned, are preferred for filing in CM/ECF. MA R USDCT CM/ECF Admin(Electronic Filing and PDF).

        ii. *Scanned PDF.* Scanned PDF documents are created from paper documents run through an optical scanner. Scanned PDF documents are generally not searchable and have a larger file size. Please note that software used to create scanned documents may (and should) be set in such a way that the document is "text-searchable." MA R USDCT CM/ECF Admin(Electronic Filing and PDF).

    b. *Title.* All pleadings filed electronically shall be titled in accordance with the approved dictionary of civil or criminal events of the CM/ECF system of this court. A list of events is available on the CM/ECF Training Information page of the court's website. The clerk's office may, when necessary and appropriate, modify the docket entry description, or delete and re-enter the docket entry in order to comply with the court's quality assurance standards. MA R USDCT CM/ECF Admin(G)(3).

    c. *Attachments to filings and exhibits.* Attachments to filings and exhibits must be filed in accordance with the court's CM/ECF User Manual, unless otherwise ordered by the court. MA R USDCT CM/ECF Admin(O)(1).

        i. Filers must submit as attachments only those excerpts of the referenced documents that are directly germane to the matter under consideration by the court. Excerpted material must be clearly and prominently identified as such. Users who file excerpts of documents do so without prejudice to their right to timely file additional excerpts or the complete document, as may be allowed by the court. Responding parties may timely file additional excerpts or the complete document that they believe are directly germane. MA R USDCT CM/ECF Admin(O)(2).

        ii. Filers shall not attach as an exhibit any pleading or other paper already on file with the court in that case, but shall merely refer to that document. (See MA R USDCT CM/ECF Admin(G) for information on using hyperlinks in PDF documents filed in CM/ECF.) MA R USDCT CM/ECF Admin(O)(3).

    d. *Redacted documents.* The parties may request or the court may require the submission of documents that have been redacted/stripped of sensitive or confidential information. The redacted document prepared for electronic filing shall include the original caption of the document, and be clearly labeled as "Redacted Document." A specific event is available for this purpose ("Redacted Document"), found under the Other Filings/Other Documents menu option. MA R USDCT CM/ECF Admin(S).

        i. Attorneys and pro se litigants are advised to take extra care when creating PDF documents intended for submission to CM/ECF. Steps shall be taken to ensure the documents are free of any hidden data (metadata) that may contain redacted information, or traces of information edited or deleted are not hidden in the final document. Even PDF content that has been encrypted may be recovered. An advisory document with additional information on this topic may be found on the court's website. MA R USDCT CM/ECF Admin(S).

    e. *Hyperlinks.* Electronically filed documents may contain the following types of hyperlinks: (1) hyperlinks to other portions of the same document; (2) hyperlinks to other documents filed within the CM/ECF system; and (3) hyperlinks to a location on the Internet that contains a source document for a citation. MA R USDCT CM/ECF Admin(G)(7).

        i. Hyperlinks to cited authority may not replace standard citation format. Complete citations must be included in the text of the filed document. Neither a hyperlink, nor any site to which it refers, shall be considered part of the

record, but are simply convenient mechanisms for accessing material cited in a document filed in CM/ECF. Instructions on creating hyperlinks may be found in the CM/ECF User Manual. MA R USDCT CM/ECF Admin(G)(7).

    ii.   The court accepts no responsibility for, and does not endorse, any product, organization, or content at any hyperlinked site, or at any site to which that site may be linked. The court accepts no responsibility for the availability or functionality of any hyperlink. MA R USDCT CM/ECF Admin(G)(7).

    iii.   One feature of PDF/A documents is that hyperlinks are commonly "masked," meaning that the full address of the referenced file is not written out; for example, clicking the word brief may open a brief which was previously filed in CM/ECF. MA R USDCT CM/ECF Admin(G)(7)(NOTE). An "unmasked" hyperlink has the full address visible to the user. MA R USDCT CM/ECF Admin(G)(7)(NOTE).

- Masked hyperlinks may or may not work in a PDF/A document, depending on how it was created. Currently, masked hyperlinks are preserved in PDF/A documents produced by the "Save As" method in Microsoft Word 2007 and 2010; the "PDFMaker" method in Microsoft Word 2007; and OpenOffice 2.4 ("PDF Export"). With other production methods, such as WordPerfect, the PDF/A document includes underlined words that appear to be links, but clicking them has no effect. MA R USDCT CM/ECF Admin(G)(7)(NOTE).

   f.   *Documents features not accepted.* CM/ECF will not accept PDF documents containing tracking tags, embedded systems commands, password protections, access restrictions or other security features, special tags or dynamic features. MA R USDCT CM/ECF Admin(G)(8).

   g.   *File size limitations.* A filing party shall limit the size of each PDF file to no more than twenty (20) megabytes. PDF files larger than seven (7) megabytes will be rejected by the CM/ECF system. The filer will see a message advising of the size limitation. MA R USDCT CM/ECF Admin(P)(2).

    i.   Larger documents or exhibits may be submitted electronically if split into separate PDF files each less than seven (7) megabytes, attached to the main document and clearly labeled. MA R USDCT CM/ECF Admin(P)(2).

    ii.   Documents submitted electronically or on paper are subject to the page limitations set by MA R USDCT LR 7.1(b)(4) or by order of the court. MA R USDCT CM/ECF Admin(P)(1).

   h.   *Accuracy and readability.* The filer shall verify the accuracy and readability of any PDF file before electronically filing it in CM/ECF. MA R USDCT CM/ECF Admin(G)(6); MA R USDCT CM/ECF Admin(P)(3).

3.   *Signing disclosures and discovery requests, responses, and objections.* FRCP 11 does not apply to disclosures and discovery requests, responses, objections, and motions under FRCP 26 through FRCP 37. FRCP 11(d).

   a.   *Signature required.* Every disclosure under FRCP 26(a)(1) or FRCP 26(a)(3) and every discovery request, response, or objection must be signed by at least one attorney of record in the attorney's own name—or by the party personally, if unrepresented—and must state the signer's address, e-mail address, and telephone number. FRCP 26(g)(1). The provisions of the Federal Rules of Civil Procedure pertaining to the form and signing of pleadings, motions, and other papers shall be applicable to all papers filed in any proceeding in this court. The board of bar overseers registration number of each attorney signing such documents, except the United States Attorney and his staff, shall be inscribed below the signature. MA R USDCT LR 5.1(a)(1).

    i.   *Electronic signing.* A filing made through a person's electronic-filing account and authorized by that person, together with that person's name on a signature block, constitutes the person's signature. FRCP 5(d)(3)(C).

    ii.   *Appearances.* The filing of an appearance or any other pleading signed on behalf of a party constitutes an entry of appearance for that party. All pleadings shall contain the name, bar admission number, address, telephone number, and e-mail address of the attorney entering an appearance. MA R USDCT LR 83.5.2(a).

- *Appearances by law firms.* When a party is represented by a law firm, the appearance must include the name and the signature of at least one individual attorney. When a party is represented by more than one attorney from the same or different law firms, the attorney entering the appearance must designate the individual attorney who is authorized to receive all notices in the case. Any notice sent to an attorney so designated shall be deemed to be proper notice unless the court finds that notice was not properly sent. MA R USDCT LR 83.5.2(b).

- For more information on appearances, refer to MA R USDCT LR 83.5.2.

    iii.   *Signatures of attorneys.* The user login and password required to submit documents to the CM/ECF system shall serve as that user's signature for purposes of FRCP 11 and for all other purposes under the Federal Rules of Civil

Procedure and the Local Rules of the United States District Court for the District of Massachusetts. All electronically filed documents must include a signature block and must set forth the attorney's name, bar number, address, telephone number and email address. The name of the CM/ECF user under whose log-in and password the document is submitted must be preceded by a "/s/" and typed in the space where the signature would otherwise appear. MA R USDCT CM/ECF Admin(M)(1). For an example, refer to MA R USDCT CM/ECF Admin(M)(1).

iv. *Signatures of pro se parties.* Any document requiring a signature that is filed by a party appearing pro se shall bear the words "pro se" following that party's signature. Any such document shall also state the party's mailing address, telephone number (if any), and e-mail address (if the party has consented to service by email). MA R USDCT LR 83.5.5(g). For more information on practice by pro se litigants, refer to MA R USDCT LR 83.5.5.

v. *Multiple signatures.* The filer of any document requiring more than one signature (e.g, stipulations, joint motions, joint status reports, magistrate judge consent forms, etc.) must list thereon all the names of other signatories by means of a "/s/ name of signatory" block for each. By submitting such a document, the filing attorney certifies that each of the other signatories has expressly agreed to the form and substance of the document and that the filing attorney has their actual authority to submit the document electronically. MA R USDCT CM/ECF Admin(M)(2). For more information, refer to MA R USDCT CM/ECF Admin(M)(2).

vi. *Affidavits.* Except as provided in MA R USDCT CM/ECF Admin(L), affidavits shall be filed electronically; however, the electronically filed version must contain a "/s/ name of signatory" block indicating that the paper document bears an original signature. MA R USDCT CM/ECF Admin(M)(3). The court will also accept a scanned version of the original, signed document. MA R USDCT CM/ECF Admin(M)(3). For more information, refer to MA R USDCT CM/ECF Admin(M)(3).

b. *Effect of signature.* By signing, an attorney or party certifies that to the best of the person's knowledge, information, and belief formed after a reasonable inquiry:

i. With respect to a disclosure, it is complete and correct as of the time it is made; and

ii. With respect to a discovery request, response, or objection, it is:

- Consistent with the Federal Rules of Civil Procedure and warranted by existing law or by a nonfrivolous argument for extending, modifying, or reversing existing law, or for establishing new law;

- Not interposed for any improper purpose, such as to harass, cause unnecessary delay, or needlessly increase the cost of litigation; and

- Neither unreasonable nor unduly burdensome or expensive, considering the needs of the case, prior discovery in the case, the amount in controversy, and the importance of the issues at stake in the action. FRCP 26(g)(1).

c. *Failure to sign.* Other parties have no duty to act on an unsigned disclosure, request, response, or objection until it is signed, and the court must strike it unless a signature is promptly supplied after the omission is called to the attorney's or party's attention. FRCP 26(g)(2).

d. *Sanction for improper certification.* If a certification violates FRCP 26(g) without substantial justification, the court, on motion or on its own, must impose an appropriate sanction on the signer, the party on whose behalf the signer was acting, or both. The sanction may include an order to pay the reasonable expenses, including attorney's fees, caused by the violation. FRCP 26(g)(3). Refer to the United States District Court for the District of Massachusetts KeyRules Motion for Discovery Sanctions document for more information.

4. *Privacy protection for filings made with the court*

a. *Redacted filings.* Unless the court orders otherwise, in an electronic or paper filing with the court that contains an individual's Social Security number, taxpayer-identification number, or birth date, the name of an individual known to be a minor, or a financial-account number, a party or nonparty making the filing may include only:

i. The last four (4) digits of the Social Security number and taxpayer-identification number;

ii. The year of the individual's birth;

iii. The minor's initials; and

iv. The last four (4) digits of the financial-account number. FRCP 5.2(a); MA R USDCT CM/ECF Admin(N).

b. *Exemptions from the redaction requirement.* The redaction requirement does not apply to the following:

i. A financial-account number that identifies the property allegedly subject to forfeiture in a forfeiture proceeding;

    ii.   The record of an administrative or agency proceeding;

    iii.   The official record of a state-court proceeding;

    iv.   The record of a court or tribunal, if that record was not subject to the redaction requirement when originally filed;

    v.   A filing covered by FRCP 5.2(c) or FRCP 5.2(d); and

    vi.   A pro se filing in an action brought under 28 U.S.C.A. § 2241, 28 U.S.C.A. § 2254, or 28 U.S.C.A. § 2255. FRCP 5.2(b).

c.   *Limitations on remote access to electronic files; Social Security appeals and immigration cases.* Unless the court orders otherwise, in an action for benefits under the Social Security Act, and in an action or proceeding relating to an order of removal, to relief from removal, or to immigration benefits or detention, access to an electronic file is authorized as follows:

    i.   The parties and their attorneys may have remote electronic access to any part of the case file, including the administrative record;

    ii.   Any other person may have electronic access to the full record at the courthouse, but may have remote electronic access only to:

       •   The docket maintained by the court; and

       •   An opinion, order, judgment, or other disposition of the court, but not any other part of the case file or the administrative record. FRCP 5.2(c).

d.   *Filings made under seal.* The court may order that a filing be made under seal without redaction. The court may later unseal the filing or order the person who made the filing to file a redacted version for the public record. FRCP 5.2(d).

e.   *Protective orders.* For good cause, the court may by order in a case:

    i.   Require redaction of additional information; or

    ii.   Limit or prohibit a nonparty's remote electronic access to a document filed with the court. FRCP 5.2(e).

f.   *Option for additional unredacted filing under seal.* A person making a redacted filing may also file an unredacted copy under seal. The court must retain the unredacted copy as part of the record. FRCP 5.2(f). For more information, refer to MA R USDCT LR 7.2.

g.   *Option for filing a reference list.* A filing that contains redacted information may be filed together with a reference list that identifies each item of redacted information and specifies an appropriate identifier that uniquely corresponds to each item listed. The list must be filed under seal and may be amended as of right. Any reference in the case to a listed identifier will be construed to refer to the corresponding item of information. FRCP 5.2(g).

h.   *Responsibility for redaction.* The clerk's office is not responsible for reviewing documents filed with the court to determine whether pleadings have been redacted and are in the proper form. MA R USDCT CM/ECF Admin(N).

i.   *Waiver of protection of identifiers.* A person waives the protection of FRCP 5.2(a) as to the person's own information by filing it without redaction and not under seal. FRCP 5.2(h).

# F. Filing and Service Requirements

1.   *Filing requirements*

a.   *Required filings.* Any paper after the complaint that is required to be served must be filed no later than a reasonable time after service. But disclosures under FRCP 26(a)(1) or FRCP 26(a)(2) and the following discovery requests and responses must not be filed until they are used in the proceeding or the court orders filing: depositions, interrogatories, requests for documents or tangible things or to permit entry onto land, and requests for admission. FRCP 5(d)(1)(A). Refer to the United States District Court for the District of Massachusetts KeyRules pleading and motion documents for information on filing with the court.

b.   *Nonfiling of discovery materials.* Discovery materials (that is, automatic or voluntary disclosure materials, depositions, deposition notices, interrogatories, requests for documents, requests for admissions, answers and responses to discovery requests, and any other requests for or products of the discovery process) shall not be filed unless so ordered by the court or for use in the proceeding. The party taking a deposition or obtaining any material through discovery is responsible for its preservation and delivery to the court if needed or so ordered. If for any reason a party or concerned citizen believes that any of the named documents should be filed, an ex parte request may be made that such document be filed, stating the reasons for the request. The court may also order filing sua sponte. MA R USDCT LR 26.6(a).

    i.   *Discovery motions.* If relief is sought under FRCP 26(c) or FRCP 37, copies of the relevant portions of disputed documents shall be filed with the court contemporaneously with any motion. MA R USDCT LR 26.6(a).

    ii.  *Motions for summary judgment.* If the moving party under FRCP 56 or the opponent relies on discovery documents, copies of the pertinent parts thereof shall be filed with the motion or opposition. MA R USDCT LR 26.6(a).

2.  *Service requirements.* Service of all pleadings subsequent to the original complaint and of all other papers required to be served shall be made in the manner specified by FRCP 5. MA R USDCT LR 5.2(a).

    a.  *Service; When required*

        i.  *In general.* Unless the Federal Rules of Civil Procedure provide otherwise, each of the following papers must be served on every party:

- An order stating that service is required;
- A pleading filed after the original complaint, unless the court orders otherwise under FRCP 5(c) because there are numerous defendants;
- A discovery paper required to be served on a party, unless the court orders otherwise;
- A written motion, except one that may be heard ex parte; and
- A written notice, appearance, demand, or offer of judgment, or any similar paper. FRCP 5(a)(1).

        ii.  *If a party fails to appear.* No service is required on a party who is in default for failing to appear. But a pleading that asserts a new claim for relief against such a party must be served on that party under FRCP 4. FRCP 5(a)(2).

        iii.  *Seizing property.* If an action is begun by seizing property and no person is or need be named as a defendant, any service required before the filing of an appearance, answer, or claim must be made on the person who had custody or possession of the property when it was seized. FRCP 5(a)(3).

    b.  *Service; How made*

        i.  *Serving an attorney.* If a party is represented by an attorney, service under FRCP 5 must be made on the attorney unless the court orders service on the party. FRCP 5(b)(1).

        ii.  *Service in general.* A paper is served under FRCP 5 by:

- Handing it to the person;
- Leaving it: (1) at the person's office with a clerk or other person in charge or, if no one is in charge, in a conspicuous place in the office; or (2) if the person has no office or the office is closed, at the person's dwelling or usual place of abode with someone of suitable age and discretion who resides there;
- Mailing it to the person's last known address—in which event service is complete upon mailing;
- Leaving it with the court clerk if the person has no known address;
- Sending it to a registered user by filing it with the court's electronic-filing system or sending it by other electronic means that the person consented to in writing—in either of which events service is complete upon filing or sending, but is not effective if the filer or sender learns that it did not reach the person to be served; or
- Delivering it by any other means that the person consented to in writing—in which event service is complete when the person making service delivers it to the agency designated to make delivery. FRCP 5(b)(2).

        iii.  *Service by electronic means.* Unless exempt or otherwise ordered by the court, all pleadings and other papers must be served on other parties by electronic means. MA R USDCT LR 5.4(C); MA R USDCT CM/ECF Admin(H)(2). Service by electronic means shall be treated the same as service by mail. MA R USDCT CM/ECF Admin(H)(4).

- *Consent to electronic service.* Registering to use CM/ECF constitutes consent to service of all documents by electronic means as provided in the Administrative Procedures for Electronic Case Filing in the United States District Court for the District of Massachusetts (MA R USDCT CM/ECF Admin) and FRCP 5(b) and FRCP 77(d). MA R USDCT CM/ECF Admin(E)(6); MA R USDCT CM/ECF Admin(H)(3).

- *Service on registered ECF users.* Transmission of the Notice of Electronic Filing (NEF) through the court's transmission facilities will constitute service of the filed document upon a registered ECF user. MA R USDCT LR 5.4(C).

- *Service on non-registered users.* The party filing the document electronically is responsible for serving a paper copy of the document by mail in accordance with FRCP 5(b) to those case participants who have not been identified on the NEF as electronic recipients. MA R USDCT CM/ECF Admin(H)(3).

- *Service of conventionally filed papers.* Documents or exhibits submitted conventionally shall be served on other parties by the filer using traditional means. MA R USDCT CM/ECF Admin(P)(4).

c. *Serving numerous defendants*

    i. *In general.* If an action involves an unusually large number of defendants, the court may, on motion or on its own, order that:

- Defendants' pleadings and replies to them need not be served on other defendants;

- Any crossclaim, counterclaim, avoidance, or affirmative defense in those pleadings and replies to them will be treated as denied or avoided by all other parties; and

- Filing any such pleading and serving it on the plaintiff constitutes notice of the pleading to all parties. FRCP 5(c)(1).

    ii. *Notifying parties.* A copy of every such order must be served on the parties as the court directs. FRCP 5(c)(2).

## G. Hearings

1. There is no hearing contemplated in the federal statutes or rules for interrogatories.

## H. Forms

### 1. Federal Interrogatories Forms

a. Interrogatories; Short form. 3A FEDFORMS § 24:18.

b. Interrogatories; Emphasis on notice. 3A FEDFORMS § 24:19.

c. Interrogatories by plaintiff; To corporation. 3A FEDFORMS § 24:20.

d. Interrogatories by plaintiff; Complete set. 3A FEDFORMS § 24:21.

e. Interrogatories by plaintiff; Requesting identification of documents and production under FRCP 34. 3A FEDFORMS § 24:22.

f. Interrogatories by plaintiff; With definition of terms used and instructions for answering. 3A FEDFORMS § 24:23.

g. Interrogatories by plaintiff; Employment discrimination case. 3A FEDFORMS § 24:24.

h. Interrogatories by defendant. 3A FEDFORMS § 24:25.

i. Interrogatories by defendant; Complete set; Accident. 3A FEDFORMS § 24:26.

j. Interrogatories by defendant; Complete set; Railroad. 3A FEDFORMS § 24:27.

k. Interrogatories by defendant; Complete set; Patent. 3A FEDFORMS § 24:28.

l. Interrogatories by defendant; Complete set; Automobile accident. 3A FEDFORMS § 24:29.

m. Interrogatories by defendant; Follow-up interrogatories to plaintiff after lapse of time since first set of interrogatories or deposition. 3A FEDFORMS § 24:30.

n. Certificate of service of interrogatories. 3A FEDFORMS § 24:32.

o. Introductory statement; Interrogatories to individual. AMJUR PP DEPOSITION § 405.

p. Introductory statement; Interrogatories to corporation. AMJUR PP DEPOSITION § 406.

q. Interrogatories; Outline form. FEDPROF § 23:343.

r. Interrogatories; To defendant; Trademark action. FEDPROF § 23:355.

s. Interrogatories; With request for documents; To defendant; Collection of royalties. FEDPROF § 23:356.

t. Interrogatories; To defendant; Copyright infringement. FEDPROF § 23:358.

u. Interrogatories; To plaintiff; Products liability. FEDPROF § 23:360.

v. Interrogatories; To plaintiff; Personal injury. FEDPROF § 23:361.

w.   Interrogatories; To defendant; Premises liability. FEDPROF § 23:364.

x.   Interrogatories; To defendant; Medical malpractice. FEDPROF § 23:365.

y.   General forms; Standard interrogatories. GOLDLTGFMS § 26:25.

z.   General forms; Civil cases. GOLDLTGFMS § 26:26.

## I. Applicable Rules

1.  *Federal rules*

    a.   Serving and filing pleadings and other papers. FRCP 5.

    b.   Privacy protection for filings made with the court. FRCP 5.2.

    c.   Computing and extending time; Time for motion papers. FRCP 6.

    d.   Pleadings allowed; Form of motions and other papers. FRCP 7.

    e.   Form of pleadings. FRCP 10.

    f.   Signing pleadings, motions, and other papers; Representations to the court; Sanctions. FRCP 11.

    g.   Duty to disclose; General provisions governing discovery. FRCP 26.

    h.   Stipulations about discovery procedure. FRCP 29.

    i.   Interrogatories to parties. FRCP 33.

    j.   Failure to make disclosures or to cooperate in discovery; Sanctions. FRCP 37.

2.  *Local rules*

    a.   Title. MA R USDCT LR 1.1.

    b.   Sanctions. MA R USDCT LR 1.3.

    c.   Form and filing of papers. MA R USDCT LR 5.1.

    d.   Service and filing of pleadings and other papers. MA R USDCT LR 5.2.

    e.   Filing and service by electronic means. MA R USDCT LR 5.4.

    f.   Alternative dispute resolution. MA R USDCT LR 16.4.

    g.   Control of discovery. MA R USDCT LR 26.1.

    h.   Sequences of discovery. MA R USDCT LR 26.2.

    i.   Phasing of discovery. MA R USDCT LR 26.3.

    j.   Uniform definitions in discovery requests. MA R USDCT LR 26.5.

    k.   Court filings and costs. MA R USDCT LR 26.6.

    l.   Settlement. MA R USDCT LR 68.2.

    m.   Office of the clerk. MA R USDCT LR 77.2.

    n.   Appearances. MA R USDCT LR 83.5.2.

    o.   Practice by pro se litigants. MA R USDCT LR 83.5.5.

    p.   CM/ECF case management/electronic case files administrative procedures. MA R USDCT CM/ECF Admin.

## Requests, Notices and Applications
## Response to Interrogatories

**Document Last Updated December 2018**

## A. Checklist

(I)   ❑ Matters to be considered by requesting party

   (a)   ❑ Required documents

      (1)   ❑ Interrogatories

    (b)  ❑  Supplemental documents

        (1)  ❑  Certificate of service

    (c)  ❑  Timing

        (1)  ❑  A party may not seek discovery from any source before the parties have conferred as required by FRCP 26(f), except in a proceeding exempted from initial disclosure under FRCP 26(a)(1)(B), or when authorized by the Federal Rules of Civil Procedure, by stipulation, or by court order

(II)  ❑  Matters to be considered by responding party

    (a)  ❑  Required documents

        (1)  ❑  Response to interrogatories

    (b)  ❑  Supplemental documents

        (1)  ❑  Certificate of service

    (c)  ❑  Timing

        (1)  ❑  The responding party must serve its answers and any objections within thirty (30) days after being served with the interrogatories

        (2)  ❑  Answers to interrogatories with respect to which objections were served and which are subsequently required to be answered shall be served within fourteen (14) days after it is determined that they should be answered, unless the court directs otherwise

## B. Timing

1. *Response to interrogatories.* The responding party must serve its answers and any objections within thirty (30) days after being served with the interrogatories. A shorter or longer time may be stipulated to under FRCP 29 or be ordered by the court. FRCP 33(b)(2).

    a.  *Answers to interrogatories following objections.* Answers to interrogatories with respect to which objections were served and which are subsequently required to be answered shall be served within fourteen (14) days after it is determined that they should be answered, unless the court directs otherwise. MA R USDCT LR 33.1(d).

2. *Computation of time*

    a.  *Computing time.* FRCP 6 applies in computing any time period specified in the Federal Rules of Civil Procedure, in any local rule or court order, or in any statute that does not specify a method of computing time. FRCP 6(a).

        i.  *Period stated in days or a longer unit.* When the period is stated in days or a longer unit of time:

- Exclude the day of the event that triggers the period;

- Count every day, including intermediate Saturdays, Sundays, and legal holidays; and

- Include the last day of the period, but if the last day is a Saturday, Sunday, or legal holiday, the period continues to run until the end of the next day that is not a Saturday, Sunday, or legal holiday. FRCP 6(a)(1).

        ii.  *Period stated in hours.* When the period is stated in hours:

- Begin counting immediately on the occurrence of the event that triggers the period;

- Count every hour, including hours during intermediate Saturdays, Sundays, and legal holidays; and

- If the period would end on a Saturday, Sunday, or legal holiday, the period continues to run until the same time on the next day that is not a Saturday, Sunday, or legal holiday. FRCP 6(a)(2).

        iii.  *Office of the clerk.* The offices of the Clerk of Court at Boston, Worcester and Springfield shall be open from 8:30 a.m. until 5:00 p.m. on all days except Saturdays, Sundays, legal holidays and other days so ordered by the court and announced in advance, if feasible. MA R USDCT LR 77.2.

        iv.  *Inaccessibility of the clerk's office.* Unless the court orders otherwise, if the clerk's office is inaccessible:

- On the last day for filing under FRCP 6(a)(1), then the time for filing is extended to the first accessible day that is not a Saturday, Sunday, or legal holiday; or

- During the last hour for filing under FRCP 6(a)(2), then the time for filing is extended to the same time on the first accessible day that is not a Saturday, Sunday, or legal holiday. FRCP 6(a)(3).

        v.  *"Last day" defined.* Unless a different time is set by a statute, local rule, or court order, the last day ends:

- For electronic filing, at midnight in the court's time zone; and

- For filing by other means, when the clerk's office is scheduled to close. FRCP 6(a)(4).

vi. *"Next day" defined.* The "next day" is determined by continuing to count forward when the period is measured after an event and backward when measured before an event. FRCP 6(a)(5).

vii. *"Legal holiday" defined.* "Legal holiday" means:

- The day set aside by statute for observing New Year's Day, Martin Luther King Jr.'s Birthday, Washington's Birthday, Memorial Day, Independence Day, Labor Day, Columbus Day, Veterans' Day, Thanksgiving Day, or Christmas Day;

- Any day declared a holiday by the President or Congress; and

- For periods that are measured after an event, any other day declared a holiday by the state where the district court is located. FRCP 6(a)(6).

b. *Computation of electronic filing deadlines.* Filing documents electronically does not alter any filing deadlines. MA R USDCT CM/ECF Admin(K); MA R USDCT LR 5.4(D). Although CM/ECF is generally available twenty-four (24) hours a day for filing, all electronic transmissions of documents must be completed prior to 6:00 PM, Eastern Standard (or Daylight Savings) Time, on the date on which it is due, in order to be considered timely filed that day. MA R USDCT CM/ECF Admin(K); MA R USDCT LR 5.4(D). When a specific time of day deadline is set by court order or stipulation, the electronic filing must be completed by that time. Documents may be filed at any time of the day on days prior to the date on which it is due. MA R USDCT CM/ECF Admin(K). A document filed electronically shall be deemed filed as of the time and date stated on the NEF received from the court. MA R USDCT CM/ECF Admin(G)(2); MA R USDCT CM/ECF Admin(K).

i. *Technical failures.* A user whose filing is made untimely as the result of a technical failure of the court's CM/ECF system may seek appropriate relief from the court. MA R USDCT CM/ECF Admin(W)(3). Technical difficulties on the filer's end, with telephone, cable lines, the filer's Internet Service Provider (ISP), or hardware or software problems, will not constitute a technical failure under the Administrative Procedures for Electronic Case Filing in the United States District Court for the District of Massachusetts (MA R USDCT CM/ECF Admin) nor excuse an untimely filing. MA R USDCT CM/ECF Admin(W)(3). As help desk support is available during normal business hours, filers are strongly urged to electronically file any documents during that period. MA R USDCT CM/ECF Admin(W)(3).

- The court has made available a public terminal (computers and scanner) in each clerk's office for registered users to scan and electronically file documents. This equipment is available during normal business hours. Users should bring their prepared document and a valid CM/ECF login and password. MA R USDCT CM/ECF Admin(W)(3).

c. *Extending time.* When an act may or must be done within a specified time, the court may, for good cause, extend the time: (1) with or without motion or notice if the court acts, or if a request is made, before the original time or its extension expires; or (2) on motion made after the time has expired if the party failed to act because of excusable neglect. FRCP 6(b)(1).

i. *Exceptions.* A court must not extend the time to act under FRCP 50(b), FRCP 50(d), FRCP 52(b), FRCP 59(b), FRCP 59(d), FRCP 59(e), and FRCP 60(b). FRCP 6(b)(2).

ii. Refer to the United States District Court for the District of Massachusetts KeyRules Motion for Continuance/Extension of Time document for more information on extending time.

d. *Additional time after certain kinds of service.* When a party may or must act within a specified time after being served and service is made under FRCP 5(b)(2)(C) (by mail), FRCP 5(b)(2)(D) (by leaving with the clerk), or FRCP 5(b)(2)(F) (by other means consented to), three (3) days are added after the period would otherwise expire under FRCP 6(a). FRCP 6(d).

## C. General Requirements

1. *General provisions governing discovery*

   a. *Discovery scope and limits*

   i. *Scope in general.* Unless otherwise limited by court order, the scope of discovery is as follows: Parties may obtain discovery regarding any nonprivileged matter that is relevant to any party's claim or defense and proportional to the needs of the case, considering the importance of the issues at stake in the action, the amount in controversy, the parties' relative access to relevant information, the parties' resources, the importance of the discovery in resolving the issues, and whether the burden or expense of the proposed discovery outweighs its likely benefit. Information within this scope of discovery need not be admissible in evidence to be discoverable. FRCP 26(b)(1).

ii. *Limitations on frequency and extent*

- *When permitted.* By order, the court may alter the limits in the Federal Rules of Civil Procedure on the number of depositions and interrogatories or on the length of depositions under FRCP 30. By order or local rule, the court may also limit the number of requests under FRCP 36. FRCP 26(b)(2)(A).

- *Specific limitations on electronically stored information.* A party need not provide discovery of electronically stored information from sources that the party identifies as not reasonably accessible because of undue burden or cost. On motion to compel discovery or for a protective order, the party from whom discovery is sought must show that the information is not reasonably accessible because of undue burden or cost. If that showing is made, the court may nonetheless order discovery from such sources if the requesting party shows good cause, considering the limitations of FRCP 26(b)(2)(C). The court may specify conditions for the discovery. FRCP 26(b)(2)(B).

- *When required.* On motion or on its own, the court must limit the frequency or extent of discovery otherwise allowed by the Federal Rules of Civil Procedure or by local rule if it determines that: (1) the discovery sought is unreasonably cumulative or duplicative, or can be obtained from some other source that is more convenient, less burdensome, or less expensive; (2) the party seeking discovery has had ample opportunity to obtain the information by discovery in the action; or (3) the proposed discovery is outside the scope permitted by FRCP 26(b)(1). FRCP 26(b)(2)(C).

iii. *Trial preparation; Materials*

- *Documents and tangible things.* Ordinarily, a party may not discover documents and tangible things that are prepared in anticipation of litigation or for trial by or for another party or its representative (including the other party's attorney, consultant, surety, indemnitor, insurer, or agent). But, subject to FRCP 26(b)(4), those materials may be discovered if: (1) they are otherwise discoverable under FRCP 26(b)(1); and (2) the party shows that it has substantial need for the materials to prepare its case and cannot, without undue hardship, obtain their substantial equivalent by other means. FRCP 26(b)(3)(A).

- *Protection against disclosure.* If the court orders discovery of those materials, it must protect against disclosure of the mental impressions, conclusions, opinions, or legal theories of a party's attorney or other representative concerning the litigation. FRCP 26(b)(3)(B).

- *Previous statement.* Any party or other person may, on request and without the required showing, obtain the person's own previous statement about the action or its subject matter. If the request is refused, the person may move for a court order, and FRCP 37(a)(5) applies to the award of expenses. A previous statement is either: (1) a written statement that the person has signed or otherwise adopted or approved; or (2) a contemporaneous stenographic, mechanical, electrical, or other recording—or a transcription of it—that recites substantially verbatim the person's oral statement. FRCP 26(b)(3)(C).

iv. *Trial preparation; Experts*

- *Deposition of an expert who may testify.* A party may depose any person who has been identified as an expert whose opinions may be presented at trial. If FRCP 26(a)(2)(B) requires a report from the expert, the deposition may be conducted only after the report is provided. FRCP 26(b)(4)(A).

- *Trial-preparation protection for draft reports or disclosures.* FRCP 26(b)(3)(A) and FRCP 26(b)(3)(B) protect drafts of any report or disclosure required under FRCP 26(a)(2), regardless of the form in which the draft is recorded. FRCP 26(b)(4)(B).

- *Trial-preparation protection for communications between a party's attorney and expert witnesses.* FRCP 26(b)(3)(A) and FRCP 26(b)(3)(B) protect communications between the party's attorney and any witness required to provide a report under FRCP 26(a)(2)(B), regardless of the form of the communications, except to the extent that the communications: (1) relate to compensation for the expert's study or testimony; (2) identify facts or data that the party's attorney provided and that the expert considered in forming the opinions to be expressed; or (3) identify assumptions that the party's attorney provided and that the expert relied on in forming the opinions to be expressed. FRCP 26(b)(4)(C).

- *Expert employed only for trial preparation.* Ordinarily, a party may not, by interrogatories or deposition, discover facts known or opinions held by an expert who has been retained or specially employed by another party in anticipation of litigation or to prepare for trial and who is not expected to be called as a witness at trial. But a party may do so only: (1) as provided in FRCP 35(b); or (2) on showing exceptional circumstances under which it is impracticable for the party to obtain facts or opinions on the same subject by other means. FRCP 26(b)(4)(D).

- *Payment.* Unless manifest injustice would result, the court must require that the party seeking discovery: (1) pay the expert a reasonable fee for time spent in responding to discovery under FRCP 26(b)(4)(A) or FRCP 26(b)(4)(D); and (2) for discovery under FRCP 26(b)(4)(D), also pay the other party a fair portion of the fees and expenses it reasonably incurred in obtaining the expert's facts and opinions. FRCP 26(b)(4)(E).

   v. *Claiming privilege or protecting trial-preparation materials*

- *Information withheld.* When a party withholds information otherwise discoverable by claiming that the information is privileged or subject to protection as trial-preparation material, the party must: (1) expressly make the claim; and (2) describe the nature of the documents, communications, or tangible things not produced or disclosed—and do so in a manner that, without revealing information itself privileged or protected, will enable other parties to assess the claim. FRCP 26(b)(5)(A).

- *Information produced.* If information produced in discovery is subject to a claim of privilege or of protection as trial-preparation material, the party making the claim may notify any party that received the information of the claim and the basis for it. After being notified, a party must promptly return, sequester, or destroy the specified information and any copies it has; must not use or disclose the information until the claim is resolved; must take reasonable steps to retrieve the information if the party disclosed it before being notified; and may promptly present the information to the court under seal for a determination of the claim. The producing party must preserve the information until the claim is resolved. FRCP 26(b)(5)(B).

b. *Protective orders.* A party or any person from whom discovery is sought may move for a protective order in the court where the action is pending—or as an alternative on matters relating to a deposition, in the court for the district where the deposition will be taken. FRCP 26(c)(1). Refer to the United States District Court for the District of Massachusetts KeyRules Motion for Protective Order document for more information.

c. *Disclosure orders.* The judicial officer may order the parties to submit at the scheduling conference, or at any subsequent time the officer deems appropriate, sworn statements disclosing certain information to every other party. At the discretion of the judicial officer, this order may direct the submission of:

   i. A sworn statement from a claimant, whether plaintiff, third-party plaintiff, cross-claimant, or counter-claimant, that:

- Itemizes all economic loss and provides a computation of damages for which recovery is sought, if any, sustained before the date of service of process;

- Identifies all persons then known to the claimant or the claimant's attorney who witnessed or participated in the transaction or occurrence giving rise to the claim or otherwise known or believed to have substantial discoverable information about the claim or defenses, together with a statement of the subject and a brief summary of that information;

- Identifies all opposing parties, and all officers, directors, and employees of opposing parties, from whom statements have been obtained by or on behalf of the claimant regarding the subject matter of the claim; and

- Identifies all governmental agencies or officials then known to the claimant or the claimant's attorney to have investigated the transaction or occurrence giving rise to the claim; and

   ii. A sworn statement from a defendant, whether the direct defendant, third-party defendant, cross-claim defendant, or counterclaim defendant, that identifies:

- All persons then known to the defendant or the defendant's attorneys who witnessed the transaction or occurrence giving rise to the claim or otherwise is known or believed to have substantial discoverable information about the claims or defenses, together with a statement of the subject and a brief summary of that information;

- All opposing parties, and all officers, directors, and employees of opposing parties, from whom statements have been obtained by or on behalf of the defendant regarding the subject matter of the claims or defenses; and

- All government agencies or officials then known to the defendant or the defendant's attorneys to have investigated the transaction or occurrence giving rise to the claims or defenses. MA R USDCT LR 26.1(b).

   iii. Noncompliance may be excused only by order of the judicial officer. MA R USDCT LR 26.1(b).

d. *Uniform definitions in discovery requests*

    i. *Incorporation by reference and limitations.* The full text of the definitions set forth in MA R USDCT LR 26.5(c) is deemed incorporated by reference into all discovery requests, but shall not preclude:

- The definition of other terms specific to the particular litigation;
- The use of abbreviations; or
- A narrower definition of a term defined in MA R USDCT LR 26.5(c). MA R USDCT LR 26.5(a).

    ii. *Effect on scope of discovery.* MA R USDCT LR 26.5 is not intended to broaden or narrow the scope of discovery permitted by the Federal Rules of Civil Procedure. MA R USDCT LR 26.5(b).

    iii. *Definitions.* The following definitions apply to all discovery requests:

- *Communication.* The term "communication" means the transmittal of information (in the form of facts, ideas, inquiries, or otherwise). MA R USDCT LR 26.5(c)(1).
- *Document.* The term "document" is defined to be synonymous in meaning and equal in scope to the usage of this term in FRCP 34(a). A draft or non-identical copy is a separate document within the meaning of this term. MA R USDCT LR 26.5(c)(2).
- *Identify (with respect to persons).* When referring to a person, "to identify" means to give, to the extent known, the person's full name, present or last known address, and, when referring to a natural person, the present or last known place of employment. Once a person has been identified in accordance with this subparagraph, only the name of that person need be listed in response to subsequent discovery requesting the identification of that person. MA R USDCT LR 26.5(c)(3).
- *Identify (with respect to documents).* When referring to documents, "to identify" means to give, to the extent known, the: (1) type of document; (2) general subject matter; (3) date of the document; and (4) author(s), addressee(s), and recipient(s). MA R USDCT LR 26.5(c)(4).
- *Parties.* The terms "plaintiff" and "defendant" as well as a party's full or abbreviated name or a pronoun referring to a party mean the party and, where applicable, its officers, directors, employees, partners, corporate parent, subsidiaries, or affiliates. This definition is not intended to impose a discovery obligation on any person who is not a party to the litigation. MA R USDCT LR 26.5(c)(5).
- *Person.* The term "person" is defined as any natural person or any business, legal, or governmental entity or association. MA R USDCT LR 26.5(c)(6).
- *Concerning.* The term "concerning" means referring to, describing, evidencing, or constituting. MA R USDCT LR 26.5(c)(7).
- *State the basis.* When an interrogatory calls upon a party to "state the basis" of or for a particular claim, assertion, allegation, or contention, the party shall: (1) identify each and every document (and, where pertinent, the section, article, or subparagraph thereof), which forms any part of the source of the party's information regarding the alleged facts or legal conclusions referred to by the interrogatory; (2) identify each and every communication which forms any part of the source of the party's information regarding the alleged facts or legal conclusions referred to by the interrogatory; (3) state separately the acts or omissions to act on the part of any person (identifying the acts or omissions to act by stating their nature, time, and place and identifying the persons involved) which form any part of the party's information regarding the alleged facts or legal conclusions referred to in the interrogatory; and (4) state separately any other fact which forms the basis of the party's information regarding the alleged facts or conclusions referred to in the interrogatory. MA R USDCT LR 26.5(c)(8).

e. *Cooperative discovery.* The judicial officer should encourage cost effective discovery by means of voluntary exchange of information among litigants and their attorneys. This may be accomplished through the use of: (1) informal, cooperative discovery practices in which counsel provide information to opposing counsel without resort to formal discovery procedures; or (2) stipulations entered into by the parties with respect to deposition notices, waiver of signing, and other matters, except that the parties may not enter into stipulations extending the time for responding to discovery requests or otherwise modify discovery procedures ordered by the judicial officer. MA R USDCT LR 26.1(a).

f. *Phasing of discovery.* In order to facilitate settlement and the efficient completion of discovery, the judicial officer has discretion to structure discovery activities by phasing and sequencing the topics which are the subject of discovery. For example, an order may be framed limiting the first phase to developing information needed for a realistic assessment of the case. If the case does not terminate, the second phase would be directed at information needed to prepare for trial. MA R USDCT LR 26.3.

g.   *Sequence of discovery.* Unless the parties stipulate or the court orders otherwise for the parties' and witnesses' convenience and in the interests of justice: (1) methods of discovery may be used in any sequence; and (2) discovery by one party does not require any other party to delay its discovery. FRCP 26(d)(3).

2.   *Response to interrogatories*

a.   *Answers and objections.* Answers and objections in response to interrogatories, served pursuant to FRCP 33 shall be made in the order of the interrogatories propounded. MA R USDCT LR 33.1(a)(1). Each answer, statement, or objection shall be preceded by the interrogatory to which it responds. MA R USDCT LR 33.1(a)(2).

   i.   *Responding party.* The interrogatories must be answered: (1) by the party to whom they are directed; or (2) if that party is a public or private corporation, a partnership, an association, or a governmental agency, by any officer or agent, who must furnish the information available to the party. FRCP 33(b)(1). It is improper for the party's attorney to answer them, though undoubtedly the common practice is for the attorney to prepare the answers and have the party swear to them. FPP § 2172.

   ii.   *Answering each interrogatory.* Each interrogatory must, to the extent it is not objected to, be answered separately and fully in writing under oath. FRCP 33(b)(3). It has been said that interrogatories should be answered directly and without evasion in accordance with information that the answering party possesses after due inquiry. FPP § 2177.

   iii.   *Objections.* Each objection and the grounds therefor shall be stated separately. MA R USDCT LR 33.1(a)(3). The grounds for objecting to an interrogatory must be stated with specificity. Any ground not stated in a timely objection is waived unless the court, for good cause, excuses the failure. FRCP 33(b)(4); MA R USDCT LR 33.1(c)(1). No part of an interrogatory shall be left unanswered merely because an objection is interposed to another part of the interrogatory. MA R USDCT LR 33.1(c)(2).

      • *Grounds for objections.* Interrogatories may be objected to on the ground that they are not within the scope of discovery as defined in FRCP 26(b), either because they seek information not relevant to the subject matter of the action, or information that is privileged, or information that is protected by the work-product rule and for which the requisite showing has not been made, or information of experts that is not discoverable. FPP § 2174. But this does not exhaust the grounds on which objection can be made. FPP § 2174.

   iv.   *Claims of privilege.* When a claim of privilege is asserted in objection to any interrogatory, or any subpart thereof, and an answer is not provided on the basis of that assertion, the attorney asserting the privilege shall identify in the objection the nature of the privilege that is being claimed. If the privilege is being asserted in connection with a claim or defense governed by state law, the attorney asserting the privilege shall indicate the particular privilege rule that is being invoked. MA R USDCT LR 33.1(e).

   v.   *Qualifying answers.* If the party to whom the interrogatory is addressed thinks that there is uncertainty in the meaning of the interrogatory, it may qualify its answer if need be. FPP § 2168.

   vi.   *Signature.* The person who makes the answers must sign them, and the attorney who objects must sign any objections. FRCP 33(b)(5). Refer to the Format section of this document for more information on signing discovery papers.

b.   *Use.* An answer to an interrogatory may be used to the extent allowed by the Federal Rules of Evidence. FRCP 33(c).

c.   *Option to produce business records.* If the answer to an interrogatory may be determined by examining, auditing, compiling, abstracting, or summarizing a party's business records (including electronically stored information), and if the burden of deriving or ascertaining the answer will be substantially the same for either party, the responding party may answer by:

   i.   Specifying the records that must be reviewed, in sufficient detail to enable the interrogating party to locate and identify them as readily as the responding party could; and

   ii.   Giving the interrogating party a reasonable opportunity to examine and audit the records and to make copies, compilations, abstracts, or summaries. FRCP 33(d).

   iii.   Whenever a party answers any interrogatory by reference to records from which the answer may be derived or ascertained, as permitted in FRCP 33(c):

      • The specification of documents to be produced shall be in sufficient detail to permit the interrogating party to locate and identify the records and to ascertain the answer as readily as could the party from whom discovery is sought;

- The producing party shall make available any computerized information or summaries thereof that it either has, or can adduce by a relatively simple procedure, unless these materials are privileged or otherwise immune from discovery;

- The producing party shall provide any relevant compilations, abstracts, or summaries in its custody or readily obtainable by it, unless these materials are privileged or otherwise immune from discovery; and

- The documents shall be made available for inspection and copying within fourteen (14) days after service of the answers to interrogatories or at a date agreed upon by the parties. MA R USDCT LR 33.1(b).

d. *Copying expense for discovery materials*

    i. *Inspection of documents.* Except as otherwise provided in an order entered pursuant to FRCP 26(c), all parties to an action shall be entitled to inspect documents produced by another party pursuant to FRCP 33(c) or FRCP 34 at the location where they are produced. MA R USDCT LR 26.6(b)(1).

    ii. *Copies of documents.* Except as otherwise provided in an order entered pursuant to FRCP 26(c), upon request of any party, and upon that party's agreement to pay the copying costs at the time of delivery, a party who produces documents pursuant to FRCP 33(c) or FRCP 34 shall provide copies of all or any specified part of the documents. No party shall be entitled to obtain copies of documents produced by another party pursuant to FRCP 33(c) or FRCP 34 without paying the costs thereof. MA R USDCT LR 26.6(b)(2).

3. *Supplementing disclosures and responses.* A party who has made a disclosure under FRCP 26(a)—or who has responded to an interrogatory, request for production, or request for admission—must supplement or correct its disclosure or response: (1) in a timely manner if the party learns that in some material respect the disclosure or response is incomplete or incorrect, and if the additional or corrective information has not otherwise been made known to the other parties during the discovery process or in writing; or (2) as ordered by the court. FRCP 26(e)(1).

4. *Sanctions for failure to cooperate in discovery.* The court where the action is pending may, on motion, order sanctions if a party, after being properly served with interrogatories under FRCP 33 or a request for inspection under FRCP 34, fails to serve its answers, objections, or written response. FRCP 37(d)(1)(A)(ii). If a motion to compel is granted, the court must, after giving an opportunity to be heard, require the party or deponent whose conduct necessitated the motion, the party or attorney advising that conduct, or both to pay the movant's reasonable expenses incurred in making the motion, including attorney's fees. But the court must not order this payment if the opposing party's nondisclosure, response, or objection was substantially justified. FRCP 37(a)(5)(A)(ii). Refer to the United States District Court for the District of Massachusetts KeyRules Motion for Discovery Sanctions document for more information.

5. *Stipulations about discovery procedure.* Unless the court orders otherwise, the parties may stipulate that: (1) a deposition may be taken before any person, at any time or place, on any notice, and in the manner specified—in which event it may be used in the same way as any other deposition; and (2) other procedures governing or limiting discovery be modified—but a stipulation extending the time for any form of discovery must have court approval if it would interfere with the time set for completing discovery, for hearing a motion, or for trial. FRCP 29.

6. *Alternative dispute resolution (ADR).* The judicial officer assigned to preside over the case shall encourage the resolution of disputes by settlement or other alternative dispute resolution programs. MA R USDCT LR 16.4(a).

a. *Settlement.* At every conference conducted under the Local Rules of the United States District Court for the District of Massachusetts, the judicial officer shall inquire as to the utility of the parties conducting settlement negotiations, explore means of facilitating those negotiations, and offer whatever assistance may be appropriate in the circumstances. Assistance may include a reference of the case to another judicial officer for settlement purposes. MA R USDCT LR 16.4(b).

    i. When a case is settled, the parties shall file with the clerk a signed agreement for judgment or stipulation for dismissal, as appropriate, within twenty-eight (28) days, unless the court otherwise orders. MA R USDCT LR 68.2.

b. *Alternative dispute resolution programs*

    i. *Discretion of judicial officer.* The judicial officer, following an exploration of the matter with all counsel, may refer appropriate cases to alternative dispute resolution programs that have been designated for use in the district court or that the judicial officer may make available. The dispute resolution programs described in MA R USDCT LR 16.4(c)(2) through MA R USDCT LR 16.4(c)(4) are illustrative, not exclusive. Moreover, nothing in MA R USDCT LR 16.4 shall preclude the parties from engaging in private dispute resolution programs as long as they comply with any schedule established by the court. MA R USDCT LR 16.4(c)(1).

ii. *Mediation.* The judicial officer may refer the case to mediation upon the agreement of all parties. MA R USDCT LR 16.4(c)(2)(A).

iii. *Other alternative dispute resolution programs.* Use of mediation is not exclusive. At the request of parties, the judicial officer may consider other forms of alternative dispute resolution including, but not limited to, mini-trial, summary jury trial and arbitration. MA R USDCT LR 16.4(c)(3).

c. For more information on alternative dispute resolution (ADR), refer to MA R USDCT LR 16.4.

7. *Sanctions.* Failure to comply with any of the directions or obligations set forth in, or authorized by, these rules may result in dismissal, default, or the imposition of other sanctions as deemed appropriate by the judicial officer. MA R USDCT LR 1.3. Except as provided by law, the court may impose sanctions as provided in MA R USDCT LR 1.3 for failure to comply with the Administrative Procedures for Electronic Case Filing in the United States District Court for the District of Massachusetts (MA R USDCT CM/ECF Admin) or with MA R USDCT LR 5.4. MA R USDCT CM/ECF Admin(C)(3).

## D. Documents

1. *Required documents*

   a. *Response to interrogatories.* Refer to the General Requirements section of this document for information on the response to interrogatories.

2. *Supplemental documents*

   a. *Certificate of service.* No certificate of service is required when a paper is served by filing it with the court's electronic-filing system. When a paper that is required to be served is served by other means: (1) if the paper is filed, a certificate of service must be filed with it or within a reasonable time after service; and (2) if the paper is not filed, a certificate of service need not be filed unless filing is required by court order or by local rule. FRCP 5(d)(1)(B).

## E. Format

1. *Form of documents.* The rules governing captions and other matters of form in pleadings apply to motions and other papers. FRCP 7(b)(2). The provisions of FRCP 10 and FRCP 11 concerning the form and signing of pleadings, motions, and other papers shall be applicable to all papers filed in any proceeding in this court. The board of bar overseers registration number of each attorney signing such documents, except the United States Attorney and his or her staff, shall be inscribed below the signature. MA R USDCT LR 5.1(a)(1).

   a. *Paper size and binding.* All papers filed in the court shall be adapted for flat filing, be filed on eight and one-half by eleven (8-1/2 x 11) inch paper without backers and be bound firmly by staple or some such other means (excluding paper or binder clip or rubber band). MA R USDCT LR 5.1(a)(2).

   b. *Spacing.* All papers, except discovery requests and responses, shall be double-spaced except for the identification of counsel, title of the case, footnotes, quotations and exhibits. Discovery requests and responses shall be single-spaced. MA R USDCT LR 5.1(a)(2).

   c. *Caption.* Every pleading must have a caption with the court's name, a title, a file number, and [an] FRCP 7(a) designation. FRCP 10(a).

   i. *Names of parties.* The title of the complaint must name all the parties; the title of other pleadings, after naming the first party on each side, may refer generally to other parties. FRCP 10(a).

   ii. *Request for special action.* When any pleading or other paper filed in the court includes a request for special process or relief, or any other request such that, if granted, the court will proceed other than in the ordinary course, the request shall, unless it is noted on the category sheet [see MA R USDCT LR 40.1(a)(1)], be noted on the first page to the right of or immediately beneath the caption. MA R USDCT LR 5.1(c).

   d. *Claims or defenses*

   i. *Numbered paragraphs.* A party must state its claims or defenses in numbered paragraphs, each limited as far as practicable to a single set of circumstances. A later pleading may refer by number to a paragraph in an earlier pleading. FRCP 10(b).

   ii. *Separate statements.* If doing so would promote clarity, each claim founded on a separate transaction or occurrence—and each defense other than a denial—must be stated in a separate count or defense. FRCP 10(b).

   e. *Adoption by reference.* A statement in a pleading may be adopted by reference elsewhere in the same pleading or in any other pleading or motion. FRCP 10(c).

   i. *Exhibits.* A copy of a written instrument that is an exhibit to a pleading is a part of the pleading for all purposes. FRCP 10(c).

f.  *Citations*

    i.  *Local rules.* These rules shall be known as Local Rules of the United States District Court for the District of Massachusetts and cited as "L.R., D. Mass." or "L.R." MA R USDCT LR 1.1.

    ii.  *Electronic case filing procedures.* The procedures governing electronic case filing shall be known as the "Administrative Procedures for Electronic Case Filing in the United States District Court for the District of Massachusetts." They shall be cited as "APECF." MA R USDCT CM/ECF Admin(A)(7).

g.  *Acceptance by the clerk.* The clerk must not refuse to file a paper solely because it is not in the form prescribed by the Federal Rules of Civil Procedure or by a local rule or practice. FRCP 5(d)(4).

    i.  Except for complaints and notices of appeal, papers that do not conform to the requirements of MA R USDCT LR 5.1(a)(2) shall be returned by the clerk. MA R USDCT LR 5.1(a)(2).

2.  *Form of electronic documents.* A paper filed electronically is a written paper for purposes of the Federal Rules of Civil Procedure. FRCP 5(d)(3)(D).

a.  *PDF/A format required.* The court will begin requiring submission of documents in PDF/A format in the foreseeable future. PDF/A is an enhanced version of the traditional PDF format. Newer versions of most PDF software will be able to convert to this format. Additional information on PDF/A documents may be found on the court's website. MA R USDCT CM/ECF Admin(Electronic Filing and PDF).

    i.  *Electronically converted PDF.* Electronically converted PDF documents are created from word processing documents (MS Word, WordPerfect, etc.) using any appropriate software. These documents are text searchable and the file size is generally smaller than a scanned document. CM/ECF users may use any brand of software to convert documents to PDF. MA R USDCT CM/ECF Admin(Electronic Filing and PDF).

        •  Documents converted to PDF, rather than scanned, are preferred for filing in CM/ECF. MA R USDCT CM/ECF Admin(Electronic Filing and PDF).

    ii.  *Scanned PDF.* Scanned PDF documents are created from paper documents run through an optical scanner. Scanned PDF documents are generally not searchable and have a larger file size. Please note that software used to create scanned documents may (and should) be set in such a way that the document is "text-searchable." MA R USDCT CM/ECF Admin(Electronic Filing and PDF).

b.  *Title.* All pleadings filed electronically shall be titled in accordance with the approved dictionary of civil or criminal events of the CM/ECF system of this court. A list of events is available on the CM/ECF Training Information page of the court's website. The clerk's office may, when necessary and appropriate, modify the docket entry description, or delete and re-enter the docket entry in order to comply with the court's quality assurance standards. MA R USDCT CM/ECF Admin(G)(3).

c.  *Attachments to filings and exhibits.* Attachments to filings and exhibits must be filed in accordance with the court's CM/ECF User Manual, unless otherwise ordered by the court. MA R USDCT CM/ECF Admin(O)(1).

    i.  Filers must submit as attachments only those excerpts of the referenced documents that are directly germane to the matter under consideration by the court. Excerpted material must be clearly and prominently identified as such. Users who file excerpts of documents do so without prejudice to their right to timely file additional excerpts or the complete document, as may be allowed by the court. Responding parties may timely file additional excerpts or the complete document that they believe are directly germane. MA R USDCT CM/ECF Admin(O)(2).

    ii.  Filers shall not attach as an exhibit any pleading or other paper already on file with the court in that case, but shall merely refer to that document. (See MA R USDCT CM/ECF Admin(G) for information on using hyperlinks in PDF documents filed in CM/ECF.) MA R USDCT CM/ECF Admin(O)(3).

d.  *Redacted documents.* The parties may request or the court may require the submission of documents that have been redacted/stripped of sensitive or confidential information. The redacted document prepared for electronic filing shall include the original caption of the document, and be clearly labeled as "Redacted Document." A specific event is available for this purpose ("Redacted Document"), found under the Other Filings/Other Documents menu option. MA R USDCT CM/ECF Admin(S).

    i.  Attorneys and pro se litigants are advised to take extra care when creating PDF documents intended for submission to CM/ECF. Steps shall be taken to ensure the documents are free of any hidden data (metadata) that may contain redacted information, or traces of information edited or deleted are not hidden in the final document. Even PDF content that has been encrypted may be recovered. An advisory document with additional information on this topic may be found on the court's website. MA R USDCT CM/ECF Admin(S).

e. *Hyperlinks.* Electronically filed documents may contain the following types of hyperlinks: (1) hyperlinks to other portions of the same document; (2) hyperlinks to other documents filed within the CM/ECF system; and (3) hyperlinks to a location on the Internet that contains a source document for a citation. MA R USDCT CM/ECF Admin(G)(7).

   i. Hyperlinks to cited authority may not replace standard citation format. Complete citations must be included in the text of the filed document. Neither a hyperlink, nor any site to which it refers, shall be considered part of the record, but are simply convenient mechanisms for accessing material cited in a document filed in CM/ECF. Instructions on creating hyperlinks may be found in the CM/ECF User Manual. MA R USDCT CM/ECF Admin(G)(7).

   ii. The court accepts no responsibility for, and does not endorse, any product, organization, or content at any hyperlinked site, or at any site to which that site may be linked. The court accepts no responsibility for the availability or functionality of any hyperlink. MA R USDCT CM/ECF Admin(G)(7).

   iii. One feature of PDF/A documents is that hyperlinks are commonly "masked," meaning that the full address of the referenced file is not written out; for example, clicking the word brief may open a brief which was previously filed in CM/ECF. MA R USDCT CM/ECF Admin(G)(7)(NOTE). An "unmasked" hyperlink has the full address visible to the user. MA R USDCT CM/ECF Admin(G)(7)(NOTE).

   - Masked hyperlinks may or may not work in a PDF/A document, depending on how it was created. Currently, masked hyperlinks are preserved in PDF/A documents produced by the "Save As" method in Microsoft Word 2007 and 2010; the "PDFMaker" method in Microsoft Word 2007; and OpenOffice 2.4 ("PDF Export"). With other production methods, such as WordPerfect, the PDF/A document includes underlined words that appear to be links, but clicking them has no effect. MA R USDCT CM/ECF Admin(G)(7)(NOTE).

f. *Documents features not accepted.* CM/ECF will not accept PDF documents containing tracking tags, embedded systems commands, password protections, access restrictions or other security features, special tags or dynamic features. MA R USDCT CM/ECF Admin(G)(8).

g. *File size limitations.* A filing party shall limit the size of each PDF file to no more than twenty (20) megabytes. PDF files larger than seven (7) megabytes will be rejected by the CM/ECF system. The filer will see a message advising of the size limitation. MA R USDCT CM/ECF Admin(P)(2).

   i. Larger documents or exhibits may be submitted electronically if split into separate PDF files each less than seven (7) megabytes, attached to the main document and clearly labeled. MA R USDCT CM/ECF Admin(P)(2).

   ii. Documents submitted electronically or on paper are subject to the page limitations set by MA R USDCT LR 7.1(b)(4) or by order of the court. MA R USDCT CM/ECF Admin(P)(1).

h. *Accuracy and readability.* The filer shall verify the accuracy and readability of any PDF file before electronically filing it in CM/ECF. MA R USDCT CM/ECF Admin(G)(6); MA R USDCT CM/ECF Admin(P)(3).

3. *Signing disclosures and discovery requests, responses, and objections.* FRCP 11 does not apply to disclosures and discovery requests, responses, objections, and motions under FRCP 26 through FRCP 37. FRCP 11(d).

a. *Signature required.* Every disclosure under FRCP 26(a)(1) or FRCP 26(a)(3) and every discovery request, response, or objection must be signed by at least one attorney of record in the attorney's own name—or by the party personally, if unrepresented—and must state the signer's address, e-mail address, and telephone number. FRCP 26(g)(1). The provisions of the Federal Rules of Civil Procedure pertaining to the form and signing of pleadings, motions, and other papers shall be applicable to all papers filed in any proceeding in this court. The board of bar overseers registration number of each attorney signing such documents, except the United States Attorney and his staff, shall be inscribed below the signature. MA R USDCT LR 5.1(a)(1).

   i. *Electronic signing.* A filing made through a person's electronic-filing account and authorized by that person, together with that person's name on a signature block, constitutes the person's signature. FRCP 5(d)(3)(C).

   ii. *Appearances.* The filing of an appearance or any other pleading signed on behalf of a party constitutes an entry of appearance for that party. All pleadings shall contain the name, bar admission number, address, telephone number, and e-mail address of the attorney entering an appearance. MA R USDCT LR 83.5.2(a).

   - *Appearances by law firms.* When a party is represented by a law firm, the appearance must include the name and the signature of at least one individual attorney. When a party is represented by more than one attorney from the same or different law firms, the attorney entering the appearance must designate the individual attorney who is authorized to receive all notices in the case. Any notice sent to an attorney so designated

shall be deemed to be proper notice unless the court finds that notice was not properly sent. MA R USDCT LR 83.5.2(b).

- For more information on appearances, refer to MA R USDCT LR 83.5.2.

iii. *Signatures of attorneys.* The user login and password required to submit documents to the CM/ECF system shall serve as that user's signature for purposes of FRCP 11 and for all other purposes under the Federal Rules of Civil Procedure and the Local Rules of the United States District Court for the District of Massachusetts. All electronically filed documents must include a signature block and must set forth the attorney's name, bar number, address, telephone number and email address. The name of the CM/ECF user under whose log-in and password the document is submitted must be preceded by a "/s/" and typed in the space where the signature would otherwise appear. MA R USDCT CM/ECF Admin(M)(1). For an example, refer to MA R USDCT CM/ECF Admin(M)(1).

iv. *Signatures of pro se parties.* Any document requiring a signature that is filed by a party appearing pro se shall bear the words "pro se" following that party's signature. Any such document shall also state the party's mailing address, telephone number (if any), and e-mail address (if the party has consented to service by email). MA R USDCT LR 83.5.5(g). For more information on practice by pro se litigants, refer to MA R USDCT LR 83.5.5.

v. *Multiple signatures.* The filer of any document requiring more than one signature (e.g, stipulations, joint motions, joint status reports, magistrate judge consent forms, etc.) must list thereon all the names of other signatories by means of a "/s/ name of signatory" block for each. By submitting such a document, the filing attorney certifies that each of the other signatories has expressly agreed to the form and substance of the document and that the filing attorney has their actual authority to submit the document electronically. MA R USDCT CM/ECF Admin(M)(2). For more information, refer to MA R USDCT CM/ECF Admin(M)(2).

vi. *Affidavits.* Except as provided in MA R USDCT CM/ECF Admin(L), affidavits shall be filed electronically; however, the electronically filed version must contain a "/s/ name of signatory" block indicating that the paper document bears an original signature. MA R USDCT CM/ECF Admin(M)(3). The court will also accept a scanned version of the original, signed document. MA R USDCT CM/ECF Admin(M)(3). For more information, refer to MA R USDCT CM/ECF Admin(M)(3).

b. *Effect of signature.* By signing, an attorney or party certifies that to the best of the person's knowledge, information, and belief formed after a reasonable inquiry:

i. With respect to a disclosure, it is complete and correct as of the time it is made; and

ii. With respect to a discovery request, response, or objection, it is:

- Consistent with the Federal Rules of Civil Procedure and warranted by existing law or by a nonfrivolous argument for extending, modifying, or reversing existing law, or for establishing new law;

- Not interposed for any improper purpose, such as to harass, cause unnecessary delay, or needlessly increase the cost of litigation; and

- Neither unreasonable nor unduly burdensome or expensive, considering the needs of the case, prior discovery in the case, the amount in controversy, and the importance of the issues at stake in the action. FRCP 26(g)(1).

c. *Failure to sign.* Other parties have no duty to act on an unsigned disclosure, request, response, or objection until it is signed, and the court must strike it unless a signature is promptly supplied after the omission is called to the attorney's or party's attention. FRCP 26(g)(2).

d. *Sanction for improper certification.* If a certification violates FRCP 26(g) without substantial justification, the court, on motion or on its own, must impose an appropriate sanction on the signer, the party on whose behalf the signer was acting, or both. The sanction may include an order to pay the reasonable expenses, including attorney's fees, caused by the violation. FRCP 26(g)(3). Refer to the United States District Court for the District of Massachusetts KeyRules Motion for Discovery Sanctions document for more information.

4. *Privacy protection for filings made with the court*

a. *Redacted filings.* Unless the court orders otherwise, in an electronic or paper filing with the court that contains an individual's Social Security number, taxpayer-identification number, or birth date, the name of an individual known to be a minor, or a financial-account number, a party or nonparty making the filing may include only:

i. The last four (4) digits of the Social Security number and taxpayer-identification number;

ii. The year of the individual's birth;

      iii.   The minor's initials; and

      iv.   The last four (4) digits of the financial-account number. FRCP 5.2(a); MA R USDCT CM/ECF Admin(N).

b.   *Exemptions from the redaction requirement.* The redaction requirement does not apply to the following:

      i.   A financial-account number that identifies the property allegedly subject to forfeiture in a forfeiture proceeding;

      ii.   The record of an administrative or agency proceeding;

      iii.   The official record of a state-court proceeding;

      iv.   The record of a court or tribunal, if that record was not subject to the redaction requirement when originally filed;

      v.   A filing covered by FRCP 5.2(c) or FRCP 5.2(d); and

      vi.   A pro se filing in an action brought under 28 U.S.C.A. § 2241, 28 U.S.C.A. § 2254, or 28 U.S.C.A. § 2255. FRCP 5.2(b).

c.   *Limitations on remote access to electronic files; Social Security appeals and immigration cases.* Unless the court orders otherwise, in an action for benefits under the Social Security Act, and in an action or proceeding relating to an order of removal, to relief from removal, or to immigration benefits or detention, access to an electronic file is authorized as follows:

      i.   The parties and their attorneys may have remote electronic access to any part of the case file, including the administrative record;

      ii.   Any other person may have electronic access to the full record at the courthouse, but may have remote electronic access only to:

          • The docket maintained by the court; and

          • An opinion, order, judgment, or other disposition of the court, but not any other part of the case file or the administrative record. FRCP 5.2(c).

d.   *Filings made under seal.* The court may order that a filing be made under seal without redaction. The court may later unseal the filing or order the person who made the filing to file a redacted version for the public record. FRCP 5.2(d).

e.   *Protective orders.* For good cause, the court may by order in a case:

      i.   Require redaction of additional information; or

      ii.   Limit or prohibit a nonparty's remote electronic access to a document filed with the court. FRCP 5.2(e).

f.   *Option for additional unredacted filing under seal.* A person making a redacted filing may also file an unredacted copy under seal. The court must retain the unredacted copy as part of the record. FRCP 5.2(f). For more information, refer to MA R USDCT LR 7.2.

g.   *Option for filing a reference list.* A filing that contains redacted information may be filed together with a reference list that identifies each item of redacted information and specifies an appropriate identifier that uniquely corresponds to each item listed. The list must be filed under seal and may be amended as of right. Any reference in the case to a listed identifier will be construed to refer to the corresponding item of information. FRCP 5.2(g).

h.   *Responsibility for redaction.* The clerk's office is not responsible for reviewing documents filed with the court to determine whether pleadings have been redacted and are in the proper form. MA R USDCT CM/ECF Admin(N).

i.   *Waiver of protection of identifiers.* A person waives the protection of FRCP 5.2(a) as to the person's own information by filing it without redaction and not under seal. FRCP 5.2(h).

## F.  Filing and Service Requirements

1.  *Filing requirements*

   a.   *Required filings.* Any paper after the complaint that is required to be served must be filed no later than a reasonable time after service. But disclosures under FRCP 26(a)(1) or FRCP 26(a)(2) and the following discovery requests and responses must not be filed until they are used in the proceeding or the court orders filing: depositions, interrogatories, requests for documents or tangible things or to permit entry onto land, and requests for admission. FRCP 5(d)(1)(A). Refer to the United States District Court for the District of Massachusetts KeyRules pleading and motion documents for information on filing with the court.

   b.   *Nonfiling of discovery materials.* Discovery materials (that is, automatic or voluntary disclosure materials, depositions, deposition notices, interrogatories, requests for documents, requests for admissions, answers and responses to discovery requests, and any other requests for or products of the discovery process) shall not be filed unless so ordered by the court or for use in the proceeding. The party taking a deposition or obtaining any material through discovery is responsible for its preservation and delivery to the court if needed or so ordered. If for any reason a party or concerned citizen believes that any of the named documents should be filed, an ex parte request may be made that such document be filed, stating the reasons for the request. The court may also order filing sua sponte. MA R USDCT LR 26.6(a).

    i.   *Discovery motions.* If relief is sought under FRCP 26(c) or FRCP 37, copies of the relevant portions of disputed documents shall be filed with the court contemporaneously with any motion. MA R USDCT LR 26.6(a).

    ii.   *Motions for summary judgment.* If the moving party under FRCP 56 or the opponent relies on discovery documents, copies of the pertinent parts thereof shall be filed with the motion or opposition. MA R USDCT LR 26.6(a).

2.   *Service requirements.* Service of all pleadings subsequent to the original complaint and of all other papers required to be served shall be made in the manner specified by FRCP 5. MA R USDCT LR 5.2(a).

  a.   *Service; When required*

    i.   *In general.* Unless the Federal Rules of Civil Procedure provide otherwise, each of the following papers must be served on every party:

- An order stating that service is required;

- A pleading filed after the original complaint, unless the court orders otherwise under FRCP 5(c) because there are numerous defendants;

- A discovery paper required to be served on a party, unless the court orders otherwise;

- A written motion, except one that may be heard ex parte; and

- A written notice, appearance, demand, or offer of judgment, or any similar paper. FRCP 5(a)(1).

    ii.   *If a party fails to appear.* No service is required on a party who is in default for failing to appear. But a pleading that asserts a new claim for relief against such a party must be served on that party under FRCP 4. FRCP 5(a)(2).

    iii.   *Seizing property.* If an action is begun by seizing property and no person is or need be named as a defendant, any service required before the filing of an appearance, answer, or claim must be made on the person who had custody or possession of the property when it was seized. FRCP 5(a)(3).

  b.   *Service; How made*

    i.   *Serving an attorney.* If a party is represented by an attorney, service under FRCP 5 must be made on the attorney unless the court orders service on the party. FRCP 5(b)(1).

    ii.   *Service in general.* A paper is served under FRCP 5 by:

- Handing it to the person;

- Leaving it: (1) at the person's office with a clerk or other person in charge or, if no one is in charge, in a conspicuous place in the office; or (2) if the person has no office or the office is closed, at the person's dwelling or usual place of abode with someone of suitable age and discretion who resides there;

- Mailing it to the person's last known address—in which event service is complete upon mailing;

- Leaving it with the court clerk if the person has no known address;

- Sending it to a registered user by filing it with the court's electronic-filing system or sending it by other electronic means that the person consented to in writing—in either of which events service is complete upon filing or sending, but is not effective if the filer or sender learns that it did not reach the person to be served; or

- Delivering it by any other means that the person consented to in writing—in which event service is complete when the person making service delivers it to the agency designated to make delivery. FRCP 5(b)(2).

    iii.   *Service by electronic means.* Unless exempt or otherwise ordered by the court, all pleadings and other papers must be served on other parties by electronic means. MA R USDCT LR 5.4(C); MA R USDCT CM/ECF Admin(H)(2). Service by electronic means shall be treated the same as service by mail. MA R USDCT CM/ECF Admin(H)(4).

- *Consent to electronic service.* Registering to use CM/ECF constitutes consent to service of all documents

393

by electronic means as provided in the Administrative Procedures for Electronic Case Filing in the United States District Court for the District of Massachusetts (MA R USDCT CM/ECF Admin) and FRCP 5(b) and FRCP 77(d). MA R USDCT CM/ECF Admin(E)(6); MA R USDCT CM/ECF Admin(H)(3).

- *Service on registered ECF users.* Transmission of the Notice of Electronic Filing (NEF) through the court's transmission facilities will constitute service of the filed document upon a registered ECF user. MA R USDCT LR 5.4(C).

- *Service on non-registered users.* The party filing the document electronically is responsible for serving a paper copy of the document by mail in accordance with FRCP 5(b) to those case participants who have not been identified on the NEF as electronic recipients. MA R USDCT CM/ECF Admin(H)(3).

- *Service of conventionally filed papers.* Documents or exhibits submitted conventionally shall be served on other parties by the filer using traditional means. MA R USDCT CM/ECF Admin(P)(4).

   c. *Serving numerous defendants*

     i. *In general.* If an action involves an unusually large number of defendants, the court may, on motion or on its own, order that:

- Defendants' pleadings and replies to them need not be served on other defendants;

- Any crossclaim, counterclaim, avoidance, or affirmative defense in those pleadings and replies to them will be treated as denied or avoided by all other parties; and

- Filing any such pleading and serving it on the plaintiff constitutes notice of the pleading to all parties. FRCP 5(c)(1).

     ii. *Notifying parties.* A copy of every such order must be served on the parties as the court directs. FRCP 5(c)(2).

## G. Hearings

1. There is no hearing contemplated in the federal statutes or rules for responses to interrogatories.

## H. Forms

### 1. Federal Response to Interrogatories Forms

   a. Answers to interrogatories. 3A FEDFORMS § 24:34.

   b. Answers to interrogatories; Complete set. 3A FEDFORMS § 24:35.

   c. Amendments to answers to interrogatories. 3A FEDFORMS § 24:36.

   d. Supplemental answer to plaintiff's interrogatories. 3A FEDFORMS § 24:37.

   e. Second supplemental answer to plaintiff's interrogatories. 3A FEDFORMS § 24:38.

   f. Supplementation of response to interrogatory. 3A FEDFORMS § 24:39.

   g. Answers by individual. 3A FEDFORMS § 24:41.

   h. Answers by corporation. 3A FEDFORMS § 24:42.

   i. Declaration; Answers by individual. 3A FEDFORMS § 24:43.

   j. Declaration; Answers by corporation. 3A FEDFORMS § 24:44.

   k. Objections to interrogatories. 3A FEDFORMS § 24:45.

   l. Objections to interrogatories; Defendant's objections. 3A FEDFORMS § 24:46.

   m. Objections to interrogatories; Corporate merger. 3A FEDFORMS § 24:47.

   n. Objections to interrogatories; With answers. 3A FEDFORMS § 24:48.

   o. Statement in answer as to interrogatory to which objection made. 3A FEDFORMS § 24:49.

   p. Introductory statement; Answer to interrogatories. AMJUR PP DEPOSITION § 407.

   q. Answers to interrogatories; Illustrative form. AMJUR PP DEPOSITION § 408.

   r. Response to interrogatories; Illustrative form. AMJUR PP DEPOSITION § 409.

   s. Verification; By defendant; Of answers to interrogatories. AMJUR PP DEPOSITION § 410.

   t. Answers; To interrogatories; Outline form. FEDPROF § 23:352.

   u. Answers; To interrogatories; By two defendants; Outline form. FEDPROF § 23:353.

    v.    Objections to interrogatories; Illustrative grounds. FEDPROF § 23:375.

    w.   Answer to interrogatories. GOLDLTGFMS § 26:72.

    x.    Answer to interrogatories; Pursuant to civil procedure rules. GOLDLTGFMS § 26:73.

    y.    Answer to interrogatories; Corporate information as basis for answers. GOLDLTGFMS § 26:74.

    z.    Answer to interrogatories; Expert not yet selected. GOLDLTGFMS § 26:75.

## I. Applicable Rules

1. *Federal rules*

   a. Serving and filing pleadings and other papers. FRCP 5.

   b. Privacy protection for filings made with the court. FRCP 5.2.

   c. Computing and extending time; Time for motion papers. FRCP 6.

   d. Pleadings allowed; Form of motions and other papers. FRCP 7.

   e. Form of pleadings. FRCP 10.

   f. Signing pleadings, motions, and other papers; Representations to the court; Sanctions. FRCP 11.

   g. Duty to disclose; General provisions governing discovery. FRCP 26.

   h. Stipulations about discovery procedure. FRCP 29.

   i. Interrogatories to parties. FRCP 33.

   j. Failure to make disclosures or to cooperate in discovery; Sanctions. FRCP 37.

2. *Local rules*

   a. Title. MA R USDCT LR 1.1.

   b. Sanctions. MA R USDCT LR 1.3.

   c. Form and filing of papers. MA R USDCT LR 5.1.

   d. Service and filing of pleadings and other papers. MA R USDCT LR 5.2.

   e. Filing and service by electronic means. MA R USDCT LR 5.4.

   f. Alternative dispute resolution. MA R USDCT LR 16.4.

   g. Control of discovery. MA R USDCT LR 26.1.

   h. Phasing of discovery. MA R USDCT LR 26.3.

   i. Uniform definitions in discovery requests. MA R USDCT LR 26.5.

   j. Court filings and costs. MA R USDCT LR 26.6.

   k. Interrogatories. MA R USDCT LR 33.1.

   l. Settlement. MA R USDCT LR 68.2.

   m. Office of the clerk. MA R USDCT LR 77.2.

   n. Appearances. MA R USDCT LR 83.5.2.

   o. Practice by pro se litigants. MA R USDCT LR 83.5.5.

   p. CM/ECF case management/electronic case files administrative procedures. MA R USDCT CM/ECF Admin.

## Requests, Notices and Applications
## Request for Production of Documents

**Document Last Updated December 2018**

## A. Checklist

(I)  ❏  Matters to be considered by requesting party

   (a)  ❏  Required documents

      (1)  ❏  Request for production of documents

(b) ❑ Supplemental documents

    (1) ❑ Subpoena

    (2) ❑ Certificate of service

(c) ❑ Timing

    (1) ❑ More than twenty-one (21) days after the summons and complaint are served on a party, a request under FRCP 34 may be delivered: (1) to that party by any other party, and (2) by that party to any plaintiff or to any other party that has been served

    (2) ❑ A party may not seek discovery from any source before the parties have conferred as required by FRCP 26(f), except in a proceeding exempted from initial disclosure under FRCP 26(a)(1)(B), or when authorized by the Federal Rules of Civil Procedure, by stipulation, or by court order

(II) ❑ Matters to be considered by responding party

  (a) ❑ Required documents

    (1) ❑ Response to request for production of documents

  (b) ❑ Supplemental documents

    (1) ❑ Certificate of service

  (c) ❑ Timing

    (1) ❑ The party to whom the request is directed must respond in writing within thirty (30) days after being served or—if the request was delivered under FRCP 26(d)(2)—within thirty (30) days after the parties' first FRCP 26(f) conference

    (2) ❑ Answers to a document request with respect to which objections were served and which are subsequently required to be answered shall be served within fourteen (14) days after it is determined that they should be answered, unless the court directs otherwise

## B. Timing

1. *Request for production of documents.* Generally, a party may not seek discovery from any source before the parties have conferred as required by FRCP 26(f), except in a proceeding exempted from initial disclosure or when authorized by the Federal Rules of Civil Procedure, by stipulation, or by court order. FEDPROC § 26:586. Discovery under FRCP 34 should ordinarily precede the trial, and a court may refuse to permit discovery shortly before the trial date. FEDPROC § 26:586.

  a. *Early FRCP 34 requests*

    i. *Time to deliver.* More than twenty-one (21) days after the summons and complaint are served on a party, a request under FRCP 34 may be delivered:

      • To that party by any other party, and

      • By that party to any plaintiff or to any other party that has been served. FRCP 26(d)(2)(A).

    ii. *When considered served.* The request is considered to have been served at the first FRCP 26(f) conference. FRCP 26(d)(2)(B).

2. *Commencement of discovery.* A party may not seek discovery from any source before the parties have conferred as required by FRCP 26(f), except in a proceeding exempted from initial disclosure under FRCP 26(a)(1)(B), or when authorized by the Federal Rules of Civil Procedure, by stipulation, or by court order. FRCP 26(d)(1).

3. *Computation of time*

  a. *Computing time.* FRCP 6 applies in computing any time period specified in the Federal Rules of Civil Procedure, in any local rule or court order, or in any statute that does not specify a method of computing time. FRCP 6(a).

    i. *Period stated in days or a longer unit.* When the period is stated in days or a longer unit of time:

      • Exclude the day of the event that triggers the period;

      • Count every day, including intermediate Saturdays, Sundays, and legal holidays; and

      • Include the last day of the period, but if the last day is a Saturday, Sunday, or legal holiday, the period continues to run until the end of the next day that is not a Saturday, Sunday, or legal holiday. FRCP 6(a)(1).

    ii. *Period stated in hours.* When the period is stated in hours:

      • Begin counting immediately on the occurrence of the event that triggers the period;

- Count every hour, including hours during intermediate Saturdays, Sundays, and legal holidays; and
- If the period would end on a Saturday, Sunday, or legal holiday, the period continues to run until the same time on the next day that is not a Saturday, Sunday, or legal holiday. FRCP 6(a)(2).

iii. *Office of the clerk.* The offices of the Clerk of Court at Boston, Worcester and Springfield shall be open from 8:30 a.m. until 5:00 p.m. on all days except Saturdays, Sundays, legal holidays and other days so ordered by the court and announced in advance, if feasible. MA R USDCT LR 77.2.

iv. *Inaccessibility of the clerk's office.* Unless the court orders otherwise, if the clerk's office is inaccessible:

- On the last day for filing under FRCP 6(a)(1), then the time for filing is extended to the first accessible day that is not a Saturday, Sunday, or legal holiday; or
- During the last hour for filing under FRCP 6(a)(2), then the time for filing is extended to the same time on the first accessible day that is not a Saturday, Sunday, or legal holiday. FRCP 6(a)(3).

v. *"Last day" defined.* Unless a different time is set by a statute, local rule, or court order, the last day ends:

- For electronic filing, at midnight in the court's time zone; and
- For filing by other means, when the clerk's office is scheduled to close. FRCP 6(a)(4).

vi. *"Next day" defined.* The "next day" is determined by continuing to count forward when the period is measured after an event and backward when measured before an event. FRCP 6(a)(5).

vii. *"Legal holiday" defined.* "Legal holiday" means:

- The day set aside by statute for observing New Year's Day, Martin Luther King Jr.'s Birthday, Washington's Birthday, Memorial Day, Independence Day, Labor Day, Columbus Day, Veterans' Day, Thanksgiving Day, or Christmas Day;
- Any day declared a holiday by the President or Congress; and
- For periods that are measured after an event, any other day declared a holiday by the state where the district court is located. FRCP 6(a)(6).

b. *Computation of electronic filing deadlines.* Filing documents electronically does not alter any filing deadlines. MA R USDCT CM/ECF Admin(K); MA R USDCT LR 5.4(D). Although CM/ECF is generally available twenty-four (24) hours a day for filing, all electronic transmissions of documents must be completed prior to 6:00 PM, Eastern Standard (or Daylight Savings) Time, on the date on which it is due, in order to be considered timely filed that day. MA R USDCT CM/ECF Admin(K); MA R USDCT LR 5.4(D). When a specific time of day deadline is set by court order or stipulation, the electronic filing must be completed by that time. Documents may be filed at any time of the day on days prior to the date on which it is due. MA R USDCT CM/ECF Admin(K). A document filed electronically shall be deemed filed as of the time and date stated on the NEF received from the court. MA R USDCT CM/ECF Admin(G)(2); MA R USDCT CM/ECF Admin(K).

i. *Technical failures.* A user whose filing is made untimely as the result of a technical failure of the court's CM/ECF system may seek appropriate relief from the court. MA R USDCT CM/ECF Admin(W)(3). Technical difficulties on the filer's end, with telephone, cable lines, the filer's Internet Service Provider (ISP), or hardware or software problems, will not constitute a technical failure under the Administrative Procedures for Electronic Case Filing in the United States District Court for the District of Massachusetts (MA R USDCT CM/ECF Admin) nor excuse an untimely filing. MA R USDCT CM/ECF Admin(W)(3). As help desk support is available during normal business hours, filers are strongly urged to electronically file any documents during that period. MA R USDCT CM/ECF Admin(W)(3).

- The court has made available a public terminal (computers and scanner) in each clerk's office for registered users to scan and electronically file documents. This equipment is available during normal business hours. Users should bring their prepared document and a valid CM/ECF login and password. MA R USDCT CM/ECF Admin(W)(3).

c. *Extending time.* When an act may or must be done within a specified time, the court may, for good cause, extend the time: (1) with or without motion or notice if the court acts, or if a request is made, before the original time or its extension expires; or (2) on motion made after the time has expired if the party failed to act because of excusable neglect. FRCP 6(b)(1).

i. *Exceptions.* A court must not extend the time to act under FRCP 50(b), FRCP 50(d), FRCP 52(b), FRCP 59(b), FRCP 59(d), FRCP 59(e), and FRCP 60(b). FRCP 6(b)(2).

      ii.   Refer to the United States District Court for the District of Massachusetts KeyRules Motion for Continuance/Extension of Time document for more information on extending time.

   d.   *Additional time after certain kinds of service.* When a party may or must act within a specified time after being served and service is made under FRCP 5(b)(2)(C) (by mail), FRCP 5(b)(2)(D) (by leaving with the clerk), or FRCP 5(b)(2)(F) (by other means consented to), three (3) days are added after the period would otherwise expire under FRCP 6(a). FRCP 6(d).

## C. General Requirements

1.   *General provisions governing discovery*

   a.   *Discovery scope and limits*

      i.   *Scope in general.* Unless otherwise limited by court order, the scope of discovery is as follows: Parties may obtain discovery regarding any nonprivileged matter that is relevant to any party's claim or defense and proportional to the needs of the case, considering the importance of the issues at stake in the action, the amount in controversy, the parties' relative access to relevant information, the parties' resources, the importance of the discovery in resolving the issues, and whether the burden or expense of the proposed discovery outweighs its likely benefit. Information within this scope of discovery need not be admissible in evidence to be discoverable. FRCP 26(b)(1).

      ii.   *Limitations on frequency and extent*

- *When permitted.* By order, the court may alter the limits in the Federal Rules of Civil Procedure on the number of depositions and interrogatories or on the length of depositions under FRCP 30. By order or local rule, the court may also limit the number of requests under FRCP 36. FRCP 26(b)(2)(A).

- *Specific limitations on electronically stored information.* A party need not provide discovery of electronically stored information from sources that the party identifies as not reasonably accessible because of undue burden or cost. On motion to compel discovery or for a protective order, the party from whom discovery is sought must show that the information is not reasonably accessible because of undue burden or cost. If that showing is made, the court may nonetheless order discovery from such sources if the requesting party shows good cause, considering the limitations of FRCP 26(b)(2)(C). The court may specify conditions for the discovery. FRCP 26(b)(2)(B).

- *When required.* On motion or on its own, the court must limit the frequency or extent of discovery otherwise allowed by the Federal Rules of Civil Procedure or by local rule if it determines that: (1) the discovery sought is unreasonably cumulative or duplicative, or can be obtained from some other source that is more convenient, less burdensome, or less expensive; (2) the party seeking discovery has had ample opportunity to obtain the information by discovery in the action; or (3) the proposed discovery is outside the scope permitted by FRCP 26(b)(1). FRCP 26(b)(2)(C).

      iii.   *Trial preparation; Materials*

- *Documents and tangible things.* Ordinarily, a party may not discover documents and tangible things that are prepared in anticipation of litigation or for trial by or for another party or its representative (including the other party's attorney, consultant, surety, indemnitor, insurer, or agent). But, subject to FRCP 26(b)(4), those materials may be discovered if: (1) they are otherwise discoverable under FRCP 26(b)(1); and (2) the party shows that it has substantial need for the materials to prepare its case and cannot, without undue hardship, obtain their substantial equivalent by other means. FRCP 26(b)(3)(A).

- *Protection against disclosure.* If the court orders discovery of those materials, it must protect against disclosure of the mental impressions, conclusions, opinions, or legal theories of a party's attorney or other representative concerning the litigation. FRCP 26(b)(3)(B).

- *Previous statement.* Any party or other person may, on request and without the required showing, obtain the person's own previous statement about the action or its subject matter. If the request is refused, the person may move for a court order, and FRCP 37(a)(5) applies to the award of expenses. A previous statement is either: (1) a written statement that the person has signed or otherwise adopted or approved; or (2) a contemporaneous stenographic, mechanical, electrical, or other recording—or a transcription of it—that recites substantially verbatim the person's oral statement. FRCP 26(b)(3)(C).

      iv.   *Trial preparation; Experts*

- *Deposition of an expert who may testify.* A party may depose any person who has been identified as an expert whose opinions may be presented at trial. If FRCP 26(a)(2)(B) requires a report from the expert, the deposition may be conducted only after the report is provided. FRCP 26(b)(4)(A).

- *Trial-preparation protection for draft reports or disclosures.* FRCP 26(b)(3)(A) and FRCP 26(b)(3)(B) protect drafts of any report or disclosure required under FRCP 26(a)(2), regardless of the form in which the draft is recorded. FRCP 26(b)(4)(B).

- *Trial-preparation protection for communications between a party's attorney and expert witnesses.* FRCP 26(b)(3)(A) and FRCP 26(b)(3)(B) protect communications between the party's attorney and any witness required to provide a report under FRCP 26(a)(2)(B), regardless of the form of the communications, except to the extent that the communications: (1) relate to compensation for the expert's study or testimony; (2) identify facts or data that the party's attorney provided and that the expert considered in forming the opinions to be expressed; or (3) identify assumptions that the party's attorney provided and that the expert relied on in forming the opinions to be expressed. FRCP 26(b)(4)(C).

- *Expert employed only for trial preparation.* Ordinarily, a party may not, by interrogatories or deposition, discover facts known or opinions held by an expert who has been retained or specially employed by another party in anticipation of litigation or to prepare for trial and who is not expected to be called as a witness at trial. But a party may do so only: (1) as provided in FRCP 35(b); or (2) on showing exceptional circumstances under which it is impracticable for the party to obtain facts or opinions on the same subject by other means. FRCP 26(b)(4)(D).

- *Payment.* Unless manifest injustice would result, the court must require that the party seeking discovery: (1) pay the expert a reasonable fee for time spent in responding to discovery under FRCP 26(b)(4)(A) or FRCP 26(b)(4)(D); and (2) for discovery under FRCP 26(b)(4)(D), also pay the other party a fair portion of the fees and expenses it reasonably incurred in obtaining the expert's facts and opinions. FRCP 26(b)(4)(E).

v.  *Claiming privilege or protecting trial-preparation materials*

- *Information withheld.* When a party withholds information otherwise discoverable by claiming that the information is privileged or subject to protection as trial-preparation material, the party must: (1) expressly make the claim; and (2) describe the nature of the documents, communications, or tangible things not produced or disclosed—and do so in a manner that, without revealing information itself privileged or protected, will enable other parties to assess the claim. FRCP 26(b)(5)(A).

- *Information produced.* If information produced in discovery is subject to a claim of privilege or of protection as trial-preparation material, the party making the claim may notify any party that received the information of the claim and the basis for it. After being notified, a party must promptly return, sequester, or destroy the specified information and any copies it has; must not use or disclose the information until the claim is resolved; must take reasonable steps to retrieve the information if the party disclosed it before being notified; and may promptly present the information to the court under seal for a determination of the claim. The producing party must preserve the information until the claim is resolved. FRCP 26(b)(5)(B).

b.  *Protective orders.* A party or any person from whom discovery is sought may move for a protective order in the court where the action is pending—or as an alternative on matters relating to a deposition, in the court for the district where the deposition will be taken. FRCP 26(c)(1). Refer to the United States District Court for the District of Massachusetts KeyRules Motion for Protective Order document for more information.

c.  *Disclosure orders.* The judicial officer may order the parties to submit at the scheduling conference, or at any subsequent time the officer deems appropriate, sworn statements disclosing certain information to every other party. At the discretion of the judicial officer, this order may direct the submission of:

i.  A sworn statement from a claimant, whether plaintiff, third-party plaintiff, cross-claimant, or counter-claimant, that:

- Itemizes all economic loss and provides a computation of damages for which recovery is sought, if any, sustained before the date of service of process;

- Identifies all persons then known to the claimant or the claimant's attorney who witnessed or participated in the transaction or occurrence giving rise to the claim or otherwise known or believed to have substantial discoverable information about the claim or defenses, together with a statement of the subject and a brief summary of that information;

- Identifies all opposing parties, and all officers, directors, and employees of opposing parties, from whom statements have been obtained by or on behalf of the claimant regarding the subject matter of the claim; and

- Identifies all governmental agencies or officials then known to the claimant or the claimant's attorney to have investigated the transaction or occurrence giving rise to the claim; and

ii. A sworn statement from a defendant, whether the direct defendant, third-party defendant, cross-claim defendant, or counterclaim defendant, that identifies:

- All persons then known to the defendant or the defendant's attorneys who witnessed the transaction or occurrence giving rise to the claim or otherwise is known or believed to have substantial discoverable information about the claims or defenses, together with a statement of the subject and a brief summary of that information;

- All opposing parties, and all officers, directors, and employees of opposing parties, from whom statements have been obtained by or on behalf of the defendant regarding the subject matter of the claims or defenses; and

- All government agencies or officials then known to the defendant or the defendant's attorneys to have investigated the transaction or occurrence giving rise to the claims or defenses. MA R USDCT LR 26.1(b).

iii. Noncompliance may be excused only by order of the judicial officer. MA R USDCT LR 26.1(b).

d. *Uniform definitions in discovery requests*

i. *Incorporation by reference and limitations.* The full text of the definitions set forth in MA R USDCT LR 26.5(c) is deemed incorporated by reference into all discovery requests, but shall not preclude:

- The definition of other terms specific to the particular litigation;

- The use of abbreviations; or

- A narrower definition of a term defined in MA R USDCT LR 26.5(c). MA R USDCT LR 26.5(a).

ii. *Effect on scope of discovery.* MA R USDCT LR 26.5 is not intended to broaden or narrow the scope of discovery permitted by the Federal Rules of Civil Procedure. MA R USDCT LR 26.5(b).

iii. *Definitions.* The following definitions apply to all discovery requests:

- *Communication.* The term "communication" means the transmittal of information (in the form of facts, ideas, inquiries, or otherwise). MA R USDCT LR 26.5(c)(1).

- *Document.* The term "document" is defined to be synonymous in meaning and equal in scope to the usage of this term in FRCP 34(a). A draft or non-identical copy is a separate document within the meaning of this term. MA R USDCT LR 26.5(c)(2).

- *Identify (with respect to persons).* When referring to a person, "to identify" means to give, to the extent known, the person's full name, present or last known address, and, when referring to a natural person, the present or last known place of employment. Once a person has been identified in accordance with this subparagraph, only the name of that person need be listed in response to subsequent discovery requesting the identification of that person. MA R USDCT LR 26.5(c)(3).

- *Identify (with respect to documents).* When referring to documents, "to identify" means to give, to the extent known, the: (1) type of document; (2) general subject matter; (3) date of the document; and (4) author(s), addressee(s), and recipient(s). MA R USDCT LR 26.5(c)(4).

- *Parties.* The terms "plaintiff" and "defendant" as well as a party's full or abbreviated name or a pronoun referring to a party mean the party and, where applicable, its officers, directors, employees, partners, corporate parent, subsidiaries, or affiliates. This definition is not intended to impose a discovery obligation on any person who is not a party to the litigation. MA R USDCT LR 26.5(c)(5).

- *Person.* The term "person" is defined as any natural person or any business, legal, or governmental entity or association. MA R USDCT LR 26.5(c)(6).

- *Concerning.* The term "concerning" means referring to, describing, evidencing, or constituting. MA R USDCT LR 26.5(c)(7).

- *State the basis.* When an interrogatory calls upon a party to "state the basis" of or for a particular claim, assertion, allegation, or contention, the party shall: (1) identify each and every document (and, where pertinent, the section, article, or subparagraph thereof), which forms any part of the source of the party's information regarding the alleged facts or legal conclusions referred to by the interrogatory; (2) identify each and every communication which forms any part of the source of the party's information regarding the alleged facts or legal conclusions referred to by the interrogatory; (3) state separately the acts or omissions to act on the part of any person (identifying the acts or omissions to act by stating their nature, time, and place and identifying the persons involved) which form any part of the party's information regarding the alleged facts or legal conclusions referred to in the interrogatory; and (4) state separately any other fact which forms the basis of the party's information regarding the alleged facts or conclusions referred to in the interrogatory. MA R USDCT LR 26.5(c)(8).

e. *Cooperative discovery.* The judicial officer should encourage cost effective discovery by means of voluntary exchange of information among litigants and their attorneys. This may be accomplished through the use of: (1) informal, cooperative discovery practices in which counsel provide information to opposing counsel without resort to formal discovery procedures; or (2) stipulations entered into by the parties with respect to deposition notices, waiver of signing, and other matters, except that the parties may not enter into stipulations extending the time for responding to discovery requests or otherwise modify discovery procedures ordered by the judicial officer. MA R USDCT LR 26.1(a).

f. *Phasing of discovery.* In order to facilitate settlement and the efficient completion of discovery, the judicial officer has discretion to structure discovery activities by phasing and sequencing the topics which are the subject of discovery. For example, an order may be framed limiting the first phase to developing information needed for a realistic assessment of the case. If the case does not terminate, the second phase would be directed at information needed to prepare for trial. MA R USDCT LR 26.3.

g. *Sequence of discovery.* Unless the parties stipulate or the court orders otherwise for the parties' and witnesses' convenience and in the interests of justice: (1) methods of discovery may be used in any sequence; and (2) discovery by one party does not require any other party to delay its discovery. FRCP 26(d)(3).

2. *Request for production of documents*

a. *In general.* A party may serve on any other party a request within the scope of FRCP 26(b):

   i. To produce and permit the requesting party or its representative to inspect, copy, test, or sample the following items in the responding party's possession, custody, or control:

   - Any designated documents or electronically stored information—including writings, drawings, graphs, charts, photographs, sound recordings, images, and other data or data compilations—stored in any medium from which information can be obtained either directly or, if necessary, after translation by the responding party into a reasonably usable form; or

   - Any designated tangible things; or

   ii. To permit entry onto designated land or other property possessed or controlled by the responding party, so that the requesting party may inspect, measure, survey, photograph, test, or sample the property or any designated object or operation on it. FRCP 34(a).

b. *Number.* Unless the judicial officer orders otherwise, the number of discovery events shall be limited for each side (or group of parties with a common interest) to. . .two (2) separate sets of requests for production. MA R USDCT LR 26.1(c).

   i. *Further discovery.* Should a party exhaust the opportunities for any type of discovery events under MA R USDCT LR 26.1(c), any requests that such party may make for additional interrogatories, depositions, admissions or the production of documents beyond that allowed pursuant to MA R USDCT LR 26.1(c) shall be by discovery motion. All requests for additional discovery events, extensions of deadlines, for the completion of discovery or for postponement of the trial must be signed by the attorney and the party making the request. MA R USDCT LR 26.2(b).

c. *Contents of the request.* The request: (1) must describe with reasonable particularity each item or category of items to be inspected; (2) must specify a reasonable time, place, and manner for the inspection and for performing the related acts; and (3) may specify the form or forms in which electronically stored information is to be produced. FRCP 34(b)(1).

   i. *Description of items.* Although the phrase "reasonable particularity" eludes precise definition and depends on the facts and circumstances in each case, at least two tests have been suggested. FEDPROC § 26:588.

   - The first test is whether the request places a party on "reasonable notice" of what is called for and what is not so that a reasonable person would know what documents or things are called for. FEDPROC § 26:588.

   - The second is whether the request gives a court enough information to enable it to rule intelligently on objections. FEDPROC § 26:588.

d. *Signature.* Though FRCP 34 does not say so, it is sufficient if the request is signed by the attorney for the party seeking discovery. FPP § 2212. Refer to the Format section of this document for more information on signing of discovery papers.

e. *Other authority on production and inspection*

   i. *Freedom of Information Act (FOIA).* Although the Freedom of Information Act (FOIA) is fundamentally designed to inform the public about agency action, and not to benefit private litigants, Congress has not acted upon proposals to forbid or limit the use of the FOIA for discovery purposes. FEDPROC § 26:559; Nat'l Presto Indus., Inc., 218 Ct. Cl. 696 (1978). However, a FOIA request may not be used to supplement civil discovery under FRCP 34, as in the case where information is privileged and therefore outside the scope of civil discovery. FEDPROC § 26:559; United States v. Weber Aircraft Corp., 465 U.S. 792, 104 S. Ct. 1488, 79 L. Ed. 2d 814 (1984).

   ii. *Hague Convention.* Under the Hague Convention, a party seeking evidence abroad must obtain and send a letter of request to the central authority of the country in which the evidence is sought, requesting service of the request on the desired person or entity; if the request complies with the Convention, the central authority will then obtain the desired evidence. FEDPROC § 26:560. [Editor's note: the Hague Convention can be found at T.I.A.S. No. 6638 and is also available in the appendix to FRCP 4].

f. *Copying expense for discovery materials*

   i. *Inspection of documents.* Except as otherwise provided in an order entered pursuant to FRCP 26(c), all parties to an action shall be entitled to inspect documents produced by another party pursuant to FRCP 33(c) or FRCP 34 at the location where they are produced. MA R USDCT LR 26.6(b)(1).

   ii. *Copies of documents.* Except as otherwise provided in an order entered pursuant to FRCP 26(c), upon request of any party, and upon that party's agreement to pay the copying costs at the time of delivery, a party who produces documents pursuant to FRCP 33(c) or FRCP 34 shall provide copies of all or any specified part of the documents. No party shall be entitled to obtain copies of documents produced by another party pursuant to FRCP 33(c) or FRCP 34 without paying the costs thereof. MA R USDCT LR 26.6(b)(2).

g. *Motion to compel.* If a party who has been requested to permit discovery under FRCP 34 makes no response to the request, or if its response objects to all or part of the requested discovery, or if it otherwise fails to permit discovery as requested, the party who submitted the request, if it still wishes the discovery that has been refused, may move under FRCP 37(a) for an order compelling inspection in accordance with the request. FPP § 2214. Refer to the United States District Court for the District of Massachusetts KeyRules Motion to Compel Discovery document for more information.

3. *Sanctions for failure to cooperate in discovery.* The court where the action is pending may, on motion, order sanctions if a party, after being properly served with interrogatories under FRCP 33 or a request for inspection under FRCP 34, fails to serve its answers, objections, or written response. FRCP 37(d)(1)(A)(ii). If a motion to compel is granted, the court must, after giving an opportunity to be heard, require the party or deponent whose conduct necessitated the motion, the party or attorney advising that conduct, or both to pay the movant's reasonable expenses incurred in making the motion, including attorney's fees. But the court must not order this payment if the opposing party's nondisclosure, response, or objection was substantially justified. FRCP 37(a)(5)(A)(ii). Refer to the United States District Court for the District of Massachusetts KeyRules Motion for Discovery Sanctions document for more information.

4. *Stipulations about discovery procedure.* Unless the court orders otherwise, the parties may stipulate that: (1) a deposition may be taken before any person, at any time or place, on any notice, and in the manner specified—in which event it may be used in the same way as any other deposition; and (2) other procedures governing or limiting discovery be modified—but a stipulation extending the time for any form of discovery must have court approval if it would interfere with the time set for completing discovery, for hearing a motion, or for trial. FRCP 29.

5. *Alternative dispute resolution (ADR).* The judicial officer assigned to preside over the case shall encourage the resolution of disputes by settlement or other alternative dispute resolution programs. MA R USDCT LR 16.4(a).

   a. *Settlement.* At every conference conducted under the Local Rules of the United States District Court for the District of Massachusetts, the judicial officer shall inquire as to the utility of the parties conducting settlement negotiations, explore means of facilitating those negotiations, and offer whatever assistance may be appropriate in the circumstances. Assistance may include a reference of the case to another judicial officer for settlement purposes. MA R USDCT LR 16.4(b).

      i. When a case is settled, the parties shall file with the clerk a signed agreement for judgment or stipulation for dismissal, as appropriate, within twenty-eight (28) days, unless the court otherwise orders. MA R USDCT LR 68.2.

    b.    *Alternative dispute resolution programs*

         i.    *Discretion of judicial officer.* The judicial officer, following an exploration of the matter with all counsel, may refer appropriate cases to alternative dispute resolution programs that have been designated for use in the district court or that the judicial officer may make available. The dispute resolution programs described in MA R USDCT LR 16.4(c)(2) through MA R USDCT LR 16.4(c)(4) are illustrative, not exclusive. Moreover, nothing in MA R USDCT LR 16.4 shall preclude the parties from engaging in private dispute resolution programs as long as they comply with any schedule established by the court. MA R USDCT LR 16.4(c)(1).

         ii.    *Mediation.* The judicial officer may refer the case to mediation upon the agreement of all parties. MA R USDCT LR 16.4(c)(2)(A).

         iii.    *Other alternative dispute resolution programs.* Use of mediation is not exclusive. At the request of parties, the judicial officer may consider other forms of alternative dispute resolution including, but not limited to, mini-trial, summary jury trial and arbitration. MA R USDCT LR 16.4(c)(3).

    c.    For more information on alternative dispute resolution (ADR), refer to MA R USDCT LR 16.4.

6.    *Sanctions.* Failure to comply with any of the directions or obligations set forth in, or authorized by, these rules may result in dismissal, default, or the imposition of other sanctions as deemed appropriate by the judicial officer. MA R USDCT LR 1.3. Except as provided by law, the court may impose sanctions as provided in MA R USDCT LR 1.3 for failure to comply with the Administrative Procedures for Electronic Case Filing in the United States District Court for the District of Massachusetts (MA R USDCT CM/ECF Admin) or with MA R USDCT LR 5.4. MA R USDCT CM/ECF Admin(C)(3).

## D. Documents

1.    *Required documents*

    a.    *Request for production of documents.* Refer to the General Requirements section of this document for information on the request for production of documents.

2.    *Supplemental documents*

    a.    *Subpoena.* As provided in FRCP 45, a nonparty may be compelled to produce documents and tangible things or to permit an inspection. FRCP 34(c). For information on the form and contents of the subpoena, refer to FRCP 45.

    b.    *Certificate of service.* No certificate of service is required when a paper is served by filing it with the court's electronic-filing system. When a paper that is required to be served is served by other means: (1) if the paper is filed, a certificate of service must be filed with it or within a reasonable time after service; and (2) if the paper is not filed, a certificate of service need not be filed unless filing is required by court order or by local rule. FRCP 5(d)(1)(B).

## E. Format

1.    *Form of documents.* The rules governing captions and other matters of form in pleadings apply to motions and other papers. FRCP 7(b)(2). The provisions of FRCP 10 and FRCP 11 concerning the form and signing of pleadings, motions, and other papers shall be applicable to all papers filed in any proceeding in this court. The board of bar overseers registration number of each attorney signing such documents, except the United States Attorney and his or her staff, shall be inscribed below the signature. MA R USDCT LR 5.1(a)(1).

    a.    *Paper size and binding.* All papers filed in the court shall be adapted for flat filing, be filed on eight and one-half by eleven (8-1/2 x 11) inch paper without backers and be bound firmly by staple or some such other means (excluding paper or binder clip or rubber band). MA R USDCT LR 5.1(a)(2).

    b.    *Spacing.* All papers, except discovery requests and responses, shall be double-spaced except for the identification of counsel, title of the case, footnotes, quotations and exhibits. Discovery requests and responses shall be single-spaced. MA R USDCT LR 5.1(a)(2).

    c.    *Caption.* Every pleading must have a caption with the court's name, a title, a file number, and [an] FRCP 7(a) designation. FRCP 10(a).

         i.    *Names of parties.* The title of the complaint must name all the parties; the title of other pleadings, after naming the first party on each side, may refer generally to other parties. FRCP 10(a).

         ii.    *Request for special action.* When any pleading or other paper filed in the court includes a request for special process or relief, or any other request such that, if granted, the court will proceed other than in the ordinary course, the request shall, unless it is noted on the category sheet [see MA R USDCT LR 40.1(a)(1)], be noted on the first page to the right of or immediately beneath the caption. MA R USDCT LR 5.1(c).

d. *Claims or defenses*

    i. *Numbered paragraphs.* A party must state its claims or defenses in numbered paragraphs, each limited as far as practicable to a single set of circumstances. A later pleading may refer by number to a paragraph in an earlier pleading. FRCP 10(b).

    ii. *Separate statements.* If doing so would promote clarity, each claim founded on a separate transaction or occurrence—and each defense other than a denial—must be stated in a separate count or defense. FRCP 10(b).

e. *Adoption by reference.* A statement in a pleading may be adopted by reference elsewhere in the same pleading or in any other pleading or motion. FRCP 10(c).

    i. *Exhibits.* A copy of a written instrument that is an exhibit to a pleading is a part of the pleading for all purposes. FRCP 10(c).

f. *Citations*

    i. *Local rules.* These rules shall be known as Local Rules of the United States District Court for the District of Massachusetts and cited as "L.R., D. Mass." or "L.R." MA R USDCT LR 1.1.

    ii. *Electronic case filing procedures.* The procedures governing electronic case filing shall be known as the "Administrative Procedures for Electronic Case Filing in the United States District Court for the District of Massachusetts." They shall be cited as "APECF." MA R USDCT CM/ECF Admin(A)(7).

g. *Acceptance by the clerk.* The clerk must not refuse to file a paper solely because it is not in the form prescribed by the Federal Rules of Civil Procedure or by a local rule or practice. FRCP 5(d)(4).

    i. Except for complaints and notices of appeal, papers that do not conform to the requirements of MA R USDCT LR 5.1(a)(2) shall be returned by the clerk. MA R USDCT LR 5.1(a)(2).

2. *Form of electronic documents.* A paper filed electronically is a written paper for purposes of the Federal Rules of Civil Procedure. FRCP 5(d)(3)(D).

a. *PDF/A format required.* The court will begin requiring submission of documents in PDF/A format in the foreseeable future. PDF/A is an enhanced version of the traditional PDF format. Newer versions of most PDF software will be able to convert to this format. Additional information on PDF/A documents may be found on the court's website. MA R USDCT CM/ECF Admin(Electronic Filing and PDF).

    i. *Electronically converted PDF.* Electronically converted PDF documents are created from word processing documents (MS Word, WordPerfect, etc.) using any appropriate software. These documents are text searchable and the file size is generally smaller than a scanned document. CM/ECF users may use any brand of software to convert documents to PDF. MA R USDCT CM/ECF Admin(Electronic Filing and PDF).

        • Documents converted to PDF, rather than scanned, are preferred for filing in CM/ECF. MA R USDCT CM/ECF Admin(Electronic Filing and PDF).

    ii. *Scanned PDF.* Scanned PDF documents are created from paper documents run through an optical scanner. Scanned PDF documents are generally not searchable and have a larger file size. Please note that software used to create scanned documents may (and should) be set in such a way that the document is "text-searchable." MA R USDCT CM/ECF Admin(Electronic Filing and PDF).

b. *Title.* All pleadings filed electronically shall be titled in accordance with the approved dictionary of civil or criminal events of the CM/ECF system of this court. A list of events is available on the CM/ECF Training Information page of the court's website. The clerk's office may, when necessary and appropriate, modify the docket entry description, or delete and re-enter the docket entry in order to comply with the court's quality assurance standards. MA R USDCT CM/ECF Admin(G)(3).

c. *Attachments to filings and exhibits.* Attachments to filings and exhibits must be filed in accordance with the court's CM/ECF User Manual, unless otherwise ordered by the court. MA R USDCT CM/ECF Admin(O)(1).

    i. Filers must submit as attachments only those excerpts of the referenced documents that are directly germane to the matter under consideration by the court. Excerpted material must be clearly and prominently identified as such. Users who file excerpts of documents do so without prejudice to their right to timely file additional excerpts or the complete document, as may be allowed by the court. Responding parties may timely file additional excerpts or the complete document that they believe are directly germane. MA R USDCT CM/ECF Admin(O)(2).

    ii. Filers shall not attach as an exhibit any pleading or other paper already on file with the court in that case, but shall merely refer to that document. (See MA R USDCT CM/ECF Admin(G) for information on using hyperlinks in PDF documents filed in CM/ECF.) MA R USDCT CM/ECF Admin(O)(3).

d. *Redacted documents.* The parties may request or the court may require the submission of documents that have been redacted/stripped of sensitive or confidential information. The redacted document prepared for electronic filing shall include the original caption of the document, and be clearly labeled as "Redacted Document." A specific event is available for this purpose ("Redacted Document"), found under the Other Filings/Other Documents menu option. MA R USDCT CM/ECF Admin(S).

  i. Attorneys and pro se litigants are advised to take extra care when creating PDF documents intended for submission to CM/ECF. Steps shall be taken to ensure the documents are free of any hidden data (metadata) that may contain redacted information, or traces of information edited or deleted are not hidden in the final document. Even PDF content that has been encrypted may be recovered. An advisory document with additional information on this topic may be found on the court's website. MA R USDCT CM/ECF Admin(S).

e. *Hyperlinks.* Electronically filed documents may contain the following types of hyperlinks: (1) hyperlinks to other portions of the same document; (2) hyperlinks to other documents filed within the CM/ECF system; and (3) hyperlinks to a location on the Internet that contains a source document for a citation. MA R USDCT CM/ECF Admin(G)(7).

  i. Hyperlinks to cited authority may not replace standard citation format. Complete citations must be included in the text of the filed document. Neither a hyperlink, nor any site to which it refers, shall be considered part of the record, but are simply convenient mechanisms for accessing material cited in a document filed in CM/ECF. Instructions on creating hyperlinks may be found in the CM/ECF User Manual. MA R USDCT CM/ECF Admin(G)(7).

  ii. The court accepts no responsibility for, and does not endorse, any product, organization, or content at any hyperlinked site, or at any site to which that site may be linked. The court accepts no responsibility for the availability or functionality of any hyperlink. MA R USDCT CM/ECF Admin(G)(7).

  iii. One feature of PDF/A documents is that hyperlinks are commonly "masked," meaning that the full address of the referenced file is not written out; for example, clicking the word brief may open a brief which was previously filed in CM/ECF. MA R USDCT CM/ECF Admin(G)(7)(NOTE). An "unmasked" hyperlink has the full address visible to the user. MA R USDCT CM/ECF Admin(G)(7)(NOTE).

  - Masked hyperlinks may or may not work in a PDF/A document, depending on how it was created. Currently, masked hyperlinks are preserved in PDF/A documents produced by the "Save As" method in Microsoft Word 2007 and 2010; the "PDFMaker" method in Microsoft Word 2007; and OpenOffice 2.4 ("PDF Export"). With other production methods, such as WordPerfect, the PDF/A document includes underlined words that appear to be links, but clicking them has no effect. MA R USDCT CM/ECF Admin(G)(7)(NOTE).

f. *Documents features not accepted.* CM/ECF will not accept PDF documents containing tracking tags, embedded systems commands, password protections, access restrictions or other security features, special tags or dynamic features. MA R USDCT CM/ECF Admin(G)(8).

g. *File size limitations.* A filing party shall limit the size of each PDF file to no more than twenty (20) megabytes. PDF files larger than seven (7) megabytes will be rejected by the CM/ECF system. The filer will see a message advising of the size limitation. MA R USDCT CM/ECF Admin(P)(2).

  i. Larger documents or exhibits may be submitted electronically if split into separate PDF files each less than seven (7) megabytes, attached to the main document and clearly labeled. MA R USDCT CM/ECF Admin(P)(2).

  ii. Documents submitted electronically or on paper are subject to the page limitations set by MA R USDCT LR 7.1(b)(4) or by order of the court. MA R USDCT CM/ECF Admin(P)(1).

h. *Accuracy and readability.* The filer shall verify the accuracy and readability of any PDF file before electronically filing it in CM/ECF. MA R USDCT CM/ECF Admin(G)(6); MA R USDCT CM/ECF Admin(P)(3).

3. *Signing disclosures and discovery requests, responses, and objections.* FRCP 11 does not apply to disclosures and discovery requests, responses, objections, and motions under FRCP 26 through FRCP 37. FRCP 11(d).

a. *Signature required.* Every disclosure under FRCP 26(a)(1) or FRCP 26(a)(3) and every discovery request, response, or objection must be signed by at least one attorney of record in the attorney's own name—or by the party personally, if unrepresented—and must state the signer's address, e-mail address, and telephone number. FRCP 26(g)(1). The provisions of the Federal Rules of Civil Procedure pertaining to the form and signing of pleadings, motions, and other papers shall be applicable to all papers filed in any proceeding in this court. The board of bar overseers registration number of each attorney signing such documents, except the United States Attorney and his staff, shall be inscribed below the signature. MA R USDCT LR 5.1(a)(1).

i. *Electronic signing.* A filing made through a person's electronic-filing account and authorized by that person, together with that person's name on a signature block, constitutes the person's signature. FRCP 5(d)(3)(C).

ii. *Appearances.* The filing of an appearance or any other pleading signed on behalf of a party constitutes an entry of appearance for that party. All pleadings shall contain the name, bar admission number, address, telephone number, and e-mail address of the attorney entering an appearance. MA R USDCT LR 83.5.2(a).

- *Appearances by law firms.* When a party is represented by a law firm, the appearance must include the name and the signature of at least one individual attorney. When a party is represented by more than one attorney from the same or different law firms, the attorney entering the appearance must designate the individual attorney who is authorized to receive all notices in the case. Any notice sent to an attorney so designated shall be deemed to be proper notice unless the court finds that notice was not properly sent. MA R USDCT LR 83.5.2(b).

- For more information on appearances, refer to MA R USDCT LR 83.5.2.

iii. *Signatures of attorneys.* The user login and password required to submit documents to the CM/ECF system shall serve as that user's signature for purposes of FRCP 11 and for all other purposes under the Federal Rules of Civil Procedure and the Local Rules of the United States District Court for the District of Massachusetts. All electronically filed documents must include a signature block and must set forth the attorney's name, bar number, address, telephone number and email address. The name of the CM/ECF user under whose log-in and password the document is submitted must be preceded by a "/s/" and typed in the space where the signature would otherwise appear. MA R USDCT CM/ECF Admin(M)(1). For an example, refer to MA R USDCT CM/ECF Admin(M)(1).

iv. *Signatures of pro se parties.* Any document requiring a signature that is filed by a party appearing pro se shall bear the words "pro se" following that party's signature. Any such document shall also state the party's mailing address, telephone number (if any), and e-mail address (if the party has consented to service by email). MA R USDCT LR 83.5.5(g). For more information on practice by pro se litigants, refer to MA R USDCT LR 83.5.5.

v. *Multiple signatures.* The filer of any document requiring more than one signature (e.g, stipulations, joint motions, joint status reports, magistrate judge consent forms, etc.) must list thereon all the names of other signatories by means of a "/s/ name of signatory" block for each. By submitting such a document, the filing attorney certifies that each of the other signatories has expressly agreed to the form and substance of the document and that the filing attorney has their actual authority to submit the document electronically. MA R USDCT CM/ECF Admin(M)(2). For more information, refer to MA R USDCT CM/ECF Admin(M)(2).

vi. *Affidavits.* Except as provided in MA R USDCT CM/ECF Admin(L), affidavits shall be filed electronically; however, the electronically filed version must contain a "/s/ name of signatory" block indicating that the paper document bears an original signature. MA R USDCT CM/ECF Admin(M)(3). The court will also accept a scanned version of the original, signed document. MA R USDCT CM/ECF Admin(M)(3). For more information, refer to MA R USDCT CM/ECF Admin(M)(3).

b. *Effect of signature.* By signing, an attorney or party certifies that to the best of the person's knowledge, information, and belief formed after a reasonable inquiry:

i. With respect to a disclosure, it is complete and correct as of the time it is made; and

ii. With respect to a discovery request, response, or objection, it is:

- Consistent with the Federal Rules of Civil Procedure and warranted by existing law or by a nonfrivolous argument for extending, modifying, or reversing existing law, or for establishing new law;

- Not interposed for any improper purpose, such as to harass, cause unnecessary delay, or needlessly increase the cost of litigation; and

- Neither unreasonable nor unduly burdensome or expensive, considering the needs of the case, prior discovery in the case, the amount in controversy, and the importance of the issues at stake in the action. FRCP 26(g)(1).

c. *Failure to sign.* Other parties have no duty to act on an unsigned disclosure, request, response, or objection until it is signed, and the court must strike it unless a signature is promptly supplied after the omission is called to the attorney's or party's attention. FRCP 26(g)(2).

d. *Sanction for improper certification.* If a certification violates FRCP 26(g) without substantial justification, the court, on motion or on its own, must impose an appropriate sanction on the signer, the party on whose behalf the signer was acting, or both. The sanction may include an order to pay the reasonable expenses, including attorney's fees, caused by the violation. FRCP 26(g)(3). Refer to the United States District Court for the District of Massachusetts KeyRules Motion for Discovery Sanctions document for more information.

4. *Privacy protection for filings made with the court*

a. *Redacted filings.* Unless the court orders otherwise, in an electronic or paper filing with the court that contains an individual's Social Security number, taxpayer-identification number, or birth date, the name of an individual known to be a minor, or a financial-account number, a party or nonparty making the filing may include only:

   i. The last four (4) digits of the Social Security number and taxpayer-identification number;

   ii. The year of the individual's birth;

   iii. The minor's initials; and

   iv. The last four (4) digits of the financial-account number. FRCP 5.2(a); MA R USDCT CM/ECF Admin(N).

b. *Exemptions from the redaction requirement.* The redaction requirement does not apply to the following:

   i. A financial-account number that identifies the property allegedly subject to forfeiture in a forfeiture proceeding;

   ii. The record of an administrative or agency proceeding;

   iii. The official record of a state-court proceeding;

   iv. The record of a court or tribunal, if that record was not subject to the redaction requirement when originally filed;

   v. A filing covered by FRCP 5.2(c) or FRCP 5.2(d); and

   vi. A pro se filing in an action brought under 28 U.S.C.A. § 2241, 28 U.S.C.A. § 2254, or 28 U.S.C.A. § 2255. FRCP 5.2(b).

c. *Limitations on remote access to electronic files; Social Security appeals and immigration cases.* Unless the court orders otherwise, in an action for benefits under the Social Security Act, and in an action or proceeding relating to an order of removal, to relief from removal, or to immigration benefits or detention, access to an electronic file is authorized as follows:

   i. The parties and their attorneys may have remote electronic access to any part of the case file, including the administrative record;

   ii. Any other person may have electronic access to the full record at the courthouse, but may have remote electronic access only to:

   • The docket maintained by the court; and

   • An opinion, order, judgment, or other disposition of the court, but not any other part of the case file or the administrative record. FRCP 5.2(c).

d. *Filings made under seal.* The court may order that a filing be made under seal without redaction. The court may later unseal the filing or order the person who made the filing to file a redacted version for the public record. FRCP 5.2(d).

e. *Protective orders.* For good cause, the court may by order in a case:

   i. Require redaction of additional information; or

   ii. Limit or prohibit a nonparty's remote electronic access to a document filed with the court. FRCP 5.2(e).

f. *Option for additional unredacted filing under seal.* A person making a redacted filing may also file an unredacted copy under seal. The court must retain the unredacted copy as part of the record. FRCP 5.2(f). For more information, refer to MA R USDCT LR 7.2.

g. *Option for filing a reference list.* A filing that contains redacted information may be filed together with a reference list that identifies each item of redacted information and specifies an appropriate identifier that uniquely corresponds to each item listed. The list must be filed under seal and may be amended as of right. Any reference in the case to a listed identifier will be construed to refer to the corresponding item of information. FRCP 5.2(g).

h. *Responsibility for redaction.* The clerk's office is not responsible for reviewing documents filed with the court to determine whether pleadings have been redacted and are in the proper form. MA R USDCT CM/ECF Admin(N).

i. *Waiver of protection of identifiers.* A person waives the protection of FRCP 5.2(a) as to the person's own information by filing it without redaction and not under seal. FRCP 5.2(h).

## F. Filing and Service Requirements

1. *Filing requirements*

   a. *Required filings.* Any paper after the complaint that is required to be served must be filed no later than a reasonable time after service. But disclosures under FRCP 26(a)(1) or FRCP 26(a)(2) and the following discovery requests and responses must not be filed until they are used in the proceeding or the court orders filing: depositions, interrogatories, requests for documents or tangible things or to permit entry onto land, and requests for admission. FRCP 5(d)(1)(A). Refer to the United States District Court for the District of Massachusetts KeyRules pleading and motion documents for information on filing with the court.

   b. *Nonfiling of discovery materials.* Discovery materials (that is, automatic or voluntary disclosure materials, depositions, deposition notices, interrogatories, requests for documents, requests for admissions, answers and responses to discovery requests, and any other requests for or products of the discovery process) shall not be filed unless so ordered by the court or for use in the proceeding. The party taking a deposition or obtaining any material through discovery is responsible for its preservation and delivery to the court if needed or so ordered. If for any reason a party or concerned citizen believes that any of the named documents should be filed, an ex parte request may be made that such document be filed, stating the reasons for the request. The court may also order filing sua sponte. MA R USDCT LR 26.6(a).

      i. *Discovery motions.* If relief is sought under FRCP 26(c) or FRCP 37, copies of the relevant portions of disputed documents shall be filed with the court contemporaneously with any motion. MA R USDCT LR 26.6(a).

      ii. *Motions for summary judgment.* If the moving party under FRCP 56 or the opponent relies on discovery documents, copies of the pertinent parts thereof shall be filed with the motion or opposition. MA R USDCT LR 26.6(a).

2. *Service requirements.* Service of all pleadings subsequent to the original complaint and of all other papers required to be served shall be made in the manner specified by FRCP 5. MA R USDCT LR 5.2(a).

   a. *Service; When required*

      i. *In general.* Unless the Federal Rules of Civil Procedure provide otherwise, each of the following papers must be served on every party:

      - An order stating that service is required;

      - A pleading filed after the original complaint, unless the court orders otherwise under FRCP 5(c) because there are numerous defendants;

      - A discovery paper required to be served on a party, unless the court orders otherwise;

      - A written motion, except one that may be heard ex parte; and

      - A written notice, appearance, demand, or offer of judgment, or any similar paper. FRCP 5(a)(1).

      ii. *If a party fails to appear.* No service is required on a party who is in default for failing to appear. But a pleading that asserts a new claim for relief against such a party must be served on that party under FRCP 4. FRCP 5(a)(2).

      iii. *Seizing property.* If an action is begun by seizing property and no person is or need be named as a defendant, any service required before the filing of an appearance, answer, or claim must be made on the person who had custody or possession of the property when it was seized. FRCP 5(a)(3).

   b. *Service; How made*

      i. *Serving an attorney.* If a party is represented by an attorney, service under FRCP 5 must be made on the attorney unless the court orders service on the party. FRCP 5(b)(1).

      ii. *Service in general.* A paper is served under FRCP 5 by:

      - Handing it to the person;

      - Leaving it: (1) at the person's office with a clerk or other person in charge or, if no one is in charge, in a conspicuous place in the office; or (2) if the person has no office or the office is closed, at the person's dwelling or usual place of abode with someone of suitable age and discretion who resides there;

      - Mailing it to the person's last known address—in which event service is complete upon mailing;

      - Leaving it with the court clerk if the person has no known address;

      - Sending it to a registered user by filing it with the court's electronic-filing system or sending it by other electronic means that the person consented to in writing—in either of which events service is complete upon filing or sending, but is not effective if the filer or sender learns that it did not reach the person to be served; or

- Delivering it by any other means that the person consented to in writing—in which event service is complete when the person making service delivers it to the agency designated to make delivery. FRCP 5(b)(2).

   iii.   *Service by electronic means.* Unless exempt or otherwise ordered by the court, all pleadings and other papers must be served on other parties by electronic means. MA R USDCT LR 5.4(C); MA R USDCT CM/ECF Admin(H)(2). Service by electronic means shall be treated the same as service by mail. MA R USDCT CM/ECF Admin(H)(4).

- *Consent to electronic service.* Registering to use CM/ECF constitutes consent to service of all documents by electronic means as provided in the Administrative Procedures for Electronic Case Filing in the United States District Court for the District of Massachusetts (MA R USDCT CM/ECF Admin) and FRCP 5(b) and FRCP 77(d). MA R USDCT CM/ECF Admin(E)(6); MA R USDCT CM/ECF Admin(H)(3).

- *Service on registered ECF users.* Transmission of the Notice of Electronic Filing (NEF) through the court's transmission facilities will constitute service of the filed document upon a registered ECF user. MA R USDCT LR 5.4(C).

- *Service on non-registered users.* The party filing the document electronically is responsible for serving a paper copy of the document by mail in accordance with FRCP 5(b) to those case participants who have not been identified on the NEF as electronic recipients. MA R USDCT CM/ECF Admin(H)(3).

- *Service of conventionally filed papers.* Documents or exhibits submitted conventionally shall be served on other parties by the filer using traditional means. MA R USDCT CM/ECF Admin(P)(4).

  c.   *Serving numerous defendants*

   i.   *In general.* If an action involves an unusually large number of defendants, the court may, on motion or on its own, order that:

- Defendants' pleadings and replies to them need not be served on other defendants;

- Any crossclaim, counterclaim, avoidance, or affirmative defense in those pleadings and replies to them will be treated as denied or avoided by all other parties; and

- Filing any such pleading and serving it on the plaintiff constitutes notice of the pleading to all parties. FRCP 5(c)(1).

   ii.   *Notifying parties.* A copy of every such order must be served on the parties as the court directs. FRCP 5(c)(2).

## G. Hearings

  1.   There is no hearing contemplated in the federal statutes or rules for requests for production of documents.

## H. Forms

### 1. Federal Request for Production of Documents Forms

  a.   Request for production, inspection and copying of documents, and inspection and photographing of things and real property. 3A FEDFORMS § 25:17.

  b.   Request for production of documents; Electronically stored information. 3A FEDFORMS § 25:18.

  c.   Request for production of documents; Business records. 3A FEDFORMS § 25:19.

  d.   Request for production of documents; Patent case. 3A FEDFORMS § 25:20.

  e.   Request for production of documents; Government records and regulations. 3A FEDFORMS § 25:21.

  f.   Request for production of documents; Government personnel files, memoranda, minutes of meetings, and statistics. 3A FEDFORMS § 25:22.

  g.   Request for production of documents; Documents to be identified in physically separate but accompanying interrogatories under FRCP 33. 3A FEDFORMS § 25:23.

  h.   Request for production of documents; Employment discrimination. 3A FEDFORMS § 25:24.

  i.   Request; Production of documents for inspection and copying. AMJUR PP DEPOSITION § 498.

  j.   Request; Production of documents, records, and objects, under FRCP 34. FEDPROF § 23:403.

   k.  Request; Production of documents for inspection and copying. FEDPROF § 23:404.

   l.  Request; Production of documents for inspection and copying; Business records. FEDPROF § 23:405.

  m.  Request; Production of objects for inspection and sampling. FEDPROF § 23:406.

   n.  Request; Production of documents for inspection and copying; Government records and files. FEDPROF § 23:407.

   o.  Request; Production of documents and things; Patent proceeding. FEDPROF § 23:408.

   p.  Request; Production of documents and things; Trademark action. FEDPROF § 23:409.

   q.  Request; Production of documents; Trademark action; Likelihood of confusion. FEDPROF § 23:410.

   r.  Request; Production of documents; Automobile negligence. FEDPROF § 23:411.

   s.  Request; Production of documents; Premises liability. FEDPROF § 23:412.

   t.  Request; Production of documents for inspection and copying; Wrongful death due to forklift accident. FEDPROF § 23:413.

   u.  Request; Production of documents; Products liability. FEDPROF § 23:414.

   v.  Request; Production of documents; Collection of tariff. FEDPROF § 23:415.

   w.  Request; Production of medical records. FEDPROF § 23:416.

   x.  Request; Production of employment records. FEDPROF § 23:417.

   y.  Request; Production of education records. FEDPROF § 23:418.

   z.  Request; Production of decedent's records. FEDPROF § 23:419.

# I. Applicable Rules

1. *Federal rules*

   a.  Serving and filing pleadings and other papers. FRCP 5.

   b.  Privacy protection for filings made with the court. FRCP 5.2.

   c.  Computing and extending time; Time for motion papers. FRCP 6.

   d.  Pleadings allowed; Form of motions and other papers. FRCP 7.

   e.  Form of pleadings. FRCP 10.

   f.  Signing pleadings, motions, and other papers; Representations to the court; Sanctions. FRCP 11.

   g.  Duty to disclose; General provisions governing discovery. FRCP 26.

   h.  Stipulations about discovery procedure. FRCP 29.

   i.  Producing documents, electronically stored information, and tangible things, or entering onto land, for inspection and other purposes. FRCP 34.

   j.  Failure to make disclosures or to cooperate in discovery; Sanctions. FRCP 37.

2. *Local rules*

   a.  Title. MA R USDCT LR 1.1.

   b.  Sanctions. MA R USDCT LR 1.3.

   c.  Form and filing of papers. MA R USDCT LR 5.1.

   d.  Service and filing of pleadings and other papers. MA R USDCT LR 5.2.

   e.  Filing and service by electronic means. MA R USDCT LR 5.4.

   f.  Alternative dispute resolution. MA R USDCT LR 16.4.

   g.  Control of discovery. MA R USDCT LR 26.1.

   h.  Sequences of discovery. MA R USDCT LR 26.2.

   i.  Phasing of discovery. MA R USDCT LR 26.3.

   j.  Uniform definitions in discovery requests. MA R USDCT LR 26.5.

   k.  Court filings and costs. MA R USDCT LR 26.6.

l. Settlement. MA R USDCT LR 68.2.

m. Office of the clerk. MA R USDCT LR 77.2.

n. Appearances. MA R USDCT LR 83.5.2.

o. Practice by pro se litigants. MA R USDCT LR 83.5.5.

p. CM/ECF case management/electronic case files administrative procedures. MA R USDCT CM/ECF Admin.

## Requests, Notices and Applications
## Response to Request for Production of Documents

### Document Last Updated December 2018

## A. Checklist

(I) ❑ Matters to be considered by requesting party

   (a) ❑ Required documents

      (1) ❑ Request for production of documents

   (b) ❑ Supplemental documents

      (1) ❑ Subpoena

      (2) ❑ Certificate of service

   (c) ❑ Timing

      (1) ❑ More than twenty-one (21) days after the summons and complaint are served on a party, a request under FRCP 34 may be delivered: (1) to that party by any other party, and (2) by that party to any plaintiff or to any other party that has been served

      (2) ❑ A party may not seek discovery from any source before the parties have conferred as required by FRCP 26(f), except in a proceeding exempted from initial disclosure under FRCP 26(a)(1)(B), or when authorized by the Federal Rules of Civil Procedure, by stipulation, or by court order

(II) ❑ Matters to be considered by responding party

   (a) ❑ Required documents

      (1) ❑ Response to request for production of documents

   (b) ❑ Supplemental documents

      (1) ❑ Certificate of service

   (c) ❑ Timing

      (1) ❑ The party to whom the request is directed must respond in writing within thirty (30) days after being served or—if the request was delivered under FRCP 26(d)(2)—within thirty (30) days after the parties' first FRCP 26(f) conference

      (2) ❑ Answers to a document request with respect to which objections were served and which are subsequently required to be answered shall be served within fourteen (14) days after it is determined that they should be answered, unless the court directs otherwise

## B. Timing

1. *Response to request for production of documents.* The party to whom the request is directed must respond in writing within thirty (30) days after being served or—if the request was delivered under FRCP 26(d)(2)—within thirty (30) days after the parties' first FRCP 26(f) conference. A shorter or longer time may be stipulated to under FRCP 29 or be ordered by the court. FRCP 34(b)(2)(A).

   a. *Answers to document request following objections.* Answers to a document request with respect to which objections were served and which are subsequently required to be answered shall be served within fourteen (14) days after it is determined that they should be answered, unless the court directs otherwise. MA R USDCT LR 34.1(d).

2. *Computation of time*

    a. *Computing time.* FRCP 6 applies in computing any time period specified in the Federal Rules of Civil Procedure, in any local rule or court order, or in any statute that does not specify a method of computing time. FRCP 6(a).

        i. *Period stated in days or a longer unit.* When the period is stated in days or a longer unit of time:

- Exclude the day of the event that triggers the period;

- Count every day, including intermediate Saturdays, Sundays, and legal holidays; and

- Include the last day of the period, but if the last day is a Saturday, Sunday, or legal holiday, the period continues to run until the end of the next day that is not a Saturday, Sunday, or legal holiday. FRCP 6(a)(1).

        ii. *Period stated in hours.* When the period is stated in hours:

- Begin counting immediately on the occurrence of the event that triggers the period;

- Count every hour, including hours during intermediate Saturdays, Sundays, and legal holidays; and

- If the period would end on a Saturday, Sunday, or legal holiday, the period continues to run until the same time on the next day that is not a Saturday, Sunday, or legal holiday. FRCP 6(a)(2).

        iii. *Office of the clerk.* The offices of the Clerk of Court at Boston, Worcester and Springfield shall be open from 8:30 a.m. until 5:00 p.m. on all days except Saturdays, Sundays, legal holidays and other days so ordered by the court and announced in advance, if feasible. MA R USDCT LR 77.2.

        iv. *Inaccessibility of the clerk's office.* Unless the court orders otherwise, if the clerk's office is inaccessible:

- On the last day for filing under FRCP 6(a)(1), then the time for filing is extended to the first accessible day that is not a Saturday, Sunday, or legal holiday; or

- During the last hour for filing under FRCP 6(a)(2), then the time for filing is extended to the same time on the first accessible day that is not a Saturday, Sunday, or legal holiday. FRCP 6(a)(3).

        v. *"Last day" defined.* Unless a different time is set by a statute, local rule, or court order, the last day ends:

- For electronic filing, at midnight in the court's time zone; and

- For filing by other means, when the clerk's office is scheduled to close. FRCP 6(a)(4).

        vi. *"Next day" defined.* The "next day" is determined by continuing to count forward when the period is measured after an event and backward when measured before an event. FRCP 6(a)(5).

        vii. *"Legal holiday" defined.* "Legal holiday" means:

- The day set aside by statute for observing New Year's Day, Martin Luther King Jr.'s Birthday, Washington's Birthday, Memorial Day, Independence Day, Labor Day, Columbus Day, Veterans' Day, Thanksgiving Day, or Christmas Day;

- Any day declared a holiday by the President or Congress; and

- For periods that are measured after an event, any other day declared a holiday by the state where the district court is located. FRCP 6(a)(6).

    b. *Computation of electronic filing deadlines.* Filing documents electronically does not alter any filing deadlines. MA R USDCT CM/ECF Admin(K); MA R USDCT LR 5.4(D). Although CM/ECF is generally available twenty-four (24) hours a day for filing, all electronic transmissions of documents must be completed prior to 6:00 PM, Eastern Standard (or Daylight Savings) Time, on the date on which it is due, in order to be considered timely filed that day. MA R USDCT CM/ECF Admin(K); MA R USDCT LR 5.4(D). When a specific time of day deadline is set by court order or stipulation, the electronic filing must be completed by that time. Documents may be filed at any time of the day on days prior to the date on which it is due. MA R USDCT CM/ECF Admin(K). A document filed electronically shall be deemed filed as of the time and date stated on the NEF received from the court. MA R USDCT CM/ECF Admin(G)(2); MA R USDCT CM/ECF Admin(K).

        i. *Technical failures.* A user whose filing is made untimely as the result of a technical failure of the court's CM/ECF system may seek appropriate relief from the court. MA R USDCT CM/ECF Admin(W)(3). Technical difficulties on the filer's end, with telephone, cable lines, the filer's Internet Service Provider (ISP), or hardware or software problems, will not constitute a technical failure under the Administrative Procedures for Electronic Case Filing in the United States District Court for the District of Massachusetts (MA R USDCT CM/ECF Admin) nor excuse an untimely filing. MA R USDCT CM/ECF Admin(W)(3). As help desk support is available during normal

business hours, filers are strongly urged to electronically file any documents during that period. MA R USDCT CM/ECF Admin(W)(3).

- The court has made available a public terminal (computers and scanner) in each clerk's office for registered users to scan and electronically file documents. This equipment is available during normal business hours. Users should bring their prepared document and a valid CM/ECF login and password. MA R USDCT CM/ECF Admin(W)(3).

c. *Extending time.* When an act may or must be done within a specified time, the court may, for good cause, extend the time: (1) with or without motion or notice if the court acts, or if a request is made, before the original time or its extension expires; or (2) on motion made after the time has expired if the party failed to act because of excusable neglect. FRCP 6(b)(1).

    i. *Exceptions.* A court must not extend the time to act under FRCP 50(b), FRCP 50(d), FRCP 52(b), FRCP 59(b), FRCP 59(d), FRCP 59(e), and FRCP 60(b). FRCP 6(b)(2).

    ii. Refer to the United States District Court for the District of Massachusetts KeyRules Motion for Continuance/Extension of Time document for more information on extending time.

d. *Additional time after certain kinds of service.* When a party may or must act within a specified time after being served and service is made under FRCP 5(b)(2)(C) (by mail), FRCP 5(b)(2)(D) (by leaving with the clerk), or FRCP 5(b)(2)(F) (by other means consented to), three (3) days are added after the period would otherwise expire under FRCP 6(a). FRCP 6(d).

## C. General Requirements

1. *General provisions governing discovery*

  a. *Discovery scope and limits*

    i. *Scope in general.* Unless otherwise limited by court order, the scope of discovery is as follows: Parties may obtain discovery regarding any nonprivileged matter that is relevant to any party's claim or defense and proportional to the needs of the case, considering the importance of the issues at stake in the action, the amount in controversy, the parties' relative access to relevant information, the parties' resources, the importance of the discovery in resolving the issues, and whether the burden or expense of the proposed discovery outweighs its likely benefit. Information within this scope of discovery need not be admissible in evidence to be discoverable. FRCP 26(b)(1).

    ii. *Limitations on frequency and extent*

- *When permitted.* By order, the court may alter the limits in the Federal Rules of Civil Procedure on the number of depositions and interrogatories or on the length of depositions under FRCP 30. By order or local rule, the court may also limit the number of requests under FRCP 36. FRCP 26(b)(2)(A).

- *Specific limitations on electronically stored information.* A party need not provide discovery of electronically stored information from sources that the party identifies as not reasonably accessible because of undue burden or cost. On motion to compel discovery or for a protective order, the party from whom discovery is sought must show that the information is not reasonably accessible because of undue burden or cost. If that showing is made, the court may nonetheless order discovery from such sources if the requesting party shows good cause, considering the limitations of FRCP 26(b)(2)(C). The court may specify conditions for the discovery. FRCP 26(b)(2)(B).

- *When required.* On motion or on its own, the court must limit the frequency or extent of discovery otherwise allowed by the Federal Rules of Civil Procedure or by local rule if it determines that: (1) the discovery sought is unreasonably cumulative or duplicative, or can be obtained from some other source that is more convenient, less burdensome, or less expensive; (2) the party seeking discovery has had ample opportunity to obtain the information by discovery in the action; or (3) the proposed discovery is outside the scope permitted by FRCP 26(b)(1). FRCP 26(b)(2)(C).

    iii. *Trial preparation; Materials*

- *Documents and tangible things.* Ordinarily, a party may not discover documents and tangible things that are prepared in anticipation of litigation or for trial by or for another party or its representative (including the other party's attorney, consultant, surety, indemnitor, insurer, or agent). But, subject to FRCP 26(b)(4), those materials may be discovered if: (1) they are otherwise discoverable under FRCP 26(b)(1); and (2) the party shows that it has substantial need for the materials to prepare its case and cannot, without undue hardship, obtain their substantial equivalent by other means. FRCP 26(b)(3)(A).

- *Protection against disclosure.* If the court orders discovery of those materials, it must protect against disclosure of the mental impressions, conclusions, opinions, or legal theories of a party's attorney or other representative concerning the litigation. FRCP 26(b)(3)(B).

- *Previous statement.* Any party or other person may, on request and without the required showing, obtain the person's own previous statement about the action or its subject matter. If the request is refused, the person may move for a court order, and FRCP 37(a)(5) applies to the award of expenses. A previous statement is either: (1) a written statement that the person has signed or otherwise adopted or approved; or (2) a contemporaneous stenographic, mechanical, electrical, or other recording—or a transcription of it—that recites substantially verbatim the person's oral statement. FRCP 26(b)(3)(C).

iv. *Trial preparation; Experts*

- *Deposition of an expert who may testify.* A party may depose any person who has been identified as an expert whose opinions may be presented at trial. If FRCP 26(a)(2)(B) requires a report from the expert, the deposition may be conducted only after the report is provided. FRCP 26(b)(4)(A).

- *Trial-preparation protection for draft reports or disclosures.* FRCP 26(b)(3)(A) and FRCP 26(b)(3)(B) protect drafts of any report or disclosure required under FRCP 26(a)(2), regardless of the form in which the draft is recorded. FRCP 26(b)(4)(B).

- *Trial-preparation protection for communications between a party's attorney and expert witnesses.* FRCP 26(b)(3)(A) and FRCP 26(b)(3)(B) protect communications between the party's attorney and any witness required to provide a report under FRCP 26(a)(2)(B), regardless of the form of the communications, except to the extent that the communications: (1) relate to compensation for the expert's study or testimony; (2) identify facts or data that the party's attorney provided and that the expert considered in forming the opinions to be expressed; or (3) identify assumptions that the party's attorney provided and that the expert relied on in forming the opinions to be expressed. FRCP 26(b)(4)(C).

- *Expert employed only for trial preparation.* Ordinarily, a party may not, by interrogatories or deposition, discover facts known or opinions held by an expert who has been retained or specially employed by another party in anticipation of litigation or to prepare for trial and who is not expected to be called as a witness at trial. But a party may do so only: (1) as provided in FRCP 35(b); or (2) on showing exceptional circumstances under which it is impracticable for the party to obtain facts or opinions on the same subject by other means. FRCP 26(b)(4)(D).

- *Payment.* Unless manifest injustice would result, the court must require that the party seeking discovery: (1) pay the expert a reasonable fee for time spent in responding to discovery under FRCP 26(b)(4)(A) or FRCP 26(b)(4)(D); and (2) for discovery under FRCP 26(b)(4)(D), also pay the other party a fair portion of the fees and expenses it reasonably incurred in obtaining the expert's facts and opinions. FRCP 26(b)(4)(E).

v. *Claiming privilege or protecting trial-preparation materials*

- *Information withheld.* When a party withholds information otherwise discoverable by claiming that the information is privileged or subject to protection as trial-preparation material, the party must: (1) expressly make the claim; and (2) describe the nature of the documents, communications, or tangible things not produced or disclosed—and do so in a manner that, without revealing information itself privileged or protected, will enable other parties to assess the claim. FRCP 26(b)(5)(A).

- *Information produced.* If information produced in discovery is subject to a claim of privilege or of protection as trial-preparation material, the party making the claim may notify any party that received the information of the claim and the basis for it. After being notified, a party must promptly return, sequester, or destroy the specified information and any copies it has; must not use or disclose the information until the claim is resolved; must take reasonable steps to retrieve the information if the party disclosed it before being notified; and may promptly present the information to the court under seal for a determination of the claim. The producing party must preserve the information until the claim is resolved. FRCP 26(b)(5)(B).

b. *Protective orders.* A party or any person from whom discovery is sought may move for a protective order in the court where the action is pending—or as an alternative on matters relating to a deposition, in the court for the district where the deposition will be taken. FRCP 26(c)(1). Refer to the United States District Court for the District of Massachusetts KeyRules Motion for Protective Order document for more information.

c. *Disclosure orders.* The judicial officer may order the parties to submit at the scheduling conference, or at any subsequent time the officer deems appropriate, sworn statements disclosing certain information to every other party. At the discretion of the judicial officer, this order may direct the submission of:

i. A sworn statement from a claimant, whether plaintiff, third-party plaintiff, cross-claimant, or counter-claimant, that:

- Itemizes all economic loss and provides a computation of damages for which recovery is sought, if any, sustained before the date of service of process;

- Identifies all persons then known to the claimant or the claimant's attorney who witnessed or participated in the transaction or occurrence giving rise to the claim or otherwise known or believed to have substantial discoverable information about the claim or defenses, together with a statement of the subject and a brief summary of that information;

- Identifies all opposing parties, and all officers, directors, and employees of opposing parties, from whom statements have been obtained by or on behalf of the claimant regarding the subject matter of the claim; and

- Identifies all governmental agencies or officials then known to the claimant or the claimant's attorney to have investigated the transaction or occurrence giving rise to the claim; and

ii. A sworn statement from a defendant, whether the direct defendant, third-party defendant, cross-claim defendant, or counterclaim defendant, that identifies:

- All persons then known to the defendant or the defendant's attorneys who witnessed the transaction or occurrence giving rise to the claim or otherwise is known or believed to have substantial discoverable information about the claims or defenses, together with a statement of the subject and a brief summary of that information;

- All opposing parties, and all officers, directors, and employees of opposing parties, from whom statements have been obtained by or on behalf of the defendant regarding the subject matter of the claims or defenses; and

- All government agencies or officials then known to the defendant or the defendant's attorneys to have investigated the transaction or occurrence giving rise to the claims or defenses. MA R USDCT LR 26.1(b).

iii. Noncompliance may be excused only by order of the judicial officer. MA R USDCT LR 26.1(b).

d. *Uniform definitions in discovery requests*

i. *Incorporation by reference and limitations.* The full text of the definitions set forth in MA R USDCT LR 26.5(c) is deemed incorporated by reference into all discovery requests, but shall not preclude:

- The definition of other terms specific to the particular litigation;

- The use of abbreviations; or

- A narrower definition of a term defined in MA R USDCT LR 26.5(c). MA R USDCT LR 26.5(a).

ii. *Effect on scope of discovery.* MA R USDCT LR 26.5 is not intended to broaden or narrow the scope of discovery permitted by the Federal Rules of Civil Procedure. MA R USDCT LR 26.5(b).

iii. *Definitions.* The following definitions apply to all discovery requests:

- *Communication.* The term "communication" means the transmittal of information (in the form of facts, ideas, inquiries, or otherwise). MA R USDCT LR 26.5(c)(1).

- *Document.* The term "document" is defined to be synonymous in meaning and equal in scope to the usage of this term in FRCP 34(a). A draft or non-identical copy is a separate document within the meaning of this term. MA R USDCT LR 26.5(c)(2).

- *Identify (with respect to persons).* When referring to a person, "to identify" means to give, to the extent known, the person's full name, present or last known address, and, when referring to a natural person, the present or last known place of employment. Once a person has been identified in accordance with this subparagraph, only the name of that person need be listed in response to subsequent discovery requesting the identification of that person. MA R USDCT LR 26.5(c)(3).

- *Identify (with respect to documents).* When referring to documents, "to identify" means to give, to the extent known, the: (1) type of document; (2) general subject matter; (3) date of the document; and (4) author(s), addressee(s), and recipient(s). MA R USDCT LR 26.5(c)(4).

- *Parties.* The terms "plaintiff" and "defendant" as well as a party's full or abbreviated name or a pronoun referring to a party mean the party and, where applicable, its officers, directors, employees, partners, corporate parent, subsidiaries, or affiliates. This definition is not intended to impose a discovery obligation on any person who is not a party to the litigation. MA R USDCT LR 26.5(c)(5).

- *Person.* The term "person" is defined as any natural person or any business, legal, or governmental entity or association. MA R USDCT LR 26.5(c)(6).

- *Concerning.* The term "concerning" means referring to, describing, evidencing, or constituting. MA R USDCT LR 26.5(c)(7).

- *State the basis.* When an interrogatory calls upon a party to "state the basis" of or for a particular claim, assertion, allegation, or contention, the party shall: (1) identify each and every document (and, where pertinent, the section, article, or subparagraph thereof), which forms any part of the source of the party's information regarding the alleged facts or legal conclusions referred to by the interrogatory; (2) identify each and every communication which forms any part of the source of the party's information regarding the alleged facts or legal conclusions referred to by the interrogatory; (3) state separately the acts or omissions to act on the part of any person (identifying the acts or omissions to act by stating their nature, time, and place and identifying the persons involved) which form any part of the party's information regarding the alleged facts or legal conclusions referred to in the interrogatory; and (4) state separately any other fact which forms the basis of the party's information regarding the alleged facts or conclusions referred to in the interrogatory. MA R USDCT LR 26.5(c)(8).

e. *Cooperative discovery.* The judicial officer should encourage cost effective discovery by means of voluntary exchange of information among litigants and their attorneys. This may be accomplished through the use of: (1) informal, cooperative discovery practices in which counsel provide information to opposing counsel without resort to formal discovery procedures; or (2) stipulations entered into by the parties with respect to deposition notices, waiver of signing, and other matters, except that the parties may not enter into stipulations extending the time for responding to discovery requests or otherwise modify discovery procedures ordered by the judicial officer. MA R USDCT LR 26.1(a).

f. *Phasing of discovery.* In order to facilitate settlement and the efficient completion of discovery, the judicial officer has discretion to structure discovery activities by phasing and sequencing the topics which are the subject of discovery. For example, an order may be framed limiting the first phase to developing information needed for a realistic assessment of the case. If the case does not terminate, the second phase would be directed at information needed to prepare for trial. MA R USDCT LR 26.3.

g. *Sequence of discovery.* Unless the parties stipulate or the court orders otherwise for the parties' and witnesses' convenience and in the interests of justice: (1) methods of discovery may be used in any sequence; and (2) discovery by one party does not require any other party to delay its discovery. FRCP 26(d)(3).

2. *Response to request for production of documents.* Answers and objections in response to requests for document production, served pursuant to FRCP 34 shall be made in the order of the requests propounded. MA R USDCT LR 34.1(a)(1). Each answer, statement, or objection shall be preceded by the request to which it responds. MA R USDCT LR 34.1(a)(2).

a. *Responding to each item.* For each item or category, the response must either state that inspection and related activities will be permitted as requested or state with specificity the grounds for objecting to the request, including the reasons. The responding party may state that it will produce copies of documents or of electronically stored information instead of permitting inspection. The production must then be completed no later than the time for inspection specified in the request or another reasonable time specified in the response. FRCP 34(b)(2)(B).

b. *Objections.* A party may waive its objections to a request for production by failing to object in a timely and effective manner. FEDPROC § 26:598. Each objection and the grounds therefor shall be stated separately. MA R USDCT LR 34.1(a)(3).

    i. When an objection is made to any document request, or subpart thereof, it shall state with specificity all grounds upon which the objecting party relies. Any ground not stated in an objection within the time provided by the Federal Rules of Civil Procedure, or any extensions thereof, shall be deemed waived. MA R USDCT LR 34.1(c)(1).

    ii. An objection must state whether any responsive materials are being withheld on the basis of that objection. An objection to part of a request must specify the part and permit inspection of the rest. FRCP 34(b)(2)(C).

    iii. No part of a document request shall be left unanswered merely because an objection is interposed to another part of the document request. MA R USDCT LR 34.1(c)(2).

iv. A response which raises no objection, but simply indicates that the information requested is "unknown" and that the records sought are "not maintained," is evasive and insufficient. FEDPROC § 26:601.

c. *Claims of privilege.* When a claim of privilege is asserted in objection to any document request, or any subpart thereof, and any document is not provided on the basis of that assertion, the attorney asserting the privilege shall identify in the objection the nature of the privilege that is being claimed with respect to each such document. If the privilege is being asserted in connection with a claim or defense governed by state law, the attorney asserting the privilege shall indicate the particular privilege rule that is being invoked. MA R USDCT LR 34.1(e).

d. *Responding to a request for production of electronically stored information.* The response may state an objection to a requested form for producing electronically stored information. If the responding party objects to a requested form—or if no form was specified in the request—the party must state the form or forms it intends to use. FRCP 34(b)(2)(D).

e. *Producing the documents or electronically stored information.* Unless otherwise stipulated or ordered by the court, these procedures apply to producing documents or electronically stored information:

   i. A party must produce documents as they are kept in the usual course of business or must organize and label them to correspond to the categories in the request;

   ii. If a request does not specify a form for producing electronically stored information, a party must produce it in a form or forms in which it is ordinarily maintained or in a reasonably usable form or forms; and

   iii. A party need not produce the same electronically stored information in more than one form. FRCP 34(b)(2)(E).

f. *Documents and things in possession, custody, or control.* FRCP 34 provides. . .that discovery may be had of documents and things that are in the "possession, custody, or control" of a party. FPP § 2210. The concept of "control" is very important in applying FRCP 34, but the application of this concept is often highly fact-specific. Inspection can be had if the party to whom the request is made has the legal right to obtain the document, even though in fact it has no copy. FPP § 2210.

   i. A party may be required to produce documents and things that it possesses even though they belong to a third person who is not a party to the action. FPP § 2210; Societe Internationale Pour Participations Industrielles Et Commerciales, S. A. v. Rogers, 357 U.S. 197, 78 S.Ct. 1087, 2 L.Ed.2d 1255 (1958). And if a party has possession, custody, or control, it must produce documents and things even though the documents and things are themselves beyond the jurisdiction of the court. FPP § 2210.

   ii. If a document or thing does not exist, it cannot be in the possession, custody, or control of a party and therefore cannot be produced for inspection. FEDPROC § 26:577.

   iii. Finally, lack of control may be considered an objection to the discovery request and, like any such objection, it may be waived. FPP § 2210.

g. *Documents made available to all parties.* Documents made available to one party to a suit must be made available to all parties. FEDPROC § 26:591.

h. *Attorney's duty to ensure compliance.* An attorney representing a party in connection with a request for the production and inspection of documents pursuant to FRCP 34 has an obligation to verify that the client has produced the documents requested, and a further obligation to [ensure] that records are kept indicating which documents have been produced. Failure to comply with these duties has been characterized as careless and inexcusable and has resulted in the imposition of sanctions. FEDPROC § 26:593.

i. *Copying expense for discovery materials*

   i. *Inspection of documents.* Except as otherwise provided in an order entered pursuant to FRCP 26(c), all parties to an action shall be entitled to inspect documents produced by another party pursuant to FRCP 33(c) or FRCP 34 at the location where they are produced. MA R USDCT LR 26.6(b)(1).

   ii. *Copies of documents.* Except as otherwise provided in an order entered pursuant to FRCP 26(c), upon request of any party, and upon that party's agreement to pay the copying costs at the time of delivery, a party who produces documents pursuant to FRCP 33(c) or FRCP 34 shall provide copies of all or any specified part of the documents. No party shall be entitled to obtain copies of documents produced by another party pursuant to FRCP 33(c) or FRCP 34 without paying the costs thereof. MA R USDCT LR 26.6(b)(2).

3. *Supplementing disclosures and responses.* A party who has made a disclosure under FRCP 26(a)—or who has responded to an interrogatory, request for production, or request for admission—must supplement or correct its disclosure or response: (1) in a timely manner if the party learns that in some material respect the disclosure or response is incomplete

or incorrect, and if the additional or corrective information has not otherwise been made known to the other parties during the discovery process or in writing; or (2) as ordered by the court. FRCP 26(e)(1).

4. *Sanctions for failure to cooperate in discovery.* The court where the action is pending may, on motion, order sanctions if a party, after being properly served with interrogatories under FRCP 33 or a request for inspection under FRCP 34, fails to serve its answers, objections, or written response. FRCP 37(d)(1)(A)(ii). If a motion to compel is granted, the court must, after giving an opportunity to be heard, require the party or deponent whose conduct necessitated the motion, the party or attorney advising that conduct, or both to pay the movant's reasonable expenses incurred in making the motion, including attorney's fees. But the court must not order this payment if the opposing party's nondisclosure, response, or objection was substantially justified. FRCP 37(a)(5)(A)(ii). Refer to the United States District Court for the District of Massachusetts KeyRules Motion for Discovery Sanctions document for more information.

5. *Stipulations about discovery procedure.* Unless the court orders otherwise, the parties may stipulate that: (1) a deposition may be taken before any person, at any time or place, on any notice, and in the manner specified—in which event it may be used in the same way as any other deposition; and (2) other procedures governing or limiting discovery be modified—but a stipulation extending the time for any form of discovery must have court approval if it would interfere with the time set for completing discovery, for hearing a motion, or for trial. FRCP 29.

6. *Alternative dispute resolution (ADR).* The judicial officer assigned to preside over the case shall encourage the resolution of disputes by settlement or other alternative dispute resolution programs. MA R USDCT LR 16.4(a).

   a. *Settlement.* At every conference conducted under the Local Rules of the United States District Court for the District of Massachusetts, the judicial officer shall inquire as to the utility of the parties conducting settlement negotiations, explore means of facilitating those negotiations, and offer whatever assistance may be appropriate in the circumstances. Assistance may include a reference of the case to another judicial officer for settlement purposes. MA R USDCT LR 16.4(b).

      i. When a case is settled, the parties shall file with the clerk a signed agreement for judgment or stipulation for dismissal, as appropriate, within twenty-eight (28) days, unless the court otherwise orders. MA R USDCT LR 68.2.

   b. *Alternative dispute resolution programs*

      i. *Discretion of judicial officer.* The judicial officer, following an exploration of the matter with all counsel, may refer appropriate cases to alternative dispute resolution programs that have been designated for use in the district court or that the judicial officer may make available. The dispute resolution programs described in MA R USDCT LR 16.4(c)(2) through MA R USDCT LR 16.4(c)(4) are illustrative, not exclusive. Moreover, nothing in MA R USDCT LR 16.4 shall preclude the parties from engaging in private dispute resolution programs as long as they comply with any schedule established by the court. MA R USDCT LR 16.4(c)(1).

      ii. *Mediation.* The judicial officer may refer the case to mediation upon the agreement of all parties. MA R USDCT LR 16.4(c)(2)(A).

      iii. *Other alternative dispute resolution programs.* Use of mediation is not exclusive. At the request of parties, the judicial officer may consider other forms of alternative dispute resolution including, but not limited to, mini-trial, summary jury trial and arbitration. MA R USDCT LR 16.4(c)(3).

   c. For more information on alternative dispute resolution (ADR), refer to MA R USDCT LR 16.4.

7. *Sanctions.* Failure to comply with any of the directions or obligations set forth in, or authorized by, these rules may result in dismissal, default, or the imposition of other sanctions as deemed appropriate by the judicial officer. MA R USDCT LR 1.3. Except as provided by law, the court may impose sanctions as provided in MA R USDCT LR 1.3 for failure to comply with the Administrative Procedures for Electronic Case Filing in the United States District Court for the District of Massachusetts (MA R USDCT CM/ECF Admin) or with MA R USDCT LR 5.4. MA R USDCT CM/ECF Admin(C)(3).

## D. Documents

1. *Required documents*

   a. *Response to request for production of documents.* Refer to the General Requirements section of this document for information on the response to request for production of documents.

2. *Supplemental documents*

   a. *Certificate of service.* No certificate of service is required when a paper is served by filing it with the court's electronic-filing system. When a paper that is required to be served is served by other means: (1) if the paper is filed, a certificate of service must be filed with it or within a reasonable time after service; and (2) if the paper is not filed, a certificate of service need not be filed unless filing is required by court order or by local rule. FRCP 5(d)(1)(B).

**E. Format**

1. *Form of documents.* The rules governing captions and other matters of form in pleadings apply to motions and other papers. FRCP 7(b)(2). The provisions of FRCP 10 and FRCP 11 concerning the form and signing of pleadings, motions, and other papers shall be applicable to all papers filed in any proceeding in this court. The board of bar overseers registration number of each attorney signing such documents, except the United States Attorney and his or her staff, shall be inscribed below the signature. MA R USDCT LR 5.1(a)(1).

   a. *Paper size and binding.* All papers filed in the court shall be adapted for flat filing, be filed on eight and one-half by eleven (8-1/2 x 11) inch paper without backers and be bound firmly by staple or some such other means (excluding paper or binder clip or rubber band). MA R USDCT LR 5.1(a)(2).

   b. *Spacing.* All papers, except discovery requests and responses, shall be double-spaced except for the identification of counsel, title of the case, footnotes, quotations and exhibits. Discovery requests and responses shall be single-spaced. MA R USDCT LR 5.1(a)(2).

   c. *Caption.* Every pleading must have a caption with the court's name, a title, a file number, and [an] FRCP 7(a) designation. FRCP 10(a).

      i. *Names of parties.* The title of the complaint must name all the parties; the title of other pleadings, after naming the first party on each side, may refer generally to other parties. FRCP 10(a).

      ii. *Request for special action.* When any pleading or other paper filed in the court includes a request for special process or relief, or any other request such that, if granted, the court will proceed other than in the ordinary course, the request shall, unless it is noted on the category sheet [see MA R USDCT LR 40.1(a)(1)], be noted on the first page to the right of or immediately beneath the caption. MA R USDCT LR 5.1(c).

   d. *Claims or defenses*

      i. *Numbered paragraphs.* A party must state its claims or defenses in numbered paragraphs, each limited as far as practicable to a single set of circumstances. A later pleading may refer by number to a paragraph in an earlier pleading. FRCP 10(b).

      ii. *Separate statements.* If doing so would promote clarity, each claim founded on a separate transaction or occurrence—and each defense other than a denial—must be stated in a separate count or defense. FRCP 10(b).

   e. *Adoption by reference.* A statement in a pleading may be adopted by reference elsewhere in the same pleading or in any other pleading or motion. FRCP 10(c).

      i. *Exhibits.* A copy of a written instrument that is an exhibit to a pleading is a part of the pleading for all purposes. FRCP 10(c).

   f. *Citations*

      i. *Local rules.* These rules shall be known as Local Rules of the United States District Court for the District of Massachusetts and cited as "L.R., D. Mass." or "L.R." MA R USDCT LR 1.1.

      ii. *Electronic case filing procedures.* The procedures governing electronic case filing shall be known as the "Administrative Procedures for Electronic Case Filing in the United States District Court for the District of Massachusetts." They shall be cited as "APECF." MA R USDCT CM/ECF Admin(A)(7).

   g. *Acceptance by the clerk.* The clerk must not refuse to file a paper solely because it is not in the form prescribed by the Federal Rules of Civil Procedure or by a local rule or practice. FRCP 5(d)(4).

      i. Except for complaints and notices of appeal, papers that do not conform to the requirements of MA R USDCT LR 5.1(a)(2) shall be returned by the clerk. MA R USDCT LR 5.1(a)(2).

2. *Form of electronic documents.* A paper filed electronically is a written paper for purposes of the Federal Rules of Civil Procedure. FRCP 5(d)(3)(D).

   a. *PDF/A format required.* The court will begin requiring submission of documents in PDF/A format in the foreseeable future. PDF/A is an enhanced version of the traditional PDF format. Newer versions of most PDF software will be able to convert to this format. Additional information on PDF/A documents may be found on the court's website. MA R USDCT CM/ECF Admin(Electronic Filing and PDF).

      i. *Electronically converted PDF.* Electronically converted PDF documents are created from word processing documents (MS Word, WordPerfect, etc.) using any appropriate software. These documents are text searchable

and the file size is generally smaller than a scanned document. CM/ECF users may use any brand of software to convert documents to PDF. MA R USDCT CM/ECF Admin(Electronic Filing and PDF).

- Documents converted to PDF, rather than scanned, are preferred for filing in CM/ECF. MA R USDCT CM/ECF Admin(Electronic Filing and PDF).

ii. *Scanned PDF.* Scanned PDF documents are created from paper documents run through an optical scanner. Scanned PDF documents are generally not searchable and have a larger file size. Please note that software used to create scanned documents may (and should) be set in such a way that the document is "text-searchable." MA R USDCT CM/ECF Admin(Electronic Filing and PDF).

b. *Title.* All pleadings filed electronically shall be titled in accordance with the approved dictionary of civil or criminal events of the CM/ECF system of this court. A list of events is available on the CM/ECF Training Information page of the court's website. The clerk's office may, when necessary and appropriate, modify the docket entry description, or delete and re-enter the docket entry in order to comply with the court's quality assurance standards. MA R USDCT CM/ECF Admin(G)(3).

c. *Attachments to filings and exhibits.* Attachments to filings and exhibits must be filed in accordance with the court's CM/ECF User Manual, unless otherwise ordered by the court. MA R USDCT CM/ECF Admin(O)(1).

i. Filers must submit as attachments only those excerpts of the referenced documents that are directly germane to the matter under consideration by the court. Excerpted material must be clearly and prominently identified as such. Users who file excerpts of documents do so without prejudice to their right to timely file additional excerpts or the complete document, as may be allowed by the court. Responding parties may timely file additional excerpts or the complete document that they believe are directly germane. MA R USDCT CM/ECF Admin(O)(2).

ii. Filers shall not attach as an exhibit any pleading or other paper already on file with the court in that case, but shall merely refer to that document. (See MA R USDCT CM/ECF Admin(G) for information on using hyperlinks in PDF documents filed in CM/ECF.) MA R USDCT CM/ECF Admin(O)(3).

d. *Redacted documents.* The parties may request or the court may require the submission of documents that have been redacted/stripped of sensitive or confidential information. The redacted document prepared for electronic filing shall include the original caption of the document, and be clearly labeled as "Redacted Document." A specific event is available for this purpose ("Redacted Document"), found under the Other Filings/Other Documents menu option. MA R USDCT CM/ECF Admin(S).

i. Attorneys and pro se litigants are advised to take extra care when creating PDF documents intended for submission to CM/ECF. Steps shall be taken to ensure the documents are free of any hidden data (metadata) that may contain redacted information, or traces of information edited or deleted are not hidden in the final document. Even PDF content that has been encrypted may be recovered. An advisory document with additional information on this topic may be found on the court's website. MA R USDCT CM/ECF Admin(S).

e. *Hyperlinks.* Electronically filed documents may contain the following types of hyperlinks: (1) hyperlinks to other portions of the same document; (2) hyperlinks to other documents filed within the CM/ECF system; and (3) hyperlinks to a location on the Internet that contains a source document for a citation. MA R USDCT CM/ECF Admin(G)(7).

i. Hyperlinks to cited authority may not replace standard citation format. Complete citations must be included in the text of the filed document. Neither a hyperlink, nor any site to which it refers, shall be considered part of the record, but are simply convenient mechanisms for accessing material cited in a document filed in CM/ECF. Instructions on creating hyperlinks may be found in the CM/ECF User Manual. MA R USDCT CM/ECF Admin(G)(7).

ii. The court accepts no responsibility for, and does not endorse, any product, organization, or content at any hyperlinked site, or at any site to which that site may be linked. The court accepts no responsibility for the availability or functionality of any hyperlink. MA R USDCT CM/ECF Admin(G)(7).

iii. One feature of PDF/A documents is that hyperlinks are commonly "masked," meaning that the full address of the referenced file is not written out; for example, clicking the word brief may open a brief which was previously filed in CM/ECF. MA R USDCT CM/ECF Admin(G)(7)(NOTE). An "unmasked" hyperlink has the full address visible to the user. MA R USDCT CM/ECF Admin(G)(7)(NOTE).

- Masked hyperlinks may or may not work in a PDF/A document, depending on how it was created. Currently, masked hyperlinks are preserved in PDF/A documents produced by the "Save As" method in

Microsoft Word 2007 and 2010; the "PDFMaker" method in Microsoft Word 2007; and OpenOffice 2.4 ("PDF Export"). With other production methods, such as WordPerfect, the PDF/A document includes underlined words that appear to be links, but clicking them has no effect. MA R USDCT CM/ECF Admin(G)(7)(NOTE).

f.  *Documents features not accepted.* CM/ECF will not accept PDF documents containing tracking tags, embedded systems commands, password protections, access restrictions or other security features, special tags or dynamic features. MA R USDCT CM/ECF Admin(G)(8).

g.  *File size limitations.* A filing party shall limit the size of each PDF file to no more than twenty (20) megabytes. PDF files larger than seven (7) megabytes will be rejected by the CM/ECF system. The filer will see a message advising of the size limitation. MA R USDCT CM/ECF Admin(P)(2).

   i.  Larger documents or exhibits may be submitted electronically if split into separate PDF files each less than seven (7) megabytes, attached to the main document and clearly labeled. MA R USDCT CM/ECF Admin(P)(2).

   ii.  Documents submitted electronically or on paper are subject to the page limitations set by MA R USDCT LR 7.1(b)(4) or by order of the court. MA R USDCT CM/ECF Admin(P)(1).

h.  *Accuracy and readability.* The filer shall verify the accuracy and readability of any PDF file before electronically filing it in CM/ECF. MA R USDCT CM/ECF Admin(G)(6); MA R USDCT CM/ECF Admin(P)(3).

3.  *Signing disclosures and discovery requests, responses, and objections.* FRCP 11 does not apply to disclosures and discovery requests, responses, objections, and motions under FRCP 26 through FRCP 37. FRCP 11(d).

a.  *Signature required.* Every disclosure under FRCP 26(a)(1) or FRCP 26(a)(3) and every discovery request, response, or objection must be signed by at least one attorney of record in the attorney's own name—or by the party personally, if unrepresented—and must state the signer's address, e-mail address, and telephone number. FRCP 26(g)(1). The provisions of the Federal Rules of Civil Procedure pertaining to the form and signing of pleadings, motions, and other papers shall be applicable to all papers filed in any proceeding in this court. The board of bar overseers registration number of each attorney signing such documents, except the United States Attorney and his staff, shall be inscribed below the signature. MA R USDCT LR 5.1(a)(1).

   i.  *Electronic signing.* A filing made through a person's electronic-filing account and authorized by that person, together with that person's name on a signature block, constitutes the person's signature. FRCP 5(d)(3)(C).

   ii.  *Appearances.* The filing of an appearance or any other pleading signed on behalf of a party constitutes an entry of appearance for that party. All pleadings shall contain the name, bar admission number, address, telephone number, and e-mail address of the attorney entering an appearance. MA R USDCT LR 83.5.2(a).

   - *Appearances by law firms.* When a party is represented by a law firm, the appearance must include the name and the signature of at least one individual attorney. When a party is represented by more than one attorney from the same or different law firms, the attorney entering the appearance must designate the individual attorney who is authorized to receive all notices in the case. Any notice sent to an attorney so designated shall be deemed to be proper notice unless the court finds that notice was not properly sent. MA R USDCT LR 83.5.2(b).

   - For more information on appearances, refer to MA R USDCT LR 83.5.2.

   iii.  *Signatures of attorneys.* The user login and password required to submit documents to the CM/ECF system shall serve as that user's signature for purposes of FRCP 11 and for all other purposes under the Federal Rules of Civil Procedure and the Local Rules of the United States District Court for the District of Massachusetts. All electronically filed documents must include a signature block and must set forth the attorney's name, bar number, address, telephone number and email address. The name of the CM/ECF user under whose log-in and password the document is submitted must be preceded by a "/s/" and typed in the space where the signature would otherwise appear. MA R USDCT CM/ECF Admin(M)(1). For an example, refer to MA R USDCT CM/ECF Admin(M)(1).

   iv.  *Signatures of pro se parties.* Any document requiring a signature that is filed by a party appearing pro se shall bear the words "pro se" following that party's signature. Any such document shall also state the party's mailing address, telephone number (if any), and e-mail address (if the party has consented to service by email). MA R USDCT LR 83.5.5(g). For more information on practice by pro se litigants, refer to MA R USDCT LR 83.5.5.

   v.  *Multiple signatures.* The filer of any document requiring more than one signature (e.g, stipulations, joint motions, joint status reports, magistrate judge consent forms, etc.) must list thereon all the names of other signatories by means of a "/s/ name of signatory" block for each. By submitting such a document, the filing attorney certifies that each of the other signatories has expressly agreed to the form and substance of the document and that the filing attorney has their actual authority to submit the document electronically. MA R USDCT CM/ECF Admin(M)(2). For more information, refer to MA R USDCT CM/ECF Admin(M)(2).

vi.   *Affidavits.* Except as provided in MA R USDCT CM/ECF Admin(L), affidavits shall be filed electronically; however, the electronically filed version must contain a "/s/ name of signatory" block indicating that the paper document bears an original signature. MA R USDCT CM/ECF Admin(M)(3). The court will also accept a scanned version of the original, signed document. MA R USDCT CM/ECF Admin(M)(3). For more information, refer to MA R USDCT CM/ECF Admin(M)(3).

b.   *Effect of signature.* By signing, an attorney or party certifies that to the best of the person's knowledge, information, and belief formed after a reasonable inquiry:

i.   With respect to a disclosure, it is complete and correct as of the time it is made; and

ii.   With respect to a discovery request, response, or objection, it is:

- Consistent with the Federal Rules of Civil Procedure and warranted by existing law or by a nonfrivolous argument for extending, modifying, or reversing existing law, or for establishing new law;

- Not interposed for any improper purpose, such as to harass, cause unnecessary delay, or needlessly increase the cost of litigation; and

- Neither unreasonable nor unduly burdensome or expensive, considering the needs of the case, prior discovery in the case, the amount in controversy, and the importance of the issues at stake in the action. FRCP 26(g)(1).

c.   *Failure to sign.* Other parties have no duty to act on an unsigned disclosure, request, response, or objection until it is signed, and the court must strike it unless a signature is promptly supplied after the omission is called to the attorney's or party's attention. FRCP 26(g)(2).

d.   *Sanction for improper certification.* If a certification violates FRCP 26(g) without substantial justification, the court, on motion or on its own, must impose an appropriate sanction on the signer, the party on whose behalf the signer was acting, or both. The sanction may include an order to pay the reasonable expenses, including attorney's fees, caused by the violation. FRCP 26(g)(3). Refer to the United States District Court for the District of Massachusetts KeyRules Motion for Discovery Sanctions document for more information.

4.   *Privacy protection for filings made with the court*

a.   *Redacted filings.* Unless the court orders otherwise, in an electronic or paper filing with the court that contains an individual's Social Security number, taxpayer-identification number, or birth date, the name of an individual known to be a minor, or a financial-account number, a party or nonparty making the filing may include only:

i.   The last four (4) digits of the Social Security number and taxpayer-identification number;

ii.   The year of the individual's birth;

iii.   The minor's initials; and

iv.   The last four (4) digits of the financial-account number. FRCP 5.2(a); MA R USDCT CM/ECF Admin(N).

b.   *Exemptions from the redaction requirement.* The redaction requirement does not apply to the following:

i.   A financial-account number that identifies the property allegedly subject to forfeiture in a forfeiture proceeding;

ii.   The record of an administrative or agency proceeding;

iii.   The official record of a state-court proceeding;

iv.   The record of a court or tribunal, if that record was not subject to the redaction requirement when originally filed;

v.   A filing covered by FRCP 5.2(c) or FRCP 5.2(d); and

vi.   A pro se filing in an action brought under 28 U.S.C.A. § 2241, 28 U.S.C.A. § 2254, or 28 U.S.C.A. § 2255. FRCP 5.2(b).

c.   *Limitations on remote access to electronic files; Social Security appeals and immigration cases.* Unless the court orders otherwise, in an action for benefits under the Social Security Act, and in an action or proceeding relating to an order of removal, to relief from removal, or to immigration benefits or detention, access to an electronic file is authorized as follows:

i.   The parties and their attorneys may have remote electronic access to any part of the case file, including the administrative record;

ii. Any other person may have electronic access to the full record at the courthouse, but may have remote electronic access only to:

- The docket maintained by the court; and

- An opinion, order, judgment, or other disposition of the court, but not any other part of the case file or the administrative record. FRCP 5.2(c).

d. *Filings made under seal.* The court may order that a filing be made under seal without redaction. The court may later unseal the filing or order the person who made the filing to file a redacted version for the public record. FRCP 5.2(d).

e. *Protective orders.* For good cause, the court may by order in a case:

i. Require redaction of additional information; or

ii. Limit or prohibit a nonparty's remote electronic access to a document filed with the court. FRCP 5.2(e).

f. *Option for additional unredacted filing under seal.* A person making a redacted filing may also file an unredacted copy under seal. The court must retain the unredacted copy as part of the record. FRCP 5.2(f). For more information, refer to MA R USDCT LR 7.2.

g. *Option for filing a reference list.* A filing that contains redacted information may be filed together with a reference list that identifies each item of redacted information and specifies an appropriate identifier that uniquely corresponds to each item listed. The list must be filed under seal and may be amended as of right. Any reference in the case to a listed identifier will be construed to refer to the corresponding item of information. FRCP 5.2(g).

h. *Responsibility for redaction.* The clerk's office is not responsible for reviewing documents filed with the court to determine whether pleadings have been redacted and are in the proper form. MA R USDCT CM/ECF Admin(N).

i. *Waiver of protection of identifiers.* A person waives the protection of FRCP 5.2(a) as to the person's own information by filing it without redaction and not under seal. FRCP 5.2(h).

## F. Filing and Service Requirements

1. *Filing requirements*

a. *Required filings.* Any paper after the complaint that is required to be served must be filed no later than a reasonable time after service. But disclosures under FRCP 26(a)(1) or FRCP 26(a)(2) and the following discovery requests and responses must not be filed until they are used in the proceeding or the court orders filing: depositions, interrogatories, requests for documents or tangible things or to permit entry onto land, and requests for admission. FRCP 5(d)(1)(A). Refer to the United States District Court for the District of Massachusetts KeyRules pleading and motion documents for information on filing with the court.

b. *Nonfiling of discovery materials.* Discovery materials (that is, automatic or voluntary disclosure materials, depositions, deposition notices, interrogatories, requests for documents, requests for admissions, answers and responses to discovery requests, and any other requests for or products of the discovery process) shall not be filed unless so ordered by the court or for use in the proceeding. The party taking a deposition or obtaining any material through discovery is responsible for its preservation and delivery to the court if needed or so ordered. If for any reason a party or concerned citizen believes that any of the named documents should be filed, an ex parte request may be made that such document be filed, stating the reasons for the request. The court may also order filing sua sponte. MA R USDCT LR 26.6(a).

i. *Discovery motions.* If relief is sought under FRCP 26(c) or FRCP 37, copies of the relevant portions of disputed documents shall be filed with the court contemporaneously with any motion. MA R USDCT LR 26.6(a).

ii. *Motions for summary judgment.* If the moving party under FRCP 56 or the opponent relies on discovery documents, copies of the pertinent parts thereof shall be filed with the motion or opposition. MA R USDCT LR 26.6(a).

2. *Service requirements.* Service of all pleadings subsequent to the original complaint and of all other papers required to be served shall be made in the manner specified by FRCP 5. MA R USDCT LR 5.2(a). The response must be served on all the parties to the action, unless the court otherwise orders, rather than only on the requesting party. FPP § 2213.

a. *Service; When required*

i. *In general.* Unless the Federal Rules of Civil Procedure provide otherwise, each of the following papers must be served on every party:

- An order stating that service is required;

- A pleading filed after the original complaint, unless the court orders otherwise under FRCP 5(c) because there are numerous defendants;

- A discovery paper required to be served on a party, unless the court orders otherwise;

- A written motion, except one that may be heard ex parte; and

- A written notice, appearance, demand, or offer of judgment, or any similar paper. FRCP 5(a)(1).

   ii. *If a party fails to appear.* No service is required on a party who is in default for failing to appear. But a pleading that asserts a new claim for relief against such a party must be served on that party under FRCP 4. FRCP 5(a)(2).

   iii. *Seizing property.* If an action is begun by seizing property and no person is or need be named as a defendant, any service required before the filing of an appearance, answer, or claim must be made on the person who had custody or possession of the property when it was seized. FRCP 5(a)(3).

b. *Service; How made*

   i. *Serving an attorney.* If a party is represented by an attorney, service under FRCP 5 must be made on the attorney unless the court orders service on the party. FRCP 5(b)(1).

   ii. *Service in general.* A paper is served under FRCP 5 by:

   - Handing it to the person;

   - Leaving it: (1) at the person's office with a clerk or other person in charge or, if no one is in charge, in a conspicuous place in the office; or (2) if the person has no office or the office is closed, at the person's dwelling or usual place of abode with someone of suitable age and discretion who resides there;

   - Mailing it to the person's last known address—in which event service is complete upon mailing;

   - Leaving it with the court clerk if the person has no known address;

   - Sending it to a registered user by filing it with the court's electronic-filing system or sending it by other electronic means that the person consented to in writing—in either of which events service is complete upon filing or sending, but is not effective if the filer or sender learns that it did not reach the person to be served; or

   - Delivering it by any other means that the person consented to in writing—in which event service is complete when the person making service delivers it to the agency designated to make delivery. FRCP 5(b)(2).

   iii. *Service by electronic means.* Unless exempt or otherwise ordered by the court, all pleadings and other papers must be served on other parties by electronic means. MA R USDCT LR 5.4(C); MA R USDCT CM/ECF Admin(H)(2). Service by electronic means shall be treated the same as service by mail. MA R USDCT CM/ECF Admin(H)(4).

   - *Consent to electronic service.* Registering to use CM/ECF constitutes consent to service of all documents by electronic means as provided in the Administrative Procedures for Electronic Case Filing in the United States District Court for the District of Massachusetts (MA R USDCT CM/ECF Admin) and FRCP 5(b) and FRCP 77(d). MA R USDCT CM/ECF Admin(E)(6); MA R USDCT CM/ECF Admin(H)(3).

   - *Service on registered ECF users.* Transmission of the Notice of Electronic Filing (NEF) through the court's transmission facilities will constitute service of the filed document upon a registered ECF user. MA R USDCT LR 5.4(C).

   - *Service on non-registered users.* The party filing the document electronically is responsible for serving a paper copy of the document by mail in accordance with FRCP 5(b) to those case participants who have not been identified on the NEF as electronic recipients. MA R USDCT CM/ECF Admin(H)(3).

   - *Service of conventionally filed papers.* Documents or exhibits submitted conventionally shall be served on other parties by the filer using traditional means. MA R USDCT CM/ECF Admin(P)(4).

c. *Serving numerous defendants*

   i. *In general.* If an action involves an unusually large number of defendants, the court may, on motion or on its own, order that:

   - Defendants' pleadings and replies to them need not be served on other defendants;

   - Any crossclaim, counterclaim, avoidance, or affirmative defense in those pleadings and replies to them will be treated as denied or avoided by all other parties; and

- Filing any such pleading and serving it on the plaintiff constitutes notice of the pleading to all parties. FRCP 5(c)(1).

    ii.  *Notifying parties.* A copy of every such order must be served on the parties as the court directs. FRCP 5(c)(2).

## G. Hearings

1. There is no hearing contemplated in the federal statutes or rules for responses to requests for production of documents.

## H. Forms

### 1. Federal Response to Request for Production of Documents Forms

a. Response to request for production. 3A FEDFORMS § 25:26.

b. Response to request for production of documents; Government personnel files, memoranda, minutes of meetings, and statistics. 3A FEDFORMS § 25:27.

c. Response; To request for production of documents and other items. AMJUR PP DEPOSITION § 523.

d. Response; To request for production and inspection of documents and other items. AMJUR PP DEPOSITION § 524.

e. Verification; By defendant; Of response to request for production of documents and other items. AMJUR PP DEPOSITION § 525.

f. Response; To request for inspection. AMJUR PP DEPOSITION § 526.

g. Response; To request for production of documents; Objection; Documents not within objecting party's possession. AMJUR PP DEPOSITION § 597.

h. Response; To request for production of documents; Objection; Documents within attorney-client privilege. AMJUR PP DEPOSITION § 598.

i. Response; To request for production of documents prepared in anticipation of litigation; Objection; Requestor may easily obtain information elsewhere. AMJUR PP DEPOSITION § 599.

j. Response; To request for production of documents and things. FEDPROF § 23:423.

k. Response; To request for production of documents; With various objections. FEDPROF § 23:424.

l. Response to request for production of documents and things; Government records. FEDPROF § 23:425.

m. Objection; To request for production of documents; Documents not within objecting party's possession. FEDPROF § 23:426.

n. Objection; To request for production of documents; Documents within attorney-client privilege. FEDPROF § 23:427.

o. Objection; To request for production of documents prepared in anticipation of litigation; Requestor may easily obtain information elsewhere. FEDPROF § 23:428.

p. Objection; To request for production of documents; Documents do not exist. FEDPROF § 23:429.

q. First notice for production; Response. GOLDLTGFMS § 28:30.

## I. Applicable Rules

1. *Federal rules*

a. Serving and filing pleadings and other papers. FRCP 5.

b. Privacy protection for filings made with the court. FRCP 5.2.

c. Computing and extending time; Time for motion papers. FRCP 6.

d. Pleadings allowed; Form of motions and other papers. FRCP 7.

e. Form of pleadings. FRCP 10.

f. Signing pleadings, motions, and other papers; Representations to the court; Sanctions. FRCP 11.

g. Duty to disclose; General provisions governing discovery. FRCP 26.

h. Stipulations about discovery procedure. FRCP 29.

i. Producing documents, electronically stored information, and tangible things, or entering onto land, for inspection and other purposes. FRCP 34.

j. Failure to make disclosures or to cooperate in discovery; Sanctions. FRCP 37.

2. *Local rules*

    a.  Title. MA R USDCT LR 1.1.

    b.  Sanctions. MA R USDCT LR 1.3.

    c.  Form and filing of papers. MA R USDCT LR 5.1.

    d.  Service and filing of pleadings and other papers. MA R USDCT LR 5.2.

    e.  Filing and service by electronic means. MA R USDCT LR 5.4.

    f.  Alternative dispute resolution. MA R USDCT LR 16.4.

    g.  Control of discovery. MA R USDCT LR 26.1.

    h.  Phasing of discovery. MA R USDCT LR 26.3.

    i.  Uniform definitions in discovery requests. MA R USDCT LR 26.5.

    j.  Court filings and costs. MA R USDCT LR 26.6.

    k.  Document production. MA R USDCT LR 34.1.

    l.  Settlement. MA R USDCT LR 68.2.

    m.  Office of the clerk. MA R USDCT LR 77.2.

    n.  Appearances. MA R USDCT LR 83.5.2.

    o.  Practice by pro se litigants. MA R USDCT LR 83.5.5.

    p.  CM/ECF case management/electronic case files administrative procedures. MA R USDCT CM/ECF Admin.

# Requests, Notices and Applications
# Request for Admissions

## Document Last Updated December 2018

## A. Checklist

  (I)  ❑ Matters to be considered by requesting party

    (a)  ❑ Required documents

      (1)  ❑ Request for admissions

    (b)  ❑ Supplemental documents

      (1)  ❑ Document(s)

      (2)  ❑ Certificate of service

    (c)  ❑ Timing

      (1)  ❑ A party may not seek discovery from any source before the parties have conferred as required by FRCP 26(f), except in a proceeding exempted from initial disclosure under FRCP 26(a)(1)(B), or when authorized by the Federal Rules of Civil Procedure, by stipulation, or by court order

  (II)  ❑ Matters to be considered by responding party

    (a)  ❑ Required documents

      (1)  ❑ Response to request for admissions

    (b)  ❑ Supplemental documents

      (1)  ❑ Certificate of service

    (c)  ❑ Timing

      (1)  ❑ A matter is admitted unless, within thirty (30) days after being served, the party to whom the request is directed serves on the requesting party a written answer or objection addressed to the matter and signed by the party or its attorney

      (2)  ❑ When there is objection to a request for admission and it is subsequently determined that the request is proper, the matter, the admission of which is requested, shall be deemed admitted unless within fourteen (14) days

after such determination such party to whom the request was directed serves a statement denying the matter or setting forth the reasons why that party cannot admit or deny the matter, as provided in FRCP 36

## B. Timing

1. *Request for admissions.* A party may not seek discovery through requests for admission before the parties have conferred as required by FRCP 26(f), except in a proceeding exempted from initial disclosure or when authorized by the Federal Rules of Civil Procedure, by stipulation, or by court order. FEDPROC § 26:657.

2. *Commencement of discovery.* A party may not seek discovery from any source before the parties have conferred as required by FRCP 26(f), except in a proceeding exempted from initial disclosure under FRCP 26(a)(1)(B), or when authorized by the Federal Rules of Civil Procedure, by stipulation, or by court order. FRCP 26(d)(1).

3. *Computation of time*

   a. *Computing time.* FRCP 6 applies in computing any time period specified in the Federal Rules of Civil Procedure, in any local rule or court order, or in any statute that does not specify a method of computing time. FRCP 6(a).

   i. *Period stated in days or a longer unit.* When the period is stated in days or a longer unit of time:
   - Exclude the day of the event that triggers the period;
   - Count every day, including intermediate Saturdays, Sundays, and legal holidays; and
   - Include the last day of the period, but if the last day is a Saturday, Sunday, or legal holiday, the period continues to run until the end of the next day that is not a Saturday, Sunday, or legal holiday. FRCP 6(a)(1).

   ii. *Period stated in hours.* When the period is stated in hours:
   - Begin counting immediately on the occurrence of the event that triggers the period;
   - Count every hour, including hours during intermediate Saturdays, Sundays, and legal holidays; and
   - If the period would end on a Saturday, Sunday, or legal holiday, the period continues to run until the same time on the next day that is not a Saturday, Sunday, or legal holiday. FRCP 6(a)(2).

   iii. *Office of the clerk.* The offices of the Clerk of Court at Boston, Worcester and Springfield shall be open from 8:30 a.m. until 5:00 p.m. on all days except Saturdays, Sundays, legal holidays and other days so ordered by the court and announced in advance, if feasible. MA R USDCT LR 77.2.

   iv. *Inaccessibility of the clerk's office.* Unless the court orders otherwise, if the clerk's office is inaccessible:
   - On the last day for filing under FRCP 6(a)(1), then the time for filing is extended to the first accessible day that is not a Saturday, Sunday, or legal holiday; or
   - During the last hour for filing under FRCP 6(a)(2), then the time for filing is extended to the same time on the first accessible day that is not a Saturday, Sunday, or legal holiday. FRCP 6(a)(3).

   v. *"Last day" defined.* Unless a different time is set by a statute, local rule, or court order, the last day ends:
   - For electronic filing, at midnight in the court's time zone; and
   - For filing by other means, when the clerk's office is scheduled to close. FRCP 6(a)(4).

   vi. *"Next day" defined.* The "next day" is determined by continuing to count forward when the period is measured after an event and backward when measured before an event. FRCP 6(a)(5).

   vii. *"Legal holiday" defined.* "Legal holiday" means:
   - The day set aside by statute for observing New Year's Day, Martin Luther King Jr.'s Birthday, Washington's Birthday, Memorial Day, Independence Day, Labor Day, Columbus Day, Veterans' Day, Thanksgiving Day, or Christmas Day;
   - Any day declared a holiday by the President or Congress; and
   - For periods that are measured after an event, any other day declared a holiday by the state where the district court is located. FRCP 6(a)(6).

   b. *Computation of electronic filing deadlines.* Filing documents electronically does not alter any filing deadlines. MA R USDCT CM/ECF Admin(K); MA R USDCT LR 5.4(D). Although CM/ECF is generally available twenty-four (24) hours a day for filing, all electronic transmissions of documents must be completed prior to 6:00 PM, Eastern Standard (or Daylight Savings) Time, on the date on which it is due, in order to be considered timely filed that day. MA R USDCT CM/ECF Admin(K); MA R USDCT LR 5.4(D). When a specific time of day deadline is set by court order or stipulation, the electronic filing must be completed by that time. Documents may be filed at any time of the day on days prior to the date on which it is due. MA R USDCT CM/ECF Admin(K). A document filed electronically shall be deemed filed as of the time and date stated on the NEF received from the court. MA R USDCT CM/ECF Admin(G)(2); MA R USDCT CM/ECF Admin(K).

    i. *Technical failures.* A user whose filing is made untimely as the result of a technical failure of the court's CM/ECF system may seek appropriate relief from the court. MA R USDCT CM/ECF Admin(W)(3). Technical difficulties on the filer's end, with telephone, cable lines, the filer's Internet Service Provider (ISP), or hardware or software problems, will not constitute a technical failure under the Administrative Procedures for Electronic Case Filing in the United States District Court for the District of Massachusetts (MA R USDCT CM/ECF Admin) nor excuse an untimely filing. MA R USDCT CM/ECF Admin(W)(3). As help desk support is available during normal business hours, filers are strongly urged to electronically file any documents during that period. MA R USDCT CM/ECF Admin(W)(3).

- The court has made available a public terminal (computers and scanner) in each clerk's office for registered users to scan and electronically file documents. This equipment is available during normal business hours. Users should bring their prepared document and a valid CM/ECF login and password. MA R USDCT CM/ECF Admin(W)(3).

  c. *Extending time.* When an act may or must be done within a specified time, the court may, for good cause, extend the time: (1) with or without motion or notice if the court acts, or if a request is made, before the original time or its extension expires; or (2) on motion made after the time has expired if the party failed to act because of excusable neglect. FRCP 6(b)(1).

    i. *Exceptions.* A court must not extend the time to act under FRCP 50(b), FRCP 50(d), FRCP 52(b), FRCP 59(b), FRCP 59(d), FRCP 59(e), and FRCP 60(b). FRCP 6(b)(2).

    ii. Refer to the United States District Court for the District of Massachusetts KeyRules Motion for Continuance/Extension of Time document for more information on extending time.

  d. *Additional time after certain kinds of service.* When a party may or must act within a specified time after being served and service is made under FRCP 5(b)(2)(C) (by mail), FRCP 5(b)(2)(D) (by leaving with the clerk), or FRCP 5(b)(2)(F) (by other means consented to), three (3) days are added after the period would otherwise expire under FRCP 6(a). FRCP 6(d).

## C. General Requirements

1. *General provisions governing discovery*

  a. *Discovery scope and limits*

    i. *Scope in general.* Unless otherwise limited by court order, the scope of discovery is as follows: Parties may obtain discovery regarding any nonprivileged matter that is relevant to any party's claim or defense and proportional to the needs of the case, considering the importance of the issues at stake in the action, the amount in controversy, the parties' relative access to relevant information, the parties' resources, the importance of the discovery in resolving the issues, and whether the burden or expense of the proposed discovery outweighs its likely benefit. Information within this scope of discovery need not be admissible in evidence to be discoverable. FRCP 26(b)(1).

    ii. *Limitations on frequency and extent*

- *When permitted.* By order, the court may alter the limits in the Federal Rules of Civil Procedure on the number of depositions and interrogatories or on the length of depositions under FRCP 30. By order or local rule, the court may also limit the number of requests under FRCP 36. FRCP 26(b)(2)(A).

- *Specific limitations on electronically stored information.* A party need not provide discovery of electronically stored information from sources that the party identifies as not reasonably accessible because of undue burden or cost. On motion to compel discovery or for a protective order, the party from whom discovery is sought must show that the information is not reasonably accessible because of undue burden or cost. If that showing is made, the court may nonetheless order discovery from such sources if the requesting party shows good cause, considering the limitations of FRCP 26(b)(2)(C). The court may specify conditions for the discovery. FRCP 26(b)(2)(B).

- *When required.* On motion or on its own, the court must limit the frequency or extent of discovery otherwise allowed by the Federal Rules of Civil Procedure or by local rule if it determines that: (1) the discovery sought is unreasonably cumulative or duplicative, or can be obtained from some other source that is more convenient, less burdensome, or less expensive; (2) the party seeking discovery has had ample opportunity to obtain the information by discovery in the action; or (3) the proposed discovery is outside the scope permitted by FRCP 26(b)(1). FRCP 26(b)(2)(C).

iii. *Trial preparation; Materials*

- *Documents and tangible things.* Ordinarily, a party may not discover documents and tangible things that are prepared in anticipation of litigation or for trial by or for another party or its representative (including the other party's attorney, consultant, surety, indemnitor, insurer, or agent). But, subject to FRCP 26(b)(4), those materials may be discovered if: (1) they are otherwise discoverable under FRCP 26(b)(1); and (2) the party shows that it has substantial need for the materials to prepare its case and cannot, without undue hardship, obtain their substantial equivalent by other means. FRCP 26(b)(3)(A).

- *Protection against disclosure.* If the court orders discovery of those materials, it must protect against disclosure of the mental impressions, conclusions, opinions, or legal theories of a party's attorney or other representative concerning the litigation. FRCP 26(b)(3)(B).

- *Previous statement.* Any party or other person may, on request and without the required showing, obtain the person's own previous statement about the action or its subject matter. If the request is refused, the person may move for a court order, and FRCP 37(a)(5) applies to the award of expenses. A previous statement is either: (1) a written statement that the person has signed or otherwise adopted or approved; or (2) a contemporaneous stenographic, mechanical, electrical, or other recording—or a transcription of it—that recites substantially verbatim the person's oral statement. FRCP 26(b)(3)(C).

iv. *Trial preparation; Experts*

- *Deposition of an expert who may testify.* A party may depose any person who has been identified as an expert whose opinions may be presented at trial. If FRCP 26(a)(2)(B) requires a report from the expert, the deposition may be conducted only after the report is provided. FRCP 26(b)(4)(A).

- *Trial-preparation protection for draft reports or disclosures.* FRCP 26(b)(3)(A) and FRCP 26(b)(3)(B) protect drafts of any report or disclosure required under FRCP 26(a)(2), regardless of the form in which the draft is recorded. FRCP 26(b)(4)(B).

- *Trial-preparation protection for communications between a party's attorney and expert witnesses.* FRCP 26(b)(3)(A) and FRCP 26(b)(3)(B) protect communications between the party's attorney and any witness required to provide a report under FRCP 26(a)(2)(B), regardless of the form of the communications, except to the extent that the communications: (1) relate to compensation for the expert's study or testimony; (2) identify facts or data that the party's attorney provided and that the expert considered in forming the opinions to be expressed; or (3) identify assumptions that the party's attorney provided and that the expert relied on in forming the opinions to be expressed. FRCP 26(b)(4)(C).

- *Expert employed only for trial preparation.* Ordinarily, a party may not, by interrogatories or deposition, discover facts known or opinions held by an expert who has been retained or specially employed by another party in anticipation of litigation or to prepare for trial and who is not expected to be called as a witness at trial. But a party may do so only: (1) as provided in FRCP 35(b); or (2) on showing exceptional circumstances under which it is impracticable for the party to obtain facts or opinions on the same subject by other means. FRCP 26(b)(4)(D).

- *Payment.* Unless manifest injustice would result, the court must require that the party seeking discovery: (1) pay the expert a reasonable fee for time spent in responding to discovery under FRCP 26(b)(4)(A) or FRCP 26(b)(4)(D); and (2) for discovery under FRCP 26(b)(4)(D), also pay the other party a fair portion of the fees and expenses it reasonably incurred in obtaining the expert's facts and opinions. FRCP 26(b)(4)(E).

v. *Claiming privilege or protecting trial-preparation materials*

- *Information withheld.* When a party withholds information otherwise discoverable by claiming that the information is privileged or subject to protection as trial-preparation material, the party must: (1) expressly make the claim; and (2) describe the nature of the documents, communications, or tangible things not produced or disclosed—and do so in a manner that, without revealing information itself privileged or protected, will enable other parties to assess the claim. FRCP 26(b)(5)(A).

- *Information produced.* If information produced in discovery is subject to a claim of privilege or of protection as trial-preparation material, the party making the claim may notify any party that received the information of the claim and the basis for it. After being notified, a party must promptly return, sequester, or destroy the specified information and any copies it has; must not use or disclose the information until the claim is resolved; must take reasonable steps to retrieve the information if the party disclosed it before being notified; and may promptly present the information to the court under seal for a determination of the claim. The producing party must preserve the information until the claim is resolved. FRCP 26(b)(5)(B).

b. *Protective orders.* A party or any person from whom discovery is sought may move for a protective order in the court where the action is pending—or as an alternative on matters relating to a deposition, in the court for the district where the deposition will be taken. FRCP 26(c)(1). Refer to the United States District Court for the District of Massachusetts KeyRules Motion for Protective Order document for more information.

c. *Disclosure orders.* The judicial officer may order the parties to submit at the scheduling conference, or at any subsequent time the officer deems appropriate, sworn statements disclosing certain information to every other party. At the discretion of the judicial officer, this order may direct the submission of:

　i. A sworn statement from a claimant, whether plaintiff, third-party plaintiff, cross-claimant, or counter-claimant, that:

- Itemizes all economic loss and provides a computation of damages for which recovery is sought, if any, sustained before the date of service of process;

- Identifies all persons then known to the claimant or the claimant's attorney who witnessed or participated in the transaction or occurrence giving rise to the claim or otherwise known or believed to have substantial discoverable information about the claim or defenses, together with a statement of the subject and a brief summary of that information;

- Identifies all opposing parties, and all officers, directors, and employees of opposing parties, from whom statements have been obtained by or on behalf of the claimant regarding the subject matter of the claim; and

- Identifies all governmental agencies or officials then known to the claimant or the claimant's attorney to have investigated the transaction or occurrence giving rise to the claim; and

　ii. A sworn statement from a defendant, whether the direct defendant, third-party defendant, cross-claim defendant, or counterclaim defendant, that identifies:

- All persons then known to the defendant or the defendant's attorneys who witnessed the transaction or occurrence giving rise to the claim or otherwise is known or believed to have substantial discoverable information about the claims or defenses, together with a statement of the subject and a brief summary of that information;

- All opposing parties, and all officers, directors, and employees of opposing parties, from whom statements have been obtained by or on behalf of the defendant regarding the subject matter of the claims or defenses; and

- All government agencies or officials then known to the defendant or the defendant's attorneys to have investigated the transaction or occurrence giving rise to the claims or defenses. MA R USDCT LR 26.1(b).

　iii. Noncompliance may be excused only by order of the judicial officer. MA R USDCT LR 26.1(b).

d. *Uniform definitions in discovery requests*

　i. *Incorporation by reference and limitations.* The full text of the definitions set forth in MA R USDCT LR 26.5(c) is deemed incorporated by reference into all discovery requests, but shall not preclude:

- The definition of other terms specific to the particular litigation;

- The use of abbreviations; or

- A narrower definition of a term defined in MA R USDCT LR 26.5(c). MA R USDCT LR 26.5(a).

　ii. *Effect on scope of discovery.* MA R USDCT LR 26.5 is not intended to broaden or narrow the scope of discovery permitted by the Federal Rules of Civil Procedure. MA R USDCT LR 26.5(b).

　iii. *Definitions.* The following definitions apply to all discovery requests:

- *Communication.* The term "communication" means the transmittal of information (in the form of facts, ideas, inquiries, or otherwise). MA R USDCT LR 26.5(c)(1).

- *Document.* The term "document" is defined to be synonymous in meaning and equal in scope to the usage of this term in FRCP 34(a). A draft or non-identical copy is a separate document within the meaning of this term. MA R USDCT LR 26.5(c)(2).

- *Identify (with respect to persons).* When referring to a person, "to identify" means to give, to the extent known, the person's full name, present or last known address, and, when referring to a natural person, the present or last known place of employment. Once a person has been identified in accordance with this subparagraph, only the name of that person need be listed in response to subsequent discovery requesting the identification of that person. MA R USDCT LR 26.5(c)(3).

- *Identify (with respect to documents).* When referring to documents, "to identify" means to give, to the extent known, the: (1) type of document; (2) general subject matter; (3) date of the document; and (4) author(s), addressee(s), and recipient(s). MA R USDCT LR 26.5(c)(4).

- *Parties.* The terms "plaintiff" and "defendant" as well as a party's full or abbreviated name or a pronoun referring to a party mean the party and, where applicable, its officers, directors, employees, partners, corporate parent, subsidiaries, or affiliates. This definition is not intended to impose a discovery obligation on any person who is not a party to the litigation. MA R USDCT LR 26.5(c)(5).

- *Person.* The term "person" is defined as any natural person or any business, legal, or governmental entity or association. MA R USDCT LR 26.5(c)(6).

- *Concerning.* The term "concerning" means referring to, describing, evidencing, or constituting. MA R USDCT LR 26.5(c)(7).

- *State the basis.* When an interrogatory calls upon a party to "state the basis" of or for a particular claim, assertion, allegation, or contention, the party shall: (1) identify each and every document (and, where pertinent, the section, article, or subparagraph thereof), which forms any part of the source of the party's information regarding the alleged facts or legal conclusions referred to by the interrogatory; (2) identify each and every communication which forms any part of the source of the party's information regarding the alleged facts or legal conclusions referred to by the interrogatory; (3) state separately the acts or omissions to act on the part of any person (identifying the acts or omissions to act by stating their nature, time, and place and identifying the persons involved) which form any part of the party's information regarding the alleged facts or legal conclusions referred to in the interrogatory; and (4) state separately any other fact which forms the basis of the party's information regarding the alleged facts or conclusions referred to in the interrogatory. MA R USDCT LR 26.5(c)(8).

e. *Cooperative discovery.* The judicial officer should encourage cost effective discovery by means of voluntary exchange of information among litigants and their attorneys. This may be accomplished through the use of: (1) informal, cooperative discovery practices in which counsel provide information to opposing counsel without resort to formal discovery procedures; or (2) stipulations entered into by the parties with respect to deposition notices, waiver of signing, and other matters, except that the parties may not enter into stipulations extending the time for responding to discovery requests or otherwise modify discovery procedures ordered by the judicial officer. MA R USDCT LR 26.1(a).

f. *Phasing of discovery.* In order to facilitate settlement and the efficient completion of discovery, the judicial officer has discretion to structure discovery activities by phasing and sequencing the topics which are the subject of discovery. For example, an order may be framed limiting the first phase to developing information needed for a realistic assessment of the case. If the case does not terminate, the second phase would be directed at information needed to prepare for trial. MA R USDCT LR 26.3.

g. *Sequence of discovery.* Unless the parties stipulate or the court orders otherwise for the parties' and witnesses' convenience and in the interests of justice: (1) methods of discovery may be used in any sequence; and (2) discovery by one party does not require any other party to delay its discovery. FRCP 26(d)(3).

2. *Request for admissions*

a. *Scope.* A party may serve on any other party a written request to admit, for purposes of the pending action only, the truth of any matters within the scope of FRCP 26(b)(1) relating to: (1) facts, the application of law to fact, or opinions about either; and (2) the genuineness of any described documents. FRCP 36(a)(1).

i. A party may serve a request for admission even though the party has the burden of proving the matters asserted therein because FRCP 36 permits requests for admission to address claims of the party seeking discovery, and generally, the party asserting a claim bears the burden of proof thereon. FEDPROC § 26:666.

b. *Number.* FRCP 36 does not limit a party to a single request, or set of requests, for admissions. But FRCP 26(b)(2)(A) authorizes courts to limit the number of requests by order or local rule. In addition, the court has power to protect a party from harassment by repeated requests for admissions, but will not bar such repeated requests when the circumstances of the case justify them. Even a second request about the same fact or the genuineness of the same document is permissible if circumstances warrant a renewed request. FPP § 2258. Unless the judicial officer orders otherwise, the number of discovery events shall be limited for each side (or group of parties with a common interest) to. . .twenty-five (25) requests for admissions. MA R USDCT LR 26.1(c).

   i. *Further discovery.* Should a party exhaust the opportunities for any type of discovery events under MA R USDCT LR 26.1(c), any requests that such party may make for additional interrogatories, depositions, admissions or the production of documents beyond that allowed pursuant to MA R USDCT LR 26.1(c) shall be by discovery motion. All requests for additional discovery events, extensions of deadlines, for the completion of discovery or for postponement of the trial must be signed by the attorney and the party making the request. MA R USDCT LR 26.2(b).

  c. *Form.* Each matter must be separately stated. FRCP 36(a)(2). The party called upon to respond should not be required to go through a document and assume the responsibility of determining what facts it is being requested to admit. FPP § 2258. Each request for an admission should be phrased simply and directly so that it can be admitted or denied without explanation. FPP § 2258; United Coal Companies v. Powell Const. Co., 839 F.2d 958, 968 (3d Cir. 1988).

   i. A request for an admission need not state the source of information about the matter for which the request is made. FPP § 2258.

  d. *Effect of an admission; Withdrawing or amending it.* A matter admitted under FRCP 36 is conclusively established unless the court, on motion, permits the admission to be withdrawn or amended. Subject to FRCP 16(e), the court may permit withdrawal or amendment if it would promote the presentation of the merits of the action and if the court is not persuaded that it would prejudice the requesting party in maintaining or defending the action on the merits. An admission under FRCP 36 is not an admission for any other purpose and cannot be used against the party in any other proceeding. FRCP 36(b).

  e. *Motion to compel.* The motion to compel discovery provided by FRCP 37(a) does not apply to a failure to respond to a request for admissions. The automatic admission from a failure to respond is a sufficient remedy for the party who made the request. If, however, a request is objected to, or the requesting party thinks that a response to a request is insufficient, it may move under FRCP 36(a)(6) to determine the sufficiency of the answers or objections. FPP § 2265.

  f. *Motion regarding the sufficiency of an answer or objection.* The requesting party may move to determine the sufficiency of an answer or objection. Unless the court finds an objection justified, it must order that an answer be served. On finding that an answer does not comply with FRCP 36, the court may order either that the matter is admitted or that an amended answer be served. The court may defer its final decision until a pretrial conference or a specified time before trial. FRCP 37(a)(5) applies to an award of expenses. FRCP 36(a)(6). Refer to the United States District Court for the District of Massachusetts KeyRules Motion for Discovery Sanctions document for more information on sanctions.

3. *Sanctions for failure to cooperate in discovery.* The pattern of sanctions for FRCP 36 is somewhat different from that for the other discovery rules. The most important sanctions are two:

  a. A failure to respond to a request is deemed an admission of the matter to which the request is directed; and

  b. A party who, without good reason, refuses to admit a matter will be required to pay the costs incurred in proving that matter. FPP § 2265. If a party fails to admit what is requested under FRCP 36 and if the requesting party later proves a document to be genuine or the matter true, the requesting party may move that the party who failed to admit pay the reasonable expenses, including attorney's fees, incurred in making that proof. The court must so order unless:

   i. The request was held objectionable under FRCP 36(a);

   ii. The admission sought was of no substantial importance;

   iii. The party failing to admit had a reasonable ground to believe that it might prevail on the matter; or

   iv. There was other good reason for the failure to admit. FRCP 37(c)(2).

  c. Refer to the United States District Court for the District of Massachusetts KeyRules Motion for Discovery Sanctions document for more information on sanctions.

4. *Stipulations about discovery procedure.* Unless the court orders otherwise, the parties may stipulate that: (1) a deposition may be taken before any person, at any time or place, on any notice, and in the manner specified—in which event it may be used in the same way as any other deposition; and (2) other procedures governing or limiting discovery be modified—but a stipulation extending the time for any form of discovery must have court approval if it would interfere with the time set for completing discovery, for hearing a motion, or for trial. FRCP 29.

5. *Alternative dispute resolution (ADR).* The judicial officer assigned to preside over the case shall encourage the resolution of disputes by settlement or other alternative dispute resolution programs. MA R USDCT LR 16.4(a).

    a. *Settlement.* At every conference conducted under the Local Rules of the United States District Court for the District of Massachusetts, the judicial officer shall inquire as to the utility of the parties conducting settlement negotiations, explore means of facilitating those negotiations, and offer whatever assistance may be appropriate in the circumstances. Assistance may include a reference of the case to another judicial officer for settlement purposes. MA R USDCT LR 16.4(b).

        i. When a case is settled, the parties shall file with the clerk a signed agreement for judgment or stipulation for dismissal, as appropriate, within twenty-eight (28) days, unless the court otherwise orders. MA R USDCT LR 68.2.

    b. *Alternative dispute resolution programs*

        i. *Discretion of judicial officer.* The judicial officer, following an exploration of the matter with all counsel, may refer appropriate cases to alternative dispute resolution programs that have been designated for use in the district court or that the judicial officer may make available. The dispute resolution programs described in MA R USDCT LR 16.4(c)(2) through MA R USDCT LR 16.4(c)(4) are illustrative, not exclusive. Moreover, nothing in MA R USDCT LR 16.4 shall preclude the parties from engaging in private dispute resolution programs as long as they comply with any schedule established by the court. MA R USDCT LR 16.4(c)(1).

        ii. *Mediation.* The judicial officer may refer the case to mediation upon the agreement of all parties. MA R USDCT LR 16.4(c)(2)(A).

        iii. *Other alternative dispute resolution programs.* Use of mediation is not exclusive. At the request of parties, the judicial officer may consider other forms of alternative dispute resolution including, but not limited to, mini-trial, summary jury trial and arbitration. MA R USDCT LR 16.4(c)(3).

    c. For more information on alternative dispute resolution (ADR), refer to MA R USDCT LR 16.4.

6. *Sanctions.* Failure to comply with any of the directions or obligations set forth in, or authorized by, these rules may result in dismissal, default, or the imposition of other sanctions as deemed appropriate by the judicial officer. MA R USDCT LR 1.3. Except as provided by law, the court may impose sanctions as provided in MA R USDCT LR 1.3 for failure to comply with the Administrative Procedures for Electronic Case Filing in the United States District Court for the District of Massachusetts (MA R USDCT CM/ECF Admin) or with MA R USDCT LR 5.4. MA R USDCT CM/ECF Admin(C)(3).

## D. Documents

1. *Required documents*

    a. *Request for admissions.* Refer to the General Requirements section of this document for information on the request for admissions.

2. *Supplemental documents*

    a. *Document(s).* A request to admit the genuineness of a document must be accompanied by a copy of the document unless it is, or has been, otherwise furnished or made available for inspection and copying. FRCP 36(a)(2).

    b. *Certificate of service.* No certificate of service is required when a paper is served by filing it with the court's electronic-filing system. When a paper that is required to be served is served by other means: (1) if the paper is filed, a certificate of service must be filed with it or within a reasonable time after service; and (2) if the paper is not filed, a certificate of service need not be filed unless filing is required by court order or by local rule. FRCP 5(d)(1)(B).

## E. Format

1. *Form of documents.* The rules governing captions and other matters of form in pleadings apply to motions and other papers. FRCP 7(b)(2). The provisions of FRCP 10 and FRCP 11 concerning the form and signing of pleadings, motions, and other papers shall be applicable to all papers filed in any proceeding in this court. The board of bar overseers registration number of each attorney signing such documents, except the United States Attorney and his or her staff, shall be inscribed below the signature. MA R USDCT LR 5.1(a)(1).

    a. *Paper size and binding.* All papers filed in the court shall be adapted for flat filing, be filed on eight and one-half by eleven (8-1/2 x 11) inch paper without backers and be bound firmly by staple or some such other means (excluding paper or binder clip or rubber band). MA R USDCT LR 5.1(a)(2).

    b. *Spacing.* All papers, except discovery requests and responses, shall be double-spaced except for the identification of counsel, title of the case, footnotes, quotations and exhibits. Discovery requests and responses shall be single-spaced. MA R USDCT LR 5.1(a)(2).

DISTRICT OF MASSACHUSETTS

c. *Caption.* Every pleading must have a caption with the court's name, a title, a file number, and [an] FRCP 7(a) designation. FRCP 10(a).

    i. *Names of parties.* The title of the complaint must name all the parties; the title of other pleadings, after naming the first party on each side, may refer generally to other parties. FRCP 10(a).

    ii. *Request for special action.* When any pleading or other paper filed in the court includes a request for special process or relief, or any other request such that, if granted, the court will proceed other than in the ordinary course, the request shall, unless it is noted on the category sheet [see MA R USDCT LR 40.1(a)(1)], be noted on the first page to the right of or immediately beneath the caption. MA R USDCT LR 5.1(c).

d. *Claims or defenses*

    i. *Numbered paragraphs.* A party must state its claims or defenses in numbered paragraphs, each limited as far as practicable to a single set of circumstances. A later pleading may refer by number to a paragraph in an earlier pleading. FRCP 10(b).

    ii. *Separate statements.* If doing so would promote clarity, each claim founded on a separate transaction or occurrence—and each defense other than a denial—must be stated in a separate count or defense. FRCP 10(b).

e. *Adoption by reference.* A statement in a pleading may be adopted by reference elsewhere in the same pleading or in any other pleading or motion. FRCP 10(c).

    i. *Exhibits.* A copy of a written instrument that is an exhibit to a pleading is a part of the pleading for all purposes. FRCP 10(c).

f. *Citations*

    i. *Local rules.* These rules shall be known as Local Rules of the United States District Court for the District of Massachusetts and cited as "L.R., D. Mass." or "L.R." MA R USDCT LR 1.1.

    ii. *Electronic case filing procedures.* The procedures governing electronic case filing shall be known as the "Administrative Procedures for Electronic Case Filing in the United States District Court for the District of Massachusetts." They shall be cited as "APECF." MA R USDCT CM/ECF Admin(A)(7).

g. *Acceptance by the clerk.* The clerk must not refuse to file a paper solely because it is not in the form prescribed by the Federal Rules of Civil Procedure or by a local rule or practice. FRCP 5(d)(4).

    i. Except for complaints and notices of appeal, papers that do not conform to the requirements of MA R USDCT LR 5.1(a)(2) shall be returned by the clerk. MA R USDCT LR 5.1(a)(2).

2. *Form of electronic documents.* A paper filed electronically is a written paper for purposes of the Federal Rules of Civil Procedure. FRCP 5(d)(3)(D).

a. *PDF/A format required.* The court will begin requiring submission of documents in PDF/A format in the foreseeable future. PDF/A is an enhanced version of the traditional PDF format. Newer versions of most PDF software will be able to convert to this format. Additional information on PDF/A documents may be found on the court's website. MA R USDCT CM/ECF Admin(Electronic Filing and PDF).

    i. *Electronically converted PDF.* Electronically converted PDF documents are created from word processing documents (MS Word, WordPerfect, etc.) using any appropriate software. These documents are text searchable and the file size is generally smaller than a scanned document. CM/ECF users may use any brand of software to convert documents to PDF. MA R USDCT CM/ECF Admin(Electronic Filing and PDF).

        • Documents converted to PDF, rather than scanned, are preferred for filing in CM/ECF. MA R USDCT CM/ECF Admin(Electronic Filing and PDF).

    ii. *Scanned PDF.* Scanned PDF documents are created from paper documents run through an optical scanner. Scanned PDF documents are generally not searchable and have a larger file size. Please note that software used to create scanned documents may (and should) be set in such a way that the document is "text-searchable." MA R USDCT CM/ECF Admin(Electronic Filing and PDF).

b. *Title.* All pleadings filed electronically shall be titled in accordance with the approved dictionary of civil or criminal events of the CM/ECF system of this court. A list of events is available on the CM/ECF Training Information page of the court's website. The clerk's office may, when necessary and appropriate, modify the docket entry description, or delete and re-enter the docket entry in order to comply with the court's quality assurance standards. MA R USDCT CM/ECF Admin(G)(3).

c. *Attachments to filings and exhibits.* Attachments to filings and exhibits must be filed in accordance with the court's CM/ECF User Manual, unless otherwise ordered by the court. MA R USDCT CM/ECF Admin(O)(1).

    i. Filers must submit as attachments only those excerpts of the referenced documents that are directly germane to the matter under consideration by the court. Excerpted material must be clearly and prominently identified as such. Users who file excerpts of documents do so without prejudice to their right to timely file additional excerpts or the complete document, as may be allowed by the court. Responding parties may timely file additional excerpts or the complete document that they believe are directly germane. MA R USDCT CM/ECF Admin(O)(2).

    ii. Filers shall not attach as an exhibit any pleading or other paper already on file with the court in that case, but shall merely refer to that document. (See MA R USDCT CM/ECF Admin(G) for information on using hyperlinks in PDF documents filed in CM/ECF.) MA R USDCT CM/ECF Admin(O)(3).

d. *Redacted documents.* The parties may request or the court may require the submission of documents that have been redacted/stripped of sensitive or confidential information. The redacted document prepared for electronic filing shall include the original caption of the document, and be clearly labeled as "Redacted Document." A specific event is available for this purpose ("Redacted Document"), found under the Other Filings/Other Documents menu option. MA R USDCT CM/ECF Admin(S).

    i. Attorneys and pro se litigants are advised to take extra care when creating PDF documents intended for submission to CM/ECF. Steps shall be taken to ensure the documents are free of any hidden data (metadata) that may contain redacted information, or traces of information edited or deleted are not hidden in the final document. Even PDF content that has been encrypted may be recovered. An advisory document with additional information on this topic may be found on the court's website. MA R USDCT CM/ECF Admin(S).

e. *Hyperlinks.* Electronically filed documents may contain the following types of hyperlinks: (1) hyperlinks to other portions of the same document; (2) hyperlinks to other documents filed within the CM/ECF system; and (3) hyperlinks to a location on the Internet that contains a source document for a citation. MA R USDCT CM/ECF Admin(G)(7).

    i. Hyperlinks to cited authority may not replace standard citation format. Complete citations must be included in the text of the filed document. Neither a hyperlink, nor any site to which it refers, shall be considered part of the record, but are simply convenient mechanisms for accessing material cited in a document filed in CM/ECF. Instructions on creating hyperlinks may be found in the CM/ECF User Manual. MA R USDCT CM/ECF Admin(G)(7).

    ii. The court accepts no responsibility for, and does not endorse, any product, organization, or content at any hyperlinked site, or at any site to which that site may be linked. The court accepts no responsibility for the availability or functionality of any hyperlink. MA R USDCT CM/ECF Admin(G)(7).

    iii. One feature of PDF/A documents is that hyperlinks are commonly "masked," meaning that the full address of the referenced file is not written out; for example, clicking the word brief may open a brief which was previously filed in CM/ECF. MA R USDCT CM/ECF Admin(G)(7)(NOTE). An "unmasked" hyperlink has the full address visible to the user. MA R USDCT CM/ECF Admin(G)(7)(NOTE).

        • Masked hyperlinks may or may not work in a PDF/A document, depending on how it was created. Currently, masked hyperlinks are preserved in PDF/A documents produced by the "Save As" method in Microsoft Word 2007 and 2010; the "PDFMaker" method in Microsoft Word 2007; and OpenOffice 2.4 ("PDF Export"). With other production methods, such as WordPerfect, the PDF/A document includes underlined words that appear to be links, but clicking them has no effect. MA R USDCT CM/ECF Admin(G)(7)(NOTE).

f. *Documents features not accepted.* CM/ECF will not accept PDF documents containing tracking tags, embedded systems commands, password protections, access restrictions or other security features, special tags or dynamic features. MA R USDCT CM/ECF Admin(G)(8).

g. *File size limitations.* A filing party shall limit the size of each PDF file to no more than twenty (20) megabytes. PDF files larger than seven (7) megabytes will be rejected by the CM/ECF system. The filer will see a message advising of the size limitation. MA R USDCT CM/ECF Admin(P)(2).

    i. Larger documents or exhibits may be submitted electronically if split into separate PDF files each less than seven (7) megabytes, attached to the main document and clearly labeled. MA R USDCT CM/ECF Admin(P)(2).

    ii. Documents submitted electronically or on paper are subject to the page limitations set by MA R USDCT LR 7.1(b)(4) or by order of the court. MA R USDCT CM/ECF Admin(P)(1).

h. *Accuracy and readability.* The filer shall verify the accuracy and readability of any PDF file before electronically filing it in CM/ECF. MA R USDCT CM/ECF Admin(G)(6); MA R USDCT CM/ECF Admin(P)(3).

3. *Signing disclosures and discovery requests, responses, and objections.* FRCP 11 does not apply to disclosures and discovery requests, responses, objections, and motions under FRCP 26 through FRCP 37. FRCP 11(d).

    a. *Signature required.* Every disclosure under FRCP 26(a)(1) or FRCP 26(a)(3) and every discovery request, response, or objection must be signed by at least one attorney of record in the attorney's own name—or by the party personally, if unrepresented—and must state the signer's address, e-mail address, and telephone number. FRCP 26(g)(1). The provisions of the Federal Rules of Civil Procedure pertaining to the form and signing of pleadings, motions, and other papers shall be applicable to all papers filed in any proceeding in this court. The board of bar overseers registration number of each attorney signing such documents, except the United States Attorney and his staff, shall be inscribed below the signature. MA R USDCT LR 5.1(a)(1).

      i. *Electronic signing.* A filing made through a person's electronic-filing account and authorized by that person, together with that person's name on a signature block, constitutes the person's signature. FRCP 5(d)(3)(C).

      ii. *Appearances.* The filing of an appearance or any other pleading signed on behalf of a party constitutes an entry of appearance for that party. All pleadings shall contain the name, bar admission number, address, telephone number, and e-mail address of the attorney entering an appearance. MA R USDCT LR 83.5.2(a).

        • *Appearances by law firms.* When a party is represented by a law firm, the appearance must include the name and the signature of at least one individual attorney. When a party is represented by more than one attorney from the same or different law firms, the attorney entering the appearance must designate the individual attorney who is authorized to receive all notices in the case. Any notice sent to an attorney so designated shall be deemed to be proper notice unless the court finds that notice was not properly sent. MA R USDCT LR 83.5.2(b).

        • For more information on appearances, refer to MA R USDCT LR 83.5.2.

      iii. *Signatures of attorneys.* The user login and password required to submit documents to the CM/ECF system shall serve as that user's signature for purposes of FRCP 11 and for all other purposes under the Federal Rules of Civil Procedure and the Local Rules of the United States District Court for the District of Massachusetts. All electronically filed documents must include a signature block and must set forth the attorney's name, bar number, address, telephone number and email address. The name of the CM/ECF user under whose log-in and password the document is submitted must be preceded by a "/s/" and typed in the space where the signature would otherwise appear. MA R USDCT CM/ECF Admin(M)(1). For an example, refer to MA R USDCT CM/ECF Admin(M)(1).

      iv. *Signatures of pro se parties.* Any document requiring a signature that is filed by a party appearing pro se shall bear the words "pro se" following that party's signature. Any such document shall also state the party's mailing address, telephone number (if any), and e-mail address (if the party has consented to service by email). MA R USDCT LR 83.5.5(g). For more information on practice by pro se litigants, refer to MA R USDCT LR 83.5.5.

      v. *Multiple signatures.* The filer of any document requiring more than one signature (e.g, stipulations, joint motions, joint status reports, magistrate judge consent forms, etc.) must list thereon all the names of other signatories by means of a "/s/ name of signatory" block for each. By submitting such a document, the filing attorney certifies that each of the other signatories has expressly agreed to the form and substance of the document and that the filing attorney has their actual authority to submit the document electronically. MA R USDCT CM/ECF Admin(M)(2). For more information, refer to MA R USDCT CM/ECF Admin(M)(2).

      vi. *Affidavits.* Except as provided in MA R USDCT CM/ECF Admin(L), affidavits shall be filed electronically; however, the electronically filed version must contain a "/s/ name of signatory" block indicating that the paper document bears an original signature. MA R USDCT CM/ECF Admin(M)(3). The court will also accept a scanned version of the original, signed document. MA R USDCT CM/ECF Admin(M)(3). For more information, refer to MA R USDCT CM/ECF Admin(M)(3).

    b. *Effect of signature.* By signing, an attorney or party certifies that to the best of the person's knowledge, information, and belief formed after a reasonable inquiry:

      i. With respect to a disclosure, it is complete and correct as of the time it is made; and

      ii. With respect to a discovery request, response, or objection, it is:

        • Consistent with the Federal Rules of Civil Procedure and warranted by existing law or by a nonfrivolous argument for extending, modifying, or reversing existing law, or for establishing new law;

- Not interposed for any improper purpose, such as to harass, cause unnecessary delay, or needlessly increase the cost of litigation; and

- Neither unreasonable nor unduly burdensome or expensive, considering the needs of the case, prior discovery in the case, the amount in controversy, and the importance of the issues at stake in the action. FRCP 26(g)(1).

c. *Failure to sign.* Other parties have no duty to act on an unsigned disclosure, request, response, or objection until it is signed, and the court must strike it unless a signature is promptly supplied after the omission is called to the attorney's or party's attention. FRCP 26(g)(2).

d. *Sanction for improper certification.* If a certification violates FRCP 26(g) without substantial justification, the court, on motion or on its own, must impose an appropriate sanction on the signer, the party on whose behalf the signer was acting, or both. The sanction may include an order to pay the reasonable expenses, including attorney's fees, caused by the violation. FRCP 26(g)(3). Refer to the United States District Court for the District of Massachusetts KeyRules Motion for Discovery Sanctions document for more information.

4. *Privacy protection for filings made with the court*

a. *Redacted filings.* Unless the court orders otherwise, in an electronic or paper filing with the court that contains an individual's Social Security number, taxpayer-identification number, or birth date, the name of an individual known to be a minor, or a financial-account number, a party or nonparty making the filing may include only:

   i. The last four (4) digits of the Social Security number and taxpayer-identification number;

   ii. The year of the individual's birth;

   iii. The minor's initials; and

   iv. The last four (4) digits of the financial-account number. FRCP 5.2(a); MA R USDCT CM/ECF Admin(N).

b. *Exemptions from the redaction requirement.* The redaction requirement does not apply to the following:

   i. A financial-account number that identifies the property allegedly subject to forfeiture in a forfeiture proceeding;

   ii. The record of an administrative or agency proceeding;

   iii. The official record of a state-court proceeding;

   iv. The record of a court or tribunal, if that record was not subject to the redaction requirement when originally filed;

   v. A filing covered by FRCP 5.2(c) or FRCP 5.2(d); and

   vi. A pro se filing in an action brought under 28 U.S.C.A. § 2241, 28 U.S.C.A. § 2254, or 28 U.S.C.A. § 2255. FRCP 5.2(b).

c. *Limitations on remote access to electronic files; Social Security appeals and immigration cases.* Unless the court orders otherwise, in an action for benefits under the Social Security Act, and in an action or proceeding relating to an order of removal, to relief from removal, or to immigration benefits or detention, access to an electronic file is authorized as follows:

   i. The parties and their attorneys may have remote electronic access to any part of the case file, including the administrative record;

   ii. Any other person may have electronic access to the full record at the courthouse, but may have remote electronic access only to:

   - The docket maintained by the court; and

   - An opinion, order, judgment, or other disposition of the court, but not any other part of the case file or the administrative record. FRCP 5.2(c).

d. *Filings made under seal.* The court may order that a filing be made under seal without redaction. The court may later unseal the filing or order the person who made the filing to file a redacted version for the public record. FRCP 5.2(d).

e. *Protective orders.* For good cause, the court may by order in a case:

   i. Require redaction of additional information; or

   ii. Limit or prohibit a nonparty's remote electronic access to a document filed with the court. FRCP 5.2(e).

f. *Option for additional unredacted filing under seal.* A person making a redacted filing may also file an unredacted copy under seal. The court must retain the unredacted copy as part of the record. FRCP 5.2(f). For more information, refer to MA R USDCT LR 7.2.

g. *Option for filing a reference list.* A filing that contains redacted information may be filed together with a reference list that identifies each item of redacted information and specifies an appropriate identifier that uniquely corresponds to each item listed. The list must be filed under seal and may be amended as of right. Any reference in the case to a listed identifier will be construed to refer to the corresponding item of information. FRCP 5.2(g).

h. *Responsibility for redaction.* The clerk's office is not responsible for reviewing documents filed with the court to determine whether pleadings have been redacted and are in the proper form. MA R USDCT CM/ECF Admin(N).

i. *Waiver of protection of identifiers.* A person waives the protection of FRCP 5.2(a) as to the person's own information by filing it without redaction and not under seal. FRCP 5.2(h).

## F. Filing and Service Requirements

1. *Filing requirements*

   a. *Required filings.* Any paper after the complaint that is required to be served must be filed no later than a reasonable time after service. But disclosures under FRCP 26(a)(1) or FRCP 26(a)(2) and the following discovery requests and responses must not be filed until they are used in the proceeding or the court orders filing: depositions, interrogatories, requests for documents or tangible things or to permit entry onto land, and requests for admission. FRCP 5(d)(1)(A). Refer to the United States District Court for the District of Massachusetts KeyRules pleading and motion documents for information on filing with the court.

   b. *Nonfiling of discovery materials.* Discovery materials (that is, automatic or voluntary disclosure materials, depositions, deposition notices, interrogatories, requests for documents, requests for admissions, answers and responses to discovery requests, and any other requests for or products of the discovery process) shall not be filed unless so ordered by the court or for use in the proceeding. The party taking a deposition or obtaining any material through discovery is responsible for its preservation and delivery to the court if needed or so ordered. If for any reason a party or concerned citizen believes that any of the named documents should be filed, an ex parte request may be made that such document be filed, stating the reasons for the request. The court may also order filing sua sponte. MA R USDCT LR 26.6(a).

      i. *Discovery motions.* If relief is sought under FRCP 26(c) or FRCP 37, copies of the relevant portions of disputed documents shall be filed with the court contemporaneously with any motion. MA R USDCT LR 26.6(a).

      ii. *Motions for summary judgment.* If the moving party under FRCP 56 or the opponent relies on discovery documents, copies of the pertinent parts thereof shall be filed with the motion or opposition. MA R USDCT LR 26.6(a).

2. *Service requirements.* Service of all pleadings subsequent to the original complaint and of all other papers required to be served shall be made in the manner specified by FRCP 5. MA R USDCT LR 5.2(a). [A request for an admission] must be served on the party from whom the admission is requested and, unless the court has otherwise ordered, a copy of the request must be served on every other party. FPP § 2258.

   a. *Service; When required*

      i. *In general.* Unless the Federal Rules of Civil Procedure provide otherwise, each of the following papers must be served on every party:

         - An order stating that service is required;
         - A pleading filed after the original complaint, unless the court orders otherwise under FRCP 5(c) because there are numerous defendants;
         - A discovery paper required to be served on a party, unless the court orders otherwise;
         - A written motion, except one that may be heard ex parte; and
         - A written notice, appearance, demand, or offer of judgment, or any similar paper. FRCP 5(a)(1).

      ii. *If a party fails to appear.* No service is required on a party who is in default for failing to appear. But a pleading that asserts a new claim for relief against such a party must be served on that party under FRCP 4. FRCP 5(a)(2).

      iii. *Seizing property.* If an action is begun by seizing property and no person is or need be named as a defendant, any service required before the filing of an appearance, answer, or claim must be made on the person who had custody or possession of the property when it was seized. FRCP 5(a)(3).

   b. *Service; How made*

      i. *Serving an attorney.* If a party is represented by an attorney, service under FRCP 5 must be made on the attorney unless the court orders service on the party. FRCP 5(b)(1).

ii. *Service in general.* A paper is served under FRCP 5 by:

- Handing it to the person;

- Leaving it: (1) at the person's office with a clerk or other person in charge or, if no one is in charge, in a conspicuous place in the office; or (2) if the person has no office or the office is closed, at the person's dwelling or usual place of abode with someone of suitable age and discretion who resides there;

- Mailing it to the person's last known address—in which event service is complete upon mailing;

- Leaving it with the court clerk if the person has no known address;

- Sending it to a registered user by filing it with the court's electronic-filing system or sending it by other electronic means that the person consented to in writing—in either of which events service is complete upon filing or sending, but is not effective if the filer or sender learns that it did not reach the person to be served; or

- Delivering it by any other means that the person consented to in writing—in which event service is complete when the person making service delivers it to the agency designated to make delivery. FRCP 5(b)(2).

iii. *Service by electronic means.* Unless exempt or otherwise ordered by the court, all pleadings and other papers must be served on other parties by electronic means. MA R USDCT LR 5.4(C); MA R USDCT CM/ECF Admin(H)(2). Service by electronic means shall be treated the same as service by mail. MA R USDCT CM/ECF Admin(H)(4).

- *Consent to electronic service.* Registering to use CM/ECF constitutes consent to service of all documents by electronic means as provided in the Administrative Procedures for Electronic Case Filing in the United States District Court for the District of Massachusetts (MA R USDCT CM/ECF Admin) and FRCP 5(b) and FRCP 77(d). MA R USDCT CM/ECF Admin(E)(6); MA R USDCT CM/ECF Admin(H)(3).

- *Service on registered ECF users.* Transmission of the Notice of Electronic Filing (NEF) through the court's transmission facilities will constitute service of the filed document upon a registered ECF user. MA R USDCT LR 5.4(C).

- *Service on non-registered users.* The party filing the document electronically is responsible for serving a paper copy of the document by mail in accordance with FRCP 5(b) to those case participants who have not been identified on the NEF as electronic recipients. MA R USDCT CM/ECF Admin(H)(3).

- *Service of conventionally filed papers.* Documents or exhibits submitted conventionally shall be served on other parties by the filer using traditional means. MA R USDCT CM/ECF Admin(P)(4).

c. *Serving numerous defendants*

i. *In general.* If an action involves an unusually large number of defendants, the court may, on motion or on its own, order that:

- Defendants' pleadings and replies to them need not be served on other defendants;

- Any crossclaim, counterclaim, avoidance, or affirmative defense in those pleadings and replies to them will be treated as denied or avoided by all other parties; and

- Filing any such pleading and serving it on the plaintiff constitutes notice of the pleading to all parties. FRCP 5(c)(1).

ii. *Notifying parties.* A copy of every such order must be served on the parties as the court directs. FRCP 5(c)(2).

## G. Hearings

1. There is no hearing contemplated in the federal statutes or rules for requests for admissions.

## H. Forms

### 1. Federal Request for Admissions Forms

a. Plaintiff's request for admission. 3B FEDFORMS § 26:60.

b. Plaintiff's request for admission; Specific examples. 3B FEDFORMS § 26:61.

c. Plaintiff's request for admission; Statements in documents. 3B FEDFORMS § 26:62.

d. Plaintiff's request for admission; Statements in documents; Letter to defendant. 3B FEDFORMS § 26:63.

e. Plaintiff's request for admission; Specific facts. 3B FEDFORMS § 26:64.

f. Plaintiff's request for admission; Specific facts; Presentation of checks. 3B FEDFORMS § 26:65.

g. Plaintiff's request for admission; Specific documents and facts. 3B FEDFORMS § 26:66.

h. Plaintiff's request for admission; Specific documents and facts; Short version. 3B FEDFORMS § 26:67.

i. Plaintiff's request for admission; True copies, filing and operational effect of government documents. 3B FED-FORMS § 26:68.

j. Plaintiff's request for additional admission. 3B FEDFORMS § 26:69.

k. Defendant's request for admission of genuineness; Specific document. 3B FEDFORMS § 26:70.

l. Defendant's request for admission of genuineness; Specific document; Copy attached. 3B FEDFORMS § 26:71.

m. Defendant's request for admission of genuineness; Specific document; Attached letters. 3B FEDFORMS § 26:72.

n. Defendant's request for admission; Truth of statement. 3B FEDFORMS § 26:73.

o. Request; For admission of facts and genuineness of documents. AMJUR PP DEPOSITION § 674.

p. Request for admissions under FRCP 36. FEDPROF § 23:555.

q. Request for admissions; General form. FEDPROF § 23:556.

r. Request for admissions; Action to collect royalties. FEDPROF § 23:557.

s. Request for admissions; Trademark action. FEDPROF § 23:558.

t. Request for admissions; Automobile negligence action. FEDPROF § 23:559.

u. Request for admissions; Motor vehicle action. FEDPROF § 23:560.

v. Request for admissions; Premises liability action. FEDPROF § 23:561.

w. Request for admissions; Products liability action. FEDPROF § 23:562.

x. Request for admissions; Medical malpractice action. FEDPROF § 23:563.

y. Request for admissions; Genuineness of documents. FEDPROF § 23:564.

z. Request for admissions; Wrongful death due to forklift accident. FEDPROF § 23:565.

# I. Applicable Rules

1. *Federal rules*

   a. Serving and filing pleadings and other papers. FRCP 5.

   b. Privacy protection for filings made with the court. FRCP 5.2.

   c. Computing and extending time; Time for motion papers. FRCP 6.

   d. Pleadings allowed; Form of motions and other papers. FRCP 7.

   e. Form of pleadings. FRCP 10.

   f. Signing pleadings, motions, and other papers; Representations to the court; Sanctions. FRCP 11.

   g. Duty to disclose; General provisions governing discovery. FRCP 26.

   h. Stipulations about discovery procedure. FRCP 29.

   i. Requests for admission. FRCP 36.

   j. Failure to make disclosures or to cooperate in discovery; Sanctions. FRCP 37.

2. *Local rules*

   a. Title. MA R USDCT LR 1.1.

   b. Sanctions. MA R USDCT LR 1.3.

   c. Form and filing of papers. MA R USDCT LR 5.1.

   d. Service and filing of pleadings and other papers. MA R USDCT LR 5.2.

   e. Filing and service by electronic means. MA R USDCT LR 5.4.

   f. Alternative dispute resolution. MA R USDCT LR 16.4.

   g. Control of discovery. MA R USDCT LR 26.1.

h.  Sequences of discovery. MA R USDCT LR 26.2.

i.  Phasing of discovery. MA R USDCT LR 26.3.

j.  Uniform definitions in discovery requests. MA R USDCT LR 26.5.

k.  Court filings and costs. MA R USDCT LR 26.6.

l.  Settlement. MA R USDCT LR 68.2.

m.  Office of the clerk. MA R USDCT LR 77.2.

n.  Appearances. MA R USDCT LR 83.5.2.

o.  Practice by pro se litigants. MA R USDCT LR 83.5.5.

p.  CM/ECF case management/electronic case files administrative procedures. MA R USDCT CM/ECF Admin.

# Requests, Notices and Applications
# Response to Request for Admissions

**Document Last Updated December 2018**

## A.  Checklist

(I)  ❏ Matters to be considered by requesting party

    (a)  ❏ Required documents

        (1)  ❏ Request for admissions

    (b)  ❏ Supplemental documents

        (1)  ❏ Document(s)

        (2)  ❏ Certificate of service

    (c)  ❏ Timing

        (1)  ❏ A party may not seek discovery from any source before the parties have conferred as required by FRCP 26(f), except in a proceeding exempted from initial disclosure under FRCP 26(a)(1)(B), or when authorized by the Federal Rules of Civil Procedure, by stipulation, or by court order

(II)  ❏ Matters to be considered by responding party

    (a)  ❏ Required documents

        (1)  ❏ Response to request for admissions

    (b)  ❏ Supplemental documents

        (1)  ❏ Certificate of service

    (c)  ❏ Timing

        (1)  ❏ A matter is admitted unless, within thirty (30) days after being served, the party to whom the request is directed serves on the requesting party a written answer or objection addressed to the matter and signed by the party or its attorney

        (2)  ❏ When there is objection to a request for admission and it is subsequently determined that the request is proper, the matter, the admission of which is requested, shall be deemed admitted unless within fourteen (14) days after such determination such party to whom the request was directed serves a statement denying the matter or setting forth the reasons why that party cannot admit or deny the matter, as provided in FRCP 36

## B.  Timing

1.  *Response to request for admissions.* A matter is admitted unless, within thirty (30) days after being served, the party to whom the request is directed serves on the requesting party a written answer or objection addressed to the matter and signed by the party or its attorney. A shorter or longer time for responding may be stipulated to under FRCP 29 or be ordered by the court. FRCP 36(a)(3).

    a.  *Statements in response to requests for admission following objections.* When there is objection to a request for admission and it is subsequently determined that the request is proper, the matter, the admission of which is requested, shall be deemed admitted unless within fourteen (14) days after such determination such party to whom the request was directed serves a statement denying the matter or setting forth the reasons why that party cannot admit or deny the matter, as provided in FRCP 36. MA R USDCT LR 36.1(b).

2.  *Computation of time*

    a.  *Computing time.* FRCP 6 applies in computing any time period specified in the Federal Rules of Civil Procedure, in any local rule or court order, or in any statute that does not specify a method of computing time. FRCP 6(a).

        i.   *Period stated in days or a longer unit.* When the period is stated in days or a longer unit of time:

             •  Exclude the day of the event that triggers the period; .

             •  Count every day, including intermediate Saturdays, Sundays, and legal holidays; and

             •  Include the last day of the period, but if the last day is a Saturday, Sunday, or legal holiday, the period continues to run until the end of the next day that is not a Saturday, Sunday, or legal holiday. FRCP 6(a)(1).

        ii.  *Period stated in hours.* When the period is stated in hours:

             •  Begin counting immediately on the occurrence of the event that triggers the period;

             •  Count every hour, including hours during intermediate Saturdays, Sundays, and legal holidays; and

             •  If the period would end on a Saturday, Sunday, or legal holiday, the period continues to run until the same time on the next day that is not a Saturday, Sunday, or legal holiday. FRCP 6(a)(2).

        iii. *Office of the clerk.* The offices of the Clerk of Court at Boston, Worcester and Springfield shall be open from 8:30 a.m. until 5:00 p.m. on all days except Saturdays, Sundays, legal holidays and other days so ordered by the court and announced in advance, if feasible. MA R USDCT LR 77.2.

        iv.  *Inaccessibility of the clerk's office.* Unless the court orders otherwise, if the clerk's office is inaccessible:

             •  On the last day for filing under FRCP 6(a)(1), then the time for filing is extended to the first accessible day that is not a Saturday, Sunday, or legal holiday; or

             •  During the last hour for filing under FRCP 6(a)(2), then the time for filing is extended to the same time on the first accessible day that is not a Saturday, Sunday, or legal holiday. FRCP 6(a)(3).

        v.   *"Last day" defined.* Unless a different time is set by a statute, local rule, or court order, the last day ends:

             •  For electronic filing, at midnight in the court's time zone; and

             •  For filing by other means, when the clerk's office is scheduled to close. FRCP 6(a)(4).

        vi.  *"Next day" defined.* The "next day" is determined by continuing to count forward when the period is measured after an event and backward when measured before an event. FRCP 6(a)(5).

        vii. *"Legal holiday" defined.* "Legal holiday" means:

             •  The day set aside by statute for observing New Year's Day, Martin Luther King Jr.'s Birthday, Washington's Birthday, Memorial Day, Independence Day, Labor Day, Columbus Day, Veterans' Day, Thanksgiving Day, or Christmas Day;

             •  Any day declared a holiday by the President or Congress; and

             •  For periods that are measured after an event, any other day declared a holiday by the state where the district court is located. FRCP 6(a)(6).

    b.  *Computation of electronic filing deadlines.* Filing documents electronically does not alter any filing deadlines. MA R USDCT CM/ECF Admin(K); MA R USDCT LR 5.4(D). Although CM/ECF is generally available twenty-four (24) hours a day for filing, all electronic transmissions of documents must be completed prior to 6:00 PM, Eastern Standard (or Daylight Savings) Time, on the date on which it is due, in order to be considered timely filed that day. MA R USDCT CM/ECF Admin(K); MA R USDCT LR 5.4(D). When a specific time of day deadline is set by court order or stipulation, the electronic filing must be completed by that time. Documents may be filed at any time of the day on days prior to the date on which it is due. MA R USDCT CM/ECF Admin(K). A document filed electronically shall be deemed filed as of the time and date stated on the NEF received from the court. MA R USDCT CM/ECF Admin(G)(2); MA R USDCT CM/ECF Admin(K).

        i.   *Technical failures.* A user whose filing is made untimely as the result of a technical failure of the court's CM/ECF system may seek appropriate relief from the court. MA R USDCT CM/ECF Admin(W)(3). Technical difficulties on the filer's end, with telephone, cable lines, the filer's Internet Service Provider (ISP), or hardware or software problems, will not constitute a technical failure under the Administrative Procedures for Electronic Case Filing in the United States District Court for the District of Massachusetts (MA R USDCT CM/ECF Admin) nor excuse an untimely filing. MA R USDCT CM/ECF Admin(W)(3). As help desk support is available during normal business hours, filers are strongly urged to electronically file any documents during that period. MA R USDCT CM/ECF Admin(W)(3).

- The court has made available a public terminal (computers and scanner) in each clerk's office for registered users to scan and electronically file documents. This equipment is available during normal business hours. Users should bring their prepared document and a valid CM/ECF login and password. MA R USDCT CM/ECF Admin(W)(3).

c. *Extending time.* When an act may or must be done within a specified time, the court may, for good cause, extend the time: (1) with or without motion or notice if the court acts, or if a request is made, before the original time or its extension expires; or (2) on motion made after the time has expired if the party failed to act because of excusable neglect. FRCP 6(b)(1).

   i. *Exceptions.* A court must not extend the time to act under FRCP 50(b), FRCP 50(d), FRCP 52(b), FRCP 59(b), FRCP 59(d), FRCP 59(e), and FRCP 60(b). FRCP 6(b)(2).

   ii. Refer to the United States District Court for the District of Massachusetts KeyRules Motion for Continuance/Extension of Time document for more information on extending time.

d. *Additional time after certain kinds of service.* When a party may or must act within a specified time after being served and service is made under FRCP 5(b)(2)(C) (by mail), FRCP 5(b)(2)(D) (by leaving with the clerk), or FRCP 5(b)(2)(F) (by other means consented to), three (3) days are added after the period would otherwise expire under FRCP 6(a). FRCP 6(d).

## C. General Requirements

1. *General provisions governing discovery*

   a. *Discovery scope and limits*

      i. *Scope in general.* Unless otherwise limited by court order, the scope of discovery is as follows: Parties may obtain discovery regarding any nonprivileged matter that is relevant to any party's claim or defense and proportional to the needs of the case, considering the importance of the issues at stake in the action, the amount in controversy, the parties' relative access to relevant information, the parties' resources, the importance of the discovery in resolving the issues, and whether the burden or expense of the proposed discovery outweighs its likely benefit. Information within this scope of discovery need not be admissible in evidence to be discoverable. FRCP 26(b)(1).

      ii. *Limitations on frequency and extent*

         - *When permitted.* By order, the court may alter the limits in the Federal Rules of Civil Procedure on the number of depositions and interrogatories or on the length of depositions under FRCP 30. By order or local rule, the court may also limit the number of requests under FRCP 36. FRCP 26(b)(2)(A).

         - *Specific limitations on electronically stored information.* A party need not provide discovery of electronically stored information from sources that the party identifies as not reasonably accessible because of undue burden or cost. On motion to compel discovery or for a protective order, the party from whom discovery is sought must show that the information is not reasonably accessible because of undue burden or cost. If that showing is made, the court may nonetheless order discovery from such sources if the requesting party shows good cause, considering the limitations of FRCP 26(b)(2)(C). The court may specify conditions for the discovery. FRCP 26(b)(2)(B).

         - *When required.* On motion or on its own, the court must limit the frequency or extent of discovery otherwise allowed by the Federal Rules of Civil Procedure or by local rule if it determines that: (1) the discovery sought is unreasonably cumulative or duplicative, or can be obtained from some other source that is more convenient, less burdensome, or less expensive; (2) the party seeking discovery has had ample opportunity to obtain the information by discovery in the action; or (3) the proposed discovery is outside the scope permitted by FRCP 26(b)(1). FRCP 26(b)(2)(C).

      iii. *Trial preparation; Materials*

         - *Documents and tangible things.* Ordinarily, a party may not discover documents and tangible things that are prepared in anticipation of litigation or for trial by or for another party or its representative (including the other party's attorney, consultant, surety, indemnitor, insurer, or agent). But, subject to FRCP 26(b)(4), those materials may be discovered if: (1) they are otherwise discoverable under FRCP 26(b)(1); and (2) the party shows that it has substantial need for the materials to prepare its case and cannot, without undue hardship, obtain their substantial equivalent by other means. FRCP 26(b)(3)(A).

- *Protection against disclosure.* If the court orders discovery of those materials, it must protect against disclosure of the mental impressions, conclusions, opinions, or legal theories of a party's attorney or other representative concerning the litigation. FRCP 26(b)(3)(B).

- *Previous statement.* Any party or other person may, on request and without the required showing, obtain the person's own previous statement about the action or its subject matter. If the request is refused, the person may move for a court order, and FRCP 37(a)(5) applies to the award of expenses. A previous statement is either: (1) a written statement that the person has signed or otherwise adopted or approved; or (2) a contemporaneous stenographic, mechanical, electrical, or other recording—or a transcription of it—that recites substantially verbatim the person's oral statement. FRCP 26(b)(3)(C).

iv. *Trial preparation; Experts*

- *Deposition of an expert who may testify.* A party may depose any person who has been identified as an expert whose opinions may be presented at trial. If FRCP 26(a)(2)(B) requires a report from the expert, the deposition may be conducted only after the report is provided. FRCP 26(b)(4)(A).

- *Trial-preparation protection for draft reports or disclosures.* FRCP 26(b)(3)(A) and FRCP 26(b)(3)(B) protect drafts of any report or disclosure required under FRCP 26(a)(2), regardless of the form in which the draft is recorded. FRCP 26(b)(4)(B).

- *Trial-preparation protection for communications between a party's attorney and expert witnesses.* FRCP 26(b)(3)(A) and FRCP 26(b)(3)(B) protect communications between the party's attorney and any witness required to provide a report under FRCP 26(a)(2)(B), regardless of the form of the communications, except to the extent that the communications: (1) relate to compensation for the expert's study or testimony; (2) identify facts or data that the party's attorney provided and that the expert considered in forming the opinions to be expressed; or (3) identify assumptions that the party's attorney provided and that the expert relied on in forming the opinions to be expressed. FRCP 26(b)(4)(C).

- *Expert employed only for trial preparation.* Ordinarily, a party may not, by interrogatories or deposition, discover facts known or opinions held by an expert who has been retained or specially employed by another party in anticipation of litigation or to prepare for trial and who is not expected to be called as a witness at trial. But a party may do so only: (1) as provided in FRCP 35(b); or (2) on showing exceptional circumstances under which it is impracticable for the party to obtain facts or opinions on the same subject by other means. FRCP 26(b)(4)(D).

- *Payment.* Unless manifest injustice would result, the court must require that the party seeking discovery: (1) pay the expert a reasonable fee for time spent in responding to discovery under FRCP 26(b)(4)(A) or FRCP 26(b)(4)(D); and (2) for discovery under FRCP 26(b)(4)(D), also pay the other party a fair portion of the fees and expenses it reasonably incurred in obtaining the expert's facts and opinions. FRCP 26(b)(4)(E).

v. *Claiming privilege or protecting trial-preparation materials*

- *Information withheld.* When a party withholds information otherwise discoverable by claiming that the information is privileged or subject to protection as trial-preparation material, the party must: (1) expressly make the claim; and (2) describe the nature of the documents, communications, or tangible things not produced or disclosed—and do so in a manner that, without revealing information itself privileged or protected, will enable other parties to assess the claim. FRCP 26(b)(5)(A).

- *Information produced.* If information produced in discovery is subject to a claim of privilege or of protection as trial-preparation material, the party making the claim may notify any party that received the information of the claim and the basis for it. After being notified, a party must promptly return, sequester, or destroy the specified information and any copies it has; must not use or disclose the information until the claim is resolved; must take reasonable steps to retrieve the information if the party disclosed it before being notified; and may promptly present the information to the court under seal for a determination of the claim. The producing party must preserve the information until the claim is resolved. FRCP 26(b)(5)(B).

b. *Protective orders.* A party or any person from whom discovery is sought may move for a protective order in the court where the action is pending—or as an alternative on matters relating to a deposition, in the court for the district where the deposition will be taken. FRCP 26(c)(1). Refer to the United States District Court for the District of Massachusetts KeyRules Motion for Protective Order document for more information.

c. *Disclosure orders.* The judicial officer may order the parties to submit at the scheduling conference, or at any subsequent time the officer deems appropriate, sworn statements disclosing certain information to every other party. At the discretion of the judicial officer, this order may direct the submission of:

    i. A sworn statement from a claimant, whether plaintiff, third-party plaintiff, cross-claimant, or counter-claimant, that:

- Itemizes all economic loss and provides a computation of damages for which recovery is sought, if any, sustained before the date of service of process;

- Identifies all persons then known to the claimant or the claimant's attorney who witnessed or participated in the transaction or occurrence giving rise to the claim or otherwise known or believed to have substantial discoverable information about the claim or defenses, together with a statement of the subject and a brief summary of that information;

- Identifies all opposing parties, and all officers, directors, and employees of opposing parties, from whom statements have been obtained by or on behalf of the claimant regarding the subject matter of the claim; and

- Identifies all governmental agencies or officials then known to the claimant or the claimant's attorney to have investigated the transaction or occurrence giving rise to the claim; and

    ii. A sworn statement from a defendant, whether the direct defendant, third-party defendant, cross-claim defendant, or counterclaim defendant, that identifies:

- All persons then known to the defendant or the defendant's attorneys who witnessed the transaction or occurrence giving rise to the claim or otherwise is known or believed to have substantial discoverable information about the claims or defenses, together with a statement of the subject and a brief summary of that information;

- All opposing parties, and all officers, directors, and employees of opposing parties, from whom statements have been obtained by or on behalf of the defendant regarding the subject matter of the claims or defenses; and

- All government agencies or officials then known to the defendant or the defendant's attorneys to have investigated the transaction or occurrence giving rise to the claims or defenses. MA R USDCT LR 26.1(b).

    iii. Noncompliance may be excused only by order of the judicial officer. MA R USDCT LR 26.1(b).

d. *Uniform definitions in discovery requests*

    i. *Incorporation by reference and limitations.* The full text of the definitions set forth in MA R USDCT LR 26.5(c) is deemed incorporated by reference into all discovery requests, but shall not preclude:

- The definition of other terms specific to the particular litigation;

- The use of abbreviations; or

- A narrower definition of a term defined in MA R USDCT LR 26.5(c). MA R USDCT LR 26.5(a).

    ii. *Effect on scope of discovery.* MA R USDCT LR 26.5 is not intended to broaden or narrow the scope of discovery permitted by the Federal Rules of Civil Procedure. MA R USDCT LR 26.5(b).

    iii. *Definitions.* The following definitions apply to all discovery requests:

- *Communication.* The term "communication" means the transmittal of information (in the form of facts, ideas, inquiries, or otherwise). MA R USDCT LR 26.5(c)(1).

- *Document.* The term "document" is defined to be synonymous in meaning and equal in scope to the usage of this term in FRCP 34(a). A draft or non-identical copy is a separate document within the meaning of this term. MA R USDCT LR 26.5(c)(2).

- *Identify (with respect to persons).* When referring to a person, "to identify" means to give, to the extent known, the person's full name, present or last known address, and, when referring to a natural person, the present or last known place of employment. Once a person has been identified in accordance with this subparagraph, only the name of that person need be listed in response to subsequent discovery requesting the identification of that person. MA R USDCT LR 26.5(c)(3).

- *Identify (with respect to documents).* When referring to documents, "to identify" means to give, to the

445

extent known, the: (1) type of document; (2) general subject matter; (3) date of the document; and (4) author(s), addressee(s), and recipient(s). MA R USDCT LR 26.5(c)(4).

- *Parties.* The terms "plaintiff" and "defendant" as well as a party's full or abbreviated name or a pronoun referring to a party mean the party and, where applicable, its officers, directors, employees, partners, corporate parent, subsidiaries, or affiliates. This definition is not intended to impose a discovery obligation on any person who is not a party to the litigation. MA R USDCT LR 26.5(c)(5).

- *Person.* The term "person" is defined as any natural person or any business, legal, or governmental entity or association. MA R USDCT LR 26.5(c)(6).

- *Concerning.* The term "concerning" means referring to, describing, evidencing, or constituting. MA R USDCT LR 26.5(c)(7).

- *State the basis.* When an interrogatory calls upon a party to "state the basis" of or for a particular claim, assertion, allegation, or contention, the party shall: (1) identify each and every document (and, where pertinent, the section, article, or subparagraph thereof), which forms any part of the source of the party's information regarding the alleged facts or legal conclusions referred to by the interrogatory; (2) identify each and every communication which forms any part of the source of the party's information regarding the alleged facts or legal conclusions referred to by the interrogatory; (3) state separately the acts or omissions to act on the part of any person (identifying the acts or omissions to act by stating their nature, time, and place and identifying the persons involved) which form any part of the party's information regarding the alleged facts or legal conclusions referred to in the interrogatory; and (4) state separately any other fact which forms the basis of the party's information regarding the alleged facts or conclusions referred to in the interrogatory. MA R USDCT LR 26.5(c)(8).

e. *Cooperative discovery.* The judicial officer should encourage cost effective discovery by means of voluntary exchange of information among litigants and their attorneys. This may be accomplished through the use of: (1) informal, cooperative discovery practices in which counsel provide information to opposing counsel without resort to formal discovery procedures; or (2) stipulations entered into by the parties with respect to deposition notices, waiver of signing, and other matters, except that the parties may not enter into stipulations extending the time for responding to discovery requests or otherwise modify discovery procedures ordered by the judicial officer. MA R USDCT LR 26.1(a).

f. *Phasing of discovery.* In order to facilitate settlement and the efficient completion of discovery, the judicial officer has discretion to structure discovery activities by phasing and sequencing the topics which are the subject of discovery. For example, an order may be framed limiting the first phase to developing information needed for a realistic assessment of the case. If the case does not terminate, the second phase would be directed at information needed to prepare for trial. MA R USDCT LR 26.3.

g. *Sequence of discovery.* Unless the parties stipulate or the court orders otherwise for the parties' and witnesses' convenience and in the interests of justice: (1) methods of discovery may be used in any sequence; and (2) discovery by one party does not require any other party to delay its discovery. FRCP 26(d)(3).

2. *Response to request for admissions*

a. *Form.* Statements and objections in response to requests for admission served pursuant to FRCP 36 shall be made in the order of the requests for admission propounded. MA R USDCT LR 36.1(a)(1). Each answer, statement, or objection shall be preceded by the request for admission to which it responds. MA R USDCT LR 36.1(a)(2). The response to a request for admissions must be in writing and signed by the party or its attorney. FPP § 2259. The response should be a single document, in which the various requests are listed in order and an admission, a denial, an objection, or a statement of inability to admit or deny made to each of the requests as is appropriate. FPP § 2259.

b. *Answer.* If a matter is not admitted, the answer must specifically deny it or state in detail why the answering party cannot truthfully admit or deny it. FRCP 36(a)(4).

   i. *Denial.* A denial must fairly respond to the substance of the matter; and when good faith requires that a party qualify an answer or deny only a part of a matter, the answer must specify the part admitted and qualify or deny the rest. FRCP 36(a)(4). It is expected that denials will be forthright, specific, and unconditional. If a response is thought insufficient as a denial, the court may treat it as an admission. FPP § 2260.

   ii. *Lack of knowledge or information.* The answering party may assert lack of knowledge or information as a reason for failing to admit or deny only if the party states that it has made reasonable inquiry and that the information it knows or can readily obtain is insufficient to enable it to admit or deny. FRCP 36(a)(4). A general statement that it can neither admit nor deny, unaccompanied by reasons, will be held an insufficient response, and the court may either take the matter as admitted or order a further answer. FPP § 2261.

c.   *Objections.* Each objection and the grounds therefor shall be stated separately. MA R USDCT LR 36.1(a)(3). Objections must be made in writing within the time allowed for answering the request. If some requests are to be answered and others objected to, the answers and objections should be contained in a single document. FPP § 2262. The grounds for objecting to a request must be stated. A party must not object solely on the ground that the request presents a genuine issue for trial. FRCP 36(a)(5). Failure to object to a request waives the objection. FPP § 2262.

d.   *Motion regarding the sufficiency of an answer or objection.* The requesting party may move to determine the sufficiency of an answer or objection. Unless the court finds an objection justified, it must order that an answer be served. On finding that an answer does not comply with FRCP 36, the court may order either that the matter is admitted or that an amended answer be served. The court may defer its final decision until a pretrial conference or a specified time before trial. FRCP 37(a)(5) applies to an award of expenses. FRCP 36(a)(6). Refer to the United States District Court for the District of Massachusetts KeyRules Motion for Discovery Sanctions document for more information on sanctions.

e.   *Effect of an admission; Withdrawing or amending it.* A matter admitted under FRCP 36 is conclusively established unless the court, on motion, permits the admission to be withdrawn or amended. Subject to FRCP 16(e), the court may permit withdrawal or amendment if it would promote the presentation of the merits of the action and if the court is not persuaded that it would prejudice the requesting party in maintaining or defending the action on the merits. An admission under FRCP 36 is not an admission for any other purpose and cannot be used against the party in any other proceeding. FRCP 36(b).

3.   *Supplementing disclosures and responses.* A party who has made a disclosure under FRCP 26(a)—or who has responded to an interrogatory, request for production, or request for admission—must supplement or correct its disclosure or response: (1) in a timely manner if the party learns that in some material respect the disclosure or response is incomplete or incorrect, and if the additional or corrective information has not otherwise been made known to the other parties during the discovery process or in writing; or (2) as ordered by the court. FRCP 26(e)(1).

4.   *Sanctions for failure to cooperate in discovery.* The pattern of sanctions for FRCP 36 is somewhat different from that for the other discovery rules. The most important sanctions are two:

a.   A failure to respond to a request is deemed an admission of the matter to which the request is directed; and

b.   A party who, without good reason, refuses to admit a matter will be required to pay the costs incurred in proving that matter. FPP § 2265. If a party fails to admit what is requested under FRCP 36 and if the requesting party later proves a document to be genuine or the matter true, the requesting party may move that the party who failed to admit pay the reasonable expenses, including attorney's fees, incurred in making that proof. The court must so order unless:

i.   The request was held objectionable under FRCP 36(a);

ii.   The admission sought was of no substantial importance;

iii.   The party failing to admit had a reasonable ground to believe that it might prevail on the matter; or

iv.   There was other good reason for the failure to admit. FRCP 37(c)(2).

c.   Refer to the United States District Court for the District of Massachusetts KeyRules Motion for Discovery Sanctions document for more information on sanctions.

5.   *Stipulations about discovery procedure.* Unless the court orders otherwise, the parties may stipulate that: (1) a deposition may be taken before any person, at any time or place, on any notice, and in the manner specified—in which event it may be used in the same way as any other deposition; and (2) other procedures governing or limiting discovery be modified—but a stipulation extending the time for any form of discovery must have court approval if it would interfere with the time set for completing discovery, for hearing a motion, or for trial. FRCP 29.

6.   *Alternative dispute resolution (ADR).* The judicial officer assigned to preside over the case shall encourage the resolution of disputes by settlement or other alternative dispute resolution programs. MA R USDCT LR 16.4(a).

a.   *Settlement.* At every conference conducted under the Local Rules of the United States District Court for the District of Massachusetts, the judicial officer shall inquire as to the utility of the parties conducting settlement negotiations, explore means of facilitating those negotiations, and offer whatever assistance may be appropriate in the circumstances. Assistance may include a reference of the case to another judicial officer for settlement purposes. MA R USDCT LR 16.4(b).

i.   When a case is settled, the parties shall file with the clerk a signed agreement for judgment or stipulation for dismissal, as appropriate, within twenty-eight (28) days, unless the court otherwise orders. MA R USDCT LR 68.2.

    b. *Alternative dispute resolution programs*

        i. *Discretion of judicial officer.* The judicial officer, following an exploration of the matter with all counsel, may refer appropriate cases to alternative dispute resolution programs that have been designated for use in the district court or that the judicial officer may make available. The dispute resolution programs described in MA R USDCT LR 16.4(c)(2) through MA R USDCT LR 16.4(c)(4) are illustrative, not exclusive. Moreover, nothing in MA R USDCT LR 16.4 shall preclude the parties from engaging in private dispute resolution programs as long as they comply with any schedule established by the court. MA R USDCT LR 16.4(c)(1).

        ii. *Mediation.* The judicial officer may refer the case to mediation upon the agreement of all parties. MA R USDCT LR 16.4(c)(2)(A).

        iii. *Other alternative dispute resolution programs.* Use of mediation is not exclusive. At the request of parties, the judicial officer may consider other forms of alternative dispute resolution including, but not limited to, mini-trial, summary jury trial and arbitration. MA R USDCT LR 16.4(c)(3).

    c. For more information on alternative dispute resolution (ADR), refer to MA R USDCT LR 16.4.

7. *Sanctions.* Failure to comply with any of the directions or obligations set forth in, or authorized by, these rules may result in dismissal, default, or the imposition of other sanctions as deemed appropriate by the judicial officer. MA R USDCT LR 1.3. Except as provided by law, the court may impose sanctions as provided in MA R USDCT LR 1.3 for failure to comply with the Administrative Procedures for Electronic Case Filing in the United States District Court for the District of Massachusetts (MA R USDCT CM/ECF Admin) or with MA R USDCT LR 5.4. MA R USDCT CM/ECF Admin(C)(3).

## D. Documents

1. *Required documents*

    a. *Response to request for admissions.* Refer to the General Requirements section of this document for information on the response to request for admissions.

2. *Supplemental documents*

    a. *Certificate of service.* No certificate of service is required when a paper is served by filing it with the court's electronic-filing system. When a paper that is required to be served is served by other means: (1) if the paper is filed, a certificate of service must be filed with it or within a reasonable time after service; and (2) if the paper is not filed, a certificate of service need not be filed unless filing is required by court order or by local rule. FRCP 5(d)(1)(B).

## E. Format

1. *Form of documents.* The rules governing captions and other matters of form in pleadings apply to motions and other papers. FRCP 7(b)(2). The provisions of FRCP 10 and FRCP 11 concerning the form and signing of pleadings, motions, and other papers shall be applicable to all papers filed in any proceeding in this court. The board of bar overseers registration number of each attorney signing such documents, except the United States Attorney and his or her staff, shall be inscribed below the signature. MA R USDCT LR 5.1(a)(1).

    a. *Paper size and binding.* All papers filed in the court shall be adapted for flat filing, be filed on eight and one-half by eleven (8-1/2 x 11) inch paper without backers and be bound firmly by staple or some such other means (excluding paper or binder clip or rubber band). MA R USDCT LR 5.1(a)(2).

    b. *Spacing.* All papers, except discovery requests and responses, shall be double-spaced except for the identification of counsel, title of the case, footnotes, quotations and exhibits. Discovery requests and responses shall be single-spaced. MA R USDCT LR 5.1(a)(2).

    c. *Caption.* Every pleading must have a caption with the court's name, a title, a file number, and [an] FRCP 7(a) designation. FRCP 10(a).

        i. *Names of parties.* The title of the complaint must name all the parties; the title of other pleadings, after naming the first party on each side, may refer generally to other parties. FRCP 10(a).

        ii. *Request for special action.* When any pleading or other paper filed in the court includes a request for special process or relief, or any other request such that, if granted, the court will proceed other than in the ordinary course, the request shall, unless it is noted on the category sheet [see MA R USDCT LR 40.1(a)(1)], be noted on the first page to the right of or immediately beneath the caption. MA R USDCT LR 5.1(c).

    d. *Claims or defenses*

        i. *Numbered paragraphs.* A party must state its claims or defenses in numbered paragraphs, each limited as far as practicable to a single set of circumstances. A later pleading may refer by number to a paragraph in an earlier pleading. FRCP 10(b).

    ii.  *Separate statements.* If doing so would promote clarity, each claim founded on a separate transaction or occurrence—and each defense other than a denial—must be stated in a separate count or defense. FRCP 10(b).

e.  *Adoption by reference.* A statement in a pleading may be adopted by reference elsewhere in the same pleading or in any other pleading or motion. FRCP 10(c).

    i.  *Exhibits.* A copy of a written instrument that is an exhibit to a pleading is a part of the pleading for all purposes. FRCP 10(c).

f.  *Citations*

    i.  *Local rules.* These rules shall be known as Local Rules of the United States District Court for the District of Massachusetts and cited as "L.R., D. Mass." or "L.R." MA R USDCT LR 1.1.

    ii.  *Electronic case filing procedures.* The procedures governing electronic case filing shall be known as the "Administrative Procedures for Electronic Case Filing in the United States District Court for the District of Massachusetts." They shall be cited as "APECF." MA R USDCT CM/ECF Admin(A)(7).

g.  *Acceptance by the clerk.* The clerk must not refuse to file a paper solely because it is not in the form prescribed by the Federal Rules of Civil Procedure or by a local rule or practice. FRCP 5(d)(4).

    i.  Except for complaints and notices of appeal, papers that do not conform to the requirements of MA R USDCT LR 5.1(a)(2) shall be returned by the clerk. MA R USDCT LR 5.1(a)(2).

2.  *Form of electronic documents.* A paper filed electronically is a written paper for purposes of the Federal Rules of Civil Procedure. FRCP 5(d)(3)(D).

a.  *PDF/A format required.* The court will begin requiring submission of documents in PDF/A format in the foreseeable future. PDF/A is an enhanced version of the traditional PDF format. Newer versions of most PDF software will be able to convert to this format. Additional information on PDF/A documents may be found on the court's website. MA R USDCT CM/ECF Admin(Electronic Filing and PDF).

    i.  *Electronically converted PDF.* Electronically converted PDF documents are created from word processing documents (MS Word, WordPerfect, etc.) using any appropriate software. These documents are text searchable and the file size is generally smaller than a scanned document. CM/ECF users may use any brand of software to convert documents to PDF. MA R USDCT CM/ECF Admin(Electronic Filing and PDF).

        •  Documents converted to PDF, rather than scanned, are preferred for filing in CM/ECF. MA R USDCT CM/ECF Admin(Electronic Filing and PDF).

    ii.  *Scanned PDF.* Scanned PDF documents are created from paper documents run through an optical scanner. Scanned PDF documents are generally not searchable and have a larger file size. Please note that software used to create scanned documents may (and should) be set in such a way that the document is "text-searchable." MA R USDCT CM/ECF Admin(Electronic Filing and PDF).

b.  *Title.* All pleadings filed electronically shall be titled in accordance with the approved dictionary of civil or criminal events of the CM/ECF system of this court. A list of events is available on the CM/ECF Training Information page of the court's website. The clerk's office may, when necessary and appropriate, modify the docket entry description, or delete and re-enter the docket entry in order to comply with the court's quality assurance standards. MA R USDCT CM/ECF Admin(G)(3).

c.  *Attachments to filings and exhibits.* Attachments to filings and exhibits must be filed in accordance with the court's CM/ECF User Manual, unless otherwise ordered by the court. MA R USDCT CM/ECF Admin(O)(1).

    i.  Filers must submit as attachments only those excerpts of the referenced documents that are directly germane to the matter under consideration by the court. Excerpted material must be clearly and prominently identified as such. Users who file excerpts of documents do so without prejudice to their right to timely file additional excerpts or the complete document, as may be allowed by the court. Responding parties may timely file additional excerpts or the complete document that they believe are directly germane. MA R USDCT CM/ECF Admin(O)(2).

    ii.  Filers shall not attach as an exhibit any pleading or other paper already on file with the court in that case, but shall merely refer to that document. (See MA R USDCT CM/ECF Admin(G) for information on using hyperlinks in PDF documents filed in CM/ECF.) MA R USDCT CM/ECF Admin(O)(3).

d. *Redacted documents.* The parties may request or the court may require the submission of documents that have been redacted/stripped of sensitive or confidential information. The redacted document prepared for electronic filing shall include the original caption of the document, and be clearly labeled as "Redacted Document." A specific event is available for this purpose ("Redacted Document"), found under the Other Filings/Other Documents menu option. MA R USDCT CM/ECF Admin(S).

   i. Attorneys and pro se litigants are advised to take extra care when creating PDF documents intended for submission to CM/ECF. Steps shall be taken to ensure the documents are free of any hidden data (metadata) that may contain redacted information, or traces of information edited or deleted are not hidden in the final document. Even PDF content that has been encrypted may be recovered. An advisory document with additional information on this topic may be found on the court's website. MA R USDCT CM/ECF Admin(S).

e. *Hyperlinks.* Electronically filed documents may contain the following types of hyperlinks: (1) hyperlinks to other portions of the same document; (2) hyperlinks to other documents filed within the CM/ECF system; and (3) hyperlinks to a location on the Internet that contains a source document for a citation. MA R USDCT CM/ECF Admin(G)(7).

   i. Hyperlinks to cited authority may not replace standard citation format. Complete citations must be included in the text of the filed document. Neither a hyperlink, nor any site to which it refers, shall be considered part of the record, but are simply convenient mechanisms for accessing material cited in a document filed in CM/ECF. Instructions on creating hyperlinks may be found in the CM/ECF User Manual. MA R USDCT CM/ECF Admin(G)(7).

   ii. The court accepts no responsibility for, and does not endorse, any product, organization, or content at any hyperlinked site, or at any site to which that site may be linked. The court accepts no responsibility for the availability or functionality of any hyperlink. MA R USDCT CM/ECF Admin(G)(7).

   iii. One feature of PDF/A documents is that hyperlinks are commonly "masked," meaning that the full address of the referenced file is not written out; for example, clicking the word brief may open a brief which was previously filed in CM/ECF. MA R USDCT CM/ECF Admin(G)(7)(NOTE). An "unmasked" hyperlink has the full address visible to the user. MA R USDCT CM/ECF Admin(G)(7)(NOTE).

      • Masked hyperlinks may or may not work in a PDF/A document, depending on how it was created. Currently, masked hyperlinks are preserved in PDF/A documents produced by the "Save As" method in Microsoft Word 2007 and 2010; the "PDFMaker" method in Microsoft Word 2007; and OpenOffice 2.4 ("PDF Export"). With other production methods, such as WordPerfect, the PDF/A document includes underlined words that appear to be links, but clicking them has no effect. MA R USDCT CM/ECF Admin(G)(7)(NOTE).

f. *Documents features not accepted.* CM/ECF will not accept PDF documents containing tracking tags, embedded systems commands, password protections, access restrictions or other security features, special tags or dynamic features. MA R USDCT CM/ECF Admin(G)(8).

g. *File size limitations.* A filing party shall limit the size of each PDF file to no more than twenty (20) megabytes. PDF files larger than seven (7) megabytes will be rejected by the CM/ECF system. The filer will see a message advising of the size limitation. MA R USDCT CM/ECF Admin(P)(2).

   i. Larger documents or exhibits may be submitted electronically if split into separate PDF files each less than seven (7) megabytes, attached to the main document and clearly labeled. MA R USDCT CM/ECF Admin(P)(2).

   ii. Documents submitted electronically or on paper are subject to the page limitations set by MA R USDCT LR 7.1(b)(4) or by order of the court. MA R USDCT CM/ECF Admin(P)(1).

h. *Accuracy and readability.* The filer shall verify the accuracy and readability of any PDF file before electronically filing it in CM/ECF. MA R USDCT CM/ECF Admin(G)(6); MA R USDCT CM/ECF Admin(P)(3).

3. *Signing disclosures and discovery requests, responses, and objections.* FRCP 11 does not apply to disclosures and discovery requests, responses, objections, and motions under FRCP 26 through FRCP 37. FRCP 11(d).

a. *Signature required.* Every disclosure under FRCP 26(a)(1) or FRCP 26(a)(3) and every discovery request, response, or objection must be signed by at least one attorney of record in the attorney's own name—or by the party personally, if unrepresented—and must state the signer's address, e-mail address, and telephone number. FRCP 26(g)(1). The provisions of the Federal Rules of Civil Procedure pertaining to the form and signing of pleadings, motions, and other papers shall be applicable to all papers filed in any proceeding in this court. The board of bar overseers registration number of each attorney signing such documents, except the United States Attorney and his staff, shall be inscribed below the signature. MA R USDCT LR 5.1(a)(1).

i. *Electronic signing.* A filing made through a person's electronic-filing account and authorized by that person, together with that person's name on a signature block, constitutes the person's signature. FRCP 5(d)(3)(C).

ii. *Appearances.* The filing of an appearance or any other pleading signed on behalf of a party constitutes an entry of appearance for that party. All pleadings shall contain the name, bar admission number, address, telephone number, and e-mail address of the attorney entering an appearance. MA R USDCT LR 83.5.2(a).

- *Appearances by law firms.* When a party is represented by a law firm, the appearance must include the name and the signature of at least one individual attorney. When a party is represented by more than one attorney from the same or different law firms, the attorney entering the appearance must designate the individual attorney who is authorized to receive all notices in the case. Any notice sent to an attorney so designated shall be deemed to be proper notice unless the court finds that notice was not properly sent. MA R USDCT LR 83.5.2(b).

- For more information on appearances, refer to MA R USDCT LR 83.5.2.

iii. *Signatures of attorneys.* The user login and password required to submit documents to the CM/ECF system shall serve as that user's signature for purposes of FRCP 11 and for all other purposes under the Federal Rules of Civil Procedure and the Local Rules of the United States District Court for the District of Massachusetts. All electronically filed documents must include a signature block and must set forth the attorney's name, bar number, address, telephone number and email address. The name of the CM/ECF user under whose log-in and password the document is submitted must be preceded by a "/s/" and typed in the space where the signature would otherwise appear. MA R USDCT CM/ECF Admin(M)(1). For an example, refer to MA R USDCT CM/ECF Admin(M)(1).

iv. *Signatures of pro se parties.* Any document requiring a signature that is filed by a party appearing pro se shall bear the words "pro se" following that party's signature. Any such document shall also state the party's mailing address, telephone number (if any), and e-mail address (if the party has consented to service by email). MA R USDCT LR 83.5.5(g). For more information on practice by pro se litigants, refer to MA R USDCT LR 83.5.5.

v. *Multiple signatures.* The filer of any document requiring more than one signature (e.g, stipulations, joint motions, joint status reports, magistrate judge consent forms, etc.) must list thereon all the names of other signatories by means of a "/s/ name of signatory" block for each. By submitting such a document, the filing attorney certifies that each of the other signatories has expressly agreed to the form and substance of the document and that the filing attorney has their actual authority to submit the document electronically. MA R USDCT CM/ECF Admin(M)(2). For more information, refer to MA R USDCT CM/ECF Admin(M)(2).

vi. *Affidavits.* Except as provided in MA R USDCT CM/ECF Admin(L), affidavits shall be filed electronically; however, the electronically filed version must contain a "/s/ name of signatory" block indicating that the paper document bears an original signature. MA R USDCT CM/ECF Admin(M)(3). The court will also accept a scanned version of the original, signed document. MA R USDCT CM/ECF Admin(M)(3). For more information, refer to MA R USDCT CM/ECF Admin(M)(3).

b. *Effect of signature.* By signing, an attorney or party certifies that to the best of the person's knowledge, information, and belief formed after a reasonable inquiry:

i. With respect to a disclosure, it is complete and correct as of the time it is made; and

ii. With respect to a discovery request, response, or objection, it is:

- Consistent with the Federal Rules of Civil Procedure and warranted by existing law or by a nonfrivolous argument for extending, modifying, or reversing existing law, or for establishing new law;

- Not interposed for any improper purpose, such as to harass, cause unnecessary delay, or needlessly increase the cost of litigation; and

- Neither unreasonable nor unduly burdensome or expensive, considering the needs of the case, prior discovery in the case, the amount in controversy, and the importance of the issues at stake in the action. FRCP 26(g)(1).

c. *Failure to sign.* Other parties have no duty to act on an unsigned disclosure, request, response, or objection until it is signed, and the court must strike it unless a signature is promptly supplied after the omission is called to the attorney's or party's attention. FRCP 26(g)(2).

d. *Sanction for improper certification.* If a certification violates FRCP 26(g) without substantial justification, the court, on motion or on its own, must impose an appropriate sanction on the signer, the party on whose behalf the signer was acting, or both. The sanction may include an order to pay the reasonable expenses, including attorney's fees, caused by the violation. FRCP 26(g)(3). Refer to the United States District Court for the District of Massachusetts KeyRules Motion for Discovery Sanctions document for more information.

4. *Privacy protection for filings made with the court*

   a. *Redacted filings.* Unless the court orders otherwise, in an electronic or paper filing with the court that contains an individual's Social Security number, taxpayer-identification number, or birth date, the name of an individual known to be a minor, or a financial-account number, a party or nonparty making the filing may include only:

      i. The last four (4) digits of the Social Security number and taxpayer-identification number;

      ii. The year of the individual's birth;

      iii. The minor's initials; and

      iv. The last four (4) digits of the financial-account number. FRCP 5.2(a); MA R USDCT CM/ECF Admin(N).

   b. *Exemptions from the redaction requirement.* The redaction requirement does not apply to the following:

      i. A financial-account number that identifies the property allegedly subject to forfeiture in a forfeiture proceeding;

      ii. The record of an administrative or agency proceeding;

      iii. The official record of a state-court proceeding;

      iv. The record of a court or tribunal, if that record was not subject to the redaction requirement when originally filed;

      v. A filing covered by FRCP 5.2(c) or FRCP 5.2(d); and

      vi. A pro se filing in an action brought under 28 U.S.C.A. § 2241, 28 U.S.C.A. § 2254, or 28 U.S.C.A. § 2255. FRCP 5.2(b).

   c. *Limitations on remote access to electronic files; Social Security appeals and immigration cases.* Unless the court orders otherwise, in an action for benefits under the Social Security Act, and in an action or proceeding relating to an order of removal, to relief from removal, or to immigration benefits or detention, access to an electronic file is authorized as follows:

      i. The parties and their attorneys may have remote electronic access to any part of the case file, including the administrative record;

      ii. Any other person may have electronic access to the full record at the courthouse, but may have remote electronic access only to:

         • The docket maintained by the court; and

         • An opinion, order, judgment, or other disposition of the court, but not any other part of the case file or the administrative record. FRCP 5.2(c).

   d. *Filings made under seal.* The court may order that a filing be made under seal without redaction. The court may later unseal the filing or order the person who made the filing to file a redacted version for the public record. FRCP 5.2(d).

   e. *Protective orders.* For good cause, the court may by order in a case:

      i. Require redaction of additional information; or

      ii. Limit or prohibit a nonparty's remote electronic access to a document filed with the court. FRCP 5.2(e).

   f. *Option for additional unredacted filing under seal.* A person making a redacted filing may also file an unredacted copy under seal. The court must retain the unredacted copy as part of the record. FRCP 5.2(f). For more information, refer to MA R USDCT LR 7.2.

   g. *Option for filing a reference list.* A filing that contains redacted information may be filed together with a reference list that identifies each item of redacted information and specifies an appropriate identifier that uniquely corresponds to each item listed. The list must be filed under seal and may be amended as of right. Any reference in the case to a listed identifier will be construed to refer to the corresponding item of information. FRCP 5.2(g).

   h. *Responsibility for redaction.* The clerk's office is not responsible for reviewing documents filed with the court to determine whether pleadings have been redacted and are in the proper form. MA R USDCT CM/ECF Admin(N).

   i. *Waiver of protection of identifiers.* A person waives the protection of FRCP 5.2(a) as to the person's own information by filing it without redaction and not under seal. FRCP 5.2(h).

## F. Filing and Service Requirements

1. *Filing requirements*

   a. *Required filings.* Any paper after the complaint that is required to be served must be filed no later than a reasonable time after service. But disclosures under FRCP 26(a)(1) or FRCP 26(a)(2) and the following discovery requests and responses must not be filed until they are used in the proceeding or the court orders filing: depositions, interrogatories, requests for documents or tangible things or to permit entry onto land, and requests for admission. FRCP 5(d)(1)(A). Refer to the United States District Court for the District of Massachusetts KeyRules pleading and motion documents for information on filing with the court.

   b. *Nonfiling of discovery materials.* Discovery materials (that is, automatic or voluntary disclosure materials, depositions, deposition notices, interrogatories, requests for documents, requests for admissions, answers and responses to discovery requests, and any other requests for or products of the discovery process) shall not be filed unless so ordered by the court or for use in the proceeding. The party taking a deposition or obtaining any material through discovery is responsible for its preservation and delivery to the court if needed or so ordered. If for any reason a party or concerned citizen believes that any of the named documents should be filed, an ex parte request may be made that such document be filed, stating the reasons for the request. The court may also order filing sua sponte. MA R USDCT LR 26.6(a).

      i. *Discovery motions.* If relief is sought under FRCP 26(c) or FRCP 37, copies of the relevant portions of disputed documents shall be filed with the court contemporaneously with any motion. MA R USDCT LR 26.6(a).

      ii. *Motions for summary judgment.* If the moving party under FRCP 56 or the opponent relies on discovery documents, copies of the pertinent parts thereof shall be filed with the motion or opposition. MA R USDCT LR 26.6(a).

2. *Service requirements.* Service of all pleadings subsequent to the original complaint and of all other papers required to be served shall be made in the manner specified by FRCP 5. MA R USDCT LR 5.2(a). A copy of the response must be served upon the party making the request. A copy of the response must also be served on all other parties to the action unless the court has ordered to the contrary. FPP § 2259.

   a. *Service; When required*

      i. *In general.* Unless the Federal Rules of Civil Procedure provide otherwise, each of the following papers must be served on every party:

      - An order stating that service is required;

      - A pleading filed after the original complaint, unless the court orders otherwise under FRCP 5(c) because there are numerous defendants;

      - A discovery paper required to be served on a party, unless the court orders otherwise;

      - A written motion, except one that may be heard ex parte; and

      - A written notice, appearance, demand, or offer of judgment, or any similar paper. FRCP 5(a)(1).

      ii. *If a party fails to appear.* No service is required on a party who is in default for failing to appear. But a pleading that asserts a new claim for relief against such a party must be served on that party under FRCP 4. FRCP 5(a)(2).

      iii. *Seizing property.* If an action is begun by seizing property and no person is or need be named as a defendant, any service required before the filing of an appearance, answer, or claim must be made on the person who had custody or possession of the property when it was seized. FRCP 5(a)(3).

   b. *Service; How made*

      i. *Serving an attorney.* If a party is represented by an attorney, service under FRCP 5 must be made on the attorney unless the court orders service on the party. FRCP 5(b)(1).

      ii. *Service in general.* A paper is served under FRCP 5 by:

      - Handing it to the person;

      - Leaving it: (1) at the person's office with a clerk or other person in charge or, if no one is in charge, in a conspicuous place in the office; or (2) if the person has no office or the office is closed, at the person's dwelling or usual place of abode with someone of suitable age and discretion who resides there;

      - Mailing it to the person's last known address—in which event service is complete upon mailing;

      - Leaving it with the court clerk if the person has no known address;

- Sending it to a registered user by filing it with the court's electronic-filing system or sending it by other electronic means that the person consented to in writing—in either of which events service is complete upon filing or sending, but is not effective if the filer or sender learns that it did not reach the person to be served; or

- Delivering it by any other means that the person consented to in writing—in which event service is complete when the person making service delivers it to the agency designated to make delivery. FRCP 5(b)(2).

iii. *Service by electronic means.* Unless exempt or otherwise ordered by the court, all pleadings and other papers must be served on other parties by electronic means. MA R USDCT LR 5.4(C); MA R USDCT CM/ECF Admin(H)(2). Service by electronic means shall be treated the same as service by mail. MA R USDCT CM/ECF Admin(H)(4).

- *Consent to electronic service.* Registering to use CM/ECF constitutes consent to service of all documents by electronic means as provided in the Administrative Procedures for Electronic Case Filing in the United States District Court for the District of Massachusetts (MA R USDCT CM/ECF Admin) and FRCP 5(b) and FRCP 77(d). MA R USDCT CM/ECF Admin(E)(6); MA R USDCT CM/ECF Admin(H)(3).

- *Service on registered ECF users.* Transmission of the Notice of Electronic Filing (NEF) through the court's transmission facilities will constitute service of the filed document upon a registered ECF user. MA R USDCT LR 5.4(C).

- *Service on non-registered users.* The party filing the document electronically is responsible for serving a paper copy of the document by mail in accordance with FRCP 5(b) to those case participants who have not been identified on the NEF as electronic recipients. MA R USDCT CM/ECF Admin(H)(3).

- *Service of conventionally filed papers.* Documents or exhibits submitted conventionally shall be served on other parties by the filer using traditional means. MA R USDCT CM/ECF Admin(P)(4).

c. *Serving numerous defendants*

i. *In general.* If an action involves an unusually large number of defendants, the court may, on motion or on its own, order that:

- Defendants' pleadings and replies to them need not be served on other defendants;

- Any crossclaim, counterclaim, avoidance, or affirmative defense in those pleadings and replies to them will be treated as denied or avoided by all other parties; and

- Filing any such pleading and serving it on the plaintiff constitutes notice of the pleading to all parties. FRCP 5(c)(1).

ii. *Notifying parties.* A copy of every such order must be served on the parties as the court directs. FRCP 5(c)(2).

# G. Hearings

1. There is no hearing contemplated in the federal statutes or rules for responses to requests for admissions.

# H. Forms

## 1. Federal Response to Request for Admissions Forms

a. Response to request for admission. 3B FEDFORMS § 26:74.

b. Response to request for admission; Admissions, qualified admissions, denials. 3B FEDFORMS § 26:75.

c. Response to request for admission; Denials and admissions of specific facts and explanatory statement of inability to admit or deny. 3B FEDFORMS § 26:76.

d. Response to request for admission; Denials and admissions of specific facts and explanatory statement of inability to admit or deny; Statement. 3B FEDFORMS § 26:77.

e. Objections to requests for admissions. 3B FEDFORMS § 26:78.

f. Objections to request for admissions; Privileged. 3B FEDFORMS § 26:79.

g. Amended response to request for admission. 3B FEDFORMS § 26:80.

h. Response; To request for admission of facts. AMJUR PP DEPOSITION § 684.

i. Response; To request for admission of facts; With verification. AMJUR PP DEPOSITION § 685.

j. Reply; To request for admissions of fact and genuineness of documents; Refusal to answer on ground of privilege. AMJUR PP DEPOSITION § 686.

k. Answer; To demand for admissions; Admission or denial not required under governing statute or rule. AMJUR PP DEPOSITION § 687.

l. Reply; Objection to request for admissions; Irrelevancy and immateriality; Answer already made in response to interrogatories. AMJUR PP DEPOSITION § 688.

m. Answer; To request for admissions; General form. FEDPROF § 23:571.

n. Answer; To request for admissions; Insurance claim. FEDPROF § 23:572.

o. Objections; To request for admissions. FEDPROF § 23:573.

p. Objections to request. GOLDLTGFMS § 30:12.

q. Reply to request for admissions. GOLDLTGFMS § 30:15.

r. Response to request; General form. GOLDLTGFMS § 30:16.

s. Response to request; Denials. GOLDLTGFMS § 30:17.

t. Response to request; Admission of genuineness of document. GOLDLTGFMS § 30:18.

u. Response to request; Admission of facts. GOLDLTGFMS § 30:19.

v. Reply and objections to request for admissions. GOLDLTGFMS § 30:20.

# I. Applicable Rules

## 1. *Federal rules*

a. Serving and filing pleadings and other papers. FRCP 5.

b. Privacy protection for filings made with the court. FRCP 5.2.

c. Computing and extending time; Time for motion papers. FRCP 6.

d. Pleadings allowed; Form of motions and other papers. FRCP 7.

e. Form of pleadings. FRCP 10.

f. Signing pleadings, motions, and other papers; Representations to the court; Sanctions. FRCP 11.

g. Duty to disclose; General provisions governing discovery. FRCP 26.

h. Stipulations about discovery procedure. FRCP 29.

i. Requests for admission. FRCP 36.

j. Failure to make disclosures or to cooperate in discovery; Sanctions. FRCP 37.

## 2. *Local rules*

a. Title. MA R USDCT LR 1.1.

b. Sanctions. MA R USDCT LR 1.3.

c. Form and filing of papers. MA R USDCT LR 5.1.

d. Service and filing of pleadings and other papers. MA R USDCT LR 5.2.

e. Filing and service by electronic means. MA R USDCT LR 5.4.

f. Alternative dispute resolution. MA R USDCT LR 16.4.

g. Control of discovery. MA R USDCT LR 26.1.

h. Phasing of discovery. MA R USDCT LR 26.3.

i. Uniform definitions in discovery requests. MA R USDCT LR 26.5.

j. Court filings and costs. MA R USDCT LR 26.6.

k. Admissions. MA R USDCT LR 36.1.

l. Settlement. MA R USDCT LR 68.2.

m. Office of the clerk. MA R USDCT LR 77.2.

n. Appearances. MA R USDCT LR 83.5.2.

o.  Practice by pro se litigants. MA R USDCT LR 83.5.5.

p.  CM/ECF case management/electronic case files administrative procedures. MA R USDCT CM/ECF Admin.

## Requests, Notices and Applications
## Notice of Deposition

### Document Last Updated December 2018

**A.  Checklist**

(I)  ❑  Matters to be considered by deposing party for depositions by oral examination

    (a)  ❑  Required documents

        (1)  ❑  Notice of deposition

    (b)  ❑  Supplemental documents

        (1)  ❑  Subpoena

        (2)  ❑  Subpoena duces tecum

        (3)  ❑  Request for production of documents

        (4)  ❑  Certificate of service

    (c)  ❑  Timing

        (1)  ❑  A party may, by oral questions, depose any person, including a party, without leave of court except as provided in FRCP 30(a)(2)

        (2)  ❑  A party must obtain leave of court, and the court must grant leave to the extent consistent with FRCP 26(b)(1) and FRCP 26(b)(2):

            (i)  ❑  If the parties have not stipulated to the deposition and: (1) the deposition would result in more than ten (10) depositions being taken under FRCP 30 or FRCP 31 by the plaintiffs, or by the defendants, or by the third-party defendants; (2) the deponent has already been deposed in the case; or (3) the party seeks to take the deposition before the time specified in FRCP 26(d), unless the party certifies in the notice, with supporting facts, that the deponent is expected to leave the United States and be unavailable for examination in this country after that time; or

            (ii)  ❑  If the deponent is confined in prison

        (3)  ❑  A party who wants to depose a person by oral questions must give reasonable written notice to every other party

(II)  ❑  Matters to be considered by deposing party for depositions by written questions

    (a)  ❑  Required documents

        (1)  ❑  Notice of deposition

        (2)  ❑  Written questions

    (b)  ❑  Supplemental documents

        (1)  ❑  Subpoena

        (2)  ❑  Certificate of service

    (c)  ❑  Timing

        (1)  ❑  A party may, by written questions, depose any person, including a party, without leave of court except as provided in FRCP 31(a)(2)

        (2)  ❑  A party must obtain leave of court, and the court must grant leave to the extent consistent with FRCP 26(b)(1) and FRCP 26(b)(2):

            (i)  ❑  If the parties have not stipulated to the deposition and: (1) the deposition would result in more than ten (10) depositions being taken under FRCP 31 or FRCP 30 by the plaintiffs, or by the defendants, or by the third-party defendants; (2) the deponent has already been deposed in the case; or (3) the party seeks to take a deposition before the time specified in FRCP 26(d); or

    (ii)  ❑  If the deponent is confined in prison

  (3)  ❑  A party who wants to depose a person by written questions must serve them on every other party, with a notice

## B. Timing

1. *Depositions by oral examination*

   a. *Without leave.* A party may, by oral questions, depose any person, including a party, without leave of court except as provided in FRCP 30(a)(2). FRCP 30(a)(1).

   b. *With leave.* A party must obtain leave of court, and the court must grant leave to the extent consistent with FRCP 26(b)(1) and FRCP 26(b)(2):

      i. If the parties have not stipulated to the deposition and: (1) the deposition would result in more than ten (10) depositions being taken under FRCP 30 or FRCP 31 by the plaintiffs, or by the defendants, or by the third-party defendants; (2) the deponent has already been deposed in the case; or (3) the party seeks to take the deposition before the time specified in FRCP 26(d), unless the party certifies in the notice, with supporting facts, that the deponent is expected to leave the United States and be unavailable for examination in this country after that time; or

      ii. If the deponent is confined in prison. FRCP 30(a)(2).

   c. *Notice of deposition.* A party who wants to depose a person by oral questions must give reasonable written notice to every other party. FRCP 30(b)(1).

2. *Depositions by written questions*

   a. *Without leave.* A party may, by written questions, depose any person, including a party, without leave of court except as provided in FRCP 31(a)(2). FRCP 31(a)(1).

   b. *With leave.* A party must obtain leave of court, and the court must grant leave to the extent consistent with FRCP 26(b)(1) and FRCP 26(b)(2):

      i. If the parties have not stipulated to the deposition and: (1) the deposition would result in more than ten (10) depositions being taken under FRCP 31 or FRCP 30 by the plaintiffs, or by the defendants, or by the third-party defendants; (2) the deponent has already been deposed in the case; or (3) the party seeks to take a deposition before the time specified in FRCP 26(d); or

      ii. If the deponent is confined in prison. FRCP 31(a)(2).

   c. *Notice of deposition with written questions.* A party who wants to depose a person by written questions must serve them on every other party, with a notice. FRCP 31(a)(3). Refer to the General Requirements section of this document for the contents of the notice.

   d. *Questions from other parties.* Any questions to the deponent from other parties must be served on all parties as follows:

      i. *Cross-questions.* Cross-questions, within fourteen (14) days after being served with the notice and direct questions;

      ii. *Redirect questions.* Redirect questions, within seven (7) days after being served with cross-questions; and

      iii. *Recross-questions.* Recross-questions, within seven (7) days after being served with redirect questions. FRCP 31(a)(5).

      iv. *Modification of timing requirements.* The court may, for good cause, extend or shorten these times. FRCP 31(a)(5).

3. *Commencement of discovery.* A party may not seek discovery from any source before the parties have conferred as required by FRCP 26(f), except in a proceeding exempted from initial disclosure under FRCP 26(a)(1)(B), or when authorized by the Federal Rules of Civil Procedure, by stipulation, or by court order. FRCP 26(d)(1).

4. *Computation of time*

   a. *Computing time.* FRCP 6 applies in computing any time period specified in the Federal Rules of Civil Procedure, in any local rule or court order, or in any statute that does not specify a method of computing time. FRCP 6(a).

      i. *Period stated in days or a longer unit.* When the period is stated in days or a longer unit of time:

      • Exclude the day of the event that triggers the period;

      • Count every day, including intermediate Saturdays, Sundays, and legal holidays; and

- Include the last day of the period, but if the last day is a Saturday, Sunday, or legal holiday, the period continues to run until the end of the next day that is not a Saturday, Sunday, or legal holiday. FRCP 6(a)(1).

ii.  *Period stated in hours.* When the period is stated in hours:

- Begin counting immediately on the occurrence of the event that triggers the period;

- Count every hour, including hours during intermediate Saturdays, Sundays, and legal holidays; and

- If the period would end on a Saturday, Sunday, or legal holiday, the period continues to run until the same time on the next day that is not a Saturday, Sunday, or legal holiday. FRCP 6(a)(2).

iii.  *Office of the clerk.* The offices of the Clerk of Court at Boston, Worcester and Springfield shall be open from 8:30 a.m. until 5:00 p.m. on all days except Saturdays, Sundays, legal holidays and other days so ordered by the court and announced in advance, if feasible. MA R USDCT LR 77.2.

iv.  *Inaccessibility of the clerk's office.* Unless the court orders otherwise, if the clerk's office is inaccessible:

- On the last day for filing under FRCP 6(a)(1), then the time for filing is extended to the first accessible day that is not a Saturday, Sunday, or legal holiday; or

- During the last hour for filing under FRCP 6(a)(2), then the time for filing is extended to the same time on the first accessible day that is not a Saturday, Sunday, or legal holiday. FRCP 6(a)(3).

v.  *"Last day" defined.* Unless a different time is set by a statute, local rule, or court order, the last day ends:

- For electronic filing, at midnight in the court's time zone; and

- For filing by other means, when the clerk's office is scheduled to close. FRCP 6(a)(4).

vi.  *"Next day" defined.* The "next day" is determined by continuing to count forward when the period is measured after an event and backward when measured before an event. FRCP 6(a)(5).

vii.  *"Legal holiday" defined.* "Legal holiday" means:

- The day set aside by statute for observing New Year's Day, Martin Luther King Jr.'s Birthday, Washington's Birthday, Memorial Day, Independence Day, Labor Day, Columbus Day, Veterans' Day, Thanksgiving Day, or Christmas Day;

- Any day declared a holiday by the President or Congress; and

- For periods that are measured after an event, any other day declared a holiday by the state where the district court is located. FRCP 6(a)(6).

b.  *Computation of electronic filing deadlines.* Filing documents electronically does not alter any filing deadlines. MA R USDCT CM/ECF Admin(K); MA R USDCT LR 5.4(D). Although CM/ECF is generally available twenty-four (24) hours a day for filing, all electronic transmissions of documents must be completed prior to 6:00 PM, Eastern Standard (or Daylight Savings) Time, on the date on which it is due, in order to be considered timely filed that day. MA R USDCT CM/ECF Admin(K); MA R USDCT LR 5.4(D). When a specific time of day deadline is set by court order or stipulation, the electronic filing must be completed by that time. Documents may be filed at any time of the day on days prior to the date on which it is due. MA R USDCT CM/ECF Admin(K). A document filed electronically shall be deemed filed as of the time and date stated on the NEF received from the court. MA R USDCT CM/ECF Admin(G)(2); MA R USDCT CM/ECF Admin(K).

i.  *Technical failures.* A user whose filing is made untimely as the result of a technical failure of the court's CM/ECF system may seek appropriate relief from the court. MA R USDCT CM/ECF Admin(W)(3). Technical difficulties on the filer's end, with telephone, cable lines, the filer's Internet Service Provider (ISP), or hardware or software problems, will not constitute a technical failure under the Administrative Procedures for Electronic Case Filing in the United States District Court for the District of Massachusetts (MA R USDCT CM/ECF Admin) nor excuse an untimely filing. MA R USDCT CM/ECF Admin(W)(3). As help desk support is available during normal business hours, filers are strongly urged to electronically file any documents during that period. MA R USDCT CM/ECF Admin(W)(3).

- The court has made available a public terminal (computers and scanner) in each clerk's office for registered users to scan and electronically file documents. This equipment is available during normal business hours. Users should bring their prepared document and a valid CM/ECF login and password. MA R USDCT CM/ECF Admin(W)(3).

c.  *Extending time.* When an act may or must be done within a specified time, the court may, for good cause, extend the time: (1) with or without motion or notice if the court acts, or if a request is made, before the original time or its extension expires; or (2) on motion made after the time has expired if the party failed to act because of excusable neglect. FRCP 6(b)(1).

    i. *Exceptions.* A court must not extend the time to act under FRCP 50(b), FRCP 50(d), FRCP 52(b), FRCP 59(b), FRCP 59(d), FRCP 59(e), and FRCP 60(b). FRCP 6(b)(2).

    ii. Refer to the United States District Court for the District of Massachusetts KeyRules Motion for Continuance/Extension of Time document for more information on extending time.

  d. *Additional time after certain kinds of service.* When a party may or must act within a specified time after being served and service is made under FRCP 5(b)(2)(C) (by mail), FRCP 5(b)(2)(D) (by leaving with the clerk), or FRCP 5(b)(2)(F) (by other means consented to), three (3) days are added after the period would otherwise expire under FRCP 6(a). FRCP 6(d).

## C. General Requirements

1. *General provisions governing discovery*

  a. *Discovery scope and limits*

    i. *Scope in general.* Unless otherwise limited by court order, the scope of discovery is as follows: Parties may obtain discovery regarding any nonprivileged matter that is relevant to any party's claim or defense and proportional to the needs of the case, considering the importance of the issues at stake in the action, the amount in controversy, the parties' relative access to relevant information, the parties' resources, the importance of the discovery in resolving the issues, and whether the burden or expense of the proposed discovery outweighs its likely benefit. Information within this scope of discovery need not be admissible in evidence to be discoverable. FRCP 26(b)(1).

    ii. *Limitations on frequency and extent*

- *When permitted.* By order, the court may alter the limits in the Federal Rules of Civil Procedure on the number of depositions and interrogatories or on the length of depositions under FRCP 30. By order or local rule, the court may also limit the number of requests under FRCP 36. FRCP 26(b)(2)(A).

- *Specific limitations on electronically stored information.* A party need not provide discovery of electronically stored information from sources that the party identifies as not reasonably accessible because of undue burden or cost. On motion to compel discovery or for a protective order, the party from whom discovery is sought must show that the information is not reasonably accessible because of undue burden or cost. If that showing is made, the court may nonetheless order discovery from such sources if the requesting party shows good cause, considering the limitations of FRCP 26(b)(2)(C). The court may specify conditions for the discovery. FRCP 26(b)(2)(B).

- *When required.* On motion or on its own, the court must limit the frequency or extent of discovery otherwise allowed by the Federal Rules of Civil Procedure or by local rule if it determines that: (1) the discovery sought is unreasonably cumulative or duplicative, or can be obtained from some other source that is more convenient, less burdensome, or less expensive; (2) the party seeking discovery has had ample opportunity to obtain the information by discovery in the action; or (3) the proposed discovery is outside the scope permitted by FRCP 26(b)(1). FRCP 26(b)(2)(C).

    iii. *Trial preparation; Materials*

- *Documents and tangible things.* Ordinarily, a party may not discover documents and tangible things that are prepared in anticipation of litigation or for trial by or for another party or its representative (including the other party's attorney, consultant, surety, indemnitor, insurer, or agent). But, subject to FRCP 26(b)(4), those materials may be discovered if: (1) they are otherwise discoverable under FRCP 26(b)(1); and (2) the party shows that it has substantial need for the materials to prepare its case and cannot, without undue hardship, obtain their substantial equivalent by other means. FRCP 26(b)(3)(A).

- *Protection against disclosure.* If the court orders discovery of those materials, it must protect against disclosure of the mental impressions, conclusions, opinions, or legal theories of a party's attorney or other representative concerning the litigation. FRCP 26(b)(3)(B).

- *Previous statement.* Any party or other person may, on request and without the required showing, obtain the person's own previous statement about the action or its subject matter. If the request is refused, the person may move for a court order, and FRCP 37(a)(5) applies to the award of expenses. A previous statement is either: (1) a written statement that the person has signed or otherwise adopted or approved; or (2) a contemporaneous stenographic, mechanical, electrical, or other recording—or a transcription of it—that recites substantially verbatim the person's oral statement. FRCP 26(b)(3)(C).

iv. *Trial preparation; Experts*

- *Deposition of an expert who may testify.* A party may depose any person who has been identified as an expert whose opinions may be presented at trial. If FRCP 26(a)(2)(B) requires a report from the expert, the deposition may be conducted only after the report is provided. FRCP 26(b)(4)(A).

- *Trial-preparation protection for draft reports or disclosures.* FRCP 26(b)(3)(A) and FRCP 26(b)(3)(B) protect drafts of any report or disclosure required under FRCP 26(a)(2), regardless of the form in which the draft is recorded. FRCP 26(b)(4)(B).

- *Trial-preparation protection for communications between a party's attorney and expert witnesses.* FRCP 26(b)(3)(A) and FRCP 26(b)(3)(B) protect communications between the party's attorney and any witness required to provide a report under FRCP 26(a)(2)(B), regardless of the form of the communications, except to the extent that the communications: (1) relate to compensation for the expert's study or testimony; (2) identify facts or data that the party's attorney provided and that the expert considered in forming the opinions to be expressed; or (3) identify assumptions that the party's attorney provided and that the expert relied on in forming the opinions to be expressed. FRCP 26(b)(4)(C).

- *Expert employed only for trial preparation.* Ordinarily, a party may not, by interrogatories or deposition, discover facts known or opinions held by an expert who has been retained or specially employed by another party in anticipation of litigation or to prepare for trial and who is not expected to be called as a witness at trial. But a party may do so only: (1) as provided in FRCP 35(b); or (2) on showing exceptional circumstances under which it is impracticable for the party to obtain facts or opinions on the same subject by other means. FRCP 26(b)(4)(D).

- *Payment.* Unless manifest injustice would result, the court must require that the party seeking discovery: (1) pay the expert a reasonable fee for time spent in responding to discovery under FRCP 26(b)(4)(A) or FRCP 26(b)(4)(D); and (2) for discovery under FRCP 26(b)(4)(D), also pay the other party a fair portion of the fees and expenses it reasonably incurred in obtaining the expert's facts and opinions. FRCP 26(b)(4)(E).

v. *Claiming privilege or protecting trial-preparation materials*

- *Information withheld.* When a party withholds information otherwise discoverable by claiming that the information is privileged or subject to protection as trial-preparation material, the party must: (1) expressly make the claim; and (2) describe the nature of the documents, communications, or tangible things not produced or disclosed—and do so in a manner that, without revealing information itself privileged or protected, will enable other parties to assess the claim. FRCP 26(b)(5)(A).

- *Information produced.* If information produced in discovery is subject to a claim of privilege or of protection as trial-preparation material, the party making the claim may notify any party that received the information of the claim and the basis for it. After being notified, a party must promptly return, sequester, or destroy the specified information and any copies it has; must not use or disclose the information until the claim is resolved; must take reasonable steps to retrieve the information if the party disclosed it before being notified; and may promptly present the information to the court under seal for a determination of the claim. The producing party must preserve the information until the claim is resolved. FRCP 26(b)(5)(B).

b. *Protective orders.* A party or any person from whom discovery is sought may move for a protective order in the court where the action is pending—or as an alternative on matters relating to a deposition, in the court for the district where the deposition will be taken. FRCP 26(c)(1). Refer to the United States District Court for the District of Massachusetts KeyRules Motion for Protective Order document for more information.

c. *Disclosure orders.* The judicial officer may order the parties to submit at the scheduling conference, or at any subsequent time the officer deems appropriate, sworn statements disclosing certain information to every other party. At the discretion of the judicial officer, this order may direct the submission of:

i. A sworn statement from a claimant, whether plaintiff, third-party plaintiff, cross-claimant, or counter-claimant, that:

- Itemizes all economic loss and provides a computation of damages for which recovery is sought, if any, sustained before the date of service of process;

- Identifies all persons then known to the claimant or the claimant's attorney who witnessed or participated in the transaction or occurrence giving rise to the claim or otherwise known or believed to have substantial discoverable information about the claim or defenses, together with a statement of the subject and a brief summary of that information;

- Identifies all opposing parties, and all officers, directors, and employees of opposing parties, from whom statements have been obtained by or on behalf of the claimant regarding the subject matter of the claim; and

- Identifies all governmental agencies or officials then known to the claimant or the claimant's attorney to have investigated the transaction or occurrence giving rise to the claim; and

ii. A sworn statement from a defendant, whether the direct defendant, third-party defendant, cross-claim defendant, or counterclaim defendant, that identifies:

- All persons then known to the defendant or the defendant's attorneys who witnessed the transaction or occurrence giving rise to the claim or otherwise is known or believed to have substantial discoverable information about the claims or defenses, together with a statement of the subject and a brief summary of that information;

- All opposing parties, and all officers, directors, and employees of opposing parties, from whom statements have been obtained by or on behalf of the defendant regarding the subject matter of the claims or defenses; and

- All government agencies or officials then known to the defendant or the defendant's attorneys to have investigated the transaction or occurrence giving rise to the claims or defenses. MA R USDCT LR 26.1(b).

iii. Noncompliance may be excused only by order of the judicial officer. MA R USDCT LR 26.1(b).

d. *Uniform definitions in discovery requests*

i. *Incorporation by reference and limitations.* The full text of the definitions set forth in MA R USDCT LR 26.5(c) is deemed incorporated by reference into all discovery requests, but shall not preclude:

- The definition of other terms specific to the particular litigation;

- The use of abbreviations; or

- A narrower definition of a term defined in MA R USDCT LR 26.5(c). MA R USDCT LR 26.5(a).

ii. *Effect on scope of discovery.* MA R USDCT LR 26.5 is not intended to broaden or narrow the scope of discovery permitted by the Federal Rules of Civil Procedure. MA R USDCT LR 26.5(b).

iii. *Definitions.* The following definitions apply to all discovery requests:

- *Communication.* The term "communication" means the transmittal of information (in the form of facts, ideas, inquiries, or otherwise). MA R USDCT LR 26.5(c)(1).

- *Document.* The term "document" is defined to be synonymous in meaning and equal in scope to the usage of this term in FRCP 34(a). A draft or non-identical copy is a separate document within the meaning of this term. MA R USDCT LR 26.5(c)(2).

- *Identify (with respect to persons).* When referring to a person, "to identify" means to give, to the extent known, the person's full name, present or last known address, and, when referring to a natural person, the present or last known place of employment. Once a person has been identified in accordance with this subparagraph, only the name of that person need be listed in response to subsequent discovery requesting the identification of that person. MA R USDCT LR 26.5(c)(3).

- *Identify (with respect to documents).* When referring to documents, "to identify" means to give, to the extent known, the: (1) type of document; (2) general subject matter; (3) date of the document; and (4) author(s), addressee(s), and recipient(s). MA R USDCT LR 26.5(c)(4).

- *Parties.* The terms "plaintiff" and "defendant" as well as a party's full or abbreviated name or a pronoun referring to a party mean the party and, where applicable, its officers, directors, employees, partners, corporate parent, subsidiaries, or affiliates. This definition is not intended to impose a discovery obligation on any person who is not a party to the litigation. MA R USDCT LR 26.5(c)(5).

- *Person.* The term "person" is defined as any natural person or any business, legal, or governmental entity or association. MA R USDCT LR 26.5(c)(6).

- *Concerning.* The term "concerning" means referring to, describing, evidencing, or constituting. MA R USDCT LR 26.5(c)(7).

461

- *State the basis.* When an interrogatory calls upon a party to "state the basis" of or for a particular claim, assertion, allegation, or contention, the party shall: (1) identify each and every document (and, where pertinent, the section, article, or subparagraph thereof), which forms any part of the source of the party's information regarding the alleged facts or legal conclusions referred to by the interrogatory; (2) identify each and every communication which forms any part of the source of the party's information regarding the alleged facts or legal conclusions referred to by the interrogatory; (3) state separately the acts or omissions to act on the part of any person (identifying the acts or omissions to act by stating their nature, time, and place and identifying the persons involved) which form any part of the party's information regarding the alleged facts or legal conclusions referred to in the interrogatory; and (4) state separately any other fact which forms the basis of the party's information regarding the alleged facts or conclusions referred to in the interrogatory. MA R USDCT LR 26.5(c)(8).

e. *Cooperative discovery.* The judicial officer should encourage cost effective discovery by means of voluntary exchange of information among litigants and their attorneys. This may be accomplished through the use of: (1) informal, cooperative discovery practices in which counsel provide information to opposing counsel without resort to formal discovery procedures; or (2) stipulations entered into by the parties with respect to deposition notices, waiver of signing, and other matters, except that the parties may not enter into stipulations extending the time for responding to discovery requests or otherwise modify discovery procedures ordered by the judicial officer. MA R USDCT LR 26.1(a).

f. *Phasing of discovery.* In order to facilitate settlement and the efficient completion of discovery, the judicial officer has discretion to structure discovery activities by phasing and sequencing the topics which are the subject of discovery. For example, an order may be framed limiting the first phase to developing information needed for a realistic assessment of the case. If the case does not terminate, the second phase would be directed at information needed to prepare for trial. MA R USDCT LR 26.3.

g. *Sequence of discovery.* Unless the parties stipulate or the court orders otherwise for the parties' and witnesses' convenience and in the interests of justice: (1) methods of discovery may be used in any sequence; and (2) discovery by one party does not require any other party to delay its discovery. FRCP 26(d)(3).

2. *Persons before whom depositions may be taken*

   a. *Within the United States.* Within the United States or a territory or insular possession subject to United States jurisdiction, a deposition must be taken before: (1) an officer authorized to administer oaths either by federal law or by the law in the place of examination; or (2) a person appointed by the court where the action is pending to administer oaths and take testimony. FRCP 28(a)(1).

      i. *Definition of "officer".* The term "officer" in FRCP 30, FRCP 31, and FRCP 32 includes a person appointed by the court under FRCP 28 or designated by the parties under FRCP 29(a). FRCP 28(a)(2).

   b. *In a foreign country.* A deposition may be taken in a foreign country: (1) under an applicable treaty or convention; (2) under a letter of request, whether or not captioned a "letter rogatory"; (3) on notice, before a person authorized to administer oaths either by federal law or by the law in the place of examination; or (4) before a person commissioned by the court to administer any necessary oath and take testimony. FRCP 28(b)(1).

      i. *Issuing a letter of request or a commission.* A letter of request, a commission, or both may be issued: (1) on appropriate terms after an application and notice of it; and (2) without a showing that taking the deposition in another manner is impracticable or inconvenient. FRCP 28(b)(2).

      ii. *Form of a request, notice, or commission.* When a letter of request or any other device is used according to a treaty or convention, it must be captioned in the form prescribed by that treaty or convention. A letter of request may be addressed "To the Appropriate Authority in [name of country]." A deposition notice or a commission must designate by name or descriptive title the person before whom the deposition is to be taken. FRCP 28(b)(3).

      iii. *Letter of request; Admitting evidence.* Evidence obtained in response to a letter of request need not be excluded merely because it is not a verbatim transcript, because the testimony was not taken under oath, or because of any similar departure from the requirements for depositions taken within the United States. FRCP 28(b)(4).

   c. *Disqualification.* A deposition must not be taken before a person who is any party's relative, employee, or attorney; who is related to or employed by any party's attorney; or who is financially interested in the action. FRCP 28(c).

3. *Depositions by oral examination*

   a. *Notice of the deposition.* A party who wants to depose a person by oral questions must give reasonable written notice to every other party. The notice must state the time and place of the deposition and, if known, the deponent's name and address. If the name is unknown, the notice must provide a general description sufficient to identify the person or the particular class or group to which the person belongs. FRCP 30(b)(1).

   i. *Notice or subpoena directed to an organization.* In its notice or subpoena, a party may name as the deponent a public or private corporation, a partnership, an association, a governmental agency, or other entity and must describe with reasonable particularity the matters for examination. The named organization must then designate one or more officers, directors, or managing agents, or designate other persons who consent to testify on its behalf; and it may set out the matters on which each person designated will testify. A subpoena must advise a nonparty organization of its duty to make this designation. The persons designated must testify about information known or reasonably available to the organization. FRCP 30(b)(6) does not preclude a deposition by any other procedure allowed by the Federal Rules of Civil Procedure. FRCP 30(b)(6).

b. *Place for taking depositions.* Unless the court orders otherwise:

   i. *Boston.* Boston is deemed a convenient place for taking of a deposition of any person who resides, is employed, or transacts business in person in Suffolk, Bristol, Essex, Middlesex, Norfolk or Plymouth Counties;

   ii. *Springfield.* Springfield is deemed a convenient place for taking the deposition of any person who resides, is employed, or transacts business in person in Berkshire, Franklin, Hampden or Hampshire Counties; and

   iii. *Worcester.* Worcester is deemed a convenient place for taking the deposition of any person who resides, is employed, or transacts business in person in Worcester County. MA R USDCT LR 30.1.

c. *Method of recording*

   i. *Method stated in the notice.* The party who notices the deposition must state in the notice the method for recording the testimony. Unless the court orders otherwise, testimony may be recorded by audio, audiovisual, or stenographic means. The noticing party bears the recording costs. Any party may arrange to transcribe a deposition. FRCP 30(b)(3)(A).

   ii. *Additional method.* With prior notice to the deponent and other parties, any party may designate another method for recording the testimony in addition to that specified in the original notice. That party bears the expense of the additional record or transcript unless the court orders otherwise. FRCP 30(b)(3)(B).

d. *By remote means.* The parties may stipulate—or the court may on motion order—that a deposition be taken by telephone or other remote means. For the purpose of FRCP 30 and FRCP 28(a), FRCP 37(a)(2), and FRCP 37(b)(1), the deposition takes place where the deponent answers the questions. FRCP 30(b)(4).

e. *Officer's duties*

   i. *Before the deposition.* Unless the parties stipulate otherwise, a deposition must be conducted before an officer appointed or designated under FRCP 28. The officer must begin the deposition with an on-the-record statement that includes: (1) the officer's name and business address; (2) the date, time, and place of the deposition; (3) the deponent's name; (4) the officer's administration of the oath or affirmation to the deponent; and (5) the identity of all persons present. FRCP 30(b)(5)(A).

   ii. *Conducting the deposition; Avoiding distortion.* If the deposition is recorded non-stenographically, the officer must repeat the items in FRCP 30(b)(5)(A)(i) through FRCP 30(b)(5)(A)(iii) at the beginning of each unit of the recording medium. The deponent's and attorneys' appearance or demeanor must not be distorted through recording techniques. FRCP 30(b)(5)(B).

   iii. *After the deposition.* At the end of a deposition, the officer must state on the record that the deposition is complete and must set out any stipulations made by the attorneys about custody of the transcript or recording and of the exhibits, or about any other pertinent matters. FRCP 30(b)(5)(C).

f. *Examination and cross-examination.* The examination and cross-examination of a deponent proceed as they would at trial under the Federal Rules of Evidence, except FRE 103 and FRE 615. FRCP 30(c)(1).

   i. *Record of the examination.* After putting the deponent under oath or affirmation, the officer must record the testimony by the method designated under FRCP 30(b)(3)(A). The testimony must be recorded by the officer personally or by a person acting in the presence and under the direction of the officer. FRCP 30(c)(1).

   ii. *Objections.* An objection at the time of the examination—whether to evidence, to a party's conduct, to the officer's qualifications, to the manner of taking the deposition, or to any other aspect of the deposition—must be noted on the record, but the examination still proceeds; the testimony is taken subject to any objection. An objection must be stated concisely in a nonargumentative and nonsuggestive manner. A person may instruct a deponent not to answer only when necessary to preserve a privilege, to enforce a limitation ordered by the court, or to present a motion under FRCP 30(d)(3). FRCP 30(c)(2).

iii. *Participating through written questions.* Instead of participating in the oral examination, a party may serve written questions in a sealed envelope on the party noticing the deposition, who must deliver them to the officer. The officer must ask the deponent those questions and record the answers verbatim. FRCP 30(c)(3).

g. *Duration.* Unless otherwise stipulated or ordered by the court, a deposition is limited to one (1) day of seven (7) hours. The court must allow additional time consistent with FRCP 26(b)(1) and FRCP 26(b)(2) if needed to fairly examine the deponent or if the deponent, another person, or any other circumstance impedes or delays the examination. FRCP 30(d)(1).

h. *Sanction.* The court may impose an appropriate sanction—including the reasonable expenses and attorney's fees incurred by any party—on a person who impedes, delays, or frustrates the fair examination of the deponent. FRCP 30(d)(2). Refer to the United States District Court for the District of Massachusetts KeyRules Motion for Discovery Sanctions document for more information on sanctions.

i. *Motion to terminate or limit.* At any time during a deposition, the deponent or a party may move to terminate or limit it on the ground that it is being conducted in bad faith or in a manner that unreasonably annoys, embarrasses, or oppresses the deponent or party. The motion may be filed in the court where the action is pending or the deposition is being taken. If the objecting deponent or party so demands, the deposition must be suspended for the time necessary to obtain an order. FRCP 30(d)(3)(A).

   i. *Order.* The court may order that the deposition be terminated or may limit its scope and manner as provided in FRCP 26(c). If terminated, the deposition may be resumed only by order of the court where the action is pending. FRCP 30(d)(3)(B).

   ii. *Award of expenses.* FRCP 37(a)(5) applies to the award of expenses. FRCP 30(d)(3)(C). Refer to the United States District Court for the District of Massachusetts KeyRules Motion for Discovery Sanctions document for more information on sanctions.

j. *Review by the witness; Statement of changes.* On request by the deponent or a party before the deposition is completed, the deponent must be allowed thirty (30) days after being notified by the officer that the transcript or recording is available in which: (1) to review the transcript or recording; and (2) if there are changes in form or substance, to sign a statement listing the changes and the reasons for making them. FRCP 30(e)(1).

   i. *Changes indicated in the officer's certificate.* The officer must note in the certificate prescribed by FRCP 30(f)(1) whether a review was requested and, if so, must attach any changes the deponent makes during the thirty (30) day period. FRCP 30(e)(2).

k. *Certification and delivery.* The officer must certify in writing that the witness was duly sworn and that the deposition accurately records the witness's testimony. The certificate must accompany the record of the deposition. Unless the court orders otherwise, the officer must seal the deposition in an envelope or package bearing the title of the action and marked "Deposition of [witness's name]" and must promptly send it to the attorney who arranged for the transcript or recording. The attorney must store it under conditions that will protect it against loss, destruction, tampering, or deterioration. FRCP 30(f)(1).

l. *Documents and tangible things.* Documents and tangible things produced for inspection during a deposition must, on a party's request, be marked for identification and attached to the deposition. Any party may inspect and copy them. But if the person who produced them wants to keep the originals, the person may: (1) offer copies to be marked, attached to the deposition, and then used as originals—after giving all parties a fair opportunity to verify the copies by comparing them with the originals; or (2) give all parties a fair opportunity to inspect and copy the originals after they are marked—in which event the originals may be used as if attached to the deposition. FRCP 30(f)(2)(A).

   i. *Order regarding the originals.* Any party may move for an order that the originals be attached to the deposition pending final disposition of the case. FRCP 30(f)(2)(B).

m. *Copies of the transcript or recording.* Unless otherwise stipulated or ordered by the court, the officer must retain the stenographic notes of a deposition taken stenographically or a copy of the recording of a deposition taken by another method. When paid reasonable charges, the officer must furnish a copy of the transcript or recording to any party or the deponent. FRCP 30(f)(3).

n. *Failure to attend a deposition or serve a subpoena; Expenses.* A party who, expecting a deposition to be taken, attends in person or by an attorney may recover reasonable expenses for attending, including attorney's fees, if the noticing party failed to: (1) attend and proceed with the deposition; or (2) serve a subpoena on a nonparty deponent, who consequently did not attend. FRCP 30(g). Refer to the United States District Court for the District of Massachusetts KeyRules Motion for Discovery Sanctions document for more information on sanctions.

o. *Limitation on number of depositions.* Unless the judicial officer orders otherwise, the number of discovery events shall be limited for each side (or group of parties with a common interest) to ten (10) depositions. MA R USDCT LR 26.1(c).

   i. *Further discovery.* Should a party exhaust the opportunities for any type of discovery events under MA R USDCT LR 26.1(c), any requests that such party may make for additional interrogatories, depositions, admissions or the production of documents beyond that allowed pursuant to MA R USDCT LR 26.1(c) shall be by discovery motion. All requests for additional discovery events, extensions of deadlines, for the completion of discovery or for postponement of the trial must be signed by the attorney and the party making the request. MA R USDCT LR 26.2(b).

4. *Depositions by written questions*

   a. *Notice of deposition.* A party who wants to depose a person by written questions must serve them on every other party, with a notice stating, if known, the deponent's name and address. If the name is unknown, the notice must provide a general description sufficient to identify the person or the particular class or group to which the person belongs. The notice must also state the name or descriptive title and the address of the officer before whom the deposition will be taken. FRCP 31(a)(3).

   b. *Questions directed to an organization.* A public or private corporation, a partnership, an association, or a governmental agency may be deposed by written questions in accordance with FRCP 30(b)(6). FRCP 31(a)(4).

   c. *Delivery to the officer; Officer's duties.* The party who noticed the deposition must deliver to the officer a copy of all the questions served and of the notice. The officer must promptly proceed in the manner provided in FRCP 30(c), FRCP 30(e), and FRCP 30(f) to:

      i. Take the deponent's testimony in response to the questions;

      ii. Prepare and certify the deposition; and

      iii. Send it to the party, attaching a copy of the questions and of the notice. FRCP 31(b).

   d. *Notice of completion.* The party who noticed the deposition must notify all other parties when it is completed. FRCP 31(c)(1).

5. *Depositions to perpetuate testimony.* For information on depositions to perpetuate testimony, refer to FRCP 27.

6. *Opening of depositions*

   a. *Pending action.* If filed, unless the court directs otherwise, depositions taken pursuant to FRCP 26 in a pending action shall be opened by the clerk and made available for inspection and copying on request of any party or counsel for any party to the proceeding. MA R USDCT LR 30.2(a).

   b. *Before action or pending appeal.* Depositions before action or pending appeal taken pursuant to FRCP 27 shall be opened by the clerk and made available for inspection and copying on request of any person served with notice pursuant to FRCP 27(a)(2), or by counsel for such person. MA R USDCT LR 30.2(b).

7. *Stipulations about discovery procedure.* Unless the court orders otherwise, the parties may stipulate that: (1) a deposition may be taken before any person, at any time or place, on any notice, and in the manner specified—in which event it may be used in the same way as any other deposition; and (2) other procedures governing or limiting discovery be modified—but a stipulation extending the time for any form of discovery must have court approval if it would interfere with the time set for completing discovery, for hearing a motion, or for trial. FRCP 29.

8. *Alternative dispute resolution (ADR).* The judicial officer assigned to preside over the case shall encourage the resolution of disputes by settlement or other alternative dispute resolution programs. MA R USDCT LR 16.4(a).

   a. *Settlement.* At every conference conducted under the Local Rules of the United States District Court for the District of Massachusetts, the judicial officer shall inquire as to the utility of the parties conducting settlement negotiations, explore means of facilitating those negotiations, and offer whatever assistance may be appropriate in the circumstances. Assistance may include a reference of the case to another judicial officer for settlement purposes. MA R USDCT LR 16.4(b).

      i. When a case is settled, the parties shall file with the clerk a signed agreement for judgment or stipulation for dismissal, as appropriate, within twenty-eight (28) days, unless the court otherwise orders. MA R USDCT LR 68.2.

   b. *Alternative dispute resolution programs*

      i. *Discretion of judicial officer.* The judicial officer, following an exploration of the matter with all counsel, may refer appropriate cases to alternative dispute resolution programs that have been designated for use in the district court or that the judicial officer may make available. The dispute resolution programs described in MA R USDCT LR 16.4(c)(2) through MA R USDCT LR 16.4(c)(4) are illustrative, not exclusive. Moreover, nothing in MA R USDCT LR 16.4 shall preclude the parties from engaging in private dispute resolution programs as long as they comply with any schedule established by the court. MA R USDCT LR 16.4(c)(1).

    ii. *Mediation.* The judicial officer may refer the case to mediation upon the agreement of all parties. MA R USDCT LR 16.4(c)(2)(A).

    iii. *Other alternative dispute resolution programs.* Use of mediation is not exclusive. At the request of parties, the judicial officer may consider other forms of alternative dispute resolution including, but not limited to, mini-trial, summary jury trial and arbitration. MA R USDCT LR 16.4(c)(3).

  c. For more information on alternative dispute resolution (ADR), refer to MA R USDCT LR 16.4.

9. *Sanctions.* Failure to comply with any of the directions or obligations set forth in, or authorized by, these rules may result in dismissal, default, or the imposition of other sanctions as deemed appropriate by the judicial officer. MA R USDCT LR 1.3. Except as provided by law, the court may impose sanctions as provided in MA R USDCT LR 1.3 for failure to comply with the Administrative Procedures for Electronic Case Filing in the United States District Court for the District of Massachusetts (MA R USDCT CM/ECF Admin) or with MA R USDCT LR 5.4. MA R USDCT CM/ECF Admin(C)(3).

## D. Documents

1. *Depositions by oral examination*

  a. *Required documents*

    i. *Notice of deposition.* Refer to the General Requirements section of this document for the form and contents of the notice of deposition.

  b. *Supplemental documents*

    i. *Subpoena.* The deponent's attendance may be compelled by subpoena under FRCP 45. FRCP 30(a)(1). For more information on subpoenas, refer to FRCP 45.

    ii. *Subpoena duces tecum.* If a subpoena duces tecum is to be served on the deponent, the materials designated for production, as set out in the subpoena, must be listed in the notice or in an attachment. FRCP 30(b)(2). For more information on subpoenas duces tecum, refer to FRCP 45.

    iii. *Request for production of documents.* The notice to a party deponent may be accompanied by a request under FRCP 34 to produce documents and tangible things at the deposition. FRCP 30(b)(2). Refer to the United States District Court for the District of Massachusetts KeyRules Request for Production of Documents document for more information.

    iv. *Certificate of service.* No certificate of service is required when a paper is served by filing it with the court's electronic-filing system. When a paper that is required to be served is served by other means: (1) if the paper is filed, a certificate of service must be filed with it or within a reasonable time after service; and (2) if the paper is not filed, a certificate of service need not be filed unless filing is required by court order or by local rule. FRCP 5(d)(1)(B).

2. *Depositions by written questions*

  a. *Required documents*

    i. *Notice of deposition.* Refer to the General Requirements section of this document for the form and contents of the notice of deposition.

    ii. *Written questions.* A party who wants to depose a person by written questions must serve them on every other party, with a notice. FRCP 31(a)(3).

  b. *Supplemental documents*

    i. *Subpoena.* The deponent's attendance may be compelled by subpoena under FRCP 45. FRCP 31(a)(1). For more information on subpoenas, refer to FRCP 45.

    ii. *Certificate of service.* No certificate of service is required when a paper is served by filing it with the court's electronic-filing system. When a paper that is required to be served is served by other means: (1) if the paper is filed, a certificate of service must be filed with it or within a reasonable time after service; and (2) if the paper is not filed, a certificate of service need not be filed unless filing is required by court order or by local rule. FRCP 5(d)(1)(B).

## E. Format

1. *Form of documents.* The rules governing captions and other matters of form in pleadings apply to motions and other papers. FRCP 7(b)(2). The provisions of FRCP 10 and FRCP 11 concerning the form and signing of pleadings, motions, and other papers shall be applicable to all papers filed in any proceeding in this court. The board of bar overseers registration number of each attorney signing such documents, except the United States Attorney and his or her staff, shall be inscribed below the signature. MA R USDCT LR 5.1(a)(1).

   a. *Paper size and binding.* All papers filed in the court shall be adapted for flat filing, be filed on eight and one-half by eleven (8-1/2 x 11) inch paper without backers and be bound firmly by staple or some such other means (excluding paper or binder clip or rubber band). MA R USDCT LR 5.1(a)(2).

   b. *Spacing.* All papers, except discovery requests and responses, shall be double-spaced except for the identification of counsel, title of the case, footnotes, quotations and exhibits. Discovery requests and responses shall be single-spaced. MA R USDCT LR 5.1(a)(2).

   c. *Caption.* Every pleading must have a caption with the court's name, a title, a file number, and [an] FRCP 7(a) designation. FRCP 10(a).

      i. *Names of parties.* The title of the complaint must name all the parties; the title of other pleadings, after naming the first party on each side, may refer generally to other parties. FRCP 10(a).

      ii. *Request for special action.* When any pleading or other paper filed in the court includes a request for special process or relief, or any other request such that, if granted, the court will proceed other than in the ordinary course, the request shall, unless it is noted on the category sheet [see MA R USDCT LR 40.1(a)(1)], be noted on the first page to the right of or immediately beneath the caption. MA R USDCT LR 5.1(c).

   d. *Claims or defenses*

      i. *Numbered paragraphs.* A party must state its claims or defenses in numbered paragraphs, each limited as far as practicable to a single set of circumstances. A later pleading may refer by number to a paragraph in an earlier pleading. FRCP 10(b).

      ii. *Separate statements.* If doing so would promote clarity, each claim founded on a separate transaction or occurrence—and each defense other than a denial—must be stated in a separate count or defense. FRCP 10(b).

   e. *Adoption by reference.* A statement in a pleading may be adopted by reference elsewhere in the same pleading or in any other pleading or motion. FRCP 10(c).

      i. *Exhibits.* A copy of a written instrument that is an exhibit to a pleading is a part of the pleading for all purposes. FRCP 10(c).

   f. *Citations*

      i. *Local rules.* These rules shall be known as Local Rules of the United States District Court for the District of Massachusetts and cited as "L.R., D. Mass." or "L.R." MA R USDCT LR 1.1.

      ii. *Electronic case filing procedures.* The procedures governing electronic case filing shall be known as the "Administrative Procedures for Electronic Case Filing in the United States District Court for the District of Massachusetts." They shall be cited as "APECF." MA R USDCT CM/ECF Admin(A)(7).

   g. *Acceptance by the clerk.* The clerk must not refuse to file a paper solely because it is not in the form prescribed by the Federal Rules of Civil Procedure or by a local rule or practice. FRCP 5(d)(4).

      i. Except for complaints and notices of appeal, papers that do not conform to the requirements of MA R USDCT LR 5.1(a)(2) shall be returned by the clerk. MA R USDCT LR 5.1(a)(2).

2. *Form of electronic documents.* A paper filed electronically is a written paper for purposes of the Federal Rules of Civil Procedure. FRCP 5(d)(3)(D).

   a. *PDF/A format required.* The court will begin requiring submission of documents in PDF/A format in the foreseeable future. PDF/A is an enhanced version of the traditional PDF format. Newer versions of most PDF software will be able to convert to this format. Additional information on PDF/A documents may be found on the court's website. MA R USDCT CM/ECF Admin(Electronic Filing and PDF).

      i. *Electronically converted PDF.* Electronically converted PDF documents are created from word processing documents (MS Word, WordPerfect, etc.) using any appropriate software. These documents are text searchable

and the file size is generally smaller than a scanned document. CM/ECF users may use any brand of software to convert documents to PDF. MA R USDCT CM/ECF Admin(Electronic Filing and PDF).

- Documents converted to PDF, rather than scanned, are preferred for filing in CM/ECF. MA R USDCT CM/ECF Admin(Electronic Filing and PDF).

ii. *Scanned PDF.* Scanned PDF documents are created from paper documents run through an optical scanner. Scanned PDF documents are generally not searchable and have a larger file size. Please note that software used to create scanned documents may (and should) be set in such a way that the document is "text-searchable." MA R USDCT CM/ECF Admin(Electronic Filing and PDF).

b. *Title.* All pleadings filed electronically shall be titled in accordance with the approved dictionary of civil or criminal events of the CM/ECF system of this court. A list of events is available on the CM/ECF Training Information page of the court's website. The clerk's office may, when necessary and appropriate, modify the docket entry description, or delete and re-enter the docket entry in order to comply with the court's quality assurance standards. MA R USDCT CM/ECF Admin(G)(3).

c. *Attachments to filings and exhibits.* Attachments to filings and exhibits must be filed in accordance with the court's CM/ECF User Manual, unless otherwise ordered by the court. MA R USDCT CM/ECF Admin(O)(1).

i. Filers must submit as attachments only those excerpts of the referenced documents that are directly germane to the matter under consideration by the court. Excerpted material must be clearly and prominently identified as such. Users who file excerpts of documents do so without prejudice to their right to timely file additional excerpts or the complete document, as may be allowed by the court. Responding parties may timely file additional excerpts or the complete document that they believe are directly germane. MA R USDCT CM/ECF Admin(O)(2).

ii. Filers shall not attach as an exhibit any pleading or other paper already on file with the court in that case, but shall merely refer to that document. (See MA R USDCT CM/ECF Admin(G) for information on using hyperlinks in PDF documents filed in CM/ECF.) MA R USDCT CM/ECF Admin(O)(3).

d. *Redacted documents.* The parties may request or the court may require the submission of documents that have been redacted/stripped of sensitive or confidential information. The redacted document prepared for electronic filing shall include the original caption of the document, and be clearly labeled as "Redacted Document." A specific event is available for this purpose ("Redacted Document"), found under the Other Filings/Other Documents menu option. MA R USDCT CM/ECF Admin(S).

i. Attorneys and pro se litigants are advised to take extra care when creating PDF documents intended for submission to CM/ECF. Steps shall be taken to ensure the documents are free of any hidden data (metadata) that may contain redacted information, or traces of information edited or deleted are not hidden in the final document. Even PDF content that has been encrypted may be recovered. An advisory document with additional information on this topic may be found on the court's website. MA R USDCT CM/ECF Admin(S).

e. *Hyperlinks.* Electronically filed documents may contain the following types of hyperlinks: (1) hyperlinks to other portions of the same document; (2) hyperlinks to other documents filed within the CM/ECF system; and (3) hyperlinks to a location on the Internet that contains a source document for a citation. MA R USDCT CM/ECF Admin(G)(7).

i. Hyperlinks to cited authority may not replace standard citation format. Complete citations must be included in the text of the filed document. Neither a hyperlink, nor any site to which it refers, shall be considered part of the record, but are simply convenient mechanisms for accessing material cited in a document filed in CM/ECF. Instructions on creating hyperlinks may be found in the CM/ECF User Manual. MA R USDCT CM/ECF Admin(G)(7).

ii. The court accepts no responsibility for, and does not endorse, any product, organization, or content at any hyperlinked site, or at any site to which that site may be linked. The court accepts no responsibility for the availability or functionality of any hyperlink. MA R USDCT CM/ECF Admin(G)(7).

iii. One feature of PDF/A documents is that hyperlinks are commonly "masked," meaning that the full address of the referenced file is not written out; for example, clicking the word brief may open a brief which was previously filed in CM/ECF. MA R USDCT CM/ECF Admin(G)(7)(NOTE). An "unmasked" hyperlink has the full address visible to the user. MA R USDCT CM/ECF Admin(G)(7)(NOTE).

- Masked hyperlinks may or may not work in a PDF/A document, depending on how it was created. Currently, masked hyperlinks are preserved in PDF/A documents produced by the "Save As" method in

Microsoft Word 2007 and 2010; the "PDFMaker" method in Microsoft Word 2007; and OpenOffice 2.4 ("PDF Export"). With other production methods, such as WordPerfect, the PDF/A document includes underlined words that appear to be links, but clicking them has no effect. MA R USDCT CM/ECF Admin(G)(7)(NOTE).

f.   *Documents features not accepted.* CM/ECF will not accept PDF documents containing tracking tags, embedded systems commands, password protections, access restrictions or other security features, special tags or dynamic features. MA R USDCT CM/ECF Admin(G)(8).

g.   *File size limitations.* A filing party shall limit the size of each PDF file to no more than twenty (20) megabytes. PDF files larger than seven (7) megabytes will be rejected by the CM/ECF system. The filer will see a message advising of the size limitation. MA R USDCT CM/ECF Admin(P)(2).

   i.   Larger documents or exhibits may be submitted electronically if split into separate PDF files each less than seven (7) megabytes, attached to the main document and clearly labeled. MA R USDCT CM/ECF Admin(P)(2).

   ii.   Documents submitted electronically or on paper are subject to the page limitations set by MA R USDCT LR 7.1(b)(4) or by order of the court. MA R USDCT CM/ECF Admin(P)(1).

h.   *Accuracy and readability.* The filer shall verify the accuracy and readability of any PDF file before electronically filing it in CM/ECF. MA R USDCT CM/ECF Admin(G)(6); MA R USDCT CM/ECF Admin(P)(3).

3.   *Signing disclosures and discovery requests, responses, and objections.* FRCP 11 does not apply to disclosures and discovery requests, responses, objections, and motions under FRCP 26 through FRCP 37. FRCP 11(d).

a.   *Signature required.* Every disclosure under FRCP 26(a)(1) or FRCP 26(a)(3) and every discovery request, response, or objection must be signed by at least one attorney of record in the attorney's own name—or by the party personally, if unrepresented—and must state the signer's address, e-mail address, and telephone number. FRCP 26(g)(1). The provisions of the Federal Rules of Civil Procedure pertaining to the form and signing of pleadings, motions, and other papers shall be applicable to all papers filed in any proceeding in this court. The board of bar overseers registration number of each attorney signing such documents, except the United States Attorney and his staff, shall be inscribed below the signature. MA R USDCT LR 5.1(a)(1).

   i.   *Electronic signing.* A filing made through a person's electronic-filing account and authorized by that person, together with that person's name on a signature block, constitutes the person's signature. FRCP 5(d)(3)(C).

   ii.   *Appearances.* The filing of an appearance or any other pleading signed on behalf of a party constitutes an entry of appearance for that party. All pleadings shall contain the name, bar admission number, address, telephone number, and e-mail address of the attorney entering an appearance. MA R USDCT LR 83.5.2(a).

   •   *Appearances by law firms.* When a party is represented by a law firm, the appearance must include the name and the signature of at least one individual attorney. When a party is represented by more than one attorney from the same or different law firms, the attorney entering the appearance must designate the individual attorney who is authorized to receive all notices in the case. Any notice sent to an attorney so designated shall be deemed to be proper notice unless the court finds that notice was not properly sent. MA R USDCT LR 83.5.2(b).

   •   For more information on appearances, refer to MA R USDCT LR 83.5.2.

   iii.   *Signatures of attorneys.* The user login and password required to submit documents to the CM/ECF system shall serve as that user's signature for purposes of FRCP 11 and for all other purposes under the Federal Rules of Civil Procedure and the Local Rules of the United States District Court for the District of Massachusetts. All electronically filed documents must include a signature block and must set forth the attorney's name, bar number, address, telephone number and email address. The name of the CM/ECF user under whose log-in and password the document is submitted must be preceded by a "/s/" and typed in the space where the signature would otherwise appear. MA R USDCT CM/ECF Admin(M)(1). For an example, refer to MA R USDCT CM/ECF Admin(M)(1).

   iv.   *Signatures of pro se parties.* Any document requiring a signature that is filed by a party appearing pro se shall bear the words "pro se" following that party's signature. Any such document shall also state the party's mailing address, telephone number (if any), and e-mail address (if the party has consented to service by email). MA R USDCT LR 83.5.5(g). For more information on practice by pro se litigants, refer to MA R USDCT LR 83.5.5.

   v.   *Multiple signatures.* The filer of any document requiring more than one signature (e.g, stipulations, joint motions, joint status reports, magistrate judge consent forms, etc.) must list thereon all the names of other signatories by means of a "/s/ name of signatory" block for each. By submitting such a document, the filing attorney certifies that each of the other signatories has expressly agreed to the form and substance of the document and that the filing attorney has their actual authority to submit the document electronically. MA R USDCT CM/ECF Admin(M)(2). For more information, refer to MA R USDCT CM/ECF Admin(M)(2).

    vi.   *Affidavits.* Except as provided in MA R USDCT CM/ECF Admin(L), affidavits shall be filed electronically; however, the electronically filed version must contain a "/s/ name of signatory" block indicating that the paper document bears an original signature. MA R USDCT CM/ECF Admin(M)(3). The court will also accept a scanned version of the original, signed document. MA R USDCT CM/ECF Admin(M)(3). For more information, refer to MA R USDCT CM/ECF Admin(M)(3).

  b.   *Effect of signature.* By signing, an attorney or party certifies that to the best of the person's knowledge, information, and belief formed after a reasonable inquiry:

    i.   With respect to a disclosure, it is complete and correct as of the time it is made; and

    ii.   With respect to a discovery request, response, or objection, it is:

- Consistent with the Federal Rules of Civil Procedure and warranted by existing law or by a nonfrivolous argument for extending, modifying, or reversing existing law, or for establishing new law;

- Not interposed for any improper purpose, such as to harass, cause unnecessary delay, or needlessly increase the cost of litigation; and

- Neither unreasonable nor unduly burdensome or expensive, considering the needs of the case, prior discovery in the case, the amount in controversy, and the importance of the issues at stake in the action. FRCP 26(g)(1).

  c.   *Failure to sign.* Other parties have no duty to act on an unsigned disclosure, request, response, or objection until it is signed, and the court must strike it unless a signature is promptly supplied after the omission is called to the attorney's or party's attention. FRCP 26(g)(2).

  d.   *Sanction for improper certification.* If a certification violates FRCP 26(g) without substantial justification, the court, on motion or on its own, must impose an appropriate sanction on the signer, the party on whose behalf the signer was acting, or both. The sanction may include an order to pay the reasonable expenses, including attorney's fees, caused by the violation. FRCP 26(g)(3). Refer to the United States District Court for the District of Massachusetts KeyRules Motion for Discovery Sanctions document for more information.

4.   *Privacy protection for filings made with the court*

  a.   *Redacted filings.* Unless the court orders otherwise, in an electronic or paper filing with the court that contains an individual's Social Security number, taxpayer-identification number, or birth date, the name of an individual known to be a minor, or a financial-account number, a party or nonparty making the filing may include only:

    i.   The last four (4) digits of the Social Security number and taxpayer-identification number;

    ii.   The year of the individual's birth;

    iii.   The minor's initials; and

    iv.   The last four (4) digits of the financial-account number. FRCP 5.2(a); MA R USDCT CM/ECF Admin(N).

  b.   *Exemptions from the redaction requirement.* The redaction requirement does not apply to the following:

    i.   A financial-account number that identifies the property allegedly subject to forfeiture in a forfeiture proceeding;

    ii.   The record of an administrative or agency proceeding;

    iii.   The official record of a state-court proceeding;

    iv.   The record of a court or tribunal, if that record was not subject to the redaction requirement when originally filed;

    v.   A filing covered by FRCP 5.2(c) or FRCP 5.2(d); and

    vi.   A pro se filing in an action brought under 28 U.S.C.A. § 2241, 28 U.S.C.A. § 2254, or 28 U.S.C.A. § 2255. FRCP 5.2(b).

  c.   *Limitations on remote access to electronic files; Social Security appeals and immigration cases.* Unless the court orders otherwise, in an action for benefits under the Social Security Act, and in an action or proceeding relating to an order of removal, to relief from removal, or to immigration benefits or detention, access to an electronic file is authorized as follows:

    i.   The parties and their attorneys may have remote electronic access to any part of the case file, including the administrative record;

    ii.   Any other person may have electronic access to the full record at the courthouse, but may have remote electronic access only to:

- The docket maintained by the court; and
- An opinion, order, judgment, or other disposition of the court, but not any other part of the case file or the administrative record. FRCP 5.2(c).

d.   *Filings made under seal.* The court may order that a filing be made under seal without redaction. The court may later unseal the filing or order the person who made the filing to file a redacted version for the public record. FRCP 5.2(d).

e.   *Protective orders.* For good cause, the court may by order in a case:

    i.   Require redaction of additional information; or

    ii.   Limit or prohibit a nonparty's remote electronic access to a document filed with the court. FRCP 5.2(e).

f.   *Option for additional unredacted filing under seal.* A person making a redacted filing may also file an unredacted copy under seal. The court must retain the unredacted copy as part of the record. FRCP 5.2(f). For more information, refer to MA R USDCT LR 7.2.

g.   *Option for filing a reference list.* A filing that contains redacted information may be filed together with a reference list that identifies each item of redacted information and specifies an appropriate identifier that uniquely corresponds to each item listed. The list must be filed under seal and may be amended as of right. Any reference in the case to a listed identifier will be construed to refer to the corresponding item of information. FRCP 5.2(g).

h.   *Responsibility for redaction.* The clerk's office is not responsible for reviewing documents filed with the court to determine whether pleadings have been redacted and are in the proper form. MA R USDCT CM/ECF Admin(N).

i.   *Waiver of protection of identifiers.* A person waives the protection of FRCP 5.2(a) as to the person's own information by filing it without redaction and not under seal. FRCP 5.2(h).

## F.  Filing and Service Requirements

1.  *Filing requirements*

a.   *Required filings.* Any paper after the complaint that is required to be served must be filed no later than a reasonable time after service. But disclosures under FRCP 26(a)(1) or FRCP 26(a)(2) and the following discovery requests and responses must not be filed until they are used in the proceeding or the court orders filing: depositions, interrogatories, requests for documents or tangible things or to permit entry onto land, and requests for admission. FRCP 5(d)(1)(A). Refer to the United States District Court for the District of Massachusetts KeyRules pleading and motion documents for information on filing with the court.

b.   *Nonfiling of discovery materials.* Discovery materials (that is, automatic or voluntary disclosure materials, depositions, deposition notices, interrogatories, requests for documents, requests for admissions, answers and responses to discovery requests, and any other requests for or products of the discovery process) shall not be filed unless so ordered by the court or for use in the proceeding. The party taking a deposition or obtaining any material through discovery is responsible for its preservation and delivery to the court if needed or so ordered. If for any reason a party or concerned citizen believes that any of the named documents should be filed, an ex parte request may be made that such document be filed, stating the reasons for the request. The court may also order filing sua sponte. MA R USDCT LR 26.6(a).

    i.   *Discovery motions.* If relief is sought under FRCP 26(c) or FRCP 37, copies of the relevant portions of disputed documents shall be filed with the court contemporaneously with any motion. MA R USDCT LR 26.6(a).

    ii.   *Motions for summary judgment.* If the moving party under FRCP 56 or the opponent relies on discovery documents, copies of the pertinent parts thereof shall be filed with the motion or opposition. MA R USDCT LR 26.6(a).

c.   *Notice of filing*

    i.   *Depositions by oral examination.* A party who files the deposition must promptly notify all other parties of the filing. FRCP 30(f)(4).

    ii.   *Depositions by written questions.* A party who files the deposition must promptly notify all other parties of the filing. FRCP 31(c)(2).

2.  *Service requirements.* Service of all pleadings subsequent to the original complaint and of all other papers required to be served shall be made in the manner specified by FRCP 5. MA R USDCT LR 5.2(a).

    a.  *Service; When required*

        i.  *In general.* Unless the Federal Rules of Civil Procedure provide otherwise, each of the following papers must be served on every party:

            ● An order stating that service is required;

            ● A pleading filed after the original complaint, unless the court orders otherwise under FRCP 5(c) because there are numerous defendants;

            ● A discovery paper required to be served on a party, unless the court orders otherwise;

            ● A written motion, except one that may be heard ex parte; and

            ● A written notice, appearance, demand, or offer of judgment, or any similar paper. FRCP 5(a)(1).

        ii.  *If a party fails to appear.* No service is required on a party who is in default for failing to appear. But a pleading that asserts a new claim for relief against such a party must be served on that party under FRCP 4. FRCP 5(a)(2).

        iii.  *Seizing property.* If an action is begun by seizing property and no person is or need be named as a defendant, any service required before the filing of an appearance, answer, or claim must be made on the person who had custody or possession of the property when it was seized. FRCP 5(a)(3).

    b.  *Service; How made*

        i.  *Serving an attorney.* If a party is represented by an attorney, service under FRCP 5 must be made on the attorney unless the court orders service on the party. FRCP 5(b)(1).

        ii.  *Service in general.* A paper is served under FRCP 5 by:

            ● Handing it to the person;

            ● Leaving it: (1) at the person's office with a clerk or other person in charge or, if no one is in charge, in a conspicuous place in the office; or (2) if the person has no office or the office is closed, at the person's dwelling or usual place of abode with someone of suitable age and discretion who resides there;

            ● Mailing it to the person's last known address—in which event service is complete upon mailing;

            ● Leaving it with the court clerk if the person has no known address;

            ● Sending it to a registered user by filing it with the court's electronic-filing system or sending it by other electronic means that the person consented to in writing—in either of which events service is complete upon filing or sending, but is not effective if the filer or sender learns that it did not reach the person to be served; or

            ● Delivering it by any other means that the person consented to in writing—in which event service is complete when the person making service delivers it to the agency designated to make delivery. FRCP 5(b)(2).

        iii.  *Service by electronic means.* Unless exempt or otherwise ordered by the court, all pleadings and other papers must be served on other parties by electronic means. MA R USDCT LR 5.4(C); MA R USDCT CM/ECF Admin(H)(2). Service by electronic means shall be treated the same as service by mail. MA R USDCT CM/ECF Admin(H)(4).

            ● *Consent to electronic service.* Registering to use CM/ECF constitutes consent to service of all documents by electronic means as provided in the Administrative Procedures for Electronic Case Filing in the United States District Court for the District of Massachusetts (MA R USDCT CM/ECF Admin) and FRCP 5(b) and FRCP 77(d). MA R USDCT CM/ECF Admin(E)(6); MA R USDCT CM/ECF Admin(H)(3).

            ● *Service on registered ECF users.* Transmission of the Notice of Electronic Filing (NEF) through the court's transmission facilities will constitute service of the filed document upon a registered ECF user. MA R USDCT LR 5.4(C).

            ● *Service on non-registered users.* The party filing the document electronically is responsible for serving a paper copy of the document by mail in accordance with FRCP 5(b) to those case participants who have not been identified on the NEF as electronic recipients. MA R USDCT CM/ECF Admin(H)(3).

            ● *Service of conventionally filed papers.* Documents or exhibits submitted conventionally shall be served on other parties by the filer using traditional means. MA R USDCT CM/ECF Admin(P)(4).

c. *Serving numerous defendants*

    i. *In general.* If an action involves an unusually large number of defendants, the court may, on motion or on its own, order that:

- Defendants' pleadings and replies to them need not be served on other defendants;
- Any crossclaim, counterclaim, avoidance, or affirmative defense in those pleadings and replies to them will be treated as denied or avoided by all other parties; and
- Filing any such pleading and serving it on the plaintiff constitutes notice of the pleading to all parties. FRCP 5(c)(1).

    ii. *Notifying parties.* A copy of every such order must be served on the parties as the court directs. FRCP 5(c)(2).

## G. Hearings

1. There is no hearing contemplated in the federal statutes or rules for the notice of deposition.

## H. Forms

### 1. Federal Notice of Deposition Forms

a. Notice to take deposition to perpetuate testimony. 3A FEDFORMS § 22:14.

b. Notice of taking of deposition to perpetuate testimony pending appeal. 3A FEDFORMS § 22:20.

c. Notice of taking deposition upon oral examination. 3A FEDFORMS § 23:72.

d. Notice of taking deposition upon oral examination; Party. 3A FEDFORMS § 23:73.

e. Notice of taking deposition upon oral examination; Naming and describing person not a party. 3A FEDFORMS § 23:74.

f. Notice of taking deposition upon oral examination; Describing deponents whose names are unknown. 3A FEDFORMS § 23:75.

g. Notice of taking deposition upon oral examination; Pursuant to order granting leave to take deposition. 3A FEDFORMS § 23:76.

h. Notice of taking of deposition of party with notice to produce documents. 3A FEDFORMS § 23:77.

i. Notice of taking of deposition of witness; Including designation of materials in related subpoena duces tecum. 3A FEDFORMS § 23:78.

j. Notice of taking deposition of witness; Including reference to materials designated in attached subpoena. 3A FEDFORMS § 23:79.

k. Notice of taking deposition upon written questions served with notice. 3A FEDFORMS § 23:99.

l. Questions to be attached to notice or served with it. 3A FEDFORMS § 23:100.

m. Notice of return and filing of deposition taken upon written questions. 3A FEDFORMS § 23:106.

n. Notice; Taking of deposition on oral examination. FEDPROF § 23:142.

o. Notice; Taking of deposition on oral examination; Patent proceedings. FEDPROF § 23:143.

p. Notice; Taking of deposition on oral examination; Corporate officer. FEDPROF § 23:144.

q. Notice; Taking of deposition on oral examination; Corporate officers to be designated by corporation. FEDPROF § 23:145.

r. Notice; Taking of deposition on written questions. FEDPROF § 23:146.

s. Notice; Taking of deposition on oral examination or on written questions; Pursuant to court order. FEDPROF § 23:147.

t. Notice; In connection with deposition on written questions; Of cross, redirect, or recross questions. FEDPROF § 23:148.

u. Attachment to notice; Taking of deposition on written questions; Questions to be propounded. FEDPROF § 23:149.

v. Attachment to notice; Cross, redirect, or recross questions to be propounded. FEDPROF § 23:150.

w. Notice; To party taking deposition; Written questions submitted in lieu of participation in oral examination. FEDPROF § 23:151.

x. Notice of taking deposition; Expert witness; Request for production of supporting documents. FEDPROF § 23:157.

y. Subpoena; To testify at taking of deposition and to produce documents or things (form AO 88). FEDPROF § 23:158.

z. Provision in subpoena; Advice to nonparty organization of its duty to designate witness. FEDPROF § 23:161.

## I. Applicable Rules

1. *Federal rules*

    a. Serving and filing pleadings and other papers. FRCP 5.

    b. Privacy protection for filings made with the court. FRCP 5.2.

    c. Computing and extending time; Time for motion papers. FRCP 6.

    d. Pleadings allowed; Form of motions and other papers. FRCP 7.

    e. Form of pleadings. FRCP 10.

    f. Signing pleadings, motions, and other papers; Representations to the court; Sanctions. FRCP 11.

    g. Duty to disclose; General provisions governing discovery. FRCP 26.

    h. Persons before whom depositions may be taken. FRCP 28.

    i. Stipulations about discovery procedure. FRCP 29.

    j. Depositions by oral examination. FRCP 30.

    k. Depositions by written questions. FRCP 31.

    l. Failure to make disclosures or to cooperate in discovery; Sanctions. FRCP 37.

2. *Local rules*

    a. Title. MA R USDCT LR 1.1.

    b. Sanctions. MA R USDCT LR 1.3.

    c. Form and filing of papers. MA R USDCT LR 5.1.

    d. Service and filing of pleadings and other papers. MA R USDCT LR 5.2.

    e. Filing and service by electronic means. MA R USDCT LR 5.4.

    f. Alternative dispute resolution. MA R USDCT LR 16.4.

    g. Control of discovery. MA R USDCT LR 26.1.

    h. Sequences of discovery. MA R USDCT LR 26.2.

    i. Phasing of discovery. MA R USDCT LR 26.3.

    j. Uniform definitions in discovery requests. MA R USDCT LR 26.5.

    k. Court filings and costs. MA R USDCT LR 26.6.

    l. Place for taking depositions. MA R USDCT LR 30.1.

    m. Opening of depositions. MA R USDCT LR 30.2.

    n. Settlement. MA R USDCT LR 68.2.

    o. Office of the clerk. MA R USDCT LR 77.2.

    p. Appearances. MA R USDCT LR 83.5.2.

    q. Practice by pro se litigants. MA R USDCT LR 83.5.5.

    r. CM/ECF case management/electronic case files administrative procedures. MA R USDCT CM/ECF Admin.

## Requests, Notices and Applications
## Application for Temporary Restraining Order

**Document Last Updated December 2018**

### A. Checklist

(I) ❏ Matters to be considered by party applying (with notice)

    (a) ❏ Required documents

        (1) ❏ Notice of motion and motion

        (2) ❏ Memorandum

        (3) ❏ Security

        (4) ❏ Certificate of service

    (b) ❏ Supplemental documents

        (1) ❏ Supporting evidence

        (2) ❏ Notice of constitutional question

        (3) ❏ Nongovernmental corporate disclosure statement

        (4) ❏ Proposed order

        (5) ❏ Compact disk with copy of document(s) in PDF format

        (6) ❏ Notice of filing with clerk's office

        (7) ❏ Additional copies

        (8) ❏ Courtesy copies

    (c) ❏ Timing

        (1) ❏ There are no specific timing requirements for applying for a temporary restraining order with notice

        (2) ❏ A written motion and notice of the hearing must be served at least fourteen (14) days before the time specified for the hearing, with the following exceptions: (i) when the motion may be heard ex parte; (ii) when the Federal Rules of Civil Procedure set a different time; or (iii) when a court order—which a party may, for good cause, apply for ex parte—sets a different time

        (3) ❏ Any affidavit supporting a motion must be served with the motion

        (4) ❏ Except as noted in FRCP 33 to FRCP 36, the original of all papers required to be served under FRCP 5(d) shall, unless otherwise submitted to the court, be filed in the office of the clerk within seven (7) days after service has been made

(II) ❏ Matters to be considered by party applying (without notice, or "ex parte")

    (a) ❏ Required documents

        (1) ❏ Motion

        (2) ❏ Memorandum

        (3) ❏ Affidavit or verified complaint

        (4) ❏ Certificate of attorney

        (5) ❏ Security

    (b) ❏ Supplemental documents

        (1) ❏ Supporting evidence

        (2) ❏ Notice of constitutional question

        (3) ❏ Nongovernmental corporate disclosure statement

        (4) ❏ Proposed order

        (5) ❏ Compact disk with copy of document(s) in PDF format

(6) ❑ Notice of filing with clerk's office

(7) ❑ Additional copies

(8) ❑ Courtesy copies

(c) ❑ Timing

(1) ❑ There are no specific timing requirements for applying for a temporary restraining order without notice, or "ex parte"

(2) ❑ Any affidavit supporting a motion must be served with the motion

## B. Timing

1. *Application for temporary restraining order*

   a. *With notice.* There are no specific timing requirements for applying for a temporary restraining order with notice.

   b. *Without notice, or "ex parte."* There are no specific timing requirements for applying for a temporary restraining order without notice, or "ex parte."

2. *Motion to dissolve or modify.* On two (2) days' notice to the party who obtained the order without notice—or on shorter notice set by the court—the adverse party may appear and move to dissolve or modify the order. The court must then hear and decide the motion as promptly as justice requires. FRCP 65(b)(4).

3. *Timing of motions, generally*

   a. *Motion and notice of hearing.* A written motion and notice of the hearing must be served at least fourteen (14) days before the time specified for the hearing, with the following exceptions:

      i. When the motion may be heard ex parte;

      ii. When the Federal Rules of Civil Procedure set a different time; or

      iii. When a court order—which a party may, for good cause, apply for ex parte—sets a different time. FRCP 6(c)(1).

   b. *Supporting affidavit.* Any affidavit supporting a motion must be served with the motion. FRCP 6(c)(2).

4. *Filing after service.* Except as noted in FRCP 33 to FRCP 36, the original of all papers required to be served under FRCP 5(d) shall, unless otherwise submitted to the court, be filed in the office of the clerk within seven (7) days after service has been made. MA R USDCT LR 5.1(b).

5. *Computation of time*

   a. *Computing time.* FRCP 6 applies in computing any time period specified in the Federal Rules of Civil Procedure, in any local rule or court order, or in any statute that does not specify a method of computing time. FRCP 6(a).

      i. *Period stated in days or a longer unit.* When the period is stated in days or a longer unit of time:

         • Exclude the day of the event that triggers the period;

         • Count every day, including intermediate Saturdays, Sundays, and legal holidays; and

         • Include the last day of the period, but if the last day is a Saturday, Sunday, or legal holiday, the period continues to run until the end of the next day that is not a Saturday, Sunday, or legal holiday. FRCP 6(a)(1).

      ii. *Period stated in hours.* When the period is stated in hours:

         • Begin counting immediately on the occurrence of the event that triggers the period;

         • Count every hour, including hours during intermediate Saturdays, Sundays, and legal holidays; and

         • If the period would end on a Saturday, Sunday, or legal holiday, the period continues to run until the same time on the next day that is not a Saturday, Sunday, or legal holiday. FRCP 6(a)(2).

      iii. *Office of the clerk.* The offices of the Clerk of Court at Boston, Worcester and Springfield shall be open from 8:30 a.m. until 5:00 p.m. on all days except Saturdays, Sundays, legal holidays and other days so ordered by the court and announced in advance, if feasible. MA R USDCT LR 77.2.

      iv. *Inaccessibility of the clerk's office.* Unless the court orders otherwise, if the clerk's office is inaccessible:

         • On the last day for filing under FRCP 6(a)(1), then the time for filing is extended to the first accessible day that is not a Saturday, Sunday, or legal holiday; or

         • During the last hour for filing under FRCP 6(a)(2), then the time for filing is extended to the same time on the first accessible day that is not a Saturday, Sunday, or legal holiday. FRCP 6(a)(3).

v. *"Last day" defined.* Unless a different time is set by a statute, local rule, or court order, the last day ends:

- For electronic filing, at midnight in the court's time zone; and

- For filing by other means, when the clerk's office is scheduled to close. FRCP 6(a)(4).

vi. *"Next day" defined.* The "next day" is determined by continuing to count forward when the period is measured after an event and backward when measured before an event. FRCP 6(a)(5).

vii. *"Legal holiday" defined.* "Legal holiday" means:

- The day set aside by statute for observing New Year's Day, Martin Luther King Jr.'s Birthday, Washington's Birthday, Memorial Day, Independence Day, Labor Day, Columbus Day, Veterans' Day, Thanksgiving Day, or Christmas Day;

- Any day declared a holiday by the President or Congress; and

- For periods that are measured after an event, any other day declared a holiday by the state where the district court is located. FRCP 6(a)(6).

b. *Computation of electronic filing deadlines.* Filing documents electronically does not alter any filing deadlines. MA R USDCT CM/ECF Admin(K); MA R USDCT LR 5.4(D). Although CM/ECF is generally available twenty-four (24) hours a day for filing, all electronic transmissions of documents must be completed prior to 6:00 PM, Eastern Standard (or Daylight Savings) Time, on the date on which it is due, in order to be considered timely filed that day. MA R USDCT CM/ECF Admin(K); MA R USDCT LR 5.4(D). When a specific time of day deadline is set by court order or stipulation, the electronic filing must be completed by that time. Documents may be filed at any time of the day on days prior to the date on which it is due. MA R USDCT CM/ECF Admin(K). A document filed electronically shall be deemed filed as of the time and date stated on the NEF received from the court. MA R USDCT CM/ECF Admin(G)(2); MA R USDCT CM/ECF Admin(K).

i. *Technical failures.* A user whose filing is made untimely as the result of a technical failure of the court's CM/ECF system may seek appropriate relief from the court. MA R USDCT CM/ECF Admin(W)(3). Technical difficulties on the filer's end, with telephone, cable lines, the filer's Internet Service Provider (ISP), or hardware or software problems, will not constitute a technical failure under the Administrative Procedures for Electronic Case Filing in the United States District Court for the District of Massachusetts (MA R USDCT CM/ECF Admin) nor excuse an untimely filing. MA R USDCT CM/ECF Admin(W)(3). As help desk support is available during normal business hours, filers are strongly urged to electronically file any documents during that period. MA R USDCT CM/ECF Admin(W)(3).

- The court has made available a public terminal (computers and scanner) in each clerk's office for registered users to scan and electronically file documents. This equipment is available during normal business hours. Users should bring their prepared document and a valid CM/ECF login and password. MA R USDCT CM/ECF Admin(W)(3).

c. *Extending time.* When an act may or must be done within a specified time, the court may, for good cause, extend the time: (1) with or without motion or notice if the court acts, or if a request is made, before the original time or its extension expires; or (2) on motion made after the time has expired if the party failed to act because of excusable neglect. FRCP 6(b)(1).

i. *Exceptions.* A court must not extend the time to act under FRCP 50(b), FRCP 50(d), FRCP 52(b), FRCP 59(b), FRCP 59(d), FRCP 59(e), and FRCP 60(b). FRCP 6(b)(2).

ii. Refer to the United States District Court for the District of Massachusetts KeyRules Motion for Continuance/Extension of Time document for more information on extending time.

d. *Additional time after certain kinds of service.* When a party may or must act within a specified time after being served and service is made under FRCP 5(b)(2)(C) (by mail), FRCP 5(b)(2)(D) (by leaving with the clerk), or FRCP 5(b)(2)(F) (by other means consented to), three (3) days are added after the period would otherwise expire under FRCP 6(a). FRCP 6(d).

## C. General Requirements

1. *Motions, generally*

a. *Requirements.* A request for a court order must be made by motion. The motion must:

i. Be in writing unless made during a hearing or trial;

ii. State with particularity the grounds for seeking the order; and

    iii.   State the relief sought. FRCP 7(b)(1).

  b.  *Notice of motion.* A party interested in resisting the relief sought by a motion has a right to notice thereof, and an opportunity to be heard. AMJUR MOTIONS § 12.

    i.   [I]n addition to statutory or court rule provisions requiring notice of a motion—the purpose of such a notice requirement having been said to be to prevent a party from being prejudicially surprised by a motion—principles of natural justice dictate that an adverse party generally must be given notice that a motion will be presented to the court. AMJUR MOTIONS § 12.

    ii.  "Notice," in this regard, means reasonable notice, including a meaningful opportunity to prepare and to defend against allegations of a motion. AMJUR MOTIONS § 12.

  c.  *Writing requirement.* The writing requirement is intended to [ensure] that the adverse parties are informed and have a record of both the motion's pendency and the grounds on which the movant seeks an order. FPP § 1191; Feldberg v. Quechee Lakes Corp., 463 F.3d 195 (2d Cir. 2006). [A] single written document can satisfy the writing requirements both for a motion and for [an] FRCP 6(c)(1) notice. FRCP 7(Advisory Committee Notes).

  d.  *Particularity requirement.* The particularity requirement [ensures] that the opposing parties will have notice of their opponent's contentions. FEDPROC § 62:358; Goodman v. 1973 26 Foot Trojan Vessel, Arkansas Registration No. AR1439SN, 859 F.2d 71 (8th Cir. 1988). That requirement ensures that notice of the basis for the motion is provided to the court and to the opposing party so as to avoid prejudice, provide the opponent with a meaningful opportunity to respond, and provide the court with enough information to process the motion correctly. FEDPROC § 62:358; Andreas v. Volkswagen of Am., Inc., 336 F.3d 789 (8th Cir. 2003).

    i.   Reasonable specification of the grounds for a motion is sufficient. The particularity requirement for motions is satisfied when no party is prejudiced by a lack of particularity or when the court can comprehend the basis for the motion and deal with it fairly. However, where a movant fails to state even one ground for granting the motion in question, the movant has failed to meet the minimal standard of "reasonable specification." FEDPROC § 62:358; Martinez v. Trainor, 556 F.2d 818 (7th Cir. 1977).

    ii.  The court may excuse the failure to comply with the particularity requirement if it is inadvertent, and where no prejudice is shown by the opposing party. FEDPROC § 62:358.

  e.  *Control of motion practice*

    i.   *Plan for the disposition of motions.* At the earliest practicable time, the judicial officer shall establish a framework for the disposition of motions, which, at the discretion of the judicial officer, may include specific deadlines or general time guidelines for filing motions. This framework may be amended from time to time by the judicial officer as required by the progress of the case. MA R USDCT LR 7.1(a)(1).

    ii.  *Motion practice.* No motion shall be filed unless counsel certify that they have conferred and have attempted in good faith to resolve or narrow the issue. MA R USDCT LR 7.1(a)(2).

    iii.  *Unresolved motions.* The court shall rule on motions as soon as practicable, having in mind the reporting requirements set forth in the Civil Justice Reform Act. MA R USDCT LR 7.1(a)(3).

2.  *Application for temporary restraining order.* Applicants for injunctive relief occasionally are faced with the possibility that irreparable injury will occur before the hearing for a preliminary injunction required by FRCP 65(a) can be held. In that event a temporary restraining order may be available under FRCP 65(b). FPP § 2951. The order is designed to preserve the status quo until there is an opportunity to hold a hearing on the application for a preliminary injunction and may be issued with or without notice to the adverse party. FPP § 2951; Granny Goose Foods, Inc. v. Bhd. of Teamsters & Auto Truck Drivers Local No. 70 of Alameda Cty., 415 U.S. 423, 94 S. Ct. 1113, 39 L. Ed. 2d 435 (1974).

  a.  *Issuing with notice.* When the opposing party actually receives notice of the application for a restraining order, the procedure that is followed does not differ functionally from that on an application for a preliminary injunction and the proceeding is not subject to any special requirements. FPP § 2951; Dilworth v. Riner, 343 F.2d 226 (5th Cir. 1965).

    i.   *Duration.* By its terms FRCP 65(b) only governs restraining orders issued without notice or a hearing. But. . .it has been argued that its provisions, at least with regard to the duration of a restraining order, apply even to an order granted when notice has been given to the adverse party but there has been no hearing. FPP § 2951.

  b.  *Issuing without notice*

    i.   *When available.* The court may issue a temporary restraining order without written or oral notice to the adverse party or its attorney only if:

        • Specific facts in an affidavit or a verified complaint clearly show that immediate and irreparable injury, loss, or damage will result to the movant before the adverse party can be heard in opposition; and

- The movant's attorney certifies in writing any efforts made to give notice and the reasons why it should not be required. FRCP 65(b)(1).

ii. *Contents.* Every temporary restraining order issued without notice must state the date and hour it was issued; describe the injury and state why it is irreparable; state why the order was issued without notice; and be promptly filed in the clerk's office and entered in the record. FRCP 65(b)(2).

iii. *Expiration.* The order expires at the time after entry—not to exceed fourteen (14) days—that the court sets, unless before that time the court, for good cause, extends it for a like period or the adverse party consents to a longer extension. The reasons for an extension must be entered in the record. FRCP 65(b)(2).

c. *Temporary restraining order versus preliminary injunction.* A temporary restraining order differs from a preliminary injunction, the core reasons being that a temporary restraining order is of limited duration and it may issue without notice to the opposing party before the adverse party can be heard in opposition. FEDPROC § 47:80.

d. *Factors considered.* As in the case of an application for a preliminary injunction, four factors must be considered in determining whether a temporary restraining order is to be granted, which are whether the moving party has established: (1) a substantial likelihood of success on the merits; (2) that irreparable injury will be suffered if the relief is not granted; (3) that the threatened injury outweighs the harm the relief would inflict on the nonmoving party; and (4) that entry of the relief would serve the public interest. FEDPROC § 47:84; Schiavo ex rel. Schindler v. Schiavo, 403 F.3d 1223 (11th Cir. 2005).

i. Plaintiffs are not required to prevail on each of these factors, rather, the factors must be viewed as a continuum, with more of one factor compensating for less of another. In each case, however, all of the factors must be considered to determine whether on balance they weigh toward granting relief. FEDPROC § 47:84.

ii. In the context of a temporary restraining order, it is particularly important for the moving party to demonstrate a substantial likelihood of success on the merits, because otherwise, there would be no justification for the court's intrusion into the ordinary processes of administration and judicial review. FEDPROC § 47:84.

iii. Refer to the United States District Court for the District of Massachusetts KeyRules Motion for Preliminary Injunction document for more information on the factors considered in moving for a preliminary injunction.

e. *Burden.* As with a preliminary injunction, the burden is on the moving party to establish that relief is appropriate. FEDPROC § 47:84.

f. *Security.* The court may issue a preliminary injunction or a temporary restraining order only if the movant gives security in an amount that the court considers proper to pay the costs and damages sustained by any party found to have been wrongfully enjoined or restrained. The United States, its officers, and its agencies are not required to give security. FRCP 65(c).

i. *Proceedings against a security provider.* Whenever the Federal Rules of Civil Procedure (including the Supplemental Rules for Admiralty or Maritime Claims and Asset Forfeiture Actions) require or allow a party to give security, and security is given with one or more security providers, each provider submits to the court's jurisdiction and irrevocably appoints the court clerk as its agent for receiving service of any papers that affect its liability on the security. The security provider's liability may be enforced on motion without an independent action. The motion and any notice that the court orders may be served on the court clerk, who must promptly send a copy of each to every security provider whose address is known. FRCP 65.1. For more information on sureties, refer to MA R USDCT LR 67.1.

g. *Contents and scope of every injunction and restraining order*

i. *Contents.* Every order granting an injunction and every restraining order must:

- State the reasons why it issued;
- State its terms specifically; and
- Describe in reasonable detail—and not by referring to the complaint or other document—the act or acts restrained or required. FRCP 65(d)(1).

ii. *Persons bound.* The order binds only the following who receive actual notice of it by personal service or otherwise:

- The parties;
- The parties' officers, agents, servants, employees, and attorneys; and
- Other persons who are in active concert or participation with anyone described in FRCP 65(d)(2)(A) or FRCP 65(d)(2)(B). FRCP 65(d)(2).

h. *Other laws not modified.* FRCP 65 does not modify the following:

    i. Any federal statute relating to temporary restraining orders or preliminary injunctions in actions affecting employer and employee;

    ii. 28 U.S.C.A. § 2361, which relates to preliminary injunctions in actions of interpleader or in the nature of interpleader; or

    iii. 28 U.S.C.A. § 2284, which relates to actions that must be heard and decided by a three-judge district court. FRCP 65(e).

i. *Copyright impoundment.* FRCP 65 applies to copyright-impoundment proceedings. FRCP 65(f).

3. *Alternative dispute resolution (ADR).* The judicial officer assigned to preside over the case shall encourage the resolution of disputes by settlement or other alternative dispute resolution programs. MA R USDCT LR 16.4(a).

    a. *Settlement.* At every conference conducted under the Local Rules of the United States District Court for the District of Massachusetts, the judicial officer shall inquire as to the utility of the parties conducting settlement negotiations, explore means of facilitating those negotiations, and offer whatever assistance may be appropriate in the circumstances. Assistance may include a reference of the case to another judicial officer for settlement purposes. MA R USDCT LR 16.4(b).

        i. When a case is settled, the parties shall file with the clerk a signed agreement for judgment or stipulation for dismissal, as appropriate, within twenty-eight (28) days, unless the court otherwise orders. MA R USDCT LR 68.2.

    b. *Alternative dispute resolution programs*

        i. *Discretion of judicial officer.* The judicial officer, following an exploration of the matter with all counsel, may refer appropriate cases to alternative dispute resolution programs that have been designated for use in the district court or that the judicial officer may make available. The dispute resolution programs described in MA R USDCT LR 16.4(c)(2) through MA R USDCT LR 16.4(c)(4) are illustrative, not exclusive. Moreover, nothing in MA R USDCT LR 16.4 shall preclude the parties from engaging in private dispute resolution programs as long as they comply with any schedule established by the court. MA R USDCT LR 16.4(c)(1).

        ii. *Mediation.* The judicial officer may refer the case to mediation upon the agreement of all parties. MA R USDCT LR 16.4(c)(2)(A).

        iii. *Other alternative dispute resolution programs.* Use of mediation is not exclusive. At the request of parties, the judicial officer may consider other forms of alternative dispute resolution including, but not limited to, mini-trial, summary jury trial and arbitration. MA R USDCT LR 16.4(c)(3).

    c. For more information on alternative dispute resolution (ADR), refer to MA R USDCT LR 16.4.

4. *Sanctions.* Failure to comply with any of the directions or obligations set forth in, or authorized by, these rules may result in dismissal, default, or the imposition of other sanctions as deemed appropriate by the judicial officer. MA R USDCT LR 1.3. Except as provided by law, the court may impose sanctions as provided in MA R USDCT LR 1.3 for failure to comply with the Administrative Procedures for Electronic Case Filing in the United States District Court for the District of Massachusetts (MA R USDCT CM/ECF Admin) or with MA R USDCT LR 5.4. MA R USDCT CM/ECF Admin(C)(3).

## D. Documents

1. *Application for temporary restraining order (with notice)*

    a. *Required documents*

        i. *Notice of motion and motion.* Refer to the General Requirements section of this document for information on the notice of motion and motion.

            • *Request for oral argument.* Any party making or opposing a motion who believes that oral argument may assist the court and wishes to be heard shall include a request for oral argument in a separate paragraph of the motion or opposition. The request should be set off with a centered caption, "REQUEST FOR ORAL ARGUMENT." MA R USDCT LR 7.1(d).

        ii. *Memorandum.* A party filing a motion shall at the same time file a memorandum of reasons, including citation of supporting authorities, why the motion should be granted. MA R USDCT LR 7.1(b)(1). Any memorandum of law or other attachment filed in support of a main document shall be filed as a separate document, using the proper event. MA R USDCT CM/ECF Admin(G)(4). Memoranda supporting or opposing allowance of motions shall not, without leave of court, exceed twenty (20) pages, double-spaced. MA R USDCT LR 7.1(b)(4).

480

iii. *Security.* Refer to the General Requirements section of this document for information on the security required.

iv. *Certificate of service.* No certificate of service is required when a paper is served by filing it with the court's electronic-filing system. When a paper that is required to be served is served by other means: (1) if the paper is filed, a certificate of service must be filed with it or within a reasonable time after service; and (2) if the paper is not filed, a certificate of service need not be filed unless filing is required by court order or by local rule. FRCP 5(d)(1)(B). Except as otherwise provided by the Federal Rules of Civil Procedure, proof of service of all pleadings and other papers required to be served (except discovery papers that in accordance with FRCP 33 to FRCP 36(f) are not to be filed) shall be filed in the office of the clerk promptly after service has been made. The proof shall show the time and manner of service, and may be made by written acknowledgment of service, a certificate of a member of the bar of this court, or an affidavit of the person who served the paper. MA R USDCT LR 5.2(b)(1). A certificate of service of a member of the bar shall appear at the bottom of or on the margin of the last page of the paper to which it relates. MA R USDCT LR 5.2(b)(2).

- *Paper service.* The certificate shall be a brief, single-spaced statement and may be in the following form: I hereby certify that a true copy of the above document was served upon (each party appearing pro se and) the attorney of record for each other party by mail (by hand) on (date). (Signature). MA R USDCT LR 5.2(b)(2).

- *Electronic service.* Any pleading or other paper served by electronic means must bear a certificate of service in accordance with MA R USDCT LR 5.2(b). MA R USDCT LR 5.4(C); MA R USDCT CM/ECF Admin(H)(2). The certificate of service shall state that the filer: (1) filed the document electronically, (2) that it will be served electronically to registered CM/ECF participants via the NEF and (3) that the filer will send paper copies to non-registered participants as indicated on the NEF. MA R USDCT CM/ECF Admin(H)(2). For example: I hereby certify that this document filed through the CM/ECF system will be sent electronically to the registered participants as identified on the NEF (NEF) and paper copies will be sent to those indicated as non registered participants on (date). MA R USDCT CM/ECF Admin(H)(2).

- *Return.* Documents not conforming to the requirements of MA R USDCT LR 5.2 (except notices of appeal) shall be returned by the clerk. MA R USDCT LR 5.2(b)(2).

- *Failure to make proof of service.* Failure to make proof of service does not affect the validity of the service. MA R USDCT LR 5.2(b)(3).

b. *Supplemental documents*

i. *Supporting evidence.* When a motion relies on facts outside the record, the court may hear the matter on affidavits or may hear it wholly or partly on oral testimony or on depositions. FRCP 43(c). Affidavits and other documents setting forth or evidencing facts on which the motion is based shall be filed with the motion. MA R USDCT LR 7.1(b)(1).

ii. *Notice of constitutional question.* A party that files a pleading, written motion, or other paper drawing into question the constitutionality of a federal or state statute must promptly:

- *File notice.* File a notice of constitutional question stating the question and identifying the paper that raises it, if: (1) a federal statute is questioned and the parties do not include the United States, one of its agencies, or one of its officers or employees in an official capacity; or (2) a state statute is questioned and the parties do not include the state, one of its agencies, or one of its officers or employees in an official capacity; and

- *Serve notice.* Serve the notice and paper on the Attorney General of the United States if a federal statute is questioned—or on the state attorney general if a state statute is questioned—either by certified or registered mail or by sending it to an electronic address designated by the attorney general for this purpose. FRCP 5.1(a).

- *No forfeiture.* A party's failure to file and serve the notice, or the court's failure to certify, does not forfeit a constitutional claim or defense that is otherwise timely asserted. FRCP 5.1(d).

iii. *Nongovernmental corporate disclosure statement*

- *Contents.* A nongovernmental corporate party must file two (2) copies of a disclosure statement that: (1) identifies any parent corporation and any publicly held corporation owning ten percent (10%) or more of its stock; or (2) states that there is no such corporation. FRCP 7.1(a).

- *Time to file; Supplemental filing.* A party must: (1) file the disclosure statement with its first appearance, pleading, petition, motion, response, or other request addressed to the court; and (2) promptly file a supplemental statement if any required information changes. FRCP 7.1(b).

iv. *Proposed order.* Proposed orders usually are not required by this court. However, the court may request the party to submit such a document. In those situations, unless otherwise directed by the clerk's office, electronically file the proposed document/order using the entry for "Proposed Documents submitted to the court," found under the Other Documents menu, or as an attachment to the motion to which it relates. MA R USDCT CM/ECF Admin(T).

v. *Compact disk with copy of document(s) in PDF format.* A filer who cannot file a document electronically because of such technical difficulty on the filer's end [with telephone, cable lines, the filer's Internet Service Provider (ISP), or hardware or software problems] shall file the document conventionally along with a copy of the document in PDF format on a compact disk or contact the clerk's office for permission to submit the PDF document via email. MA R USDCT CM/ECF Admin(W)(3). Refer to the Timing section of this document for more information on technical failures.

vi. *Notice of filing with clerk's office.* When documents or exhibits (other than those filed ex parte or under seal) are submitted conventionally, a "Notice of Filing with clerk's office" shall be filed electronically and attached to the main document. A paper copy of the "Notice of Filing with clerk's office" must accompany the documents submitted to the court. The "Notice of Filing with clerk's office" (see MA R USDCT CM/ECF Admin(Appendix I)) shall describe each of the documents that will be filed as paper copies in the clerk's office, or shall include an index of the documents if those documents are voluminous. MA R USDCT CM/ECF Admin(P)(5).

vii. *Additional copies.* Whenever, because of the nature of a proceeding, such as a proceeding before a three-judge district court under 28 U.S.C.A. § 2284, additional copies of a paper required to be filed are necessary either for the use of the court or to enable the clerk to carry out his duties, it is the responsibility of the party filing or having filed the paper to provide the necessary copies. MA R USDCT LR 5.1(d).

viii. *Courtesy copies.* COURTESY COPIES OF DOCUMENTS FILED ELECTRONICALLY SHALL NOT BE SUBMITTED ROUTINELY. MA R USDCT CM/ECF Admin(J). Judicial officers, on a case-by-case basis, may require courtesy copies for specific cases, or types of motions, etc. A few Judicial Officers have entered Standing Orders, which may be found on their respective pages on the court's website (under Divisions). Any document filed on paper with the court as a courtesy copy must be clearly labeled as such (Example: COURTESY COPY—DO NOT SCAN). Documents delivered to the court as a courtesy copy will not be maintained in the official court record. MA R USDCT CM/ECF Admin(J).

2. *Application for temporary restraining order (without notice, or "ex parte")*

   a. *Required documents*

   i. *Motion.* All papers filed pursuant to MA R USDCT LR 7.1(b) shall be served unless the moving party indicates in writing on the face of the motion that ex parte consideration is requested. MA R USDCT LR 7.1(c). Refer to the General Requirements section of this document for information on the motion.

      • *Request for oral argument.* Any party making or opposing a motion who believes that oral argument may assist the court and wishes to be heard shall include a request for oral argument in a separate paragraph of the motion or opposition. The request should be set off with a centered caption, "REQUEST FOR ORAL ARGUMENT." MA R USDCT LR 7.1(d).

   ii. *Memorandum.* A party filing a motion shall at the same time file a memorandum of reasons, including citation of supporting authorities, why the motion should be granted. MA R USDCT LR 7.1(b)(1). Any memorandum of law or other attachment filed in support of a main document shall be filed as a separate document, using the proper event. MA R USDCT CM/ECF Admin(G)(4). Memoranda supporting or opposing allowance of motions shall not, without leave of court, exceed twenty (20) pages, double-spaced. MA R USDCT LR 7.1(b)(4).

   iii. *Affidavit or verified complaint.* The applicant for an ex parte restraining order must present to the court, in an affidavit or a verified complaint, facts that clearly show irreparable injury. FPP § 2952.

   iv. *Certificate of attorney.* [T]he applicant's attorney must certify in writing any efforts made to give notice and the reasons why it should not be required. FEDPROC § 47:81.

   v. *Security.* Refer to the General Requirements section of this document for information on the security required.

   b. *Supplemental documents*

   i. *Supporting evidence.* When a motion relies on facts outside the record, the court may hear the matter on affidavits or may hear it wholly or partly on oral testimony or on depositions. FRCP 43(c). Affidavits and other documents setting forth or evidencing facts on which the motion is based shall be filed with the motion. MA R USDCT LR 7.1(b)(1).

ii. *Notice of constitutional question.* A party that files a pleading, written motion, or other paper drawing into question the constitutionality of a federal or state statute must promptly:

- *File notice.* File a notice of constitutional question stating the question and identifying the paper that raises it, if: (1) a federal statute is questioned and the parties do not include the United States, one of its agencies, or one of its officers or employees in an official capacity; or (2) a state statute is questioned and the parties do not include the state, one of its agencies, or one of its officers or employees in an official capacity; and

- *Serve notice.* Serve the notice and paper on the Attorney General of the United States if a federal statute is questioned—or on the state attorney general if a state statute is questioned—either by certified or registered mail or by sending it to an electronic address designated by the attorney general for this purpose. FRCP 5.1(a).

- *No forfeiture.* A party's failure to file and serve the notice, or the court's failure to certify, does not forfeit a constitutional claim or defense that is otherwise timely asserted. FRCP 5.1(d).

iii. *Nongovernmental corporate disclosure statement*

- *Contents.* A nongovernmental corporate party must file two (2) copies of a disclosure statement that: (1) identifies any parent corporation and any publicly held corporation owning ten percent (10%) or more of its stock; or (2) states that there is no such corporation. FRCP 7.1(a).

- *Time to file; Supplemental filing.* A party must: (1) file the disclosure statement with its first appearance, pleading, petition, motion, response, or other request addressed to the court; and (2) promptly file a supplemental statement if any required information changes. FRCP 7.1(b).

iv. *Proposed order.* Proposed orders usually are not required by this court. However, the court may request the party to submit such a document. In those situations, unless otherwise directed by the clerk's office, electronically file the proposed document/order using the entry for "Proposed Documents submitted to the court," found under the Other Documents menu, or as an attachment to the motion to which it relates. MA R USDCT CM/ECF Admin(T).

v. *Compact disk with copy of document(s) in PDF format.* A filer who cannot file a document electronically because of such technical difficulty on the filer's end [with telephone, cable lines, the filer's Internet Service Provider (ISP), or hardware or software problems] shall file the document conventionally along with a copy of the document in PDF format on a compact disk or contact the clerk's office for permission to submit the PDF document via email. MA R USDCT CM/ECF Admin(W)(3). Refer to the Timing section of this document for more information on technical failures.

vi. *Notice of filing with clerk's office.* When documents or exhibits (other than those filed ex parte or under seal) are submitted conventionally, a "Notice of Filing with clerk's office" shall be filed electronically and attached to the main document. A paper copy of the "Notice of Filing with clerk's office" must accompany the documents submitted to the court. The "Notice of Filing with clerk's office" (see MA R USDCT CM/ECF Admin(Appendix I)) shall describe each of the documents that will be filed as paper copies in the clerk's office, or shall include an index of the documents if those documents are voluminous. MA R USDCT CM/ECF Admin(P)(5).

vii. *Additional copies.* Whenever, because of the nature of a proceeding, such as a proceeding before a three-judge district court under 28 U.S.C.A. § 2284, additional copies of a paper required to be filed are necessary either for the use of the court or to enable the clerk to carry out his duties, it is the responsibility of the party filing or having filed the paper to provide the necessary copies. MA R USDCT LR 5.1(d).

viii. *Courtesy copies.* COURTESY COPIES OF DOCUMENTS FILED ELECTRONICALLY SHALL NOT BE SUBMITTED ROUTINELY. MA R USDCT CM/ECF Admin(J). Judicial officers, on a case-by-case basis, may require courtesy copies for specific cases, or types of motions, etc. A few Judicial Officers have entered Standing Orders, which may be found on their respective pages on the court's website (under Divisions). Any document filed on paper with the court as a courtesy copy must be clearly labeled as such (Example: COURTESY COPY—DO NOT SCAN). Documents delivered to the court as a courtesy copy will not be maintained in the official court record. MA R USDCT CM/ECF Admin(J).

## E. Format

1. *Form of documents.* The rules governing captions and other matters of form in pleadings apply to motions and other papers. FRCP 7(b)(2). The provisions of FRCP 10 and FRCP 11 concerning the form and signing of pleadings, motions, and other papers shall be applicable to all papers filed in any proceeding in this court. The board of bar overseers

registration number of each attorney signing such documents, except the United States Attorney and his or her staff, shall be inscribed below the signature. MA R USDCT LR 5.1(a)(1).

a. *Paper size and binding.* All papers filed in the court shall be adapted for flat filing, be filed on eight and one-half by eleven (8-1/2 x 11) inch paper without backers and be bound firmly by staple or some such other means (excluding paper or binder clip or rubber band). MA R USDCT LR 5.1(a)(2).

b. *Spacing.* All papers, except discovery requests and responses, shall be double-spaced except for the identification of counsel, title of the case, footnotes, quotations and exhibits. Discovery requests and responses shall be single-spaced. MA R USDCT LR 5.1(a)(2).

c. *Caption.* Every pleading must have a caption with the court's name, a title, a file number, and [an] FRCP 7(a) designation. FRCP 10(a).

    i. *Names of parties.* The title of the complaint must name all the parties; the title of other pleadings, after naming the first party on each side, may refer generally to other parties. FRCP 10(a).

    ii. *Request for special action.* When any pleading or other paper filed in the court includes a request for special process or relief, or any other request such that, if granted, the court will proceed other than in the ordinary course, the request shall, unless it is noted on the category sheet [see MA R USDCT LR 40.1(a)(1)], be noted on the first page to the right of or immediately beneath the caption. MA R USDCT LR 5.1(c).

d. *Claims or defenses*

    i. *Numbered paragraphs.* A party must state its claims or defenses in numbered paragraphs, each limited as far as practicable to a single set of circumstances. A later pleading may refer by number to a paragraph in an earlier pleading. FRCP 10(b).

    ii. *Separate statements.* If doing so would promote clarity, each claim founded on a separate transaction or occurrence—and each defense other than a denial—must be stated in a separate count or defense. FRCP 10(b).

e. *Adoption by reference.* A statement in a pleading may be adopted by reference elsewhere in the same pleading or in any other pleading or motion. FRCP 10(c).

    i. *Exhibits.* A copy of a written instrument that is an exhibit to a pleading is a part of the pleading for all purposes. FRCP 10(c).

f. *Citations*

    i. *Local rules.* These rules shall be known as Local Rules of the United States District Court for the District of Massachusetts and cited as "L.R., D. Mass." or "L.R." MA R USDCT LR 1.1.

    ii. *Electronic case filing procedures.* The procedures governing electronic case filing shall be known as the "Administrative Procedures for Electronic Case Filing in the United States District Court for the District of Massachusetts." They shall be cited as "APECF." MA R USDCT CM/ECF Admin(A)(7).

g. *Acceptance by the clerk.* The clerk must not refuse to file a paper solely because it is not in the form prescribed by the Federal Rules of Civil Procedure or by a local rule or practice. FRCP 5(d)(4).

    i. Except for complaints and notices of appeal, papers that do not conform to the requirements of MA R USDCT LR 5.1(a)(2) shall be returned by the clerk. MA R USDCT LR 5.1(a)(2).

2. *Form of electronic documents.* A paper filed electronically is a written paper for purposes of the Federal Rules of Civil Procedure. FRCP 5(d)(3)(D).

a. *PDF/A format required.* The court will begin requiring submission of documents in PDF/A format in the foreseeable future. PDF/A is an enhanced version of the traditional PDF format. Newer versions of most PDF software will be able to convert to this format. Additional information on PDF/A documents may be found on the court's website. MA R USDCT CM/ECF Admin(Electronic Filing and PDF).

    i. *Electronically converted PDF.* Electronically converted PDF documents are created from word processing documents (MS Word, WordPerfect, etc.) using any appropriate software. These documents are text searchable and the file size is generally smaller than a scanned document. CM/ECF users may use any brand of software to convert documents to PDF. MA R USDCT CM/ECF Admin(Electronic Filing and PDF).

    • Documents converted to PDF, rather than scanned, are preferred for filing in CM/ECF. MA R USDCT CM/ECF Admin(Electronic Filing and PDF).

    ii. *Scanned PDF.* Scanned PDF documents are created from paper documents run through an optical scanner.

Scanned PDF documents are generally not searchable and have a larger file size. Please note that software used to create scanned documents may (and should) be set in such a way that the document is "text-searchable." MA R USDCT CM/ECF Admin(Electronic Filing and PDF).

b. *Title.* All pleadings filed electronically shall be titled in accordance with the approved dictionary of civil or criminal events of the CM/ECF system of this court. A list of events is available on the CM/ECF Training Information page of the court's website. The clerk's office may, when necessary and appropriate, modify the docket entry description, or delete and re-enter the docket entry in order to comply with the court's quality assurance standards. MA R USDCT CM/ECF Admin(G)(3).

c. *Attachments to filings and exhibits.* Attachments to filings and exhibits must be filed in accordance with the court's CM/ECF User Manual, unless otherwise ordered by the court. MA R USDCT CM/ECF Admin(O)(1).

    i. Filers must submit as attachments only those excerpts of the referenced documents that are directly germane to the matter under consideration by the court. Excerpted material must be clearly and prominently identified as such. Users who file excerpts of documents do so without prejudice to their right to timely file additional excerpts or the complete document, as may be allowed by the court. Responding parties may timely file additional excerpts or the complete document that they believe are directly germane. MA R USDCT CM/ECF Admin(O)(2).

    ii. Filers shall not attach as an exhibit any pleading or other paper already on file with the court in that case, but shall merely refer to that document. (See MA R USDCT CM/ECF Admin(G) for information on using hyperlinks in PDF documents filed in CM/ECF.) MA R USDCT CM/ECF Admin(O)(3).

d. *Redacted documents.* The parties may request or the court may require the submission of documents that have been redacted/stripped of sensitive or confidential information. The redacted document prepared for electronic filing shall include the original caption of the document, and be clearly labeled as "Redacted Document." A specific event is available for this purpose ("Redacted Document"), found under the Other Filings/Other Documents menu option. MA R USDCT CM/ECF Admin(S).

    i. Attorneys and pro se litigants are advised to take extra care when creating PDF documents intended for submission to CM/ECF. Steps shall be taken to ensure the documents are free of any hidden data (metadata) that may contain redacted information, or traces of information edited or deleted are not hidden in the final document. Even PDF content that has been encrypted may be recovered. An advisory document with additional information on this topic may be found on the court's website. MA R USDCT CM/ECF Admin(S).

e. *Hyperlinks.* Electronically filed documents may contain the following types of hyperlinks: (1) hyperlinks to other portions of the same document; (2) hyperlinks to other documents filed within the CM/ECF system; and (3) hyperlinks to a location on the Internet that contains a source document for a citation. MA R USDCT CM/ECF Admin(G)(7).

    i. Hyperlinks to cited authority may not replace standard citation format. Complete citations must be included in the text of the filed document. Neither a hyperlink, nor any site to which it refers, shall be considered part of the record, but are simply convenient mechanisms for accessing material cited in a document filed in CM/ECF. Instructions on creating hyperlinks may be found in the CM/ECF User Manual. MA R USDCT CM/ECF Admin(G)(7).

    ii. The court accepts no responsibility for, and does not endorse, any product, organization, or content at any hyperlinked site, or at any site to which that site may be linked. The court accepts no responsibility for the availability or functionality of any hyperlink. MA R USDCT CM/ECF Admin(G)(7).

    iii. One feature of PDF/A documents is that hyperlinks are commonly "masked," meaning that the full address of the referenced file is not written out; for example, clicking the word brief may open a brief which was previously filed in CM/ECF. MA R USDCT CM/ECF Admin(G)(7)(NOTE). An "unmasked" hyperlink has the full address visible to the user. MA R USDCT CM/ECF Admin(G)(7)(NOTE).

        • Masked hyperlinks may or may not work in a PDF/A document, depending on how it was created. Currently, masked hyperlinks are preserved in PDF/A documents produced by the "Save As" method in Microsoft Word 2007 and 2010; the "PDFMaker" method in Microsoft Word 2007; and OpenOffice 2.4 ("PDF Export"). With other production methods, such as WordPerfect, the PDF/A document includes underlined words that appear to be links, but clicking them has no effect. MA R USDCT CM/ECF Admin(G)(7)(NOTE).

f. *Documents features not accepted.* CM/ECF will not accept PDF documents containing tracking tags, embedded systems commands, password protections, access restrictions or other security features, special tags or dynamic features. MA R USDCT CM/ECF Admin(G)(8).

g. *File size limitations.* A filing party shall limit the size of each PDF file to no more than twenty (20) megabytes. PDF files larger than seven (7) megabytes will be rejected by the CM/ECF system. The filer will see a message advising of the size limitation. MA R USDCT CM/ECF Admin(P)(2).

　　i. Larger documents or exhibits may be submitted electronically if split into separate PDF files each less than seven (7) megabytes, attached to the main document and clearly labeled. MA R USDCT CM/ECF Admin(P)(2).

　　ii. Documents submitted electronically or on paper are subject to the page limitations set by MA R USDCT LR 7.1(b)(4) or by order of the court. MA R USDCT CM/ECF Admin(P)(1).

h. *Accuracy and readability.* The filer shall verify the accuracy and readability of any PDF file before electronically filing it in CM/ECF. MA R USDCT CM/ECF Admin(G)(6); MA R USDCT CM/ECF Admin(P)(3).

3. *Signing of pleadings, motions and other papers*

a. *Signature.* Every pleading, written motion, and other paper must be signed by at least one attorney of record in the attorney's name—or by a party personally if the party is unrepresented. The paper must state the signer's address, e-mail address, and telephone number. FRCP 11(a). The provisions of the Federal Rules of Civil Procedure pertaining to the form and signing of pleadings, motions, and other papers shall be applicable to all papers filed in any proceeding in this court. The board of bar overseers registration number of each attorney signing such documents, except the United States Attorney and his staff, shall be inscribed below the signature. MA R USDCT LR 5.1(a)(1).

　　i. *Electronic signing.* A filing made through a person's electronic-filing account and authorized by that person, together with that person's name on a signature block, constitutes the person's signature. FRCP 5(d)(3)(C).

　　ii. *Appearances.* The filing of an appearance or any other pleading signed on behalf of a party constitutes an entry of appearance for that party. All pleadings shall contain the name, bar admission number, address, telephone number, and e-mail address of the attorney entering an appearance. MA R USDCT LR 83.5.2(a).

　　　　• *Appearances by law firms.* When a party is represented by a law firm, the appearance must include the name and the signature of at least one individual attorney. When a party is represented by more than one attorney from the same or different law firms, the attorney entering the appearance must designate the individual attorney who is authorized to receive all notices in the case. Any notice sent to an attorney so designated shall be deemed to be proper notice unless the court finds that notice was not properly sent. MA R USDCT LR 83.5.2(b).

　　　　• For more information on appearances, refer to MA R USDCT LR 83.5.2.

　　iii. *Signatures of attorneys.* The user login and password required to submit documents to the CM/ECF system shall serve as that user's signature for purposes of FRCP 11 and for all other purposes under the Federal Rules of Civil Procedure and the Local Rules of the United States District Court for the District of Massachusetts. All electronically filed documents must include a signature block and must set forth the attorney's name, bar number, address, telephone number and email address. The name of the CM/ECF user under whose log-in and password the document is submitted must be preceded by a "/s/" and typed in the space where the signature would otherwise appear. MA R USDCT CM/ECF Admin(M)(1). For an example, refer to MA R USDCT CM/ECF Admin(M)(1).

　　iv. *Signatures of pro se parties.* Any document requiring a signature that is filed by a party appearing pro se shall bear the words "pro se" following that party's signature. Any such document shall also state the party's mailing address, telephone number (if any), and e-mail address (if the party has consented to service by email). MA R USDCT LR 83.5.5(g). For more information on practice by pro se litigants, refer to MA R USDCT LR 83.5.5.

　　v. *Multiple signatures.* The filer of any document requiring more than one signature (e.g, stipulations, joint motions, joint status reports, magistrate judge consent forms, etc.) must list thereon all the names of other signatories by means of a "/s/ name of signatory" block for each. By submitting such a document, the filing attorney certifies that each of the other signatories has expressly agreed to the form and substance of the document and that the filing attorney has their actual authority to submit the document electronically. MA R USDCT CM/ECF Admin(M)(2). For more information, refer to MA R USDCT CM/ECF Admin(M)(2).

　　vi. *Affidavits.* Except as provided in MA R USDCT CM/ECF Admin(L), affidavits shall be filed electronically; however, the electronically filed version must contain a "/s/ name of signatory" block indicating that the paper document bears an original signature. MA R USDCT CM/ECF Admin(M)(3). The court will also accept a scanned version of the original, signed document. MA R USDCT CM/ECF Admin(M)(3). For more information, refer to MA R USDCT CM/ECF Admin(M)(3).

    vii.   *No verification or accompanying affidavit required for pleadings.* Unless a rule or statute specifically states otherwise, a pleading need not be verified or accompanied by an affidavit. FRCP 11(a).

    viii.  *Unsigned papers.* The court must strike an unsigned paper unless the omission is promptly corrected after being called to the attorney's or party's attention. FRCP 11(a).

  b.  *Representations to the court.* By presenting to the court a pleading, written motion, or other paper—whether by signing, filing, submitting, or later advocating it—an attorney or unrepresented party certifies that to the best of the person's knowledge, information, and belief, formed after an inquiry reasonable under the circumstances:

    i.   It is not being presented for any improper purpose, such as to harass, cause unnecessary delay, or needlessly increase the cost of litigation;

    ii.  The claims, defenses, and other legal contentions are warranted by existing law or by a nonfrivolous argument for extending, modifying, or reversing existing law or for establishing new law;

    iii.  The factual contentions have evidentiary support or, if specifically so identified, will likely have evidentiary support after a reasonable opportunity for further investigation or discovery; and

    iv.  The denials of factual contentions are warranted on the evidence or, if specifically so identified, are reasonably based on belief or a lack of information. FRCP 11(b).

  c.  *Sanctions.* If, after notice and a reasonable opportunity to respond, the court determines that FRCP 11(b) has been violated, the court may impose an appropriate sanction on any attorney, law firm, or party that violated FRCP 11(b) or is responsible for the violation. FRCP 11(c)(1). Refer to the United States District Court for the District of Massachusetts KeyRules Motion for Sanctions document for more information.

4.  *Privacy protection for filings made with the court*

  a.  *Redacted filings.* Unless the court orders otherwise, in an electronic or paper filing with the court that contains an individual's Social Security number, taxpayer-identification number, or birth date, the name of an individual known to be a minor, or a financial-account number, a party or nonparty making the filing may include only:

    i.   The last four (4) digits of the Social Security number and taxpayer-identification number;

    ii.  The year of the individual's birth;

    iii.  The minor's initials; and

    iv.  The last four (4) digits of the financial-account number. FRCP 5.2(a); MA R USDCT CM/ECF Admin(N).

  b.  *Exemptions from the redaction requirement.* The redaction requirement does not apply to the following:

    i.   A financial-account number that identifies the property allegedly subject to forfeiture in a forfeiture proceeding;

    ii.  The record of an administrative or agency proceeding;

    iii.  The official record of a state-court proceeding;

    iv.  The record of a court or tribunal, if that record was not subject to the redaction requirement when originally filed;

    v.  A filing covered by FRCP 5.2(c) or FRCP 5.2(d); and

    vi.  A pro se filing in an action brought under 28 U.S.C.A. § 2241, 28 U.S.C.A. § 2254, or 28 U.S.C.A. § 2255. FRCP 5.2(b).

  c.  *Limitations on remote access to electronic files; Social Security appeals and immigration cases.* Unless the court orders otherwise, in an action for benefits under the Social Security Act, and in an action or proceeding relating to an order of removal, to relief from removal, or to immigration benefits or detention, access to an electronic file is authorized as follows:

    i.   The parties and their attorneys may have remote electronic access to any part of the case file, including the administrative record;

    ii.  Any other person may have electronic access to the full record at the courthouse, but may have remote electronic access only to:

      •  The docket maintained by the court; and

      •  An opinion, order, judgment, or other disposition of the court, but not any other part of the case file or the administrative record. FRCP 5.2(c).

  d.  *Filings made under seal.* The court may order that a filing be made under seal without redaction. The court may later unseal the filing or order the person who made the filing to file a redacted version for the public record. FRCP 5.2(d).

e. *Protective orders.* For good cause, the court may by order in a case:

    i.   Require redaction of additional information; or

    ii.   Limit or prohibit a nonparty's remote electronic access to a document filed with the court. FRCP 5.2(e).

f. *Option for additional unredacted filing under seal.* A person making a redacted filing may also file an unredacted copy under seal. The court must retain the unredacted copy as part of the record. FRCP 5.2(f). For more information, refer to MA R USDCT LR 7.2.

g. *Option for filing a reference list.* A filing that contains redacted information may be filed together with a reference list that identifies each item of redacted information and specifies an appropriate identifier that uniquely corresponds to each item listed. The list must be filed under seal and may be amended as of right. Any reference in the case to a listed identifier will be construed to refer to the corresponding item of information. FRCP 5.2(g).

h. *Responsibility for redaction.* The clerk's office is not responsible for reviewing documents filed with the court to determine whether pleadings have been redacted and are in the proper form. MA R USDCT CM/ECF Admin(N).

i. *Waiver of protection of identifiers.* A person waives the protection of FRCP 5.2(a) as to the person's own information by filing it without redaction and not under seal. FRCP 5.2(h).

## F. Filing and Service Requirements

1. *Filing requirements*

a. *Required filings.* Any paper after the complaint that is required to be served must be filed no later than a reasonable time after service. FRCP 5(d)(1).

    i.   Except as noted in FRCP 33 to FRCP 36, the original of all papers required to be served under FRCP 5(d) shall, unless otherwise submitted to the court, be filed in the office of the clerk within seven (7) days after service has been made. MA R USDCT LR 5.1(b). Except as otherwise provided by the Federal Rules of Civil Procedure, proof of service of all pleadings and other papers required to be served (except discovery papers that in accordance with FRCP 33 to FRCP 36(f) are not to be filed) shall be filed in the office of the clerk promptly after service has been made. MA R USDCT LR 5.2(b)(1).

b. *Nonelectronic filing.* A paper not filed electronically is filed by delivering it: (1) to the clerk; or (2) to a judge who agrees to accept it for filing, and who must then note the filing date on the paper and promptly send it to the clerk. FRCP 5(d)(2).

c. *Electronic filing.* Unless exempt or otherwise ordered by the court, all pleadings and other papers submitted to the court must be filed, signed, and verified by electronic means as provided in MA R USDCT LR 5.4. MA R USDCT LR 5.4(A); MA R USDCT CM/ECF Admin(A)(1). All electronic filings must be made in accordance with the Administrative Procedures for Electronic Case Filing in the United States District Court for the District of Massachusetts (MA R USDCT CM/ECF Admin). MA R USDCT LR 5.4(B). The court may deviate from the Administrative Procedures for Electronic Case Filing in the United States District Court for the District of Massachusetts (MA R USDCT CM/ECF Admin) in specific cases, without prior notice, if deemed appropriate in the exercise of discretion, considering the need for the just, speedy, and inexpensive determination of matters pending before the court. MA R USDCT CM/ECF Admin(C)(1). The court may excuse a failure to comply with any administrative procedure whenever justice so requires. MA R USDCT CM/ECF Admin(C)(2).

    i.   *By a represented person; Generally required; Exceptions.* A person represented by an attorney must file electronically, unless nonelectronic filing is allowed by the court for good cause or is allowed or required by local rule. FRCP 5(d)(3)(A).

    ii.   *By unrepresented person; When allowed or required.* A person not represented by an attorney: (1) may file electronically only if allowed by court order or by local rule; and (2) may be required to file electronically only by court order, or by a local rule that includes reasonable exceptions. FRCP 5(d)(3)(B).

    iii.   *Exemptions from electronic filing*

        • *Documents that should not be filed electronically.* The following types of documents must not be filed electronically, and will not be scanned into the ECF system by the clerk's office: (1) sealed documents; (2) ex parte motions; (3) documents generated as part of an alternative dispute resolution (ADR) process; (4) the administrative record in Social Security and other administrative proceedings; (5) the state court record in proceedings under 28 U.S.C.A. § 2254; and (6) such other types of documents as the clerk may direct in the Administrative Procedures for Electronic Case Filing in the United States District Court for the District of Massachusetts (MA R USDCT CM/ECF Admin). MA R USDCT LR 5.4(G)(1); MA R USDCT CM/ECF Admin(L).

- *Documents that need not be filed electronically.* The following types of documents need not be filed electronically, but may be scanned into the ECF system by a filing party or the clerk's office: (1) handwritten pleadings; (2) documents filed by pro se litigants who are incarcerated or who are not registered ECF users; (3) indictments, informations, criminal complaints, and the criminal JS45 form; (4) affidavits for search or arrest warrants and related documents; (5) documents received from another court under FRCRP 20 or FRCRP 40; (6) appearance bonds; (7) any document in a criminal case containing the original signature of a defendant, such as a waiver of indictment or a plea agreement; (8) petitions for violations of supervised release; (9) executed service of process documents under FRCP 4; and (10) such other types of documents as the clerk may direct in the Administrative Procedures for Electronic Case Filing in the United States District Court for the District of Massachusetts (MA R USDCT CM/ECF Admin). MA R USDCT LR 5.4(G)(2); MA R USDCT CM/ECF Admin(L).

- For more information on exemptions from electronic filing, refer to MA R USDCT CM/ECF Admin(L).

   iv. *Consequences of electronic filing.* Electronic transmission of a document to the CM/ECF system, together with the transmission of a Notice of Electronic Filing (NEF) from the court at the completion of the transaction, constitutes the filing of the document for all purposes of the Federal Rules of Procedure and constitutes entry of the document on the docket maintained by the clerk pursuant to FRCP 58 and FRCP 79. MA R USDCT CM/ECF Admin(G)(1).

   v. *Payment of filing fees.* When electronically filing any pleading or paper through CM/ECF that requires a fee, all registered ECF users are to pay the fee electronically through the Treasury Department's Internet payment process. MA R USDCT LR 67.4(d); MA R USDCT CM/ECF Admin(A)(1). Pro se filers and those who have been exempted from electronic filing and/or electronic payment of fees may submit payments by check or money order made payable to "Clerk, U.S. District Court". MA R USDCT LR 67.4(d). For more information on filing fees, refer to MA R USDCT LR 67.4 and MA R USDCT CM/ECF Admin(I).

   vi. For more information on electronic filing, refer to MA R USDCT CM/ECF Admin.

  d. *Email or fax filing.* In general, the court does not accept documents by email or by fax. If the court, in special circumstances, does authorize the submission of a document in that manner, the document shall not be considered filed until an NEF is generated by CM/ECF at the completion of the transaction. MA R USDCT CM/ECF Admin(H)(5).

2. *Service requirements.* All papers filed pursuant to MA R USDCT LR 7.1(b) shall be served unless the moving party indicates in writing on the face of the motion that ex parte consideration is requested. Motions filed "ex parte" and related papers need not be served until the motion has been ruled upon or the court orders that service be made. MA R USDCT LR 7.1(c). Service of all pleadings subsequent to the original complaint and of all other papers required to be served shall be made in the manner specified by FRCP 5. MA R USDCT LR 5.2(a).

  a. *Service; When required*

   i. *In general.* Unless the Federal Rules of Civil Procedure provide otherwise, each of the following papers must be served on every party:

- An order stating that service is required;

- A pleading filed after the original complaint, unless the court orders otherwise under FRCP 5(c) because there are numerous defendants;

- A discovery paper required to be served on a party, unless the court orders otherwise;

- A written motion, except one that may be heard ex parte; and

- A written notice, appearance, demand, or offer of judgment, or any similar paper. FRCP 5(a)(1).

   ii. *If a party fails to appear.* No service is required on a party who is in default for failing to appear. But a pleading that asserts a new claim for relief against such a party must be served on that party under FRCP 4. FRCP 5(a)(2).

   iii. *Seizing property.* If an action is begun by seizing property and no person is or need be named as a defendant, any service required before the filing of an appearance, answer, or claim must be made on the person who had custody or possession of the property when it was seized. FRCP 5(a)(3).

  b. *Service; How made*

   i. *Serving an attorney.* If a party is represented by an attorney, service under FRCP 5 must be made on the attorney unless the court orders service on the party. FRCP 5(b)(1).

- *Nonresident attorney.* On application of a party, the court may order an attorney who represents any other

party and who does not maintain an office within this district where service can be made on him by delivery as provided by FRCP 5(b), to designate a member of the bar of this court who does maintain such an office to receive service of all pleadings and other papers in his behalf. MA R USDCT LR 5.2(c)(1).

ii. *Serving a party acting pro se.* On application of a party, the court may order any other party who is appearing without an attorney and who does not maintain an office or residence within this district where service can be made on him by delivery as provided by FRCP 5(b), to designate an address within the district at which service can be made on him by delivery. MA R USDCT LR 5.2(c)(2).

iii. *Service in general.* A paper is served under FRCP 5 by:

- Handing it to the person;

- Leaving it: (1) at the person's office with a clerk or other person in charge or, if no one is in charge, in a conspicuous place in the office; or (2) if the person has no office or the office is closed, at the person's dwelling or usual place of abode with someone of suitable age and discretion who resides there;

- Mailing it to the person's last known address—in which event service is complete upon mailing;

- Leaving it with the court clerk if the person has no known address;

- Sending it to a registered user by filing it with the court's electronic-filing system or sending it by other electronic means that the person consented to in writing—in either of which events service is complete upon filing or sending, but is not effective if the filer or sender learns that it did not reach the person to be served; or

- Delivering it by any other means that the person consented to in writing—in which event service is complete when the person making service delivers it to the agency designated to make delivery. FRCP 5(b)(2).

iv. *Service by electronic means.* Unless exempt or otherwise ordered by the court, all pleadings and other papers must be served on other parties by electronic means. MA R USDCT LR 5.4(C); MA R USDCT CM/ECF Admin(H)(2). Service by electronic means shall be treated the same as service by mail. MA R USDCT CM/ECF Admin(H)(4).

- *Consent to electronic service.* Registering to use CM/ECF constitutes consent to service of all documents by electronic means as provided in the Administrative Procedures for Electronic Case Filing in the United States District Court for the District of Massachusetts (MA R USDCT CM/ECF Admin) and FRCP 5(b) and FRCP 77(d). MA R USDCT CM/ECF Admin(E)(6); MA R USDCT CM/ECF Admin(H)(3).

- *Service on registered ECF users.* Transmission of the Notice of Electronic Filing (NEF) through the court's transmission facilities will constitute service of the filed document upon a registered ECF user. MA R USDCT LR 5.4(C).

- *Service on non-registered users.* The party filing the document electronically is responsible for serving a paper copy of the document by mail in accordance with FRCP 5(b) to those case participants who have not been identified on the NEF as electronic recipients. MA R USDCT CM/ECF Admin(H)(3).

- *Service of conventionally filed papers.* Documents or exhibits submitted conventionally shall be served on other parties by the filer using traditional means. MA R USDCT CM/ECF Admin(P)(4).

c. *Serving numerous defendants*

i. *In general.* If an action involves an unusually large number of defendants, the court may, on motion or on its own, order that:

- Defendants' pleadings and replies to them need not be served on other defendants;

- Any crossclaim, counterclaim, avoidance, or affirmative defense in those pleadings and replies to them will be treated as denied or avoided by all other parties; and

- Filing any such pleading and serving it on the plaintiff constitutes notice of the pleading to all parties. FRCP 5(c)(1).

ii. *Notifying parties.* A copy of every such order must be served on the parties as the court directs. FRCP 5(c)(2).

## G. Hearings

1. *Hearings, generally.* If the court concludes that there should be a hearing on a motion, the motion will be set down for hearing at such time as the court determines. MA R USDCT LR 7.1(e).

a. *Oral argument.* Due process does not require that oral argument be permitted on a motion and, except as otherwise

provided by local rule, the district court has discretion to determine whether it will decide the motion on the papers or hear argument by counsel (and perhaps receive evidence). FPP § 1190; F.D.I.C. v. Deglau, 207 F.3d 153 (3d Cir. 2000).

    i.   *Evidence on a motion.* When a motion relies on facts outside the record, the court may hear the matter on affidavits or may hear it wholly or partly on oral testimony or on depositions. FRCP 43(c).

b.   *Providing a regular schedule for oral hearings.* A court may establish regular times and places for oral hearings on motions. FRCP 78(a).

c.   *Providing for submission on briefs.* By rule or order, the court may provide for submitting and determining motions on briefs, without oral hearings. FRCP 78(b). Motions that are not set down for hearing as provided in MA R USDCT LR 7.1(e) will be decided on the papers submitted after an opposition to the motion has been filed, or, if no opposition is filed, after the time for filing an opposition has elapsed. MA R USDCT LR 7.1(f).

2.   *Hearing on motion for preliminary injunction after temporary restraining order is issued without notice*

a.   *Expediting the preliminary injunction hearing.* If the order is issued without notice, the motion for a preliminary injunction must be set for hearing at the earliest possible time, taking precedence over all other matters except hearings on older matters of the same character. At the hearing, the party who obtained the order must proceed with the motion; if the party does not, the court must dissolve the order. FRCP 65(b)(3). Refer to the United States District Court for the District of Massachusetts KeyRules Motion for Preliminary Injunction document for more information on the hearing on the motion for preliminary injunction.

3.   *Conflict of court appearances.* For information on conflict of court appearances, refer to MA R USDCT LR 40.2.

## H.   Forms

### 1.   Federal Application for Temporary Restraining Order Forms

a.   Motion for temporary restraining order. 4A FEDFORMS § 47:75.

b.   Motion for temporary restraining order; Enforcement of statute. 4A FEDFORMS § 47:76.

c.   Motion for temporary restraining order; Restraining attorney. 4A FEDFORMS § 47:77.

d.   Motion for temporary restraining order; Restraining defendant from refusing to admit plaintiffs to school. 4A FEDFORMS § 47:78.

e.   Motion for temporary restraining order; Requesting expedited hearing; Athletic eligibility. 4A FEDFORMS § 47:79.

f.   Motion for temporary restraining order; Without notice. 4A FEDFORMS § 47:80.

g.   Motion for temporary restraining order; Without notice; Reciting attempts to give notice. 4A FEDFORMS § 47:81.

h.   Motion for temporary restraining order; Without notice; Encumbering property. 4A FEDFORMS § 47:82.

i.   Certificate of attorney's efforts to give notice; School board. 4A FEDFORMS § 47:83.

j.   Certificate of attorney's efforts to give notice; Telephone call to opposing counsel. 4A FEDFORMS § 47:84.

k.   Certificate of attorney's efforts to give notice; Hand-delivered to attorney. 4A FEDFORMS § 47:85.

l.   Motion to extend temporary restraining order and for amendment of order. 4A FEDFORMS § 47:86.

m.   Motion to dissolve or modify temporary restraining order. 4A FEDFORMS § 47:87.

n.   Motion to dissolve temporary restraining order; Material change in circumstances. 4A FEDFORMS § 47:88.

o.   Motion to dissolve temporary restraining order; Various grounds. 4A FEDFORMS § 47:89.

p.   Motion to dissolve temporary restraining order and dismiss complaint. 4A FEDFORMS § 47:93.

q.   Ex parte motion; For temporary restraining order and order to show cause; Interference with property rights. AMJUR PP INJUNCTION § 42.

r.   Affidavit; In support of ex parte motion for temporary restraining order. AMJUR PP INJUNCTION § 48.

s.   Certificate of attorney; In support of ex parte motion for temporary restraining order. AMJUR PP INJUNCTION § 50.

t.   Affidavit; In support of ex parte motion for temporary restraining order; Interference with property rights. AMJUR PP INJUNCTION § 51.

u.   Motion for temporary restraining order and preliminary injunction. GOLDLTGFMS § 13A:6.

v.   Motion for temporary restraining order; General form. GOLDLTGFMS § 13A:11.

w.   Motion for temporary restraining order; Ex parte application. GOLDLTGFMS § 13A:12.

x.   Motion for temporary restraining order; Ex parte application; Supporting affidavit by party. GOLDLTGFMS § 13A:13.

y.   Motion for temporary restraining order; Ex parte application; Supporting affidavit by party; Copyright infringement. GOLDLTGFMS § 13A:14.

z.   Motion for temporary restraining order; Ex parte application; Certificate by counsel. GOLDLTGFMS § 13A:15.

2.   **Forms for the District of Massachusetts**

a.   Notice of filing with clerk's office. MA R USDCT CM/ECF Admin(Appendix I).

# I.   Applicable Rules

1.   *Federal rules*

a.   Serving and filing pleadings and other papers. FRCP 5.

b.   Constitutional challenge to a statute; Notice, certification, and intervention. FRCP 5.1.

c.   Privacy protection for filings made with the court. FRCP 5.2.

d.   Computing and extending time; Time for motion papers. FRCP 6.

e.   Pleadings allowed; Form of motions and other papers. FRCP 7.

f.   Disclosure statement. FRCP 7.1.

g.   Form of pleadings. FRCP 10.

h.   Signing pleadings, motions, and other papers; Representations to the court; Sanctions. FRCP 11.

i.   Taking testimony. FRCP 43.

j.   Injunctions and restraining orders. FRCP 65.

k.   Proceedings against a security provider. FRCP 65.1.

l.   Hearing motions; Submission on briefs. FRCP 78.

2.   *Local rules*

a.   Title. MA R USDCT LR 1.1.

b.   Sanctions. MA R USDCT LR 1.3.

c.   Form and filing of papers. MA R USDCT LR 5.1.

d.   Service and filing of pleadings and other papers. MA R USDCT LR 5.2.

e.   Filing and service by electronic means. MA R USDCT LR 5.4.

f.   Motion practice. MA R USDCT LR 7.1.

g.   Alternative dispute resolution. MA R USDCT LR 16.4.

h.   Payments and deposits made with the clerk. MA R USDCT LR 67.4.

i.   Settlement. MA R USDCT LR 68.2.

j.   Office of the clerk. MA R USDCT LR 77.2.

k.   Appearances. MA R USDCT LR 83.5.2.

l.   Practice by pro se litigants. MA R USDCT LR 83.5.5.

m.   CM/ECF case management/electronic case files administrative procedures. MA R USDCT CM/ECF Admin.

# Requests, Notices and Applications
# Pretrial Conferences, Scheduling, Management

## Document Last Updated December 2018

**A. Checklist**

(I) ❑ Matters to be considered by parties for the pretrial conference

   (a) ❑ Documents to consider

      (1) ❑ Joint case management statement

      (2) ❑ Compact disk with copy of document(s) in PDF format

      (3) ❑ Notice of filing with clerk's office

      (4) ❑ Additional copies

      (5) ❑ Courtesy copies

   (b) ❑ Timing

      (1) ❑ The court determines at what stage in the action to hold a pretrial conference

      (2) ❑ [The joint case management] statement is to be filed with the court no later than seven (7) days before the case management conference

(II) ❑ Matters to be considered by parties for the scheduling conference

   (a) ❑ Required documents

      (1) ❑ Joint statement containing proposed pretrial schedule

      (2) ❑ Settlement proposals

   (b) ❑ Supplemental documents

      (1) ❑ Request for scheduling conference

      (2) ❑ Compact disk with copy of document(s) in PDF format

      (3) ❑ Notice of filing with clerk's office

      (4) ❑ Additional copies

      (5) ❑ Courtesy copies

   (c) ❑ Timing

      (1) ❑ If a scheduling conference is called, it is important to recognize that, unlike the ordinary pretrial conference, the scheduling conference occurs before the substantive issues have been defined and is directed toward organizing the processing of the action by setting deadlines for the completion of the various pretrial phases

      (2) ❑ In every civil action, except in categories of actions exempted by MA R USDCT LR 16.2 as inappropriate for scheduling procedures, the judge or, in the interests of the efficient administration of justice, a designated magistrate judge shall convene a scheduling conference as soon as practicable, but in any event within sixty (60) days after the appearance of a defendant and within ninety (90) days after the complaint has been served on a defendant

         (i) ❑ In cases removed to this court from a state court or transferred from any other federal court, the judge or designated magistrate judge shall convene a scheduling conference within sixty (60) days after removal or transfer

      (3) ❑ Unless otherwise ordered by the judge, the plaintiff shall present written settlement proposals to all defendants no later than fourteen (14) days before the date for the scheduling conference

(III) ❑ Matters to be considered by parties for the final pretrial conference

   (a) ❑ Required documents

      (1) ❑ Joint pretrial memorandum

   (b) ❑ Supplemental documents

      (1) ❑ Compact disk with copy of document(s) in PDF format

    (2)  ❏  Notice of filing with clerk's office

    (3)  ❏  Additional copies

    (4)  ❏  Courtesy copies

(c)  ❏  Timing

    (1)  ❏  Unless otherwise ordered by the judicial officer to whom the case is assigned for trial, counsel for the parties shall confer no later than fourteen (14) days before the date of the final pretrial conference for the purpose of jointly preparing a pretrial memorandum for submission to the judicial officer

    (2)  ❏  Unless otherwise ordered by the judicial officer to whom the case is assigned for trial, the parties are required to file, no later than seven (7) days prior to the pre-trial conference, a joint pretrial memorandum

(IV)  ❏  Matters to be considered by parties for the discovery planning conference

(a)  ❏  Required documents

    (1)  ❏  Written report outlining proposed discovery plan

(b)  ❏  Supplemental documents

    (1)  ❏  Compact disk with copy of document(s) in PDF format

    (2)  ❏  Notice of filing with clerk's office

    (3)  ❏  Additional copies

    (4)  ❏  Courtesy copies

(c)  ❏  Timing

    (1)  ❏  Except in a proceeding exempted from initial disclosure under FRCP 26(a)(1)(B) or when the court orders otherwise, the parties must confer as soon as practicable—and in any event at least twenty-one (21) days before a scheduling conference is to be held or a scheduling order is due under FRCP 16(b)

    (2)  ❏  Within fourteen (14) days after the conference, the attorneys of record are responsible for submitting a written report outlining the plan

## B. Timing

1. *Pretrial conferences, generally.* The court determines at what stage in the action to hold a pretrial conference. When only one conference is involved, the most favored practice seems to be to wait until after the case has been prepared for trial. FPP § 1524. Although there rarely will be any need to hold a conference in a relatively simple case until after the preliminary motions have been disposed of, the only inherently logical limitation on the court's discretion as to when to hold a conference is that it should not be held before all the necessary and indispensable parties are served. FPP § 1524.

    a. *Joint case management statement.* [The joint case management] statement is to be filed with the court no later than seven (7) days before the case management conference. MA R USDCT LR 16.3(b).

2. *Scheduling conference.* If a scheduling conference is called, it is important to recognize that, unlike the ordinary pretrial conference, the scheduling conference occurs before the substantive issues have been defined and is directed toward organizing the processing of the action by setting deadlines for the completion of the various pretrial phases. FPP § 1522.1. In every civil action, except in categories of actions exempted by MA R USDCT LR 16.2 as inappropriate for scheduling procedures, the judge or, in the interests of the efficient administration of justice, a designated magistrate judge shall convene a scheduling conference as soon as practicable, but in any event within sixty (60) days after the appearance of a defendant and within ninety (90) days after the complaint has been served on a defendant. MA R USDCT LR 16.1(a).

    a. *Removed or transferred cases.* In cases removed to this court from a state court or transferred from any other federal court, the judge or designated magistrate judge shall convene a scheduling conference within sixty (60) days after removal or transfer. MA R USDCT LR 16.1(a).

    b. *Joint statement containing proposed pretrial schedule.* Unless otherwise ordered by the judge, the parties are required to file, no later than seven (7) days before the scheduling conference and after consideration of the topics contemplated by FRCP 16(b) and FRCP 16(c) and FRCP 26(f), a joint statement containing a proposed pretrial schedule. MA R USDCT LR 16.1(d).

    c. *Settlement proposals.* Unless otherwise ordered by the judge, the plaintiff shall present written settlement proposals to all defendants no later than fourteen (14) days before the date for the scheduling conference. MA R USDCT LR 16.1(c).

3. *Final pretrial conference*

   a. *Obligation of counsel to confer.* Unless otherwise ordered by the judicial officer to whom the case is assigned for trial, counsel for the parties shall confer no later than fourteen (14) days before the date of the final pretrial conference for the purpose of jointly preparing a pretrial memorandum for submission to the judicial officer. MA R USDCT LR 16.5(d).

   b. *Joint pretrial memorandum.* Unless otherwise ordered by the judicial officer to whom the case is assigned for trial, the parties are required to file, no later than seven (7) days prior to the pre-trial conference, a joint pretrial memorandum. MA R USDCT LR 16.5(d).

4. *Discovery planning conference.* Except in a proceeding exempted from initial disclosure under FRCP 26(a)(1)(B) or when the court orders otherwise, the parties must confer as soon as practicable—and in any event at least twenty-one (21) days before a scheduling conference is to be held or a scheduling order is due under FRCP 16(b). FRCP 26(f)(1); MA R USDCT LR 16.1(b).

   a. *Submission of written report outlining proposed discovery plan.* The attorneys of record and all unrepresented parties that have appeared in the case are jointly responsible for arranging the conference, for attempting in good faith to agree on the proposed discovery plan, and for submitting to the court within fourteen (14) days after the conference a written report outlining the plan. FRCP 26(f)(2).

   b. *Expedited schedule.* If necessary to comply with its expedited schedule for FRCP 16(b) conferences, a court may by local rule: (1) require the parties' conference to occur less than twenty-one (21) days before the scheduling conference is held or a scheduling order is due under FRCP 16(b); and (2) require the written report outlining the discovery plan to be filed less than fourteen (14) days after the parties' conference, or excuse the parties from submitting a written report and permit them to report orally on their discovery plan at the FRCP 16(b) conference. FRCP 26(f)(4).

5. *Computation of time*

   a. *Computing time.* FRCP 6 applies in computing any time period specified in the Federal Rules of Civil Procedure, in any local rule or court order, or in any statute that does not specify a method of computing time. FRCP 6(a).

      i. *Period stated in days or a longer unit.* When the period is stated in days or a longer unit of time:

         - Exclude the day of the event that triggers the period;

         - Count every day, including intermediate Saturdays, Sundays, and legal holidays; and

         - Include the last day of the period, but if the last day is a Saturday, Sunday, or legal holiday, the period continues to run until the end of the next day that is not a Saturday, Sunday, or legal holiday. FRCP 6(a)(1).

      ii. *Period stated in hours.* When the period is stated in hours:

         - Begin counting immediately on the occurrence of the event that triggers the period;

         - Count every hour, including hours during intermediate Saturdays, Sundays, and legal holidays; and

         - If the period would end on a Saturday, Sunday, or legal holiday, the period continues to run until the same time on the next day that is not a Saturday, Sunday, or legal holiday. FRCP 6(a)(2).

      iii. *Office of the clerk.* The offices of the Clerk of Court at Boston, Worcester and Springfield shall be open from 8:30 a.m. until 5:00 p.m. on all days except Saturdays, Sundays, legal holidays and other days so ordered by the court and announced in advance, if feasible. MA R USDCT LR 77.2.

      iv. *Inaccessibility of the clerk's office.* Unless the court orders otherwise, if the clerk's office is inaccessible:

         - On the last day for filing under FRCP 6(a)(1), then the time for filing is extended to the first accessible day that is not a Saturday, Sunday, or legal holiday; or

         - During the last hour for filing under FRCP 6(a)(2), then the time for filing is extended to the same time on the first accessible day that is not a Saturday, Sunday, or legal holiday. FRCP 6(a)(3).

      v. *"Last day" defined.* Unless a different time is set by a statute, local rule, or court order, the last day ends:

         - For electronic filing, at midnight in the court's time zone; and

         - For filing by other means, when the clerk's office is scheduled to close. FRCP 6(a)(4).

      vi. *"Next day" defined.* The "next day" is determined by continuing to count forward when the period is measured after an event and backward when measured before an event. FRCP 6(a)(5).

      vii. *"Legal holiday" defined.* "Legal holiday" means:

         - The day set aside by statute for observing New Year's Day, Martin Luther King Jr.'s Birthday, Washington's

Birthday, Memorial Day, Independence Day, Labor Day, Columbus Day, Veterans' Day, Thanksgiving Day, or Christmas Day;

- Any day declared a holiday by the President or Congress; and

- For periods that are measured after an event, any other day declared a holiday by the state where the district court is located. FRCP 6(a)(6).

b. *Computation of electronic filing deadlines.* Filing documents electronically does not alter any filing deadlines. MA R USDCT CM/ECF Admin(K); MA R USDCT LR 5.4(D). Although CM/ECF is generally available twenty-four (24) hours a day for filing, all electronic transmissions of documents must be completed prior to 6:00 PM, Eastern Standard (or Daylight Savings) Time, on the date on which it is due, in order to be considered timely filed that day. MA R USDCT CM/ECF Admin(K); MA R USDCT LR 5.4(D). When a specific time of day deadline is set by court order or stipulation, the electronic filing must be completed by that time. Documents may be filed at any time of the day on days prior to the date on which it is due. MA R USDCT CM/ECF Admin(K). A document filed electronically shall be deemed filed as of the time and date stated on the NEF received from the court. MA R USDCT CM/ECF Admin(G)(2); MA R USDCT CM/ECF Admin(K).

  i. *Technical failures.* A user whose filing is made untimely as the result of a technical failure of the court's CM/ECF system may seek appropriate relief from the court. MA R USDCT CM/ECF Admin(W)(3). Technical difficulties on the filer's end, with telephone, cable lines, the filer's Internet Service Provider (ISP), or hardware or software problems, will not constitute a technical failure under the Administrative Procedures for Electronic Case Filing in the United States District Court for the District of Massachusetts (MA R USDCT CM/ECF Admin) nor excuse an untimely filing. MA R USDCT CM/ECF Admin(W)(3). As help desk support is available during normal business hours, filers are strongly urged to electronically file any documents during that period. MA R USDCT CM/ECF Admin(W)(3).

  - The court has made available a public terminal (computers and scanner) in each clerk's office for registered users to scan and electronically file documents. This equipment is available during normal business hours. Users should bring their prepared document and a valid CM/ECF login and password. MA R USDCT CM/ECF Admin(W)(3).

c. *Extending time.* When an act may or must be done within a specified time, the court may, for good cause, extend the time: (1) with or without motion or notice if the court acts, or if a request is made, before the original time or its extension expires; or (2) on motion made after the time has expired if the party failed to act because of excusable neglect. FRCP 6(b)(1).

  i. *Exceptions.* A court must not extend the time to act under FRCP 50(b), FRCP 50(d), FRCP 52(b), FRCP 59(b), FRCP 59(d), FRCP 59(e), and FRCP 60(b). FRCP 6(b)(2).

  ii. Refer to the United States District Court for the District of Massachusetts KeyRules Motion for Continuance/Extension of Time document for more information on extending time.

d. *Additional time after certain kinds of service.* When a party may or must act within a specified time after being served and service is made under FRCP 5(b)(2)(C) (by mail), FRCP 5(b)(2)(D) (by leaving with the clerk), or FRCP 5(b)(2)(F) (by other means consented to), three (3) days are added after the period would otherwise expire under FRCP 6(a). FRCP 6(d).

## C. General Requirements

1. *Pretrial conferences, generally*

   a. *Purposes of a pretrial conference.* FRCP 16 provides an important mechanism for carrying out one of the basic policies of the [Federal Rules of Civil Procedure]—the determination of disputes on their merits rather than on the basis of procedural niceties or tactical advantage. FPP § 1522. In any action, the court may order the attorneys and any unrepresented parties to appear for one or more pretrial conferences for such purposes as:

      i. Expediting disposition of the action;

      ii. Establishing early and continuing control so that the case will not be protracted because of lack of management;

      iii. Discouraging wasteful pretrial activities;

      iv. Improving the quality of the trial through more thorough preparation; and

      v. Facilitating settlement. FRCP 16(a).

   b. *When appropriate.* FRCP 16 specifically provides that the court "may order the attorneys and any unrepresented parties to appear for one or more pretrial conferences." This language makes it clear that the utilization of the pretrial conference procedure lies within the discretion of the district court both as a matter of general policy and in terms of whether and when the rule should be invoked in a particular case. FPP § 1523; Mizwicki v. Helwig, 196 F.3d 828 (7th Cir. 1999). There is no requirement that any pretrial conferences be held or not held in certain types of actions. FPP § 1523.

c.   *Obligation of counsel to confer.* The judicial officer may require counsel for the parties to confer before the case management conference for the purpose of preparing a joint statement containing: (1) an agenda of matters that one or more parties believe should be addressed at the conference; and (2) a report advising the judicial officer whether the case is progressing within the allotted time limits and in accord with the specified pretrial steps. MA R USDCT LR 16.3(b).

d.   *Attendance at a pretrial conference.* A represented party must authorize at least one of its attorneys to make stipulations and admissions about all matters that can reasonably be anticipated for discussion at a pretrial conference. If appropriate, the court may require that a party or its representative be present or reasonably available by other means to consider possible settlement. FRCP 16(c)(1).

e.   *Matters for consideration at a pretrial conference.* At any pretrial conference, the court may consider and take appropriate action on the following matters:

i.   Formulating and simplifying the issues, and eliminating frivolous claims or defenses;

ii.   Amending the pleadings if necessary or desirable;

iii.   Obtaining admissions and stipulations about facts and documents to avoid unnecessary proof, and ruling in advance on the admissibility of evidence;

iv.   Avoiding unnecessary proof and cumulative evidence, and limiting the use of testimony under FRE 702;

v.   Determining the appropriateness and timing of summary adjudication under FRCP 56;

vi.   Controlling and scheduling discovery, including orders affecting disclosures and discovery under FRCP 26 and FRCP 29 through FRCP 37;

vii.   Identifying witnesses and documents, scheduling the filing and exchange of any pretrial briefs, and setting dates for further conferences and for trial;

viii.   Referring matters to a magistrate judge or a master;

ix.   Settling the case and using special procedures to assist in resolving the dispute when authorized by statute or local rule;

x.   Determining the form and content of the pretrial order;

xi.   Disposing of pending motions;

xii.   Adopting special procedures for managing potentially difficult or protracted actions that may involve complex issues, multiple parties, difficult legal questions, or unusual proof problems;

xiii.   Ordering a separate trial under FRCP 42(b) of a claim, counterclaim, crossclaim, third-party claim, or particular issue;

xiv.   Ordering the presentation of evidence early in the trial on a manageable issue that might, on the evidence, be the basis for a judgment as a matter of law under FRCP 50(a) or a judgment on partial findings under FRCP 52(c);

xv.   Establishing a reasonable limit on the time allowed to present evidence; and

xvi.   Facilitating in other ways the just, speedy, and inexpensive disposition of the action. FRCP 16(c)(2).

xvii.   Case management conferences shall be presided over by a judicial officer who, in furtherance of the scheduling order required by MA R USDCT LR 16.1(f) may:

- Explore the possibility of settlement;

- Identify or formulate (or order the attorneys to formulate) the principal issues in contention;

- Prepare (or order the attorneys to prepare) a specific discovery schedule and discovery plan that, if the presiding judicial officer deems appropriate, might: (1) identify and limit the volume of discovery available in order to avoid unnecessary or unduly burdensome or expensive discovery; (2) sequence discovery into two or more stages; and (3) include time limits set for the completion of discovery;

- Establish deadlines for filing motions and a time framework for their disposition;

- Provide for the "phased resolution" or "bifurcation of issues for trial" consistent with FRCP 42(b); and

- Explore any other matter that the judicial officer determines is appropriate for the fair and efficient management of the litigation. MA R USDCT LR 16.3(a).

f. *Pretrial orders.* After any conference under FRCP 16, the court should issue an order reciting the action taken. This order controls the course of the action unless the court modifies it. FRCP 16(d).

g. *Additional case management conferences.* Nothing in MA R USDCT LR 16.3 shall be construed to prevent the convening of additional case management conferences by the judicial officer as may be thought appropriate in the circumstances of the particular case. In any event, a conference should not terminate without the parties being instructed as to when and for what purpose they are to return to the court. MA R USDCT LR 16.3(c).

h. *Sanctions.* On motion or on its own, the court may issue any just orders, including those authorized by FRCP 37(b)(2)(A)(ii) through FRCP 37(b)(2)(A)(vii), if a party or its attorney: (1) fails to appear at a scheduling or other pretrial conference; (2) is substantially unprepared to participate—or does not participate in good faith—in the conference; or (3) fails to obey a scheduling or other pretrial order. FRCP 16(f)(1).

   i. *Imposing fees and costs.* Instead of or in addition to any other sanction, the court must order the party, its attorney, or both to pay the reasonable expenses—including attorney's fees—incurred because of any noncompliance with FRCP 16, unless the noncompliance was substantially justified or other circumstances make an award of expenses unjust. FRCP 16(f)(2).

2. *Scheduling conference.* A scheduling conference may be requested by the judge or by the parties, but it is not mandatory. FPP § 1522.1. In every civil action, except in categories of actions exempted by MA R USDCT LR 16.2 as inappropriate for scheduling procedures, the judge or, in the interests of the efficient administration of justice, a designated magistrate judge shall convene a scheduling conference. MA R USDCT LR 16.1(a).

   a. *Joint statement containing proposed pretrial schedule.* Unless otherwise ordered by the judge, the parties are required to file, no later than seven (7) days before the scheduling conference and after consideration of the topics contemplated by FRCP 16(b) and FRCP 16(c) and FRCP 26(f), a joint statement containing a proposed pretrial schedule, which shall include:

      i. A joint discovery plan scheduling the time and length for all discovery events, that shall:

         - Conform to the obligation to limit discovery set forth in FRCP 26(b), and

         - Take into account the desirability of conducting phased discovery in which the first phase is limited to developing information needed for a realistic assessment of the case and, if the case does not terminate, the second phase is directed at information needed to prepare for trial; and

      ii. A proposed schedule for the filing of motions; and

      iii. Certifications signed by counsel and by an authorized representative of each party affirming that each party and that party's counsel have conferred:

         - With a view to establishing a budget for the costs of conducting the full course—and various alternative courses—of the litigation; and

         - To consider the resolution of the litigation through the use of alternative dispute resolution programs such as those outlined in MA R USDCT LR 16.4. MA R USDCT LR 16.1(d).

      iv. To the extent that all parties are able to reach agreement on a proposed pretrial schedule, they shall so indicate. To the extent that the parties differ on what the pretrial schedule should be, they shall set forth separately the items on which they differ and indicate the nature of that difference. The purpose of the parties' proposed pretrial schedule or schedules shall be to advise the judge of the parties' best estimates of the amounts of time they will need to accomplish specified pretrial steps. The parties' proposed agenda for the scheduling conference, and their proposed pretrial schedule or schedules, shall be considered by the judge as advisory only. MA R USDCT LR 16.1(d).

   b. *Settlement proposals.* Unless otherwise ordered by the judge, the plaintiff shall present written settlement proposals to all defendants no later than fourteen (14) days before the date for the scheduling conference. Defense counsel shall have conferred with their clients on the subject of settlement before the scheduling conference and be prepared to respond to the proposals at the scheduling conference. MA R USDCT LR 16.1(c).

   c. *Conduct of scheduling conference.* At or following the scheduling conference, the judge shall make an early determination of whether the case is "complex" or otherwise appropriate for careful and deliberate monitoring in an individualized and case-specific manner. The judge shall consider assigning any case so categorized to a case management conference or series of conferences under MA R USDCT LR 16.3. The factors to be considered by the judge in making this decision include:

i. The complexity of the case (the number of parties, claims, and defenses raised, the legal difficulty of the issues presented, and the factual difficulty of the subject matter);

ii. The amount of time reasonably needed by the litigants and their attorneys to prepare the case for trial;

iii. The judicial and other resources required and available for the preparation and disposition of the case;

iv. Whether the case belongs to those categories of cases that:

- Involve little or no discovery,
- Ordinarily require little or no additional judicial intervention, or
- Generally fall into identifiable and easily managed patterns;

v. The extent to which individualized and case-specific treatment will promote the goal of reducing cost and delay in civil litigation; and

vi. Whether the public interest requires that the case receive intense judicial attention. MA R USDCT LR 16.1(e).

vii. In other respects, the scheduling conference shall be conducted according to the provisions for a pretrial conference under FRCP 16 and for a case management conference under MA R USDCT LR 16.3. MA R USDCT LR 16.1(e).

d. *Disclosure orders.* The judicial officer may order the parties to submit at the scheduling conference, or at any subsequent time the officer deems appropriate, sworn statements disclosing certain information to every other party. At the discretion of the judicial officer, this order may direct the submission of:

i. A sworn statement from a claimant, whether plaintiff, third-party plaintiff, cross-claimant, or counter-claimant, that:

- Itemizes all economic loss and provides a computation of damages for which recovery is sought, if any, sustained before the date of service of process;
- Identifies all persons then known to the claimant or the claimant's attorney who witnessed or participated in the transaction or occurrence giving rise to the claim or otherwise known or believed to have substantial discoverable information about the claim or defenses, together with a statement of the subject and a brief summary of that information;
- Identifies all opposing parties, and all officers, directors, and employees of opposing parties, from whom statements have been obtained by or on behalf of the claimant regarding the subject matter of the claim; and
- Identifies all governmental agencies or officials then known to the claimant or the claimant's attorney to have investigated the transaction or occurrence giving rise to the claim; and

ii. A sworn statement from a defendant, whether the direct defendant, third-party defendant, cross-claim defendant, or counterclaim defendant, that identifies:

- All persons then known to the defendant or the defendant's attorneys who witnessed the transaction or occurrence giving rise to the claim or otherwise is known or believed to have substantial discoverable information about the claims or defenses, together with a statement of the subject and a brief summary of that information;
- All opposing parties, and all officers, directors, and employees of opposing parties, from whom statements have been obtained by or on behalf of the defendant regarding the subject matter of the claims or defenses; and
- All government agencies or officials then known to the defendant or the defendant's attorneys to have investigated the transaction or occurrence giving rise to the claims or defenses. MA R USDCT LR 26.1(b).

iii. Noncompliance may be excused only by order of the judicial officer. MA R USDCT LR 26.1(b).

e. *Scheduling order.* Except in categories of actions exempted by local rule, the district judge—or a magistrate judge when authorized by local rule—must issue a scheduling order: (1) after receiving the parties' report under FRCP 26(f); or (2) after consulting with the parties' attorneys and any unrepresented parties at a scheduling conference. FRCP 16(b)(1). Following the conference, the judge shall enter a scheduling order that will govern the pretrial phase of the case. MA R USDCT LR 16.1(f).

i. *Exemptions from FRCP 16(b).* The following categories of actions (based upon the numbered "Nature of Suit" list on form JS 44) are exempted in this district from the scheduling and planning provisions of FRCP 16(b), as inappropriate actions for such scheduling and planning:

- CONTRACT: 150 Recovery of Overpayment & Enforcement of Judgment; 152 Recovery of Defaulted Student Loans; 153 Recovery of Overpayment of Veterans Benefits. MA R USDCT LR 16.2.

- REAL PROPERTY: 210 Condemnation; 220 Foreclosure; 230 Rent Lease & Ejectment; 245 Tort Product Liability—Asbestos Cases Only. MA R USDCT LR 16.2.

- PRISONER PETITIONS: 510 Vacate Sentence (2255); 530 Habeas Corpus; 535 Death Penalty; 540 Mandamus & Other; 550 Civil Rights; 555 Prison Condition Cases; 560 Civil Detainee—Conditions of Confinement. MA R USDCT LR 16.2.

- FORFEITURE/PENALTY: 625 Drug Related Seizure. MA R USDCT LR 16.2.

- BANKRUPTCY: 422 Appeal (22 U.S.C.A. § 158); 423 Withdrawal (28 U.S.C.A. § 157). MA R USDCT LR 16.2.

- SOCIAL SECURITY: 861 HIA (1395ff); 862 Black Lung (923); 863 DIWC/DIWW (405(g)); 864 SSID Title XVI; 865 RSI (405(g)). MA R USDCT LR 16.2.

- TAX SUITS: 871 IRS—Third Party (26 U.S.C.A. § 7609). MA R USDCT LR 16.2.

- OTHER SUITS: 400 State Reapportionment; 450 Commerce. MA R USDCT LR 16.2.

ii. *Required contents of the order.* The scheduling order must limit the time to join other parties, amend the pleadings, complete discovery, and file motions. FRCP 16(b)(3)(A). Unless the judge determines otherwise, the scheduling order shall include specific deadlines or general time frameworks for:

- Amendments to the pleadings;

- Service of, and compliance with, written discovery requests;

- The completion of depositions, including, if applicable, the terms for taking and using videotape depositions;

- The identification of trial experts;

- The sequence of disclosure of information regarding experts contemplated by FRCP 26(b);

- The filing of motions;

- A settlement conference, to be attended by trial counsel and, in the discretion of the judge, their clients;

- One or more case management conferences and/or the final pretrial conference;

- A final pretrial conference, which shall occur within eighteen months after the filing of the complaint;

- The joinder of any additional parties;

- Any other procedural matter that the judge determines is appropriate for the fair and efficient management of the litigation. MA R USDCT LR 16.1(f).

iii. *Permitted contents of the order.* The scheduling order may:

- Modify the timing of disclosures under FRCP 26(a) and FRCP 26(e)(1);

- Modify the extent of discovery;

- Provide for disclosure, discovery, or preservation of electronically stored information;

- Include any agreements the parties reach for asserting claims of privilege or of protection as trial-preparation material after information is produced, including agreements reached under FRE 502;

- Direct that before moving for an order relating to discovery, the movant must request a conference with the court;

- Set dates for pretrial conferences and for trial; and

- Include other appropriate matters. FRCP 16(b)(3)(B).

f. *Time to issue.* The judge must issue the scheduling order as soon as practicable, but unless the judge finds good cause for delay, the judge must issue it within the earlier of ninety (90) days after any defendant has been served with the complaint or sixty (60) days after any defendant has appeared. FRCP 16(b)(2).

g. *Modifying a schedule.* A schedule may be modified only for good cause and with the judge's consent. FRCP 16(b)(4).

The scheduling order shall specify that its provisions, including any deadlines, having been established with the participation of all parties, can be modified only by order of the judge, or the magistrate judge if so authorized by the judge, and only upon a showing of good cause supported by affidavits, other evidentiary materials, or references to pertinent portions of the record. MA R USDCT LR 16.1(g).

h. *Definition of judge.* As used in MA R USDCT LR 16.1, "judge" refers to the United States District Judge to whom the case is assigned or to the United States Magistrate Judge who has been assigned the case pursuant to 28 U.S.C.A. § 636(c), if the Magistrate Judge has been assigned the case prior to the convening of the scheduling conference mandated by MA R USDCT LR 16.1. MA R USDCT LR 16.1(h).

3. *Final pretrial conference.* The court may hold a final pretrial conference to formulate a trial plan, including a plan to facilitate the admission of evidence. FRCP 16(e).

a. *Timing and attendance.* The conference must be held as close to the start of trial as is reasonable, and must be attended by at least one attorney who will conduct the trial for each party and by any unrepresented party. FRCP 16(e).

i. *Schedule of conference.* The judicial officer to whom the case is assigned for trial may set a new date for the final pretrial conference if that judicial officer determines that resolution of the case through settlement or some other form of alternative dispute resolution is imminent. MA R USDCT LR 16.5(a).

ii. *Representation by counsel; Settlement.* Unless excused by the judicial officer to whom the case is assigned for trial, each party shall be represented at the final pretrial conference by counsel who will conduct the trial. Counsel shall have full authority from their clients with respect to settlement and shall be prepared to advise that judicial officer as to the prospects of settlement. MA R USDCT LR 16.5(b).

b. *Disclosures preliminary to the pretrial conference.* As provided in MA R USDCT LR 26.4(a), the disclosure regarding experts required by FRCP 26(a)(2) shall be made at least ninety (90) days before the final pretrial conference. No later than twenty-eight (28) days before the date of the pretrial conference the parties shall make the pretrial disclosures required by FRCP 26(a)(3). Any objections to the use of the evidence identified in the pretrial disclosure required by FRCP 26(a)(3) shall be made before counsel confer regarding the pretrial memorandum, shall be a subject of their conference and shall not be filed with the court unless the objections cannot be resolved. Filing of such objections shall be made pursuant to MA R USDCT LR 16.5(d)(12). MA R USDCT LR 16.5(c).

c. *Obligation of counsel to confer and prepare pretrial memorandum.* Unless otherwise ordered by the judicial officer to whom the case is assigned for trial, counsel for the parties shall confer no later than fourteen (14) days before the date of the final pretrial conference for the purpose of jointly preparing a pretrial memorandum for submission to the judicial officer. Unless otherwise ordered by the judicial officer to whom the case is assigned for trial, the parties are required to file, no later than seven (7) days prior to the pre-trial conference, a joint pretrial memorandum which shall set forth:

i. A concise summary of the evidence that will be offered by: (1) plaintiff; (2) defendant; and (3) other parties, with respect to both liability and damages (including special damages, if any);

ii. The facts established by pleadings or by stipulations or admissions of counsel;

iii. Contested issues of fact;

iv. Any jurisdictional questions;

v. Any questions raised by pending motions;

vi. Issues of law, including evidentiary questions, together with supporting authority;

vii. Any requested amendments to the pleadings;

viii. Any additional matters to aid in the disposition of the action;

ix. The probable length of the trial;

x. The names, addresses and telephone numbers of witnesses to be called (expert and others) and whether the testimony of any such witness is intended to be presented by deposition;

xi. The proposed exhibits; and

xii. The parties' respective positions on any remaining objections to the evidence identified in the pretrial disclosure required by FRCP 26(a)(3). MA R USDCT LR 16.5(d).

d. *Conduct of conference.* The agenda of the final pretrial conference, when possible and appropriate, shall include:

i. A final and binding definition of the issues to be tried;

   ii.   The disclosure of expected and potential witnesses and the substance of their testimony;

   iii.   The exchange of all proposed exhibits;

   iv.   A pretrial ruling on objections to evidence;

   v.   The elimination of unnecessary or redundant proof, including the limitation of expert witnesses;

   vi.   A consideration of the bifurcation of the issues to be tried;

   vii.   The establishment of time limits and any other restrictions on the trial;

   viii.   A consideration of methods for expediting jury selection;

   ix.   A consideration of means for enhancing jury comprehension and simplifying and expediting the trial;

   x.   A consideration of the feasibility of presenting direct testimony by written statement;

   xi.   The exploration of possible agreement among the parties on various issues and encouragement of a stipulation from the parties, when that will serve the ends of justice, including:

- That direct testimony of some or all witnesses will be taken in narrative or affidavit form, with right of cross-examination reserved;

- That evidence in affidavit form will be read to the jury by the witnesses, or by counsel or another reader with court approval; and

- That time limits shorter than those set forth in MA R USDCT LR 43.1 be used for trial; and

   xii.   A consideration of any other means to facilitate and expedite trial. MA R USDCT LR 16.5(e).

e.   *Setting terms and conditions for handling experts.* At the final pretrial conference, the judge shall consider:

   i.   Precluding the appearance of expert witnesses not timely identified;

   ii.   Precluding use of any trial testimony by an expert at variance with any written statement or any deposition testimony;

   iii.   Making a ruling concerning the use of expert depositions, including videotaped depositions at trial; and

   iv.   Making any other ruling on the admissibility of expert testimony at the trial. MA R USDCT LR 26.4(b).

f.   *Modification of final pretrial order.* The court may modify the order issued after a final pretrial conference only to prevent manifest injustice. FRCP 16(e).

4.   *Discovery planning conference*

a.   *Conference content.* In conferring, the parties must consider the nature and basis of their claims and defenses and the possibilities for promptly settling or resolving the case; make or arrange for the disclosures required by FRCP 26(a)(1); discuss any issues about preserving discoverable information; and develop a proposed discovery plan. FRCP 26(f)(2). Unless otherwise ordered by the judge, counsel for the parties must, pursuant to FRCP 26(f), confer at least twenty-one (21) days before the date for the scheduling conference for the purpose of:

   i.   Preparing an agenda of matters to be discussed at the scheduling conference,

   ii.   Preparing a proposed pretrial schedule for the case that includes a plan for discovery, and

   iii.   Considering whether they will consent to trial by magistrate judge. MA R USDCT LR 16.1(b).

b.   *Parties' responsibilities.* The attorneys of record and all unrepresented parties that have appeared in the case are jointly responsible for arranging the conference, for attempting in good faith to agree on the proposed discovery plan, and for submitting to the court within fourteen (14) days after the conference a written report outlining the plan. The court may order the parties or attorneys to attend the conference in person. FRCP 26(f)(2).

c.   *Discovery plan.* A discovery plan must state the parties' views and proposals on:

   i.   What changes should be made in the timing, form, or requirement for disclosures under FRCP 26(a), including a statement of when initial disclosures were made or will be made;

   ii.   The subjects on which discovery may be needed, when discovery should be completed, and whether discovery should be conducted in phases or be limited to or focused on particular issues;

   iii.   Any issues about disclosure, discovery, or preservation of electronically stored information, including the form or forms in which it should be produced;

   iv.   Any issues about claims of privilege or of protection as trial-preparation materials, including—if the parties agree on a procedure to assert these claims after production—whether to ask the court to include their agreement in an order under FRE 502;

    v.   What changes should be made in the limitations on discovery imposed under the Federal Rules of Civil Procedure or by local rule, and what other limitations should be imposed; and

    vi.   Any other orders that the court should issue under FRCP 26(c) or under FRCP 16(b) and FRCP 26(c). FRCP 26(f)(3).

  d.  *Sanctions.* If a party or its attorney fails to participate in good faith in developing and submitting a proposed discovery plan as required by FRCP 26(f), the court may, after giving an opportunity to be heard, require that party or attorney to pay to any other party the reasonable expenses, including attorney's fees, caused by the failure. FRCP 37(f).

5.  *Scheduling and procedures in patent infringement cases.* For additional items for consideration by the court and parties in patent infringement cases, refer to MA R USDCT LR 16.6.

6.  *Alternative dispute resolution (ADR).* The judicial officer assigned to preside over the case shall encourage the resolution of disputes by settlement or other alternative dispute resolution programs. MA R USDCT LR 16.4(a).

  a.  *Settlement.* At every conference conducted under the Local Rules of the United States District Court for the District of Massachusetts, the judicial officer shall inquire as to the utility of the parties conducting settlement negotiations, explore means of facilitating those negotiations, and offer whatever assistance may be appropriate in the circumstances. Assistance may include a reference of the case to another judicial officer for settlement purposes. MA R USDCT LR 16.4(b).

    i.   When a case is settled, the parties shall file with the clerk a signed agreement for judgment or stipulation for dismissal, as appropriate, within twenty-eight (28) days, unless the court otherwise orders. MA R USDCT LR 68.2.

  b.  *Alternative dispute resolution programs*

    i.   *Discretion of judicial officer.* The judicial officer, following an exploration of the matter with all counsel, may refer appropriate cases to alternative dispute resolution programs that have been designated for use in the district court or that the judicial officer may make available. The dispute resolution programs described in MA R USDCT LR 16.4(c)(2) through MA R USDCT LR 16.4(c)(4) are illustrative, not exclusive. Moreover, nothing in MA R USDCT LR 16.4 shall preclude the parties from engaging in private dispute resolution programs as long as they comply with any schedule established by the court. MA R USDCT LR 16.4(c)(1).

    ii.   *Mediation.* The judicial officer may refer the case to mediation upon the agreement of all parties. MA R USDCT LR 16.4(c)(2)(A).

    iii.   *Other alternative dispute resolution programs.* Use of mediation is not exclusive. At the request of parties, the judicial officer may consider other forms of alternative dispute resolution including, but not limited to, mini-trial, summary jury trial and arbitration. MA R USDCT LR 16.4(c)(3).

  c.  For more information on alternative dispute resolution (ADR), refer to MA R USDCT LR 16.4.

7.  *Sanctions.* Failure to comply with any of the directions or obligations set forth in, or authorized by, these rules may result in dismissal, default, or the imposition of other sanctions as deemed appropriate by the judicial officer. MA R USDCT LR 1.3. Except as provided by law, the court may impose sanctions as provided in MA R USDCT LR 1.3 for failure to comply with the Administrative Procedures for Electronic Case Filing in the United States District Court for the District of Massachusetts (MA R USDCT CM/ECF Admin) or with MA R USDCT LR 5.4. MA R USDCT CM/ECF Admin(C)(3).

## D.  Documents

1.  *Pretrial conference*

  a.  *Documents to consider*

    i.   *Joint case management statement.* The judicial officer may require counsel for the parties to confer before the case management conference for the purpose of preparing a joint statement. MA R USDCT LR 16.3(b). Refer to the General Requirements section of this document for the contents of the joint case management statement.

      •  Even though it is not specifically mentioned in FRCP 16, most courts require the attorney for each side to file a pretrial memorandum or statement prior to the conference, which, if adopted by the court, may be binding at trial. FPP § 1524. The purpose of the memorandum is to reveal the lawyer's theory of the case and the issues counsel believes are in contention in order to aid the court in determining what matters should be considered at the conference itself. FPP § 1524; Manbeck v. Ostrowski, 384 F.2d 970 (D.C. Cir. 1967).

ii. *Compact disk with copy of document(s) in PDF format.* A filer who cannot file a document electronically because of such technical difficulty on the filer's end [with telephone, cable lines, the filer's Internet Service Provider (ISP), or hardware or software problems] shall file the document conventionally along with a copy of the document in PDF format on a compact disk or contact the clerk's office for permission to submit the PDF document via email. MA R USDCT CM/ECF Admin(W)(3). Refer to the Timing section of this document for more information on technical failures.

iii. *Notice of filing with clerk's office.* When documents or exhibits (other than those filed ex parte or under seal) are submitted conventionally, a "Notice of Filing with clerk's office" shall be filed electronically and attached to the main document. A paper copy of the "Notice of Filing with clerk's office" must accompany the documents submitted to the court. The "Notice of Filing with clerk's office" (see MA R USDCT CM/ECF Admin(Appendix I)) shall describe each of the documents that will be filed as paper copies in the clerk's office, or shall include an index of the documents if those documents are voluminous. MA R USDCT CM/ECF Admin(P)(5).

iv. *Additional copies.* Whenever, because of the nature of a proceeding, such as a proceeding before a three-judge district court under 28 U.S.C.A. § 2284, additional copies of a paper required to be filed are necessary either for the use of the court or to enable the clerk to carry out his duties, it is the responsibility of the party filing or having filed the paper to provide the necessary copies. MA R USDCT LR 5.1(d).

v. *Courtesy copies.* COURTESY COPIES OF DOCUMENTS FILED ELECTRONICALLY SHALL NOT BE SUBMITTED ROUTINELY. MA R USDCT CM/ECF Admin(J). Judicial officers, on a case-by-case basis, may require courtesy copies for specific cases, or types of motions, etc. A few Judicial Officers have entered Standing Orders, which may be found on their respective pages on the court's website (under Divisions). Any document filed on paper with the court as a courtesy copy must be clearly labeled as such (Example: COURTESY COPY—DO NOT SCAN). Documents delivered to the court as a courtesy copy will not be maintained in the official court record. MA R USDCT CM/ECF Admin(J).

2. *Scheduling conference*

   a. *Required documents*

      i. *Joint statement containing proposed pretrial schedule.* Refer to the General Requirements section of this document for the contents of the joint statement containing proposed pretrial schedule.

      ii. *Settlement proposals.* Unless otherwise ordered by the judge, the plaintiff shall present written settlement proposals to all defendants no later than fourteen (14) days before the date for the scheduling conference. MA R USDCT LR 16.1(c).

   b. *Supplemental documents*

      i. *Request for scheduling conference.* A scheduling conference may be requested by the judge or by the parties, but it is not mandatory. FPP § 1522.1.

      ii. *Compact disk with copy of document(s) in PDF format.* A filer who cannot file a document electronically because of such technical difficulty on the filer's end [with telephone, cable lines, the filer's Internet Service Provider (ISP), or hardware or software problems] shall file the document conventionally along with a copy of the document in PDF format on a compact disk or contact the clerk's office for permission to submit the PDF document via email. MA R USDCT CM/ECF Admin(W)(3). Refer to the Timing section of this document for more information on technical failures.

      iii. *Notice of filing with clerk's office.* When documents or exhibits (other than those filed ex parte or under seal) are submitted conventionally, a "Notice of Filing with clerk's office" shall be filed electronically and attached to the main document. A paper copy of the "Notice of Filing with clerk's office" must accompany the documents submitted to the court. The "Notice of Filing with clerk's office" (see MA R USDCT CM/ECF Admin(Appendix I)) shall describe each of the documents that will be filed as paper copies in the clerk's office, or shall include an index of the documents if those documents are voluminous. MA R USDCT CM/ECF Admin(P)(5).

      iv. *Additional copies.* Whenever, because of the nature of a proceeding, such as a proceeding before a three-judge district court under 28 U.S.C.A. § 2284, additional copies of a paper required to be filed are necessary either for the use of the court or to enable the clerk to carry out his duties, it is the responsibility of the party filing or having filed the paper to provide the necessary copies. MA R USDCT LR 5.1(d).

      v. *Courtesy copies.* COURTESY COPIES OF DOCUMENTS FILED ELECTRONICALLY SHALL NOT BE SUBMITTED ROUTINELY. MA R USDCT CM/ECF Admin(J). Judicial officers, on a case-by-case basis, may require courtesy copies for specific cases, or types of motions, etc. A few Judicial Officers have entered Standing

504

Orders, which may be found on their respective pages on the court's website (under Divisions). Any document filed on paper with the court as a courtesy copy must be clearly labeled as such (Example: COURTESY COPY—DO NOT SCAN). Documents delivered to the court as a courtesy copy will not be maintained in the official court record. MA R USDCT CM/ECF Admin(J).

3. *Final pretrial conference*

   a. *Required documents*

      i. *Joint pretrial memorandum.* Refer to the General Requirements section of this document for the contents of the joint pretrial memorandum.

   b. *Supplemental documents*

      i. *Compact disk with copy of document(s) in PDF format.* A filer who cannot file a document electronically because of such technical difficulty on the filer's end [with telephone, cable lines, the filer's Internet Service Provider (ISP), or hardware or software problems] shall file the document conventionally along with a copy of the document in PDF format on a compact disk or contact the clerk's office for permission to submit the PDF document via email. MA R USDCT CM/ECF Admin(W)(3). Refer to the Timing section of this document for more information on technical failures.

      ii. *Notice of filing with clerk's office.* When documents or exhibits (other than those filed ex parte or under seal) are submitted conventionally, a "Notice of Filing with clerk's office" shall be filed electronically and attached to the main document. A paper copy of the "Notice of Filing with clerk's office" must accompany the documents submitted to the court. The "Notice of Filing with clerk's office" (see MA R USDCT CM/ECF Admin(Appendix I)) shall describe each of the documents that will be filed as paper copies in the clerk's office, or shall include an index of the documents if those documents are voluminous. MA R USDCT CM/ECF Admin(P)(5).

      iii. *Additional copies.* Whenever, because of the nature of a proceeding, such as a proceeding before a three-judge district court under 28 U.S.C.A. § 2284, additional copies of a paper required to be filed are necessary either for the use of the court or to enable the clerk to carry out his duties, it is the responsibility of the party filing or having filed the paper to provide the necessary copies. MA R USDCT LR 5.1(d).

      iv. *Courtesy copies.* COURTESY COPIES OF DOCUMENTS FILED ELECTRONICALLY SHALL NOT BE SUBMITTED ROUTINELY. MA R USDCT CM/ECF Admin(J). Judicial officers, on a case-by-case basis, may require courtesy copies for specific cases, or types of motions, etc. A few Judicial Officers have entered Standing Orders, which may be found on their respective pages on the court's website (under Divisions). Any document filed on paper with the court as a courtesy copy must be clearly labeled as such (Example: COURTESY COPY—DO NOT SCAN). Documents delivered to the court as a courtesy copy will not be maintained in the official court record. MA R USDCT CM/ECF Admin(J).

4. *Discovery planning conference*

   a. *Required documents*

      i. *Written report outlining proposed discovery plan.* Refer to the General Requirements section of this document for information on the parties' responsibilities for submitting a written report outlining the proposed discovery plan.

   b. *Supplemental documents*

      i. *Compact disk with copy of document(s) in PDF format.* A filer who cannot file a document electronically because of such technical difficulty on the filer's end [with telephone, cable lines, the filer's Internet Service Provider (ISP), or hardware or software problems] shall file the document conventionally along with a copy of the document in PDF format on a compact disk or contact the clerk's office for permission to submit the PDF document via email. MA R USDCT CM/ECF Admin(W)(3). Refer to the Timing section of this document for more information on technical failures.

      ii. *Notice of filing with clerk's office.* When documents or exhibits (other than those filed ex parte or under seal) are submitted conventionally, a "Notice of Filing with clerk's office" shall be filed electronically and attached to the main document. A paper copy of the "Notice of Filing with clerk's office" must accompany the documents submitted to the court. The "Notice of Filing with clerk's office" (see MA R USDCT CM/ECF Admin(Appendix I)) shall describe each of the documents that will be filed as paper copies in the clerk's office, or shall include an index of the documents if those documents are voluminous. MA R USDCT CM/ECF Admin(P)(5).

      iii. *Additional copies.* Whenever, because of the nature of a proceeding, such as a proceeding before a three-judge district court under 28 U.S.C.A. § 2284, additional copies of a paper required to be filed are necessary either for the use of the court or to enable the clerk to carry out his duties, it is the responsibility of the party filing or having filed the paper to provide the necessary copies. MA R USDCT LR 5.1(d).

iv. *Courtesy copies.* COURTESY COPIES OF DOCUMENTS FILED ELECTRONICALLY SHALL NOT BE SUBMITTED ROUTINELY. MA R USDCT CM/ECF Admin(J). Judicial officers, on a case-by-case basis, may require courtesy copies for specific cases, or types of motions, etc. A few Judicial Officers have entered Standing Orders, which may be found on their respective pages on the court's website (under Divisions). Any document filed on paper with the court as a courtesy copy must be clearly labeled as such (Example: COURTESY COPY—DO NOT SCAN). Documents delivered to the court as a courtesy copy will not be maintained in the official court record. MA R USDCT CM/ECF Admin(J).

# E. Format

1. *Form of documents.* The rules governing captions and other matters of form in pleadings apply to motions and other papers. FRCP 7(b)(2). The provisions of FRCP 10 and FRCP 11 concerning the form and signing of pleadings, motions, and other papers shall be applicable to all papers filed in any proceeding in this court. The board of bar overseers registration number of each attorney signing such documents, except the United States Attorney and his or her staff, shall be inscribed below the signature. MA R USDCT LR 5.1(a)(1).

   a. *Paper size and binding.* All papers filed in the court shall be adapted for flat filing, be filed on eight and one-half by eleven (8-1/2 x 11) inch paper without backers and be bound firmly by staple or some such other means (excluding paper or binder clip or rubber band). MA R USDCT LR 5.1(a)(2).

   b. *Spacing.* All papers, except discovery requests and responses, shall be double-spaced except for the identification of counsel, title of the case, footnotes, quotations and exhibits. Discovery requests and responses shall be single-spaced. MA R USDCT LR 5.1(a)(2).

   c. *Caption.* Every pleading must have a caption with the court's name, a title, a file number, and [an] FRCP 7(a) designation. FRCP 10(a).

      i. *Names of parties.* The title of the complaint must name all the parties; the title of other pleadings, after naming the first party on each side, may refer generally to other parties. FRCP 10(a).

      ii. *Request for special action.* When any pleading or other paper filed in the court includes a request for special process or relief, or any other request such that, if granted, the court will proceed other than in the ordinary course, the request shall, unless it is noted on the category sheet [see MA R USDCT LR 40.1(a)(1)], be noted on the first page to the right of or immediately beneath the caption. MA R USDCT LR 5.1(c).

   d. *Claims or defenses*

      i. *Numbered paragraphs.* A party must state its claims or defenses in numbered paragraphs, each limited as far as practicable to a single set of circumstances. A later pleading may refer by number to a paragraph in an earlier pleading. FRCP 10(b).

      ii. *Separate statements.* If doing so would promote clarity, each claim founded on a separate transaction or occurrence—and each defense other than a denial—must be stated in a separate count or defense. FRCP 10(b).

   e. *Adoption by reference.* A statement in a pleading may be adopted by reference elsewhere in the same pleading or in any other pleading or motion. FRCP 10(c).

      i. *Exhibits.* A copy of a written instrument that is an exhibit to a pleading is a part of the pleading for all purposes. FRCP 10(c).

   f. *Citations*

      i. *Local rules.* These rules shall be known as Local Rules of the United States District Court for the District of Massachusetts and cited as "L.R., D. Mass." or "L.R." MA R USDCT LR 1.1.

      ii. *Electronic case filing procedures.* The procedures governing electronic case filing shall be known as the "Administrative Procedures for Electronic Case Filing in the United States District Court for the District of Massachusetts." They shall be cited as "APECF." MA R USDCT CM/ECF Admin(A)(7).

   g. *Acceptance by the clerk.* The clerk must not refuse to file a paper solely because it is not in the form prescribed by the Federal Rules of Civil Procedure or by a local rule or practice. FRCP 5(d)(4).

      i. Except for complaints and notices of appeal, papers that do not conform to the requirements of MA R USDCT LR 5.1(a)(2) shall be returned by the clerk. MA R USDCT LR 5.1(a)(2).

2. *Form of electronic documents.* A paper filed electronically is a written paper for purposes of the Federal Rules of Civil Procedure. FRCP 5(d)(3)(D).

   a. *PDF/A format required.* The court will begin requiring submission of documents in PDF/A format in the foreseeable future. PDF/A is an enhanced version of the traditional PDF format. Newer versions of most PDF software will be able to convert to this format. Additional information on PDF/A documents may be found on the court's website. MA R USDCT CM/ECF Admin(Electronic Filing and PDF).

      i. *Electronically converted PDF.* Electronically converted PDF documents are created from word processing documents (MS Word, WordPerfect, etc.) using any appropriate software. These documents are text searchable and the file size is generally smaller than a scanned document. CM/ECF users may use any brand of software to convert documents to PDF. MA R USDCT CM/ECF Admin(Electronic Filing and PDF).

         • Documents converted to PDF, rather than scanned, are preferred for filing in CM/ECF. MA R USDCT CM/ECF Admin(Electronic Filing and PDF).

      ii. *Scanned PDF.* Scanned PDF documents are created from paper documents run through an optical scanner. Scanned PDF documents are generally not searchable and have a larger file size. Please note that software used to create scanned documents may (and should) be set in such a way that the document is "text-searchable." MA R USDCT CM/ECF Admin(Electronic Filing and PDF).

   b. *Title.* All pleadings filed electronically shall be titled in accordance with the approved dictionary of civil or criminal events of the CM/ECF system of this court. A list of events is available on the CM/ECF Training Information page of the court's website. The clerk's office may, when necessary and appropriate, modify the docket entry description, or delete and re-enter the docket entry in order to comply with the court's quality assurance standards. MA R USDCT CM/ECF Admin(G)(3).

   c. *Attachments to filings and exhibits.* Attachments to filings and exhibits must be filed in accordance with the court's CM/ECF User Manual, unless otherwise ordered by the court. MA R USDCT CM/ECF Admin(O)(1).

      i. Filers must submit as attachments only those excerpts of the referenced documents that are directly germane to the matter under consideration by the court. Excerpted material must be clearly and prominently identified as such. Users who file excerpts of documents do so without prejudice to their right to timely file additional excerpts or the complete document, as may be allowed by the court. Responding parties may timely file additional excerpts or the complete document that they believe are directly germane. MA R USDCT CM/ECF Admin(O)(2).

      ii. Filers shall not attach as an exhibit any pleading or other paper already on file with the court in that case, but shall merely refer to that document. (See MA R USDCT CM/ECF Admin(G) for information on using hyperlinks in PDF documents filed in CM/ECF.) MA R USDCT CM/ECF Admin(O)(3).

   d. *Redacted documents.* The parties may request or the court may require the submission of documents that have been redacted/stripped of sensitive or confidential information. The redacted document prepared for electronic filing shall include the original caption of the document, and be clearly labeled as "Redacted Document." A specific event is available for this purpose ("Redacted Document"), found under the Other Filings/Other Documents menu option. MA R USDCT CM/ECF Admin(S).

      i. Attorneys and pro se litigants are advised to take extra care when creating PDF documents intended for submission to CM/ECF. Steps shall be taken to ensure the documents are free of any hidden data (metadata) that may contain redacted information, or traces of information edited or deleted are not hidden in the final document. Even PDF content that has been encrypted may be recovered. An advisory document with additional information on this topic may be found on the court's website. MA R USDCT CM/ECF Admin(S).

   e. *Hyperlinks.* Electronically filed documents may contain the following types of hyperlinks: (1) hyperlinks to other portions of the same document; (2) hyperlinks to other documents filed within the CM/ECF system; and (3) hyperlinks to a location on the Internet that contains a source document for a citation. MA R USDCT CM/ECF Admin(G)(7).

      i. Hyperlinks to cited authority may not replace standard citation format. Complete citations must be included in the text of the filed document. Neither a hyperlink, nor any site to which it refers, shall be considered part of the record, but are simply convenient mechanisms for accessing material cited in a document filed in CM/ECF. Instructions on creating hyperlinks may be found in the CM/ECF User Manual. MA R USDCT CM/ECF Admin(G)(7).

      ii. The court accepts no responsibility for, and does not endorse, any product, organization, or content at any

hyperlinked site, or at any site to which that site may be linked. The court accepts no responsibility for the availability or functionality of any hyperlink. MA R USDCT CM/ECF Admin(G)(7).

    iii.   One feature of PDF/A documents is that hyperlinks are commonly "masked," meaning that the full address of the referenced file is not written out; for example, clicking the word brief may open a brief which was previously filed in CM/ECF. MA R USDCT CM/ECF Admin(G)(7)(NOTE). An "unmasked" hyperlink has the full address visible to the user. MA R USDCT CM/ECF Admin(G)(7)(NOTE).

- Masked hyperlinks may or may not work in a PDF/A document, depending on how it was created. Currently, masked hyperlinks are preserved in PDF/A documents produced by the "Save As" method in Microsoft Word 2007 and 2010; the "PDFMaker" method in Microsoft Word 2007; and OpenOffice 2.4 ("PDF Export"). With other production methods, such as WordPerfect, the PDF/A document includes underlined words that appear to be links, but clicking them has no effect. MA R USDCT CM/ECF Admin(G)(7)(NOTE).

    f.   *Documents features not accepted.* CM/ECF will not accept PDF documents containing tracking tags, embedded systems commands, password protections, access restrictions or other security features, special tags or dynamic features. MA R USDCT CM/ECF Admin(G)(8).

    g.   *File size limitations.* A filing party shall limit the size of each PDF file to no more than twenty (20) megabytes. PDF files larger than seven (7) megabytes will be rejected by the CM/ECF system. The filer will see a message advising of the size limitation. MA R USDCT CM/ECF Admin(P)(2).

    i.   Larger documents or exhibits may be submitted electronically if split into separate PDF files each less than seven (7) megabytes, attached to the main document and clearly labeled. MA R USDCT CM/ECF Admin(P)(2).

    ii.   Documents submitted electronically or on paper are subject to the page limitations set by MA R USDCT LR 7.1(b)(4) or by order of the court. MA R USDCT CM/ECF Admin(P)(1).

    h.   *Accuracy and readability.* The filer shall verify the accuracy and readability of any PDF file before electronically filing it in CM/ECF. MA R USDCT CM/ECF Admin(G)(6); MA R USDCT CM/ECF Admin(P)(3).

3.   *Signing of pleadings, motions and other papers*

    a.   *Signature.* Every pleading, written motion, and other paper must be signed by at least one attorney of record in the attorney's name—or by a party personally if the party is unrepresented. The paper must state the signer's address, e-mail address, and telephone number. FRCP 11(a). The provisions of the Federal Rules of Civil Procedure pertaining to the form and signing of pleadings, motions, and other papers shall be applicable to all papers filed in any proceeding in this court. The board of bar overseers registration number of each attorney signing such documents, except the United States Attorney and his staff, shall be inscribed below the signature. MA R USDCT LR 5.1(a)(1).

    i.   *Electronic signing.* A filing made through a person's electronic-filing account and authorized by that person, together with that person's name on a signature block, constitutes the person's signature. FRCP 5(d)(3)(C).

    ii.   *Appearances.* The filing of an appearance or any other pleading signed on behalf of a party constitutes an entry of appearance for that party. All pleadings shall contain the name, bar admission number, address, telephone number, and e-mail address of the attorney entering an appearance. MA R USDCT LR 83.5.2(a).

- *Appearances by law firms.* When a party is represented by a law firm, the appearance must include the name and the signature of at least one individual attorney. When a party is represented by more than one attorney from the same or different law firms, the attorney entering the appearance must designate the individual attorney who is authorized to receive all notices in the case. Any notice sent to an attorney so designated shall be deemed to be proper notice unless the court finds that notice was not properly sent. MA R USDCT LR 83.5.2(b).

- For more information on appearances, refer to MA R USDCT LR 83.5.2.

    iii.   *Signatures of attorneys.* The user login and password required to submit documents to the CM/ECF system shall serve as that user's signature for purposes of FRCP 11 and for all other purposes under the Federal Rules of Civil Procedure and the Local Rules of the United States District Court for the District of Massachusetts. All electronically filed documents must include a signature block and must set forth the attorney's name, bar number, address, telephone number and email address. The name of the CM/ECF user under whose log-in and password the document is submitted must be preceded by a "/s/" and typed in the space where the signature would otherwise appear. MA R USDCT CM/ECF Admin(M)(1). For an example, refer to MA R USDCT CM/ECF Admin(M)(1).

    iv.   *Signatures of pro se parties.* Any document requiring a signature that is filed by a party appearing pro se shall

bear the words "pro se" following that party's signature. Any such document shall also state the party's mailing address, telephone number (if any), and e-mail address (if the party has consented to service by email). MA R USDCT LR 83.5.5(g). For more information on practice by pro se litigants, refer to MA R USDCT LR 83.5.5.

v. *Multiple signatures.* The filer of any document requiring more than one signature (e.g, stipulations, joint motions, joint status reports, magistrate judge consent forms, etc.) must list thereon all the names of other signatories by means of a "/s/ name of signatory" block for each. By submitting such a document, the filing attorney certifies that each of the other signatories has expressly agreed to the form and substance of the document and that the filing attorney has their actual authority to submit the document electronically. MA R USDCT CM/ECF Admin(M)(2). For more information, refer to MA R USDCT CM/ECF Admin(M)(2).

vi. *Affidavits.* Except as provided in MA R USDCT CM/ECF Admin(L), affidavits shall be filed electronically; however, the electronically filed version must contain a "/s/ name of signatory" block indicating that the paper document bears an original signature. MA R USDCT CM/ECF Admin(M)(3). The court will also accept a scanned version of the original, signed document. MA R USDCT CM/ECF Admin(M)(3). For more information, refer to MA R USDCT CM/ECF Admin(M)(3).

vii. *No verification or accompanying affidavit required for pleadings.* Unless a rule or statute specifically states otherwise, a pleading need not be verified or accompanied by an affidavit. FRCP 11(a).

viii. *Unsigned papers.* The court must strike an unsigned paper unless the omission is promptly corrected after being called to the attorney's or party's attention. FRCP 11(a).

b. *Representations to the court.* By presenting to the court a pleading, written motion, or other paper—whether by signing, filing, submitting, or later advocating it—an attorney or unrepresented party certifies that to the best of the person's knowledge, information, and belief, formed after an inquiry reasonable under the circumstances:

i. It is not being presented for any improper purpose, such as to harass, cause unnecessary delay, or needlessly increase the cost of litigation;

ii. The claims, defenses, and other legal contentions are warranted by existing law or by a nonfrivolous argument for extending, modifying, or reversing existing law or for establishing new law;

iii. The factual contentions have evidentiary support or, if specifically so identified, will likely have evidentiary support after a reasonable opportunity for further investigation or discovery; and

iv. The denials of factual contentions are warranted on the evidence or, if specifically so identified, are reasonably based on belief or a lack of information. FRCP 11(b).

c. *Sanctions.* If, after notice and a reasonable opportunity to respond, the court determines that FRCP 11(b) has been violated, the court may impose an appropriate sanction on any attorney, law firm, or party that violated FRCP 11(b) or is responsible for the violation. FRCP 11(c)(1). Refer to the United States District Court for the District of Massachusetts KeyRules Motion for Sanctions document for more information.

4. *Privacy protection for filings made with the court*

a. *Redacted filings.* Unless the court orders otherwise, in an electronic or paper filing with the court that contains an individual's Social Security number, taxpayer-identification number, or birth date, the name of an individual known to be a minor, or a financial-account number, a party or nonparty making the filing may include only:

i. The last four (4) digits of the Social Security number and taxpayer-identification number;

ii. The year of the individual's birth;

iii. The minor's initials; and

iv. The last four (4) digits of the financial-account number. FRCP 5.2(a); MA R USDCT CM/ECF Admin(N).

b. *Exemptions from the redaction requirement.* The redaction requirement does not apply to the following:

i. A financial-account number that identifies the property allegedly subject to forfeiture in a forfeiture proceeding;

ii. The record of an administrative or agency proceeding;

iii. The official record of a state-court proceeding;

iv. The record of a court or tribunal, if that record was not subject to the redaction requirement when originally filed;

v. A filing covered by FRCP 5.2(c) or FRCP 5.2(d); and

vi. A pro se filing in an action brought under 28 U.S.C.A. § 2241, 28 U.S.C.A. § 2254, or 28 U.S.C.A. § 2255. FRCP 5.2(b).

c. *Limitations on remote access to electronic files; Social Security appeals and immigration cases.* Unless the court orders otherwise, in an action for benefits under the Social Security Act, and in an action or proceeding relating to an order of removal, to relief from removal, or to immigration benefits or detention, access to an electronic file is authorized as follows:

i. The parties and their attorneys may have remote electronic access to any part of the case file, including the administrative record;

ii. Any other person may have electronic access to the full record at the courthouse, but may have remote electronic access only to:

- The docket maintained by the court; and

- An opinion, order, judgment, or other disposition of the court, but not any other part of the case file or the administrative record. FRCP 5.2(c).

d. *Filings made under seal.* The court may order that a filing be made under seal without redaction. The court may later unseal the filing or order the person who made the filing to file a redacted version for the public record. FRCP 5.2(d).

e. *Protective orders.* For good cause, the court may by order in a case:

i. Require redaction of additional information; or

ii. Limit or prohibit a nonparty's remote electronic access to a document filed with the court. FRCP 5.2(e).

f. *Option for additional unredacted filing under seal.* A person making a redacted filing may also file an unredacted copy under seal. The court must retain the unredacted copy as part of the record. FRCP 5.2(f). For more information, refer to MA R USDCT LR 7.2.

g. *Option for filing a reference list.* A filing that contains redacted information may be filed together with a reference list that identifies each item of redacted information and specifies an appropriate identifier that uniquely corresponds to each item listed. The list must be filed under seal and may be amended as of right. Any reference in the case to a listed identifier will be construed to refer to the corresponding item of information. FRCP 5.2(g).

h. *Responsibility for redaction.* The clerk's office is not responsible for reviewing documents filed with the court to determine whether pleadings have been redacted and are in the proper form. MA R USDCT CM/ECF Admin(N).

i. *Waiver of protection of identifiers.* A person waives the protection of FRCP 5.2(a) as to the person's own information by filing it without redaction and not under seal. FRCP 5.2(h).

## F. Filing and Service Requirements

1. *Filing requirements*

a. *Required filings.* Any paper after the complaint that is required to be served must be filed no later than a reasonable time after service. FRCP 5(d)(1).

i. Except as noted in FRCP 33 to FRCP 36, the original of all papers required to be served under FRCP 5(d) shall, unless otherwise submitted to the court, be filed in the office of the clerk within seven (7) days after service has been made. MA R USDCT LR 5.1(b). Except as otherwise provided by the Federal Rules of Civil Procedure, proof of service of all pleadings and other papers required to be served (except discovery papers that in accordance with FRCP 33 to FRCP 36(f) are not to be filed) shall be filed in the office of the clerk promptly after service has been made. MA R USDCT LR 5.2(b)(1).

b. *Nonelectronic filing.* A paper not filed electronically is filed by delivering it: (1) to the clerk; or (2) to a judge who agrees to accept it for filing, and who must then note the filing date on the paper and promptly send it to the clerk. FRCP 5(d)(2).

c. *Electronic filing.* Unless exempt or otherwise ordered by the court, all pleadings and other papers submitted to the court must be filed, signed, and verified by electronic means as provided in MA R USDCT LR 5.4. MA R USDCT LR 5.4(A); MA R USDCT LR 5.4(B); MA R USDCT CM/ECF Admin(A)(1). All electronic filings must be made in accordance with the Administrative Procedures for Electronic Case Filing in the United States District Court for the District of Massachusetts (MA R USDCT CM/ECF Admin). MA R USDCT LR 5.4(B). The court may deviate from the Administrative Procedures for Electronic Case Filing in the United States District Court for the District of Massachusetts (MA R USDCT CM/ECF Admin) in specific cases, without prior notice, if deemed appropriate in the exercise of discretion, considering the need for the just, speedy, and inexpensive determination of matters pending before the court. MA R USDCT CM/ECF Admin(C)(1). The court may excuse a failure to comply with any administrative procedure whenever justice so requires. MA R USDCT CM/ECF Admin(C)(2).

i. *By a represented person; Generally required; Exceptions.* A person represented by an attorney must file

electronically, unless nonelectronic filing is allowed by the court for good cause or is allowed or required by local rule. FRCP 5(d)(3)(A).

ii.    *By unrepresented person; When allowed or required.* A person not represented by an attorney: (1) may file electronically only if allowed by court order or by local rule; and (2) may be required to file electronically only by court order, or by a local rule that includes reasonable exceptions. FRCP 5(d)(3)(B).

iii.   *Exemptions from electronic filing*

- *Documents that should not be filed electronically.* The following types of documents must not be filed electronically, and will not be scanned into the ECF system by the clerk's office: (1) sealed documents; (2) ex parte motions; (3) documents generated as part of an alternative dispute resolution (ADR) process; (4) the administrative record in Social Security and other administrative proceedings; (5) the state court record in proceedings under 28 U.S.C.A. § 2254; and (6) such other types of documents as the clerk may direct in the Administrative Procedures for Electronic Case Filing in the United States District Court for the District of Massachusetts (MA R USDCT CM/ECF Admin). MA R USDCT LR 5.4(G)(1); MA R USDCT CM/ECF Admin(L).

- *Documents that need not be filed electronically.* The following types of documents need not be filed electronically, but may be scanned into the ECF system by a filing party or the clerk's office: (1) handwritten pleadings; (2) documents filed by pro se litigants who are incarcerated or who are not registered ECF users; (3) indictments, informations, criminal complaints, and the criminal JS45 form; (4) affidavits for search or arrest warrants and related documents; (5) documents received from another court under FRCRP 20 or FRCRP 40; (6) appearance bonds; (7) any document in a criminal case containing the original signature of a defendant, such as a waiver of indictment or a plea agreement; (8) petitions for violations of supervised release; (9) executed service of process documents under FRCP 4; and (10) such other types of documents as the clerk may direct in the Administrative Procedures for Electronic Case Filing in the United States District Court for the District of Massachusetts (MA R USDCT CM/ECF Admin). MA R USDCT LR 5.4(G)(2); MA R USDCT CM/ECF Admin(L).

- For more information on exemptions from electronic filing, refer to MA R USDCT CM/ECF Admin(L).

iv.    *Consequences of electronic filing.* Electronic transmission of a document to the CM/ECF system, together with the transmission of a Notice of Electronic Filing (NEF) from the court at the completion of the transaction, constitutes the filing of the document for all purposes of the Federal Rules of Procedure and constitutes entry of the document on the docket maintained by the clerk pursuant to FRCP 58 and FRCP 79. MA R USDCT CM/ECF Admin(G)(1).

v.     *Payment of filing fees.* When electronically filing any pleading or paper through CM/ECF that requires a fee, all registered ECF users are to pay the fee electronically through the Treasury Department's Internet payment process. MA R USDCT LR 67.4(d); MA R USDCT CM/ECF Admin(A)(1). Pro se filers and those who have been exempted from electronic filing and/or electronic payment of fees may submit payments by check or money order made payable to "Clerk, U.S. District Court". MA R USDCT LR 67.4(d). For more information on filing fees, refer to MA R USDCT LR 67.4 and MA R USDCT CM/ECF Admin(I).

vi.    For more information on electronic filing, refer to MA R USDCT CM/ECF Admin.

d.  *Email or fax filing.* In general, the court does not accept documents by email or by fax. If the court, in special circumstances, does authorize the submission of a document in that manner, the document shall not be considered filed until an NEF is generated by CM/ECF at the completion of the transaction. MA R USDCT CM/ECF Admin(H)(5).

2.  *Service requirements.* Service of all pleadings subsequent to the original complaint and of all other papers required to be served shall be made in the manner specified by FRCP 5. MA R USDCT LR 5.2(a).

a.  *Service; When required*

i.    *In general.* Unless the Federal Rules of Civil Procedure provide otherwise, each of the following papers must be served on every party:

- An order stating that service is required;

- A pleading filed after the original complaint, unless the court orders otherwise under FRCP 5(c) because there are numerous defendants;

- A discovery paper required to be served on a party, unless the court orders otherwise;

- A written motion, except one that may be heard ex parte; and

- A written notice, appearance, demand, or offer of judgment, or any similar paper. FRCP 5(a)(1).

ii. *If a party fails to appear.* No service is required on a party who is in default for failing to appear. But a pleading that asserts a new claim for relief against such a party must be served on that party under FRCP 4. FRCP 5(a)(2).

iii. *Seizing property.* If an action is begun by seizing property and no person is or need be named as a defendant, any service required before the filing of an appearance, answer, or claim must be made on the person who had custody or possession of the property when it was seized. FRCP 5(a)(3).

b. *Service; How made*

  i. *Serving an attorney.* If a party is represented by an attorney, service under FRCP 5 must be made on the attorney unless the court orders service on the party. FRCP 5(b)(1).

    - *Nonresident attorney.* On application of a party, the court may order an attorney who represents any other party and who does not maintain an office within this district where service can be made on him by delivery as provided by FRCP 5(b), to designate a member of the bar of this court who does maintain such an office to receive service of all pleadings and other papers in his behalf. MA R USDCT LR 5.2(c)(1).

  ii. *Serving a party acting pro se.* On application of a party, the court may order any other party who is appearing without an attorney and who does not maintain an office or residence within this district where service can be made on him by delivery as provided by FRCP 5(b), to designate an address within the district at which service can be made on him by delivery. MA R USDCT LR 5.2(c)(2).

  iii. *Service in general.* A paper is served under FRCP 5 by:

    - Handing it to the person;

    - Leaving it: (1) at the person's office with a clerk or other person in charge or, if no one is in charge, in a conspicuous place in the office; or (2) if the person has no office or the office is closed, at the person's dwelling or usual place of abode with someone of suitable age and discretion who resides there;

    - Mailing it to the person's last known address—in which event service is complete upon mailing;

    - Leaving it with the court clerk if the person has no known address;

    - Sending it to a registered user by filing it with the court's electronic-filing system or sending it by other electronic means that the person consented to in writing—in either of which events service is complete upon filing or sending, but is not effective if the filer or sender learns that it did not reach the person to be served; or

    - Delivering it by any other means that the person consented to in writing—in which event service is complete when the person making service delivers it to the agency designated to make delivery. FRCP 5(b)(2).

  iv. *Service by electronic means.* Unless exempt or otherwise ordered by the court, all pleadings and other papers must be served on other parties by electronic means. MA R USDCT LR 5.4(C); MA R USDCT CM/ECF Admin(H)(2). Service by electronic means shall be treated the same as service by mail. MA R USDCT CM/ECF Admin(H)(4).

    - *Consent to electronic service.* Registering to use CM/ECF constitutes consent to service of all documents by electronic means as provided in the Administrative Procedures for Electronic Case Filing in the United States District Court for the District of Massachusetts (MA R USDCT CM/ECF Admin) and FRCP 5(b) and FRCP 77(d). MA R USDCT CM/ECF Admin(E)(6); MA R USDCT CM/ECF Admin(H)(3).

    - *Service on registered ECF users.* Transmission of the Notice of Electronic Filing (NEF) through the court's transmission facilities will constitute service of the filed document upon a registered ECF user. MA R USDCT LR 5.4(C).

    - *Service on non-registered users.* The party filing the document electronically is responsible for serving a paper copy of the document by mail in accordance with FRCP 5(b) to those case participants who have not been identified on the NEF as electronic recipients. MA R USDCT CM/ECF Admin(H)(3).

    - *Service of conventionally filed papers.* Documents or exhibits submitted conventionally shall be served on other parties by the filer using traditional means. MA R USDCT CM/ECF Admin(P)(4).

   c.   *Serving numerous defendants*

      i.  *In general.* If an action involves an unusually large number of defendants, the court may, on motion or on its own, order that:

- Defendants' pleadings and replies to them need not be served on other defendants;

- Any crossclaim, counterclaim, avoidance, or affirmative defense in those pleadings and replies to them will be treated as denied or avoided by all other parties; and

- Filing any such pleading and serving it on the plaintiff constitutes notice of the pleading to all parties. FRCP 5(c)(1).

     ii.  *Notifying parties.* A copy of every such order must be served on the parties as the court directs. FRCP 5(c)(2).

## G. Hearings

1. Refer to the General Requirements section of this document for information on pretrial conferences, scheduling conferences, and discovery planning conferences.

## H. Forms

**1. Federal Pretrial Conferences, Scheduling, Management Forms**

   a.  Plaintiff's informal summary of status of case to court before pretrial conference in complex case. 2C FEDFORMS § 15:31.

   b.  Joint pretrial report. 2C FEDFORMS § 15:32.

   c.  Joint statement of undisputed facts. 2C FEDFORMS § 15:33.

   d.  Joint statement of disputed facts. 2C FEDFORMS § 15:34.

   e.  Joint report of counsel prior to pretrial conference. 2C FEDFORMS § 15:35.

   f.  Plaintiff's list of exhibits to be offered at trial. 2C FEDFORMS § 15:38.

   g.  Defendant's list of prospective witnesses. 2C FEDFORMS § 15:39.

   h.  Designation of witnesses whom plaintiff intends to call at trial pursuant to pretrial conference oral stipulation. 2C FEDFORMS § 15:40.

   i.  Defendant's list of prospective exhibits. 2C FEDFORMS § 15:42.

   j.  Report of parties' planning meeting. 3A FEDFORMS § 21:93.

   k.  Report of parties' discovery conference. 3A FEDFORMS § 21:94.

   l.  Report of parties' discovery conference; Outline structure. 3A FEDFORMS § 21:95.

   m.  Joint scheduling report. 3A FEDFORMS § 21:96.

   n.  Stipulation and order regarding discovery conference discussions. 3A FEDFORMS § 21:97.

   o.  Pretrial statement; By plaintiff; Automobile collision involving corporate defendant. FEDPROF § 1C:295.

   p.  Pretrial statement; By defendant; Automobile collision. FEDPROF § 1C:296.

   q.  Pretrial statement; By parties jointly; Automobile collision. FEDPROF § 1C:297.

   r.  Pretrial statement; Provision; Waiver of abandoned claims or defenses. FEDPROF § 1C:298.

   s.  Status report. GOLDLTGFMS § 34:2.

   t.  Preliminary pretrial checklist. GOLDLTGFMS § 34:3.

   u.  Pretrial memorandum. GOLDLTGFMS § 34:4.

   v.  Pretrial memorandum; Plaintiff. GOLDLTGFMS § 34:5.

   w.  Pretrial memorandum; Defendant. GOLDLTGFMS § 34:6.

   x.  Pretrial memorandum; Short form. GOLDLTGFMS § 34:7.

   y.  Pretrial memorandum; Civil action. GOLDLTGFMS § 34:8.

   z.  Pretrial memorandum; Worker's compensation case. GOLDLTGFMS § 34:9.

**2. Forms for the District of Massachusetts**

   a.  Notice of scheduling conference. MA R USDCT App. D.

b. Notice of filing with clerk's office. MA R USDCT CM/ECF Admin(Appendix I).

# I. Applicable Rules

1. *Federal rules*

   a. Serving and filing pleadings and other papers. FRCP 5.

   b. Privacy protection for filings made with the court. FRCP 5.2.

   c. Computing and extending time; Time for motion papers. FRCP 6.

   d. Pleadings allowed; Form of motions and other papers. FRCP 7.

   e. Form of pleadings. FRCP 10.

   f. Signing pleadings, motions, and other papers; Representations to the court; Sanctions. FRCP 11.

   g. Pretrial conferences; Scheduling; Management. FRCP 16.

   h. Duty to disclose; General provisions governing discovery. FRCP 26.

   i. Failure to make disclosures or to cooperate in discovery; Sanctions. FRCP 37.

2. *Local rules*

   a. Title. MA R USDCT LR 1.1.

   b. Sanctions. MA R USDCT LR 1.3.

   c. Form and filing of papers. MA R USDCT LR 5.1.

   d. Service and filing of pleadings and other papers. MA R USDCT LR 5.2.

   e. Filing and service by electronic means. MA R USDCT LR 5.4.

   f. Early assessment of cases. MA R USDCT LR 16.1.

   g. Exemptions from FRCP 16(b). MA R USDCT LR 16.2.

   h. Case management conferences. MA R USDCT LR 16.3.

   i. Alternative dispute resolution. MA R USDCT LR 16.4.

   j. Final pretrial conference. MA R USDCT LR 16.5.

   k. Control of discovery. MA R USDCT LR 26.1.

   l. Special procedures for handling experts. MA R USDCT LR 26.4.

   m. Payments and deposits made with the clerk. MA R USDCT LR 67.4.

   n. Settlement. MA R USDCT LR 68.2.

   o. Office of the clerk. MA R USDCT LR 77.2.

   p. Appearances. MA R USDCT LR 83.5.2.

   q. Practice by pro se litigants. MA R USDCT LR 83.5.5.

   r. CM/ECF case management/electronic case files administrative procedures. MA R USDCT CM/ECF Admin.

# Appendix - Related Court Documents

# Complaint

2015 WL 13665887 (D.Mass.)

**Westlaw Query>>**

To find more Complaint filings on Westlaw: access Massachusetts Civil Trial Court Documents (from the Home page, click Trial Court Documents, then Massachusetts), click the Advanced Search link, select Complaint, and click Search. Use the Jurisdiction filter on the left to narrow results to Federal.

United States District Court, D. Massachusetts.

Joseph POZZATO, Jr., Plaintiff,

v.

Elizabeth A. Tynan MORIARTY and Paul C. Tynan, Defendants.

No. 15CV14150.

December 16, 2015.

## Complaint

Timothy L. O'Keefe, BBO No. 561873, Kenny, O'Keefe & Usseglio, P.C., 21 Oak Street, Suite 208, Hartford, CT 06160, (860) 246-2700, tokeefe@kou-law.com, for the plaintiff, Joseph Pozzato.

### Jurisdiction and Venue

1. The plaintiff, Joseph Pozzato, Jr., is a citizen of the State of Connecticut.

2. The defendants, Elizabeth A. Tynan Moriarty and Paul C. Tynan are citizens of the Commonwealth of Massachusetts.

3. Jurisdiction of the Court is based on diversity of citizenship of parties, 28 U.S.C. § 1332.

4. The amount in controversy exceeds $75,000.00, exclusive of interest and costs.

5. Venue is this District is based on 28 U.S.C. § 1391.

### Factual Allegations

1. On May 9, 2013, at approximately 3:00 p.m., the plaintiff, Joseph Pozzato, Jr., in his capacity as an invitee, was in the process of exiting his vehicle, which had been parked in a designated parking space, in a parking lot located at 535 College Highway, Southwick, Massachusetts,

2. After the plaintiff stepped out of his motor vehicle, he was caused to lose his footing, fall backwards and roll down the paved embankment abutting the parking space where he had parked his car due to a hazardous condition, namely a steep surface slope.

3. At all relevant times, the defendants, Elizabeth A. Tynan Moriarty and Paul C. Tynan, owned, controlled, maintained, managed, operated, and/or possessed the bcation where the plaintiff fell.

4. The plaintiffs fall and resulting injuries were caused by the negligence and carelessness of the defendants, Elizabeth A. Tynan Moriarty and Paul C. Tynan, in one or more than one of the following ways:

    a. In that the defendants failed to remedy or correct the hazardous condition in the parking lot when they could and should have done so;

    b. In that the defendants failed to warn the plaintiff and other patrons of the hazardous condition in the parking lot;

    c. In that the defendants failed to utilize cones, barriers, signs or other visible means of warning the plaintiff and other patrons of the presence of the hazardous condition;

    d. In that the defendants failed to conduct, or caused to be conducted, proper inspections of the parking lot; and

e. In that the defendants knew, or had reason to know, of the hazardous condition but failed to take proper steps to repair and/or remedy same.

5. As a result of this incident, the plaintiff was caused to sustain and suffer painful injuries to his head, right knee, right elbow, left ankle and left elbow as well as an aggravation or exacerbation of a pre-existing injury and/or condition of his left ankle. Some or all of these injuries and their effects are, or will likely prove to be, permanent in nature.

6. As a result, the plaintiff has been caused to suffer from shock, fright, nervousness, anxiety and emotional distress, and will likely suffer from same for the rest of his life.

7. As a further result, the plaintiff's ability to enjoy life and carry on his usual activities, hobbies and recreations have been impaired, and will likely continue to be Impaired for the rest of his life.

8. As a further result, the plaintiff has been forced to incur expenses for hospital and medical care, x-rays, medicines, physical therapy and the like, and will likely be forced to incur further expenses for the same purposes in the future.

9. As a further result, the plaintiff has suffered, and may continue to suffer for he rest of his life from fear, anxiety and emotional distress relative to his concern that here may be additional or continued medical problems, surgeries, procedures, complications and/or impairments as a result of the incident of May 9, 2013.

10. As a further result, the plaintiff has increased likelihood of future medical problems, complications, impairments and/or surgeries.

## JURY DEMAND

The plaintiff hereby demands a jury trial.

**WHEREFORE,** the Plaintiff demands:

1. Compensatory damages in the amount of $500,000.00;

2. Any and all other equitable relief, in accordance with the claims of the Plaintiff, as the Court deems appropriate.

THE PLAINTIFF,

JOSEPH POZZATO

BY: <<signature>>

Timothy L. O'Keefe

BBO No. 561873

Kenny, O'Keefe & Usseglio, P.C.

21 Oak Street, Suite 208

Hartford, CT 06160

(860) 246-2700

tokeefe@kou-law.com

# Answer

2018 WL 3596794 (D.Mass.)

United States District Court, D. Massachusetts.

Drew KATZ and Melissa Silver, individually and as the co-Personal Representatives of the Estate of Lewis A. Katz, deceased, Plaintiffs,

v.

SPINIELLO COMPANIES, a New Jersey Corporation; SK Travel, LLC, a North Carolina Limited Liability Company; Arizin Ventures, LLC, a Delaware Limited Liability Company; Carol McDowell, in her capacity as Personal Representative of the Estate of James McDowell, deceased, a resident of Delaware; Shelly De Vries, in her capacity as Personal Representative of the Estate of Bauke De Vries, deceased, a resident of New Jersey; Gulfstream Aerospace Corporation, a Georgia Corporation; Gulfstream Aerospace Corporation, a Delaware Corporation; Gulfstream Aerospace Services Corporation, d/b/a Gulfstream Aerospace Corporation, a Delaware Corporation; Rockwell Collins, Inc., an Iowa Corporation; Honeywell International, Inc., a Delaware Corporation; and the Massachusetts Port Authority, an independent public authority of the Commonwealth of Massachusetts, Defendants,

SK TRAVEL, LLC, Spiniello Companies, and Arizin Ventures, LLC, Third-Party Plaintiffs,

v.

UNITED STATES OF AMERICA, Third-Party Defendant.

No. 16-cv-11380- DJC.

June 5, 2018.

Arizin Ventures, LLC's Answer to Crossclaims of Defendant Carol McDowell, in Her Capacity as Personal Representative of the Estate of James McDowell

James A. Ruggieri, Esq., #433770, Higgins, Cavanagh & Cooney, LLP, 10 Dorrance Street, Suite 400, Providence, RI 02903, Tel: 401-272-3500, jruggieri@hcc-law.com, for defendant, Arizin Ventures, LLC.

J. Denny Shupe, Esquire (admitted pro hac vice), Schnader Harrison Segal & Lewis LLP, 1600 Market Street, Suite 3600,

Philadelphia, PA 19103, Tel: 215-751-2300, Fax: 215-972-7413, Of Counsel.

Defendant Arizin Ventures, LLC ("Arizin"), by and through its undersigned counsel, responds to the Crossclaims of Defendant Carol McDowell, in her capacity as Personal Representative of the Estate of James McDowell (the "McDowell Estate"), as follows:

539. Arizin admits that Arizin had a lease agreement with SK Travel relating to the subject aircraft at the time of the accident. The lease agreement with SK Travel is set forth in a document that speaks for itself and any characterization of it is therefore denied. The remaining allegations in paragraph 539 are conclusions of law to which no response is required.

540. Arizin admits that Arizin had a lease agreement with SK Travel relating to the subject aircraft at the time of the accident. The lease agreement with SK Travel is set forth in a document that speaks for itself and any characterization of it is therefore denied. The remaining allegations in paragraph 540 are conclusions of law to which no response is required.

541. Arizin admits that Arizin had a lease agreement with SK Travel relating to the subject aircraft at the time of the accident. The lease agreement with SK Travel is set forth in a document that speaks for itself and any characterization of it is therefore denied. The remaining allegations in paragraph 541 are conclusions of law to which no response is required.

542. Arizin admits that plaintiffs' decedent, Lewis Katz, selected the itinerary for the accident flight and that on May 30, 2014, Kathleen Palella, Executive Assistant to Lewis Katz, sent the itinerary for the accident flight to SK Travel to fly Lewis Katz roundtrip from Atlantic City International Airport in Atlantic City, New Jersey, to L.G. Hanscom Field in Bedford, Massachusetts. The remaining allegations in paragraph 542 are conclusions of law to which no response is required.

543. Paragraph 543 is comprised of conclusions of law to which no response is required.

544. Admitted.

545. Paragraph 545 is comprised of conclusions of law to which no response is required.

546. Arizin denies that the McDowell Estate is entitled to a judgment against Arizin for common law and contractual indemnification.

547. Arizin restates and incorporates by reference its answers to Paragraphs 539 through 546 as if set forth fully herein.

548. Paragraph 548 is comprised of conclusions of law to which no response is required.

549. Paragraph 549 is comprised of conclusions of law to which no response is required.

550. Paragraph 550 is comprised of conclusions of law to which no response is required.

Arizin denies that the McDowell Estate is entitled to judgment in its favor over Arizin for contribution and indemnification and denies that the McDowell Estate is entitled to any damages, costs or other relief as alleged in its prayer for relief.

### AFFIRMATIVE DEFENSES

Arizin asserts the following affirmative defenses, and reserves the right to assert additional defenses to the extent such defenses become known through discovery or otherwise.

### FIRST AFFIRMATIVE DEFENSE

The McDowell Estate's crossclaims have failed to state a claim against Arizin upon which relief can be granted.

### SECOND AFFIRMATIVE DEFENSE

To the extent that the McDowell Estate's crossclaims for contribution and indemnification are based upon plaintiffs' claims against Arizin as alleged in plaintiffs' Second Amended Complaint, Arizin incorporates all of its affirmative defenses to plaintiffs' Second Amended Complaint as if fully set forth herein and asserted against the McDowell Estate.

### THIRD AFFIRMATIVE DEFENSE

Arizin alleges that it presently has insufficient knowledge or information regarding other affirmative defenses, and therefore Arizin reserves the right to assert additional defenses that may be discovered through the course of litigation and discovery.

WHEREFORE, Defendant Arizin Ventures, LLC demands judgment dismissing the McDowell Estate's crossclaims against it, with prejudice, in their entirety or, alternatively, judgment limiting its liability pursuant to the foregoing, and that this Court grant Arizin Ventures, LLC an award of the costs and disbursements of the within action and any other relief this Court may deem just and proper.

Date: June 5, 2018

Respectfully submitted,

Attorneys for Defendant, Arizin Ventures, LLC

*/s/ James A. Ruggieri*

James A. Ruggieri, Esq., #433770

**HIGGINS, CAVANAGH & COONEY, LLP**

10 Dorrance Street, Suite 400

Providence, RI 02903

Tel: 401-272-3500

jruggieri@hcc-law.com

*Of Counsel:*

J. Denny Shupe, Esquire (admitted *pro hac vice*)

**SCHNADER HARRISON SEGAL & LEWIS LLP**

1600 Market Street, Suite 3600

Philadelphia, PA 19103

Tel: 215-751-2300

Fax: 215-972-7413

# Amended Pleading

2018 WL 6039401 (D.Mass.)

**Westlaw Query>>**

To find more Amended Pleading filings on Westlaw: access Massachusetts Civil Trial Court Documents (from the Home page, click Trial Court Documents, then Massachusetts), enter "DT(amended and complaint answer)" in the search box, and click Search. Use the Jurisdiction filter on the left to narrow results to Federal.

United States District Court, D. Massachusetts.

Andre VYSEDSKIY, Plaintiff,

v.

ONSHIFT, INC.; and Company A, Defendants.

No. 1:16-cv-12161-MLW.

July 26, 2018.

## First Amended Complaint

For this Complaint, the Plaintiff, Andre Vysedskiy, by undersigned counsel, states as follows:

### JURISDICTION

1. This Court has jurisdiction over this matter pursuant to the Telephone Consumer Protection Act, 47 U.S.C. § 227, *et. seq.* (the "TCPA"), and under the doctrine of supplemental jurisdiction as set forth in 28 U.S.C. § 1367.

2. Venue is proper in this District pursuant to 28 U.S.C. § 1391(b), in that the Defendants transact business in this District and a substantial portion of the acts giving rise to this action occurred in this District.

### PARTIES

3. The Plaintiff, Andre Vysedskiy ("Plaintiff"), is an adult individual residing in Brookline, Massachusetts, and is a "person" as defined by 47 U.S.C. § 153(39).

4. Defendant OnShift, Inc. ("OnShift"), is an Ohio business entity with an address of 1621 Euclid Avenue, #1500, Cleveland, Ohio 44115, and is a "person" as defined by 47 U.S.C. § 153(39).

5. OnShift is in the business of providing software that assists OnShift's customers with their needs for hiring and scheduling shifts.

6. OnShift's customers are long-term care and senior living facilities.

7. Twenty (20) such customers are located within the Commonwealth of Massachusetts, comprising about 5% of OnShift's total customer base.

8. OnShift regularly solicits customers in Massachusetts.

9. Currently OnShift derives about 3-3.5% of its revenue from Massachusetts.

10. Defendant COMPANY A (hereafter "COMPANY A," and together with OnShift, the "Defendants") is one of OnShift's Massachusetts-based customers.[1]

"In response to your question below, yes, the OnShift customer who made the alleged calls does business and is located in both Suffolk and Essex counties."

---

1. As set forth in Dk. 55, for purpose of resolving pending discovery disputes pending before Judge Cabell, OnShift has represented by email dated May 11, 2018, OnShift's Counsel has confirmed as follows:

Plaintiff was satisfied with this representation for purposes of resolving the jurisdictional discovery disputes. Plaintiff reserved the right to compel OnShift to identify the customer, by name.

11. COMPANY A does business and is located in Massachusetts; it does business and is located in both Suffolk and Essex counties.

12. COMPANY A will be joined as a party once its identity is disclosed through discovery.

## *FACTS*

### A. *COMPANY A's Use of OnShift's Software*

13. OnShift is a developer and seller of software that provides its customers with predictive tools to assist with the scheduling of employees, forecasting overtime to lower costs, mitigating risk with labor budget management, and filling openings to staff shifts appropriately.

14. COMPANY A, a long term care facility, uses OnShift's software.

15. Specifically, COMPANY A used OnShift's software to compile information from its employees regarding those employees' preferred dates and times for working open shifts.

16. COMPANY A then uploaded that information into OnShift's software, which then matched open shifts with employees who previously expressed a preference for those particular shifts.

17. COMPANY A then used OnShift's software to contact individuals directly via robocalls and pre-recorded and artificial messages delivered to cellular telephones.

### B. *Robocalls to Plaintiff*

18. For an unknown reason, Plaintiff's cellular telephone number 617-xxx-1916 made its way into COMPANY A's database and then into OnShift's computer dialing system.

19. Plaintiff has no business relationship of any sort with OnShift or COMPANY A. Plaintiff has never had such a relationship.

20. Thereafter and within the last four years, Defendants placed more than 200 calls to Plaintiff's cellular telephone, number 617-xxx-1916, by using an automated telephone dialer system ("ATDS") and/or by using an artificial or prerecorded voice. Attached as *Exhibit A* is Plaintiff's call history log reflecting him receiving over 150 calls from the Defendants.

21. Plaintiff received calls from Defendants from telephone numbers 216-820-9202 and 216-438-5120, several of which appear in Plaintiff's call log, *Illustration 1*.

22. According to public databases, these numbers belong to OnShift.

23. Defendants left prerecorded messages on Plaintiff's cellular telephone which stated in part the following:

> "Hello, this is a call from OnShift, opening at 'COMPANY A' for [north] shift from 11:00 PM to 7:30 AM on January 31. Press '1' for 'YES', '2' for 'NO', or '3' to repeat this message, or, if this is a voice mail, please call your scheduler for more information."

24. OnShift's software controls COMPANY A's capability to generate such prerecorded message and COMPANY A generated such pre-recorded message.

25. The messages were delivered from Massachusetts, by COMPANY A, using OnShift's computer dialing system.

26. In the alternative, the messages were delivered by OnShift on behalf of COMPANY A to Plaintiff.

27. The pre-recorded messages Plaintiff received did not state a phone number to reach a "scheduler."

28. The pre-recorded messages Plaintiff received always stated, "This is a call from OnShift" and informed of a shift opening at "COMPANY A."

29. Defendants' pre-recorded messages failed to present Plaintiff with an option to opt out of receiving Defendants' robocalls.

30. When Plaintiff called the phone numbers that appeared on his caller ID and cellular telephone logs, 216-820-9202 and 216-438-5120, he heard a recording stating "You have reached an unattended line at OnShift. Please contact your scheduler for more information."

31. Plaintiff then called OnShift and directed Defendants to cease all calls to his cellular telephone, but the calls continued, as OnShift failed cease calling and failed to instruct COMPANY A to cease all calls to Plaintiff.

32. In August of 2016 Plaintiff, through his counsel, contacted OnShift and instructed it to cease all calls to his cellular telephone.

33. The calls from OnShift nonetheless persisted.

34. Plaintiff never provided his cellular telephone number to OnShift or COMPANY A and never provided his consent to Defendants to be contacted on his cellular telephone.

## COUNT I

### VIOLATIONS OF THE TCPA - 47 U.S.C. § 227, et seq.

35. The Plaintiff incorporates by reference all of the above paragraphs of this Complaint as though fully stated herein.

36. Without prior express consent, Defendants contacted Plaintiff on his cellular telephone using an automatic telephone dialing system ("ATDS") and/or by using artificial messages in violation of 47 U.S.C. § 227(b)(1)(A)(iii).

37. The calls from Defendants to Plaintiff were not placed for "emergency purposes" as defined by 47 U.S.C. § 227(b)(1)(A)(i).

38. Plaintiff never provided express consent to Defendants to place automated calls to his cellular telephone number.

39. Moreover, Plaintiff directed Defendants to cease all calls to his cellular telephone.

40. Defendants placed automated calls to Plaintiff's cellular telephone knowing that it lacked consent to call his telephone number. As such, each call placed to Plaintiff was made in knowing and/or willful violation of the TCPA and is subject to treble damages pursuant to 47 U.S.C. § 227(b)(3)(C).

41. Plaintiff is entitled to an award of $500.00 in statutory damages for each call placed in violation of the TCPA pursuant to 47 U.S.C. § 227(b)(3)(B).

42. As a result of each call made in knowing and/or willful violation of the TCPA, Plaintiff is entitled to an award of treble damages in an amount up to $1,500.00 pursuant to 47 U.S.C. § 227(b)(3)(B) and 47 U.S.C. § 227(b)(3)(C).

## COUNT II

### VIOLATION OF THE MASSACHUSETTS CONSUMER PROTECTION ACT, M.G.L. c. 93A § 2, et seq. (as to OnShift)

43. The Plaintiff incorporates by reference all of the above paragraphs of this Complaint as though fully stated herein.

44. The Defendants employed unfair or deceptive acts in trade or commerce, in violation of M.G.L. c. 93A § 2.

45. Defendant's failure to comply with these provisions constitutes an unfair or deceptive act under M.G.L. c. 93A § 9 and, as such, the Plaintiff is entitled to double or treble damages plus reasonable attorney's fees.

## COUNT III

### INVASION OF PRIVACY BY INTRUSION UPON SECLUSION (as to both Defendants)

46. The Plaintiff incorporates by reference all of the above paragraphs of this Complaint as though fully stated herein.

47. The Restatement of Torts, Second, § 652(b) defines intrusion upon seclusion as, "One who intentionally intrudes...upon the solitude or seclusion of another, or his private affairs or concerns, is subject to liability to the other for invasion of privacy, if the intrusion would be highly offensive to a reasonable person."

48. Massachusetts further recognizes the Plaintiff's right to be free from invasions of privacy, thus Defendants violated Massachusetts state law.

49. The Defendants intentionally intruded upon Plaintiff's right to privacy by continually harassing the Plaintiff with continues pre-recorded messages to his cellular telephone despite Plaintiff's request for the calls to stop.

50. The telephone calls made by Defendants to the Plaintiff were so persistent and repeated with such frequency as to be considered, "hounding the plaintiff," and, "a substantial burden to her existence," thus satisfying the Restatement of Torts, Second, § 652(b) requirement for an invasion of privacy.

51. The conduct of the Defendants in placing over 200 robocalls to his cellular telephone resulted in multiple invasions of privacy in such a way as would be considered highly offensive to a reasonable person.

52. As a result of the intrusions and invasions, the Plaintiff is entitled to actual damages in an amount to be determined at trial from Defendants.

53. All acts of Defendants were committed with malice, intent, wantonness, and recklessness, and as such, Defendants are subject to punitive damages.

## COUNT IV

### INTENTIONAL INFLICTION OF EMOTIONAL DISTRESS (as to both Defendants)

54. The Plaintiff incorporates by reference all of the above paragraphs of this Complaint as though fully set forth herein at length.

55. The acts, practices and conduct engaged in by the Defendants vis-a`-vis the Plaintiff was so outrageous in character, and so extreme in degree, as to go beyond all possible bounds of decency, and to be regarded as atrocious, and utterly intolerable in a civilized community.

56. The foregoing conduct constitutes the tort of intentional infliction of emotional distress under the laws of the State of Massachusetts.

57. All acts of Defendants complained of herein were committed with malice, intent, wantonness, and recklessness, and as such, Defendants are subject to imposition of punitive damages.

### PRAYER FOR RELIEF

WHEREFORE, the Plaintiff prays that judgment be entered against the Defendants as follows:

   A.  Find Defendants jointly and severally liable on all causes of action;

   B.  Statutory damages of $500.00 for each violation determined to be negligent pursuant to 47 U.S.C. § 227(b)(3)(B);

   C.  Treble damages for each violation determined to be willful and/or knowing pursuant to 47 U.S.C. § 227(b)(3)(C);

   D.  Punitive damages;

   E.  Reasonable attorney fees and costs; and

   F.  Such other and further relief as may be just and proper.

**TRIAL BY JURY DEMANDED ON ALL COUNTS**

Dated: July 26, 2018

*/s/ Sergei Lemberg*

Sergei Lemberg, Esq. (BBO# 650671)

LEMBERG LAW L.L.C.

43 Danbury Road

Wilton, CT 06897

Telephone: (203) 653-2250

Facsimile: (203) 653-3424

slemberg@lemberglaw.com

# Motion to Strike

2018 WL 3579382 (D.Mass.)

United States District Court, D. Massachusetts.

DESKTOP METAL, INC., Plaintiff and Counterclaim Defendant,

v.

MARKFORGED, INC. and Matiu Parangi, Defendants and Counterclaim Plaintiff (Markforged, Inc.),

v.

Ricardo FULOP, Jonah Myerberg, Boston Impact LLC, and Amy Buntel, Third-Party Defendants.

No. 1:18-cv-10524-WGY.

May 11, 2018.

Plaintiff Desktop Metal, Inc.'s Memorandum of Law in Support of Motion to Strike Defenses from Defendant Matiu Parangi's Answer

William Trach (Bar No. 661401), Charles H. Sanders (Bar No. 646740), Christopher Henry (Bar No. 676033), Nathanial J. McPherson (Bar No. 697666), Latham & Watkins LLP, 200 Clarendon Street, Floor 27, Boston, MA 02116, T: (617) 948-6000; F: (617) 948-6001, charles.sanders@lw.com, william.trach@lw.com, christopher.henry@lw.com, nathanial.mcpherson@lw.com; Adam M. Greenfield (pro hac vice), Latham & Watkins LLP, 555 Eleventh Street, NW, Suite 1000, Washington, DC 20004, T: (202) 637-2200; F: (202) 637-2201, adam.greenfield@lw.com, for plaintiff and counterclaim defendant, Desktop Metal, Inc.

Pursuant to Federal Rule of Civil Procedure 12(f), Plaintiff and Counterclaim Defendant Desktop Metal, Inc. ("Desktop Metal") submits this memorandum in support of its Motion to Strike certain defenses asserted by Defendant Matiu Parangi ("Mr. Parangi") in his Answer to Desktop Metal's Complaint.

On March 19, 2018, Desktop Metal filed this action against Markforged and Mr. Parangi, a former employee of Desktop Metal. Desktop Metal asserted claims for misappropriation of trade secrets, unfair business practices, and breach of non-disclosure and non-competition agreements, among others. Although Desktop Metal's claims against Mr. Parangi are based largely on a discrete incident in October 2016 where Mr. Parangi surreptitiously downloaded Desktop Metal documents containing proprietary information—documents that he had no reason to view, no less download, in his role as an intern on the "print farm"—through discovery, Desktop Metal will investigate where Mr. Parangi engaged in other instances of misconduct as well.

On April 20, Mr. Parangi filed his Answer to Desktop Metal's Complaint, asserting 18 affirmative and other defenses. *See* Dkt. No. 44 (Answer). These defenses fall far short of the requisite pleading standard, do not given Desktop Metal adequate notice of how Mr. Parangi will defend against the claims, and should be stricken from Mr. Parangi's Answer: unclean hands (First Defense), lack of standing (Second Defense), no entitlement to injunctive relief (Third Defense), more definite statement required (Fifth Defense), invalid trade secret (Sixth Defense), no misappropriation (Seventh Defense), no breach of contract (Eighth Defense), no unfair competition (Ninth Defense), express and/or implied license and permission (Tenth Defense), unenforceable obligations (Eleventh Defense), no breach of the covenant of good faith and fair dealing (Twelfth Defense), no enhanced, punitive, or fee shifting damages are warranted (Thirteenth Defense), waiver and/or estoppel (Fourteenth Defense), acquiescence (Fifteenth Defense), failure to mitigate (Sixteenth Defense), innocent and non-willful (Seventeenth Defense), and invalid or illegal contracts (Eighteenth Defense).[1]

Rule 12(f) permits the Court to "strike from a pleading an insufficient defense or any redundant, immaterial, impertinent, or scandalous matter." Fed. R. Civ. P. 12(f). A motion to strike under this rule is "governed by the same standards as a motion to dismiss filed pursuant to Fed. R. Civ. P. 12(b)(6)" and thus should be granted "if the pleadings fail to support a plausible entitlement to relief." *E.g., Bryan Corp. v. Chemwerth, Inc.*, 2013 WL 6489785, at *1 (D. Mass. Dec. 9, 2013) (internal quotations and citations omitted). Under Rule 12(b)(6), a complaint must allege "factual content that allows the court to draw the reasonable inference that the defendant is liable for the misconduct alleged," *Ashcroft v. Iqbal*, 129 S. Ct. 1937, 1949 (2009), and "to raise a right to relief above the speculative level." *Bell Atl. Corp. v. Twombly*, 550 U.S. 544, 555 (2007). "[T]hreadbare recitals of a cause of action's elements, supported by mere conclusory statements . . . are not entitled to the assumption of truth." *Iqbal*, 556 U.S. at 662 (citation omitted). Thus, a complaint that "tenders 'naked assertion[s]' devoid of 'further factual enhancement'" will not survive a motion to dismiss. *Iqbal*, 556 U.S. at 678 (quoting *Twombly*, 550 U.S. at 557).

The Court should strike all of the defenses listed above because they consist of nothing more than mere "labels and conclusions" without any reference to, let alone satisfaction of, the subsidiary elements of each defense. *Twombly*, 550 U.S. at 555. The First Defense for unclean hands, for example, alleges nothing more than, "Desktop Metal's claims and/or requested relief are barred, in whole or in part, under the doctrine of unclean hands." Dkt. No. 44 at 12 (Answer). Mr. Parangi does not plead any factual allegations regarding alleged wrongful conduct by Desktop Metal.[2] Moreover, he has pleaded no "immediate and necessary relation to the equity that [Desktop Metal] seeks in respect of the matter in litigation." *Gilead Scis.*, No. 2016-2302, slip op. at 13; *see also Bryan*, 2013 WL 6489785, at *2-3 (striking unclean hands defense and quoting *Amerada Hess Corp. v. Garabedian*, 617 N.E.2d 630, 634 (Mass. 1993)). Unlike in *Gilead* where the unclean hands defense had "a direct connection to the ultimate patent litigation" because the "knowledge" "acquired improperly" "influenced" "filing of narrowed [patent] claims," which "held the potential for expediting patent issuance and for lowering certain invalidity risks," slip op. at 13, here Mr. Parangi alleges *no connection whatsoever* to the claims against him in the Complaint. Dkt. No. 44 at 12 (Answer). Every one of Mr. Parangi's defenses is a similarly bare bones legal conclusion, without subsidiary factual allegations "to raise a right to relief above the speculative level." *Twombly*, 550 U.S. at 555. For example, there is no explanation of what Mr. Parangi's Second Defense for "Lack of Standing" is based on, or what the Fifth Defense for a "More Definite Statement Required" is seeking. Dkt. No. 44 at 12-13 (Answer). The same is true with respect to all of the defenses listed above. Desktop Metal cannot adequately defend against Mr. Parangi's arguments if it has no notice of what Mr. Parangi seeks to establish.

Desktop Metal respectfully requests that the Court strike the First through Third and Fifth through Eighteenth Defenses from Mr. Parangi's Answer.

Dated: May 11, 2018

Respectfully submitted,

LATHAM & WATKINS LLP

*/s/ William J. Trach*

William Trach (Bar No. 661401)

Charles H. Sanders (Bar No. 646740)

Christopher Henry (Bar No. 676033)

Nathanial J. McPherson (Bar No. 697666)

LATHAM & WATKINS LLP

200 Clarendon Street, Floor 27

Boston, MA 02116

T: (617) 948-6000; F: (617) 948-6001

charles.sanders@lw.com

---

1. The only defense that this motion does not seek to strike is the Fourth Defense for failure to state a claim, because Mr. Parangi has already filed a motion to dismiss under Rule 12(b)(6).

2. To the extent that Mr. Parangi's unclean hands defense is based on alleged "fraud or mistake," he needed to "state with particularity the circumstances constituting fraud or mistake." Fed. R. Civ. P. 9(b); *see also PetEdge, Inc. v. Marketfleet Sourcing, Inc.*, 2017 WL 2983086, at *4—5 (D. Mass. July 12, 2017).

william.trach@lw.com

christopher.henry@lw.com

nathanial.mcpherson@lw.com

Adam M. Greenfield (pro hac vice)

LATHAM & WATKINS LLP

555 Eleventh Street, NW, Suite 1000

Washington, DC 20004

T: (202) 637-2200; F: (202) 637-2201

adam.greenfield@lw.com

ATTORNEYS FOR PLAINTIFF AND COUNTERCLAIM DEFENDANT

DESKTOP METAL, INC.

# Motion to Dismiss for Improper Venue

2017 WL 6760273 (D.Mass.)

United States District Court, D. Massachusetts.

REALTIME DATA LLC,

v.

CARBONITE, INC., et al.

No. 1:17CV12499.

June 7, 2017.

Defendant EVault, Inc's Motion to Dismiss Under Rule 12(b)(3) for Improper Venue

Max Ciccarelli, State Bar No. 00787242, Max.Ciccarelli@tklaw.com, Michael E. Schonberg, State Bar No. 00784927, Mike.Schonberg@tklaw.com, Nadia E. Haghighatian, State Bar No. 24087652, Nadia.Haghighatian@tklaw.com, Thompson & Knight LLP, One Arts Plaza, 1722 Routh Street, Suite 1500, Dallas, Texas 75201, 214.969.1700, 214.969.1751 (Fax), for defendant EVault, Inc.

Note: This document was obtained from the above titled case. (PDF information below.)

Court: United States District Court, E.D. Texas, Tyler Division.

Title: REALTIME DATA LLC d/b/a Ixo, Plaintiff, v. CARBONITE, INC. and EVault, Inc., Defendants.

Docket Number: No. 6:17-cv-121.

Date: June 7, 2017.

## TABLE OF CONTENTS

## TABLE OF AUTHORITIES
### Cases

## I. Introduction

Realtime cannot bear its burden of establishing that venue is proper as to EVault in the Eastern District of Texas under 28 U.S.C. § 1400(b) and the Supreme Court's recent holding in *TC Heartland*.[1] To do so, Realtime must show that EVault either (1) resides in this district, or (2) committed acts of infringement *and* has a regular and established place of business in this district. But EVault does not reside in this district because it is not incorporated in Texas, nor does EVault have a regular and established place of business in this district because it does not have a permanent and continuous presence here. Thus, venue in this district is improper as to EVault, and the Court should dismiss all of Realtime's claims against EVault pursuant to Rule 12(b)(3) of the Federal Rules of Civil Procedure.

## II. Statement of the Issue to be Decided

Whether the Court should dismiss all of Realtime's claims against EVault in this case because venue is improper as to EVault in the Eastern District of Texas.[2]

## III. Legal Standards

### A. Standard for motion to dismiss under Rule 12(b)(3).

Dismissal is appropriate under Rule 12(b)(3) when the plaintiff has initiated a lawsuit in an improper venue. When ruling on a motion to dismiss pursuant to Rule 12(b)(3), a court should resolve all factual allegations in the complaint in the plaintiff's favor. *Braspetro Oil Servs. Co. v. Modec (USA), Inc.*, 240 F. App'x 612, 615 (5th Cir. 2007). *However*, once a defendant has objected to the plaintiff's chosen venue, "the burden shifts to the plaintiff to establish that the district he chose is a proper venue." *Mass Eng'g, Inc. v. 9X Media, Inc.*, No. 2--09--cv--358, 2010 WL 2991018, at *1 (E.D. Tex. July 28, 2010).

Also, because venue requirements exist for the benefit of defendants, when there are multiple defendants in an action, venue is considered as to each defendant individually. *See Hoover Grp., Inc. v. Custom Metalcraft, Inc.*, 84 F.3d 1408, 1410 (Fed. Cir. 1996) ("When the cause of action is personal to the individual defendant, the venue requirement must be met as to that defendant."); *see also, e.g.*, *Pope v. Chase/EMC Mortg.*, No. 4:15cv20, 2015 WL 1926022, at *2 (E.D. Tex. Apr. 27, 2015) (holding that "once a defendant has objected to venue, the burden shifts to the plaintiff to establish that venue is proper *as to each defendant and each claim*" (emphasis added)).

### B. Standard for proper venue in a patent-infringement case.

The patent-venue statute, 28 U. S. C. § 1400(b), provides that venue is proper only in the judicial districts (1) "where the defendant resides," or (2) "where the defendant has committed acts of infringement and has a regular and established place of business." For purposes of § 1400(b), where the defendant resides "refers only to the State of incorporation." *TC Heartland*, 2017 WL 2216934, at *8.

---

1. *See TC Heartland LLC v. Kraft Foods Group Brands LLC*, No. 16--341, 2017 WL 2216934 (May 22, 2017).

2. There are two defendants in this case--Carbonite and EVault. The instant motion relates only to Realtime's claims against EVault; however, Carbonite separately filed its own Motion to Dismiss for Improper Venue based on similar grounds. *See* Dkt. No. 32.

## IV. Argument

### A. The Court should dismiss all claims against EVault pursuant to Rule 12(b)(3) for improper venue under 28 U.S.C. § 1400(b).

Venue is improper in the Eastern District of Texas under the Supreme Court's recent holding in *TC Heartland*, because Realtime has not alleged, and cannot establish, that EVault either "resides" or has a "regular and established place of business" in this district for purposes of establishing proper venue under § 1400(b).[3]

In *TC Heartland*, the defendant was organized under Indiana law and headquartered in Indiana. *TC Heartland*, 2017 WL 2216934, at \*3. Instead of filing suit in Indiana, the plaintiff filed its patent-infringement lawsuit against the defendant in Delaware. *Id*. As here, the defendant in *TC Heartland* moved to dismiss the case under Rule 12(b)(3), arguing that venue was improper in Delaware because the defendant (1) did not "reside" in Delaware for purposes of the first clause of § 1400(b), and (2) had no "regular and established place of business" in Delaware for purposes of the second clause. *Id*. In particular, relevant to the second clause (requiring a "regular and established place of business"), the defendant had "no meaningful local presence" in Delaware. *Id*. At most, it shipped the allegedly infringing products into the state, which did not rise to the level of a "regular and established place of business." *See id*. The question then turned on whether the defendant "resided" in Delaware under the first clause of § 1400(b). The Supreme Court agreed the defendant did not--holding that for purposes of the patent-venue statute, a corporation "resides" only in its State of incorporation. *Id*. Because the defendant was not incorporated in Delaware, venue in Delaware was improper. This case is just like *TC Heartland*.

### 1. EVault does not reside in this district.

With respect to the first clause of the patent-venue statute, Realtime has not alleged, and cannot establish, that EVault "resides" in the Eastern District of Texas. As previously explained, for purposes of § 1400(b), a corporation resides only in its State of incorporation. *Id*. EVault is not incorporated in Texas. Ex. 1, Small Decl. ¶ 3. Rather, as Realtime's Complaint admits, EVault is incorporated in *Delaware*. *See* Dkt. No. 1 at ¶ 3; Ex. 1, Small Decl. ¶ 2 (explaining that EVault was incorporated in Delaware on August 3, 2000, and has remained incorporated there). Thus, EVault resides only in Delaware, and Realtime cannot establish proper venue under the first clause of § 1400(b).

### 2. EVault does not have a regular and established place of business in this district.

Turning to the second clause of the patent-venue statute, Realtime likewise has not borne its burden of establishing proper venue based on EVault having a "regular and established place of business" in this district. Realtime's Complaint alleges that EVault is headquartered in *California* at 6001 Shellmound Street, Emeryville, California 94608. *See* Dkt. No. 1 at ¶ 3. But the Complaint does not allege that EVault has any regular and established place of business in *Texas* (much less this district), and neither the facts nor the law support such a finding.

The Federal Circuit's decision in *In re Cordis Corp.*, 769 F2d 733 (Fed. Cir. 1985), represents controlling law in the interpretation of a "regular and established place of business" under § 1400(b). In *Cordis*, the court stated "the appropriate inquiry is whether the corporate defendant does its business in that district *through a permanent and continuous presence there*." *Id*. at 737 (emphasis added). Here, EVault does not have a permanent and continuous presence in the Eastern District of Texas that would give rise to a regular and established place of business. For example, EVault does not have any buildings, offices, or leases to facilities in this district; does not have a listed phone number or address within this district; does not have any officers or employees in this district; and does not maintain any inventory, equipment, or other property in this district. Ex. 1, Small Decl. ¶¶ 4--7. Rather, just as the defendant in *TC Heartland* had no meaningful local presence in the District of Delaware, EVault has no meaningful local presence in the Eastern District of Texas.

Realtime's Complaint merely purports that venue is proper because EVault has at some point allegedly "transacted business in the Eastern District of Texas" and "committed acts of direct and indirect infringement in the Eastern District of Texas." Dkt. No. 1 at ¶ 8. But bare-bones allegations of "transacting business" and alleged acts of infringement are not enough. *See, e.g., Roblor Mktg. Grp., Inc. v. GPS Indus., Inc.*, 645 F. Supp. 2d 1130, 1146 (S.D. Fla. 2009) (explaining that "[t]he standard 'regular and established place of business,' is quite narrow: it involves more 'than doing business' "); *Hsin Ten Enter. USA, Inc. v. Clark Enters.*, 138 F. Supp. 2d 449, 461 (S.D.N.Y. 2000) (holding that a " 'regular and established place of business' involves more than 'doing business' "); *see also*

---

3. Although Realtime alleges that "[v]enue is proper in this district under 28 U.S.C. §§ 1391(b), 1391(c) and 1400(b)" (Dkt. No. 1 at ¶ 8), the Supreme Court has made clear that § 1400(b) is the exclusive provision controlling venue in patent-infringement cases. *See TC Heartland*, 2017 WL 2216934, at \*5--7.

*TC Heartland*, 2017 WL 2216934, at *3 (remarking the defendant had "no meaningful local presence" despite shipping the accused products into the state). Under *TC Heartland*, Realtime must show that EVault either (1) is incorporated in Texas, or (2) has committed acts of infringement *and* has a "regular and established place of business" in the Eastern District of Texas. Realtime has shown neither. Venue is therefore improper in this district.

## V. Conclusion

Realtime cannot establish proper venue in the Eastern District of Texas under § 1400(b) and *TC Heartland* because EVault is not incorporated in Texas and does not have a regular and established place of business in this district. EVault therefore respectfully requests that the Court dismiss all claims against EVault in Realtime's Complaint pursuant to Rule 12(b)(3).

Dated: June 7, 2017

Respectfully submitted,

*/s/ Max Ciccarelli*

Max Ciccarelli

State Bar No. 00787242

Max.Ciccarelli@tklaw.com

Michael E. Schonberg

State Bar No. 00784927

Mike.Schonberg@tklaw.com

Nadia E. Haghighatian

State Bar No. 24087652

Nadia.Haghighatian@tklaw.com

Thompson & Knight LLP

One Arts Plaza

1722 Routh Street, Suite 1500

Dallas, Texas 75201

214.969.1700

214.969.1751 (Fax)

**Attorneys for Defendant EVault, Inc.**

# Motion for Leave to Amend

2018 WL 3117093 (D.Mass.)

**Westlaw Query>>**

To find more Motion for Leave to Amend filings on Westlaw: access Massachusetts Civil Trial Court Documents (from the Home page, click Trial Court Documents, then Massachusetts), enter "DT(leave and amend!)" in the search box, and click Search. Use the Jurisdiction filter on the left to narrow results to Federal.

United States District Court, D. Massachusetts.

Arian DINAPOLI d/b/a Ari Family Dental, Plaintiff,

v.

YELP, INC., Defendant.

No. 1:18-cv-10776.

May 29, 2018.

## Plaintiff's Motion for Leave to Amend First Amended Complaint

The Cohen Law Group, 500 Commercial Street, Suite 4R, Boston, MA 02109, Tel: (617) 523-4552, Fax: (617) 723-9211; David C. Farrell; BBO# 693022, E-mail: dave@cohenlawgroupboston.com, for plaintiff Arian DiNapoli.

Plaintiff Arian DiNapoli d/b/a Ari Family Dental, through undersigned counsel, respectfully seeks leave of Court to amend the Complaint pursuant to Fed. R. Civ. P. 15(a).

## INTRODUCTION

Plaintiff submits that the allegations in the First Amended Complaint plausibly suggest an entitlement to relief. However, plaintiff seeks leave to amend the First Amended Complaint to clarify existing factual allegations as presently filed. Plaintiff's Proposed Second Amended Complaint is attached hereto as *Exhibit A*.

## ARGUMENT

Pursuant to Fed. R. Civ. P. 15(a) "leave [to amend] shall be freely given when justice so requires." *United States v. General Hospital Corporation*, 2018 WL 1586027, *8 (D. Mass.) ("Rule 15(a) reflects a liberal amendment policy ... and provides that a court should freely give leave when justice so requires, providing the district court with significant latitude in deciding whether to grant leave to amend."), quoting *United States ex rel. Edward L. Gagne, et al. v. City of Worcester, et al.*, 565 F.3d 40, 48 (1st Cir. 2009) (Internal quotations omitted).

> Reasons for denying leave [to amend] include undue delay in filing the motion, bad faith or dilatory motive, repeated failure to cure deficiencies, undue prejudice to the opposing party, and futility of amendment.

Id., QUOTING *Forman v. Davis*, 371 U.S. 178, 182 (1962) (If the underlying facts or circumstances relied upon by a plaintiff may be a proper subject of relief, he ought to be afforded an opportunity to test his claim on the merits.").

## I. PLAINTIFF FILES THE PRESENT MOTION IN GOOD FAITH TO CLARIFY EXISTING ALLEGATIONS AND NOT FOR THE PURPOSE OF CURING REPEATED DEFICIENCIES.

Here, plaintiff moves to amend the First Amended Complaint in a good faith effort to clarify existing factual allegations. SEE GENERALLY *Green v. Cosby*, 99 F.Supp. 3d 223 (D. Mass. 2015) (Court warranted in allowing leave to amend Complaint to clarify dates of factual allegations).

Plaintiff's present motion is not an attempt to cure repeated deficiencies. See *Abel v. AT&T*, 2003 WL 21077050, *2 (1st Cir. 2003) ("Although Rule 15(a) does not prescribe a particular time limit for a motion to amend, it is well established that such a motion should be made as soon as the necessity for altering the pleading becomes apparent.").

Here, the "necessity" to clarify the factual allegations, See *Id.*, did not become apparent until defendant filed its second "motion to dismiss for failure to state a claim and special motion to strike, SEE CM/ECF Dkt. No. 12 (05/14/2018) at 3 ¶ 4 ("According to DiNapoli's [C]omplaint, Yelp [initially] displayed the review on the Ari Family Dental review page as one that was "not recommended" by Yelp"). In fact, Yelp initially "characterized the January 29, 2016 Review as 'Reliable' and 'Recommended' thereby causing the Review to overshadow pre-existing five-star reviews of plaintiff's dental practice." See *Plaintiff's Proposed Second Amended Complaint*, attached hereto as Exhibit A at 2 ¶ 12.

Thus plaintiff's present motion to amend is "made as soon as the necessity for altering the pleadings" became apparent, *Abel*, 2003 WL at *3 (1st Cir. 2003), and does not constitute a "repeated failure to cure deficiencies by amendments previously allowed," *Forman*, 371 U.S. at 182 (1962).

## II. PLAINTIFF FILES THE PRESENT MOTION PROMPTLY WITH NO DELAY AND NO DILATORY INTENT.

Plaintiff originally filed suit against the defendant in Suffolk Superior Court on March 22, 2018. Defendant then waited the full twenty-one (21) days after receiving service of process before removing this matter to the United States District Court for the District of Massachusetts on April 23, 2018. See CM/ECF Dkt. No. 1 (03/23/2018). On April 30, 2018, defendant filed a "motion to dismiss for failure to state a claim and special motion to strike," SEE CM/ECF Dkt. No. 6 (04/30/2018), despite actual knowledge of plaintiff's intent to amend the Complaint, see CM/ECF Dkt. No. 11 (04/30/2018), see also CM/ECF Dkt. No. 17-1 (04/30/2018) at 3 (procedural confusion here is due at least in-part to defendant's failure to comply with Local Rule 7.1 (D. Mass)). On the other hand, plaintiff's present motion to amend does not suggest any dilatory motive.

Furthermore, plaintiff did not unduly delay filing the present motion to amend. "Undue delay" may justify the Court's denial of a motion to amend when a "considerable time" has elapsed between the filing of the Complaint and the filing of the motion to amend. *Moore v. NStar Electric & Gas Co.*, 264 F.Supp. 3d 292, 295 (D. Mass. 2017), QUOTING *Invest Almaz v. Temple-Inland Forest Production Corp.*, 243 F.3d 57, 71 (1st Cir. 2001). "Periods of fourteen months, fifteen months, and seventeen months have been deemed to constitute 'considerable time.' " *Moore*, 264 F.Supp. 3d at 295 (D. Mass. 2017), quoting *In re Lombardo*, 755 F.3d 1, 3 (1st Cir. 2014).

Here, just one month has elapsed since the defendant removed this matter from Suffolk Superior Court., See CM/ECF Dkt. No. 1 (04/23/2018), Contrast *Moore*, 264 F.Supp. 3d at 295 (D. Mass. 2017) (finding "undue delay" where eighteen (18) months elapsed between filing Complaint and moving to amend). Thus the Court should allow plaintiff's motion for leave to amend the First Amended Complaint because it does not pose a threat of undue delay to the underlying proceedings and nothing in the record suggests plaintiff is filing the present motion with dilatory intent.

## III. PLAINTIFF'S PROPOSED SECOND AMENDED COMPLAINT IS NOT FUTILE AND WILL NOT PREJUDICE THE DEFENDANT.

The First Circuit has long recognized that a proposed amended Complaint - when filed prior to the commencement of discovery -- is not futile unless it "could not withstand a 12(b)(6) motion to dismiss." *Hatch v. Department for Children, Youth and Their Families*, 274 F.3d 12, 19 (1st Cir. 2001), quoting *Rose v. Hartford Underwriters Ins. Co.*, 203 F.3d 417, 421 (6th Cir. 2000). Here, plaintiff's proposed Second Amended Complaint clarifies that (1) on January 29, 2016, defendant characterized the Review as "Reliable" and "Recommended," (2) throughout the month of February, 2016 plaintiff repeatedly attempted to contact defendant to resolve his grievances regarding the Review, (3) on or about March 1, 2016, defendant re-categorized the Review as "Not Recommended" and "Not Reliable," and (4) on January 26, 2018, defendant re-categorized the Review as "Reliable" and "Recommended," after two years of fruitless attempts to sell the plaintiff advertising space on defendant's website. See *Plaintiff's Proposed Second Amended Complaint*, attached hereto as Exhibit A at 4 ¶¶ 12 - _.

Furthermore, allowing plaintiff's present motion to amend the First Amended Complaint will not prejudice the defendant. The Sixth Circuit has defined a prejudicial motion to amend as that which "would produce 'a grave injustice to the defendants.' " *Pendley v. Komori Printing Machinery Co., Ltd.*, 1990 WL 17152, *3 (D. Rhode Island), quoting *Hageman v. Signal L.P. Gas, Inc.*, 486 F.2d 479, 484 (6th Cir. 1973). The First Circuit recognizes a three-part test for determining whether or not a motion to amend will impermissibly prejudice a defendant:

> As the First Circuit has explained: the district court may deny leave to amend where (1) discovery would have to be reopened after the accumulation of an extensive and expensive record and after the legal issues involved had already been developed; (2) the additional allegations contained no newly discovered evidence of facts of a different character that would change the basic claims; and (3) the threshold issues of justifiable reliance would still prove an insurmountable obstacle to recovery.

*Abel v. AT&T*, 2003 WL 21077050, *3 (1st Cir. 2003), quoting *Kennedy v. Josephthal & Co.*, 814 F.2d 798, 806 (1st Cir. 1987) (internal quotations omitted).

This Court has specifically declined to recognize such prejudice where "trial is not imminent." *Lucas v. United States*, 133 F.Supp. 3d 284, 288 (D. Mass. 2015), see also *Abel*, 2003 WL at *4 (1st Cir. 2003) (allowing motion to amend where "[t]he amount of additional discovery is relatively limited and a trial is not on the horizon.").

Here, plaintiff promptly files the present motion to clarify existing factual allegations plausibly entitling him to judicial relief from and against the defendant prior to the commencement of discovery. Thus the Court should allow the present motion because it is neither futile nor prejudicial to the defendant.

WHEREFORE, plaintiff respectfully requests that the Court:

I. Grant plaintiff's Motion for Leave to Amend First Amended Complaint;

II. Deem plaintiff's Proposed Second Amended Complaint filed, attached hereto as Exhibit A; and

III. Issue any additional order(s) deemed necessary to maintain fairness and justice.

Respectfully submitted,

Plaintiff Arian DiNapoli,

By his attorneys,

THE COHEN LAW GROUP

500 Commercial Street, Suite 4R

Boston, MA 02109

Tel: (617) 523-4552

Fax: (617) 723-9211

*/s/ David C. Farrell*

David C. Farrell; BBO# 693022

E-mail: *dave@cohenlawgroupboston.com*

# Motion for Continuance/Extension of Time

2015 WL 10551207 (D.Mass.)

**Westlaw Query>>**

To find more Motion for Continuance/Extension of Time filings on Westlaw: access Massachusetts Civil Trial Court Documents (from the Home page, click Trial Court Documents, then Massachusetts), enter "DT(motion and continu! exten!)" in the search box, and click Search. Use the Jurisdiction filter on the left to narrow results to Federal.

United States District Court, D. Massachusetts.

Patricia WRIGHT, Substitute Plaintiff,

v.

CSX TRANSPORTATION, INC., Defendant.

No. 11-30161-MGM.

May 12, 2015.

Plaintiff's Motion for Continuance of Trial Date

Thomas J. O'Connor, Jr. Esq., BBO # 640433, S. Thomas Martinelli, Esq., BBO# 322920, 1391 Main Street, Suite 1022, Springfield, MA 01103-1649, Tel.: 413-781-5311, Fax: 413-746-2707, Email: attorneytomoconnor@gmail.com, Email: stm@omcp-law.com.

Now comes Patricia Wright, substitute plaintiff in this action as the duly appointed personal representative of the Estate of Mark Menard, and hereby moves this court for a continuance of the trial date in this matter for a period of at least 150 days, from the presently scheduled date of June 15, 2015, to November 15, 2015. As grounds for this motion, the plaintiff states that a continuance is warranted for the following reasons:

1. Mr. Menard's untimely and sudden death has hampered plaintiff's counsel's ability to prepare the case for trial and meet other deadlines, as scheduled, and denial of a continuance would work an injustice on the present plaintiff;

2. The plaintiff needs time to obtain information about the cause of Mr. Menard's death from the medical examiner's autopsy, which may be relevant to the determination of damages in the present case;

3. Substitute plaintiff seeks time to pursue amendment of the complaint in this action to include a claim for wrongful death, pursuant to M.G.L. c. 229, § 2, which claim is related to the present action, arises largely from the same set of facts, and considerations of fairness and judicial economy dictate that the plaintiff be permitted to bring any such viable claims in the present action rather than filing suit in state court at a later date (once the cause of death is established) and fighting claims of res judicata.

4. The delays in bringing this case to trial fall to date are not generally attributable to the plaintiff and, therefore, concerns about further delay is not a basis to deny the plaintiff's current motion.

As further grounds for this motion, plaintiff states as follows.

## ARGUMENT

### I. Mr. Menard's Untimely and Sudden Death Hampered Plaintiff's Counsel's Ability To Prepare the Case for Trial and Meet Other Deadlines

The original plaintiff in this matter, Mark Menard, died an unexpected and unattended death on or about January 24, 2015, the cause of which has yet to be determined by the medical examiner's office. Mr. Menard's death left plaintiff's counsel without a client with whom to consult on the progress of the case, including decisions to be made regarding expert disclosures, which were required to be disclosed by March 18, 2015;

Mr. Menard's personal representative, the present substituted plaintiff, Patricia Wright, was appointed by the Probate and Family Court on March 11, 2015. Ms. Wright hired present counsel to represent her in her capacity as Personal Representative of the Estate of Mark Menard on or about March 23, 2015. During the interim period of time, Ms. Wright, who is Mr. Menard's sister and served as his caretaker following his injuries that are the subject of this suit, was grieving her brother's death. Ms. Wright was substituted as plaintiff on April 23, 2015.

For approximately three months, from January 24, 2015, to April 23, 2015, plaintiff's counsel were without a client to authorize decisions and actions in this case. That period of time fell within the critical six months leading up to the presently scheduled trial date. As a consequence, counsel were unable to make decisions and take actions in the case that required client input, including decisions about expert costs and disclosures and motions challenging CSX's expert. A continuance of the trial date and establishment of new deadlines for expert disclosures and depositions is appropriate to remedy this disadvantage resulting from these tragic and unpredictable circumstances.

CSX's counsel suggested at the status conference held on April 28, 2015, that plaintiff's counsel should have simply continued making trial preparations without a client, intimating that if the likely personal representative were known, she could authorize the conduct of counsel without formally being appointed to act on behalf of the estate. CSX's assertion that family members dealing with the sudden and tragic death of a loved one should be expected to simply step in and begin making decisions about the deceased's pending case without legal authority to do so is hardly worthy of comment. The suggestion demonstrates a lack of appreciation of the tragedy the family suffered. It also calls on plaintiff's counsel to act in a way that would have exposed them to ethical jeopardy and professional liability. A member of the bar was suspended from the practice of law for continuing to pursue the claims of a deceased plaintiff without authorization and without disclosing the death. *See In Re Alan B. Goodman*, Order for Suspension, January 3, 2007, Supreme Judicial Court, No. BD-2006-069; *Chandler v. Dunlop*, 311 Mass. 1, 5 (1947). Contrary to CSX's assertions at the status conference, the reality is that plaintiff's counsel could not make decisions about the case without a client to authorize them.

It would be a gross injustice if this Court were to require the substituted plaintiff who has only recently entered this case to digest the death of her brother, learn the issues in the case, familiarize herself with the facts, and make all of the decisions that must be made in advance of trial without any delay. Counsel for the plaintiff also would be disadvantaged in their preparation for trial if this continuance were not allowed. During the time since Mr. Menard's death, plaintiff's counsel has been preoccupied addressing issues associated with Mr. Menard's death, including assisting in the probating of the will to expedite the process of substituting the plaintiff, meeting with the newly appointed personal representative to discuss engagement for the continuation of the case, contacting the medical examiner's office to determine when the autopsy report will issue and to request that the assessment be expedited, educating the substituted plaintiff as to the convoluted history of the case, the facts established during discovery and the legal issues at play, preparing the suggestion of death and motion for substitution of parties, and now preparing this motion for a continuance of the case. Plaintiff's counsel also has been in discussions with Mr. Menard's personal representative regarding bringing a potential wrongful death action against CSX in the event that Mr. Menard's death is shown to be related to the injuries he suffered in CSX's railroad yard.

As this Court surely can imagine, it was not socially appropriate for plaintiff's counsel to push those issues too quickly with Mr. Menard's bereaved family. But plaintiff's counsel was able to accomplish a significant amount of work necessary to keep this case moving forward following Mr. Menard's death. Any delays that have resulted are minimal under the circumstances, which are unusual, could not have been planned for, were beyond plaintiff's counsel's control, but have been appropriately and promptly addressed by them. A continuance of the trial date in light of these unfortunate events is warranted.

By contrast, CSX's counsel were *not* without a client following Mr. Menard's death and, therefore, and were fully capable of consulting with their client during this critical trial preparation time. CSX's counsel was able to continue trial preparations unimpeded without having to deal with the same distractions presented to the plaintiff, giving the defendant an unfair advantage if this Court were to require the parties to go to trial as scheduled. Surely the Court can see that CSX's demand that the present trial date be maintained is little more than an attempt to take unfair advantage of the disarray that Mr. Menard's death temporarily caused for the plaintiff's case. A fair trial requires that both parties have a reasonably equal opportunity to prepare their cases. And common decency dictates that one party not be permitted to gain advantage from its opponent's misfortune. The trial should be continued to afford plaintiff's counsel time to recover from the shocking news of Mr. Menard's death and to refocus on the adequate preparation of the case for presentation to the jury.

## II. Continuation of the Trial Is Necessary To Permit the Plaintiff To Obtain Information About the Cause of Mr. Menard's Death, Which Is Relevant To the Determination of Damages In the Present Case

Mr. Menard suffered from a broad array of ailments that arose as a result of the catastrophic injuries he sustained in CSX's railroad yard in 2008. He died an unattended death at a young age. It is the substituted plaintiff's good faith belief that his death may have been the result of complications attributable to his injuries. The medical examiner has performed an autopsy, but reports that it may be number of months before the results of the autopsy are made available. Counsel for the plaintiff was in frequent contact with the medical examiner's office early in the process to urge an expedited report, without success.

CSX argued at the status conference that plaintiff's counsel should have arranged for their own pathologist to conduct the autopsy so that the results could be made available in this case more quickly. At the time the autopsy was being conducted, plaintiff's counsel did not have a client to authorize the hiring of a pathologist to conduct an autopsy. CSX's counsel did. CSX's argument in this regard, therefore, is also disingenuous. CSX could have hired its own pathologist and sought authorization to conduct an expedited autopsy but did not do so. CSX should not now be heard to complain or to blame the plaintiff for the delay.

Because Mr. Menard's death was quite possibly the result of complications of his injuries suffered in CSX's railroad yard, the substituted plaintiff should be permitted a reasonable continuance of the trial date to try to obtain the autopsy results necessary to establish these new damages. Otherwise, the plaintiff would be denied a legitimate avenue of recovery.

### III. Substitute Plaintiff Seeks Time to Pursue Amendment of the Complaint in This Action To Include a Claim for Wrongful Death, Pursuant to M.G.L. c. 229, § 2

Massachusetts law provides a separate cause of action for wrongful death to enumerated relatives of an individual whose injuries result in death. M.G.L. c. 229, § 2. Here, it is reasonable to believe that Mr. Menard's death was the result of complications related to the injuries he sustained in CSX's railroad yard. To prove the connection, however, the plaintiff needs to obtain the autopsy results, which the medical examiner's office has indicated will take a number of months to release.

Allowing the plaintiff's motion to continue the trial would permit the plaintiff the time needed to obtain the results of the autopsy and to evaluate the potential claim for wrongful death. In the event that there is a basis for the claim discovered after the presently set trial date, and this Court were to deny the plaintiff's requested continuance, the plaintiff would be in the difficult of later having to file suit for wrongful death and fend off CSX's inevitable claim that the claim is precluded as a result of the trial in the present matter. Such a scenario would place the plaintiff at a legal and financial disadvantage — having to incur the costs of multiple litigations of related topics — and would violate principles of judicial economy. For those reasons, this motion to continue should be allowed.

CSX argued at the recent status conference that a claim for wrongful death is precluded by the First Circuit's opinion remanding this case and by this Court's prior orders addressing claims sounding in willful, wanton and reckless conduct. It is CSX's apparent contention that because the wrongful death statute requires that a claimant seeking recovery from a railroad show that the death resulted from willful, wrongful or reckless conduct, any such claims by Mr. Menard's family members in the present action are prohibited. CSX's position in this regard is not persuasive and, at a minimum, is not a basis to deny this requested continuance.

The question of whether entirely separate plaintiffs — in this case, Mr. Menard's next of kin — seeking to assert their statutory rights under the wrongful death statute against a defendant in a pending action can be precluded from doing so by developments in the case prior to the accrual of their claim is a complex one. It is one that warrants briefing by the parties and careful consideration of the Court, which is a further basis for the granting of a continuance of the trial.

CSX's contention is that the First Circuit's opinion upheld the dismissal of Mr. Menard's willful, wanton and reckless claim, and that any and all claims by whatever potential plaintiff or plaintiffs that require proof of willful, wanton or reckless behavior, therefore, are also precluded as a matter of law. Giving a Rule 12(b)(6) dismissal such broad preclusive effect is not justified, particularly against plaintiffs who were not parties to the pleadings so dismissed. Furthermore, CSX overstates the doctrine of law of the case, which is not absolute, *see* United States v. Rivera-Martinez, 931 F.2d 148, 150-51 (1st Cir. 1991)("[t]o be sure, the law of the case doctrine is neither an absolute bar to reconsideration nor a limitation on a federal court's power"). The plaintiff should have an opportunity to be heard on that issue, which is a further basis for this Court to grant the requested continuance of the scheduled trial.

### IV. The Plaintiff Has Not Sought Any Unjustified Continuances In This Case and Has Not Otherwise Caused Undue Delay In This Matter Going To Trial

The plaintiff in this matter is sensitive to the Court's expressed concerns as to the age of this case. But age of the case alone does not warrant a denial of this requested continuance, particularly where the continuance is being requested by a substitute plaintiff for compelling reasons that could not have been anticipated. That is particularly true where, as here, the party requesting the continuance was not responsible for the bulk of the delays in this case proceeding to trial to date.

This case was initiated in the state court by the original plaintiff, Mark Menard, alleging willful, wanton and reckless conduct and negligence by the defendant, CSX Transportation, Inc., resulting in severe injuries, including the severance of his left leg, the degloving of his left arm and the loss of his right foot. As is permitted under the Massachusetts civil rules, Mr. Menard served his initial requests for discovery at the time of the filing and service of his complaint. Mr. Menard's conduct demonstrated his interest in an expeditious resolution of this matter.

CSX sought removal of the action to this court, which was granted. Subsequently Mr. Menard and CSX engaged in automatic disclosures in accordance with the Local Rules. CSX's automatic disclosures, however, failed to disclose certain relevant information, setting the tone for a hard fought and sometimes acrimonious discovery process that has lasted throughout the course of this case.

Before that matter could be addressed, however, CSX moved for dismissal of Mr. Menard's claims on the grounds that his complaint failed to state a claim pursuant to Rule 12(b)(6) of the Federal Rules of Civil Procedure. The motion was allowed and Mr. Menard's claims were dismissed on January 3, 2012, without the benefit of the discovery process. (Doc. # 21 and 22). Mr. Menard was — and remained — fully prepared to engage in the expeditious production of discovery as would have been required under the applicable rules had his claims survived.

The court's dismissal of Mr. Menard's complaint was appealed by Mr. Menard to the First Circuit, resulting in a significant delay in the progress of this case towards trial — a delay that can hardly be placed at the feet of the plaintiff. Ultimately, on October 24, 2012, nearly 11 months from the date of the dismissal, the First Circuit reversed the order of dismissal, vacating the judgment and remanding the case to the district court for further proceedings. (Doc. # 27, 28).

Specifically, the First Circuit ordered that the plaintiff be permitted to "explain to the district judge what basis he has to believe that narrow discovery is warranted for the interval between the switch incident that limited discovery would yield and Menard's fall under the wheels of the train." *Menard v. CSX Transp., Inc.*, 698 F.3d 40, 45-46 (2012). The First Circuit further instructed that, "[i]f anything beyond speculation supports Menard's "information and belief allegation, that too can be disclosed." *Id.* at 46. Finally, and significantly, the First Circuit stated, "[a]fter that, the matter is *confided to the discretion* of the district judge" consistent with the opinion. *Id.* (emphasis added).

Following reversal of the dismissal of Mr. Menard's case, the original district judge recused himself from the case on October 31, 2012 (Doc. # 29), and the matter was reassigned on December 6, 2012 (Doc. # 32). Again, the delay due to the reassignment of the case cannot justly be attributed to any conduct of the plaintiff.

On December 19, 2012, without hearing, the newly assigned district judge ordered that "the *parties* are granted ninety (90) days . . . during which to conduct discovery on plaintiff's peril-and-negligence allegation." (Doc. # 34) (emphasis added).

Mr. Menard then embarked on a diligent effort to obtain the discovery necessary to prove his claims against CSX, seeking written discovery and taking numerous depositions. CSX resisted Mr. Menard's efforts strenuously, frequently claiming that all requests for information outside of the brief interval between Mr. Menard's first injury and his subsequent injuries were outside the scope of ordered discovery. CSX took that position even when Mr. Menard sought discovery of information that was technically outside of the limited time frame (like manuals and rulebooks prepared long before Mr. Menard's accident) but that had bearing on the conduct of the company's employees during the "brief interval."

Mr. Menard was forced to defend a motion for a protective order filed by CSX, seeking to avoid production of such information. (Doc. # 36). Ultimately, this court ordered Mr. Menard to limit his requests to the "brief interval" and required the parties to confer on that matter. (Doc. # 45). Mr. Menard then sought and received one extension of the discovery deadline to complete limited discovery. (Doc. # 45). CSX continued to resist Mr. Menard's discovery efforts, leading to another motion for the extension of the discovery deadlines that was denied by this court. (Doc. # 46 and 57).

Notably, despite this court order granting the *parties* limited discovery regarding the peril-and-negligence claim (Doc. # 34), CSX conducted *no* discovery during this time period.

On June 17, 2013, CSX filed a motion to reinstate the initial order of dismissal on the grounds that discovery had not yielded evidence sufficient to support Mr. Menard's negligence claim. (Doc. # 58). The court treated CSX's motion as one for summary judgment and requested further briefing. (Doc. # 63). In doing so, the court referred to the "*now-complete* discovery process." (Doc. # 63)(emphasis added). CSX's motion for summary judgment was denied on September 9, 2013, in open court. (Doc. # 89). That unsuccessful motion caused a three month delay in the progress of this case towards trial that also cannot be attributable to conduct of the plaintiff.

CSX immediately requested time to conduct discovery despite its having sat on its rights during what the district judge described as the "now-complete" limited discovery phase that had just closed. Mr. Menard opposed CSX's request, but the court allowed CSX's request for continued discovery, ruling from the bench without briefing of the issue. (Doc. # 89).

CSX gained a significant advantage by waiting to conduct its discovery until it had seen all of Mr. Menard's efforts to develop his theory of the case.

On December 12, 2013, after deposing Mr. Menard and conducting a series of depositions of Mr. Menard's treating physicians and other ancillary witnesses frequently on matters outside of the scope of Judge Stearns' limited discovery order, CSX moved for a protective order from Mr. Menard's requests for various relevant documents and discovery partially on the grounds that the requests had already been denied as being outside the scope of limited discovery or had already been produced. (Doc. # 112). Mr. Menard opposed the motion for a protective order and sought a motion to compel the production.

After excoriating the plaintiff for failing to abide by the court's limitations on discovery, the court granted Mr. Menard virtually every single item of discovery requested. (Doc. # 121). The court ironically also reiterated in its ruling its view that it was Mr. Menard who misunderstood the limitations on discovery that still applied in the case, apparently unaware that CSX's counsel had aggressively taken the position that CSX was not subject to such limitations. The result of the order was a brief extension of time for Mr. Menard to obtain the discovery to which he was entitled. The court also reminded CSX that it could again petition the court for summary judgment if it believed that the evidence adduced during this secondary phase of discovery did not support Mr. Menard's claims.

Following the court's ruling, counsel for CSX withdrew from the case and present counsel filed appearances in substitution. (Doc. # 124-130). On March 27, 2014, the parties filed a joint motion to continue the discovery deadline, which was allowed. (Doc. # 131, 132). CSX then filed a motion for leave to file yet another motion for summary judgment on March 26, 2014, which also was granted over Mr. Menard's objection. (Doc. # 133, 136, 137). The motion raised no new significant undisputed facts and was denied on May 30, 2014, after working another delay in the progress of the case of more than two months. (Doc. # 170).

Subsequently, Mr. Menard realized that CSX had shared important locomotive data recorder information with its expert that had never been produced to Mr. Menard. As a result, on June 28, 2014, Mr. Menard filed a motion seeking sanctions, pointing out — among other things — that he had been deprived an opportunity to present such data to his own potential expert for examination. (Doc. # 171). CSX admitted to the violation and initially claimed inadvertence. In open court, however, counsel for CSX later conceded awareness of the issue as early as January of that year and further admitted that nothing was done to remedy the matter until Mr. Menard raised the issue.

On October 16, 2014, this court found that no discovery violation had been committed but permitted the plaintiff to seek to reopen expert discovery to address the previously undisclosed data. (Doc. # 198). Mr. Menard filed such a motion on October 27, 2014. (Doc. # 199). It was opposed. (Doc. # 202). This court allowed the motion on November 18, 2014, granting Mr. Menard 120 days to disclose his experts and affording CSX an additional 30 days to conduct expert depositions. (Doc. # 205).

The delays from December, 2013, to November, 2014, and through the re-opened expert discovery period reaching to March, 2015, again are not attributable to any improper conduct by the plaintiff or any dilatory efforts to pursue these claims. To the contrary, they are largely attributable to CSX's poorly supported renewed motion for summary judgment and its failure to produce clearly relevant data in a timely manner — even after its failure to produce the data had been discovered by its new counsel.

To hold now that a continuance of the trial in this matter is not warranted because of the age of this case would work a gross injustice on the plaintiff. Accordingly, this Court should allow this motion and continue the trial data in this matter for the reasons stated above.

WHEREFORE, Ms. Wright, the duly substituted plaintiff in this action hereby requests that this Court allow this motion to continue the trial to at least November 15, 2015, or such later date as is convenient for the Court and the parties.

*Local Rule 7.1 Certification.* Counsel for the plaintiff in this matter has conferred with counsel for defendant CSX Transportation, Inc., for purposes of attempting to resolve or narrow the issues addressed in this motion, without success.

Respectfully submitted,

Plaintiff,

*/s/ Thomas J. O'Connor, Jr.*

Thomas J. O'Connor , Jr. Esq.

BBO # 640433

S. Thomas Martinelli, Esq.

BBO# 322920

1391 Main Street, Suite 1022

Springfield, MA 01103-1649

Tel.: 413-781-5311

Fax: 413-746-2707

Email: attorneytomoconnor@gmail.com

Email: stm@omcp-law.com

# Motion for Summary Judgment

2018 WL 3579345 (D.Mass.)

United States District Court, D. Massachusetts.

DESKTOP METAL, INC., Plaintiff and Counterclaim Defendant,

v.

MARKFORGED, INC. and Matiu Parangi, Defendants and Counterclaim Plaintiff (Markforged, Inc.),

v.

Ricardo FULOP, Jonah Myerberg, Boston Impact LLC, and Amy Buntel, Third-Party Defendants.

No. 1:18-CV-10524-WGY.

June 26, 2018.

Memorandum in Support of Markforged, Inc.'s Motion for Summary Judgment on Desktop Metal, Inc.'s Alleged Monetary Damages

Harvey J. Wolkoff (BBO# 532880), Patrick D. Curran (BBO# 568701), Aliki Sofis (BBO# 675777), Kaitlyn M. O'Connor (BBO# 687527), Quinn Emanuel Urquhart & Sullivan, LLP, 111 Huntington Avenue, Suite 520, Boston, MA 02199, Tel: (617) 712-7100, harveywolkoff@quinnemanuel.com, patrickcurran@quinnemanuel.com, alikisofis@quinnemanuel.com, kaitoconnor@quinnemanuel.com; Steven Cherny (pro hac vice), James Baker (pro hac vice), Elinor Sutton (pro hac vice), Jeremy Baldoni (pro hac vice), Brendan Carroll (pro hac vice), Quinn Emanuel Urquhart & Sullivan, LLP, 51 Madison Avenue, 22nd Floor, New York, NY 10010, Tel: (212) 849-7000, stevencherny@quinnemanuel.com, jamesbaker@quinnemanuel.com, elinorsutton@quinnemanuel.com, jeremybaldoni@quinnemanuel.com, brendancarroll@quinnemanuel.com, for Markforged, Inc.

Howard J. Susser (BBO# 636183), Eric G. J. Kaviar (BBO# 670833), Laura Carroll (BBO# 076180), Burns & Levinson LLP, 125 Summer Street, Boston, MA 02110, (617) 345-3000, hsusser@burnslev.com, ekaviar@burnslev.com, lcarroll@burnslev.com, for Matiu Parangi.

## TABLE OF CONTENTS

## TABLE OF AUTHORITIES

*Cases*

**Statutes**

35 U.S.C. 271 . . . 2, 3

## INTRODUCTION

Desktop Metal bases its sole damages claim of $47,100 to $63,900 on one sale of a Markforged Metal X printer to Stanley, Black & Decker ("Stanley"). But, because every asserted claim in this action is a method claim, selling a machine does not suffice to support a finding of liability or damages—Desktop Metal must show that Stanley actually performed the claimed methods and that Markforged induced or contributed to that infringing use. It is black letter law that a patentee cannot show indirect infringement of a method unless it can show direct infringement. Desktop Metal, however, has identified no evidence, ***none***, that Stanley ever used its Metal X to perform any method claimed in the asserted patents. Desktop Metal's own experts testified that they do not know whether Stanley ever used any of the claimed methods.

Desktop Metal's damages witness, Dr. Christopher Vellturo, unequivocally testified at his deposition (which was not able to be conducted until last Friday, June 22, 2018 because of scheduling issues): "I don't know what they [Stanley] have actually done with the [Metal X] system since they received it." Similarly, Desktop Metal's technical witness, Dr. Kenneth Gall (whose deposition was conducted just today, again because of scheduling issues), likewise acknowledged that he is not aware of any evidence showing that Stanley used the Metal X in any infringing way. Indeed, the Stanley presentation that he appended to his report explicitly states that they did not. Desktop Metal also never sought discovery from Stanley to find out if and how they used the Metal X. And the one Stanley document Desktop Metal cites specifically identifies a part as being made without supports (and therefore could not have been made with any claimed method), and says nothing about how any other part was made using the Metal X.

There is no genuine issue of material fact, disputed or otherwise, here. Desktop Metal has identified no evidence of direct infringement and therefore cannot meet its burden of showing indirect infringement. Desktop Metal has not even identified a specific claim in either patent which Stanley purportedly infringed. Desktop Metal thus is unable as a matter of law to prevail on its claims under 35 U.S.C. 271(b) and (c), requiring summary judgment for Markforged on Desktop Metal's damages claim.

## BACKGROUND

The following background is drawn from the undisputed facts set forth in Markforged's Local Rule 56.1 Statement Of Undisputed Material Facts and the exhibits thereto.

Desktop Metal alleges that Markforged infringed "methods claimed in the '839 patent," for "fabricating an interface layer for removable support[s] object," and the "methods claimed in the ' 118 patent," for "fabricating multi-part assemblies." (SUMF ¶ 3.) As described by Desktop Metal's damages witness, Dr. Vellturo, the allegedly infringed method is the use of "supports separated by a release layer and interlocking parts separated by an interface layer." (SUMF ¶ 4).

Dr. Vellturo opined as to a single basis for monetary damages on Desktop Metal's claims: alleged lost profits of "$47,100 to $63,900" based on the fact that in April 2018, "Markforged shipped a complete Metal X system (comprised of a printer, washer, and furnace) to Stanley" that allegedly "would have instead been made by Desktop Metal" but for the alleged infringement. (SUMF ¶¶ 5-6.) Desktop Metal's technical witness, Dr. Gall, asserts that Stanley's use of the Metal X system constituted infringement giving rise to a claim for damages against Markforged because Stanley is an example (Desktop Metal's only example) of "third parties using Markforged's Metal X 3D Print System [to] perform methods that literally satisfy every element of the asserted claims of the '118 and '839 patents." (SUMF ¶ 10.) In asserting this third party infringement, Dr. Gall cites a case study performed by Stanley regarding parts printed using the Metal X. (SUMF ¶ 11.) It is undisputed, however, that the case study specifically states that the "redesigned part [made using the Metal X] prints in one piece without support material," meaning that it does not use the asserted method. (SUMF ¶ 12.)

At deposition, Dr. Vellturo conceded that he "literally can't know" whether Stanley used the accused component of the Metal X System, a "support separated by a release layer and interlocking parts separated by an interface layer feature to print any part at any time." (SUMF ¶ 13.) He further testified that "at the time [of his report], [he] had no information that told me what they [Stanley] were actually using [the accused component] for," (SUMF ¶ 14.) To the contrary, he testified that as far as he knew, the Metal X printer system at Stanley "may still be in the testing and set up phase." (SUMF ¶ 16.)Thus, while Vellturo attributed "$47,100 to

$63,900" in lost profits damages to Stanley's alleged use of the patents' methods in his damages report, he admits that he did so even though he "d[oes]n't know what they [Stanley] have actually done with the system since they received it." (SUMF ¶ 15.) When shown the Stanley case study cited by Dr. Gall demonstrating that Stanley does not use the purportedly infringing supports, Dr. Vellturo testified that he had never seen it before. (SUMF ¶ 17.) Additionally, Dr. Gall admitted at his deposition today that he can identify no direct infringement of the patents by Stanley or any other third party. (SUMF ¶ 18.)

## ARGUMENT

Desktop Metal's indirect infringement claims under 35 U.S.C. §§ 271(b) and (c) require proof that Stanley not only used the Metal X printer, but used it in a way that directly infringed the claimed methods asserted here. Desktop Metal fails to identify evidence of a single instance when Stanley directly infringed the methods claimed in the '118 and '839 patents. This failure requires judgment in Markforged's favor on the sole damages claim at issue—the claim that Markforged caused Desktop Metal lost profits by inducing or contributing to third-party infringement.

Proof of Stanley's direct infringement is an absolute prerequisite to these claims, because "[a]bsent direct infringement of the patent claims, there can be neither contributory infringement nor inducement of infringement." *Jansen v. Rexall Sundown, Inc.*, 342 F.3d 1329, 1334 (Fed. Cir. 2003) (quoting *Met—Coil Sys. Corp. v. Korners Unlimited, Inc.*, 803 F.2d 684, 687 (Fed.Cir. 1986)). Under either 271(b) (inducement) or (c) contributing infringement, "indirect infringement of a patent requires direct infringement." *In re Bill of Lading Transmission & Processing Sys. Patent Litig.*, 681 F.3d 1323, 1333 (Fed. Cir. 2012).

Under these rules, Desktop Metal's claims must fail. The evidentiary record is devoid of any support for the allegation that Stanley directly infringed the claimed method at issue by using "supports separated by a release layer and interlocking parts separated by an interface layer." In his expert report, Dr. Gall affirmatively asserts only that Stanley purchased a Metal X printer, not that Stanley used that printer in an infringing manner. (SUMF ¶ 10.) That is not enough. Nor do the documents Dr. Gall cites support an inference of any infringing use. Indeed, as previously noted, the Stanley case study he cites expressly states that a part made using the Metal X printer "prints in one piece without support material." (SUMF ¶¶ 11-12.) Dr. Gall even admitted at deposition today that he can identify no direct infringement of the patents by Stanley or any other third party. (SUMF ¶ 18.) Desktop Metal thus has no evidence that Stanley (or any third party) actually used the Metal X in a way that infringes any patented method at issue. Neither Desktop Metal nor Dr. Gall references any other entity besides Stanley as an alleged example of Markforged inducing or contributing to third-party infringement. This failure to provide evidence of any third party engaging in direct infringement of any claim in the patents puts an end to Desktop Metal's damages claim based on alleged indirect infringement by Markforged.

Nor has Desktop Metal produced any evidence of record that Markforged was aware, another required element for indirect infringement, that Stanley was using the purported infringing method in printing any parts. *See Global-Tech Appliances, Inc. v. SEB S.A.*, 563 U.S. 754, 760-761 (2011). In any event, it is black letter law that "[a]bsent direct infringement of the claims of a patent, there can be neither contributing infringement nor inducement of infringement." *Carborundum Co. v. Molten Metal Equipment Innovations, Inc.*, 72 F. 3d 872, 876 n. 4 (Fed. Cir. 1995). Because the record is devoid of support for Desktop Metal's sole damages claim, the July 9 trial should be limited to the question of Markforged's alleged infringement and the availability of injunctive relief. As a result, Desktop Metal has no right to a jury. *See Tegal Corp. v. Tokyo Electron Am., Inc.*, 257 F.3d 1331, 1340-41 (Fed. Cir. 2001) (where a "case is a claim of patent infringement, seeking an injunction and no damages," holding that "the nature of Tegal's action is equitable" and the parties had no right to a jury trial) (citing *Tull v. United States*, 481 U.S. 412, 417 (1987)).

## CONCLUSION

The Court should grant summary judgment in favor of Markforged on Desktop Metal's claims for damages based on alleged lost profits with respect to their infringement causes of action.

Dated: June 26, 2018

*/s/ Harvey J. Wolkoff*

Harvey J. Wolkoff (BBO# 532880)

Patrick D. Curran (BBO# 568701)

Aliki Sofis (BBO# 675777)

Kaitlyn M. O'Connor (BBO# 687527)

QUINN EMANUEL URQUHART & SULLIVAN, LLP

111 Huntington Avenue, Suite 520

Boston, MA 02199

Tel: (617) 712-7100

harveywolkoff@quinnemanuel.com

patrickcurran@quinnemanuel.com

alikisofis@quinnemanuel.com

kaitoconnor@quinnemanuel.com

Steven Cherny (*pro hac vice*)

James Baker (*pro hac vice*)

Elinor Sutton (*pro hac vice*)

Jeremy Baldoni (*pro hac vice*)

Brendan Carroll (*pro hac vice*)

QUINN EMANUEL URQUHART & SULLIVAN, LLP

51 Madison Avenue, 22nd Floor

New York, NY 10010

Tel: (212) 849-7000

stevencherny@quinnemanuel.com

jamesbaker@quinnemanuel.com

elinorsutton@quinnemanuel.com

jeremybaldoni@quinnemanuel.com

brendancarroll@quinnemanuel.com

*Attorneys for Markforged, Inc.*

*/s/ Eric G. J. Kaviar*

Howard J. Susser (BBO# 636183)

hsusser@burnslev.com

Eric G. J. Kaviar (BBO# 670833)

ekaviar@burnslev.com

Laura Carroll (BBO# 076180)

lcarroll@burnslev.com

BURNS & LEVINSON LLP

125 Summer Street

Boston, MA 02110

(617) 345-3000

*Attorneys for Matiu Parangi*

# Motion for Sanctions

2015 WL 9809970 (D.Mass.)

United States District Court, D. Massachusetts.

SERKAN CABI, Ph.D., Isin Cakir, Ph.D., and Safak Mert, Ph.D., Plaintiffs,

v.

BOSTON CHILDREN'S HOSPITAL, The Children's Hospital Corporation and Its Affiliated Entities, Umut Ozcan, M.D., Joseph Majzoub, M.D., Sandra L. Fenwick, Michele Garvin, and Erx Pharmaceuticals, Inc., Defendants.

No. 1:15-cv-12306.

October 16, 2015.

Defendant Umut Ozcan, M.D.'s Memorandum in Support of His Amended Motion for Sanctions Pursuant to Rule 11 of the Federal Rules of Civil Procedure

Umut Ozcan, M.D., By his attorneys, Tracy A. Miner, BBO No. 547137, Demeo LLP, 200 State Street, Boston, MA 02109, Tel: (617) 263-2600, Fax: (617) 263-2300, Email: tminer@demeollp.com; Bruce A. Singal, BBO #464420, Callan G. Stein, BBO #670569, Donoghue Barrett & Singal, P.C., One Beacon Street, Suite 1320, Boston, Massachusetts 02108, Tel: (617) 720-5090, Fax: (617) 720-5092, Email: bsingal@dbslawfirm.com, Email: cstein@dbslawfirm.com.

### Introduction

This Amended Complaint represents the most recent salvo fired in the longstanding and baseless campaign waged by the Plaintiffs--Drs. Cabi, Cakir, and Mert--to destroy the professional career and reputation of Dr. Umut Ozcan. In seeking to advance this campaign, the Plaintiffs have asserted claims in Counts I, II, III, V, VI, and VII of their Amended Complaint that are, on their face, frivolous. These claims only could have been brought to smear, harass, and embarrass Dr. Ozcan.

Plaintiffs refused to withdraw these frivolous counts, even after each of the Defendants expressed their concerns about their lack of factual and legal bases and requested that they do so. In an apparent admission that some of their claims were in fact frivolous, Plaintiffs dropped several claims in an Amended Complaint, including their Title VII claim against Dr. Ozcan, their spoliation claim, and their claims for intentional or reckless and negligent infliction of emotional distress. However, Plaintiffs simply reasserted most of the frivolous counts, without remedying the fatal defects in those claims, and added more defendants. In the face of Plaintiffs' obstinate refusal to withdraw these Counts, Dr. Ozcan hereby moves for sanctions pursuant to Rule 11 of the Federal Rule of Civil Procedure for the frivolous claims filed in Counts I, II, III, V, VI, and VII of the Amended Complaint.

### Background

Plaintiffs' campaign to discredit and damage Dr. Ozcan began in late February/early March 2014 when they (falsely) accused Dr. Ozcan of committing research misconduct. *See* Am. Compl. ¶¶ 30-35. More specifically, Plaintiffs complained to Boston Children's Hospital ("BCH") and the Harvard Medical School ("HMS") that Dr. Ozcan forced them to fabricate and falsify research data while working in his laboratory. Am. Compl. ¶¶ 33-35. Dr. Ozcan vehemently denied ever directing the Plaintiffs to commit such misconduct, and filed counter-allegations of research misconduct based largely on the Plaintiffs' admissions that they had, indeed, falsified and fabricated certain data. *See* Am. Compl. ¶ 95. These research misconduct proceedings are ongoing at BCH and HMS. Am. Compl. ¶ 47.

This was only the first battle in the full-fledged war that the Plaintiffs have waged against Dr. Ozcan. Shortly after they filed their research misconduct allegations, the Plaintiffs initiated additional internal investigations/processes at BCH and HMS by falsely accusing Dr. Ozcan of a litany of human resources violations, Am. Compl. ¶ 155, Exhibit C, Exhibit Q and falsely claiming that Dr. Ozcan made no contributions to certain patents owned by HMS and should, therefore, be removed as a named inventor, Am. Compl. ¶ 66, Exhibit C, Exhibit Q.

After each of these investigations/processes was resolved in Dr. Ozcan's favor, *see, e.g.*, Am. Compl. ¶ 63, Exhibit I (BCH/HMS investigation concluded that Dr. Ozcan would remain an inventor on the patents but that the Postdocs would be removed as inventors), each of the Plaintiffs filed an unsupported Complaint with the Massachusetts Commission Against Discrimination accusing Dr. Ozcan (who, like them, is of Turkish ancestry) of discrimination and retaliation. Am. Compl. Exhibit C. The Plaintiffs filed the MCAD Complaints, like the present lawsuit, to denigrate Dr. Ozcan, and to improperly publicize the BCH/HMS research misconduct proceedings which federal law (and BCH/HMS policies) requires be kept strictly confidential. *See* 42 U.S.C. § 93.108.

Next, Plaintiffs filed their original 336-paragraph Complaint contending that Dr. Ozcan's alleged research misconduct and his accusing them of research misconduct violates myriad federal and state statutes and common law. Plaintiffs included in this Complaint a litany of purported "facts" that have nothing to do with any of the claims they bring and are, instead, designed solely to publicly embarrass Dr. Ozcan. One of the most egregious examples of this is Plaintiffs' completely irrelevant accusations in ¶¶ 137 and 156 that Dr. Ozcan made disparaging remarks about groups to which Plaintiffs do not belong.[1]

In response to Plaintiffs' original Complaint, Defendants served Rule 11 letters on Plaintiffs, filed Motions to Dismiss the Complaint, and served Motions for Sanctions under Rule 11 detailing the egregious nature of Plaintiffs' claims and frivolous allegations. Acknowledging that at least some of their claims were frivolous, Plaintiffs' filed an Amended Complaint dropping several claims, including their Title VII claim against Dr. Ozcan their spoliation claim, and their claims for intentional or reckless and negligent infliction of emotional distress. Plaintiffs did not, however, withdraw their Complaint in its entirety, and instead reasserted the vast majority of their original claims in a 312-paragraph Amended Complaint.

Plaintiffs' entire lawsuit is meritless, and is the subject of a renewed Motion to Dismiss. The Counts Plaintiffs bring against Dr. Ozcan--Counts I, II, III, V, VI, and VII--qualify as frivolous, however, and, therefore, violate Rule 11. Those Counts are based on neither fact nor existing law. Even the most basic inquiry into applicable law would have revealed as much to counsel. Dr. Ozcan made Plaintiffs and their counsel aware of the frivolousness of each of these claims in his Rule 11 letter dated July 14, 2015. In that letter, Dr. Ozcan implored Plaintiffs to withdraw these claims, and warned them that further pursuit of them violated Rule 11. Plaintiffs never responded to that letter. Defendants also laid out the hopeless nature of Plaintiffs' claims in their original Motions to Dismiss and Rule 11 Motions. Plaintiffs have not withdrawn many of their claims, and should be sanctioned for their waste of Dr. Ozcan's and the Court's resources.

## *Argument*

### I. Rule 11 Standard

Rule 11 of the Federal Rules of Civil Procedure prohibits frivolous filings by setting forth substantive obligations for persons submitting pleadings to the Court. *See Young v. City of Providence ex rel. Napolitano*, 404 F.3d 33, 39 (1st Cir. 2005). Rule 11 requires an attorney to certify that "to the best of the [attorney's] knowledge, information, and belief" the legal claims submitted are done so with some basis in law and fact. That is, that the claim is not submitted "for any improper purpose," that "the claims, defenses, and other legal contentions are warranted by existing law," and that the "factual contentions have evidentiary support or . . . will likely have evidentiary support after a reasonable opportunity for further investigation or discovery." Fed. R. Civ. P. 11(b)(1)-(3). Rule 11 further requires that an attorney conduct "an inquiry reasonable under the circumstances" before signing his or her name to a pleading. Fed. R. Civ. P. 11(b).

The Court must view objectively whether an attorney's position is well-grounded in fact and warranted under the existing law sufficient to meet the Rule 11 requirements. *See Cruz v. Savage*, 896 F.2d 626, 631-632 (1st Cir. 1990). If the court determines that Rule 11(b) has been objectively violated, the court may impose an appropriate sanction. Fed. R. Civ. P. 11 (c)(1). Where an attorney does not act reasonably under the circumstances in initiating or litigating a cause of action, sanctions are warranted. *See Cruz*, 896 F.2d at 631; *Hochen v. Bobst Grp., Inc.*, (D. Mass. 2000) aff'd sub nom. *Nyer v. Winterthur Int'l*, 290 F.3d 456 (1st Cir. 2002) (attorney liable for costs and reasonable attorneys' fees incurred by other party in opposing motion and moving for sanctions).

Even the most basic inquiry into the facts and law applicable to Counts I, II, III, V, VI, and VII--let alone a "reasonable inquiry" as

---

1. Plaintiffs are well aware of Dr. Ozcan's objections to them including allegations like this in their public complaints. While the MCAD actions were still pending Dr. Ozcan filed Motions to this effect and identified by paragraph number the offending allegations. Plaintiffs have disregarded those objections by re-asserting them in their original Complaint.

required by Rule 11--reveals that all six Counts are frivolous on their face. Even if Plaintiffs failed to make this inquiry prior to filing their Complaint as they were required to do, Defendants identified each claim at issue in this Motion as frivolous in their Rule 11 letters, Rule 11 Motions, and Motions to Dismiss and gave Plaintiffs an opportunity to withdraw them. Plaintiffs, however, simply ignored this request. By pursuing such obviously frivolous claims, Plaintiffs and Plaintiffs' counsel have violated Rule 11 and the imposition of sanctions is warranted.[2]

## II.  Counts I and II: Plaintiffs cannot meet, and in fact do not even allege, the fundamental element of state action required to bring a claim pursuant to 42 U.S.C. § 1983, or federal action required to bring a *Bivens* claim, because under no view of the facts is Dr. Ozcan even arguably a state or federal actor.

Plaintiffs original Complaint failed to allege that Dr. Ozcan acted under color of state law, as required to state a claim under 42 U.S.C. § 1983. Plaintiffs alleged no facts suggesting that Dr. Ozcan, who they acknowledge is a private individual, Compl. at ¶¶ 4-6, acted under color of law. The Amended Complaint fares no better.

The Amended Complaint brings Counts I and II against Dr. Ozcan for violating their constitutional rights while acting under color of both state and federal law in violation of 42 U.S.C. § 1983 and *Bivens v. Six Unknown Agents of the Fed. Bureau of Narcotics*, 403 U.S. 388 (1971). To state a claim against Dr. Ozcan under § 1983 or *Bivens*, Plaintiffs must allege that he violated their constitutional rights while acting under color of state or federal law, respectively. *See* 42 U.S.C. § 1983; *DeMayo v. Nugent*, 517 F.3d 11, 14 (1st Cir. 2008) ("A claimant who seeks relief under *Bivens* must prove the violation of a constitutional right by a federal agent acting under color of federal law."). It is not enough to simply assert that a private individual has had some connection with the state or federal government at some time. Plaintiffs must connect Dr. Ozcan's alleged violations of their constitutional rights with his alleged status as a state or federal actor. *See Redondo-Borges v. U.S. Dep't of Housing and Urban Dev.*, 421 F.3d 1, 7 (1st Cir. 2005) (affirming dismissal of *Bivens* claim where complaint did not connect alleged federal oversight with due process deprivation); *Ferlisi v. Galvin*, 787 F. Supp. 2d 111, 117 (D. Mass. 2011) (dismissing § 1983 claim where defendant made disparaging statement before he was state actor).

Plaintiffs' amended Count I and II are frivolous. Plaintiffs make no effort to connect their conclusory allegations that Dr. Ozcan acted under color of state or federal law with his purported violations of their constitutional rights. For the reasons stated in BCH's Rule 11 motion, Plaintiffs do not allege that BCH or any of its affiliates are state or federal actors. Moreover, to the extent that Plaintiffs allege BCH collaborates with a quasi-public state agency, they make no effort to connect that collaboration to Dr. Ozcan or any of the events underlying the Amended Complaint. Am. Compl. ¶ 3.

The claims against Dr. Ozcan are even less plausible. For example, while the Amended Complaint asserts that BCH is acting under color of federal law in conducting a research misconduct investigation pursuant to federal regulations, they do not allege that Dr. Ozcan performed a quasi-judicial investigatory or disciplinary role in the research misconduct investigation. Am. Compl. ¶ 241. It is clear from Plaintiffs' allegations that Dr. Ozcan's role in the investigation is limited to that of complainant. Am. Compl. ¶ 45. Reporting information to an investigatory body is not acting under color of law. *See Meuse v. Stults*, 421 F. Supp. 2d 358, 362 (D. Mass. 2006).

Plaintiffs have had multiple opportunities to withdraw the § 1983 and *Bivens* against Dr. Ozcan. However, they have refused to withdraw those claims in response to Dr. Ozcan's Rule 11 letter (Exhibit A), his original Rule 11 motion (Exhibit B), and his motion to dismiss (Docket Nos. 31-32). In fact, they never responded to the Rule 11 letter let alone offer any reasonable justification for including these claims in the Amended Complaint.

Plaintiffs lack any basis to assert § 1983 and *Bivens* claims against Dr. Ozcan because under no circumstances can they meet the fundamental requirement of state or federal action. The impropriety of asserting these claims against Dr. Ozcan would have been unambiguously apparent from *any* reasonable inquiry into the law. Plaintiffs' failure to conduct such an inquiry renders Counts I and II frivolous, and warrants the imposition of sanctions.

## III.  Count III: Plaintiffs do not allege Dr. Ozcan interfered with their protected rights by means of threats, intimidation, or coercion under M.G.L. c. 12, §§ 11H and 11I.

Count III of the Amended Complaint is likewise frivolous and unsupported by Plaintiffs' allegations. To state a claim under M.G.L. c. 12, §§ 11H and 11I against Dr. Ozcan, Plaintiffs must allege that he interfered with their protected rights "by threats, intimidation, or coercion." M.G.L. c. 12 § 11H. Threats, intimidation, or coercion require "something akin to duress which causes the victim to relinquish [his] rights." *Butler v. TMS Techs., Inc.*, 741 F. Supp. 1008, 1011 (D. Mass 1990) (citing *Layne v. Superintendent, Massachusetts Corr. Inst.*, 406 Mass. 156 (1989)). The Amended Complaint contains no allegation that Dr. Ozcan threatened, intimidated, or coerced them.

---

2. Dr. Ozcan incorporates by reference the arguments contained in the other defendants' Motions for Sanctions.

The sole allegation regarding any action taken by Dr. Ozcan in Count III is that he contacted Dr. Cakir's new principal investigator. Am. Compl. ¶ 253. Plaintiffs make no effort to show that this allegation is sufficient to state a claim under § 11H. The Amended Complaint claims that this contact was "inappropriate[ ]," Am. Compl. ¶ 190, but does not suggest that this contact caused Dr. Cakir to relinquish any rights under duress or identify any specific rights that were impacted by this contact. Nor does it allege that Dr. Ozcan made any threats, intimidation, or coercion directed at Drs. Cabi and Mert.

Dr. Ozcan notified Plaintiffs of the defects in Count III in its Motion to Dismiss the original Complaint. Plaintiffs' continued failure to allege a single right that Dr. Ozcan interfered with through threats, intimidation, or coercion is frivolous and sanctionable.

## IV.  Count V: Plaintiffs do not and cannot allege that Dr. Ozcan discriminated against them or created a hostile work environment because of their membership in a protected class under M.G.L. c. 151B.

Count V is also frivolous and unsupported by law or fact. In an effort to smear Dr. Ozcan's reputation, Plaintiffs once again allege that he engaged in a variety of offensive behaviors unrelated to their discrimination or sexual harassment claims. However, they do not allege, as they must, that Dr. Ozcan took any discriminatory actions against them or created a hostile work environment because of Plaintiffs' membership in a protected class.

At most, Plaintiffs' Amended Complaint alleges that Dr. Ozcan engaged in certain general, rude behavior directed toward them. But even if these allegations were true (which they are not), they fall far short of violating M.G.L. ch. 151B. Chapter 151B prohibits discrimination against an individual "because of the race, color, national origin, sex, gender identity, sexual orientation, . . ., genetic information, or ancestry of any individual." M.G.L. ch. 151B § 4(1). Plaintiffs do not allege that Dr. Ozcan took discriminatory actions or created a hostile work environment as a result of Plaintiffs' status as Turkish men, a group of which he is also a member. To the contrary, Plaintiffs repeatedly attribute Dr. Ozcan's anger towards them as stemming from their reporting him for research misconduct. Am. Compl. ¶¶ 45, 166-69.

Dr. Ozcan advised Plaintiffs that their chapter 151B claim was frivolous in his Rule 11 letter, his original Rule 11 Motion, and his motion to dismiss. Plaintiffs have repeatedly refused to withdraw this claim. Even worse, Plaintiffs continue to embarrass Dr. Ozcan by alleging he made certain remarks that have no bearing on Plaintiffs' race or gender. *See, e.g.*, Am. Compl. ¶¶ 127, 144. Plaintiffs' conduct in pursuing Count V is sanctionable.

## V.  Count VI: The Amended Complaint makes clear that the entire basis for Plaintiffs' Count VI is that Dr. Ozcan retaliated against them for reporting his research misconduct. But on its face, reporting research misconduct is not protected activity under any of the statutes they list in Count VI.

Count VI makes clear that Plaintiffs' retaliation claim is tied to their report that Dr. Ozcan engaged in research misconduct. As Plaintiffs allege, "But for making that report, the alleged retaliatory acts would not have happened." Am. Compl. ¶ 277. Even a cursory glance at the provisions Plaintiffs cite in Count VI would demonstrate that they provide no cause of action for retaliation for reporting research misconduct.

Four of the provisions to which Plaintiffs refer do not even provide a private right of action against Dr. Ozcan for retaliation. 42 U.S.C. § 289b simply establishes the federal Office of Research Integrity. 42 C.F.R. § 93 is the Public Health Service's Policies and Final Rule on Research Misconduct, which the Amended Complaint acknowledges does not create a cause of action. Am. Compl. ¶ 272. Title VII, including 42 U.S.C. § 2000e-3(a) also does not provide a cause of action against individuals. *See Fantini v. Salem State Coll.*, 557 F.3d 22, 31 (1st Cir. 2009). Likewise, the First Amendment of U.S. Constitution does not provide a cause of action against a private individual. *See Orell v. UMass Mem'l Med. Ctr., Inc.*, 203 F. Supp. 2d 52, 71 (D. Mass. 2002).

The remaining statutes do not cover the conduct alleged here. 41 U.S.C. §§ 1981 and 1983 do not apply because, as previously discussed, Dr. Ozcan is not a state or federal actor. M.G.L. c. 149 § 185 provides a private cause of action for public employees who suffer retaliation for disclosing an unlawful activity, policy or practice of a state government employer. Plaintiffs do not allege that they are state employees, or that Dr. Ozcan is a state government employer. Finally, M.G.L. ch. 151B prohibits only retaliation against a plaintiff who has opposed any forbidden employment discrimination or participated in any employment discrimination proceedings. That chapter does not apply to complainants who bring charges of research misconduct.

Plaintiffs have ignored repeated warnings that Count VI is baseless in Dr. Ozcan's Rule 11 letter, his original Rule 11 Motion, and Defendants' motions to dismiss. The Court should sanction Plaintiffs for their refusal to withdraw this frivolous claim.

## VI.  Count VII: Plaintiffs do not allege that Defendants engaged in a conspiracy for the purpose of depriving Plaintiffs of the equal protection of the laws, or of equal privileges and immunities under the laws under 42 U.S.C. § 1985.

Among other things, § 1985 prohibits conspiring to deprive "any person or class of persons of equal protection of the laws, or of equal privileges and immunities under the laws." 42 U.S.C. § 1985(3). The Amended Complaint contains only cursory allegations that Defendants conspired. Am. Compl. ¶ 283 ("Defendants are parties to a conspiracy. . . ."). At best, the Amended Complaint alleges that Dr. Ozcan and the other Defendants had a shared financial interest in the intellectual property that was developed in his laboratory. These allegations fall far short of a conspiracy.

Even if Plaintiffs had alleged a conspiracy, the Amended Complaint does not even attempt to allege a conspiracy to deprive them of the equal protection of the law or of equal privileges and immunities under the law. Section 1985 requires "some racial, or perhaps otherwise class-based, invidiously discriminatory animus behind the conspirators' action." *Griffin v. Breckenridge*, 403 U.S. 88, 102-03 (1971). Plaintiffs were well aware that failure to do so would render Count VII frivolous. Plaintiffs failure to retract their conspiracy claim is therefore sanctionable.

### VII. The Court should exercise its discretion under Fed. R. Civ. P. 11(c) and impose sanctions on Plaintiffs.

The purpose of Rule 11 is to deter frivolous filings in Federal Court. *McCarty v. Verizon New England, Inc.*, 731 F. Supp. 2d 123, 133 (D. Mass. 2010). Rule 11 also seeks to curb filings that are made for an "improper purpose, such as to harass or to cause unnecessary delay or needless increase in the cost of litigation." Fed. R. Civ. P. 11(b)(1). Given Plaintiffs' lengthy history of harassing and smearing Dr. Ozcan, and their inability to allege any facts that could possibly support Counts I, II, III, V, VI, and VII, there is little question that the claims are frivolous and were brought solely for purposes that violate Rule 11.

Indeed, other federal courts have imposed Rule 11 sanctions under strikingly similar circumstances to those presented here. For example, in *Elsman v. Standard Fed. Bank (Michigan)*, 238 F. Supp. 2d 903, 909 (E.D. Mich. 2003), the U.S. District Court for the Eastern District of Michigan imposed sanctions on an attorney for filing a § 1983 claim even though the Defendants were clearly not state actors:

> Elsman did not allege that Defendants' actions as private citizens could be attributed to the state. The complaint lacks any factual or legal support that Elsman's claims involved state actors, a necessary element for his constitutional and § 1983 claims...A competent attorney's careful investigation would have revealed that none of the Defendants are state actors and, therefore, that there were no plausible legal grounds on which to file a complaint asserting constitutional claims against them.

*See also Levine v. County of Westchester*, 164 F.R.D. 372, 375 (S.D.N.Y. 1996) (imposing Rule 11 sanctions for alleging constitutional and § 1983 claims against a non-state actor); *Soler v. Puerto Rico Tel. Co.*, 230 F. Supp. 2d 232 (D.P.R. 2002) (imposing Rule 11 sanctions where plaintiffs filed Title VII action but never identified the plaintiff's protected class).

On its face, Plaintiffs' improper conduct warrants the imposition of sanctions. But sanctions are even more appropriate here given the extensive efforts by Dr. Ozcan and each of the other Defendants to send letters explaining why each of these Counts is frivolous, as well as drafting motions to dismiss explaining the fatal deficiencies of Plaintiffs Complaint, and also providing notice that if Plaintiffs did not withdraw those Counts they would be pursuing a Rule 11 Motion. But Plaintiffs ignored these warnings. Plaintiffs' refusal to withdraw or explain these clearly-frivolous claims confirms that they are no more than vehicles for the Plaintiffs to continue their campaign of harassment and abuse against Dr. Ozcan.

In light of these circumstances, it is particularly appropriate for the Court to impose Rule 11 sanctions here. Plaintiffs never should have brought these claims in the first place as even a minimal inquiry into their merits would have revealed them to be frivolous. Plaintiffs not only filed these claims but also forwent the many opportunities Defendants afforded them to remedy that initial failure and avoid Rule 11 sanctions. At a minimum, this Court should require Plaintiffs to bear all expenses and reasonable attorneys' fees Dr. Ozcan has incurred as a result of Plaintiffs' frivolous claims, including, but not limited to, all fees and costs related to: (i) drafting and sending his Rule 11 letter; (ii) drafting and arguing his original and amended Rule 11 Motions; and, (iii) drafting and arguing his original and amended Motions to Dismiss the frivolous Counts.

### Conclusion

Plaintiffs have had many chances to avoid being subjected to Rule 11 sanctions. Had they made any inquiry at all, let alone the type of "reasonable inquiry" Rule 11 requires, they would have recognized the Counts at issue in this Motion as meritless. Had they genuinely considered Dr. Ozcan's and each of the other Defendants' explanations and arguments in their Rule 11 letters, they would have withdrawn those frivolous Counts. Had they then genuinely considered Defendants' arguments in their respective Motions to Dismiss the original Complaint, they would not have filed an Amended Complaint. Plaintiffs were absolutely required to do all of these things but failed. Had they complied with their obligations they could have avoided this Motion and Rule 11 sanctions. But Plaintiffs did not. They instead continued to pursue these improper claims against Dr. Ozcan to continue to harass and defame him and to force him to use his resources to prepare and file motions to dismiss these claims that should never have been filed in the first place.

As the 1993 Advisory Committee on the Federal Rules of Civil Procedure noted, litigation is not a game. Rule 11 requires litigants and, perhaps more importantly, attorneys to "stop and think" before filing claims. Here neither the Plaintiffs nor their counsel heeded this warning. Instead, they filed numerous Counts that are obviously frivolous without any inquiry and without any justification. This type of abuse of the legal process is precisely the conduct Rule 11 was enacted to prevent and punish.

Respectfully submitted,

UMUT OZCAN, M.D.

By his attorneys,

*/s/ Tracy A. Miner*

Tracy A. Miner, BBO No. 547137

DEMEO LLP

200 State Street

Boston, MA 02109

Tel: (617) 263-2600

Fax: (617) 263-2300

Email: tminer@demeollp.com

*/s/ Bruce A. Singal*

Bruce A. Singal, BBO #464420

Callan G. Stein, BBO #670569

DONOGHUE BARRETT & SINGAL, P.C.

One Beacon Street, Suite 1320

Boston, Massachusetts 02108

Tel: (617) 720-5090

Fax: (617) 720-5092

Email: bsingal@dbslawfirm.com

Email: cstein@dbslawfirm.com

Dated: August 26, 2015

# Motion to Compel Discovery

2018 WL 3596799 (D.Mass.)

United States District Court, D. Massachusetts.

MEDINA, et al.,

v.

SUN PRODUCTS CORPORATION., et al.

No. 1:16-cv-11675.

July 9, 2018.

Motion to Compel

Elizabeth Tully, BBO No. 685855, Julie Ferraro, BBO No. 665364, Anthony Tarricone, BBO No. 492480, Kreindler & Kreindler LLP, 855 Boylston Street, Boston, MA 02116, Tel. (617) 424-9100, Fax (617) 424-9120, atarricone@kreindler.com, jferraro@kreindler.com, etully@kreindler.com.

Dear Judge Burroughs:

This is a complex product liability action involving single-dose detergent pods manufactured by Defendant Sun Products Corporation and sold by Defendant Costco Whole Corporation that caused serious injury to a thirteen-month old child. This letter concerns a discovery dispute the parties have been unable to resolve. Notwithstanding Plaintiffs' requests, Defendant Sun Products ("Defendant") has withheld several studies involving single-dose detergent pods subject to attorney-client privilege and work product protection. Defendant asserts that because these studies were prepared at the request of an attorney in order to comply with a Consumer Product Safety Commission Investigation ("CPSC") the studies are privileged. However, Defendant's assertions of attorney-client privilege and work-product privilege are misplaced and inconsistent with the governing law. With regard to work-product privilege, Defendant has failed to demonstrate that the studies at issue were prepared in anticipation of litigation. *United States v. Textron Inc. & Subsidiaries,* 577 F.3d 21 (1st Cir.2009). With regard to attorney-client privilege, Defendant has failed to demonstrate that the withheld documents were confidential or made for the purpose of seeking legal advice. *In re Keeper of the Records (Grand Jury Subpoena Addressed to XYZ Corp.),* 348 F.3d 16, 22 (1st Cir. 2003). Accordingly, Plaintiffs request the Court Order Defendants to produce the withheld documents.

## Background

On April 21, 2017 Plaintiffs served Defendant Sun Products Corporation ("Sun Products") with documents requests. On June 30, 2017 Defendants responded to Plaintiffs' discovery requests. Below are the relevant discovery requests and responses:

**Request No. 14:** All Documents, including studies, evaluations, and analysis that evaluate the risks of use and foreseeability of use of the Subject Product by children.

**Response No. 14**: Sun Products objects to this request on the ground and to the extent it seeks the attorney's/party's undiscoverable work product, including thoughts, impressions, views, strategy, conclusions and other similar information produced in anticipation of litigation. Sun Products also objects to the extent this requests seeks material protected by attorney-client privilege.

Subject to and without waiving these objections, please refer to Correspondence and Data from Industry Organization, Bates Nos. SPC0001231-0001719; CPCS Correspondence and Documents, Bates Nos. SPC 0001720-0002130, SPC0003383-0008767; and Regulatory Affairs Documents, Bates Nos. SPC0002131-0002529.

**Request No. 25:** All Documents relating to any studies concerning laundry detergent pods or pacs.

**Response No. 25:** Sun Products objects to this request on the ground and to the extent it seeks the attorney's/party's undiscoverable work product, including thoughts, impressions, views, strategy, conclusions and other similar information produced in anticipation of litigation. Sun Products also objects to the extent this requests seeks material protected by attorney-client privilege. Sun Products further objects on the basis that the term "studies" is vague and undefined, and a clearer request would be required before Sun Products could reasonably respond.

Subject to and without waiving these objections, please refer to Pre- Production Documents and General Reports, Bates Nos. SPC0000001-0000523; Studies Conducted on Single Dose Packs, Bates Nos. SPC000674-0001127; Correspondence and Data from Industry Organization, Bates Nos. SPC0001231-0001719; CPCS Correspondence and Documents, Bates Nos. SPC 0001720-0002130, SPC0003383-0008767; and Regulatory Affairs Documents, Bates Nos. SPC0002131-0002529; Correspondence and Data from Industry Organization, Bates Nos. SPC0001231-0001719; CPCS Correspondence and Documents, Bates Nos. SPC 0001720-0002130, SPC0003383-0008767; and Regulatory Affairs Documents, Bates Nos. SPC0002131-0002529.

(Exhibit A, Defendant Sun Products' Responses to Plaintiffs' Requests for Production).

On May 21, 2018 Sun Products produced a supplemental privilege log identifying for the first time that they are withholding relevant documents relating to studies, risk assessments, product safety summaries and product safety reviews from 2015 to 2017 on the basis of attorney-client privilege and work product. (Exhibit B, Sun Products Supplemental Privilege Log, dated May 21, 2018). The documents identified in the supplemental privilege log are directly responsive to Plaintiffs' Request Nos. 14 and 25.[1] (Exhibit B, Sun Products Supplemental Privilege Log, dated May 21, 2018).

Additionally, Plaintiffs have a basis for concluding that Defendant has withheld responsive documents not identified in the privilege log. On June 5, 2018, Attorney Ferraro took the deposition of Rule 30(b)(6) designee Ms. Jillaine Dellis, the Director of Product Safety and Regulatory Affairs at Sun Products. Ms. Dellis testified that Sun Products consulted with a toxicologist who Defendant had contracted in 2013 and 2014 with regard to single-dose detergent pods and that Defendant had conducted safety testing on single-dose detergent pods in 2015 and 2016. (Exhibit D, Dellis Depo. at 27-31;80-82; 234-241). Counsel for Sun Products instructed Ms. Dellis not to answer questions relating to studies the company conducted on the basis of attorney-client privilege. (Exhibit D, Rule 30(b)(6) Deposition of Jillaine Dellis at 27-31; 80-82; 234-241). Furthermore, a Sun Products letter dated July 23, 2012 represents that Sun Products had conducted an intensive review of toxicity and safety issues associated with single-dose detergent pods. (Exhibit E, letter dated July 23, 2012). Although Defense Counsel has represented that there is no documentation of the referenced studies, Defendants have been unable to explain the representations made in the letter, raising a potential issue of spoliation. The studies references in the privilege log, Ms. Dellis's Deposition and July 2012 letter are directly responsive to Plaintiffs' Request for Production of Documents Nos. 14 and 25.

On July 2, 2018 the parties held a conference regarding discovery issues in dispute by telephone. Attorneys Ferraro and Tully participated on Plaintiffs' behalf and Attorney Aronsson participated on Defendants' behalf. The central issue in dispute was the discoverability of the studies references in this motion. The parties were unable to reach a resolution.

## Work Product

Defendant's sweeping claims of work product privilege is baseless and is inconsistent with the narrow standard applied by the First Circuit in determining whether a document was "prepared in anticipation of litigation." *United States v. Textron Inc. & Subsidiaries,* 577 F.3d 21, 29 (1st Cir.2009). The relevant test asks whether the documents or materials at issue were "prepared *for use* in possible litigation." *Id.* at 27 (emphasis in original); *See also Id.* at 32 (Torruella, J., dissenting) (explaining the majority's abandonment of the test asking whether the documents were prepared "because of the prospect of litigation" in favor of a narrower "prepared for use in possible litigation" test). The "prepared for use in possible litigation" standard protects only "materials that lawyers typically prepare for the purpose of litigating cases." *Textron, supra* at 26. As the First Circuit reasoned:

From the outset, the focus of work product protection has been on materials prepared for use in litigation, whether the litigation was underway or merely anticipated. . . It is not enough to trigger work product protection that the *subject matter* of a document relates to a subject that might conceivably be litigated. Rather, as the Supreme Court explained, 'the literal language of [Rule 26(b)(3)] protects materials *prepared for* any litigation or trial as long as they were prepared by or for a party to the subsequent litigation.'

---

1. Plaintiffs' counsel had previously attempted to confirm if Defendant was withholding studies of the Subject Product. On April 20, 2018, Counsel for Sun Products confirmed that no documents were withheld subject to Sun Product's objections, except for one document that was addressed to an attorney at the company. (See Exhibit C, Email from Attorney Tully to Attorney Aronsson dated April 20, 2018). Notably, the supplemental privilege log produced by Defendants included several additional studies appear to be responsive to Plaintiffs' Request No. 14.

Nor is it enough that the materials were prepared by lawyers or represent legal thinking. . . .It is only work done in anticipation of or for trial that is protected. Even if prepared by lawyers and reflecting legal thinking, '[m]aterials assembled in the ordinary course of business, or pursuant to public requirements unrelated to litigation, or for other nonlitigation purposes are not under the qualified immunity provided by [Rule 26(b)(3)].'

*Textron, supra,* at 29-30, quoting in part *Federal Trade Comm'n v. Grolier Inc.,* 462 U.S. 19, 25 (1983) (emphasis in original).

Therefore, no protection attaches to "documents that are prepared in the ordinary course of business or that would have been created in essentially similar form irrespective of the litigation, even if the documents would aid in the preparation of litigation." *Maine v. United States Dep't of the Interior,* 298 F.3d 60, 70 (1st Cir. 2002).

The party claiming work product protection has the burden of proof. *United States v. Wilson,* 798 F.2d 509, 512 (1st Cir. 1986). Conclusory allegations that the documents were prepared in anticipation of litigation are not sufficient: it must be shown by evidence and facts that the work product privilege applies. *Mullins v. Department of Labor of Puerto Rico,* 269 F.R.D. 172, 175-176 (D. Puerto Rico 2010). A party's burden to explain why the privilege applies cannot be "brush[ed] . . .aside or satisfied . . .with vague generalities." *Maine v. United States Dep't of the Interior,* 298 F.3d at 69.

Sun Products has not even attempted to meet its burden. The studies at issue were created in the ordinary course of business and according to counsel in response to the Consumer Product Safety Commission investigation into single-dose detergent pods. While litigation was, of course, a possibility, the studies, risk assessments and product safety summaries were not prepared for use in litigation. Rather, the studies would have been conducted in the ordinary course of Sun Products business even in the absence of the possibility of litigation. *Janicker v. George Washington Univ.,* 94 F.R.D. 648, 650 (D.C. 1982).

Further, the mere fact that Sun Products' in-house counsel Brian Del Buono was the recipient of those studies does not render these documents immune from production. The involvement of Mr. Brian Del Buono in the studies does not magically transform those studies into documents "prepared for use in possible litigation." *Textron Inc. & Subsidiaries,* 577 F.3d at 29-30 (it is not enough that the materials were prepared by lawyers or represent legal thinking).

Rather, Sun Products has the burden to show that *each* individual document withheld "was prepared for litigation" and to "correlate the documents to the lawsuit[]." *Maine v. United States Dep't of the Interior,* 298 F.3d at 69. In this regard, Sun Products privilege log is woefully deficient. The log fails to identify each individual document with specificity and merely describes the documents generally which does not allow Plaintiffs or the Court to determine whether a document was prepared for use in litigation. These generalized statements are facially deficient to establish work product protection. *Maine v. United States Dep't of the Interior,* 298 F.3d at 69; *Mullins v. Department of Labor of Puerto Rico,* 269 F.R.D. at 175-176.

## Attorney-Client Privilege

Similarly, Defendant's claim of attorney-client privilege is without merit. The attorney-client privilege "protects only those communications that are confidential and are made for the purpose of seeking or receiving legal advice." *In re Keeper of the Records (Grand Jury Subpoena Addressed to XYZ Corp.),* 348 F.3d 16, 22 (1st Cir. 2003). The mere fact that the communication is between a client and an attorney does not render the communication confidential. *Maine v. United States Dep't of the Interior,* 298 F.3d 60, 71-72. The attorney-client privilege "'does not allow the withholding of documents simply because they are a product of an attorney-client relationship. *It must be demonstrated that the information is confidential.*'" *Id.* at 71-72, quoting *Mead Data Central, Inc. v. U.S. Dept. of Air Force,* 566 F.2d 242, 253 (D.C. Cir. 1977)(emphasis in original). A party must "demonstrate that the withheld documents contain or relate to information that the client intended to keep confidential . . ." *Maine, supra* at 72.

The party asserting protection has the burden of further showing "that the [document] relates to facts communicated for the purpose of securing a legal opinion, legal services or assistance in a legal proceeding. . ." *United States v. Bay State Ambulance and Hosp. Rental Services,* 874 F.2d 20, 27—28 (1st Cir. 1989). The attorney must be acting as a lawyer in connection with the document. *See Texaco Puerto Rico, Inc. v. Department of Consumer Affairs,* 60 F.3d 867, 884 (1st Cir. 1995)("The attorney-client privilege attaches only when the attorney acts in that capacity."). *See Sneider v. Kimberly—Clark Corp.,* 91 F.R.D. 1, 4 (N.D.Ill.1980) (counsel must be "involved in a legal, not business capacity" for the privilege to apply).

Further, documents prepared by non-attorneys and addressed to non-attorneys with copies routed to counsel are generally not privileged since they are not communications made "primarily for legal advice." *Pacmor Bearings, Inc. v. Minebea Co., Ltd.,* 918 F.Supp. 491, 511 (D.N.H. 1996). Sun Products does not obtain this broad protection simply by adding an attorney to the email's list of recipients. Id; *See also Towne Place Condominium Ass'n v. Philadelphia Ind. Ins. Co.,* 284 F.Supp. 3d 889, 895 (N.D.Ill. 2018)(merely communicating with a lawyer or copying a lawyer on an otherwise non-privileged communication does not transform the document into a privileged one, even if the communication was at the behest of the lawyer); *Terra Foundation for Amer. Art v. Solomol+Bauer+Giambastiani, Architects,* 2015 WL 1954459 (April 29, 2015, N.D. Ill.)(the mere presence of a lawyer's name on a document nor the copying of counsel on an email automatically makes the document privileged).

Sun Products has failed to meet its burden. There is no indication that the studies, risk assessments, safety reviews, memorandums and product safety summaries were done for the purpose of securing a legal opinion or advice, legal services, or assistance in a legal proceeding. Defense counsel has not represented that the documents and studies conducted by toxicologists were conducted for the purpose of obtaining a legal opinion, legal services, or legal advice.

For the forgoing reasons, Plaintiffs request that this Court order Sun Products to: (1) produce all documents identified in the privilege log concerning any studies, evaluations, memorandums, and analysis that evaluate safety and risks of use (those documents highlighted in in Exhibit C); (2) produce any other documents or studies responsive to Plaintiff's requests Nos. 14 and 25 that have been withheld, including documentation of any consultation with toxicologists regarding safety or risk of use of single-dose detergent pods references in Ms. Dellis's deposition, and documentation of the toxicity review and safety studies referenced in Mr. Larson's letter; and (3) allow Plaintiffs to continue all depositions for the purposes of questioning witnesses regarding the withheld studies.

Respectfully,

Kreindler & Kreindler LLP

*/s/ Elizabeth Tully*

Elizabeth Tully, BBO No. 685855

Julie Ferraro, BBO No. 665364

Anthony Tarricone, BBO No. 492480

KREINDLER & KREINDLER LLP

855 Boylston Street

Boston, MA 02116

Tel. (617) 424-9100

Fax (617) 424-9120

atarricone@kreindler.com

jferraro@kreindler.com

etully@kreindler.com

# Motion for Protective Order

2018 WL 6068485 (D.Mass.)

United States District Court, D. Massachusetts.

COMERICA BANK & TRUST, N.A. as Personal Representative of the Estate of Prince Rogers Nelson, Plaintiff,

v.

Kian Andrew HABIB, Defendant.

No. 1:17-CV-12418.

August 29, 2018.

## Plaintiff's Memorandum in Support of Its Motion for a Protective Order

Craig R. Smith (BBO No. 636,723), Eric P. Carnevale (BBO No. 677,210), Lando & Anastasi, LLP, Riverfront Office Park, One Main Street — 11th Floor, Cambridge, MA 02142, Tel: (617) 395-7000, Fax: (617) 395-7070, Email: csmith@lalaw.com, ecarnevale@lalaw.com; Lora M. Friedemann, (admitted pro hac vice), Fredrikson & Byron, P.A., 200 South Sixth Street, Ste. 40000, Minneapolis, MN 55402, Tel: (612) 492-7185, Fax: (612) 492-7077, Email: lfriedemann@fredlaw.com, for plaintiff Comerica Bank & Trust, N.A. as Personal Representative of the Estate of Prince Rogers Nelson.

In cases with small amounts in controversy, such as this one, efficient discovery is critical. Under these circumstances, contention interrogatories are an effective means for gathering information while also minimizing costs. Instead, Defendant Kian Andrew Habib has noticed five inefficient and improper deposition topics for a Rule 30(b)(6) witness, seeking legal conclusions, strategies, and attorney mental impressions. Plaintiff Comerica Bank & Trust, N.A. as Personal Representative of the Estate of Prince Rogers Nelson respectfully seeks a protective order for deposition topics that seek to pry into the basis for Comerica's claims and legal theories. Furthermore, because Comerica has already answered contention interrogatories on the same subjects, the deposition topics are not only improper, they are unnecessary.

## BACKGROUND

Plaintiff Comerica Bank & Trust, N.A. commenced this action in its capacity as Personal Representative of the Estate of Prince Rogers Nelson ("Prince") when Defendant Kian Andrew Habib posted videos of live Prince performances on YouTube and refused to take them down. The Amended Complaint asserts claims for copyright infringement and violation of the civil anti-bootlegging statute. 17 U.S.C. § 1101; ECF No. 27.

Discovery is currently ongoing. On July 23, 2018, counsel for Habib served a Notice of Taking Deposition of Comerica Bank & Trust, N.A. pursuant to Rule 30(b)(6) of the Federal Rules of Civil Procedure. Declaration of Lora M. Friedemann ("Friedemann Dec."), Ex. A. The notice included the following five topics, which are at issue in this motion:

**TOPIC 2**: The Works Plaintiff claims, in connection with the Lawsuit, are protected by the Copyright Act.

**TOPIC 3**: The Performance Plaintiff claims Habib infringed and the manner of the alleged infringement.

**TOPIC 4**: The Works Plaintiff claims Habib infringed and the manner of the alleged infringement.

**TOPIC 13**: Damages the Estate claims to have suffered arising from the events that are the subject of the Lawsuit.

**TOPIC 14**: The Estate's discovery responses.

*Id.* Habib's first set of interrogatories, to which Comerica responded on July 2, 2018, request similar information. Friedemann Dec., Ex. B (see Interrogatories 3-8, 18-20).

Comerica objected to each of these five topics on July 26, 2018, for improperly seeking legal conclusions, legal opinions and strategies, as well as the factual basis for Comerica's contentions. *Id.*, Ex. C.

Counsel for Comerica, Lora Friedemann, and for Habib, Seth Salinger, met and conferred on these objections, among others, via telephone for twenty-five minutes beginning at 2:15 p.m. on August 13, 2018. *Id.*, ¶ 5. Although the parties were able to resolve disagreements related to noticed deposition topics 5, 6, and 8-11, the parties did not resolve Comerica's objections as to proposed topics 2-4, 13 and 14. *Id.* Accordingly, Comerica brings the present motion for a protective order regarding these topics.

## ARGUMENT

Federal Rule of Civil Procedure 30(b)(6) allows deposition discovery directed to an organization. The organization must designate a person or persons who will testify on its behalf about information "known or reasonably available to the organization." Fed. R. Civ. P. 30(b)(6). But the scope of this discovery is limited by Rule 26, which permits a court to limit the extent of discovery otherwise allowed under the Federal Rules if it concludes that the discovery sought is "unreasonably cumulative or duplicative"; "can be obtained from another source that is more convenient, less burdensome, or less expensive"; if "the party seeking discovery has had ample opportunity to obtain the information by discovery"; or if the court determines that the burden of producing the discovery outweighs its likely benefit. Fed. R. Civ. P. 26(b)(2)(C). The court must also "protect against disclosure of the mental impressions, conclusions, opinions, or legal theories of a party's attorney or other representative concerning the litigation." Fed. R. Civ. P. 26(b)(3)(B). Courts may enforce these discovery limits by entering a protective order on matters relating to a deposition. Fed. R. Civ. P. 26(c). Specifically, a court may issue a protective order for good cause to protect a party "from annoyance, embarrassment, oppression, or undue burden or expense." *Id.*

A protective order is warranted in this case to prevent Habib from taking a deposition on legal topics that are inappropriate for a Rule 30(b)(6) deposition and an inefficient use of discovery, given the needs of the case.

Courts in this district have consistently held that "a Rule 30(b)(6) witness may not be expected to testify about the factual basis of legal theories." *SEC v. Present*, No. 14-14692-LTS, 2016 WL 10998439, at *2 (D. Mass. May 12, 2016) (citing *Cooper v. Charter Commc'ns, Inc.*, No. 12-10530-MGM, 2016 WL 128099, at *2 (D. Mass. Jan. 12, 2016)). To begin with, deposition topics asking a 30(b)(6) witness about the factual basis for a party's legal claims quickly run into issues of work-product privilege. Such questions "make[] it extremely difficult to distinguish between 'facts' (not protected) and the issue of why those facts have legal consequences, which usually has a work-product (lawyer's mental impressions) dimension." *Fid. Mgmt. & Res. Co. v. Actuate Corp.*, 275 F.R.D. 63, 64 (D. Mass. 2011) (noting that the problem is even more acute because a lawyer is likely the source of information which was provided to the 30(b)(6) witness so that he or she could answer the questions on behalf of the organization).

Moreover, a party may properly object to a Rule 30(b)(6) deposition "on the grounds that the information sought is more appropriately discoverable through other discovery devices." *Present*, 2016 WL 10998439, at *2 (citing *SmithKline Beecham Corp. v. Apotex Corp.*, No. 00-CV-1393, 2004 WL 739959, at *4 (E.D. Pa. Mar. 23, 2004)). A 30(b)(6) deposition is often an "inefficient and unreasonable means of discovering an opponent's factual and legal basis for its claims." *Id.*

Habib's notice of deposition pursuant to Rule 30(b)(6) contains five such topics that improperly seek the factual basis for Comerica's legal theories:

**TOPIC 2**: The Works Plaintiff claims, in connection with the Lawsuit, are protected by the Copyright Act.

Topic 2 seeks the factual information underlying Comerica's claims of copyright infringement and violations of the civil anti-bootlegging statute—in particular, which of the Prince songs owned by Comerica are protected by the Copyright Act. This topic is inappropriate for a 30(b)(6) deposition because it plainly seeks the factual basis of Comerica's legal theories. *See Present*, 2016 WL 10998439, at *2. A lay witness "should not be expected to testify as to how any. . .facts form the basis of a legal [theory]." *Cooper*, 2016 WL 128099, at *2.

Further, such information is more appropriately sought through other discovery means. Indeed, Habib has already requested this information through his first set of interrogatories—and Comerica provided the requested information. Friedemann Dec., Ex. B. Specifically, in response to Habib's Interrogatory No. 3, which explicitly asks Comerica to "[i]dentify the work or works. . . [it] claims is protected by the Copyright Act," Comerica provided a chart of copyrighted works it is asserting by title and registration number. *Id.* at 3.

A deposition on this topic would be inefficient, unreasonable, and inappropriate.

**TOPIC 3**: The Performance Plaintiff claims Habib infringed and the manner of the alleged infringement.

Topic 3 seeks the factual basis for Comerica's claims of copyright infringement and violations of the civil anti-bootlegging statute. Courts have found that similar topics—seeking the basis for allegations that a party does (or does not) infringe a patent—are "more appropriately discoverable through contention interrogatories" because a Rule 30(b)(6) deposition is an "overbroad, inefficient, and unreasonable means of discovering an opponent's factual and legal basis for its claims." *Trustees of Boston Univ. v. Everlight Elecs.*

*Co.*, No. 12-CV-11935-PBS, 2014 WL 5786492, at *4 (D. Mass. Sept. 24, 2014); *see also SmithKline Beecham*, 2004 WL 739959, at *4. It would be difficult for a non-attorney witness to answer such questions at a deposition.

Moreover, Comerica has already provided this information in response to Habib's Interrogatory Nos. 5 and 7, which request that Comerica "[id]entify all the ways that Plaintiff is aware of that Habib infringed the work . . . identified" and asks, in short, whether Comerica contends that "all parts of a Prince concert performance. . .are subject to copyright protection." Friedemann Dec., Ex. B at 4-5. Comerica identified the URLs in which Habib publicly posted live Prince concerts on YouTube and explained that the musical compositions that Prince performed in these live concerts are protected by the Copyright Act and the Civil Anti-Bootlegging Statute. *Id.* Thus, Habib has already received the information sought in this topic.

**TOPIC 4**: The Works Plaintiff claims Habib infringed and the manner of the alleged infringement.

Topic 4 seeks information analogous to Topic 3, relating to the copyrighted works Comerica claims Habib has infringed. As the Courts found in *Trustees of Boston Univ.*, 2014 WL 5786492, and *SmithKline Beecham*, 2004 WL 739959, this topic is not proper for a 30(b)(6) witness. Further, Comerica has already provided a chart of copyrighted works it claims Habib has infringed in response to Habib's Interrogatory No. 4 ("Identify the work or works that the Plaintiff claims Habib infringed."), and explained the manner of the infringement in response to Habib's Interrogatory No. 5. Friedemann Dec., Ex. B at 4-5. A deposition on any of these first three topics would be inefficient, unreasonable, and inappropriate. As a result, good cause exists for entry of a protective order to prevent Habib from deposing Comerica's 30(b)(6) witness as to Topics 2-4.

**TOPIC 13**: Damages the Estate claims to have suffered arising from the events that are the subject of the Lawsuit.

Topic 13 is improper because it seeks information regarding Comerica's legal claim for damages. A court in this district considering an analogous topic requesting factual information underlying the party's damages theory from a Rule 30(b)(6) witness concluded that the topic is "unnecessary" because the "information requested can be adequately provided by written discovery, interrogatories, and a deposition of the . . . expert on damages." *E.E.O.C. v. Texas Roadhouse, Inc.*, No. 11-11732-DJC, 2014 WL 4471521, at *3-4 (D. Mass. Sept. 9, 2014). Moreover, Comerica has already provided this information in its response to Interrogatories 18-20, which asks whether Comerica contends that it "suffered any monetary damages as a result of any act or omission on the part of Habib"; "the total amount of damages that the Plaintiff calculates it has incurred to date"; and "all facts known that support the damages calculation." Friedemann Dec., Ex. B at 8-9. Comerica is seeking statutory damages and an award of attorney's fees and costs under 17 U.S.C. § 505. Because Comerica is not seeking to recover actual damages incurred as a result of Habib's actions, Topic 13 is inappropriate and unnecessary.

**TOPIC 14**: The Estate's discovery responses.

Finally, Topic 14 seeks information regarding Comerica's discovery responses. Because Comerica's discovery responses were prepared with the assistance of an attorney, it would be difficult—if not impossible—for Comerica's 30(b)(6) witness to answer questions on this topic without divulging information protected by attorney-client or work-product privilege. *See Present*, 2016 WL 10998439, at *3 ("Such questioning inappropriately veers into the territory of . . . attorney work product."). Furthermore, as noted above, several of Comerica's discovery responses articulate the legal basis for the claims it is asserting — subjects that are not appropriate for a Rule 30(b)(6) deposition.

Topic 14 also fails to identify the subject matter for questioning with enough specificity to allow Comerica to prepare a witness. Habib propounded discovery requests that address all aspects of the case, and Comerica's responses therefore address all aspects of the case. The Topic as worded is hopelessly broad, and fails to identify the subject for examination "with reasonable particularity," as required under Fed. R. Civ. P. 30(b)(6).

## CONCLUSION

Depositions "are designed to discover facts . . . not legal theories." *Cooper*, 2016 WL 128099, at *2. Habib's proposed deposition Topics 2-4, 13, and 14 are legally improper and an inefficient use of the parties' discovery resources. Comerica respectfully requests that the Court issue a protective order preventing Habib from taking a deposition of Comerica's 30(b)(6) witness on Topics 2-4, 13, and 14.

Dated: August 29, 2018

Respectfully submitted,

By: */s/ Lora M. Friedemann*

Craig R. Smith (BBO No. 636,723)

Eric P. Carnevale (BBO No. 677,210)

**LANDO &ANASTASI, LLP**

Riverfront Office Park

One Main Street — 11th Floor
Cambridge, MA 02142
Tel: (617) 395-7000
Fax: (617) 395-7070
Email: csmith@lalaw.com
ecarnevale@lalaw.com
Lora M. Friedemann
(*admitted pro hac vice*)
**FREDRIKSON &BYRON, P.A.**
200 South Sixth Street, Ste. 40000
Minneapolis, MN 55402
Tel: (612) 492-7185
Fax: (612) 492-7077
Email: lfriedemann@fredlaw.com
*Attorneys for Plaintiff Comerica Bank &Trust, N.A. as Personal Representative of the Estate of Prince Rogers Nelson*

# Motion for Discovery Sanctions

2018 WL 6039412 (D.Mass.)

**Westlaw Query>>**

To find more Motion for Discovery Sanctions filings on Westlaw: access Massachusetts Civil Trial Court Documents (from the Home page, click Trial Court Documents, then Massachusetts), enter "DT(discovery and sanction!)" in the search box, and click Search. Use the Jurisdiction filter on the left to narrow results to Federal.

United States District Court, D. Massachusetts.

Andre VYSEDSKIY, Plaintiff,

v.

ONSHIFT, INC.; and Does 1-10, inclusive, Defendants.

No. 1:16-cv-12161-MLW.

February 9, 2018.

Plaintiff's Second Motion to Compel and for Discovery Sanctions

Sergei Lemberg, Esq., Lemberg Law, LLC, 43 Danbury Road, Wilton, CT 06897, Telephone: (203) 653-2250, Facsimile: (203) 653-3424, for plaintiff.

Plaintiff Andre Vysedskiy ("Plaintiff"), by and through undersigned counsel, moves this Court pursuant to Fed. R. Civ. Pr. 37 to enter sanctions against the Defendant OnShift, Inc. ("OnShift").[1] Plaintiff moves to compel testimony on deposition topics 1, 2, 8, and 9[2] related to jurisdictional discovery specifically ordered by the Court. In response to Plaintiff's Rule 30(b)(6) notice of deposition OnShift produced two corporate designees: Michael Rich and Adam Wallace. Both corporate designees failed to answer many of the questions posed. Following the parties' Rule 37.1 pre-motion discovery conference OnShift agreed to produce Mr. Rich for re-deposition, but refused to produce Mr. Wallace or produce discovery in unredacted form, prompting Plaintiff to file his first Motion to Compel and for Discovery Sanctions on January 12, 2018. (Doc. No. 25). OnShift has subsequently withdrawn its offer to produce Mr. Rich for re-deposition, prompting Plaintiff to file yet another motion.

## I. PROCEDURAL HISTORY AND BACKGROUND

When the Court ordered that jurisdictional discovery could commence, it ordered discovery on:

- "OnShift's conduct - in particular, the sales of its software to Massachusetts residents -may constitute a 'purposeful availment' of Massachusetts' economy or the protection of its laws, such that the exercise of jurisdiction would be fundamentally fair." Doc. No. 14 Pg. 16.

- "evidence of any 'specific effort' by OnShift to sell its product in Massachusetts, such as advertising or solicitations directed to Massachusetts residents." *Id.* at 16.

- "evidence of how OnShift's Massachusetts customers purchased the software or whether OnShift knew that the customers lived in Massachusetts when it sold them the product." *Id.*

- "evidence of the total number of customers who reside in Massachusetts." *Id.*

- "total revenue OnShift derives from those customers." *Id.*

- circumstances surrounding OnShift's sales of its software to Massachusetts residents, the volume of such sales, and the revenue derived from those sales. *Id.* at 18.

---

1. On January 12, 2018, Plaintiff moved this Court to compel Defendant to produce discovery in unredacted form and to compel re-deposition of Defendant on notice topics 4, 5, and 6. (Doc. No. 25).

2. *Exhibit A* to Declaration of Sergei Lemberg - Deposition Notice.

Plaintiff's Fed. R. Civ. Pr. 30(b)(6) deposition notice lists the following topics, which closely track the Order's exemplary listing of permissible areas of inquiry. Specifically, Plaintiff sought the following:

- *Topic 1*: The circumstances surrounding Defendant's sale(s) of its software to Massachusetts residents, including how Defendant's Massachusetts customers came to purchase Defendant's software;

- *Topic 2*: The volume of Defendant's sale(s) of its software to Massachusetts residents;

- *Topic 8*: Whether Defendant knew that these customers were located in Massachusetts when it sold them the product; and

- *Topic 9*: Any specific efforts taken by Defendant to sell its product in Massachusetts, including advertising campaigns.

During the December 14, 2017, deposition, Plaintiff questioned OnShift's corporate representative Michael Rich on deposition topics above. Mr. Rich lacked knowledge to answer many of the questions posed and noticed in the 30(b)(6) notice.

## II. PLAINTIFF SATISFIED HIS DUTY TO MEET AND CONFER

On January 5, 2018, Plaintiff sought to meet and confer pursuant to Local Rule 37.1 regarding failure of OnShift's 30(b)(6) designee to provide answers.[3] On January 11, 2018, parties conferred over the telephone, with Vlad Hirnyk representing the Plaintiff and Julie Crocker representing the Defendant. In the course of the conference OnShift agreed to make Mr. Rich available for re-deposition via video-conference to answer questions for which he claimed no knowledge and to answer such other questions concerning relevant facts or facts that could lead to relevant evidence. Pursuant to OnShift's request to provide re-deposition topics, Mr. Hirnyk sent OnShift on January 30, 2018, a list of deposition topics with sub-topics and inquired of Mr. Rich's availability for re-deposition.[4] On February 5, 2018, OnShift responded that in light of Plaintiff's Motion to Compel re-deposition of Mr. Wallace, it no longer saw sense in making Mr. Rich available for the re-deposition.[5]

## III. DEFENDANT MUST PRODUCE MR. RICH OR ANOTHER 30(b)(6) DESIGNEE FOR RE-DEPOSITION ON TOPICS 4, 5, & 6

OnShift had a duty to prepare and produce a knowledgeable person for the Rule 30(b)(6) deposition. *Booker v. Massachusetts Dep't of Pub. Health*, 246 F.R.D. 387, 389 (D. Mass. 2007). Such witness(es) have an obligation to educate himself as to the matters regarding the corporation so that he may give knowledgeable and binding answers for the corporation. *Booker*, 246 F.R.D. at 389; *Calzaturficio S.C.A.R.P.A. s.p.a. v. Fabiano Shoe Co.*, 201 F.R.D. 33, 36 (D. Mass. 2001); *see also Briddell v. St. Gobain Abrasives Inc.*, 233 F.R.D. 57, 60 (D. Mass. 2005) ("If necessary, the deponent must use documents, past employees, and other resources in performing this required preparation."). "Producing an unprepared witness is tantamount to a failure to appear at a deposition." *Calzaturficio S.C.A.R.P.A. s.p.a.*, 201 F.R.D. at 39; *citing Starlight Int'l v. Herlihy*, 186 F.R.D. 626, 639 (D. Kan., 1999); *see also Black Horse Lane Assoc, P.P. v. Dow Chemical Corp.*, 228 F.3d 275, 303 (3 Cir., 2000) ("If the agent [of a corporation] is not knowledgeable about relevant facts, and the principal has failed to designate an available, knowledgeable, and readily identifiable witness, then the appearance is, for all practical purposes, no appearance at all."). The Court can order the corporation to re-designate its witnesses and mandate their preparation for re-deposition at the corporation's expense. *Calzaturficio S.C.A.R.P.A. s.p.a.*, 201 F.R.D. at 41.

A party conducting a 30(b)(6) deposition is not strictly limited to topics identified in the deposition notice, but is entitled to discovery of any information that 'is discoverable if there is any possibility it might be relevant to the subject matter of the action,' *EEOC v. Electro--Term, Inc.*, 167 F.R.D. 344, 346 (D. Mass. 1996), even if it 'is not directly related to the subject of the underlying litigation,' *Cabana v. Forcier*, 200 F.R.D. 9, 17 (D.Mass.2001). *Gulbankian v. MW Mfrs., Inc.*, 2013 WL 2146868, at *1 (D. Mass. May 15, 2013); Fed. R. Civ. P. 26(b)(1). A deponent who objects to a deposition notice carries the burden of filing a motion to terminate or limit a deposition; it is insufficient to simply object to the deposition notice. *New England Carpenters Health Benefits Fund v. First DataBank, Inc.*, 242 F.R.D. 164, 166 (D. Mass. 2007). Further, the Fed. R. Civ. P. 30(c)(2) provides that objections during depositions must be noted on the record, but "the examination still proceeds" and "the testimony is taken subject to any objection."

Plaintiff's Rule 30(b)(6) deposition notice was strictly limited to areas of inquiry the Court deemed appropriate. It aimed at exploring OnShift's activities and connections with Massachusetts-based entities which might constitute "a 'purposeful availment' of Massachusetts' economy or the protection of its laws, such that the exercise of jurisdiction would be fundamentally fair." Doc. No. 14 Pg. 16.

---

3. *Exhibit B* to Declaration of Sergei Lemberg - a January 5, 2018, letter outlining the areas of disagreement.

4. *Exhibit C* to Lemberg Decl. - a January 30, 2018, letter listing re-deposition topics.

5. *Exhibit D* to Lemberg Decl. - a February 5, 2018, letter from OnShift.

### A. Mr. Rich Lacked Knowledge to Answer Questions on Topics "1", "2", "8" & "9"

OnShift designated Mr. Michael Rich, OnShift's [Text redacted in copy.] to testify about "Topic 1" (The circumstances surrounding Defendant's sale(s) of its software to Massachusetts residents, including how Defendant's Massachusetts customers came to purchase Defendant's software), "Topic 2" (The volume of Defendant's sale(s) of its software to Massachusetts residents), "Topic 8" (Whether Defendant knew that these customers were located in Massachusetts when it sold them the product) and "Topic 9" (Any specific efforts taken by Defendant to sell its product in Massachusetts, including advertising campaigns). Mr. Rich testified he [Text redacted in copy.]. (Deposition Transcript of Michael Rich 7:5-8:6, 11:4-6; 13:16-25).[6]

During the deposition, Mr. Rich, admitted he lacked answers to many of the questions posed. Mr. Rich testified [Text redacted in copy.] (Rich Tr. 15:1-15). Mr. Rich further testified that [Text redacted in copy.]. (Rich Tr. 15:25-16:5). Further, Mr. Rich had no knowledge whether Defendant [Text redacted in copy.] (Rich Tr. 17:13-18:20). Similarly, Mr. Rich did not know [Text redacted in copy.]. (Rich Tr. 20:7-31:3).

Mr. Rich also testified that [Text redacted in copy.]. (Rich Tr. 22:22-23:21; 24:10-18). Further, Mr. Rich testified that [Text redacted in copy.]. (Rich Tr. 25:2-16).

On "Topic 2," Mr. Rich did not know when [Text redacted in copy.]. (Rich Tr. 36:6-19). When discussion turned to [Text redacted in copy.]. (Rich DePo. 41:3-8).

As such, Mr. Rich's lack of knowledge and/or lack of preparation denied Plaintiff his right to discover facts about extent of Defendant's contacts with the Commonwealth of Massachusetts which Plaintiff believes are extensive and sufficient for the Court to exercise specific personal jurisdiction over the Defendant. The Court, therefore, should compel Defendant to continue the 30(b)(6) deposition due to Mr. Rich's admitted lack of answers on numerous noticed topics.

## IV. DEFENDANT SHOULD BEAR COSTS ASSOCIATED WITH CONTINUED 30(b)(6) DEPOSITION

Fed. R. Civ. Pr. 37(b)(2)(C) provides that the Court may award reasonable costs associated with the motion, including costs attendant to subsequent depositions. *Baker v. St. Paul Travelers Ins. Co.*, 670 F.3d 119, 124 (1st Cir. 2012) ("[T]he corporation should be subject to sanctions if it designates a witness who is not knowledgeable about the relevant facts."); *Signature Breads, Inc. v. Signature Bakery, Inc.*, 2010 WL 3044066, at *1 (D. Mass. July 29, 2010) (defendant's Rule 30(b)(6) witness ordered to appear for continued deposition and ordered to bear the costs of the deposition after it refused to answer questions about deposition topics and refused to produce documents).

Here, the extent of OnShift's contacts with the Commonwealth of Massachusetts is an area of inquiry specifically ordered by the Court and for which OnShift produced an unprepared and unknowledgeable witness. Plaintiff would not have needed to file this motion had OnShift originally proffered a knowledgeable witness and complied with its written discovery obligations. *Foster-Miller, Inc. v. Babcock & Wilcox Canada*, 210 F.3d 1, 17 (1st Cir. 2000) (sanctions order upheld against defendant who failed to comply with its Rule 30(b)(6) obligations).

## V. CONCLUSION

For the foregoing reasons, Plaintiff respectfully requests that the Court grant this Motion and enter an Order granting the following relief:

1. Order OnShift to appear for re-deposition in Boston on Topics 1, 2, 8 & 9;

2. Order OnShift to pay all fees and costs associated with such re-deposition(s);

3. Award Plaintiff costs and fees upon the granting of such motion;

4. Extend all applicable discovery deadlines by 60 days from the date of entry of an Order granting such motion.

Dated: February 9, 2018

Respectfully submitted,

By: /s/ *Sergei Lemberg*

Sergei Lemberg, Esq.

Lemberg Law, LLC

43 Danbury Road

---

6. *Exhibit E* to Lemberg Decl.

Wilton, CT 06897

Telephone: (203) 653-2250

Facsimile: (203) 653-3424

*Attorney for Plaintiff*

# Motion for Preliminary Injunction

2018 WL 3549116 (D.Mass.)

**Westlaw Query>>**

To find more Motion for Preliminary Injunction filings on Westlaw: access Massachusetts Civil Trial Court Documents (from the Home page, click Trial Court Documents, then Massachusetts), click the Advanced Search link, select Motion for Preliminary Injunction, and click Search. Use the Jurisdiction filter on the left to narrow results to Federal.

United States District Court, D. Massachusetts.

FRIENDS OF RUTH& EMILY, INC.,

v.

CITY OF NEW BEDFORD, MASSACHUSETTS.

No. 117CV11809.

June 19, 2018.

## Memorandum in Support of Renewed Preliminary Injunction

This renewal to the preliminary injunction is sought under Rule 65 of the Federal Rules of Civil Procedure.

Plaintiff brought an Endangered Species Act complaint to the Court on September 21, 2017. On December 12, 2017, Plaintiff filed a preliminary injunction to allow Asian elephant Ruth to be examined and removed from Buttonwood Park Zoo (Dkt. #16). On February 15, 2018, Plaintiff Joyce Rowley was substituted for Friends of Ruth & Emily, Inc. (Dkt. #23).

The merits of the case are likely to succeed because additional and continuous harm has occurred to Asian elephant Ruth since the suit was filed which substantiates the claims made in the complaint.

This renewed preliminary injunction meets Rule 65 requirements for a preliminary injunction as follows.

1. Without receiving the preliminary injunction, irreparable harm has and will continue to occur to Ruth, one of the two endangered species of Asian elephants held captive by Defendant. Plaintiff has suffered and will suffer irreparable harm from Ruth's continued injury and likely death at the zoo.

2. The threat is imminent. If this were a dog kept under these conditions, there would be no doubt that the dog was in imminent danger and that there was sufficient evidence to remove the dog. The Defendant's Animal Control Officer routinely removes animals if they are found to be kept standing in its own waste.

3. Old injuries are not healing well and Ruth has incurred new injuries.

4. The records, as noted previously and as described in the Declaration of Julia Allen, D.V.M., Ph.D.[1], show that Ruth's injury had not healed after five months of various treatments and continues to require treatment as her ear tissue sloughs off. It appears Ruth will lose half of her ear to this injury[2].

5. There is additional direct evidence that Ruth's living quarters caused her to get staphylococcus and streptococcus infections on the painfully raw tissue of her ear as the skin sloughed off (Dkt. 17-2 through 17-5).

6. On April 7, 2018, Ruth suffered a more recent injury on her trunk of unknown origin that gouged out a 4" by 2" chunk of her trunk[3].

---

1. Ex. 1, Declaration of Julia Allen, DVM, PhD.

2. Ex. 2, Photo of Ruth's ear dated June 13, 2018.

3. Ex. 3, Clinical records for Ruth, secured through MGL 66, Public Records Access Act from the City of New Bedford, MA, dated April 1, 2018 through April 30, 2018.

7. On May 28, 2018, Ruth suffered a trauma or injury to her rear left leg which now requires treatment[4].

8. On June 13, 2018, Ruth was observed with a large 3 in. diameter laceration on her left cheek, of unknown origin[5].

9. Ruth is not receiving adequate care throughout the day to alleviate her suffering due to her inability to regulate her temperature. In 80°F weather on June 14, 2018, Ruth did not have access to adequate shade, mud, or water.

10. Her untreated lameness makes her unable to access the concrete water feature, even when it is not contaminated with duck feces, as it often is. The barn doors were closed as she must be on exhibit to show people what an elephant looks like. And, standing in the barn day and night will only increase her lameness and pain.

11. On that day, Ruth exhibited stereotype behavior for over an hour, swaying and rocking her head back and forth while standing facing the barn door and then standing near the door[6].

12. Elephants can die from overheating, and are subject to heat stroke and other heat-illnesses as are dogs and humans.

13. The fact that Ruth is surviving yet more calamities due to her captivity at Buttonwood Park Zoo makes the risk of harm no less imminent--it only increases the risk of further life-threatening injuries.

14. There is no harm to the Defendant to have Asian elephant Ruth examined or removed. The Defendant has already claimed that it will not replace her if she dies at the zoo.

15. There is no other remedy available to plaintiff.

16. The grant of the injunction will serve the public interest in protecting this captive zoo elephant, and upholding the Endangered Species Act. An online petition that over 120,000 people have signed asking that both elephants, including Asian elephant Ruth, be removed from the zoo as a result of filing this lawsuit. (www.thepetitionsite.com/101/458/190/new-bedford-send-zoos-incompatible-elephants-ruth-and-emily-to-a-sanctuary/). Over 70 people donated to a legal fund for the lawsuit to go forward and for Asian elephants Ruth and Emily to be removed from the zoo and relocated to The Elephant Sanctuary (www.gofundme.com/R-ELegalFund). Previously, over 2,500 New Bedford residents signed a petition for both Buttonwood Park Zoo elephants to be removed and sent to The Elephant Sanctuary.

17. Should Ruth die at the zoo, no public interest would be served.

## I. FACTUAL BACKGROUND

18. Two days after the complaint was filed on September 21, 2017, Asian elephant Ruth contracted vasculitis on her right ear. This painful condition has resulted in sloughing of the skin on her ear and destroyed parts of her ear tissue. It requires painful "debridement" and physical cutting of the skin with tissue scissors and a scalpel to remove decaying tissue. This injury was described in full in the original preliminary injunction (Dkt. 16, 17).

19. Briefly, on September 23, 2017, Defendant's elephant staff injected Ketaprofen as prescribed in Ruth's right ear vein. According to the record, only 50% of the drug was used. On October 3, 2017, clinical records for Ruth indicated that her right ear had a 2-inch infected lesion.

20. By October 30, 2017, the Defendant's veterinarian made a diagnosis of vasculitis.

21. Elephant ears are thermoregulators and control the elephant's temperature through a complex vascular system. As noted in Dr. Allen's declaration, Ruth will have difficulty in the future controlling her temperature.

22. The threat of this becoming a fatal injury is seen in the unsanitary conditions in which Ruth is kept.

23. Elephants "dust" frequently by throwing dirt on themselves to protect themselves from insects.

24. The barn floor is dirt, (Cplt 1:59) leading to staphylococcus and streptococcus skin infections in Ruth in 2014, and staphylococcus skin infections in Emily in 2016.

25. Ruth must spend a minimum of 16 hours standing, walking, sleeping and eating in her own waste (Cplt. 1:64). She cannot escape it.

26. Due to inclement weather, and shorter zoo hours of operation, her confinement increased to 18-20 hours after November 1st. As

---

4. Ex. 4, Clinical records for Ruth, secured through MGL 66, Public Records Access Act from the City of New Bedford, MA, dated May 1, 2018 through May 31, 2018.

5. Ibid, Ex. 2, Photo of Ruth's ear dated June 13, 2018.

6. Ex. 6, Videos taken at 2:49 p.m. and 3:50 p.m., June 14, 2018, at https://youtu.be/IbvSk-K4e4w and https://youtu.be/vbJqbi4q6uc, respectively.

temperatures dropped to freezing and snow prevented the elephants from exiting the barn or being allowed outside, Ruth spent less than 4 hours per day outside. Between December 26, 2017 and January 7, 2018, Ruth spent 13 days continuously inside the barn as temperatures dropped to -11°F at times during the day.

27. Ruth's new stall is a mere 750 s.f., proportionately the equivalent of a 160-lb. person kept in a 15 s.f. closet. Ruth cannot avoid contaminating her injured and infected ear with waste-laden dirt when she dusts in the barn.

28. Regardless of causation, Ruth's painful and dangerous condition is a direct result of her captivity at defendant's Buttonwood Park Zoo. After eight months and multiple treatments, Ruth's ear is not better, and apparently she will lose at least half of it.

29. Now Ruth is subjected to extreme heat without relief.

30. Ruth will not be subjected to unsanitary and dangerous environmental conditions at The Elephant Sanctuary. The Sanctuary has specialized areas in its elephant barns to treat sick elephants. The barn floors are concrete, and can be kept sanitary through daily powerwashing.

31. Although concrete floors can cause harm to elephants' feet in the long term, the climate is such that the elephants can be outside on natural ground for much of the day, and throughout most of the winter. When it does snow in Tennessee, it rarely lasts more than a day.

32. Because the Sanctuary is closed to the public and they have 24-hour staffing, the elephants do not need to be put inside of the barn. Instead, they can remain outside at night if they so choose, weather permitting.

33. In hot weather, elephants can maintain mobility by accessing the barn during the day and accessing the 2,000 acre habitat at night. There are multiple opportunities for cooling during hot weather--ponds, streams, lakes, and deep forest shade.

34. For these reasons, relocation to The Elephant Sanctuary would be more likely to result in healing Ruth's vasculitis and secondary infections, addressing environmental issues relative to temperature control, monitoring, and veterinary care.

35. Left at the defendant's zoo, Ruth's condition will likely worsen and likely lead to premature euthanasia.

## II. RELIEF

Plaintiff seeks a preliminary injunction against the Defendant's continued keeping of Ruth under these dangerous conditions.

Plaintiff seeks the Court order the City to allow Ruth's assessment by Plaintiff's transpor experts. Several elephant veterinary familiar with transporting an elephant and a transport company have been contacted regarding her safe removal from Buttonwood Park Zoo and transfer to The Elephant Sanctuary. Should the Court allow it, Plaintiff will pay for the assessment for the transport.

Plaintiff seeks the Court order the City to pay the full cost of Ruth's transport to The Elephant Sanctuary.

Respectfully submitted on June 15, 2018,

*/s/Joyce Rowley*

Joyce Rowley, *pro se*

PO Box 50251

New Bedford, MA 02745

(508)542-8297

# Motion to Dismiss for Failure to State a Claim

2018 WL 3579376 (D.Mass.)

United States District Court, D. Massachusetts.

DESKTOP METAL, INC., Plaintiff and Counterclaim Defendant,

v.

MARKFORGED, INC. and Matiu Parangi, Defendants and Counterclaim Plaintiff (Markforged, Inc.),

v.

Ricardo FULOP, Jonah Myerberg, Boston Impact LLC, and Amy Buntel, Third-Party Defendants.

No. 1:18-cv-10524-WGY.

May 14, 2018.

Memorandum in Support of Third-Party Defendants Jonah Myerberg's, Boston Impact LLC's, and Amy Buntel's Motion to Dismiss Under Federal Rule of Civil Procedure 12(B)(6)

Russell Beck, BBO No. 561031, Laura M. Raisty, BBO No. 640400, Hannah T. Joseph, BBO No. 688132, Lauren C. Schaefer, BBO No. 696628, Beck Reed Riden LLP, 155 Federal Street, Suite 1302, Boston, Massachusetts 02110, Telephone: (617) 500-8660, Facsimile: (617) 500-8665, rbeck@beckreed.com.

Pursuant to Rule 12(b)(6) and this Court's Orders at the hearings on April 12 and May 3, Third-Party Defendants Jonah Myerberg ("Myerberg"), Boston Impact LLC ("Boston Impact"), and Amy Buntel ("Buntel") (collectively, the "Myerberg/Buntel Parties") hereby submit this memorandum in support of their Motion to Dismiss (the "Motion") all claims filed against them in the Third-Party Complaint (Dkt. No. 45) by Third-Party Plaintiff Markforged, Inc. ("Markforged").

## I. INTRODUCTION

Plaintiff Desktop Metal, Inc. ("Desktop Metal") filed this action on March 19, 2018 against Markforged and a former employee. The Complaint alleged (among other things) two counts of patent infringement relating to its 3D metal printing technology, for which Desktop Metal sought preliminary injunctive relief. On April 12, the Court, in consultation with the three then-existing parties, ordered consolidation of the preliminary injunction hearing with the trial on the merits in July.

Shortly thereafter — despite having agreed to an expedited schedule without disclosing its intent to join four new parties to the action — Markforged brought third-party claims against Ricardo Fulop ("Fulop") and the Myerberg/Buntel Parties, and asserted a host of counterclaims against Desktop Metal. The nine counts against the Myerberg/Buntel Parties rely on two core allegations: (1) starting in July 2014, Myerberg (acting through his consulting company, Boston Impact) "infiltrated" Markforged as a "beta tester" for its 3D printers and then misappropriated trade secrets for the benefit of Desktop Metal; and (2) in January 2016, Buntel ordered a Markforged Mark One 3D printer to her home so that Desktop Metal could analyze it for the purpose of incorporating Markforged's proprietary technology into Desktop Metal's printers, in violation of a purported user license agreement (the "License Agreement").

These allegations fail, as a matter of law, to support Markforged's claims against the Myerberg/Buntel Parties.

As a threshold matter, Markforged has not alleged with sufficient specificity — much less the "exquisite detail of a patent claim" as

**Westlaw Query>>**

To find more Motion to Dismiss for Failure to State a Claim filings on Westlaw: access Massachusetts Civil Trial Court Documents (from the Home page, click Trial Court Documents, then Massachusetts), enter "DT("state a claim" 12(b)(6))" in the search box, and click Search. Use the Jurisdiction filter on the left to narrow results to Federal.

ordered by this Court — what trade secrets it claims were misappropriated or even who among the Third-Party Defendants (or Counter Defendant) is alleged to have taken what. As the Court indicated at a hearing on May 3, Markforged's trade secret identification statement is "woefully inadequate." At the same hearing, Markforged admitted that it could not meet its pleading requirements without inspecting Desktop Metal's 3D metal printer. Consistent with that admission and despite having since added more vague and irrelevant verbiage to its trade secret identification statement, Markforged has continued to fail to comply with the Court's Order or to satisfy its pleading requirements in connection with its trade secret-related claims.

In addition, Markforged's contract-related claims against Buntel fail because Markforged does not allege any act by Buntel that violates any provision of the purported License Agreement (or even that she saw, much less read and agreed to, the License Agreement). Rather, the Third-Party Complaint simply concludes that, because Buntel ordered a Markforged 3D printer, she must have disassembled, reverse engineered, analyzed, or otherwise used it in order to incorporate Markforged's proprietary technology into Desktop Metal's printers, all purportedly in violation of the License Agreement. Such allegations fail as a matter of law to satisfy applicable pleading requirements. Indeed, the hollowness of Markforged's claims against Buntel are again underscored by its own admission that, without inspecting Desktop Metal's 3D printer (which it has not), Markforged cannot identify which of its trade secrets or other proprietary technologies have been incorporated into Desktop Metal's printers, *i.e.*, whether it even has an articulable breach of contract claim against Buntel at all.

Having apparently failed to conduct a reasonable investigation in advance of joining the Myerberg/Buntel Parties, Markforged should not now be permitted to embark on a fishing expedition to discover what claims it may or may not have.[1] Accordingly, the Third-Party Complaint should be dismissed as against the Myerberg/Buntel Parties.

## II. RELEVANT FACTUAL ALLEGATIONS AND PROCEDURAL BACKGROUND

### INSUFFICIENT FACTUAL ALLEGATIONS[2]

The factual allegations set forth in the Third-Party Complaint that are relevant to the Myerberg/Buntel Parties can be summarized as follows:

- In 2014, Markforged became the first midmarket retailer of 3D carbon fiber printers. Third-Party Complaint ("Compl."), ¶¶ 137, 142-43.
- Starting in July 2014, Markforged retained Myerberg as a beta tester for its 3D printers through his company, Boston Impact. In connection with his role, Myerberg signed a nondisclosure agreement (the "NDA") on behalf of Boston Impact. *Id.*, ¶ 158.
- Myerberg worked at Markforged's facility and met with its engineers and product developers, received "information relating to Markforged's specific technical know-how and processes" including "the method and manner" in which 3D printers worked, and learned about the functions of Markforged's 3D printers from "head to toe." *Id.*, ¶¶ 159-60, 164.
- Later, in 2015, Myerberg co-founded Desktop Metal and became its Chief Technology Officer. *Id.*, ¶ 162.
- On or about January 12, 2016, at the direction of Fulop and Myerberg, Buntel (a Desktop Metal employee) ordered a Markforged Mark One 3D printer to her home using her personal information. *Id.*, ¶ 178.

Conspicuously omitted from the Third-Party Complaint is any factual allegation describing what confidential and proprietary information the Myerberg/Buntel Parties misappropriated for Desktop Metal's benefit.[3]

From these sparse, threadbare allegations, the Third-Party Complaint assumes that Myerberg misappropriated Markforged's trade secrets on behalf of Desktop Metal and speculates that Desktop Metal disassembled, reverse engineered, analyzed, and used the Markforged printer purchased by Buntel, so it could incorporate Markforged's technology into its 3D metal printers. *Id.*, ¶¶ 165, 179.

---

1. To avoid unnecessary duplication, the Motion and this supporting memorandum incorporate by reference the arguments set forth in Plaintiff and Counterclaim Defendant Desktop Metal, Inc.'s Motion To Dismiss Under Federal Rule Of Civil Procedure 12(B)(6) and its supporting memorandum (Dkt. Nos. 81 and 82) to extent that they support dismissal of the claims against Third-Party Defendants Myerberg, Boston Impact, and Buntel.

2. As required by Federal Rule of Civil Procedure Rule 12(b)(6), the Myerberg/Buntel Parties treat the facts alleged in the Third-Party Complaint as true solely for purposes of this Motion.

3. The closest the Third-Party Complaint comes to alleging misappropriation is its allegation that Desktop Metal filed patent applications incorporating certain features of 3D printers, including a heat drive wheel, soft rollers, ultrasonic disruption, a dynamic monitoring system, and a hard nozzle tip. *Id.*, ¶ 166. Notwithstanding the fact that these descriptions are vague and overly broad, the features are generally known within the 3D printing industry (and therefore are not trade secrets).

Based on this speculation, Markforged asserts a total of nine claims against the Myerberg/Buntel Parties: two for trade secret misappropriation against Myerberg and Boston Impact under state and federal law (Counts II and V), two for breach of contract claims against Boston Impact and Buntel (Counts XIII and XIV), and five for related claims against the Myerberg/Buntel Parties (Counts X, XI, XVII, XXII, and XXIV).

## FAILURE TO IDENTIFY TRADE SECRETS

Prior to Markforged's filing of the Third-Party Complaint, the Court, on April 12, in anticipation of a trade secret counterclaim against Desktop Metal, ordered Markforged to describe its trade secrets "to the exquisite detail of a patent claim." Transcript of April 12, 2018 Hearing ("Apr. 12, 2018 Hearing Tr."), relevant pages attached to the Declaration of Russell Beck in Support of [the Motion] ("Beck Decl.") as *Exhibit* 1, pp. 11-12. After receiving the Court's directive, however, Markforged filed under seal and produced on an attorneys' eyes only basis a trade secret identification statement (the "Initial Identification") that the Court would later characterize as "woefully inadequate," lacking so much in substance that no person could defend against it, and "very vulnerable to a prompt motion to dismiss." Hearing Transcript for May 3, 2018 Hearing ("May 3, 2018 Hearing Tr."), relevant pages attached to Beck Decl. as *Exhibit* 2, pp. 8-9, 15.

Consistent with that failing, Markforged admitted during the May 3 hearing that it could not yet identify which (purported) trade secrets Desktop Metal and the Third-Party Defendants had purportedly taken. Accordingly, counsel for Markforged asked the Court to allow him to make an oral application to inspect Desktop Metal's 3D metal printer, stating:

> I mean one of the issues, your Honor, we have with "What do they take from our product?" from our 3D metal printer . . . *it's difficult to know because we haven't seen their 3D metal printer.* Their 3D metal printer has not hit the market, as I understand it, they haven't had any sales. *We would like to see it, to inspect it, and that way we can sharpen, into exquisite detail hopefully, your Honor, consistent with your Honor's requirements, what we say they've taken. Right now we're shooting without a target.*

May 3, 2018 Hearing Tr., p. 13 (emphasis added).

On May 9, Markforged filed a supplemental trade secret identification statement under seal (the "Supplemental Identification," and together with the Initial Identification, the "Identification Statements"), again producing it on an attorneys' eyes only basis. While the Supplemental Identification is certainly more verbose, it fails to cure Markforged's fatal pleading deficiencies. Among other things, the Supplemental Identification, which lists 72 categories of information ranging from business and customer information to technical know-how, remains vague and overly broad. Indeed, it even includes general industry information and information that exists in the public domain or that can be easily ascertained from observing most 3D printers. Moreover, neither the Third-Party Complaint nor the Initial or Supplemental Identification specifies, as among Desktop Metal, Fulop, and the Myerberg/Buntel Parties, who took what or the basis for Markforged's allegations.

## III. ARGUMENT

To survive a motion to dismiss under Rule 12(b)(6), a complaint "must contain sufficient factual matter, accepted as true, to state a claim to relief that is plausible on its face." *Ashcroft v. Iqbal*, 556 U.S. 662, 678 (2009) (citation and internal quotation marks omitted). Its factual allegations must "raise a right to relief above the speculative level," *Bell Atl. Corp. v. Twombly*, 550 U.S. 544, 545 (2007), and establish "more than an unadorned, the-defendant-unlawfully-harmed-me accusation," *Iqbal*, 556 U.S. at 678. Neither "naked assertion[s]" nor "conclusory statements" are sufficient to state a claim. *Id.* Accordingly, "threadbare recitals of a cause of action's elements, supported by mere conclusory statements . . . are not entitled to the assumption of truth" and will fail as a matter of law. *Id.* at 662 (citation omitted). Markforged's claims against the Myerberg/Buntel Parties fail to satisfy this standard.

### A. *The Court Should Dismiss Markforged's Claims Against Myerberg and Boston Impact Because the Third-Party Complaint Fails to Adequately Allege Markforged's Trade Secrets at Issue or Any Act of Misappropriation*

This Court should dismiss Markforged's trade secret-related claims (Counts II, V, X, XIII, XVII, XXII, and XXIV) against Myerberg and Boston Impact because the Third-Party Complaint (even as read in light of the Identification Statements) fails to allege with sufficient specificity — much less the "exquisite detail of a patent claim" as required by this Court's April 12 Order — its trade secrets at issue in this action. Moreover, the Third-Party Complaint does not allege any facts that plausibly suggest that Myerberg, in his own capacity or acting on behalf of Boston Impact, misappropriated Markforged's information for the benefit of Desktop Metal. Having failed to allege these essential elements of its claim, Markforged has failed to state a *prima facie* case for trade secret misappropriation under either federal or state law. Because the remaining counts against Myerberg and/or Boston Impact are derivative of Markforged's misappropriation claim, they likewise should be dismissed.

To state a claim for trade secret misappropriation under both federal and Massachusetts state law, Markforged must allege: (1) the existence of a trade secret; (2) that the plaintiff took reasonable steps to protect the secret; and (3) that the defendant acquired the trade secret by improper means or through breach of a confidential relationship. *Blake v. Prof'l Coin Grading Serv.*, 898 F. Supp. 2d 365, 393 (D. Mass. 2012) (analyzing M.G.L. c. 93, § 42); 18 U.S.C. 1836(b)(1) (establishing a private right of action for trade secret misappropriation under federal law) & 1839(3) & (5) (defining "trade secret" and "misappropriation"); *see also, e.g., N. Am. Deer Registry, Inc. v. DNA Sols., Inc.*, No. 4:17-CV-00062, 2017 WL 2402579, at *7-8 (E.D. Tex. June 2, 2017), *appeal dismissed*, No. 17-40814, 2017 WL 7240613 (5th Cir. Aug. 15, 2017) (discussing the elements of a DTSA claim); *Dichard v. Morgan*, No. 17-CV-00338-AJ, 2017 WL 5634110, at *2 (D.N.H. Nov. 22, 2017) (same); *Yager v. Vignieri*, No. 16CV9367(DLC), 2017 WL 4574487, at *3 (S.D.N.Y. Oct. 12, 2017).

"The party asserting the claim must identify with *adequate specificity* the trade secret or proprietary information that was allegedly misappropriated by the defendant." *Ferring Pharm. Inc. v. Braintree Labs., Inc.*, 38 F. Supp. 3d 169, 175 (D. Mass. 2014) (citing *Sutra, Inc. v. Iceland Exp., ehf*, 2008 WL 2705580, at *3-4 (D. Mass. July 10, 2008)) (emphasis added). At the very least, "[t]he description must be made 'with clarity that can be understood by a lay person . . . *and distinguish what is protectable from that which is not.*'" *Sutra, Inc.*, 2008 WL 2705580, at *4 (quoting *Staffbridge, Inc. v. Gary D. Nelson Assocs., Inc.*, No. 024912BLS, 2004 WL 1429935 (Mass. Super. June 11, 2004)) (emphasis added).[4] Accordingly, trade secret claims premised on overly broad descriptions, publicly available information, industry know-how, and/or readily observable material fail. *See, e.g., Tr. Safe Pay, LLC v. Dynamic Diet, LLC*, No. CV 17-10166-MPK, 2017 WL 3974949, at *9 (D. Mass. Sept. 8, 2017); *Solomon v. Khoury*, No. CV 16-10176, 2017 WL 598758, at *5 (D. Mass. Feb. 13, 2017); *Ferring Pharm. Inc.*, 38 F. Supp. 3d at 175; *Sutra, Inc.*, 2008 WL 2705580, at *3-4. Consistent therewith, at the April 12 hearing, this Court ordered that Markforged describe its alleged trade secrets with precision. Apr. 12, 2018 Hearing Tr., pp. 11-12.

The Third-Party Complaint falls fatally short of satisfying these requirements. With respect to Myerberg and Boston Impact, the Third-Party Complaint alleges merely that Myerberg worked for Markforged, received information related to Markforged's "specific technical know-how and processes," and learned about the functions of Markforged's 3D printers from "head to toe" before leaving to join Desktop Metal, which was an indirect competitor at the time. Compl., ¶¶ 158-60. The Third-Party Complaint goes on to allege that Desktop Metal's patent applications for its 3D metal printing technology included certain features found in 3D printers. *Id.*, ¶ 166. Such broad descriptions of its alleged trade secrets are the exact kind of allegations courts have found cannot make out a claim for misappropriation. *See, e.g., Tr. Safe Pay, LLC*, 2017 WL 3974949, at *9 (allegations that defendants acquired and used plaintiff's marketing algorithm failed to state a claim for trade secret misappropriation where the complaint did not explain the algorithm or what it did, or how it was confidential to plaintiff rather than common to the industry); *Solomon*, 2017 WL 598758, at *5 ("Solomon has not sufficiently alleged what his trade secret is or how it has been misappropriated. Defendants cannot be required to guess the trade secret Solomon is referencing."); *Ferring Pharm. Inc.*, 38 F. Supp. 3d at 175 (counterclaimant failed to state a claim for misappropriation of trade secret where the claim was based on its entire set of training materials, which contained publicly available information, without differentiating what was proprietary to counterclaimant); *Blake*, 898 F. Supp. 2d at 394 (plaintiff failed to state a claim with respect to a coin-grading system, where he failed to allege with sufficient particularity which portion of the system remained a secret at the time of the alleged misappropriation).

Markforged's Initial and Supplemental Identifications do not cure its fatal pleading deficiencies. As an initial matter, the Court should not consider the Identification Statements when analyzing this Motion, as they are wholly outside of the four corners of the Third-Party Complaint, and are not referenced by or expressly linked to the Third-Party Complaint.[5] *See, e.g., Penney v. Deutsche Bank Nat'l Tr. Co.*, No. 16-CV-10482-ADB, 2017 WL 1015002, at *3 (D. Mass. Mar. 15, 2017) (citing 1st Circuit cases).

Even if the Court were inclined to consider the Identification Statements in analyzing this Motion, however, Markforged's trade secret misappropriation claims still fail as a matter of law. The Court has already found Markforged's Initial Identification to be "woefully inadequate" and "vulnerable to a prompt motion to dismiss." May 3, 2018 Hearing Tr., p. 9. The Supplemental

---

4. Courts have identified at least four policy reasons for requiring plaintiffs to sufficiently allege their trade secrets at issue prior to seeking discovery on their claims, which are germane to this case: (1) such identification is necessary to ensure that plaintiffs do not use unmeritorious lawsuits to discover their competitors' trade secrets; (2) until the plaintiff has identified the trade secrets at issue with some specificity, there is no way to know whether the information sought in discovery is relevant; (3) it is difficult for a defendant to mount a defense until it has some indication of the trade secrets allegedly misappropriated, and (4) requiring the plaintiff to state its claimed trade secrets prior to engaging in discovery ensures that it will not mold its cause of action around the discovery it receives. *See, e.g., DeRubeis v. Witten Techs.*, Inc., 244 F.R.D. 676, 680-81 (N.D. Ga. 2007) and cases cited therein.

5. Exacerbating this failure is the fact that the Identification Statements were produced on an *attorneys' eyes only* basis, and — if merged into the pleadings — would undermine the purpose of the notice pleading requirement under Rule 8(a) altogether. *See Twombly*, 550 U.S. at 555 (the purpose of Rule 8(a)'s pleading requirement is to "give the defendant fair notice of what the . . . claim is and the grounds upon which it rests.").

Identification, which takes the "kitchen sink" approach, listing 72 categories of information ranging from business and customer information to technical know-how, is vague, imprecise, and overly broad. It also includes general industry information and information in the public domain or that can be easily ascertained from observing most 3D printers.[6] Moreover, it does not distinguish what information is protectable from that which is not with any kind of specificity. While this memorandum will not address in detail the alleged trade secrets set forth in the Identification Statements (because they are under seal and were produced on an attorneys' eyes only basis), the following analogy is apt: If Markforged's product were a car, its Identification Statements would list its grooved rubber tires, round steering wheel, leather seats, and a list of dealerships (which also appear on its website) among its alleged trade secrets.

Markforged also identifies information related to "power consumption" as a protected trade secret, yet aspects of this purported trade secret are displayed on its very own website. *Compare* Supplemental Identification No. 52 (claiming power consumption components as protected trade secret), *with* Markforged Q&A: Power Consumption (last updated May 19, 2017), https://support.markforged.com/hc/en-us/articles/207304750-Power-Consumption (last visited May 14, 2018). PDF printouts of these articles as they existed on May 13, 2018 are attached to the Beck Declaration as *Exhibit 3*.

Also fatal to Markforged's claims, neither the Third-Party Complaint nor the Identification Statements identify, as among Desktop Metal, Fulop, and the Myerberg/Buntel Parties, who took what, and the basis for Markforged's allegations. Rather, the Third-Party Complaint merely assumes that, because Myerberg worked at a 3D carbon fiber printer company (where he was exposed to its information) and then went to start a 3D metal printer company, he must have misappropriated Markforged's trade secrets and incorporated them into his new products. Markforged's conclusory and groundless allegation is not enough to make out a claim for misappropriation. *See, e.g., Solomon*, 2017 WL 598758, at *5 (trade secret claim dismissed where plaintiff merely alleged that defendant assisted in filing patent on behalf of another company that covered similar technology as plaintiff's information); *Gillette Co. v. Provost*, No. 1584CV00149-BLS2, 2016 WL 2610677, at *8 (Mass. Super. May 5, 2016) (Gillette's claims against its former in-house patent attorney were dismissed with prejudice where Gillette's allegations that the lawyer disclosed and used "privileged information with respect to Gillette's patent, trade secret, and litigation strategy" were merely "conclusory and unexplained"); *see also All Bus. Sols., Inc. v. NationsLine, Inc.*, 629 F. Supp. 2d 553, 558-59 (W.D. Va. 2009) (plaintiff's trade secret claim was dismissed where it was premised on the "single, conclusory assertion that [defendant] 'sought . . . to appropriate and disclose the names of [plaintiff's] customers, along with other [plaintiff's] trade secrets and confidential information.'"); *Washburn v. Yadkin Valley Bank & Tr. Co.*, 190 N.C. App. 315, 327 (2008) (affirming dismissal of trade secret claim where allegations did "not identify with sufficient specificity either the trade secrets [p]laintiffs allegedly misappropriated or the acts by which the alleged misappropriations were accomplished"); *Lycoming Engines v. Superior Air Parts, Inc.*, No. 3:13-CV-1162-L, 2014 WL 1976757, at *8 (N.D. Tex. May 15, 2014) (affirming lower court's dismissal with prejudice of trade secret claim where second amended complaint included no allegation linking any particular misconduct to any particular alleged trade secret contained within plaintiff's long list of parts).

As Markforged admitted in open court, the crux of its deficiencies is not a matter of drafting. Rather, absent inspecting Desktop Metal's 3D metal printer, Markforged is unable to articulate which, if any, of its alleged trade secrets made it into Desktop Metal's products. May 3, 2018 Hearing Tr., p. 13. This was later reaffirmed by Third-Party Plaintiff's submission of the Supplemental Identification, which still falls far short of the mark. Markforged should not now be permitted to mold its cause of action around the discovery it receives while Myerberg and Boston Impact attempt to mount a defense with one arm tied behind their backs. *See supra*, note 4. Accordingly, the Court should dismiss Markforged's trade secret claims as to Myerberg and Boston Impact (Counts II and V) with prejudice. *See, e.g., Solomon*, 2017 WL 598758, at *5; *Gillette*, 2016 WL 2610677, at *8; *Lycoming Engines*, 2014 WL 1976757, at *11.

Because Markforged's trade secret claims as to Myerberg and Boston Impact fail, so must its claims of M.G.L. c. 93A (Count X), breach of contract (the NDA) (Count XIII), breach of covenant of good faith and fair dealing (Count XVII), civil conspiracy (Count XXII), and unjust enrichment (Count XXIV), which are all premised on the alleged misappropriation of trade secrets. *See* Compl., ¶¶ 255, 275-78, 312, 343-45, 355. Accordingly, Counts X, XIII, XVII, XXII, and XXIV should also be dismissed with prejudice.

---

6. For example, Markforged again claims that its channel resellers and customer identities are protected trade secrets, yet some of this so-called confidential information is already in the public domain and has been since 2015. *Compare, e.g.*, Supplemental Identification No. 61 (claiming Markforged's channel resellers as protected trade secrets), *with* T.E. Halterman, *3HTi Signs Deal with MarkForged to Sell the Mark One 3D Printer* (Feb. 19, 2015), https://3dprint.com/45660/3hti-markforged-partnership/ (last visited May 13, 2018); *NovaCopy named flagship reseller for Markforged Mark One 3D printer* (Feb. 12, 2015), https://www.tctmagazine.com/3d-printing-news/novacopy-named-flagship-reseller-for-markforged-3d-printer/ (last visited May 13, 2018); *compare* Supplemental Identification No. 58-A (claiming Markforged's customer identities as protected trade secrets), *with EVCO Plastics Adds Advanced 3D Carbon Fiber Printer to Innovation Center. New technology from MarkForged prints composite parts as strong as metal* (Nov. 17, 2014), https://www.evcoplastics.com/latest-news/evco-plastics-adds-advanced-3d-carbon-fiber-printer (last visited May 13, 2018).

## B. *The Court Should Dismiss Markforged's Claims Against Buntel Because the Third-Party Complaint Fails to Allege Any Act by Buntel that Violated the License Agreement*

Markforged's claims against Buntel for breach of contract (Count XIV) and M.G.L. c. 93A (Count XI) should also be dismissed because Markforged has failed to allege any act by Buntel that breached the License Agreement or otherwise constitutes unfair or deceptive conduct. Indeed, with respect to Buntel, the Third-Party Complaint alleges *only* that in January 2016, Buntel ordered a Markforged 3D printer to her home, without disclosing her affiliation with Desktop Metal, and that she agreed to the License agreement as a condition of her order. Compl., ¶¶ 178, 180. That's all.[7]

From this mere ordering of a printer, the Third-Party Complaint jumps to the conclusion that "Buntel . . . violated Markforged's [License Agreement] by using, and allowing Desktop Metal to use, the Markforged 3D printer that she ordered to disassemble, reverse engineer, analyze and copy more completely Markforged's proprietary engineering methodologies and to print metal so as to advance Desktop Metal's own 3D printer design." Compl., ¶ 287; *see* Compl., ¶ 179. These assumptions are based on no information; they are pure speculation.[8] Moreover, as discussed above, the Third-Party Complaint fails to allege which of "Markforged's proprietary engineering methodologies" have been incorporated in or otherwise "advance[d] Desktop Metal's own 3D printer design." Without more, Markforged's threadbare recitals, supported by mere conclusory statements, should be rejected, and its contract claim as to Buntel should be dismissed. *Iqbal*, 556 U.S. at 678 ("Threadbare recitals of the elements of a cause of action, supported by mere conclusory statements, do not suffice." Such conclusory statements are "not entitled to the assumption of truth.").

Likewise, Markforged's derivative Chapter 93A claim against Buntel fails. Even if the breach of contract claim survives the dismissal stage, Markforged has not alleged any act by Buntel that would rise to the rise to the level of "egregiously wrong." *GMO Tr. ex rel. GMO Emerging Country Debt Fund v. ICAP plc*, No. CIV.A. 12-10293-DPW, 2012 WL 5197545, at *10 (D. Mass. Oct. 18, 2012). Even if the Court accepts Markforged's conclusory allegations against Buntel, the consequences of her actions would be no worse than the simple breach of the License Agreement itself. Indeed, it is well settled that a plaintiff's Chapter 93A claim that is premised merely on its allegations that a defendant breached a contract falls well short of the Chapter 93A liability threshold. *Brooks v. AIG SunAmerica Life Assur. Co.*, 480 F.3d 579, 590 (1st Cir. 2007) (affirming dismissal of Chapter 93A claim based solely on an alleged breach of contract); *GMO Tr. ex rel. GMO Emerging Country Debt Fund*, 2012 WL 5197545, at *10 (dismissing 93A claim premised on conduct with "consequences no worse than the simple breach of the commercial obligation itself").

## CONCLUSION

For the reasons set forth above, Third-Party Defendants Jonah Myerberg, Boston Impact LLC, and Amy Buntel respectfully request that the Court dismiss the Counts II, V, X, XI, XIII, XIV, XVII, XXII, and XXIV, as set forth against them, in Markforged's Third-Party Complaint.

Dated: May 14, 2018

Respectfully submitted,

JONAH MYERBERG, BOSTON IMPACT LLC, and AMY BUNTEL,

By their attorneys,

*/s/ Russell Beck*

Russell Beck, BBO No. 561031

Laura M. Raisty, BBO No. 640400

Hannah T. Joseph, BBO No. 688132

Lauren C. Schaefer, BBO No. 696628

BECK REED RIDEN LLP

155 Federal Street, Suite 1302

---

7. The Third-Party Complaint noticeably omits any allegation that Buntel was obligated to disclose her affiliation with Desktop Metal as a precondition for purchasing the printer. Further, the Third-Party Complaint omits any allegation that Buntel actually saw, much less read and accepted, the License Agreement.

8. While it may be customary in the industry (and many industries) to inspect competitors' products, there is simply no basis to suggest that Buntel — an administrative assistant — "used" the printer in any of the ways alleged. Such a throwaway conclusion as to Buntel's "use" is based on nothing more than the fact that she purchased the printer; such allegation of use is therefore devoid of any good faith basis.

Boston, Massachusetts 02110

Telephone: (617) 500-8660

Facsimile: (617) 500-8665

rbeck@beckreed.com

# Motion to Dismiss for Lack of Subject Matter Jurisdiction

2017 WL 6886387 (D.Mass.)

United States District Court, D. Massachusetts.

Sean EISNOR; John Freeman; Ronald Urnetta; Mallory Salvaggio; Suzan Khan; Bradley Waxer; Jose Harris; and Robert Nash, Plaintiffs,

v.

ADMIRAL'S BANK and Lee Pollock, Defendants.

No. 1:17-cv-11433-IT.

October 31, 2017.

## Memorandum in Support of Defendant Admirals Bank's Motion to Dismiss Non-Diverse Plaintiffs for Lack of Subject-Matter Jurisdiction

Mark A. Pogue (#550807), Pierce Atwood LLP, 72 Pine Street, Providence, RI 02903, (401) 490-3416, (40l) 588-5166 (Fax), mpogue@pierceatwood.com.

Defendant Admirals Bank ("Admirals") submits this memorandum in support of its motion to dismiss the six non-diverse Plaintiffs in this action (Sean Eisnor, Mallory Salvaggio, Suzan Khan, Bradley Waxer, Jose Harris and Robert Nash) (collectively, the "Massachusetts Plaintiffs") for lack of subject-matter jurisdiction.

To bring a civil action under 28 U.S.C. § 1332(a)(1), the matter in controversy must: (1) exceed $75,000 and (2) be between citizens of different states. The Massachusetts Plaintiffs and Admirals are citizens of Massachusetts for purposes of Section 1332(a)(1). Therefore, this Court does not have subject-matter jurisdiction over the Massachusetts Plaintiffs in this diversity action. The Court does, however, have subject-matter jurisdiction over plaintiffs John Freeman and Ronald Umetta, who reside in New Hampshire (the "New Hampshire Plaintiffs"). Accordingly, to preserve diversity jurisdiction over the New Hampshire Plaintiffs, the Massachusetts Plaintiffs should be dismissed.

### *Factual Background*

This action was originally filed in this Court. Plaintiffs asserted that this Court had subject-matter jurisdiction because "the parties are diverse in citizenship and the amount in controversy exceeds $75,000." Complaint, ¶ 5.

In an Order To Show Cause issued August 4, 2017, this Court questioned whether complete diversity of citizenship existed among the plaintiffs and defendants. Noting the limited information provided in the Complaint concerning Defendant Admirals' citizenship, the Court directed Plaintiffs to show cause why the lawsuit should not be dismissed for lack of subject- matter jurisdiction.

In response, Plaintiffs clarified that plaintiffs John Freeman and Ronald Urnetta reside in New Hampshire, not Massachusetts.[1] Plaintiffs asserted that Admirals has places of business in Rhode Island and California, and "a corporate office" located in Boston, Massachusetts. Response, ¶ 2. Plaintiffs provided no information concerning the state in which Admirals' main office is located, even though, as the Court correctly pointed out in its Show Cause Order, this was the relevant fact for determining the citizenship of a national bank such as Admirals for diversity purposes.

---

1. Response To Show Cause Why The Case Should Not Be Dismissed For Lack Of Jurisdiction ("Response"), p. 1.

571

In fact, Admirals' main office is located in Boston, Massachusetts. Declaration of Dimitri Nionakis, ¶ 2. Admirals is therefore a citizen of Massachusetts for diversity purposes. Consequently, diversity of citizenship does not exist between Admirals and the Massachusetts Plaintiffs. It does exist, however, between Admirals and the New Hampshire Plaintiffs.

### *Argument*

The Massachusetts Plaintiffs should be dismissed in order to preserve diversity jurisdiction over the New Hampshire Plaintiffs.

### I. *This Has Court Has Authority To Dismiss The Massachusetts Plaintiffs In Order To Preserve Diversity Jurisdiction*

"The Supreme Court has stated that 'Rule 21 invests district courts with authority to allow a dispensable nondiverse party to be dropped at any time.'" *Garber Bros., Inc. v. Troilo*, 2015 WL 13389919, C.A. No. 15-cv-10148-IT (D. Mass. June 25, 2015) (Talwani, J.), *quoting Newman-Green, Inc., v. Alfonzo-Larrain*, 490 U.S. 826, 832 (1989). Based on this authority, both district courts and the court of appeals in this Circuit have dismissed non-diverse parties in order to preserve diversity jurisdiction over the remaining parties. For example, in *Gorfinkle v. U.S. Airways, Inc.*, 431 F.3d 19 (1st Cir. 2005), the plaintiff added a non-diverse party as a defendant and the original defendant (on appeal) moved to dismiss the non-diverse party in order to preserve diversity jurisdiction. The court granted the motion and dismissed the non-diverse party. It did so after considering two points: whether the non-diverse party was dispensable, and whether dismissing it would prejudice any of the remaining parties. *Id.* at 22 ("We conclude that we can preserve diversity jurisdiction by dismissing [the non-diverse defendant] because he is a dispensable party and his dismissal will not prejudice any of the remaining parties.").

As another example, in *Erickson v. Johnson Controls, Inc.*, 912 F. Supp.2d 1, 3 (D. Mass. 2012), an action was removed to federal court based on diversity jurisdiction, after which two non-diverse parties were added as defendants. Upon motion of one of these defendants, the district court dismissed the non-diverse defendants in order to preserve diversity jurisdiction over the remaining parties. Again, the court considered two factors: whether the non-diverse parties were dispensable, and whether dismissing them would prejudice the remaining parties. *Id.*

Dismissing non-diverse parties in order to preserve diversity jurisdiction in an ongoing federal case creates the possibility that related litigation will be filed in another court, thereby creating the possibility of inconsistent judgments. *Garber Bros.*, 2015 WL at *3. Where a case is in its early stages, however, this Court has not found that concern to be dispositive. *Erickson*, 912 F. Supp. 2d at 3 (dismissing non-diverse parties despite possibility of related litigation; "The possibility of piecemeal litigation is, of course, vexing to the parties and to the judicial system. Nonetheless, this litigation is in its early stages and pretrial deadlines have recently been further postponed.").

### II. *The Massachusetts Plaintiffs Should Be Dismissed Because They Are Not Indispensable And Their Dismissal Would Not Prejudice The New Hampshire Plaintiffs*

Application of the factors discussed above leads to the conclusion that the Massachusetts Plaintiffs should be dismissed in order to preserve diversity jurisdiction over this case and the New Hampshire Plaintiffs.

### A. *The Massachusetts Plaintiffs Are Dispensable*

First, the Massachusetts Plaintiffs are dispensable. Their presence in this case as plaintiffs is in no way necessary for the New Hampshire Plaintiffs to prove their claims or to recover any damages they can establish against Admirals. Just as joint tortfeasors and co- conspirators named as defendants are not considered indispensable parties because they are not necessary for a plaintiff to obtain full relief from the remaining defendants, *see, e.g., Casas Office Machines, Inc. v. Mita Copystar America, Inc.*, 42 F.3d 668, 677 (1st Cir. 1994), parties named as co-plaintiffs are not indispensable because they are not needed for the other plaintiffs to obtain full relief.

### B. *Dismissing The Massachusetts Plaintiffs Will Not Prejudice The New Hampshire Plaintiffs*

Dismissing the Massachusetts Plaintiffs will in no way prejudice the New Hampshire Plaintiffs. As noted, the presence of the Massachusetts Plaintiffs in this case is not necessary for the New Hampshire Plaintiffs to obtain any relief to which they are entitled. Their departure therefore will not prejudice the plaintiffs who remain.

Significantly, in this case the factual predicate of each plaintiff's claim is different. The Complaint attaches notarized affidavits from each of the eight plaintiffs in support of their claims. Those affidavits (which Admirals accepts as true for present purposes only) tell widely divergent stories regarding the factual basis of each plaintiff's claim against Admirals. What Admirals supposedly said to each plaintiff; who said it; when it was said; and how the plaintiff responded to the alleged statements vary substantially from one plaintiff to the next. Because each plaintiff's story is unique, the New Hampshire Plaintiffs simply will not be affected by the dismissal of the Massachusetts Plaintiffs.

### C. *The Possibility That The Massachusetts Plaintiffs Will Refile In Another Court Should Not Deter This Court From Preserving Diversity Jurisdiction Over The New Hampshire Plaintiffs*

If the Massachusetts Plaintiffs are dismissed, it may be that they will sue in another court. That possibility should not cause this Court to dismiss this entire action.

First, "federal courts have a strict duty to exercise the jurisdiction that is conferred upon them by Congress." *Quackenbush v. Allstate Ins. Co.*, 517 U.S. 706, 716 (U.S. 1996); *Colorado River Water Conservation Dist. v. United States*, 424 U.S. 800, 817 (1976) (noting the "virtually unflagging obligation of the federal courts to exercise the jurisdiction given them.").

Second, as discussed above, the factual predicate underlying the claims differs from one Plaintiff to the next. For that reason, it is far from clear that permitting the Massachusetts Plaintiffs to proceed in a different forum, while retaining jurisdiction over the New Hampshire Plaintiffs in this court, would create a risk of inconsistent judgments. Nor would adjudicating the Plaintiffs' claims in two different courts necessarily lead to redundancy or duplication of effort. Each Plaintiff will have to be deposed once, whether in this or another court. Each Admirals witness will have to be deposed once, whether in this or another court.

Finally, unlike in cases where an action was removed to federal court and the court was then asked to dismiss a non-diverse party,[2] this action was *originally* filed in this court. *This* is the Plaintiffs' chosen forum. Accordingly, dismissing the Massachusetts Plaintiffs and retaining jurisdiction over the New Hampshire Plaintiffs does less violence to the Plaintiffs' choice of forum than does dismissing the entire case.

### *Conclusion*

For the foregoing reasons, this Court should dismiss the Massachusetts Plaintiffs and retain jurisdiction over the New Hampshire Plaintiffs.

ADMIRALS BANK

By its Attorneys,

*/s/Mark A. Pogue*

Mark A. Pogue (#550807)

PIERCE ATWOOD LLP

72 Pine Street

Providence, RI 02903

(401) 490-3416

(401) 588-5166 (fax)

mpogue@pierceatwood.com

Dated: October 31, 2017

---

2. In *Gorfinkle, supra*, 431 F.3d at 21; *Garber Bros., supra*, 2015 WL at *1; *Casas Office Machines, Inc., supra*, 42 F.3d at 670; and *Erickson, supra*, 912 F. Supp.2d at 2, the plaintiff initially sued in state court and the lawsuit was removed to federal court based on diversity jurisdiction, at which point the court was asked to dismiss one or more non-diverse parties.

# Motion to Dismiss for Lack of Personal Jurisdiction

2017 WL 8727653 (D.Mass.)

**Westlaw Query>>**

To find more Motion to Dismiss for Lack of Personal Jurisdiction filings on Westlaw: access Massachusetts Civil Trial Court Documents (from the Home page, click Trial Court Documents, then Massachusetts), click the Advanced Search link, select Motion to Dismiss for Lack of Jurisdiction, and click Search. Use the Jurisdiction filter on the left to narrow results to Federal.

United States District Court, D. Massachusetts.

Sheena GRICE, Plaintiff,

v.

VIM HOLDINGS GROUP, LLC, Michael D'Ambrose, Hirsch Mohindra, B Financial, LLC, John Bartlett, U Solutions Group, LLC, Theresa D'Ambrose, Global Service Group, LLC, Ruth Poutanen, KRW Attorneys & Associates, LLC, and George Wahbeh, Defendants.

No. 1:17-cv-10944-WGY.

October 10, 2017.

## Memorandum of Law in Support of Defendants' Joint Motion to Dismiss for Lack of Personal Jurisdiction

Susan E. Cohen, BBO # 553353, Steven E. DiCairano, BBO # 694228, Peabody & Arnold LLP, Federal Reserve Plaza, 600 Atlantic Avenue, Boston, MA 02210-2261, Telephone: (617) 951-2100, scohen@peabodyarnold.com, sdicairano@peabodyarnold.com.

Defendants VIM Holdings Group LLC ("VIM Holdings"), Michael D'Ambrose, John Bartlett, Theresa D'Ambrose, Global Service Group LLC ("Global Service"), Ruth Poutanen, KRW Attorneys and Associates, LLC ("KRW"), and George Wahbeh (collectively, "Moving Defendants"), by and through their respective undersigned attorneys, and hereby submit this Memorandum of Law in support of its motion to dismiss pursuant to Rule 12(b)(2) of the Federal Rules of Civil Procedure because the Court lacks personal jurisdiction over Defendants.

## BACKGROUND FACTS[1]

On July 14, 2015, the Plaintiff, Sheena Grice, applied for and received a $200 loan through the www.guaranteedcashnow.net website. *Compl.* ¶ 31. As Plaintiff expressly acknowledges, the *Consumer Line of Credit Agreement* ("*Agreement*") "govern[s] the Loan" and indicates that B Financial LLC ("B Financial") is the lender. *Compl.* ¶ 33, Exhibit A[2] Global Service began making automatic debits on behalf of B Financial from her Citibank account shortly after she received the $200 loan. *Compl.* ¶¶ 12, 41. At some unspecified time she closed her Citibank account to prevent further debits from her account. *Compl.* ¶ 42. Upon her closing of her Citibank account, she began receiving phone calls from representatives of U Solutions Group LLC ("U Solutions") on behalf of B Financial seeking her authorization to make automatic withdrawals from her new bank account. *Compl.* ¶¶ 10, 43. Plaintiff also alleges that on June 14, 2016, George Wahbeh sent her a letter under KRW letterhead via email seeking her authorization to make automatic withdrawals from her new bank account. *Compl.* ¶¶ 45, 114.

Plaintiff brings causes of action against all defendants for violation of the Massachusetts Debt Collection Practices Act, *Mass. Gen.*

---

1. The following facts are assumed to be true for the sole purpose of the instant motion and in no way constitute admissions in this case.

2. The Moving Defendants properly rely on facts set forth in "documents the authenticity of which are not disputed by the parties, official public records, documents central to the plaintiff's claim, and documents sufficiently referred to in the complaint." *See Wilborn v. Walsh*, 584 F. Supp. 2d 384, 386 (D. Mass. 2008) (quoting *Watterson v. Page*, 897 F.2d 1, 3-4 (1st Cir. 1993)).

*Laws* ch. 93 § 24 (Count II), Fraud (Count IV), Civil Conspiracy to Commit Fraud (Count V), and violation of the Massachusetts Consumer Protection Act, *Mass. Gen. Laws* ch. 93A § 2 (Count VI). Plaintiff also asserts claims against VIM Holdings and B Financial for violation of the Massachusetts Small Loans Law, *Mass. Gen. Laws* ch. 140 §§ 96-113 (Count I) and against VIM Holdings, B Financial, U Solutions, Global Service, KRW, and George Wahbeh for violation of the Federal Fair Debt Collection Practices Act, 15 *U.S.C.* § 1692 (Count III).

VIM is a limited liability company organized under the laws of the state of Delaware with its principal place of business in the state of Illinois. *Compl.* ¶ 5. Global Service is a limited liability company organized under the laws of the state of Delaware with its principal place of business in the state of Illinois. *Compl.* ¶ 12. KRW is a limited liability company organized under the laws of the state of Illinois with its principal place of business in the state of Illinois. *Compl.* ¶ 14. Neither Michael D'Ambrose, nor John Bartlett, nor Theresa D'Ambrose, nor Ruth Poutanen, nor George Wahbeh is domiciled in Massachusetts. *See Defendants' Notice of Removal* [Dkt. # 1].

The only involvement George Wahbeh and KRW had in this matter was the drafting of a single piece of correspondence dated June 14, 2016, which was addressed generically to Plaintiff's "employer." *Declaration of George Wahbeh* (*Wahbeh Dec.*), ¶ 4, attached hereto as **Exhibit 1**. The correspondence did not contain a mailing address. *Id.* at ¶ 5. Mr. Wahbeh did not cause to be mailed or otherwise transmitted the June 14, 2016 correspondence or any communication to Plaintiff or her employer. *Id.* at ¶ 6. He has never communicated with Plaintiff directly by phone or any other means. *Id.* at ¶ 7.

VIM Holdings Group LLC had no involvement in the origination, servicing, or any other activity related to Plaintiff's loan. *Declaration of Michael D'Ambrose* (*D'Ambrose Dec.*), ¶ 14, attached hereto as **Exhibit 2**. John Bartlett had no involvement in the origination, servicing, or any other activity related to Plaintiff's loan. *Id.* at ¶ 15. Theresa D'Ambrose had no involvement in the origination, servicing, or any other activity related to Plaintiff's loan. *Id.* at ¶16. Ruth Poutanen had no involvement in the origination, servicing, or any other activity related to Plaintiff's loan. *Id.* at ¶ 17.

### *ARGUMENT*

### I. THIS COURT DOES NOT HAVE PERSONAL JURISDICTION OVER MOVING DEFENDANTS.

#### A. It is Plaintiff's Burden to Establish that this Court has Personal Jurisdiction.

It is well established that the plaintiff bears the burden of proving that a court has *in personam* jurisdiction over the defendant. *Walsh v. National Seating Co.*, 411 F. Supp. 564, 568 (D. Mass. 1976); *Diamond Group, Inc. v. Selective Distribution Intern., Inc.*, 84 Mass. App. Ct. 545, 548 (2013). The plaintiff must make a *prima facie* case that jurisdiction is appropriate by "go[ing] beyond the pleadings" to "make affirmative proof" of jurisdiction. *Dodora Unified Commc'n, Inc. v. Direct Info. Pvt. Ltd.*, 379 F. Supp. 2d 10, 13 (D. Mass. 2005) (quoting *Boit v. Gar-Tec Prods., Inc.*, 967 F.2d 671, 675 (1st Cir. 1992)). Furthermore, "[p]laintiffs may not rely on unsupported allegations in their pleadings," *Boit*, 967 F.2d at 675, but are "obliged to adduce evidence of specific facts. . ." *Foster-Miller, Inc. v. Babcock & Wilcox Can.*, 46 F.3d 138, 145 (1st Cir. 1995).

"For a nonresident to be subject to personal jurisdiction in Massachusetts, there must be a statute authorizing jurisdiction and the exercise of jurisdiction must be consistent with basic due process requirements mandated by the United States Constitution." *Bulldog Inv'rs Gen. P'ship v. Sec'y of Com.*, 457 Mass. 210, 215, 929 (2010). Separate analysis of the Massachusetts long-arm statute is not necessary because Plaintiff must demonstrate that the exercise of jurisdiction pursuant to that statute comports with Due Process. *Shirokov v. Dunlap, Grubb & Weaver, PLLC*, No. CIV.A. 10-12043-GAO, 2012 WL 1065578, at *12 (D. Mass. Mar. 27, 2012); *see also Hannon v. Beard*, 524 F.3d 275, 278 (1st Cir. 2008) ("Because we have construed the Massachusetts long-arm statute to be coextensive with the limits allowed by the United States Constitution, we often sidestep the statutory inquiry and proceed directly to the constitutional analysis.").

This Court has held that the Due Process Clause requires that "in order to subject a defendant to a judgment *in personam*. . . he [must] have certain minimum contacts with it such that maintenance of the suit does not offend traditional notions of fair play and substantial justice." *Kim v. Veglas*, 607 F. Supp. 2d 286, 294 (D. Mass. 2009) (quoting *Phillips v. Prairie Eye Center*, 530 F.3d 22, 27 (1st Cir. 2008) (quoting *International Shoe Co. v. Washington*, 326 U.S. 310, 319 (1945)). It is the nonresident's contacts with the *forum state* that are of interest in determining if in personam jurisdiction exists, not its contacts with a resident.

#### B. There is no basis for general jurisdiction.

"For an individual, the paradigm forum for the exercise of general jurisdiction is the individual's domicile; for a corporation, it is an equivalent place, one in which the corporation is fairly regarded as at home." *Goodyear Dunlop Tires Operations, S.A. v. Brown*, 564 U.S. 915, 924, 131 S.Ct. 2846, 180 L.Ed.2d 796 (2011). For business entities, the inquiry is not just whether the in-forum contacts are "continuous and systematic," but rather, "whether that corporation's 'affiliations with the State are so continuous and systematic as to render [it] essentially at home in the forum State.'" *Daimler AG v. Bauman*, — U.S. —, 134 S.Ct. 746, 761, 187 L.Ed.2d 624 (2014) (quoting *Goodyear*, 564 U.S. at 919, 131 S.Ct. 2846). Thus, "the place of incorporation and principal place of business are paradigm bases for general jurisdiction" in all but the most "exceptional" cases. *Id.* at 760-61, n.19 (quotation omitted).

As discussed above, none of the corporate defendants operates a "continuous and systematic" portion of its business in Massachusetts as to make it "at home" in this forum. Moreover, none of the individual defendants is domiciled in Massachusetts. Accordingly, there is no general jurisdiction over any of the Moving Defendants.

## C. There is no basis for specific jurisdiction.

The First Circuit uses a three-part inquiry to determine whether the Constitution permits the exercise of specific jurisdiction. First, the claims "must relate to or arise out of the defendant's contacts in the forum." *EMC Corp. v. Petter*, 104 F. Supp. 3d 127, 133 (D. Mass. 2015). Second, the defendant's contacts must constitute "purposeful availment of the benefits and protections" of the forum's laws. *Id.* Third, the exercise of jurisdiction must be reasonable, in light of the First Circuit's "gestalt factors." *Id.* The "gestalt factors" are: (1) the defendant's burden of appearing; (2) the forum state's interest in adjudicating the dispute; (3) the plaintiff's interest in obtaining convenient and effective relief; (4) the judicial system's interest in obtaining the most effective resolution of the controversy; and (5) the common interests of all sovereigns in promoting substantive social policies. *Id.* at 134, n.4. Plaintiff cannot satisfy these Due Process requirements as against Moving Defendants.

### 1. The Exercise of Jurisdiction Over George Wahbeh and KRW Would Violate the Minimum Contacts Requirement of the Due Process Clause.

Plaintiff has made no showing that KRW or Wahbeh "invok[ed] the benefits and protections of Massachusetts law, thereby rendering foreseeable and reasonable its compelled presence before the courts in this state." *See Pritzker v. Yari*, 42 F.3d 53, 60, 61 (1st Cir. 1994); *Nowak v. Tak How Investment Ltd.*, 899 F. Supp. 25, 32 (D. Mass. 1995). The conduct alleged against KRW and Wahbeh amounts to a single email to Plaintiff. *Compl.* ¶¶ 45, 114. Plaintiff does not even allege that Wahbeh was aware Plaintiff was a Massachusetts resident or worked in Massachusetts when he prepared this correspondence. *Id.* In fact, the correspondence was addressed generically to Plaintiff's employer, did not contain a mailing address, and was not mailed or otherwise transmitted by Wahbeh or KRW to anyone in Massachusetts. *Wahbeh Dec.*, ¶¶ 4-7. This isolated contact is insufficient to confer jurisdiction. *See Pandey v. Giri*, 457 F. Supp. 2d 94, 101 (D. Mass. 2006) (single letter did not subject attorney or his law firm to the court's jurisdiction); *see also Rimmer v. John Doe, Inc.*, No. CIV. 13-548 JNE/JJG, 2013 WL 5655865, at *7 (D. Minn. Oct. 16, 2013) (while "numerous telephone calls, letters, or wire communications could conceivably establish personal jurisdiction in a case arising under the FDCPA . . . a single email without more, cannot establish personal jurisdiction."); *Krambeer v. Eisenberg*, 923 F.Supp. 1170 (D.Minn. 1996) (collection attorney in Connecticut who sent single letter to debtor in Minnesota was not subject to personal jurisdiction in FDCPA action brought in federal district court in Minnesota); *Ernst v. Jesse L. Riddle, P.C.*, 964 F.Supp. 213 (M.D.La. 1997) (where basis of FDCPA claim was letter sent from corporate debt collector in Utah to consumer in Louisiana, court did not have personal jurisdiction over principal of corporation who was in Louisiana only once in previous five years and other contacts with Louisiana came as representative of corporation); *Hawkins v. Harston*, No. 93-CV-72031, 1994 WL 902366, at *3 (E.D. Mich. Jan. 31, 1994) (the transmittal of two debt collection letters were "insufficient to establish the requisite minimum contacts with the state to make the exercise of personal jurisdiction reasonable"); *see also Eubanks v. Filipovich*, No. CIV.A. 12-4299, 2012 WL 6731123, at *5 (E.D. Pa. Dec. 27, 2012) ("minimal exchange of emails and phone calls [does] not subject the defendant to jurisdiction in the forum state").

The facts of *Krambeer* are nearly identical to this case. In *Krambeer*, a Connecticut attorney who was not licensed to practice law in Minnesota and did not own property there sent a letter to a Minnesota resident regarding a debt owed to a third party. *Krambeer*, 923 F. Supp. At 1172. The plaintiff filed suit alleging violations of the Fair Debt Collection Practices Act as a result of this letter. *Id.* at 1173. The District Court of Minnesota found that the attorney's "contacts with Minnesota consist of a single debt collection letter sent to Plaintiff." *Id.* at 1174. The court further found that the single letter to the plaintiff in Minnesota was insufficient to establish that the attorney should reasonably anticipate being haled into court in Minnesota, noting that "the use of interstate mail or telephone alone is insufficient to establish minimum contacts with the forum state" and this "rule applies even with the item mailed into the forum state is the basis for the ensuing lawsuit." *Id.* at 1175. Finding personal jurisdiction based on such limited contacts would be constitutionally impermissible, the court therefore granted the attorney's motion to dismiss for lack of personal jurisdiction. *Id.* at 1176. The Court should reach the same result here.

### 2. The Exercise of Jurisdiction Over VIM Holdings and Global Service Would Violate the Minimum Contacts Requirement of the Due Process Clause.

Nearly all of Plaintiff's allegations against VIM Holdings are all made in the alternative with respect to B Financial and they all arise from the $200 loan she applied for and received through the www.guaranteedcashnow.net website on July 14, 2015. *Compl.* ¶ 31.

The *Agreement*, which Plaintiff alleges "govern[s] the Loan," provides that B Financial was the lender. *Compl.* ¶ 33, Exhibit A. As has been demonstrated in Defendants' Motion to Dismiss under Rule 12(b)(6), Plaintiff's agreement was formed with B Financial not VIM Holdings. *D'Ambrose Dec.*, ¶¶ 6-13. Moreover, VIM Holdings had no involvement in the origination, servicing, or any other activity related to Plaintiff's loan. *Id.* at ¶ 14. Accordingly, exercising personal jurisdiction on VIM Holdings would be constitutionally impermissible.

Plaintiff's allegations against Global Service are limited to the automatic account withdrawals that Plaintiff authorized under the *Agreement. Compl.* ¶¶ 41, 47. Such routine banking activity is plainly insufficient to confer jurisdiction over Global Service. *See Randall D. Jones D.D.S., P.A. v. E-Z Pay Servs., Inc.*, No. CIV. 06-6043, 2006 WL 2927479, at *2 (W.D. Ark. Oct. 12, 2006) ("to the extent that [the defendant] is merely debiting bank accounts of Arkansas residents, the Court finds such activity does not confer personal jurisdiction over [it]"). Accordingly, exercising personal jurisdiction over Global Service would be constitutionally impermissible.

### 3. The Exercise of Jurisdiction over Michael D'Ambrose, John Bartlett, Theresa D'Ambrose and Ruth Poutanen Would Violate the Minimum Contacts Requirement of the Due Process Clause.

Plaintiff does not allege that Michael D'Ambrose, John Bartlett, Theresa D'Ambrose, and Ruth Poutanen took any actions in relation to Plaintiff nor or does she allege that any of them reside or have substantial contacts in Massachusetts. Nor could she. Therefore, personal jurisdiction can only exist over these defendants on a theory of agency—specifically, that B Financial or U Solutions acted as their agent in their alleged interactions with Plaintiff. It is axiomatic that "jurisdiction over the individual officers of a corporation may not be based on jurisdiction over the corporation." *Johnson Creative Arts, Inc. v. Wool Masters, Inc.*, 573 F.Supp. 1106, 1111 (D. Mass. 1983); *see La Vallee v. Parrot—Ice Drink Products of America, 280 Inc.*, 193 F. Supp. 2d 296, 300 (D. Mass. 2002).[3] "For jurisdictional purposes, employees are 'not to be judged according their employer's activities [but by whether they were] primary participants in the alleged wrongdoing intentionally directed at the forum.'" *M-R Logistics, LLC v. Riverside Rail, LLC*, 537 F. Supp. 2d 269, 279—80 (D. Mass. 2008) (quoting *La Vallee,* 193 F. Supp. 2d at 301)). This requires Plaintiff to show that B Financial or U Solutions engaged in conduct in Massachusetts relating to Plaintiff for the benefit of and with the knowledge and consent of each of the individual defendants and that each individual defendant exercised some control over B Financial or U Solutions in the matter. *Id.*

Plaintiff has not met that burden. *See N. Laminate Sales, Inc. v. Matthews*, 249 F. Supp. 2d 130, 139 (D.N.H. 2003) ("the forum-state contacts of a corporation may be attributed to an individual who is an officer, director, or shareholder of the corporation when evidence is presented that shows that the corporation is the alter ego of the individual, or where other circumstances permit the court to pierce the corporate veil); *see also Gingras v. Rosette*, No. 5:15-CV-101, 2016 WL 2932163, at *9 (D. Vt. May 18, 2016) ("But Plain Green's contacts with Vermont are not vicariously attributed to its officials any more than directors of a corporation are subject to suit personally in any forum where the actions of the corporation satisfy the minimum contacts test."); *Karabu Corp. v. Gitner,* 16 F.Supp.2d 319, 324 (S.D.N.Y.1998) (Sotomayor, J.) (Plaintiff "must sufficiently detail [each] defendant's conduct so as to persuade a court that the defendant was a 'primary actor' in the specific matter in question"—"conclusory allegations that the defendant controls the corporation" will not suffice). Indeed, courts "routinely" grant 12(b)(2) motions by individuals where the allegations about the individual's participation in the specific matter at hand are "broadly worded and vague." *Gerstle v. Nat'l Credit Adjusters, LLC*, 76 F. Supp. 3d 503, 510 (S.D.N.Y. 2015). Plaintiff has made only conclusory allegations against Michael D'Ambrose and no allegations against the remaining individuals. Accordingly, all of the individual defendants should be dismissed from this case.

### CONCLUSION

For the foregoing reasons, and those that may be advanced at oral argument, defendants VIM Holdings Group LLC, Michael D'Ambrose, John Bartlett, Theresa D'Ambrose, Global Service Group LLC, Ruth Poutanen, KRW Attorneys and Associates, LLC, and George Wahbeh respectfully request that the Court dismiss the *Complaint* against them for lack of personal jurisdiction.

Dated: October 10, 2017

Respectfully Submitted,

The Defendants

---

3. To the extent that Plaintiff asserts personal jurisdiction on the basis of her conspiracy allegations, the First Circuit has never accepted the conspiracy doctrine of personal jurisdiction. *New Motor Vehicles Canadian Exp. Antitrust Litig.*, No. MDL 1532, 2004 WL 1571617 (D. Me. Apr. 20, 2004) ("The Supreme Court has labeled the conspiracy doctrine in the venue context as having 'all the earmarks of a frivolous albeit ingenious attempt to expand the statute.'") (citing *Bankers Life & Cas. Co. v. Holland,* 346 U.S. 379, 384, 74 S.Ct. 145, 98 L.Ed. 106 (1953)); *see also Openrisk, LLC v. Roston*, 90 Mass. App. Ct. 1107, 59 N.E.3d 456 (2016) (noting Massachusetts rejects the theory as well).

VIM Holdings Group LLC, Michael

D'Ambrose, B Financial LLC, John

Bartlett, U Solutions Group LLC, Theresa

D'Ambrose, Global Service Group LLC,

Ruth Poutanen,

By their attorneys:

*/s/ Mark Rossi*

Mark C. Rossi, Esq. (BBO: 662376)

Bostonian Legal Group, LLC

One Boston Place, 26th Floor

Boston, Massachusetts 02108

617-956-0956 (telephone)

877-266-0957 (facsimile)

MCR@BostonianLegal.com

The Defendant KRW Attorneys and Associates, LLC, and George Wahbeh By their attorneys,

*/s/ Susan E. Cohen*

Susan E. Cohen, BBO # 553353

Steven E. DiCairano, BBO # 694228

PEABODY & ARNOLD LLP

Federal Reserve Plaza

600 Atlantic Avenue

Boston, MA 02210-2261

Telephone: (617) 951-2100

scohen@peabodyarnold.com

sdicairano@peabodyarnold.com

Dated: October 10, 2017

# Motion for Judgment on the Pleadings

2018 WL 1896387 (D.Mass.)

**Westlaw Query>>**

To find more Motion for Judgment on the Pleadings filings on Westlaw: access Massachusetts Civil Trial Court Documents (from the Home page, click Trial Court Documents, then Massachusetts), click the Advanced Search link, select Motion for Judgment on the Pleadings, and click Search. Use the Jurisdiction filter on the left to narrow results to Federal.

United States District Court, D. Massachusetts.

SECURITIES AND EXCHANGE COMMISSION, Plaintiff,

v.

Patrick MURACA, NanomolecularDX, LLC (a/k/a NMDX, LLC), and MetaboRX, LLC, Defendants.

No. 1:17-cv-11400-FDS.

March 18, 2018.

ORAL ARGUMENT REQUESTED

NanomolecularDX, LLC's Motion for Judgment on the Pleadings

Colin R. Hagan, BBO No. 684798, David J. Shlansky, BBO No. 565321, James. P. McEvilly, III,[*] Shlansky Law Group, LLP, 1 Winnisimmet Street, Chelsea, MA 02150, Phone: (617) 370-8321, Fax: (866) 257-9530, E-mail: Colin.Hagan@slglawfirm.com, David.Shlansky@slglawfirm.com, James.McEvilly@slglawfirm.com.

Defendant NanoMolecularDX, LLC ("NMDX" or "Company"), by and through its undersigned counsel, hereby moves for judgment on the pleadings pursuant to Fed. R. Civ. P. 12(c) on all counts of the Complaint filed by the Plaintiff United States Securities and Exchange Commission ("SEC") against NMDX.

## I. PRELIMINARY STATEMENT

The SEC's allegations against Defendants fail to establish any actionable violations of the federal securities laws by NMDX, and the Company is entitled to entry of judgment in its favor dismissing all claims against it with prejudice. This memorandum explains that the SEC's claims against NMDX should be dismissed for four reasons:

● First, investor funds solicited and raised by Patrick Muraca ("Mr. Muraca") for NMDX were used primarily for acquiring business assets and Company inventory. This is what was represented to investors in NMDX, and it is accurate based on the SEC's own allegations regarding the primary use of investor funds.

● Second, Mr. Muraca was permitted to compensate and reimburse himself for expenses by the terms of his employment agreement, multiple assignment and sale agreements with NMDX, as well as reimbursement for personal expenditures on operating expenses for NMDX. The SEC fails to show that Mr. Muraca was allegedly using or expending NMDX funds in an unauthorized or false and misleading manner.

● Third, the investors in NMDX have overwhelmingly re-affirmed their investments in the Company despite being given the opportunity to rescind after robust disclosures regarding the SEC's allegations. This demonstrates that the false and misleading acts and omissions alleged by the SEC are not material to NMDX's investors, and that all claims against the Company should be dismissed.

● Fourth, assuming, *arguendo*, that the SEC's allegations that Mr. Muraca stole Company funds are true, basic principles of agency law dictate that the SEC may not impute those actions to NMDX for liability purposes.

There are no materially false and misleading acts or omissions on which the SEC's claims against Mr. Muraca are based, and there

---

FN* pro hac vice

are no viable claims to attribute to NMDX through his alleged actions. Accordingly, the claims against the Company set forth in the Complaint must be dismissed with prejudice.

## II. FACTUAL BACKGROUND

The SEC brought this action by filing a Complaint on July 31, 2017, alleging that Mr. Muraca, the former Chief Executive Officer and President of NMDX, had violated the Securities Act, 15 U.S.C. § 77q(a), and the Exchange Act, 14 U.S.C. § 78j(b) and Rule 10b-5. [ECF No. 1]. The SEC also sued NMDX and MetaboRX, LLC ("Metabo"), another company operated by Mr. Muraca. On August 25, 2017, Mr. Muraca, NMDX, and Metabo filed an Answer to the Complaint, and NMDX seeks dismissal of the claims against it now that the pleadings are closed.

### A. Mr. Muraca's Statements to NMDX's Investors.

Pursuant to its Operating Agreement, NMDX was formed for the business purpose of pharmaceutical development. Declaration of Mark Albers, ECF No. 1-3, ("Albers Dec."), at 6. The SEC's Complaint alleges that Mr. Muraca solicited investors for NMDX beginning in or around April through July of 2016 and continuing through June 2017. Complaint ("Compl."), ¶ 14. NMDX is focused on the development of IVD and RUO diagnostic assays and kits for early detection and monitoring of biomarkers in oncology and endocrinology. *Id.* ¶ 15. On or about September 6, 2016, Mr. Muraca e-mailed investors in NMDX a letter to solicit investment in the Company. *Id.* ¶ 20. In his letter, Mr. Muraca told investors that the proceeds from the offering would be used *primarily* for the development and manufacturing of FAS and HER-2 for the commercialization of testing kits, and other ongoing regulatory and operational efforts for commercialization. *Id.* The Complaint also alleges that, on or about October 21, 2016, Mr. Muraca solicited additional investment in NMDX and told investors that "the use of proceeds from this offering will be used primarily for manufacturing of pre-clinical test assays, commercialization of the tissue repository and clinical histochemistry products and for ongoing regulatory effort to support our NanoMolecularDX development." *Id.* ¶ 21; *See Exhibits A and B.* In subsequent letter updates to NMDX investors on November 3, 2016, March 16, 2017, and April 3, 2017, Mr. Muraca detailed to investors the efforts underway to raise strategic financing up to a maximum of $1,000,000 in aggregate to acquire, develop and commercialize cancer testing kits. *Id.* ¶¶ 22— 24. These statements were factually true when made.

### B. Investor Funds Were Used Primarily for NMDX's Business Purposes.

NMDX issued a press release on July 5, 2017, announcing the closing of the $1 million seed funding started in or around April 2016, and informed investors that the funds were being "used to finance the commercialization of NMDX's diagnostic tests, the development of additional diagnostic clinical trials, and expand operational capabilities." Compl., ¶ 23. During the period between February 17, 2017, and March 22, 2017, Mr. Muraca spent $330,000 from NMDX's bank account to purchase assets legitimately related to the business of NMDX. *Id.* ¶ 40. The Declaration of the Forensic Accountant filed in support of the Complaint further alleges that Mr. Muraca used investor funds to make a significant asset purchase of $300,000 from the bankruptcy proceedings of a company that he had previously worked with, Nuclea Biotechnologies, Inc. ECF No. 1-2, Albers Dec., ¶ 16. These assets, purchased by the Company for the benefit of the investors, were valued, even in bankruptcy, at over $3,000,000 approximately one year earlier. *Exhibit C.* The purchase of these specific assets in the areas of biotechnology and immunohistochemistry in which NMDX conducts business brought significant value to the investors through Mr. Muraca's efforts.

NMDX agreed to compensate Mr. Muraca for his work on behalf of the Company, as well as his contributions of intellectual property. The Complaint and its supporting exhibits show that Mr. Muraca and NMDX were parties to an employment agreement entered into as of April 25, 2016. ECF No. 1-3, ("Employment Agreement"), at 25—29. Pursuant to the Employment Agreement, NMDX agreed to pay $4,000 per month to Mr. Muraca in compensation, $1,000 per month for business insurance and car expenses, and $47,000 remaining from funds used to begin NMDX. *Id.* at Section 3(a). NMDX also had legitimate operating expenses throughout its existence which further required payment from investor funds, and which were legitimate uses of the investments. Expenses such as rent, utilities, salaries and storage all required investor funds to be paid until such a time as the company was cash flow positive. While the SEC and its forensic accountant, Mr. Albers, focused their attention on Mr. Muraca's allegedly personal transactions, the Complaint completely ignored all of the legitimate transactions that show NMDX as an operational company. The SEC and Mr. Albers also ignored the value of Mr. Muraca's allegedly personal transactions as compared to the amounts legitimately owed to Mr. Muraca by the Company. To the degree that the SEC is implying that the "Company" blessing the transactions with Mr. Muraca was effectively Mr. Muraca serving himself, the current position of NMDX herein affirms these dealings, and have fully ratified them. The "victim" is speaking clearly that it does not need the ambulance and the sirens can be turned off. There is no public interest to be served by further damaging the Company or imposing penalties on it.

### C. NMDX Is a Legitimate Operating Company.

It is only now that Mr. Muraca has been removed from exercising any control over the Company's business that the SEC does not dispute that NMDX is actually a legitimate company selling diagnostic cancer testing kits to its customers. On January 19, 2018, NMDX filed a Motion for Modification of the Preliminary Injunction ("First Assented-to Motion"), which was assented to by the SEC after discussions between NMDX and the SEC. (ECF No. 33). The purpose of the First Assented-to Motion was to permit NMDX to ship product — the very product Mr. Muraca purchased with investor funds as stated in the Company's funding solicitation — to three customers, the University of Texas, Martell Diagnostic Laboratories, Inc. ("Martell"), and NanoDetection Technology, Inc. ("NDT"). *Id.* ¶ 3. The SEC assented to the modification of the original Preliminary Injunction to permit NMDX to ship product to these customers and to accept funds paid by customers into NMDX's bank account, provided that Mr. Muraca had no access or control over the bank account. *Id.* ¶ 4. The First Amended Preliminary Injunction was entered by Order of the Court on January 22, 2018, to permit NMDX to ship product and accept funds into its bank account. (ECF. No. 35).

In February 2018, the SEC and NMDX agreed to modify the First Amended Preliminary Injunction, in the form of a Second Assented-to Motion for Preliminary Injunction ("Second Assented-to Motion"), to permit NMDX to ship additional product requested by two customers, Martell and NDT. (ECF No. 39). Again, the Court entered a Second Amended Preliminary Injunction Order on February 9, 2018, authorizing NMDX to ship products and accept payment in furtherance of its business purpose. (ECF. No. 41).

These two modifications to the original Preliminary Injunction, assented to by the SEC, show that NMDX is a legitimate company with live business due to the prior efforts of Mr. Muraca. The modifications to the injunction also make clear that Mr. Muraca acted in accordance with statements that he made to the investors in soliciting their investments, and as mentioned in passing in the SEC's Complaint regarding the purchase of business assets by Mr. Muraca with investor funds. (Compl., ¶ 40).

### D. NMDX's Investors Affirm Their Investments in the Company.

The actions of the investors in NMDX do not support the SEC's characterization of events as reflected in the Complaint. All investors in NMDX were provided an opportunity to rescind their investments in the Company after corporate governance changes were implemented during the pendency of the SEC and DOJ civil and criminal actions against Mr. Muraca. The letter accompanying the NMDX Investor Package, dated February 26, 2018, informed all investors as follows:

> This letter is in regard to an opportunity to participate in the reformation of NanoMolecularDX, LLC. As you know, there have been certain events that have intruded on the Company's progress, including litigation initiated by the United States Government alleging that there have been issues in the funding and operation of the Company. In an abundance of caution, we are offering each and every investor in the Company the opportunity to participate as an investor by opting in, with a default assumption that they wish to rescind their initial investment. In fact, we have had an overwhelming indication of interest in past investors continuing on as investors, but we are eager to preclude any claims that there is a need for further interference with the Company's progression as a going concern.

*Exhibit D*, NMDX Investor Package, dated Feb. 26, 2018, Ex. 1, Cover Letter dated Jan. 16, 2018. The investor packages included a Subscription Agreement with disclosures about the allegations in the instant litigation. After having the opportunity to review this information and consider their options in light of the SEC's allegations, all but two of the investors have opted in and reaffirmed their investments in NMDX. Only Ram V. Chary and Philip Seligmann, for entirely personal reasons extrinsic to the allegations against Mr. Muraca, rescinded their investments by execution of Mutual Rescission Agreements with NMDX. *See Exhibit E*, Mutual Rescission Agreement between NMDX and Philip Seligmann, dated Feb. 28, 2018; *Exhibit F*, Mutual Rescission Agreement between NMDX and Ram V. Chary, dated Feb. 28, 2018. The Mutual Rescission Agreements specifically confirm that Messrs. Chary and Seligmann did not rescind their agreements due to concerns regarding the allegations filed by the SEC or the disclosures made by NMDX, but, rather, for other personal reasons.

NMDX is entitled to judgment in its favor and dismissal of the claims against it in the Complaint. The SEC's allegations fail to establish that Mr. Muraca's alleged omissions regarding investor funds were material, or that any statements made concerning the *primary* purpose for which investor funds were being raised and used, were fraudulent or misleading when made, or were made with the requisite *scienter.* Further, the SEC also fails to establish that Mr. Muraca's alleged acts and omissions should be imputed to NMDX as a corporate entity since it is the target of Mr. Muraca's alleged scheme and there are no specific allegations of wrongdoing by NMDX.

### III. ARGUMENT

"After the pleadings are closed — but early enough not to delay trial — a party may move for judgment on the pleadings." Fed. R. Civ. P. 12(c). The Court reviews motions for judgment on the pleadings under substantially the same standard as that for a motion to dismiss for failure to state a claim under Rule 12(b)(6), except that "[a] Rule 12(c) motion, unlike a Rule 12(b)(6) motion, implicates the pleadings as a whole." *Aponte-Torres v. Univ. of P.R.*, 445 F.3d 50, 54-55 (1st Cir. 2006). On a motion for judgment on the pleadings, the Court "may consider 'documents the authenticity of which are not disputed by the parties; . . . documents central to plaintiffs' claim; [and] documents sufficiently referred to in the complaint.'" *Curran v. Cousins*, 509 F.3d 36, 44 (1st Cir.

2007) (quoting *Watterson v. Page*, 987 F.2d 1, 3) (1st Cir. 1993). Judgment on the pleadings is appropriate if the uncontested and properly considered facts conclusively establish the movant's entitlement to a favorable judgment. *Zipperer v. Raytheon Co., Inc.*, 493 F.3d 50, 53 (1st Cir. 2007) (quoting *Aponte-Torres*, 445 F.3d at 54).

In addition to facts and documents included in or incorporated into the complaint, on a motion for judgment on the pleadings, the court "may also consider 'documents incorporated by reference in [the complaint], matters of public record, and other matters susceptible to judicial notice.'" *Giragosian v. Ryan*, 547 F.3d 59, 65 (1st Cir. 2008) (alteration in original) (quoting *In re Colonial Mortg. Bankers Corp.*, 324 F.3d 12, 20 (1st Cir. 2003)). The fact that a party has submitted additional materials outside the pleadings is sufficient notice that the motion may be converted to a summary judgment motion. *Gulf Coast Bank & Trust Co. v. Reder*, 355 F.3d 35, 38 (1st Cir. 2004). In this case, the SEC cannot credibly dispute any of the factual circumstances presented here.

## A. NMDX Investor Funds Were Used Primarily for Acquiring Business Assets and Company Inventory.

To state a claim under section 10(b) and its corresponding rule, Rule 10b-5, a plaintiff must allege: "(1) a material misrepresentation or omission; (2) scienter; (3) a connection with the purchase or sale of a security; (4) reliance; (5) economic loss; and (6) loss causation." *Miss. Pub. Employees Retirement Sys. v. Boston Scientific Corp.*, 523 F.3d 75, 85 (1st Cir. 2008). *Scienter* is a "mental state embracing intent to deceive, manipulate, or defraud." *Ernst & Ernst v. Hochfelder*, 425 U.S. 185, 193 n.12 (1976). A defendant may also have the requisite mental state if it "acted with a high degree of recklessness." *Aldridge v. A.T. Cross Corp.*, 284 F.3d 72, 82 (1st Cir. 2002). "Recklessness, as used in this context, 'does not include ordinary negligence, but is closer to being a lesser form of intent.'" *Fire & Police Ass'n of Colo. v. Abiomed, Inc.*, 778 F.3d 228, 240 (1st Cir. 2015). Thus, "a defendant can be held liable for 'a highly unreasonable omission, involving not merely simple, or even inexcusable, negligence, but an extreme departure from the standards of ordinary care, and which presents a danger of misleading buyers or sellers that is either known to the defendant or is so obvious the actor must have been aware of it.'" *City of Dearborn Heights Act 345 Police & Fire Ret. Sys. v. Waters Corp.*, 632 F.3d 751, 757 (1st Cir. 2011) (quoting *Greebel*, 194 F.3d at 198). Courts should look at the complaint "as a whole" and weigh "competing inferences" in a "comparative evaluation" of the complaint's allegations and alternative inferences from those allegations. *ACA Fin. Guar. Corp. v. Advest, Inc.*, 512 F.3d 46, 59 (1st Cir. 2008).

The allegations in the Complaint regarding Mr. Muraca's use of funds raised from investors fail to demonstrate that Mr. Muraca acted with the requisite *scienter* to establish liability under Rule 10b-5 or Section 17(a)(1) of the Securities Act, 15 U.S.C. § 77q(a). The SEC's Complaint quotes Mr. Muraca as telling investors that the proceeds from the offerings for NMDX would be used *primarily* for the development and manufacturing of FAS and HER-2 for the commercialization of testing kits, and other ongoing regulatory and operational efforts for commercialization. Compl. ¶ 20. These statements about the primary use of investor funds raised through the offering are repeated in the Complaint as to NMDX's "manufacturing of pre-clinical test assays, commercialization of the tissue repository and clinical histochemistry products and for ongoing regulatory efforts to support our NanoMolecularDX development." *Id.* ¶ 21. The SEC does not allege that Mr. Muraca's statements regarding the primary use of funds raised from investors were false or misleading in the context in which they were made. And NMDX and its investors concur.

Instead, the SEC's Complaint admits that funds raised from NMDX investors were used to purchase NMDX assets worth $330,000 legitimately related to NMDX's business. This is demonstrated by the fact that the SEC has twice modified the Preliminary Injunction to permit NMDX to ship product to customers and accept payment, and the SEC has admitted as much in conferences to modify the Preliminary Injunction. If Mr. Muraca's efforts to raise funds from investors was little more than a sham or a fraud, there would not be any products for NMDX to ship now that it is controlled by its outside investors. Far from showing that Mr. Muraca used NMDX funds for his own benefit in an unauthorized manner, the Complaint and First and Second Amended Preliminary Injunctions show that Mr. Muraca used investor funds for the primary purpose of purchasing company assets, manufacturing inventory, and creating a demand for NMDX's test kits and components.

Other claims by the SEC as to Mr. Muraca's allegedly false or misleading acts and omissions brought forth in the Complaint are not grounded in fact. Paragraph 46 of the SEC's Complaint references Mr. Muraca's initial contribution of $150,000 to NMDX which the SEC claims was never made. However, it is clear that Mr. Muraca instead assigned intellectual property to the Company with an assigned value of $150,000, and justifying an independent valuation of $747,000. *Exhibits G and H*. These assignments of intellectual property by Mr. Muraca to the Company in 2016 clearly refute the allegations in paragraphs 46 and 47 of the Complaint that Mr. Muraca failed to make contributions to NMDX. In paragraph 48 of the Complaint, the SEC references a July 5, 2017, press release stating that "the company is already generating revenue through sales of its HER-2 blood testing kits, acquired through their acquisition of Nuclea Biotechnologies," and claims that this press release is false. The press release is true as evidenced by the June 7, 2017, Purchase Order from Martell in the Company's records and available to the SEC. *Exhibit J*. As the SEC and its forensic accountant are no doubt aware, revenue is routinely recognized on an accrual basis at the time of sale, not on a cash basis when the funds are received. In reality, it is the actions of the SEC in obtaining a temporary restraining order on July 31, 2017, and a Preliminary Injunction on August 28, 2017, that caused the Company to fail to deposit the revenue from the sale to Martell, not any wrongdoing by Mr. Muraca.

In any event, the allegations against Mr. Muraca are not actionable, and the claims against the Company should be dismissed for the reasons stated herein to the extent that the SEC seeks to impute them to NMDX.

## B. The SEC Fails to Allege or Show that Mr. Muraca Was Not Authorized to Use NMDX Funds for Compensation and Expense Reimbursement.

Mr. Muraca is not alleged by the SEC to have been working at NMDX without being compensated and reimbursed for expenses, and the Complaint ignores the assignment and sale agreements Mr. Muraca had with the Company. Nor does the SEC allege or show that Mr. Muraca was transferring investor funds from NMDX in excess of any compensation or expenses to which he may have been entitled under his Employment Agreement or other assignment and sale agreements with the Company, or without investors' knowledge. The SEC does not allege that Mr. Muraca's statements to investors regarding the business purposes for which investor funds were *primarily* being used prevented Mr. Muraca from using NMDX for legitimate compensation and expense reimbursement purposes. Further, there are no allegations by the SEC that NMDX's investors did not believe that Mr. Muraca was permitted to compensate and reimburse himself with NMDX funds in the manner and to the extent that he was allegedly doing so.

Compelling evidence of *scienter* most often includes "clear allegations of admissions, internal records or witnessed discussions" that suggest that defendants were "aware that they were withholding vital information or at least were warned by others that this was so" when they made the allegedly misleading statements. *In re Boston Scientific Corp. Sec. Litig.*, 686 F.3d 21, 31 (1st Cir. 2012). The SEC's allegations against Mr. Muraca amount to claims of failing to disclose what he was doing with *all* investor funds. Under the recklessness standard, a defendant can be held liable for "a highly unreasonable omission, involving not merely simple, or even inexcusable, negligence, but an extreme departure from the standards of ordinary care, and which presents a danger of misleading buyers or sellers that is either known to the defendant or is so obvious the actor must have been aware of it." *Greebel v. FTP Software, Inc.*, 194 F.3d 185, 198 (1st Cir. 1999) (quoting *Sundstrand Corp. v. Sun Chem. Corp.*, 553 F.2d 1033, 1045 (7th Cir. 1977)) (internal quotation mark omitted); *see also SEC v. Ficken*, 546 F.3d 45, 47-48 (1st Cir. 2008); *SEC v. Fife*, 311 F.3d 1, 9—10 (1st Cir. 2002). The SEC has made no such allegation against Mr. Muraca here. Despite having access to NMDX's books and records in preparing the Complaint filed in July 2017, the SEC does not make any specific allegations that Mr. Muraca had reason to believe that he might be misleading NMDX's investors.

The SEC also fails to provide any supporting statements from any witnesses who warned or claimed that investors were being misled by Mr. Muraca because he was compensating and reimbursing himself with Company funds. No investor has rescinded his or her investment on the belief or suspicion of any wrongdoing by Mr. Muraca — after reading the SEC's allegations — nor has any investor demanded or requested repayment to the Company from Mr. Muraca as a condition for remaining an investor.

## C. Mr. Muraca's Allegedly False or Misleading Acts and Omissions Were Not Material to Investors in NMDX.

Proof of *scienter* is required to establish violations of § 17(a)(1), § 10(b), or Rule 10b-5, while negligence is sufficient to establish liability under § 17(a)(2) or § 17(a)(3). *See Aaron v. S.E.C.*, 446 U.S. 680, 694—97, 100 S.Ct. 1945, 64 L.Ed.2d 611 (1980); *S.E.C. v. Ficken*, 546 F.3d 45, 47 (1st Cir. 2008); *SEC v. Fife*, 311 F.3d 1, 9—10 (1st Cir. 2002). The SEC is unable to allege or establish liability under § 17 (a)(2) or § 17 (a)(3), because the statements attributed to Mr. Muraca are immaterial to investors in NMDX, and the SEC fails to demonstrate otherwise. A fact is material when there is "a substantial likelihood" that a reasonable investor would have viewed it as "significantly alter[ing] the 'total mix' of information made available." *Basic Inc. v. Levinson*, 485 U.S. 224, 231-32 (1988) (quoting *TSC Indus., Inc. v. Northway, Inc.*, 426 U.S. 438, 449 (1976)) (internal quotation mark omitted). A statement can be "false or incomplete" but not actionable "if the misrepresented fact is otherwise insignificant." *Id.* at 238.

The actions of NMDX's investors show that the omitted facts in the statements made by Mr. Muraca are immaterial to NMDX's investors. Mr. Muraca's statements regarding the primary use of investor funds raised did not cause investors to abandon NMDX due to the SEC's allegations. On the contrary, NMDX's investors sent two letters to the SEC requesting that the company be permitted to move forward, funded its life support and ongoing operations, and hired counsel to free it from these proceedings — all with the SEC's and DOJ's complaints in public view. NMDX's investors were required to face rescission of their investments in the Company after an additional full disclosure of the SEC's allegations in the instant litigation, and all but two opted in (and in their case, for other personal reasons). After having the opportunity to review this information and consider their options in light of the SEC's allegations, all but two of the investors have opted in and reaffirmed their investments in NMDX. The two NMDX investors who did rescind their investments in NMDX did not do so due to concerns regarding the allegations filed by the SEC or the disclosures made by NMDX, but, rather, for other personal reasons. *Exhibits D and E*. Despite the initiation of this action against Defendants in July 2017, the SEC has not come forward with any showing of any specific NMDX investors claiming that they were misled by the statements or actions set forth in the Complaint by the SEC. Thus, the actions of NMDX's investors demonstrate that the SEC's allegations are immaterial and not actionable under the federal securities laws under the circumstances present here.

## D. Mr. Muraca's Alleged Acts and Omissions are Not Imputed to NMDX.

The SEC's Complaint alleges that Mr. Muraca improperly used Company funds for his personal benefit and deceived investors. For the reasons stated above, the SEC's allegations are insufficient and misguided. Even assuming, *arguendo*, that there is some merit to the SEC's allegations against Mr. Muraca, any liability flowing from those allegations should not be imputed to NMDX. It is true that Section 10(b) and Rule 10b-5 can be violated by any "person," natural or legal, including corporations. *See* 15 U.S.C. § 78c(a)(9) (defining "person" under the Securities Exchange Act to include corporations); *see also Cent. Bank of Denver, N.A. v. First Interstate Bank of Denver*, 511 U.S. 164, 191 (1994) ("Any person or entity . . . may be liable as a primary violator under 10b-5."). Further, it is axiomatic that a corporation acts through its employees and agents and can only have *scienter* through them. *See Suez Equity Investors, L.P. v. Toronto-Dominion Bank*, 250 F.3d 87, 101 (2d Cir. 2001).

Under the rule of imputation, it is "fundamental that an employer is liable for the torts of his employee committed while acting in the scope of his employment." *Fields v. Synthetic Ropes, Inc.*, 215 A.2d 427, 432 (Del.1965); *see also Belmont v. MB Inv. Partners, Inc.*, 708 F.3d 470, 494 (3d Cir. 2013) ("[T]he imputation doctrine recognizes that principals generally are responsible for the acts of agents committed within the scope of their authority.") (internal citation omitted) (alteration in original). Under the circumstances present here, however, the rule of imputation does not apply due to the adverse interest exception under the common law. Under this exception, an agent's actions or knowledge are "not imputed to the principal if the agent acts adversely to the principal in a transaction or matter, intending to act solely for the agent's own purposes or those of another person." Restatement (Third) of Agency § 5.04 (2006); *Baena v. KPMG LLP*, 453 F.3d 1, 8 (1st Cir. 2006) ("Adverse interest in the context of imputation means that the manager is motivated by a desire to serve himself or a third party, and not the company, the classic example being looting.") (citation omitted); *see also Hecksher v. Fairwinds Baptist Church, Inc.*, 115 A.3d 1187, 1205 (Del. 2015) ("[T]he adverse interest doctrine may prevent a court from imputing knowledge of wrongdoing to an employer when the employee has totally abandoned the employer's interests, such as by stealing from it or defrauding it.").

Here, the adverse interest doctrine prevents application of the rule of imputation between Mr. Muraca and NMDX as to the alleged false acts, omissions, and misappropriation set forth in the SEC's Complaint. Mr. Muraca is alleged by the SEC to have been acting adverse to the interests of the Company through theft of its funds and concealment. There should be no liability imputed to NMDX. According to the SEC's alleged version of events, the Company is a victim of Mr. Muraca's alleged scheme and directly harmed by his alleged actions. This is consistent with the SEC's own position in the recent action filed by the SEC against Elizabeth Holmes and Theranos, Inc., in the Northern District of California. *See S.E.C. v. Elizabeth Holmes and Theranos, Inc.*, Case 5:18-cv-001602 (N.D. Cal.). In that SEC enforcement action filed in March 2018, the SEC did not seek any penalties against Theranos, Inc. Steven Peikin, the co-director of the SEC's Enforcement Division, said that Theranos avoided paying any penalties in part because the misconduct was perpetrated by the individual defendants, Holmes and Balwani. "[A] corporate penalty would harm investors who had already been defrauded," Mr. Peikin said. *https://www.bloomberg.com/news/articles/2018-03-14/theranos-ceo-holmes-accused-of-fraud-by-sec-jeraxw6a*. The same is true here. The SEC should not be seeking to punish NMDX's investors by pursuing this matter against the Company. In seeking to impute liability to NMDX in this action, the SEC seeks to punish the Company for being the target of Mr. Muraca's alleged wrongdoing. That is the wrong result, at odds with established agency law, and contrary to the SEC's own policy approach, particularly given the absence of specific allegations against NMDX itself.

## IV. CONCLUSION

For the reasons explained above, the SEC does not allege or establish that Mr. Muraca made any materially false or misleading statements to investors in the Company while raising funds from investors or drawing compensation and expense reimbursements from NMDX. Absent any predicate violations by Mr. Muraca, the SEC's claims against NMDX must be dismissed with prejudice as non-actionable under the federal securities laws as alleged in the Complaint. Alternatively, Mr. Muraca's alleged acts and omissions may not be imputed to NMDX for purposes of establishing the Company's liability in this action. Accordingly, NMDX respectfully requests that the Court enter an Order in the form set forth at *Exhibit I*, dismissing all claims against NMDX in this matter.

Respectfully Submitted,

**NANOMOLECULARDX, LLC**

By its attorneys,

*By: /s/ James P. McEvilly, III*

Colin R. Hagan, BBO No. 684798

David J. Shlansky, BBO No. 565321

James. P. McEvilly, III*

SHLANSKY LAW GROUP, LLP

1 Winnisimmet Street

Chelsea, MA 02150

Phone: (617) 370-8321

Fax: (866) 257-9530
E-mail: Colin.Hagan@slglawfirm.com
David.Shlansky@slglawfirm.com
James.McEvilly@slglawfirm.com
*pro hac vice*
DATED: March 18, 2018

# Motion for More Definite Statement

2016 WL 8577939 (D.Mass.)

United States District Court, D. Massachusetts.

Drew KATZ, et al., Plaintiffs,

v.

SPINIELLO COMPANIES, et al., Defendants,

SK TRAVEL, LLC, Third-Party Plaintiff,

v.

UNITED STATES OF AMERICA, Third-Party Defendant.

No. 16-cv-11380.

December 27, 2016.

### Memorandum of Law in Support of United States' Motion to Dismiss Crossclaims or Alternatively Motion for More Definite Statement

Benjamin C. Mizer, Principal Deputy Assistant, Attorney General; Carmen M. Ortiz, United States Attorney; Michael W. Kerns, Orla M. Brady, Trial Attorneys, United States Department of Justice, Torts Branch, Civil Division, P.O. Box 14271, Washington D.C. 20044-4271, (202) 616-4020 (MK), (202) 514-0372 (OB), (202) 616-4159 (fax), michael.kerns@usdoj.gov, orla.m.brady@usdoj.gov, for third-party defendant, United States.

The United States respectfully submits this memorandum of law in support of its motion to dismiss the crossclaims made by Arizin Ventures, LLC, and Spiniello Companies ("cross-claimants") for failure to state a claim upon which relief can be granted. Fed. R. Civ. P. 12(b)(6). In the alternative, the United States moves for a more definite statement. Fed. R. Civ. P. 12(e).

## I. Relevant Procedural History

SK Travel filed a third-party claim against employees of the United States in state court. ECF No. 1-1. The United States certified, under the Westfall Act, that the employees were acting within the scope of their employment at the time of the conduct alleged and removed the case to this Court. ECF No. No. 1. Defendant Spiniello Companies filed a crossclaim against the United States for contribution and indemnification. ECF No. 102. Defendant Arizin Ventures, LLC filed an amended answer with affirmative defenses and a crossclaim against the United States for contribution and indemnification. ECF No. 107. The language of both defendants' crossclaims are, in relevant part, identical.

The cross-claimants allege no facts in their claims against the United States. Rather, they claim they are entitled to contribution, under Mass. Gen. Law Ch. 231B, § 1:

> [I]f any judgment is recovered herein by Plaintiffs against [the cross-claimants], concerning which any such negligence . . . is denied, then [the cross-claimants] will be damaged . . . and . . . [they] demand[] judgment for contribution from . . . [the] United States . . . and that [cross-claimants] have judgment over . . . [the] United States for all or part of any verdict or judgment obtained by Plaintiffs . . . ECF No. 102, 107.

And, cross-claimants demand common law indemnity:

[I]f Plaintiffs sustained damages as alleged in the Amended Complaint, said damages were caused . . . by the intentional conduct, carelessness, negligence, acts and/or omissions of . . . [the] United States . . . in the event Plaintiffs recover any sum or judgment against [cross-claimants], then [they] are entitled to indemnification by operation of the common law . . . for the full amount of any such sum or judgment. *Id.*

The crossclaims set forth no facts alleging why the United States is liable in contribution or indemnity. The bare allegations against the United States fail to comply with Rule 8 of the Federal Rules of Civil Procedure, and fail to state a claim for which relief can be granted, pursuant to Rule 12(b)(6).

## II. Argument

### A. The Crossclaims Should be Dismissed Because They Fail to Meet the Barest Pleading Standards.

At a minimum, a complaint must include a "short and plain statement of the claim showing that the pleader is entitled to relief." Fed. R. Civ. P. 8(a)(2). While Rule 8 does not require "detailed factual allegations," it does require more than "unadorned, the defendant-unlawfully-harmed-me accusation." *Ashcroft v. Iqbal*, 556 U.S. 662, 678 (2009) (citing *Bell Atlantic Corp. v. Twombly*, 550 U.S. 544, 556 (2007)). Although the crossclaims make reference to both contribution and indemnification claims, they put forth no facts and should be dismissed. ECF No. 102, 107.

A court cannot be expected to "read the cross-claim in light of what may be proved at the trial, but only as it stands upon the record." *Coates v. Potomac Elec. Power Co.*, 95 F. Supp. 779, 783 (D.D.C. 1951); *see also Washington Building Realty Corp. v. Peoples Drug Stores, Inc.*, 161 F.2d 879 (D.D.C. 1947)(crossclaim that alleged only facts that constituted a defense to the original tort was properly dismissed because it contained no factual allegations against the crossclaimed defendant). *Cf. Goldring v. Ashland Oil & Refining Co.*, 59 F.R.D. 487, 490 (N.D. W. Va. 1973) (rule 12(b)(6) motion to dismiss crossclaim denied where crossclaim alleged sufficient facts.) Because the crossclaims contain no facts or factual allegations, the United States cannot provide an informed responsive pleading, as required under the rules, and the crossclaims should be dismissed. Fed. R. Civ. P. 8(b).

### B. The Crossclaims Fail to State a Cognizable Claim and Should be Dismissed.

Even if the crossclaims were sufficient under Rule 8(a)(2), they fail to state a cognizable claim and should be dismissed pursuant to Federal Rule of Civil Procedure 12(b)(6). To survive a motion to dismiss pursuant to Fed. R. Civ. P. 12(b)(6), a complaint must allege a plausible entitlement to relief. *Twombly*, at 555. A claim is plausible when there are factual allegations sufficient "enough to raise a right to relief above the speculative level." *Id.* at 545. The complaint must include "factual content that allows the court to draw the reasonable inference that the defendant is liable" for the alleged misconduct. *Iqbal*, at 678. Here, the crossclaims have provided no factual allegations upon which this Court or the United States could use to glean the basis of the claims.

If the Court is not inclined to dismiss the crossclaims, the United States respectfully moves for a more definite statement. "A party may move for a more definite statement of a pleading . . . which is so vague or ambiguous that the party cannot reasonably prepare a response." Fed. R. Civ. P. 12(e). A motion for a more definite statement is appropriate where a complaint fails to provide a "clear way for . . . [a] defendant to determine exactly which acts are attributed to him." *Thompson v. Worcester County,* No. 10-40126-FDS, 2011 WL 2633270, at *3 (D. Mass. July 1, 2011). The crossclaims are completely devoid of facts and the United States cannot effectively respond. Therefore, the United States moves for a more definite statement if the Court does not find dismissal appropriate.

Third-Party Defendant United States prays that the crossclaims brought by Arizin Ventures, LLC and Spiniello Companies be dismissed. Alternatively the United States moves for a more definite statement.

Dated: December 27, 2017

Respectfully submitted,

BENJAMIN C. MIZER

Principal Deputy Assistant

Attorney General

CARMEN M. ORTIZ

United States Attorney

*s/ Orla M. Brady*

Michael W. Kerns

Orla M. Brady

Trial Attorneys
United States Department of Justice
Torts Branch, Civil Division
P.O. Box 14271
Washington D.C. 20044-4271
(202) 616-4020 (MK)
(202) 514-0372 (OB)
(202) 616-4159 (fax)
michael.kerns@usdoj.gov
orla.m.brady@usdoj.gov
Attorneys for Third-Party Defendant
United States

# Motion for Post-Trial Relief

2018 WL 3117006 (D.Mass.)

**Westlaw Query>>**

To find more Motion for Post-Trial Relief filings on Westlaw: access Massachusetts Civil Trial Court Documents (from the Home page, click Trial Court Documents, then Massachusetts), enter "DT(motion and (trial and post new) (judgment and relief alter amend))" in the search box, and click Search. Use the Jurisdiction filter on the left to narrow results to Federal.

United States District Court, D. Massachusetts.

Cheryl CARNEVALE, Kimberly Colombo, Stephen Daniels, Hezron Farrell, Gwendolyn Farrell, and Adriana Guzman, Plaintiffs,

v.

THE BOEING COMPANY, a Delaware Corporation, and Does 1-100, Defendants.

No. 1:13-cv-12615-JGD.

May 17, 2018.

### Plaintiff's Memorandum in Support of Her Motion To Alter or Amend Judgment

Adriana Guzman, by her Attorneys, Randy M. Hitchcock, Elaine Whitfield Sharp, BBO #56552, Randy Hitchcock, BBO # 561511, Whitfield Sharp & Hitchcock, LLC, 196 Atlantic Avenue #546512, Marblehead, MA 01945, Tel: 781 639-1862, Fax: 781.486.9156, E-mail: elainesharp@sharplaw.net, randyhitchcock@sharplaw.net.

## I. Factual Background

The Plaintiff, Adriana Guzman, after a trial by jury, received an award of $2,200,000 for her injuries and damages caused by Defendant, The Boeing Company. Exhibit 2 (Docket #348). However, the jury reduced the amount of the award by $726,000, in response to a special verdict slip question:

> Do you find that the Plaintiff failed to mitigate her damages (by failing to seek treatment?), and if so, how much reduction in her damages would this have caused?

(*Id.*).

The Plaintiff requests that the Court reduce the amount of the mitigation found by the jury, and as grounds states that, there was never any evidence presented during the trial which would have allowed the jury to assess the amount of $726,000 as mitigation.

The testimony at trial given by Defendant The Boeing Company's expert, Charles Marmar, MD, was that the Plaintiff could have been cured with four to six psychiatric sessions if addressed immediately, or 18 or so treatments at the time of trial, seven and one half years after the triggering event. Exhibit 3 (Docket # 364 - Trial Transcript Day 7, pgs. 73 and 116). However, Dr. Marmar offered no testimony as to the costs of these 18 or so treatments that Dr. Marmar claimed would cure the plaintiff. If the jury believed Dr. Marmar's testimony that Plaintiff failed to mitigate her damages and could be cured with 18 or so treatments' presently, they would have had to value each individual treatment at approximately $40,333 in order to reach the total amount of $726,000 for the reduction. There simply was no testimony from any of Defendant's witnesses to support this amount of reduction.

The only other testimony regarding future treatment came from the Plaintiffs expert, Jhilam Biswas, MD, who testified that the Plaintiff had a "fair to good" prognosis for recovery with treatment; that when one had first acquired an acute traumatic injury, intensive therapy would be short-lived; but that once a condition became chronic, the treatment would probably take as long as chronic condition had persisted had (7 and 1/2 years, or 90 months by the time of trial) Exhibit 4 (Docket #360 - Trial Transcript Day 3, pgs. 116-117). Even using Dr. Biswas' much longer treatment time, the mitigation amount stated by the jury breaks down to $8,066 per month, or $1,861 per week. There was simply no evidence to suggest that treatment would be that expensive over the months or years of treatment.

## II. Legal Argument

A motion under Rule 59(e) should be granted to correct a clear error, whether of law or of fact, and to prevent a manifest injustice. *Crawford v. Clarke,* 578 F.3d 39, 44 (1st Cir. 2009); *Aybar v. Crispin-Reyes,* 118 F.3d 10, 16 ( st Cir. 1997); *Firestone v. Firestone,* 76 F.3d 1205, 1208 (D.C. Cir. 1996) (the four grounds under Rule 59(e) include: to prevent manifest injustice, to accommodate for an intervening change in controlling law, to account for newly discovered evidence, or to correct clear error of fact or law); *EEOC v. Lockheed Martin Corp.,* 116 F.3d 110, 112 (4th Cir. 1997); *see also* Wright *et al.,* Federal Practice & Procedure § 2810.1. The majority of courts recognize all four grounds as a basis to grant a motion under Rule 59(e). *See e.g., Lazaridis v. Wehmer,* 591 F.3d 666, 669 (3d Cir. 2010) *(per curiam); Pac. Ins. Co. v. Am. Nat'l Fire Ins. Co.,* 148 F.3d 396, 403 (4th Cir. 1998); *GenCorp, Inc. v. Am. Int'l Underwriters,* 178 F.3d 804, 834 (6h Cir. 1999). So long as the Rule 59(e) motion is timely filed, the courts have considerable discretion. *Lockheed Martin Corp.,* 116 F.3d at 112. Although the courts are not required to consider new legal arguments or mere restatements of old facts or arguments, the court can and should correct clear errors in order to "preserve the integrity of the final judgment." *Turkmani v. Republic of Bolivia,* 273 F. Supp. 2d 45, 50 (D.D.C. 2002).

Additionally, failure to mitigate damages is in the nature of an affirmative defense. *See, Allied Int'l, Inc. v. Int'l Longshoremen's Ass'n,* 814 F.2d 32, 38-39 (1st Cir. 1987). Thus, the defendant has the burden to prove by a preponderance of the evidence that the Plaintiff "failed to take reasonable steps to hold down [his or her] losses." *Id.*

Here the Defendant failed to put forth any testimony that would support a reduction by $726,000 for failure to mitigate damages, or anything even close to that amount. While there was testimony regarding symptom validity, or a tendency to exaggerate or over-report her symptoms while under-reporting her faults, that alone could not have formed a basis for reducing the verdict along the lines of failure to mitigate damages. Instead, the jury's verdict appears to be completely based on speculation as to the alleged mitigation of damages because there simply was no evidence or testimony testimony upon which that amount could be based. As such, the verdict and judgment are based on a fatal mistake of fact - that there was any testimony to support a mitigation of damages by $726,000.00. As such, a judgment based on this mistaken fact results in a manifest injustice on the Plaintiff because her damages are reduced by an amount wholly without support in the evidence at trial. Under the power of Rule 59(e), Plaintiff respectfully requests the Court amend the judgment to correct this mistake of fact.

## III. Conclusion

For the foregoing reasons, Plaintiff Adriana Guzman, respectfully requests that the Court grant her motion to alter or amend the judgment, thereby correcting the factual mistake that there was any testimony to support a $726,000 reduction for her alleged failure to mitigate damages.

Respectfully submitted,

ADRIANA GUZMAN

By her Attorneys,

/S/ Randy M. Hitchcock

Elaine Whitfield Sharp, BBO #56552

Randy Hitchcock, BBO # 561511

Whitfield Sharp & Hitchcock, LLC

196 Atlantic Avenue #546512

Marblehead, MA 01945

Tel: 781 639-1862

Fax: 781.486.9156

E-mail: elainesharp@sharplaw.net

randyhitchcock@sharplaw.net

# Application for Temporary Restraining Order

2015 WL 13446383 (D.Mass.)

**Westlaw Query>>**

To find more Application for Temporary Restraining Order filings on Westlaw: access Massachusetts Civil Trial Court Documents (from the Home page, click Trial Court Documents, then Massachusetts), click the Advanced Search link, select Motion for TRO, and click Search. Use the Jurisdiction filter on the left to narrow results to Federal.

United States District Court, D. Massachusetts.

178 LOWELL STREET OPERATING COMPANY, LLC, d/b/a Lexington Health Care Center, Plaintiff,

v.

Dana NICHOLS, Denise Belliveau, Integrated Health Services, Inc., d/b/a Medford Rehabilitation and Nursing Center; and MRNC Operating, LLC, d/b/a Medford rehabilitation and nursing center, Defendants.

No. 1:15-cv-13547-NMG.

December 23, 2015.

## Plaintiff's Refiled Motion for Temporary Restraining Order

178 Lowell Street Operating, Company, LLC, d/b/a Lexington Health Care Center, By its attorneys, Danielle Y. Vanderzanden (BBO #563933), Francesco A. DeLuca (BBO #692138), Ogletree, Deaknis, NASH, Smoak & Stewart, P.C., One Boston Place, Suite 3220, Boston, MA 02108, Telephone: 617-994-5700, Fax: 617-994-5701.

Pursuant to Rule 65 of the Federal Rules of Civil Procedure and this Court's order dated December 16, 2015 (ECF Doc. 70), Plaintiff 178 Lowell Street Operating Company, LLC, d/b/a Lexington Health Care Center ("Lexington") respectfully moves this Court to enter a Temporary Restraining Order ("TRO") against Defendants Dana Nichols ("Nichols"), Denise Belliveau ("Belliveau"), and MRNC Operating, LLC, d/b/a Medford Rehabilitation and Nursing Center ("Medford") to preserve the status quo and protect Lexington's contractual, statutory, and common law rights.[1] The grounds for this Motion are detailed in Lexington's Complaint; the affidavit(s) filed in this matter; and the Memorandum of Law submitted in support of this Motion. As those documents establish, Lexington is entitled to the injunctive relief it seeks because:

1. Nichols solicited, hired and now employs Belliveau and Jennifer Gorell ("Gorell"), former Lexington employees, in violation of her contractual obligations to Lexington.

2. Nichols hires and now employs other individuals who formerly worked for Lexington between June 13, 2015 and September 11, 2015, in violation of her contractual obligations to Lexington.

3. Nichols breached her contractual obligations, and Nichols, Belliveau, and Medford violated Massachusetts law, by misappropriating Lexington's trade secrets and confidential information.

4. Bruce Bedard, Medford's Chief Executive Officer, knowingly colluded with Nichols in soliciting Belliveau and Gorell in breach of Nichols's non-solicitation covenant with Lexington.

5. Medford, through its chief executive officer, willfully and knowingly participated in Nichols's breach of her contractual obligations to Lexington in violation of statutory and common law.

6. For a period of nearly six (6) weeks, by written agreement of the parties and order of the Court (ECF Docs. 47, 57 and 59),

---

1. Lexington cites court filings, including supporting documents, with the Court's electronic court filing docket references, as "ECF Doc. _."

Medford refrained from allowing Nichols to employ Belliveau and/or Gorell. Absent equitable relief, Nichols, Belliveau, and Medford will return to the above-referenced breaches of contract and violations of M.G.L. c. 93A.

7. Without equitable relief, Lexington will be irreparably harmed by ongoing damage to or destruction of Lexington's relationships with current employees and its employee non-solicitation covenants would be rendered meaningless.

8. Lexington has no adequate remedy at law.

9. Lexington will suffer greater hardship if the TRO is not issued than Defendants will experience if the Court provides the relief that Lexington seeks.

10. The public interest in the consistent enforcement of contractual obligations outweighs any potential countervailing interest and mandates entry of the requested TRO.

**WHEREFORE**, Lexington respectfully requests that this Court issue a TRO, substantially in the form attached hereto as **Exhibit 1** ordering that, for fourteen (14) days:

1. Nichols shall:

(a) not directly or indirectly hire, employ or solicit for employment, for any purpose or on behalf of any entity, any individual employed by Lexington between June 13, 2015 and September 11, 2015;

(b) not directly or indirectly, in any capacity whatsoever solicit, sell to, or receive any business from a customer, client, or prospect of Lexington with whom Lexington had or expected to have an exclusive contractual relationship during Nichols's employment therewith;

(c) not, whether acting alone or in concert or participation with others, including, without limitation, any officer, agent, employee, attorney, or representative of Medford, use or disclose, for any purpose, any confidential, proprietary, or trade secret information belonging to Lexington;

(d) be required to identify to Lexington's counsel any and all documents and information taken from Lexington; and

(e) be required to provide to Lexington's counsel a detailed accounting of how Nichols, Belliveau, and/or Gorell, or anyone acting in concert or participation with them, have used any and all documents and information taken from Lexington.

2. So long as Medford continues to employ Nichols, Medford, including its officers, agents, employees, attorneys, and representatives, shall:

(a) refrain from encouraging and/or assisting Nichols in soliciting Lexington employees;

(b) prohibit Nichols, on Medford's behalf, from soliciting or hiring any individual(s) who performed services of any kind for Lexington between June 13, 2015 and September 11, 2015;

(c) refrain from encouraging and/or assisting Nichols in soliciting, selling to, or receiving any business from a customer, client, or prospect of Lexington with whom Lexington had or expected to have an exclusive contractual relationship during Nichols's employment therewith;

(d) prohibit Nichols, on Medford's behalf, from soliciting, selling to, or receiving any business from a customer, client, or prospect of Lexington with whom Lexington had or expected to have an exclusive contractual relationship during Nichols's employment therewith;

(e) prohibit Nichols, on Medford's behalf, from engaging in any conduct, that violates of her contractual duties to Lexington;

(f) prohibit Belliveau from performing services for Medford and/or Nichols;

(g) prohibit Gorell from performing services for Medford and/or Nichols;

(h) be enjoined from using or disclosing, for any purpose, any confidential, proprietary, or trade secret information belonging to Lexington;

(i) be required to take any and all actions necessary to ensure that Medford is not using Lexington's confidential, proprietary, or trade secret information, and to provide independent third-party verification that it has taken such action; and

(j) prohibit any other individual who performed services for Lexington between June 13, 2015 and September 11, 2015 from performing services for Medford and/or Nichols.

3. Belliveau shall:

(a) be enjoined from performing services for Medford and/or Nichols;

(b) be required to provide to Lexington's counsel a detailed accounting of how Nichols, Belliveau, and/or Gorell, or anyone acting in concert or participation with them, have used any and all documents and information taken from Lexington.

4. Gorell shall:

(a) be enjoined from performing services for Medford and/or Nichols; and

(b) be required to provide to Lexington's counsel a detailed accounting of how Nichols, Belliveau, and/or Gorell, or anyone acting in concert or participation with them, have used any and all documents and information taken from Lexington.

5. Any other individual who performed services for Lexington between June 13, 2015 and September 11, 2015 shall be enjoined from being directly in directly employed by Nichols or by Medford, so long as Nichols works as the Administrator at Medford.

Respectfully submitted,

178 LOWELL STREET OPERATING COMPANY, LLC, d/b/a LEXINGTON HEALTH CARE CENTER,

By its attorneys,

/s/ Francesco A. DeLuca

Danielle Y. Vanderzanden (BBO #563933)

Francesco A. DeLuca (BBO #692138)

OGLETREE, DEAKNIS, NASH

SMOAK & STEWART, P.C.

One Boston Place, Suite 3220

Boston, MA 02108

Telephone: 617-994-5700

Fax: 617-994-5701

Dated: December 23, 2015

# Table of Laws and Rules

## FEDERAL RULES OF CIVIL PROCEDURE—Continued

## FEDERAL RULES OF CIVIL PROCEDURE—Continued

# FEDERAL RULES OF CIVIL PROCEDURE—Continued

# FEDERAL RULES OF CIVIL PROCEDURE—Continued

## FEDERAL RULES OF CIVIL PROCEDURE—Continued

## FEDERAL RULES OF CIVIL PROCEDURE—Continued

# FEDERAL RULES OF CRIMINAL PROCEDURE

# FEDERAL RULES OF EVIDENCE

# RULES OF THE U.S. DISTRICT COURT OF MASSACHUSETTS

## RULES OF THE U.S. DISTRICT COURT OF MASSACHUSETTS—Continued

## RULES OF THE U.S. DISTRICT COURT OF MASSACHUSETTS—Continued

## ORDERS OF THE U.S. DISTRICT COURT FOR THE DISTRICT OF MASSACHUSETTS